Encyclopedia of the Holocaust

Encyclopedia of the Holocaust

ROBERT ROZETT   SHMUEL SPECTOR

YAD VASHEM

Facts On File, Inc.

Library of Congress Cataloging-in-Publication Data

Encyclopedia of the Holocaust / Robert Rozett, Shmuel Spector, editors.
    p. cm
    Includes bibliographical references (p.) and index
    ISBN 0-8160-4333-7
1. Holocaust, Jewish (1939–1945)—Encyclopedias. I. Title: Facts On File encyclopedia of
the Holocaust. II. Rozett, Robert. III. Spector, Shmuel.
D804.25 .E53 2000
940.53'18'003–dc21

                                00-030917

TABLE OF CONTENTS

INTRODUCTION

The Holocaust has become the symbol of modern man's ability to do evil and echoes of the Holocaust are ever present in our daily lives. Box office hits, like Schindler's List, have brought the Holocaust to the attention of millions of people the world over, who may otherwise have never encountered it. In the media, current events are compared to the Holocaust, or are themselves termed "Holocausts." On any given day news stories about the Holocaust and its repercussions may be found in the pages of major newspapers and magazines the world over. Former Nazis and their accomplices are still being brought to trial for crimes they committed over 55 years ago, and some of these trials have engendered great public debate. As we begin the twenty-first century many new-old issues have reared their heads. The compensation of forced laborers used by the Nazis — among them many Jews, the theft of Jewish property, the concealing of Jewish bank accounts in Switzerland, and the non-payment of insurance policies to the heirs of Holocaust victims are receiving much attention. The Internet is replete with thousands of web pages about the Holocaust, most trying to present a faithful picture of it and a relative few seeking to distort and deny it. Nearly all of this sea of information helps serve the memory of the six million Jews who were ruthlessly murdered by the Nazis. But sometimes words and even images are so misused that the memory of the victims is trivialized, even desecrated.

The key to ensuring that the memory of the victims remains untarnished and that the Holocaust is not trivialized, is education. Teaching about the Holocaust has made great strides in the last decade or so. Governments such as Israel, Sweden, Britain, and the United States have joined an international task force to foster education about the Holocaust and its repercussions. The teaching of the history of the Holocaust is mandatory in several states in the United States, and in others, it is touched upon as part of courses on world history. In light of this, the need for reliable basic reference information, in the classroom and outside of it, has not diminished but has grown.

Given the multitude of fragments — events, organizations, people, and concepts — that together constitute the story of the Holocaust, it would take thousands upon thousands of pages to discuss them all in the detail that they deserve. Such a compendium would be overwhelming for student and teacher alike. The purpose of this Encyclopedia is to set forth the main themes of the history of the Holocaust, from its roots through its aftermath. The introductory essays were written to provide a broad portrait of the Holocaust and to put the rest of the smaller entries in their historical context. The entries themselves are concise and touch upon the most salient facts, and are not meant to be exhaustive. They are intended to provide basic information for students and their teachers, as they grapple with the history of the Holocaust in the classroom or other educational settings. The photographs and other illustrations throughout the book serve as documents from the period, and help make the now distant events more tangible to the reader. There is no question that the Holocaust is a highly charged subject that summons up deep emotions and much thought. Although the style of this Encyclopedia is academic, the emotional charge lies just under its surface ready to be released through the reflection of the reader.

This Encyclopedia is an important tool for pupils and teachers alike. Its eight opening essays provide a survey of the history of the Holocaust written by scholars for pupils. The first two essays depict the Jewish world on the eve of the Holocaust. It is clear that one cannot understand the great impact of the Holocaust on Jews and on Western culture without understanding how the Jews lived in their communities before the Nazis destroyed them. One of the central questions concerning the Holocaust is how could human beings do such a thing? Part of the answer may be found in the essays on the nature of Nazi ideology and the regime the Nazis created. Another part of the answer may be found in an analysis of the development of Nazi policies against the Jews; policies that culminated in the "Final Solution." Given the abyss of time and space between the generation born at the end of the twentieth century and the experience of the Jews in the Holocaust, it is not a simple matter to help young people approach an understanding of that terrible epoch. The experience of Jews, their families, and their communities lies at the core of the Holocaust; and so this too is a subject of one of the opening essays. It is true that in many ways Auschwitz can be best understood as a kind of surreal planet, where the brutal exploitation, dehumanization, and death of the prisoners reigned. But it is equally true that Auschwitz was established in the heart of modern Europe, and both the perpetrators and victims had grown up in a world that in many ways was similar to our own.

Especially in the Western democracies, the question how did the Allied Nations respond to the unfolding murder of the Jews is of central importance. Like so many seminal questions, the answer is not simple, and the essay on this subject tries to place the reaction of those governments in the context of the war and the worldview of different government officials. Lastly, the repercussions of the Holocaust on our society have been broad and deep. The fact that there was a Holocaust has brought us to question our most cherished beliefs about the nature of man and our modern world. This is the subject of the last essay presented in the Encyclopedia.

Because the events of the Holocaust touched so many places with a complex geopolitical and linguistic history, it is important to note both how spellings were chosen, and the method used for rendering various names and proper nouns from foreign languages into English. The place names used are those that were in use on the eve of World War II or those that are most commonly used in English. Accents and diacritical marks have been omitted. In the case of the German umlaut, the letter "e" has been given after the vowel that customarily carries the umlaut above it.

This Encyclopedia provides well beyond an introduction to the history of the Holocaust, but it is our hope that students will not consider it the last book they ever read about it. For students, as well as teachers who would like to continue learning about the Holocaust, we have provided a selected bibliography arranged by subject.

As in all projects of this magnitude many people deserve thanks for their contribution to the finished product. First and foremost, we would like to thank our colleagues at Yad Vashem. In addition to the people who appear below as part of the staff, many individuals generously gave of their time and expertise to ensure that this Encyclopedia would be published. The directorate of Yad Vashem, Avner Shalev, the Chairman, and Yishai Amrami, the Director-General, gave their unswerving backing to the project. The staff of the International School for Holocaust Studies at Yad Vashem, and in particular Amos Goldberg, provided important source material for the Encyclopedia. The staff of the Library and Archives helped in finding additional material. The Library staff in particular showed great understanding and patience when their director was submerged in Encyclopedia entries instead of attending to the Library. Last, but certainly not least, Dana Porat kindly read and commented on several of the opening essays.

Without basic information put into context we cannot have knowledge. Only with knowledge can we have wisdom. Only with wisdom can we prevent future tragedies of the magnitude of the Holocaust.

Robert Rozett and Shumel Spector
The Editors

CONTRIBUTORS

Editors

ROBERT ROZETT PH.D.
Director of the Library, Yad Vashem

SHMUEL SPECTOR, PH.D.
Director of the Encyclopedia of Jewish Communities Project, Yad Vashem

Educational Editor

AVIVA GOLBERT

Managing Editor

RACHEL GILON

Contributing Authors

DAVID CESARANI PH.D.
Professor of Modern Jewish History, University of Southampton, United Kingdom

DANIEL FRAENKEL PH.D.
Editor, Encyclopedia of Jewish Communities - Germany, Yad Vashem

GUY MIRON PH.D.
Researcher Yad Vashem and Lecturer, Department of Modern Jewish History, Hebrew University of Jerusalem, Israel

DAVID SILBERKLANG, MA
Editor Yad Vashem Studies and Lecturer, School for Overseas Students—Hebrew University of Jerusalem, Israel

AHARON WEISS PH.D.
Researcher and Former Editor, Yad Vashem Studies

Photo Research

DANIEL UZIEL; REUVEN KUPFER; AYALA FELSENTHAL

Supporting Staff

SHOSHANA LEWIS; JOAN MATHIS; INBAL MOR-YOSEF; GALIA SCHNEIDER; AMI GREEN; JEN SUNDICK; VERONIKA MOSTASLAVSKY

Photographs

Unless otherwise cited, all photographs were provided by the Yad Vashem Archives in Jerusalem

THE CONTRIBUTION OF EUROPEAN JEWRY TO MODERN CULTURE

Guy Miron

The integration of the Jews into European society and culture, starting with the birth of the Jewish Enlightenment (*Haskala*) in the late eighteenth century, brought with it a gradual but profound change in the identity and culture of a large segment of Europe's Jews. While traditional Jewish society operated on the margins of Christian society in Europe, integrating for the most part economically but maintaining a separate identity in everything else, the *Haskala* movement introduced a basic change. Its advocates (the *maskilim*), the most prominent of whom was Moses Mendelssohn of BERLIN, called for Jewish openness to the social and cultural life around them. This process, which reached its peak in Europe on the eve of the HOLOCAUST, significantly changed the face of European Jewry and produced a variety of cultural achievements in different fields, some of which remain to this day cornerstones of Jewish and Western culture.

By adopting the language of their surroundings (French, German, and later the languages of Eastern Europe) and familiarizing themselves with the culture of the countries they were living in, the Jews were in effect meeting the expectations of those who wished to grant them equal rights. The liberals who were in favor of Jewish integration did not wish to see the Jews as a minority alienated from the local culture but as participating in it and even making a contribution, just as they would in economic and social life. The effort at integration also extended to personal relations. Thus the close friendship between Mendelssohn and the German philosopher Gotthold Ephraim Lessing exemplified the beginning of coexistence between the Jews and European culture and became a symbol for German and European Jewry as a whole. Others besides Mendelssohn were active. Among them the best known was Solomon Maimon, who left the Hasidic life in POLAND to become a leading German philosopher in Berlin.

Mendelssohn, Maimon, and the others belonged at first to a small Jewish elite but in the course of time succeeded in spreading their ideas among a broader Jewish public. By the second half of the nineteenth century, within two or three generations, European culture was the common possession of most of the Jews of Western and Central Europe. In Eastern Europe, where progress was slow and Jewish society more tradi-tional, cultural integration was also slower and more gradual, but there too it ultimately bore fruit.

Acceptance of the basic idea that the Jew is not only a member of his community but also of the brotherhood of mankind, not only produced increasing involvement in the surrounding culture but also caused some Jews to seek new ways of looking at their Jewishness. Indeed, there were those among the *maskilim* whose enthusiasm for European culture led them to turn away from their Jewish identity, becoming indifferent to it and sometimes converting to Christianity. However, others sought only to modernize Judaism. Here too Mendelssohn came to symbolize the breakthrough. Alongside his work as a German philosopher, he also worked on a translation of the Hebrew Bible into German and even added a commentary of his own. In the second half of the nineteenth century several Jewish thinkers sought a formula that would best express Jewish nationalism. Simon Dubnow, for example, believed the Jews needed autonomy in Europe itself. Others spoke of the need for a return to Zion. Men like Asher Ginsberg (Ahad Ha-Am) wrote of spiritual Zionism, whereas Theodore Herzl and his followers worked to establish a Jewish national home in Palestine.

Striking a balance between involvement in the surrounding culture and loyalty to the Jewish heritage, and even the effort to modernize it, was the chief concern of Jews active in European culture in the nineteenth century. In 1819 the Society for Jewish Culture and Science was founded in Berlin. Its members were young Jewish students whose aim was to investigate and represent Judaism using the methods of modern science and to improve its image in the eyes of the Christian world. This enormous undertaking produced impressive results. The scholars active in the nineteenth century—and first and foremost Leopold Zunz, who was one of the founders of the Society—succeeded in giving Judaism a new image on the basis of critical historical study, investigating its origins with tools borrowed from the scientific historical research taking place all around them. Nonetheless, not all of the Society's founding fathers persevered; some despaired of creating a synthesis and concluded that it was impossible to reconcile loyalty to Judaism with European culture. The most famous of them, Heinrich Heine, and others as well, reached what they took to be the inevitable conclusion and converted. Heine, who afterwards achieved fame as one of GERMANY'S greatest poets, characterized his baptism as an admission ticket to European culture. Other converts of Jewish origin who were prominent in European culture in this period were the composer Felix Mendelssohn-Bartholdy and later also Karl Marx, who was born into a family that had converted.

Toward the middle of the nineteenth century, as the process of modernization progressed in Central Europe, there emerged a number of religious movements within Judaism whose influence is still felt. One was the liberal Reform movement, whose outstanding leader was Rabbi Abraham Geiger. It was rivaled by the Modern Orthodox movement, led by Rabbi Raphael Samson Hirsch. Still another movement was the positivist-historical school of Zacharias Frankel—the ancestor of modern Conservative Judaism. The period also saw the beginning of modern Jewish historical literature, noteworthy primarily for the work of Heinrich Graetz. Jews also contributed to the world of art. The German-Jewish artist Moritz Oppenheim was one of the more prominent of the painters. Also beginning to appear in Central and Western Europe toward the middle of the nineteenth century were Jewish periodicals in the local language. In Eastern Europe as well— in Galicia under the Austrians and in Czarist Russia— there were signs of a Jewish renaissance at the time, but here the unfriendly social atmosphere and the attitude of the authorities—especially in Russia—served to discourage the assimilation of local language and culture. Nonetheless, in the second half of the nineteenth century groups of Jewish intellectuals began publishing periodicals in Russian, Polish, and even Hungarian.

Toward the end of the nineteenth century a new generation of Jews came of age in Central and Western Europe, belonging for the most part to the second or third generation after Jews were granted equal rights in many parts of Europe. Out of a certain segment of this generation, primarily from among those who had dropped out of their communities and were known as "marginal Jews," came a number of figures who made a vital contribution to the evolution of European science and culture and whose influence is still being felt.

Albert EINSTEIN, whose name more than any other is associated with the breakthrough in the natural sciences at the beginning of the twentieth century, did not spring from the scientific establishment of his time but in fact from its fringes. The development of the

theory of relativity is of course first and foremost to be attributed to his scientific capacity and intellectual brilliance, but it is difficult to separate them from the social and cultural factors that shaped his world, including his Jewish background. It is just this marginality, both in regard to the scientific establishment and to the social reality of the Jews of Central Europe at the time, which produced in Einstein's great mind the revolutionary way of thinking that made possible the scientific revolution that he brought about.

Another scientific breakthrough associated with the creativity of the Jews of Central Europe is the psychoanalysis of Sigmund Freud. Freud, a native of Moravia, began his career as a student of medicine at the University of Vienna, where he found himself rejected as a Jew by many. It was this rejection, which prevented his advancement in the academic establishment, that caused him to start a private practice as a doctor. It was his practice that provided him with a framework for developing his theory of the unconscious and the interpretation of dreams. Freud defined himself as a Jew "prepared to be in opposition and dispense with the time-honored majority view." As such, he met with fierce opposition to his discoveries on the part of the scientific establishment and had to deal with open antisemitic attacks, but like Einstein he was not intimidated and went on courageously advocating what he believed to be the truth.

Jews were also prominent in other social sciences, especially in sociology, where Emile Durkheim of

Sigmund Freud at his desk, reading "Der Mann Moses und die Monotheistische Religion," London, 1938
(Photo: A. W. Freud et al, by arrangement with Mark Paterson & Associates)

FRANCE and Georg Simmel of Germany may be numbered among the founding fathers of the discipline, followed in the next generation by Maurice Halbwachs and Karl Mannheim. It is interesting to note that Simmel addressed the question of the place of the Jew in European culture, arguing in his *Soziologie* (1908) that the Jews of Europe could serve as a perfect example of the "stranger" (*Fremde*) who is assimilated into the environment but remains on its edges, enabling him to view it critically and sometimes call into question its basic assumptions and forge new directions.

The early twentieth century also saw the appearance of works of Jewish writers, scholars, and artists in a wide variety of fields. The works of Franz Kafka of PRAGUE, especially *The Trial, The Castle,* and stories like "The Metamorphosis," symbolize perhaps better than any other literary creations the existential dilemma of man in the modern age. Kafka, who died of tuberculosis at 41, owes much of his world fame to the devotion of his friend Max Brod, also a writer of note. During the same period Stefan Zweig was publishing his novels in VIENNA and winning a broad audience, and in Berlin Alfred Doeblin, a medical doctor by profession, was one of the pioneers of expressionistic writing with novels like *Berlin-Alexanderplatz.* Jews were also prominent in other fields of art and culture

Franz Kafka and his fiancee, Felice Bauer, 1917
(Diaspora Museum, Tel-Aviv)

in Central Europe. The paintings of Max Liebermann received wide recognition in Germany and he was even elected president of the Prussian Academy of the Arts. The composer Arnold Schoenberg was recognized as a pioneer of modern music in his own time and Walter Benjamin was recognized after his death as an outstanding literary critic.

The Jews of Central Europe displayed their creativity within the realm of Judaism as well. The outstanding Jewish philosophers were Hermann Cohen, Martin Buber, and Franz Rosenzweig. The last two even took up the challenge which Moses Mendelssohn had undertaken at the outset of the Enlightenment period, and tried their hand at a new and updated German translation of the Bible. What is notable in this period is the cultural flowering of East European Jewry. Alongside the traditional works one can also find more secular efforts. Here Hayyim Nahman Bialik and Shmuel Yosef Agnon, the two giants of modern Hebrew poetry and fiction, began their writing careers. As a scholar Simon Dubnow, who has already been mentioned, met the challenge of producing an overview of Jewish history, with an interpretation differing from his predecessor Graetz's.

The destruction of European Jewry in the Holocaust also brought to an end, to a large extent, this multifaceted cultural world. Einstein, Freud, Zweig, and others managed to leave the European continent before it was too late and continued to produce their work in the West. Others, like Bialik and Agnon as well as Buber, who won world acclaim as a philosopher, turned to Zionism and reached the shores of Palestine, some long before the Nazi threat appeared on the horizon. Some could not bear being torn away from Europe, a state of affairs symbolized by the tragedy of Stefan Zweig, who immigrated to South America and committed suicide there. And some, like Dubnow, were swallowed up in the Nazi death machine, either in the 1930s as political dissenters or in the Holocaust itself.

Looking back at this cultural heritage one cannot help asking to what extent it was Jewish. There is no dispute that the 150 years from the beginning of Jewish integration into European society to the Holocaust have produced Jewish cultural works of enormous value—from the Bible translation of Mendelssohn through the Jewish philosophy and scholarship of the nineteenth century and up to the works of Bialik, Agnon, and Buber in the twentieth century. But it still may be asked: can we regard the work of Einstein, Freud, and

Kafka as Jewish? This is not a simple question. There is no dispute that Einstein, Freud, and Kafka, and many others as well, were not deeply involved in Judaism and did not write for Jews. At the same time, for the Nazis, the physics of Einstein was "Jewish physics" and this was how they saw the psychoanalysis of Freud too. In May 1933, when thousands of books were cast into the flames in the middle of Berlin and the Nazi Minister of Propaganda, Joseph GOEBBELS, declared an "end to the age of sophisticated Jewish intellectualism" no distinction was made between works of a "Jewish" character and "universal" works produced by Jews.

A distinction should nonetheless be made. The work of Einstein, Freud, and Kafka did not in fact stem directly from Judaism and cannot therefore be thought of as Jewish. However, it is hard to think of the enormous Jewish involvement in local culture and its role in shaping it—far beyond the weight of the Jews in the local population—as coincidental. In no way can this be attributed to some kind of biological inheritance; this kind of thinking borders on RACISM. On the other hand,

there is much to be said for the argument that certain foundations of the Jewish heritage, such as the impulse to study and know the Bible, served as an excellent starting point for scholarly and artistic pursuits in the modern world. The unique position of the Jews in Europe during this period—denied complete acceptance as they were by broad sectors of the population—served on the one hand to spur them to greater efforts to win a place in the inhospitable culture, and on the other kept them outside the more conservative establishments. It would seem that this produced a unique blend of the creative impulse and the intellectual openness that fed it.

European Jewry was nearly destroyed in the Holocaust and with it part of its cultural heritage, never to return. At the same time, there is hardly an area of contemporary Jewish life that is not influenced by this cultural heritage. This is also true in the world at large, where Jewish scientific and cultural creativity continues to make itself felt in many fields, based on the foundations left behind by the Jews of Europe.

THE JEWS OF EUROPE BETWEEN THE TWO WORLD WARS

Shmuel Spector

The First World War changed the geopolitical map of Europe. The three great empires—Russia, GERMANY, and Austria-Hungary—were dismantled. Russia lost large parts of its western territory, from the Arctic Ocean in the north down to BUKOVINA and BESSARABIA in the south. These regions saw the creation of a number of buffer states, namely FINLAND and the Baltic republics (ESTONIA, LATVIA, LITHUANIA, and POLAND), while Bukovina and Bessarabia became part of ROMANIA. All this was the direct result of the Bolshevik Revolution erupting in Russia in October 1917, at the end of World War I, and the violent civil war that followed it, completing the total destruction of the state, especially from an economic standpoint. A Communist dictatorship arose and the name of the country was changed; hereafter it was to be the Union of Soviet Socialist Republics—or, for short, the SOVIET UNION.

As for Germany, the borders of the empire were shortened, the army was cut back in size, and the French sent an army of occupation to the important industrial region on the Rhine River (the Rhineland). The Germans were also made to pay a large fine for damages and losses incurred during the war, imperial rule was eliminated, and in its stead the Weimar Republic was created.

The Austro-Hungarian Empire ceased to exist altogether. In HUNGARY there was a short-lived Communist takeover and afterwards Miklos HORTHY established himself on the throne as regent. YUGOSLOVIA was created in the Balkans; Czechoslovakia in the northern part of the Austro-Hungarian Empire, including the Czech and Slovak districts and the TRANSCARPATHIAN UKRAINE; and in the reduced area of AUSTRIA a republic was set up.

All these new states, with the exception of the Soviet Union, were founded as democratic republics. Democratic principles were generally honored in their constitutions, but due to the absence of democratic traditions, the practice of democracy left much to be desired. Usually a large number of political parties formed the government, continually splitting apart and realigning themselves, so that it was often impossible to get stable rule and pass vital laws in parliament. The political instability in these young countries left its mark on their citizens.

The Treaty of Paris, signed on the conclusion of WWI, guaranteed the rights of national minorities through appropriate clauses in the constitutions of the new countries. But the same unstable political situation in these countries, and their own national aspirations, kept these terms from being implemented, so that they mostly existed only on paper.

The three great European empires were not only broken up politically, they were also devastated economically. The worst off was Russia, where in addition to fighting the world war, the country had to deal with a civil war in 1917–1920 that wiped out nearly the entire economy. Germany, which was the most highly developed of the three, had to pay a huge fine to the victors. The Austro-Hungarian Empire was carved into a number of states, which also affected the economy negatively.

Subsequently, in the second half of the 1920s and in the early 1930s severe economic crises afflicted Europe as a whole, but especially the new states and Germany. Runaway inflation, accompanied by mass unemployment, cutbacks in production, and soaring prices, struck hard at large segments of the population. Many were on the verge of starvation. This led to widespread social unrest and influenced domestic policy in various countries. Radical political parties, mostly on the right, exploiting the public's distress, launched unrestrained propaganda campaigns and succeeded in broadening their base of voters. They proposed curing the sick economies of their countries through strong leadership—dictatorships based on single-party rule in place of multi-party parliamentary democracy. To persuade the people they used various means, among them ANTISEMITISM. The Jews were accused of bringing on the economic crisis in order to rule the world (in the style of the PROTOCOLS OF THE ELDERS OF ZION). The outstanding example was the National Socialist (Nazi) Party in Germany.

There were about 10 million Jews in Europe between the world wars, over half of them in Poland and the Soviet Union. The process of urbanization continued at a quick pace, involving in particular an exodus from small towns and settlements to big cities with populations of 100,000 and up. Natural increase among the Jews declined as a result of the living conditions in these cities. In Eastern Europe, Jews continued to engage mainly in trade and crafts but the educated class also expanded, despite the many obstacles placed in the way of Jewish students in various countries (such as Poland). Countries like Poland, Romania, Hungary, and the Baltic States drastically limited the number of Jews in the public sector. In the Soviet Union, on the other hand, where private enterprise was banned, the number of Jews attracted to the public service was large and the process of academization was also stepped up.

While Jewish political activity in the Soviet Union was banned, in other countries it flourished, with numerous movements operating among the Jews. Many Jews, especially in the West, also belonged to the general liberal and socialist parties. The Jewish parties fell into three categories: Zionist, socialist, and religious. The parties competed vigorously during elections for community leadership, for seats on city councils, and for places in parliament.

The process of secularization in the Jewish educational system in Western Europe began after the Emancipation in the middle of the nineteenth century (when Jews were given equal rights in many areas), while in Eastern Europe it began in the early twentieth century. The process intensified and broadened in the period between the wars. In Poland tens of thousands of children attended Jewish schools where the language of instruction was Hebrew, with a minority being taught in Yiddish and Polish. In the Soviet Union a large number of the Jewish schools used only Yiddish as the language of instruction. Their contribution to Jewish culture was minimal, however, because the language was only a means while the curriculum was in the Soviet spirit.

The Soviet Union. Jews in the Russian Empire had suffered discrimination in every area of life. They were restricted as to where they could live, meaning that they could only live in a single geographic area—the Pale of Settlement in western Russia. They could not live in villages or in big cities and were thus crowded into towns where they sometimes made up a majority of the population. Thus was born the *shtetl* (a small community with a large Jewish minority or a Jewish majority) with its popular image. The exclusion of Jews from the civil service and restrictions in high school and higher education forced the Jews to engage mainly in trade and crafts. Confinement to the Pale of Settlement, however, began to give way in WWI,

when the czar was forced to allow large numbers of Jews who had been expelled from frontline areas to settle in the interior of the country. All restrictions were formally canceled during the February 1917 Revolution. Subsequently, after the October Revolution of 1917 and the civil war that followed, numerous changes, both for better and for worse, occurred in the lives of the Jews.

The negative changes involved the restriction of Jewish national life through the cancellation of recognized communities and the nationalization of their institutions (hospitals, old age homes, orphanages, etc.). Jewish political parties, Zionist and religious, were also done away with. Some of the Zionist YOUTH MOVEMENTS like *He-Halutz* and *Ha-Shomer ha-Tsa'ir* continued to operate secretly until the second half of the 1920s, when many of their members were arrested and exiled. The BUND, some of whose members founded the Communist *Bund* (*Kombund*), attached itself to the Communist Party. *Kombund* activists operated in the *Yevsektsiya* (the Jewish section of the Communist Party) and *Ozet* (the Society for the Promotion of Jewish Settlement). During the purges of the mid-1930s many were arrested and some executed.

The war against religion, as such declared by the Communist Party, seriously affected the Jewish religion. *Yevsektsiya* officials conducted anti-religious campaigns among the Jews, closing synagogues and converting them into clubrooms and warehouses or tearing them down. Rabbis and other religious officials were left without a means of livelihood, declared part of the hated middle class, and stripped of civil rights.

Private enterprise in trade and crafts was liquidated. During the period of the New Economic Policy (NEP) small trade was allowed, but when the NEP was canceled in the late 1920s high taxes were imposed upon shopkeepers and artisans were forced to join producer cooperatives under total government control. Those providing services were placed under city government control. In the second half of the 1920s merchants, self-employed artisans, and religious officials, labeled middle class, were denied rights like free education for their children, state medical assistance, and the right to vote. This affected a large portion of the Jewish population, which would have collapsed entirely if not for the aid extended from abroad. In their distress the Jews turned to new occupations: in the civil service, in commercial services, and in farming. New agricultural colonies were established in the UKRAINE, Crimea, BE-LORUSSIA, and Birobidzhan. New and older colonies served as a basis for the creation of self-ruling Jewish regions in the Ukraine: Kalinindorf in March 1927, Nai-Zlatopol in July 1929, and Stalindorf in 1930. Two such regions were established in Crimea: Fraidorf in October 1930 and Larindorf in 1935. These regions continued to exist until the beginning of the HOLOCAUST period but according to the January 1939 census, the Jews were already a minority there. In Kalinindorf, for example, the Jews numbered 7,717 out of a total 19,480 and in Larindorf the Jews comprised only a third of the population. Aside from colonies, *kolkhozes* (collective farms) were also set up in the towns and next to the cities in these regions. The number of Jews engaged in agriculture in the Soviet Union at the time reached 10 percent.

The demographic distribution of the Jews in the Soviet Union underwent a change between the world wars. From concentration in the Pale of Settlement, which ended after the February 1917 Revolution, they dispersed into the interior of the country and increasingly moved from the towns to the big cities and new industrial regions.

According to the January 1939 census, the number of Jews in the entire Soviet Union was 3,280,538, or 1.8 percent of the total population. About two-thirds lived in the Ukraine and Belorussia. Over a third lived in large cities: 303,433 lived in Moscow, 224,336 in Kiev, 219,553 in Leningrad, 200,931 in ODESSA, and 130,230 in Kharkov.

The lifting of all legal restrictions against the Jews resulted, as in the West, in the onset of a process of assimilation, particularly in language. The January 1939 census still shows a high percentage of Jews declaring Yiddish to be their mother tongue in the former Pale of Settlement. In the Vinnitsa district, for example, the figure was 70 percent. Linguistic assimilation was marked in the big cities, where 40 percent and less declared Yiddish to be their mother tongue. In new settlement areas in the eastern provinces the percentage was around 25 percent.

The end of restrictions in institutes of higher learning accelerated the process of academization among the Jews. By the second half of the 1930s Jews were to be found in various academic fields in percentages much higher than their share in the population. According to the January 1939 figures, Jewish representation in selected fields was as follows:

Profession/Area	Ukraine	Belorussia	Russia (RSFSR)
Doctors	47%	51%	20%
Dentists	72%	54%	34%
Pharmacists	55%	65%	18%
Technicians	18%	20%	5%
Lecturers and research workers in universities	29%	33%	14%

In traditional occupations, Jewish representation remained high:

Profession/Area	Ukraine	Belorussia	Russia (RSFSR)
Tailors	28%	54.5%	less than 1%
Shoemakers	16%	43%	2%

In state commerce Jews were also well represented: 33 percent in the Ukraine, 45 percent in Belorussia, and five percent in Russia.

Jewish schools at various levels were opened in many settlements. The language of instruction was Yiddish and in order to distance it from the Hebrew language, Hebrew words were transliterated phonetically according to Yiddish usage and Hebrew final letters were done away with. Most of the schools had up to seven grades but the cities also had high schools, trade schools, and teachers' seminaries. There were also institutes and chairs for Yiddish language and culture at the universities of Minsk, Moscow, Kiev, and others. In the Soviet Ukraine the number of Jewish schools in 1927 was 392, including 1,536 teachers and 61,222 students. Until the early 1930s departments of Jewish education were attached to the minorities section of the *Commissariat* (department) of Education of the U-kraine and Belorussia. Given their limited budgets and the overall economic situation in the country, it would seem that these Jewish departments had to struggle to survive in the face of a perpetual shortage of teachers, textbooks, and facilities. The curriculum was in the Soviet spirit, ruling out anything connected with religious or Jewish national education, so that neither the Bible nor Jewish history was taught. The Jewish authors selected for study were those who described the hard times of the Jews in the Pale of Settlement, such as Mendele Mokher Seforim and Shalom Aleichem. In the 1930s both the authorities and parents exerted pressure, concerned that the children would not qualify for higher education, and the number of Jewish schools declined. After WORLD WAR II and the liquidation of Jewish culture, not a single Jewish school remained in the Soviet Union.

Until the late 1920s the Yiddish language had a semi-official status wherever there were large concentrations of Jews. In towns with a Jewish majority the local council, law courts, and militia offices all conducted their business in Yiddish. In big cities like Kharkov or Zhitomir militia offices in Jewish neighborhoods also used Yiddish. This was done because *Yevsektsiya* officials claimed that the Jews were not yet fluent in the national languages and that Yiddish was their primary language. All this ended in the early 1930s.

Newspapers and periodicals also appeared in Yiddish. The most important among them were *Der Emes* in Moscow, *Der Shtern* in Kiev, and *Der Shtern* in MINSK. Until the late 1920s there were still remnants of Yiddish culture to be found in these and other publications. Among the leading Yiddish writers were Peretz Markish, Itzik Fefer, Leib Kvitko, David Hofstein, and Der Nister (Pinhas Kaganovich). From the early 1930s the Jewish newspapers and periodicals became merely Yiddish translations of the major Soviet party organs. Little remained of Jewish culture and what little there was, was infused with the Soviet spirit.

The last cultural artifact of Yiddish was the theater. In addition to the regional theaters and traveling ensembles, the national theater of Shlomo Michoels in Moscow should be mentioned, which because of his talent became a major institution in the Soviet Union and appeared throughout the country. The Ukrainian Jewish National Theater, founded in Kharkov and later moving to Kiev, is also worthy of note. The problem with all the theaters and troupes was one of repertoire, which was obligated to reflect so-called socialist realism. In the beginning Goldfaden, Mendele Mokher Seforim, Shalom Aleichem, Y. L. Peretz, and translations from other languages were presented. Subsequently, following criticism mainly of the ideological content of the plays, the number of classics was pared down and writers were encouraged to produce plays in the spirit of socialist realism.

Like all residents of the Soviet Union, the Jews suffered from two phenomena: collectivization and the Stalinist purges. The first began in the late 1920s and forced farmers to join collectives (large state-owned farms comprised of formerly smaller individually-owned farms). The wealthy and the resistant among them were labeled enemies of the state and exiled or executed. Since most Jewish farm settlements were new they lacked a wealthy class and therefore suffered less. The purges struck at the heads of the *Yevsektsiya,* senior party officials, and senior army officers, among them Yan Gamarnik, the writer Hayyim Nahman Bialik's brother-in-law.

After the annexation of eastern Poland to the Soviet Union in September 1939, another 1.5 million Jews were added to the population of the Soviet Union, bringing the total up to about five million.

Poland. The end of WWI saw the reconstitution of Poland after its division for over 100 years between Russia, Germany, and Austria. After its final borders were fixed, fully a third of its population turned out to consist of big national minorities: Ukrainians, Belorussians, Jews, and Germans. The Treaty of Versailles of April 1919 and an additional treaty signed there guaranteed full civil and political rights to national minor-

Members of the Jewish socialist Bund protesting Nazi discrimination of German Jews

ities along with cultural and religious freedoms, including state-supported schools.

The liberation of Poland was accompanied by a wave of pogroms against the Jews. In the eastern districts, where General Haller's army passed through, the Jews were murdered, robbed, and abused. In a pogrom in LVOV in late 1918, 72 Jews were killed and about 300 injured. In all, pogroms were staged in over 100 localities in November–December 1918 and in 52 places in 1919, with a total of about 200 Jews killed. The Paris Peace Conference dispatched a commission of investigation and through foreign pressure the disturbances ceased.

The Polish Constitution of 1921 as well as of 1935 guaranteed equal rights and cultural freedom to the minorities, but all this existed only on paper. In the elections to the Polish Parliament (*Sejm*) of 1919, 11 Jewish representatives were elected and duly formed a Jewish bloc. These representatives were treated with hostility by representatives of both the right-wing and socialist parties. A democratic constitution, as stated, was indeed adopted in 1921, but its implementation was made dependent on further legislation. Those laws that were intended to bolster minority rights were never passed; on the contrary, laws were passed restricting minority rights. In the matter of elections, especially in areas where Poles were a minority (the eastern borderlands), the non-Jewish voter base was swelled by geographic manipulation, by attaching rural districts to towns and cities. In the matter of civil law as it was to be applied to hundreds of thousands of Jews, deliberations were stretched out for years, allowing local authorities to act randomly, often according to laws dating back to the days of the czar. The Sabbath Law was manipulated to force Jews to close their businesses twice a week, on both the Jewish and Christian Sabbath (Saturday and Sunday), and in this way to undermine their livelihoods. In the 1922 elections, 35 Jews were elected to the *Sejm* and 12 to the Senate—the largest number of Jewish representatives between the wars. The *Sejm* continued to discuss the removal of czarist discriminatory laws, but without completing its deliberations; it also discussed restriction of the number of Jews in institutes of education and would have acted, if not for the intervention of the president of FRANCE. Another law that discriminated against the Jews made tobacco production a state monopoly, nationalizing the factories where about 6,000 Jews were employed, all of whom were dismissed within a few years.

In 1924 Wladislaw Grabski took office as finance minister, stabilizing the currency but also raising taxes, the burden of which fell mainly on the Jews, many of whom went bankrupt. Jews with a little property sought to emigrate and many reached Palestine ("the Gbarski exodus"). However, because of the difficult conditions in Palestine and the unsuitability of the newcomers, about half returned to Poland within a short time. With inflation setting in at the end of 1925 and the government changing hands with increasing rapidity, Marshal Jozef Pilsudski staged a coup and took control of affairs in mid-May 1926. His stand-in, Prime Minister Bartel, published a declaration sympathetic to the Jews but after about a year and a half, Jewish policy began to change. Pilsudski's Sanatia Party gradually became antisemitic, especially after the marshal's death in 1935. At that time the group of colonels who surrounded him founded the OZON (National Unity) Party. Government support for the "Polonization" of trade and crafts increased through credit facilities and other benefits given to Poles while nationalist and antisemitic circles worked to boycott Jewish businesses.

The rise of Nazism in Germany and the signing of the agreement between Germany and Poland in 1936 intensified antisemitism. This time anti-Jewish riots erupted in Minsk-Mezowiecki, Brest-Litovsk, Przytyk, and other places, claiming Jewish victims and resulting in the destruction and pillaging of much Jewish property. The government's stand was expressed in the words of Prime Minister Slavoi-Skladkovski: "It is not permissible to beat up the Jews, but boycotting them is fine." Attacks on Jewish students at the universities increased, forcing them into a kind of ghetto—all this with the blessing of university authorities. The law against ritual slaughter, legislated for supposed humanitarian reasons, affected mainly Jewish butchers. Finally, the law depriving people who had spent extended time abroad of their citizenship was exploited by the Nazis to expel thousands of Jewish citizens of Poland from Germany. The Poles would not let them in and in the fall of 1938 they were forced to camp along the border waiting for some country to give them refuge.

As mentioned, every third citizen in the Polish state was not a Pole and in the eastern borderlands the Poles were a minority. The country's rulers and the nationalist parties were interested in assimilating the non-Polish areas and did this through economic pressure, discrimination in education, etc. The process of "Polonization" struck hard particularly at Jewish livelihoods.

Jews in Warsaw before the war

According to the 1931 census (the last in Poland before WWII) there were 3,137,000 Jews in the country, representing 9.8 percent of the population. About 10 percent (352,659) lived in WARSAW, the capital; 202,497 lived in LODZ; 99,595 in Lvov; 58,611 in VILNA (in 1937); and 56,515 in CRACOW. Most lived in towns, sometimes making up a majority of the population, while only four percent lived in villages. Natural increase was about 0.9 percent, less than in the non-Jewish population. The rate of emigration dropped off in the 1930s. Between 1927 and 1937, about 400,000 Jews emigrated.

In the beginning of the 1930s about a third of the Jews of Poland worked in trade, a third in crafts and industry, nearly 10 percent in agriculture, over four percent in the professions, about five percent in domestic services, and over seven percent were unemployed. This picture was not much different from the one that had prevailed at the turn of the nineteenth century. Jewish craftsmen were mainly artisans working alone and barely eking out a living, especially during the years of economic crisis. They required financial assistance to purchase raw materials and were in fact helped by loan and charity funds. The number employed in industry was smaller than in crafts, most of them being factory hands, mainly in the textile centers of Lodz and BIALYSTOK. Their wages were low and during economic crises there were large-scale layoffs and many were on the brink of starvation. On the other hand, Jewish industrialists were dominant in a number of fields: paper (85 percent), chemicals (70 percent), and fine metals (69 percent). In trade most of the Jews were shopkeepers and peddlers, of limited income, and also in need of cheap or interest-free loans to replenish their stocks. Nearly 60 percent of the commerce in Poland was in Jewish hands and in many towns, especially in the eastern borderlands, the percentage was even higher. In central and eastern Poland, where most of the Jews lived, Jewish doctors comprised 35 percent of the total and Jewish lawyers over half. Economic activity was aided and supported by a Jewish financial system including hundreds of charity funds set up by local Jews and helped at first by *Landsmannschaft* organizations in the UNITED STATES (Polish Jews who had moved to the US and grouped themselves according to city or town of origin), and by hundreds of mutual aid funds set up by officials in merchant and artisan associations. Most were officially recognized by the Cooperative Center in Warsaw and assisted by the American Jewish JOINT DISTRIBUTION COMMITTEE (the Joint). The funds provided loans at low interest and on easy payment terms. Wealthy industrialists and merchants were assisted by private banks and by the state bank.

As a result of the dismantling of the Russian Empire and the liquidation of Jewish national life in the Soviet Union, Poland became the leading center of Jewish life after WWI.

What was most striking there was the development of a Jewish national educational system, mostly secular and modern, which served tens of thousands of children from kindergarten up through elementary school, secondary school, and teachers' seminaries, and culminating in the Institute of Judaic Sciences in Warsaw. In accordance with the Treaty of Versailles (June 1919), the new Polish government was committed to supporting Jewish schools, but in fact did nothing of the sort. Jewish educational institutes had to fight to survive. While state education was free, Jewish parents had to cover 70 percent of Jewish school costs from out of their own pockets. Part of the balance was covered by the Joint, the Jewish community, and the municipalities, leaving about 20 percent as a deficit. The payment of tuition was a great burden on the parents, most of whom were living under difficult economic circumstances. From the mid-1930s the Polish authorities made things even harder on Jewish secondary schools by revoking state benefits. A graduate of a Jewish secondary school could no longer gain admission to a Polish institute of higher learning and had to attend a university abroad.

In the 1934–1935 school year, 425,566 Jewish children were attending school, about 82,000 (19 percent) in the Jewish educational system. This system was divided into a number of school networks characterized by language of instruction and the political movement that had founded them. Two networks used Hebrew as the language of instruction: *Tarbut* (the Zionist Organization) and *Yavne* (religious Zionist). These operated 77 kindergartens, 335 elementary schools, 12 secondary schools, six teachers' seminaries, and an agricultural high school. The Yiddish-language school networks included the CYSHO (the *Bund*), the *Shulkult* (rightist *Po'alei Zion*), and *Horev* (*Agudat Israel*). The CYSHO and *Shulkult* organizations ran 17 kindergartens, 93 elementary schools, and two secondary schools (belonging to the CYSHO). They also operated two teachers' seminaries for a while. The *Horev* system included 649 educational institutions, nearly all at the primary school level—for boys, for girls (Beth Jacob), *heders*, *talmud torah* Hebrew school programs, and small *yeshivas*. The bilingual system (Polish and Hebrew) included 41 institutions: 18 elementary schools, 21 secondary schools, and two trade schools. In addition, ORT and the ICA (Jewish Colonization Agency) operated trade schools and classes for boys and girls. At the top of the pyramid stood the Institute of Judaic Sciences in Warsaw, whose students were required simultaneously to take a course of humanistic studies at Warsaw University. The Institute turned out rabbis with a general educational background but mainly produced teachers for Jewish secondary schools. Outstanding teachers lectured there, like Meir Balaban, Moses Schorr, Yitzhak Schiffer, etc. Among the graduates were future scholars in the field of Jewish studies.

Jewish journalism was also a highly active field in Poland. Dozens of newspapers and periodicals appeared in Warsaw and in provincial cities like Vilna, Lvov, Bialystok, Grodno, Pinsk, and Rovno. The three major newspapers were *Haynt* (with a circulation of 100,000), *Moment* (60,000), and the Polish-language *Nasz Przeglad* (50,000). Also noteworthy were the Hebrew daily *Ha-Zefira* and the Hebrew literary journal *Ha-Tekufa*.

Jews were also very active in literature, publishing extensively in the periodicals. The well-known poets include Uri Zvi Greenberg, Yaakov Kohen, Jacob Fich-

Street scene in a pre-war Jewish neighborhood, Warsaw

mann, and Yizhak Lamdan. Other writers include Nahum Sokolow, Sholem Asch, Alter Katzizne, Hillel Zeitlin, Yehoshua Perle, and Nobel Prize winner Isaac Bashevis-Singer. Those writing in Polish include the poet Julian Tuwim, Bruno Schulz, and the children's writer and great educator Dr. Henryk Goldszmit (Janusz KORCZAK). All Jewish writers belonged to the Jewish Writers and Journalists Association of Poland. Within its walls, poets, novelists, and journalists with different outlooks on life and representing different political parties and movements were brought together.

Six Jewish theater companies operated between the wars, most of them in Warsaw. Dozens of amateur groups could be found in the provincial towns and cities. The best-known professional groups were the Vilna Troupe, which started operating in Warsaw in 1917; the Vikt Theater, managed by Esther Rachel Kaminska and featuring her daughter Ida Kaminska, Zygmunt Turkow, and Y. Godik; and the Ararat satirical theater in Lodz, founded by Moshe Broderzon and touring the big towns and cities of Poland to appear before Jewish audiences.

All the Jewish political parties and movements were active in Poland, while Jews also belonged to Poland's left-wing parties. The leading Zionist parties were the General Zionists, *Po'alei Zion, Hitahdut*, the Revisionists, *Mizrachi*, and the youth movements—*Ha-Shomer ha-Tsa'ir, Dror, Ha-No'ar ha-Tsiyyoni, Betar, Gordonia*, and *He-Halutz*. The *Bund* gained strength in the 1930s and *Agudat Israel* was supported by Orthodox circles. Among the welfare agencies were TOZ, the health organization for needy children, CENTOS for orphans, ORT for vocational training, and the ICA aiding Jewish farmers.

Germany. The defeat of Germany in WWI had as its result the dismantling of the German Empire. The emperor (*Kaiser*) was dethroned and the Weimar Republic was created. During this period stark contradictions emerged in Jewish life. On the one hand, Jews made unprecedented strides and were integrated into many areas of German life. On the other hand, political anti-semitism intensified. The latter phenomenon expressed itself in the platforms and propaganda campaigns of the right-wing parties and organizations, the most radical of which was the National Socialist Party (NAZI PARTY).

Jewish achievements were many and varied. Among the outstanding figures were Max Reinhardt in theater, Max Liebermann in art, Arnold Schoenberg in music, and Albert EINSTEIN in science. By 1938 Jews had been awarded nine Nobel Prizes (a quarter of the total for Germany).

Jews were also prominent in German politics. Hugo Heze and Gustav Landauer were members of the first postwar German government and Jews like Rosa Luxemburg were among the leaders of the left-wing parties. The outstanding personality among them was Walter Rathenau, who served as Germany's foreign minister and was murdered in 1922 by right-wing extremists. In the early 1920s Jews were blamed for Germany's defeat in the war. It was argued that they had "stabbed the country in the back" (see also STAB IN THE BACK MYTH). Jewish apologetics, citing the number of Jewish soldiers in the emperor's army, the number of Jewish dead, and their heroism, did little good.

The economic crises and soaring inflation of 1922 and 1923 served to provoke anti-Jewish agitation even more. The most extreme of the right-wing parties, the Nazis, featured in their political platform a call for the nullification of Jewish civil rights and removal of the Jews from economic, social, and cultural life, peaking in their expulsion from the country.

According to the 1925 census there were 564,379 Jews in Germany, constituting 0.9 percent of the total population. About half of them lived in the six big cities: 180,000 in Berlin and 90,000 in FRANKFURT, HAMBURG, Breslau, Leipzig, and Cologne. Most worked in trade or belonged to the professional class. The integration of Jews in different areas of German life quickened assimilation and religious conversion. In 1927, 54 percent of Jewish marriages were mixed and about 1,000 Jews left Judaism.

During the Weimar period Jewish political, social, and religious organizations continued to develop. The leading organizations were the *Centralverein* (CENTRAL UNION OF GERMAN CITIZENS OF JEWISH BELIEF), the Zionist Organization, the Union of Orthodox Jews, and the HILFSVEREIN DER DEUTSCHEN JUDEN (Aid Association of German Jews), to which were added such new organizations as the *Reichsbund Juedischer Frontsoldaten* (REICH UNION OF JEWISH FRONTLINE SOLDIERS), the Zionist youth movements, which covered the entire political spectrum, youth and sports clubs, and student associations. Immigrant communities began to organize societies on the basis of country of origin (*Laender*). Germany also became one of the centers of Jewish scholarship and culture. The two rabbinical seminaries in Berlin and Breslau continued to operate. Franz Rosenzweig and Martin Buber worked to involve large segments of the adult Jewish population in Jewish studies via the so-called *Lehrhaus*. Jewish publishers were also very active, putting out newspapers and periodicals as well as two encyclopedias: the Jewish Lexicon and the Encyclopedia Judaica.

The Great Depression of 1929–1932 hit Germany hard and led among other things to the strengthening of the Nazi Party, which increased its share of the vote from three percent in the 1928 elections to 37 percent in 1932. The economic crisis and antisemitic agitation, accompanied by violence at the hands of the Nazi SA (Storm Troopers), undermined the position of the Jews in Germany and produced an identity crisis.

On January 30, 1933 President Paul von HINDENBURG appointed Adolf HITLER chancellor after a prolonged political and economic crisis. Immediately the Nazi Party and its paramilitary organizations (the SS and the SA) organized a reign of terror against political opponents and began to take over state institutions. Among the targets were many Jews. Various decrees and laws led to the separation of Jews from the general society. The Nazis' idea was to convince the Jews that they had no future in Germany, so that they would leave.

These laws met no opposition in the German public. Many Jews, abruptly awakened from their peaceful existence, began to flee the country in panic, with tens of thousands emigrating in 1933. The removal of the Jews from public life served to intensify the community's inner life. The *Reichsvertretung der Deutschen Juden* (REICH REPRESENTATION OF GERMAN JEWS), founded in May 1933 and headed by Leo BAECK and Otto HIRSCH, became the representative body of German Jewry. The *Centralverein* and the Jewish War Veterans Association wanted to fight for Jewish rights within Germany, while the Zionist movement wished to prepare the public for emigration to Palestine. Thus the Zionist movement also supported the YOUTH ALIYA organization founded by Recha Freier. The *Reichsvertretung* centralized activities relating to education, economic assistance, employment, and emigration.

Antisemitic agitation was stepped up still further in the beginning of 1935. In the summer of 1935 the NUREMBERG LAWS were passed. In late 1936 the seizure of Jewish businesses, or so-called "ARYANIZATION" began. On October 28, 1938 about 17,000 former Jewish citizens of Poland were expelled to the Polish border. On the night between November 9–10, 1938 a mass pogrom was carried out in which hundreds of synagogues and thousands of Jewish places of business were burned or destroyed, scores of Jews were murdered, and about 30,000 were sent to CONCENTRATION CAMPS. This was KRISTALLNACHT. In its wake, over the course of the following year, over 100,000 Jews emigrated from Germany.

Austria. In 1934, some 191,000 Jews were living in the territories that remained part of Austria after WWI, about 176,000 of them in VIENNA, the country's capital. The mainly political antisemitism that had flourished there since the beginning of the century continued undiminished between the world wars, as well.

On March 11, 1938 the Germans took over the country without armed resistance, and within a few days annexed it to the German Reich. Jewish community institutions were shut down and hundreds of community leaders were sent to the DACHAU concentration camp. Jews' homes were pillaged, valuables and art collections seized. By the end of March Jews were dismissed from public service and from the universities, and in June they were expelled from the private sector as well. Jewish businesses were "Aryanized," being sold to non-Jews for a fraction of their value with the proceeds seized as fines.

In May 1938 Adolf EICHMANN arrived in Vienna and instituted a reign of terror against the Jews. In August he opened the Central Office for Jewish Emigration (ZENTRALSTELLE FUER JUEDISCHE AUSWANDERUNG), and through intimidation and force and with Jewish funds made large numbers of Jews leave the country. Until war broke out, roughly 126,500 Jews emigrated, and by November 1941 another 2,000 had left the country. Emigration was then halted.

Latvia. In November 1918 the Latvians, previously part of the Russian Empire, declared their independence. The young republic was faced with serious economic problems, mainly as a result of being cut off from its Russian market, and with cultural problems as well, stemming from the existence of a number of large minorities (such as Russians, who made up 12 percent of the population). There were also political problems resulting from the huge number of political parties—until Victor Ulmanis seized power in 1934 and put an end to the party system, replacing it with an authoritarian regime. In September 1939 the Soviets took over the country. At first they only established military bases there, but in June 1940 they turned it into a Soviet Socialist Republic and made it part of the Soviet Union.

In 1920 the Jewish population of Latvia was about 80,000 (about five percent of the total population). About half the Jews lived in RIGA, the country's capital. In accordance with the guarantee of cultural freedom, a Jewish educational system with Hebrew and Yiddish as the languages of instruction was set up at state expense. The state also financed religious and welfare services. Over 80 percent of Jewish children attended Jewish schools. In addition, Jewish newspapers appeared and Jewish political parties represented the Jewish voters in parliament.

In 1934 Ulmanis abolished cultural freedom, liquidated the political parties, and nationalized banks and factories belonging to Jews as well as to others. Between the world wars, 5,000 Jews immigrated to Palestine. With the annexation of Latvia to the Soviet Union, Jewish life came to an end, with about 5,000 Jews exiled to Siberia. When the Germans overran Latvia in June 1941, there were about 70,000 Jews in the country.

Lithuania. Founded in February 1918, independent Lithuania was committed to granting cultural freedom also to the Jews. In March 1939 it was forced to give up the port city of MEMEL to the Germans and in October 1939 it was given its ancient capital of Vilna (and the surrounding area) by the Soviet Union. In June 1940 the Soviets took over the country and incorporated it into the Soviet Union as a Soviet Socialist Republic.

In the early years of Lithuanian independence Lithuanian Jews enjoyed cultural autonomy, with a Jewish minister looking after their affairs. They developed a Jewish educational system in Hebrew and Yiddish, mostly Zionist in character and encompassing most Jewish children. In 1924 Jewish autonomy was revoked, but the educational system continued to operate. Meanwhile the government pushed the Jews out of various sectors of the economy and antisemitism increased, mainly in the second half of the 1930s. About 20,000 Jews emigrated between the world wars, half of them to Palestine. At the time the republic was founded the Jewish population of Lithuania was 150,000. In the early 1920s many previously expelled Jews returned to the country and after the annexation of the Vilna area and the arrival of numerous REFUGEES from Poland, the number of Jews rose to 250,000. In 1940–1941 the Soviets expelled thousands of Jews and on the outbreak of war between the Soviet Union and Germany in June 1941 another few thousand managed to flee to the east.

Hungary. At the end of WWI the Hapsburg (Austro-Hungarian) Empire was dismantled. In accordance with the Treaty of Trianon, two-thirds of Hungary's territory was handed over to others. Northern TRANSYLVANIA was given to Romania; BACKA (Delvidek) to Yugoslavia; TRANSCARPATHIAN UKRAINE and a strip of southern SLOVAKIA (Felvidek) to Czechoslovakia; and part of Burgenland to Austria. These territories included three million Hungarians out of a population of 11 million. In March–August 1919 a Soviet republic under Bela Kun took control of Hungary, but it was overthrown by the White Army of Admiral Miklos Horthy, who declared himself regent of Hungary. For economic and political reasons close ties were established between Hungary and Germany, which became stronger in the 1930s. These ties benefited Hungary, which got back its lost territories with German help: the Felvidek in November 1938, Transcarpathian Ukraine in May 1939, northern Transylvania in August 1940, and Delvidek (Backa) in April 1941.

In WWI about 10,000 Jews died fighting in the Hungarian army. This did not prevent the murder of about 3,000 Jews in the White Terror that followed the suppression of the Soviet republic in 1919. According to the 1930 census, 445,000 Jews were living in the pared down Hungarian State. Their general tendency was toward assimilation, despite official antisemitism. Already in 1920 the *numerus clausus* restriction was applied to the admission of Jewish students to institutes of higher education. Under German influence, Hungarian newspapers called for restrictions on Jews in different areas of life. In 1938 the first anti-Jewish law was passed, limiting the number of Jews in commercial, industrial, and professional occupations to 20 percent. In May 1939 the figure became six percent and

in 1941 legislation resembling the Nuremberg Laws was passed. In 1939–1940 a system of substitute labor was instituted for young Jews in place of army service. In June 1941 Hungary joined Germany in its attack on the Soviet Union. It sent an army to the Ukrainian front, accompanied by a large number of Jewish labor brigades. The brutality of Hungarian officers, lack of food and clothing, the hard work, which included clearing minefields by hand, substandard living quarters, and the harsh winter all contributed to the toll of 42,000 Jewish dead there by the end of the war.

Including the Jews in the returned territories, the Jewish population of Hungary in 1941 was 725,000 (not including Jews by a Nazi racial definition). About 18,000 Jews were expelled, based on the excuse that they were not Hungarian citizens, most to the KAMENETS-PODOLSKI Ghetto in the Ukraine, where most were murdered together with the local Jews. Another 1,000 were murdered in the Delvidek area.

Until Germany occupied Hungary in March 1944, the Hungarian government was able to sidestep the German demand that it implement the FINAL SOLUTION on its territory. The German occupation brought Adolf Eichmann and his people to Hungary and with him the concentration of Jews in GHETTOS and their DEPORTATION to the EXTERMINATION CAMPS.

Romania. Following WWI, Romania annexed Transylvania, Bukovina, and Bessarabia. This increased the minority population to one-third of the total and produced claims for the return of these territories to their former occupiers. About 80 percent of the country's population was rural. The economy was backward and the political situation unstable. Extreme right-wing parties came into existence, among them the IRON GUARD, which was close to the Nazis in Germany. Following the collapse of parliamentary government, King Carol II suspended the constitution, dispersed the political parties, and established a dictatorship. On his orders a number of Iron Guard leaders were executed. An ally of France, Romania saw its situation deteriorate. In late 1939 Bukovina and Bessarabia were annexed by the Soviet Union, in August northern Transylvania was transferred to Hungary, and in September the southern Dobruja district was handed over to BULGARIA. The regime collapsed, King Carol II gave up his throne in favor of his son, Mihai, and entrusted Ion ANTONESCU with the task of forming a government. Antonescu became dictator and the government became Fascist, consisting of Iron Guardists and army officers. German influence increased, with real power in the hands of the German embassy in BUCHAREST. Romanian divisions took part in the German attack on the Soviet Union in June 1941. Romania then got back Bukovina and Bessarabia as well as a strip of the southwestern U-kraine, which it called TRANSNISTRIA, with its capital at Odessa.

In 1930 the Jewish population of Romania was about 760,000 (4.2 percent of the total). The terms of the Treaty of Versailles intended to guarantee equal rights to minorities were never implemented, while increasing nationalization undermined Jewish econom-ic life. The *numerus clausus* restriction was instituted at the universities and Jews were excluded from various professions, including the civil service. The Jewish party sitting in parliament tried to fight discrimination but had little success.

The Jews developed an independent educational system and Jewish writing in Hebrew, Yiddish, and Romanian flourished. The Zionist movement attracted large numbers of Jews and many of the young be-longed to the Zionist youth movements and under-went pioneer training. In 1937, during the 40 days of the antisemitic GOGA-CUZA government, legislation was introduced to strip Jews of their citizenship and im-plement antisemitic principles. Under the dictatorship of Carol II the situation grew worse. The constitution of 1938 included terms that legalized racial discrimi-nation, and the removal of Jews from all areas of economic and social life continued at a fast pace. In 1940 the Romanian army retreating from Bessarabia murdered 200 Jews in Dorohoi and hundreds more in the villages. After Romania was stripped of its terri-tories, 342,000 Jews remained in the now diminished country. The Antonescu government and its "legion-naire" (Iron Guard) cohorts instituted a reign of terror, seizing Jewish businesses and property. A law enacted in October 1940 confiscated all rural Jewish property. It was followed by the seizure of forests, wood-proces-sing plants, distilleries, boats, etc. On January 21–23, 1941 the Iron Guard staged a pogrom against the Jews of Bucharest, killing 127 and looting many homes and stores. By June 1941, when the Soviet Union was invaded, the Antonescu government had passed laws, under German inspiration, enabling it to seize about 41,000 Jewish houses and subject the Jews to FORCED LABOR. On the outbreak of war, about 40,000 Jews were expelled from the towns and villages on the Soviet border, their property was confiscated, some

were sent to concentration camps, others to towns and cities where they became charity cases. The Ro-manians and Germans then perpetrated a bloody slaughter of the Jews of Bessarabia, Bukovina, and Transnistria.

Yugoslavia. Yugoslovia was established in 1918 as a centralized state ruled by a king. It was made up of a number of regions inhabited by Slavic peoples, mostly Serbs and Croats, Serbs being Eastern Orthodox in religion, the Croats Catholic. The conflicting national aspirations and religious differences produced tension and political instability. Political assassinations heated up the atmosphere. Among the victims were the Croa-tian leader Stepjan Radic in 1928 and King Alexander, who had set up a dictatorship, in 1934. After Yugoslavia was forced to align itself with the AXIS powers (Ger-many, ITALY, and Japan) on March 25, 1941, a counter-revolution was staged and on April 6 the Germans invaded the country, marking the end of Yugoslavia as a political entity.

In 1931 the Jewish population of Yugoslavia was 73,000, rising to 80,000 in 1941, including refugees. The Jews were concentrated in the cities: BELGRADE (11,000), Zagreb (11,000), and Sarajevo (10,000). About 18 percent engaged in crafts and 59 percent in commerce and banking, while 12 percent belonged to the professional class. Their economic situation was good, aside from a few impoverished communities in MACEDONIA. The Jewish public was organized in a Fed-eration of Jewish Communities, which represented the Jews before the government. The chief rabbi, Dr. Yitz-hak Alkalay, was a member of the Senate. The Jews maintained a network of organizations dealing with welfare, education, and culture, with Zionist activity at the center of community life. Until the Nazi rise to power in Germany, antisemitism was barely felt in Yugoslavia. It was worsened by German-financed pro-paganda, particularly after the outbreak of war. Under German pressure the government passed a *numerus clausus* restriction and a law prohibiting Jews from sell-ing certain food items. About 50,000 Jewish refugees passed through Yugoslavia, aided by the Jewish organi-zations.

Greece. Modern Greece was founded as a monarchy in 1830. In 1924 the monarchy was abolished, only to be reestablished in 1935. A year later Prime Minister Me-taxas established a dictatorship. In foreign policy he leaned toward GREAT BRITAIN but entered into no agree-ments. In October 1940 the Italians invaded Albania and then struck into Greece, but the Greek army blocked their advance and even occupied some territory in Albania. On April 6, 1941 Hitler came to the assistance of the Italians. At first the Greek army, together with British troops, succeeded in stopping the Germans, but finally it was forced to surrender. The king fled abroad with his government and from 1943 resided in Cairo.

According to the 1928 census the Jewish population of Greece was about 73,000 (1.2 percent of the total) and on the eve of the war rose to about 77,000. About 76 percent of the Jews resided in SALONIKA and about 62,000 Jews declared Ladino (Judeo-Spanish) as their mother tongue, the rest mostly Greek. Their occupational distribution was as follows: salaried laborers 65 percent; artisans and small traders 25 percent; merchants, industrialists, and professional people 10 percent. Living conditions were difficult, especially in Salonika, with over half the Jews struggling under poor economic circumstances.

In 1920 the Greek government approved a set of regulations for the Jewish communities. The chief rabbi of Salonika was recognized as the chief rabbi of Greece. The communities were to be responsible for religion, charity, welfare, and maintenance of Jewish schools.

In 1917 a devastating fire struck the Jews of Salonika, leaving 30,000 homeless and burning down 32 synagogues and other public buildings. In 1931 riots broke out in the Cambell quarter of Salonika. Antisemitism intensified in the 1920s but declined under Prime Minister Metaxas.

In 1925–1940 Zionism and *aliya* to Palestine reached their peak. In elections to the Salonika community council in the 1930s the Zionists reached an absolute majority (70–84 percent). In addition to the Sephardi communities, there were also Romaniots—the original Greek Jews. Their largest communities were in Janina, which numbered 1,970 Greek-speaking Jews in 1928, and in ATHENS, where most of the 3,200 Jews were Romaniots. They engaged in import and export. The period between the world wars saw a flowering of Jewish culture, which found expression in school activities, cultural clubs, and various societies. Most Jewish literature was written in Ladino and five daily Jewish newspapers appeared in Salonika in French.

Italy. The Jews of Italy had attained equality and were well integrated into the country's social and political life.

In the early twentieth century Jews had served as minister of war (Giuseppe Ottolenghi) and prime minister (Luigi Luzzatti). Assimilation was on the rise, intermarriage widespread, and the birthrate in decline. Jews constituted 0.1 percent of the total population. After Fascist leader Benito MUSSOLINI seized power in 1922, Jews were apprehensive that his party would prove to be antisemitic. Mussolini, however, met with the chief rabbi of Rome in 1923 and assured him that neither his government nor the Fascist Party had an antisemitic policy—and as it turned out the Jews and the Fascist regime coexisted peacefully until 1933.

In 1933–1936 Mussolini wavered between declarations sympathetic to the Jews and unofficial antisemitic measures, along with expressions of admiration for Nazi Germany. During this period the legal status of the Jews was unaffected. In the fall of 1938 racial laws were published and in June 1940 anti-Jewish decrees were issued. Mussolini refused to hand over Italian Jews to the Germans, and the Italian occupation authorities in Albania and Yugoslavia gave the Jews refuge. After Pietro BADOGLIO signed the cease-fire agreement with the Allies in September 1943, the Germans overran the country. The Jewish population of Italy at the time, including the island of RHODES, was 44,500. The Germans began rounding up the Jews for deportation to the extermination camps.

The Netherlands. The Jews of the NETHERLANDS enjoyed complete equality and were active in politics and in the Dutch labor movement. In 1940 their population was 140,000, including 15,000 refugees. The latter, along with tens of thousands of Jewish refugees who passed through the country, were aided by a special committee set up by Prof. David COHEN, who raised about a million dollars for the purpose, mostly from local sources. Refugees entering the country illegally were held in the WESTERBORK camp. Refugees also contributed to the Netherlands' economy, mainly in the textile, fashion, and film industries. During the 1930s, under German influence, antisemitism made inroads, its banner raised by the Dutch Nazi Party (see also NATIONAL SOCIALIST MOVEMENT, NETHERLANDS). About 75,000 Jews resided in Amsterdam (53 percent of all the Jews in the Netherlands), their synagogues outstanding in design and beauty.

France. France was among the victors in WWI but at a terrible price. A spirit of pacifism prevailed there, along with no movement demographically and an outdated economy. The country was also politically unstable, with many radical parties, from the Communists on the left to the ACTION FRANCAISE on the right.

The Jews had won Emancipation (equal rights) in the late eighteenth century and since then had become integrated into French society through assimilation and intermarriage. Not even the Dreyfus Trial (in which a Jewish officer was falsely accused of treason) had slowed the process. From the second half of the nineteenth century through the twentieth century, mainly between the world wars, large numbers of Jews had immigrated to France, mostly from Eastern Europe, until they made up half of the 350,000 Jews in France in 1940. Over half the Jews in France did not hold French citizenship. About two-thirds of the Jews lived in PARIS. The native French Jews were organized in *Consistoires,* through which they participated in different areas of Jewish life. The foreign Jews had their own independent cultural and welfare organizations, along with Yiddish newspapers and social clubs. In the second half of the 1930s entry of refugees was restricted and those filtering through were held in detention centers.

Belgium. The Jewish community in BELGIUM grew in the early twentieth century through an inflow of immigrants from Eastern and Central Europe. The Jewish population on the eve of the German invasion was about 66,000, with just 10 percent of them Belgian citizens. They were mainly concentrated in BRUSSELS and ANTWERP. The immigrant non-citizens were organized in independent communities and organizations and spoke Yiddish. Most of the Jewish political parties were active among Belgian Jews, but mainly the socialist parties. In the later period Jews had ties to the Belgian parties as well, and this assumed importance during the German occupation for rescue and resistance.

Other countries. Apart from the above countries there

Members of the religious Zionist youth movement Bnei Akiva, Belgium

were small concentrations of Jews in the following places: DENMARK—about 6,000, mostly in Copenhagen, the capital. They enjoyed full equality and were prominent in science, literature, and the arts. The rate of assimilation and intermarriage was high. After Hitler came to power in Germany, about 2,000 refugees reached Denmark (bringing the Jewish population to 8,000.) NORWAY—1,700 in 1940, mainly in Oslo and Trondheim. They enjoyed full equality and were integrated into Norwegian society. LUXEMBOURG—3,500 on the eve of WWII, most from Eastern Europe. Estonia—4,500 between the world wars, about half in TALLINN, the capital. From the mid-1930s an upsurge of nationalism made itself felt in the country, with demands to restrict Jews in the economy and in the universities. In 1940 the Soviets turned the country into a Soviet Socialist Republic and annexed it to the Soviet Union.

NAZI IDEOLOGY AND ITS ROOTS

Daniel Fraenkel

The Role of Ideology: Some Preliminary Remarks. Ideology may be defined as an abstract system of ideals, values, or beliefs, which guides or underlies the concrete political agenda and actions of political movements, especially in the twentieth century. In its historical usage—especially in the writings of Karl Marx and his followers—the word ideology often has a negative connotation, as it is associated with a false consciousness, a kind of smokescreen designed by those who promote it to form a shield between the masses and the true perception of reality. This is why Nazi leaders themselves preferred to talk about their ideology as a "worldview" or *Weltanschauung.* Be that as it may, in the present article we shall take ideology to mean a subjectively believed system of ideas concerning politics, without implying anything about its objective truth-value. The importance of understanding the underlying ideological motivation of a twentieth century movement and regime, which committed some of the most horrendous crimes in recorded history, does not need much justification or elaboration. It is based on the fact that, both chronologically and logically, the formation of the concrete political goals and objectives of Nazism, especially the genocidal drive against millions of civilians during WORLD WAR II, was preceded by the ideology. It was the ideology, rather than any concrete political interests or passing military needs, which determined both the Nazis' choice of the Jews as their victims and their decision to launch an extermination campaign against them. However, in saying as much, let us be careful about the implications. First of all, we should not accord Nazism a dignity that it does not deserve by claiming for it any inherent philosophical value as an abstract system of ideas. In fact, Nazism was never able to develop a logically connected system of ideas at all comparable to that of Communism, the other great anti-democratic movement of the twentieth century. Nazi ideology consisted, rather, of a loose cluster of ideas about race, human society, and German history which had been borrowed freely by HITLER and other Nazi leaders from the writings of various nineteenth century anti-rationalist philosophers, self-proclaimed prophets, and downright eccentrics, without regard to their inner consistency. Some of these ideas are indeed bound to strike us as bizarre, obscure, and esoteric. However, the need to explore Nazi ideology does not depend at all upon its intellectual originality or place of honor in the world of ideas. It is a measure of the fact that—however obviously absurd, worthless, and offensive Nazi ideology may strike us—for twelve critical years this ideology functioned as the underlying motivation of a political movement which seized power in one of the most technologically advanced and militarily powerful nations in the world. Furthermore, by insisting on the role of ideological motivation in Nazism, we do not mean yet to claim that the Nazis' Jewish policy after 1933 or even after 1939 is to be regarded as the simple, straightforward implementation of ideological convictions. Far from it, there was no direct and predictable progression from the foundation of the NAZI PARTY in 1920 or from its seizure of power in 1933 to the genocidal campaign in World War II. Not only were the Nazi decisionmakers subject to practical considerations and constraints of political reality, but, moreover, even for them there was at first a wide, almost uncrossable gulf between their abstract ideological image of the Jew as the mortal racial enemy of GERMANY and their readiness to launch into operation the wholesale murder of millions of human beings. This notwithstanding, it would appear that the failure of most observers at that time to take Nazi ideology seriously enough was in itself one of the most important reasons for that "fatal underestimation" of Nazism which Dietrich Bracher, the renowned German historian, would identify as the root cause of Nazism's early successes.

Origins of the Term "Nazi" or "National Socialist." "Nazi" is the widely used abbreviation for the somewhat bulky German term *Nazionalsozialistisch* (National Socialist), which derives from the official name of the Nazi Party: "The National Socialist German Workers' Party" (*Nationalsozialistische Deutsche Arbeiterpartei* or NSDAP). It is worth noting that the abbreviated name was first applied to the Nazi Party by its political opponents: in the original German the abbreviated term carries with it a negative connotation, conveying a sense of disrespect. The origin of the term "National Socialist" dates back to pre-World War I ethnic politics in Bohemia, which at that time belonged to the Austro-Hungarian Empire. The term surfaced for the first time in 1904 in the Sudeten German Workers' Party, which renamed itself in May 1918 the "German National Socialist Workers Party" (*Deutsch Nationalsozialistische Arbeiterpartei*). One of its ideologists, the Sudeten German political activist Rudolf Jung, published in 1919 a detailed text entitled "National Socialism." The German Nazi Party adopted from the Sudeten party both its name and its political program. The Nazi Party was founded in MUNICH in January 1919 by Karl Harrer and Anton Drexler under the name "The German Workers' Party." Hitler joined the two co-founders in September 1919 and in February 1920 the party renamed itself the "National Socialist German Workers' Party." The term "national socialism" refers to the Nazi Party's claim to combine within itself the foundations of two great competing ideologies of the twentieth century: nationalism and socialism. This in turn was connected to the Nazis' ideological claim of providing for the German people a "third way" as an alternative to the two opposite extremes of capitalism or communism. The promise to fulfill the wishes and satisfy the needs of the most diverse sectors and interests in Germany, especially the reconciliation of the working masses with modern nationalism, comes across very clearly in the "25 points" party program, the only official program of the Nazi Party ever to be published. The program, read by Hitler in February 1920 at the first mass meeting of the party, consists of a peculiar mixture of pseudo-socialist, anti-capitalist ideas, racist and antisemitic principles, nationalistic declarations, and demands for territorial expansion. However, in contrast to the other ingredients of the program, the anti-capitalist, pseudo-socialist element was not much more than a superficial dressing designed to make Nazism attractive to the unemployed masses and the discontented lower-middle class. It stopped playing a serious role in the history of the party after 1926, when Hitler succeeded in neutralizing the power of the brothers Otto and Georg Strasser, who led the leftist segment in the party. In any case, the socialist element of national socialism never prevented Hitler from flirting with big business, nor stopped big business from offering Nazism its support, both before and after 1933.

Nazism as a Form of Fascism. Nazism is a form of FASCISM, a twentieth century nationalist ideology that surfaced in many European countries between the two world wars, and gained control of the government in ITALY in 1922 and in Germany in 1933. The term

German soldiers saluting at a swearing-in ceremony surrounded by Nazi symbols, 1940

fascism derives from the Latin *fasces,* a bundle of sticks or rods bound to an ax, which symbolized authority in ancient Rome. Transmitted into Italian as *fascio,* meaning "union" or "league," it was adopted in 1919 by the Italian Fascist leader, Benito MUSSOLINI, as the name of his movement, called *Fasci Italiani di Combattimento* (Italian Combat Veteran's League). Fascism is characterized by its disdain for liberal democracy and democracy's sacred institutions, such as the parliamentary system, the constitution, and the sanctity of the rights of man. Instead of them, it puts forward the overpowering figure of the leader (*Duce* in Italian, *Fuehrer* in German), as the sole legitimate representative of the nation. In its relationship to modernity, fascism tends to be ambivalent: on the one hand, it is romantic and backward-looking in its authoritarianism; opposition to modernity and rationalism; adoption of pre-modern myths such as the superiority of the simple rural life to urban civilization; and the use of mythical symbols (such as the *fasces* or SWASTIKA) associated with the people's ancient past. On the other hand, fascism can also be intensely modern, forward-looking, and even pioneering in its use of state of the arts technology; in its manipulative use of modern media such as the radio and film; and the use of advanced means of transportation such as the airplane for the purpose of spreading its political propaganda and gaining an edge over its opponents. German Nazism shared with Italian Fascism this inconsistent relationship to modernity as well as many other related features, such as an aggressive nationalist position, the glorification of war and warfare, the cult of the leader as a central structural principle, the extensive use of ritualized ceremonies and political mass rallies for inciting the masses, and the unrestrained use of internal political violence or terror as the most efficient means of attaining its ends. However, despite these similarities, the intellectual and social roots of Nazism were uniquely German, grounded in its distinctly German setting and history. What set the German development apart was that the late nineteenth century romantic revolt against positivism (a philosophical doctrine which focuses on the concrete, factual, and real, ignoring all phenomenon that go beyond actual experience) and rationalism (a theory of perception which rejects any knowledge that does not derive from reason alone), which took place in many countries, took off in Germany in directions and dimensions not met elsewhere. In contrast to modern nation-states such as England or France, Germany was a "belated" nation whose centuries-long quest for political unity was only partially satisfied in 1871 with the establishment of the German empire under Wilhelm I. The frustrations resulting from this situation of a nation *manque* (unfulfilled), coupled with the social and economic problems brought about by too rapid industrialization, were more sharply felt in Germany than in the rest of Europe. In 1873, the extended economic crisis that had been caused by the collapse of the unhealthy economic boom following Germany's victory in the war with France, aggravated the plight of the lower-middle class and heightened its anxieties. All this made Germany a fertile breeding ground for the formation of various mystical and supernatural cults centering on the "mystique of the blood" and a glorified Germanic, Aryan past. In rejecting industrial society and its associated urban culture as incompatible with true national unity, those cults fell back upon an idealized and imaginary past, in which the hated Jews, who were thought

of as the agents of corruption and decay, played no part.

World War I (1914–1918) and the humiliating terms of the peace treaty of Versailles (signed on June 28, 1919; came into effect in January 1920), furthered these escape-from-reality attitudes, casting a gloom over the public atmosphere. The treaty, which charged Germany with sole responsibility for the war, imposed on it extremely severe reparations and forced it to surrender various disputed territories to its western and eastern neighbors. The treaty was never accepted by the majority of the German people. The fact that military defeat was never conclusively settled on the battlefield—Germany itself was not invaded and German armies were to be found at the end of the war still stationed on enemy territory—contributed to the STAB IN THE BACK LEGEND. According to this theory, which was advocated by rightist circles after the end of the war, not the army but the home front, manipulated by the treacherous Socialists and their Jewish allies, was responsible for Germany's defeat. Severe inflation, caused by the payment of heavy reparations and trauma of the defeat, crippled the economy of the Weimar Republic, destroying the German middle class. This in turn played into the hands of the nationalist-racist right, whose ideology of hate found a responsive chord amongst the despairing middle class.

The *Voelkisch* Tradition as a Forerunner of Nazism.
The most important stream of thinking which helped

Adoring crowds, some dressed in the "Voelkisch" style, salute Hitler's passing entourage

prepare the ground for the appearance of Nazi ideology—and in part seamlessly merged into it—was associated with that inexhaustible source of racist principles and antisemitic stereotypes: the German *voelkisch* tradition. It is true that it was only in the wake of the trauma of the German defeat in World War I and the alienation caused by the politics of the Weimar Republic that the *voelkisch*-based movement or movements were first able to move from the margins of society into the mainstream and make deep inroads into German society as a whole. However, the mass political following which the organized *voelkisch* movement was able to acquire during the Weimar period (1919–1932) was preceded by a long intellectual development in the course of which *voelkisch* thinking and attitudes had been profoundly imprinted on the minds of many Germans.

Some clarification of word origins may be in order here. The German word *Volk* (meaning people or folk)—from which the adjective *voelkisch* derives—carries with it a wealth of connotations that are not even hinted at in its English translation: people. The word, which in the original Old High German used to denote a troop of warriors or a human crowd, in the eighteenth century gathered to it the largely negative connotation of referring to the common folk or people. However, with the shift of attitudes and mentality brought about by the age of romanticism in Germany (which came about during the first half of the nineteenth century), the word lost its negative connotation and came to signify the very desirable condition of a people rooted in its natural environment. The culture of the *Volk* living in harmony with nature was contrasted with the corrupt and mechanical civilization of the modern town. In the course of time the word came to denote an idealized condition: the extraordinary union of a people with its natural surroundings and the long succession of generations preceding it. In Nazi propaganda, which adopted various themes from German romanticism, *Volk* and the many words derived from it acquired the status of a catch-all ideological root concept. Thus, during the THIRD REICH, the *Volk* Community (*Volksgemeinschaft*) became the official designation for the "community of blood" and race, which Nazism strove to set up. The true *Volk* Community was one which, according to Hitler, would rise above "classes and social orders, occupations, religious denominations, and all the usual confusion of life—" (1940). From the beginning, a central element of that

mythic community was to be the exclusion from its ranks—ultimately, the physical extermination—of all those who by reason of their contaminated, non-Aryan blood were considered unsuitable to partake in the Community. Hence the term "*Volk* vermin" (*Volksschaedlinge*) became in Nazi speech a synonym for Jews and other social undesirables. By the same token, "*Volk* fury" (*Volkszorn*) was Nazi propaganda's common explanation for the crimes committed during the infamous KRISTALLNACHT pogrom of November 1938. Relatively more innocent derivations of the same term were the famous *Volkswagen* (literally the "*Volk's* car") and the Nazi radio set, *Volksempfaenger* (the "*Volk's* receiver").

The Founding Fathers of *Voelkisch* Thought: Paul de Lagarde and Julius Langbehn. Although various *voelkisch* concepts may be traced back to the romantic movement of the early nineteenth century—notably to Friedrich Ludwig Jahn, the Berlin professor who founded the German fraternity movement in order to strengthen "Germanic culture" through gymnastics—the first significant crystallization of *voelkisch* thinking into a coherent system of ideas only occurred in the late nineteenth century. The most important names to keep in mind in this context were the German expert on eastern culture, Paul de Lagarde (1827–1891; until 1854, known as Paul de Boetticher), and the German culture critic, Julius Langbehn (1851–1907). Although not unsuccessful as scholars, both men were in fact disappointed academics, working for the better part of their lives on the fringes of the academic establishment of their day. Their special achievement was their ability to transform the disappointments and frustrations of their personal lives into a sharp critique of contemporary civilization and its social decline. Most significant to us is the fact that in the writings of both authors, Jews and Judaism figure prominently as the major symbol of the decline of modern civilization. Lagarde's main contribution to *voelkisch* thought is to be found in his collection of essays titled *German Writings* (*Deutsche Schriften*, 1878). In it he criticized the lack of true spirituality and unity in contemporary Germany. He proposed to correct this by a drastic revision of traditional Christianity, replacing it with a new Germanic faith centering on the spiritual rebirth of the German *Volk*. With regard to the Jews, he asserted that their essential nature and their keep-to-themselves religion made them incompatible foreign elements on German soil and a barrier to true German unification. Lagarde appeared to believe in the myth that Jews ritually murdered Christian children in order to use their blood in religious ceremonies, and even went so far as entertaining plans for their mass resettlement—an idea that foretold some of the later Nazi expulsion designs.

Much more widely read than Lagarde's academic collection of essays was Langbehn's *Rembrandt as Teacher: By a German* (*Rembrandt als Erzieher. Von einem Deutschen*). Published in 1890, the book went through 40 editions in two years and continued to be read widely into the 1930s. Langbehn, who shared with Lagarde his criticism of the materialistic and rationalistic nature of modern German society, chose the famous Dutch painter, Rembrandt, because he regarded him as the outstanding example of an artist who relied on his subjective intuition and mystical creative impulses as inspiration for his work. Langbehn sought to elevate these qualities into a new mystical religion, an ecstatic celebration of the vital and organic life-force that he considered as the true remedy for the materialistic, mechanical spirit that had overtaken Europe. As regards the Jews, he pictured them as the perverted arch-enemy of true spirituality, the embodiment of all that was harmful to the authentic Germanic *Volk*.

In their respective writings, Lagarde and Langbehn offered for the first time a systematic critique of society that laid the ideological groundwork for the further development of *voelkisch* thought.

Christian Germanism. The antisemitic prejudices of *voelkisch* thought were naturally reinforced by traditional Christian prejudices. After all, Christianity had its own religious biases which it by no means abandoned or renounced after the Jews were given equal rights in many parts of Europe. With the growth of the *voelkisch* movement and the systematic consolidation of its ideas in the writings of Lagarde and Langbehn, traditional religious ANTISEMITISM was absorbed into *voelkisch* thinking, resulting in a synthesis of thought known by historians as Christian Germanism. According to the advocates of Germanic Christianity, the Jew was a being with no soul, consumed by lust and greed and incapable of truly moral behavior.

In 1879 Wilhelm Marr (1819–1904), an unemployed journalist who had sacrificed his job and career in order to fight what he regarded as the "threat of world Jewish domination" founded the *Antisemiten Liga* (Antisemite League), the first organization explicitly dedicated to the pursuit of antisemitism. In a pamphlet that ran into twelve editions, Marr ranted against the threat of Judaism and called for a life and death struggle between it and Germanism. Marr's league had close links with the *voelkisch* movement. In 1881 Eugen Duehring (1833–1921), a respected Berlin professor, published a book entitled *Die Judenfrage* (*The Jewish Question*), in which he set out to analyze the "Jewish question" in Germany in racial terms. Duehring attributed alleged Jewish corruption and wickedness to inborn Jewish racial traits. He denounced the efforts of certain Jews to assimilate through outward conversion to Christianity as a fraud, claiming that their baptism was just an attempt at masking their destructive intentions. He denied that Christianity was undeniably interwoven with Judaism, claiming that it was the first duty of every Christian to fight Judaism with all his might. According to Duehring a struggle unto death between the Germans and the Jewish invaders was decreed by fate. However, the Germans were bound to prevail in the end thanks to their superior racial strength. Another advocate of antisemitism who based his theories on traditional Christian ideas was Emperor Wilhelm's royal court preacher, Adolf Stoecker (1835–1909). Ultra-conservative in his political outlook, Stoecker accused the Jews of trying to undermine the existing social order and of being the enemies of the Protestant German state which he sought to defend. Although as a gifted public speaker Stoecker foreshadowed the antisemitic campaign of pre-1933 Nazi speakers, the concept of an all-out racial war against the Jews went beyond his conservative Christian outlook.

Already in the late nineteenth century it would appear that there was a readiness by some writers to cross the threshold from theoretical preaching to actual violence. Hermann Ahlwardt is a case in point. In 1890 he published *Der Verzweiflung-kampf der arischen Voelker mit den Judentum* (*The Desperate Struggle Between the Aryan Peoples and Judaism*). Basing himself on the doctrines of the Germanic prophets, Ahlwardt stated that a people who rid itself of Jews freed itself for the natural development of the *Volk* and thereby attained world domination—in dealing with the Jews, Christian mercy was definitely out of place. Instead, Ahlwardt asserted, the nation must act with determination to combat the Jewish threat. Nonetheless, when it came to concrete proposals to carry out such measures, he displayed reservations that were still typical of his times. When he drew up an actual program, Ahlwardt did not go further than calling for the placing of stringent restrictions upon Jews, a decree proclaiming them foreigners on German soil, and excluding them from all walks of German life.

The ideological basis of *voelkisch* antisemitism was summarized by Theodor Fritsch (1852-1933), a publicist who attained something of a cult status among the Nazis with his *Antisemitischer Cateschismus* (1887), which later appeared under the name *Handbuch der Judenfrage* (*The Handbook on the Jewish Question*). Dietrich Eckart, young Hitler's friend and mentor, called it in 1920 "our whole intellectual arsenal." Coming from a middle class background, Fritsch took up the fight against the Jews to save the German middle classes from the new wave of industrialism and capitalism which he typically identified with the Jews. However, this social/economic-based antisemitism developed into racial hatred.

The demonization of the Jew was perhaps the most fateful single result of the development of *voelkisch* ideology. Along with its depiction of the Jew as an inhuman, un-German intruder, *voelkisch* antisemitism helped popularize a state of mind that regarded the Jewish victims of Nazi persecution as less than fully human.

The evil nature of the Jew, depicted in *voelkisch* thought as having originally been perpetuated by his depraved inner drives, was further reflected in a stereotyped depiction of his outward appearance. The mutant physical features of the Jews were contrasted with the Germanic ideal of beauty: a stocky and grotesquely twisted figure with short legs and a typical "Jewish" nose was set against the idealized symmetry of the Nordic man. The fear of racial defilement with its erotic-sexual associations became an obsession with *voelkisch* thinkers. The image of the dark, sly, lustful Jew seducing the innocent, blond, German maiden haunted the minds of these self-appointed defenders of the German *Volk*.

Scientific Racism: Gobineau and the Development of Racial Anthropology. Yet another stream of thought that was to have a decisive influence on Nazi ideology and especially on Hitler's mind, was the nineteenth century doctrine of RACISM. In contrast to the Germanic-romantic vision of the VOELKISCH movement, which was mystical in its origins and came into being in the first place as a revolt against the spiritually-lacking eighteenth century theories of positivism and rational-

ism, racism started out from the world of science. German antisemitism became truly deadly when these two distinct strands of thought—mystic visions of Germanic-Aryan past greatness on the one hand, and pseudo-scientific speculations on the racial foundations of civilization on the other hand—were fused into one.

Eighteenth century anthropology had already occupied itself with the racial classification of nations, while Franz Joseph Gall (1758-1828) had founded the science of phrenology, a psychological theory claiming the ability to know a person's character and mental abilities from the size and shape of his skull. However, "scientific" racism came into its own only in the mid-nineteenth century with the publication of Gobineau's *Essay on the Inequalities of the Human Race*. In his four-volume work, Count Arthur de Gobineau (1816-1882), French diplomat and poet, made race the lone determining factor in human history, dismissing such human institutions as religion, governments, and ideas as "superstitions." According to Gobineau, mankind is inherently unequal, consisting of "lower" races—mainly blacks and Semites—and "higher" "purer" races such as the "Aryans" or "Teutons." The "higher" races alone possess creative power and their rise to prominence in history depends on their racial purity. However, they are bound to leave the stage of history once they become contaminated by the "lower" races.

Although the French racist's ideas were destined to play a far more important and fateful role in Germany than they ever did in his native land, their effect on the German scene was not immediate and had to wait for the 1890s. Ludwig Schenmann (1852-1938), Gobineau's German translator, founder of the Gobineau society in 1894, and its chairman until 1920, was a typical *voelkisch* activist who thought that all the evils which he associated with modernity and Jewish influence could be set right by the application of Gobineau's racial principles. Even so, Gobineau's own writings never became widely popular in Germany; instead, they owed their impact to their enthusiastic adoption by the aging Richard Wagner (1813-1883) and the Bayreuth circle. Wagner, the famous German composer, admired by Hitler as no other artist, became a central figure in Nazi tradition due to both his antisemitic writings—most notably, *Jewry in Music* (1850)—and the thematic contents of his musical works—especially *The Ring of the Niebelungs*, regarded by Nazi interpreters as a Gospel of the German race, and *Die Meistersinger von Nuernberg*, praised by them as

Y AVEZ-VOUS PENSÉ ?...

Un Chinois catholique?

Pourquoi pas?
mais **JAUNE**...

Un Juif catholique?

Pourquoi pas - si c'est son intérêt?
mais **JUIF!**...

French poster depicting Nazi racial ideology: "Have you ever thought about this?... A Chinese Catholic? Why Not? But yellow... A Jewish Catholic? Why not—if this is his interest? But Jewish!..."

a "profession of Germanness" which celebrates the *Volk* and the ancient Germanic heroic past. Wagner's son-in-law and fervent admirer, Houston Stewart CHAMBERLAIN (1855–1927), became in time the most significant advocate of racial doctrine in Germany. English by birth, Chamberlain was drawn into Germany by his early admiration for Wagner's music. Following his (second) marriage to Wagner's daughter Eva, he settled permanently in Bayreuth and became a German citizen in 1916. Chamberlain's major work, *The Foundations of the Nineteenth Century,* which came out in Germany in 1899, used many of Gobineau's ideas but also expanded them and went beyond them. Where Gobineau was content to offer an objective analysis of the history of civilization from the perspective of race, Chamberlain, a hopeless optimist, posed himself as the prophet of the future, making race the future hope of mankind. In this respect he was a true romantic and his vision fitted in very nicely with the romantic mystique of the *voelkisch*

tradition, adding to it the aura of scientific respectability. His interpretation of history was dualistic, in that he viewed history as the arena of a struggle of opposites—between the forces of absolute good, represented by the Teutonic or Indo-European races, and those of absolute evil, represented by the dehumanized Semitic or Jewish anti-race. The Jews were incapable of any creative, culture-building activity. While the Indo-Europeans were anxious to maintain the "spotless" purity of their own race, the Jews were at the same time strenuously striving to infect the Indo-Europeans with Jewish blood. Chamberlain "rescued" Christianity for Germanism by proposing to show by pseudo-scientific arguments that Jesus could not have been a Jew since the Galilee, where he lived, was inhabited by non-Jewish tribes. Similarly, with regard to science and technology, he did not simply reject them like some of the other mystic visionaries, but proposed to rid them of their Jewish presence. Chamberlain's book, which climaxed with a passage predicting the imminent victory of the German race, became immensely popular with the *voelkisch* movement, counting Adolf Hitler among its readers. Indeed the two men admired each other and in 1924, three years before Chamberlain's death, the future German *Fuehrer* came to pay his respects to his much revered and already ailing mentor.

Social Darwinism. Meanwhile, the anthropologically-based racism of Gobineau fused with another distinct trend of racial thinking, which had its roots in Charles Darwin's theory of the process of evolution through natural selection. The British biologist published his revolutionary study *On the Origin of the Species by means of Natural Selection, or the Preservation of Favoured Races in the Struggle for Life* in 1859, only four years after the publication of Gobineau's essay. However, while Gobineau's contribution to science, were it not for his lethal influence on the development of racial doctrine, would hardly have merited even a footnote in intellectual history, Darwin's classic study ranks as one of the major scientific achievements of his age. The question arises: how did scientific work of such high quality end up being misused by the most vulgar of racial ideology? The middle step that we need here is that of the so-called "Social Darwinism"—that is, the controversial application of the Darwinian laws to humankind and society. Darwin's original theory of evolution set out to show that all living species—including the human—are subject to and are a result of natural selection, that is the survival of the fittest and the strongest. Darwin arrived at his findings by making the following observations: (a) in every biological population the individual members have their own personal traits and possess the potential for new traits (b) the overall size of a given population remains stable although the number of offspring is larger than that which is necessary for maintaining the size. From these observations, he inferred that the result of the various forces acting upon the population—competition, diseases, climate—is the survival of those individuals most adapted to their natural environment. He termed this process "natural selection." The survivors reproduce, passing on to their descendants their most useful acquired qualities. With the passage of time, and in the course of the gradual change of the environment, the process of selection will have effected a change in the population as a whole and a new species will be formed. The explosive force of Darwin's revolution-

ary work lay in the fact that, for the first time, it provided a natural and self-regulating explanation for the fact that there are so many different kinds of species, and thus did away with the need to include in the scheme any supernatural factors. Nor could Darwin's carefully worded conclusions be dismissed as mere speculations: they were based on a solid body of carefully gathered evidence. However, with Social Darwinism, the adaptation of Darwin's theory for social and political purposes, we move to a completely different ethical and scientific plane. One of the earliest promoters of Social Darwinism in Germany was Ernst Haeckel, a professor of zoology at the University of Jenna, Thuringia, who already in the 1860s used Darwin's theory for developing a universal philosophy, which applied not only to biological but also to psychological and social phenomena. While Haeckel himself, in spite of his attack on the Church and Christianity, did not use his theory to undermine the ethical norms associated with Jewish-Christian civilization, later advocates of Social Darwinism did. They stated that human society was itself like a biological organism and that therefore the principles of selection, "Culling Out" and the "Right of the Stronger" which occur in nature, should also govern relations between human individuals and groups. While Social Darwinism was by no means an exclusively German phenomenon, nowhere else was it raised, even before Hitler came on the scene, to the status of a world religion. Its spread in Germany was facilitated by an essay competition sponsored in 1900 by the head of the powerful Krupp Corporation on the topic: "What can we learn from the principles of Darwinism for application to inner political development and the laws of the state?" The winner of the first prize, Wilhelm Schallmayer, looked at all human institutions in terms of the struggle for survival. His close associate and supporter, Dr. A. Ploetz, maintained that the Aryan race alone stood at the peak of racial development. As a way of ensuring the race's health he suggested that at a child's birth, a consultation of doctors should be held to determine his right to live. Another disciple of Ploetz, Adolf Lenz, produced in 1917 for his professor a thesis fittingly entitled "An Ethic Revised." In this thesis, Lenz ranted at the "naive assumption that all men have equal rights." He further asserted that "there could be no greater fallacy than the belief that human nature abhors war—the exact contrary is true." Lenz argued that the object of the State is not to see to it that "the individual gets his right but to serve the race."

According to the views of the Social Darwinists, modern civilization and its humanitarian principles were in fact a double-edged sword, favoring the weak and threatening the process of natural selection as a healthy regulator of human affairs. Social Darwinists saw it as their task to reverse this "unhealthy" interference with the natural process. They demanded that the modern State stop supporting the "incapable elements" and favor instead the biologically valuable elements on whom the survival of the race depends. The supporters of the racial hygiene school (Eugenics) went even further in demanding the forcible sterilization, if not the physical elimination, of all those believed to be suffering from hereditary diseases or weaknesses. Moreover, the same principle of the preservation of the species could be carried over from the individual society to relations between human groups like nations and races. Thus, the more fanatical Social Darwinists like Alexander Tille could demand—in the name of the same principle of self-preservation of the species—the right of the stronger races to destroy the weaker. Once the Nazis seized power in Germany, especially after World War II had loosened all normal inhibitions and taboos, these fantastical, insane-sounding ideological fixations could become stark realities, programs to be put into operation. Hitler himself said in his book, MEIN KAMPF, that "in the search for self-preservation so-called humanitarian ideals melt away like snow in the March sunshine." Heinrich HIMMLER, head of the SS, the major implementer of Nazi ideology, thought of the mission of his organization in the following terms:

> We are like the plant-breeding specialist who, when he wants to breed a pure new strain from a well-tried species that has been exhausted by too much cross-breeding, first goes over the field to cull the unwanted plants. We, too, shall begin by weeding out the people who, in our opinion, are not suitable SS material.

The 1933–1934 syllabus for the philosophical education of the SS distinguished between inferior and "high-value races" which were defined as "the culminating entities of the biological process." The primary representatives of the "high-value races" were the people of Nordic stock. They had survived in the struggle for existence despite a low rate of fertility because of an inborn creative ability that brought them forward in the process of natural selection. They thus provided "the most striking evidence that the basic law of the eternal struggle, in which all the weak and the less valuable must succumb, holds good." By contrast, the main representatives of people of inferior racial stock, the Jews, did well living in cities, which suited their special characteristics but were harmful to the majority of people and especially to the high-value races. The Nazi State, which had taken note of these biological facts, had therefore turned its attention to "measures for promoting greater discrimination in reproduction."

Nazi Racism and the Occult. One further ideological link must be considered apart from the *voelkisch* and the scientific-racial schools in order to cover the range of intellectual influences that fed into the making of the ideology of Nazism: the occult or esoteric racial philosophies that took root in German-speaking countries from the 1890s to the 1920s, thus coinciding with the years in which Nazism was being formed. Occultism differs from the more traditional mystical thinking of *voelkisch* racism in two important respects: (1) It has to do with highly complex theories of cosmology, history, and spiritual instruction rather than with racial myths. (2) It is advocated by secret societies or sects who organize themselves around an esoteric philosophy. One of the best known occult groups was the Theosophical Society built around the esoteric philosophy of the Russian emigre, Madame Helena Petrovna Blavatsky. She named the philosophy developed by her, Theosophy (Wisdom of Gods), claiming that it derived from an earlier, advanced civilization in which religious knowledge was unified with scientific knowledge. The first Theosophic lodge was established in Germany in 1894, multiplying rapidly thereafter. Blavatsky's esoteric work is especially relevant to the formation of Nazi ideology in that it gives the concept of race a place of prominence. Blavatsky described all human evolution in terms of the mystical unfolding of seven root races, each with its own sub-race. Each of the seven root races is made up of a unique combination of physical and spiritual ingredients. In earliest times man was pure spirit, having supernatural, psychic powers which he had lost, but was destined to regain at the end of the full cycle of development. The present stage of the development is the fifth stage, with the Aryan race standing in the forefront of cultural and spiritual progress and embodying all that is humanly valuable. At the end of the sixth and seventh rounds man will return to the earlier pure stage of spiritual existence, which is also a state of being one with nature. All this in itself should have made Blavatsky's Theosophic vision favorable and pleasing to the Nazi mind. However, there was an additional prominent feature in her teachings that gave her high marks in the eyes of Nazism: she was blatantly antisemitic. Just as the Aryan race in her writings symbolizes all that is culturally and spiritually valuable in present civilization, so the Jew is the height of all that is negative: the incarnation of base materialism, sly rationalism, and vulgar sensuality. It is also worth noting that the source material of the PROTOCOLS OF THE ELDERS OF ZION—an infamous antisemitic invention accusing the Jews of world conspiracy—was first brought to Russia by one of Blavatsky's devoted followers. There are indeed some striking verbal and thematic echoes of Blavatsky in the writings and recorded pronouncements of both Hitler and Alfred ROSENBERG, the self-appointed ideologist of the Nazi movement, whose *Myth of the Twentieth Century* (1930) claimed to be a guidebook of Nazi ideological thinking. At the same time there were also important differences between Theosophy and the Nazi racial doctrine, differences which should not be glossed over. First, Blavatsky did not identify the Aryan Race with the current Germanic peoples. Even more importantly, hers was an essentially peaceful vision. She did not advocate racial violence, nor did she call for the vanquishing of the lower races by the higher ones. We thus need to establish a further link between Nazism and the occult to account for the inherent violence of Nazi racial ideology. This link may well have been provided by Ariosophy, a philosophy of the occult that combined its esoteric ideas with *voelkisch* nationalism and *voelkisch* racism.

The central figure in Ariosophy was the occultist writer Guido von List (1848–1919), whose followers included such celebrities as Franz Hartmann, the chief of staff of the Austro-Hungarian army, the painter Moench, and Joerg Lanz von Liebenfels (1874–1954), the self-styled "racial researcher, philosopher of religion and sexual mystic." In 1903, List's supporters, who included wealthy businessmen, founded the Guido von List's Society in Vienna. An undeniable relationship existed between Theosophy and Ariosophy: many of List's followers were at the same time pledged admirers of Madame Blavatsky's teachings. Likewise, some of the contributors to *Prana,* an occult journal published by the Theosophic society in Leipzig, were Ariosophists.

List wrote about his occult views in a series of books, notably in *The Religion of the Ario-Germans* and *The Armanen Caste of the Ario-Germans,* which became the chief ideological texts of Ariosophy. According to List's philosophy only the Aryans, the race furthest removed from modern rationalistic and materialistic society, were capable of perceiving the spiritual life-force which pervades the universe. The Jews, by contrast, were the prime example of a people removed from nature, infected as they are with the excessive materialism and rationalism of modern civilization. List proposed establishing an Ario-Germanic State, which would reflect in its constitution and organization the inborn superiority of the Aryan race. In this futuristic utopian state, only Ario-Germans could hold leading positions in government and society and the purity of the Aryan race would be protected by appropriate laws that would ban interracial marriages. List, who took an interest in occult symbols, found the swastika (which he believed to be the secret symbol of salvation) in occult writings. He chose to interpret it as symbolizing the victory of the Aryan over the lower races. Hitler wrote something quite similar in *Mein Kampf:* "the swastika symbolizes the victory of the Aryan man and simultaneously the victory of the idea of creative work which itself has always been antisemitic and will always remain antisemitic."

Even more sinister similarities exist between the Nazi program and the occult writings of von Liebenfels, List's student. Liebenfels identified Jews with animals, and promoted selective breeding for Jews "for the extirpation of the animal man and the propagation of the new man" by means of sterilization, deportation, liquidation by FORCED LABOR, and even murder. As may be judged by the title of one of his occult "researches"—*The Zoological and Talmudic Origins of Bolshevism*—von Liebenfels further identified Judaism with Bolshevism, a typical aspect of Hitler's worldview. Whether or not the future German *Fuehrer* met von Liebenfels in person during his days living in Vienna—as von Liebenfels claimed in 1932—it is hardly conceivable that the occult climate in Vienna and later in Munich did not have some impact on Hitler. An even more direct link between occultism and Nazism was probably the Thule Society, which was founded in Munich on January 1, 1918 by the occultist Rudolf von Sebottendorff. The name "Thule" was taken from the mythic Germanic Kingdom of Ultima Thule, alleged to be the original home of the German race. The Thule Society was a direct continuation of the Germanen Order, an occult group preaching German supremacy. Ostensibly a study group devoted to "the research of German history and the promotion of German art" the Thule was in fact a rebellious organization of *voelkisch* militants who were active in Munich in the immediate aftermath of World War I. It was thus involved in the founding of the Free Corps, the volunteer para-military units made up of former German soldiers and officers, and published an antisemitic paper, the *Munich Observer*. In 1920, Eckart, Hitler's personal friend and mentor, acquired the paper. Renamed the *Voelkischer Beobachter* (*Voelkisch Observer*), it became the central mouthpiece of the Nazi Party. The announcement published on that occasion stated that the Nazi Party had taken over the paper "in order to develop it into a relentless weapon for Germanism against hostile un-German efforts." Several prominent Thule members besides Eckart became leading Nazis, amongst them Alfred Rosenberg and Rudolf HESS, Hitler's deputy. In his already mentioned *Myth of the Twentieth Century,* Rosenberg set out to develop an occult history of mankind based on the lost Atlantis continent, while Hess dabbled in astrology and astrological prophecies. Thus, the story of an occult society that combined radical racist ideology with a commitment to militant action became undeniably involved with the fortunes of the Nazi Party.

Hitler's Worldview. At this stage it may be in place to tie together the different threads. One may well wonder: how did this bizarre mixture of mystical *voelkisch* thinking on the one hand, and scientific-biological racism on the other hand, fit together into one ideological framework? What was its effect on the Nazi mind and on that of Hitler in particular? Nazi ideology—it should be clear—has no claim to originality or systematic unity, consisting rather of an eclectic—at times downright bizarre—assortment of irrational beliefs about the Germanic past and pseudo-scientific ideas about the biological foundations of the human race. However, worthless as this ideology may appear to us from the point of view of the history of ideas, the fact that it influenced the political agenda of the Nazi movement is enough to justify its most serious consideration. Arguably, the unprecedented criminality of the Nazi regime would itself have been inconceivable and incomprehensible without our taking

into account that the Nazi perpetrators were implementing the principles of an ideology in which they believed.

The case of Hitler's world picture is crucial in this respect. Ever since the publication in 1938 of Hermann RAUSCHNING'S *The Revolution of Nihilism,* the point has been repeatedly made that the Nazis, and Hitler in particular, were a gang of unprincipled upstarts who cared only about advancing their own self-interests, and who lacked any coherent program apart from the naked pursuit of power. Although the most revealing single source on Hitler's worldview—the two volumes of his autobiographical *Mein Kampf*—had already been published in 1925, this complicated and wordy confession of faith did not encourage close reading at the time. However, an unbiased examination of the programmatic passages in *Mein Kampf* and of Hitler's published speeches (such as has been undertaken by Eberhard Jaeckel) leaves little doubt that—however crude and misguided—Hitler did possess an internally logical and self-coherent ideology, and that he remained faithful to its warped principles and goals to the closing day of his criminal career.

The central element of Hitler's "biological" view of politics and human nature was the absolute supremacy of race in history. "Race is the key to world history." The true subjects of history were thus neither social classes, as in Marxist thought, nor human institutions, cultures, or individuals as they appear in traditional historical literature, but race and *Volk* alone, which were synonymous concepts in Hitler's worldview. Hitler's theory of history was the most vulgar application of Social Darwinism, moving freely from zoological observations to laws which allegedly governed human affairs and human societies. Darwin's principles of "natural selection" and "survival of the fittest" became the reference point of all human progress, and the logic of "nature red in tooth and claw" replaced the morality of the humanistic and Jewish-Christian traditions. In the universal struggle for existence, there was only one right and one justice: that of the stronger. The "ridiculous fetters of so-called humanity" had to give way to "the humanity of Nature, which destroys the weak in order to make way for the strong." Hitler's racial ideology started out from the assumption of the "internal exclusivity of the species among all living beings on earth." The instinct of the self-preservation of the species, he said, caused "every animal to mate only with its own kind. Titmouse goes to titmouse, finch to finch, stork to stork, field mouse to field mouse, house mouse to house mouse, wolf to wolf, and so on and so forth." Every departure from this law, he argued, was contrary to nature: "Every crossing of two unequal individuals will produce something which is between the level of the two parents. That is to say, the offspring will indeed be superior to the racially inferior parental half, but not as advanced as the superior one. As a result it will later lose out in the struggle against the superior type. Such a mating contradicts Nature's will to improve breeds. [...]The result of this universally valid racial purity in Nature is not merely the sharp outside demarcation of individual races, but also their own internally uniform nature. The fox is always a fox, the goose a goose, the tiger a tiger and so on."

The lesson to be learned from this for humankind is clear: "The experience of history has countless proofs for this. It shows with frightening clarity, that every time that the blood of Aryans mixed with that of inferior peoples the end of the bearers of culture came about." In Hitler's picture of history, the original sin was the mixing of blood through intermarriage: "The mixing of blood and the consequent decline in racial purity is the sole cause of the dying out of all cultures." Following the teachings of Gobineau and Chamberlain, Hitler distinguished between races that create culture and races that destroy culture. The primary example of the first was the Aryan race, and Hitler praised its immeasurable contribution to civilization: "Everything we see today in the way of human culture, the products of art, science and technology, is almost exclusively the creative product of the Aryan... If one were to do away with him a profound darkness would descend upon earth, human culture would cease, and the world become desolate." In contrast, the Jew, "the most powerful antithesis of the Aryan" is the culture-destroying race par excellence. Completely devoid of any culture-creating ability, the Jews, in the interest of their own self-preservation, could only sponge upon their superiors or live "as parasites in the body of other peoples." And just as he waxed eloquent in describing the contributions of the Aryan race, so Hitler became crudely and violently abusive when he referred to the Jew: "He is and remains the typical parasite, a sponger, which spreads more and more like a pernicious bacillus, as soon as a favorable culture medium offers itself. But the result of its presence resembles that of a sponger: where he appears: the host people dies sooner or later." Furthermore, Hitler argued, the Jew could not main-

tain his parasitic existence within the body of other peoples, without deceiving them as to his true nature. This is why, according to him, the Jews liked to present themselves as a religious community, masking their identity as a race. Thus lying and deception became second nature to Jews. One of the most persuasive proofs of their lying nature, claimed Hitler, were their tireless efforts to deny the supposed truth of the *Protocols of the Elders of Zion*. For Hitler, when the historical development of the last hundred years was viewed from the right perspective, there could be no doubt at all that the allegations about a world Jewish conspiracy were true. Thus, the image of the Jew in Hitler's conceptual world assumed a contradictory character: a biologically inferior being and at the same time an all-powerful schemer, conspiring to achieve world domination. In this context, the (alleged) Jewish presence behind pacifism, democracy, socialism, and Marxism as interpreted by Hitler as maneuvers in the Jewish world struggle for domination. In Hitler's view, because the Jew, on account of his inferior racial nature, was incapable of creating a territorial state, he had to resort to other means in his drive for power. Hitler considered it as his most important task, his literally holy mission, to ward off the danger of the culture-destroying Jew. He even used religious language in depicting it: "By defending myself against the Jew, I am fighting for the work of the Lord."

While the Jews as the racial enemy of the German *Volk* was the central thrust of Hitler's worldview, his second ideological obsession was LEBENSRAUM, the conquest of "living space" for the German master-race. The starting point here—so Hitler argued in 1925—was a "simple" fact: "Germany has an annual population increase of 900,000." There were four different ways of dealing with this increase: population control, internal colonization, development of the export industry, or "the acquisition of new land and soil." Hitler chose the fourth possibility, dismissing the first three out of hand. He furthermore rejected the return to Germany's pre-1914 boundaries—a major part of the German demand for the revision of the Versailles peace treaty—as "political nonsense." These outdated boundaries could never satisfy the German hunger for land and soil.

Therefore, the only sensible solution which suggested itself to him was an expansion eastward, to that huge reservoir of land and soil: Russia. However, because Hitler believed that the Jewish Bolshevists (Communists) had taken control of Russia in the 1917 October Revolution, a war of expansion against the SOVIET UNION was associated in his mind with a war against the mortal racial enemy, the Jew. In this way, the two central ideological essentials in Hitler's worldview, the removal of Jews and the conquest of *Lebensraum* for the master race, came together in the Nazi invasion of the Soviet Union in June 1941.

Let us conclude: the unleashing of the HOLOCAUST against the Jews during World War II was not just an accident of history; it was a logical end-result of the Nazi worldview and of the antisemitic contamination that prevailed in Germany in the century preceding the Nazi takeover.

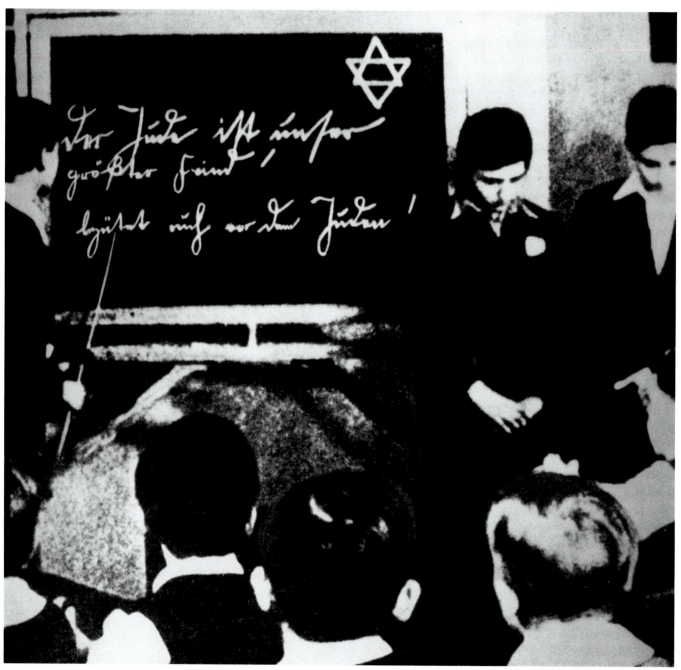

Lesson in Nazi ideology. Two Jewish students are made to demonstrate Jewish racial characteristics, Vienna, 1938

THE NAZI RISE TO POWER AND THE NATURE OF THE NAZI REGIME

Daniel Fraenkel

Causes of the Nazi Takeover: Some Preliminary Reflections. How could the Nazis have come to power in GERMANY? How did a nation of eighty million in the geographical and cultural heartland of mid-twentieth century Europe give in so easily, as it were without offering resistance, to one of the worst dictatorial regimes in the history of mankind? Was the Nazi takeover an inevitable, predestined result of the entire course of German history? Could it have been prevented? As January 30, 1933, the day HITLER was appointed chancellor of Germany by aging President Paul von HINDENBURG, finally recedes from living memory into the status of another date in recorded history, these questions will still continue to haunt the imagination and exercise the mind of all those interested in German and twentieth century history. The sheer volume of historical literature and the amount of controversy that these issues have generated are proof not only of the interest that they are capable of arousing, but also of the fact that they cannot be resolved by a simple and definitive solution. One thing appears certain: the Nazi rise to power had more than one root cause and lends itself to more than one reasonable explanation. There are those who would go as far back as the religious reformation of the sixteenth century in trying to unravel what they consider to be the basic structural flaw in the German national psyche and its warped conception of national politics. Others prefer to focus their attention on the twentieth century phenomena of the rise and fall of fascist movements and emphasize the common European roots of Nazism. Be that as it may, one would still have to explain why the ideological forerunners of the Nazi movement, extremist splinter groups with similar *voelkisch* and antisemitic worldviews, stood no chance of making a serious impact on German political life before World War I, let alone seizing control of the government. In seeking to clarify the *specific* circumstances which underlay and made possible Hitler's rise to power, it would thus seem advisable not to stretch the evidence too far back but to focus our attention on the history of the crisis-ridden democracy of the Weimar Republic, the immediate predecessor of the Nazi regime.

The 14 years of the Weimar Republic, which existed from November 1919 to January 1933, and its troubled political scene, are the immediate historical backdrop against which we should view both the early climb of the NSDAP (NAZI PARTY) from anonymity in its native Bavaria and its rise to the status of a victorious contender for power during the years 1930–1932. No other party, not even the Communists, thrived as much on the tragic misfortunes and recurring internal and external crises of the ill-fated republic. In fact, the electoral successes of the Nazi Party before 1933 were a mirror image of the external and internal political setbacks suffered by the Weimar Republic. Rather than creating themselves the crises which afflicted the Republic, Hitler and his cronies were the first to reap the benefits from them. For most of the time period of which we speak, the Nazi Party was no more than a marginal political group, little known outside its Bavarian home turf. It was only beginning in 1929—coinciding and clearly connected with the worldwide economic crisis that came to be known as the Great Depression—that the Nazis, overcoming years of no forward movement and virtual political insignificance, were able to break through to new national importance and ultimately rise to power in Germany.

The Weimar Republic and its Drawbacks. Named after the German town where it was founded, the Weimar Republic was born under the double sign of German defeat in World War I on the one hand, and an unfinished Socialist revolution on the other hand. Prompted by a popular anti-war revolt that had begun with a naval mutiny in Kiel on October 29, 1918, the leaders of the Social Democratic Party (SPD) demanded that the warmongering Kaiser Wilhelm II step down from his throne. On November 9, 1918, the Reich Chancellor Max von Baden gave in to the demands, announcing the abdication of the emperor and appointing the chairman of the Social Democratic Party, Friedrich Ebert, as chancellor. On the same day, Ebert's colleague, Philipp Scheidemann, quickly proclaimed the German Republic (without Ebert's agreement), in order to stop the developing revolution which threatened to be violent. Two days later, German representatives signed the armistice agreements that put the final seal on the humiliating German defeat. Under the harsh terms of the Versailles peace treaty, which Germany was forced to sign on June 28, 1919, the country had to surrender all its overseas colonies to the authority of the League of Nations. In the west, Germany had to give ALSACE-LORRAINE to FRANCE and the Saarland was placed under the administration of the League of Nations pending a region-wide vote on its status. In 1923 the strategically vital industrial center of the Ruhr region was occupied by the French and the Belgians. In the east, Posen (Poznan) and West Prussia were lost to POLAND, and MEMEL to LITHUANIA (seized by it in 1923). The German-speaking city of DANZIG became a "Free City." A "Polish Corridor" which linked Poland to the Baltic Sea at Danzig, separated Germany from East Prussia and became a visible and bitter symbol of crippled German rule. Militarily, Germany was severely weakened, with the German army limited to a maximum of 100,000, the navy reduced to 15,000, the air force disbanded and the Rhineland demilitarized. To the loss of territory and the insult to German military pride was added direct economic punishment. Accused by the victorious powers of responsibility for the war it had lost, Germany had to shoulder the heavy burden of reparations. These amounted to some 20 billion Gold marks for the period from 1919 to April 1921 alone. The payment of reparations was a major contributing factor to the huge rate of inflation in the early 1920s. At its peak, on November 15, 1923, one dollar was worth 4.2 billion Reich marks, having escalated during the course of the year from a one to 1,800 ratio.

The first all-German republic was thus born under the shadow of defeat in war and national humiliation. The new constitutional system, solemnly adopted by the German National Assembly in its meeting in the National Theater of Weimar on July 31, 1919, became permanently associated in the minds of the German people with the disgrace of an undeserved military defeat and an unpatriotic democratic revolution.

The majority of the population never gave the new constitutional system their fullhearted support. While the "scandalous" peace treaty of Versailles was rejected by practically all Germans, no matter what political affiliation, the three parties that had joined together to form the coalition which stood at the cradle of the Weimar constitution—the Social Democratic Party (SPD), the Center Party, and the German Democratic Party (DDP)—were soon destined to find themselves reduced to a minority status amongst the German voters. In fact, the so-called "Weimar coalition" had already lost its majority in June 1920, never to regain it again. In the first regular REICHSTAG (parliamentary)

elections held at that date, the former majority of 76 percent that the coalition still enjoyed in January 1919 was reduced to a mere 46 percent. Only 11 million German voters (instead of the former 19 million) gave their voice to the three parliamentarian parties, while their opponents on the right and left practically doubled their vote from 7.7 to 14.4 million, with the right receiving 9.1 million votes and the radical left (the Communists) 5.3 million.

The early loss of the people's electoral support was evidence of the phenomenon of a "republic without republicans." The German elites—the civil service, the judiciary, the industrial tycoons, and the officer corps—never gave the Weimar Republic their undivided loyalty; they remained loyal to the Kaiser or at least believed at heart that an authoritarian regime should be in control, rather than a democratic government. The parties that represented them, the Conservatives and right Liberals, while formally accepting the rules of the game dictated by the constitution, favored the pre-1918 authoritarian form of government. The rank-and-file population, especially the lower-middle class, lacking any firm democratic convictions and driven to panic by its downward spiral into poverty, became fair game to the rabble-rousing propaganda of the radically anti-democratic parties on the extreme left and extreme right of the political scene.

This potentially explosive political situation was made even worse by a structural flaw which seemed to be built into the Weimar form of government. This flaw consisted of an unresolved question as to the center of real sovereignty: does it reside in the parliament (*Reichstag*) or in the president? On the one hand, the Weimar constitution provided for a system of parliamentary democracy in which the party representatives were democratically elected by universal vote and the executive branch and its head, the Reich Chancellor, were dependent on a *Reichstag* majority. On the other hand, it also contained elements of a presidential system of government with a strong, popularly elected president. Thus, the president was the supreme commander of the armed forces and was empowered to appoint and dismiss the Reich Chancellor and his ministers. Moreover, Article 48 of the constitution provided that in cases of emergency the president was entitled to take whatever steps he deemed necessary to restore law and order. He alone decided when a state of emergency had been reached and what steps were necessary to take. Since no single political party ever had an absolute majority in the Weimar Republic and since even most of the coalition governments had only minority support in the *Reichstag,* the president's position, as opposed to those of the *Reichstag* and the chancellor, became even stronger, to the point of threatening the democratic basis of government. The authoritarian and conservative parties tended to regard the presidential system as a sort of substitute monarchy or empire. In 1925 they scored a victory when ultra-conservative Field Marshal Paul von Hindenburg was elected president. In 1928, the democratic forces had their own victory when they succeeded in nominating a Social Democrat, Hermann Mueller, as chancellor. It was the continuing constitutional deadlock caused by the breakup of Mueller's coalition in March 1930, rather than any terrorist takeover, which brought about the downfall of the Weimar Republic.

The Nazi Party's Progress, 1919–1929. The troubled history of the embattled Weimar Republic, which never won either the love or full agreement of the majority of its citizens, formed the background against which the Nazi movement began to shape its tortuous path to power. A basic irony of the situation—which should not be missed in hindsight—was that the democratic system itself granted to its bitterest and self-proclaimed enemies the legal tolerance and the democratic tools with which they eventually toppled it. Because the progress of the Nazi Party mirrored so closely the weaknesses and failures of the first German democracy, its pre-1933 history was a faithful reflection of the state of the republic. Thus, it scored its initial political successes during the first four crisis-ridden years which peaked in the occupation of the Ruhr region and the rising inflation in 1923; it lay low during the subsequent period, 1924–1929, which was characterized by economic and political consolidation and stability; it reared its head again with the onset of the global economic crisis in late 1929, scoring its greatest electoral gains during the final years of political and constitutional disintegration, 1930–1933, which eventually led to Hitler being invited to become chancellor in January 1933.

The rise of Nazism was closely connected with the life of Adolf Hitler. This holds true particularly for the earlier history of the Nazi Party, which, were it not for Hitler's evil political genius and his powers as a propaganda spouting agitator, would have probably ended up as just another locally-based extremist splinter group with no effect at all on the national political scene.

Both Hitler and the Nazi Party, founded in 1919, were in a real sense products of the German defeat in World War I. It was the German defeat, news of which had reached him in the field hospital where he was being treated for gas poisoning, which prompted Hitler to turn to politics in the first place. From then on, he dedicated his life to preparing Germany for another European war in which it would redeem the undeserved defeat in the first one, which—so he believed—had been brought about by the Jewish "stab in the back" (see also STAB IN THE BACK MYTH). Moreover, he transferred to the political sphere both the principle of hierarchical military command and the front-line experience of male camaraderie that he had learned in the war. From the early days of the Nazi movement, the so-called "leader principle" (FUEHRERPRINZIP) and the cult of the leader became integral parts of the movement's organizational structure and political practice.

The setting for the early history of the Nazi movement was post-World War I MUNICH, with the conservative, counter-revolutionary regime which gained power there after the suppression of the Communist rising (Soviet republic) and the many paramilitary groups (known as Free Corps) which gathered in the city in the wake of the Versailles treaty. Joining the 40-member strong German Workers' Party (DAF) in September 1919, which had been founded in January by the former locksmith Anton Drexler and Karl Harrer, Hitler soon carved a name for himself as a star speaker who attracted large audiences and many new members. He achieved his first decisive upset on July 29, 1921, when an extraordinary membership meeting of the party—renamed the National Socialist Workers' Party in February 1920—voted Drexler out of active office (he was made honorary chairman) and made Hitler first chairman with dictatorial powers. Another major step was the setting up in spring 1920 of a party troop organized along military lines with the active help of officers from the rightist Defense Leagues and the paramilitary Free Corps. This troop was known as the SA (*Sturmabteilung,* or Storm Troopers). It was the SA that first gave the small Nazi Party the qualitative edge over similar *voelkisch* rabble-rousing groups, which multiplied in the muddled political climate of the first postwar years. The SA enabled the Nazi Party to control the streets, terrorize opponents, and stage provocative demonstrations and flamboyant military parades that galvanized the spellbound masses. Under the command of retired army major Ernst ROHM, the SA became a formidable instrument of political terror, growing from 3,000 members in 1923 to about 500,000 in 1932—five times the size of the weakened German army. The number of political opponents murdered by the SA during the so-called time of struggle (*Kampfzeit*) ran into the hundreds. As no other party, the Nazis excelled in using state of the art propaganda techniques, putting up mass meetings with columns of taut marching men, martial music, *Heil* salutes, and flying banners. The choice of visual symbolism was also significant, with signs and emblems from the ancient Indo-Germanic past being deliberately manipulated for new political use. The sign of the SWASTIKA, the symbol of the sun disk, was adopted as the official banner of the Nazi Party at the Salzburg conference of August 7, 1920. After 1933 the swastika acquired the semi-religious status of a cult object. The brown shirt became the official uniform of the SA in 1926, its earthly color apparently symbolizing the Nazi "movement's connections with sod and soil."

A street decorated with Nazi flags

Although its transformation into a mass movement still lay far ahead in the future, the relatively small Nazi Party of the early 1920s and its upstart leader already became involved with influential sectors in Munich. Hitler became friendly with local notables, amongst them Gustav Ritter von Kahr, the chief administrator for Upper Bavaria, Otto von Lossow, the commander of the Bavarian division of the German army (*Reichswehr*), and Erich Ludendorff, retired general and legendary

World War I hero. After the summer of 1921, when Hitler grasped the helm of the movement firmly in his hands, financial contributions from big industrialists like Fritz Thyssen and Emil Kirdorf began to pour in. These patrons did not necessarily share the fanatical, antisemitic RACISM of Hitler's worldview and took exception to some of the wilder visions and methods of Nazism, but as Ian Kershaw has written, they still regarded Hitler as a "national drummer" who would proclaim and advance the patriotic cause dear to their hearts. Together with corrupt politicians of the nationalist-conservative camp, they were destined to play a disastrous role in opening to Hitler the doors of influence and power and in smoothing his path to the chancellorship.

With all its remarkable progress, the Nazi Party of the early 1920s was still little more than another rightist splinter group on the extreme fringe of German politics. It was the political and social crisis generated by the occupation of the Ruhr region by French and Belgian forces and the soaring inflation of 1923 which appeared to give Hitler the first opportunity to make his entry into the mainstream of national politics. On November 8–9, 1923, Hitler and his then comrade-in-arms, General Erich Ludendorff, taking advantage of the general political unrest, attempted to overthrow the Bavarian state government and the national government in BERLIN. The takeover attempt ended in a fiasco, with the conspirators arrested and later put on trial for high treason. However, with the help of a sympathetic judge and a half-hearted prosecutor, Hitler managed to turn the sham trial into a master propaganda performance, blasting against the "Jew republic" and the corrupt "system." The ridiculously short prison terms to which Hitler and his fellow conspirators were sentenced—five years' imprisonment—ended prematurely in December 1924 with a pardon. During his detention, Hitler's cell in the Landsberg castle became a place of pilgrimage for admirers and sympathizers from all over the Reich.

Meanwhile, the republic appeared to enter upon a phase of consolidation and stability. The galloping inflation was tamed with the introduction of a new currency in November 1923. The burden of reparations was eased somewhat after the adoption of the Dawes scheme of annual payments in August 1924, and France agreed to withdraw from the Ruhr region. In his capacity as chancellor and later as foreign minister, Gustav Stressemann, leader of the German People's Party, conducted a moderate foreign policy which peaked in a series of agreements signed by Germany, GREAT BRITAIN, France, ITALY, Poland, and Czechoslovakia at Locarno, SWITZERLAND in October 1925. A French-German reconciliation opened up prospects of an early evacuation of the occupied Rhineland. All these seemed to bode well for the republic and its democratic institutions. However, there were also some ominous signs pointing to a darker future. Throughout 1924–1928, the Social Democrats, the strongest *Reichstag* party and the staunchest supporters of democracy, were in the opposition and the quick succession of governments—there were 21 of them between June 1920 and March 1930—increasingly alienated the voters from the parties. The most harmful consequence by far was the disillusionment and distancing from the republic of the lower-middle classes and the small landholders, who had been hardest hit by inflation and by the structural effects of the process of economic modernization. The special importance of this development may be appreciated when we take into account that the sudden mass swing of the vote to the Nazi Party after 1929 was achieved through the mobilization of non-voters and middle class voters, who had become alienated from the democratic parties. The shift to the right was signaled by the election of Hindenburg as president in 1925. Anti-democratic and supremely conservative, the aging field marshal contributed greatly only a few years before his election to the spread of the stab-in-the-back legend, which put the blame for the German collapse in World War I on the home front. He was destined to play a fateful role both in dismantling the democratic constitution of the republic and in handing power to Hitler on a silver platter.

For the Nazi Party, the years 1924–1928 were mainly a period of internal organization and political incubation. After his release from prison, Hitler devoted himself to the task of organizing the party and concentrating his dictatorial authority. His supreme command was confirmed after he had successfully displaced the two other contenders for the leadership position, Gregor Strasser, the leader of the left wing in the party, and Ernst Rohm, the ruthless SA chief. Both men were later murdered during the "Night of the Long Knives" on June 30, 1934. A new star who joined the Nazi Party in this period was Joseph GOEBBELS, the *Gauleiter* (head of a Nazi administrative unit) of Berlin and future Reich Propaganda Minister. One of the lessons that Hitler drew from the failure of his 1923 takeover attempt and the subsequent (temporary) ban imposed on the

Nazi Party, was the adoption of a new strategy of pseudo-legality, that is the tactic of taking full advantage of the opportunities and legal protection afforded by the democratic system in order to undermine it from within. As Goebbels himself was to neatly summarize it later: "It will remain forever one of the biggest jokes of the history of democracy that she herself supplied the weapons with which she was brought down." This new political strategy was to pay off handsomely by paving Hitler's way to power a few years later. For the time being, however, the success was very moderate. In the *Reichstag* elections of May 1928, the Nazi Party received a mere 2.6 percent of the vote. The party did comparatively well in the rural areas of Bavaria, Franconia, and north Germany, but received very few votes in the industrial areas in Prussia east of the Elbe (including the capital, Berlin). The Social Democrats, who received in the same elections almost 30 percent of the vote, came out of their four year slump in the opposition and put up a new Great Coalition government, resting on the two pillars of the Social Democratic Party and the German People's Party (DVP)—the so-called "wing parties"—with the Catholic Center Party, and headed by the Social Democrat Hermann Mueller as Reich Chancellor.

It is worth emphasizing that the final destabilization of the Weimar democracy and the extraction of the Nazi genie from the bottle of the political doldrums into which the Weimar Republic had fallen, came about through a cluster of external forces over which the Nazi leaders themselves had no control. First and foremost amongst the warnings of decay was the onset of the world economic crisis in 1929, which was set off by the New York Stock Market crash on Black Friday (October 29, 1929). Germany was especially hard hit because of the economic burden it carried from the lost war and its resulting dependence on short-term loans, which were now being massively withdrawn. The unavoidable result was a growing rate of unemployment that reached six million in 1932. The fact that the memories of the inflation of 1922–1923 were still fresh only contributed to intensifying the psychological effect and to the spread of panic amidst the German population. The feeling of panic was all the more potent amongst the "declassed" middle class who felt threatened not only economically, but also socially. It was above all members of the middle classes who became susceptible to the hate propaganda of the Nazis, who were quick to take advantage of the subjective anxieties of those who felt disadvantaged and threatened. The phantom of the betrayal on the home front and the disgrace of Versailles were revived. Behind them all, the Nazis declared, were the Jews.

The looming economic crisis found the Nazi Party very well prepared to reap the political benefits. In August 1929 it held with great fanfare an impressive party rally at NUREMBERG which was attended by an unprecedented number of delegates, followers, and SA formations from all parts of Germany. The painstakingly organized Nuremberg rally marked the recovery of the Nazi Party from the low ebb of the 1928 election defeat and its successful adaptation to the era of mass organization and mass demonstrations. Wealthy supporters of Hitler from business and industry who were invited to the Nazi Party rally as honorary guests went away highly impressed. One of the earliest strongholds of the Nazi movement were the German universities. The Ring, the *voelkisch*-antisemitic oriented student organization, won a majority of student votes in numerous universities as early as 1924, and the ASTA, the student self-government organization, came under Nazi influence in 1929, well before the general elections of September 1930. By that time, Nazi student groups were moving forward into the forefront almost everywhere, winning an absolute majority in the universities of Erlangen and Greifswald (already in 1929) and in the universities of Breslau, Berlin's Technical and Veterinary institutes, Giessen, Rostock, Jena, and even in the University of Koenigsberg, the philosopher Immanuel Kant's *alma mater*. Least infected by the Nazi disease—for the time being at least—were the universities of Bonn, Munich, Wuerzburg, and HAMBURG.

During the summer and fall of 1929, the Nazis took part—alongside the Steel Helmet (or *Stahlhelm,* a veteran soldiers' league founded in December 1918 that identified with the nationalist-*voelkisch* viewpoint and fought against the democratic institutions of the Weimar Republic) and the German National People's Party (DNVP)—in a boisterous campaign of the right-wing opposition against the proposed settlement of the German reparations dispute by the Young Plan. The heart of the campaign, headed by the DNVP politician Alfred Hugenberg, was the call for a plebiscite (direct vote of the people on political issues). The Nazis, the much junior partner at that stage, were the real winners of the campaign, which ended in a dismal failure for the forces of the self-dubbed "National Opposition." It gave their superb propaganda machine an incomparable opportunity to present the Hitler movement as the spearhead of the anti-Weimar camp and rescued the much despised Nazi Party from the role of political pariah to which it had previously been condemned. In the state elections held in this period, the Nazis registered strong gains in north and east Germany, foreshadowing the great breakthrough in the *Reichstag* elections of September 1930. The masses started streaming into the party, which from the end of 1929 to March 1930, increased its membership from 178,000 to 210,000. The anti-Young campaign set an important precedent for the Harzburg Front of October 1931, in which the Nazi Party, no longer in the role of the junior partner, joined forces with the German National People's Party, the Steel Helmet, and other rightist associations to present a united front against the reigning government of Heinrich Bruening, and in fact against the Weimar Republic itself. The aura of respectability which Hitler acquired for himself by collaborating with the middle

Nazi Party Day in prewar Germany

class right wing opposition proved an invaluable asset in clearing the way for his eventual nomination as chancellor.

The Breakup of the Weimar Republic, 1930–1933. In analyzing the process that brought the Weimar Republic to its final collapse, smoothing the way for the Hitler dictatorship, we should distinguish between long-term, background causes, and the circumstances and individual decisions which functioned as the immediate trigger. The young republic may have been afflicted from its birth by a "permanent structural crisis" inherent in the psychological and economic burden of a lost war, in the absence of a true democratic tradition among its people, and in the faulty constitution with its unresolved tension between the role of the president and the role of the parliament (*Reichstag*). However, despite all these drawbacks, the crisis-ridden democracy had proven remarkably strong and capable of sustaining blows until 1930, when the final crisis began to envelop it. No less important than to distinguish between the long-term, background causes and the immediate circumstances that quickened the catastrophe is to recognize the role played by individual actors. A decisive contributing factor in advancing the Nazi rise to power was the subjective conduct of President Hindenburg and the scheming of a small group of conservative, non-Nazi politicians—primarily Franz von Papen and Kurt von Schleicher—who had managed to capture the ears and confidence of the 84-year-old president. Their monumental shortsightedness regarding Hitler and his real intentions and their repeated political miscalculations assumed under the circumstances truly historic importance.

The most important background factor for the breakup of the republic was the growing economic crisis which had a spreading, ripple effect on all spheres of German life. In the winter months of 1931–1932 and 1932–1933, unemployment reached such drastic proportions that one out of two German families was affected. The psychological effects on the lower-middle classes, who lived in constant fear of proletarianization (meaning descent into the lowest social rung), were even graver than those operating on the working classes who, after all, had nowhere else to descend. The dislike, indeed revulsion, that the middle class felt for the democratic system was intensified by the spectacle of prolonged governmental crisis. The middle class parties were unable to rise above the party crisis and offer the

disaffected and fractured middle classes a new rallying point. Both the Nazi and the Communist parties reaped profits from the growing disenchantment of the German masses with democracy. However, the appeal of the unrestrained Nazis, who quickly adapted themselves to every situation and promised all things to all men, was much wider in scope than that of the Communists who were handicapped by their rigid class ideology and inflexible Marxist teachings.

The superiority of the Nazi propaganda machine was clearly demonstrated in the phenomenal advance of the Nazi Party in the elections of September 14, 1930, which surpassed even the expectations of the Nazi leaders themselves. The Nazi vote in these elections increased eight-fold in relation to the results it registered only two years earlier—18.3 percent, compared to 2.6 percent in 1928—an amazing feat in the history of democratic mass elections. Its number of parliamentary seats increased nine-fold (from 12 to 107). The Nazi Party (which received 18.3 percent of the vote) came out of these elections as the second strongest party after the SPD (Social Democrats; 24.5 percent) and before the KPD (Communists; 13.1 percent). The middle class, liberal parties were the big losers, with the DVP (German People's Party) and the State Party (former DDP or German Democratic Party) reduced to splinter parties (4.5 percent and 3.8 percent respectively). The DNVP (German National People's Party) also suffered a heavy setback (from 13 percent in 1928 to 8.5 percent). The Catholic Center Party (15 percent) was the only middle class party to remain stable.

Potentially even more deadly than the setback suffered by the democratic forces in the parliamentary elections, was the helplessness of the democratic state in the face of the illegal challenge of Nazism. Not only did Nazi bad-mouthing of the "system" go on unchecked, but a minor civil war developed in the country without the effective interference of either the police or the courts. Bands of SA thugs stalked the streets, breaking up assemblies of the left and terrorizing their political opponents. The unemployed workers flocked into the ranks of the brown-shirted hoards (the SA), drawn by the promise of pay and solidarity. The countermeasures taken by the central authorities were feeble and half-hearted at best. Thus, in the fall of 1931, the attorney general refused to begin criminal proceedings against Werner BEST, the future deputy-chief of the GESTAPO, and his associates, for writing the "Boxheim

Documents" in which they set up elaborate schemes for a terrorist regime following a Nazi takeover of the government. The temporary ban on the SA (April–June 1932) came too late to restrain it; it only had the effect of spurring it on to a new wave of terror. The SA's membership increased from 260,000 at the end of 1931 to 600,000–700,000 at the threshold of the Nazi takeover in January 1933. The lack of firmness and determination on the part of the democratic state and its institutions in the face of the concerted attack that was being mounted against them fitted in very well with Hitler's two-pronged tactic of pseudo-legality and terrorist force. One of the ironies was that the Nazis gained much of their electoral support on the strength of the promise to restore law and order to a situation of anarchy, for the creation of which they were responsible more than any other.

This unprecedented growth of the Nazi Party in the early 1930s took place against the background of a thickening constitutional crisis which created a power vacuum at the very top level of the German state. During the two final years of its existence, the Weimar Republic was governed by a series of non-parliamentary, presidential cabinets, who did not enjoy the support of the majority of the *Reichstag*. This semi-dictatorial nature of the government weakened the parties and drained the life out of the democratic system even before the formal demise of the Weimar Republic. The immediate trigger of the crisis was the breakup of the Great Coalition government under Chancellor Hermann Mueller. The issue over which the coalition, which had been in office just over 21 months, finally broke up, was the proposal to raise the contributions for the unemployment fund. In face of the unresolved dispute between the two "wing parties" of the coalition, the Social Democratic Party, standing mainly for the interests of the laborers, and the German People's Party, representing the interests of the employers, Chancellor Mueller submitted his resignation on March 27, 1930. His was the last government to rest on a parliamentary basis. On March 30, Reich President von Hindenburg, making use of the powers granted him by Article 53 of the constitution, appointed Heinrich Bruening of the Center Party as Mueller's successor. Bruening headed a middle class minority government that did not enjoy the confidence of the majority of the *Reichstag*. When the *Reichstag* passed in middle July a vote of no confidence in Bruening's government, Bruening responded by having Hindenburg dissolve the

Reichstag on July 18 and declare a new general election. The day set for the elections, September 14, 1930, was the last legally permissible date, to give Bruening the longest possible time period to govern without the interference of the *Reichstag*. The September elections provided Bruening with an unpleasant surprise. When the *Reichstag* reconvened again, he found that his parliamentary basis had shrunk even further. An alliance with the Nazi Party, the real winner of the elections, was still unthinkable at that stage; an open alliance with the Social Democratic Party, the largest party, was overruled by the authoritarian president and his associates who did not want to see the Socialists in the government again. The only possible course of action that suggested itself was to govern without a parliamentary majority, with the help of the extraordinary powers conferred on the president by the constitution. The fact that the Bruening administration could last 18 months, until Bruening was finally dismissed by Hindenburg, was due to its unspoken support by the Social Democratic Party. In order to prevent the possible promotion of Hitler to the chancellorship, the majority of the *Reichstag* chose the lesser of two evils and refrained from challenging the authority of the dictatorial Bruening by a vote of no confidence. However, the longer this policy of tolerating a non-democratic cabinet continued, the higher the price it exacted. First of all, by deliberately refraining from playing the democratic game of constituting an opposition to the government, the Social Democrats in fact left the arena free to the Nazis, who could pose as the only true champions of the rights of the people against a government that had taken power without the consent of the people. Second, the fact that for most of this crucial period the *Reichstag* remained out of session, meeting only on rare occasions, meant that the real political confrontation moved to the street where the Nazis had the upper hand. Third, the paralysis of the *Reichstag* served to further discredit the parliamentary system in the eyes of the masses, preparing them for radically undemocratic solutions. Hitler had frequently denounced parliamentary democracy as a foreign intrusion, alien to the spirit of the German people, but it was only the self-imposed deprivation of power by the *Reichstag* delegates which gave the Nazi leaders the chance to present themselves as the true spokesmen of the people.

In spring 1932, the seven year term of office of the 84-year-old president came to an end. Bruening prevailed on the reluctant Hindenburg to run again. The

Nazis had a good chance of having their representative elected in the second round, in which a relative majority of the votes was sufficient. To prevent this danger, the Social Democratic leadership told its supporters to vote for the authoritarian Hindenburg, a choice of the lesser of two evils. The move paid off when Hindenburg was elected in the second round with a majority of 53 percent, against Hitler's 36.8 percent and the Communists' candidate Ernst Thaelemann's 10.2 percent. However, the fact that he could only be reelected thanks to the support of the "Sozis" (Social Democrats) and the Catholics (Center Party) embittered the autocratic Hindenburg. In the coming months he fell out with Bruening and was persuaded by the entourage around him to dismiss him on May 30, 1932. The new chancellor appointed by Hindenburg on June 1 was Franz von Papen, a former member of the Center Party and representative of the extreme right wing there.

With the appointment of von Papen, another essential step in the downhill course that led to Hitler's summons in January 1933 was taken. Unlike his predecessor, von Papen was neither a member of parliament nor the leader of a political party. In fact, he was a private person, accountable to no one except the president. He owed his new office to a chance encounter with General Kurt von Schleicher, another of Hindenburg's favorites. The *Reichstag,* which could not be expected to tolerate the ultra-conservative cabinet of von Papen, was dissolved—prematurely—by Hindenburg, who set the date of the new election for July 31, 1932. This proved an even greater miscalculation than the *Reichstag* election of September 1930. Compared with the 1930 elections, the Nazis had more than doubled their gains, becoming with 37.3 percent of the vote the strongest party by far, well ahead of the Social Democrats, who slid into second position with 21.6 percent. The number of Nazi seats in the *Reichstag* rose from 107 to 230. The biggest losers again were the right wing non-Nazi parties, the so-called middle class parties, who had lost some 5.3 million votes to the Nazis, and who, with the exception of the Catholic Center, practically disappeared from the political scene.

Shortly before the *Reichstag* election, von Papen had dealt a death blow to the last home base of parliamentary democracy in Germany: Prussia. To Hindenburg's chagrin, Otto Braun, the head of the government of Prussia and his two ministers, Carl Severing and Otto Abegg, continued to defend the democratic constitutional order in this largest region of the Reich. On July 20, 1932, von Papen, with the help of the emergency powers of the president, dissolved the democratically elected government of Prussia. Von Papen's governmental overthrow in Prussia set a clear precedent for the Nazi seizure of power less than a year later. Von Papen's decision (on June 4, 1932) to lift the ban on the SA, another of his ill-advised moves, threatened to plunge the country into civil war.

At any rate, when the new *Reichstag* was finally convened on August 30, it passed an overwhelming vote of no confidence against von Papen. To rescue him, Hindenburg again dissolved the parliament and set a new election for November 6. In that election, which took place less than five months after the Nazi landslide victory in July, a very remarkable development took place: the Nazi vote sank from 37.3 percent to 33.1 percent and the number of Nazi seats from 230 to 196. Even though the Nazis remained the strongest party, their upward trend was clearly reversed. And yet, ironically, it was only following this electoral setback and at a time when the economic crisis had already passed its lowest point that Hitler came to power. The role of the midwife in this process of delivering the monstrosity belonged to that tireless schemer, von Papen. Neither he nor Hindenburg had initially wanted to see Hitler in control of the government; they only wanted to use him for their authoritarian plans to reform the republican constitution. In fact, as late as November 24, 1932, Hindenburg stated with remarkable insight that he feared that "a presidential cabinet led by Hitler would necessarily develop into a party dictatorship with all the attendant consequences for an extreme aggravation of the conflicts within the German people." Yet only two months later he was persuaded to summon Hitler to head a new government.

The missing link in the chain of events was Schleicher's short-lived government, which lasted from December 2, 1932 to January 28, 1933. Schleicher, the wily "political general" had persuaded Hindenburg to dismiss his former ally on the grounds that von Papen had no chance of winning widespread popular support. Schleicher's own plan for widening the basis of the government—an outmaneuvering of Hitler in his own party by negotiations with Gregor Strasser—rested on a complete misconception about the realities of power in the Nazi Party and turned out very soon to be a delusion. In the meantime, the ousted von Papen, working tirelessly behind the scenes for his own return to power, was carrying on simultaneous negotiations with Hitler, the conservative party under Hugenberg, and certain German economic leaders (most of whom really favored Schleicher). Finally, after ingratiating himself with Hindenburg's son, Oskar, von Papen managed to turn the tables on his rival and overcome Hindenburg's resistance to the appointment of a Hitler-led government. The pill was sweetened somewhat by having the so-called "cabinet of national concentration" consist of only two Nazi ministers aside from Hitler, with von Papen himself as vice-chancellor, and Hindenburg's own choice as defense minister. The die was cast when Schleicher, who had failed to rally a majority, was forced to resign on Saturday, January 28. On Monday, January 30, Hindenburg appointed Hitler as chancellor.

Two things stand out from the confusion of maneuvers and counter-maneuvers: Hitler's accession to power was neither the result of a violent government takeover nor the outcome of a free democratic election. At the time of his nomination, the Nazi Party was indeed still the largest party with 33.1 percent of the vote, but still far short of an absolute majority. Moreover, it was already on the decline, having lost some 4.2 percent of the vote in relation to its performance in the previous July election. The Nazi coming to power would not have been possible without the breakup of the Weimar Republic and the breakdown of its democratic parliamentary system. Likewise, the manner in which it occurred would have been inconceivable without the structural flaws in the constitution, with the "authoritarian loophole" which permitted the president to appoint governments that did not have parliamentary support. Nevertheless, our understanding of the process of the Nazi rise to power is not furthered by seeing it as either inevitable or unavoidable. There was nothing inevitable about the development that led to Hitler's summons to the chancellorship. The chain of events could probably have been reversed at any single moment before January 30, 1933, but once in the saddle Hitler could no longer be dislodged. The unscrupulous individuals—none of them real supporters of Hitler and his movement—who through their short-sightedness and monumental miscalculations helped smooth Hitler's path to power, had freedom of choice to the very end. They are accountable to history.

The Nazi Consolidation of Power, 1933–1934. The day that Hitler was appointed chancellor by Hindenburg became henceforth known in Nazi lore as "the seizure of power" and was adopted as such by historians of the Nazi period. The term, however, can be doubly misleading. In the first place, the Nazis neither seized nor conquered power. It was delivered to them on a silver platter by Hindenburg, von Papen, and the unholy conservative-national clique around them. Secondly, the 30th of January was not the end of the transfer of power but its beginning. It took the Nazis not one day but 18 months—from January 30, 1933 to August 3, 1934—to consolidate their grip over state and society. The breakthrough of the undertaking was that once in power, the Nazis—like Fascists everywhere—refused to abide by the rules of the old political game and stopped at nothing in their drive to establish total control. Let us be clear about the power relations at the point of departure: January 1933. The so-called seizure of power was in reality a form of political power-sharing between the Nazi movement and the anti-democratic conservative right, represented by Hindenburg, von Papen, and Hugenberg (leader of the German National People's Party). In this "cabinet of national concentration" the Nazis were in a minority position, having only three ministers, as opposed to the eight ministers of the conservatives. The conservatives, with von Papen as vice-chancellor, controlled such important posts as the Ministries of Defense under Werner von Blomberg, Economics and Agriculture under Hugenberg (who as of February 4 also had provisional control of the Prussian Department of Agriculture, Economics, and Labor), and Foreign Affairs under Konstantin von NEURATH. The only two Nazi members of the cabinet—aside from Hitler himself as chancellor—included Wilhelm FRICK, minister of the interior, and the minister without portfolio, Hermann GOERING, who as Reich Commissioner for the Ministry of the Interior in Prussia was nominally under Vice-Chancellor von Papen. In constitutional-parliamentary terms, the first Hitler government was an emergency cabinet like its forerunners, dependent for its existence on the extraordinary powers of the president. The two coalition partners, the Nazi Party (with 33.1 percent of the vote) and the DNVP (8.9 percent), mustered together only 42 percent. On paper at least, the non-Nazi elements in the coalition appeared perfectly capable of taming Hitler. "We have fenced him in" von Papen is reported to have stated triumphantly. This principle of "fencing in" or "containing" Hitler was soon to prove itself a dangerous delusion.

In analyzing the path which the Nazis took to consolidate their monopoly of power, we can distinguish three distinct elements of their strategy: (1) the deliberate dismantling of the remaining foundations of the democratic constitutional system; (2) the exclusion of actual or potential rivals—in the first place, the direct political-ideological opponents of Nazism, in the second place, also its former coalition partners; (3) the administrative leveling ("coordination") of the political, economic, social, and cultural spheres through the infiltration of Nazi principles and Nazi supporters. Hitler sought to lend this three-pronged revolutionary, profoundly unconstitutional process the camouflage of fake legality by calling it "the legal revolution" or "national revolution." However, it was the cooperation of his conservative allies that made it possible to disguise the terrorist, essentially illegal nature of the proceedings.

The first blow against the constitutional multi-party state was cleverly struck on February 1, when, in accordance with the agreement made in forming the government, Hindenburg dissolved the *Reichstag* and set fresh elections for March 5. The upshot was that for the next seven critical weeks, during which the constitutional state was effectively torn down, the supreme legislative body (the *Reichstag*), in which the Nazis were still a minority, was shut out of the political game. When it finally reconvened on March 21, it was already too late; the constitutional order had already been fatally ravaged. On February 4 "an emergency decree of the Reich President for the protection of the German people" made it possible to bring the election campaign of the leftist parties to a standstill by suppressing press activities and public meetings. A far more drastic step was taken with the emergency "Decree of the Reich President for the Protecting of the People and the State" issued the day after the *Reichstag* fire, for which the Communists were blamed. To ward off the alleged Communist danger, the decree set aside the basic rights guaranteed by the Weimar constitution, notably the personal liberties: sanctity of home, privacy of communication, freedom of opinion and assembly, and the guarantee of private property. Public opinion watched silently as the Communist party was smashed and thousands of Communists arrested and imprisoned in the first CONCENTRATION CAMPS without the benefit of trial. However, the declared legal state of emergency—which was in effect never suspended—could be turned at will against anything and anybody deemed harmful to the regime.

Despite the massive Nazi propaganda barrage and the severe restrictions imposed on the campaigns of the left parties, the *Reichstag* elections on March 5 still failed to give the Nazis the desired absolute majority. The Nazi Party won 288 seats out of 647, with 43.9 percent of the vote, so that it still needed the 52 seats of the conservatives (DNVP) for an absolute majority. On March 23, only two days after the festive inauguration of the new *Reichstag,* it passed by a vote of 441 against the 94 of the SPD the "Law to Relieve the Distress of People and Reich." The law, known as the Enabling Law, set the seal on the parliamentary constitutional state as such, by allowing the government to legislate without the consent of the *Reichstag.* It was prolonged by Hitler in 1937, 1941, and 1943.

The "*Reichstag* Fire Decree" also provided the new rulers with a pseudo-legal basis for "coordinating" the individual states (*Laender*), that is taking away their right of self-rule and bringing them in line with the centralist Nazi state. The legal excuse used was the right of the national Reich government to "temporarily assume" the powers of the *Land* governments in case they failed to implement the necessary emergency measures to restore the state of law and order. The legal basis for the "coordination" of Prussia, the biggest state by far, had already been established in the presidential decree of February 6, "For the Restoration of Orderly Government in Prussia." This followed the termination of the Prussian provincial diets (legislative assemblies) and district assemblies as well as all other electoral bodies on the previous day. The next most powerful stronghold of federal autonomy, Bavaria, fell during the second week of March after a concerted campaign of political intimidation followed by the appointment of a Nazi *Commissar* according to the terms of the "*Reichstag* Fire Decree." The coordination of the remaining *Laender* followed in quick order. The law of March 31 regarding the "Coordination (*Gleichschaltung*) of the States (*Laender*) with the Reich" provided legal camouflage for an already existing state of affairs. On April 4 a further coordination law ordered the appointment of Reich governors to be appointed by the Reich President on Hitler's recommendation. With one exception, all these governors, who had a right to appoint the state governments and their officials, were all party *Gau* leaders, as well (after 1933 the *Gau* was the highest "sovereign territory" below the Reich. The *Gau* was directed by a *Gauleiter*, a Nazi Party official).

The legal basis for coordinating the public administration and the professional associations was provided on April 7 with the "Law for the Restoration of the

Professional Civil Service." The euphemistically titled law was the instrument for purging the civil service of all those considered either politically unreliable or racially undesirable. It was extended also to the sphere of culture and to professional and voluntary associations.

The multi-party system was the next target of the "coordination" efforts of the regime. The first victims were naturally the Communists, who were officially banned only after the *Reichstag* elections of March 5. The SPD was able to prolong its existence somewhat by way of its demonstrative—if self-deluding—tactic of adhering to strict legality, but it too was outlawed on June 22 as a "party hostile to the nation and the state." The remaining national and liberal parties obligingly dissolved themselves in the next days: on June 27 the German National People's Party (DNVP), on June 28 the State Party (previously named the German Democratic Party), on July 3 the Center Party, and on July 4 the Bavarian People's Party. With the issuing of the "Law Against the Formation of New Parties" (July 14, 1933), Germany had become a one-party state.

The last logical step was to remove all challenges to Hitler's authority from within the ranks of the Nazi movement. The SA had outlived its usefulness to the regime and had been growing all too strong to the *Fuehrer's* taste. Its unbridled rowdiness and the arrogant ambition of its leader, Rohm, were felt to be a threat to the stability of the new government and to the authority of the established army, the *Reichswehr,* which was considered vital to Hitler's war plans. As an instrument of political terror, the loyal and disciplined SS under Heinrich HIMMLER was considered much superior. Accordingly, between June 30 and July 2, 1934, Ernst Rohm and other SA leaders were summarily executed on Hitler's orders. The SA had now become a leaderless mass-organization, outside the political power game. Its place was taken by the SS, the embodiment and the executive organ *par excellence* of Nazi ideology. Finally, after Hindenburg's death on August 2, 1934, the offices of the president and the chancellor were united by law in the person of Hitler, who had become the all-powerful dictator of the Reich and supreme commander of the armed forces. The law, which set aside any form of division of power, was approved in a plebiscite run on August 19.

The Nature of the Nazi Regime. The complex, unruly process by which the Nazis consolidated their power in Germany between January 30, 1933 and August 2,

1934 was reflected in the two-faced character of the regime. On the one hand, the law that combined the offices of the president and the chancellor and united them in the person of Hitler as the *"Fuehrer* (leader) of the German Reich and *Volk* (people)" confirmed the absolutist nature of the Hitler state. In this state, the *Fuehrer* became the embodiment of the political will of the German people, the sole source of authority and sovereignty, his personal decisions assuming the authority of law. On the other hand, the unsystematic process of the seizure of power, which was by no means completed by August 1934, failed to solve the disputed question as to the proper division of power between the party and the state bureaucracy. A confusion of competing power centers and authorities continued to exist and grow under the shadow of this all-powerful dictatorship. In this system personal relations, especially personal access to Hitler, could be much more important than objective considerations. Hitler's own dislike of the state as such and his wish to see the old order disappear nourished and fortified these anarchic tendencies. The above perceptions work well with the findings of postwar historical scholarship which has considerably modified the popular image of the THIRD REICH as a "well-oiled super state" guaranteed to make everything run in place and on time. Far from guaranteeing an orderly and smooth process of decision-making and policy-implementation, the process of government under the Hitler state—it was felt—resembled a model of "institutional Darwinism," a confusion of competing authorities and private empires that strove for the favor of the dictator. This state of affairs was actively encouraged by Hitler who was guided by the "divide and rule" tactic.

One of the most distinctive outgrowths of the Nazi system of government, which in the end almost became synonymous with the Nazi state as such, was Heinrich Himmler's SS empire. The SS originated from the Personal Headquarters Guard, which Hitler had created in 1922–1923. It was reformed in 1925 as *Schutzstaffeln,* or Protection Squads to protect party leaders and party meetings. The SS only assumed real importance with the appointment of Heinrich Himmler as the new Reich SS Leader on January 6, 1929. Under Himmler the SS grew from a few hundred to about 52,000 members at the end of 1932, and 209,000 by the end of 1933. Dedicated to a *voelkisch* ideology of blood, race, and soil, the former agricultural engineer set about transforming the old bodyguard into an elite corps that would be set apart from the mass army of the SA. The SS had its own insignia and its own unique code of honor, which consisted of absolute and unswerving loyalty to Hitler. The guidelines for the selection of recruits included racial criteria such as strict Aryan ancestry and health, physique, and appearance. Having proven its nerve and strength in the liquidation of the SA leadership on the Night of the Long Knives (June 30, 1934), the SS was rewarded by being granted an independent status within the Nazi Party. Free of SA control, Himmler was now free to build his own power base, which rested on three pillars. First was the monopoly which he and his protege, Reinhard HEYDRICH, had achieved over police functions in the Reich. This was first formalized in Himmler's designation as "Reich *Fuehrer*' of the SS and Chief of the German Police" on June 17, 1936, and finally institutionalized in the foundation of the Reich Security Main Office (REICHSSICHERHEITSHAUPTAMT, RSHA) on September 27, 1939. During the war, the RSHA became the main

instrument of Nazi terror, implementing the Nazi policy of racial GENOCIDE. The second pillar of SS power was the monopoly that its Security Service (SD) had achieved over intelligence-gathering in the Nazi Party. Third was the concentration camp system that had been taken over from the SA after June 1934 and was vastly expanded during the war. The cancerous spread of the SS through all spheres of public life and its growing absorption of normal state functions has given rise to the designation of Nazi Germany as the SS state.

From yet another perspective, the duality of the Nazi state can best be understood in terms of what Ernst Fraenkel, the German-Jewish emigre, analyzed long ago as the phenomenon of the "Dual State." That is, the simultaneous coexistence within one totalitarian system of the "Prerogative State" (*Massnahmenstaat*), characterized by "unlimited arbitrariness and violence unchecked by any legal guarantees" with the "Normative State," characterized by its respect for the courts and the rule of law in general. The "Prerogative State"

Destroying opposition by burning books that are not in accordance with Nazi ideology, Berlin, 1933

embodied above all in the institution of the *Gestapo,* could intervene at any moment and annul the powers of the "Normative State." With the increasing radicalization of the Nazi system in the later 1930s, there was a decisive shift towards the arbitrary and violent component in this uneasy balance. Another German-Jewish emigre, Franz Neumann, writing in 1942, characterized the structure of the Nazi state as *Behemoth,* after the mythological biblical monster. According to Neumann, German society consisted of four centralized groups, each operating according to the leader principle and in accordance with its own legislative, administrative, and judicial powers: the Nazi movement, the higher bureaucracy, the armed forces, and the monopolistic economy. The only thing that united these four competing power centers in the way of compromise was the need to defend their common interests against the oppressed masses. In this early analysis, Hitler's decisions were seen as mere confirmations of previously thought out "compromises" between the competing systems of power. This tendency to take Hitler out of the decision-making process in the Third Reich has been carried even further in later studies, which have described the Nazi system by terms such as "authoritarian anarchy" or "organizational chaos" and termed Hitler himself as "the weak dictator." In the face of these extravaganzas of the "structuralist" approach, it is important to reaffirm that although the Nazi state was not the monolithic *Fuehrer* state wildly talked up by Nazi propaganda—and fixed as such in the popular imagination—it was still, whether at the top or at the lower ranks, an ideology-driven system, dedicated to the implementation of the goals dictated by the Nazi program and its supreme, charismatic advocate, Hitler.

A show of revived German military might under the Nazi regime, Munich, 1935

THE DESTRUCTION OF EUROPEAN JEWRY, 1933–1945

Aharon Weiss

Nazi policy toward the Jews began with acts of terror, social isolation, economic restrictions, denial of human and civil rights, and pressure to remove them from GERMANY—and ended with the almost total destruction of the Jews in occupied Europe. This policy was carried out by the NAZI PARTY and various authorities in the German state, as well as with the active assistance of pro-Nazi and antisemitic forces in the territories conquered by the Germans in WORLD WAR II. Germany's satellite countries also played their part in the process. Hostility to the Jews in this period was indeed fueled by traditional ANTISEMITISM, but it was mainly based on the racist antisemitism that was at the heart of the National Socialist ideology (see also RACISM and NATIONAL SOCIALISM). In its view there was no place for the Jews in human society. The stages in the implementation of Nazi policy were determined by a variety of factors: Nazi Germany's political position in the international community; the extent to which Nazi ideology was accepted in German society and among other nations in occupied Europe; economic considerations; and the course of the war. But in the final analysis it was the Nazis' racist antisemitic ideology that tipped the scales—and the result was the destruction of about six million Jews, approximately one-third of the Jewish people. The HOLOCAUST saw the liquidation of hundreds upon hundreds of Jewish communities with all their material and spiritual treasures. In its scope and nature it was the greatest tragedy that had befallen the Jewish people in its entire history.

The First Stage Of Nazi Anti-Jewish Policy (1933–1939).
With the rise of the Nazis to power in Germany on January 30, 1933, policy toward the Jews took two directions: formal constitutional measures calculated to eliminate the Jews from public and social life, take away their civil rights, and crush them economically; and at the same time smear campaigns, harassment, and violence in every area of life, the overall aim being to force the Jews to leave Germany.

Already in March 1933 Jews were being attacked on the main streets of Germany's cities. Storm Troopers (SA) and excited mobs physically removed Jews from public positions—judges from their courtrooms, lawyers from their offices, teachers from schools, and doc-

tors from the public health service. On April 1, 1933 an economic boycott was instituted against the Jews of Germany, involving among other things boycott watches in front of Jewish business establishments to keep away German patrons (see also BOYCOTT, ANTI-JEWISH). Officially it was a one-day boycott, but unofficially it continued for some time. The boycott was temporarily discontinued, in part, because of world reaction, among both Jews and non-Jews. A law passed on April 7, 1933 brought about the dismissal of many hundreds of Jews from the civil service. In the same year the number of Jewish students at institutes of higher education was adjusted downward to correspond to the percentage of Jews in the total population—less than one percent—far below the actual percentage of Jewish students until the Nazis came to power. On September 29, 1933 Jewish artists were thrown out of the German Artists Association. Jews were also expelled from the media and cultural frameworks: newspapers, the film industry, and the theater.

The year 1935 saw the strengthening of the German state and the Nazi regime, reflected in a corresponding step-up of anti-Jewish policy. On September 15, 1935 the racist NUREMBERG LAWS were issued, fixing the infer-

A Jewish shop on the day of the Boycott, marked with the word Jew (in German) and the Star of David. The sign reads: "Germans! Beware! Don't buy from Jews!"

ior status of the Jews in two ways: 1) by officially revoking the civil equality won by the Jews in the period of the Emancipation; 2) by giving legal force to racist principles. The upshot of these laws was to separate the Jews as individuals and as a group from the rest of the population. Only full-blooded Germans could now be citizens of the German state, and only they had full political rights. Jews were forbidden to enter into marital or sexual relations with those of German blood. Jews could not employ German women under the age of 45 as maids or raise a German flag. In an addition to the law there was a definition setting forth who was a Jew, a definition which would serve in the future as a basis for Nazi policy with regard to the Jews.

Attacks against Jews fell off somewhat in 1936 because of the Berlin Olympics (see also OLYMPIC GAMES OF 1936), but by early 1938 anti-Jewish legislation moved ahead again at a quick pace and attacks orchestrated by various Nazi bodies were stepped up. The drive to take over Jewish businesses and property, ARYANIZATION, was carried out with greater intensity. A decree made property registration mandatory for Jews in order to facilitate confiscation. Many Jews were forced to sell their businesses to Aryans for a fraction of their value.

On another front, a law from 1938 required Jewish men and women to add the name "Israel" or "Sarah" to their own, if they did not bear a so-called "Jewish name" in accordance with a list the Nazis compiled. Thus, Jews could be clearly identified from their names alone. On June 15, 1938 about 1,500 Jews were sent to CONCENTRATION CAMPS, and in October arrests of Jews holding Polish citizenship began, peaking within a short while with the expulsion of about 17,000 Jews to the Polish border. The Polish government refused to admit them and some were herded into the border town of ZBASZYN under extremely difficult conditions.

All this persecution made many Jews want to leave Germany, but numerous countries refused to take them in. To solve the problem of Jewish REFUGEES from Germany, the EVIAN CONFERENCE was convened in FRANCE in July 1938 with the aim of finding places of refuge for them. Deliberations produced no real results. Seeing that the countries of the world were not about to volunteer to accept large numbers of Jews, the Nazis came to the conclusion that their principal aim of getting the Jews out of Germany would not be realized through "legal" measures alone. Therefore they decided to step up the acts of violence and terror against the

Jews. Nazi leaders exploited the assassination of a German embassy worker in PARIS by a young Jew named Herschel GRYNSZPAN to unleash the riots that came to be known as KRISTALLNACHT. On the night of November 9–10, 1938 rioters throughout Germany smashed windows in Jewish homes and stores, pillaged Jewish property, and set over 250 synagogues on fire. Thousands of Jews were beaten and humiliated, and dozens were murdered or injured. Over 7,500 Jewish business establishments were destroyed and about 30,000 Jews were sent to CONCENTRATION CAMPS.

It should be noted that the Jewish response to persecution was twofold: increased efforts at emigration, on the one hand, and attempts to strengthen the internal organization of the community in the fields of education, culture, and welfare, and by deepening Jewish identity, on the other.

AUSTRIA was annexed to the German Reich in March 1938, drawing its 185,000 Jews as well into the web of persecution that was the lot of Germany's Jews. With the final dismemberment of Czechoslovakia on March 15, 1939, another 118,000 Jews, inhabitants of the newly created Protectorate of Bohemia and Moravia, also came under direct Nazi rule and were subjected to pressure to emigrate (see also BOHEMIA AND MORAVIA, PROTECTORATE OF). In all, nearly 450,000 Jews left Germany with its expanded borders, representing over half the pre-1933 Jewish population. With the outbreak of WWII, those who remained behind and those in other European countries now faced a reality at the heart of which lay the threat of annihilation.

The Second Stage Of Nazi Anti-Jewish Policy (September 1939–June 1941). With the outbreak of war on September 1, 1939, the Germans conquered western POLAND, and in accordance with the terms of the NAZI-SOVIET PACT, eastern Poland was annexed to the SOVIET UNION. German-occupied territory, under the name GENERALGOUVERNEMENT, contained about two million Jews. Subsequently, within less than two years, the Germans also conquered DENMARK, NORWAY, the NETHERLANDS, BELGIUM, LUXEMBOURG, France, YUGOSLAVIA, and GREECE, and the Jews there came under German rule. During the same period the persecution of Jews in Germany's satellites also increased: in SLOVAKIA, HUNGARY, ROMANIA, CROATIA, BULGARIA, and in Vichy-ruled (French) North Africa. The situation of the Jews also deteriorated in ITALY, Germany's ally. The nature and extent of antisemitic policy in these countries was to a large degree the function of the influence of local antisemites and the nonstop pressure exercised by Germany.

In the period between September 1939 (when Germany invaded Poland) and June 1941 (marking the invasion of the Soviet Union) Nazi policy toward the Jews underwent a distinct change. The possibility of emigrating, which in any case had been unpromising on the eve of the war, was now practically eliminated. The world was divided into two enemy camps engaged in a war. The deep-seated hatred of the Jews that was part and parcel of the Nazi ideology deepened. World opinion with regard to the situation of the Jews was no longer a factor for the Nazis in determining their policy toward the Jews. Under these circumstances, the Nazi leadership began coming up with various "solutions" for the Jewish problem in areas under Nazi control. At this stage their policy was based on total denial of human and civil rights to the Jews, their humiliation and their isolation from their surroundings, restriction of all economic activity, exploitation of the Jews for FORCED LABOR, and starvation. To achieve these ends the Jews were concentrated in GHETTOS. This period saw the expulsion of the Jews from the territory of the Reich, Bohemia, and Moravia to occupied Poland and from 1940, the concentration of thousands of Jews in forced labor camps, as well. Even if the scheme of mass destruction had not yet crystallized, thousands of Jews began to fall victim to the general deterioration in their living conditions, to backbreaking labor, starvation, disease, the inhuman conditions in the ghettos, and the terror in the labor camps. This stage of Nazi policy toward the Jews can rightly be called "indirect destruction."

Numerous measures were applied against the Jews in the Polish *Generalgouvernement* in the first months of the occupation: forced labor for those between the ages of 14 and 60; a ban on changing places of residence; wearing of a white band marked with the Star of David on the right arm (see also BADGE, JEWISH); confiscation of property; and group fines. From the fall of 1939 the Germans began expelling Jews to the *Generalgouvernement* territory from the parts of Poland annexed to the Reich: DANZIG (Gdansk), western Prussia, Poznan, and Eastern Upper Silesia (see also SILESIA, EASTERN UPPER). Between October 1939 and March 1940 the Germans concentrated about 95,000 Jews, some from VIENNA, around the town of Nisko, near LUBLIN. They were brought to a deserted area, cold and hungry, and ordered to build a camp. This was part of the German effort to create a Jewish "reservation" in the Nisko-Lublin area (see also NISKO AND LUBLIN PLAN). Jews were to be brought there from areas earmarked for "cleansing" of Jews. Confinement of the Jews in this area was meant to facilitate their supervision, their exploitation for forced labor, and their elimination through starvation and disease. The plan was scrapped, most probably, because of a dispute over the division of responsibility among different branches of the Nazi administration, and DEPORTATIONS to the so-called reservation were consequently stopped in March 1940.

Another plan for the "solution of the Jewish problem" in territories controlled by the Germans was connected to the French colony of Madagascar (see also MADAGASCAR PLAN). In the middle of 1940, after the fall of France, a German foreign ministry official proposed concentrating four million European Jews in Madagascar, where they would be under full German control. After the British captured the island the scheme was abandoned. Following all these developments, with the option of emigration eliminated by the war and with the Nisko-Lublin and Madagascar plans scrapped, the Nazi leadership began to arrive at the conclusion that other ways would have to be sought to deal with the Jews of Europe. In the unfolding of their plans the ghettos, the concentration camps, and the labor camps were to play a central role. At this stage officials in the SS still hoped that pushing Jews into the Soviet interior would also contribute to the solution. Some regard this as an intermediate stage on the road to mass systematic murder, which began to be implemented after the German invasion of the Soviet Union on June 22, 1941.

The Ghettos. Ghettos were first set up in Poland and, after June 1941, in the occupied territories of the Soviet Union, for the purpose of isolating the Jewish population and making it easier to relieve them of their property and exploit them for forced labor. The ghettos were mainly established in poorer quarters or in overcrowded Jewish neighborhoods. Many were surrounded by walls or fences, or utilized other means to eliminate contact with the outside world. The Jews were moved to the ghettos quickly and allowed to take only personal possessions with them, resulting in the loss of their remaining property. The ghettos were overcrowded and without basic hygienic facilities. Official food rations were inadequate to support life. Under these circumstances, life in the ghetto was characterized by aggravated hunger and high rates of death and disease. In the year 1941, for example, over 43,000 people died in the

A scene from the Warsaw Ghetto, September 1941

WARSAW Ghetto, representing ten percent of the Jewish population there. The death rate rose much higher up to the mass deportations of summer 1942. The Germans took severe measures against food smugglers, including execution.

THERESIENSTADT in Czechoslovakia occupies a special place in the ghetto landscape. First Czech Jews and then selected groups of German, Austrian, Danish, Dutch, Belgian, and Slovak Jews were housed there, and the place was billed as a "model Jewish settlement" to throw sand in the eyes of the public opinion. In reality, the circumstances in Theresienstadt were very bad, and many Jews died there before they were ever deported to Nazi camps. Despite these terrible conditions, in Theresienstadt, as in many of the other ghettos, Jews engaged in a great variety of cultural activities—expressions of their humanity in the face of Nazi inhumanity.

Labor Camps. Jews were mobilized for forced labor from the first days of the German occupation. The Jews were not paid for their labor, being subjected instead to abuse and physical attacks. In the summer of 1940 German policy went a step further and tens of thousands of Jews were separated from their families and communities and sent to forced labor camps, which were sealed off and well-guarded. The first of these camps was established in the Lublin area. Over the course of time, the camp network spread throughout the entire *Generalgouvernement* and other occupied territories. Inmates were put to work building fortifications, roads, and bridges, or laboring in factories. Work conditions, housing, and food were terrible and a backbreaking regime was instituted in the

camps that caused its inhabitants to lose their strength, their health, and often their lives.

Concentration Camps. Concentration camps were established in Germany soon after the Nazi rise to power and were intended for opponents of the regime as a means of breaking them, and often of eliminating them physically. Many Jews were among the party and trade union members, the professionals, and academics who became objects of Nazi terror and were sent to the various camps in the early years. After *Kristallnacht,* the concentration camps served mainly as another of the deadly weapons in the arsenal of anti-Jewish policy. Among the better-known camps operating in the 1933–1939 period were DACHAU, ORANIENBURG, SACHSENHAUSEN, BUCHENWALD, and RAVENSBRUECK. After 1939 some of these were integrated into the larger system of camps where millions of Jews and other peoples in occupied Europe were imprisoned, exploited in backbreaking slave labor, and murdered. With the expansion of the system, the nature and function of the camps also changed, so that a distinction must be made between transit camps, concentration camps, labor camps, and—with the arrival of the "FINAL SOLUTION" at the stage of mass murder—EXTERMINATION CAMPS, as well.

The Third Stage: The "Final Solution" (*Endloesung*), or Mass Destruction (June 1941–Summer 1943). As part of the preparations for the invasion of the Soviet Union in spring 1941, principles and practical measures were developed for the mass destruction of, mainly, the Jews. German documents from the time earmarked a number of specific groups for mass murder, such as Communist *commissars* and members of the Soviet intellectual class who were considered to be dangerous to efforts to control the soon to be conquered areas. Jews were considered dangerous by definition, since in the Nazi view of the world they were not only the creators of Bolshevism—they were seen as its most fervent adherents. The ideological and political principles of the Nazis, which had until then been applied to the Jews in the occupied territories by means of denial of rights, humiliation, starvation, robbery, and forced labor, began to receive their most extreme expression: the murder of the Jews as Jews without differentiation.

Responsibility for implementing the plan for the total destruction of the Jews was placed in the hands of the SS and the Reich Security Main Office (REICHSSICHERHEITSHAUPTAMT, RSHA). Among the more prominent directors of the machinery of mass murder were Heinrich HIMMLER, head of the SS; Reinhard HEY-DRICH, head of the RSHA; and after his assassination by Czech partisans in 1942, Ernst KALTENBRUNNER. From 1939 Adolf EICHMANN was head of the Department of Jewish Affairs in the GESTAPO and a central figure in the organization of the "Final Solution." HITLER himself was closely involved in the policy of the mass systematic murder of the Jews. The central role of the RSHA was confirmed in a letter from Hermann GOERING to Heydrich dating from July 31, 1941, in which he wrote: "The final solution of the Jewish problem must be implemented in the German sphere of influence in Europe."

On June 22, 1941, the German armed forces invaded the Soviet Union. Within days, special units of the SS, the *Einsatzgruppen*, began "pacifying" the newly occupied areas as they had been ordered to do in the spring. From the start Jews were the main target of the killings. In addition to the SS, regular German army units, various police units, and local collaborators all had a hand in the murder. At first Jewish women and children were not shot, but by mid-August the mass murder had spread to them as well. This apparently

came about after Heinrich Himmler visited the front, where it became clear that a territorial solution to the Jewish problem no longer existed, which in turn opened the door to systematic mass murder in Nazi territory. It also was determined that Jewish women and children would be of no labor value and thus should be disposed of as "useless eaters." All Jews in these areas were now under sentence of death.

Here we see clearly the interplay between ideology and a distorted Nazi sense of pragmatism, and how several different lines now began to be tied together. First, Jews were not considered a part of the German community (*Volksgemeinschaft*) and moreover were considered to be "biologically" dangerous: therefore they need not be treated humanely. Second, solving the Jewish problem was of high priority, and when the war began against the Soviet Union, all plans for pushing Jews out of Nazi territory ceased being considered. Third, the Nazis had sweeping plans for resettling populations, and as part of this the Jewish presence in a particular area was considered a serious problem. Fourth, Nazi forces engaged in mass murder from early in the war onward; in the AB AKTION thousands of Poles

Jew being beaten by civilians, Riga, Latvia, 1941

had been murdered, and before the advent of the "Final Solution," thousands of Jews had also been murdered, albeit not systematically. With the entry into the Soviet Union, systematic mass murder became institutionalized. Once systematic mass murder became an accepted and wide spread tool, any combination of supposedly practical considerations, such as food distribution or housing shortages could be invoked as triggers or justifications for specific murder *Aktionen*. This was the case in Stanislavov, in newly occupied Galicia. According to the research of Thomas Sandkuehler, on Yom Kippur in October of 1941 over half of the Jewish community of 20,000 was murdered because the site designated for the ghetto was too small to hold them all. Later, with the establishment of the extermination camps, various "practical" considerations, along with local fluctuations in the need for Jewish labor, or infighting among different German authorities, could determine when specific deportations occurred and exactly which Jews they affected. But once the "Final Solution" had become policy, all Jews were eventually to be murdered.

With the German invasion of the Soviet Union on June 22, 1941, the entire Soviet military apparatus broke down, and within a few weeks the German army had occupied vast areas in which large numbers of Jews were concentrated. These were both original Soviet territories (the UKRAINE, BELORUSSIA, and the western parts of the Russian SFSR) and territories annexed by the Soviet Union in 1939–1940 (eastern Poland, LITHUANIA, LATVIA, ESTONIA, BESSARABIA, and northern BUKOVINA). The combined Jewish population in all these territories on the eve of the German invasion was about 3,900,000.

Hundreds of thousands of Jews succeeded in fleeing to the interior of the Soviet Union but most were trapped by the Germans and became victims of murders carried out by the *Einsatzgruppen,* the WEHRMACHT, various police units, and local collaborators. By early 1942 about one million Jews had been put to death by the Germans and their helpers. The massacres generally took place in forests, valleys, and empty buildings near the homes of the victims. The procedure was usually the same: SS or army officers would order the Jews to report on a certain date to an assembly point with a few belongings only. Sometimes they were told that they were being evacuated to labor camps, but very often no explanations were given at all. Hiding and mass flight were prevented by the threat to execute immediately anyone who failed to report at the desig-

nated place on time. It should be remembered that in the first months of the occupation the Jews did not know and could not have known what was in store for them. From the assembly points the Jews were marched to previously prepared burial pits. In some instances the murderers used natural sites like gullies and ravines or army trenches. The first victims were murdered on the way there as guards shot anyone who could not keep up. At a certain distance from the mass graves the Jews were ordered to undress and hand over all valuables. They were then taken in groups to the pits, and shot. Many fell into the pits wounded and were buried alive. The firing squads were made up of Germans and collaborators like the Ukrainian and Lithuanian police. Only a few of the wounded were able to climb out of the pits at night and, either on their own or with the help of neighboring peasants, rejoin the remnant of the community or hide out in the villages or the forest. It was only through the eyewitness accounts of these survivors that the Jews left behind learned what had befallen those members of their communities taken away "to an unknown destination."

In the summer and fall of 1941, Lithuania was soaked in blood. Here, local collaborators played a particularly active role. In Latvia the Jews in the provincial towns were killed off within a few weeks, excluding the Jews of Dvinsk, RIGA, and Liepaja. In late November and early December 1941, 27,000 of Riga's 33,000 Jews were murdered at RUMBULA, not far from the city. The ghetto was then filled with Jews from Germany, some of whom were also murdered within a short time.

Most of the 5,000 Jews of Estonia managed to escape. Out of the approximately 1,000 who remained, about 500 were murdered in September 1941 and the rest later. But in Belorussia, proportionately fewer Jews were able to flee east owing to the quick Nazi armed advance there. In eastern Galicia and Volhynia, which comprised the western Ukraine, the Germans and the local populace (mostly the Ukrainians) staged pogroms against the Jews throughout the entire month of July 1941, and in the entire area about 28,000 were murdered in this way. In the Soviet Ukraine some Jews were able to escape to the east before the arrival of the Germans. Those who remained behind shared the fate of the rest of the Jews in the region.

While fighting was going on in late June and early July 1941, the German army and its Romanian allies

Jews awaiting deportation

began the mass destruction of the Jews of Bessarabia and northern Bukovina. About 150,000 Jews were massacred in July and August, representing about half the prewar Jewish population in these regions. The murders were accompanied by various acts of abuse and the pillaging of Jewish property. Those who remained alive for the time being were deported to TRANSNISTRIA in September and October. Participating in the Transnistrian massacres were SS units, Romanian soldiers, the Romanian *gendarmerie* (police), and local collaborators such as the Ukrainian police and ethnic Germans (VOLKSDEUTSCHE).

In the meantime, toward the end of 1941, the Germans realized that the war was going to be a long, drawn-out affair and that the German army would require a workforce for its duration, especially skilled labor, and thus decided to set up temporarily, in a number of big cities, ghettos whose inhabitants could be exploited for the war effort. This was what happened, for example, in Riga, VILNA, KOVNO, MINSK, BIALYSTOK,

and other places. However, other than in such places, the wave of mass destruction was renewed in all its fury in the occupied territories of the Soviet Union in the spring of 1942. By the winter of 1942–1943, most of the Jews of western Belorussia and the western Ukraine had been liquidated, including thousands in the Lida and Slutsk districts, in the Novogrudok and BARANO-VICHI ghettos, in the city of Grodno and its environs, and in the Polesie region—about 17,000 Jews in Pinsk on October 29–November 1, 1942—and all the Jews in the Brest-Litovsk Ghetto in October 1942. Most of the ghettos in the western Ukraine were also liquidated in 1942 and their remnants were converted into labor camps. It should be noted that beginning in 1942 the Jews of the western Ukraine were liquidated in two ways: by the established method and by deportation to extermination camps.

The Establishment Of The Extermination Camps And Their Operation. As has been seen, upon the invasion of the Soviet Union the mass murder of the Jews was carried out within the occupied territories of the country. However, at the same time, the plan for the total destruction of Europe's Jews was beginning to be elaborated. Nazi and SS leaders kept a close watch on the mass murders in the east, but even if hundreds of thousands were being liquidated by the conventional method of execution—firing squads—it was clear that this would not suffice to destroy all the Jews of Europe. It would seem that the Nazis had a number of reasons for setting up the extermination camps, including both the desire to speed up the process and improve its efficiency and the wish to hide the crime of GENOCIDE from the eyes of Europe and the world. While it is true that as the war unfolded Nazi sensitivity to public opinion declined, the perpetrators nonetheless still wished to hide the crime in all its immensity.

As early as summer 1941, Rudolf HESS, commander of the AUSCHWITZ (Oswiecim) concentration camp, was ordered to test new methods of mass destruction. The idea arrived at was the use of GAS CHAMBERS. The Germans had already tried gassing in 1939–1941 as part of their EUTHANASIA PROGRAM, putting to death 70,000–90,000 of the disabled and mentally ill in Germany. The practice had been greeted with a public outcry in Germany and was therefore canceled, but the experience acquired served as a basis for improving methods and extending the system to the extermination camps.

The first experiment in mass extermination in a gas chamber was conducted in Auschwitz in September 1941. The victims were Soviet PRISONERS OF WAR. A chemical substance called ZYKLON B was introduced into a sealed chamber, causing their death within a short time. Additional experiments were carried out and in the end, a network of extermination camps was created where over three million Jews were sent to their deaths in 1942–1944. With the principle of gassing established, various methods were tried simultaneously. In late 1941 the Germans tried out sealed GAS VANS, usually disguised as ambulances, in the occupied territories of the Soviet Union. A few dozen Jews would be packed into the van, the engine would be run, and the exhaust gases would be piped into the sealed vehicle. The process took 20–30 minutes. The bodies were then removed and thrown into previously dug pits.

Widespread use of this method was made in the first extermination camp, which was set up on Polish soil near the village of CHELMNO in the LODZ area on December 8, 1941. The Jews were brought to an assembly point not far from Chelmno and ordered to undress and

The selektion of Hungarian Jews on the arrival platform in Auschwitz, 1944

get into the sealed vans for what they were told was the ride to the baths. They were gassed to death during the three-mile ride to the burial pits. Burial was handled by a special group of prisoners. In all, about 300,000 Jews were murdered at Chelmno, most from the Lodz Ghetto and other ghettos in the same area.

In late 1941 the Germans began planning practical steps for the mass destruction of the Jews in the *Generalgouvernement* territory. At around the same time, the second extermination camp in Poland was established, BELZEC, midway between LVOV and Lublin. It was completed in early 1942 and in March the first transports of Jews arrived from the Lublin district and from eastern Galicia (the latter being part of the western Ukraine from fall 1939, but transferred by the Germans to the *Generalgouvernement* in August 1941).

Thus the first units in the machinery of destruction were put into operation for the annihilation of the Jews of Poland and afterwards the Jews of other countries in occupied Europe. According to the research of the historian Christian Gerlach, based on Himmler's meetings' diary, on December 12, 1941 Hitler told some of his intimates that the murder would include the German Jews as well, which now meant the murder was to encompass all Jews everywhere.

To speed up the construction of the extermination camp network and create the organizational framework for the transfer of millions of Jews to the killing grounds, Heydrich convened a conference in Wannsee, a suburb of BERLIN, on January 20, 1942. Present were government and Nazi Party representatives and the heads of the SS and police. The WANNSEE CON-

FERENCE may be regarded as one more important stage in the elaboration of the "final solution of the Jewish problem" in Europe.

Following the conference, two new extermination camps were established in the Lublin area in addition to the Belzec camp: SOBIBOR and TREBLINKA. Sobibor began operating in March 1942 and Treblinka in June. The three camps together were called the Operation Reinhard camps, named for the slain head of the RSHA, Reinhard Heydrich (see also AKTION REINHARD). All three camps used the same method of extermination: gas pumped into hermetically sealed chambers by big diesel engines. The victims, who were packed naked into the chambers, died quickly. Afterwards the bodies were thrown into giant pits. Later, to obliterate all traces of the crime, the bodies were dug up and burned while special machines ground up the bones. These three camps were in effect "death factories," with the entire process, from the arrival of the victims to their extermination, taking about two hours and thus making possible the immediate disposition of additional transports with new victims.

In these camps, no SELEKTIONEN were made between those slated to die and those able to work. Only small groups of Jews were picked to take part in certain aspects of the extermination process, such as sorting and packing the victims' clothes, removing hair from the bodies, emptying the gas chambers, burying the dead, and burning the corpses. These Jews were part of what was called the SONDERKOMMANDO, and they worked under a reign of terror, some being gassed after a short time and replaced by others.

Each of these camps was staffed by 25–30 SS personnel and 100–120 Ukrainians chosen for the work from among Soviet prisoners of war. These Ukrainian "volunteers" received special training in an SS camp at TRAWNIKI, near Lublin. The three extermination camps themselves were situated in isolated areas and closely guarded so that no one on the outside, near or far, might guess what was going on there. In the final count, over a million and a half Jews were murdered in the three camps.

The most infamous of all the extermination camps was Auschwitz, in Silesia. In 1940 a concentration camp was set up at the old Polish army barracks on the site to imprison Polish opponents of the occupation. In October 1941 the Germans began constructing a camp nearby at the Polish village of Brzezinka (in German: Birkenau), intended from the outset to serve as an extermination camp, and also known as "Auschwitz II." Mass extermination began in March 1942, and eventually its four big, improved gas chambers were capable together of killing about 12,000 people simultaneously with the use of Zyklon B. The bodies were burned in crematoria next to the gas chambers. Transports from all over occupied Europe brought the victims to Birkenau, where an immediate *selektion* was made with some chosen for work in local factories and the rest taken to the gas chambers. The number of Jewish dead at Birkenau is estimated to be at least one million.

Another extermination camp was MAJDANEK in the suburbs of Lublin. It began in 1941 as a Soviet prisoner of war camp and later held thousands of Poles as well. In 1942 Jews too were sent there in large numbers, with about 150,000 perishing. As mentioned, dozens of labor and concentration camps were in effect transformed during the war into death camps for thousands of Jews. In 1942 the stage was thus set for the implementation of the "final and total solution," not only through mass executions by firing squads but now also in "death factories" which within a short while would claim millions of lives.

The largest of the ghettos set up in Europe was Warsaw. The course of events there can serve as a broad example of those that overtook the Jews of Poland once the "Final Solution" had been ordered, although in the small details the history of each ghetto was unique. In late 1941 and the first half of 1942 terror was stepped up against the Jews of Warsaw. Jews who were accused of smuggling food were executed along with dozens suspected of belonging to the underground. These operations were intended to pacify the ghetto prior to mass deportations. On July 22, 1942 notice was given of the evacuation of the Jews of Warsaw. Considerable unrest resulted in the ghetto and many tried to get work permits to avoid the scheduled deportation. The JUDENRAT was ordered to help assemble the daily quota of 9,000 deportees but its chairman, Adam CZERNIAKOW, refused to give in to the demand, committing suicide instead. Deportations continued until September 12, 1942, with about 260,000 Jews sent to Treblinka. At that point the ghetto area was reduced and only Jews with work permits were permitted to reside there. About 60,000 Jews now remained in the ghetto, some "illegally." In October the Jewish Fighting Organization (ZOB) was officially established (see also JEWISH FIGHTING ORGANIZATION, WARSAW). Upon the resumption of deportations on

January 18, 1943, the ZOB clashed with the Nazis, causing deportations to be halted. The WARSAW GHETTO UPRISING began on April 19, 1943, when the Germans moved to liquidate the entire ghetto. Despite the overwhelming superiority of German forces the Jewish fighters engaged them boldly in battle for about three weeks. To defeat the Jewish fighters, the Nazis burned down the ghetto area. The WARSAW GHETTO UPRISING became a symbol of Jewish resistance against the Nazis.

By the fall of 1943, most of the Jews of Poland had been liquidated. In the same period the deportation and destruction of the Jews in other European countries also gained momentum. Deportation to the east continued from Germany, Austria, and Bohemia and Moravia. Some were murdered shortly after their arrival and the rest shared the fate of the local Jews later on. From November 1941 through 1942 and into 1943, about 60,000 Jews from the territory of the Reich and about 70,000 from the Protectorate of Bohemia and Moravia were sent to the Theresienstadt Ghetto. Most were subsequently transferred to other camps and fewer than 20,000 survived.

The Jews from Slovakia were among the first group deported to Poland, beginning in March 1942. During the first wave of deportations, until October of that year, some two-thirds of the 90,000 Jews living in the country were deported to Poland, where they were murdered. Another 13,000 were deported after the failed SLOVAK NATIONAL UPRISING in the fall of 1944.

The Jews of Western Europe were deported at different times between the summer of 1942 and 1944 to a variety of camps, chief among them Auschwitz. From France, they were sent to the east via the transit camp at DRANCY, in large part owing to the collaboration of certain segments of French society. The Dutch Jews were deported via WESTERBORK, and the Belgian Jews via MECHELEN. The Jews of Scandinavia had a different experience. Most of Danish Jewry and half of Norwegian Jewry reached safety in SWEDEN, and almost all of the small Finnish Jewish community was safe-guarded in FINLAND. Slightly under two-thirds of the 3,500 Jews of Luxembourg were deported. In Italy, thousands of Jews were interned in local camps, and about 7,500 of the 57,000 Jews who lived in Italy before the war died during the Holocaust.

In the other areas of Europe, different communities had different fates, and sometimes in the same country, different groups of Jews were treated differently by the local regimes. In both Romania and Bulgaria, most of the Jews killed were those who lived in territories acquired by those countries during the war. The Jews of pre-war Bulgaria were saved by a combined effort of Jewish leaders and Bulgarian leaders, whereas those living in MACEDONIA AND THRACE were deported to extermination camps by the Germans with the cooperation of the Bulgarian regime. The Romanians murdered a great many Jews in the areas they occupied (Bessarabia, Bukovina, and Transnistria), but largely spared the Jews of their heartland, known as the Regat. The Jews of northern TRANSYLVANIA, an area relinquished by the Romanians under German pressure and awarded to the Hungarians, shared the terrible fate of Hungarian Jewry—almost three-quarters of whom were murdered during the last 14 months of the war, with the collaboration of the Hungarian regime. Most of the Jews of Greece, including the large Jewish community of SALONIKA, were sent to their deaths primarily in the spring and summer of 1943, although some transports were sent to Poland as late as the summer of 1944. In Yugoslavia, which the Germans dismembered, the Croatian USTASA puppet regime had a hand in the murder and by spring 1943, almost all the Jews had been killed. In SERBIA, the Jews were murdered by the Germans, often locally in gas vans. The situation of the Jews was better along the Adriatic shore, where the Italians were in control. Almost all of them survived.

The Fourth And Final Stage In The Process Of Destruction (Fall 1943–May 1945). Starting in spring 1943 a definite turn in the fortunes of the war could be perceived. Germany had been disastrously defeated at Stalingrad and a slow retreat was in process along the entire Eastern Front. The Allies too had had successes. However, even under these circumstances the destruction of the last remnants of the Jews in the ghettos and in the concentration and extermination camps continued unabated. Owing to their lack of military success and the need to draft new recruits into the army, the Germans felt a serious shortage in the manpower needed to keep the war economy going. Against this background, part of the military and economic leadership proposed the exploitation of able-bodied Jewish workers. On the other hand, the Nazi leadership wished to continue with its implementation of the "Final Solution" irrespective of economic considerations. In its view, absolute priority was to be given to ideological considerations and the process of destruction even stepped up. It should be pointed out that even at this stage, those who wished to call a temporary halt to the murder of able-bodied Jews had no basic objection to their destruction nor any humanitarian purpose in mind; they were acting out of practical considerations. Thus, alongside direct and unrestrained extermination, there evolved a policy of "extermination through labor" for part of the able-bodied Jewish population.

Coinciding with the Soviet advance westward, the Germans began to liquidate the last ghettos and labor camps. Special units were also created to obliterate all traces of Nazi crimes by digging up bodies from the mass graves and burning them (see also AKTION 1005).

The Vilna Ghetto was liquidated in September 1943. About 6,000 Jewish men were sent to camps in Estonia and about 2,000 women were transferred to the KLOOGA camp near TALLINN. The Kovno Ghetto existed as a labor camp until mid-August 1944. About two weeks before the Soviet army entered the city, the last Jews were moved to various camps in the west. The remnants of the Jews of Latvia were concentrated in the KAISERWALD camp, where most perished. The remnants of the Jews in the Estonian camps were transferred to the STUTTHOF camp near Gdansk (Danzig) in 1944. In the second half of 1944 the Germans assembled about 50,000 Jews in the latter camp and in January 1945 sent them on a "DEATH MARCH" to the west. The last ghettos of Belorussia were liquidated in fall 1943. The Minsk Ghetto ceased to exist on September 23, 1943. The Bialystok Ghetto was one of the last to survive in eastern Poland. Up to August 1943 it had about 35,000 inhabitants. The head of the *Judenrat* there, Efraim BARASZ, set up extensive industrial facilities, hoping to prolong the life of the ghetto by making it vital to the German war economy. He also hoped that the Soviet advance would lead to the collapse of the German front and pave the way for the Soviet army to reach Bialystok and rescue the Jews in the ghetto. But here too, ideological considerations were put before economic necessity and on August 16, 1943 the Germans began to liquidate the ghetto. As in dozens of other ghettos throughout Eastern Europe, the Jewish underground resisted, but the uprising was brutally suppressed. The Lvov Ghetto was liquidated in June 1943. The CRACOW Ghetto was liquidated in March 1943 and in September 1943 all the others in the area were likewise liquidated.

With the Soviet army nearing the Polish border, the Germans also sped up the liquidation process in the camps. Most of the inmates were murdered on the spot while others were evacuated to the west. The elimination of the Jews in the camps of the Lublin area began in November 1943, under the code name ERNTEFEST, meaning harvest festival. After the wave of deportations in summer 1942 the remnant of the Jewish communities of central Poland was concentrated in such ghettos as RADOM, KIELCE, Czestochowa, and PIOTRKOW TRYBUNALSKI. By mid-1943 all had been liquidated. Able-bodied workers were confined in the labor camps around Czestochowa and Piotrkow. These were evacuated to German camps in late 1944. On August 23, 1944 the Lodz Ghetto was liquidated, most of its 70,000 inhabitants being deported to Auschwitz.

The Jews In The Last Months Of The German Reich. In fall 1944 and early winter 1945 the evacuation of the inmates of camps, known as the Death Marches, began. On November 25, 1944 Himmler gave the order to dismantle the mass murder facilities at Auschwitz and in January 1945 the order to evacuate all the camps near the front and march their inmates to Germany. At that time death marches from Auschwitz to GROSS-ROSEN, Sachsenhausen, MAUTHAUSEN, Dachau, Ravensbrueck, Buchenwald, and BERGEN-BELSEN began. Auschwitz was liberated by the Soviet army on January 20, 1945. Meanwhile, thousands and thousands of Jews—sick and exhausted—were dying in the Nazi death marches. It is estimated that 200,000 Jews took part in these marches and that 80,000 perished on German soil, all this just a few weeks, a few days, before the end of the war. In Bergen-Belsen alone the toll was about 40,000.

In early May 1945, in the final hours of Nazi Germany, before putting an end to his life in his Berlin bunker, Adolf Hitler composed his "political testament," calling for the war against "International Jewry" to continue. This document personifies the poisonous hatred of the Jewish people whose end result was the murder of six million Jews during his regime.

After the war, the Nazi leadership was brought before an international tribunal at Nuremberg to answer for its crimes against peace and humanity (see also NUREMBERG TRIALS). Much of the trial focused on Nazi crimes against the Jewish people, which had been so central to the Nazi worldview and regime. The survivors of the Holocaust began the painful but deter'mined and hope-inspired task of rebuilding their lives.

ON BEING A JEW IN THE HOLOCAUST

Robert Rozett

Introduction. Since the events of the HOLOCAUST, the circumstances that led up to it, and its aftereffects were played out on a vast canvas of history, it is impossible to present one model for understanding the experience of Jews in the whirlpool of the Holocaust. At best it is possible to point out commonalities or similarities in the experiences of Jews that sometimes cut across space or time. Some of these experiences share only their general form but differ significantly in the details. Others sometimes share many of the details as well. Most Jews in Nazi-dominated Europe were ultimately subjected to profound physical hardship—hunger, thirst, cold, extreme heat, debilitating disease, cruel beatings, and physical injuries—during the Holocaust years. The Nazi system of dehumanization added a biting psychological component to physical suffering, as did the almost inevitable death of loved ones.

The Jewish experience during the Holocaust may be explored from a variety of points of reference: the fate of the Jews of an entire country; the fate of the Jews of a specific locality; the fate of a specific Jewish family; or the fate of the individual. On each of these levels, the fate of the Jews was influenced by diverse factors that in turn could be additional angles from which Jewish experience during the Holocaust could be examined. First, and of foremost importance, is the progression of events that were experienced and their impact. In broad terms Jews were not the initiators of events in the Holocaust, but were forced to respond to them. Clearly, the evolution of events differed from country to country and even from locality to locality. The course of events that German Jews faced under the Nazis, spanning the years 1933 to 1945, was very different from that encountered by Polish Jews, who experienced Nazi domination from 1939 to 1945. The span of years alone indicates one aspect of that difference. German Jews suffered Nazi persecution during the entire 12-year period of the Nazi rise and decline. They were faced with the entire long, drawn out, twisted path of Nazi discrimination that climaxed in the mass and systematic murder of the Jews. By the same token, they had more time than other Jewish communities to try to come to terms with their circumstances. Polish Jewry, however, experienced between three and six years of Nazi rule, depending on which part of POLAND they

found themselves in shortly after the Nazi attack in September 1939, and when they experienced LIBERATION at the hands of the Soviet armed forces. Nazi persecution caught Polish Jews at a more advanced stage than it did German Jews and it was accordingly more intense, harsher, and deadly to the community as a whole. Both of these situations differed from the course of events experienced by Hungarian Jews, who felt indirect Nazi influence by the Hungarian authorities from 1938 through early 1944 and the direct effect of Nazi occupation from early 1944 through spring 1945. In 1944 Hungarian Jews were caught by the Nazi machinery of murder at its high point, and suffered more intensely than most other Jewish communities. Nevertheless, the large-scale rescue operation that unfolded in HUNGARY that led to the survival of many Jews in BUDAPEST happened to a large extent precisely because the Nazis began destroying Hungarian Jewry so late in the war. The war situation in 1944 and early 1945 offered more possibilities of rescue than earlier stages would have.

In addressing Jewish experience during the Holocaust, we must also bear in mind other important factors. The regime in which Jews found themselves differed from country to country and sometimes from city to city. Some Jews were under direct Nazi domination, such as in the Reich itself, occupied Poland, or the occupied areas of the SOVIET UNION. Other Jews found themselves living in puppet regimes manipulated by the Nazis from a certain distance, such as SLOVAKIA or CROATIA. Yet others lived in countries that were independent partners of the Nazis (at least for part of the war years), such as BULGARIA, ITALY, Hungary, and ROMANIA, or for a time found themselves in regions occupied by those partners. Each of these different scenarios affected how Jews lived and died.

In the areas they occupied and administered, the Nazis did not always set up the same type of regime or maintain the same attitude toward the native population. Some places, such as BELGIUM, were ruled by the German military; others like the GENERALGOUVERNEMENT (part of Nazi-occupied Poland) had a civil administration with much SS influence. Within a given country, or region, different elements in the Nazi domain—the military, the SS, the civil administration—

often vied for power and the upper hand shifted from one to the other. These differences could influence the fate of the Jews and their experiences. In DENMARK for example, until mid-1943, the Nazis were interested in convincing the Danes (whom they considered to be of the same racial group as the Germans) to voluntarily join the Nazi new order in Europe. Thus, their relatively light rule allowed the Danes to maintain some amount of political freedom and self-respect. This in turn is seen as an important factor in the mostly successful attempt by the Danish underground to rescue the Jews of Denmark in October 1943. The struggle for power among Nazi officials apparently was a critical factor in the decision to deport the Danish Jews in the first place, and also was crucial for the leaking of that decision to the Danish underground which organized the aforementioned rescue. Nazi rule in Denmark may be contrasted to the ironfisted rule in the *Generalgouvernement,* and the correspondingly high death rate and low rescue rate of Polish Jews that resulted to some extent from that unrelenting and merciless rule.

The particular history of a countrywide Jewish community, the web of relations between that community and the surrounding people, and the attitudes of the non-Jewish population to the Jews, also played a role in determining Jewish fate and experience during the Holocaust. In regions where there was a long established tradition of open ANTISEMITISM, such as the UKRAINE or LITHUANIA, Jews could rely on little show of support or help from their neighbors (although there were certainly exceptions; hundreds of people in these places risked their lives to rescue Jews. See also RIGHTEOUS AMONG THE NATIONS). The almost incomprehensible hatred encountered by Jews seeking help or the decisions made on the grounds that they could expect no help, are important components of their common experience in these areas. In regions where Jewish relations had followed a smoother course, such as Italy, Bulgaria, or Denmark, rescue activity was more pronounced, and many more Jews experienced acts of selfless, life-saving generosity from their neighbors and even strangers.

Factors of timing and geography significantly influenced the options of response that Jews had. Before the outbreak of the war (and formally until October 1941), Jews living in the Reich had the option of emigrating. Although this was by no means a simple matter, many did so. During the heart of the war, flight from Nazi-dominated territory was not always possible, and when it was possible it was many times more difficult than it

had been before the outbreak of the war. Whether flight was possible or not had a lot to do with geography—obviously it was somewhat easier (although far from easy) to flee from countries that bordered on the neutral states of Europe—SWITZERLAND, SWEDEN, SPAIN, or Turkey (neutral Portugal had no common borders with the warring countries). Geography also was crucial for flight from the GHETTOS of Eastern Europe. Ghettos that bordered on large forests or swampland provided a better possibility of flight than did those far from such natural hiding places. Flight to these places, which usually meant joining the PARTISANS, ironically offered a better chance of rescue later in the war when partisan activity was more organized. The tragic irony is that in the later stages of the war many fewer Jews remained alive to flee.

Each and every Jew who went through the Holocaust, whether he or she survived or was murdered, had a unique personal experience. This personal experience was determined by many factors, from the broad and often intertwined factors mentioned above, to intensely personal factors, such as the age, gender, family status, education, responsibilities, personality, and cumulative life experience of the individual. Although many elements influenced personal experience, there are some overarching circumstances that need to be kept in mind when considering how individual Jews went through the Holocaust period: 1. Nazi persecution was aimed at every person they considered to be a Jew by their racial definition. After the beginning of the "FINAL SOLUTION," every Jew living within reach of the Nazi machinery of murder was sentenced to death. 2. No matter how hard he struggled, a Jew caught in the Nazis' web could not really be the master of his own destiny. The forces of destruction arrayed against him were far stronger than any drive for survival that an individual could muster. 3. Survival was mostly a matter of luck, since the standard ground-rules by which decisions would have been made before the Holocaust period were often irrelevant during it. The evolving, unprecedented situation was exceptionally difficult to interpret or understand precisely because it was unprecedented. The fluidity of the situation often made recently learned lessons unhelpful. In many circumstances it was simply impossible to accurately predict the outcome of a given decision or strategy for rescue.

Since it is not possible to portray an archetype of Jewish experience during the Holocaust, the following are several examples of that experience, each focusing on a different period and locale. The emphasis of the following sections is not on countrywide or community-wide response, but on that of the individual. Of course, since the story of each Jew who went through the Holocaust cannot be presented here, certain generalizations are unavoidable.

Germany Before the War, 1933–1939. Following the Nazi rise to power in 1933, German Jewry was faced with a policy of discrimination that evolved and became harsher over time. In outline form that policy can be seen as one that moved from separation of the Jews from other Germans—a policy that was directed toward showing the Jews that they had no place in GERMANY—to the use of violence after 1938 to pressure Jews to emigrate from Germany.

One of the most notable experiences of many German Jews was that which has been so aptly described by the historian Marion Kaplan as "social death." Social death included both public and private aspects for the individual. The public exclusion of the Jews greatly undermined, if it did not completely destroy, their generally deeply held self-identification as Germans. The dismissal of Jews from various organizations, professional, social, and cultural, was painful. Many Jews felt betrayed by the Fatherland for which they or their family members had fought in World War I. They felt betrayed by their exclusion from the society and culture they had called their own, and which they had cherished and passed on to their children. Children were often confused by their exclusion from society—from organizations like the Hitler Youth (HITLERJUGEND). Even though on some level they knew that such organizations fostered hatred, many Jewish children simply longed to belong, to take part in the outings and other social events. There are testimonies of Jewish children who were so swept up in the passion of the crowd when HITLER came to town, that they offered the Nazi salute, although it was forbidden them. The many daily insults and even worse to which German Jews were subjected often took their toll both physically and psychologically. Again, Jewish children suffered especially, since they were routinely taunted and beaten up by their non-Jewish peers.

In the private sphere many of these same feelings were also felt. Non-Jewish friends often abandoned their Jewish friends, or at best would visit them in secret. As time went by such visits became fewer and fewer. Men, who had been the pillars of their families, were often deeply wounded by their loss of status,

especially because Nazi economic decrees made it increasingly difficult for them to make a living, or find any gainful employment. Some of these men had previously held positions honored by society (professors, physicians, judges, etc.). Indeed the constantly deteriorating economic situation of the great majority of Jews who remained in Germany went well beyond psychological effects, and especially after the outbreak of the war reduced many to a bleak, hungry, and (in winter) cold existence.

Although with the perspective and hindsight of history, the deteriorating situation of German Jewry looks clear, it sometimes was very difficult for German Jews to draw an accurate picture of their new situation. This was especially true in the first years of the Nazi regime when their neighbors sometimes treated them in a contradictory fashion. For example, on the day of the Nazi boycott in April 1933 (see also BOYCOTT, ANTI-JEWISH), SA men picketed most Jewish enterprises, warning patrons not to buy from Jews, whereas at the same time some non-Jewish customers intentionally did business with those very establishments. After the many anti-Jewish decrees of 1933 and 1934, some Jews felt relieved with the issuing of the NUREMBERG LAWS in September 1935, which sought to define who was a Jew and diminished Jews to a secondary status of German subjects but not of citizens. They believed their position in German society, although reduced, was now clear and not subject to modification. But this was far from the case—neither Jewish property nor Jewish life was sacred. The violent riot against the Jews in November 1938 (KRISTALLNACHT) resulted in more than the destruction of community property and businesses. During the rioting people's homes were violated by the rampaging crowd, and along with the mass arrest of Jewish men and their imprisonment in CONCENTRATION CAMPS, the last remnants of personal security were torn to pieces.

Throughout the Nazi period, individual Jews had to assess not only their situation, but also their options. Very early on many German Jews chose to end their lives by their own hands. Feeling isolated, betrayed, humiliated, and abandoned, suicides occurred so frequently that they became a common topic of conversation. Increasingly suicide, despite the traditional Jewish view that it is a sin, was seen as a reasonable alternative to the situation.

Many Jews agonized over the alternative of emigration. Leaving one's homeland is never a simple matter, and for Jews who felt thoroughly German it was often an excruciating choice. Parents frequently encouraged their sons to leave, seeing rather early on that they in particular had no future in Nazi Germany. But, it was not long before daughters were also sent abroad, often to work as household help. The separation of closely-knit families brought about its own set of problems. For children or adults with older parents, leaving family members behind often led to delay in emigration or decisions to remain despite the deteriorating situation.

Once emigration was decided upon, the obstacle course that had to be passed through to arrange exit from Germany and entry into another country required strength, determination, and great patience. Financing emigration was also a problem, especially since the Nazi regime severely limited Jews' ability to leave with their assets. Even after emigration was arranged, people worried about how they would live in their country of exile: how would they cope with a foreign language and society, and how would they make a living? German Jewish organizations made a great effort to prepare Jews for life outside of Germany.

Not every German Jew wanted to emigrate, especially before *Kristallnacht,* or if he wanted to he was not necessarily able to do so. But as time went on, coping with the situation in Germany became harder and harder. Many individual Jews greatly benefited from the activities of the Jewish community organizations. In addition to receiving financial and material aid, they found temporary spiritual refuge and human warmth in the many classes and cultural activities sponsored by the Jewish community. But especially after the war had begun, impoverishment, longing for departed family members, constant public humiliation, isolation, grinding poverty, and hard, monotonous physical labor made life unbearable. For almost all the Jews who had remained in Germany after the start of the war, the start of the DEPORTATIONS to the east in the fall of 1941 signaled the start of the last phase of their suffering.

The Ghettos of Poland—Before the Murder. Soon after the Germans invaded Poland in September 1939,

A scene from the Jewish theater production "The Eternal Jew" in the Vilna Ghetto

they began dealing with the so-called Jewish problem. For the part of Poland that remained under German control until the summer of 1941 when the Germans occupied the remaining areas, they ordered, among other things, that Jews be concentrated in larger cities. Reinhard HEYDRICH'S well-known order of September 21, 1939 provided the basis for what came to be the ghettos of Eastern Europe under the Nazis. The ghettos would be established between fall 1939 and spring 1943. The conditions in them varied from a sealed, almost concentration camp-like environment, to more open ghettos. Some like WARSAW and LODZ were immense and crowded, housing hundreds of thousands of Jews, whereas others contained only a few thousand. In some of the ghettos, hunger and disease took a great toll, whereas in some of the smaller ghettos in the countryside, starvation was less common. Jews lived in the various ghettos for different lengths of time and the deportations did not strike all the ghettos at exactly the same time or in exactly the same way. Smaller ghettos were often liquidated in one or two swift blows, whereas the liquidation of the larger ghettos might take several weeks, months, or in the case of Lodz, years. Given the variety of the ghettos, it is difficult to generalize about Jewish experience in them.

At the time of the German invasion of Poland and in the period before ghettos were established in large numbers, barbaric Nazi violence against the Jews frequently erupted. Jews were routinely humiliated and beaten in public—especially religious bearded Jews wearing traditional clothing and Jews randomly chosen for FORCED LABOR. Although statistics vary, it is clear that thousands of Jews were killed in the course of this arbitrary ungoverned savagery.

During the invasion and in the weeks following it, many Jews tried to find a haven from the turmoil, although others had good memories of a humane German presence during World War I that inspired them with the hope that the occupation would be harmless. Since Jews had no way of really knowing what place might prove safer, at first they tended to flee away from the fast approaching front. As the front caught up with them, already displaced Jews either tried to find a way home or make their way to places where they had relatives. When it became clear that part of Poland was to be under Soviet rule, some 300,000 Jews fled to that area, hoping to find refuge. Thus, before the ghettos were even established many Jews felt deep panic and fear, owing to the general chaos of the war

and Nazi savagery against Jews. Many suddenly found themselves among hoards of fleeing people traveling the roads of Poland, or they became homeless REFUGEES, deprived of the normal community ties that might have lent them support in a time of turbulence.

The process of entering the ghettos was accompanied by strong feelings of upheaval for the large majority of Jews. Belongings had to be chosen, since it was not usually possible to move an entire household and people were sometimes limited to that which could be carried. The piles of chosen belongings then had to be brought to the ghetto area quickly. Most Jews were forced to abandon their homes in order to enter the ghetto, which meant new housing had to be found. Many of those who remained in their homes, which were in the area of the ghetto, suddenly found themselves living with additional people, frequently complete strangers. This was particularly true when an entire small community was confined to the ghetto of the nearest larger city. Sometimes the entry into the ghetto was accompanied by cruelty on the part of overseeing policemen or guards, and when this was the case, the new arrivals reached the ghetto with their senses reeling from vicious encounters. From the moment they entered the ghetto, the living circumstances of most Jews plummeted sharply, another reason for feeling hopeless and lost.

After the initial shock of entry, the Jews' main concern was to find a way to obtain the necessities of life. Finding employment was of utmost importance. In the world of the ghetto, former social hierarchies were abruptly transformed. Intellectuals, artists, and professionals usually had little to offer in the ghetto economy, which was based on light manufacture and "illegal" trade and bartering; their struggle for survival could be harrowing, accompanied by a deep sense of degradation. Many a person of moderate means slowly sold off his last possessions until nothing was left. It was the craftsmen, small traders, and people who had experience bypassing the law who often rose to the top along with high level ghetto officials. In this topsy-turvy world, where obeying the law frequently meant death, those who enforced the law were the criminals and those who broke the law did so more in the name of survival and morality than greed.

Not all ghettos were plagued by hunger or suffered starvation and epidemics to the same extent. But especially in those ghettos where there was little opportunity to supplement the meager rations allocated by the German administration, a great many inhabitants suffered constant hunger pangs, the deterioration of their health, and ultimately death by starvation or disease that attacked their broken bodies. The crowded conditions made hygiene on both a personal and public level almost impossible to maintain in many localities. This provided a breeding ground for disease and epidemics. In the largest ghettos of Poland (Warsaw and Lodz), death, owing to the conditions, was a massive phenomenon. Public deaths in the ghetto streets became so common as to go virtually unnoticed. Proper burial was often impossible; and in Warsaw, bodies were thrown into huge mass graves. Most inhabitants of the larger ghettos were either in a state of mourning or deeply fearful that death would reach their door anytime.

The family was hit hard in the ghetto. On the one hand, family was a source of comfort and support for many ghetto inhabitants. On the other hand, Nazi measures led to the breaking up of families by separation and death. From the first days of the occupation, Jewish men were rounded up for forced labor. Although this process became more organized after many of the JUDENRAETE took it over in the hope of making it less random, forced labor, especially in camps, came to mean long term separation from family. If they were lucky enough to survive the ordeal, when fathers and elder sons returned, they were often broken in body and spirit. Because the men had been taken away or could not find employment, many Jewish women in Poland became the heads of their households as other women in Germany had done and were doing. Young people also frequently became heads of their families, being the more employable members of the family or finding it somewhat easier to adapt to the ways of the ghetto.

Residents of the larger ghettos sometimes found temporary relief from the pervading dreariness, sadness, and dehumanization of their lives in the cultural, educational, and political activities that were held both openly and in secret. Attending performances, learning, or discussing politics, especially those concerned with the far off and much longed for land of Israel, allowed people to feel normal again. For religious Jews, the daily observance of the law, some aspects of which were extremely hard or even impossible under the Nazis, provided the same feeling. Study sessions about the Torah and holy books helped people transcend their daily problems—if only for a short while. Prayer, both public and private, could give the individual a feeling that he was doing something to help improve his situation. It is part of ancient Jewish wisdom that when some one is in trouble he should pray as if help can only come from heaven and at the same time, take action as if he alone can make things better.

Some ghetto residents found an important outlet in writing about their experiences. Diaries were kept, and those that have survived are an important source for our understanding about how people coped with life and death in the ghetto (see also DIARIES, HOLOCAUST). We know from diarists like Chaim Kaplan and Emanuel RINGELBLUM (the moving force behind the secret Warsaw Ghetto archive, ONEG SHABBAT) how important the act of writing was for them. The underground press was a source of information and inspiration for many residents of the larger ghettos.

The attitude of individual ghetto residents toward the official Jewish leadership, the *Judenrat,* obviously varied greatly from ghetto to ghetto, changed over the course of time, and above all varied from person to person. In a well-known study about *Judenrat* members, Aharon Weiss showed that most of them refused to carry out clearly immoral acts, although some gave in to Nazi demands, often under the threat of their personal safety. Residents of the ghettos were not always aware of the inner workings of their *Judenrat,* but they were deeply affected by the results of those workings. Some diarists and SURVIVORS have expressed an understanding of the dilemmas faced by the Jewish leadership and generally praised them, whereas others put much of the blame for the horror they encountered on those leaders. The issue of the behavior of the Jewish leadership and the attitude of the Jews toward them is a complex subject of ongoing research. The formation of armed underground organizations, an important aspect of life in many ghettos, will be discussed below.

Jews in the Western Soviet Union After the German Invasion. For Jews in the Baltic States (ESTONIA, LATVIA, and Lithuania) and parts of Poland that fell under Soviet control at the beginning of the war, life changed dramatically. The imposition of the Soviet regime meant the end of the vibrant community life of the pre-war period. Everything and everyone was made to conform to Soviet ideology, and barring the minority of Jews who supported the Soviet way, these changes were painful. Nevertheless the lot of Jews in the Soviet areas of influence was decidedly better than that of their peers under German occupation. Only Jews who the Soviets believed would not conform or belonged to groups the Soviets believed would never conform, were openly persecuted. Many of them were deported to the Soviet interior, a move that unknowingly would later help save their lives by keeping them out of reach of the Germans.

When the German armed forces invaded the western Soviet Union in June 1941, an even more abrupt and lethal change occurred in the lives of the Jews. As the front approached, panic-stricken masses of Jews and non-Jews alike tried to flee eastward, into the Soviet interior. Most were blocked, although from areas that had been part of the Soviet Union before 1939, there was an ongoing organized process of removing people and equipment to the Soviet interior. Entire factories were rebuilt deep in Soviet territory, and some five million people—among them about one million Jews—were evacuated. Even during the fighting, some holes existed in BELORUSSIA and the Ukraine by which people could flee from the front.

As the Germans gobbled up territory, local inhabitants, often at the urging of the conquerors, ferociously attacked the Jews of numerous communities, killing many in pogroms. Soon thereafter the EINSATZ-GRUPPEN, supplemented by regular army units, police units, and local residents, began killing the Jews in a mass and systematic fashion. Jews, who had been living more or less normal lives under the Soviets, suddenly found themselves dragged out of their homes. They were herded under a hail of insults and blows to the edges of their towns, frequently by their neighbors, and were made to stand along pits they had dug or were made to stand at the edge of a ravine. There, the Germans ruthlessly massacred them by gunfire. This vicious surprise attack, carried out with zealous intensity, left little room for response. Were it not for the testimony of a chosen few, who instead of being killed somehow survived the ordeal, we would be left only with our imaginations to understand what these Jews experienced in the last moments of their lives.

During the course of this murderous drive, and in some places directly after the first murder *aktion,* the Germans set up ghettos. The ghettos were similar to those in which Polish Jews were kept captive. However, there was one crucial difference: the Jews in these new ghettos had already experienced the extensive murder of beloved family, friends, and neighbors. A few had even heard the stories of those who had miraculously survived the shootings. When these new ghettos were set up the fabric of life had already been torn to pieces. In addition to having to deal with the severity of ghetto existence, the Jews in these areas had to come to terms

with the initial murderous rampages that they had experienced. Some believed they were truly pogroms, violent events that had come and were now gone.

For most ghetto inhabitants, however, life became a daily struggle for survival: to put food on the table, to remain clothed, to keep warm in winter, and to maintain their human dignity. In TRANSNISTRIA, which was under Romanian administration, Jews who had been deported from BESSARABIA and BUKOVINA and had survived the first wave of murder found themselves living among the remnants of the native Jewish population. In the winter of 1941–1942 the deported Romanian Jews began receiving some aid from the Jews of the Romanian heartland. Romanian Jewish leaders among the deportees faced the dilemma of keeping the meager aid they received for their community, in the hope that it would help get them through the winter, or dividing it with the local Jews, in which case nobody would have enough. This was one more difficult dilemma faced by Jews in a "no win" situation.

Throughout the Soviet areas, Jews hoped that the murder had come and gone. However, a few, especially younger people, came to believe that they had not experienced isolated incidents of murder. At a now famous meeting in a convent outside of VILNA, Abba KOVNER and his colleagues in the Zionist YOUTH MOVEMENT debated the meaning of the wave of murder they had experienced in Vilna. The young Kovner was perhaps one of the first Jewish leaders to make a leap of understanding based on fragmentary information about events in nearby communities; he concluded that the Nazis sought to systematically murder the Jews and that Jews must fight against this death sentence with arms. In the Vilna Ghetto, however, even after subsequent smaller murder *aktionen,* the official leadership took a different course of action. They, and especially the head of the *Judenrat,* Jacob GENS, believed that by making the ghetto work force valuable to the Germans, the Jews would be treated better and many would survive to see the liberation.

In Vilna, Gens and the ghetto residents worked hard and tried their best to make their lives normal with cultural activities and education for the remaining children. Kovner and his people continued to organize, but decided not to engage in armed resistance within the ghetto confines, unless the ghetto was on the verge of final liquidation. They realized the great responsibility they bore. They knew that revolt could not lead to the rescue of all the ghetto residents, and that many who had not chosen this way of response would die immediately because of it. They also had learned that flight to the partisans would bring down fierce German vengeance upon innocent family members and neighbors, who would be executed in retaliation for the escape. Nonetheless, when they believed the liquidation was at hand, they staged a revolt. The revolt was short-lived because the ghetto inhabitants did not support the fighting. Kovner and his people, like younger people from many of the other ghettos in former Soviet territory, then fled to the forests to continue fighting as partisans. Kovner's escape from the ghetto was accompanied by a wrenching personal decision: he told his mother she could not accompany the young fighters, because she might slow them down and endanger everyone. The Germans, who had not intended to do so before the revolt, shut down the ghetto and deported the remaining Vilna Jews to forced labor camps.

Deportation to Extermination Camps. While the youth from Vilna were debating the significance of the six-month long wave of bloodshed they had experienced, the German machinery of murder extended its reach to the ghettos of Poland, and from there to the rest of Nazi-dominated Europe. In many Polish ghettos, the Germans ordered the *Judenraete* to organize the arrival of Jews to the collection points. Frequently, JEWISH POLICE were forced to round up the ill-fated Jews; sometimes, Polish police units or various German units also took part in these initial round-ups. As time went on the round-ups became more and more violent; fre-

Saying goodbye during a deportation from the Lodz Ghetto

quently the old, the sick, and those who did not go willingly were shot in cold blood by the Germans and their henchmen. Many Jewish leaders gave in to Nazi demands to assist in the deportations, but some refused and were killed on the spot. The story of the head of the Warsaw Ghetto, Adam CZERNIAKOW, is well known. When faced with the order to supply deportation lists of Jews to the Nazis, he committed suicide instead.

In the face of the deportations, Jews scrambled for protection. Sometimes the fact that they were employed, or employed in an enterprise considered valuable to the German authorities, offered a lifeline. In many cases such protection was limited to a specific number of individuals per family. The decision of who would remain and who would not was unbearable—how many families could not make such an impossible choice and instead were deported together will probably never be known. Other Jews turned to members of the *Judenraete* or Jewish police for protection—the results of such requests were as varied as the requests themselves. The only constant was that at most, an individual or his family received a short-term reprieve from execution.

Sometimes all the Jews of a given ghetto were required to gather at the collection point and there were subjected to a SELEKTION by the Germans. Such *selektionen* occurred more frequently during later deportation drives. At the collection point, the Jews sometimes waited for many hours and even days until the Germans met their quota. Invariably the Jews waited without food or water, in the hot summer sun, the drenching rain, or the freezing cold of winter. Many are the stories of parents who chose to accompany children or children who chose to accompany their parents on the deportation trains.

It is hard to know if or when Jews in Eastern Europe realized that deportations meant death. Such knowledge varied from place to place, from time to time, and from individual to individual. But from the beginning and despite Nazi lies to the contrary, many Jews in the ghettos understood that deportation was evil, based on, if on nothing else, their experience with forced labor round-ups.

Some Jews tried to flee from the collection point. Where the forest was nearby, sometimes only meters away, daring individuals ran toward it. Such a decision could be life saving, or result in a bullet in the back. Others tried to sneak away and hide, especially after long hours of waiting lessened the attentiveness of the guards. There are records of mass resistance both spontaneous and planned, which invariably resulted in an on-the-spot slaughter, with few survivors. For the Jews awaiting deportation, they were really in a situation without clear choices and in which a gamble could lead to immediate death.

Sometimes after the ordeal of the round-up and interminable wait, boarding the deportation train seemed a relief. But any such relief was short-lived. The Germans and their helpers packed the Jews into the trains, usually freight cars or open cattle cars. Almost all survivor testimony about the train rides emphasizes the terrible suffering of the journey itself. The ride might have taken hours, days, or even weeks, depending on the point of departure, the distance to the camps, and the general conditions of the rail traffic. The distance covered by the Jews of SALONIKA, for example, was immense. In transports that left between March and August 1943, they were shipped in cattle cars from Greece, through SERBIA and Croatia, by way of VIENNA, AUSTRIA to Poland.

Other than for some transports of German Jews, there was no place in the cars to sit or lie down and nothing but the foulest air to breathe. Owing to the terrible conditions in the cars—with only a single bucket to serve as a toilet for all the passengers in the car, without food or sufficient water, and with the miserable terror of the unknown before them—many Jews died. When the train pulled into the camp and the doors of the cars were opened, a gust of air usually entered the car and provided again a fleeting moment of relief for the suffering passengers.

Armed underground organizations generally came into being after the first experience with deportations (or, as we have seen in the Soviet areas, after the first murder drives). The establishment of most armed ghetto underground organizations was fraught with obstacles. Jews from different ideological and political points of view had to come to agreement regarding a range of dilemmas. They had to decide if they wanted to take the responsibility for supporting armed resistance when they knew it would lead to the immediate death of many who did not support the idea. They had to decide if it was better to fight in the ghetto, or escape to the forest to join the partisans, or fight with the intention of escaping to the forest during the revolt. They had to determine when the time was appropriate for staging a revolt and if, until that time, they would support or oppose the official Jewish leadership. Often decisions were shaped in the melting pan of the depor-

tation *aktionen.* That pan also melted down many differences that had earlier prevented agreement.

The most troublesome dilemmas of the individual revolved around their responsibilities to family and friends. Joining an armed underground put not only the person who joined it, but his entire family and household in grave danger. Discovery could lead, and sometimes led, to collective punishment of anyone associated with the underground member. It is not surprising that many who joined the underground were young—they had less family responsibilities than older adults did. It is also not surprising that most underground organizations were formed at the point when ghetto inhabitants began to feel they had nothing to lose by opposing their oppressors with the use of arms. They felt they were under a death sentence and many no longer had family responsibilities, since their loved ones had been deported or murdered already. Most Jews fought for the sake of honor, for revenge, for future generations, or simply in the hope of bringing down as many of their enemies as possible before they

Jews hiding in a bunker during the Warsaw Ghetto Uprising, spring 1943

fell. Few believed that fighting could lead to mass rescue, although many harbored some hope that after combat in the ghetto, some fighters might survive to continue fighting and perhaps someone would live to tell their story.

Being a Jewish partisan was extremely difficult. Many Jews reached the forests of Eastern Europe before partisan activity came under the wings of the Soviet authorities, and thus they did not have a framework for support. Jewish partisans suffered from the rough outdoor living, for which many were not equipped, having not known the forest very well before the war and having arrived there in a state of physical and mental exhaustion. Many fled in panic at the time of murder *aktionen* or deportations, dazed with the fear that they would never see family and friends again. Moreover, unlike non-Jewish partisans, Jewish partisans rarely were treated sympathetically by local peasants on whom they had to depend for basic supplies. Some local inhabitants made a living out of discovering Jews in the forest and turning them in to the Germans. Non-Jewish partisans also frequently robbed or killed Jews they encountered. The Jews who fled to the forest were not only fighters, frequently they were elderly or the very young. Caring for those who could not fight added to the concerns of Jewish fighters, some of whom established family camps for them (see also FAMILY CAMPS IN THE FORESTS). Given all these obstacles it is not surprising that most Jews who fled to the forests did not survive the ordeal. But it also must be noted that hundreds of Jewish partisans received decorations for their heroics, miraculously survived scrapes with death, and lived to tell their stories.

Another kind of resistance many Jews chose was to hide outside the boundaries of the ghetto. Hiding was no less difficult than flight to the forests, although some of the problems were different. The first problem was to leave the confines of the ghetto undetected. Next, finding a safe haven required either a very trusted person to provide housing and the basic necessities of life, or false papers that could provide a convincing cover for a Jew trying to pass as a non-Jew. Not all Jews had the connections and money necessary to arrange these things before their flight, and many quickly fell victim to their enemies. Some Jews managed to arrange things before they fled the ghetto, but bad luck stalked them and finally caught up with them. Relatively few were the Jews who managed to hide from their oppressors and greet the liberation. Those who succeeded were usually helped selflessly by non-Jews, many of whom were later honored as Righteous among the Nations.

Hiding was usually a very difficult experience. If it was with the use of false papers, the fear of discovery was everpresent. In various hideouts, Jews experienced not only the fear of discovery, but frequently almost indescribable physical discomfort. Many are the stories of Jews who were hidden behind false walls, in damp, dark, bug-infested cellars or barns, or in places where they could not stand upright. The mental anguish that accompanied this physical agony could be immense, but the will to survive was usually just as great.

Western Europe. Between April and June 1940, the Nazis swiftly conquered and occupied most of Western Europe from NORWAY in the north to FRANCE in the south. In each of the countries that came under their control there were aspects of the conquest, occupation, and persecution of the Jews that had common features. Sealed ghettos were not set up in any of these countries; the closest thing to an Eastern European-type ghetto was the Jewish living district in Amsterdam, the NETHERLANDS. The Jews in the countries of Western Europe suffered neither the degradation nor physical depravation of ghetto life. Their material suffering was more similar to that of the rest of the population, than that of the Jews of the east, as long as they were not imprisoned.

In France, Belgium, the Netherlands, and Italy, camps were set up locally. Some of these were internment camps for foreign Jews that were later put under German control, and were used as transit camps to the camps of Eastern Europe. The conditions in these Western European camps varied from camp to camp, and also during different periods in each camp's individual history. Generally, however, life in them was char-

The wedding of Mauritz and Bertah Levie, The Hague, Netherlands, during the Nazi occupation

acterized by poor physical surroundings, poor food, and often mind-numbing labor. Under Nazi commandants, the general situation frequently deteriorated. During the period of the deportations, there was the added stress of waiting to be sent on a transport to the unknown. In some camps families were together, or at least could meet, and there was a small amount of social support. As awful as they were, most of these camps did not rival the camps of Germany itself and the east for their brutal and deadly atmosphere.

The Jewish badge was imposed on the Jews of Belgium, France, and the Netherlands in spring 1942, just prior to the beginning of mass deportations to the EXTERMINATION CAMPS (see also BADGE, JEWISH). The badge was crucial to the Nazi attempt to separate the Jews from society and dispose of them. In Western Europe, however, there were expressions of sympathy for Jews because of the badge. A Dutch underground newspaper printed 300,000 badges, proclaiming "Jews and non-Jews are one and the same" in May 1942. The legend about the Danish king riding a white horse through Copenhagen with the Jewish badge on his chest is indeed a legend, but it reflects the real attitude of the Danes that led to the rescue of the Danish Jews.

It also must be kept in mind that each country had its own unique set of circumstances that greatly affected the fate of the Jews. According to the historian Maxime Steinberg, these various factors, in their different configurations, account for such basic differences as the fact that in the Netherlands 80 percent of the Jews were deported, in Belgium over 40 percent were deported, and in France about 25 percent were deported. But not all of the factors carried the same weight in each country.

Each of the Western European countries had a different type of regime, with its own cast of characters running it. Belgium was under German military rule, there was a Belgian government-in-exile in London, and the Belgian senior civil servants that remained in Belgium were not supportive of the Nazi "new order" in Belgium. The Netherlands was under German civilian rule run by an Austrian SS clique, and the remaining Dutch senior civil servants towed the line the Germans set. In France the regime was more complex, with German occupation in the north and the Vichy government in the south. On the one hand, France sought to gain as much independence as possible from Germany, and was willing to give in to many of their demands regarding Jews in order to achieve the right of self-rule in areas they considered more important. On the other hand,

since they had more independence than either Belgium or the Netherlands, this also expressed itself regarding the treatment of the Jews. The French had much influence on the timing and focus of anti-Jewish measures.

Sometimes an important element in the fate of the Jews was their citizenship. In both France and Belgium, citizens were protected better than refugees who did not hold citizenship of their country of residence. In both countries most of the deported Jews were not citizens. Indeed the French set up internment camps for Jews who were not citizens even before the period of the deportations. In Belgium, it was the German authorities who began imprisoning Jewish refugees, before the period of the "Final Solution." In the Netherlands, Denmark, and Norway, however, citizenship had little to do with the fate of the Jews. In Denmark most of the Jews, 7,200 out of 8,000, were rescued whether they were citizens or not. In Norway about half the Jews were deported and the other half fled to Sweden, without citizenship really having any effect since the percentage of rescued refugees was the same as that of rescued citizens. In the Netherlands, citizens and non-citizens alike were mostly deported by way of the transit camp WESTERBORK.

There was a great variety of responses by individual Jews in these countries. In those countries that collaborated or in which the German "new order" took hold, native Jews often felt bitterly betrayed whereas refugees often viewed things differently. In France, for example, the barrage of antisemitic propaganda was particularly painful to native Jews. Refugees, however, who had not really been a part of the society beforehand, did not always suffer the same feelings. Highly assimilated French Jews often felt they had no community on which to lean. Jews who had not been born in France, however, had a more dynamic pre-war community life in many ways. That community life helped them through the war as well. Refugees also tended to be more willing to go underground or to try to flee or fight—at least in part this was a function of the fact that they were more at risk.

It should also be noted that some Western European countries presented more options for rescue attempts than did others. For example, France offered more options for rescue attempts than did the flat Netherlands, which was surrounded by German-dominated territory. For much of the time the Southern Zone of France was safer than the North, and thus was a place of refuge. For a time, the Italian Zone of France was safer than the German-occupied areas and also afforded refuge. Neutral Spain and neutral Switzerland had common borders with France. Lastly, French peasants often hid Jews, especially children, either out of humanitarian concerns or in defiance of the Germans. Yet despite different circumstances we know that relatively many Dutch citizens also tried to help their Jewish neighbors, but were unsuccessful.

In many ways the personal dilemmas faced by Jews in Western Europe were similar to those in Eastern Europe. Taking part in any kind of underground activity carried with it basically the same responsibility for reprisals against family members as it did in Eastern Europe. Since family life was less disrupted in the West, until the beginning of the deportations, the dilemmas posed by fragmented families was a less dominant feature of Jewish life. Hiding and escape, for example, were attempted not only by individuals, but by the family unit. Nevertheless, the rescue of children alone—a common occurrence—carried with it the deep anxiety of separation, a separation that could be and often was permanent.

In the Camps. The Nazis and their partners set up a variety of camps that are generically known as concentration camps and included labor camps, transit camps, and of course extermination camps. Although all of the camps were noted for their brutality, dehumanization, and otherworld reality, camp regimes differed and even in the same camp, conditions could change over time. The living circumstances in a particular camp were affected by changes in Nazi policies, the makeup of the camp staff, the inflow, removal, or death of inmates, or the evolving war situation. Jews entered the camps with different experiences as well. Some reached Nazi camps after a long period of suffering in a ghetto or local transit camp (such as the Dutch- or French-run transit camps). Some never set foot in a ghetto or were deported directly from their homes. Some German and Hungarian Jews reached the camps after having been confined in special Jewish houses in their cities of residence. As has already been noted, the length of the journey to the camp also varied, although the train ride itself was as a rule a harrowing experience. Despite these differences, there was a certain commonality of camp experience for Jews: appalling physical and psychological hardships, and the all-pervasive presence of death.

In the camps individual prisoners had to cope with a world that was essentially the direct opposite of their normal prewar circumstances. In almost all the Nazi camps, almost all of the time, human life was of little value and the lives of Jews were the least precious to the Nazis. Dehumanization was a constant aspect of camp life. Inmates were not referred to by name, but by number. The roll call, usually held early in the morning before work began and again late in the day when work ended, was both dehumanizing and cruel. Inmates were made to stand silently as numbers were called out and all were accounted for by the guards. If someone was missing the procedure continued, sometimes for hours, until it was clear why. Inmates had to endure the elements, hungry, thirsty, and exhausted until the procedure was over.

Constant physical suffering prevailed in the Nazi camps. Beatings were a permanent facet of life, although some guards and *Kapos* were more cruel than others. Beatings, sometimes to the death, were doled out for major and minor rule violations, or for no reason at all other than unprovoked cruelty.

The camps lacked any resemblance to civilized lodgings. Inmates generally slept on rough wooden bunks, sometimes with a bit of rancid, lice-infested straw, or a threadbare and soiled blanket. There were never enough latrines, and those that existed were invariably filthy and let off an indescribable stench. Since dysentery was epidemic in the Nazi camp system, prisoners were in constant need of latrines—and rarely reached them in time. So the same stench that came from the latrines was everywhere in the camps.

Hunger was king in the Nazi camps. Inmates were usually given only a fraction of the food adults normally need to perform labor, and that which was served was often inedible. Where and when the Nazis were more interested in squeezing labor out of the inmates, the food situation might improve somewhat. Drinkable water was also almost always scarce. Survivors from AUSCHWITZ-Birkenau have told of the double frustration of feeling bone dry and seeing water all around, but knowing that drinking the water would be deadly because it was so foul. Because water was so scarce, keeping clean was impossible. Primo LEVI writes of an inmate who ceremoniously washed everyday, with a rag and a bit of water. When Levi asked him why he bothered since he remained filthy after the ceremony, Levi began to understand that washing was less for the sake of keeping clean than it was for trying to retain a trace of human dignity.

Labor was another constant of camp life and inmates engaged in a large scope of work activities. The worst

אין געראַנגל פאַר ברויט,אין געראַנגל פאַרן טויט ·

Camp inmates risking death for some bread, Berl Friedlander, 1946

kind of work was heavy outdoor labor under the watchful eyes of barbaric guards. Inmates in such a situation could expect to live only a short while. Probably the best assignment was to work in food preparation, a position that customarily offered opportunities for supplementing a meager diet—the most important facet to remaining alive. Other indoor or skilled work was also considered good. In the extermination camps, inmates of the SONDERKOMMANDO who worked in the GAS CHAMBERS and crematorium had the most paradoxical of jobs. Their job was indescribably gruesome and they worked with the knowledge that their turn would come. But working at the heart of the Nazi murder apparatus afforded inmates the opportunity to secrete away items that had belonged to the victims and trade them for food, medicine, or other essential items that could be

had in the camps' often lively underground economy. It is no wonder that at Birkenau the area where the victims' belongings were sorted and stored, next to the crematoria, was dubbed Kanada, the German spelling of Canada—a country that symbolized abundance.

Due to the effects of the general conditions in the camps, the hard labor, and poor nutrition, many inmates suffered from disease. Dysentery struck almost everyone, and because it contributed to the weakening of already broken bodies, it could prove deadly. Many a prisoner struck with dysentery was either selected for murder by the camp staff, or simply collapsed and died. Typhus also caused thousands and thousands of deaths in the camps. When the British liberated BERGEN-BELSEN and saw piles of bodies and thousands of sick and dying prisoners, they were sure that they had stumbled upon an extermination camp. In reality they had come upon a concentration camp, in which prisoners had been dumped at the end of the war and in which a typhus epidemic was raging.

Inmate committing suicide on the electrified fence, Mauthausen

The emotional anguish of camp existence could be as great as the physical strain. Since inmates were separated by sex, except in a very few exceptional family camps, and since in most camps the sexes could have no contact, families who may have arrived together were broken up. Of course families may have arrived together to the extermination camps and may have died on the same day, but never would have remained whole in the labor sections of the camps. Most prisoners lived with a terrible sense of loss, for their family, friends, and communities. Sometimes two or more family members were together, or sometimes friends bonded into family-like groups. As a unit, inmates had a better chance of survival. But most inmates lived with death—the past death of loved ones, the ongoing death of those around them, and their own imminent death. These feelings, along with the dehumanization and physical hardship, were the lot of all the Jewish inmates. Some Jews looked to the more distant past for comfort and some tried to imagine a

brighter future. Some inmates acquired "camp smarts" and learned how to help themselves as much as possible in their virtually helpless situation. Others, so beaten down, gave up and became what were known in camp jargon as the MUSELMAENNER.

In the camps, resistance to the Nazis took many forms. In several of the camps, underground organizations formed and armed revolt even broke out. But more commonly the resistance was to the constant, grinding dehumanization. It could be found in the daily routine of washing as described by Primo Levi, or it could center around the daily study of a fragment of the Talmud found in the camp, as David Weiss-Halivny has written in his memoirs. It could be found in an attempt to obtain medicine for a loved one, or in simply holding their hand at the moment of their death. When they could, many inmates engaged in sabotage at work, especially when they knew that the product of their work was supposed to help the German war effort. Relatively few of the total inmate population in the camps, but still thousands of individual inmates, attempted to escape. Most never got beyond the camp perimeter (indeed some failed on purpose in order to commit suicide). But there were successes. It was through two successful escape attempts that the first detailed eyewitness reports about Auschwitz-Birkenau reached the world in spring 1944, and were spread as the AUSCHWITZ PROTOCOLS.

Hungary. One of the most important aspects of the Auschwitz Protocols was that they warned that the camp was being prepared to receive the Jews of Hungary for extermination. Until March 19, 1944, Hungary was a relatively safe haven for Jews. The large community of over 800,000 Jews (by a racial definition) had faced only a few early incidents of murder, at KAMENETS-PODOLSKI and in the Hungarian occupied area of YUGOSLAVIA. These incidents were well known; since they had not been repeated and the Hungarian government had even made a show of prosecuting the murders in the Yugoslav region, most Hungarian Jews felt their government would protect them. The dismal, often deadly, lot of the Jewish men who served in the HUNGARIAN LABOR SERVICE SYSTEM (the auxiliary units that accompanied the Hungarian armed forces) was also known; but seems not to have led to a feeling that Hungarian Jewry as a whole stood in mortal danger. Indeed until 1944, the Jews within Hungary's borders did not stand in mortal danger since the government deflected German pressure to deal with Hungarian Jewry once and for all. Only with the German occupation in March 1944 did the situation change drastically for the worse.

One of the most central questions regarding Hungarian Jewry at the time of the German occupation is, what did they know? Until they actually reached Auschwitz, saw and smelled the smoke rising from the crematoria at Birkenau, and were told by veteran inmates that the smoke was from their relatives' burning bodies, many Hungarian survivors have testified that they did not know about the "Final Solution." Nevertheless, there is much evidence that a lot of information about the murder of the Jews was available in Hungary before the German occupation. Thousands of Jewish refugees from Poland and Slovakia told of their personal experiences and offered the information they had about the murderous activities of the Nazis. Hungarian soldiers and some Jewish forced laborers returning from the Soviet areas also told about atrocities they had seen or about which they had heard. Hungarian Jewish leaders had been in touch with the Slovak Jewish underground WORKING GROUP, from whom they learned about the murder of Slovak Jews and others in Poland. The Zionist RELIEF AND RESCUE COMMITTEE OF BUDAPEST, headed by Rezso KASZTNER and Otto KOMOLY, as well as the Zionist youth movements, had been pipelines for sending information about the murder to the "free world." Zionist youth movement representatives had even tried, mostly unsuccessfully, to warn various communities outside of Budapest about what they could expect if the Nazis were to arrive in Hungary.

How is it possible that there was information but not necessarily knowledge? There is no simple answer to this question. In part, the unprecedented nature of the Holocaust made it very difficult for anybody anywhere to digest information and come out with a comprehensible picture of the Nazi mass systematic murder of the Jews. Many Hungarian Jews felt the news they received about murder was greatly exaggerated. There were also people who felt that even if other Jews were being murdered, the murder would not strike them. Many held that the Hungarians might not like Jews but they would not be a party to mass systematic murder; or it was too late in the war, so the murder would not reach their doorsteps. So the "ignorance" of Hungarian Jews was not faked and certainly did not result from stupidity, but was largely a product of a failure in imagination.

The intense period of persecution, deportation, and murder also made it harder to come to grips with the reality of the murder. Unlike the Jews of Germany or Poland who experienced a long period of Nazi persecution that culminated in murder and which allowed them some time to learn about their persecutors, Hungarian Jews were faced with murder almost immediately after the Germans entered Hungary—only two months after the occupation started. The brutal process of stripping Jews of their property and driving them into ghettos, followed very swiftly by deportations, gave individuals little or no time to attempt to hide or escape. Moreover, the more dynamic segment of the community, the young men who had been drafted for forced labor long ago, were not on the scene to help their families. However, many of the refugee youth who were living underground and individuals from the Orthodox communities living near the border fled to relative safety in Romania.

By July 1944, after the first wave of deportations, the only remaining Jews were either in forced labor units or in Budapest. In Budapest a large-scale rescue operation came into being, in which neutral diplomats and Jews—mostly Zionist youth—combined to help the remnant of the community. Since this rescue was based on the protection provided to Jews by the various diplomats, their countries, and their international organizations, individuals clamored to receive the protective papers issued by those bodies. The Zionist youth also manufactured some 100,000 false papers and distributed them. In fall 1944, the atmosphere of rescue and the fact that the Soviet army was advancing gave Budapest Jews hope that they might survive. Although tens of thousands of Jews were deported from Budapest by foot to the Austrian border, and tens of thousands were murdered in Budapest itself, the individual, with the help of the rescuers, needed to remain safe for only a matter of weeks to survive the war. If he could stay out of the hands of the Hungarian fascist ARROW CROSS PARTY, and if he could keep body and soul together in the freezing Budapest winter, where heat, medicine, and food were scarce, a Jew had the chance of surviving. Unlike the Jews of the Eastern European ghettos, the Jews in Budapest retained hope that they might live to see their city free from the Nazis, and in such a case what amounted to a suicidal show of armed resistance never seemed to be a serious option.

The Death Marches. During the height of the deportation of Hungarian Jewry, in June 1944, the Nazis were already setting the stage for the evacuation of camp inmates from territory that was soon to be the scene of fighting between the German military and Soviet forces.

Most of the major evacuations, however, which came to be known by the name DEATH MARCHES, began in January 1945, and subsequent evacuations continued until the end of the war in Europe in May. Camp inmates were sometimes transported by train or boat, but at some point during the process of retreat, they were made to march by foot.

During these forced marches, tens of thousands died. Many thousands simply collapsed from exhaustion; they received little or no food or water during the course of the withdrawal and they were exposed to the elements, still harsh in the winter and spring months of 1945. Others, by order from above, were shot by their guards for not keeping up with the column. Guards also shot down other inmates before the start of the marches, since they were considered too weak to even attempt the forced march. Among the few prisoners who had the strength to attempt escape, many were shot at the outset of their flight. Others were found later and then shot by the guards, and still other escaped prisoners were turned in by local inhabitants to the guards, who then shot them. A relatively few escaped prisoners found refuge in the homes of the local population. There are other recorded incidents of great kindness, when local inhabitants provided food and drink to the passing ragged columns. But there were also incidents of wanton slaughter—some carried out by local people who had been recruited into the civil guard or on the orders of local Nazi leaders.

If until the period of the death marches Jews were singled out for especially murderous treatment, during the forced marches both Jewish and non-Jewish prisoners were subject to the same inhumane treatment. Yet, there was one significant difference. It stands to reason since Jewish prisoners generally began the death marches weaker than other inmates, they were more likely to be murdered or to die along the way.

The terrible tragedies that were played out along the route of the death marches are expressed in the testimonies and memoirs of almost every Jew who found himself marching, often aimlessly, during the last months, weeks, and even days of the war. Many are the stories of Jews who lost their last family member or dearest friend during the death marches. Many Jews with such experiences could tell the exact date and place where the death happened, unlike the previous deaths of their other dear ones. Others tell of their terrible physical suffering and being reduced to eating herbs and grass that they gathered, and some have written about how they collapsed and managed to summon a supreme will to rise at the last moment to stave off a murderous gun shot.

Those who survived the marches were dumped in camps deep inside German territory, and some were sent on further death marches from those camps. In the camps the Jews generally encountered even worse conditions than they had experienced before the death marches had begun. Generally the camps into which they were dumped were so overflowing, that they could not provide even the barest degree of shelter or sustenance to the new arrivals. It is no wonder that epidemics raged in these camps, and during the first weeks after liberation, thousands upon thousands of inmates died from the cumulative effects of their ordeal.

Liberation. Over the course of 1944 and 1945, liberation greeted Jews in innumerable places and situations, the variety of which mirrors the great range of experience Jews suffered during the Holocaust. Jews who retained enough strength might have felt short-lived jubilation at the moment of their liberation. However, in many cases prisoners were so near death that they were not aware that the liberators had arrived. Thousands died immediately after liberation without ever really knowing they had been freed of the Nazi yoke.

Most camp survivors' first concern was to find food and drink. Often, well-meaning liberators gave them food, and many prisoners died from eating things their bodies could no longer process. Enraged by their ordeal, some liberated prisoners went on rampages, storming through the town near their camp. But from survivor testimony and memoirs, it seems that the thirst for vengeance never dominated.

Most Holocaust survivors, of the camps and in other venues, embarked on searches for family that frequently proved futile. Whether at the point of liberation or shortly thereafter, most survivors began digesting the fact that they had lost everyone and everything that had been dear to them before the war. It would be wrong to talk about liberation as the happy ending to a terrible nightmare. It was simply the end of the immediate threat of death and intense physical deprivation, but the nightmare of loss tormented many survivors during both their waking and sleeping hours for a long time to come. Even though the great majority of survivors built new lives, those lives could never really be said to have balanced out their dreadful experiences and irreversible losses during the Holocaust.

THE ALLIES AND THE HOLOCAUST

David Silberklang

On a dark mid-September night in 1942, in the semi-ruins of a "safe-house" in WARSAW maintained by the Polish underground, a young Polish courier code-named Jan KARSKI met with two political leaders from the underground groups in the Warsaw GHETTO—one a Bundist, the other a Zionist. Being both very well educated and politically aware, Karski was well impressed by the fact that these two hardened political adversaries had come to meet him together, bearing a joint Jewish message from the depths of the Warsaw Ghetto. Clearly they had something of the greatest importance to relate.

The Polish underground had decided to send Karski on a mission to London, bearing messages from the Polish political parties operating secretly in POLAND to their parent bodies in the POLISH GOVERNMENT-IN-EXILE in London. He was to meet with Polish government leaders in London, as well as with British government leaders and the American ambassador to the governments-in-exile. Through their connections with various Polish underground groups, particularly with the Polish Socialists, leaders of the Jewish Socialist BUND party had learned of the upcoming mission of a Polish courier and asked permission to send a Jewish message as well. The Polish underground agreed, as did Karski, and sometime during the last days of the massive DEPORTATIONS from the Warsaw Ghetto to the TREBLINKA extermination camp or shortly thereafter, Karski met with the two Jewish representatives. For hours they related to him in great detail all that had been happening to the Jews of Warsaw during the previous months and to the Jews in Poland in general. As they came to the end of their long tale of agony and woe, Karski asked what their message was. Did they wish him simply to relate the story, which, given his photographic memory, he could do very reliably, or was there a specific message? One of them responded: "We want that nobody after the war will be able to say he was not informed."

Karski then agreed to be smuggled into the Warsaw Ghetto so that he could be an eyewitness, rather than presenting only hearsay evidence. After spending a full day in the ghetto, he agreed to be smuggled into one of the camps. The notion that starving Jews locked up behind ghetto walls could actually smuggle a Pole *into* an EXTERMINATION CAMP and bring him out again is astounding. Yet, in a true-life story beside which the espionage stories of popular fiction pale by comparison, these Jews activated a long chain of connections which ended with a bribe to a non-commissioned officer at a camp who would bring Karski into the camp for a day disguised as a guard. The non-commissioned officer had no idea of the real source of the bribe, nor did he realize the identity of his client. Karski was to spend a full day in the camp, but, as he reports it, he suffered a nervous breakdown there within forty minutes. The horrible scene before him became foggy and the world began to sway. As his knees began to buckle, his escort, who had been watching him from a distance, ran over and began yelling at him as though disciplining an errant guard. He grabbed Karski by the collar and marched him out of the camp, thereby saving both of them from certain death.

In London Karski seems to have reported that he had been in BELZEC, but in actuality he seems to have been in one of the transit camps on the way to Belzec—perhaps at the town of Izbica. Of course, what is relevant is not the exact details of where he had been, but rather his eyewitness account of the "Final Solution."

Before departing for the West, Karski met again with the same two underground leaders from the Warsaw Ghetto, who now equipped him with specific messages and requests for the Polish government and for Jewish leaders in the West. Karski crossed Poland into GERMANY, and from there into BELGIUM, FRANCE, and SPAIN, where he boarded a small fishing boat which transferred him to another boat for Scotland. He arrived in Scotland on November 14, 1942, and was in London meeting with Polish leaders within a few days. Shortly thereafter, he began his meetings with several British Cabinet ministers, including Foreign Minister Anthony Eden. Karski faithfully fulfilled his mission for the Jews, as well, reporting all he had seen and heard.

Karski's testimony came at the peak of a wave of reports from Europe regarding the murder of the Jews, and appeared at the same time as reports in Palestine from Jews who had just been released from Poland in a prisoner exchange between Germany and GREAT BRITAIN, and the American State Department's confirmation to Stephen WISE of "your deepest fears." These reports put all the mass murder reports of the previous 16 months into the context of a premeditated Nazi plan to murder all the Jews under their rule. The impact of the eyewitness reports led the Polish government-in-exile and outraged citizens and members of Parliament to pressure the Allies for a response. The result was the Allied Declaration of December 17, 1942:

> The attention of the Governments...has been drawn to numerous reports from Europe that the German authorities...are now carrying into effect Hitler's oft-repeated intention to exterminate the Jewish people in Europe. From all the occupied countries, Jews are being transported, in conditions of appalling horror and brutality, to Eastern Europe. In Poland, which has been made the principal Nazi slaughter-house, the ghettos established by the Nazi invaders are being systematically emptied of all Jews...None of those taken away are ever heard of again...The number of victims of these bloody cruelties is reckoned in many hundreds of thousands.... The above-mentioned Governments...condemn in the strongest possible terms this bestial policy of cold-blooded extermination...They reaffirm their solemn resolution to ensure that those responsible for those crimes shall not escape retribution...

This forthright condemnation was read simultaneously by Undersecretary of State Sumner Welles before a joint session of Congress, over Radio Moscow by Soviet Foreign Minister Viacheslav MOLOTOV, and before the House of Commons by Foreign Secretary Eden. Following Eden's reading of the declaration, in a singular and unusual tribute, the House rose for a minute of silence in honor of the victims. The declaration received wide media coverage and was reported on the front pages of many newspapers the following day. This was the first Allied joint declaration regarding the murder of the Jews. It was also the last. Reflecting back on these events decades later, Karski has said that all mankind during the HOLOCAUST was guilty of the second original sin, "committed by commission, by omission, or by self-imposed ignorance."

Prerequisites. By what criteria can we today, nearly sixty years later, assess the responses of the Allied powers to the Holocaust? There has been much good research and many fine books and articles have been written on the subject during the last 30 years. Nearly all of them have felt compelled by the difficult evidence to reach much the same conclusion as Karski's harsh accusation. Certainly Karski himself is in a unique position to assess the Allied responses, being perhaps the only person in the world to have been eyewitness both to the Jews' fate and to the Allied leaders' responses to it. A number of issues should be clarified as prerequisites to reassessing the Allies' responses.

The Roles of the Actors. As with many crimes, there were three types of "actors" involved in the Holocaust. These may be generally categorized as Perpetrators, Victims, and Bystanders. For the purposes of this essay, the identities and roles of the first two seem clear. The perpetrators were the Nazis and those who helped them in committing one of the greatest crimes in history. The victims of the "Final Solution" were the Jews, including anyone whom the Nazis believed was a Jew by their racist definition. The bystanders were the third and largest party.

In a sense, at the moment at which the crime was committed in each place, the bystanders were neutral. They had neither chosen the crime, nor were they chosen by its perpetrators to be its victims. Yet, from the moment the crime began to unfold, we begin to ask questions of these bystanders. They will be assessed by later observers based on their reactions and behavior once they became aware of the crime, whether it took place in their backyards or far away from view. Those who tried to intervene on the victims' behalf, the "RIGHTEOUS AMONG THE NATIONS" are rightly remembered in heroic proportions. Many of them paid with their own lives, and in that sense, too, they joined the victims. Those who tried to intervene on the perpetrators' side, aiding and abetting the murder and engaging in murder themselves, abandoned their initial "neutrality" and are rightly remembered, and sometimes prosecuted, as perpetrators in their own right. But what of those who tried to remain "neutral?" Clearly, it is difficult, perhaps impossible, to speak in terms of neutrality in the face of such a horrendous crime, and it is on this basis that the bystanders have been judged by those who have come afterward.

There were many groups who could be theoretically included under the general heading "Bystanders" such as the civilian populations of the occupied countries; elements in the governments, armed forces, and civilian populations of the AXIS countries; and the same groups among the neutral countries, the Vatican, the International Red Cross, and many more (see also RED CROSS, INTERNATIONAL). The Allied powers—their governments, military forces, civilian non-Jewish populations, and Jewish populations—can be included among the bystanders, at least in the general terms presented above. Of course, different questions will be asked and different expectations assumed for a Pole seeing his neighbor being dragged away than for British or American leaders receiving reports from Nazi-occupied Europe. For one, the information was immediate and clear, yet the resources were sorely limited, while for the other, the resources were far vaster, but the information came from a great distance and with uncertain significance.

Regardless of how the Allies as bystanders are judged, even if serious accusations are thrust at them, one thing must remain clear. By the very nature of things, it was the perpetrators who initiated the action. The bystanders, including the Allies, were mainly in a position to respond. Perhaps the Allies were guilty of callousness, or even criminal indifference, but care should be taken not to confuse apparent moral failure with murderous action.

The Nature of the Crime. During WORLD WAR II, it can be argued, the Nazis were engaged in two parallel wars. One was a military conflict fought between opposing armed forces along thousands of miles of front, with infantry, tanks, artillery, airplanes, and warships on all sides. The arm of Nazi Germany responsible for planning strategy and tactics and for waging war on the battlefield was the WEHRMACHT. The reasons behind this war were in part similar to the classic reasons for wars: desire for territorial expansion, exploitation of natural resources, political domination, etc. For the Nazis, there were clearly also ideological motivations for this war, and these may have been the primary motivations. However, on the face of it, this was a military conflict similar to others before it.

Parallel to this was an ideological war—the war against the Jews—whose opposing forces and battlefields were very different. The SS was the main body responsible for planning and waging this war. In it a heavily armed force, deeply motivated ideologically on the one side, faced an unarmed civilian population of young and old, healthy and frail, of families living peacefully in their homes at the moment that the attack began. The arena of warfare was unique—ghettos, FORCED LABOR camps, killing fields, GAS CHAMBERS, and the routes of the DEATH MARCHES. Certainly, one regime stood behind these two parallel wars, and there was extensive overlapping and mutual assistance rendered between the two bodies chiefly responsible for each.

Still, a question that must exercise anyone examining Allied responses to the Holocaust is: While the Nazis were engaged in two parallel wars, which war did the Allies fight?

The Prejudices of the Observer. Nearly all the literature and discussions of Allied responses to the Holocaust have focused on two of the three major Allied powers, Great Britain and the UNITED STATES. The reasons for this are obvious. Citizens of democratic countries are allowed to publicly ask such questions of their governments, and the historical documents that might contain the answers to these questions are accessible. It is not known whether Soviet citizens ever addressed such questions to their government. The terms of reference for discussing the "Great Patriotic War" (the Soviet name for World War II) have been very different there from the West. Moreover, archives in the former SOVIET UNION were closed to historical researchers until very recently, so that those who might have raised the questions had no access to the documents that might provide the hints of answers.

In addition to the accessibility of primary sources and interest in raising such questions as the responses of a country to the Holocaust, citizens of these two Western democracies have a liberal humanitarian self-perception of their societies. Therefore, they may publicly demand that humanitarian concerns play a role in foreign policy. Moreover, they believe their societies to be not only moral, but morally superior to the former Communist countries. That the citizens of the Communist countries (while they still existed as such) may also have seen themselves as morally superior, and that such perceptions may be entirely misleading, are not the point here. Rather, the point is the implication of such perceptions in the West, where the historical literature on this subject has been written. In the light of their self-perception, citizens of the West may expect and demand more morally of their countries than of others. Therefore, whereas penetrating questions have been raised regarding the presence or absence of humanitarian concerns in British and American government responses to the Holocaust, none of the Western historical literature on this subject has expected that STALIN would have troubled his mind over such concerns. Since the sources, the writers, the perspectives, and the biases have been Western, the Soviet Union has rarely been discussed, and when it has entered the discussion, it has been for a brief, cameo appearance. However, two qualifications must be noted. First, clearly it was the Soviet army that was closest to the scenes of the crime and might theoretically have been in the best position to intervene militarily to stop the murder. Yet, no one in 1944 or since seriously considered demanding that the Soviets bomb AUSCHWITZ, for example (see also AUSCHWITZ, BOMBING OF). Second, whereas humanitarianism does sometimes play a role in the foreign policies of democratic countries, ultimately it is national interests that determine foreign policy. The reactions of governments to major world crises in the 1990s—such as the Iraqi occupation of Kuwait, the genocide in Rwanda, and the repeated crises in the former YUGOSLAVIA—reflect this to a great extent. Leaders of major powers who seem to be carrying humanitarianism to an extreme in determining foreign policy, tend not to be taken seriously. President Jimmy Carter in the late 1970s is one example of such a leader. Humanitarian concerns tend to play a role in foreign policy only to the extent that they do not seriously conflict with defined national interests. The primary national interest of the Western Allies during World War II is easy to ascertain—victory.

Conflicting Timetables. The Holocaust and World War II did not unfold along the same timetable. By the time the Western Allies were near enough to the scenes of the crime perhaps to consider military intervention of some sort, in 1944, most of the Jews were already dead. When questions of reactions are addressed to the Allies, the period in question must be kept in mind. Certainly, there will be different expectations of the countries of the world during the war years than in the 1933–1939 period, when there were no Allies and no war, and when the numbers being persecuted and the extent of the persecution, great and shocking as they were, were clearly of a lesser magnitude than what followed. Similarly, the same responses cannot be expected to the harsh persecution and the murders that characterized the September 1939–June 1941 period, as opposed to the period following the Joint Declaration of December 17, 1942. That was the point at which the Allies seem to have said openly and publicly, "we know."

In addressing questions to the Western Allies, we must look for the turning points following which a new stage in the Holocaust or in the Allies' capabilities to respond was reached. The military turning point in the war came during the latter part of 1942 and the first part of 1943, with the Soviet victory at Stalingrad and the Western Allies' invasion of North Africa. However,

turning points evolve, and they have contexts and consequences that might become clear or bear fruit only considerably later than the definable turning point itself. The turning point in the war might have begun arguably with the German invasion of the Soviet Union, a military adventure too large for the German armed forces to sustain. With the American entry into the war nearly six months later, Germany was faced with overwhelming military prowess arrayed against it on two fronts. Still, the Allies' first major military victories came much later, and their vanquishing of the *Wehrmacht* was years away.

When were the turning points for the Jews? Operation Barbarossa (the German invasion of the Soviet Union), which began on June 22, 1941, brought with it the beginning of the systematic mass murder of the Jews. This was clearly the beginning of the end for the Jews under Nazi rule. However, in an ironic sense, the same factor that dramatically changed the military odds against Germany also snatched away the Jews' last possible hope for aid—the US entry into the war. Until December 7, 1941, at least in theory, the United States and American Jews could have contact with the Jews of Europe because the United States was a neutral country. The American Jewish JOINT DISTRIBUTION COMMITTEE and other organizations sent care packages to Poland and subsidized the Jews' existence there to a significant degree at least until the fall of 1941. There was limited correspondence and some individual packages were sent as well. For example, on June 5, 1941, the Deutsche Bank in BERLIN wrote to the JUDENRAT in LUBLIN that it had received a check in the sum of $13, drawn from Liberty National Bank in Chicago, for the Polish-Jewish PRISONER OF WAR, Benjamin Rogaczewski. The German bank was willing to forward the sum in zloty from its Warsaw branch, once Rogaczewski completed the enclosed forms. There was a bureaucratic delay, but apparently, this POW in the Lipowa 7 POW camp received the said amount in late July 1941. Thirteen American dollars could go a long way for a Jew in occupied Poland. But more significantly, someone in Chicago knew of Mr. Rogaczewski's whereabouts deep in occupied Europe. It is not known how many letters, packages, or checks were sent from the US to Poland, but Rogaczewski was certainly not the only Jew of his kind. As of December 7, 1941, this last significant lifeline was cut. In the year that elapsed until the tide of war began to turn, nearly all of Polish Jewry was murdered.

National Interests 1933–1939. The Nazi and Jewish

problems facing the world in the prewar years were not of the same proportions as during the war. The numbers of Jews under Nazi rule were "limited" to the hundreds of thousands, and what they suffered was loss of civil freedoms, loss of citizens' rights, severe economic dislocation, and other forms of persecution. Many were arrested at various points; some were killed. As a result, many Jews sought to leave Germany for more hospitable areas. But where would they go?

The countries of the world were caught up in the throes of the Great Depression when the Nazis came to power, and most countries remained so for many years afterward. The United States, according to many American historians, did not fully emerge from the Great Depression until its entry into the war. One of the primary national interests for most countries, including those later to constitute the Allies, was economic recovery. This was accompanied by an overwhelming desire among the former victorious powers in World War I to maintain the peace at almost any cost.

Near the end of the nineteenth century the United States began passing a series of laws designed to limit immigration to the country. This culminated with the National Origins Immigration Act of 1924, which set strict quota limitations on immigration, based upon national origin. These severe limitations on immigration were further tightened by President Herbert Hoover's September 1930 administrative order to consular officials to exercise the strictest possible interpretation of the "likely to become a public charge clause." This clause in the 1917 Immigration Act gave the consular officials the right to deny a visa to a prospective immigrant who they believed was likely to become dependent on public funds. Hoover's order meant that consular officials could now deny immigration visas to anyone whom they believed had any chance of someday becoming a public charge. The result was a drastic decrease in immigration to the United States, and quotas were never even nearly filled until 1938. These restrictions preceded the Nazi rise to power and were clearly unconnected to the Nazis' persecution of the Jews. Rather, they were based on the American government's perception of its responsibility to its own citizens and on the perception that immigrants would unfairly compete for jobs with unemployed American citizens. These severe immigration restrictions were not affected by Nazi policies towards German Jews, but they had a devastating impact upon the availability of safe havens for Jews seeking to flee Germany.

Accompanying the economic crisis was a strong current of isolationism in the United States. Americans were tired of Europe and were happy to leave the Europeans to deal with their own problems. There was a growing sense of American nativism, a dislike of everything and everyone foreign, and an ever-growing ANTISEMITISM. Other countries were similarly suspicious of foreigners and shared a growing popular antisemitism, which was influenced by a variety of factors, such as the deep economic depression, the development of an intense nationalism deeply connected to the hatred of anything foreign, the rise of the radical right and of FASCISM throughout Europe, and the rise of the Nazis in Germany. In such an atmosphere, few countries were willing to take in dirt-poor REFUGEES (and this was the condition in which the Jews were permitted to leave Germany), especially if these were Jewish refugees. In addition, it was not only Germany that looked forward to being rid of its Jews, and not only Jews in Germany who felt a need to emigrate during the 1930s. Many Jews in Poland and ROMANIA also found their conditions unbearable. To these factors must be added the reluctance of governments to become involved in what was perceived at least until 1938 as an internal German matter. Moreover, the intense desire prevalent especially in the democratic countries to maintain the peace at all costs took precedence over nearly all kinds of intervention in Germany's policies towards its Jews. The laws and sentiments around the world did not leave much room for most of the potential emigrants.

A turning point in Western responses to the plight of German Jewry occurred during 1938. This turning point had two axes, the "ANSCHLUSS" (annexation) of AUSTRIA in March and the "KRISTALLNACHT" pogrom in November. In the wake of the "*Anschluss*" President ROOSEVELT issued invitations to a July conference in Evian, France, to discuss the problem of refugees from Germany and Austria. Thirty-two countries sent representatives and 24 voluntary organizations presented papers and suggestions for dealing with the problem. The conference discussed actual and "potential" refugees, which meant it was at least theoretically expecting to have to deal with a long-range problem that was still growing.

In terms of expanding immigration possibilities, the results of the EVIAN CONFERENCE were practically worthless. Britain was unwilling to discuss the possibility of expanded immigration to Palestine, where Jewish immigration had been seriously limited following the Arab uprising in 1936. European countries that had received refugees were unwilling to receive any more. The United States announced its willingness to fill its quotas for immigration from Germany and Austria (27,230), and the Dominican Republic offered to take in up to 100,000 refugees. The Dominican Republic's offer was widely viewed as a public relations ploy to win favor and to get the developed countries to invest in its underdeveloped infrastructure. It was also designed to increase the white population of the country. It was clear that the Dominican Republic was equipped to absorb only a small fraction of the numbers of immigrants it was suggesting. No other country was willing to change or adjust its immigration regulations or practices. Most countries expressed their concern for the plight of the persecuted Jews and others who might feel the need to emigrate, but regretted that they were unable to do more than they had already done. The delegate from Australia, Lt. Col. Thomas Walter White, was more blunt: "As we have no racial problem, we are not desirous of importing one." Thus, the doors of the world remained politely closed.

However, one thing that did emerge from the Evian Conference was the Intergovernmental Committee on Refugees (ICR), which was given the responsibility to search for potential places of refuge and to negotiate with the German government regarding allowing Jews to emigrate without having to leave all their money behind. The ICR's Executive Director, George Rublee, took this mandate seriously and soon opened negotiations with the president of the Reichsbank and German Economics Minister, Hjalmar SCHACHT. By January 1939, an arrangement was in the works whereby Jews would be permitted to leave with a small amount of their assets, which would actually be provided by the Jews of the world in a huge ransom. To some degree, the arrangement was based on the "transfer agreement" between the Jewish Agency for Palestine and the German government. Schacht was dismissed from his ministerial post before the deal could be signed, and Rublee then continued the negotiations with Schacht's replacement, Helmuth Wohltat. By early summer, a deal was ready and awaited the approval of the ICR's participating governments and the Jews of the world, particularly American Jewry, in order to begin carrying it out. Jews outside Germany were profoundly disturbed by the arrangement, which, for all intents and purposes, was a colossal ransoming of hostages based on the unspoken recognition that the German government was within its rights to steal the capital of its Jewish citizens. President Roosevelt pressured American Jewish leaders to accept the arrangement. The funding body that was to stand behind the organized emigration, the Coordinating Foundation, was established in July 1939, but the war broke out before anything could be done with it.

The pogrom on November 9–10, 1938, brought a more dramatic change in the responses of some Western governments. Expressions of condemnation and outrage were widespread. On November 15 the United States recalled its ambassador to Germany, Hugh Wilson. There was not to be an American ambassador in Germany for eleven years. In addition, President Roosevelt issued an order to extend indefinitely 15,000 tourist visas, held mostly by German Jews who had fled Germany and who would soon have had to have left the United States. American immigration quotas for Germany and Austria were finally filled that year, for the first time that decade. Britain allowed some 50,000 refugees to enter its shores during the months before the outbreak of the war, many times the number allowed into Britain in the previous five-and-a-half years combined. Among these refugees were more than 9,000 unaccompanied children, most of them Jewish, sent to Britain in the "KINDERTRANSPORT," for whom voluntary foster homes were found all across Britain.

As dramatic as these changes were, they were also very limited in scope and duration. At the same time as Britain opened its shores to refugees, it closed the doors of Palestine, the only territory on Earth with a society hungry to receive Jewish refugees. The British WHITE PAPER of May 1939 made the closing of Palestine to Jewish immigration official policy. With war just a matter of time, Britain felt the need to secure peace among the Arabs of the Middle East and to secure oil supplies. Once the war broke out, some of the Jewish refugees allowed into Britain were subsequently deported to Australia and CANADA in 1940, on suspicion of being potential enemies. The United States did not continue to fill its immigration quotas and made no serious effort to reach out to find those seeking to leave Germany. The outbreak of the war put an end to this flash of humanitarian concern for refugees, but the results were far from insignificant. Tens of thousands of German and Austrian Jews owed their lives to this eleventh hour limited change of heart.

Wartime: Information vs. Knowledge. The reactions of the wartime Western Allies to the Holocaust can be examined through the prism of two dialectic historical questions: information vs. knowledge, and willingness vs. ability. That is, in order to understand the Allied reactions to the Holocaust, we must first try to understand what they believed they were reacting to. At what point did information about the "Final Solution" begin to reach the Allies, and at what point did that information coalesce into a reasonably clear picture, not of a rash of unconnected massacres, but of a deliberate, systematic, methodical operation designed to murder every Jew the Nazis could lay their hands on? In order to organize and implement the "Final Solution" the Nazis had to undergo a leap of imagination into the realm of unprecedented criminality. The question here, then, will be at what point did Allied leaders undergo a parallel leap of imagination that would enable them to grasp the meaning of the crime unfolding in occupied Europe?

The other side of these questions is the accompanying dialectic between the willingness and the ability to rescue Jews. There are historians and politicians who have argued that there was nothing the Allies could have done to rescue the Jews. Regardless of Allied actions on behalf of the Jews, the Nazis would have continued to pursue their murderous intentions. However, the question here is twofold. It is not only one of capabilities, but also one of intent. Ultimately, any discussion of the Allies' responses to the Holocaust must come back to the same, fundamental issue. Did the Allies consider any attempt to rescue European Jewry at any time, in any way, shape, or form? The answer to this question can be sought not only in the battlefield, but also in the planning rooms.

Until mid or late summer 1941, the Jews' plight in ghettos and forced labor camps was familiar to the Western powers. The neutrality of the United States until December 7, 1941 enabled contact to be maintained with occupied Europe. Neutral journalists had limited access to the occupied countries, and the German government was neither able nor wanted to hide all of its actions taken against Jews during the first 21 months of the war. Thus, the uprooting of populations, the Nazi plans for a Jewish "reservation," the wholesale denial of basic rights to Jews, the extensive starvation, the widespread disease, the harsh conditions of forced labor, and the large numbers of Jews killed were at times reported in Western newspapers. They were also familiar to British and American government officials. However, during this period, we cannot ask how these two governments reacted to the murder of

the Jews because that had not happened yet. The concept of Allies—and therefore of an Allied reaction to the Nazi treatment of Jews—was also not yet what it came to be during the second half of 1941, as both the United States and the Soviet Union remained officially neutral.

Soon after the beginning of Operation Barbarossa, chilling reports began to reach the West regarding massacres of Jews or of civilians in general. British intelligence was regularly intercepting German police reports from the Soviet Union about massacres of Jews. Escapees and underground reports also reached the West. Among the most astonishing were the November 1941 reports of up to 50,000 shot dead in Kiev the previous September in what is known as the murder at BABI YAR. These reports did not refer to any murder plan or pattern, and some of them seemed too fantastic to be believed. Yet, these reports continued to arrive, with increasing frequency. As the weeks and months passed, it became clear that Germans were committing outrageous atrocities against civilians.

The first public attempt to combine these reports into one picture of sorts was that by Soviet Foreign Minister Molotov, in a January 7, 1942 note to the embassies in Moscow. But who among Western leaders would take such a report from the Soviet government at face value? On March 13, 1942, S. Bertrand Jacobson, Joint Distribution Committee representative in HUNGARY, told a press conference in the United States of special Nazi killing squads in Eastern Europe and of at least 300,000 Jews murdered by that point. Among his chief sources were Hungarian soldiers returning from the Soviet front. However, neither Molotov nor Jacobson drew the conclusion that the Nazis had embarked on the murder of all the Jews.

The first report that actually referred to a Nazi plan to murder all Jews was the secret report from the *Bund* in Warsaw, smuggled out to the West in late May 1942. The *Bund* Report referred to 700,000 Jews murdered on Polish soil and related specific places, numbers, and methods. The report received some media coverage, including foreign language broadcasts over the BBC, a June 25, 1942 report in the London *Daily Telegraph,* and later reports in other newspapers in Britain and the United States. This might have led to the beginning of a clearer understanding of the Holocaust, but apparently it did not. A joint press conference was called on July 8, 1942 by the British and Polish governments to present the data in the *Bund* report officially. The Poles sent appropriate representation for such a serious matter,

Deputy Prime Minister and Interior Minister Stanislaw Mikolajczyk and the two Jewish representatives on the Polish National Council, the Bundist Samuel ZYGELBOJM, and the Zionist Ignacy SCHWARZBART. Representing the British was Brendan Bracken, the minister for information, who was responsible for propaganda. The nature of the British representation reflects ambivalence regarding the information being discussed and could only have led observers to relate to the report as good propaganda that might be partly true.

Many historians have pointed to the now famous cable sent by Gerhart Riegner to Stephen Wise on August 8, 1942, as the decisive report (see also RIEGNER CABLE). Neutral SWITZERLAND, and especially Geneva, had become an important listening post for war information and for news regarding the Jews. Representatives of Jewish organizations, such as Riegner of the WORLD JEWISH CONGRESS and Richard Lichtheim of the Jewish Agency, were especially attuned to information regarding the Jews of Europe. Yet, Riegner was not willing to commit completely to the information in his report; this is reflected in his statement that a Nazi plan "being discussed" for the fall to kill up to four million Jews with prussic acid "at one blow" should be taken with "all necessary reservation as exactitude cannot be confirmed." The cable was sent to Wise via US diplomatic mail, and to Sidney Silverman in London via the British diplomatic pouch. State Department officials determined that the American government did not have evidence to confirm Riegner's information and therefore decided not to forward the cable to Wise. British Foreign Office officials reached the same conclusion regarding Riegner's information, but decided to pass on the cable together with a cover note disclaiming possession of any corroborative evidence. Silverman then forwarded the cable to Wise through regular telegraph channels.

Despite the qualification that Riegner inserted into the cable, the information, coming on the heels of numerous massacre reports and of the *Bund* report, shocked its Jewish recipients in Britain and the US. Wise took the information to Sumner Welles at the State Department as soon as he received the cable at the end of August. Welles requested that Wise give him a short time to verify the report before going public with it. Wise agreed, and on November 24 Welles summoned Wise to his office and confirmed the information in the report. Wise immediately called a press conference and made the information public.

Eleven days earlier, 78 Polish Jewish refugees arrived in Palestine as part of a civilian prisoner exchange between Britain and Germany. These Jews were interviewed by Jewish Agency officials and related the entire horrible story of the Holocaust as eyewitnesses. Their reports appeared in Palestinian Jewish newspapers on November 23, beneath black-bordered front-page headlines. When taken together, it would seem that convincing evidence of the Holocaust reached three continents from three different sources almost simultaneously. The American and British governments had access to all three reports. Public pressure and Polish government pressure produced the Joint Declaration of December 17, 1942. It would seem, therefore, that from at least that point onward attempts at rescue action could be expected of the Allies.

Wartime: Willingness vs. Ability. At the time that the Western Allies seemingly grasped finally the true nature of the Holocaust, in December 1942, their armed forces were too far away to intervene. Although a major battle had been won in North Africa, the battle at Stalingrad had not yet been decided. The American forces had only at that time begun to be fully integrated into the war effort, and the impact of millions of fresh soldiers entering the fray had yet to be felt in Europe. However, this is not the only question being asked of the Allies at this point in time. In the wake of the terrible realization to which they had arrived regarding the fate of the Jews, did the Allied leaders, in their moral outrage and horror, immediately appoint a task force to examine possibilities for rescuing the threatened Jews? Did such a hypothetical committee work day and night, tearing their hair out and banging their heads against the wall searching for some way to rescue Jews, only to throw their hands up in despair because nothing could yet be done? Or, was rescue not on the agenda to begin with?

Here, as before, the answer to the question might seem self-evident. "They did nothing" is a common conclusion. However, even if this could be demonstrated, the reasons for the inaction must be examined, and such an examination must begin with national interests.

A country's main national interest during a war is obvious—victory. Following the defeat of France in June 1940, there was effectively only one Allied power left in the fray against Germany: Great Britain. In a brief nine months, Germany had succeeded in overwhelming nearly all of Europe, whether by occupation, alliance, or the fear and wariness imposed upon the neutral powers of Europe. Switzerland, for example, was now an island in a sea of Nazi rule on all sides, while SWEDEN feared a German attempt to conquer this final piece of Scandinavia. Britain itself seemed an unworthy foe in the summer of 1940. Its infantry had been smashed, only remnants escaping in the evacuation of Dunkirk. It seemed as though Germany was poised in the summer of 1940 to invade a weakened Britain and put an end to the farce. Survival was Britain's highest priority, and it could be persuasively argued that the European Jews' fate hinged at least in part on Britain's achieving that aim. Luckily for Britain, and for all of mankind it might be added, it was the *Luftwaffe* that was knocked out of the skies in the Battle of Britain, and Great Britain had survived to fight another day. However, even this Allied victory hardly turned the tide of war. Britain was crippled militarily and was in no position to intervene on the Jews' behalf, or anyone else's for that matter.

Once the Soviet Union and the United States had entered the war, Allied energies were focused on achieving victory in the swiftest and most convincing way possible. As the tide of war turned in early 1943 and rescue pressure mounted among the American and British publics, the US and Great Britain felt constrained to convene a conference to address the issue.

Great hopes were placed on the BERMUDA CONFERENCE at first. The Western Allies, who had by now affirmed their knowledge of the Holocaust, who had defined the Nazi enemy as the embodiment of evil in this war waged to rescue the world, and who were now ready to become victorious on all fronts, were in a strong position from which to launch a rescue program. American Jewish groups prepared detailed rescue proposals for the consideration of the conference, and massive public demonstrations advocating rescue of the Jews were taking place all across the United States. Yet, the Bermuda Conference, which convened ironically on April 19, 1943, the same day on which the WARSAW GHETTO UPRISING broke out, proved very quickly to be a major disappointment to rescue advocates.

The historian Henry Feingold aptly referred to the Bermuda Conference as "Mock Rescue for Surplus People." Indeed, when the meager results of the conference are examined, it becomes evident that it was planned not so much to rescue Jews as to rescue the Allied governments from the growing pressure of the rescue advocates. The Bermuda Conference was a meeting of middle level officials representing only two countries, the United States and Great Britain, convened on the closed military island of Bermuda, far away from the public eye and from the prying press. Only a handful of journalists were allowed onto the island, and they were not permitted to observe the meetings. They would receive only daily briefings full of vague generalizations. Voluntary organizations concerned with rescue were not represented at all, and any rescue proposals they had were apparently never really discussed. The conference determined that no ships could be spared to transport refugees who might have escaped to temporary havens, there could be no negotiations with the enemy for the sake of rescue, and nothing could be done that would divert supplies from the war effort. The conference proved such an embarrassment, that no report or closing statement was issued for weeks after its conclusion.

The most tangible result of the Bermuda Conference was to bring more pressure to bear on the Allied governments to rescue the Jews of Europe. At the same time, Allied forces continued to advance on all fronts, but until September 1943, when the Western Allies occupied the southern half of ITALY, actual rescue operations were still a military impossibility. Allied planes could not make the round trip from their nearest bases to the extermination camps and ghettos. Most other actions that might have been undertaken on behalf of the Jews and were raised by rescue advocates were generally not even considered.

The rescue pressure came from many different sources, not all of them working in harmony. The major American Jewish organizations, which had been working together since January 1943 to organize demonstrations and meetings aimed at heightening public awareness about rescue and getting rescue placed onto the American agenda, succeeded in maintaining their temporary coalition through the summer of 1943. At that time, the differences between Zionists and non-Zionists surfaced again to divide their forces, but rescue advocacy continued from both camps. At the same time, the rival BERGSON GROUP, an outgrowth of a delegation of the Revisionist Zionist-related *Irgun Tsevaʾi Leʾummi* organization, heightened its competing publicity campaign for rescue, which culminated in a July 1943 Emergency Conference to Save the Jewish People of Europe. Many public figures in the United States and Great Britain, including members of Congress and Parliament, also called on their governments repeatedly to undertake rescue activities. In the United States, public concern over the fate of Europe's Jews led to public hearings in the House of Representatives, beginning in November 1943, to consider a congressional resolution calling on the government to undertake rescue action. The subcommittee hearings were well publicized, as was the embarrassing testimony of the State Department's official in charge of immigration, Breckenridge Long. Long had created a false impression regarding American generosity in supposedly allowing hundreds of thousands of refugees into the United States. Had the resolution come to a vote in the House as planned in January 1944, it might well have passed. Although such a resolution would have been non-binding on the executive branch of the government, it would have been an embarrassment. At the same time, Treasury officials had discovered that the State Department had been actively blocking rescue attempts and the passing of information regarding the fate of the European Jews. Treasury Secretary Henry MORGENTHAU brought this to the attention of the president in January 1944 in a damning report prepared by three of his deputies, and Roosevelt immediately issued an Executive Order creating the WAR REFUGEE BOARD (WRB). Ironically, the Bermuda Conference itself had created that significant combination of rescue pressure from rival Jewish groups, congressional hearings, public figures, and, most importantly, from the Treasury Department in late 1943, that pushed President Roosevelt in January to change precisely that rescue policy that Bermuda was meant to perpetuate.

The creation of the WRB represented a marked departure from previous American rescue policy. The WRB's mandate was to do all it could to rescue those in danger of being murdered by the Nazis or their collaborators, including activities that were previously expressly forbidden, such as negotiating with the enemy, or sending money into enemy territory. Although seriously hampered by a lack of cooperation from other government agencies and the minimal budget allotted to it by Roosevelt, the Board pursued its rescue mandate energetically. Its energies were concentrated on four types of activity: evacuating Jews from enemy territory; finding places to which these people could be sent; applying psychological pressure, especially threats of war crimes trials, on officials in Axis countries; and trying to send relief supplies into CONCENTRATION CAMPS.

The historian David Wyman estimates that the WRB played a crucial role in the rescue of some 200,000 Jews. This is a very significant number and leads to the obvious conclusion that it was too little too late. If only the WRB had been created a year or two earlier, how many more lives might have been saved? How many extermination camps may never have succeeded in completing their ghoulish tasks? Yet, it must be kept in mind that the timing of the creation of the WRB probably had a great deal to do with its success. Threats from an American agency in 1942 would have had little impact on European countries noting the stark difference between an overwhelmingly powerful and nearby Germany and a distant United States whose power was as yet unproven. Such threats could have carried more weight in 1943, but Germany was still in occupation and America still too far away to do much. Only the occupation of southern Italy in the fall of 1943 and the progressing retreat of German forces on all fronts going into 1944 lent credence to WRB threats during the first months of its activity. These factors were not present earlier. Moreover, the Allies' invasion of France in June 1944 brought the threats to the doorsteps of the Axis powers, except Germany herself. Therefore, even had the WRB been created much earlier, it is not at all clear that it would have accomplished much more than it did during its brief existence near the end of the war. In this sense, the two separate schedules of the war and the Holocaust began to meet again in 1944, as Allied victories began to liberate some surviving Jews and to hold out the possibility of liberating still more.

The occupation of southern Italy and the advance of Soviet troops on the eastern front enabled the Allies to begin considering bombing military targets in western Poland. By early 1944, they had established absolute air superiority and were bombing German military targets regularly. During the spring and summer of 1944, American reconnaissance planes flying out of Italy flew over the Auschwitz complex of camps to photograph the labor camps where synthetic rubber and oil were being produced for the German war effort. Beginning in August, these industrial installations were bombed several times.

At the same time, public pressure began to build on Allied leaders to bomb the extermination camp of Auschwitz as well as the rail lines leading to it from Hungary, based on detailed reports on the camp received from several escapees from Auschwitz in the spring and summer (see also AUSCHWITZ PROTOCOLS). The American and British governments consistently refused to undertake the bombing mission for a number of reasons. First, it was argued that the bombing missions were technically impossible because there were no Allied bombers that could fly the round-trip distance laden with bombs. The inaccuracy of this argument is obvious from the fact that the Auschwitz camp complex was being bombed at the very same time that the claim of technical impossibility was put forward. Of course, this was a contradiction that the rescue advocates could not have been aware of. It could also be argued that the Allies did not have adequate maps of the extermination camp or its whereabouts to justify a bombing mission. However, it is not clear that the information available on the extermination camp was ever seriously examined, or that the additional information that might have been necessary to carry out a bombing mission was ever clearly defined or sought. Since January 1944 the War Department's policy was to avoid getting the armed forces involved in rescue activities. Thus, the bombing requests in summer 1944 were never examined on their merits in the United States prior to their rejection by the War Department. Similarly, in Great Britain, the Air Ministry nixed the bombing request without examination, despite support for the request expressed by Winston CHURCHILL and Foreign Minister Eden. It is also apparent that those forces based in Italy who prepared the bombing missions of the industrial complexes so close to the extermination camp were not the same people responsible for refusing this mission. Those who took the aerial photographs for the Americans in relation to bombing the industrial targets were unaware of the murderous nature of the large camp very close by that also appeared in several photographs. These photographs were not examined by policymakers with an awareness of the Holocaust until the late 1970s. In addition, it was argued that flying such distances left the air crews greatly exposed for a mission whose potential to be effective was dubious at best. If the Germans wanted to kill the Jews in the camps, then they would do so even if the murder installations were partially destroyed by an air strike. Moreover, rather than rescuing Jews, bombing the camp would serve only as a symbolic act of Allied concern while it would in fact make the Allied bombers into the Jews' murderers because the bombings could not avoid the prisoners. The Allies were also reluctant to single out any particular group for rescue. To single out Jews would be like admitting that the Nazis were correct—the Jews are different. The Allies were not interested in living down to Nazi propaganda.

Allied reluctance to undertake any military action can be summed up in two related Allied slogans: rescue through victory, and no diversion from the war effort. A speedy victory, it was argued, was the best way to rescue the maximum number of people. Therefore, all energies must go into the undertaking of the war effort, and any military action that would divert from the war effort would be counterproductive and would result in a later rescue of fewer people. It was difficult to fight such logic in wartime, and the WRB ultimately adopted the same reasoning.

If this was the end of the story of Allied responses to the Holocaust, then we might reach the conclusion that there was logic to the Allied approach to rescue, at least in 1944, and that the absence of greater rescue was as much the result of grand strategy as of moral failure. However, the grand strategy that left no room for rescue operations for Jews was not adhered to in all cases. For example, when the Polish uprising broke out in Warsaw in August 1944 and the Soviet army sat idly by from a distance of a few miles, the Western Allies decided to undertake to parachute supplies to the Polish fighters, despite the risks involved in such a long flight and despite their estimation that most of the airlifted supplies would fall into enemy hands or be lost. There was important symbolic significance in helping the long suffering Poles.

Why were the Jews different? Or was it the Poles who were different? A serious study of all Allied rescue and aid missions during the war would have to be undertaken to determine what was the exception and what the rule. Nonetheless, it is clear that in the summer of 1944, the Allies viewed the Poles differently from the remaining Jews in Poland. Perhaps with the winds of the Cold War already beginning to blow from the east, this was an attempt to remind the Poles who their friends were and which camp had come to their assistance in their time of need. If so, the political hopes attached to the airlift were realized only 45 years later, if at all. The Jews, of course, not only knew who their friends were, but also had nothing to offer to the postwar political realignment of the world.

Assessments. At times, a willingness to rescue could produce rescue seemingly out of thin air. The thousands of "Righteous among the Nations" are examples of this. Most of them were ordinary people who had no power to speak of, other than the willingness to help those in danger. Raoul WALLENBERG is one of the most famous of the "Righteous." Yet, it must be remembered that his heroic activities were backed by his government, and it is doubtful if such backing would have been forthcoming before mid-1943. The timing is important here, too. Moreover, Wallenberg's activities were largely subsidized by the WRB, an American government agency. Much of these WRB funds, in turn, came from American Jewry, particularly the Joint Distribution Committee. Where is credit due, in addition to Wallenberg the hero, himself? This is difficult to assess, but a small piece of credit is perhaps due to the government which, however reluctantly, created the agency that channeled the funds.

In sharp contrast to the "Righteous" the Allies' rescue efforts seem rather to have been a case of unwillingness eliminating most opportunities to exercise whatever rescue ability there might have been. Why were the Allies unwilling to rescue the Jews? The reasons seem to be many. A few will be discussed briefly below.

The Allies' national interests must be taken seriously. Victory was the overwhelming interest, and when victory seemed in sight, postwar planning came into play. In order for the Jews, who had no state and no real political power, to be considered in these postwar arrangements, they needed to thrust themselves onto the Allied agenda. They succeeded in doing this only to a limited degree during the war and more so after it, when Jewish Displaced Persons forced the Allies to consider them and pressured them to be allowed to emigrate, mostly to Palestine (see also DISPLACED PERSONS, JEWISH). The slogans "rescue through victory" and "no diversion from the war effort" were not merely slogans. They can be seen as a direct offshoot of Allied interests, unless future research demonstrates otherwise. It is also arguable that there has been little change in the way the world reacts to the suffering of others at the hands of powerful murderers. National interests, not humanitarian concerns, seem to determine whether the world's democratic powers become involved in the former Yugoslavia, Somalia, Ethiopia, Cambodia, Burundi, Rwanda, or other areas where massive crimes have apparently been committed. These post-Holocaust events are not the Holocaust, and in all the cases just cited, the Western democracies were not at war with the perpetrators. Still, the importance of national interests vs. humanitarianism cannot be overlooked, even if we might wish things were different.

Attached to the Allies' interests was their perception of the war as a war of good against evil, light against darkness. This perception did not necessarily benefit the Jews conceptually. In a war against the devil, there can be no negotiations with the devil. In other words, there must be an unconditional surrender by the enemy. Negotiations to rescue one group or another would not be undertaken by the Allies because this would come into conflict with the unconditional surrender goal. It also would anger the ever-suspicious Stalin. Moreover, in a war of good against evil, the Allies sought to avoid being infected by that evil. They tried, in their own terms, to adhere to their liberal humanist official perception of humanity. That meant that the Jews were just like all other people, contrary to what the Nazis and their cohorts argued. The Allies would not favor one group over another, at least officially. In this regard, the Jews fell victim to the limited perceptions of Western liberalism.

One of the most common explanations for apparent Allied indifference to the fate of the Jews is antisemitism. There is no doubt that antisemitism existed both among the populations at large and in government circles. Breckenridge Long was an antisemite, and British Foreign Office official Arminius R. Dew used blatantly antisemitic language when he complained in September 1944 about the time wasted "dealing with these wailing Jews." But Long was ultimately dismissed and Dew was reprimanded for his disparaging remarks made privately. Such language and behavior was unbecoming to government officials in the eyes of their superiors. Antisemitism played a role, but not in the sense of joy at the Jews' fate, nor even in the sense of absolute indifference to their fate. Rather, it seems to have played a role in inhibiting the ability of many officials to make rescue a high priority and to relate to the Jews as a distinct member of the Allied side of the war, and not merely as citizens of their countries suffering like their fellow citizens who were not Jewish.

There were many additional factors that went into determining the Allied responses to the Holocaust, but one that is often overlooked should be raised here in conclusion. It was established early in this article that the Allies knew clearly about the Holocaust by December 1942. Perhaps this needs to be qualified somewhat; the two examples below will suffice to illustrate the point. When interviewed for the "Genocide" segment of the 1970s Thames television series, "The World at War" Anthony Eden, then the Earl of Avon, was asked to discuss Allied responses to news of the murder of the Jews. He told of the Allied Joint Declaration that he had read before the House of Commons on December 17, 1942 and of the House rising for a minute of silence in honor of the victims. Visibly moved by the recollection of the scene, Eden concluded, "Now *there* was something we could do."

Jan Karski was originally to return to Poland in 1942, but he was ordered by his government to remain in the West because the Germans had in the meantime discovered his identity. He subsequently went public, with his government's approval, and went on a series of lecture tours and meetings in Britain and the United States. As he related it afterward, wherever he went, people were interested to hear his eyewitness report on the Jews. In the summer of 1943 he went to the United States and met with government officials, including President Roosevelt, other public figures, and Jewish leaders. Among the Jewish leaders he met was Supreme Court Justice Felix Frankfurter, in the offices of the Polish ambassador to Washington. Frankfurter, too, was interested in hearing Karski's report on the Jews. As Karski spoke, Frankfurter became agitated and began pacing across the room. When Karski completed his story, a heavy, tense silence fell over the room, and Frankfurter continued his agitated pacing. Finally, Frankfurter stopped pacing, wheeled around, looked Karski in the face, and broke the silence, saying: "When a man like me talks to a man like you, he must be perfectly candid. Young man, I cannot believe you!" Karski and Ambassador Ciechanowski were taken aback, and the ambassador protested Karski's trustworthiness and honesty. The Polish government stood behind everything he said. "How can you call him a liar?" "Oh no! Oh no!" replied Frankfurter. "I did not call him a liar. I merely said I am unable to believe him."

Neither Eden nor Frankfurter was a fool. Eden must have realized, more than twenty years after the war, that Allied political and military power enabled more response than one moment of silence during the entire war. And by the time Frankfurter met Karski, he had access to seven months' additional information about the Jews, both from the press and from the White House. We can only be left somewhat baffled and wonder: Did they ever really know?

Joseph Stalin, Franklin Roosevelt, and Winston Churchill at the Tehran Conference, 1943

THE AFTERMATH OF THE HOLOCAUST

David Cesarani

Although the persecution and mass murder of the Jews ended with the defeat of HITLER, the physical and psychological effects linger while the social, cultural, and political consequences seem endless. It has taken decades to set right the destruction and plunder of Jewish communities or to achieve a measure of justice against those responsible. One reason for the delay was the lack of understanding about what had occurred in Europe in 1939–1945 and the slow dawning of awareness about the "FINAL SOLUTION." The delay was due to social, cultural, but mainly political circumstances—the Cold War, in particular. Consequently, it was not until the 1980s that the full impact of the events that have now become known as the HOLOCAUST penetrated fully into public consciousness around the world. Then, with astonishing speed, the Holocaust became a central feature of global culture and a universal metaphor for evil. The universalization of the Holocaust has proceeded so far that the Holocaust is now in danger of losing its specifically Jewish connotations.

When the THIRD REICH surrendered on May 8, 1945 some 50,000 Jews were alive, many barely clinging to life, on pre-war German territory. A few thousand had survived in hiding or with false papers. Thousands more, like the diary author Victor Klemperer, had avoided DEPORTATION because they were in mixed marriages. The majority were the surviving Jewish inmates of the labor and CONCENTRATION CAMPS that dotted GERMANY. This multi-national assortment grew to 157,000 as Jews from the areas conquered by the Soviet army moved to the zones of British and American occupation in Germany. They were the Jewish DISPLACED PERSONS, DPs, who had no homes to go back to or no desire to return to the countries where their communities had been destroyed. By mid-1947, following the attack on Jewish returnees at KIELCE, in POLAND, a wave of panic-stricken Polish Jews increased the number of Jewish DPs in Germany to 182,000.

The Jewish DPs mainly congregated in the US zone of occupation. Initially they were held in camps that also contained the far larger numbers of non-Jewish camp survivors, forced laborers, ethnic German refugees fleeing the Soviet army, and Nazi collaborators from Central and Eastern Europe. This unhappy mix-

ture led to frequent incidents of anti-Jewish violence. A few months after the end of hostilities, therefore, the US authorities recognized that Jews had endured a quite different ordeal under the Nazis and set up separate DP camps for them. The British military administration, which was responsible for a large population of survivors from the BERGEN-BELSEN concentration camp, took much longer to reach the same conclusion. They were afraid that giving separate status to the Jews would in effect be an admission that the Zionist argument was right, that the Jews were a nation and, consequently, were entitled to immigrate to Palestine. Since Palestine was under British rule and the British were desperately trying to keep the peace there between the Jews and the Palestinian Arabs, this was the last thing they wanted. As a result, when Jews fled Poland they tended to move into the US zone where the authorities were perceived to be more sympathetic.

Inmates celebrating their liberation, Dachau, 1945

Outside aid slowly reached the survivors. The JOINT DISTRIBUTION COMMITTEE (Joint) sent aid from the UNITED STATES, while the Jewish Relief Unit channeled help from British Jews. With this assistance the DP camps turned into recuperation centers. Health and welfare systems were set up, schools were opened, and cultural life developed. In several of the camps there were large numbers of children and orphans: their education became a priority. Jewish army chaplains helped set up religious education and soon Jewish learning was once again underway. A lively Yiddish press was established. Papers like *Undzer Shtimme,* published in Hohne Camp (Bergen-Belsen), and *Undzer Hofenung* (Eschwege camp, Kassel) discussed the Jewish future, every possible cultural topic, and carried the first eyewitness accounts of Jewish experiences under Nazi rule. Political life flourished and the dominant role was taken by the Zionist movement. In April 1946, when the Anglo-American Committee of Inquiry on the Palestine issue asked Jewish DPs where they wanted to go, 118,570 out of the 138,320 who were surveyed said Palestine. Probably not all of them really saw their future in the emerging Jewish state and they may have opted for Palestine since no other country seemed willing to have them, but the Zionist message seemed irrefutable in the light of all that had happened since 1933. From April 1948 and Israel's independence, the number of Jewish DPs in the British and American zones fell rapidly. Within half a year there were only around 80,000 left. But many of these were too old, too sick, or just unwilling to immigrate to a raw, young country that was at war with its neighbors. Some moved to the United States, taking advantage of the 1948 DP Act. Several thousand were cared for in camps in Germany until the mid-1950s. Others were absorbed into the new German Jewish community.

One of the most remarkable features of the aftermath of the Holocaust is the rebirth of Jewish life in West Germany. The German Jews who survived were mainly older people, who had been sent to the THERESIENSTADT Ghetto, or lived in mixed marriages in Germany. This was not a promising basis for reconstructing communities. However, between 1945 and 1959 about 12,000 Jewish emigres returned to Germany. They reestablished communal organizations, synagogues, and Jewish schools. The relations between the German Jews and the larger number of East European Jewish DPs who settled in West Germany were often tense. By 1960 there were 23,000 Jews in Germany. Their number rose to 30,000 by the start of the 1980s, mainly due to natural increase. The young German Jews, predominantly the children of SURVIVORS and emigrants, struggled to define an identity and a place for themselves in post-war Germany (see also SURVIVORS, SECOND GENERATION OF). Intellectuals such as Mischa Brumlik, Maxim Biller, Irene Dische, and Henryk Broder came to take a leading role in determining a Jewish position in Germany and probing Germany's relationship to the Jews and to its tormented past.

The 180,000–200,000 Jews of FRANCE who had been liberated from German rule in the summer of 1944 faced problems that were similar to those confronting Germany's Jews. Their communal institutions had been plundered and wrecked. Thousands of children who had been hidden with non-Jews were now orphans. Only three percent of the approximately 75,000 Jewish deportees returned, many in a terrible state. Along with the Jewish REFUGEES who began to pass through France en route to other countries, they added to the burden on the community. In 1946, 47,500 Jews of all ages received welfare that was provided by the Joint. The French government offered little in the way of recognition or aid to the "racial deportees." While resistance fighters who had been caught and sent to the concentration camps, PRISONERS OF WAR (POWs), and forced laborers were welcomed back and given some assistance to restart their lives, a veil of silence fell over the Jewish survivors. Their fate provoked too many awkward questions about the conduct of the Vichy regime and the French population which the new government, intent on creating social and political harmony, was unwilling to ask. The returnees published numerous memoirs, mainly in Yiddish, and produced YIZKOR BOOKS (memorial books) for the destroyed communities in Poland and Russia from which they had emigrated to France before 1933, but few of these reached a French audience.

French Jews were amongst the first to establish an institute devoted to documentation of the "Final Solution," the *Centre de Documentation Juive Contempor-*

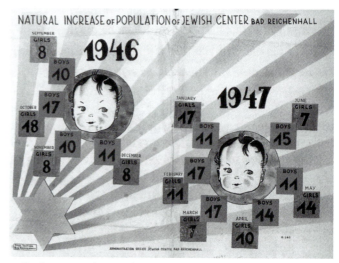

Poster portraying survivor attempts to rebuild their families, Reichenhall, Germany, 1947 (YIVO Institute for Jewish Research, New York)

aine (see also DOCUMENTATION CENTERS). In 1950 a memorial to the murdered Jews was dedicated in PARIS. However, the attitude of French society towards the survivors remained cool. It was sometimes necessary to fight long, expensive legal battles to recover Jewish children from Christian families. The process of restitution of property was partial and prolonged. A wave of conversions to Christianity and name-changing amongst Jews in France indicated the level of unease amongst those who chose to reconstruct their lives there. Much later, survivor writers and activists of French origin or living in France, such as Serge Klarsfeld, Claude Lanzmann, and Elie WIESEL, had a decisive role in raising the awareness of the Holocaust in French society.

The marginalization of survivors was repeated in the NETHERLANDS. The country was not fully liberated until the very end of the war and the part which remained under occupation in the winter of 1944–1945 suffered from terrible famine. About 25,000 Jews finally emerged from hiding, to be joined by 6,000 survivors of the deportations. But the Jewish returnees were swamped by the returning home of 600,000 Dutch men and women who had been shipped to the Reich as POWs or laborers. The devastated country faced a food shortage and in view of the "Hunger Winter," Jewish suffering went unrecognized. The Jews who came back were placed in processing camps alongside Dutch pro-Nazi collaborators. German-born Jews who had arrived in the Netherlands as refugees before 1939 were treated as "enemy aliens." The emaciated, unkempt survivors were feared as carriers of disease. Responsibility for their care was placed on the remnant of Dutch Jews, whose resources were all but exhausted. A bitter struggle took place over the fate of 2,000 Jewish orphans, of whom over half remained in the care of non-Jews and were lost to the Jewish community. It says much about the awareness of Jewish suffering and attitudes towards the survivors that Otto Frank, father of Anne FRANK, when he prepared his daughter's diary for publication, toned down her comments about the Dutch collaborators and stressed its universal, rather than its specifically Jewish message.

By contrast, BELGIUM'S left-wing government was more sympathetic towards the suffering of Jewish deportees and survivors. For a while they received assistance for rehabilitation and efforts. This was very necessary since up to one-third of the 30,000 Jews who survived in Belgium, including those who re-turned from the camps or from countries of refuge, were homeless or penniless. Even so, German-born Jews were excluded from state aid. Until the liberation government fell from power, efforts were also made to memorialize the murdered Jews of Belgium.

In ITALY the vast numbers of returning POWs, imprisoned resistance fighters, and those deported to Germany to do FORCED LABOR overshadowed the fate of the 1,000 Jews, including the author Primo LEVI, who straggled back from the camps. The country was torn by political conflict and the left took care to glorify those deported for resistance activity as one element in their propaganda. The experience of the Jews did not fit this narrative and was overlooked. When Primo Levi sought a publisher for his memoir about AUSCHWITZ, he encountered a wall of indifference. *If This is a Man* (also published as *Survival in Auschwitz*, was eventually published in 1947, in a run of under 3,000 copies. It was out of print until 1958 when it finally achieved recognition as a masterpiece.

A soldier of the Jewish Brigade with child survivors, Florence, Italy

The political situation in Poland in 1944–1946 was rather similar. The low-level civil war between the Communist Poles, backed by the SOVIET UNION, and the non-Communist nationalists, put Jews in an awkward situation. Some 50,000 Jews emerged into freedom in 1944–1945, including 20,000 who had lived underground. They were joined by around 13,000 Jews who had been recruited into the Polish armed forces under Russian control and about 160,000 who had fled to the Soviet Union in 1939. Because some prominent pro-Moscow Poles were Jewish, many right-wing, nationalist Poles believed that the Jews were agents of Soviet rule. Their hostility was bolstered by the widespread fear that Jews would reclaim looted property. As a result, anti-Jewish feeling was intense and numerous violent attacks were launched against the survivors: some 150 Jews were killed by Poles in March 1945, 116 in September–November 1945, and 42 were murdered at the pogrom in KIELCE in July 1946.

As a consequence, approximately 180,000 Polish Jews emigrated. The majority went to Palestine, later Israel. Others went to Western Europe, the United States, and Australia. By the mid-1950s there were only 55,000 Jews in Poland. Yet with the aid of the Joint Distribution Committee the survivors rebuilt communal life; welfare bodies, schools, and synagogues rose from the ruins. Cultural and political life was, of course, restricted by the establishment of Communist rule after 1948. But it suited the new rulers of Poland to allow Jews to record the horrors of Nazi occupation, especially if in the process they blackened right-wing, nationalist Poles accused of collaboration. In 1947 a Jewish Historical Institute was set up in WARSAW, an offshoot of state-sponsored efforts to chronicle Nazi war crimes. A Yiddish theater and Yiddish press maintained a less pronounced but prolonged existence.

Throughout the rest of the Eastern Bloc, as in Poland, the recognition of Jewish suffering and the scope for commemorative activity by the survivors was strictly limited on Moscow's orders. Hence, STALIN'S attitude towards the Jews was all-important. In 1943–1944, as the Soviet army liberated territory from the German occupiers, Stalin wanted Jewish writers attached to the Moscow-sponsored JEWISH ANTIFASCIST COMMITTEE to research and record Nazi cruelty. Two brilliant Jewish writers, Vasily Grossman and Ilya Ehrenburg, took the lead in this project. However, in 1945 Stalin changed his mind. He and his aides disliked the evidence of widespread collaboration between supposedly loyal Soviet citizens and the Nazi invaders. Work on the BLACK BOOK OF SOVIET JEWRY, which Grossman and Ehrenburg were editing, was suspended; in 1948, the proofs, and the plates used by the printer, were seized by the secret police and destroyed. This step was part and parcel of Stalin's onslaught against Jews in the Soviet Union, whom he increasingly saw as agents of Western imperialism and Zionism. Between 1948 and 1953, when Stalin died, a string of Yiddish writers and creative personalities were arrested and shot, while cultural institutions were shut down. Memoirs and histories of the Nazi period that could be seen as courting sympathy for the Jews and Zionism were suppressed. Nevertheless, it remained possible to publish such material in the Soviet Yiddish press. The truth about the massive slaughter of the Soviet Jews was never denied, but it was systematically distorted and disguised. Accounts of the war referred to the mass murder of innocent Soviet civilians, never to Jews, even when the massacre in question was an event such as BABI YAR. This line was imposed on ROMANIA, BULGARIA, HUNGARY, Czechoslovakia, Poland, and the Baltic States that were incorporated into the Soviet Union. It suffocated any chance that survivors in these places had to acquaint a large public with their experiences. Survivors who reached GREAT BRITAIN and the US after 1945 faced no such constraints, but that does not mean they entered societies that were particularly well disposed towards them. The British government was so afraid that survivors would demand the right to go to Palestine that it did its utmost to keep them out of the British zones of Germany and AUSTRIA, and restricted their access to the United Kingdom. Only about 2,000 survivors reached Britain between 1945 and 1950, mostly under the Distressed Relatives schemes. About 750 children and teenagers were also admitted. These figures stand in contrast to the 110,000 Poles who had served in the British army and who, with their families, were permitted to settle in Britain, plus the 90,000 East Europeans recruited from DP camps in 1947–1949 under a series of foreign labor schemes. Amongst them were thousands of pro-Nazi collaborators, ex-*Waffen*-SS soldiers, and many war criminals. Little was known about the wartime activity of these East Europeans; rather, they were seen in a sympathetic light as victims of Soviet tyranny and a potential asset in the Cold War. By contrast Jews were seen as a problem. The British public had been poorly informed about the atrocities committed against the Jews during the war, a deficit of information that was not set straight after 1945. Instead, they were soon being fed on stories of atrocities committed by Jews against British troops in Palestine. There was actually a substantial revival of FASCISM and ANTISEMITISM in

Britain in 1946–1947. Many of the survivors who were able to settle in Britain remarked on the indifference towards them and ignorance of all they had been through, even amongst the Jewish community. The large community of Jewish refugees who had arrived between 1933 and 1939 and the survivors who came after the war were severely intimidated by this unsympathetic atmosphere and were mostly silent.

However, the group of 750 youngsters that arrived in 1945—subsequently known as "The Boys"—received excellent, organized care. With the help of counselors and youth workers who were attached to the reception centers and hostels, the young survivors were able to recover with speed. The friendships that they made in those days lasted throughout their lives. In 1963 they formed the "45 Aid Society to promote the welfare of survivors in Britain and raise awareness of the Holocaust. Their numbers included figures such as Rabbi Hugo Gryn, the rabbi of the West London Synagogue who, until his death in 1996, was one of Britain's most popular and influential broadcasters.

Although the United States administration supported the Zionist movement's efforts to open Palestine to Jewish immigration, it did not display equal enthusiasm about Jewish immigration to the US. The 1948 DP Act actually discriminated against Jews from Eastern Europe and was not revised until 1950. Eventually, about 160,000 Holocaust survivors made new homes in the United States. By 1990, they and their descendants made up eight percent of the entire US Jewish population. Despite their numerical size, the survivors found it hard to make an initial impact on Jewish and non-Jewish perceptions of what had happened in Europe. For example, even though after the Holocaust New York was the largest Jewish city in the world, in 1947–1950 a committee of East European immigrants and survivors was unable to raise enough interest and funding in the city for a memorial to the murdered Jews of Europe. They were told that because Russia was now the enemy and Germany an ally, it was wrong to dredge up memories of German wrongdoing. Israel was a better cause to support. In the 1960s Polish Holocaust survivors in New York tried again. Even though they lived amidst the largest, wealthiest Jewish community the world had ever known, their efforts failed. It was not until the 1970s that survivors were able to shape a memorial culture in America.

In other respects the survivors were immensely successful. Several made large fortunes, notably in property.

Some entered politics and attained prominence, such as Congressman Tom Lantos. Abe Foxman, director of the Anti-Defamation League, Miles Lerman, a guiding light of the US Holocaust Memorial Museum, and Ben Meed, a moving force behind the New York memorial, are just a few of these success stories. Survivors also had a big impact on scholarship and Jewish learning. In 1945, YIVO, the Institute for Jewish Research, was resurrected in New York and has since provided a line of continuity with the great tradition of research and teaching that was the glory of Europe's Jews.

Between 1948 and 1953, Israel received over 300,000 survivors of European Jewry. The first arrivals, mainly GHETTO fighters and PARTISANS, many from the pre-war Zionist YOUTH MOVEMENTS, were welcomed as heroes. But their tales of ideologically motivated resistance cast a shadow over those who followed. Other survivors had not fought back with arms and they came to Israel simply because they had nowhere else to go. The thousands of ordinary survivors streamed into a country at war. Everyone was poor and, as losses in the fighting mounted, no one had a special claim to personal suffering. The survivors held their peace and a wide gap developed between them and the native-born Israelis or immigrants who had arrived under happier circumstances. The gulf was widened even more by the physical isolation of many survivor communities. They were channeled into towns and villages where there was poor infrastructure and little in the way of work. Some people who had overcome incredible hardship and shown enormous energy and initiative in the DP camps finally succumbed to apathy. They presented a picture of despair to Israeli officials who began to form a contemptuous view of their human wreckage. The burden that the sick and the old placed on the young state led to resentment amongst the struggling inhabitants of new towns and settlements.

Although the worst medical cases received good care, there was little provision for the rehabilitation of survivors. Some fragile cases were even thrown into combat units of the Israeli army. Substantial numbers emigrated from Israel once they had the means to do so. Nevertheless, survivors did help to shape Israel's emerging culture and politics. They formed associations and institutions, most notably Kibbutz Lohamei HaGettaot and Kibbutz Yad Mordecai and were active from the start in YAD VASHEM. They led the public debates in the 1950s over reparations (see also REPARATIONS AND RESTITUTION) and their experiences stood at the heart of the Kasztner case, a legal and political battle revolving around the accusation that certain Jews had collaborated with the Nazis (see also KASZTNER, REZSO). Yet it was not until the EICHMANN TRIAL of 1961 that survivors were given a platform and national attention. This marked a turning point in recognition of their experiences. By the 1970s survivors had penetrated into every corner of Israeli society and politics and some had amassed fortunes in business. By 1995 the speaker of the *Knesset,* Shevach Weiss, the president of the Supreme Court, Aharon Barak, and the Chief Rabbi, Israel Lau, were all survivors. Three years earlier, Ehud Barak, the then chief-of-staff of the Israeli Army, made a special trip to Auschwitz-Birkenau and expressed a new attitude of compassion and respect for the experience of the survivors.

The silence and marginalization of the survivors in the post-war world is often given as a reason for the slow and partial progress made on restitution, reparation, and compensation issues. However, recent research in this area shows that in the immediate aftermath of the war survivors made great efforts to recover property and assets stolen from them or their families by the Nazis and their accomplices. They were thwarted by the powerful opposition they faced and the indifference of the victorious powers. Jewish organizations were only able to help up to a point, and they too faced overwhelming obstacles.

The Western Allies were aware of the systematic robbery the Jews had endured. However, their immediate and chief concern was to recover the gold taken by the Nazis from the central banks of the countries they had occupied and to seize control of German assets to ensure that they were not available to Nazis who had fled abroad. Non-monetary gold looted from Jews and so-called "dental gold" (that is to say, gold that was taken from the mouths of murdered Jews) was not part of their claim. At the Allied Reparations Conference in Paris in November–December 1945, 18 Allied nations gathered to solve the problem of the nearly two million DPs. There was little agreement about what funds should be used to help them and the British resisted any steps that would channel money to Jewish organizations for the settlement of Jews in Palestine. Under American pressure, it was decided that all non-monetary gold found in Germany (worth an estimated five million dollars, plus 25 million dollars to be raised from the liquidation of German assets abroad), and all heirless assets left by the victims of Nazism, would be allotted to the relief and resettlement of genuine refugees and former subjects of Nazi persecution.

In June 1946 the Western Allies followed up with a Conference on Non-Repatriable Victims of National Socialism. The so-called non-repatriables were refugees who could not or would not return to their countries of origin. Some, like the Jews, had been driven out and had no desire to go back. Others had collaborated with the Nazis and fled before the advancing Soviet army. This distinction was one bone of contention that frustrated the efforts to bring aid to the DPs. Another was the refusal of the British to accept the WORLD JEWISH CONGRESS (WJC) or the Jewish Agency for Palestine as partners in relief work. It was finally agreed to nominate the Inter-Governmental Committee on Refugees as the recipient of the funds to be made available from the recovered gold and German assets. It was given the freedom to work with "appropriate field organizations" that might include the Joint and the Jewish Agency. It was also agreed to give priority to assisting Jews: only five percent of the funds would be allotted to non-Jewish refugees. However, for the Jews the monies received under the Paris Agreement proved a drop in the ocean. The sums it raised did not even cover the spending of the Jewish refugee and relief agencies since 1933, let alone current and future spending.

The Allies faced nothing but frustration when it came to raising the 25 million dollars from German assets in neutral countries. The Swiss, who contested the Allies' claim to control German assets abroad, never implemented the accord. They got away with this because the increasing tension between the Western Allies and the Soviet Union persuaded American negotiators that any settlement was better than none, if it helped to get the European economy moving again. If the Swiss were able to reject the combined efforts of the Allies it can be seen that Jewish organizations or individual claimants had little chance of success. The Swiss banking authorities made it almost impossible for survivors to obtain the contents of accounts opened by deceased relatives before 1939. Bank officials demanded account numbers from the heirs of claimants who knew only the name of the account holder, and legal proof of demise, such as a death certificate, which was hardly likely to have been issued in a place like TREBLINKA. As a result, thousands of so-called dormant accounts opened by Jews before the Holocaust sat in Swiss banks. This was not unique to SWITZERLAND. The same pattern was evident wherever Jewish individuals, communities, or restitution agencies sought to recover the assets of Jews who had perished at the hands of the Nazis.

In 1939 the British government had frozen enemy assets in the United Kingdom. As Nazi control extended over Europe, the Custodian of Enemy Property applied the same controls to assets belonging to individuals or corporations from occupied countries. Initially, the goal was simply to deprive the enemy of these assets. But as Britain's economic situation worsened, the Treasury began to sell off "enemy" assets to raise cash for the war. By 1944 the treasury regarded the frozen "enemy" assets as a potential contribution to any postwar reparations scheme. As a result, the government developed an interest in preventing claimants from recovering their assets. In the years after the war the government reached agreements with friendly West European states to send assets back to their rightful place of origin or assist heirs to claim them, but it dragged its feet over similar treaties with countries which had fallen under Soviet domination. Since British-owned property in these countries was being nationalized, the Treasury wanted to hold back assets in Britain to encourage the successful completion of compensation deals. Survivors of the Holocaust in Britain, Israel, or Eastern Europe found it almost impossible to gain access to bank accounts or assets deposited before 1939 in the United Kingdom. The standards of proof needed to make a claim were no less inappropriate than those applied in the better known case of Switzerland. An "ex-belligerent enemy," even if they were Jewish, had to prove that they had been deprived of their liberty by the Nazis. Detention in a ghetto was not enough: they had to give proof of detention in a concentration camp. Even then, some officials claimed that imprisonment in a concentration camp might not necessarily signify racial persecution.

Survivors in Germany did not find things easier. In October 1947 the British, US, Soviet, and French military governments required Germans to register property and assets acquired since 1933 and froze transactions in such property prior to its return to its rightful owners. In November 1947 the Office of the Military Government, US (OMGUS), passed a law—OMGUS Law 59—that enabled German Jews to recover property which had been stolen by the Nazi regime. It provided for the establishment of the Jewish Restitution Successor Organization (JRSO) which was empowered to act in the case of heirless private and communal property. But OMGUS Law 59 was not adopted in the British

zone until May 1949. It was delayed by the British to avoid Jews recovering assets that would finance their migration to Palestine or feed into the Zionist movement.

The JRSO and the Jewish Trust Corporation (in the British zone) were formed to investigate and file claims, but they faced immense obstacles. Few Jews remained in Germany who could identify the property in question, if it was still standing, and many records had been destroyed. Germans who had acquired such properties argued that they had acted "in good faith." Finally, the submission of thousands of contested claims had to be made by June 30, 1950. So the Jewish Trust Corporation and JRSO concentrated only on property and businesses and simply ignored household goods, gold and silver, bank accounts, securities, insurance policies, rent, debts, and mortgages owed to Jews. Instead, they accepted a global settlement of 88 million deutsche marks from the West German government in place of these assets.

Law 59 had other weaknesses. It only applied to German claimants of property in Germany. Restitution and reparations to Jewish individuals and collective claimants outside Germany had to await the conclusion of a separate reparations agreement between the Federal Republic of Germany (FRG) and Jewish organizations in the 1950s. Yet the Allies, eager to see the new FRG on its feet, were unwilling to support the claims of world Jewry. It was left to increasingly desperate representatives of the State of Israel, the American Jewish Congress, the WJC, the Joint, and the Jewish Agency to consider how best to approach West Germany. In November 1949, a statement by Chancellor Konrad Adenauer expressing remorse for Nazi crimes and seeking a means of making good, *wiedergutmachung,* opened the door to negotiations.

The subsequent negotiations were marked by an imbalance of power. The Germans wanted to win reentry into the community of Western nations, but the Jewish organizations faced more pressing calls for funds to resettle Jewish refugees in Israel. The German negotiators knew this and drove a hard bargain. Nahum Goldman, representing the Jewish organizations that combined for this purpose to form the Conference on Jewish Material Claims against Germany, came initially with a claim of 1.5 billion dollars (six billion deutsche marks) as a global settlement for Israel for the cost of resettling half a million refugees, and 1.1 billion dollars as a global settlement of the claims of world Jewry. In the face of stout German opposition and pleas of poverty, this was quickly scaled back to one billion dollars and 500 million dollars respectively. Under the Luxembourg Agreement on reparations, signed in 1952, Israel and the representatives of the Diaspora accepted the FRG final offer of three billion deutsche marks (one billion dollars) to Israel and 450 million deutsche marks or 110 million dollars to the Claims Conference for use in the Diaspora. Subsequent agreements in 1953 and 1957 created procedures for individuals to lodge claims for injury, unjust detention, loss of income, loss of schooling, pensions, and household furnishings, personal valuables, and bank accounts left heirless. By 1990, individual payments by West Germany to Jewish victims of Nazi persecution exceeded 100 billion dollars. This would seem to be a tribute to the effectiveness of the process, but the global total masks years of obstacles placed before and anguish inflicted on claimants. The mechanics of *wiedergutmachung* were designed to frustrate claimants in Germany and abroad and were administered with breathtaking insensitivity. For example, in order to prove physical injury sustained in a concentration camp, claimants had to undergo a medical examination. Frequently the doctor who looked them over had served in the WEHRMACHT or the *Waffen*-SS. Not surprisingly, a far higher percentage of the claims from refugees in the US or the UK, who were examined by doctors from the refugee community, tended to be successful.

The struggle for restitution and compensation was continued by the Claims Conference throughout the 1950s and 1960s. It employed a small legal team headed by Benjamin Ferencz, who fought a series of prolonged and largely fruitless legal battles in German courts to win compensation on behalf of former Jewish slave laborers. His targets included I.G. FARBEN, Krupp, AEG, Siemens, Telefunken, Rheinmetall AG, and the Flick family interests. By 1970, when the Claims Conference gave up the legal fight, just 15,000 out of 100,000 potential claimants had received compensation. The sums ranged from $500 to $1,700. Ferencz was unsuccessful partly because he was working in German courts, which were hardly sympathetic, but the Claims Conference declined to apply much public pressure because it was afraid of endangering its relationship with the German government.

Nor did the question of dormant accounts in Swiss banks escape attention. During the early 1950s, the SIG, the Swiss Jewish Community organization, lobbied for legislation to enable the identification of "heirless assets" and cut through the inappropriate regulations for the establishment of demise and the lodging of a claim. In 1952 the Swiss Federal Council drafted a bill to this end and negotiations were held between the government, Swiss Jewish representatives, and the Swiss Bankers Association (SBA). However, the SBA insisted on sticking by existing practice and argued that its members were acting in good faith as legal guardians of the so-called "heirless accounts." The SBA merely suggested sending a circular letter to its members to initiate a general call for declaring a person dead or missing. The Jewish negotiators pointed out that frequently there was no one left who could declare this or that person missing or dead. They proposed the setting up of a trust company to register unclaimed assets and conduct a worldwide appeal for heirs. The banks retorted that a registration process could not be enforced on its members. It also raised the possibility of foreign governments laying claim to "heirless assets." Indeed, under international law there was a genuine risk that Communist regimes would exercise this right. In 1949 and 1950 the Swiss government had already concluded arrangements that transferred the contents of dormant accounts to the Polish and Hungarian governments which, quite legally, claimed ownership of the assets of their citizens who had died abroad and left no heirs.

The issue dragged on through the late 1950s. The Israeli government and the Jewish Agency stepped in to add to the pressure and in 1959 the Swiss Parliament formally requested that action be taken. A draft law was drawn up after discussions involving the SIG, the SBA, the insurance companies, and representatives of the legal profession. As the bill progressed members of the Swiss Federal Council argued that if a person was declared missing or dead who turned out to be alive and well, but living in a Communist country, their well-being would be endangered rather than enhanced. Consequently, if there were reasons for believing that a person who owned assets might be resident behind the Iron Curtain that name should be omitted from any public call for owners or heirs to claim assets. Moreover, the process should be carried out under Swiss local law to avoid it being seen as a violation of international agreements and giving foreign powers rights over the unclaimed assets. After many delays, a Federal Law of December 20, 1962 established a central agency to register "heirless assets." An advisory bureau was set up to handle the registered assets and to seek rightful owners or claimants, and after a six-month search 8,540,023 Swiss francs worth of assets were registered. Between 1966 and 1977 the bureau received 7,000 applications by potential claimants. All but 700 were speedily dismissed on the grounds of inadequate information. In 132 instances the owner or heir was successfully located. It proved impossible to locate 228 asset holders and 151 were traced to Eastern Bloc countries, whereupon no further action was taken. By 1977, when the procedure was terminated, about 10 million Swiss francs had been uncovered. Of this, 75 percent was restored to the rightful owners or heirs. The rest was placed in a trust fund, of which 60 percent was put at the disposal of the SIG. The remainder was presented to the Swiss Refugee Aid Society.

Despite a good deal of press attention to this issue, particularly at the time of the Eichmann trial in 1960–1961, no steps were taken to apply the lessons to other former neutral states that were in a similar position to Switzerland. SWEDEN and Portugal took no parallel action over the proceeds they had earned through the gold trade with Germany or the absorption of German assets that they had received. It was not until 1995 that the issue resurfaced. The eruption of post-Holocaust issues—including the investigation and prosecution of Nazi-era war criminals, restitution of property, reparations, and compensation for slave laborers—was largely a result of the end of the Cold War, the collapse of the Soviet Bloc, and the breakup of the Soviet Union.

The original decision to try Nazi war criminals was made by the Allied powers in 1944. As a result, the International Military Tribunal (IMT) was established at Nuremberg in October 1945 (see also NUREMBERG TRIALS). Over the following year 22 leading Nazis, generals, and industrialists were tried. The selection reflected the priorities of the Allies rather than the monstrousness of the crimes for which the defendants were charged. The main intention of the Allies was to prove that Germany had planned and waged a war of aggression. Several of the defendants were charged with war crimes and a new offense, CRIMES AGAINST HUMANITY, but the Nazi persecution and mass murder of the Jews were submerged in a long list of other vile deeds.

To its credit, the IMT established the principle that political leaders and military commanders could be held accountable for their acts and that the defense of obedience to superior orders would only count in helping to lessen punishment rather than as a legitimate excuse.

It established a record of the Nazi regime on which many histories drew for years to come. However, the IMT was highly controversial and its work was not universally accepted. Many Germans regarded it as "victors' justice." The inclusion of Soviet prosecutors and judges, acting on behalf of a regime that had also committed massive atrocities and gross abuses of human rights, crippled its legitimacy in Western countries. To most people, however, the IMT was a bore and a distraction from the business of reconstruction. It had relatively little impact on the understanding of how Jews had suffered, apart from establishing in most people's minds the figure of six million victims.

The British conducted independent trials under Royal Warrant in their zone, including the trials of those responsible for the horrors of Bergen-Belsen and the manufacturers of ZYKLON B poison gas. In 1949 the British government decided not to mount any more prosecutions of their own because public opinion was turning against them. The United States mounted a series of 12 major trials between December 1946 and April 1949. Those tried included civil servants who had written up and implemented Nazi race laws, Nazi doctors, the SS administration responsible for the concentration camps, industrialists who had used slave labor, and EINSATZGRUPPEN commanders. However, a backlash also developed in the US. By 1950, the Western Allies were appeasing German and domestic opinion in the light of the Cold War and revising the sentences of those already tried and convicted. Sentences were reduced and by the late-1950s most of those convicted were discharged.

The French, the Dutch, and the East European states also conducted war crimes trials (see also TRIALS OF WAR CRIMINALS). The French, however, did not confront the persecution of the Jews by the Vichy regime and only tried those responsible for "treason" by virtue of collaborating with the occupier. The Dutch tried Jews accused of cooperating with the Nazis as well as Dutch citizens who had assisted in the deportations. Many of those responsible for mass shootings and the running of ghettos and camps in the east were tried in the Soviet Union and Poland. In both countries commissions were set up to collect evidence and to interview survivors. The Jewish dimension of the crimes was never openly acknowledged, although the hearings provided a huge volume of valuable documentation.

After 1950 the Allies handed over the prosecution of Nazi-era war criminals to the West German courts. The rules of the IMT never applied in Germany, though, and prosecutions were made according to the old German criminal code. This meant that it was extremely difficult to successfully prosecute "desk killers" for murder because it was necessary to show a "thirst for blood," cruelty, or maliciousness. Most of those who organized and implemented the deportation of Jews simply said that they had been obeying orders and had acted like decent, law-abiding bureaucrats without any personal feeling. To have any hope of securing a conviction such men could only be charged with manslaughter, but the statute of limitations prevented prosecutions for manslaughter after 15 years. This meant that by 1960 it was almost impossible to secure convictions against Nazi criminals. Nor did the German authorities look very hard for alleged war criminals. The presence in the judicial system of many policemen and judges who had loyally served the Nazis acted as a major obstacle to any progress.

In 1958, as a result of routine investigations, a trial of several officers and men who had been involved in mass murders in LITHUANIA was held in Ulm, Germany. The trial exposed the scale of crimes and the number of perpetrators that had so far gone unpunished. The West German government consequently set up the Central Office for the Prosecution of National Socialist Crimes at Ludwigsburg (see also CENTRAL OFFICE OF JUDICIAL ADMINISTRATION, LUDWIGSBURG). This office collected materials, launched investigations, and coordinated cases. As a result of its successes, and due to external pressure, in 1965, 1969, and 1979 the statute of limitations on prosecutions for murder was extended, then lifted permanently. From 1958 onward the office mounted nearly 5,000 prosecutions, including the case of guards at Treblinka and Franz STANGL, its commandant, personnel at MAJDANEK, and one of the last surviving ghetto commanders from Poland, Josef Schwammberger.

During the late 1970s the focus of war crimes investigations shifted to the Allied countries where East Europeans who had collaborated with the Nazis had settled after the war. In 1978 the US Congress passed a law enabling the Immigration and Naturalization Service to investigate immigrants and strip them of their citizenship if they were found to have entered the US under false pretenses and to have collaborated with the Nazis. Since the mid-1980s the OFFICE OF SPECIAL INVESTIGATIONS has investigated 1,500 cases, successfully instituted denaturalization proceedings in 50, and secured deportation orders against 48 individuals.

The case of John Demjanjuk, believed to be a notorious guard at the Treblinka death camp, was probably the most famous of these, although it proved very problematic (see also DEMJANJUK TRIAL). Demjanjuk was deported to Israel in 1988 and put on trial in Jerusalem. He was found guilty, but on appeal the conviction was overturned and it was shown that he had been misidentified.

CANADA, Australia, and the United Kingdom followed the American example, revising existing law or introducing new laws to enable the prosecution of individuals suspected of Nazi-era war crimes committed when they were outside the jurisdiction of the state in which they now resided. Investigative units were set up in Canada and Australia and a handful of prosecutions were mounted, but none with any success. By 1998 these countries had abandoned further efforts. The British authorities successfully brought two cases to court. The first, against Szymion Serafinowicz, a former Belorussian police officer, had to be suspended due to the age and feebleness of the defendant. In 1999 Anthony Sawoniuk, a former police commander in White Russia, was convicted of murders committed in 1942 and sentenced to life imprisonment. Soon afterwards the British authorities announced that there would be no further prosecutions, despite the evidence that Nazi war criminals remained at large in the United Kingdom.

In the 1980s and 1990s a series of trials took place in France, largely thanks to the persistence of the "Nazi hunters" Serge and Beate Klarsfeld. They tracked down and exposed Klaus Barbie, former head of the Lyons GESTAPO, who had fled to Bolivia. He was arrested in 1983, extradited to France, and tried in 1987 (see also BARBIE TRIAL). Two years later Paul Touvier, a senior officer in the collaborationist *Milice* group, was arrested after his protectors at the highest levels of the French state lost power. He was tried in 1992–1994 and became the first French national to be convicted of crimes against humanity (see also TOUVIER TRIAL). In 1993 Rene BOUSQUET, former head of the Vichy police and a confidant of many French politicians, was assassinated three days before he was due to stand trial. In 1999 Maurice Papon, the wartime secretary of the Gironde district and subsequently a high-flying politician who was a friend of French President Francois Mitterrand, was found guilty of authorizing the deportation of some 1,600 Jews from Bordeaux (see also PAPON TRIAL).

Following the end of Soviet domination in Eastern

Europe the war crimes issue became an issue there, too. In Lithuania and LATVIA men who had served with collaborationist units were celebrated as anti-Soviet heroes and any possibility that they had committed war crimes was conveniently overlooked. In the cases of suspects identified by Jewish organizations abroad, the authorities dragged their feet. By contrast, they have acted with promptness against individuals accused of committing atrocities in the service of the Soviet regime.

The end of East/West superpower rivalry had many other ramifications for the history of the Nazi era. Countries in the Western alliance now felt able to look more critically at their own and each other's histories. Formerly closed collections of documents, especially those dealing with intelligence, were opened to scrutiny. These made it possible to fill in aspects of the intelligence and economic war against the Nazis. In 1995 representatives of the World Jewish Congress who were alerted to the issue of dormant accounts in Swiss banks made use of this fresh documentation to reopen the matter. This, in turn, led to scrutiny of how Switzerland and other neutral countries had profited from the gold trade with Nazi Germany and how it had avoided paying back more than a tiny fraction of the profits of business in looted gold. These inquiries went on to reveal how little effort the Allies made to recover gold stolen from the Jews. They were left to pursue their case for recompense through civil courts and banking procedures that often demanded unrealistic standards of proof of entitlement to assets.

During 1996 the World Jewish Congress, with the Jewish Agency and the World Jewish Restitution Organization, mounted a powerful campaign to force the Swiss banks to open their records to outside examination in order to establish once and for all the number and content of heirless accounts of Holocaust victims. They enlisted the support of Senator Alfonse D'Amato, the powerful chairman of the US Senate Banking Committee, who held dramatic hearings in April 1996. The powerful financial comptrollers of several American states threatened to boycott Swiss financial institutions unless they reached a settlement with the claimants. In October 1996 the first of several class action suits were launched in American courts against the banks. To appease their critics, in May 1996 the Swiss Bankers Association agreed to set up an independent commission under Paul Volcker, former head of the US Federal Reserve Bank, and in December 1996 the Swiss govern-

ment established an international committee of experts to oversee an exhaustive investigation of Swiss dealings with Nazi Germany. By February 1997 the Swiss were wilting under the relentless pressure of foreign criticism. Admitting that Switzerland had to make amends for its wartime corruption, the government announced the creation of two funds, one for Holocaust victims and a humanitarian solidarity fund. Finally, in summer 1998, after officials in half a dozen states in the US prepared economic sanctions on Swiss banks and blocked Swiss business, and the class actions approached a decisive phase, the Swiss banks, the Swiss government, and Jewish representatives reached a settlement. All action against the banks was dropped in return for a payment of 1.25 billion dollars into a fund to compensate the owners or heirs of stolen property in the possession of Swiss banks and the owners or heirs of dormant accounts.

As a consequence of the furor over the gold trade, in December 1997 an international conference on "Nazi gold" was convened in London. On the initiative of the British and the Americans, the member states of the Tripartite Gold Commission (TGC, which had handled gold looted by the Nazis from the countries they occupied during the war) agreed to set up a fund drawing on the remainder of the TGC gold stock to compensate the victims of Nazism. But the TGC refused to reopen the 1946 agreement on the fate of the gold, despite evidence that it had included gold looted from Jews.

The 1997 conference focused attention on all sorts of other property and assets that were sold by the Germans via Switzerland, such as art works. It also exposed the role of insurance companies that had never paid out on the insurance policies of Jews murdered by the Nazis and left heirless (see also INSURANCE COMPANIES AND THE HOLOCAUST). In March 1997, a class action suit was filed in New York against 10 leading European insurance firms that had been active in the 1930s. Following intense pressure from US financial regulatory officers and the threat of legislative action, four of the largest insurance companies agreed to the formation of a commission under former US Secretary of State Lawrence Eagleburger to investigate the question of insurance policies. The first task was to establish who held a policy and who was a Holocaust victim. With the cooperation between the leading insurance companies in the field, forensic accountants, and Holocaust archives, a huge effort was made to assemble lists of all those who had perished at the hands of the Nazis and to cross check this against the names of deceased policy holders.

The London conference on "Nazi gold" was followed up by one in Washington in November–December 1998. This gathering considered the insurance issue and the question of returning or compensating for looted art. In April 1999 a deal was reached between the major insurance companies—Alliance (Germany), Axa (France), Generali (Italy), and Winterhur (Switzerland)—and Jewish representatives to establish a fund to compensate claimants who could locate the names of relatives on this list. After a similar campaign against the German corporations that took advantage of slave labor, a 5.1 billion dollar fund was set up to compensate Jewish and non-Jewish survivors. Since early 1999, international efforts have been made to search through art collections in the public and the private sectors to locate works of art with suspicious origin, to publicize their existence, and to seek claimants or heirs. Certain countries, notably France, Israel, Germany, and Austria, have returned stolen works of art to their owners immediately. In the US and Britain, long legal battles have been fought and mediation procedures are only slowly being introduced. In France and the Netherlands, scandals developed when it was revealed that property of Jews had been taken over by the state or sold off during or after the war, without compensation ever being paid to the victims or their communities. As a result of the light shed on the confiscation and theft of Jewish property and the extensive dealing in these stolen assets, investigative commissions were set up in Belgium, Brazil, France, the Netherlands, NORWAY, Portugal, SPAIN, Sweden, Britain, and the United States. Many have still to report their findings.

The end of Communist rule in Eastern Europe made it possible for Jews and other victims of Nazi persecution to make individual claims for reparations. It also became possible for survivor emigres to seek the restitution of property confiscated from their families by the Nazis and taken over by the post-war Communist regimes. In the former German Democratic Republic, the government of reunited Germany simply applied existing restitution laws and practices. The process there was relatively smooth and free of conflict. But in Poland, Hungary, and the Czech Republic, where there were potentially huge numbers of claimants who had lost property at the hands of Nazis and/or Communists, the problem took on massive dimensions and caused both social and political controversy. Laws were

gradually introduced to enable Jews to reclaim property, but usually only under limited circumstances and without damaging the interests of tenants. Frequently the process was hardly worth the effort and costs involved.

The reopening of restitution, reparation, and compensation issues and the pursuit of war criminals did not occur simply due to the end of the Cold War. The importance these issues gained in the perception of Jews and non-Jews, without whom little progress could have been made, was a register of the increasing awareness of the Holocaust and the significance placed on it. This amounted to nothing less than a revolution in public consciousness about the recent past. The "Holocaust" as a subject did not come into existence until the 1970s, which was when the word itself gained wide use. Before then, the fate of the Jews was a secondary part of the history of Nazi Germany and WORLD WAR II. There was very little understanding of the unique catastrophe that had overtaken the Jews until the 1960s and the late 1970s when greater efforts were made to institutionalize the memory of Jewish suffering and struggles in the Nazi era.

In the post-war United States of America, the Jewish communities were more preoccupied by domestic anti-semitism and the struggle for Palestine than studying or memorializing Nazi atrocities. At a time when West Germany was being treated as a valuable member of the NATO alliance, there was little motivation for Jews to revive memories of German misdeeds. In any case, most American Jews were more interested in assimilating into the mainstream and the survivors were busy making new lives for themselves. Only scholars from the immigrant and refugee communities, such as Raul Hilberg, Hannah Arendt, and Lucy Dawidowicz, wrote or researched about the Holocaust. The Eichmann trial in 1960–1961 began to change this. The trial, which Americans could watch on television, created much interest. Hannah Arendt caused a major controversy when she published a book about Eichmann and the trial in which she accused the wartime Jewish leadership of aiding the Nazis in the destruction of the Jews (see also ARENDT CONTROVERSY). The efforts to refute these charges spurred the development of Holocaust Studies in universities in the US and Israel.

By the 1960s American Jews were wealthier and more confident about expressing their Jewish identity. The Arab-Israeli crisis in the spring of 1967 and the Six-Day War in June 1967 revived memories of the wartime isolation of the Jews and made American Jews more aggressive in the defense of Jewish interests at home and abroad. They also became more critical of the behavior of the US during the war. In 1978 the TV miniseries *Holocaust* made millions of Americans aware of the history of the Holocaust. It now became a focal point of American-Jewish identity. In 1978 President Jimmy Carter established the Presidential Commission on the Holocaust which led in 1979 to the Holocaust Memorial Council and ultimately to the United States Holocaust Memorial Museum. President Jimmy Carter was motivated by the desire to counteract the unpopularity of his Middle East policy amongst American Jews. He also saw the Holocaust in universalistic terms and wanted to integrate it into his human rights campaign. This led to a series of public debates about the meaning of the Holocaust, with Elie Wiesel insisting on the total uniqueness of the Holocaust as a Jewish experience even if it had universal implications.

During the 1980s, American novelists and filmmakers "discovered" the Holocaust. Films such as *Sophie's Choice* in 1982 were highly influential. When during a state visit to Germany in 1985, President Ronald Reagan attended a memorial ceremony at a cemetery at Bitburg that contained the graves of *Waffen*-SS men, there was an outcry which, in turn, stimulated further debate about the meaning and memorialization of the Holocaust. By 1981 there were 12 Holocaust education centers in the US and 93 university courses on the subject. A decade later, there were over 70 museums, memorials, and educational centers and countless courses. Interest in the Holocaust was heightened still further by Steven Spielberg's much honored 1992 film *Schindler's List*. In April 1993, the United States Holocaust Memorial Museum opened to immense acclaim and immediate popularity. American Jewish organizations, aided by President Bill Clinton's administration, have been the driving force behind the campaigns to secure restitution of dormant accounts from Swiss banks and to achieve compensation for slave laborers used by German corporations.

In Britain at the end of the war there was little detailed appreciation of the specific fate of the Jews. In line with wartime guidelines from the Ministry of Information, reports of the LIBERATION of the camps avoided mention of the Jews even though they were the majority of survivors in Bergen-Belsen. The conflict in Palestine between 1945 and 1948 tended to overshadow reports from the Nuremberg trials and actually fueled hostility towards the Jews. During the

years of the Cold War, the German Federal Republic was perceived as a loyal ally and as early as the 1950s a string of memoirs, novels, and feature films about the German General Rommel and the war in general spread the myth that the German army had been an "honorable" opponent. When Anne Frank's diary was offered to a British Jewish publishing house in 1952 they were reluctant to publish it and printed a run of just 2,000 copies. The capture and trial of Eichmann provoked much interest during 1961–1962, but it was temporary. Historians and writers only began to take an enduring interest in the Holocaust in the late 1970s, in the wake of developments in the US. In the mid-1980s, aided by the fortieth and fiftieth anniversaries of wartime events, refugee and survivor groups became more vocal and assertive in demanding public recognition of their experiences. They campaigned successfully for a Holocaust memorial that was dedicated in Hyde Park in 1988. They also fought for the inclusion of the Holocaust in the school history curriculum. In summer 2000 the Imperial War Museum opened a specially designed Holocaust Exhibition funded by a grant from the Heritage Lottery Fund and Jewish donors. The exhibition will be the focus for a sustained educational program.

In post-liberation France the fate of the Jews was deliberately concealed since it called into question the role of thousands of Frenchmen during the occupation. The first post-Vichy head of government, Charles de GAULLE, spread the myth that France had always resisted the Nazis. However, the Vichy era returned to haunt French political life. In the 1970s the work of two North American historians, Michael Marrus and Robert Paxton, exposed the extent of native French antisemitism and the degree of voluntary cooperation between the Vichy government and the Nazis. Their work was followed by the controversial film *Le Chagrin et la Pitie* by Max Ophuls, which triggered debate about the occupation. From the late 1970s a series of scandals and war crimes trials kept the Holocaust at the top of the national agenda. The expansion of Holocaust denial in France also focused attention on its "repressed" past. It became the subject for numerous films, such as Louis Malle's *Lacombe Lucien* and Joseph Losey's *Monsieur Klein*, which explored the deportations and the phenomena of collaboration. During the 1980s, the French Jewish community became more assertive over Jewish issues, insisting that France needed to face up to its anti-Jewish past if it was to have a healthy future. In 1993 President Francois Mitterrand, who had served in the Vichy administration before entering the resistance, publicly indicted Vichy and created a Memorial Day to the Jewish deportees. On July 16, 1994, for the first time, the French officially remembered the deportation of 77,000 Jews from their country. A year later, after his election as president, Jacques Chirac publicly apologized to French Jews for the crimes of the Vichy regime.

Germany was forced to come to terms with its past much faster, although not more thoroughly. The process began in the Western zones of occupation where the Allies enforced a policy of DENAZIFICATION and reeducation from 1945 to 1949. However, this did not penetrate very deeply. By the 1950s films and novels in Germany routinely depicted the Germans as victims of Allied bombing and of atrocities perpetrated by the Soviet army, and showed German prisoners of war in Russian camps in terms intended to evoke the plight of inmates in Nazi camps. Konrad Adenauer, the conservative German chancellor from 1949 to 1969, on the surface acknowledged his country's guilt and agreed to pay reparations to Israel and the victims of Nazi persecution. His government adopted a stance of philosemitism—being a friend to the Jews—yet this functioned as a substitute for confronting the past. It was not until the youth revolt in 1968 that the older generation faced tough questions about its behavior during the Nazi era. This soul-searching became possible after Willi Brandt became chancellor at the head of a left-leaning coalition government in 1969. Germany then pursued a path of reconciliation with countries in Eastern Europe and in 1970, during a state visit to Poland, Brandt made a dramatic gesture of remorse at the site of the Warsaw

Commemorating prisoners who died in the Natzweiler camp, Walldorf, Germany

Ghetto. A new atmosphere of democratization and openness in German academic and public life resulted in a wave of research and publications on the THIRD REICH. In 1979 the screening of the TV miniseries *Holocaust* evoked a massive response and contributed to the decision to suspend indefinitely the statute of limitations for prosecution of murders committed in the Nazi era.

In 1983 a crucial mood change occurred when Helmut Kohl became chancellor at the head of a conservative coalition government. Kohl fostered the revival of German national pride and supported historians who sought to "normalize" the Third Reich. An expression of the new mood was Edgar Reitz's 1984 film *Heimat*. Made as an antidote to the *Holocaust* miniseries, it showed the life of a German village from 1919 to 1945 in loving detail, but the fate of German Jews over this time was hardly mentioned. The attempt to normalize and consider as relative the Nazi part led to the "historian quarrel" or *Historikerstreit,* which raged in the German press during 1986 and 1987. It was triggered when the prominent historian Ernst Nolte attributed Nazism to German fears of Bolshevism and suggested that Hitler merely copied Stalin's atrocities. The historian Andreas Hillgruber added to the debate by suggesting that the German nation suffered a catastrophe in 1944–1945 when it was invaded from the east, at the same time as a separate and almost incidental catastrophe, that of the Jews, was reaching its end. Chancellor Kohl's national revival was bolstered by the fall of the Berlin Wall and German reunification between 1989 and 1991. In order to integrate the two halves of Germany, he stressed the continuities of oppression from the Nazi era through the Soviet era. The plan for a memorial to the Jews in the heart of BERLIN, destined again to be the capital of Germany, aroused years of debate until a design for it was finally agreed upon in 1999. The mayor of Berlin boycotted the groundbreaking ceremony in January 2000 in protest against the attempt to identify the city forever with the Nazi past and the Holocaust.

In Israel, several years passed before the State of Israel formally adopted ways of commemorating Europe's murdered Jews and the past. Survivors and other groups had been holding memorial events since wartime, but there was no single, national event. An official Holocaust memorial day was finally established partly because some religious Jews wanted a date on which to say a communal mourning prayer. There was much argument about what was to be commemorated, when, and how: whether it should be a secular event or coincide with a religious fast day. The Israeli parliament finally declared 27 Nissan to be *Yom Ha-Shoah VeHaGvurah,* Day of Holocaust and Heroism. This date falls close to *Pesach* (Passover), *Yom HaZikkaron,* the day of memorial for the fallen of Israel's wars, and *Yom HaAztmaut,* Independence Day. On *Yom HaShoah* cafes, restaurants, cinemas, and theaters close; flags fly at half mast; and synagogues, kibbutzim, schools, and survivors hold memorial meetings. In 1953 the government decreed the establishment of YAD VASHEM in Jerusalem to commemorate the Jews who died in the Holocaust, collect documentation and published information about the Holocaust, and educate the generations born since. In 1957 the archive, library, and educational center opened. It is now a huge, modern complex with exhibitions, library, archive, teaching facilities, and memorials.

In Poland during the period of Stalinist rule from 1948 to 1953, the fate of the Jews was discussed and commemorated, but mainly as a way of blackening the reputation of right-wing Poles. The years from 1954 to 1966 saw a National-Communist experiment in which Polish national pride was given more expression. As Jews were associated with the regime of the Stalinist period, the suffering of the Jews under Nazi rule was played down. In 1967–1968 an internal crisis led to a thinly disguised antisemitic campaign that gave way to chauvinistic versions of the past that suppressed almost any writing on the Jewish fate. During the 1970s and 1980s only dissidents investigated Poland's Jewish past and the Holocaust era. Since then, freedom from Soviet control has allowed Poles to celebrate their nationalist resistance to the Nazis and secure recognition of their country's wartime suffering. Increased openness has also allowed non-Poles to intervene in debates about memorials and Polish memory, often with clashing effects. In 1984 a Carmelite Convent was set up in one of the buildings at Auschwitz. The nuns wished to pray for the souls of those who had been murdered there, but Jews objected that most of the victims in Auschwitz-Birkenau had been Jews. Jewish protestors provoked angry Polish reactions, tinged with antisemitism. Mediation by groups involved in Christian-Jewish dialogue eventually led to a compromise in 1993, but the convent controversy exposed the continuing gulf between Jewish memory of the Holocaust and Polish memory. The fiftieth anniversaries of the WARSAW GHETTO UPRISING

and the liberation of Auschwitz were major media events and helped Jews and Poles confront their respective, tragic histories in a spirit of reconciliation. Jews from around the world now have a greater input into the establishment and running of museums and memorial sites in Poland.

In the Soviet Union memory of the Holocaust was almost totally suppressed. The occurrence of the Holocaust was never denied, but Soviet policy sought to hide the specific suffering of the Jews in order to avoid creating sympathy for Jews or for Israel. Soviet writers even accused Zionists of collaborating with the Nazis. Individual Soviet authors and artists fought this policy and some produced major artistic works with Holocaust themes, such as Vasily Grossman's *Life and Fate* and Yevgeny Yevtushenko's poem on the Babi Yar massacre. The poem was powerfully set to music by Dimitri Shostakovitch. Since *glasnost* and the collapse of the Soviet Union, contradictory strands have appeared in official and collective memory. In the independent UKRAINE, former Nazi collaborators have been rehabilitated. Yet there has been increased scope for the establishment of Jewish memorials and Holocaust museums. The Ukrainian government made major efforts in 1991 to mark the massacre at Babi Yar, while the Belorussian legal authorities have given much help to Western war crimes investigators. In Russia, a revival of antisemitism and even NEO-NAZISM coexists with a much greater openness about the past.

The struggles over memory of the Holocaust are evidence of the Holocaust's centrality to contemporary Jewish identity and its significance for the wider public. Since the 1970s commentators have noted that the Holocaust has become part of the "civil religion" of Jews in America, especially. The Jewish thinker Emil Fackenheim was partly responsible for this by suggesting in March 1967 that one more commandment should be added to the 613 that observant Jews are bound to observe: "Thou shalt not give Hitler a posthumous victory." Fackenheim meant this as a warning to young Jews who considered marrying out of the faith or assimilating totally that they were unintentionally fulfilling Hitler's goal of eliminating the Jewish people. Rabbis and Jewish educators seized on this notion as a powerful tool to fight assimilation, and communal institutions began to invest heavily in Holocaust education. This turn came at the same time as American Jews were becoming disillusioned with the civil rights movement and the progressive ideology that had reigned in

Jewish circles since the time of the New Deal. The memory of the Holocaust and the lessons to be drawn from it appeared to be a new, unifying idea.

However, other Jewish thinkers have criticized the investment in education about the Holocaust, university Holocaust Studies programs, Holocaust museums, and trips to extermination camp sites in Poland. Theological thinkers such as Eliezer Berkovits have insisted that the Holocaust can be located in the Jewish historical experience of catastrophe and renewal and offers no special challenge to Jewish belief. Others have complained that there is more to Jewish history and culture than death and destruction. Why should Jewish college students learn only about Jews as victims? Why not teach them about Jewish achievements and the glories of Jewish civilization? More recently, the campaign against the Swiss banks, the quest for restitution in Eastern Europe, and the demands for compensation for slave laborers have led to the concern that Jews appear as merely interested in money. The preoccupation with hunting down and prosecuting Nazi-era war criminals has been labeled revenge, not a quest for justice.

The very prominence of the Holocaust has led to controversy, which has alarmed some Jews. Other victims of the Nazis, such as GYPSIES and homosexuals, protest that Jewish claims on memory have overshadowed their suffering. Peoples who have suffered GENOCIDE or lesser atrocities in the twentieth century and in contemporary times object that the world seems obsessed with Jewish suffering of 60 years ago. The descendants of African slaves, victims of the transatlantic slave trade, complain that their suffering deserves recognition and amends. Palestinian Arabs complain that the world knows about the deportation and mass murder of Jews, but ignores the suffering of Palestinians who have lived in refugee camps since 1948. They argue that Jews use the Holocaust to shield Israel from international criticism. In countries that were once under the yoke of Stalinism, there is impatience with the West's apparent fixation on the Holocaust. Ukrainians express annoyance that the artificial famine in the Ukraine in 1932–1933 that led to the death of millions of people is barely known. Lithuanians and Latvians object that their suffering under Stalinism in 1940–1941 and after the war is all but ignored. These attacks on the prominence of the Holocaust are interpreted by some Jews as an attack on a central part of Jewish identity and amount to nothing less than antisemitism. Hence, the centrality of the Holocaust has become tangled up with debates about Jewishness, political arguments, and antisemitism.

Since the 1970s, the Holocaust has emerged as a magnetic subject for artists, filmmakers, novelists, and dramatists. It has come to embody evil and to dramatize human choices in the most extreme circumstances. But every effort to represent the Holocaust, in novels such as Anne Michael's *Fugitive Pieces* (1997) or in films such as Roberto Benigni's *Life is Beautiful* (1999), raises the question of whether it can be represented at all. Yet the very indescribability of the subject, the magnitude of the evil, and the incomprehensible scale of suffering are to artists what mountains are to climbers: they feel compelled to make the attempt. Paradoxically, the more popular the Holocaust becomes as a subject, the more universal its message has to be. By using Auschwitz as a metaphor for "absolute evil," by making the camps a scenario for exploring human relations in the most extreme of situations, the specific fate of the Jews becomes irrelevant. The presence of the Holocaust in popular culture has ensured that it is no longer a marginal subject, confined to the collective memory of the Jewish people; but the price that has been paid for this is a blurring of what made it happen in the first place, why the Germans were responsible for it, and why it happened to the Jews in particular. In this sense, ignorance may be replaced by incomprehension and remembrance may lead to forgetting.

A demonstration against German reparation payments, Jerusalem, 1952 (State of Israel, Government Press Office)

A

AB-AKTION (*Ausserordenliche Befriedungsaktion;* Extraordinary Pacification Operation), campaign to exterminate Polish resistance leaders in 1940, in order to subdue Polish opposition to the Germans and unnerve the Polish people. The *AB-Aktion* was raised as a war crime at the NUREMBERG TRIALS and the war crimes trials held by the Supreme People's Court in POLAND.

The *Reichsverteidigungsrat* (the Reich's military planning committee) planned the *AB-Aktion* during February and March 1940. Hans FRANK ordered the beginning of the *aktion* on May 16, 1940, days after the Germans initiated their military offensive in Western Europe. The Germans arrested about 3,500 Poles in the GENERALGOUVERNEMENT whom they considered to be activist leaders and 3,000 suspected of criminal activities. They then massacred the entire group at sites including the Palmiry Forest.

The Nazis had originally hoped to end the *AB-Aktion* by the middle of 1940; it continued, however, into the fall. German military successes in Western Europe probably brought about the extension.

In spite of the Nazis' intentions, the *AB-Aktion* did not achieve its goal of destroying the Polish resistance movement. For a short while, the membership of the resistance organizations was brought down by a third. However, they soon regained their strength and moved on with their activities.

ABETZ, OTTO (1903–1958), GERMANY'S ambassador to Vichy (unoccupied) FRANCE during WORLD WAR II.

An art teacher, Abetz gave his support to the NAZI PARTY in 1931. In 1935 he joined the German Foreign Office as a French expert. He spent a lot of time in France, but was thrown out of the country in 1939 when the French cracked down on a secret fascist association called the *Cagoulards*.

Germany invaded France in May 1940. Abetz returned that year and in August was named ambassador to the Vichy government. He served in that position for four years. His obligations as ambassador included dealing with all political matters in both occupied and unoccupied France and counseling the German military and police administration in PARIS, the capital of Nazi-occupied France. His main responsibility was to make sure the French collaborated with the Nazis in furthering their antisemitic goals. He played a large part in the DEPORTATION of both foreign Jewish REFUGEES and French-born Jews, particularly after Germany occupied southern France in the fall of 1942.

After the war Abetz was tried for war crimes and sentenced to 20 years doing hard labor. He served just five years. (for more on Vichy, see also FRANCE.)

ABWEHR (full name: *Amt Ausland/Abwehr im Oberkommando der* WEHRMACHT; Foreign Bureau/ Defense of the Armed Forces High Command), intelligence service of the German military. Until 1944, Adm. Wilhelm CANARIS was head of the *Abwehr*.

ACTION FRANCAISE Radical French right-wing antisemitic movement. The *Action Francaise* was founded by Charles Maurras during the Dreyfus Affair in 1894, to oppose the liberal intellectuals who supported the Jewish army captain accused of treason; it was dissolved at the end of WORLD WAR II.

Action Francaise was a nationalistic movement that regarded FRANCE as a superior motherland that deserved the utmost allegiance. Members advocated the removal of the republic and return to monarchy. They also believed that France had four enemies constantly trying to destroy her: Jews, foreigners, Protestants, and FREEMASONS. The nation had to expel those enemies, and other destructive elements such as democracy. For nearly 50 years, Maurras's movement was a frontrunner of French ANTISEMITISM.

During World War II, Maurras considered himself the idea man behind the Vichy government's "national revolution." He gladly received the anti-Jewish laws (STATUT DES JUIFS) passed in October 1940, which attempted to do exactly what *Action Francaise* had been calling for since 1894: exclude the Jews from French life.

When the war ended Maurras was sentenced to life in jail for collaboration. Despite its relatively small size, *Action Francaise* had enjoyed an inordinately large amount of intellectual influence both in France and other European countries. (for more on Vichy, see also FRANCE.)

ADAMOWICZ, IRENA
(1910–1963), Polish non-Jew who aided various GHETTO underground movements during WORLD WAR II.

Born in WARSAW, Adamowicz was a religious Catholic and one of the leaders of the Polish scout movement. She earned her social work degree at the University of Warsaw. During the 1930s she developed an attachment to the *Ha-Shomer ha-Tsa'ir* Jewish Zionist YOUTH MOVEMENT, and she even took part in its educational and social work activities.

During the summer of 1942 Adamowicz risked her life by carrying out perilous missions for the Jewish underground organizations in the Warsaw, BIALYSTOK, VILNA, KOVNO, and Siauliai ghettos. She both carried important messages between the different ghettos and boosted the morale of the Jews imprisoned in them. She also helped to establish contact between the Jewish underground organizations and the HOME ARMY (the Polish underground militia).

After the war, Adamowicz stayed in close contact with the surviving members of the Zionist pioneer movements she had worked with and aided. She was designated as RIGHTEOUS AMONG THE NATIONS by YAD VASHEM.

AHNENERBE
(*Studiengesellschaft fuer Geistesurgeschichte Deutsches Ahnenerbe*), the Society for Research into the Spiritual Roots of GERMANY's Ancestral Heritage. *Ahnenerbe* was founded in BERLIN on July 1, 1935 by SS chief Heinrich HIMMLER, Nazi ideologist Richard Walther DARRE, and German-Dutch lecturer Herman Wirth. The society's purpose was to establish support for Wirth's "Germandom" cult by studying aspects of Germany's spiritual and historical heritage. However, from the beginning, the society delved into all sorts of esoteric subjects that did not have much scientific basis, such as research of ancient Germanic letters of the alphabet and interpretation of German symbols, like the SWASTIKA.

Himmler took charge of *Ahnenerbe* in 1937. All kinds of new projects were initiated, including the listing of "Jewish scientists or scientists related to Jews by marriage," and the confiscation of Jewish libraries. It was quite hard to tell which of the projects were scientifically motivated, which were politically motivated, and which were downright ridiculous.

In 1942 *Ahnenerbe* began sponsoring pseudo-scientific MEDICAL EXPERIMENTS that were performed on CONCENTRATION CAMP victims. These included freezing and high altitude experiments conducted by Dr. Sigmund Rascher in DACHAU, and the extermination of Jews and GYPSIES from AUSCHWITZ so that their skulls could be studied by Dr. August Hirt as examples of the "sub-human prototype."

AKTION 1005
(Operation 1005), code name for the large-scale campaign to destroy all evidence of the mass extermination of European Jewry at the hands of the Nazis. The operation began in June 1942 and lasted until late 1944.

By the summer of 1942, countries in the West had begun receiving reports of the mass murders going on in Europe. This caused the Nazis to try to find a way to conceal the evidence of their horrific activities. In June 1942 SS-*Standartenfuehrer* Paul BLOBEL was appointed head of *Aktion* 1005, and the first corpses were burnt in the CHELMNO extermination camp.

The dirty work of *Aktion* 1005 was carried out mainly by Jewish prisoners. They were forced to dig up the mass graves and remove the corpses. They built pyres made out of long wooden beams, soaked them with flammable liquid, arranged the corpses in layers between the beams, and burnt them. When this was finished, the area was flattened out, plowed, and replanted. After the work was done, the prisoners who

Burning bodies in the Klooga camp to destroy the evidence of murder

had participated were themselves murdered in order to keep the operation secret. In some cases, the *Aktion 1005* prisoners tried to escape this fate.

Between the summers of 1942 and 1943, corpses were burnt in BELZEC, TREBLINKA, SOBIBOR, and AUSCHWITZ. In June 1943 the Germans began burning corpses in the occupied SOVIET UNION and POLAND. Two SONDERKOMMANDO prisoner units were organized. One worked in areas such as Berdichev and Zamosc, the other in areas including RIGA and Dvinsk. *Aktion 1005* was also carried out in BELORUSSIA and the Baltic countries, where the corpses of Soviet PRISONERS OF WAR were burnt. By mid-1944, *Aktion 1005* activities were focused on the GENERALGOUVERNEMENT—a *Sonderkommando* unit was established in each of its districts. Soon, similar actions were also performed in those parts of Poland annexed to GERMANY. *Aktion 1005* was also carried out in YUGOSLAVIA.

The destruction of the mass graves in Eastern Europe made it difficult to determine the number of victims exterminated by the Nazis, and fueled the flames of HOLOCAUST denial. (see also HOLOCAUST, DENIAL OF THE.)

AKTION REINHARD   Code name for the Nazi operation to exterminate the 2,284,000 Jews living in the five districts of the GENERALGOUVERNEMENT, including the WARSAW, Lublin, Radom, Cracow, and Lvov districts. During the last few months of 1942 the operation was extended to the Bialystok district, adding some 210,000 Jews. *Aktion Reinhard* was named after Reinhard HEYDRICH, the main organizer of the "FINAL SOLUTION" in Europe, who had been assassinated by Czech resistance fighters.

The Nazis began planning *Aktion Reinhard* in the fall of 1941. SS chief Heinrich HIMMLER appointed Odilo GLOBOCNIK (SS and Police Leader of the Lublin district) to head up *Aktion Reinhard*, and SS-*Hauptsturmfuehrer* Hans Hofle as chief of operations. They were assigned a staff of 450 Germans, including 92 men who had previously worked for the EUTHANASIA PROGRAM. In addition, the *Aktion Reinhard* headquarters recruited a special unit made up of Ukrainian volunteers, most of whom had been Soviet PRISONERS OF WAR.

Three EXTERMINATION CAMPS were established for *Aktion Reinhard*: BELZEC, SOBIBOR, and TREBLINKA. Belzec, situated along the LUBLIN-LVOV railway, was constructed between November 1941 and March 1942.

The extermination process began there on March 17, 1942. Sobibor, located east of Lublin, was built in March and April 1942, and was opened for operations in early May 1942. Treblinka, located 50 miles northeast of Warsaw, was set up in June and July 1942 and began functioning on July 23, 1942—in conjunction with the mass DEPORTATION of Jews from the Warsaw GHETTO.

The Nazis set up a deportation process that they used unwaveringly in most parts of Eastern Europe. Their main goal was to keep the victims in the dark about where they were going until they got there. In the smaller ghettos, the Nazis carried out this process in just one or two days. In the large ghettos, which sometimes contained hundreds of thousands of Jews, the deportation could not be carried out in one day only. Thus, the JUDENRAT would be instructed to gather several thousand people each in several smaller *aktionen*. If the *Judenrat* could not or would not provide the Germans with the number of people they had asked for, German and Ukrainian troops would be sent in to break into the houses and courtyards where the Jews were hiding and drag them out.

After being removed from the ghetto, the Jews were marched to a railroad station, where they were jammed into cattle cars. The trip to the extermination camp sometimes only took a few hours, but often took days. The long trip and the insufferable conditions in the train cars (including overcrowding, terrible heat in the summer months and cold in the winter, and lack of water or sanitation) resulted in many people dying en route.

In July 1942 Himmler visited the *Aktion Reinhard* camps. Afterwards, he ordered that the deportation of the *Generalgouvernement's* Jews was to be completed by December 31 of that year. However, the army appealed his order, citing its need for Jewish manpower for the war effort. As a result, it was decided to keep some Jewish laborers in several of the large ghettos for the time being.

During *Aktion Reinhard* the Germans confiscated huge amounts of Jewish property, worth more than 178 million reichsmarks. The cash and valuables gathered in the extermination camps were sent to the SS Economic-Administrative Main Office (WIRTSCHAFTSVERWALTUNGSHAUPTAMT, WVHA), while other items were spread out among the Economy Ministry, the army, SS workshops, and the ethnic Germans (VOLKSDEUTSCHE) living in the occupied territories.

Aktion Reinhard continued until early November

1943, when the last *Generalgouvernement* Jews in the MAJDANEK, PONIATOWA, and TRAWNIKI camps were exterminated as part of Operation ERNTEFEST. Altogether, more than two million Jews in the *Generalgouvernement* were killed during *Aktion Reinhard*.

ALBANIA   Country in the Balkans. On the eve of WORLD WAR II, there were about 600 Jews in Albania, of whom 400 were REFUGEES. The largest community was in Kavaje. Most of the refugees were German and Austrian Jews who had reached Albania in the hope of making their way to the UNITED STATES or South American countries. Traditionally there was no discrimination of Jews in Albania.

On April 7, 1939, Italian troops entered Albania, beginning their occupation of the country. Soon thereafter Jews were forbidden from leaving Albania for their studies in ITALY, and Jews were removed from the coastal port cities to the country's interior. But on the whole the Italian regime did not persecute the Jews harshly.

Following the fall of YUGOSLAVIA in spring 1941, the Kosovo province was annexed to Italian controlled Albania. The Germans demanded that the Jews of Pristina be handed over to them. The Italians refused, but eventually agreed to hand over prisoners from the jails to them. Among the prisoners were 60 Jews, who were then murdered. Jewish refugees from other parts of Yugoslavia who had reached Pristina were transported to the older areas of Albania, where they were housed in a camp at Kavaje. Eventually some 200 refugees were in this camp. The conditions there were poor, but the inmates could leave the camp during the day. About 100 Jewish men from Pristina, later joined by their families, were taken to Berat. In Berat, many were aided and protected by local Albanians. Smaller numbers of Jewish refugees could also be found in other localities, including the capital Tirana.

In September 1943, after the change in Italy's government, Albania came under German control. The situation of the Jews became worse. Albanian clerks gave identity papers to many of the Jews of Kavaje, so they could go to Tirana as part of an Italian convoy and hide there.

Early in 1944 the GESTAPO ordered Jews in Tirana to register. Many Jews took this as a signal to flee to the PARTISANS outside the capital. Other Jews obtained false papers from Albanian friends, and thus avoided attempts by the Gestapo to round up Jews. The Germans also demanded that Albanian officials give them lists of Jews living in Albania, but the officials did not comply. Rather they warned the Jews. Christian and Muslim Albanians alike regarded it as a matter of national pride to help Jews, both native Albanian and refugees. Thus no Jews were turned over to the Germans and the community survived the war, except for one family of six that was discovered by the Germans and sent to Pristina. Only one member of that family survived.

ALGERIA   Country in central North Africa that, from the mid-nineteenth century, was governed by FRANCE. In 1870 the Jews of Algeria received French citizenship. At that time, and from the 1920s through WORLD WAR II, ANTISEMITISM was rampant in Algeria. On the eve of the war, there were 120,000 Jews living there.

In June 1940 France was divided into north and south—the north conquered and governed by the Nazis, the south unoccupied by the Nazis, but controlled by the pro-Nazi Vichy government. Under the French-German cease-fire agreement, North Africa was considered part of unoccupied Vichy France, and most of the Europeans in North Africa supported the Vichy regime. All French laws were activated in Algeria, including those that restricted the legal status of Algerian Jews. On October 7, 1940, the Jews lost their citizenship, and a few days later, were subjected to the racial STATUT DES JUIFS—just like the Jews of France. Over the next two years, France's OFFICE FOR JEWISH AFFAIRS ordered many more anti-Jewish measures that were enacted both in Vichy France and in Algeria. These included the establishment of an ARYANIZATION office in Algeria that confiscated Jewish property; the institution of strict quotas on the number of Jews who could work in the professions, including doctors, registered nurses, druggists, lawyers, and others; severe restrictions on the number of Jewish students who could study at university; and the exclusion of Jewish children from elementary and secondary schools. The Bedeau camp located near the town of Sidi-bel-Abbes acted as a CONCENTRATION CAMP for Algerian Jewish soldiers. These men had been placed in a special unit called the Jewish Work Group, and made to do extremely hard FORCED LABOR. The authorities also planned to set up a JUDENRAT based on the UNION OF FRENCH JEWS, and the Germans intended to begin deporting Jews to EXTERMINATION CAMPS in Europe. All these anti-Jewish measures were devised both in accordance with the antisemitic Vichy philosophy, and in order to gain the favor of the North African Muslim population.

The Jews of Algeria believed that the Germans pressured the French authorities into instituting racist laws. Thus, many joined the Algerian underground after it was formed in 1940 by a group of young Jews, some of whom were former French army officers. Other Jewish underground groups were also established and joined the organized resistance, which made contact with certain French officials who had come to Algeria to get ready to continue the battle against the Germans. At the end of October 1942, the American authorities told the Algerian resistance about their plans to land in Algeria and MOROCCO, and asked them to participate in the fight by seizing control of strategic locations in Algiers, Oran, and Casablanca. The underground was not successful in Oran or Casablanca, but fully succeeded in its part of the capture of Algiers on November 7–8. There were 377 resistance members who took Algiers—of whom 315 were Jews. Thus, the Algerian Jewish community survived due to this early Allied LIBERATION of Algeria in November 1942.

However, the Jews were not truly "liberated." The Americans agreed to appoint a Vichy official named Francois DARLAN as High Commissioner of North Africa in exchange for a cease-fire, and allowed Vichy law, including its anti-Jewish regulations, to remain intact. When Darlan was murdered in December 1942, Jewish resistance leaders were arrested for collaboration—on the orders of their former French comrades in the resistance. In March 1943 only some of the anti-Jewish laws were cancelled. General Charles DE GAULLE took control of Algeria in May, and three months later, he reinstated citizenship for the country's Jews and revoked its ANTI-JEWISH LEGISLATION. (for more on Vichy, see also FRANCE.)

ALIYA BET   ("Illegal Immigration," *Ha'apala*), the organized entry of Jews into Palestine during the period of the British Mandate in direct defiance of the British government's restriction on Jewish immigration.

By the early 1920s, GREAT BRITAIN had publicly committed to helping establish a Jewish state in Palestine. However, as the British authorities were strongly af-

The arrival in Haifa harbor of the "Haim Arlozorov" with "illegal" refugees

fected by Arab pressure, they began withdrawing their support for the Jews. In the early 1930s they put severe quotas on Jewish immigration. Zionist groups responded with a policy called *Aliya Bet,* meaning illegal immigration. The Jews in Palestine called these immigrants *ma'apilim,* from the word *ha'apala,* meaning upward struggle. The British called them illegal immigrants. Most reached Palestine by boat and tried to enter the country secretly. Approximately 530,000 immigrants entered Palestine before the State of Israel was established; one-quarter of that number entered by way of *Aliya Bet.*

The first ship of illegal immigrants reached Palestine in 1934. At that point, the Jewish Agency leadership did not approve of illegal methods of immigration. However, by 1939, David BEN-GURION realized that *Aliya Bet* was the only real option for Jews to reach Palestine. The *Mossad le-Aliya Bet*—the official *Aliya Bet* organization—was then created.

During WORLD WAR II, *Aliya Bet* became one of the principle ways of rescuing Jews. However, the *Mossad* had to contend with many problems, including the restriction of ship use, lack of funds, the continuing British blockade of Palestine, and unsafe conditions. This led to the slowing down of *Aliya Bet,* and by 1942, its complete postponement. The *Mossad* resumed operations in 1944 when the Jews of Palestine became aware of the extent of the "final solution."

After the war, *Aliya Bet* became the crux of Zionist activity, focusing the world's attention on the plight of those Holocaust SURVIVORS who wanted to immigrate to a Jewish state. Tens of thousands of would-be immigrants arrived at the shores of Palestine on dozens of ships (among them the EXODUS 1947), only to be caught by the British and interned in detention camps. About half were held in Cyprus until the State of Israel was established in May 1948.

ALSACE-LORRAINE Two provinces located in northeastern FRANCE that share a border with GERMANY. For centuries, Alsace-Lorraine was a major topic of conflict between France and Germany, as both countries claimed the region as their own. Alsace-Lorraine belonged to France during the seventeenth and eighteenth centuries; from 1871–1918 it was controlled by Germany. In 1919, after World War I, the area was returned to France. For most of WORLD WAR II Germany again held control; after the Allies re-conquered France in the fall of 1944, Alsace-Lorraine reverted to France.

In 1939 there were 20,000 Jews living in Alsace-Lorraine. The largest Jewish community was in Strasbourg; the second largest in Metz.

After the MUNICH CONFERENCE of September 1938 there were riotous demonstrations in Alsace-Lorraine, during which Jewish shops were attacked. In addition, Strasbourg soon became a center for distribution of antisemitic propaganda that was smuggled in by NAZI PARTY members. In response, Jewish YOUTH MOVEMENTS in the city established a committee to deal with such ANTISEMITISM. At the same time, Jewish relief organizations were also established in Strasbourg in order to aid the Jewish REFUGEES from central and eastern Europe who were seeking shelter in the city.

World War II began in September 1939. At that point, the French government evacuated the people living in areas very close to Germany, such as Alsace-Lorraine. Among the evacuees were 14,000 Jews, who were sent to central-western France. After Germany invaded and conquered northern France in mid-1940, another 5,000 Jews from Alsace-Lorraine escaped to southern France. The Germans expelled the rest of the Jews of Alsace-Lorraine in July, and declared the region "Jew-free." Later on in the war, a German professor in Strasbourg, August Hirt, began a collection of Jewish skulls and skeletons in order to study racial theory. In June 1943 nearly 100 Jews were transferred from AUSCHWITZ to a CONCENTRATION CAMP in Alsace-Lorraine, where they were gassed. Their corpses were then sent to Hirt to be studied.

Many of the Jews from Alsace-Lorraine who had been evacuated or evicted became active members of the French Jewish resistance. Approximately 2,000 Alsace-Lorraine Jews perished in the HOLOCAUST.

ALTHAMMER CONCENTRATION CAMP located in POLAND, about 10 miles west of the city of Katowice. Althammer was established in September 1944 as a satellite camp of AUSCHWITZ.

About 500 Jewish prisoners were interned at Althammer, including a large group from the LODZ Ghetto, and smaller groups from HUNGARY, FRANCE, and Greece. There was also a small number of German prisoners who were considered to be "privileged" and held positions of authority within the prisoner hierarchy. The inmates at Althammer worked at building a power station close by. They were treated brutally, worked to the bone, and given inadequate food rations. As a result, one-third of the prisoners fell sick.

In addition, the camp commandant, Josef Mirbeth, tortured the prisoners and even murdered some of them himself.

On January 19, 1945 the Germans sent 400 prisoners on a DEATH MARCH towards Gliwice. Most were killed along the way. The rest of the prisoners had been left behind in the camp because they were sick. The German staff murdered most of them before fleeing the camp; the survivors eventually reached the Nordhausen camp in Saxony. A few managed to escape Nordhausen and were liberated by Soviet troops.

AMELOT   Jewish welfare association in PARIS whose goal was to provide relief for the Jewish community in FRANCE during WORLD WAR II. *Amelot* was established in June 1940, soon after the German army invaded France. It was founded by a group of Jewish immigrant activists, including members of the FEDERATION OF JEWISH SOCIETIES OF FRANCE, the BUND, and the *Po'alei Zion* Zionist movement.

Amelot did not want to join the Coordinating Committee of Jewish Welfare Societies, which had been instituted in January 1941 due to Nazi pressure. However, it decided to cooperate with the committee in order to further the needs of the community. Nonetheless, when the Nazis tightened their grip on the committee, *Amelot* would have nothing more to do with it. From then on, *Amelot* acted independently.

In mid-1941, 8,000 Jewish males were arrested; *Amelot* expanded its aid activities to help them. The group also provided relief for Jews who had escaped DEPORTATION, who thus could not be helped by the UNION OF FRENCH JEWS, a Jewish umbrella organization established by the Vichy government. Furthermore, *Amelot* hid children and gave out forged identity papers. In all, *Amelot* assisted thousands of Jews, rescued more than 1,000 children, and handed out thousands of meals to the needy.

AMERICAN FRIENDS SERVICE COMMITTEE (AFSC)   Relief organization established in 1917 by the Quakers, also known as the Society of Friends, as a forum for doing service to humanity in a moral fashion. The Quakers make up one of the smallest religious groups in the UNITED STATES.

During the first years after Adolf HITLER rose to power, the Quakers were afraid to jeopardize their reputation in GERMANY, so they did relatively little to help REFUGEES escaping the Nazis. However, after the KRIS-TALLNACHT pogrom of 1938, the AFSC opened a Refugee Division, which provided services for European refugees who immigrated to the US. The AFSC concentrated on Americanizing the new arrivals and adjusting them to their new country.

The Foreign Service Section of the AFSC did even more than the Refugee Division. Cooperating with Jewish relief agencies, in 1939 the organization sent a delegation to Germany to check on the situation of Jews and Christians and provide relief if necessary. They mainly assisted Christian refugees, but they also helped Jews. Among other activities, they fed and saved children in FRANCE, assisted Jews who had reached Portugal, and organized the activities of relief agencies in SPAIN.

In 1947 the AFSC won the Nobel Peace Prize for helping refugees during and after WORLD WAR II.

AMERICAN JEWISH CONFERENCE   American Jewish organization created in August 1943 to unify American Jewry for the purpose of planning their postwar policy.

In January 1943, two months after the UNITED STATES State Department confirmed reports that the Nazis intended to annihilate all of European Jewry, representatives of 32 American Jewish organizations met to organize a conference to be held later that year. The conference agenda was to include Jewish rights after the war; the Jewish right to Palestine; and the election of a group that would carry out the conference's decisions. In late July the rescue of European Jewry was added to the proposed agenda.

The American Jewish Conference was convened in August 1943. The first topic of discussion was rescue, but no new solutions were found. However, when the Palestine issue was raised, American Jewish leader Stephen WISE delivered a fiery speech that called for the establishment of a Jewish state in Palestine. The conference was completely caught up in Wise's furor, and passed a resolution in favor of a Jewish state.

Despite its good intentions, the American Jewish Conference did not successfully unify American Jewry or gain the recognition of the US government as the American Jewish authority on rescue, Palestine, or postwar matters. The conference was dissolved in 1949.

AMERICAN JEWRY AND THE HOLOCAUST   When the Nazis rose to power in GERMANY during the early 1930s, the Jews living in the UNITED STATES were not prepared to confront the threat to the Jews of Europe.

Most Jews in America at that time were either new immigrants themselves or first generation Americans, reluctant to stand up with confidence as citizens with a say in government policies. In addition, American Jewry was not united and lacked a central representative organization like those that existed in other countries. In fact, it could be said that in the 1930s and 1940s there was no one American Jewish community. Instead, there were small communities that were loosely linked together because they were all Jewish. Partly as a result of the fact that the Jews of America were not unified into one cohesive group with one voice, they were ineffective at rescuing their Jewish brethren in Europe during the HOLOCAUST.

The first evidence of disunity within American Jewry with regard to the Nazi threat was in its failure to agree on how to evaluate that threat when it first reared its head in early 1933. Certain Jewish organizations, like the Jewish Labor Committee, refused to have any dealings with the Nazi government. The American Jewish Committee, which represented the wealthier, more Americanized German Jews, believed that the best way to deal with HITLER was diplomatically and quietly, with behind-the-scenes negotiations. On the other hand, the American Jewish Congress, which represented the less Americanized Eastern European Jewish immigrants, felt that holding protest rallies, demonstrations, and boycotts was a better way to affect the Nazis (see also BOYCOTTS, ANTI-NAZI). Some Jews were Zionists, who demanded a Jewish homeland in Palestine. Others were non-Zionists, who did not call for a Jewish state per se, but wanted Palestine to be opened up for Jewish immigration. Anti-Zionists strenuously opposed a Jewish state in Palestine. American Ultra-Orthodox Jews established their own rescue organization, the VA'AD HA-HATSALA (Rescue Committee of United States Orthodox Rabbis), which until 1944 concentrated on rescuing Orthodox Jews, mainly rabbis and rabbinical students. A group of Palestinian Jews active in the United States, called the BERGSON GROUP, took its own particular route: as the group's militant members did not feel that they owed allegiance to any one Jewish leader or group in the United States, they felt free to pursue unconventional methods of prodding President Franklin D. ROOSEVELT to rescue European Jews, such as mass demonstrations and public advertisements on the subject. This led to a grave rift between them and American Jewish leaders.

Boycotting against German goods sold in Woolworth's and HH. Kress in New York City, 1937

With such disparate ways of dealing with the issue, there was no single American Jewish voice to appeal to the American government for help. The president of the American Jewish Congress, Rabbi Stephen S. WISE, did not have direct channels to President Roosevelt, and was forced to appeal to Jews close to the president. Many of those American Jews working in the government were often more American than Jewish, and did not want to take on the responsibility of representing all of American Jewry, nor did they want to risk their jobs on a purely Jewish issue. The only case of a Jew highly placed in the American government speaking out for his fellow Jews was Henry J. MORGENTHAU, Roosevelt's Secretary of the Treasury. In early January 1944, Morgenthau received written proof that the American State Department was actively sabotaging rescue efforts for Jewish REFUGEES. Morgenthau brought this news to the president, who decided to avoid scandal and give in to Morgenthau's pressure, and establish a government agency that would work on rescuing refugees. Thus, the WAR REFUGEE BOARD (WRB) was born, but in the words of the WRB's director, John Pehle, their ability to make a difference came "too little, too late."

If they were not able to unite on a level of joint leadership, the American Jews were able to cooperate, if only in name, to raise funds for Jews in Europe and Palestine. The United Jewish Appeal, which was established just before the war in 1939, collected $124 million during the war years. Even more important, the American Jewish JOINT DISTRIBUTION COMMITTEE was able to stay out of politics and do what it needed to do to fund the rescue and sheltering of thousands of Jews who had made their way to the neutral countries of Europe.

Another reason that American Jews were reluctant to take a stand regarding the Nazi threat in Europe was their numbing fear of the ANTISEMITISM that existed in the United States at that time. Many prominent Americans were avowed antisemites, including Charles Lindbergh, America's aviation hero; Henry Ford, the automobile millionaire; and radio personalities Gerald L.K. Smith and Father Charles Coughlin, who broadcast their antisemitic tirades over the airwaves to millions of Americans. Some American Jews did not want to emphasize their Jewishness by speaking out against antisemitism abroad, for fear of losing their jobs or being shunned by their neighbors because of antisemitism close to home.

Nonetheless, after the US government confirmed reports of the "FINAL SOLUTION" in the fall of 1942, the American Jewish community felt compelled to do something. An organization called the AMERICAN JEWISH CONFERENCE was created in August 1943 by the major American Jewish organizations for the purpose of planning their postwar policy. Despite its good intentions, however, the American Jewish community was too divided on the issues to be unified—the American Jewish Conference did not successfully coalesce American Jewry, nor did it gain the recognition of the US government as an authority.

Even if the Jews living in America during the 1930s and 1940s had been a cohesive, unified group with an effective leadership, it is unlikely that they themselves could have altered American war policies. No ethnic group in America possessed that sort of power. The US government wanted, first and foremost, to win the war against Germany, and no other issue was going to get in the way.

AMERICAN ZIONIST EMERGENCY COUNCIL (AZEC)

Council created at the beginning of WORLD WAR II to represent Zionist leadership in the UNITED STATES, in case the activities of Zionist leaders in London and Jerusalem were to be restricted because of the war. The council's original members included representatives of the Zionist Organization of America and other American Zionist leaders.

Until 1941, the council had a weak and disorganized leadership. It did not protest the British WHITE PAPER OF 1939, which placed further restrictions on Jewish immigration to Palestine. As long as the United States stayed out of the war, the council was afraid to sponsor the establishment of a Jewish fighting organization.

AZEC did not rescue Jews being persecuted by the Nazis; this was mainly done by the American Jewish Congress. AZEC's job was to deal with issues related to the Zionist movement and Palestine, such as immigration. One of its major responsibilities was to convince the American public of the importance of Palestine to the future of the Jewish people.

After the war, AZEC turned its attention to supporting the "illegal immigration" of Holocaust SURVIVORS to Palestine and lobbying the United States for a Jewish state. In 1949, AZEC became the American Zionist Council.

ANIELEWICZ, MORDECAI

(1919 or 1920–1943), Commander of the WARSAW GHETTO UPRISING. Kibbutz Yad Mordecai is named after Anielewicz.

Born in WARSAW, Anielewicz became a leader of the *Ha-Shomer ha-Tsa'ir* Zionist YOUTH MOVEMENT at a young age. When the war started, Anielewicz fled Warsaw for VILNA in Soviet-occupied eastern POLAND. He tried to set up an escape route to Palestine, but was caught by Soviet officials. After his release, Anielewicz spearheaded an effort to send a group back to German-occupied Poland to continue the movement's activities in secret. Anielewicz was among the first to volunteer. He helped publish an underground newspaper and organized meetings and seminars. He also made illegal trips outside Warsaw to visit comrades in other GHETTOS.

In June 1941, upon hearing reports of the mass murder of Jews, Anielewicz set up a self-defense organization in the Warsaw Ghetto. In the summer of 1942 the Germans deported all but 60,000 of Warsaw's Jews. Anielewicz saw that the Jewish Fighting Organization (*Zydowska Organizacja Bojowa*, ZOB) was very weak.

He rejuvenated the group. Most other Jewish underground groups then merged with the ZOB. In November 1942, Anielewicz became their commander.

On January 18, 1943, the Germans surprised the ZOB with a second DEPORTATION. The ZOB staged a street battle, commanded by Anielewicz. Four days later, the Germans stopped the deportation. The Jews interpreted this as a victory for the resistance. For the next three months, Anielewicz led the ZOB in intensive preparations for the next round of fighting.

The final deportation of Warsaw's Jews began on April 19, 1943. This deportation was a cue for the resistance to launch the Warsaw Ghetto Uprising, which Anielewicz commanded. After a fierce battle, Anielewicz and many of his soldiers retreated to the bunker at 18 Mila Street. Although he understood the end was near, Anielewicz wrote: "My life's dream has come true; I have lived to see Jewish resistance in the ghetto in all its greatness and glory." The bunker fell on May 8. Most of the ZOB members, including Aniele-

Mordecai Anielewicz

wicz, were killed. (see also JEWISH FIGHTING ORGANIZATION, WARSAW and RESISTANCE, JEWISH.)

ANSCHLUSS   German word meaning connection or annexation that is used to refer to the takeover of AUSTRIA by GERMANY in March 1938. In German political jargon, the term *Anschluss* came into use at the end of World War I to denote the desire to include Austria in a united Greater Germany. However, based on the peace treaty made in 1919 between Austria and the allies who won the war, known as the Treaty of St. Germain, Austria was forbidden to unite with Germany, and instead was made into an independent country—the Republic of Austria.

During the 1930s the leader of Austria's Christian Socialist Party, Engelbert Dollfuss, allied himself with Fascist ITALY and set himself up as Austria's dictator. Dollfuss was strongly opposed both to Austria's Social Democrats and to its NAZI PARTY. In July 1934 the Nazis tried to take over the government, but failed when the Italian authorities stopped them. Nonetheless, the Nazis did succeed in assassinating Dollfuss right in his own

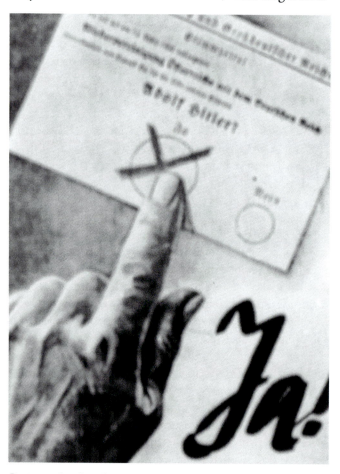

Poster urging Austrians to vote "yes" for the annexation of Austria to Germany after the arrival of German troops in 1938

office. Dollfuss's successor, Kurt von Schuschnigg, tried to reach a compromise with HITLER, but Hitler would not back down: he wanted to annex Austria to the Reich and nothing else.

Over the next few years Austrian support for the Nazi Party increased greatly and, as a result of the German-Italian alliance of 1938, Italy withdrew its support for an independent Austria. Thus, Austria was not strong enough to defy Hitler for long. On March 13, 1938 German troops marched into Austria, and declared the country a part of the German Reich.

The *Anschluss* was supported by many Austrians, among them Austrian Nazis, who saw it as a political, social, and cultural reunification with their brother country, Germany. Thousands turned out to greet Adolf Hitler, the native son who was returning to his homeland. On the other hand, the leaders of the West saw the *Anschluss* as an invasion, pure and simple. Despite this, not one government made a move to stop Hitler who, without interference, felt free to embark upon the next step in his scheme to conquer all of Europe.

ANTI-JEWISH LEGISLATION   The more than 2,000 anti-Jewish measures put into effect in GERMANY under Nazi rule.

A park bench in Germany marked "for Jews only"

When the NAZI PARTY was formed in 1920, its party platform included four anti-Jewish goals: Jews should not be citizens, and should be given the legal status of foreigners; Jews should not be public officials; Jews should be forbidden to immigrate to Germany; and Jewish owners or editors of German newspapers should

be removed from their positions. These declarations were similar to the platforms of other antisemitic groups active at that time.

The Nazis rose to national power in Germany in January 1933. During their rule, which lasted from 1933–1945, three separate groups of anti-Jewish legislation were enacted. The first began in March–April 1933, peaking with the Law for the Restoration of the Professional Civil Service. This law legalized firing "non-Aryan" government employees. It also acted as a precedent for the exclusion of Jews from other jobs. Most "non-Aryan" students were barred from attending German schools and "non-Aryans" were forbidden to take final state exams for many occupations. This last clause was also adopted by private firms, societies, and clubs. Another set of laws discriminated against the Jewish religion. By 1935, Jewish life had been severely restricted in Germany.

The second wave of anti-Jewish legislation began in September 1935, with the passage of two laws by the German parliament, termed the NUREMBERG LAWS. According to the first law, Jews were stripped of their citizenship and were denied the right to vote. Within a few months 13 additional decrees were attached to this law. The second law, the Law for the Protection of German Blood and German Honor, prohibited marriage and sexual contact between Germans and Jews. This legislation led the Germans to clearly define who was an "Aryan," Jew, or part-Jew (and to what degree; see also MISCHLINGE).

The third group of anti-Jewish laws restricted Jews from the German economy. The Germans began issuing this legislation as early as 1936 and 1937, but timed most severe measures to coincide with the KRISTALLNACHT pogrom of November 1938. The government made it legal to confiscate Jewish property through ARYANIZATION. On November 9, 1938 Reinhard HEYDRICH became the chief of the Central Office for Jewish Emigration (ZENTRALSTELLE FUER JUEDISCHE AUSWANDERUNG). The creation of this office empowered the SS to make all decisions regarding the Jews and their fate.

WORLD WAR II broke out in September 1939. At that time, the Germans expanded all existing anti-Jewish measures. Later, in September 1941, the Jews were forced to wear the Jewish badge any time they went out in public (see also BADGE, JEWISH), and by October 23 of that year Jewish emigration from Germany was strictly forbidden. On December 12, 1941 HITLER told a gathering of his intimates that the murder of the Jews, which had begun in the east, would be extended to German Jews as well.

Within the countries that allied themselves with Germany and those that were invaded and occupied by Germany, anti-Jewish laws were enacted to different degrees based on the type of occupation regime established by the Germans, how much pressure Germany put on the country, how antisemitic the country's government was to begin with, or how successfully the country could convince Germany to leave it alone to make its own rules. Racial laws were enacted at lightning speed in AUSTRIA, the Protectorate of Bohemia and Moravia (see also BOHEMIA AND MORAVIA, PROTECTORATE OF), and POLAND. In Germany's satellite states or in countries defeated by the German army, Jews were generally excluded from economic activities, and laws were made which defined exactly who was to be considered a Jew. Only in DENMARK, where the government did not resist German occupation but insisted on protecting its Jews, were no anti-Jewish measures put into effect, until the attempt to deport the Jews in October 1943.

ANTISEMITISM

Hatred of Jews as a group or of "the Jew" as a concept. The term antisemitism was first coined in the late 1870s, and since then it has come to be used with reference to all types of Jew-hatred, both historical and modern. The word itself comes from the idea that Hebrew belongs to the Semitic language family, and thus Jews must be "Semites." Many other languages also belong to the Semitic language family, such as Arabic and Ethiopic, and by the same token other groups of people could also be called "Semites." However, there is no such thing as "semitism," and no other groups have ever been included in the hatred and prejudice denoted by antisemitism. The word itself is a good example of how, during the late nineteenth century, Jew haters pretended that their hatred had its basis in scholarly and scientific ideas.

Jew-hatred is not a modern phenomenon—it goes all the way back to ancient times. Traditional antisemitism is based on religious discrimination against Jews by Christians. Christian doctrine was ingrained with the idea that Jews were responsible for the death of Jesus, and thus deserved to be punished (this is known as the Deicide, or killing of god, Myth). Another concept that provoked hatred of Jews among Christians was the Supercession Myth, which claimed that Christianity

Burning Jews at the stake, a fifteenth century woodcut

had replaced Judaism, as the Jews had failed in their role as the chosen people of God—and thus deserved to be punished, specifically by the Christian world. Over the centuries various stereotypes about Jews came into being. Individual Jews were not judged based on their personal achievements or merits, but rather were seen on the whole as greedy, devilish, standoffish, lazy, money-grubbing, and over-sexed. At some points, Jews were even falsely accused of using the blood of Christian children as part of the Passover holiday ritual (known as the Blood Libel).

The nineteenth century gave the world the Enlightenment—a philosophical movement that based its ideas on reason rather than traditional, religious dogma, and was accompanied by social, humanitarian, and political progress. However, antisemitism did not disappear during the Enlightenment, it just changed

An antisemitic sign: "Attention, Jews," Germany, November 1938

forms. At that time Jews were awarded equal rights in many European countries, and many people expressed Jew-hatred in their questioning of whether Jews could ever be truly loyal to the newly emerging nation states. In addition, people who did not approve of the modernization and political changes being made accused the Jews of being behind the changes.

During the 1870s the new political antisemitism was joined by "racial" antisemitism. Based on the new ideas on evolution posited by the English naturalist Charles Darwin—who himself never meant them to leave the realm of science—Jew haters began saying that Jews were an inferior "race" on the evolutionary scale. Since their problem was physical, or genetic, it could never be changed, despite assimilation. Included in this new form of antisemitism was the idea that Jews were responsible for the world's troubles because of their race.

In GERMANY, this type of thinking found expression in a political, nationalist movement called the *voelkisch* movement. This group's representatives opposed the industrialization and secularism that accompany modernization, because they believed that industrialization and secularism would destroy traditional German culture. They blamed the Jews for undermining the Germans' traditional way of life, and stated that German Jews were not really part of the German people. At the end of the nineteenth century many antisemitic political parties sprung up in Germany, which were further revitalized after Germany's loss in World War I.

In FRANCE, antisemitism reared its ugly head in the 1890s during the Dreyfus Affair, in which a Jewish army officer was falsely accused of treason by Jew haters. In Russia, throughout the reign of the Czars, antisemitism was official government policy. Jewish movement was restricted to certain areas, and pogroms were encouraged by the ruling class. Only after the February Revolution in 1917 were Jews granted equal rights. Many Jews took part in the October Revolution, and this gave antisemites throughout Europe another excuse to hate Jews—because Jews were now associated with the hated Communists.

The NAZI PARTY, which was created in 1919 and came to national power in Germany in 1933, was one of the first political movements that was fundamentally based on racist antisemitism. The Nazis discriminated against the Jews from the very beginning of their regime, first by instituting racial laws that separated Jews from the rest of the society, and later by exterminating members of the "inferior" race. In the countries that collaborated with or were occupied by the Nazis, the local manifestations of antisemitism—whether traditional, political, or racial—helped determine the Jews' fate. Even in the countries that opposed HITLER and the Nazis, antisemitism still existed to some degree, and some experts believe that those antisemitic attitudes inhibited those nations from doing more to rescue Jews from the clutches of the Nazis.

After WORLD WAR II, when the West realized what had happened in Europe, antisemitism was greatly weakened. Many churches admitted their huge mistake in cultivating traditional Christian antisemitism (Pope John Paul II termed antisemitism a sin,) and some governments no longer allowed the enactment of antisemitic policies. However, antisemitism was revitalized in the Soviet Union just a few years after the war's end, when Joseph STALIN became paranoid about his country's Jews and began persecuting them.

In addition, over the years, antisemites (especially Muslims who opposed the existence of the State of Israel) began camouflaging their Jew-hatred in "antiZionism." The United Nations even showed its approval of such antisemitic sentiment in 1975 when it passed a resolution which stated that "Zionism is racism." This resolution was finally canceled in 1994. Holocaust denial and NEO-NAZISM are other ways of expressing antisemitism in the modern world, in that they seek to absolve Nazism of its crimes or to glorify Nazism and Jew-hatred as it existed in the past. (see also HOLOCAUST, DENIAL OF THE.)

ANTONESCU, ION (1882–1946), Leader of ROMANIA from 1940–1944. In 1937 Antonescu served as defense minister in the short-lived Goga-Cuza government. When GERMANY forced Romania to give large parts of its territory to the SOVIET UNION, HUNGARY, and BULGARIA in 1940, Antonescu was made prime minister. Along with Horia SIMA, the head of the antisemitic fascist IRON GUARD movement, Antonescu instituted the pro-German National Legionary Government. In January 1941 the Iron Guard revolted against Antonescu, who crushed the rebellion with HITLER'S help. From then on, Antonescu ruled Romania as a dictator.

Regarding his Jewish policy, Antonescu differentiated between the Jews living in pre-World War I Romania and southern TRANSYLVANIA, whom he considered to be real Romanians, and those living in BESSARABIA and southern BUKOVINA. He ordered the rural Jews of Bessarabia and Bukovina exterminated, and the ur-

Ion Antonescu

ban Jews imprisoned in GHETTOS and CONCENTRATION CAMPS. In the summer of 1941 he exiled 150,000 Bessarabian and Bukovinan Jews to TRANSNISTRIA, where many died or were murdered. In the rest of Romania, the Jews were concentrated in urban centers and their property was confiscated. However, Antonescu refused to surrender them to the Nazis.

Antonescu's government toppled in August 1944 when Romania broke its ties with Germany. He was executed as a war criminal in June 1946.

ANTONESCU, MIHAI (1907–1946), Deputy premier and foreign minister in the government of Romanian leader Ion ANTONESCU. Mihai Antonescu enforced the persecution of Romanian Jewry, including the extermination and DEPORTATION to TRANSNISTRIA of the Jews of BESSARABIA and BUKOVINA.

ANTWERP City in northern BELGIUM. On the eve of the German invasion of Belgium in May 1940, about 50,000 Jews lived in Antwerp. Of those, only 20 percent held Belgian citizenship; the rest were recent immigrants from Eastern Europe and GERMANY. Soon after the occupation, about 20,000 of Antwerp's Jews fled the country.

For the first few months of the occupation, daily life continued as usual. One of Antwerp's economic mainstays was the diamond industry, in which Jews were very involved. The industry was reactivated during the first part of the occupation. However, things began to change for the worse in December 1940. Based on a German decree that foreigners could be removed from certain areas of Belgium, the German military administration began expelling Jews from Antwerp who had immigrated to Belgium after 1938. Ultimately, a total of 3,334 Jews were exiled from Antwerp in this way.

On April 10, 1941 a pogrom broke out in Antwerp's Jewish quarter. The rioters were members of right-wing movements who had been spurred on by the local German authorities. They attacked two synagogues and a rabbi's home, and were not restrained by the fire department or police.

That summer, the German military administration launched an ARYANIZATION drive. During 1942, four transports of Jews were sent to northern FRANCE and from there to Nazi camps. In August of that year, the first mass arrest of Jews took place: first, Romanian citizens were taken, and soon others were rounded up. In September 1942, Jews were arrested on the streets, and only those who could prove that they held Belgian citizenship were let go. By September 1943, the Nazis began arresting and deporting Belgian nationals.

The Jews of Antwerp proactively tried to save themselves and others from the Germans. Zionist YOUTH MOVEMENTS became very active during the occupation; in 1942–1943 they helped smuggle members into SWITZERLAND and SPAIN. More than 3,000 Jews hid in

Antwerp Jews loaded on trucks for deportation

the Antwerp area during the war, including about 1,000 Dutch Jews. Many Antwerp Jews, including members of the Belgian resistance, found hiding places for Jewish children and adults. Antwerp was liberated on September 4, 1944.

ARENDT CONTROVERSY   Public debate incited by the 1963 book *Eichmann in Jerusalem,* written by philosopher and political scientist, Hannah Arendt. Arendt had been sent by *The New Yorker* magazine to cover the 1961 trial of Nazi leader Adolf EICHMANN in Jerusalem. Her subsequent report dealt with the Nazis' attempt to annihilate European Jewry, Eichmann's part in it, and the trial itself.

What provoked public controversy was Arendt's assessment of Eichmann's motivations and behavior on one hand, and her depiction of Jewish behavior during the HOLOCAUST on the other. Arendt looked at Eichmann within the context of Nazi GERMANY, a society that had accepted evil behavior as a value. She saw his actions as a totally normal result of that society, and Eichmann as an ordinary bureaucrat who exemplified the "banality of evil." At the same time, Arendt denounced Jewish communities all over Europe for their behavior: she claimed that European Jews and their leaders were morally irresponsible in their protection of certain elements of their society and their willingness to forfeit other elements.

Arendt's work was alternately condemned and praised. A main topic of debate was the boundaries of moral judgement with regard to the persecutors and the victims. The controversy provides an interesting reflection of the public perception of the Holocaust during the early 1960s, and it was the jumping-off point for a large body of research about the nature of Jewish response and Nazi evil.

ARIERPARAGRAPH   see ARYAN PARAGRAPH.

ARISIERUNG   see ARYANIZATION.

ARMEE JUIVE   see JEWISH ARMY, FRANCE.

ARMIA KRAJOWA   see HOME ARMY.

ARROW CROSS PARTY   (in Hungarian, *Nylas*), Hungarian fascist party and movement established in 1937 by Ferenc SZALASI. The Arrow Cross ideology included Hungarian nationalism, the elevation of

Arrow Cross propaganda—"we will win"

agriculture as a value, anti-capitalism, anti-Communism, and militant ANTISEMITISM.

In the 1939 Hungarian national election the Arrow Cross Party won more than 25 percent of the vote. Subsequently it became HUNGARY'S most important opposition party. The party's foreign policy was faithfully pro-Nazi; despite this, it was not included in Hungary's pro-Nazi government, even after GERMANY occupied Hungary in March 1944. However, in October of that year, government leader Miklos HORTHY declared that Hungary would no longer be a partner of Germany. The German authorities promptly dismissed him and set up a new government led by Szalasi.

Under the Arrow Cross, Hungarian Jews were terrorized: DEPORTATIONS were renewed and nearly 80,000 Jews were expelled from Hungary in a DEATH MARCH to the Austrian border. Many died on the way. At the same time, thousands of Jews were murdered in BUDAPEST.

The Arrow Cross government was dissolved when the Soviet army liberated Budapest in January 1945.

Many Arrow Cross leaders were put on trial as war criminals, while most of the party's regular members resumed normal civilian life.

ART OF THE HOLOCAUST   The first reactions through painting and sculpture to the Nazi persecution of Jews were produced soon after Adolf HITLER rose to power in the early 1930s. Artists continued to express their feelings about the HOLOCAUST throughout the Holocaust period, and still do so today. Holocaust art can be classified by the type of artist, whether camp inmate, SURVIVOR, liberator, or nonparticipant; the artist's goal in creating his work, ranging from eyewitness testimony to the memorializing of the victims or the condemnation of the atrocities perpetrated by the Nazis; and the artist's style, such as realist, surrealist, abstract, or expressionist.

One of the most important types of Holocaust art is that which was created during the Holocaust itself by prisoners in the camps and GHETTOS. These artists risked their lives to produce art in the most insufferable of conditions. Some were forced by the Germans to create "official art." However, most ghetto and camp artists produced their art in secret, in defiance of the Nazis, in order to achieve two main goals. The first goal was to create an eyewitness report of the horrors going on all around them, in direct opposition to the Nazi desire to keep their murderous activities hidden from the rest of the world. The second was to resist the Nazis' systematic efforts to dehumanize the Jews: the prisoner artists struggled to maintain their sense of self through art in the face of Nazi dehumanization, and their art served to provide them with a reason to live.

The inmates who created art from within the confines of ghettos and camps almost always dealt with the Holocaust as a theme. After the war, some survivor-artists continued to depict their Holocaust experiences in art, either as a type of therapy or as a manifestation of their need to memorialize those who did not survive. Others, however, tried to put the past behind them and move on to different artistic subjects. Some of those survivors later returned to Holocaust topics in their work, sometimes as a result of events that reminded them of the past, such as the EICHMANN TRIAL, the wars in Israel, or genocidal massacres similar to the Holocaust.

A different type of eyewitness also portrayed the Holocaust in art. This was the liberator, who came into the camps to free the surviving prisoners, and found an

Charcoal drawing by W. Simek,
"Never say you are travelling your last road"

unimaginable state of being: huge piles of dead bodies, prisoners still alive but on the brink of death, filth, and degradation. Some liberators artistically portrayed the camps in an objective manner, showing just what they saw with their own eyes. Others created art based on interviews with the surviving inmates, or based on their subjective feelings of revulsion and repulsion. Still others took photographs at the newly liberated camps. Their photos were published far and wide, in magazines and newsreels, allowing people in even the remotest areas to become eyewitnesses to the Holocaust.

Another type of artist to represent the Holocaust in his work is the Jewish artist who did not himself experience the Holocaust. Some of these artists had initially left all things Jewish behind, but in the wake of the Holocaust returned openly to Judaism and Jewish themes in their work, such as biblical motifs, scenes of the European *shtetl*, or the Jew at prayer. Others reclaimed their Jewish identity not by utilizing tradi-

Drawing by Hirsh Szylis, "Hauling Bread in the Lodz Ghetto," 1942

tional Jewish motifs, but by dealing with the Holocaust in their art as an expression of their Judaism. This exhibits the growing phenomenon—not only among artists, but among many Jews—of the Holocaust as the defining aspect of their Jewish identity.

The children of Holocaust survivors constitute another group of artists who did not experience the Holocaust but are deeply affected by it. Some children of survivors use their art to try to put themselves in their parents' shoes and imagine how they would have reacted to life and death in the camps (see also SURVIVORS, SECOND GENERATION OF). Some young German artists have also started using their art to deal with and heal their country's painful past.

Common motifs, or themes, run through all categories of Holocaust art. The photographs taken by the liberators allowed the world to see, up close and personaly, the decomposing piles of corpses lying around the camps and the sickly, starving survivors herded together behind ominous-looking barbed wire fences. Thus, these most commonly known Holocaust images of corpses, survivors, and barbed wire are used quite often throughout Holocaust-related art. These images are so often associated with the Holocaust that they are sometimes used to depict totally different subjects, which the artist means to be understood through an analogy to the Holocaust. For instance, one Soviet Jewish artist used the image of barbed wire wrapped around a Soviet Jew to portray the idea that his imprisonment in Russia is like a Nazi CONCENTRATION CAMP. Another potent symbol of the Holocaust is the crematorium chimney. This symbol is so well known that even when used alone in art, without the surrounding context of a crematorium or concentration camp, the noxious aura of the Holocaust is implicitly understood.

Another group of themes found in Holocaust art is employed in an attempt to deal with the moral questions associated with the subject. These themes are the victims, the perpetrators, and resistance to the Nazis. The victim is often portrayed through various biblical symbols, such as the sacrifice of Isaac, or as Job, who questions God in a world full of suffering. Sometimes the victims are even depicted as the crucified Jewish Jesus. Resistance to Nazism often employs biblical images, as well, such as David slaying a Nazi Goliath, or mythical images, such as Prometheus slaying the vulture. The portrayal of the Nazis is more difficult. On one hand, a realistic depiction can never effectively express their evil. On the other hand, a surrealist portrayal of the Nazis as monsters or demons does not do justice to the fact that those who carried out the Holocaust were human beings.

ARYANIZATION (*Arisierung*), the transfer of Jewish-owned businesses to German ownership throughout GERMANY and German-occupied countries. The Aryanization process included two stages: from 1933–1938 the Jews were gradually removed from German economic life, termed by the Nazis as "voluntary" exclusion; after 1938, Jewish businesses and property were forcibly confiscated by the Nazis.

Before the Nazis rose to power in January 1933, Jews owned 100,000 businesses in Germany, including stores, factories, publishing houses, newspapers, and private professional practices. Soon after taking over the German government, the Nazis imposed unofficial economic boycotts on the Jews (see also BOYCOTT, ANTI-JEWISH). They first targeted stores and then the professions. The Nazis tried to intimidate Jews into selling their businesses by publishing advertisements that denounced Germans who bought from Jews. Uniformed guards were posted outside Jewish businesses to harass customers, and public institutions were forbidden to patronize them. Thus, Jewish businesses either went under, or were forced into being sold for a fraction of their value. Of the 50,000 Jewish-owned stores that existed in 1933, only 9,000 remained in 1938.

Aryanization was organized by government economic counselors within each district in order to ensure that the best businesses were given to longstanding NAZI

Removing a Jewish store name to be replaced by a German name (Photo: Stadtarchive Hof, Germany)

PARTY members. In some cases, Jewish business owners were jailed until they agreed to give up their ownership; in others, the government just confiscated the businesses. After the 1936 Olympics, Aryanization was intensified. During the summer of 1938 Jewish professionals were banned from their jobs.

After the KRISTALLNACHT pogrom of November 1938, the Nazis legalized forced Aryanization—allowing the forcible confiscation of Jewish property. The German Jewish community had to pay a fine of one billion reichsmarks for the damage inflicted upon them during the pogrom. Jewish businesses not yet sold were put under government trusteeship, and Jews were forced to register all their property with the Nazis. Their money was put into blocked accounts from which they could only draw small amounts each month. Jews who emigrated had to leave most of their valuables behind. Those Jews deported to THERESIENSTADT had to sign away their property. Eventually, all those monies were confiscated by the Nazis and used to finance the DEPORTATION of the Jews.

ARYAN PARAGRAPH (*Arierparagraph*), a type of regulation that blocked "non-Aryans" (Jews) from becoming members in German economic establishments, political parties, social clubs, volunteer organizations, student groups, sports groups, and other institutions. Regulations of this kind made their first appearance in GERMANY during the nineteenth century. They were included in the constitutions of racist and nationalist student associations, political groups, and social organizations, and were used to exclude Jews from their ranks.

After the Nazi rise to national power in January 1933, the Aryan Paragraph was used as a legal stepping-stone to increased persecution. In April 1933 it was included in a group of laws that permitted the removal of Jews from various aspects of German society, such as the government, professional groups, universities, and other places of academic learning. When the racial NUREMBERG LAWS were passed in September 1935, the Aryan Paragraph became a basic fundamental of German law. (see also ANTI-JEWISH LEGISLATION.)

ASSCHER, ABRAHAM (1880–1950), Dutch Jewish public figure and spokesman for Dutch Jewry.

Asscher owned Amsterdam's most prestigious diamond company, was a member of the Amsterdam Chamber of Commerce, and a leader of the Liberal party. He also chaired the Amsterdam Jewish Community Council and the Union of Ashkenazic Communities.

Asscher responded to the Nazis' anti-Jewish activities by forming the Committee for Special Jewish Affairs. When the Germans occupied the NETHERLANDS, they used Asscher as their contact to the Jewish community. They asked him to form a Jewish Council, which he did, and even did him certain favors despite his consistent criticism of the Nazi regime (many of his relatives and friends were not deported to POLAND). Asscher wanted to protest the extermination of Europe's Jews, but his close friend, David COHEN, convinced him to keep quiet.

Despite his cooperation, Asscher was sent to BERGEN-BELSEN in September 1943. He survived the war and returned to Holland, where he was arrested for collaboration. He was exonerated by the Dutch, but the Jewish community found him guilty and ostracized him. Asscher then broke off all ties with the Jewish community and was even buried in a non-Jewish cemetery.

ASSOCIATION DES JUIFS EN BELGIQUE see ASSOCIATION OF JEWS IN BELGIUM.

ASSOCIATION OF JEWS IN BELGIUM (in French, *Association des Juifs en Belgique*, AJB; in Flemish, *Jodenvereeiniguing van Belgie*), JUDENRAT-like organization forced upon the Jews of BELGIUM by the Nazis during WORLD WAR II.

The Germans invaded Belgium in May 1940. That fall, the Jews of Belgium set up their own coordinating committee. However, on November 25, the Security Police ordered the creation of the AJB. Officially, the association was supposed to take care of the needs of the Jewish community. In reality, however, its main function was to register the country's Jews for FORCED LABOR and DEPORTATIONS to EXTERMINATION CAMPS.

In December 1941 an executive board was appointed, with the chief rabbi of Belgium, Rabbi Salomon Ullmann, as its chairman. Four local committees worked under the executive board, in BRUSSELS, ANTWERP, Charleroi, and Liege—the cities with the largest Jewish communities.

From the beginning, the AJB was not liked, trusted, or respected by Belgian Jewry. In May 1942 the Germans ordered the Jews to wear the Jewish badge (see also BADGE, JEWISH). In July the association's executive director, Maurice Benedictus, was made responsible to help the Germans deport the Jews. That summer, the AJB listed many new people as its employees in order to help them avoid being sent to do forced labor in FRANCE. This helped improve the association's reputation.

In August 1943 the first five transports left Belgium for AUSCHWITZ. The AJB's standing quickly deteriorated. Rabbi Ullmann left his job as chairman in early September, and the Charleroi local association committee decided to dissolve itself. The weakened association mainly dealt with welfare and educational work. After many Belgian Jews were arrested in September, the AJB deteriorated even further. Most of the Jews left in Belgium either worked for the association or lived in one of its institutions. At that point, many of the AJB's employees worked for the underground.

In August 1944 the AJB decided to stop its operations, and hid 600 orphans who had been living under its care. They were saved when Allied forces entered Brussels in early September.

ATHENS   Capital of Greece. Italian troops occupied Athens in April 1941; at that time, 3,500 Jews lived in the city. The Italian occupying authorities did not enact any anti-Jewish measures. They were generally friendly to the Jews, and spurned attempts made by the GESTAPO to put anti-Jewish laws into effect. However, the Italians could not stop the *Gestapo* from arresting Jewish leaders and plundering libraries and archives. During the rule of the Italians, many Jews from the German- and Bulgarian-occupied regions of Greece fled to Athens; the city's Jewish population grew to 8,000–10,000.

The Allies invaded ITALY in September 1943; five days later the German army occupied Athens. SS officer Dieter WISLICENY soon arrived and set up a JUDENRAT. The Jews were made to register and much Jewish property was confiscated. The first transport of Greek Jews to AUSCHWITZ left Athens on April 2, 1944. Another transport arrived at the camp on June 6.

Many well-known Greeks objected to the Germans' treatment of the Jews, including Archbishop Damaskinos. As a result, the church protected hundreds of children, the police gave out false identity papers, and citizens hid Jews and helped them escape. In general, the Greek tendency was to aid its Jewish population.

ATLAS, YEHESKEL   (1913–1942), Doctor and PARTISAN commander. Born near WARSAW, Atlas studied medicine in both FRANCE and ITALY. When WORLD WAR II

broke out in September 1939, Atlas was in Kozlovshchizna (in the Novogrudok district), which was located in Soviet-occupied eastern POLAND. The Germans attacked the SOVIET UNION and Soviet-occupied territories in June 1941; they massacred hundreds of thousands of Jews and then set up GHETTOS for those who survived that first round of extermination. Atlas's parents and sister died in the ghetto in Kozlovshchizna in November 1941. Atlas stayed in the area, serving as a doctor for the nearby farmers and for the Soviet troops who had escaped the Germans and survived in the forest.

When the nearby Derechin Ghetto was liquidated in July 1942, Atlas formed a Jewish partisan company with 120 of the ghetto's survivors. The company, headed by Atlas, was put under the authority of a Soviet partisan commander named Bulat who led a battalion that was active in the Lipiczany Forest. On August 10, 1942 Atlas and his company successfully attacked German policemen in Derechin; they caught and killed 44. Despite the fact that the Soviet authorities wanted Atlas to serve as the partisans' doctor, the partisan leadership saw how talented he was as a fighter, and chose to continue using him as a combat commander instead.

Atlas continued to impress with his bold achievements: he and his men blew up a German train, burned down a bridge, and initiated an attack on Kozlovshchizna in which more than 30 Germans were killed. They also participated in a battle on October 10, 1942, in which the partisans killed 127 Germans, captured 75, and took a large amount of war materials, which they desperately needed. Atlas also provided medical help for the family camp attached to his company that took in refugees from ghettos nearby.

On December 5, 1942 Atlas was injured in a battle that took place in Wielka Wola. He gave over the command of his company to Eliyahu Lipshowitz, and then died from his wounds. (see also FAMILY CAMPS IN THE FORESTS.)

AUERSWALD, HEINZ   (b. 1908), German governor of the WARSAW Ghetto from March 1941 to November 1942. Auerswald enlisted in the SS in mid-1933, but only joined the NAZI PARTY in the late 1930s. He fulfilled his army service by working for the regular German police.

After WORLD WAR II broke out, Auerswald was sent to Warsaw with the police. He was soon relocated to the

German civil administration that was set up to run the city, and was put in charge of ethnic German (VOLKSDEUTSCHE) affairs. In March 1941 he was given the job of running the Warsaw GHETTO. In this post Auerswald was responsible for a population of over 400,000 Jews. His main goal was to turn the ghetto into an efficient and productive moneymaker for the German war economy by taking advantage of Jewish slave labor. In addition, he wanted to stop the spread of epidemics, and to that end he made the ghetto boundaries even smaller and imposed the death penalty on any Jew found outside the ghetto (who, presumably, could be carrying infectious diseases).

After the mass DEPORTATIONS from the ghetto in the summer of 1942, Auerswald was appointed district administrator in the Ostrow area. In January 1943 he was drafted into the army. He was never convicted of war crimes.

AUSCHWITZ (in Polish, Oswiecim), largest Nazi concentration and EXTERMINATION CAMP, located in the Polish town of Oswiecim, 37 miles west of CRACOW. One-sixth of all Jews murdered by the Nazis were gassed at Auschwitz.

In April 1940 SS chief Heinrich HIMMLER ordered the establishment of a new CONCENTRATION CAMP in Oswiecim, a town situated within the part of POLAND that was annexed to GERMANY at the beginning of WORLD WAR II. The first Polish political prisoners arrived in Auschwitz in June 1940. By March 1941 there were 10,900 prisoners, still mostly Polish. Auschwitz soon became known as the most brutal of the Nazi concentration camps.

In March 1941 Himmler ordered that a second, much larger section of the camp be built 1.9 miles from the original camp. This site was to be used as an extermination camp. It was named Birkenau, or Ausch-

The rail lines entering Birkenau (Auschwitz II)

witz II. Eventually, Birkenau held the most prisoners in the Auschwitz complex, including Jews, Poles, Germans, and GYPSIES. It also had the worst, most inhuman conditions—and contained the complex's GAS CHAMBERS and crematoria.

A third section, Auschwitz III, was constructed in nearby Monowitz, and consisted of a FORCED LABOR camp called Buna-Monowitz and 45 other forced labor sub-camps. The name Buna was based on the Buna synthetic rubber factory on the site, owned by I.G. FARBEN, Germany's largest chemical company. The mainly Jewish inmates who worked at that factory and others owned by German firms were pushed to the point of total exhaustion, at which time they were replaced by new laborers.

Auschwitz was first run by camp commandant Rudolf HOESS, and was guarded by a cruel regiment of the SS's DEATH'S HEAD UNITS. The staff was assisted by several privileged prisoners who were given better food, better conditions, and an opportunity to survive if they agreed to enforce the brutal order of the camp.

Auschwitz I and II were surrounded by electrically-charged four-meter high barbed wire fences, which were guarded by SS men armed with machine guns and rifles. The two camps were further closed in by a series of guard posts located two-thirds of a mile beyond the fences.

In March 1942 trains carrying Jews began arriving daily. Sometimes several trains would arrive on the same day, each carrying one thousand or more victims coming from the GHETTOS of Eastern Europe, as well as from Western and Southern European countries. During 1942 transports arrived from Poland, SLOVAKIA, the NETHERLANDS, BELGIUM, YUGOSLAVIA, and THERESIENSTADT. Jews continued to arrive throughout 1943, as did Gypsies. Hungarian Jews were brought to Auschwitz in 1944, as were Jews from the last Polish ghettos to be liquidated.

By August 1944 there were 105,168 prisoners in Auschwitz. Another 50,000 Jewish prisoners lived in Auschwitz's satellite camps. The camp's population constantly grew, in spite of the high mortality rate caused by exterminations, starvation, hard labor, and contagious diseases.

When Jews arrived at the platform in Birkenau, they were thrown out of their train cars without their belongings and forced to make two lines, men and women separately. SS officers, including the infamous Dr. Josef MENGELE, would conduct selections among these

Prisoners after liberation in Auschwitz

lines, sending most victims to one side, condemning them to death in the gas chambers (see also SELEKTION). A minority was sent to the other side, destined for forced labor. Those who were sent to their deaths were killed that same day and their corpses were burnt in the crematoria. Those not sent to the gas chambers were taken to "quarantine," where their hair was shaved, they were given striped prison uniforms, and were registered as prisoners. Their registration numbers were tattooed on their left arms. Most prisoners were then sent to perform forced labor in Auschwitz I, III, sub-camps, or other concentration camps, where their life expectancy usually was a few months. Prisoners who stayed in quarantine had a life expectancy of a few weeks.

The prisoners' camp routine consisted of many duties to perform. The daily schedule included waking at dawn, straightening one's sleep area, morning roll call, the trip to work, long hours of hard labor, standing in line for a pitiful meal, the return to camp, block inspection, and evening roll call. During roll call, prisoners were made to stand completely motionless and quiet for hours, in the thinnest of clothing, no matter what the weather. Whoever fell or even stumbled was sent to die. Each prisoner, in his own way, had to focus all his energy on just getting through the day's tortures.

The gas chambers in the Auschwitz complex constituted the largest and most efficient extermination method used by the Nazis. Four chambers were in use at Birkenau, each with the potential to kill 6,000 people every day. They were built to look like shower rooms in order to confuse the victims: new arrivals at Birkenau were told that they were being sent to work, but first needed to shower and be disinfected. They would be led into the shower-like chambers, where they were quickly gassed to death with the highly poisonous ZYKLON B gas.

Some prisoners at Auschwitz, including twins and dwarfs, were used as the subjects of torturous MEDICAL EXPERIMENTS. They were tested for endurance under terrible conditions such as heat and cold, or sterilized.

Despite the horrible conditions, prisoners in Auschwitz managed to resist the Nazis, including some instances of escape and armed resistance. In October 1944, members of the SONDERKOMMANDO, who worked in the crematoria, succeeded in killing several SS men and destroying one gas chamber. All of the rebels died, leaving behind diaries that provided authentic documentation of the atrocities committed at Auschwitz.

By January 1945 Soviet troops were advancing towards Auschwitz. The Nazis, desperate to withdraw, sent most of the 58,000 remaining prisoners on a DEATH MARCH. Most prisoners were killed en route to Germany. The Soviet army liberated Auschwitz on January 27; soldiers found just 7,650 barely living prisoners throughout the entire camp complex. In all, some one million Jews had been murdered there.

AUSCHWITZ, BOMBING OF   In the spring and early summer of 1944, some 435,000 Hungarian Jews were deported to AUSCHWITZ. By that time, the Allied governments knew a lot about the mass annihilation going on at Auschwitz, the largest of the Nazi EXTERMINATION CAMPS. In fact, in mid-April, two men had escaped Auschwitz and brought specific information about the camp, including detailed maps, to the leaders of the WORKING GROUP, a Jewish rescue organization in SLOVAKIA (see also AUSCHWITZ PROTOCOLS). In the wake of the Hungarian DEPORTATIONS, those Jewish leaders and others begged the Allies to

bomb the camp, including the GAS CHAMBERS and the railroad tracks leading up to it, but their requests were not fulfilled.

The first of the requests made to the UNITED STATES War Department was turned down in June 1944. War Department officials claimed that they would not allow the bombing of Auschwitz because it could only be done by using air support that was needed elsewhere for the war effort. Their decision, however, was not based on war strategies or analyses. The department never thoroughly investigated the possibility of bombing the camp, and never even consulted their air force commanders based in ITALY, who were in the best possible position to strike. Instead, when the War Department authorities were first asked to consider bombing Auschwitz, they fell back on the secret policy their department had established months before: a policy of noninvolvement in rescue actions. This policy was cre-

The Holocaust Revisited

Photo 1: The Auschwitz-Birkenau Complex, 26 June 1944

Aerial photograph of the Auschwitz complex, taken by the Americans in summer 1944

ated in January 1944, after President ROOSEVELT had instituted the WAR REFUGEE BOARD. At the time, the president charged the US State, Treasury, and War departments with doing their utmost to further the rescue efforts. War Department officials feared this meant that military forces necessary elsewhere in the war would be taken away for the rescue effort. At a crucial point in the pursuit of victory, the War Department developed a blanket policy of noninvolvement, in direct defiance of the president's order—and when requests were made to bomb, the War Department kept rejecting them with the statement that it would "divert military power from essential war operations."

In GREAT BRITAIN, Prime Minister Winston CHURCHILL supported a proposal made by the Jewish Agency to bomb Auschwitz and the railroad tracks leading up to it. However, the British Air Ministry and the Foreign Office kept stalling in order to avoid bombing operations. The British government's official reply to the Jewish Agency employed the phrase that "technical difficulties" made carrying out the operations impossible, meaning perhaps that Auschwitz was not in the range of Allied bombers.

In fact, by mid-1944, the Allied forces controlled European skies and definitely had the range to bomb Auschwitz and its railroad lines. The United States Air Force could even have carried out the operation in conjunction with other war operations. The Auschwitz complex, which included a major industrial zone and armaments factories, was itself a military target. A specific military goal was to destroy the synthetic oil refinery in Auschwitz. The Germans had seven other such plants in the area, all within 45 miles of Auschwitz. From July–November 1944, more than 2,800 American planes bombed the oil factories—on their way, flying right over or along the railways leading up to Auschwitz. On August 20 and September 13, American bombers hit the industrial zone at Auschwitz itself, just five miles from the camp's four gas chambers. The killing installations at Birkenau, however, were never bombed. Post-war experts on bombing disagree as to how feasible it would have been to bomb only the gas chambers. Some also point to fears at the time that such a raid would have been accompanied by the killing of many people. Real and imagined obstacles not withstanding, the fact that Auschwitz was not bombed to save Jewish lives shows that the Allies' desire to help Jews was not nearly as strong as the Nazis' desire to murder them.

AUSCHWITZ PROTOCOLS
Two reports about the mass murders taking place at AUSCHWITZ based on information provided by four escapees from the camp in 1944.

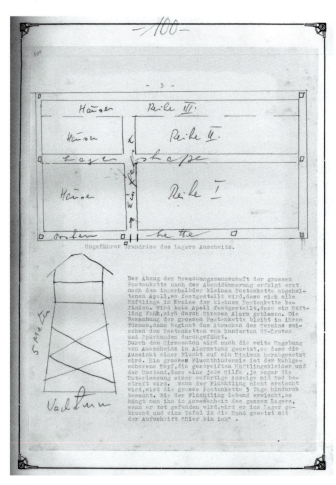

First page of the report known as the "Auschwitz Protocols"

In April 1944 two Slovak Jews, Rudolf Vrba (originally Walter Rosenberg) and Alfred Wetzler, successfully escaped the infamous EXTERMINATION CAMP at Auschwitz with the help of the camp's underground. They made their way to SLOVAKIA, where they contacted Erwin Steiner, a member of the Jewish Council in Zilina. They met at Steiner's home, where they gave detailed testimony about the goings-on at Auschwitz, including how the camp worked, the number of Jews who had already been killed, and the Nazis' plans to deport and exterminate the 800,000 Jews of HUNGARY and 3,000 Czech Jews, who had been transferred to Auschwitz six months earlier. Steiner wrote a 30 page report based on the testimony, and sent it to Rabbi Michael Dov WEISSMANDEL, a leader of the Slovak WORKING GROUP in BRATISLAVA.

In mid-May the Working Group managed to send a message with a shortened version of the report to the representative of the Orthodox VA'AD HA-HATSALA (Rescue Committee) in SWITZERLAND. The message also contained a plea to the Allies to help save Hungarian Jewry—the only major community that had not yet been annihilated—and to bomb Auschwitz and the railroad tracks leading up to it.

Rezso KASZTNER of the RELIEF AND RESCUE COMMITTEE OF BUDAPEST also received a copy of Steiner's report. However, he did not publicize it, perhaps because he did not want to jeopardize the rescue negotiations between Hungarian Jewish leaders and Nazi representatives. Copies were also forwarded to the Jewish Council of Hungary, the Regent of Hungary, Miklos HORTHY, and the Vatican.

In late May two more Jews, Czeslaw Mordowicz and Arnost Rosin, also escaped Auschwitz and reached Slovakia. New information about Auschwitz that they provided was added to the initial report. The expanded protocols were then sent through various channels to the West. The news reached the US State Department on June 16, while the BBC broadcast parts of the report on June 18. Finally, the free world knew the truth about Auschwitz.

AUSTRALIA, JEWISH REFUGEES IN

After the Nazis rose to power in 1933, Australia was considered to be an appropriate safe haven for Jewish REFUGEES trying to escape persecution in Europe. However, Australia had an immigration policy that was designed to keep out immigrants of non-British origin. Only "aliens" who had 500 pounds sterling for landing money or relatives of aliens already living in Australia were allowed to enter the country.

In 1937 the Australian government showed an interest in Jewish refugees, and encouraged the establishment of the Australian Jewish Welfare Society to organize aid for Jewish refugees. Nonetheless, at the EVIAN CONFERENCE in June 1938, Australia's delegate refused to increase the country's immigration quotas. Five months later, the KRISTALLNACHT pogroms broke out all over GERMANY. The horrors of that one night of destruction convinced the Australian government to change its policy. It announced that over the next three years, it would accept 15,000 Jewish refugees. By the outbreak of WORLD WAR II in September 1939, more than 7,000 Jewish refugees had arrived in Australia.

In December 1942 the Allies, including Australia, issued a joint announcement about their recognition of the massacre of the Jews in POLAND. Soon, the United Jewish Emergency Committee was instituted in Sydney, while the United Jewish Overseas Relief Fund was founded in Melbourne. In 1943 all the Jewish communities in Australia presented a joint resolution to Prime Minister John Curtin, asking him to support Jewish immigration to both Australia and Palestine and to take part in international relief efforts for the SURVIVORS of Nazi horrors. However, the government responded negatively to these requests; most people were not aware of the true extent of Nazi atrocities, and thus were not empathetic to the cause. The lack of understanding in Australia is reflected in the label given to Jewish refugees from Europe: "enemy aliens." Some refugees were interned at camps. Even the Jewish community treated the refugees coldly; they encouraged the refugees to keep as low a profile as possible.

Altogether, 8,200 Jewish refugees reached Australia between 1933 and 1945; eventually, their status was changed to "friendly aliens."

AUSTRIA

Country in central Europe that gained independence in 1918 after the breakup of the Austro-Hungarian Empire.

On March 11, 1938 the German army marched into Austria and annexed the country to the German Reich. Most of the Austrian population happily accepted this move, which was termed the ANSCHLUSS, meaning annexation or union. Their enthusiasm for unification with the Reich was also manifested in rampant anti-Jewish rioting. Members of the Austrian NAZI PARTY quickly began the process of excluding the country's Jews from Austria's economy, culture, and social life.

By March 18 the authorities had closed down the offices of the Jewish community and Zionist organizations in VIENNA, and imprisoned their officers. During the first weeks after the *Anschluss,* Jews were fired from their jobs in theaters, community centers, public libraries, and universities. Throughout Austria, Jews were arrested and imprisoned. In fact, the situation was so miserable for the Jews that from February to March 1938, the number of Jewish suicides multiplied 20 times.

Soon, an office was established in Vienna to implement the confiscation of Jewish property. In late June Jews and all non-Jews married to Jews who worked in the private sector were fired from their jobs. The Germans' immediate goal was to "encourage" the Jews to leave the country. Senior SS officer Adolf EICHMANN was in charge of Jewish emigration from Austria. In August 1938 Eichmann established the Central Office for Jewish Emigration (ZENTRALSTELLE FUER JUEDISCHE AUSWANDERUNG) in the Rothschild palace, which the Nazis had seized from its owners.

During the KRISTALLNACHT pogrom of November 1938, Jews and Jewish businesses were attacked all over GERMANY and Austria. Many synagogues were desecrated and Jewish homes were vandalized. After *Kristallnacht,* Eichmann began detaining Austrian Jews in Nazi CONCENTRATION CAMPS in order to blackmail them for money and to convince them to leave the country. When this type of inmate was released, he was given a limited amount of time to get out of the country. If he was still in Austria at the end of his grace period, he was put back in jail. The pogrom also helped speed up the liquidation of Austria's Jewish communities. By May

1939, 27 of 33 Jewish community councils had been dissolved.

Before the war began, 126,445 Jews managed to escape Austria, leaving 58,000 Jews in the country. Of the remaining Jews, some 2,000 were able to emigrate by October 1941, when the Nazis halted all Jewish emigration from the Reich.

In October 1939, 1,584 Austrian Jews were deported to the Lublin district of POLAND, as part of a grand plan to concentrate all of Europe's Jews in one area of the GENERALGOUVERNEMENT (see also NISKO AND LUBLIN PLAN). In February and March 1941 some 5,000 Austrian Jews were deported to KIELCE in Poland; during 1942 they were exterminated in BELZEC and CHELMNO. In October 1941 the Nazis began deporting the Jews of Austria en mass. Thousands of Jews were sent to LODZ and GHETTOS in the Baltic region. After the WANNSEE CONFERENCE of January 1942, during which steps were taken to better coordinate the murder of Europe's Jews,

Jews forced to clean city streets in Vienna, 1938

DEPORTATIONS from Austria were sped up. Thousands were transported to RIGA, MINSK, and LUBLIN. During the second half of 1942 nearly 14,000 Jews were sent to the THERESIENSTADT concentration camp. The Jewish community of Vienna was liquidated in November 1942, leaving only 7,000 Jews in Austria—most of whom were married to non-Jews. All those strong enough to work were made to do FORCED LABOR. Small-scale deportations continued into 1943; by the end of 1944 only about 1,000 Jews remained in Vienna.

Altogether, including Austrian Jews who had fled to countries the Nazis later occupied, over 65,000 Austrian Jews died in the ghettos and concentration camps of Eastern Europe. After the war, Austria became the center for the BERIHA movement.

AUTONOMOUS REFUGEE AID COMMITTEE, ROMANIA
(*Comisia Autonoma de Ajutorare*), organization established in BUCHAREST, ROMANIA, after the unsuccessful IRON GUARD revolt and accompanying pogroms of January 1941. The committee was instituted by leaders of the Union of Jewish Communities, Zionists, businessmen, and women known for their aid activities, in order to amass funds and supplies for the pogrom victims.

After the Germans invaded the SOVIET UNION in mid-1941 and the Romanian authorities began deporting Jews to the region of TRANSNISTRIA, many new volunteers joined the committee. They provided aid to victims of other persecutions, including the IASI pogrom and the transfer of Jews from their small villages to large cities. They also supplied the Jews who had been drafted into FORCED LABOR battalions with money, food, tools, kitchen utensils, and medicine.

The Romanians launched the mass extermination of the Jews of BESSARABIA and BUKOVINA in the summer of 1941. The committee tried to send aid to the Jews there, to no avail. After the Union of Jewish Communities was dissolved in December 1941, the committee got permission to send aid to the Jews interned in Transnistria. When those Jews were allowed to come home in 1943, the committee helped organize their return.

AXIS (in German, *Achse*), the military, ideological, and political alliance of Nazi GERMANY and Fascist ITALY. Later the alliance grew to include Japan, and during WORLD WAR II, the term "Axis countries" came to refer to other countries allied with Germany such as HUNGARY, ROMANIA, SLOVAKIA, and BULGARIA.

When the Nazis first came to power in Germany in 1933, the Italian Fascists, who had risen to power in 1922, did not share HITLER'S political aspirations, despite many shared elements in their ideology. In fact, Fascist leader Benito MUSSOLINI was so concerned about Hitler's desire for territorial expansion that he made a pact with GREAT BRITAIN and FRANCE against Germany. However, when the League of Nations condemned Italy's invasion of Ethiopia in 1935, Mussolini broke off with the two countries and improved his relationship with Germany. The reconciliation was further boosted when both countries supported the same side in the Spanish Civil War. Mussolini first used the term "Rome-Berlin Axis" in 1936. In the beginning, although Italy and Germany both opposed democracy, Mussolini was not ready to adopt Hitler's racist and antisemitic views. Nonetheless, in 1938, after Germany had grown very powerful, Italy initiated anti-Jewish measures. Germany and Italy formally signed the military "Pact of Steel" in May 1939.

BABI YAR   Ravine in northwestern Kiev, the capital of the UKRAINE, where some 50,000 Jews were murdered in 1941.

The Germans captured Kiev on September 19, 1941. A week later, they decided to massacre the city's Jews. On September 28, the Jews were ordered to assemble the next morning for resettlement. They were marched to the ravine, and as they reached the site, were forced to surrender any valuables. Then they were made to take off their clothes, and move towards the edge of the ravine in groups of ten. As they reached the edge, they were shot by *Einsatzkommando 4a* and German and Ukrainian police. At the end of the day, the bodies were covered with a thin layer of dirt. After two days of shooting, 33,771 Jews were dead.

Over the next few months, thousands more were murdered at Babi Yar, including Jews, GYPSIES, and Soviet PRISONERS OF WAR. In all, about 100,000 people were killed there. Those who attempted to hide were turned over to the Germans by the Ukrainians. In July 1943 the Germans returned to destroy the evidence of mass murder as part of AKTION 1005.

A memorial to those who died there was finally erected at Babi Yar in 1974.

BACH-ZELEWSKI, ERICH VON DEM   (1899–1972), SS commander. Bach-Zelewski joined the NAZI PARTY in 1930 and the SS in 1931. After the Nazis came to power in GERMANY in January 1933, Bach-Zelewski rose quickly through the party ranks. In 1938 he became SS commander in Silesia. After WORLD WAR II broke out in September 1939, the Polish part of Silesia was annexed to his area of authority. Bach-Zelewski later was in charge of deporting tens of thousands of Jews from the region.

Germany invaded the SOVIET UNION in June 1941. At that point, Bach-Zelewski was named Higher SS and Police Leader in central Russia, and several months later became general of police. In this capacity he was responsible for the EINSATZGRUPPE B unit that massacred Jews in BELORUSSIA. In 1942 Heinrich HIMMLER made Bach-

Zelewski his representative in the fight against the PARTISANS and in 1943 Bach-Zelewski became the head of all anti-partisan forces in Eastern Europe. From August to October 1944 he led the troops that put down the WARSAW POLISH UPRISING. His troops were known for their brutality and the massacre of innocent civilians.

After the war, Bach-Zelewski served as a witness for the prosecution at various war crimes trials, including the NUREMBERG TRIALS. He himself was sentenced to several years in jail.

BACKA   Region in YUGOSLAVIA. Before Yugoslavia was invaded by GERMANY in 1941, there were 16,000 Jews in Backa, constituting 20 percent of the country's entire Jewish population.

In 1940, under pressure from the Nazis, the Yugoslav government began issuing anti-Jewish laws. The Jews of Backa protested the measures, and supported the new anti-Nazi regime that seized power in late March 1941. Most young Jewish men volunteered for the Yugoslav army to fight the Nazis, who invaded the country in April 1941. Dozens of Jewish soldiers were wounded, killed, or made PRISONERS OF WAR.

Germany quickly defeated Yugoslavia, and divided up the country amongst its allies. The Backa region was given to HUNGARY. Just as soon as the Hungarian authorities occupied Backa, they began inventing incidents which they used as excuses to murder Jews and Serbs. Other Jews were exiled from Backa or handed over to the Germans, while thousands of Jews were stripped of their citizenship and property. Jewish community and Zionist movement leaders were taken hostage by the authorities, and the various Jewish communities were forced to pay a war tax. By May 1941, males Jews were forced to do hard labor—during which many were tortured and beaten.

In July 1941 Hungary joined Germany in its war against the SOVIET UNION. At that point, the Hungarians in Backa intensified their attacks on Jews and Serbs. Many Jews responded by joining the Yugoslav PARTI-

SAN movement, led by TITO. By the end of 1941 all male Jews under the age of 60 were forcibly drafted into units of the HUNGARIAN LABOR SERVICE SYSTEM. In general, these units were linked to the Hungarian forces fighting the Soviets in the UKRAINE; the Jewish men were often treated deplorably and many died. Some of the men successfully fled to the Soviet side, where they created a Yugoslav unit within the Soviet army.

During the winter of 1941–1942, the Hungarian authorities in Backa used partisan activity as another excuse to massacre Jews and Serbs. Two special units were created to execute the massacre. During January 1942 some 5,000 men were slaughtered, more than half Jewish; six Jewish communities were completely wiped out; and thousands of Jews were subjected to the whims of Hungarian "selection commissions" which chose the way they were to die, either by hanging, shooting, or other awful techniques. Altogether, one-third of the entire Jewish population in Backa was destroyed. Only due to the intervention of moderates in the government did the massacre come to an end.

News of the massacre in Backa led to protests all over the world and in Hungary itself. The Hungarian premier was forced to admit that innocent people had been slaughtered needlessly, and that those responsible should pay. However, "those responsible" escaped Hungary for Germany, where they were given refuge, and when Germany occupied Hungary in 1944, they were returned to their homes and even helped deport Hungarian Jewry to EXTERMINATION CAMPS.

Those Backa Jews who survived the massacre found a slightly better situation during 1943. Many joined the partisans at that time, and Zionist leaders took the opportunity to step up rescue operations. Dozens of Backa Jews managed to escape to Palestine.

German troops invaded Hungary in March 1944. SS units and the Hungarian GENDARMERIE entered Backa and began the DEPORTATION of the surviving Jews to AUSCHWITZ and other camps. Over a third were sent to their deaths by May 1944; others died while serving in the Yugoslav army in its last battles against SS units or fascist forces in CROATIA. Of the 16,000 Jews living in Backa in early 1941, only 2,500 survived.

BADGE, JEWISH   Symbol that Jews were forced to wear during the HOLOCAUST, so that they could be identified as Jews. The Germans used the Jewish badge, often in the form of a yellow Star of David, to harass and isolate the Jews. In that way, they were able to

A woman selling Jewish badges in the Warsaw Ghetto

create a wide rift between the Jews and the rest of the population. Sometimes, other opponents of the Nazis were also forced to wear special identification badges. The Nazis' inspiration for the Jewish badge came from medieval times, when both Muslims and Christians decreed that Jews must wear articles of clothing that would set them apart and shame them for being different.

Reinhard HEYDRICH first suggested the Jewish badge concept after the KRISTALLNACHT pogrom of November 1938. In September 1939, after the German invasion of POLAND, the Nazis decreed that Jewish stores should be branded with a distinctive mark. Soon after, the head of the GENERALGOUVERNEMENT, Hans FRANK, ordered that the Jews themselves be marked: all Jews over the age of 12 were to don white armbands, at least four inches wide, inscribed with a blue Star of David. From then on the idea spread to all territory held by the Nazis.

The Jews were responsible to buy and distribute the badges. If a Jew was caught without a badge, he was fined, imprisoned, or shot. In some GHETTOS, certain groups were given different badges to identify them as being unique among the Jews. These included Jewish police, doctors, JUDENRAT employees, and factory workers, who no longer had to wear the regular Jewish badge and thus felt more favored than the rest of the Jews.

Different symbols, all variations on the same theme, were introduced in different areas of the *Generalgouvernement* and the Polish territories occupied by GERMANY. In 1941 the SS ordered the Jews to wear a yellow six-pointed star, four inches high, on the left side of the breast and on the back. When Germany invaded the SOVIET UNION, Jews there were also forced to wear Jewish badges. By September 1941 Jews within the Reich were ordered to wear the "Jewish star."

The Jewish badge also became the norm in other areas controlled by or allied with the Nazis, such as SLOVAKIA, part of ROMANIA, and in HUNGARY after the Nazi occupation. The Germans had a harder time, however, convincing their satellite countries in Western Europe to force Jews to wear Jewish badges. The French Vichy government refused to implement the order in the unoccupied zone, saying that the anti-Jewish measures they had already taken were enough, and that a distinguishing mark would "shock" the French people. The decree was carried out, though, in occupied FRANCE, BELGIUM, and the NETHERLANDS.

The Nazis did not even try to make the Jewish badge obligatory in DENMARK, due to the Danes' strong opposition to anti-Jewish measures. A story is told that King Christian X himself donned the Jewish badge in solidarity with the Jews of Denmark. The story is fictional (as Danish Jewry was never forced to wear badges), but it powerfully demonstrates the Danish king's courage and commitment to his country's Jews.

Both Jews and non-Jews reacted strongly to the Jewish badge decree. Almost all Polish Jews cooperated with the law, in fear of severe punishment; however, diaries from the time speak with unabashed bitterness about having to wear the badge. In Germany, the introduction of the badge was followed by a wave of suicides. Many French Jews refused to wear the badge, and some French non-Jews expressed their empathy for the Jewish plight by wearing stars themselves. Even the French police did not enforce the decree. In Holland, an underground newspaper expressed its soli-

darity with the Jews by printing 300,000 stars, inscribed with the words, "Jews and non-Jews are one and the same."

BADOGLIO, PIETRO (1871–1956), Italian general who served as prime minister of ITALY for a year after the downfall of Italian leader Benito MUSSOLINI. Badoglio accepted Italy's Jews as full citizens, but supported his government's racial programs to stay in favor with Mussolini and GERMANY.

BAECK, LEO (1873–1966), Reform rabbi, philosopher, and leader of German Jewry in Nazi GERMANY.

Baeck studied at the Jewish Theological Seminary in Breslau and the College for Judaic Studies in BERLIN. He was ordained a rabbi in 1897 and led congregations in Oppeln, Dusseldorf, and Berlin. He also taught in the Reform rabbinical seminary. During World War I Baeck served as a chaplain.

Baeck was a creative scholar who published articles on many Jewish subjects. Although he considered himself a non-Zionist, he took a stand against a group of

Leo Baeck

German rabbis who opposed Zionism and served on several Zionist committees. He was a leader of many German Jewish organizations, such as the General Association of German Rabbis, of which he was elected chairman in 1922.

When HITLER came to power in 1933, Baeck was made president of an umbrella German Jewish organization called the REICH REPRESENTATION OF GERMAN JEWS. He thus acted as the official representative of all German Jewry. He was deported to the THERESIENSTADT Ghetto in 1943 where he served as a member of the Jewish camp leadership. His spiritual inspiration greatly boosted the morale of the other inmates. After the war, Baeck moved to London, where he pursued teaching, research, and communal work.

BAKY, LASZLO (1889–1946), Hungarian antisemitic politician who helped implement the annihilation of Hungarian Jewry in 1944.

During the 1920s Baky was an activist in many radical right-wing organizations. As a member of the Hungarian officers' corps, Baky was remarkably candid about his antisemitic views, and in 1938 he left his post in the *gendarmerie* to devote himself fully to the extreme right (see also GENDARMERIE, HUNGARIAN). In May 1939 he was elected to the Hungarian parliament as a leading member of the Hungarian National Socialist Party— HUNGARY'S equivalent of the NAZI PARTY.

Soon after GERMANY occupied Hungary on March 19, 1944, Baky was appointed undersecretary of state in the collaborating Hungarian government led by Dome SZTOJAY. After the Germans gave control of the government to Ferenc SZALASI and his ARROW CROSS PARTY in October of that year, Baky took on a major role in that regime. In both governments of which he was a member, Baky played a leading role in the DEPORTATION of Hungarian Jewry.

At the end of the war, Baky escaped from Hungary, but was captured by American forces who sent him back in October 1945. He was sentenced to death for war crimes and executed.

BANDERA, STEFAN (1909–1959), Ukrainian nationalist leader. Bandera joined the ORGANIZATION OF UKRAINIAN NATIONALISTS (OUN) in his twenties, and quickly became one of the organization's leaders in the western UKRAINE, which was under Polish rule at the time.

During the early 1930s Bandera took control of the OUN, which encouraged armed revolt for the cause of Ukrainian independence. When the Polish Minister of the Interior was assassinated in 1936, Bandera was arrested and sentenced to life imprisonment. However, when the Germans invaded POLAND in September 1939, he was set free by the Soviets and he moved to German-occupied Poland.

At the 1940 national OUN conference, Bandera caused a breach in the organization; his supporters, the group's majority, wanted to bring about an armed revolt. Before the Germans invaded the SOVIET UNION in June 1941, Bandera helped the Nazis set up two Ukrainian intelligence battalions within their army. He also organized units that accompanied German troops into the Ukraine to form the local government and police. Bandera and his people considered the Soviets and the Jews their main enemies.

After the German invasion of the Soviet Union, Bandera's representatives declared the establishment of an independent Ukrainian government in LVOV on June 30, 1941. The Germans were completely opposed to this, so they deported Bandera to SACHSENHAUSEN. He kept in contact with his comrades, and was finally released in September 1944. He led the OUN until his assassination in 1959.

BARANOVICHI (in Polish, Baranowicze), city in BELORUSSIA and site of a GHETTO and labor camps. Before WORLD WAR II, Baranovichi was part of POLAND. The Germans invaded Poland in September 1939, and divided the country into three parts. The easternmost third, including Baranovichi, was given to the SOVIET UNION. However, the Germans then invaded the Soviet Union in June 1941 and took control of Soviet territories. They entered Baranovichi on June 27. At that time, there were 10,000 Jews living there.

Just a few days after the invasion, the Germans killed 73 Jews who they said were Communists. Another 350 Jews were murdered soon thereafter, and 759 Jews were sent to be killed at the Koldichevo camp.

The Germans formed a JUDENRAT and named Yehoshua Isikson its chairman. They then ordered him to supply them with Jews for FORCED LABOR, but he refused. On March 3, 1942, 2,300 Jews were murdered in retaliation. Isikson was forced to watch the killing, and was then murdered himself. Following the massacre, Jews from surrounding towns were brought to the Baranovichi Ghetto.

An underground organization was formed in Baranovichi in mid-1942 with 200 members. Their major dilemma was whether to fight the Germans from inside the ghetto or from the forests. The underground decided to launch a ghetto uprising on July 19, 1942. They made a detailed plan and acquired weapons, but decided at the beginning of July to postpone the uprising, out of consideration for the rest of the ghetto. After that, the members of the underground concentrated on simply escaping the ghetto.

In late summer 1942, the Germans began arresting, killing, and deporting Jews from the Baranovichi Ghetto. The underground again discussed the possibility of an uprising, but abandoned the idea when they realized that they did not have the full support of the rest of the ghetto population. When the *aktion* ended, Jews began to run from the ghetto. In December 1942 the Germans initiated a final *aktion* in Baranovichi, murdering 3,000 Jews and totally liquidating the ghetto. After December 17, only 700 Jews remained in Baranovichi as forced laborers. (see also RESISTANCE, JEWISH.)

BARASZ, EFRAIM

(1892–1943), Chairman of the JUDENRAT in the BIALYSTOK Ghetto of northeast POLAND.

Barasz, a long-time Zionist, moved to Bialystok in 1934. From that time on, he was very active in the city's Jewish affairs, serving as the executive director of the Jewish community. After the Germans occupied Bialystok in June 1941, they named Rabbi Gedaliah Rosenmann chairman of the *Judenrat*. However, it was actually Barasz, acting as Rosenmann's deputy, who ran the council. A month later he officially took over the job.

In the fall of 1942 the Nazis began liquidating the other GHETTOS in the region and deporting the Jews to EXTERMINATION CAMPS. Barasz knew what was happening to Jews all around Bialystok, and he thought that the only way the Jews in his ghetto could avoid the same fate would be to become indispensable to the Germans as productive laborers. Thus, he did all he could to create industrial jobs for the inhabitants of the ghetto. He also cooperated with the Germans in the DEPORTATION of February 1943, in which 9,000–10,000 "nonproductive" Jews were taken away. At the same time, Barasz was in close contact with the ghetto's underground and cooperated with Mordechai TENENBAUM, who later became the head of Bialystok's Jewish Fighting Organization (*Zydowska Organizacja Bojowa,* ZOB) and led the ghetto's uprising. Barasz helped the resistance by funding the manufacture of weapons. However, soon before the ghetto uprising, Barasz and the underground broke off relations.

The Germans began the final liquidation of the Bialystok Ghetto on August 16, 1943 with large-scale deportations. This led to an uprising in the ghetto, which was put down by the Germans after five days of fighting. Between August 21 and 27, 25,000 Jews were deported to TREBLINKA. Several hundred Jews, including Barasz and other *Judenrat* members, were separated from the deportees and put into a small ghetto. In September these Jews were transferred to MAJDANEK. From there, the last surviving Jews from Bialystok were sent to PONIATOWA, where they were exterminated during the ERNTEFEST operation of November 1943. Exact details of Barasz's death are not known.

BARBIE TRIAL

Trial of SS officer Klaus Barbie, who was known as "the butcher of Lyons." The trial, which aroused interest and controversy all over the world, was held in Lyons, FRANCE, from May to July 1987.

Barbie joined the NAZI PARTY in 1932 and the SS in

Klaus Barbie, during the war

1935. In 1942 he began working for the GESTAPO. In November of that year he was sent to Lyons to serve as the city's *Gestapo* chief. During the 21 months in that post, Barbie was responsible for many horrific actions; he even carried out some of the atrocities himself (hence his nickname). One of the most notorious things he did was to torture to death the famed hero of the French Resistance, Jean Moulin.

After the war Barbie worked for the United States government as a secret agent in Germany. He moved to La Paz, Bolivia in 1951, and became a Bolivian citizen in 1957 under the false name, Klaus Altmann. Despite the fact that Barbie was safely settled in South America, the French government tried him for war crimes twice during the 1950s. In both cases he was convicted and sentenced to death.

In 1971 French Nazi hunter Beate Klarsfeld tracked Barbie to La Paz. Over the next few years the French government repeatedly requested that the Bolivian authorities extradite Barbie to France; they finally agreed to cooperate in 1983, and Barbie was returned to France.

Barbie was charged with various CRIMES AGAINST HUMANITY, including a raid on the Lyons headquarters of the UNION OF FRENCH JEWS on February 9, 1943, in which 85 Jews were arrested and sent to AUSCHWITZ; the DEPORTATION of 44 Jewish children whom Barbie's *Gestapo* men found to be hiding in the village of Izieu, more than 43 miles from Lyons; and ordering the last deportation from Lyons to Auschwitz on August 11, 1944. Altogether, Barbie was charged with being responsible for the deportation of 842 people from Lyons, some Jewish and the rest French resistance fighters. Barbie was convicted and sentenced to life in prison. He died in jail in 1990.

BARTOSZEWSKI, WLADYSLAW (b. 1922), A Pole who opposed the Nazis and helped Polish Jews during the HOLOCAUST.

Bartoszewski was held in AUSCHWITZ from September 1940 to April 1941. From 1942–1945 he was a member of the Polish HOME ARMY, the underground organization of young Catholics, and the Front for the Rebirth of Poland. In September 1942 Bartoszewski helped establish a temporary committee that later became ZEGOTA, the Polish Council for Aid to Jews. After a permanent *Zegota* council was formed in December 1942, Bartoszewski served as one of two delegates from the DELEGATURA—the underground

representative of the POLISH GOVERNMENT-IN-EXILE active in POLAND—who regularly attended *Zegota* meetings. He was also an underground activist who sent the London-based Polish government-in-exile reports on the atrocities committed by the Nazis against the Poles and the Jews.

Bartoszewski was designated as RIGHTEOUS AMONG THE NATIONS by YAD VASHEM in 1963. He is both an historian and a writer who has published several books. Most deal with the history of WARSAW during WORLD WAR II, the Jews of Poland, and the rescue of Jews by Polish non-Jews. A professor at the Catholic University in LUBLIN, he also served as an ambassador and as foreign minister of Poland.

BAUBLYS, PETRAS (d. 1974), Pediatrician and head of an orphanage in KOVNO, LITHUANIA. During the war, an underground Jewish organization active in the Kovno GHETTO asked Baublys if the orphanage, situated in the same section of the city as the ghetto, could be used as a temporary place of refuge for Jewish children and a steppingstone for moving Jewish children to safer, permanent locations. Baublys agreed; over time, tens of Jewish babies and children were admitted into the orphanage. Some were even left on the orphanage's doorstep by their mothers. Children who could speak a bit of Lithuanian were kept in the orphanage for longer amounts of time, while children who could not speak the language or were older than the rest of the orphans were quickly sent to live with Lithuanian families. Whenever Baublys would visit a sick child, he would treat him for free. Only a few members of the orphanage staff were told about Baublys' rescue activities, in order to decrease the chances of getting caught or being betrayed.

In 1977 Baublys was posthumously awarded the title RIGHTEOUS AMONG THE NATIONS by YAD VASHEM. His brother Sergejus and sister-in-law Jadvyga were also recognized as "Righteous among the Nations" for hiding a Jewish child in their home.

BAUM GRUPPE (Baum Group), underground anti-Nazi organization in BERLIN. The *Baum Gruppe*, led by Herbert and Marianne Baum, was made up mainly of Jews who belonged to YOUTH MOVEMENTS. Most were Communist, although some were left-wing Zionists. Almost all of the *Baum Gruppe's* members were quite young.

In 1936 the Communist underground asked the

group's Jewish members to start an independent group and set up Communist units in Jewish youth organizations. From 1937–1942 the group concentrated on giving out illegal literature; organizing political training courses, cultural events, and educational evenings; and bolstering the morale of those Jews who were to be deported. In May 1942 members of the *Baum Gruppe* set fire to an anti-Bolshevik exhibit set up in Berlin by the Nazi Ministry of Propaganda. This action was considered to be a major offense against the Nazis; most of the group's members were arrested, as were 500 other Berlin Jews. Half were executed on the spot, and the rest were sent to SACHSENHAUSEN and killed a few months later. Herbert Baum was tortured to death, and the rest of the *Baum Gruppe* members were put on trial. Some were executed, while others were deported to AUSCHWITZ, where they were murdered.

BECHER, KURT   (1909-) Nazi official. During the first years of WORLD WAR II, Kurt Becher fought on the Russian front. In 1944, he arrived in HUNGARY. His official SS assignment was to buy horses and horse-drawn vehicle equipment for the *Waffen-SS*. However, he played a key role in acquiring the huge Weiss Manfred Works for the Germans. He also represented the SS in negotiations with the RELIEF AND RESCUE COMMITTEE of BUDAPEST concerning the fate of Hungarian Jewry. Dr. Israel Rezso KASZTNER, a committee leader, depended on Becher to transport Hungarian Jews from BERGEN-BELSEN to SWITZERLAND (called the "Kasztner transport"). With the approval of Heinrich HIMMLER, Becher also met with the head of the American Jewish JOINT DISTRIBUTION COMMITTEE in Switzerland, Saly MAYER, and the WAR REFUGEE BOARD representative, Roswell McClelland, on November 4, 1944. Becher considered the meeting to be extremely important, as he was encountering President ROOSEVELT'S intermediary.

In January 1945 Himmler appointed Becher Special Reich Commissioner for all CONCENTRATION CAMPS. Becher and Kasztner worked together to prevent the liquidation of the camps during the last few weeks of the war. After GERMANY surrendered, Becher was arrested by the Allies and imprisoned in NUREMBERG. However, Kasztner testified on his behalf, and he was released from jail.

BELGIUM   Country in Western Europe that was occupied by German forces on May 10, 1940, and

Anti-Jewish propaganda, "The Jewish Plot Against Europe"

surrendered on May 28 on the orders of King Leopold III. The king stayed in Belgium, but the prime minister and many cabinet members fled the country for London where they set up a government-in-exile. The German occupiers formed a military administration, which was replaced by a civil administration in July 1944. While the military had control over Belgium, the SS and its Reich Security Main Office (REICHSSICHERHEITSHAUPTAMT, RSHA) tried very hard to extend their power in the country. However, the military administration made all attempts to restrain them.

Shortly after the occupation, 66,000 Jews lived in Belgium; only 10 percent of those were Belgian citizens. The rest were mostly immigrants who had fled to Belgium from Eastern Europe and GERMANY. The Jewish population was found mostly in BRUSSELS and ANTWERP, with large groups also residing in Liege and Charleroi. Of those 66,000 Jews, 34,801 were imprisoned or deported during the HOLOCAUST, and of those, 28,902 perished.

The anti-Jewish policies in Belgium were similar to those in other countries occupied by the Nazis. However, due to the competition for power in Belgium between the German military administration and the SS representatives, anti-Jewish measures were enacted more slowly. In November 1940 Hermann GOERING ordered that the Belgian economy be "Aryanized"— that Jewish businesses and property be confiscated and given to Germans. Many German businesses were indeed interested in buying Jewish-owned enterprises, but the ARYANIZATION process only started a year later in late 1941. In fact, "Aryanization" was never fully completed in Belgium: many large Jewish businesses and real estate properties stayed under the control of their Jewish owners. However, the Germans did pillage other types of Jewish property. Those Jews who were deported had their possessions confiscated by Operational Staff Rosenberg (EINSATZSTAB ROSENBERG). Operational Staff Rosenberg also pillaged Jewish institutions, libraries, and art collections.

Over the first two years of the occupation, 18 anti-Jewish decrees were issued and carried out by the military administration. These regulations included removing Jews from government positions and the professions, subjecting them to night curfews, forcing them to wear the yellow Jewish badge (see also BADGE, JEWISH), and concentrating them in the four major cities. In November 1941 the Germans instituted a kind of JUDENRAT called the ASSOCIATION OF JEWS IN BELGIUM (*Association des Juifs en Belgique,* AJB), to which every Jew was forced to belong. Soon, all Jewish children were kicked out of the public school system, and the AJB was made to set up its own schools. In January 1942 Jews were forbidden to leave Belgium. In March the Germans instituted a general labor draft, and the Jews of Belgium were subjected to FORCED LABOR. Most Belgian Jews engaged in forced labor were sent to build fortifications along the coast of northern FRANCE under the auspices of ORGANIZATION TODT. A total of 2,252 Belgian Jews were forced to work there.

The "final solution" was launched in Belgium in the spring of 1942. At that time, the SS's RSHA took control of the country's Jewish affairs. DEPORTATIONS from Belgium were ordered in the summer of that year. Adolf EICHMANN and his Jewish affairs department in the RSHA made the plans for the transports, which began on August 4 and lasted for over a year. The last deportations took place in September 1943 during "Operation Iltis" when Jews with Belgian citizenship were deported. Until then, only immigrants and RE-FUGEES had been sent away. The deportees were rounded up by the German military police, and most were sent to their deaths in AUSCHWITZ. Smaller groups were sent to BUCHENWALD, RAVENSBRUECK, and BERGEN-BELSEN.

BELGRADE   Capital of SERBIA during the nineteenth century and the capital of YUGOSLAVIA since 1918. In early April 1941 GERMANY and its allies invaded Yugoslavia. At that time, Belgrade had approximately 11,000 Jewish inhabitants. About 3,000 inhabitants of Belgrade were killed during the invasion, including Jews. Soon after the Germans took over the city they ordered a census; 9,000 Jews were counted. Most of the Jewish males were forced to do hard labor, clearing away the city's rubble.

Over the next few months, the German military government issued anti-Jewish decrees which gradually isolated the Jews from the rest of the population. The Serbs rebelled against the Germans in July 1941; as a result, many Jewish men were arrested and imprisoned in a CONCENTRATION CAMP right outside the city. From September to November most were executed by firing squad. In December all the Jewish women and children in Belgrade were deported to another concentration camp outside the city. A GAS VAN was then brought in and by May all the women and children had been murdered by gassing. By August 1942 the German authorities claimed that the Jewish problem had been eradicated in Serbia; more than 90 percent of Belgrade's Jews had been exterminated.

BELORUSSIA   (White Russia), region in Eastern Europe between Russia and POLAND, located to the south of LATVIA and LITHUANIA and to the north of the UKRAINE. After World War I, Belorussia was divided in two: the western part was ceded to Poland, while the eastern part became a republic in the SOVIET UNION. When WORLD WAR II broke out in September 1939 and the Germans invaded Poland, the Soviets occupied most of Western Belorussia, according to the agreement made between the two countries in the pre-war NAZI-SOVIET PACT. However, the Nazis turned on their former allies in June 1941 when they invaded the Soviet Union. By July, they had occupied both Eastern and Western Belorussia.

On the eve of the 1941 German invasion of the Soviet Union, there were 670,000 Jews living in Western Belorussia, including REFUGEES who had fled western Poland after the German invasion of 1939. By the end of June the Germans were in control of the region. The local population initiated a series of pogroms. The Germans themselves launched a wave of *aktionen,* in which EINSATZGRUPPEN units murdered 40 percent of the region's Jews. They were shot to death in pits near their cities and towns, and were immediately buried in these mass graves. This first group of *aktionen* lasted from July–December 1941; a second wave began in the spring of 1942 and continued until the end of that year. By that time, only 30,000 Jews were left in Western Belorussia outside of the Bialystok district, which the Germans had annexed to the Reich immediately upon invasion of the Soviet Union. The last Western Belorussian GHETTOS to be liquidated were Glubokoye and Lida in late summer 1943.

In Eastern Belorussia, there was a population of 405,000 Jews including refugees at the time of the 1941 German invasion of the Soviet Union. The Germans quickly conquered the main cities of Belorussia: MINSK fell to them on June 28, and Vitebsk on July 11. About 120,000 Jews were able to flee eastward into the Soviet interior; the rest were not so lucky. The Germans began exterminating the Jews en mass, without any resistance on the part of the local population. By the end of 1941, the Germans had murdered the Jews of 35 ghettos, including Gomel, Vitebsk, Mogilev, and Bobruisk. Only the Minsk Ghetto, (which originally held 100,000 Jewish inhabitants), was allowed to exist until October 1943.

The mass murder of the Jews of Eastern Belorussia took place in large pits located close to the ghettos, and was carried out by *Einsatzgruppen* units, two police battalions, and units of Lithuanian, Belorussian, and Ukrainian policemen. In certain cases, the Germans utilized GAS VANS to kill the Jews.

From November 1941 to October 1942, the Germans deported many Jews from the Reich and from Poland to Belorussia. More than 35,000 Jews from the Reich and the Protectorate of Bohemia and Moravia were sent to the Minsk Ghetto, and 2,000 from WARSAW and other places in Poland were brought to a transit camp in Bobruisk. Any Jews left in Bobruisk were killed in September 1943. Another transit camp was set up in Mogilev, where 196 Jews were killed.

In both Eastern and Western Belorussia, Jews offered resistance to the Nazis. In Western Belorussia, there were both organized undergrounds and resistance

Jews in the Minsk region, 1941

without the help of an organization. Thousands of Jews hid from the Nazis, while at least 25,000 escaped to the forests. In Eastern Belorussia, Jews resisted in their ghettos; in Minsk, an organized underground functioned until the ghetto was liquidated. About 10,000 Jews from Minsk fled to the forests. Many joined PARTISAN units, and two Jewish battalions operated there: that of the BIELSKI brothers and that of Shalom ZORIN. The local population was quite hostile to the Jews. Only a very small number of people tried to rescue Jews. (see also RESISTANCE, JEWISH and FAMILY CAMPS IN THE FORESTS.)

BELZEC EXTERMINATION CAMP located in the Lublin district of southeastern POLAND, along the Belzec railway line. The Nazis began building Belzec in November 1941 as a result of AKTION REINHARD, the Nazi plan to exterminate the two million Jews in the GENERALGOUVERNEMENT. Altogether, 600,000 people, mostly Jews and a few hundred GYPSIES, were murdered at Belzec.

Belzec was first run by camp commandant Christian WIRTH. He was assisted by 20–30 German SS men, and 90–120 Ukrainian guards who volunteered from among the PRISONERS OF WAR in the TRAWNIKI camp. Belzec measured 886 square feet and was surrounded by a barbed-wire fence. Watchtowers were situated at the corners of the camp. It was camouflaged so those on the outside could not tell what was going on inside. Belzec was divided into two sections, one in which the Jews were murdered.

In February 1942 the camp's three GAS CHAMBERS were tested on several groups of Jews. On March 17,

Belzec officially opened its doors as an extermination center. In its first few weeks of operation, 80,000 Jews were murdered there, over half from LUBLIN and LVOV. The camp halted operations in mid-April, but began receiving transports again in mid-May, when thousands of Jews arrived from CRACOW and the Cracow district.

The Jews were transported by freight trains and traveled for hours or even days under intolerable con-

bers by screaming Germans and Ukrainians who beat them along the way. Then they were gassed. At first, this whole process lasted three or four hours, but as the Germans gained more experience, they cut it down to 60–90 minutes.

The Germans, however, were still not satisfied. In mid-June, they halted transports so they could enlarge the gas chambers, in an effort to kill more efficiently. The transports started again in July 1942 and continued

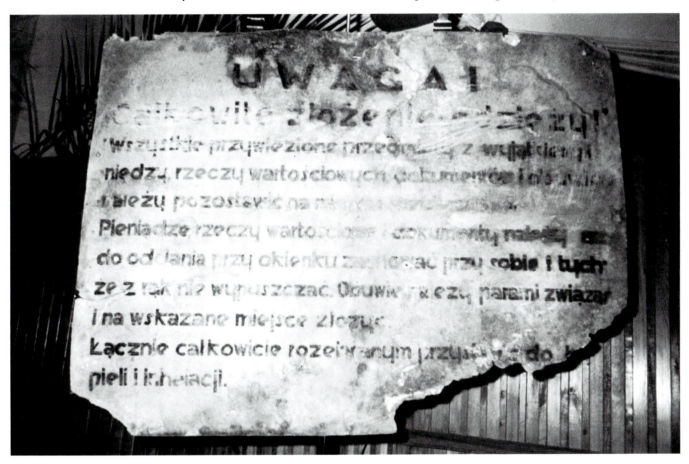

Sign posted outside the gas chambers in Belzec: "Attention, all personal property that is to be kept with you, with the exception of money, documents, and other valuables must be handed over in the hut. Shoes should be tied together in pairs and placed in the area designated for shoes. Afterward you must enter the showers completely naked"

ditions. Many died on the way. Each train consisted of 40–60 cars. When they arrived at Belzec, 20 cars with more than 2,000 Jews would be detached from the train and pulled into the camp. The Jews were pulled out of the cars, and told that they had arrived in a transit camp, so they were to be disinfected and showered. They were forced to hand over their valuables. Men and women were separated, and all were told to strip. They were marched on the run to the gas cham-

arriving regularly until December, when they were stopped because most of the Jews in the *Generalgouvernement* had already been murdered. During those five months, 130,000 Jews had been brought from the Cracow district, 225,000 from the Lvov area, and many others from the Lublin and Radom districts.

Not all Jews were immediately killed upon arrival: during the camp's first few weeks, some of the strong young men were selected to do FORCED LABOR. As time went on, 700–1,000 people were kept alive for longer periods so that they could work. One group worked on the trains: they cleaned the freight cars, helped down those Jews who could not disembark on their own, and removed the bodies of Jews who had not survived the trip. Another group worked on the victims' property, making it usable for the Germans. This even included processing women's hair. Another group of several hundred Jews removed the corpses from the gas chambers and buried them in pits. A group of "dentists" was responsible to remove gold teeth from the corpses' mouths. All these laborers were also subjected to brutality and selections from time to time (see also SELEKTION).

Between late 1942 and spring 1943, the mass graves were opened and the corpses cremated in an effort to conceal evidence of mass extermination. The camp was then closed, and the last 600 prisoners sent to SOBIBOR. The site was turned into a farm and given to a Ukrainian guard.

BENES, EDVARD (1884–1948), President of Czechoslovakia from 1935 and head of the London-based CZECHOSLOVAK GOVERNMENT-IN-EXILE during WORLD WAR II. Benes condemned the annihilation of European Jewry and supported Jewish aspirations for a Jewish state in Palestine.

BEN-GURION, DAVID (1886–1973), Zionist leader and first prime minister of Israel. Born in POLAND, Ben-Gurion moved to Palestine in 1906. From 1935 to 1948 he served as chairman of the Jewish Agency and Zionist Executive.

As the situation in Europe deteriorated during the late 1930s, Ben-Gurion became increasingly desperate to devise a plan for mass Jewish immigration to Palestine. During the first two years of WORLD WAR II, Ben-Gurion traveled around the UNITED STATES, rallying the support of American Jewry for a bold new program called the Biltmore Resolution. This program called for Palestine to be opened up for large-scale immigration after the war and for it to become a Jewish state, under Jewish control. The Zionists would deal with the political side of the Biltmore program, while Jewish organizations throughout the free world would be responsible to fund the project and provide immediate assistance for the Jews of Europe.

Ben-Gurion returned to Palestine in October 1942. By that time, he had confirmed reports of the systematic

Ben-Gurion in a Displaced Persons' camp in Zeilsheim, Germany

mass murder of European Jewry. From then on, he worked at organizing the YISHUV'S rescue operations. He encouraged the Jews of Palestine to mobilize for the war effort, and called for the creation of Jewish units in the British army. He did not let the Jewish Agency set up its own wide-reaching rescue committee, preferring that the *Yishuv* run its own official committee. However, he did allow the Jewish Agency to coordinate political action.

Many historians view Ben-Gurion's actions during the war as rather controversial; they believe that he was dispassionate and did not try hard enough to save European Jews. It seems that Ben-Gurion believed that the *Yishuv* could not feasibly save many lives, because of the strength of the German war machine and because the Allied powers were not willing to support most rescue plans. Thus, Ben-Gurion decided to turn his attention to smaller, more practical rescue operations that could actually succeed. In fact, he was not apathetic at all to the plight of European Jewry—he was deeply touched by the tragedy, and thus tried to develop policies that would allow for long-term solutions.

BENOIT, MARIE (b. 1895), French Catholic Capuchin monk who rescued Jews during the HOLO-CAUST.

Benoit decided to rescue Jews after witnessing Vichy authorities arrest thousands of non-French Jewish RE-FUGEES and surrender them to the Nazis. Benoit helped Jews reach SPAIN or SWITZERLAND; working with various Christian and Jewish organizations, he developed a far-reaching rescue network.

GERMANY occupied Vichy FRANCE in November 1942, making the escape routes to Switzerland and Spain much less accessible. At that point, Benoit decided to focus his efforts on getting French Jews to the safe haven of Italian-occupied territories. He met with the Italian commissioner for Jewish affairs and persuaded him to permit the rescue of 30,000 Jews from Nice, France. In July 1943 Benoit managed to see Pope PIUS XII and inform him of a plan to move the Jews of Nice to northern ITALY. However, the plan subsequently failed.

Benoit then tried to help save the Jews of ROME, using the Vatican's Capuchin College as his headquarters. While avoiding arrest by the GESTAPO, Benoit procured ration cards and documents from various consulates, which allowed Jews to move around Rome freely.

After the war, Benoit was lauded by the Jewish community. In 1966, he was designated as RIGHTEOUS AMONG THE NATIONS by YAD VASHEM. (for more on Vichy, see also FRANCE.)

BERGEN-BELSEN CONCENTRATION CAMP located in northern GERMANY. Bergen-Belsen was established in April 1943 as a detention camp for prisoners who were to be exchanged with Germans imprisoned in Allied countries.

The first prisoners to arrive at Bergen-Belsen were not candidates for prisoner swaps, but rather 500 Jewish prisoners from the BUCHENWALD and NATZWEILER-STRUTHOF camps who were brought in to build the campsite. Over the next year and a half, five sub-camps were set up at Bergen-Belsen. The first was a "prisoners' camp" which housed those 500 prisoners who had come to construct the camp. This sub-camp was shut down in February 1944, and the few surviving prisoners were sent to SACHSENHAUSEN.

The second sub-camp was called the "special camp." This camp barracked two transports of Jews from PO-LAND (some 2,400 Jews mostly from WARSAW, LVOV, and

CRACOW) that arrived in mid-June 1943. These Jews were bearers of special documents, passports or entry papers, which had been issued by various countries, mostly South American. Despite the documents, which their holders had considered a ticket to life, these Jews were deported to their deaths at AUSCHWITZ in late 1943 and early 1944.

The third sub-camp in Bergen-Belsen was called the "neutral camp." This section contained some 350 Jews who were citizens of neutral countries, such as SPAIN, Turkey, Argentina, and Portugal, and who lived at Bergen-Belsen from July 1944 to early March 1945. The conditions in the "neutral camp" were better than in any other Bergen-Belsen sub-camp.

The fourth sub-camp was the "star camp" which housed those Jewish prisoners who were designated as exchange candidates. The prisoners living in this sub-camp, the largest of the five, did not have to wear prison uniforms, but were made to wear the Jewish badge—a star of David—hence, the camp's name (see also BADGE, JEWISH). Most of these prisoners were from the NETH-ERLANDS, with smaller groups from TUNISIA, Tripoli, Benghazi, FRANCE, YUGOSLAVIA, and Albania. In July 1944 there were 4,100 Jews in the "star camp." Only a small number of the Jews brought to Bergen-Belsen as prisoner exchange candidates were actually set free in such swaps.

Bergen-Belsen shortly after liberation

Bergen-Belsen shortly after liberation

The last of the sub-camps was the "Hungarian camp," which was established in July 1944 to house the 1,684 Jews from HUNGARY who had been allowed to leave Hungary on the "KASZTNER train" and would eventually reach safety in SWITZERLAND.

From March 1944 Bergen-Belsen slowly became a "regular" concentration camp, with new prisoners arriving who were considered to be too sick to work at other camps. The first such prisoners arrived in late March from DORA-MITTELBAU. They were barracked in a new section of the camp where the living conditions were awful; most died shortly after arrival. Similar groups of prisoners, mainly from Hungary, kept arriving throughout 1944.

In August 1944 a new section was added to serve as a

women's camp for 4,000 Jewish female prisoners from Hungary and Poland. In early fall thousands of prisoners arrived from PLASZOW and Auschwitz. They were put in the "star" sub-camp with almost no living facilities. Among this group were Anne FRANK and her sister Margot, who both died of typhus in March 1945.

The conditions at Bergen-Belsen, which were already abominable, got even worse when tens of thousands of prisoners arrived in early 1945, after horrific DEATH MARCHES from camps in the east that had been evacuated by the Germans. In March 1945 alone some 18,000 prisoners died in the camp.

Bergen-Belsen was liberated by the British army on April 15, 1945. The soldiers were totally shocked at what they found, including 60,000 prisoners in the camp, many on the brink of death, and thousands of unburied bodies lying about. After its LIBERATION, Bergen-Belsen became a Displaced Persons' camp, which was in existence until 1951. (see also DISPLACED PERSONS, JEWISH.)

BERGSON GROUP   Several members of the *Irgun Tseva'i Le'umi,* a Zionist Revisionist underground movement based in Palestine. They were active in the UNITED STATES between 1940 and 1948. The group was named for its leader, Hillel Kook, who called himself Peter H. Bergson in the United States.

Because the Bergson Group consisted of Jews from Palestine, it did not owe allegiance to any one Jewish leader or group in the United States, or suffer from dual loyalty hesitations like many American Jews. Thus, Bergson Group members were able to be more forward and unconventional in their methods of rescuing European Jews—leading to a grave rift between them and American Jewish leaders.

In late 1941 the group formed the "Committee for a Jewish Army of Stateless and Palestinian Jews." However, when information about the mass murder of Jews in Europe went public in November 1942, the group decided to scrap its campaign for a Jewish army and focus all its energies on rescue efforts. The Bergson Group chose to use American public opinion to pressure the United States government into helping European Jewry. They riled up public response through mass demonstrations, like the one at Madison Square Garden in March 1943, which rallied around the motto "We Will Never Die."

After the unsuccessful BERMUDA CONFERENCE on REFUGEES in April 1943, the Bergson Group instituted the "Committee to Save the Jewish People in Europe." The committee's goal was to convince the US government to create an official agency that would deal solely with the rescue of Jews. Many public personalities, such as Congressman Will Rogers, New York Mayor Fiorello La Guardia, Secretary of the Interior Harold Ickes, and publisher William Randolph Hearst supported the committee.

The committee's lobbying for a government rescue agency was seemingly successful. In November 1943, committee supporters introduced resolutions to establish a rescue commission. Soon, Secretary of the Treasury Henry MORGENTHAU revealed that the State Department was sabotaging rescue efforts. Public calls for action, plus the looming State Department sabotage

scandal, led President Franklin D. ROOSEVELT to establish the WAR REFUGEE BOARD (WRB) in January 1944.

BERIHA   The postwar movement of 250,000 SURVIVORS of the HOLOCAUST to Displaced Persons' camps in GERMANY, AUSTRIA, and ITALY. Their aim was to reach the Mediterranean and Black Sea coasts, so that they could set off for Palestine. The Hebrew word *Beriha* means "flight" or "escape."

Jewish survivors attempting to cross borders illegally

The first stage of the organized *Beriha* began in 1944 when groups of Jewish PARTISAN survivors decided that they wanted to go to Palestine. They had heard that they could reach Palestine by way of ROMANIA, but when that avenue failed, these groups gathered in LUBLIN. They were joined there by Jews who had found refuge in the SOVIET UNION during the war. In January 1945 survivors from the WARSAW Ghetto also joined them.

Soon, the *Beriha* gained a budding formal structure under the leadership of Abba KOVNER. The group traveled west to Italy, where the JEWISH BRIGADE had set up a central aid agency for survivors. The two groups got together in July 1945, at the same time that the *Beriha* leadership in POLAND began sending survivors to Italy. By August, about 15,000 survivors had arrived in Italy. However, only a restricted number of people could leave for Palestine from Italy, so the stream of survivors from the Soviet Union was directed towards Displaced Persons' camps in Germany. Survivors from other countries were sent either to Italy or Germany. The flight from Poland was motivated mainly by ANTISEMITISM, peaking with the KIELCE pogrom of July 1946.

The first Jews from Palestine arrived to help organize the *Beriha* in September 1945 and tie it to the ALIYA BET organization. The *Beriha* movement was funded by the American Jewish JOINT DISTRIBUTION COMMITTEE.

Once in Italy, the survivors were taken to the south of the country to wait for boats to Palestine. Those ships that evaded the British blockade of Palestine landed secretly and successfully. However, those ships that were detected by the British were sent to Cyprus, and their passengers put into detention camps until the State of Israel was established in 1948. At that point, the *Beriha* was also dismantled. (see also DISPLACED PERSONS, JEWISH.)

BERLIN   Capital of GERMANY. When Adolf HITLER rose to national power in January 1933, about 160,000 Jews lived in Berlin, constituting one-third of German Jewry. The city's Jewish leaders had to deal with many new challenges, such as creating expanded school and social welfare systems after Jewish students were banned from public schools and Jewish professionals were fired from their jobs. One of the Jewish community's main responsibilities was to organize emigration. By the outbreak of WORLD WAR II in September 1939, half of Berlin's Jewish population had left the country.

Anti-Jewish measures reached a new high in 1938. On the night of November 9, a preplanned pogrom, KRISTALLNACHT, was launched in Berlin, and spread throughout Germany. Most of the city's synagogues were burnt to the ground, Jewish stores and businesses were pillaged, and Jewish institutions were attacked. Tens of Jews were murdered and thousands were deported to CONCENTRATION CAMPS. In the aftermath, Jewish institutions were shut down and their property was taken away. Over 1,200 Jewish businesses were confiscated as part of the ARYANIZATION process. In December, the Nazis began taking over Jewish homes in the wealthier areas of Berlin, and restrictions were put on Jewish movement.

In September 1941 the Jews were forced to wear the Jewish badge (see also BADGE, JEWISH). When Jewish emigration was totally forbidden in October 1941, the Nazis immediately began deporting Jews from Berlin. From October 1941 to January 1942, 10,000 Berlin Jews were deported to RIGA, LODZ, KOVNO, and MINSK.

A street scene showing the celebration of Berlin's 700th year, 1937

In June 1942 the Germans launched transports to THERESIENSTADT, and in July, they initiated direct DEPORTATIONS to AUSCHWITZ. In November 1942, Alois BRUNNER, an SS officer and representative of Adolf EICHMANN, took control of the deportations. By January 1943, the GESTAPO called for the total liquidation of the Berlin Jewish community. Within the next two months, thousands of Jews were deported to Auschwitz. Berlin was declared free of Jews in June 1943, although 7,000 Jews remained in the city. In all, over 55,000 Berlin Jews perished in the HOLOCAUST.

BERMAN, ADOLF ABRAHAM (1906–1978), Zionist active in the WARSAW Ghetto underground, and one of the leaders of ZEGOTA, the Polish Council for Aid to Jews. After the Germans occupied POLAND in September 1939, Berman directed the Warsaw GHETTO branch of the Federation of Associations for the Care of Orphans in Poland. He also helped found the Antifascist Bloc, which later became the Jewish Fighting Organization (ZOB), Warsaw's main Jewish fighting alliance. In September 1942 Berman and his wife Batya moved out of the ghetto to the Polish side of Warsaw. Because of his non-Jewish looks, Berman was able to pass for a Pole and move freely around Warsaw. He lived among Poles until the end of the war, and tried to help the Jews in his positions as secretary of *Zegota* and representative of the Jewish National Committee. He rescued many Jews who hid in Warsaw after the suppression of the WARSAW GHETTO UPRISING and the liquidation of the ghetto. He also preserved records written in the ghetto.

In January 1944 Berman was captured by Polish blackmailers, but his Polish friends paid his ransom, and he was set free. After the war Berman moved to Israel, where he served in the *Knesset* (parliament) and was active in survivors' associations. (see also JEWISH FIGHTING ORGANIZATION, WARSAW.)

BERMUDA CONFERENCE Conference convened by the UNITED STATES and GREAT BRITAIN in Bermuda on April 19, 1943. The purpose of the conference, supposedly, was to deal with the issue of wartime REFUGEES. The real reason the conference was called, however, was to shush the growing public outcries for the rescue of European Jewry without actually having to find any solutions to the problem.

By the end of 1942, reports confirmed that the Nazis intended to exterminate all of European Jewry.

Both in the United States and Britain, Jewish groups demanded that their governments take a stand against the atrocities. The two governments then planned the conference to quiet public opinion, but arranged it so that they would not have to actually make a serious effort to save any Jews. They chose inaccessible Bermuda as the conference's venue in order to control the number of reporters and private representatives attending. Members of the JOINT DISTRIBUTION COMMITTEE and the WORLD JEWISH CONGRESS were not permitted to attend.

The organizers also severely limited the issues that could be discussed. They insisted that the Jewish aspect of the problem not be mentioned, and neither government was willing to discuss the "final solution." Furthermore, the Americans refused to consider changing their strict immigration quotas to let in more Jewish refugees, while the British refused to consider Palestine as a safe haven for Jewish refugees. They would not even discuss sending food packages to CONCENTRATION CAMP prisoners. The Americans also betrayed their lack of seriousness by not sending a high-ranking delegation with the authority to make decisions.

At the conference itself, the attendees spent much time talking about renewing the Intergovernmental Committee on Refugees, which had been created at the 1938 EVIAN CONFERENCE for the purpose of negotiating with the Germans about refugees. However, the point was moot because, as negotiating with the Nazis was no longer an option, no one was willing to fund the committee. No other solution suggested was deemed acceptable by the two governments, either. Thus, nothing was accomplished, and the Bermuda Conference did not save one Jew.

BERNADOTTE, FOLKE (1895–1948), Swedish count and diplomat. During WORLD WAR II, Bernadotte served as the representative of the Swedish Red Cross during prisoner exchanges between GERMANY and the Allies. In 1943 he was named vice president of the Swedish Red Cross, and president in 1946.

Bernadotte negotiated with SS leader Heinrich HIMMLER as a Red Cross representative. In March and April 1945 Bernadotte convinced Himmler to release over 7,000 Scandinavians who were imprisoned in Nazi CONCENTRATION CAMPS (including more than 400 Danish Jews interned in THERESIENSTADT). After Himmler met with the representative of the WORLD JEWISH CONGRESS, Norbert Masur, in SWEDEN, Bernadotte also suc-

Members of the Swedish Red Cross meet Count Folke Bernadotte in Luebeck, Germany

cessfully organized the release of 10,000 women from the RAVENSBRUECK concentration camp, including 2,000 Jews. Most of the women were then brought to Sweden.

Just days after the establishment of the State of Israel, the United Nations appointed Bernadotte to negotiate between Israel and the Arab countries which had invaded the fledgling state. He worked out a settlement between the two sides, but was assassinated in September 1948 by the Fatherland Front, an organization associated with the Jewish underground group, *Lehi*.

BERNHEIM PETITION   Petition presented to the League of Nations in May 1933 in an effort to protest Nazi ANTI-JEWISH LEGISLATION.

Soon after HITLER'S rise to power, Jews outside GERMANY began looking for ways to protect the civil rights of German Jews. In May, a group of Jews turned to the League of Nations. In their appeal, they cited the German-Polish Geneva Convention of 1922, under which the two countries agreed to protect the civil rights of minorities in Upper Silesia and named the League of Nations as judge if anyone felt the treaty was being violated. The group then presented a petition signed

by a Jewish resident of Upper Silesia, Franz Bernheim, in which he complained of the anti-Jewish laws in his region.

The League soon affirmed the complaint's validity, and ruled that Germany should stop discriminating against Jews in Upper Silesia. In September, Germany announced that all anti-Jewish laws in Upper Silesia had been cancelled. The German-Polish treaty expired in May 1937, and until that time the Germans did not even activate the NUREMBERG LAWS in the Upper Silesia region. However, after the expiration date, Germany and POLAND excluded the League of Nations from making any decisions regarding Upper Silesia, and the Germans began to systematically strip the Jews there of their civil rights.

BESSARABIA   Region in Eastern Europe that today covers parts of Moldavia and the UKRAINE. Bessarabia was governed by ROMANIA from the end of World War I until 1940, at which time about 200,000 Jews were living there. In June 1940 the SOVIET UNION took Bessarabia in accordance with the terms of the NAZI-SOVIET PACT. However, when GERMANY invaded the Soviet Union in June 1941, Bessarabia was once again awarded to Germany's ally, Romania.

The Romanian dictator, Ion ANTONESCU, immediately called for the "cleansing" of Bessarabia. This translated into the extermination of all Jews living in villages, and the compression of city Jews into GHETTOS. Romanian police and soldiers took part in the annihilation of Bessarabian Jewry. The deputy prime minister, Mihai ANTONESCU, instituted a special unit to kill Jews. Along with German army units and an EINSATZGRUPPE unit, the "Special Echelon" murdered more than 150,000 Jews between July and August 1941.

In August 1941 the Romanian and German authorities began setting up ghettos and camps for the remaining Jews of Bessarabia. Most of these camps were constructed on sites where thousands of Jews had already been killed, or in the ruined Jewish quarters of the cities of Bessarabia, including Balti, Soroca, Kishinev, and Khotin.

At the beginning of September 1941, 64,176 Jews were still left in Bessarabia; by the end of the month, there were only 43,397. The other 20,000 had mostly been deported, along with Jews from BUKOVINA, to TRANSNISTRIA, an area in the Ukraine also under Romanian rule. Almost all of the remaining 43,000 Jews were also deported to Transnistria and in all, about 25,000

Jews being deported to Transnistria, 1941

Jews died just during the period of DEPORTATIONS: the authorities moved them around for an entire month, without any specific destination or purpose other than to cause the deaths of as many Jews as possible. Anyone who could not keep up with the others was shot by the Romanian guards on the spot. Those that finally arrived in Transnistria were either killed or made to do FORCED LABOR.

By May 1942, only 227 Jews were left in Bessarabia. The region was liberated by Soviet troops in August 1944 and made part of the Soviet Union.

BEST, WERNER (1903–1989), Nazi official who was a senior member of the SS and served as the representative (plenipotentiary) of the German government in DENMARK from 1942 to 1945.

Trained as a lawyer, Best became a judge in 1929. In 1930 he joined the NAZI PARTY and enlisted in the SS in 1931. Soon after the Nazis rose to national power in 1933, Best was named both state commissioner for the

police force and police president in the German province of Hesse. Over the next few years, Best advanced quickly through the Nazi hierarchy. He served as the GESTAPO'S legal advisor, and deputy to both Reinhard HEYDRICH and SS chief Heinrich HIMMLER. From 1935 to 1940 Best worked as a bureau chief in the headquarters of the SS's Security Service (SD) in BERLIN. From September 1939 to June 1940 he also headed a section in the Reich Security Main Office (REICHSSICHERHEITSHAUPTAMT, RSHA). In this post, he was involved in the mass murder in POLAND of Jews and Polish intellectuals. From June 1940 to August 1942 Best was the head of the military administration in German-occupied FRANCE. In that position, he helped exclude Jews from French life and tried to put down the French Resistance.

In November 1942 Best was transferred to German-occupied Denmark, where he served as German plenipotentiary until 1945. Some experts believe that Best tried to lighten the persecution of Jews in Denmark, almost all of whom survived the "final solution" by escaping to SWEDEN.

In 1949 a Danish court sentenced Best to death; however, the sentence was then changed to 12 years in prison. Despite the fact that he had several years left of his sentence, Best was released in 1951. He then returned to Germany and resumed a normal civilian job. In 1958 he was fined 70,000 marks as punishment for his service as an SS leader; in 1969 he was re-arrested for his involvement in the mass murders in Poland. However, he was released in 1972 for health reasons—and then went on to live for many more years.

BIALYSTOK   City in northeastern POLAND. Before WORLD WAR II, 50,000 Jews lived in Bialystok, representing more than half of the city's population.

The Germans invaded Bialystok on September 15, 1939. A week later, they transferred the city to the Soviets, as promised in the NAZI-SOVIET PACT. However, when the Germans attacked the Soviets in June 1941, they retook control of Bialystok. June 27 was named "Red Friday" because on that day Nazi EINSATZGRUPPEN murdered 2,000 Jews there. Over the next two weeks, another 4,000 Jews were killed in an open field near Pietraszek.

On June 29 the Nazis ordered the Jews to establish a JUDENRAT; Efraim BARASZ eventually became its chairman. On August 1, 50,000 Bialystok Jews were restricted to a GHETTO. Within three months, the *Judenrat* was ordered to transfer 4,500 of the ghetto's inhabitants to the town of Pruzhany. Most of them were killed when the Pruzhany Ghetto was destroyed in January 1943.

The Bialystok Ghetto was divided into two parts, on the east and west sides of the Biala River. It quickly became an industrial center where textiles and weapons were manufactured for the Germans. Most of the Jews worked in these industries; a handful worked in German factories outside the ghetto. Within this setup, the Jews also managed to secretly manufacture products for their own use. The Germans gave the Jews very little food, so they grew their own food in "*Judenrat* gardens." The *Judenrat* instituted aid organizations in the ghetto. These included soup kitchens, two hospitals, an outpatient clinic, pharmacies, a gynecological clinic, a first aid organization, two schools, and a court. They also established a Jewish police force.

There were several Jewish YOUTH MOVEMENTS in the ghetto that split into two undergrounds. These even-

Jews performing forced labor, June 1941

tually united in July 1943 under the command of Mordechai TENENBAUM and Daniel Moskowicz. Tannenbaum also established a secret archive in the ghetto that functioned until April 1943. The archive's documents, which included many from the *Judenrat*, were hidden on the Polish side of Bialystok.

From February 5–12, 1943 the Germans carried out a massacre in the ghetto. Two thousand Jews were shot and 10,000 were deported to TREBLINKA. One of the two resistance movements tried to fight the Nazis and lost many of its members. *Judenrat* chairman Barasz believed that the Nazis would be satisfied with those Jews they deported, and would therefore leave the rest of the ghetto alone. However, in August 1943, the Nazis ordered the final liquidation of the ghetto. At that point, the ghetto had 30,000 inhabitants. On the night of August 15, German troops and Ukrainian collaborators surrounded the ghetto. The next morning, the Jews were ordered to gather for evacuation. At 10:00 a.m. the underground revolted. The main goal of the uprising was to create an opening in the German lines, allowing the fighters to escape to the forest. However, they only had a few weapons and over 300 died per day. At one point, German troops even entered the ghetto with tanks and armored cars. The fighting lasted until August 20, when the resistance fighters' last defenses fell. The resistance leaders, Tannenbaum and Moszkowicz, fell back to the last stronghold where they committed suicide.

DEPORTATIONS began on August 18 and lasted for

three days. Most of the Jews of the ghetto were deported to Treblinka, MAJDANEK, PONIATOWA, Blizyn, and AUSCHWITZ, while 1,200 children were sent to THERE-SIENSTADT, and later to Auschwitz. About 150 fighters from Bialystok joined the PARTISANS. Only 2,000 Jews were left in the ghetto; they were deported to Majdanek three weeks later. In all, about 200 Jews from Bialystok survived the camps and several dozen survived by hiding on the Polish side of the city; 60 Jews who had joined the partisans also survived. Bialystok was liberated by Soviet troops in August 1944. (see also RESISTANCE, JEWISH.)

BIEBOW, HANS (1902–1947), Head Nazi administrator of the LODZ Ghetto. Biebow was a businessman and Nazi from Bremen. When the Lodz Ghetto was erected in 1940, Biebow was appointed head of the GHETTO'S food and economic office (soon renamed the "ghetto administration"). Biebow and his staff of 250 Germans controlled all business activity in the ghetto.

Hans Biebow in the Lodz Ghetto, on left looking at a necktie

Biebow got rich by setting up factories within the ghetto and forcing the Jews of Lodz to work there for almost no pay. He also robbed the Jews of their property. The ghetto was sealed shut according to Biebow's instructions; the Jews could not leave or buy food.

The clothes and personal items belonging to the Jews from Lodz who had been deported to CHELMNO were stored by Biebow in warehouses in the town of Pabianice. Then they were sent to GERMANY to be used by the German population. Nonetheless, Biebow also

wanted to continue making money off the ghetto factories, so he kept the ghetto running for as long as he could. When the Germans called for the ghetto's elimination in summer 1944, Biebow got very involved in arranging the fatal transports from Lodz and nearby ghettos to Chelmno and AUSCHWITZ. After the war Biebow was executed by order of a Polish court in Lodz.

BIELSKI, TUVIA (1906–1987), Jewish PARTISAN commander who set up a family camp and a fighting unit in a Belorussian forest.

Tuvia Bielski and some members of his family camp, Bielski is crouching at the extreme right

Bielski lived in eastern POLAND which, at the beginning of WORLD WAR II, was annexed by the SOVIET UNION. In June 1941 German troops invaded the Soviet Union and began massacring the Jews who lived there. After Bielski's parents and other relatives were murdered in the Novogrudok GHETTO, he and his brothers, Zusya, Asael, and Aharon fled to the forest, where they set up a small partisan unit. They also sent a message back to the ghetto: "Organize as many friends and acquaintances as possible. Send them to us in the woods. We will be waiting for you." Over the next two years, 1,200 men, women, and children joined Bielski's family camp. Those who were able joined his partisan group.

Unlike other partisan commanders, Bielski did not consider fighting the enemy his only goal. Instead, he held saving Jewish lives as his highest value, and unlike other partisans, he took in all Jews and refused to abandon the weak and the old. Nonetheless, he also successfully fought the Belorussian police and local farmers who collaborated with the Nazis, and gained the trust of the Soviet partisans in his area. The Germans grew so frustrated by their inability to catch him that they offered a 100,000 marks reward for his capture.

When the Germans launched an extensive hunt for Bielski and other partisans, the region's Soviet commander ordered Bielski to cut all but essential fighters from his group and send away all women, married men, and children. Bielski refused, knowing that if he abandoned his people they would almost certainly die. His soldiers protected the rest of the group from the Germans until the region was liberated in 1944. At that point, the Bielski brothers and the 1,200 Jews from their family camp returned, alive, to Novogrudok.

Asael Bielski was killed in battle in 1944. After the war, Tuvia Bielski returned to Poland, and then immigrated to Palestine. In 1954 he settled in the United States, along with his surviving brothers and their families. (see also FAMILY CAMPS IN THE FORESTS.)

BLACK BOOK OF SOVIET JEWRY, THE A book, originally compiled during WORLD WAR II by well-known Soviet Jewish writers Ilya Ehrenburg and Vasily Grossman, about the crimes committed by the Nazis in the SOVIET UNION. The *Black Book* includes personal statements and documents such as letters, diary excerpts, and descriptions that were contributed by Soviet writers and poets who were either Jewish survivors of the HOLOCAUST or non-Jewish eyewitnesses. According to the book's subtitle, the book deals with "the ruthless murder of Jews by fascist German invaders throughout the temporarily occupied regions of the Soviet Union and in the EXTERMINATION CAMPS of POLAND during the war of 1941 to 1945."

In 1943 Ehrenburg decided to publish a book of testimony about the Nazi persecutions of Soviet Jewry. By late 1944 the book's first draft was complete; at that time Ehrenburg published pieces of the book in a two-volume work called *Merder fun Felker,* which translates as *Murder of Peoples.* In early 1945 he gave the composition to the Soviet JEWISH ANTIFASCIST COMMITTEE, which modified the manuscript and made additions. In 1946 copies of the revised manuscript were sent to the UNITED STATES, ROMANIA, and Israel. Parts of the manuscript were published in English in the United States in a book called *Black Book,* which dealt with the extermination of all of European Jewry.

Parts were also published in Romania in 1946. According to Ehrenburg, the book was also printed in the Soviet Union, but the manuscript and the entire edition were destroyed in 1948 when the Jewish Antifascist Committee was dissolved.

The copy of the manuscript that had been sent to Israel (which was missing the chapter on LITHUANIA) was given to YAD VASHEM in 1965. The book was published in Russian in 1980, in English in 1981, in Yiddish in 1984, and in Hebrew in 1991. The Yiddish version included a redone chapter on Lithuania. In the mid 1980s Ehrenburg's daughter passed on his archive to Yad Vashem which included most of the material on which the Black Book was based and much material that Ehrenburg did not include in the book.

BLECHHAMMER (in Polish, Blachownia Slaska), CONCENTRATION CAMP located near the Polish town of Kozle. Blechhammer was originally established in April 1942 as a FORCED LABOR camp for Jews. The first prisoners to arrive at the camp worked on the construction of a chemical-products plant. Soon, a typhus epidemic broke out. The 120 prisoners who became ill with the disease were sent to AUSCHWITZ, where they were murdered. The remaining prisoners were moved to a new, larger site nearby.

New prisoners were then brought to Blechhammer; most were Jews from Upper SILESIA, but there were also Jews there from 15 other countries. The number of prisoners peaked at 5,500. They lived in wooden barracks without running water. Diarrhea and tuberculosis affected many of the prisoners, and all were malnourished. A Jew from VIENNA named Karl Demerer served

Prisoner sleeping in a storeroom

as the "camp elder." In various instances he stood up to the camp authorities and helped the other prisoners.

In April 1944 Blechhammer became a satellite camp of Auschwitz. In January 1945 some 4,000 prisoners were sent on a DEATH MARCH; 800 were executed along the way. The survivors reached the GROSS-ROSEN camp, and then moved on to BUCHENWALD. Prisoners who tried to hide in Blechhammer during the evacuation were killed immediately.

BLITZKRIEG (German for "lightning war"), theory of swift, large-scale offensive warfare developed by the German army during WORLD WAR II, whose goal was a quick victory. GERMANY successfully used the *Blitzkrieg* method in conquering POLAND, FRANCE, DENMARK, NORWAY, YUGOSLAVIA, and Greece.

BLOBEL, PAUL (1894–1951), SS officer. Blobel joined the NAZI PARTY in 1931 and the SS in 1932. In 1934 he began serving in the SD. Blobel quickly rose through the ranks of the SS and was promoted to SS-*Standartenfuehrer* in January 1941.

In June 1941 Blobel was asked to come to the town of Pretzsch, where mobile killing units called EINSATZGRUPPEN were being formed. These units were on their way to German-occupied territories in the SOVIET UNION. Blobel was made commander of *Einsatzkommando 4a* assigned to the UKRAINE; his group carried out murderous *aktionen* all over the region. After the Germans occupied Kiev, Blobel's unit massacred the city's Jews in a two-day bloodbath at BABI YAR. In December Blobel's unit executed an *aktion* in Kharkov in which 21,685 Jews were murdered.

In January 1942 Blobel took a leave of absence for health reasons. After his recovery, the Reich Security Main Office (REICHSSICHERHEITSHAUPTAMT, RSHA) put him in charge of AKTION 1005, an operation to destroy all evidence of mass murder in Eastern Europe by burning the victims' corpses. In late 1944 Blobel took command of a unit that fought the Yugoslavian PARTISANS.

After the war, Blobel was tried as a war criminal. He was hanged in June 1951.

BLUM, ABRAHAM (1905–1943), A leader of the BUND Jewish-Socialist Party and member of the Jewish Fighting Organization (ZOB) in WARSAW.

At the beginning of WORLD WAR II, Blum, known as Abrasha, was one of the few *Bund* leaders who did not flee Warsaw. He was very active in the *Bund's* under-

ground operations, such as its soup kitchens, welfare services, underground press, and political training. In mid-1942 Blum encouraged the *Bund* to join Warsaw's Zionist groups in a fighting alliance. In October the *Bund* joined the ZOB; Blum was made his party's delegate to the ZOB's political leadership.

The WARSAW GHETTO UPRISING broke out on April 19, 1943. Blum and a group of young *Bund* members defended a GHETTO section called the "Brushmakers" district. Blum then managed to escape the ghetto through the city's sewers. He hid in the forest for several days; he then returned to Warsaw and went into hiding. When he was discovered, he tried to escape from the fourth floor of a building by tying sheets together and sliding down. However, the sheets tore, and Blum was injured and captured by the Germans. He was taken to the GESTAPO, and was never heard from again. (see also JEWISH FIGHTING ORGANIZATION, WARSAW.)

BLUM, LEON (1872–1950), First Jew and first socialist to serve as prime minister of FRANCE. Blum was sent to BUCHENWALD in 1943, and then transferred to DACHAU. After the war, he returned to French politics.

BOARD OF DEPUTIES OF BRITISH JEWS Council representing the Jews of GREAT BRITAIN. After the Nazis rose to power in GERMANY in 1933, the board had to decide how to react to the persecution of German Jewry and how to absorb German Jewish REFUGEES. There were no easy answers to these dilemmas, as board members often had to choose between their British and Jewish loyalties, which frequently evoked conflicting interests.

Throughout the 1930s, the board requested that the British Foreign Office step in to stop the persecution of German Jewry, and bring the refugee problem to the world's attention. However, the British authorities refused to do anything that might be seen as barging in on Germany's internal affairs. The board itself did not join the anti-Nazi boycott or the WORLD JEWISH CONGRESS (see also BOYCOTTS, ANTI-NAZI). Board members were also hesitant about protesting the British fascist movement's antisemitic campaign.

During the war, the board again asked the British government to intercede on behalf of the Jews trapped in Nazi-occupied countries; publicize Nazi atrocities; help refugees inside Britain and neutral countries; and bomb AUSCHWITZ. The board also tried to convince the British government to lighten their Palestine immigration restrictions. However, the British authorities rejected all their pleas. (see also AUSCHWITZ, BOMBING OF.)

BOGAARD, JOHANNES (1881–1974), Dutch farmer who rescued 300 Jews during the HOLOCAUST. Taught by his father to respect the Jews as the people of the Bible, Bogaard felt responsible to help Jews running from the Nazis. He hid Jews on his farm and on the farms of relatives and neighbors.

When the Nazis began deporting Jews from the NETHERLANDS in July 1942, the Bogaard family decided to help Jews escape DEPORTATION. When Bogaard heard of Jews who needed his help, he would travel to Amsterdam to get them and bring them to his farm. He did this once or twice a week. At some points, Bogaard, known to those he rescued as "Uncle Hannes" had 100 Jews living at his family farm. He also helped Jews by handing out money, ration cards, and identity papers.

In November 1942 Bogaard's farm was stormed by Dutch Nazis. Over the next few months the Nazis raided his farm another two times, capturing tens of Jews. Bogaard's father, brother, and son were all deported to a German CONCENTRATION CAMP where they were killed. By the end of 1943, Bogaard moved most of the Jews under his care to safer locations.

In 1963 Bogaard was designated as RIGHTEOUS AMONG THE NATIONS by YAD VASHEM.

BOGDANOVKA (in Romanian, Bogdanovca), camp located on the Bug River, in the village of Bogdanovka in TRANSNISTRIA. It was established in October 1941 by the Romanian occupation authorities. By December 1, 1941, over 54,000 Jews from BESSARABIA and ODESSA were imprisoned in the camp.

In mid-December, typhus broke out in Bogdanovka. At that point, the Romanians and Germans decided to destroy the entire camp population. The extermination began on December 21. Romanian soldiers and police, Ukrainian police, and local civilians took part, under the command of the local Ukrainian police chief. Approximately 5,000 sick and handicapped prisoners were locked into two stables which were then burnt down. The rest of the prisoners were marched in groups of 300–400 to the river. They were forced to remove their clothing and kneel. Then they were shot or hit with hand grenades. The killing continued for four days, during which 30,000 Jews were murdered.

The killing was stopped temporarily on Christmas Eve, while the remaining Jews were left outside, freezing and waiting to die. The massacre began again on December 28; 11,000 Jews were killed by December 31. Two hundred were kept alive to burn the bodies, after which most of them were either killed or died from exposure.

BOHEMIA AND MORAVIA, PROTECTORATE OF
Western region of Czechoslovakia, occupied by German troops on March 15, 1939 and declared by Adolf HITLER to be a German "protectorate" (a euphemistic term for a subjugated state) belonging to the Reich. On the eve of the German occupation, 118,310 Jews lived in the region, whose capital was PRAGUE.

Immediately after the occupation, a wave of arrests began, mostly of REFUGEES from GERMANY, Czech public figures, and Jews. Fascist organizations began harassing Jews: synagogues were burnt down and Jews were rounded up and attacked in the streets. In June Adolf EICHMANN arrived in PRAGUE to establish the Central Office for Jewish Emigration (ZENTRALSTELLE FUER JUEDISCHE AUSWANDERUNG), to encourage the Jews to leave the country. In fact, 26,629 Jews managed to emigrate, legally or not, before emigration was completely banned in October 1941.

Also in June, a decree was issued barring Jews in the protectorate from almost all economic activity, and much Jewish property was seized. Jewish businesses were "bought" by Germans using force and threats. In all, the Germans seized about a half-billion dollars worth of Jewish property in the Protectorate of Bohemia and Moravia.

WORLD WAR II broke out in September 1939; the Jews were immediately subjected to a brutal series of persecutions. Jews were fired from their jobs; they were denied certain ration items, such as sugar, tobacco, and clothing; and their freedom of movement was restricted. Many prominent Jews were taken hostage and sent to CONCENTRATION CAMPS. In October, the first DEPORTATION took place: 3,000 Jewish men were exiled to the LUBLIN area (see also NISKO AND LUBLIN PLAN). Some managed to return home with reports of the atrocities being committed there. By November, Jewish children had been expelled from their schools and Jewish use of telephones and public transportation had been restricted. The Jews were forced to provide their own education, relief for the elderly and ill, and welfare

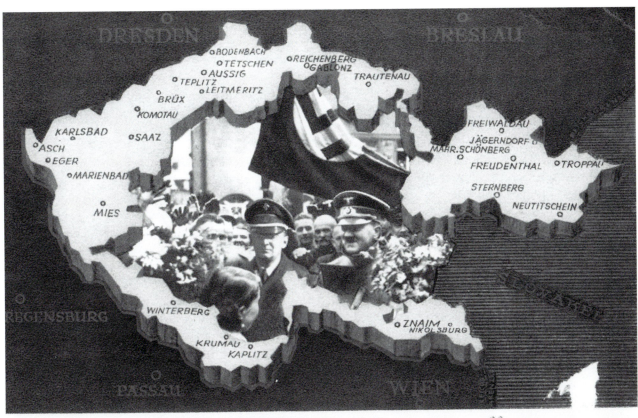

Postcard commemorating Hitler's acquisition of Czech territory

programs. Paramount was language and job training so Jews could leave for other countries.

A JUDENRAT-like organization called the Jewish Religious Congregation of Prague (JRC) was soon established. Gradually, the JRC turned into the obedient puppet of the German authorities, charged with responsibilities such as seizing Jewish assets, assigning Jews to do FORCED LABOR, and aiding deportations. In September 1941 the JRC was ordered to take a census of the Jewish population of the protectorate. They came up with 88,105 people, who were then forced to wear the Jewish badge and live totally separate from the rest of the population (see also BADGE, JEWISH).

Reinhard HEYDRICH was appointed acting governor of the Protectorate of Bohemia and Moravia in 1942. He immediately began to persecute the Jews in the protectorate. He decided to move all the Jews to THERESIENSTADT, in the hope that many of them would die there; the remaining Jews would then be deported to the east. However, first Heydrich sent five transports of Jews from Prague to LODZ and one transport from Brno to MINSK and RIGA. Most of these Jews were ultimately murdered.

From November 1941 to March 1945, more than 73,000 Jews from the protectorate were sent to Theresienstadt. Between 1942 and 1944 approximately 60,000 of them were sent on to AUSCHWITZ and other EXTERMINATION CAMPS. Only 3,277 survived the war.

Czechoslovakia was liberated on May 5, 1945. At that time, only 2,803 Jews were left in the Protectorate of Bohemia and Moravia. Of the 92,199 Jews living there before the deportations began, 78,154 died during the HOLOCAUST and 14,045 survived.

Throughout the war, the Nazis collected many Jewish religious and cultural articles from communities in the protectorate. They intended to display them in a planned "Central Museum of the Extinguished Jewish Race." Instead, their pillage turned into the most valuable Judaica collection in Europe, now exhibited in the Jewish Museum of Prague.

BONHOEFFER, DIETRICH (1906–1945), German Protestant theologian who opposed the Nazis. Despite the fact that Bonhoeffer came from a Christian tradition that viewed the Jews as a cursed people, he saw how poisonous and extreme the Nazis were. Thus, in 1933 he became a frank critic of the "German Christian" section of the German Evangelical Church, which supported Adolf HITLER and the NAZI PARTY. Because of his opposition to the government, his church decided to get him out of harm's way; they sent him to England to be a chaplain in the German church in south London. He served there until 1935, but was then asked to return to train ordination candidates for the anti-Nazi Confessing Church. This work was illegal, and it was put to an end by the GESTAPO in 1938.

During the war Bonhoeffer supported the German resistance movement. Several members of his immediately family were directly involved in resisting the Nazis, and some were later executed for their activities. Bonhoeffer himself tried to help Jews escape GERMANY; in 1942 he smuggled a group of 15 Jews into SWITZERLAND. This led to his arrest in April 1943, and subsequent imprisonment in BERLIN. Bonhoeffer was executed at the Flossenburg CONCENTRATION CAMP in April 1945.

BOR-KOMOROWSKI, TADEUSZ (1895–1966), Polish army officer who was appointed commander of the Polish HOME ARMY in WARSAW in 1943 by the POLISH GOVERNMENT-IN-EXILE, and led the WARSAW POLISH UPRISING in 1944.

BORKOWSKA, ANNA (d. 1988), Mother superior of a small convent of Dominican nuns located in Kolonia Wilenska, a town near VILNA, LITHUANIA. During WORLD WAR II, Borkowska aided Jews in her area who were being persecuted by the Nazis.

The Germans invaded Lithuania in mid-1941 and began murdering the Jews there almost immediately. During the summer, thousands of Jews were massacred in PONARY, a site about six miles from Vilna. At that time, Borkowska agreed to hide in her convent 17 members of Jewish Zionist youth groups for short periods of time. Later, she helped the Vilna GHETTO underground by sneaking weapons into the ghetto. Abraham SUTZKEVER, the Yiddish poet and PARTISAN fighter active in the Vilna Ghetto, later recalled that the first four grenades obtained by the Vilna underground were a gift from Borkowska—and she even showed resistance

leader Abba KOVNER how to use them. She also provided them with other weapons.

The Nazis found out about Borkowska's activities in 1943; in September she was arrested, the convent was closed down, and the other nuns moved elsewhere. One was sent to a labor camp. Borkowska survived the war, and in 1984 was designated as RIGHTEOUS AMONG THE NATIONS by YAD VASHEM in Jerusalem.

BORMANN, MARTIN (1900–1945?), Nazi leader and trusted aide to HITLER. In 1942 Bormann was appointed head of the NAZI PARTY, and in 1943 became Hitler's personal secretary. Bormann wielded tremendous power, for he controlled who could see the *Fuehrer*. For years after the war, there were rumors that Bormann had escaped to South America. At the TRIALS OF WAR CRIMINALS at Nuremberg, he was tried in absentia and sentenced to death. However, it is now generally accepted that he died in Berlin a few days after Hitler's death, during the Soviet bombardment of that city.

Martin Bormann, disembarking from a ship, 1935

BOTHMANN, HANS (1911–1946), Commandant of the CHELMNO extermination camp.

Bothmann joined the Hitler Youth (HITLERJUGEND) in 1932. In 1933 he enlisted in the SS. After GERMANY invaded POLAND in September 1939, kicking off WORLD WAR II, Bothmann was transferred to the Security Police in Poznan, an area of Poland annexed to Germany.

In the spring of 1942 Bothmann was named camp commandant at Chelmno. He served at the camp for a year, during which time he oversaw the extermination of hundreds of thousands of Jews. In March 1943 the DEPORTATION of Jews to Chelmno was halted. At that point, Bothmann and 85 members of the Chelmno staff were moved to YUGOSLAVIA, where Bothmann founded a SONDERKOMMANDO unit that fought the Yugoslav PARTISANS.

In mid-1944 Bothmann and his unit were sent back to Chelmno to renew the gassing campaign there. In August Bothmann's *Sonderkommando* unit participated in the liquidation of the LODZ Ghetto. The unit then took part in AKTION 1005 at Chelmno, the Nazis' attempt to conceal any evidence of the killings that took place there.

Bothmann fled to western Germany in January 1945. He was caught by the British and imprisoned; he committed suicide in jail in April 1946.

BOUSQUET, RENE (1909–1993), Chief of the FRENCH POLICE during the period of Nazi occupation. Bousquet was responsible for the collaboration of the police in the rounding up of Jews and their dispatch to DRANCY and other French transit camps. This included the infamous round up of some 12,000 Jews at the Velodrome d'Hiver stadium in PARIS in July 1942. The Jews were deported from the French camps to Nazi camps, where most were murdered. It was Bousquet who negotiated with the SS and came to an agreement with them that the French authorities would hand over to them all foreign Jews. Bousquet was not an adherent of Nazi ideology; instead, he acted as an authoritarian, xenophobic, arrogant, and callous bureaucrat of the Vichy regime. His main concern was not deporting Jews, but expanding the role and enhancing the prestige of the French Police. Bousquet was tried as a collaborator in 1949, and was given a suspended sentence as a reward for acts of resistance. He then pursued a successful career in banking. In the late 1980s and early 1990s, Bousquet's actions were again the subject of a court inquiry and public debate. In June 1993, several months before his trial was to begin, Bousquet was shot to death in his apartment by Christian Didier, an unbalanced man. (For more on Vichy, see also FRANCE.)

BOYCOTT, ANTI-JEWISH First officially-sanctioned national attack on German Jewry. A one-day boycott on Jewish businesses and shops was held on April 1, 1933,

SA men at the entrance to a Jewish store on the day of the Boycott, April 1, 1933. The sign in German reads:
"Germans Beware, Do Not Buy From Jews"

just months after HITLER rose to national power in GERMANY.

Joseph GOEBBELS, the Nazis' main propagandist, launched the anti-Jewish boycott in response to what he called horror propaganda, which he claimed the Jews were spreading about the Germans. The day was also meant to be a counter-boycott to the anti-Nazi boycotts already initiated by the world community.

The boycott, organized by Nazi leader Julius STREICHER, was to commence all over Germany at 10:00 a.m. That morning, uniformed and sometimes armed Nazi guards were posted in front of every Jewish business; they tried to block all clients from entering; but some insisted on patronizing Jewish establishments. The businesses themselves were marked with yellow Stars of David, and trucks drove through the streets sporting anti-Jewish signs. Despite the fact that the boycott was supposed to be peaceful, in many places store windows were shattered, business owners attacked, and stores plundered. In addition, although the order had gone out not to hurt businesses belonging to non-Germans, many were also attacked. Even Jewish doctors and lawyers had guards blocking their practices, and in several cities, Jewish lawyers and judges were kicked out of courtrooms.

The declaration of a boycott—originally slated for an unlimited period of time—aroused a strong response around the world. American Jews in particular protested strenuously and even called a protest rally in New York on March 27. This might have been one of the reasons that the Nazis then limited the boycott to one day only, after threatening to renew it if the situation did not change. In addition, the boycott of Jewish businesses also hurt Aryans who worked in those businesses.

Some scholars believe that the Nazis issued the boycott as a way to appease party members who demanded extreme economic steps against the Jews as they had been promised in the party's platform. Others view the boycott as the cue to begin harassing the Jews—a legal precedent for racial discrimination that could only lead downhill. In addition to the official one-day boycott, an unofficial boycott continued throughout Germany. (see also BOYCOTTS, ANTI-NAZI.)

BOYCOTTS, ANTI-NAZI

Economic actions taken by groups in many countries, especially the UNITED STATES, against Nazi GERMANY before WORLD WAR II in protest of the persecution of Jews.

The Jewish War Veterans established a boycott in the United States on March 19, 1933. In May the American League for the Defense of Jewish Rights was founded by the Yiddish journalist, Abraham Coralnik. Six months later Samuel Untermyer took charge of the organization; he soon became a leading figure in the boycott movement and was active until the United States entered the war in 1941. Untermyer changed his organization's name to the Non-Sectarian Anti-Nazi League to Champion Human Rights to emphasize that the cause did not only apply to Jews.

Untermyer and Coralnik also organized the World Jewish Economic Conference in Amsterdam in an unsuccessful effort to create an international Jewish boycott movement. The American Jewish Congress (AJC) declared a boycott in August 1933. In 1935 the AJC set up a joint boycott council with the Jewish labor committee; it developed into one of two major boycott organizations in the US. Nevertheless, Untermyer's league and the joint council did not succeed in joining forces.

Despite the fact that much support was expressed for the boycotts, many important organizations and leaders (both Jewish and among the American public) did not back the movement. Some, such as the American Jewish Committee and B'nai B'rith in the US, the BOARD OF DEPUTIES OF BRITISH JEWS in England, and the Alliance Israelite Universelle in FRANCE, even opposed the movement. In Britain, a group of board members under the leadership of Lord Melchett (Henry Mond) broke away to form their own movement. However, the group soon split up. The Jewish Agency could not support the boycott movement because of the TRANSFER AGREEMENT it had made with Germany, allowing them to help German Jews leave for Palestine, but forfeiting their right to protest Germany's activities.

The boycott was somewhat successful: it stopped the fur trade between Germany and Britain; several American department stores stopped buying German goods; and some leading Nazis even showed concern about the boycott's effects on the economy.

BRACK, VICTOR

(1904–1948), High-ranking SS officer who served as one of the head administrators in the EUTHANASIA PROGRAM and helped run the gassing campaign in the Nazi EXTERMINATION CAMPS during WORLD WAR II.

Brack studied economics in MUNICH. He was a friend of SS leader Heinrich HIMMLER, and even worked as

Himmler's driver before he took on the position of liaison officer between the SS and HITLER'S office in 1936. He was soon promoted to the post of deputy to the head of the office; in that position he was in charge of the extermination of tens of thousands of Jews and German citizens in the Euthanasia Program between 1939 and 1941. Brack himself personally handpicked the medical staff who worked in the Euthanasia Program.

In mid-1941 the mass murder of European Jewry began. Brack later helped the cause by volunteering his knowledge of medical experiments and murder to the program to sterilize Jews in x-ray clinics and kill them in GAS CHAMBERS in extermination camps.

After the war, Brack was tried in the "Medical Case," one of the NUREMBERG TRIALS. An American military court sentenced him to death in 1947; he was executed in 1948.

BRAND, JOEL (1907–1964), Member of the RELIEF AND RESCUE COMMITTEE of BUDAPEST. Brand and his wife Hansi organized rescue and relief actions for REFUGEES from GERMANY, AUSTRIA, Czechoslovakia, and POLAND. When the Relief and Rescue Committee was instituted formally in 1943, Brand was responsible for smuggling Jews into HUNGARY.

When Germany invaded Hungary in March 1944, Brand was approached by Adolf EICHMANN, who offered a deal whereby "one million" Hungarian Jews would be spared in exchange for certain goods, including 10,000 trucks. This deal was termed "Blood for goods." Eichmann sent Brand to Istanbul in May 1944 to consult with Jewish leaders there. The details of his mission were soon revealed to American and British authorities.

On June 7 Brand was arrested by the British in Syria. On June 10 he was allowed to promote the deal to Jewish Agency leader, Moshe Shertok (Sharett), and to Ira Hirschmann of President ROOSEVELT'S WAR REFUGEE BOARD; they were both convinced. However, the British refused to pursue Eichmann's offer and broadcast details to the public, killing any hopes of its success.

Brand was imprisoned in Cairo and finally released to Palestine in October—despondent at losing the chance to save the lives of so many Hungarian Jews.

BRATISLAVA (in German, Pressburg; in Hungarian, Pozsony), city in Czechoslovakia and capital of independent SLOVAKIA from 1939–1945 and after

1993. In 1940, 15,000 Jews lived in Bratislava. The city also housed important Jewish organizations, including the Jewish Center (*Ustredna Zidov*, UZ), as well as nationalist groups which often attacked the Jews.

The Jews of Bratislava aided many fellow Jews who needed their help. These included Austrian Jews persecuted by the Nazis, and Slovakian Jews who lived in areas annexed to HUNGARY. Many Jews, including both REFUGEES and native Czechoslovakians, escaped to Palestine through the port of Bratislava.

From fall 1941 to spring 1942, 6,700 Jewish residents of Bratislava were expelled from certain parts of the city and sent to the provinces. Their property was seized and their homes were given away.

The Nazis launched large-scale deportations from Slovakia to EXTERMINATION CAMPS in March 1942. Jews remaining in Bratislava continued their rescue efforts through the officially recognized UZ and through the underground WORKING GROUP. After the outbreak of the SLOVAK NATIONAL UPRISING in August 1944, the Germans occupied Bratislava. Jews either fled or hid; those who hid were found and sent to labor camps. When the Soviets liberated Bratislava in April 1945, only a few Jews remained. (see also JEWISH CENTER, SLOVAKIA.)

BREENDOCK Internment camp located in the Belgian village of Breendock, south of ANTWERP. In the early 1900s a fortress was built on the site as part of a string of fortifications.

The Germans occupied BELGIUM in May 1940. In August they turned the Breendock fortress into an internment camp. In mid-September the first group of 20 prisoners arrived at the camp, mostly consisting of political prisoners and non-Belgian Jews.

At first, the majority of prisoners were Jewish. However, during 1942 the Germans began deporting Jews from Belgium, so the number of Jewish prisoners ebbed. The non-Jews who arrived were mostly members of the leftist Belgian underground, hostages, and people who operated the black market. Altogether, about 3,000–3,600 prisoners passed through the camp. About 300 died there as a result of torture and the intolerable conditions; 450 were shot to death and 14 were hanged; and 54 Jews were transferred to AUSCHWITZ.

The physical conditions at Breendock were among the worst in Western European camps. In addition, the camp commanders subjected the prisoners to terrible cruelty and violence. From late 1942 until the camp's

LIBERATION in the summer of 1944, political prisoners in Breendock were executed.

BRIZGYS, VINCENTAS

(1903–1992), Lithuanian Catholic priest. During the 1930s, Brizgys was one of the heads of the Catholic Center in KOVNO. During WORLD WAR II, he became the city's assistant archbishop.

In June 1941 GERMANY invaded the SOVIET UNION and Soviet-held territories, including LITHUANIA. At that time, Brizgys allowed himself to be associated with several written statements that gave thanks to Nazi Germany for liberating Lithuania from the Soviets and pledged allegiance to the Nazis. However, during the years of Nazi control over his country, Brizgys met with Kovno's Jewish leaders on several occasions and expressed his compassion for them. In addition, he supported the idea of rescuing children from the Kovno GHETTO. On the other hand, he refused to personally help the children by appealing to the Nazis on their behalf. His excuse for not getting involved in rescue activities was that he did not want to risk the position and reputation of Lithuania's Catholic church.

When the German army withdrew from Lithuania in 1944, Brizgys left the country for Germany. After the war he settled in the UNITED STATES, where he was active in Lithuanian immigrant circles.

BRUNNER, ALOIS

(b. 1912), SS officer who served as one of Adolf EICHMANN'S assistants.

Originally from AUSTRIA, Brunner joined the NAZI PARTY in 1931 and the SS in 1938. After the ANSCHLUSS—the annexing of Austria by GERMANY in March 1938—Brunner began working for the SS's Security Service (SD) and Security Police in VIENNA. In August he was appointed director of the Central Office for Jewish Emigration (ZENTRALSTELLE FUER JUEDISCHE AUSWANDERUNG) in Vienna, an office established by Eichmann whose purpose was to "encourage" the Jews of Austria to leave the country.

WORLD WAR II broke out in September 1939; in October and November Brunner was responsible for deporting groups of Jews from Vienna and Moravia to Nisko, in the Lublin district of POLAND. In February and March 1941 Brunner was put in charge of the DEPORTATION of Jews from Vienna to the KIELCE area in south central Poland. In October 1941 he deported more Viennese Jews to the east.

In March 1943 Brunner was transferred to Greece, where he took charge of the deportation of the Jews of

SALONIKA and of those from MACEDONIA AND THRACE, regions occupied by BULGARIA during the war. In July 1943 Brunner moved on to FRANCE. He took control of the DRANCY detention camp, which had previously been run by the French. After his arrival, the inmates' conditions deteriorated rapidly, and deportations to AUSCHWITZ were stepped up. While in France, Brunner also went to the part of southern France which, until that time, had been under Italian control. Brunner oversaw the deportation of the Jews from that area to Drancy, and then on to Auschwitz. In September 1944 Brunner traveled to BRATISLAVA, SLOVAKIA, in order to finish the job of deporting the Jews of that country.

After the war, Brunner disappeared. Despite his absence, the French authorities conducted a trial against him and sentenced him to death in 1954. He later reappeared in Syria, where he was granted asylum, and settled there under a new name. It is not known if he is still living or not. (see also BOHEMIA AND MORAVIA, PROTECTORATE OF and NISKO AND LUBLIN PLAN.)

BRUSSELS

Capital of BELGIUM. When the Germans invaded Belgium in May 1940, 33,000 Jews lived in Brussels, most of whom were recent immigrants from Eastern Europe. After the German invasion, many of Brussels' Jewish community leaders fled, disrupting community services.

Communal life was somewhat revitalized in the summer of 1940. However, by mid-1941, the German occupational authorities began issuing ANTI-JEWISH LEGISLATION. Jewish children were kicked out of Belgian schools, and the Jews were forced to establish the ASSOCIATION OF JEWS IN BELGIUM (AJB), a JUDENRAT-like organization. In 1942 the Germans began confiscating Jewish property, drafted Jews into FORCED LABOR units, and made them wear the Jewish badge (see also BADGE, JEWISH). Many non-Jewish residents of Brussels wore badges in solidarity.

During the summer of 1942, the Jews were rounded up for DEPORTATION to the MECHELEN camp. Many resisted the deportations. In September the Jewish Defense Committee was formed by Jewish Communists and Zionists; it helped hide Jews, provided assistance for them, and kept in contact with the Belgian resistance movement. Many Jews were also active in Belgian resistance organizations, and 12,000 Jews hid all over Brussels.

After the LIBERATION, Brussels was a center for the reorganization and restoration of Belgium's Jews.

BUCHAREST Capital of ROMANIA. In 1941, 102,018 Jews lived in Bucharest. In addition, many Jewish REFUGEES sought shelter in the city throughout the war years.

In the late 1930s, the Jews' situation in Bucharest deteriorated. In 1938, Jewish workers were excluded from the chamber of commerce and trade unions. When Ion ANTONESCU took power in Romania in September 1940, the IRON GUARD terrorized the city's Jews. During the three-day Iron Guard rebellion against the Antonescu government in January 1941, 127 Jews were murdered, and many wounded. Jewish homes and businesses were destroyed by furious mobs.

After GERMANY invaded the SOVIET UNION in June 1941, Antonescu continued to persecute Bucharest's Jews. Recent arrivals to Bucharest were banished. Some 395 Jews were sent to TRANSNISTRIA and murdered. Harsh taxes were exacted from the Jews, and almost 30,000 were made to do FORCED LABOR. Those who evaded forced labor were deported to Transnistria. The Jews were also told to wear the Jewish badge, but Romanian Jewish leader Wilhelm FILDERMAN managed to get the decree canceled (see also BADGE, JEWISH).

Bucharest's Jews were saved from extermination in August 1944 when the king arrested Antonescu and broke off Romania's alliance with Germany. Adolf EICHMANN, who had intended to visit Bucharest to begin DEPORTATION preparations, was forced to cancel his trip—sparing the lives of the city's Jews.

BUCHENWALD One of the largest CONCENTRATION CAMPS in GERMANY, located five miles north of the city of Weimar. It was founded on July 16, 1937 and liberated on April 11, 1945. During its existence 238,980 prisoners from 30 countries passed through Buchenwald. Of those, 43,045 were killed, including Soviet PRISONERS OF WAR.

Jews after the liberation on the wooden planks that served as their beds during the Nazi period

Bucharest Jews in line to receive food for Passover during the war

Buchenwald was divided into three sections: the "large camp" which housed prisoners of higher standing; the "small camp" where prisoners were kept under restriction; and the "tent camp" set up in 1939 for Polish prisoners. There was also the administrative area, SS barracks, camp factories, and 130 satellite camps. Two different commandants ran the camp: SS-Standartenfuehrer Karl KOCH from 1937–1941, and SS-Oberfuehrer Hermann Pister from 1942–1945.

The first group of 149 prisoners arrived at Buchenwald in July 1937. They were mostly political prisoners and criminals. Soon after, large groups of prisoners began to arrive. By the end of 1937, there were 2,561 prisoners, mostly political. In the spring of 1938 prisoners who were considered asocial were brought to the site. The first transports of German Jews also came at that time. By July there were 7,723 prisoners in Buchenwald. On September 23, 1938, 2,200 Jews arrived from AUSTRIA. After KRISTALLNACHT (November 9–10), 10,000 more Jews were imprisoned.

The Jews were treated very cruelly; they were forced to work 14–15 hours a day, and lived under terrible conditions. At this point, the Germans' goal was to pressure the Jews to leave Germany. At the end of 1938 they released 9,370 Jews from Buchenwald after their families and Jewish and international organizations arranged for them to leave the country. During the short time such prisoners were kept at Buchenwald, 600 were killed, committed suicide, or died.

After the war broke out, thousands of political enemies were arrested and brought to Buchenwald. The number of Jewish prisoners rose again when Jews from Germany and the Protectorate of Bohemia and Moravia were deported to Buchenwald; in September 1939 the camp held 2,700 Jews. Next, thousands of Poles were brought in and held in the tent camp.

On October 17, 1942 the Nazis ordered that all Jewish prisoners in the Reich be transferred to AUSCHWITZ except for 204 workers. However, in 1944, Hungarians Jews were transported in the opposite direction, from Auschwitz to Buchenwald. They stayed a short time in the main camp, and were then moved to the satellite camps. Jews were treated much worse than the other prisoners and were used in MEDICAL EXPERIMENTS.

In 1943 the Germans finished building weapons factories on the site. This swelled the population. By the end of 1944 there were 63,048 prisoners, and 86,232 in February 1945.

On January 18, 1945 the Germans began to evacuate Auschwitz and other camps in Eastern Europe. This brought thousands of Jewish prisoners to Buchenwald, including hundreds of children. A special barracks, called "Children's Block 66" was set up for them in the tent camp, and most survived.

An underground movement that included Jews was formed in 1943, called the International Underground Committee. The movement succeeded in undermining some of the work done in the weapons factory and smuggling weapons and ammunition into the camp.

The Germans began evacuating Jewish prisoners on April 6, 1945. The next day, thousands of other prisoners were also evacuated. Some 25,500 prisoners died during the camp's evacuation. During Buchenwald's last days, resistance members were able to slow down the evacuation. By April 11 most of the SS had fled. The underground members took control of the camp and trapped the remaining SS. On that day 21,000 prisoners were liberated in Buchenwald, including 4,000 Jews and 1,000 children.

In 1947, 31 members of the camp staff were brought to trial, as part of the NUREMBERG TRIALS. Two were sentenced to death, and four to life in prison.

BUDAPEST   Capital of HUNGARY. The 200,000 member strong Jewish community of Budapest was first subjected to ANTI-JEWISH LEGISLATION in 1938 and 1939, as was the rest of Hungarian Jewry. They also suffered from the expansion of the HUNGARIAN LABOR SERVICE SYSTEM in 1941.

Despite this, from the outbreak of WORLD WAR II in September 1939 to the German occupation of Hungary on March 19, 1944, the Jews of Budapest were generally shielded from Nazi atrocities. Thousands of REFUGEES from AUSTRIA, POLAND, and SLOVAKIA streamed into Budapest in search of a safe haven. However, when the Nazis invaded, the situation became unbearable very quickly. Despite warnings from various world leaders, Hungarian regent Miklos HORTHY chose to give in to German demands to deport his country's Jews. First, the GESTAPO set up a JUDENRAT (in Hungarian, *Zsido Tanacs*) under the leadership of Samu STERN. This council was charged with governing the Jews of Budapest and informing Jewish Councils in the provinces about decrees made by the Nazi authorities. Next, Jewish shops were closed down, and many Jews were imprisoned in the Kistarcsa camp. By April 12, 1944, 1,500 Jewish-owned apartments had been taken away to be used by non-Jews.

At the end of June, instead of being confined to a GHETTO, the Jews of Budapest were transferred to 2,639 buildings, scattered all over the city, which were marked by the Star of David as being for Jews. Some 17,500

Jews were sent to AUSCHWITZ, just before Horthy halted the first wave of DEPORTATIONS.

Horthy decided to end the deportations on July 7, mostly as a result of pressure from Western governments. This respite gave the Jews left in Budapest time to consider rescue and escape options. Foreign diplomats sponsored, in part, by the American government's WAR REFUGEE BOARD began setting the stage for the rescue of Budapest's Jews. These included Raoul WALLENBERG from SWEDEN, Carl LUTZ from SWITZERLAND, and others. The diplomats often complained to the authorities about their terrible treatment of the Jews, and helped Jewish rescue groups supply food, fuel, and medicine to the Jewish community. They also attempted to protect Jews from being deported by giving them "protective passports." Some Jews also obtained false identity papers from the church, while others tried to get deportation exemptions from the government. Those Jews who held protective documents were put under diplomatic protection, and housed in safe residences provided by the diplomats. Often, Jews holding false protective documents—many of which were issued by the Zionist youth movement underground—were also protected by the rescuers.

In October 1944 the Germans overthrew Horthy's government and gave authority to the ARROW CROSS PARTY. This group of Hungarian fascists quickly embarked upon a reign of terror. During the first few days of their rule, 600 Jews were murdered in Budapest. Next, many Jews were forced to build fortifications. By November 8, deportations were resumed, full steam ahead. On November 13 a ghetto was established and 70,000 Jews were gradually moved into it. At the same time, the foreign diplomats set up an "international ghetto" as a safe haven for those Jews who held protective documents. From November 8 to December 24, nearly 80,000 Jews were sent on a DEATH MARCH toward the Austrian border. The rescuing diplomats followed the columns and removed those Jews with protective passports.

During December 1944 and January 1945, the Arrow Cross violence increased, and 20,000 Jews were

Jews being arrested in Budapest, 1944

shot and thrown into the Danube River. The Germans planned to liquidate the Budapest Ghetto, but the Soviet army reached the city first, conquering Pest in mid-January and Buda a month later. Some 120,000 Budapest Jews had survived.

BUDZYN FORCED LABOR and CONCENTRATION CAMP in the Lublin district of POLAND. In the summer of 1942, 500 Jews were brought to the camp from nearby towns. That fall, 400 PRISONERS OF WAR arrived from the Konska Wola camp and from the Lipowa Street camp in LUBLIN, while 100 sick, elderly, and very young inmates were deported to BELZEC. By mid-1943, there were 3,000 people imprisoned in the camp, including 300 women and children. The prisoners worked in military factories, in construction, and in general services.

In August 1943, 200 of the camp's prisoners were sent to MAJDANEK. On October 22, 1943 Budzyn was declared a concentration camp, and on February 8, 1944, tens of prisoners were massacred by Ukrainian guards.

Conditions in Budzyn were somewhat bearable, due to the efforts of the camp elder, Noah Stockman. In one case, some prisoners stole weapons from the military factories where they worked and escaped to the forest to join the PARTISANS. Stockman was able to convince the camp authorities not to retaliate against the Jews. On Passover 1944, Stockman managed to have *matza* (ritual unleavened bread) baked in the camp and hold a *seder* ceremony.

In May 1944, Budzyn was evacuated and the prisoners were sent to other nearby camps.

BUKOVINA Region in east-central Europe, today divided between ROMANIA and the UKRAINE. Bukovina was annexed by Romania after World War I. In June 1940 the SOVIET UNION took control of northern Bukovina. During the annexation process and the furious retreat of Romanian troops, Romanian soldiers murdered hundreds of Jews. Under the Soviets, traditional Jewish life was restricted and many Jewish leaders were deported to FORCED LABOR camps.

GERMANY invaded the Soviet Union in June 1941, including northern Bukovina. Organized groups of peasant thugs, mainly Ukrainians, tortured, raped, and robbed Jews before the Germans and their Romanian allies even arrived. When the Nazis entered the region they immediately began killing Jews: German and Romanian soldiers carried out pogroms killing thousands of Jews, while an EINSATZGRUPPE unit murdered thousands more. The remaining Jews were forced to wear the Jewish badge (see also BADGE, JEWISH) and move into GHETTOS. Jews were deported in brutal fashion from there to camps in northern BESSARABIA, where many died. The survivors were sent to TRANSNISTRIA, where they were made to do forced labor under extremely harsh conditions.

Right before the Germans entered northern Bukovina, Romanian leader Ion ANTONESCU also ordered that the Jews in southern Bukovina be sent to camps in Romania. From there they were sent on to Transnistria. By November 1941, 57,000 Jews from all over Bukovina had arrived in Transnistria. DEPORTATIONS were then halted, but began again in summer 1942; at that point, 4,000 more Jews were sent to Transnistria.

In October 1943 the Jewish badge decree was cancelled and Jews were allowed to move freely around the main city of northern Bukovina, Chernovtsy. In February 1944 the Romanians left Chernovtsy to the Germans, who planned to finish off the city's Jews. However, the Soviet army quickly arrived to liberate the city, and rescued the Jews from almost certain death. Thousands of deportees returned to the city in late 1944 and early 1945. In all, about half the Jewish population of Bukovina had perished. After the war, most of the SURVIVORS fled to Romania, and later settled in Israel.

BULGARIA Country in Eastern Europe. On the eve of WORLD WAR II some 50,000 Jews lived in Bulgaria; more than half lived in the country's capital, Sofia.

For hundreds of years there was almost no ANTISEMITISM in Bulgaria. This changed during the 1930s, when certain political groups began expressing anti-Jewish sentiments. In late 1940 a pro-German government passed Bulgaria's first ANTI-JEWISH LEGISLATION. These laws were vigorously protested by many Bulgarians, but to no avail—they were still passed by the Bulgarian parliament. Jewish teachers were fired from their jobs, all Jews were forced to don the Jewish badge (see also BADGE, JEWISH), and they were made to live in terribly overcrowded conditions. In addition, Jews were not allowed to frequent main streets or places of entertainment, their radios, cars, and other valuable possessions were confiscated, and most Jewish males were drafted into doing FORCED LABOR.

King Boris signing friendship pact with Germany

In March 1941 Bulgaria allied itself with GERMANY and ITALY; its main hope in doing so was that the AXIS powers would help it regain territories lost during World War I. As part of the package Bulgaria declared war on the Western Allies, and was rewarded by the Germans with its former provinces of MACEDONIA AND THRACE. German army units were stationed in Bulgaria, but the Bulgarian government was not completely taken over by the Nazis.

In September 1942 the Bulgarians established a *Commissariat* (office) for Jewish Affairs and appointed a well-known antisemite, Alexandr Belev, to run it. The *Commissariat*, which was funded by money taken from blocked Jewish bank accounts, soon became Bulgaria's main address for dealing with Jewish affairs.

During the winter of 1943 SS officer Theodor DANNECKER came to Bulgaria to direct its anti-Jewish measures. At that point, the DEPORTATION of Jews to EXTERMINATION CAMPS became a distinct and frightening possibility. In February of that year the Bulgarian government agreed to deport 20,000 Jews from Macedonia and Thrace. However, there were nowhere near 20,000 Jews in the two regions combined, so the extra 6,000 were to be taken from Bulgaria itself. As a first step, more than 11,000 Jews were sent from Macedonia and Thrace to holding camps, where they were kept for about a week before they were handed over to the Germans, who deported them to TREBLINKA.

The first group of Jews set aside for deportation from Bulgaria itself came from the town of Kyustendil. Dimiter Peshev, a deputy speaker of the parliament, quickly launched a campaign to stop the deportation. Peshev met with Minister of the Interior Peter Gabrovski, who agreed to cancel the deportation order for the Jews of Bulgaria itself, but not for those from Macedonia and Thrace. Peshev then turned to the prime minister, and demanded that all anti-Jewish persecution be halted. Prime Minister Bogdan Filov promptly fired Peshev, and the Germans stepped up their demand for the deportation of Bulgarian Jewry. In late May the Bulgarian government decided to expel the Jews of Sofia to the provinces, pending their deportation. However, this turned out to be the furthest the government would go, and the threat of deportation disintegrated (although all Jewish men between the ages of 20 and 46 were drafted into forced labor battalions and made to do backbreaking work).

As the Germans slowly began losing the war, conditions improved for the Jews of Bulgaria. While the Jews from Macedonia and Thrace had been murdered by the Germans with Bulgarian assistance, the Jews who had been expelled from Sofia were allowed to go home on short visits and were given certain other privileges. When the Soviet army reached Bulgaria in August 1944 all anti-Jewish decrees were cancelled. The Jews of pre-war Bulgaria had been persecuted, but they had been spared the fate of most other Jews in Europe—death. After the establishment of the State of Israel in 1948, 90 percent of Bulgaria's Jews settled there.

BUND (*Yidisher Arbeter-Bund in Russland, Lite un Poiln;* League of Jewish Workers in Russia, LITHUANIA, and POLAND), Jewish Socialist party founded in VILNA in 1897.

Originally, the *Bund* aimed to organize Jewish workers and encourage their involvement in the Russian Socialist movement. However, after the Bolshevik Revolution of 1917, the *Bund* disintegrated in the SOVIET UNION when most of its members joined the Communist party. The *Bund* flourished in Poland after World War I and became an important force among Poland's Jews. Small branches were also active in Lithuania, ROMANIA, BELGIUM, FRANCE, and the UNITED STATES.

The *Bund* completely opposed Zionism and Hebrew culture and language; it viewed Yiddish as the national language of Eastern European Jewry. It called for equal rights for Jews within a Socialist framework in which Jews would be given cultural freedom.

Prior to WORLD WAR II, the *Bund* fought ANTISEMITISM in Poland, and even empowered its self-defense units to

Underground publications of the Bund from the Warsaw Ghetto

respond aggressively against attacks on Jews. *Bund* members also extended their influence by joining Polish city councils.

When World War II broke out most of the *Bund's* leaders fled Poland. Many members were arrested, exiled, or murdered. In WARSAW, the party elders refused to join forces with any Zionist parties or movements in creating a united Jewish fighting alliance, claiming they had ties with the underground outside the GHETTO. Younger leaders did support an umbrella organization. However, only after the major DEPORTATIONS from Warsaw in October 1942 did the young members join the Jewish Fighting Organization. A similar thing happened in Vilna, when the younger members defied the party elders by joining the United Partisan Organization. Four *Bund* squads also joined the fighting in the WARSAW GHETTO UPRISING in April 1943.

Samuel ZYGELBOJM, a *Bund* leader who had fled to the US, was appointed to the Polish National Committee in London in 1942. After receiving reports of the mass murder of Polish Jewry, Zygelbojm desperately tried to enlist the help of international and Jewish organizations. After failing to garner support, however, Zygelbojm committed suicide in 1943. (see also JEWISH FIGHTING ORGANIZATION, WARSAW and UNITED PARTISAN ORGANIZATION, VILNA.)

CANADA   Country in North America that joined the war against GERMANY just one week after the German invasion of POLAND in September 1939. Despite the fact that Canada fought resolutely for the Allied cause, the country did very little to help rescue European Jewry during the HOLOCAUST.

Canada closed its doors to Jews long before the Nazis rose to power. During the early 1920s the farmlands of western Canada attracted many Europeans, including Jews. This provoked many Canadians to oppose an open immigration policy, and in 1923 the Canadian government restricted its immigration quotas for all Eastern Europeans. Particularly strict rules limited the immigration of Jews to Canada, except those from GREAT BRITAIN or the UNITED STATES. After 1923, only Jews who had very close relatives in Canada or could convince the authorities to give them an entry permit—which almost never happened—were admitted into the country.

The Great Depression of the 1930s made matters even worse. Despite the rise of ANTISEMITISM in Europe, especially in Germany, Canada's conditions for immigration were further restricted. Canada's small Jewish community—which made up less than 1.5 percent of the country's entire population—responded to the immigration restrictions by lobbying the government for change. Their national Jewish organization, the Canadian Jewish Congress, also responded to the Nazi threat by arranging a national boycott of goods manufactured in Germany (see also BOYCOTTS, ANTI-NAZI). The boycott may have been somewhat successful, but the lobbying accomplished nothing. Canadian delegates attended the international EVIAN CONFERENCE on REFUGEES in July 1938, but not to offer their country's support in helping the Jews desperately seeking a safe haven from the Nazis. Rather, totally unaffected by the Jews' plight and the lobbying efforts of Canada's own Jews, the delegates were present at the conference in order to ensure that other delegates did not suggest Canada as a possibility for some Jewish refugee resettlement plan.

When WORLD WAR II broke out in September 1939,

Canada's Jewish community both completely supported the war effort, and continued trying to convince the Canadian government to allow in European Jews who could still be saved. On a very few occasions, the Canadian Jewish Congress did manage to persuade the authorities to admit into Canada small groups of Jews. In late 1941 the government agreed to accept 1,000 Jewish children from Vichy FRANCE whose parents had already been deported to EXTERMINATION CAMPS in Poland. However, their hard-won efforts came too late to actually save those children: before the children could leave for Canada, the Nazis took control of Vichy France, and the orphans were deported to their deaths. Later on in the war, the Canadian authorities allowed into Canada several hundred Jewish refugees who had made their way to SPAIN and SWITZERLAND.

A third group of Jewish refugees arrived in Canada during the war, but not due to the efforts of the Jewish community or by the good graces of the Canadian government. These refugees came from England, where they had already found a safe haven from the Nazis. After France was vanquished by the Germans in mid-1940, the British started to fear an invasion of their island. They began to believe that German and Austrian refugees in Britain—including Jews who were simply trying to escape with their lives—were a danger, and might aid the enemy from within. Thus, the British began deporting such refugees to Australia and Canada. Only after two years of pressure from the Canadian Jewish community were the Jewish refugees among the group finally released.

After the war, Canada still refused to change its immigration regulations, even with its recognition of the atrocities that had occurred in Europe. Only during the late 1940s did the Canadian government open its doors wide to Jewish SURVIVORS of the Holocaust.

CANARIS, WILHELM   (1887–1945), Chief of the German military's intelligence department (ABWEHR) from 1935–1944. Originally a Nazi supporter, Canaris opposed their treatment of the Polish clergy and

Wilhelm Canaris (on the right)

aristocracy. He eventually connected with opponents of HITLER, and was executed in 1945 for treason.

CENTRAL COMMITTEE OF GERMAN JEWS FOR HELP AND RECONSTRUCTION   (*Zentralausschuss der Deutschen Juden fuer Hilfe und Aufbau*), center that coordinated economic and social assistance for German Jews from 1933 to 1938. The committee was created in April 1933, just three months after HITLER rose to national power, as a collaboration of various German Jewish communal, political, and social-welfare organizations. Its goal was to take care of those Jews who had lost their jobs or businesses as a result of the Nazis' ANTI-JEWISH LEGISLATION. In addition, Jewish welfare organizations outside of GERMANY had requested the creation of such a committee to deal with all the monies being donated to help German Jewry.

At first, the committee concentrated on providing job training for those Jews who needed to find new professions, as they did not yet see emigration as the necessary solution to their problems. In April 1934 the committee was incorporated into the REICH REPRESENTATION OF GERMAN JEWS. At that point, the committee became even more efficient in its welfare activities, and took responsibility for the Reich Representation's finances. In that capacity, the committee consolidated all the aid funds donated by Jewish organizations abroad, such as the JOINT DISTRIBUTION COMMITTEE and the Central British Fund, and continued to collect donations from German Jews.

CENTRAL CONSISTORY OF THE JEWS OF FRANCE
(*Consistoire Central des Israelites de France*), representative body of French Jewry, established in 1808, which was historically responsible for Jewish religious life in FRANCE.

When GERMANY occupied France in mid-1940, the *Consistoire* moved its headquarters from PARIS to Lyons, in the unoccupied zone. At first, the *Consistoire* leadership counseled French Jewry to cooperate with the anti-Jewish restrictions set in place by the Vichy government, in order to preserve their dignity. At the same time, the *Consistoire* protested the racial laws, and opposed the establishment of the UNION OF FRENCH JEWS, an organization set up by the Vichy government to represent French Jewry.

The *Consistoire* was not dissolved by the Vichy authorities; throughout the war it kept its synagogues open and promoted welfare activities. In October 1943, when the SS intensified its campaign to deport Jews from France, the *Consistoire* agreed to join forces with immigrant and Communist Jewish organizations in order to present a united front against the Nazis. In 1944 the REPRESENTATIVE COUNCIL OF FRENCH JEWS was established, headed by *Consistoire* president, Leon Meiss. This new umbrella organization represented all of French Jewry until the LIBERATION of France. (for more on Vichy, see also FRANCE.)

CENTRAL OFFICE OF JUDICIAL ADMINISTRATION, LUDWIGSBURG   (*Ludwigsburger Zentralstelle*), office established in December 1958 in the West German city of Ludwigsburg, whose goal was to investigate Nazi crimes, committed between 1933 and 1945, which were based on Nazi ideology and which were now punishable according to West German law. Many of the members of EICHMANN'S office, for example, were investigated by the *Zentralstelle*. The *Zentralstelle* was staffed by judges and prosecuting attorneys from the 11 states that made up West Germany.

When it was originally established, the *Zentralstelle* only dealt with crimes that were committed outside the borders of West Germany. In 1964 that ruling was changed to include all Nazi crimes, no matter where they took place, as long as they were committed in the name of Nazi ideology. Thus, the office did not and does not deal with war crimes, by definition.

The *Zentralstelle* is responsible to collect any available information about Nazi crimes, sort the crimes into categories, and determine where to find the criminals.

Once the *Zentralstelle* locates a Nazi criminal within West Germany, it passes the case on to public prosecutors in the appropriate area for indictment. During the 1990s the *Zentralstelle* initiated fewer and fewer investigations, whereas its importance as an archive about Nazi crimes grew.

CENTRAL RESETTLEMENT OFFICE (*Umwanderer-zentralstelle*),

German office that oversaw the expulsion of Poles from the Polish territories annexed to the Reich at the beginning of WORLD WAR II and from the Zamosc province in the GENERALGOUVERNEMENT. The office also ran the transit camps in which these Polish exiles were held, and decided how to racially classify them.

In November 1939 the Germans established an office in the region of POLAND annexed to the Reich, which they called the Special Staff for the Resettlement of Poles and Jews. Soon this evolved into the Office of the Higher SS and Police Leader for the Resettlement of Poles and Jews, which was renamed the Transfer Office in the spring of 1940, and the Central Resettlement Office just weeks later.

In 1942 the Central Resettlement Office was opened in LUBLIN and a sub-office was opened in Zamosc. These two offices, which had 30 branches all over Poland, were under the authority of the Higher SS and Police Leader of each region, and were supervised by the Jewish affairs department of the Reich Security Main Office (REICHSSICHERHEITSHAUPTAMT, RSHA). In all, some 920,000 Poles and Jews from the Polish regions attached to the Reich were expelled by these two offices, as were 116,000 Poles from the Zamosc region of the *Generalgouvernement*.

CENTRAL UNION OF GERMAN CITIZENS OF JEWISH BELIEF (*Centralverein Deutscher Staatsbuerger Juedischen Glaubens*, CV),

organization dedicated to protecting the civil and social rights of Jews in GERMANY, while at the same time, cultivating their German identity. The union, active from 1893 to 1938, was originally established in response to the rise of political ANTISEMITISM. Part of the union's platform was to view Jews as a religious group only—not a national group. Thus, it was anti-Zionist for a long time. However, its young leaders supported settlement in Palestine.

When the NAZI PARTY rose to national power in 1933, the union opened a legal office to fight for Jewish rights, and initiated an information campaign, which at first tried to calm German Jews. After the anti-Jewish boycott of April 1933, the union began organizing educational and religious activities, hoping to convince the Nazi government to recognize the Jews as a separate but equal group within Germany (see also BOYCOTT, ANTI-JEWISH). After the racial NUREMBERG LAWS were issued in 1935, the union was forced to change its name to *Centralverein der Juden in Deutschland* (Central Union of Jews in Germany). The organization increasingly made emigration and job training its main priorities.

After the KRISTALLNACHT pogrom of November 1938, the union was no longer independently active, and was assimilated into the new Reich Association of Jews in Germany.

CENTRALVEREIN DEUTSCHER STAATSBUERGER JUEDISCHEN GLAUBENS see CENTRAL UNION OF GERMAN CITIZENS OF JEWISH BELIEF.

CENTRAL WELFARE COUNCIL, POLAND (*Rada Glowna Opiekuncza*, RGO),

social welfare organization manned by Polish volunteers that was active in the GENERALGOUVERNEMENT from 1940–1945. The RGO was supervised by the German occupying authorities, but helped both Poles and Jews. The RGO was also in contact with the Polish underground. In 1941 one million people received aid from the council; in the fall of 1944, 1.2 million people were aid recipients. The first chairman of the RGO was Adam Ronikier, who was succeeded by Konstanty Tchorznicki in October 1943.

The RGO's headquarters were located in WARSAW, while Polish Welfare Committees worked in the *Generalgouvernement's* districts under the RGO's direction. Council representatives provided food, clothing, health services, fuel, and money. They ran welfare institutions and set up special services to take care of children, prisoners, and exiles. Public contributions and Polish institutions funded the council. Clothing and other supplies were sent from abroad; bought on the free market; donated by generous Poles; and given as gifts by various *Generalgouvernement* government offices.

The RGO had very good connections with the Polish underground and with groups within the Polish community. It did not give in to the German authorities who wanted their cooperation. In addition, as the council was officially regulated by the German occupying government, it tried to convince the authorities to better the living circumstances of the *Generalgouvernement* population.

Other welfare organizations were also active within the *Generalgouvernement* at this time. These included the Jewish Self-Help Society (*Zydowska Samopomoc Spoleczna*, ZSS), and the Ukrainian Central Council (*Ukrainska Rada Glowna*), which was part of the Main Welfare Council (*Naczelna Rada Opiekuncza*). There were Jewish workers within the RGO, and RGO leaders supported the ZSS. In addition, the council defended Jews before the German authorities on several occasions. After the ZSS was shut down in the fall of 1942, the RGO continued to hand out contributions from overseas to the Jews. The council also gave funding to the Jewish Welfare Bureau (*Juedische Unterstuezungsstelle*), and in CRACOW it worked with the ZEGOTA organization (the underground Council for Aid to Jews) on its rescue activities.

CENTRALA EVREILOR   see JEWISH CENTER, ROMANIA.

CHAMBERLAIN, HOUSTON STEWART   (1855–1927), Racial ideologist who served as a conceptual link between older theories of RACISM and Nazism. Chamberlain was British but chose German as his nationality. He believed that Adolf HITLER was just the man to implement his racial theories.

Chamberlain viewed the clash between two races, the superior Aryans and the inferior Jews, as the basis of European history. In his major work, "The Foundations of the Nineteenth Century" (1899), Chamberlain reached back to the time of Jesus to begin proving his theories. He maintained that the Jews had contaminated Jesus' Aryan doctrine, and that since then there has been a constant war waging between the two races. According to Chamberlain, the Germans are fated to destroy the Jews, as they are the highest cultural achievers and saviors of humanity, while the Jews are a bastard race of greedy, inferior foreigners whose interference in the world can only lead to cultural degeneration. All of Western history since Jesus' time leads to the resolution of this race struggle, with the Aryans completely destroying Judaism and rescuing the world from racial chaos.

These theories appealed to the Nazis because Chamberlain provided "historical" proof of their "duty" to rid the world of Judaism.

CHELMNO   (in German, Kulmhof), EXTERMINATION CAMP located in the Polish village of Chelmno, 47 miles

west of LODZ. Chelmno was the first Nazi camp where gassing was used to exterminate Jews on a large-scale basis, and the first place outside the SOVIET UNION where Jews were slaughtered en mass as part of the "final solution." It was created to serve as the extermination center for the Jews in the Lodz GHETTO as well as those from the entire WARTHEGAU region. In all, some 320,000 people were murdered at Chelmno.

Chelmno encompassed two sites 2.5 miles apart. The first was located inside the village in an old palace. This site was where the prisoners were received and gassed, and where the camp staff was housed. The second site was located in a nearby forest, and consisted of mass graves and later, crematoria ovens.

The first group of prisoners arrived at Chelmno on December 7, 1941, and the first exterminations began the next day. The camp's early victims included Jews from throughout the area, as well as 5,000 GYPSIES who had been imprisoned in the Lodz Ghetto. No railroad tracks reached Chelmno directly, so the deportees were brought by train to a nearby station, and then loaded onto trucks that delivered them straight to the reception area at Chelmno. The Nazis then gathered the victims in the palace's courtyard, and told them that they were being sent to a work camp, and thus had to get washed up. Groups of 50 were then sent to the building's ground floor, where they were made to give up their valuables and undress—men, women, and children together. Next, they were taken to the cellar, where they were reassured by signs that they were heading "To the Washroom" but in fact were forced down a ramp into a GAS VAN. After the van was filled to the brim, the driver locked the doors and turned on the motor. After 10 minutes, the gas fumes had suffocated all those inside the van.

Throughout 1942 Jews from the Lodz Ghetto and from the 32 other towns and villages in the Warthegau were deported to their deaths at Chelmno. In addition, several Poles were also sent there, as were Soviet PRISONERS OF WAR and 88 children from the Czech village of LIDICE. The possessions that had been brought by victims to Chelmno were given or sold to Germans living in the region. On January 19, 1942 an inmate, Jacob Grojanowski, succeeded in escaping and reached the WARSAW Ghetto, where he gave detailed information to the underground ONEG SHABBAT Archives. By June 1942, through the channels of the Polish underground, his report reached London and was published (see also GROJANOWSKI REPORT).

Jewish slave laborers digging their own graves in Chelmno

In March 1943 the Nazis stopped the DEPORTATIONS to Chelmno, as all of the Jews in the Warthegau, except for those left in the Lodz Ghetto, had already been annihilated. The camp was dismantled, and the camp staff was transferred to YUGOSLAVIA to fight Yugoslav PARTISANS. However, the Nazis reopened the camp in April 1944 in conjunction with their plan to liquidate the Lodz Ghetto. Members of the Chelmno staff were brought back from Yugoslavia to resume their work at the camp, to which crematoria had been added. Transports to Chelmno were renewed on June 23, 1944, and by mid-July, more than 7,000 Jews had been exterminated. At that point, the Nazis decided to step up the liquidation process, so they halted the transports to Chelmno and began deporting the remaining ghetto inhabitants to AUSCHWITZ, where extermination by ZYKLON B gas was quicker and more efficient.

In early September 1944, as part of AKTION 1005, the Nazis began destroying all evidence of mass murder at Chelmno by digging up and cremating the bodies that

had been buried in mass graves. On January 17, 1945, as Soviet troops drew near, the Nazis began evacuating Chelmno. While the Nazis were murdering the last 48 Jewish prisoners in the camp, the Jews put up a fight and three escaped. The rest were killed.

CHETNICKS Armed groups of Serb fighters who were active in YUGOSLAVIA during the German occupation, from 1941–1945. Their goal was to return Yugoslavia's (Serb) royal family to power.

The Chetnicks began their activities soon after Yugoslavia succumbed to GERMANY in April 1941. They participated in the Yugoslav revolt against the Germans in the summer of that year, and even cooperated with the PARTISANS under the leadership of TITO. However, after the revolt was brutally suppressed, the Chetnicks decided that there was no point in fighting the Germans, because the struggle was hopeless and unattainable. Their most important conclusion was that the real enemy was not Germany, but rather the pro-Communist partisans, who would attempt to take over Yugoslavia after the war. Therefore, the Chetnicks turned on the partisans. They even collaborated with their former enemies, the Germans and Italians, against the partisans.

When the Chetnicks began cooperating with the occupying forces, any Jews among their ranks left. There were even instances where the Chetnicks killed Jews or surrendered them to the Germans.

After the war, most of the Chetnicks were caught and executed.

CHOMS, WLADYSLAWA (1891–1966), Pole, nicknamed the "Angel of LVOV," who rescued Jews during the HOLOCAUST. When the Germans occupied Lvov in eastern POLAND in June 1941, Choms created a charitable fund for needy Jews. She also gathered around her a group of other devoted rescuers, who helped her provide food, money, and medical care to Jews both inside and outside the GHETTO; forge false identity papers for Jews living illegally outside the ghetto; and hide both children and adults in the safe havens of convents and private families. She personally watched over some 60 Jewish children herself.

Choms' husband (an officer in the Polish army) and son had fled to GREAT BRITAIN and joined the fight against the Nazis from there. In retaliation, the Germans sought to arrest Choms. Thus she was constantly moving from place to place and changing her name.

In November 1942 the ZEGOTA (Polish Council for Aid to Jews) asked Choms to set up a local office in Lvov. She continued her rescue activities until the end of 1943, when she was sent to WARSAW by her underground commanders in order to ensure her safety.

After the war, Choms was designated as RIGHTEOUS AMONG THE NATIONS by YAD VASHEM.

CHRISTIAN CHURCHES When Adolf HITLER and the NAZI PARTY rose to power in early 1933, many church groups in GERMANY, both Catholic and Protestant, supported the new government. They did so for several reasons. First, the Nazis claimed that they would support "positive Christianity" and thus won the backing of many Christian groups. Second, many Christians, especially Catholics, were violently opposed to Soviet Communism and its anti-religion ideology, and they believed that the Nazis would suppress the spread of Communism. Third, many Christians supported the Nazis' anti-Jewish stance. For nearly 2,000 years, Christians had been persecuting Jews due to their belief that Jews were responsible for the crucifixion of Jesus; because of their ingrained notion that Jews deserved to be punished for failing in their role as the original chosen people; and because of the idea that Christianity had replaced Judaism.

However, soon the Nazis began showing their true colors when it came to religion: they started interfering in various church matters, such as religious education. The idea that the government was free to decide what the church would teach was unacceptable to both Catholic and Protestant leaders. The Catholic church tried to solve the problem by making an official agreement with the Nazis. In July 1933 the Vatican's secretary of state, Eugenio Pacelli, signed a *Reich Concordat* with Nazi Germany, which stated that the Vatican recognized the political legitimacy of Nazi Germany, in exchange for a guarantee that the Nazis would not interfere with Catholic institutions and religious schools. Just six years later, that very same man who signed the pact—Eugenio Pacelli—was elected Pope PIUS XII in Rome.

The German Protestant church dealt with the problem of Nazi interference into its affairs differently: it split. Supporters of the Nazis, called "German Christians" were prepared to follow the Nazis' orders at all costs, and even demanded that all Jewish elements be removed from Christian prayers and rituals. Opponents of the Nazis created a breakaway church, called the Confessing Church. Members of this new church vehemently opposed the Nazi regime, but they did not challenge the Nazis for passing ANTI-JEWISH LEGISLATION and were more interested in saving Jews who had converted to Christianity, than all Jews. Only a small group of Confessing Christians made active efforts to hide Jews or help them escape the country. Moderates in the Protestant church may have opposed the Nazis' actions, but they wanted to avoid a fight, so they were willing to compromise with the German government. Some Protestants, such as the bishop of Wurttemberg, Theophil WURM, supported the "German Christians" at first, but turned away from the Nazis in late 1933, when Nazi efforts to impose their world view on society grew stronger. An expression of this was the Nazi attempt to put church institutions under their control and subject them to Nazi ideology. At that point, Wurm joined other prominent Protestants in the anti-Nazi Confessing Church, such as Dietrich BONHOEFFER and Martin NIEMOLLER, all of whom were later imprisoned for their opposition to the Nazis.

In general, the Catholic church's attitude towards the Nazi persecution of Jews during the HOLOCAUST was rather ambivalent. The official agreement made between the Vatican and the Reich in mid-1933 made it impossible for large groups of German Catholics to get together and protest the Nazis' activities. As a rule, the church was more interested in protecting itself and its members than in saving Jews. Thus, the church was silent both during the issuing of the NUREMBERG LAWS of 1935 and during the massive KRISTALLNACHT pogrom of November 1938.

Pope Pius XII himself was mixed in his attitude towards the Jews. Soon after his appointment in 1939, he procured 3,000 visas to Catholic Brazil for Jews who had been baptized. However, a year later he ignored requests to intervene on behalf of Jews in SPAIN and LITHUANIA who were in danger of being sent back to Germany. In addition, the Pope refused to directly condemn the Nazis in his pronouncements. It is possible that the Pope was not willing to speak out publicly in defense of the Jews, but supported the rescue of Jews from behind the scenes. Catholic clergy in ITALY played a very large role in hiding Italian Jews, while representatives of the Vatican stationed in SLOVAKIA, HUNGARY, and ROMANIA did their best to pressure the governments of those countries to stop DEPORTATION of Jews to EXTERMINATION CAMPS, and in fact, these efforts led to the rescue of some Jews.

In other countries, the Christian reaction to Nazi persecution of Jews was also mixed. In FRANCE, many Catholic clergy were held back by the traditional idea that they were not obligated to help the Jews, classically considered to be an inferior group, and their hatred of foreigners, which many of the Jews in France were. However, some younger clergy decided that helping the Jews was a natural part of resisting the German occupiers, so they and their constituents helped hide many Jews, especially children, and organized escape routes to Spain and SWITZERLAND.

The Reformed (Calvinist) churches in France, Switzerland, the NETHERLANDS, and Hungary were also more helpful to the Jewish victims of the Nazis. Throughout their history, members of these churches had also been victims of persecution, so they identified with the Jews' plight, and were more willing to come to the rescue.

One notable example was the French Protestant village of LE CHAMBON-SUR-LIGNON, whose inhabitants protected some 3,000–5,000 Jews from the Nazis at the encouragement of their pastor, Andre Trocme. In addition, the Lutheran churches of NORWAY, SWEDEN, and DENMARK loudly protested the persecution and extermination of European Jewry.

After the war, both the Catholic and Protestant churches admitted the fact that Christians had not done enough to help the Jews during the Holocaust. This recognition has led them to rethink Christianity's attitude towards and relationship with Judaism and Jews.

CHURCHILL, WINSTON   (Winston Leonard Spencer Churchill; 1874–1965), Prime minister of GREAT BRITAIN from May 1940 until the end of WORLD WAR II.

Winston Churchill (on right) in Italy during the war

During the 1930s, Churchill was one of the few British politicians who spoke out against then Prime Minister Neville Chamberlain's policy of appeasement of Adolf HITLER. He also called for an active buildup of the British army in the face of the threat of Nazi GER-

MANY. In addition, he supported Jewish immigration to Palestine, and opposed the WHITE PAPER OF 1939, which limited Jewish immigration to Palestine and the purchase of land there by Jews.

When Britain declared war on Germany after the Nazis invaded POLAND in September 1939, Churchill was invited to reprise his World War I position as the head of the British navy. After the fall of FRANCE in May 1940, the British parliament chose Churchill over Chamberlain as prime minister.

On several occasions during the war, Prime Minister Churchill announced his intentions of supporting the creation of an independent Jewish state in Palestine after Germany was defeated. A Cabinet Committee on Palestine was even formed, which recommended the partition of the mandate between Arabs and Jews. The British cabinet accepted this decision in January 1944.

However, Churchill's attitude of "after Germany is defeated" also colored his efforts to save European Jewry, of whose situation he was fully aware. He wanted to help, but felt that the best way to rescue the Jews would be to totally vanquish Nazi Germany. Helping the Jews would and could only come after this was achieved. In a letter dated February 1943, Churchill outlined the reasons why Britain would not actively take part in the rescue efforts: transportation of the REFUGEES would present a major problem, as the escape routes would cross through military areas and thus interfere with the war effort; and it would not be possible to save Jewish refugees while deserting the other citizens of German-occupied areas. In July 1944 Churchill approved the Jewish Agency's pleas to bomb AUSCHWITZ. This never happened, though, due to obstacles caused by the Allied military and bureaucracy. (see also AUSCHWITZ, BOMBING OF.)

CLAUBERG, CARL (1898–1957), SS doctor who conducted brutal sterilization experiments on Jewish and GYPSY women at AUSCHWITZ and at the women's CONCENTRATION CAMP of RAVENSBRUECK during WORLD WAR II. Arrested by the Russians at the end of the war, Clauberg was tried in 1948 for his role in the "mass extermination of Soviet citizens." He was sentenced to twenty-five years' imprisonment, but was released in 1955 under the German-Soviet prisoner repatriation agreement. The Kiel police in West Germany put him under arrest, but he died in a hospital shortly before the date of the trial.

COHEN, DAVID (1882–1967), Dutch Jewish public figure and Zionist leader. Cohen was a professor of ancient history who provided assistance to German Jewish refugees during World War I and served as secretary of the Committee for REFUGEES. He was a member of the Jewish Council in THE HAGUE and later in Amsterdam. In 1934 he joined the Standing Committee of the Union of Ashkenazic Communities.

When HITLER came to power, Cohen called for the establishment of the Committee of Special Jewish Affairs. He was then made executive chairman of its subcommittee on refugees. After the Germans occupied the NETHERLANDS in May 1940, Cohen backed the establishment of the Jewish Coordinating Committee.

In February 1941 Cohen and his close friend, Abraham ASSCHER, formed the Jewish Council at the Germans' request. Throughout the rest of the war, former supreme court justice Lodewijk Ernst VISSER and others criticized the council for cooperating with the Nazis.

Cohen was arrested and sent to THERESIENSTADT in September 1943. He survived the war and returned home, where the Dutch regime charged him with collaboration. He was exonerated, but found guilty by the Jewish community, which banned him from serving in any Jewish institutions. His sentence was later annulled, but he never returned to Jewish public life.

COHN, MARIANNE (1924–1944), French Jewish underground activist. Cohn helped smuggle into SWITZERLAND Jewish children whose parents had been deported from FRANCE. She was murdered by a pro-Nazi French militia while on a rescue mission.

COLUMBIA HAUS CONCENTRATION CAMP located in BERLIN, used mainly to hold prisoners under interrogation at the GESTAPO headquarters. Columbia Haus was only in use for the first few years of the Nazi regime in GERMANY.

In mid-1933 the prisoner cells at the *Gestapo* headquarters could only hold about 50 people at a time. At that point, the *Gestapo* began using Columbia Haus, a concentration camp set up by the SS, to hold its prisoners while under investigation. Soon the concentration camp became infamous for the torture methods used there.

The administration of Columbia Haus was taken over by the Inspectorate of Concentration Camps in 1934. In January 1935 it was taken under the direct administration of the *Gestapo*.

In late 1935 the *Gestapo* decided to increase the size of the prisoner cells at its headquarters. Around the same time, the SS dissolved all the concentration camps it had been using to persecute enemies of the state during the first few years of Nazi power, except DACHAU, and in their place, began building larger camps. Thus, Columbia Haus was no longer needed by the *Gestapo,* and was shut down on November 5, 1935.

COMISIA AUTONOMA DE AJUTORARE   see AUTONOMOUS REFUGEE AID COMMITTEE, ROMANIA.

COMMISSARIAT GENERAL AUX QUESTIONS JUIVES   see OFFICE FOR JEWISH AFFAIRS.

CONCENTRATION CAMPS   (in German, *Konzentrationslager*), camps where the Nazis imprisoned their opponents without trial. Although the term "concentration camp" is often used as a term for all Nazi camps, there were in fact several types of camps in the Nazi system, of which concentration camp was just one. Other types include labor and hard labor camps, EXTERMINATION CAMPS, transit camps, and PRISONER OF WAR camps. As time went on the distinction between concentration camps and labor camps became blurred, since hard labor was performed in the concentration camps. The concentration camp network assumed an important role within the Nazi regime, which evolved over time.

Chronologically, the use of concentration camps can be divided into three distinct periods, from 1933 to 1936; 1936 to 1942; and 1942 to 1944–1945. The first period corresponds to the Nazis' rise to and consolidation of power. During this time, concentration camps were established for the detention of political opponents of the NAZI PARTY. Soon after HITLER came to power in January 1933, the Nazis began arresting political adversaries and placing them in camps. By the end of July some 27,000 people had been taken into what the Nazis called "protective custody." In Prussia alone, there were 20 camps for these prisoners. Beginning in the fall of 1933, the Nazis began detaining other people besides political prisoners, including persons whom the Nazis considered to be "asocial elements" such as beggars, tramps, and chronic criminals.

In July 1934 SS chief Heinrich HIMMLER named Theodor EICKE (who was serving at the time as commandant at the DACHAU concentration camp) the Inspector of Concentration Camps and SS Guard Units. These guard units, which became known as DEATH'S

Prisoners during roll call in Dachau, 1938

Prisoners at work in Sachsenhausen

HEAD UNITS, did the brutal work of guarding the concentration camps. In his new post, Eicke was in charge of the concentration camp prisoners' routine and punishments. During this phase the main goal of the camp system was to break the opposition to the Nazi regime.

In the second period (1936–1942), almost all of the concentration camps established during the first period were shut down, except Dachau, and newer, larger camps were built to accommodate the growing number of prisoners. These included SACHSENHAUSEN, BUCHENWALD, MAUTHAUSEN, Flossenburg, RAVENSBRUECK, AUSCHWITZ, MAJDANEK, NATZWEILER, NEUENGAMME, and STUTTHOF. During this period, in the middle of which WORLD WAR II broke out, the Nazis also established labor, hard labor, and "reeducation" camps. From 1937 onward many companies used German Jews, then Austrian Jews, and then Jews from throughout Nazi territory for FORCED LABOR, housing them in camp-like conditions or in camps themselves. From the summer of 1938, Jews were imprisoned in the camps simply for being Jews, especially after KRISTALLNACHT, when

36,000 were detained. Throughout this period, the number of prisoners detained in concentration camps rose constantly. When the war began, some 25,000 were housed in the camps; by the end of 1941 some 60,000 prisoners were included in the concentration camp system. That number rose even higher after Germany invaded the Soviet Union in June 1941; tens of thousands of Soviet prisoners of war were imprisoned in Nazi concentration camps. Many were soon murdered.

In late 1941 and early 1942, after the Nazis decided upon an official policy of extermination with regards to European Jewry, they set up extermination camps at CHELMNO, TREBLINKA, SOBIBOR, and BELZEC. Majdanek and Auschwitz, originally built as concentration camps, were expanded to serve as extermination centers, as well. Birkenau, or Auschwitz II, was the extermination center while the rest of Auschwitz and its subcamps functioned as forced labor camps. In Majdanek, prisoners who were not murdered immediately were part of the concentration camp population.

During the third period, beginning in February 1942, concentration camp prisoners were officially exploited as laborers forced to work in the German armaments industry, manufacturing weapons and other essential items for the German war economy. Previously, forced labor had often been used as a punishment. At this point, the SS created a special Economic-Administrative Main Office (WIRTSCHAFTS-VERWALTUNGSHAUPTAMT, WVHA) to oversee the use of concentration camp prisoners as manpower for both government-owned and private companies. The WVHA even built many sub-camps next to industrial factories to house the prisoner-laborers.

The level of the living conditions in the Nazi concentration camps varied from period to period and from camp to camp. From 1933 to 1936, the work, food, and housing were bearable, and most prisoners were only detained for about a year. During the second period and the start of the third period, many prisoners died in the camps as a result of brutal treatment, harsh working conditions, malnutrition, and overcrowding. In 1943 the living conditions improved slightly as the Nazis wanted the prisoners to work for the armaments industry in a productive manner.

Concentration camp prisoners did not have much personal choice; the SS told them exactly what to do throughout the day. If a prisoner did not follow an order, he would be severely punished, whether by whipping, solitary confinement, losing his food rations, etc.

The prisoners were classified according to their country of origin and according to the reason they were interned. Some prisoners were given supervisory or administrative positions, such as room, block, and camp "elders" or as *kapos* (work foremen). In general, German prisoners were given the top positions, and thus received the most privileges. In the Auschwitz camp complex, Polish prisoners were accorded this higher status. Jews and Soviets were on the very bottom of the prisoner totem pole. The Jews were treated much worse than any other prisoner group, and after the war broke out, Jewish prisoners had very poor prospects for survival. By October 1942 the WVHA ordered the removal of Jews from all concentration camps inside the Reich. The Jewish prisoners were deported to Auschwitz or Majdanek, in Poland, where most were exterminated.

By the fall of 1944 the Germans were clearly losing the war. The Allies were approaching from all directions. The Nazis gradually closed the concentration camps outside of the Reich and sent their prisoners on insufferable DEATH MARCHES towards camps that were still in operation in Germany and AUSTRIA.

CONSEIL REPRESENTATIF DES JUIFS DE FRANCE

see REPRESENTATIVE COUNCIL OF FRENCH JEWS.

CONSISTOIRE CENTRAL DES ISRAELITES DE FRANCE   see CENTRAL CONSISTORY OF THE JEWS OF FRANCE.

CORFU   Northernmost Greek island in the Ionian Sea.

ITALY occupied Corfu in April 1941. When the Italians surrendered to the Allies in September 1943, German troops invaded the island. They bombed Corfu's Jewish quarter and several Jews were killed.

Despite the fact that the Italians had warned the Jews of Corfu of the impending danger and advised them to run, the Jews—unaware of the horrors of the HOLOCAUST—had not believed that the Germans would cross over to their island, and stayed put. The Germans immediately shut down the Jewish school and put restrictive measures into effect.

The German commander posted in Corfu, Karl JAEGER, reported that the DEPORTATION of Corfu's Jews was not possible, because of the Red Cross representatives stationed there and because the local Greek population might intercede on the Jews' behalf. However, 1,795 Jews—almost all of Corfu's Jewish population—were arrested on June 9, 1944 by German army police units and the local Greek police. They were moved into an old fortress, and then sent on an arduous seven-day trip to ATHENS. From there the Jews were deported to AUSCHWITZ. Two-thirds were murdered immediately upon arrival on June 30, 1944. Only about 200 Jews returned to Corfu after the war.

COUNCIL FOR GERMAN JEWRY (CFGJ)   British Jewish organization established in 1936 to help German Jews leave GERMANY. British Jewish leaders instituted the CFGJ in response to the racial NUREMBERG LAWS of 1935; they designed an emigration plan whereby 100,000 German Jews aged 17–35 could leave Germany in an organized manner. Half were to move to Palestine, and half to other countries. The CFGJ also hoped that another 100,000 German Jews would emigrate without their help.

The CFGJ held its first meeting in London in March 1936. Two American groups, the JOINT DISTRIBUTION COMMITTEE and the United Palestine Appeal, formally joined the council in August.

The CFGJ was never able to achieve the prominence to which it had aspired. It was blocked by many obstacles, including Britain's restrictive Palestine immigration policy; German barriers to emigration; the growing poverty among German Jews due to Germany's oppressive ANTI-JEWISH LEGISLATION; and the deterioration of the situation in the Reich after Germany annexed AUSTRIA in March 1938. Nonetheless, the CFGJ was able to help almost 100,000 Jews leave Germany by the time WORLD WAR II broke out. It also financed several work-training programs in Germany and other countries. During the war, the CFGJ was limited to helping REFUGEES already in Britain.

CRACOW   (in Polish, Krakow), city in southern POLAND. On the eve of WORLD WAR II 60,000 Jews lived in Cracow, out of a total population of 250,000. During the first days of the war thousands of Jews fled from Cracow.

German troops occupied Cracow on September 6, 1939 and immediately began persecuting the city's Jews. In late October the Nazis made Cracow the capital of the GENERALGOUVERNEMENT; this made the persecution even worse for Cracow's Jews. Soon a Jewish committee was set up; it was declared to be a JUDENRAT on November 28. In early December the Germans carried out a terror action in which several synagogues were burnt down and much Jewish property was seized.

In May 1940 the Germans began expelling the Jews of Cracow to nearby towns in an effort to make the capital of the *Generalgouvernement* "free of Jews." By March 1941 some 40,000 Jews had been kicked out of their homes, and only 11,000 remained. During the expulsions, the Germans stripped the Jews of all their property. That same month, the German authorities established a GHETTO in the southern part of Cracow. On March 20 the ghetto was closed off with a wall and a barbed-wire fence. The remaining Cracow Jews were packed inside, as were several thousand Jews from nearby communities. By late 1941 about 18,000 Jews were imprisoned in the ghetto. They were subjected to terrible overcrowding and unsanitary conditions. In addition, the Germans installed several factories inside the ghetto so that they could take advantage of the cheap Jewish manpower.

Within the ghetto, several Jewish organizations were created to improve the awful conditions. Outstanding among them were the Jewish Social Self-Help Society and the Federation of Associations for the Care of Orphans.

On March 19, 1942 the Germans initiated a terror operation against the ghetto's intellectual class. During this *Intelligenz Aktion,* about 50 well known Jews were deported to their deaths at AUSCHWITZ. At the end of May the Germans began deporting the rest of the ghetto population to EXTERMINATION CAMPS. The *aktion* began on May 28, and was carried out by the GESTAPO, the regular police, and army units. During the operation, which lasted until June 8, 300 Jews were killed on the spot and 6,000 were deported to BELZEC. Among them was the chairman of the *Judenrat,* Artur Rosenzweig, who had refused to collaborate with the Germans and was thus punished.

After the *aktion* the *Judenrat* was abolished and a *Kommissariat* was established instead. The area comprising the ghetto was decreased by half (this despite the fact that there were still 12,000 Jews living there). In late October, following the *Kommissariat*'s refusal to collaborate with the Germans, the authorities began a second *aktion,* during which they deported 7,000 Jews to Belzec and Auschwitz and shot 700 on the spot. After this *aktion* the Germans further reduced the ghetto's area and divided the remaining part in two, one part for the working Jews, and the other for the rest of the prisoners.

Jewish children in the ghetto standing with a member of the ghetto's public health committee

In March 1943 the Germans transferred the 2,000 working Jews to the PLASZOW camp, and then proceeded to liquidate the rest of the ghetto, murdering 700 Jews on the spot and deporting 2,300 to Auschwitz. Only a few hundred of the Jews who had been transferred to Plaszow survived the war.

Throughout its existence, several resistance organizations were active in the Cracow Ghetto. In October 1942 many of the groups united under one underground organization, called the Jewish Fighting Organization. The organization's leaders decided that instead of launching an uprising inside the ghetto, where space was limited, they would move the fight to the Polish side of Cracow. They managed to launch 10 operations outside the ghetto, most notably an attack on a cafe in the city center, in which 11 Germans were killed and 13 wounded. In late 1943 two of the underground leaders, Shimshon and Tova Draenger, were caught in the apartment of a man who smuggled Jews to HUNGARY. They apparently were executed by the Germans and the underground dissolved after their disappearance. (see also RESISTANCE, JEWISH.)

CRIMES AGAINST HUMANITY   One of the three categories of crime used by the International Military Tribunal (IMT, the court that conducted the NUREMBERG TRIALS) as a basis for convicting war criminals. Besides crimes against humanity, the IMT was authorized to convict Nazis and Nazi collaborators of war crimes and crimes against peace.

According to the IMT's legal code, the definition of crimes against humanity is "murder, extermination, enslavement, deportation, and other inhumane acts committed against any civilian population, before or during the war; or persecution on political, racial, or religious grounds in execution of or in connection with any crime within the jurisdiction of the tribunal, whether or not in violation of the domestic law of the country where perpetrated." This last clause means that the court could only convict a person of crimes against humanity if those crimes were committed in conjunction with war crimes or crimes against peace. In addition, crimes against humanity, as opposed to war crimes, were also defined as criminal acts committed against a population at any time—during times of war, and during times of peace. Most, but not all, of the victims of the Nazi crimes against humanity were Jews.

CROATIA   Region of YUGOSLAVIA until spring 1941 and after the end of WORLD WAR II. Croatia was a puppet state ruled by the fascist USTASA movement but supervised by the Germans during most of the war; since 1991, it is a separate state.

GERMANY invaded Yugoslavia in April 1941, and divided the country amongst its allies. The region of Croatia was united with Bosnia and Herzegovina into the Independent State of Croatia, and put under the control of the *Ustasa* movement. Almost immediately, the *Ustasa* embarked upon a campaign to "purge Croatia of foreign elements." This mainly referred to the Eastern Orthodox Serb minority living in Croatia, greatly despised by the Catholic *Ustasa*. More than 500,000 Serbs were murdered in horribly sadistic ways (mostly in the summer of 1941), 250,000 were expelled, and another 200,000 were forced to convert to Catholicism.

Another group of "foreign elements" whom the *Ustasa* wanted to destroy was Croatia's Jewish popula-

tion, numbering some 37,000. Just days after taking control of the Croatian government, the *Ustasa* began issuing ANTI-JEWISH LEGISLATION. Over the next few months, Jews were stripped of their property and jobs, their freedom of movement was restricted, and they were forced to wear the Jewish badge (see also BADGE, JEWISH).

In June 1941 the Croatians began arresting the Jews en mass and transferring them to camps. A camp called JASENOVAC was established in August; from then on, most arrested Jews were sent there or to smaller camps. By the end of 1941, two-thirds of the Jews of Croatia had been sent to Croatian camps. Almost all were murdered upon arrival.

For several months the Germans allowed the Croatians to go about killing their country's Jews without much interference. However, at the beginning of 1942, it seemed that the Croatians might halt their murder spree, so the Nazis felt compelled to step in. During the spring the Croatians agreed to let the Nazis deport the remaining Jews in Croatia to the east. In August 1942 and again in May 1943 thousands of Jews were sent to their deaths at AUSCHWITZ. In all, some 30,000 of Croatia's Jews died during the HOLOCAUST—80 percent of the country's Jewish population.

CULTURAL UNION OF GERMAN JEWS   (*Kulturbund Deutscher Juden*), organization that promoted culture and the arts among the Jews of GERMANY from 1933 to 1941. The *Kulturbund* was founded in BERLIN as a response to the exclusion of Jews from German cultural life after the Nazis rose to power; its goals were to allow German Jews to maintain the level of culture they were used to, and provide work for the thousands of Jewish musicians and theater artists who had lost their jobs as a result of the Nazis' ANTI-JEWISH LEGISLATION.

In October 1933 the *Kulturbund* in Berlin opened a theater company, a symphony orchestra, an opera, a cabaret group, and a lecture program. Jewish communities all over Germany followed Berlin's lead and established their own cultural societies. In April 1935 all of Germany's Jewish cultural societies united into one umbrella organization, called the Reich Association of Jewish Cultural Societies (*Reichsverband der Juedischen Kulturbuende*). After the KRISTALLNACHT pogrom of 1938, the German authorities ordered the organization to take charge of all Jewish cultural activities, including the remaining publishing houses and the one remaining Jewish newspaper. In September 1941 the *Kulturbund* was abolished. During its eight years of existence, the society provided German Jewry with spiritual support, and served as a form of moral resistance in the face of persecution and humiliation.

CUZA, ALEXANDRU (1857–1946), Romanian political leader, a founder of the fascist, antisemitic IRON GUARD movement in 1927, and a leader of the short-lived GOGA-Cuza government in 1937. During his reign, Cuza stripped Romania's Jews of their citizenship and instituted other anti-Jewish measures

CZECHOSLOVAK GOVERNMENT-IN-EXILE Government established in FRANCE by the president of Czechoslovakia, Edvard BENES, after his country was overrun by GERMANY. In 1940 the government-in-exile moved to London, where it attempted to gain legal recognition for the Czechoslovak republic. It also tried to assist Czechoslovak Jews.

CZERNIAKOW, ADAM (1880–1942), Chairman of the Warsaw JUDENRAT. Born in WARSAW, Czerniakow was trained as a chemical engineer. He served on the

Warsaw Municipal Council from 1927–1934, and was elected to the Polish Senate in 1931. Even though Czerniakow was a member of the Jewish community's executive council before WORLD WAR II, the Jews of Warsaw did not consider him to be one of their leaders. He was not a member of any Jewish political party, was considered to be an assimilated Jew, and could not speak Yiddish very well.

In spite of this, when the Nazis invaded Warsaw and the chairman of the Jewish community council fled the city, the mayor asked Czerniakow to take his place as the leader of the Jews. The Germans ordered him to establish a *Judenrat* in October 1939. During the first few months of the occupation, some leading *Judenrat* members managed to leave the country. Czerniakow also had this opportunity, but he refused to shirk his leadership duties and criticized those who did.

The Warsaw GHETTO was established in October 1940. At this point, the *Judenrat*, led by Czerniakow, took on many new municipal-like responsibilities, including food, work, sanitation, housing, culture, and health services for the inhabitants of the ghetto. The *Judenrat* grew to encompass 25 different departments

Adam Czerniakow reading a document in his office in the Warsaw Ghetto

and 6,000 employees—more than 11 times the number of workers in Warsaw's Jewish Council before the war.

Czerniakow was strenuously criticized by Warsaw's underground resistance for what they saw as collaboration with the Nazis. However, Czerniakow's policy of trying to work within the system was his attempt at saving lives. He tried to keep the Germans out of the internal affairs of the ghetto as much as possible; this enabled Jews to illegally smuggle food and other necessities restricted by the Nazis. In his daily contact with the German police, Czerniakow tried to arouse some sympathy for the plight of his ghetto's Jews and extract aid from them. This did not usually work, though, and Czerniakow was even beaten up twice for his efforts. He was able to get some help from the ghetto *commissar*, Heinz AUERSWALD. But, Auerswald also betrayed Czerniakow when he hid the truth about plans for mass DEPORTATIONS.

Czerniakow was also criticized by the ghetto's lead historian, Emanuel RINGELBLUM, who felt that because of his assimilated background, Czerniakow could not fully identify with his Jewish constituents in the ghetto. It is true that Czerniakow appointed other assimilated Jews to important positions, such as Joseph Szeryns-ki—a police officer who had converted to Christianity—whom Czerniakow made commander of the ghetto police. However, unlike other *Judenrat* chairmen, Czerniakow did not use his position for personal gain, and would only go so far in cooperating with Nazi demands.

The Germans began a two-month wave of deportations to the TREBLINKA EXTERMINATION CAMP during the summer of 1942. On July 22 Czerniakow was ordered to round up Jews for "resettlement in the east." He knew what that innocuous term really meant, and was not prepared to surrender the Jews of his ghetto to certain death. The next day, at 4:00 p.m., Czerniakow took his own life. Some say that he left a note to his wife explaining his actions: "They are demanding that I kill the children of my people with my own hands. There is nothing for me to do but to die."

Czerniakow kept a diary from September 1939 until the day he died; it can be found today at YAD VASHEM in Jerusalem. This public diary, which serves as a vital primary source, consists of 1,009 pages that chronicle the current events in Warsaw from the German invasion, through the establishment of the ghetto, to the beginning of the deportations.

D

DACHAU   First Nazi CONCENTRATION CAMP. The camp was located in the small German town of Dachau, about 10 miles northwest of MUNICH. It was established in March 1933 and liberated in April 1945. Altogether, more than 200,000 prisoners passed through the camp, and over 30,000 officially died there, although the true figure is certainly much higher.

The original purpose of the camp was to silence any opponent of the Nazis; it was also meant to scare the people of GERMANY into obeying and supporting the Nazi regime. The commandant of Dachau, Theodor EICKE, ran the camp according to a strict system of rules and regulations. He was aided by a staff that consisted of members of the SS's DEATH'S HEAD UNITS, known for their brutality. When he was later made inspector general for all concentration camps, Eicke used those same regulations to run other camps. In that way, Dachau was an effective training ground for the Nazis' cruel agenda.

Dachau was opened in March 1933, soon after HITLER rose to national power in Germany. The first prisoners interned at the camp were known political enemies of the Nazi regime, mostly Communists and Social Democrats. According to the Nazis, they had been taken into "protective-custody." These political prisoners, who had arrived first and knew the camp best, held most of the important positions in the prisoners' internal government, set up by the SS. From 1935

Registration of prisoners in Dachau

on, people who had been condemned in court were immediately sent to a concentration camp such as Dachau. The first Jews brought to the camp were also political enemies of the Reich. However, they were treated worse than other inmates.

Soon other groups were imprisoned, including GYPSIES who, like the Jews, were considered to be an inferior race; homosexuals; Jehovah's Witnesses, who refused to serve in the army; clergymen, who protested the way the Nazis controlled the churches; and many others who had criticized the Nazis.

More and more Jews were brought to Dachau as the Nazis' systematic persecution of Jews picked up speed. After the KRISTALLNACHT pogrom of November 9–10, 1938, more than 10,000 German Jews were imprisoned. In 1942, when the "final solution" began in earnest, Jews were sent from Dachau and other camps within the Reich to EXTERMINATION CAMPS in POLAND.

Several thousand Austrians were brought to Dachau during the summer of 1939. This signaled the beginning of the transports that would come throughout the war from each country as it was occupied by the German army. The Austrian prisoners included Jews, resistance fighters, clergymen, and others who would not cooperate with the Nazi occupations.

Dachau was surrounded by an electrified fence and a large ditch filled with water. Upon arrival at the camp, prisoners lost all legal rights and their possessions were taken away. Their hair was shaved off and they were dressed in striped prison uniforms. Each prisoner was given an identification number and a colored triangle that signified what prisoner category they belonged to (Jew, Gypsy, homosexual, etc.). They were worked to the bone, given minute amounts of food, and lived under the threat of horribly cruel treatment at the hands of the prison guards.

The Nazis took merciless advantage of the cheap labor provided by the prisoners. The prisoners were forced to build roads, work in quarries, and drain marshes. As the war continued, weapons production became more and more important to the Nazis, so thousands of Jewish prisoners from HUNGARY, Poland, Czechoslovakia, and the SOVIET UNION were brought to Dachau to work on armaments. Thirty-six large camps were added at Dachau to house 37,000 prisoners working at its arms factories. Private firms could also hire slave laborers from Dachau; those firms paid the SS directly and the laborers saw none of their wages. Prisoners would work until they became too sick to continue, at which point other, healthier inmates would replace them.

Like at some other camps, MEDICAL EXPERIMENTS were performed on prisoners at Dachau; they were used as human guinea pigs. Dr. Sigmund Rascher, an SS physician, conducted "decompression" and "high-altitude" experiments, while Professor Dr. Claus Schilling, a well-known tropical medicine researcher, ran a malaria experiment station at the camp. He infected about 1,100 inmates with malaria, in hopes of finding an immunization against the disease. In addition, other pseudo-medical experiments were performed on Dachau prisoners: some had inflammations and poisoned states induced in them to test reactions to different medicines; others were cut to test anti-bleeding medications. Tests were also done to see if seawater could be made drinkable, and there was a tuberculosis experiment station on site.

During the last few months before Dachau was liberated, the prisoners lived under even worse conditions than before. Thousands of prisoners were brought from other camps that had been evacuated with the knowledge that the Allies were quickly advancing. Barracks meant to house 200 prisoners were jammed with more than 1,600. A typhus epidemic swept Dachau, killing 100–200 prisoners a day. Inmates formed an underground committee to help their fellow prisoners survive and resist SS plans to liquidate the camp. On April 26, 1945 the SS force-marched 7,000 prisoners south. Those who fell behind were shot, and many died from hunger, exhaustion, or cold. The marchers who survived were overtaken by American troops at the beginning of May—after the SS guards had disappeared.

Dachau was liberated on April 29, 1945 by the Seventh Army of the United States Armed Forces. At that point, there were more than 60,000 prisoners in the camp; they had come from more than 30 countries and by that time, there was only a small minority of Germans. About 30 percent of the inmates were Jewish.

After the war, 40 members of Dachau's SS staff were caught. An American court put them on trial at the camp between November 15 and December 14, 1945. Of the 40 tried, 36 were sentenced to death.

DALUEGE, KURT (1897–1946), Nazi official. In 1916 Daluege enlisted in the German army and became a lieutenant. He then served in the infamous *Rossbach Freikorps,* one of many private German armies

Police commander, SS-Gruppenfuehrer Kurt Daluege

commanded by former World War I officers, which conducted guerilla actions against FRANCE. He later worked as an engineer.

In 1926 Daluege joined the Storm Troopers (SA), but transferred to the SS in 1928 after becoming commander of SS Group East. He became a member of the German parliament (REICHSTAG) in January 1933. In May he was appointed chief of the Prussian police department which he filled with SS men. In 1934, after the SA leadership was destroyed during the "Night of the Long Knives" and Heinrich HIMMLER became chief of German police, Daluege was given command over the main office of the regular uniformed police.

Daluege was not an intellectual nor was he interested in ideology, but he was a good organizer and content to execute orders while leaving "Jewish affairs" to Reinhard HEYDRICH. After Heydrich's assassination in June 1942, Daluege took over as acting governor of the Protectorate of Bohemia and Moravia (see also BOHEMIA AND MORAVIA, PROTECTORATE OF). Daluege was executed

in 1946 for crimes such as the LIDICE massacre, the Nazi response to Heydrich's death.

DANNECKER, THEODOR (1913–1945), SS officer who helped organize the DEPORTATION of Jews from Nazi-occupied Europe.

Born in Tuebingen, Dannecker was trained as a lawyer. In 1937 he joined the staff of SS officer Adolf EICHMANN, who ran the Jewish affairs department of the Reich Security Main Office (REICHSSICHERHEIT-SHAUPTAMT, RSHA). In 1940 Dannecker was sent to PARIS as Eichmann's representative advisor on Jewish affairs. In this position, he oversaw the amassing of names of French Jews who were then arrested in May and August 1941. In 1942 Dannecker came up with a set of regulations regarding the deportation of both native-born French Jews and Jewish immigrants, referring to the latter as "stateless" Jews. An extreme antisemite, Dannecker also strenuously encouraged the Vichy authorities to step up their deportation of Jews to the east. (for more on Vichy, see also FRANCE.)

At the end of 1942 Eichmann called Dannecker back to the BERLIN office as a punishment for Dannecker's abuses of power. He was quickly transferred to BULGARIA, where he arranged for the deportation of 11,000 Jews from MACEDONIA AND THRACE. In October 1944 Dannecker was appointed by Eichmann as Jewish Commissioner in ITALY. He stayed in Italy until the end of the war. In December 1945 Dannecker took his own life in an American prison camp.

DANZIG (GDANSK) City on the Baltic Sea. Over centuries, Danzig was passed back and forth between GERMANY and POLAND. After World War I, the League of Nations designated Danzig a "free city" that did not belong to any specific country. Ninety-six percent of the city's population was German. Thousands of Jews moved to Danzig, increasing the city's Jewish population five-fold, despite the fact that the government had begun to restrict Jewish rights. In addition, the German majority was strongly nationalistic and antisemitic. They were very influenced by the Nazis after HITLER came to power in January 1933.

In May 1933 the NAZI PARTY became the leading power in Danzig. Hermann RAUSCHNING, a Christian conservative, was elected head of the senate. He was opposed to racial ANTISEMITISM for both ideological and practical reasons. In November 1934 he was fired by the Nazi leader, Albert FORSTER. The next man in the post, Arthur GREISER, also believed that he was obligated to respect Danzig's international character and not completely associate the city with the anti-Jewish policies of Nazi Germany.

In 1935 the Jewish community of Danzig turned to the League of Nations for help, but by that time the organization was too weak to have enough influence. The League's High Commissioner for Danzig did attempt to get antisemitic actions postponed, and in September 1937, he was able to convince Hitler to postpone the activation of the NUREMBERG LAWS in Danzig. However, after the KRISTALLNACHT pogrom of November 1938, the Nuremberg Laws were put into effect, with just a few changes.

As the ANTI-JEWISH LEGISLATION became more severe, most of the Jews of Danzig emigrated, leaving only 4,000. The Jewish community and the government decided to cooperate with regard to Jewish emigration, and on December 17, 1938, the Jews announced

Poster commemorating the Nazi takeover of Danzig: "Danzig is German"

publicly that they were willing to leave. When the war broke out in September 1939 and Danzig united with Germany, only 1,600 Jews were left. Emigration continued until the fall of 1940. At the end of February 1941, the city's remaining 600 Jews were deported to their deaths in Poland.

DARLAN, FRANCOIS   (1881–1942), Prime minister of unoccupied (Vichy) FRANCE from 1940 to April 1942 and chief of state in North Africa after the Allied invasion in November 1942. Darlan upheld Vichy law in North Africa, including its ANTI-JEWISH LEGISLATION. On December 24, 1942, Darlan was killed by an anti-Vichy assassin.

DARQUIER DE PELLEPOIX, LOUIS   (also known as Louis Darquier; 1897–1980), Coordinator of the Vichy government's anti-Jewish program from 1942–1944.

Darquier was an infamous and devout antisemite who believed that all Jews should either be kicked out of FRANCE or exterminated. In May 1942 he was appointed to head the Vichy government's OFFICE FOR JEWISH AFFAIRS. He replaced Xavier VALLAT in that position, who had been removed because the SS in France had considered Vallat to be too moderate in his views and actions.

Darquier persecuted French Jewry in a brutal and violent fashion. In conjunction with the German authorities in PARIS, he accelerated the confiscation of Jewish property and helped coordinate the DEPORTATION of French Jews to AUSCHWITZ. However, the Germans soon found that Darquier's administration was inefficient, incompetent, and corrupt. Thus, he was also removed from his position in February 1944.

After the war, Darquier fled to SPAIN, where he lived until his death in 1980. In 1978 he was interviewed in his home by a French reporter. During the interview Darquier denied any involvement in the persecution of France's Jews during the HOLOCAUST, and even denied that the Holocaust ever took place.

DARRE, RICHARD WALTHER   (1895–1953), Nazi ideologist and German minister of food and agriculture from 1933–1942. Darre depicted a connection between the blood of the German race and the soil, and helped develop the idea of LEBENSRAUM—acquiring more "living space" for GERMANY. The Nuremberg Military Tribunals sentenced him to five years' imprisonment, but he was released in 1950.

DEATH'S HEAD UNITS (*Totenkopfverbaende*), SS units assigned to guard CONCENTRATION CAMPS; later they also served as elite combat units.

The Death's Head Units were established in 1934 by Theodor EICKE, the first commandant of DACHAU and later inspector of concentration camps. They were named for the skull-and-cross-bones symbol worn on the right collar of their uniforms. Eicke trained the units to conduct themselves with strict discipline and cruelty, and to view the prisoners under their guard as enemies of the state who should be destroyed if possible. Thus, he forged a group known for their extreme brutality.

At the beginning of WORLD WAR II, the Death's Head Units had 24,000 members, including reservists; by January 1945 that number had increased to 40,000. In 1938 HITLER announced that they were to become military units. Some groups were then discharged from guarding the camps for combat duty, serving in POLAND and the SOVIET UNION. Just as Eicke had trained the units to be barbaric in their treatment of camp prisoners, so did they act on the field of combat. They were known to be cruel and ferocious warriors.

After the war, the Death's Head Units were declared to be a criminal organization, and its members subject to war crimes trials.

DEATH MARCHES (in German, *Todesmaersche*), the forced marches of prisoners over long distances, under unbearable conditions, during which the prisoners were abused by their accompanying guards, and many killed by them. The Nazis conducted death marches many times during the HOLOCAUST, mostly near the war's end during the evacuation of CONCENTRATION CAMPS. The term death march was used originally by prisoners in Nazi concentration camps, and later employed by Holocaust historians.

The first large-scale death march took place in the summer of 1941, following the German invasion of the SOVIET UNION. Hundreds of thousands of Soviet PRISONERS OF WAR were forced to walk along the highways of the UKRAINE and BELORUSSIA while being transferred from one camp to another. Masses of prisoners were murdered along the way, or at prearranged execution sites. Around the same time, Romanians (who were

Theodor Eicke (second from left) and members of the Death's Head Unit in Lichtenburg, March 1936. The emblem of the unit, the skull and cross bones is visible on the collar of the officer standing on the far left

Death march of prisoners from Dachau

then German allies) marched Jews from BESSARABIA and BUKOVINA to TRANSNISTRIA. Thousands were shot along the way by the Romanian and German guards.

Most death marches took place near the end of WORLD WAR II. During the summer of 1944, as the Allies advanced in the West and the Soviets advanced in the east, the Nazis began liquidating the concentration camps in earnest. The first camps to be emptied were those in eastern and central POLAND and in the Baltic States.

That fall, Nazi leaders decided to expedite the DE-PORTATION of the Jews of BUDAPEST to their deaths. Thus, a death march from Budapest began on November 8, 1944; 76,000 Jewish men, women, and children were forced to walk to the Austrian border, accompanied by Hungarian guards. The march lasted a month, during which time thousands died from starvation, disease, exhaustion, and cold. Thousands more were shot along the way. Several hundred were rescued by neutral diplomats like Raoul WALLENBERG from SWEDEN, who pulled Jews out of the marching lines, took them into his custody, and accompanied them back to Buda-

pest. Most were not so lucky, though—those prisoners who reached the Austrian border were turned over to German soldiers, who led them to various concentration camps, such as DACHAU and MAUTHAUSEN, and forced them to build fortifications.

During the winter of 1944–1945, the Germans knew that they had essentially lost the war. This led them to evacuate the Polish concentration camps, and force-march their prisoners to GERMANY. The Jews themselves lived in constant fear of being murdered during the last stages of the war, because they were no longer needed for work.

The evacuation of AUSCHWITZ and its satellite camps began on January 18, 1945, when about 60,000 mostly Jewish prisoners were marched to Wodzislaw (called Loslau in German). At that point they were put on terribly crowded freight trains and shipped to other concentration camps further west, such as GROSS-RO-SEN, BUCHENWALD, Dachau, and Mauthausen. At least 15,000 people died or were killed on that death march.

Three days later, on January 21, 4,000 prisoners, mostly Jews, were sent off from the BLECHHAMMER camp. During that month the Germans also began to empty the STUTTHOF camp complex—a network that at that time held 47,000 prisoners, over 35,000 of them Jews, most of them female. A total of 7,000 Jews—6,000 women and 1,000 men—were force-marched for 10 days. Seven hundred were murdered en route. Those who survived the march itself arrived at the Baltic Sea on January 31. That very day, the Nazis pushed the remaining prisoners into the sea and shot them—only 13 survived.

The evacuation of the main camp of Gross-Rosen and its sub-camps began in February 1945. Altogether, 40,000 prisoners were marched off, and thousands were murdered along the way. Also in February, the 20,000 Jewish prisoners who worked in the FORCED LABOR camps at Eulengebirge were either murdered right before the evacuation or during the death march away from the camps.

Throughout March and April 1945, as the war drew to a close, the Nazis evacuated camp after camp, sending at least 250,000 of their 700,000 concentration camp prisoners on death marches. Some of those marches lasted for weeks, causing thousands of deaths along the highways of western AUSTRIA and central Germany. Often, the prisoners would be marched on foot part of the way, and then crowded onto trains—70 people to a car—where they were denied food and water.

The evacuation of the main Buchenwald camp began on April 6, 1945; 3,100 Jewish prisoners were marched off, of whom 1,400 were murdered en route. Over the next four days, another 40,000 prisoners were kicked out of the camp, of whom 13,500 were killed. Just over 20,000 prisoners remained in the camp, including a few Jews. One of the last of the Buchenwald sub-camps to be emptied was Rehmsdorf, which was evacuated on April 13. More than 4,000 prisoners left the camp—but no more than 500 survived until the end of the march. The DORA-MITTELBAU camp evacuation also started in April. Most of the camp's prisoners were marched for two weeks towards BERGEN-BELSEN. One group of prisoners was forced into a barn that was then set on fire. American troops arrived the next day to find hundreds of burnt bodies.

By the end of April, the Nazis had initiated death marches from Flossenburg, SACHSENHAUSEN, NEUEN-GAMME, Magdeburg, Mauthausen, RAVENSBRUECK, and from several of the Dachau sub-camps. During those marches, which lasted literally until the day of the Nazi surrender two weeks later, tens of thousands of prisoners died or were executed. Those who fell behind or stopped to rest, even for a minute, were shot. In one instance, thousands of mostly Hungarian prisoners were buried along a short 37-mile stretch of road between Gunskirchen and Mauthausen. In all, about 250,000 concentration camp prisoners were murdered or died on the forced death marches that were conducted throughout the last ten months of World War II.

DEFFAUGT, JEAN   Mayor of Annemasse, a French town on the Swiss border, who was designated as RIGHTEOUS AMONG THE NATIONS by YAD VASHEM in 1965 for his rescue activities during WORLD WAR II.

Secret escape routes to SWITZERLAND used by fleeing Jews intersected in Annemasse. Some Jews whom the Germans caught trying to escape were imprisoned in an annex of the Pax Hotel, where they underwent torturous interrogation by the GESTAPO. Deffaugt made it a practice to visit the Jews incarcerated in the *Gestapo* prison; he brought them food, blankets, medical supplies, and other necessary items. He also tried to intercede on the Jews' behalf.

In one instance, the *Gestapo* agreed to release a young group of children into Deffaugt's care, after he agreed to return them if the *Gestapo* requested it. He soon put them in the care of a priest, who hid them until the Allies came to liberate the area just weeks later. After the LIBERATION, Deffaugt brought all the children back together and returned them to Jewish hands.

DELEGATURA   Underground representatives of the POLISH GOVERNMENT-IN-EXILE active in POLAND from 1940–1945. The *Delegatura* was both an advisory committee and a decision-making group. It had different names at different times. The *Delegatura* was considered to be an "underground state" which had its own law and education systems and its own army, called the HOME ARMY (*Armia Krajowa*). The *Delegatura* went out of existence after the war, when Poland's Provisional Government of National Unity was created in July 1945.

Until the fall of 1942, the *Delegatura* did not confront the horrific persecution of Jews in occupied Poland. However, in September of that year, the group announced that in addition to the slaughter of the Polish people by the Germans, Poland had been the site of the systematic massacre of the Jews. In their declaration they protested the crimes against the Jews and called for "all political and public organizations to join in this protest." In early 1943 the *Delegatura* set up a Jewish affairs bureau, which was responsible to organize the group's activities with regard to the Jews, stay in constant contact with ZEGOTA (the Polish Council for Aid to Jews), and process materials about the Jews, which were then sent to the Polish government-in-exile in London.

DEMJANJUK TRIAL   Trial of accused collaborator and war criminal, John Iwan Demjanjuk, which took place in 1987 in Jerusalem. This was the second trial in Israel in which the death sentence was called for under the Nazis and Nazi Collaborators (Punishment) Law; the first was the EICHMANN TRIAL of 1961.

John Demjanjuk (on left) at his trial in Israel

In 1975 the US Department of Justice learned that Demjanjuk, a resident of Ohio who had immigrated to the UNITED STATES from the UKRAINE in the early 1950s, had collaborated with the SS and served as a guard in the SOBIBOR camp during the HOLOCAUST. He was also identified by SURVIVORS in Israel as "Ivan the Terrible" a Ukrainian staff member at TREBLINKA. In 1981 an Ohio court ruled that Demjanjuk had indeed worked at both Treblinka and Sobibor. The court found that Demjanjuk had lied on his immigration application, and had hidden the fact that he was an SS member. His Amer-

ican citizenship was taken away, and in 1987, Demjanjuk was extradited to Israel.

The trial began on February 16, 1987. Demjanjuk was charged with crimes against the Jewish people, CRIMES AGAINST HUMANITY, war crimes, crimes against persecuted individuals, and murder. During the course of the trial, it was found that the Ukrainian Demjanjuk had been drafted into the Soviet army in 1940 and taken prisoner by the Germans in 1942. Soon, he volunteered for service at the TRAWNIKI SS training camp, and several months later, was posted in Treblinka, where he supervised the GAS CHAMBER operations. He was horribly brutal, forcing the victims into the chambers with whips, pipes, swords, knives, or guns. He served at Treblinka until September 1943, except for a short assignment at Sobibor.

The defense claimed that the wrong man had been put on trial, that in fact, Demjanjuk was not "Ivan the Terrible" of Treblinka. In April 1988, the court found Demjanjuk guilty and sentenced him to death. However, the ruling was overturned by the Israeli Supreme Court, which accepted that there was serious doubt about Demjanjuk's identity. Demjanjuk was set free.

DENAZIFICATION   Process instituted by the Allies after WORLD WAR II to remove all traces of Nazism from GERMANY.

Even before the war ended, the Allied leaders met at the Yalta Conference where they agreed to wipe out the NAZI PARTY and its influence. This view was restated in the Potsdam Agreement of August 1945. By that time, the Allies had created a list of 178,000 suspected Nazis who were put under "mandatory arrest" while the Soviets arrested 67,000 people. Their aim was to remove all Nazi officials from public life.

After the war, the UNITED STATES, GREAT BRITAIN, FRANCE, and the SOVIET UNION each occupied a part of Germany—and each occupier went about "denazifying" its zone differently. The Americans were very strict about not allowing former Nazis to fill any public posts. They wanted to help the Germans learn to function in a democratic society, but they also distrusted them and considered them to be guilty of terrible crimes. The British were more moderate about allowing former Nazis to hold important positions; to rebuild their zone's destroyed economy, they decided to let anyone familiar with the area, even Nazis, take on public responsibilities. The main goal of the French was to weaken their former enemy (Germany) and use the resources in their zone to rebuild France's destroyed economy, so they allowed Nazis from other zones to work in their area. The Soviets aimed to make their zone into a Communist society; those former Nazis who were willing to conform to Communism were not removed from public life.

In October 1946 the Allies began classifying former Nazis into five categories, intending to punish those in the first four: Major Offenders; Offenders; Lesser Offenders; Followers; and Persons Exonerated. Nazis were made to fill out a questionnaire and classify themselves; most true major offenders lied about their participation in Nazi actions, and were not punished at all. By the beginning of the Cold War, the denazification process was turned over to German authorities (except in the Soviet zone, where it ended altogether), and many Nazis began returning to important positions.

DENMARK   The southernmost country in Scandinavia. Approximately 7,800 Jews lived in Denmark right before WORLD WAR II. Of that number, about 6,000 were native Danes, and the rest were REFUGEES, many of whom were children from the YOUTH ALIYA and Zionist YOUTH MOVEMENTS. Many other refugees had fled to Denmark in the years proceeding the war. However, between 1934 and 1938 the rules regarding foreign refugees were tightened, so most of the 4,500 Jews who had sought shelter in Denmark left the country.

The German army occupied Denmark on April 9, 1940. The Danes did not challenge German control, so the Germans agreed to let them continue running their government and army themselves. Included in the agreement was a clause that called for the protection of the Danish Jews, a point that the Danes stubbornly insisted upon. Thus, for the next few years, the status of the Jews did not change.

However, by the spring of 1943, the situation deteriorated. Encouraged by the victories of the Allied forces against the Germans, Danish resistance groups increased their activities. This caused tension between the Danes and the Germans, which led the Germans to rethink the status of the Danish Jews. When the Zionist youth found out what was happening, many tried to escape the country. Some tried to flee to southern Europe by hiding under train cars, but their attempt failed. Others succeeded in escaping to SWEDEN from Bornholm Island by boat.

After refusing to go along with the Germans' new demands regarding the Jews, the Danish government

One of the boats used by Danish fishermen to transfer Jews from Denmark to Sweden in fall 1943

resigned in late August 1943. Werner BEST, the German minister in the Danish capital of Copenhagen, decided that the time was now right to propose to the Nazi leadership in BERLIN that the Jews be deported. He then developed second thoughts, for fear that his own relationship with the Danes would be ruined. Despite this, the German police began arresting Jews on the night of October 1–2, 1943. However, several German sources, chief among them the German legation's attachee for shipping affairs, Georg Ferdinand DUCKWITZ, had leaked this information to Danish groups, who immediately warned the Jews. The Danes—reacting spontaneously and humanely—helped the Jews reach the beach, and Danish fisherman crossed them to Sweden on their boats. The Swedish government announced that it would accept all refugees from Denmark, and the Danish resistance organized the escape of the rest of the Jews. The king of Denmark, Christian X, and the heads of the Danish churches also objected to the DEPORTATION. Within three weeks, 7,200 Jews and about 700 of their non-Jewish relatives were taken to Sweden.

Even though Rolf Guenther, Adolf EICHMANN'S assistant, failed in his general mission to deport Danish Jewry, about 500 Jews were still arrested. These, among them some Zionist Youth and Youth Aliya children, were sent to THERESIENSTADT. The Danish government strongly protested the deportations, and demanded that a group of Danish representatives be allowed to visit Theresienstadt. In the summer of 1944 the Nazis set up a fake "model ghetto" for the visit of the Danes and an International Red Cross group (see also RED CROSS, INTERNATIONAL). Even so, no Danish Jews were sent to AUSCHWITZ. Most were moved to Sweden just before the war ended.

The way the Danes took care of and saved "their" Jews is considered one of the most heroic and humane aspects of World War II, and is still admired today. Legend has it that King Christian X himself donned a Jewish badge in solidarity with the Jews of Denmark (see also BADGE, JEWISH). The story is fictional (as Danish Jews were never forced to wear badges), but it powerfully depicts the Danish king as a model of courage and a symbol of commitment to his country's Jews.

DEPORTATIONS In 1919 Adolf HITLER wrote of his desire for the complete removal of Jews from GERMANY, and his belief that methodical measures were needed in order to achieve that goal. By the mid-1930s, the SS transformed that theoretical goal into a policy that called for a Germany that was physically "cleansed" (*Judenrein*) or "free" (*Judenfrei*) of Jews. After the annexation of AUSTRIA (ANSCHLUSS) in March 1938 and even more so after the KRISTALLNACHT pogrom of November 1938, the Nazis began pressuring Jews to emigrate.

Soon after the Germans invaded POLAND in September 1939, they began the first stage of deportation by forcing Jews out of their homes and into GHETTOS. There were also attempts to drive the Jews into Soviet territory. The Nazis then decided to deport all the Jews living within the Reich to an area in Poland's GENERALGOUVERNEMENT called the Lublin Reservation. This scheme was part of the Nazis' larger plan to move around the populations of Europe: besides these designs for the Jews, they intended to remove many Poles from Poland, and resettle the area with ethnic Germans (VOLKSDEUTSCHE) primarily from the SOVIET UNION. Adolf EICHMANN was put in charge of the deportations of Jews and Poles, as the SS expert on "Jewish affairs and

Monument to deportees, Yad Vashem

Deportation of Jewish children from the Lodz Ghetto

evacuations." However, the so-called NISKO AND LUBLIN PLAN faltered. Germany's resettlement plans halted completely in mid-1941, during preparations to invade the Soviet Union. Thus, Hitler's goal to expel all Jews from German-occupied areas had not yet been achieved.

The next stage of deportation was the result of a shift in the Nazi's Jewish policy from expulsion to mass extermination. After invading the Soviet Union in June 1941, the Germans began to massacre Soviet Jewry by firing squad. However, this method could not reasonably be used in the cities of Eastern and Western Europe. Thus, the Nazis decided to deport Jews to extermination centers in the east. Deportations from the LODZ Ghetto to the first EXTERMINATION CAMP, called CHELMNO, began in December 1941. The other major extermination camps were ready for operation by mid-1942.

The Jews were transferred to the camps by train. The German Transport Ministry and German Railways helped the Nazis in their murderous goal by providing special trains for the Jews. In most cases, the Jews were crowded into cattle cars; in northern Europe some Jews paid for their tickets, and sometimes even upgraded to first-class. In the end, though, however they got there, the Jews deported to the east suffered a similar fate.

The Jews of Poland were transported to extermination camps throughout 1942. In March 1942 nearly 60,000 Slovak Jews were deported to Poland to their deaths. In July 1942 mass deportations were launched from FRANCE, BELGIUM, and the NETHERLANDS—at first consisting mostly of foreign Jewish refugees. In August, 5,000 Jews from CROATIA were deported. Starting in late October, more than 700 Norwegian Jews were arrested and taken to the extermination camps. Deportations continued in 1943 from all those countries, but the Germans began to concentrate mainly on deporting the Jews in the Balkans.

ROMANIA carried out the deportation of Jews to TRANSNISTRIA from the territories it had taken from the Soviet Union, including BESSARABIA and BUKOVINA. Nonetheless, the Romanians refused to deport their own Jews. The Italian government protected the Jews within its jurisdiction, such as in southern Greece and France, and parts of YUGOSLAVIA. However, most Greek Jews lived in northern Greece, in SALONIKA, which was occupied by Germany. Thus, some 44,000 Greek Jews were deported to extermination camps between March and August 1943, the rest following later.

The Germans also tried to deport the Jews of DENMARK in October 1943. However, the local population foiled their plan by hiding their country's Jews and then smuggling them to neutral SWEDEN.

In 1944 most of the remaining Jews were deported from SLOVAKIA and from the last ghetto, Lodz. But the Nazis' main efforts at that time were focussed upon the destruction of Hungarian Jewry. After Germany occupied HUNGARY in March 1944, 437,000 Jews were deported to their deaths at AUSCHWITZ.

DEUTSCHE AUSRUSTUNGSWERKE   see GERMAN ARMAMENT WORKS.

DEUTSCHER VORTRUPP, GEFOLGSCHAFT DEUTSCHER JUDEN   see GERMAN VANGUARD, GERMAN JEWISH FOLLOWERS.

DIARIES, HOLOCAUST   Personal journals written by victims of the HOLOCAUST. These diaries are very useful to historians as reliable primary sources. Unlike Holocaust literature written after the fact, they provide a direct window into the lives of those who endured the day-to-day horrors of the Holocaust. They describe the genuine feelings of those who experienced the Holocaust, without the drawbacks of 20-20 hindsight.

Holocaust diaries were kept for several reasons. Some Jews, including many teenagers and children, felt the need to record their feelings of pain and humiliation as an outlet of expression. Others wrote diaries so that there would be some historical evidence of what was happening, which could help ensure that what they were going through would never happen again. Some even wrote as an act of resistance—their way of showing that they could not be defeated.

Jews kept diaries in all countries, in every situation—in GHETTOS, camps, and in hiding. Many of the diaries have been lost, so it is impossible to estimate how much was written during the Holocaust and by whom. However, the many writings that were found and preserved have served as important reminders of the legacy of those who perished.

Several different kinds of diaries were written during the Holocaust. These include daily records of events, public diaries, private diaries, and children's diaries. Those journals that recorded day-to-day happenings did not usually include personal thoughts or observations about the events described, but rather presented a drier type of record. One example of this was the chronicles of the LODZ Ghetto JUDENRAT. *Judenrat* members charged some of the council's employees with recording the current events that took place in their ghetto from January 1940 to July 1944.

Public diaries were similar to daily chronicles in that they did not record private feelings, but rather concentrated on public events that affected many. However, unlike daily chronicles, public diaries emphasized those specific details that the author associated with historical trends. One such diary is that of the historian Emanuel RINGELBLUM of the WARSAW Ghetto, who kept both his own public chronicles and organized the writings and testimonies of others in the ONEG SHABBAT Archives. Other public diaries were written by Adam CZERNIAKOW, the head of the Warsaw Ghetto *Judenrat;* Raymond-Raoul (Heshel) Lambert, a leader of the UNION OF FRENCH JEWS; and Tova Draenger, a leader of the *Akiva* movement and the Fighting *Halutz* resistance movement in CRACOW.

In private diaries, the authors concentrated on their

The original of Holocaust survivor Abba Gefen's diary
(Photo: Aba Gefen)

own feelings, observations, and experiences, or on their relatives' experiences. They did not generally describe current events; rather they wrote about those happenings in which they themselves were involved. Some such diaries were found in CONCENTRATION CAMPS—several, whose authors were members of the SONDERKOMMANDO units, were discovered in the ruins of the AUSCHWITZ-Birkenau crematorium. These men wrote about the horrors of being in daily contact with murder, and begged the world to understand how they had been forced by the Nazis to participate in the extermination process. They also disclose many details about the *Sonderkommando* uprising in Birkenau, for which there is very little other primary source material.

Children's diaries are a special type of private diary. They help us see the horrors of the Holocaust through the observant eyes of children who quietly protested what was happening, and struggled to find the good in the world in even those darkest of times. The most famous of these diaries is that of Anne FRANK, the young Dutch teenager who kept a diary while hiding from the Nazis in Amsterdam. Her father published her diary after the war, and it has served as an important testament and reminder to millions of readers around the world.

DIATLOVO (in Polish, Zdzienciol; in Yiddish, Zhetl), town in BELORUSSIA. At the beginning of WORLD WAR II, Diatlovo was annexed by the SOVIET UNION. At that point, 4,000 Jews lived there.

In June 1941 GERMANY invaded the Soviet Union. German troops entered Diatlovo on June 30; over the next three weeks, they murdered more than 120 Jews. About 400 Jews were sent to a labor camp in Dvorets, while Jews from other towns were brought into Diatlovo. Soon, the Germans established a GHETTO, formed a JUDENRAT, and appointed Alter DVORETSKI as its chairman.

In late 1941 Dvoretski formed an underground with 60 members, whose goals were to revolt if the Germans staged an *aktion* against the Jews, and to promote escape to the forest. On April 30, 1942, 1,200 Jews were removed from the ghetto and executed. The underground did not start an uprising because the Soviet PARTISANS in the area would not cooperate. Dvoretski then tried to establish a strong Jewish partisan force to save the ghetto's remaining Jews, but he was killed by the Soviet partisans.

Another *aktion* began in August 1942. About 600

Jews attempted to escape to the forest; some who survived founded Jewish partisan units. About 370 Diatlovo Jews survived the war, most by escaping to the forest.

DIBELIUS, OTTO (1880–1967), German Protestant bishop and theologian who participated in the German church's anti-Nazi resistance.

Dibelius was a proud German nationalist, and after the Nazis rose to national power in January 1933, he gave the sermon at the opening service for the 1933 REICHSTAG. He spoke in a cautiously generous manner about the Nazis, but he also stressed the fact that dictatorship was not the will of God. As a result, he was fired from his position as general superintendent of the Lutheran church in a Prussian district. He soon joined the Confessing Church, which was anti-Nazi in orientation.

During WORLD WAR II Dibelius struggled for freedom of religious expression and criticized the Nazis' church policy. This led to his arrest on several occasions; he was also forbidden to preach. In addition, he was in contact with some of the people who took part in the failed bid to assassinate HITLER in 1944 (but did not himself take part in the plot). However, despite the fact that he knew about the mass murder of Jews in POLAND, Dibelius never spoke out against the killings, preferring to stay within the perimeters of what was considered appropriate by the church.

After the war, Dibelius became bishop of Berlin-Brandenburg.

DIRLEWANGER, OSKAR (1895–1945), High-ranking SS officer. Dirlewanger joined the NAZI PARTY for the first of three times in 1923; he finalized his membership in 1932. In 1934 Dirlewanger was arrested for indecent behavior and sent to jail for two years.

Dirlewanger joined the SS in 1940 and immediately offered to train a special battalion within the DEATH'S HEAD UNITS. In early 1941 Dirlewanger and his battalion were sent to the Lublin district, where Dirlewanger was appointed commandant of a Jewish labor camp, oversaw the building of fortifications in the BELZEC area, and fought the Polish PARTISANS in the GENERAL-GOUVERNEMENT. In February 1942 Special Battalion Dirlewanger was moved to BELORUSSIA to fight the partisans active there. Dirlewanger and his men were so savage in their murder of civilians and their destruction of civilian sectors that even the Nazis were offended; an investigation into Dirlewanger's activities was initiated, but he was never tried.

In August 1944 Dirlewanger was sent to WARSAW to help suppress the WARSAW POLISH UPRISING, during which he again proved himself to be a brutal killer. That same month he was promoted. In late 1944 Dirlewanger and his unit were stationed in SLOVAKIA to put down the SLOVAK NATIONAL UPRISING.

Dirlewanger died mysteriously in June 1945.

DISPLACED PERSONS, JEWISH

At the end of WORLD WAR II, between seven and nine million people had been uprooted from their homes by the Nazis. By the end of 1945, more than six million had returned home to begin life anew. However, many Jews who had survived FORCED LABOR camps, EXTERMINATION CAMPS, CONCENTRATION CAMPS, and DEATH MARCHES did not want to go home. After experiencing the horrors of the HOLOCAUST, they wanted to leave Europe altogether and rebuild their broken lives elsewhere. Some did return home, only to leave again after finding their homes and property stolen by their former neighbors. None of these Jews had anywhere to go. Thus, they congregated in Displaced Persons' (DP) camps located within the central European areas controlled by the Allies. They organized themselves under the Hebrew name *She'erit ha-Pletah* a biblical term meaning "surviving remnant." The *She'erit ha-Pletah* organization existed from the end of the war until December 1950.

Those Western European Jews who survived generally returned to their countries of origin, while those from Eastern Europe flocked to DP camps in the Allied zones of Europe. Soon, thousands more Polish, Soviet, Czechoslovakian, Hungarian, and Romanian Jews who had tried to go home began to flee westward to the DP camps when they realized that nothing was left for them in Eastern Europe. By the end of 1946, there were approximately 250,000 Jewish DPs—185,000 in GERMANY, 45,000 in AUSTRIA, and 20,000 in ITALY.

A year and a half earlier, in the summer of 1945, public interest in the DP camps had influenced President Harry S. TRUMAN to send Earl G. Harrison as his personal emissary to check into the conditions of the Jewish DPs in the camps of the American zone in Germany. Harrison reported that the conditions in the DP camps were terrible. He accused the Americans

Passover seder for Displaced Persons in Stuttgart, 1947

of being responsible for the awful situation, and declared that the only solution was to let the Jewish DPs immigrate to Palestine. Harrison advised that the Americans work to improve the conditions in their camps, and that the British allow 100,000 DPs to move to Palestine. Most of the DPs did want to immigrate to Palestine, but Britain, afraid of upsetting the Arabs, refused to open Palestine's doors to them.

Following Harrison's visit, conditions in the American zone DP camps improved. The Jewish DPs were put in separate camps and recognized as a special group with its own needs. They were also given the freedom to govern themselves. Each camp elected a camp committee that took responsibility for running the camp; these committees took care of sanitation, hygiene, cultural activities, education, and religious life. They were supported financially by the American Jewish JOINT DISTRIBUTION COMMITTEE and the Jewish Agency.

Many groups of Palestinian Jews worked in the DP camps. The first group arrived in June 1945. Emissaries of Jewish YOUTH MOVEMENTS and agricultural settlement organizations, a group of Jewish teachers from Palestine, and a Jewish Agency delegation came to help run the camps and train the DPs for life in Palestine. They also helped set up a school system, and taught the DPs how to farm in preparation for the agricultural life in Palestinian *kibbutzim*.

The Jews of the DP camps developed a culture all their own. More than 70 newspapers were published, commemoration projects were initiated, and even theaters and orchestras were established. People married and had children, and waited to begin their new lives outside of Europe.

The need for DP camps dwindled with the establishment of the State of Israel; about two-thirds of the DPs emigrated to Israel, while most of the rest moved to the UNITED STATES, which had loosened its immigration quotas. The last Jewish DP camp in Germany was closed in 1953.

DOCUMENTATION CENTERS   Archival centers that collect and maintain documentation about the HOLOCAUST.

The BERLIN Documents Center is an archive that contains two sets of Holocaust materials. The first set was discovered by the UNITED STATES army in a paper factory in MUNICH (slated for recycling), while the second set consists of documents that the Nazis hid in the Harz and Tirol Mountains. The center houses some 30

million files, questionnaires, and information sheets about the people who established and ran the THIRD REICH, from the lowest level to the very top of the Nazi echelons. Thus, the Berlin Documents Center is one of the most important sources of documented materials for the study of the Nazi regime's structure.

The Center of Contemporary Jewish Documentation (*Centre de Documentation Juive Contemporaine,* CDJC) was founded surreptitiously in Grenoble in 1943 and today is located in PARIS, FRANCE. Its goal is to preserve for future generations the evidence of the crimes committed by the Nazis. The CDJC conducts basic research; publishes information; works on bringing Nazi war criminals to justice; and seeks restitution for all types of victims of the Nazis. Aside from its documents collection, the CDJC also contains a large library that focuses on the Holocaust period.

ITALY's Center for Contemporary Jewish Documentation (*Centro di Documentazione Ebraica Contemporanea,* CDEC) in Milan was instituted in 1955 to study the history of the persecution of Jews by the Nazis and the Italian Fascists and the role of the Jews in the Italian resistance movement. Over time, the CDEC's activities have expanded to include the collecting of documentation on the Jews in Italy from the late nineteenth century to today, focusing mainly on the Holocaust period; the study of ANTISEMITISM in modern-day Italy; and the collecting of books and articles in Italian and other languages on various Jewish historical subjects.

The Leo BAECK Institute (LBI) is a research institute that deals with the history of the Jews in GERMANY and of German-speaking Jews in other countries, beginning with the nineteenth century Emancipation period. It was founded in 1955 in Jerusalem by the Council of Jews from Germany, and has branches in Israel, the United States, and GREAT BRITAIN—the three major areas where German Jews have settled over the years. The LBI both collects archival materials and funds research. The archives and library in its New York branch are among the largest and most extensive on the subject of German Jewish history. Its yearbook is an important source of information about German Jewry.

The NETHERLANDS State Institute for War Documentation (*Rijksinstituut voor Oorlogsdocumentatie*), located in Amsterdam, includes an official research institute, records annex, and library. The records annex contains hundreds of archives and document collections. Those relating to the Holocaust include the archives of the Committee for Jewish REFUGEES, the Dutch *Joodse Raad* (JUDENRAT), the WESTERBORK transit camp, the VUGHT concentration camp, the Jewish affairs office of the Dutch branch of the Reich Security Main Office, and various other bodies.

The Wiener Library is a research center on Nazism that was originally founded by the CENTRAL UNION OF GERMAN CITIZENS OF JEWISH BELIEF in order to gather material about the NAZI PARTY. In 1939 it moved to London and during WORLD WAR II the library's materials were used by the British government, especially its Ministry of Information. Later, it came to contain a significant book collection, eyewitness testimonies, 40,000 prosecution documents from the NUREMBERG TRIALS, and much other archival material pertaining to antisemitism and Nazism. The collection is divided between London and Tel-Aviv.

The Jewish Historical Institute (*Zydowski Instytut Historyczny*) is a research institute located in WARSAW that deals with the history of the Jews of POLAND, specifically during the Holocaust. Originally founded in LUBLIN in 1944, the institute collects historical documentation and Jewish books and art that survived the war, and records testimony from Holocaust SURVIVORS. One of the institute's most important collections is that of documents from the Warsaw Ghetto's ONEG SHABBAT Archives.

DOENITZ, KARL   (1891–1980), Commander of the German navy. On April 30, 1945, just hours before committing suicide (and having broken ties with other Nazi leaders such as GOERING and HIMMLER), Adolf HITLER appointed Doenitz his successor, a post Doenitz filled for one week.

DOLCHSTOSSLEGENDE   see STAB IN THE BACK MYTH.

DOMANEVKA   Capital of the Golta district in TRANSNISTRIA, and site of one of the three mass-murder camps established in that district in October 1941 (the others were BOGDANOVKA and Akhmetchetka). The camp was instituted on the orders of the district governor, Col. Modest Isopescu, and run by Romanian police.

Between November 1941 and January 1942, 20,000 Ukrainian and Bessarabian Jews were deported to Domanevka. In December 1941 Isopescu ordered their extermination. By February 1942, Romanian sol-

diers and police, Ukrainian militiamen, and a SONDERKOMMANDO unit of ethnic Germans had murdered 18,000 Jews in groups of 500 each. The remaining 2,000–3,000 Jews were not murdered, but many died of diseases, starvation, and cold.

Those prisoners that were left alive lived in dilapidated stables, pigsties, and several houses without roofs. The guards would only feed those prisoners strong enough to work; the rest were left to starve, and indeed, several dozen died per day.

In the spring of 1942, Jewish prisoners were forced to burn the corpses to conceal evidence of mass extermination. At the end of 1942, 1,000 Jews were left. Most were transferred to the Akhmetchetka camp a year later, where they were murdered.

Soviet troops liberated Domanevka on March 28, 1944; 500 Jews, mostly Romanian, had survived.

DORA-MITTELBAU   (also known as Dora-Nordhausen), CONCENTRATION CAMP in the Harz Mountains of eastern GERMANY. Dora-Mittelbau was built in August 1943 as a satellite camp of BUCHENWALD. In October 1944 it became an independent concentration camp with 23 satellites of its own.

In mid-1943, 10,000 prisoners, mostly from Buchenwald, were brought to the Dora-Mittelbau site to dig tunnels for a huge underground arms factory where V-2 missiles were to be manufactured. Until late spring of the following year, the prisoners had no above ground barracks, and lived inside the tunnels with no fresh air, inadequate food and water, and terribly unsanitary conditions. They were forced to work at breakneck speed without safety precautions. This led to a mortality rate that was higher than at any other camp in Germany.

When the factories were put into production in the fall of 1944, barracks were finally built above the ground, but the prisoners still had to work 12 hour days. Over 12,000 prisoners lived in the main camp and 20,000 more in the satellites. When Jewish prisoners became too exhausted to work, they were sent to their deaths in AUSCHWITZ and MAUTHAUSEN.

A strong underground functioned in Dora-Mittelbau, which sabotaged production in the weapons factories and thus disturbed weapons deliveries to the Nazis. Many prisoners were executed for taking part in the sabotage. Over 200 were publicly hanged as a punishment and warning to other prisoners.

In March 1945 there were 34,500 prisoners in the entire camp compound. The Nazis began evacuating them on April 1. Within days most of the prisoners had been sent away, most to BERGEN-BELSEN; thousands were murdered en route. In one case, several thousand prisoners, mostly Jews, were burned to death in a barn near the village of Gardelegen. On April 9 American troops arrived to liberate Dora-Mittelbau; they found but a handful of prisoners left on the site.

Nineteen members of the Dora-Mittelbau staff were tried by an American military court between August and December 1947. Fifteen were found guilty—one was sentenced to hanging, while the rest received varying prison sentences.

DOUWES, ARNOLD (b. 1906), Member of the Dutch underground who rescued hundreds of Jews during the HOLOCAUST. Douwes carried out most of his activities near the town of Nieuwlande where, due to his efforts, almost every family hid a Jew. Douwes also recruited the help of several hundred Dutch families in the countryside near Nieuwlande.

After being summoned for DEPORTATION, Jewish families would be directed to Douwes by the underground. He would pick them up himself in Amsterdam or at the train station in his district, and place them in safe havens. He would then personally take care of all their needs, including food, money, and false identity papers. When the Germans raided homes in the area, Douwes would use his bicycle to move Jews to safety.

The Nazis sought to arrest Douwes, so he disguised his appearance with a mustache, glasses, and hat. Nonetheless, he was caught and imprisoned in January 1945; the underground managed to break him out of jail before his execution.

After the war Douwes moved to South Africa, and then settled in Israel in 1956. He was designated as RIGHTEOUS AMONG THE NATIONS by YAD VASHEM in 1965. Later on, over 200 inhabitants of the town of Nieuwlande were also given the title.

DRANCY Assembly and detention camp for French Jews, located in a northeastern suburb of PARIS. From Drancy, Jews were sent to FORCED LABOR and EXTERMINATION CAMPS. The camp was established in August 1941 and liberated in August 1944. It could hold 4,500 inmates at a time; altogether, about 70,000 prisoners passed through it.

Drancy was run like a Nazi CONCENTRATION CAMP, but until July 1, 1943, it was managed by the French (under the supervision of the German Security Police

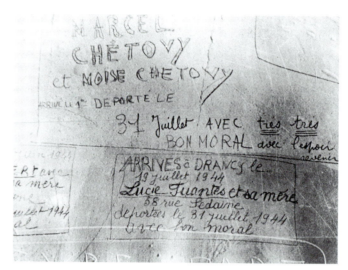

Names of prisoners in Drancy and their deportation dates inscribed on a wall in the camp

and Security Service). Food rations were small, but the prisoners were aided by the Red Cross and French Jewish organizations. On July 2 Alois BRUNNER, an SS officer, took over the camp. Under his charge, the inmates' conditions declined rapidly and DEPORTATIONS to AUSCHWITZ increased. From June 1942 to July 1944, 64 transports with 61,000 French, Polish, and German Jews left Drancy—61 for Auschwitz and three for SOBIBOR.

In spite of the terrible conditions at Drancy, cultural and religious life endured. The Jewish High Holidays were observed in a synagogue that was established in 1941, and many prisoners attended Sabbath services regularly despite German prohibitions. A school was instituted, books were brought into the camp, and cultural evenings were conducted.

Drancy was liberated on August 17, 1944, after the Allies reached Paris.

DUBNOW, SIMON (1860–1941), Jewish professor and historian who developed the theory of autonomous Jewish national life in the Diaspora. Dubnow founded the Jewish Peoples Party in 1906, so that Jews could represent themselves within Russian politics. Confined to the RIGA Ghetto in July 1941, he was shot to death in December 1941.

DUCKWITZ, GEORG FERDINAND (1904–1973), German diplomat, designated by YAD VASHEM as RIGHTEOUS AMONG THE NATIONS for his role in the rescue of the Jews of DENMARK during the HOLOCAUST. During

Georg Duckwitz at the eternal flame in the Hall of Remembrance, Yad Vashem, upon being proclaimed a Righteous among the Nations

the early 1930s Duckwitz was a businessman in Copenhagen, Denmark. He joined the NAZI PARTY in 1932 and served in its foreign-policy department. However, he quit the job in 1935 and went to work for a private shipping firm.

At the beginning of WORLD WAR II Duckwitz returned to Denmark to work for a German intelligence organization. When GERMANY occupied Denmark in April 1940, Duckwitz was named German shipping attache. At the same time, he made contact with many Danish politicians who did not support the Nazis. In the late summer of 1943 the Germans decided to begin deporting Danish Jewry to EXTERMINATION CAMPS. Duckwitz immediately warned his Danish contacts of the plan, and they in turn organized a rescue operation whereby almost all of Danish Jewry was smuggled into SWEDEN. Duckwitz even visited the prime minister of Sweden to ensure his cooperation with the rescue effort.

Never caught by the German authorities, Duckwitz went on to a successful foreign service career in West Germany, including an ambassadorship to Denmark and the post of Foreign Ministry director-general.

DVORETSKI, ALTER   (1906–1942), PARTISAN commander in BELORUSSIA. Born in the town of DIATLOVO (Zhetl), Dvoretski became a lawyer in Novogrudok. When the Germans occupied Diatlovo in June 1941, Dvoretski returned to the town and was appointed chairman of its JUDENRAT. Unlike some other *Judenrat* chairmen, Dvoretski quickly set up an underground partisan group in his GHETTO. He came up with a plan to arm the young Jews of the surrounding towns and take them to the Lipiczany Forest to fight the Germans.

Dvoretski managed to obtain weapons and smuggle them into the ghetto. He also gave weapons to a group of escaped Soviet PRISONERS OF WAR, and sent them to the forest. In addition, he helped young Jewish REFUGEES with no family leave the ghetto to join the partisans in the forest.

Dvoretski devised a detailed plan for armed resistance in case the Germans tried to liquidate the ghetto. However, someone betrayed Dvoretski to the Nazis, and he was forced to flee to the forest, where he met escaped Soviet PRISONERS OF WAR who had become partisans. These men, many who hated Jews, did not have enough weapons and were not really willing to fight the Germans. Nonetheless, Dvoretski tried to convince their commanders to attack Diatlovo in order to free the young Jews trapped inside. On the night of April 29, 1942, the partisans went to the ghetto, only to learn that a large number of German troops had arrived to massacre the Jews of the ghetto the next day. The Soviet partisans were not willing to risk their lives by attacking, so they returned to their base in the forest. The partisan commanders were both afraid and jealous of Dvoretski—so they set up an ambush and murdered him and one of his comrades.

In the end, despite his death, the plans Dvoretski had laid helped more than 600 Jews escape from the Diatlovo Ghetto and flee to the forest during the ghetto's liquidation on August 6, 1942. Those Jews formed a fighting partisan unit, which eventually became the third Jewish company in the Soviet Orlianski-Borba battalion. (see also RESISTANCE, JEWISH.)

E

EBENSEE Sub-camp of the MAUTHAUSEN concentration camp. Located in upper AUSTRIA, Ebensee was established in November 1943 to house inmates forced to build a tunnel system in the side of a mountain that would eventually contain a rocket-research factory.

Most of the prisoners came to Ebensee from the main camp at Mauthausen or from its other sub-camps. At its peak, Ebensee held 18,437 prisoners. The first Jews arrived at Ebensee in early June 1944. They were subjected to extremely cruel treatment, and as a result their mortality rate was much higher than that of the rest of the camp population. By April 1945 the overcrowding was so bad at Ebensee that more prisoners died daily than could be handled by the crematorium. That month, 4,547 prisoners out of a total population of 16,000 perished.

On April 30 the Nazis released most of the German prisoners and halted all FORCED LABOR. On May 5 the camp commandant tried to get the remaining prisoners to enter one of the mountain tunnels; they refused, and the camp staff left. On May 6 American troops liberated Ebensee, and found that same tunnel full of explosives. By refusing to enter the tunnel, the prisoners had saved themselves from being blown up by the Germans.

Altogether, about 11,000 prisoners died at Ebensee.

ECLAIREURS ISRAELITES DE FRANCE   see FRENCH JEWISH SCOUTS.

EDELMAN, MAREK   (b. 1921), One of the commanders of the WARSAW GHETTO UPRISING. Marek Edelman was also one of its few SURVIVORS.

Edelman was born in WARSAW. As a teenager, he joined the *Zukunft*, the YOUTH MOVEMENT associated with the Jewish-Socialist BUND Party. When the Nazis occupied POLAND in 1939, Edelman was deported to the Warsaw Ghetto. He soon became a leader of the GHETTO'S underground resistance. When the young people in the underground began to distinguish themselves as influential activists, Edelman became a member of the *Bund*'s central administration.

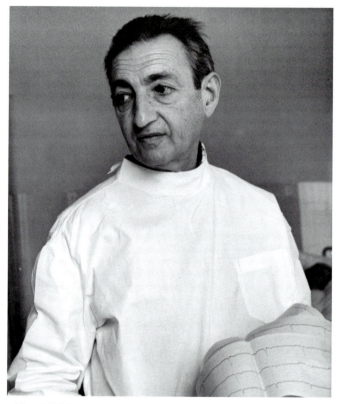

Marek Edelman, a commander of the Warsaw Ghetto Uprising

Edelman joined the ghetto's Jewish Fighting Organization (*Zydowska Organizacja Bojowa,* ZOB) in November 1942. Soon thereafter he was selected to serve as the *Zukunft* representative in the ZOB's management.

The Warsaw Ghetto Uprising broke out on April 19, 1943, on the first night of Passover. Edelman helped lead the Jewish resistance when the Nazis began to close in on the fighters. At first, Edelman and his soldiers were in charge of defending the "Brushmakers" ghetto district. After the ZOB forces began to withdraw, Edelman and his men joined the fighters centered at 30 Franciszkanska Street. The Nazis progressively destroyed the Warsaw Ghetto and cut the Jewish fighters off from one another. Edelman was among one of the last groups to hold out in the ZOB's headquarters at 18 Mila Street. On May 10 he was able to cross over to the non-Jewish side of Warsaw by way of the city's sewers.

Edelman and other members of the ZOB took part in the WARSAW POLISH UPRISING, which broke out on August 1, 1944 and was only put down on October 2 of that year.

Right after the war, Edelman published a book called "The *Bund*'s Role in the Defense of the Warsaw Ghetto" in Polish and Yiddish. A year later, he published a short history of the Warsaw Ghetto Uprising in Polish, Yiddish, and English, called "The Ghetto Fights." Edelman chose to stay in Poland after WORLD WAR II, and became a cardiologist. During the early 1980s he was active in Lech Walesa's Solidarity Trade Union Movement. (see also JEWISH FIGHTING ORGANIZATION, WARSAW and RESISTANCE, JEWISH.)

EDELSTEIN, JACOB   (1903–1944), Chairman of the JUDENRAT in the THERESIENSTADT Ghetto.

When GERMANY took over Bohemia and Moravia in March 1939, Edelstein, as the most prominent Zionist leader in PRAGUE, was put in charge of emigration to Palestine. Soon, he also became the Jews' official spokesman in their dealings with the Germans.

Over the next two and a half years, Edelstein went on many trips abroad in search of ways to accelerate Jewish emigration. On each trip he met with Jewish community and Zionist leaders, whom he warned about the troubles to come. Throughout his travels, Edelstein had many opportunities to stay away from Nazi-occupied Bohemia and Moravia, but he always returned to Prague, to honor what he felt was his duty to his fellow Jews.

In October 1939 Edelstein was part of a group sent to an area in POLAND called Nisko. This DEPORTATION was part of a German plan to resettle Jews in one area near LUBLIN (see also NISKO AND LUBLIN PLAN). However, the plan was unsuccessful, and some of the men were allowed to return home, among them Edelstein, who returned to Prague in November 1939.

Jacob Edelstein (right) watching the burial of inmates in Theresienstadt

In October 1941 the Germans established the Theresienstadt GHETTO to detain the Jews of the Protectorate of Bohemia and Moravia until such time that they would be deported to the east. Edelstein did not know that Theresienstadt was really just a temporary holding place; he believed that the Nazis had been successfully convinced not to deport his country's Jews. Edelstein arrived at Theresienstadt in December 1941 and was named chairman of its Jewish Council. In this post, he focused on education and on making the ghetto an indispensable labor force for the Germans. Historians disagree about Edelstein's role at Theresienstadt. Some say that he cooperated with the Nazis or fault him for misunderstanding the situation at hand. Others consider him to have been a model human being who gave his life for his fellow Jews.

Edelstein was fired from the *Judenrat* in January 1943. In December he and his family were sent to AUSCHWITZ, where they were executed. (see also BOHEMIA AND MORAVIA, PROTECTORATE OF.)

EICHMANN, ADOLF   (1906–1962), SS officer who played a major role in the annihilation of European Jewry.

Eichmann was born in the German Rhineland, but grew up in AUSTRIA and joined the Austrian NAZI PARTY in 1932. A year later he arrived in GERMANY and joined the SS's Austrian unit. In October 1934 Eichmann moved on to the headquarters of the Security Service (SD). In 1935 he joined the SD's new Jewish section, and became one of the SS's main planners and executors of anti-Jewish policy.

In 1937 Eichmann traveled to Palestine, and concluded that the establishment of a Jewish state would not be in Germany's best interests. After the ANSCHLUSS—the annexing of Austria by Germany in March 1938—Eichmann was charged with organizing the emigration of Austria's Jews. He devised a method that would force the Jews to emigrate: he stripped them of their property and thus destroyed their economic situation, forcing them to go elsewhere; terrorized them into leaving; and grabbed control of Jewish community institutions and forced their leaders to cooperate with the emigration plans. Despite his previous position on Jewish immigration to Palestine, Eichmann began cooperating with ALIYA BET agencies. To make the forced emigration process more efficient and consolidated, Eichmann set up the Central Office for Jewish Emigration (ZENTRALSTELLE FUER JUEDISCHE AUSWAN-

Adolf Eichmann during the Nazi period

DERUNG) in VIENNA in August 1938. A few months later, after the KRISTALLNACHT pogrom of November 1938, Hermann GOERING established a similar office in Germany. Eichmann also set up a *Zenstralstelle* in PRAGUE in 1939.

With the establishment of the Reich Security Main Office (REICHSSICHERHEITSHAUPTAMPT, RSHA) in September 1939, Eichmann became head of the Jewish section in the GESTAPO. In that position, Eichmann had more power than any other section chief—he worked under Reinhard HEYDRICH, and sometimes even worked directly with Heinrich HIMMLER.

In 1939 and 1940 Eichmann oversaw the DEPORTATION of Poles and Jews from those areas of POLAND that had been annexed by the Reich. One of the first ideas to be brought up was the NISKO AND LUBLIN PLAN, in which the SS envisioned the mass deportation and resettlement of Jews in the GENERALGOUVERNEMENT. Though the plan quickly failed, it became a prototype

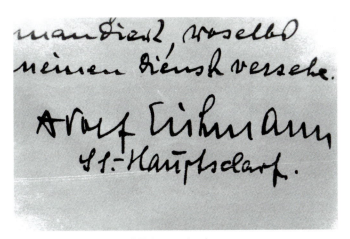

Adolf Eichmann's signature

for mass deportations of Jews throughout the rest of the war.

By the end of 1940 Eichmann's office controlled all the Jews within the Reich. He sent his representatives, including Alois BRUNNER, Theodor DANNECKER, Dieter WISLICENY, and his deputy, Rolf Guenther, to act as advisors on Jewish affairs to various governments; their job was to encourage the execution of anti-Jewish policy. His representatives were active all over Nazi-dominated Europe, except in Scandinavia and in the areas where the EINSATZGRUPPEN functioned.

In October 1941 Eichmann participated in the initial discussions concerning the "final solution." On Heydrich's orders, Eichmann organized the WANNSEE CONFERENCE to coordinate the murders; the conference took place in BERLIN in January 1942. Once the "Final Solution" was launched, Eichmann's office issued the orders regarding when and where deportations were to happen. He and his staff also designed the regimen for rounding up Jews and taking away their property. Eichmann himself paid several visits to EX-TERMINATION CAMPS to check on their efficiency and progress, and was directly responsible for the THERE-SIENSTADT Ghetto.

Eichmann personally directed the 1944 deportations from HUNGARY where, as in other countries, he was confronted with many rescue attempts. In some cases he foiled rescue plans, as in ROMANIA and BULGARIA; in Hungary he tried to make a deal, to exchange Jewish lives for goods or money.

After the war, Eichmann escaped to Argentina. He lived there undetected until May 1960, when the Israeli Security Service captured him. He was tried in a sensational trial in Jerusalem in April 1961. Eichmann was found guilty and sentenced to death; he was hanged on June 1, 1962.

EICHMANN TRIAL   Trial of Adolf EICHMANN, Nazi SS officer in charge of the Jewish affairs department in the Reich Security Main Office. The trial was held in Jerusalem in 1961 and 1962.

In May 1960 Israeli secret service agents had found Eichmann living in Argentina under a false name. They kidnapped him and brought him to Israel to stand trial under the Nazis and Nazi Collaborators (Punishment) Law of 1950. He was indicted on 15 counts, including crimes against the Jewish people, CRIMES AGAINST HUMANITY, war crimes, and membership in various criminal organizations, including the SS, the Security Service (SD), and the GESTAPO. The charges against Eichmann also included crimes against the Poles, Slovenes, GYPSIES, and Czechs.

The trial began on April 10, 1961. It was conducted by the District Court of Jerusalem, with three judges presiding: Supreme Court justice Moshe Landau, who headed the bench; Jerusalem District Court president Benjamin Halevi; and Tel Aviv District Court judge Yitzhak Raveh. The chief prosecuting attorney was Gideon HAUSNER, Israel's attorney general, and a German lawyer who had previously defended Nazis at the NUREMBERG TRIALS, Dr. Robert Servatius, defended Eichmann.

The court was packed with spectators throughout the trial, which lasted four months. For his own safety, Eichmann sat inside a bulletproof glass booth. Members of the audience, which included many survivors, were frequently so moved by the sessions that some would stand up and begin shouting. One survivor who testified passed out on the stand.

The prosecution opened with a summary of the history of the HOLOCAUST. Hausner brought 112 witnesses who testified about the events of the Holocaust and Eichmann's involvement in coordinating and carrying out the "final solution" to the "Jewish question." He brought 1,600 documents that provided details of the persecution of European Jewry in all its phases, and attested to Eichmann's personal involvement in the extermination plans and process. Many documents even contained Eichmann's signature. The Nazi officer was proved to be the head of the RSHA's office of Jewish affairs, whose main goal was to annihilate European Jewry.

The defense did not challenge the facts presented by

Eichmann standing in his bulletproof glass booth during his trial in Jerusalem, 1961

the prosecution, nor did they challenge the genuineness of Hausner's documents. Instead, they argued that Jewish Israeli judges would be prejudiced and thus could not produce a fair trial for Eichmann; that the trial itself was illegal because Eichmann had been illegally kidnapped and taken to Israel; that the law under which the trial was called—the Nazis and Nazi Collaborators (Punishment) Law of 1950—was unjust as it had been passed after the Holocaust had happened; and that the trial should not be taking place in Israel, as the crimes had been committed outside of the country, before it was even established. However, the judges rejected each of these arguments. Eichmann then pleaded "in the sense of the indictment, not guilty" to each count. The defense also claimed that Eichmann had not acted out of his own will, but was just obeying HITLER'S orders; this claim was also rejected. Eichmann was found guilty on all counts as a key figure in the "Final Solution." On December 15, 1961 he was sentenced to death.

Eichmann appealed the guilty verdict, but the Israeli Supreme Court upheld the lower court's decision. Eich-

mann than appealed for clemency, but this was denied by Israel's president, Itzhak Ben-Zvi. Eichmann was hanged in Ramleh prison on the night between May 31 and June 1, 1962. His body was cremated, and the ashes scattered at sea, outside of Israel's waters.

The Eichmann trial led to a heightened awareness of the Holocaust and to an interest in Holocaust research, both within Israel and throughout the world. It also induced the prosecution of other war criminals, especially in West Germany.

EICKE, THEODOR (1892–1943), SS Lieutenant General, commandant of CONCENTRATION CAMPS, and commander of the SS DEATH'S HEAD UNITS (*Totenkopfverbaende*), an armed SS troop that guarded the concentration camps.

Eicke was born in Huddington, GERMANY. He served in the German army from 1909 until the end of World War I. He then became a police officer. In 1928 he joined the NAZI PARTY and the Storm Troopers (SA), at that time led by Ernst ROHM. In 1930 Eicke switched over from the SA to the SS. He had a very good relationship with SS chief Heinrich HIMMLER, and despite his sometimes difficult personality, he quickly advanced through the SS's chain of command.

In June 1933 Eicke was made commandant of the first concentration camp, DACHAU, and was awarded the rank of *Oberfuehrer*. His personal motto was "Tolerance is a sign of weakness." His brutal style of command at Dachau was soon to become a model for other camp administrators. This included the torture of prisoners and encouragement of the Death Head Units' barbarous behavior.

On June 30, 1934, nicknamed "The Night of the Long Knives" Himmler's SS men destroyed the leadership of the SA. It was Eicke who actually shot Ernst Rohm in his cell. His involvement in that purge earned Eicke a promotion to Inspector for Concentration Camps and Commander of the Death's Head Units. He was also advanced to the rank of *Brigadefuehrer*.

In November 1939 Eicke was made commander of the *Waffen*-SS, which were the SS's military units. Under his leadership, they took part in the fighting in FRANCE and on the Russian front. Eicke's brutal style extended to the *Waffen*-SS; their first war crime was the murder of about 100 British PRISONERS OF WAR in FRANCE on May 26, 1940. At the end of the war the Allies labeled the *Waffen*-SS a "criminal organization."

Eicke was killed on the Russian front on February

16, 1943 when his plane was shot down. At that time, he was serving as an SS-*Obergruppenfuehrer* in the *Waffen-SS*.

EINSATZGRUPPEN (full name: *Einsatzgruppen der Sicherheitsdienstes* [SD] *und der Sicherheitspolizei* [SIPO]), German term, meaning "action-groups," that originally referred to Nazi police intelligence units that worked with the German army after the invasion of AUSTRIA, Czechoslovakia, and POLAND. Later, the term referred to mobile SS killing units that traveled with the German forces that invaded the SOVIET UNION in 1941.

the invasion, the *Einsatzgruppen* were instructed on how to deal with Jews in the newly conquered regions: they were to arrest the Jews and put them in GHETTOS near railway lines to facilitate future population movement, and set up JUDENRAETE (Jewish Councils). These *Einsatzgruppen* were disbanded in November 1939; their members joined the permanent Security Services and Security Police offices in occupied Poland.

As GERMANY prepared to invade the Soviet Union in June 1941, HITLER made it clear to the army that the upcoming war was based on a fundamental conflict

Units of the Einsatzgruppen murdering Jews

When the Germans invaded Austria in March 1938 and Czechoslovakia in March 1939, the job of the *Einsatzgruppen* was to follow the advancing military, and act as portable offices of the Nazis' Security Service and Security Police until permanent offices could be set up. The *Einsatzgruppen* were in charge of security in these regions, which meant finding and imprisoning opponents of the Nazis.

In preparation for the Nazi invasion of Poland in September 1939, the *Einsatzgruppen* were commanded to combat elements that were hostile to the Reich; they interpreted that as an order to murder thousands of Jews and members of the Polish upper-class. Soon after

between two completely opposing ideologies. It was imperative to destroy those elements that perpetuated the conflicting ideology. Thus, special units called *Einsatzgruppen* were formed to accompany the advancing military forces. Their job was to search for opponents of the Reich, including Communists and all Jews—and execute them.

When Operation "Barbarossa" began, the *Einsatzgruppen* followed the German army WEHRMACHT right in to the Soviet Union. Four units had been established, *Einsatzgruppen* A, B, C, and D. Each one was assigned to liquidate the Jews in its own region and each was divided into sub-units called SONDERKOMMANDOS or

Einsatzkommandos. Einsatzgruppe A, the largest group with about 1,000 men, was attached to Army Group North. They operated in the Baltic States (LITHUANIA, LATVIA, and ESTONIA) and the area between their eastern borders and Leningrad. *Einsatzgruppe* B, 655 men attached to Army Group Center, worked in BELORUSSIA and the Smolensk district, east of Moscow. *Einsatzgruppe* C, a group of 700 attached to Army Group South, covered the northern and central UKRAINE. *Einsatzgruppe* D, with 600 men attached to the Eleventh Army, operated in the southern Ukraine, the Crimea, and Ciscaucasia. These groups did not carry out the destruction of Soviet Jewry alone—wherever they went, regular German soldiers, German police units, and local collaborators helped get their murderous job done. By the spring of 1943, the *Einsatzgruppen* had exterminated 1.25 million Jews and hundreds of thousands of Soviets, including PRISONERS OF WAR.

The *Einsatzgruppen* killed their victims—men, women, and children—by gathering them in ravines, mines, quarries, ditches, or pits dug specifically for this purpose. First they would force the Jews to hand over their possessions and remove their clothing. Then they would shoot them, and throw the bodies into the ditch. The commanders filed daily reports of their murderous activities.

The constant up-close contact with murder had a terribly destructive effect on the *Einsatzgruppen* members, despite the large amounts of alcohol they were plied with. This led the Nazis to search for other execution alternatives. Soon the *Einsatzgruppen* were given GAS VANS for the murder of the remaining Jews.

After the war, leaders of the *Einsatzgruppen* were tried at NUREMBERG and at later trials. Of 24 defendants, 14 were sentenced to death. Only four were actually executed; the rest had their sentences reduced.

EINSATZSTAB ROSENBERG (Operational Staff Rosenberg), organization established by Alfred ROSENBERG for the systematic plunder of the art and cultural objects belonging to Jews in Europe.

Right after the Nazis occupied FRANCE in June 1940, HITLER announced his wish to pillage the artistic treasures belonging to France's Jews. The first repossessions were carried out in France by the Special Operational Staff for the Arts (*Sonderstab Bildende Kunst*), created by Hitler on September 17, 1940. The FRENCH POLICE, German Security Police, and the German Embassy in PARIS all assisted in the operation (Rosenberg nonethe-

Torah scrolls seized by Einsatzstab Rosenberg

less complained that the French authorities involved kept works of art for themselves). Unit members raked through the collections of the Rothschild family and others, and looked for hidden art storehouses. They also searched through the shipments of overseas removal companies, claiming that they wanted to ensure that no art treasures would be smuggled out of France.

From 1940–1944 almost 22,000 items, including pieces of art, furniture, paintings, and antiques, were transferred to GERMANY in 29 shipments. The objects stolen—relocated by 137 freight cars holding 4,174 crates—represented all kinds of art from world over, from different periods. Besides those items, many distinctive pieces were taken to decorate the homes of Hitler, Hermann GOERING, and other Nazi leaders.

At the same time the Jewish art of France was being plundered, Operational Staff Rosenberg administered the seizure of furniture (*Mobel Aktion*) in the NETHERLANDS and BELGIUM, similar to the appropriation done previously in Germany. Tens of thousands of Jewish homes were stripped of their furniture; the homeowners had either left the country or had been deported to Eastern Europe. The possessions were relocated to Germany in 735 freight trains. Some of the Dutch property, which included linens and clothing, was transported down the Rhine River on rafts. On October 3, 1942 Rosenberg reported to Hitler that 40,000 tons of furniture had been confiscated and brought to Germany.

The pillage in Eastern Europe was less methodical; however, many ritual objects and artworks were stolen. Jewish libraries all over Europe were also looted.

EINSTEIN, ALBERT (1897–1955), German Jewish physicist who left GERMANY when HITLER rose to power in 1933. Einstein postulated the famed "theory of relativity" and won the Nobel Prize in Physics in 1921.

EISENHOWER, DWIGHT DAVID (1890–1969), American military leader and president of the UNITED STATES from 1953–1961. During WORLD WAR II Eisenhower organized and commanded the Allied invasion of Europe, and served as commander in chief of the Allied forces in Europe. When the war ended, he was appointed commander in chief of the American occupation forces in Europe.

In 1945 Eisenhower's forces liberated tens of thousands of Jews from CONCENTRATION CAMPS and FORCED LABOR camps. He personally visited several newly-liberated camps, and ordered that as many American soldiers as possible visit the camps to see the remnants of the Nazis' horrible crimes with their own eyes. Over and over, Eisenhower reiterated to the public his feelings of shock and loathing regarding the Nazis' genocidal activities.

As head of the American occupation forces in Europe after the war, Eisenhower faced the problem of Jewish displaced persons (DPs), Holocaust SURVIVORS with nowhere to go. He created the position of advisor on Jewish affairs as an address to deal with the DP issue, and sanctioned the building of separate Jewish DP camps in the American zone in GERMANY. Later, Eisenhower allowed in thousands of Holocaust survivors who

General Dwight D. Eisenhower (center) viewing human remains at the Ohdruf concentration camp in Germany

illegally reached the American zone from Eastern Europe. (see also DISPLACED PERSONS, JEWISH.)

ELKES, ELCHANAN (1879–1944), Physician and chairman of the *Aeltestenrat* (Council of Elders) in the KOVNO Ghetto in LITHUANIA.

From the early 1920s, Elkes chaired the internal medicine department in Kovno's Bikkur Holim Jewish Hospital; he was one of the best doctors in Lithuania and a Zionist.

The Germans attacked the SOVIET UNION in June 1941. They occupied Kovno on June 24 and murdered several thousand Jews. The remaining 30,000 Jews were forced into a GHETTO and ordered to designate a head for the *Aeltestenrat*. Elkes became its leader on August 4. All who knew him affirmed that he was completely devoted to the Jewish cause, courageous and dignified in his dealings with the Nazis, an ethical and modest leader, and comfortable with his fellow Jews. Elkes supported the ghetto's resistance movement and helped gather supplies for the General Jewish Fighting Organization (*Yidishe Algemeyne Kamf Organizatsye*, JFO).

In July 1944, the Soviet army was advancing towards Kovno. At that point, the Nazis began liquidating the ghetto and relocating its inhabitants to GERMANY. Elkes risked his life by approaching the commander of the ghetto, Wilhelm Goecke, to suggest that Goecke change his plan to transfer the Jews to Germany. Elkes argued that in the end, Goecke would be praised for dropping the transfer. Goecke refused Elkes' suggestion, but let him leave without punishment.

The ghetto was emptied a few days later. Elkes was sent to the Landsberg CONCENTRATION CAMP in Germany, and put in charge of the camp's hospital hut. Elkes soon got sick, and he died on October 17, 1944. A year before, almost to the day, Elkes wrote these words to his children in England: "With my own ears I have heard the awful symphony of weeping, wailing and screaming of tens of thousands of men, women, and children, which have rent the heavens. No one throughout the ages has heard such a sound. Along with many of these martyrs I have quarreled with my Creator, and with them I cried out from a broken heart, 'Who is as silent as you, O lord.'"

ENDRE, LASZLO (1895–1946), Hungarian politician who helped plan and implement the annihilation of Hungarian Jewry in 1944. Endre was an activist in many extreme right-wing organizations, and was the founder of the "Race-protecting Socialist Party" (*A Fajvedo Szocialista*). A career policeman, he was appointed deputy chief of police for all of Pest County in 1937.

Endre was in close contact with the German Nazis, and after GERMANY occupied HUNGARY on March 19, 1944, he developed a strong, personal relationship with Adolf EICHMANN. On April 9 of that year Endre became undersecretary of state in the Hungarian government led by Dome SZTOJAY. He held the position until September 5, 1944. During his five months in the government, Endre played a major role in the extermination of his country's Jews.

At the end of the war Endre fled Hungary with the withdrawing German troops. He was captured by American soldiers and sent back to Hungary in October 1945. He was tried, convicted, and sentenced to death as a war criminal, and was hanged on March 29, 1946.

EPPSTEIN, PAUL (1901–1944), A leader of the Jewish community in GERMANY during the HOLOCAUST.

A sociology professor, Eppstein became principal of an adult education college in 1929. However, when

Paul Eppstein (standing)

HITLER rose to national power in 1933, the Nazis closed down the college. At that point, Eppstein was invited to come to BERLIN to work for the Jewish community. His first positions in Berlin were with the CENTRAL COMMITTEE OF GERMAN JEWS FOR HELP AND RECONSTRUCTION and the Union of Jewish Communities of Prussia.

Soon, Eppstein joined the board of the REICH REPRESENTATION OF GERMAN JEWS, where he dealt with social activities and administration. After the KRISTALLNACHT pogrom of November 1938, he was invited to England to lecture there on sociology. However, he refused to leave Germany as long as the Jews there needed him. He continued his work for the Reich Representation, whose name by that time had been changed to the Reich Association of Jews in Germany, and was given even more responsibilities, including being in close contact with the German authorities and dealing with emigration. By the end of 1940, Eppstein became the organization's executive director.

During his time with the Reich Representation/Association, Eppstein was arrested several times by the GESTAPO. In October 1940 he was released from a stint in prison that had followed his arrest in the summer of that year. At that point, the Reich Security Main Office (REICHSSICHERHEITSHAUPTAMT, RSHA) warned him to stop his emigration activities. From then on, Eppstein kept to administrative duties. In January 1943 Eppstein was deported to the THERESIENSTADT Ghetto, where he replaced Jacob EDELSTEIN as leader of the GHETTO'S Jewish Council. Historians disagree about Eppstein's role in Theresienstadt. Some fault him for not challenging the German authorities enough and for giving in to their demands, while others believe that he was a loyal and resolute spokesman for the Jews, both in Germany and in the ghetto.

Eppstein was put in prison in the summer of 1944, and executed the day after the Jewish High Holiday of Yom Kippur.

ERNTEFEST ("Harvest Festival"), German codename for the operation to eliminate the last Jews in the TRAWNIKI, PONIATOWA, and MAJDANEK camps. *Erntefest* was the last *aktion* in the GENERALGOUVERNEMENT area, beginning on November 3, 1944 and lasting for several days.

After the SOBIBOR uprising, Heinrich HIMMLER worried that the Jews might attempt to revolt elsewhere. He thus ordered the execution of all Jews in the labor camps in the *Generalgouvernement*. At that time, there were 15,000 Jews in Poniatowa and between 8,000–10,000 in Trawniki.

At dawn on November 3, 1943, thousands of SS and police surrounded Poniatowa and Trawniki, took the Jews out in groups, and shot them in pits. In Majdanek, the Jews were also shot after being separated from the other prisoners at the morning assembly. In Trawniki and Majdanek, music was blared to drown out the killing. Jews from other camps in LUBLIN were also brought to Majdanek to be executed. Between 17,000–18,000 Jews were killed there on the first day. In all, 42,000–43,000 Jews were murdered during *Erntefest*.

Some Jews attempted to fight back in Poniatowa, but were defeated. Jews who tried to hide were found and shot. Hundreds of Jews were left behind to burn the corpses, after which they were also killed.

ESTONIA The northernmost and the smallest of the three Baltic states. On the eve of WORLD WAR II, there were 4,500 Jews in Estonia, out of a total population of more than one million.

Estonia was an independent country between the two world wars and again since 1991. In August 1940 the Soviets took control of the country as a result of the NAZI-SOVIET PACT. However, when the Nazis invaded the SOVIET UNION in mid-1941, they entered and conquered Estonia. The Germans included it in REICHSKOMMISSARIAT OSTLAND, an administrative area that encompassed the Baltic states and BELORUSSIA, but allowed an extreme nationalistic Estonian movement to rule the country.

Before the war, about half of Estonia's Jews lived in the capital city, TALLINN, while the rest lived in large towns. They were considered to be an important Estonian minority, and were allowed a certain amount of self-rule. When the Soviets took control of Estonia in 1940, however, the right of self-rule was taken away from the Jews and many were arrested. When the Germans arrived, many Jews fled eastward. Those who had not escaped were immediately treated to harsh restrictions: they were forced to wear the Jewish badge and stripped of their property (see also BADGE, JEWISH). Then the EINSATZGRUPPEN arrived and began murdering Jews, with the help of right-wing Estonian units (*Omakaitse*). By October 1941, almost all Jewish males over 16 had been killed. At the January 1942 WANNSEE CONFERENCE in BERLIN, the authorities in charge of Estonia noted that the region was Jew-free.

In the fall of 1942 the Germans began sending tens of thousands of Jews to Estonia from other occupied areas, including THERESIENSTADT, VILNA, KOVNO, and camps in LATVIA. They were imprisoned in 20 labor camps. Those prisoners too sick to work were killed, while many others died of torture, malnourishment, and disease. By the fall of 1944 the Soviet army was once again advancing towards Estonia; the Germans quickly removed the last Jews from the labor camps and moved them across the Baltic Sea to STUTTHOF, a Polish CONCENTRATION CAMP. On September 18–19, 1944, the remainder were killed in the Lagedi and KLOOGA camps.

Since the end of the 1990s, the Estonian government has tried to document the fate of all Estonian victims of the Nazi period.

EUROPA PLAN   Plan devised by the Slovakian WORKING GROUP to rescue European Jewry from extermination by paying ransom.

In the summer of 1942 activists from the Slovakian Jewish Center wanted to stop the DEPORTATION of Slovakian Jews to POLAND. They bribed Dieter WISLICENY, SS advisor on Jewish affairs; he agreed to a sum of US $40,000–$50,000. The deportations did halt after Wisliceny was bribed, but there is no proof that his influence stopped them. Even so, the group believed this was the case. Encouraged, a Working Group leader named Rabbi Michael Dov WEISSMANDEL suggested repeating their success regarding other Jewish communities. This plan called for the end of the deportation of Jews from Nazi-dominated Europe to Poland in exchange for US $2–$3 million to be paid by the Jews of the free world. Negotiations lasted from fall 1942 to August 1943. However, the plan ultimately deteriorated. The Working Group believed that they failed because the Jews of the free world, who claimed the money was not available or could not be transferred, would not provide the needed funds.

The "Blood for Goods" negotiations concerning the rescue of Hungarian Jews were a direct follow-up to the Europa Plan. (see also JEWISH CENTER, SLOVAKIA.)

EUTHANASIA PROGRAM   (*Aktion* T4, T4 Operation), program of "mercy killings" which the Nazis used to euphemistically refer to their systematic extermination of certain groups including the mentally ill, aged, disabled, and others. The Euthanasia Program, code-named T4, was part of the Nazis' attempt to preserve

the purity of the master race—in order to create a superior group of "Aryans" the Nazis needed to destroy all those with racial defects.

The Nazis first began cutting out undesirable elements of their society in the 1930s, with the forced sterilization of children of black fathers, those with genetic diseases, and repeat criminals. By late 1939, HITLER appointed Dr. Karl Brandt and Philip Bouhler heads of the Euthanasia Program. These men hired a staff of medical doctors and established four euthanasia centers in GERMANY during the first half of 1940, in Grafeneck, Brandenburg, Hartheim, and Sonnenstein. Residents of welfare institutions, some CONCENTRATION CAMP inmates, the chronically sick, the mentally and physically disabled, homosexuals, and even sick German soldiers were brought to these centers and gassed, shot, or killed by lethal injection. By the end of that year, almost 27,000 Germans had been killed as part of the program; by August 1941, more than 35,000 additional people had been exterminated.

The Euthanasia Program was officially closed down on September 1, 1941, due to growing public pressure, including a sermon delivered by Bishop Clemens GALEN in Muenster on August 3. However, the Nazis secretly continued their "mercy killings" all the way up to the end of the war. The Euthanasia Program staff was transferred to AKTION REINHARD, and different Nazi institutions took over the killing. According to sources at the NUREMBERG TRIALS, there were 275,000 victims of the Euthanasia Program; other sources estimate about 200,000 victims.

One of the most heinous aspects of the Euthanasia Program was the fact that its staff members were trained medical doctors, sworn to help care for their patients, not destroy them because of a racial difference. At its inception, the program was even illegal—and yet the Euthanasia practitioners seemed to have no moral, religious, or legal doubts about what they were doing.

EVIAN CONFERENCE   Conference convened by President Franklin D. ROOSEVELT to deal with the Jewish REFUGEE problem. It was held in Evian, FRANCE, from July 6–15, 1938.

After GERMANY annexed AUSTRIA in March 1938, Roosevelt called for an international conference to promote the emigration of Austrian and German Jewish refugees and create an international organization whose purpose would be to deal with the general refugee problem. The president invited delegates from 32 coun-

Illustration from the New York Times about the Evian Conference, July 3, 1938

tries, including the UNITED STATES, GREAT BRITAIN, France, CANADA, six small European democratic nations, the Latin American nations, Australia, and New Zealand. When he proposed the conference, Roosevelt made it clear that no country would be forced to change its immigration quotas, but would instead be asked to volunteer changes.

During the conference, it became painfully obvious that no country was willing to volunteer anything. The British delegate claimed that Britain was already fully populated and suffering from unemployment, so it could take in no refugees. His only offer consisted of British territories in East Africa, which could take in small numbers of refugees. The French delegate declared that France had reached "the extreme point of saturation as regards admission of refugees." Myron C. Taylor, the American delegate, allowed that the United States would make the previously unfilled quota for Germans and Austrians available to these new refugees. Other countries claimed the Depression as their excuse for not accepting refugees. Only the Dominican Republic, a tiny country in the West Indies, volunteered to take in refugees—in exchange for huge amounts of money.

The one thing accomplished at the conference was the establishment of the Intergovernmental Committee on Refugees (ICR). Its goals were to help safe haven candidate countries develop opportunities for refugee settlement, and to try and convince Germany to allow organized emigration. However, ICR member countries did not give the organization either the funding or authority it needed to make a real difference. Thus, whatever good the Evian Conference set out to do was buried in the sand—and the world's democracies had made it extremely clear that they were not willing to help European Jewry.

EXODUS 1947   An "illegal" immigration ship that attempted to bring Jewish SURVIVORS to Palestine in

The "illegal" immigration ship "Exodus 1947"

1947, only to be turned back to Europe by the British Mandate authorities. The *Exodus 1947* became an international symbol of the need for free Jewish immigration to Palestine.

In July 1947 the *Mosad le-Aliya Bet,* the main illegal immigration agency, loaded 4,500 Jewish REFUGEES onto a re-outfitted American ship, which sailed from Marseilles, FRANCE. When it reached the open sea, the ship renamed itself *Exodus 1947.* British warships picked up on the ship before it even reached Palestine's waters and forced it to advance into Haifa. As soon as the boat reached the port, British soldiers forcibly removed the refugees, killing three and wounding many others. On July 20 the refugees were dragged onto three British ships and sailed back to France. The ships sat off the coast of France for a month, while the French authorities refused to remove the Jews, but also refused them refuge. The Jews organized a hunger strike that attracted world attention to their terrible situation. Nonetheless, to the world's astonishment, the British decided to send the Jews back to DISPLACED PERSONS camps in GERMANY. The refugees remained in the camps until 1948, when the State of Israel was established.

EXTERMINATION CAMPS (in German, *vernichtungslager*), Nazi camps located in occupied POLAND whose sole purpose was to murder the Jews brought there. Altogether, about 3.5 million Jews were killed in extermination camps as part of the "FINAL SOLUTION."

The Nazis began systematically mass murdering Jews when they invaded the SOVIET UNION in June 1941. At first, hundreds of thousands of Jews were shot to death by EINSATZGRUPPEN and other units. However, this method quickly proved cumbersome, and the Nazis began searching for other murder methods. They soon began experimenting with poison gas at AUSCHWITZ and other camps. After these experiments showed gas to be a successful technique, Nazi leaders ordered the establishment of extermination camps where gas would be used for the murder of Jews.

The extermination camps were constructed in the region of Poland occupied by GERMANY in 1939. They included the Birkenau (Auschwitz II) section of Auschwitz, CHELMNO, BELZEC, SOBIBOR, and TREBLINKA. Some experts also include MAJDANEK with its 360,000 victims, as there was a time when the Jews who arrived there were subjected to selections, as at Auschwitz, and most sent to their deaths (see also SELEKTION).

Crematoria III in Birkenau (Auschwitz II)

Chelmno was the first extermination camp to be established. Located near LODZ, it was put into operation on December 8, 1941, and disbanded in the summer of 1944. Victims were killed by GAS VANS; about 320,000 people were murdered there.

Auschwitz was both a CONCENTRATION CAMP and an extermination camp. Its extermination section in Birkenau was instituted in March 1942, and finally closed in November 1944. About one million Jews were murdered in the camp's GAS CHAMBERS, which used ZYKLON B gas. In addition, tens of thousands of GYPSIES and Soviet PRISONERS OF WAR were also murdered there.

Belzec, Sobibor, and Treblinka were all set up in 1942 as a result of AKTION REINHARD. Belzec was in operation from March to December 1942, during which time 600,000 Jews were murdered there; Sobibor operated from April 1942 to October 1943, with 250,000 victims; and Treblinka operated from July 1942 to August 1943, encompassing 870,000 murders. Those annihilated at these camps were suffocated to death by carbon monoxide gas.

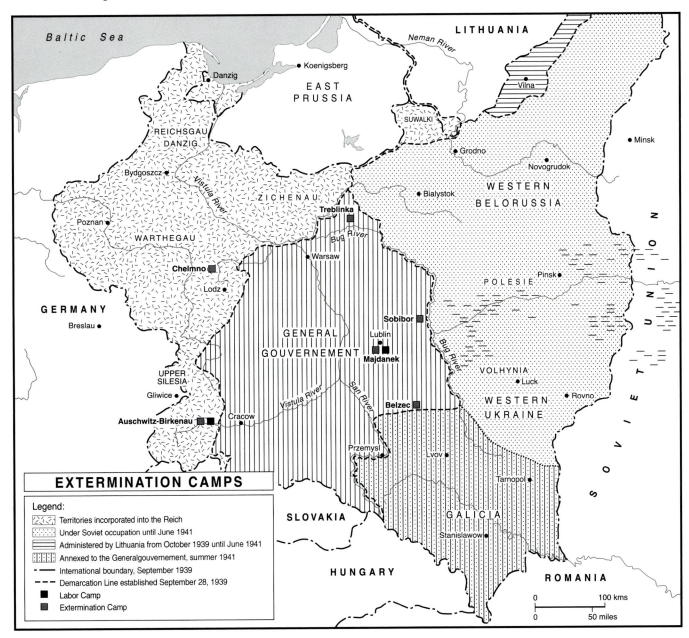

Map of the six extermination camps

F

FAMILY CAMPS IN THE FOREST   Groups of Jewish men, women, and children who fled to the forests of Eastern Europe to escape the Nazis. Most family camps were established between the summer of 1942 and the spring of 1943, during the mass exterminations in western BELORUSSIA and the western UKRAINE.

Family camps ranged from just a few families to hundreds of Jews, such as Tuvia BIELSKI'S camp, which involved 1,200 people. Camps could only exist in regions with large forests; most were located deep inside the Naliboki Forest of western Belorussia. Most Jews in family camps came from nearby towns and villages, although there were also Jews from other areas, such as MINSK and VILNA.

Each camp had a group of armed men who protected the camp and procured food for them. The men would raid neighboring villages and seize food by force. This caused resentment and hostility towards the family camps on the part of the village peasants. However, some did help the Jews. During the winter, the family camp Jews built wooden huts, stuck deep into the ground. In summer, they lived in lean-tos made of branches. When it seemed as if they were about to be discovered, camps moved elsewhere.

The establishment of family camps happened around the time that Jewish PARTISAN groups began operating in the forests. In most places where there were partisans, a family camp also existed. Sometimes family units were combined with partisan units. The main difference between the two groups was that the purpose of the family camp was to provide refuge and save lives, while the partisans' main purpose was to fight the enemy.

In most of the forests, the Jews lived alongside Soviet partisans. They both had to fight the same enemies and steal food from the same sources. This led to a strange interrelationship that included both competition and cooperation. In some areas, family camps were persecuted by non-Jewish partisans.

The Jews in the forest had to contend with a freezing climate, starvation, disease, and discovery by the Nazis. Probably less than 10,000 Jews survived in the forests.

FAREYNEGTE PARTIZANER ORGANIZATSYE (FPO) see UNITED PARTISAN ORGANIZATION, VILNA.

FASCISM   A political, cultural, and intellectual movement that flourished in twentieth century Europe. Most notably, adherents of Fascism ruled ITALY from 1922 to 1945, but in fact, the word "fascism" actually describes a range of extreme right-wing movements that were active in various countries throughout Europe and in other parts of the world.

Fascism developed as a result of the social changes and intellectual revolution that took place in the Western world at the turn of the twentieth century. It was a type of original, modern thought that reflected change and the need for something new and different amongst the young people of Europe, who disdained their parents' middle class values. Fascist ideas spread all over Europe and gained force during the Depression of the 1920s and 1930s.

As an ideology, Fascism represents a synthesis of nationalism (devotion to one's nation as the highest ideal) and socialism (communal ownership of economic enterprises), and the rejection of materialism, liberalism, Marxism, and democracy. It calls for the absolute political rule of the leaders, and deplores the democratic ideal of the common people making important decisions. The state government is how national unity—the major Fascist value—is manifested. Fascism tries to create a new civilization, based on the total community, in which all sectors and classes of the population will find their niche. As a result, the nation will be revitalized and strengthened, and each individual will be nothing more than a cell in the communal organism. Fascism even poses as a type of spiritual revolution.

Fascism came up with two tools that would help maintain "the unity of the nation"—corporatism and totalitarianism. In a corporative state, a country's political, social, and economic power is held by a group of corporations, made up both of employers and employees. This group of corporations plans the economy and settles differences between social classes. In a totalitarian state, the government has total control over and can intervene in every aspect of an individual's life. Using these two instruments, the nation would easily be maintained as the highest ideal.

The phenomenon of Fascism evolved out of an awareness of a major societal problem: the exclusion of the working man from the community ideal. According to Fascist ideology, the nation will not become a complete unit as long as the working class is not assimilated into it, and until a way is found to harness each individual in a joint effort to achieve the common good. Fascism is also a reflection of certain values of the time, namely, emotions and spontaneity as opposed to reason—reason being the basis of democratic thought. In Fascism, the idea that emotions and the subconscious are more important in politics than reason is totally acceptable. An offshoot of this "cult of the emotions" is the Fascist philosophy of action, energy, intuition, and violence.

Although Fascism was put into power in Italy under the Fascist leader, Benito MUSSOLINI, the movement made waves all over Europe—and was different in each country it visited. Fascism was found in FRANCE, where the first Fascist movement outside Italy was founded in 1925; in GREAT BRITAIN; BELGIUM; SPAIN, where the Fascist Francisco Franco won the Spanish Civil War and took control of the government in 1939; and ROMANIA. Nazism was an extreme form of Fascism, whose adherents took on ANTISEMITISM as a central component of their ideology. However, antisemitism is not a fundamental element in pure Fascist ideology. The racist nationalism invoked in Fascism is definitely receptive to antisemitic tendencies, but not a necessary part of Fascist belief. In its early period, Italian Fascism did not include antisemitism, and only when Mussolini allied himself with HITLER did he begin touting antisemitic rhetoric.

FEDERATION DES SOCIETES JUIVES DE FRANCE
see FEDERATION OF JEWISH SOCIETIES OF FRANCE.

FEDERATION OF JEWISH SOCIETIES OF FRANCE
(*Federation des Societes Juives de France*, FSJF), umbrella organization of Jewish immigrant societies in FRANCE, established in 1913. These societies, divided into groups according to geographical origin, were made up of Jews who had immigrated to France from Central and Eastern Europe. The fact that the FSJF existed at all points to the conflict between Jewish immigrants to France and native-born French Jews, who had their own umbrella organization. By the late 1930s the FSJF included over 200 immigrant societies.

After the Germans occupied northern France in 1940, most FSJF leaders fled to unoccupied southern France. They created underground FSJF committees in many areas, which took care of tens of thousands of Jews, and provided them with forged identity papers. When the Germans invaded southern France in late 1942, the FSJF set up an absorption center in the part of France occupied by ITALY, where Jews were protected by the Italians from the Nazis and French authorities. The FSJF also funded Jewish youth organizations that smuggled Jewish children into SWITZERLAND and sent young underground fighters to Palestine via SPAIN. In addition, the organization set up PARTISAN units in several French cities. In August 1942 the FSJF helped institute the Jewish Defense Committee, which encompassed all Jewish underground organizations.

FEGELEIN, HERMANN (1906–1945), *Gruppenfuehrer* in the *Waffen*-SS and confidant of Adolf HITLER. Previously, Fegelein had served as cavalry inspector in

Hermann Fegelein during World War II

the REICHSSICHERHEITSHAUPTAMT, commanded *Kampf-gruppe Fegelein,* and worked for Heinrich HIMMLER as an SS liaison officer.

FEINER, LEON (1888–1945), Active member of the BUND and the Jewish underground in POLAND, and chairman of ZEGOTA. Feiner prepared most of the *Bund*'s reports that were sent to the Free World to plead for help in saving Polish Jewry.

FERRAMONTI DI TARSIA Internment camp for Jews in southern ITALY. Ferramonti, officially a CONCENTRA-TION CAMP, was the largest of 15 internment camps established by Italian Fascist leader, Benito MUSSOLINI, during the summer of 1940.

Ferramonti di Tarsia, 1942

The Italians began building Ferramonti on June 4, less than a week before Italy entered WORLD WAR II. The arrest of Jews began on June 15, and prisoners began arriving at the camp on June 20. From 1940–1943, over 3,800 Jews were imprisoned at the camp: 3,682 were foreign-born Jews, and 141 were Italians. In general, Italian-born Jews were not imprisoned unless they participated in anti-Fascist activities.

At first, the physical conditions at the camp were not that bad. However, as the situation of the Jews went downhill, so did the living conditions. Despite all this, Ferramonti was never a concentration camp like those that the Nazis ran: the relationship between the prisoners and camp staff was rather peaceful, the prisoners were not tortured or executed, and they were allowed to receive packages of food, visit sick relatives, and participate in cultural activities. In fact, four couples got married at the camp and 21 children were born.

The prisoners at Ferramonti were released on September 4, 1943, six weeks after Mussolini was overthrown by his own Fascist Grand Council.

FILDERMAN, WILHELM (1882–1963), Romanian Jewish leader active in the rescue of his country's Jews.

Born in BUCHAREST, Filderman studied law and served in the Romanian parliament. He also acted as chairman of most of the important Jewish organizations in ROMANIA, such as the Federation of Jewish Communities, the Union of Jewish Communities in the Regat [pre–World War I Romania], the UNION OF ROMANIAN JEWS, the JOINT DISTRIBUTION COMMITTEE'S Romanian headquarters, and the Jewish Council.

In the fall of 1941 Filderman tried to stop the DEPORTATION of Jews from BESSARABIA and BUKOVINA to TRANSNISTRIA, but was unsuccessful. He did succeed, though, in getting the government to cancel the order for Jews to wear the Jewish badge (see also BADGE, JEWISH). From 1941–1943 he sent aid to those Jews interred in Transnistria, and was even somewhat successful later on in getting them returned to their homes.

During spring and summer of 1942 Filderman established a secret Jewish leadership called the Jewish Council. This council was active in averting the Nazis' plan to deport the Jews of Romania to POLAND during that fall. Filderman was able to turn the deportation into a national Romanian issue by convincing government officials that if they agreed to the Germans' demand, they would be dishonoring the institution of Romanian self-rule. Throughout the war, Filderman was in contact with important government officials, including the premier, Ion ANTONESCU, and his close colleague, Mihai ANTONESCU. He used those contacts to help improve the situation of his fellow Jews. However, his activities led to his deportation to Transnistria in May 1943. He continued working tirelessly for Jewish rights while there, and was allowed to return home in August. During that time the government had created a leadership alternative to Filderman, called the Jewish Center (*Centrala Evreilor*). However, they ultimately returned to Filderman and recognized him as the true leader of the Jewish community.

After Ion Antonescu was kicked out of office in 1944, Filderman continued his public activities. He fought for Jewish rights from 1944–1947, but was forced to resign his posts and flee to FRANCE in 1948 after Jewish Communists took control of Romania's Jewish organizations. (see also JEWISH CENTER, ROMANIA.)

FILMS, NAZI ANTISEMITIC   Films used by the Nazis to help spread their antisemitic ideology and psychologically prepare the German people for the extermination of European Jewry. In late 1938, the German Propaganda Ministry asked the country's film companies to begin making movies with antisemitic content. In 1939 two anti-Jewish films were produced, which used comedy to make fun of the Jews and portray them as sub-human.

Poster advertising the Nazi antisemitic film, "The Eternal Jew"

During 1940, three anti-Jewish movies appeared in GERMANY. The first to come out was *Die Rothschilds* (The Rothschilds). The subject of this film was the Rothschilds, a wealthy Jewish family of bankers who originally came from Germany. The German propagandists attempted to portray Jews as greedy parasites who suck in more and more of the world's money while others die for their country (Germany) on the battle-field. The film was unsuccessful in the theaters and was withdrawn soon after its premier.

The next antisemitic film was called *Jued Suss* (Jew Suss), which told the story of an eighteenth century banker named Suss Oppenheimer who served as a financial advisor to a German duke. Oppenheimer is depicted as a horrible person who rapes the blonde Aryan heroine, while the other Jews in the film are dirty, immoral, and ugly. Ultimately, Oppenheimer is arrested and executed. Unlike *The Rothschilds,* this film was wildly successful. SS chief Heinrich HIMMLER ordered all members of the SS and police to see it. It was also shown to CONCENTRATION CAMP guards, who were then spurred on to treat their Jewish prisoners as the sub-humans portrayed in the film.

The third and most despicable of the three propaganda films was *Der ewige Jude* (The Eternal Jew). This film was touted as a documentary, which supposedly "revealed" the Jews to be filthy and parasitic leeches who thus deserve to be wiped out. The producers "proved" their claims with maps and statistics, and closed with "footage" of a Jewish ritual murder, perpetrating the medieval lie that Jews use the blood of Christian children on Passover. Nonetheless, the film was also a failure at the box office.

FILMS ON THE HOLOCAUST   Because the HOLOCAUST was such a unique and painful event in the history of human interactions, many filmmakers have dealt with the subject in their films. As the topic is so large, filmmakers all over the world, from the 1940s to our day, have chosen to depict diverse aspects of the Holocaust in both fiction and nonfiction films.

During the first years after WORLD WAR II, fiction films about the Holocaust were made in those Eastern European countries that suffered very badly under the Nazis. In some of the films from that time, the Nazi persecution of Jews plays a minor role, while the war and the ensuing hardship take the films' major focus. An example of this phenomenon is the trilogy of films made by Polish director Andrzej Wajda, which describe Polish life in occupied WARSAW.

Since that time, a number of films have been produced that focus on Jewish characters and the specifically Jewish experience during the Holocaust. *The Diary of Anne Frank* (1959) depicts a young Dutch girl who hid with her family for years until they were discovered by the Nazis (see also FRANK, ANNE). *Kapo* (1960) hits on the compelling moral issues surrounding a Jewish labor foreman in a CONCENTRATION CAMP. *Jacob the Liar,* first made in Germany in 1978 and remade in the United States in 1999, is the tale of a GHETTO Jew who cheers his fellow Jews by telling them the lie that the Germans are losing the war.

A different type of fictionalized Holocaust film is that which uses the Holocaust as a backdrop for the film's main story line, rather than a major focus. For example, *Judgement at Nuremberg* (1961) is a portrayal of the trial of German judges at Nuremberg, and focuses on the moral issues of guilt and responsibility. *Cabaret* (1972), which tells the story of a German nightclub, is set in 1932, right before the Nazis' rise to national power. *The Tin Drum* (1979) depicts a young man in Germany who simply refuses to continue growing under the Nazis.

The documentary is another important category of films on the Holocaust. As almost all film footage from the Holocaust was taken in an amateur fashion by the Nazis or shot by the liberating armies, filmmakers face the difficulty of trying to make their documentaries compelling without much actual footage. In *Night and Fog* (1955) the problem is solved by using black and white footage from the concentration camps, and then showing scenes in color that were filmed on the same sites 10 years later. The monumental documentary *Shoah* (1985) skips archival footage altogether. Instead, this almost ten-hour film builds the horrific story of the "final solution" through interviews with SURVIVORS, bystanders, and perpetrators. Another documentary is the 1970 French film *The Sorrow and the Pity.* This film created great controversy in France, as it shattered the myth that the French on a whole resisted the Nazis, and instead depicted the widespread French collaboration with the Nazis. Scores of other documentaries have been made about the Holocaust and the THIRD REICH. The films *Genocide* (1981) and *The Long Way Home* (1994), produced by the Simon Wiesenthal Center, received Oscars in the category of Documentary Films.

In 1978 American television presented a new type of Holocaust film: the mini-series. *Holocaust,* which told the fictionalized story of one family whose members each represented a different element of the Holocaust experience, provoked much criticism for being like a soap opera. However, it also introduced the Holocaust as an acceptable subject matter on television.

Two more recent Academy Award winning films have once again brought the Holocaust to a world-wide

A scene from the film "Schindler's List"

audience. Based on the real-life RIGHTEOUS AMONG THE NATIONS German businessman Oskar SCHINDLER, director Steven Spielberg's *Schindler's List* (1994) depicted both the horrors and the saviors of the Holocaust. The 1998 Italian film *Life Is Beautiful* from director Roberto Benigni became famous as the "Holocaust comedy" but actually told a life-affirming story of a father and son surviving together in a concentration camp.

FINAL SOLUTION   Code-name for the Nazis' plan to solve the "Jewish question" by murdering all the Jews in Europe. The "Final Solution" was the culmination of many years of evolving Nazi policy: from HITLER'S earliest writings about the need for a solution to the Jewish question in Europe; through the Nazis' attempts to induce mass emigration during the 1930s; to the plan for collective exile to a specific destination during the first war years; and by 1941, the mass extermination of Jews.

In September 1919 Hitler penned his first political document. In it, he stated that the Jewish question would eventually be solved by the removal of the Jews from Europe altogether. According to Hitler, this removal would not be carried out in an emotional fashion, with pogroms and such, but executed with typical German thoroughness and efficient planning. For Hitler, the Jewish question was the essential question for all Nazis. In fact, Hitler was obsessed with Jews and was determined to find a "final solution" for getting rid of them. However, his early writings and statements can not be viewed as a blueprint for the murders put into effect so many years later.

Throughout the 1930s, Hitler believed that mass emigration was the answer to the Jewish problem. The ANTI-JEWISH LEGISLATION passed in GERMANY from the time Hitler rose to national power in January 1933 to the outbreak of WORLD WAR II in September 1939 was designed to convince and later coerce the Jews to leave the country. In January 1939 Hitler spoke before the German parliament. He criticized the Free World for not taking in Jewish immigrants and warned that the consequences of war would include the "annihilation" of European Jewry. Experts debate whether that statement should be interpreted as a direct articulation of Hitler's intention to murder the Jews, or whether it was just Hitler's manipulative way of leaning on the Free World to take in Jewish immigrants.

When Germany invaded POLAND, launching World War II, an additional 1.8 million Jews came under German control. Hitler did not immediately order their extermination. Instead, a plan was formulated whereby all Jews living within the Reich were to be exiled to a reservation in the LUBLIN district of the GENERALGOUVERNEMENT. The Nazis tried to implement this NISKO AND LUBLIN PLAN, but it never came to fruition. By the spring of 1940, it was clear that the Lublin program was no longer the answer to the Jewish question, as Poland did not have enough territory to spare for the Jews.

The next phase in anti-Jewish policy, introduced in May 1940, was the MADAGASCAR PLAN—a plan to deport all of Europe's Jews to the island of Madagascar, a French colony in Africa. However, the Germans were defeated in the Battle of Britain just a few months later, rendering the Madagascar idea unfeasible.

The Germans attacked their former ally, the SOVIET UNION, in June 1941. Mobile killing units called EINSATZGRUPPEN, along with regular army, police units, and local collaborators, immediately began the systematic murder of the Jews in the Soviet Union. This was the first time that mass systematic extermination was used as a method of solving the Jewish question.

In July, Hermann GOERING authorized the preparation for the "Final Solution." At the end of 1941 and early in 1942, the Nazis established EXTERMINATION CAMPS, began DEPORTATIONS to them, and perfected killing methods. The first gassing experiment was performed in AUSCHWITZ in September 1941, and extermination camps at BELZEC and CHELMNO were constructed in late fall. SOBIBOR, TREBLINKA, MAJDANEK and Auschwitz became extermination centers in the spring of 1942. In the meantime, on December 12, 1941, Hitler told his intimate circle that the murder was to be extended to include German Jews, thereby including all the Jews of Europe in the plans for the "Final Solution."

At the WANNSEE CONFERENCE in January 1942, German government and SS leaders met to coordinate the extermination of every Jew in Europe. From then until the end of the war in 1945, the "Final Solution" was official Nazi policy and meant one thing only—death to the Jews.

FINLAND   Country in Scandinavia. In 1939 there were some 2,000 Jews living in Finland, including about 300 REFUGEES from GERMANY, AUSTRIA, and Czechoslovakia. Most of the local Jews had arrived in Finland from Russia in the nineteenth century.

Before and during WORLD WAR II there was almost no ANTISEMITISM in Finland, and in fact, the Finnish government refused to condone the Nazis' anti-Jewish platform. When Finland also refused to cooperate with the SOVIET UNION in late 1939, Soviet troops attacked Finland. As equal Finnish citizens, the country's Jews joined the army to fight the Soviets; some 15 were killed and many others were wounded. After holding out for several months, Finland surrendered to the Soviet Union in March 1940 and was forced to hand over some of its territory to the Soviets.

In 1941 Germany occupied Finland; Finland then joined Germany in its attack on the Soviet Union in order to recapture the land it had lost to the Soviets the previous year. Some 300 Jews served in the Finnish army during the war. The German authorities requested that the Finnish government hand over its

Jewish community, but the Finns refused. Reportedly, when SS chief Heinrich HIMMLER brought up the "Jewish question" with Prime Minister Johann Wilhelm Rangell in mid-1942, Rangell replied that there was no Jewish question in Finland; he firmly stated that the country had but 2,000 respected Jewish citizens who fought in the army just like everyone else, and thus closed the issue to discussion. The Germans did not press the issue, as they were afraid to lose Finnish cooperation against the Soviets.

However, later that year, GESTAPO chief Heinrich MUELLER convinced the head of the Finnish State Police, Arno Anthoni, to deport eight Jewish refugees. Ultimately, only one of the eight Jews survived. Many clergymen and politicians condemned the DEPORTATION, and as a result the Finnish government refused to surrender any more Jews to the Germans. Apart from that one incident and those Finnish Jews who died on the battlefield, the Jews of Finland, both local Jews and refugees, went through the war unharmed.

FISCHER, LUDWIG   (1905–1947), Governor of the GENERALGOUVERNEMENT'S WARSAW district from 1939 until the German retreat from Warsaw in January 1945. Fischer joined the NAZI PARTY in 1926 and enlisted in the SA in 1929. In 1937 he was elected to the German parliament (REICHSTAG).

WORLD WAR II broke out in September 1939 after the Germans invaded and occupied POLAND. They divided Poland into thirds, the western third annexed to GERMANY, the eastern third annexed to the SOVIET UNION, and the middle third turned into a semi-independent administrative unit, called the *Generalgouvernement,* which was run by German authorities. The *Generalgouvernement* was divided into four districts, one of them being the Warsaw district.

In October 1939 Fischer became the governor of the Warsaw district, a post which he filled until Germany withdrew from the area in January 1945. Fischer established the Warsaw GHETTO in November 1940 and other ghettos in his district as well. He also organized terror actions against both Jews and Poles in the district, and called for the liquidation of the ghettos in 1942 and 1943. In April and May 1943 Fischer also stood in as acting governor of the *Generalgouvernement's* LUBLIN district.

After the war Fischer was arrested in West Germany. He was extradited to Poland in 1946, where he was put on trial and hanged.

FLEISCHMANN, GISI   (1897–1944), Jewish leader in SLOVAKIA. Fleischmann was a leader of the Women's International Zionist Organization and of the WORKING GROUP.

Gisi Fleischmann (on the right) sitting with friends on the Sabbath eve

When Slovakia's Jewish Center (*Ustredna Zidov*) was established in 1940, Fleischmann took over its *aliya* (immigration to Palestine) department. She used this section as camouflage for Zionist youth activities and job training. In early 1940 she helped bring 326 men from Sosnowiec, POLAND to Slovakia, and ultimately got most of them to Palestine. Fleischmann's position provided her with the opportunity to obtain an immigration certificate for Palestine. She sent her daughters, but declined to join them in favor of staying to help her community.

Early in 1942, it became painfully clear to Slovakian Jewish leaders that their community was to be deported shortly. Fleischmann and others created a semi-underground rescue committee called the Working Group, which made attempts to prevent and later halt the DEPORTATIONS. That summer, the Working Group approached Adolf EICHMANN'S representative in BRATISLAVA, Dieter WISLICENY, with a bribe of US $40,000–$50,000 to stop the deportations. Fleischmann worked on raising the money for Wisliceny. When the deportations were stopped in October, Fleischmann played a major part in creating an even bolder rescue proposal, called the EUROPA PLAN. This plan called for the termination of all deportations from German-occupied Europe to Poland in exchange for huge amounts of money. However, these negotiations petered out in the autumn of 1943.

Fleischmann was soon arrested and held for four months. She refused to allow her friends to get her out of Slovakia, and upon release, devotedly continued her work. In the fall of 1944 she once again tried to persuade SS leaders to stop the deportations, which had been renewed. She was unsuccessful, and was arrested by the SS on September 28. She was allowed to stay in Bratislava for a short time to wind down the Jewish Center's affairs. In October, she was sent to the SERED camp and then on to AUSCHWITZ with the instructions "return undesirable." She was sent to the GAS CHAMBERS upon arrival. (see also JEWISH CENTER, SLOVAKIA.)

FOMENKO, WITOLD (1905–1961), Pole from the town of Lutsk, designated as RIGHTEOUS AMONG THE NATIONS by YAD VASHEM, who rescued Jews during the HOLOCAUST. During his childhood, Fomenko had much positive contact with Jews and even spoke Yiddish. As a music teacher and barber, many of his students and customers were Jews.

The Germans occupied Lutsk in 1941 and set up a GHETTO. Fomenko immediately began bringing food, firewood, and medicines to the Jews in the ghetto. He paid for these supplies out of his own pocket, and whenever he visited the ghetto he tried to cheer up the Jews by singing to them and telling them jokes.

Right before the liquidation of the Lutsk Ghetto, Fomenko began helping Jews leave the ghetto with forged identity papers he obtained for them. Fomenko himself was arrested after one of the Jews he had helped was captured and tortured into revealing his name. However, the city's military commander, one of Fomenko's customers, released him. After the ghetto's liquidation Fomenko continued helping Jews interned in a labor camp in Lutsk. That camp was destroyed in December 1942; at that point, Fomenko began hiding Jews in Christian homes around the city.

After the war, Fomenko married one of the Jewish women he had rescued, and together they moved to Israel.

FORCED LABOR Work performed under coercion for the Nazi regime by Jews and others. It included work done within the Reich by laborers brought from German-occupied territories or from GERMANY'S satellite

Jews performing forced labor under guard in Poland

countries. In German, these laborers were called *Fremdarbeiter*, meaning "foreign workers."

The first forced laborers brought to Germany were 100,000 Austrians, who arrived after the ANSCHLUSS— the annexing of AUSTRIA by Germany in March 1938. By August 1, 1939, another 70,000 forced laborers had been brought from the Protectorate of Bohemia and Moravia. (see also BOHEMIA AND MORAVIA, PROTECTORATE OF)

One month later, WORLD WAR II broke out. Germany began using PRISONERS OF WAR as forced laborers, which was illegal according to international law. During the fall of 1939, 340,000 Polish prisoners of war were put to work. In the spring of 1940 the Germans created a work draft in the GENERALGOUVERNEMENT, and by August 1942 they decreed that forced laborers were to be taken from all occupied countries and prisoner of war camps. In the Western European countries controlled by Germany, the local administration would sometimes cooperate with the Germans in their drafting of forced laborers, in exchange for the freedom of some of their prisoners of war, or at least a change in their status from prisoners of war to foreign workers.

Jews performing forced labor under guard

In September 1944, 5.5 million foreign workers and two million prisoners of war were working in Germany; 38 percent of those were Soviet and 20 percent were Polish. By the end of that year, another 1.5 million forced laborers had been recruited.

Nazi leaders held various opinions about forced laborers. Albert SPEER, who was appointed the minister of armaments and war production in February 1942, and Fritz SAUCKEL, who was appointed chief plenipotentiary for the labor effort in March 1942, understood that in order to keep up recruitment and productivity, they would have to provide better work conditions. However, in most cases it was the GESTAPO and German Security Police who were in charge of the supervision of the workers, and they were not concerned with productivity. Thus, they treated the foreign workers brutally.

Eastern European forced laborers were treated much worse than those from Western Europe. Germans who had sexual relations with those workers were punished with the death penalty for race defilement. Although

Western European workers had better living and working conditions, they also complained that they were treated like slaves.

By the middle of the war, Germany had severe labor shortages, leading Nazi leaders to begin hunting seriously for workers. However, their cruel treatment of the forced laborers, poor working conditions, and the obviousness of Germany's imminent defeat led to a rise in organized resistance. Ironically, during the last year of the war, as Germany's territory shrank and many of its factories were destroyed by Allied bombing raids, labor quotas were largely filled.

Beginning with the annexation of Austria, Jews were taken by the Nazi authorities for forced labor. After the invasion of POLAND, Jews were first taken for tasks such as clearing rubble, and soon afterward were sent to forced labor camps. From the moment the Nazis began using Jews for forced labor, they were treated terribly. Throughout the period of the HOLOCAUST, the performance of forced labor by Jews in the GHETTOS and camps was a dominant feature of their experience. In most cases the authorities had no regard for the lives of their Jewish laborers, and many were worked to their deaths intentionally. In a few instances, however, especially later in the war, some Jewish forced laborers were treated somewhat better.

FORT ONTARIO   "Emergency refugee shelter" established in New York by the UNITED STATES government in 1944.

In 1944 WAR REFUGEE BOARD director John Pehle and others began pressuring President ROOSEVELT to establish temporary shelters in the United States for European REFUGEES. At first, due to opposition from the State and War Departments, President Roosevelt dismissed the idea. However, during his reelection campaign later that year, he agreed to create one "emergency refugee shelter" in a former US army base in the upstate New York town of Oswego.

President Roosevelt's decision did not reflect a major change in US refugee policy. The shelter was to house no more than 1,000 refugees, who would return to Europe at war's end. These refugees were not even brought from Nazi-occupied territories; rather, they came from an internment camp in ITALY, where their lives were not in immediate danger.

A group of 982 refugees arrived at Fort Ontario in August. They were not allowed to leave the shelter for school or work, and tensions rose between the different nationalities. By the winter, the refugees were extremely discouraged about their situation. At war's end, most of the refugees did not want to return "home" as stipulated by President Roosevelt. In December 1945, President Harry TRUMAN agreed to let them remain in the US.

FOUR-YEAR PLAN   (*Vierjahresplan*), economic program written by Adolf HITLER in August 1936 for the revitalization of the German army and economy within four years, in anticipation of war. This was the first time Hitler intervened in German economic policy.

Hitler intended to quickly rearm and create an independent economy strong enough to endure enemy blockades and war conditions. He aspired to create a self-sufficient GERMANY not dependent on raw materials from the outside world. Thus, he established the Goering Reich Works, aluminum factories, oil refineries, and sought to develop a synthetic-materials industry to eliminate the need for some raw materials. Hermann GOERING was put in charge of the Four-Year Plan; he was awarded exceptional powers in the economic do-

main despite his ignorance of economics. During the war Goering robbed German-occupied countries of their raw materials in order to further Germany's economic goals. He also had millions of people deported for FORCED LABOR.

Hitler kept the plan secret for fear of opposition from economic circles. In making Germany more self-sufficient, Hitler provided the foundation for speeding up his anti-Jewish policies. In an attempt to bolster the economy, he even tried to pass a law making the Jews responsible for the sorry state of the German economy after World War I.

FRANCE   Country in Western Europe. France entered WORLD WAR II in September 1939 to join its ally, POLAND, in its struggle against GERMANY. The German army invaded France itself in May 1940; in June the French surrendered and signed an armistice with the Nazis. France was then divided in two: northern France (the occupied zone) was put under German control, while southern France (the unoccupied zone) was put under the control of a new French

German victory parade through Paris after the fall of France, June 1940

government that was established in the spa town of Vichy. The Vichy government was headed by Marshal Philippe PETAIN, a World War I hero who was revered by the French people. At the same time French general Charles de GAULLE, who bitterly opposed Petain's surrender to the Germans, fled to GREAT BRITAIN, where he set up a French government-in-exile and rallied around him other Frenchmen who wanted to free France from the tyranny of the Germans and the collaborating Vichy government.

ment was restricted, and many were arrested. At the same time, the Vichy government also actively went ahead with persecuting the Jews. In October 1940 it passed a set of anti-Jewish laws called the STATUT DES JUIFS. These laws strictly defined who was to be considered a Jew, and called for the drastic cutback of Jewish involvement in French society. In March 1941 the Vichy authorities, under pressure from the Germans, set up an OFFICE FOR JEWISH AFFAIRS under the direction of Xavier VALLAT. The office was responsible to institute

Jewish women wearing the Jewish badge, France

In the summer of 1940, after France fell to Germany, there were 350,000 Jews living in France; more than half were not French citizens, but Jews who had moved to France after World War I and Jewish REFUGEES from Germany and other areas taken over by the Nazis. Almost immediately after the occupation, both the Jews living in the occupied zone and those in the unoccupied zone were subjected to the first wave of anti-Jewish measures. In the German-controlled zone, Jews were stripped of their jobs, their freedom of move-

and carry out France's ANTI-JEWISH LEGISLATION, including the confiscation of Jewish property and businesses (see also ARYANIZATION). In November 1941 Vallat created the UNION OF FRENCH JEWS under the impetus of Adolf EICHMANN's representative in France, Theodor DANNECKER.

At first, the anti-Jewish measures put into effect by the Vichy government were mainly directed against those Jews who were not native French citizens. Thousands were sent to FORCED LABOR camps or imprisoned.

However, at the end of April 1942 Pierre LAVAL joined the Vichy government as prime minister; Laval was proactively committed to collaborating fully with the Nazis. In May, the Office for Jewish Affairs' Vallat was replaced with a rabid antisemite named Louis DARQUIER DE PELLEPOIX, who willingly persecuted all the Jews in France, those with and without citizenship. Then, after two years of inflicting suffering upon the Jews, the Germans and the Vichy authorities began DEPORTATIONS.

The FRENCH POLICE agreed to round up and arrest the Jews for deportation in exchange for a great deal of independence. In June 1942 the Germans forced the Jews in the occupied zone to wear the Jewish badge for easy identification, began arresting large groups, and restricted the movements of the rest (see also BADGE, JEWISH). The roundups, carried out mostly by the French police, continued throughout the summer. In one horrible *aktion* that took place on July 16–17, they rounded up about 12,000 Jews in PARIS, jamming some 7,000 of them into the *Velodrome d'Hiver* sports stadium for days without food, water, or toilets. Many thousands of Jews were arrested and sent by cattle car to a transit camp in the Paris suburb of DRANCY, from which they were deported to the east. The Vichy authorities also arrested and deported Jews from their zone. Altogether, 42,500 Jews were sent to the east during 1942.

In November 1942 German and Italian forces took over the Vichy zone. ITALY took control of a small area of southeast France, and protected the Jews who fled there seeking refuge from the Germans and Vichy authorities. The Italians even refused to implement any anti-Jewish laws in their zone. However, in September 1943, when Italy tried to surrender to the Allies, the Germans took over the Italian part of France, and began arresting the Jews who had found shelter there. Some Jews tried to escape southward to SPAIN or eastward to SWITZERLAND, but the journey to those countries was extremely dangerous, and few Jews made it successfully. Some Jews were aided by French non-Jews, who hid the Jews at great risk to themselves and their families.

Despite Laval's stated commitment to collaborate with the Nazis, he faced protests from the French people when the deportation of Jews began to include French citizens, and not just Jewish refugees from other countries. In August 1943 Laval refused to strip French Jews of their citizenship in order to expedite their deportation. However, in spite of this and other minor protests, the deportations continued in 1943 and into 1944. In all, some 80,000 Jews were deported from France during the war, and all but 2,000 of them perished. Approximately 70,000 Jews were sent to AUSCHWITZ, while the rest were sent to MAJDANEK, SOBIBOR, and a small number to BUCHENWALD.

Throughout the war, a French resistance movement (the *Maquis*) under the leadership of Jean Moulin was active against the Nazis and the Vichy government; Moulin was the representative of General Charles de Gaulle. The Jews of France also participated in underground activities, both in the general French Resistance and in Jewish resistance organizations, such as a Jewish militia called the *Armee Juive* (see also JEWISH ARMY, FRANCE). The Jewish underground worked very hard at hiding fellow Jews, especially Jewish children.

The Allies landed at Normandy in northwestern France on June 6, 1944. Two months later France was liberated, and de Gaulle marched victorious into Paris; the leaders of the defunct Vichy government fled to Germany.

FRANK, ANNE (1929–1945), A young Dutch victim of the HOLOCAUST and author of a famous diary.

Anne Frank

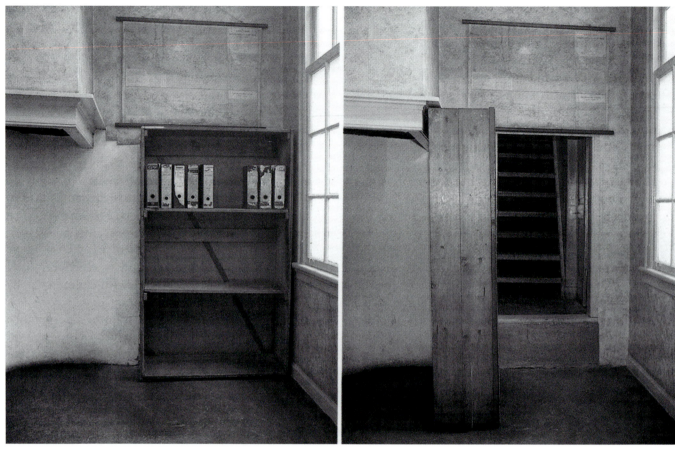

The Frank family's hiding place

In 1933 the Nazis rose to national power in GER-MANY. Soon after, Anne Frank and her family left Germany for Amsterdam, Holland. When the Germans then occupied the NETHERLANDS in October 1940, Anne's father, Otto, began to prepare for the eventuality of having to go into hiding. On July 5, 1942 Anne's older sister, Margot, received a summons from the Central Office for Jewish Emigration (ZENTRALSTELLE FUER JUEDISCHE AUSWANDERUNG), which ordered her to appear for FORCED LABOR. The very next day, the Franks moved into the empty annex of Otto's office at Prinsengracht 263. Four of Otto's employees knew about the plan and helped the Franks hide: Victor Kugler, Johannes Kleiman, Elli Voskuijl, and Miep Gies. A week later, the Franks were joined by the family of Otto's partner, Hermann van Pels. An eighth person, Fritz Pfeffer, came to hide in the annex on November 16, 1942.

Anne had turned 13 one month before she went into hiding; for her birthday she had received a diary. She immediately began to record entries, addressed to an imaginary friend named Kitty. She continued to write while living in the annex. She wrote about her family relationships, her own development, both physical and emotional, and about how it felt to be in hiding. She described the events that occurred in the annex and her reactions to them. She also penned stories and a "Book of Beautiful Phrases" which was full of quotations to which she had taken a liking.

On August 4, 1944, after more than two years of hiding, the Security Service (SD) in Amsterdam found out that Jews were living at Prinsengracht 263. They immediately came and arrested the Franks, van Pels, and Pfeffer. They also arrested and imprisoned Kleiman and Kugler. The eight Jews were sent to the Dutch transit camp at WESTERBORK, and the Franks were transferred to AUSCHWITZ on the last transport from the camp. Anne's mother, Edith, died in Auschwitz. Anne and Margot were moved to BERGEN-BELSEN at the end of October 1944. Both died there of typhus in March 1945. Their father, Otto, survived Auschwitz and was liberated by Soviet troops on January 27, 1945.

When Otto returned from Auschwitz, Miep Gies gave him the papers she had saved from the annex; among them was Anne's diary. Otto published the diary in 1947, under the name *The Annex.* Since then, 20 million copies have appeared in more than 50 editions, in many languages. A stage version of the diary premiered on Broadway on October 5, 1955; it won the Pulitzer Prize for Best Play of the Year. A film version appeared in 1959.

The diary, now known as "Anne Frank—The Diary of a Young Girl" has had a very strong impact on people all over the world. For some, it is their first contact with the Holocaust. Many view Anne as a tangible symbol of the millions of victims of the Holocaust. Eleanor Roosevelt said that the diary is "a remarkable book. Written by a young girl—and the young are not afraid of telling the truth—it is one of the wisest and most moving commentaries on war and its impact on human beings that I have ever read."

In 1960 the annex where Anne hid during the war was made into a museum about the struggle against RACISM and ANTISEMITISM. The Anne Frank Foundation has a DOCUMENTATION CENTER, creates teaching aids, and organizes traveling exhibits about those subjects. The original diary is on display there.

FRANK, HANS (1900–1946), Nazi governor of the GENERALGOUVERNEMENT from 1939–1945. Trained as a lawyer, Frank joined the NAZI PARTY in 1923. Throughout the 1920s, Frank served as Adolf HITLER'S personal lawyer. However, when Hitler seized power in 1933, Frank lost his importance within the party. He was given a number of positions without power, including minister without portfolio.

When the Germans invaded POLAND in September 1939, they split the country into three: the western third was annexed to the THIRD REICH; the eastern third was given to the SOVIET UNION; and the central third was made into the *Generalgouvernement,* a semi-independent administrative unit. At that point, Frank ostensibly achieved prominence once more when Hitler appointed him governor-general of the *Generalgouvernement.* However, Frank did not hold great power there. He was the most important administrator in the region; but while he managed to get Hermann GOERING to cooperate with him regarding the region's economy, the SS took charge of the extermination of Jews in the *Generalgouvernement.* Hitler meant for the *Generalgouvernement* to be used as a "racial dumping

Hans Frank (front left) shaking the hand of an officer in Galicia

ground," an endless supply of slave labor, and a site for the mass extermination of European Jewry. Frank did not oppose these goals, but he hated others infringing on his domain. Thus, he went back and forth, sometimes opposing and sometimes supporting the inflow of Jews and Poles who had been expelled from German-occupied areas and the mass murder of Jews. He very much wanted to please Hitler, but he also wanted to build up his own power base. This conflict led to his downfall.

In March 1942 Frank was stripped of all power over racial and police issues. He then began to openly criticize SS policies, leading Hitler to relieve Frank of his party positions. Hitler, though, would not allow Frank to resign, so Frank stayed in the position of governor-general until he was forced to flee from the advancing Soviet army. After the war, Frank was tried and hanged at Nuremberg. His official diary still serves as an important source for WORLD WAR II historians.

FRANK, KARL HERMANN (1898–1946), Deputy leader of the Sudetenland after the MUNICH CONFERENCE of 1938 and virtual leader of the Protectorate of Bohemia and Moravia from 1943. In these posts Frank persecuted Czech Jewry. At the end of the war he fled to the West, but the Americans extradited him to Czechoslovakia, where a Czech court sentenced him to death. He was executed by public hanging. (see also BOHEMIA AND MORAVIA, PROTECTORATE OF.)

The execution of Karl Hermann Frank, Prague, 1946

FRANKFURT AM MAIN   City in western GERMANY. In 1933, more than 26,000 Jews lived in Frankfurt, making the city the second largest Jewish community in Germany.

As soon as the Nazis rose to national power in January 1933, the Jews of Frankfurt, like Jews all over Germany, were subjected to discrimination. The city's Jewish mayor was immediately kicked out of office and many Jewish workers were fired from their jobs. The Nazis in Frankfurt began their anti-Jewish boycott earlier than the rest of the country, and continued boycotting Jewish enterprises after the official one-day boycott of April 1, 1933 (see also BOYCOTT, ANTI-JEWISH).

The Jews of Frankfurt responded to their community's seriously deteriorating economic circumstances by establishing a widespread welfare system. By 1935, almost 20 percent of the Jews in Frankfurt were being assisted by the welfare network. The Jewish community also boosted morale by setting up its own cultural activities, including a symphony, theater groups, and sports programs.

During the KRISTALLNACHT pogrom of November 9–10, 1938, many of the city's synagogues were burnt down, Jewish stores were attacked and pillaged, and homes were ransacked. The Frankfurt *yeshiva* was also destroyed. Soon, thousands of Jews were arrested and over 2,000 were sent to BUCHENWALD. The grave violence led many Jews to flee the country, and by May 1939, only about 14,000 Jews were left in Frankfurt.

Just a few months after WORLD WAR II broke out in September 1939, the GESTAPO began the ARYANIZATION process of confiscating Jewish property. The Frankfurt municipality bought Jewish community property for much less than its true worth, and the Jewish cemeteries were vandalized. In March 1941 Jews were made to do FORCED LABOR, and in October, the first Jews were deported to LODZ. On November 11, 1,052 Jews were sent to MINSK, and another 902 were deported to RIGA on November 22. During 1942, 2,952 Jews from Frankfurt were sent to THERESIENSTADT. More Jews were deported eastward in late 1942 and throughout 1943. The last transport of Jews from Frankfurt was transferred to Theresienstadt in January 1944. Altogether, only 600 Jews from Frankfurt survived the war.

FRANKFURTER, DAVID   (1909–1982), Assassin of a Nazi leader in SWITZERLAND. Frankfurter was born in Daruvar, CROATIA to a local Orthodox rabbi. In 1929 he began medical school in Leipzig and then at FRANKFURT; in 1934 he moved to Switzerland to continue his studies.

The racial NUREMBERG LAWS were passed in GERMANY in September 1935; these and other anti-Jewish steps convinced Frankfurter that he needed to take a stand against the Nazis. He soon began to track Switzerland's leading Nazi, Wilhelm Gustloff. On the evening of February 4, 1936, Frankfurter entered Gustloff's lodgings at the famous Alpine resort town of Davos, and shot him dead. He then immediately surrendered to the police.

Many in Switzerland approved of Frankfurter's act, but the government was afraid of Nazi Germany and thought that German Jewry would only be punished if Frankfurter were to go free. Thus, the trial ignored the political issues and stuck to the criminal elements of Frankfurter's deed. The young medical student was convicted and sentenced to 18 years in jail.

At the end of WORLD WAR II Frankfurter was granted a pardon, but banished from Switzerland. He settled in Palestine, and only 24 years later, in September 1969, did the Swiss government lift his expulsion order.

David Frankfurter, after the war

FRANZ, KURT (b. 1914), SS officer who served as deputy commandant at TREBLINKA. Franz joined the German army in 1935; after his service he enlisted in the SS. At first he worked at the BUCHENWALD concentration camp. In late 1939 he moved to the EUTHANASIA PROGRAM. In April 1942 he was transferred to the BELZEC extermination camp, and in late summer he was sent to the EXTERMINATION CAMP at Treblinka, where he served as deputy to camp commandant Franz STANGL.

Franz was the most prominent and most terrifying figure at Treblinka. He would inspect the camp and its prisoners on a regular basis, hitting, abusing, and shooting them at random. Such service was considered "excellent" by the SS, and Franz was promoted to a higher rank in June 1943.

A revolt broke out in Treblinka that August, and subsequently the camp was closed down. Stangl left, leaving Franz to take apart the camp and destroy all evidence of the mass murders that had taken place there. In November the Jews who had been forced to help raze Treblinka were themselves killed.

After the war Franz was tried along with other offi-

cers who had worked at Treblinka. In 1965 he was sentenced to life in prison.

FREEMASONS Secret fraternity associated with Jews, and thus persecuted during the HOLOCAUST.

The Masonic movement was founded in England in 1717. Jews were admitted to its English lodges by 1732, and later on in the NETHERLANDS, GERMANY, FRANCE, and other European countries. The lodges were open to Jews until the 1870s; with the advent of political ANTI-SEMITISM in the 1880s, Jews were forced out. This led to the growth of Jewish fraternities such as B'nai B'rith. However, the association between Jews and Freemasons was already being touted by right-wing organizations in Germany as early as the 1840s. Soon the notion of their alliance spread to France, and then throughout the world.

Catholic groups strongly believed that the Masonic lodges were a cover for a Jewish plot to eradicate Christianity. An anti-Masonic world congress met in Trent, ITALY, in September 1894; it was supported by Pope Leo XIII.

After World War I anti-Jewish literature, such as the PROTOCOLS OF THE ELDERS OF ZION, repeated these false claims of Jewish-Masonic brotherhood. Freemasonry was considered an enemy of Nazi ideology, so a special section of the Security Service was designated to deal with it. Some Masons were sent to CONCENTRATION CAMPS.

FRENCH JEWISH SCOUTS (*Eclaireurs Israelites de France*, EIF), French Jewish scouting movement, created by Robert GAMZON in 1923, which rescued thousands of Jews in FRANCE during WORLD WAR II.

Soon after war broke out in September 1939, the EIF established several children's homes in southwest France. After France fell to the German army in mid-1940, the EIF moved south to the unoccupied zone of France while still continuing to function illegally in PARIS. Its children's homes soon began to take in the children of Jews imprisoned in Nazi camps.

In 1941 the EIF was forced to join the UNION OF FRENCH JEWS (UGIF), the organization established by the Vichy government to consolidate all French Jewish organizations into one unit. However, the EIF's status was improved when Gamzon was appointed to the UGIF's administration and the EIF became the UGIF's young people's department.

The Germans began deporting the Jews of France in

March 1942. That summer the EIF established a social service that evolved into a rescue organization; it supplied Jewish children with forged identity papers, placed them in safe homes, or moved them out of France. During the winter of 1943 the EIF set up an underground fighting group, which participated in the LIBERATION of southwest France. (for more on Vichy, see also FRANCE.)

FRENCH POLICE (*Police et Gendarmerie Francaises*), French police serving in both occupied and unoccupied (Vichy) FRANCE. The entire French police force, about 100,000 police officers, acted under the authority of the Vichy government. In the fall of 1941 a special police section was established to deal with Jewish matters. It was supervised by the Vichy government's OFFICE FOR JEWISH AFFAIRS.

The French police cooperated with the German occupiers. They were responsible to maintain public order, stop crime, and implement anti-Jewish policy. In July 1942 they helped round up thousands of Jews in PARIS; some Jews were saved after humane police officers warned them of the imminent arrests. During 1943 the French police registered Jews for DEPORTATION, confiscated their property, made mass arrests, and forced the Jews to wear the Jewish badge (see also BADGE, JEWISH) and get their identity cards stamped with the word *Juif* (Jew). The police also built and operated French CONCENTRATION CAMPS and accompanied transports of Jews to the German border.

In the summer of 1943 PARTISAN groups intensified their activities against the German occupiers and French police. The police eventually stopped arresting Jews, and the French administration at the DRANCY camp was replaced by the GESTAPO. From then on, the Germans and the French fascist militia carried out operations against the Jews. (for more on Vichy, see also FRANCE.)

FREUDIGER, FULOP (1900–1976), Hungarian Jewish leader. In 1939 Freudiger succeeded his father as head of the Orthodox Jewish community in BUDAPEST. In 1943 he helped found the RELIEF AND RESCUE COMMITTEE OF BUDAPEST, and in 1944, he aided many REFUGEES who had illegally entered HUNGARY in search of a safe haven.

German troops occupied Hungary in March 1944 and established a JUDENRAT in Budapest, to which Freudiger was appointed. Later that spring Rabbi Michael

Dov WEISSMANDEL of the Slovakian WORKING GROUP sent Freudiger a copy of the AUSCHWITZ PROTOCOLS—a report about AUSCHWITZ made by two Jews who had escaped the camp. Based on the report, Freudiger spread the news of the killings going on at Auschwitz to both Jewish and non-Jewish Hungarian leaders. With Weissmandel's help, Freudiger established contact with Dieter WISLICENY, the SS officer sent by Adolf EICHMANN to act as advisor to the Hungarian government on Jewish affairs. Freudiger successfully bribed Wisliceny into releasing 80 well-known Orthodox Jews from Hungarian GHETTOS.

With Wisliceny's help, Freudiger and his family managed to escape to ROMANIA in August 1944. After the war they moved to Israel, where Freudiger was considered a controversial figure due to his *Judenrat* job, his escape, and the issue of whether or not he had sufficiently warned Hungarian Jewry about Auschwitz. In 1961 Freudiger was a witness in the EICHMANN TRIAL in Jerusalem.

FRICK, WILHELM (1877–1946), German minister of the interior from January 1933 to August 1943 and governor of the Protectorate of Bohemia and Moravia from 1943 until the end of the war. As interior minister, Frick issued most of GERMANY'S racial laws. He was one

Wilhelm Frick in Nazi uniform

of the major war criminals hanged on October 16, 1946. (see also BOHEMIA AND MORAVIA, PROTECTORATE OF.)

FUEHRERPRINZIP   German term, meaning "leadership principle" which refers to the Nazi value of revering and even worshiping the leader, or *Fuehrer*. Authority was to flow from the top to the bottom and responsibility in the opposite direction.

FUNK, WALTHER   (1890–1960), Adolf HITLER'S personal advisor on economic affairs, German minister of economics beginning in 1937, and president of the state bank (*Reichsbank*) beginning in 1939. Funk helped confiscate Jewish property and money and transfer them to the SS.

He was sentenced to life imprisonment, but was released in 1957 because of ill health.

G

GALEN, CLEMENS AUGUST GRAF VON (1878–1946), German Catholic archbishop who was one of the most outstanding Catholic opponents of Nazism and Adolf HITLER.

When the Nazis rose to national power in GERMANY in 1933, Galen pledged his allegiance to them, in the hope that they would win back the country's honor, which had been lost during World War I. However, he changed his mind after discovering the Nazis' anti-Catholic propaganda campaign, and after reading *The Myth of the Twentieth Century* by chief Nazi ideologist Alfred ROSENBERG. Galen immediately denounced the book for its pagan, racist, and anti-Catholic content.

Galen's most famous anti-Nazi action was his condemning of the EUTHANASIA PROGRAM as clear-cut murder in a sermon he delivered on August 3, 1941. Some scholars believe that Galen's very public denunciation led Hitler to abandon the "mercy killings" of the mentally ill, aged, disabled, homosexuals, and others. Even so, Galen's opposition was considered to be an act of treason, and he was only saved from execution because Hitler did not want to risk a public battle with the Catholic church.

After a group of officers tried to assassinate Hitler in July 1944, Galen was sent to SACHSENHAUSEN, where he was imprisoned until the end of the war.

GAMZON, ROBERT (1905–1961), Founder of the Jewish scout movement in FRANCE and PARTISAN commander.

Gamzon established the FRENCH JEWISH SCOUTS in 1923; his organization brought in young Jews from all sorts of backgrounds. During 1939 and 1940, Gamzon served as a communications officer in the French army. After GERMANY vanquished France in June 1940, Gamzon moved his movement's institutions to southern France, which was not yet occupied by the Germans, and to French-governed ALGERIA. He began setting up children's homes, workshops, welfare centers, and training farms, and organized Jewish tradition and culture courses for youth leaders. In January 1942

Robert Gamzon during the war

Gamzon joined the executive board of the UNION OF FRENCH JEWS (UGIF), which was a consolidation of all the Jewish organizations in France. In that capacity, Gamzon went to PARIS in May 1943 to help organize underground actions there.

In the summer of 1942 Gamzon instituted a secret rescue network called "The Sixth" whose purpose was to help Jews escape the GESTAPO. The Sixth provided Jews with false identity papers, hid young people in non-Jewish institutions and homes, and smuggled Jews of any age into SPAIN and SWITZERLAND.

In December 1943 Gamzon set up a Jewish partisan unit in the Tarn district of southwestern France. Those who joined the unit were mainly young people who had been part of the Jewish scout movement or had participated in Gamzon's workshops. Gamzon attached his partisan unit to the Jewish Army, which was a major French Jewish resistance and fighting organization. By joining the Jewish Army, Gamzon helped unite all of France's Jewish underground militias.

By June 1944 Gamzon's partisan unit, named for the leader of "The Sixth" (Marc Haguenau) who had taken his own life after being captured by the *Gestapo*, was a serious and disciplined group of 120 fighters. On August 19 of that year Gamzon and his unit captured an armored German train, and two days later they liberated the cities of Castres and Mazamet.

In 1949 Gamzon moved to Israel along with a group of 50 alumni of the French Jewish scouts. (see also JEWISH ARMY, FRANCE.)

GANZENMULLER, ALBERT (1905–1973), Nazi who served from 1942–1945 as the state secretary of the Reich Transportation Ministry. During that time, some three million Jews were carried by the German train system to their deaths at Nazi EXTERMINATION CAMPS.

An engineer, Ganzenmuller began working for the German railways in 1928. Ganzenmuller was not just a simple man doing his job: he had engaged in anti-Jewish activities in his youth and joined the NAZI PARTY and the Storm Troopers (SA) in 1931. In 1937 he transferred to the Reich Transportation Ministry's railway section.

GERMANY invaded the SOVIET UNION in June 1941. Ganzenmuller volunteered to serve on the eastern war-front, and was charged with renovating the Main Railway Directorate East. After successfully completing this task, he was made state secretary of the Reich's Transportation Ministry. In this post, Ganzenmuller played a vital part in the "Final Solution" by supplying the SS with the trains used to deport Jews to extermination camps.

After the war Ganzenmuller escaped to Argentina, and only returned to Germany in 1955. He was finally brought to trial in 1973, but he had a heart attack soon after the trial began, and the proceedings did not continue.

GAS CHAMBERS Method of mass murder used by the Nazis.

The Nazis first began using poison gas as a means for mass murder in December 1939, when an SS SONDERKOMMANDO unit used carbon monoxide to suffocate Polish mental patients. One month later, the head of the EUTHANASIA PROGRAM decided to use carbon monoxide to kill the handicapped, chronically ill, aged, and others who had been put in his charge. By August 1941 some 70,000 Germans had been murdered in five euthanasia centers, which were equipped either with stationary gas chambers or with mobile GAS VANS.

In the summer of 1941 the Germans began murdering Jews in a systematic and mass fashion. After several months, it became clear to them that the mass murder method they had been using, shooting, was neither quick nor efficient enough for their needs. Thus, based on the experience gained in the Euthanasia Program, they began using gas chambers to annihilate European Jewry.

In December 1941 the SS inaugurated the large-scale use of gas vans at the CHELMNO extermination camp. These worked by piping exhaust fumes into the closed cab through a special tube. Forty to sixty victims were jammed into the van at a time, and after several minutes, they were suffocated. However, this method was insufficient for the millions of Jews that the Nazis hoped to kill, so when they built three exterminations camps in 1942 as part of AKTION REINHARD—the program to exterminate the Jews in the GENERALGOUVERNEMENT—they equipped them with large, stationary gas chambers. BELZEC, which opened for operation in March, had three gas chambers located in a wooden barrack; SOBIBOR, where the killings began in May, housed its gas chambers in a brick building; and TREBLINKA, which was established in July, had three gas chambers that could be hermetically sealed. At each of the three camps, hundreds of thousands of Jews were murdered by exhaust gas from diesel engines. During the summer and fall of 1942 the Nazis enlarged the existing gas chambers and added new ones.

When transports arrived at Sobibor, Treblinka, and Belzec, a few of the victims were chosen to join *Sonderkommando* units, while a few others with various skills were selected to work in repair shops that served the camp staff. The rest of the victims were sent on an assembly line, where they were stripped of their possessions and clothing and their hair was cut. They were then pushed into the gas chambers with their arms raised so the maximum number of people could be jammed in. Babies and young children were thrown in on top of the heap. After the victims had died, the *Sonderkommando* men would remove the bodies from the chamber and bury them.

The Nazis continued to look for a still more efficient method of mass murder. After some experimentation done on Soviet PRISONERS OF WAR, the Nazis found a commercial insecticide called ZYKLON B to be an appropriate gas for their needs. Zyklon B, a form of hydrogen

Gas chamber in Majdanek (Photo: Geoffrey Wigoder)

cyanide, was put to use in the extermination center at AUSCHWITZ. Over its four years of existence, more than one million people were gassed to death there. However, the Nazis were never satisfied with the rate of extermination. During the summer of 1942 plans were made to build newer, more efficient gas chambers and crematoria ovens to dispose of the corpses. The project was completed under the direction of *JA Topf und Soehne* by the spring of 1943, allowing Auschwitz to become the Nazis' main killing center.

Some of the Nazis' other camps also contained gas chambers, but they were not used on a regular basis for mass extermination. Gas chambers functioned at MAUTHAUSEN, NEUENGAMME, SACHSENHAUSEN, STUTTHOF, and RAVENSBRUECK. All of these gas chambers utilized Zyklon B.

GAS VANS Vans used by the Nazis to murder Jews and other prisoners through asphyxiation by carbon monoxide. About 700,000 people were victims of gas vans.

The Nazis first experimented with gas vans in 1940 in Kochanowka, POLAND; they locked mentally ill children inside a sealed van and choked them to death with carbon monoxide. Soon, the Nazis performed further experimentation that involved piping carbon monoxide from a truck's engine into a sealed chamber. When the EINSATZGRUPPEN began the extermination of Soviet Jewry in mid-1941, they shot their victims to death. However, this was not a quick or secret enough method. Thus, the Reich Security Main Office (REICHSSICHERHEITSHAUPTAMT, RSHA) ordered that gas vans be employed for murder on a large scale. The first gas vans in the SOVIET UNION were used in Poltava, in November 1941, and in Kharkov in December. That same month, gas vans were also used in the CHELMNO EXTERMINATION CAMP. By June 1942 there were 20 gas vans in operation, and another ten were being prepared. Some of the trucks could hold up to 50–60 victims; others could only handle 25–30 people.

In March 1942, 7,000 prisoners, mostly Jewish women and children, were put to death by gas van in

Gas van in Chelmno

the Yugoslavian CONCENTRATION CAMP called SAJMISTE. Vans were also employed in LUBLIN, where they were used to kill Polish and Jewish prisoners in the Lublin fortress prison. The vans were then driven to MAJDANEK, where the corpses were burned in the crematorium.

Fifteen vans were put at the disposal of the *Einsatzgruppen* operating in German-occupied Soviet Union. However, after several months of use, the Germans realized that the gas van method of extermination was rather troublesome. The men who unloaded the vans suffered mental stress due to their extremely close contact with murder. In addition, the back roads of the Soviet Union were very bad and caused the vans to break down quite frequently. Ultimately, the gas vans could not handle the large number of Jews that the Nazis intended to murder, so the more effective GAS CHAMBERS were developed.

GAULLE, CHARLES DE (1890–1970), French army general and political leader. During WORLD WAR II de Gaulle headed the Free French Movement and resistance forces in German-occupied and Vichy FRANCE.

GERMANY invaded France in May 1940. After the French army was defeated, de Gaulle was appointed deputy minister of war and strenuously opposed French Prime Minister Philippe PETAIN'S surrender to Germany. He then went to London, where he formed the Free French Movement for all those French soldiers and civilians who did not accept the truce with Germany.

In 1941 de Gaulle led Free French troops in battle against Vichy forces in Syria and Lebanon to free those French colonies from the Nazis. However, during the 1942 battle to liberate North Africa, the Allies did not confer with de Gaulle; instead they relinquished ALGERIA to Vichy officials such as Francois DARLAN who had surrendered to them. De Gaulle soon overwhelmed his enemies in Algeria and abolished the anti-Jewish laws instituted there by the Vichy government.

General Charles de Gaulle

De Gaulle became prime minister of the provisional French government established after France was liberated in August 1944. He cancelled all racial laws and made sure the Jews received their property and rights. De Gaulle served as president of France from 1958–1969. (for more on Vichy, see also FRANCE.)

GEBIRTIG, MORDECAI (1877–1942), Yiddish folk poet. Gebirtig was the poet's pen name—his real name was Mordecai Bertig.

Born in WARSAW, Gebirtig was trained as a carpenter.

Much of his poetry, about 100 hundred poems in all, focused on simple Jewish folk, the type of people Gebirtig saw around him every day. Many of his poems were put to music. They were sung and performed in concert halls, theaters, at public meetings, on the radio, by street singers, and by regular Jews like those about whom he wrote. During WORLD WAR II, Gebirtig's poems were sung in the CRACOW Ghetto (where he was imprisoned), in other GHETTOS, and in CONCENTRATION CAMPS.

The poems Gebirtig wrote during the war reflect three distinct periods that he and other Jews in Cracow experienced. The first was from September 5, 1939 to October 24, 1940; during that year, Gebirtig lived in occupied Cracow. His writings from that time express his anger at the Poles for collaborating with the Nazis. The second period corresponds to the time when Gebirtig hid in a nearby village called Lagiewniki. His poems from that stage describe feelings of revenge, hope, and longing. The third period covers the few months he lived inside the Cracow Ghetto—from April 1942 to June 4, 1942, the day he was killed by the Nazis. His poems at that point mirror his gloom and fear near the end of his life.

About 15–20 of the poems Gebirtig wrote during the war are known. Most were published in 1946 in Cracow in a special volume titled *S'Brent*. The book includes a forward by Joseph Wolf, a member of the Cracow underground. The poem *S'Brent* was written in 1938 after a pogrom took place in Przytyk; it influenced many young people to resist the Nazis.

In 1967, a volume called *Ha-Ayara Bo'eret* (The Town Is Burning) was published in Israel. The book contains several of Gebirtig's Yiddish poems, along with Hebrew translations. It also includes photocopies of some of Gebirtig's original manuscripts and chronicles the manuscripts' history and how they were saved.

GENDARMERIE, HUNGARIAN

Police force whose job was to maintain law and order in the Hungarian countryside. During WORLD WAR II, the *Gendarmerie* was supposed to destroy any opponents of the Hungarian regime and was responsible for carrying out the regime's anti-Jewish policies.

The *Gendarmerie* consisted of 3,000–5,000 policemen who were divided into 10 districts. At the time of the DEPORTATIONS of Hungarian Jewry in 1944, the country was divided into six zones, each with one or two *Gendarmerie* districts.

In the summer of 1941 the *Gendarmerie* partici-

pated in the roundup of Jews that resulted in massacres in KAMENETS-PODOLSKI by the EINSATZGRUPPEN. It was also involved in the murder in February 1942 of 3,300 Serbs and Jews in the Novi-Sad area. After the Germans occupied HUNGARY in March 1944, the *Gendarmerie* was charged with putting the Jews in GHETTOS and then deporting them to EXTERMINATION CAMPS. Special *Gendarmerie* investigative units, located in the larger ghettos, were in charge of confiscating Jewish property. They set up a "mint" in each of the ghettos, where Jews were tortured into revealing where they had hidden their supposed valuables. The *Gendarmerie* men were so cruel in their treatment of Hungary's Jews that even some Nazis were shocked at their barbarity.

The *Gendarmerie* was disbanded by the Provisional National Government of Hungary in June 1945.

GENERALGOUVERNEMENT

(General Government), territorial unit in POLAND with its own administration, created by the Nazis on October 26, 1939. When the Germans invaded Poland in September 1939, they split the country into three parts: the western third was annexed to the THIRD REICH; the eastern third was occupied by the SOVIET UNION; and the central third was made into the *Generalgouvernement*, a semi-independent unit which the Nazis intended to use as a place to do all their racial "dirty work." The *Generalgouvernement* was to serve as a "racial dumping ground," an endless supply of slave labor, and ultimately, as a site for the mass extermination of European Jewry.

The *Generalgouvernement* was divided into four districts: CRACOW, WARSAW, RADOM, and LUBLIN, with Cracow serving as the administrative center. These areas, which had a total population of 12 million of which 1.5 million were Jews, were further divided into sub-districts. After the Germans attacked the Soviet Union in the summer of 1941, they attached Eastern Galicia to the *Generalgouvernement*, making it the fifth district and adding between three and four million people to the population.

The head of the *Generalgouvernement* was Hans FRANK, who held the position of governor-general. However, he was not free to govern as he pleased. The racial policies carried out in the *Generalgouvernement* were the responsibility of the SS and the police, which were first headed by SS-*Obergruppenfuehrer* Friedrich Kruger, and then by Wilhelm Koppe.

The Nazis treated the Poles of the *Generalgouverne-*

ment in a terrible fashion. They only allowed a handful of Polish institutions to continue functioning, including the bank that put out the country's currency; the Polish Police, known as *Granatowa,* meaning "blue"; and the Central Relief Committee. These were not allowed to operate however they wanted: they were subject to the strict supervision of the *Generalgouvernement* authorities. The Nazis viewed the Poles living within the *Generalgouvernement* as a cheap labor source, to be taken advantage of at any occasion. Later, the Germans tried to deal with the Poles by distinguishing between those who were of German origin (*Deutschstammig*) and those whom they regarded as inferior (see also VOLKSDEUTSCHE).

The Germans tried to make sure that the Poles would obey them by terrorizing the population. If the Polish underground killed a German, 50–100 Poles were executed as a punishment and warning. Two acts of terror that the Nazis inflicted on Polish citizens were particularly barbaric. In November 1939 the Nazis performed *Sonderaktion Krakau* (Special Action Cracow), in which they arrested 183 school and college staff members who were attending a meeting with the German police. These Poles were deported to SACHSENHAUSEN; most never returned. The second act was carried out in LVOV, where 38 Polish professors were executed soon after German troops entered the city.

The Germans also destroyed Polish scientific and cultural institutions, and pillaged artistic and archaeological treasures. In addition, they stripped the Poles of their financial infrastructure, leaving them to support themselves with only small businesses and agriculture. The Poles were made to turn over food to the Germans, and were forbidden to trade foodstuffs. Thus, those Poles living in urban areas were limited to the pitiful food rations provided—a veritable starvation diet. They were forced to smuggle food illegally just to stay alive.

The Jews of the *Generalgouvernement* were subject to terribly harsh decrees. From the very beginning, the Germans confiscated their property and made them perform FORCED LABOR. From late 1939, the Jews were put in GHETTOS, where they were totally isolated from the outside world and severely restricted. In the spring of 1942 the Germans began deporting the Jews from the ghettos to EXTERMINATION CAMPS located in the Lublin district, and by 1944 all ghettos in the *Generalgouvernement* had been liquidated.

The *Generalgouvernement* was completely liberated by Soviet troops by January 1945.

GENERALPLAN OST (General Plan East), plan devised by Nazi leaders in 1941–1942 to resettle Eastern Europe with Germans, and move about other "inferior" groups within the Nazis' domain.

In 1941 the Nazis fully believed that they were going to win WORLD WAR II and maintain control over all the lands they had conquered. Thus, they came up with a long-term scheme for the fate of those territories: the expulsion or enslavement of most non-Aryans, the extermination of the Jews living in the conquered territories, and the resettlement of the empty areas with Germans and VOLKSDEUTSCHE (ethnic Germans).

The territories involved included the occupied areas of POLAND, the Baltic states (LITHUANIA, LATVIA, and ESTONIA), BELORUSSIA, and parts of Russia and the UKRAINE. There were about 45 million people living in those areas in the early 1940s, including five to six million Jews. The Nazis came up with an elaborate racial classification system by which to decide who would be enslaved, expelled, murdered, or resettled. Some 31 million of the territories' inhabitants, mostly of Slavic origin, were to be declared "racially undesirable" and expelled to western Siberia. The Jews were to be annihilated, euphemistically referred to as "total removal." The rest of the local population would be enslaved, "Germanized," or killed. After the area was cleared out, 10 million Germans and people of German origin, called ethnic Germans, were to be moved in.

During the war, many of the Nazis' activities were carried out with *Generalplan Ost* in mind. They massacred millions of Jews in Eastern Europe, in addition to millions of Soviet PRISONERS OF WAR. Millions more were sent to GERMANY to do FORCED LABOR, and two million Poles living in the areas that had been annexed to the Reich were treated to a "Germanization" process. Approximately 30,000 Germans who had been living in the Baltic countries were moved from their homes and prepared for resettlement in Poland. From November 1942 to August 1943, Poles living in the Zamosc region of Poland were kicked out of their homes and replaced by Germans.

The Nazis quickly lost interest in *Generalplan Ost* after the battle of Stalingrad, when they realized that their victory in the war was not a sure thing.

GENOCIDE The annihilation of a racial, ethnic, political, or religious group or its destruction to the extent that it no longer exists as a group. The term "genocide" was first used in 1933 at a conference in

Madrid by a Jewish judge named Raphael Lemkin. Lemkin proposed to the League of Nations that they create an international agreement to condemn vandalism and barbaric crimes. He then went on to define and analyze the crime of genocide in books he wrote during WORLD WAR II. He explained that genocide does not necessarily mean the immediate and complete destruction of a group; rather, it may also involve a series of planned actions that are meant to destroy basic elements of the group's existence, including its language, culture, national identity, economy, and the freedom of its individuals.

On December 9, 1948 the United Nations approved the Genocide Convention, an agreement to prevent genocide and punish those who design and carry it out. Lemkin himself played an important part in drafting the convention. The convention lists several actions that are defined as genocide when carried out against a religious, ethnic, national, or racial group in order to destroy part or all of that group: 1) killing people belonging to the group; 2) causing severe bodily or spiritual harm to members of the group; 3) deliberately forcing a group to live under conditions that could lead to the complete or partial destruction of the group; 4) taking measures to prevent births among a group; and 5) forcibly removing children from the group and transferring them to another group. This list of genocide crimes is very similar to those Nazi crimes that were dealt with at the first of the NUREMBERG TRIALS. The crimes brought up at Nuremberg, defined as "crimes against humanity" included murder, cruel treatment, and persecution of a group based on its race or ethnicity in order to destroy the group. However, the Nazis tried at Nuremberg were not accused specifically of "genocide" since that crime was not included in the agreement that launched the International Military Tribunal.

The accusation of genocide was included during the later war crimes trials held at Nuremberg and at many of the Nazi criminal trials held in POLAND. For example, in the July 1946 trial of Arthur GREISER, a Polish court convicted him of crimes of genocide committed against the Polish people.

The government of Israel joined the Genocide Convention soon after the State of Israel was established, and in 1950 passed its own Genocide Prevention and Punishment Law. The definition of genocide used in that law was the same as that of the Genocide Convention. The Israeli government also used that definition in

another law it passed in 1950, the Nazis and Nazi Collaborators (Punishment) Law. This law included the definitions of "crimes against humanity" and "war crimes" which had been established before the Nuremberg Trials, and also contained the definition of a newly coined crime—"Crimes against the Jewish People." To explain this crime, the Israelis took the Genocide Convention's list of genocide crimes, but adapted it specifically to the Jewish people. Thus, "Crimes against the Jewish People" consist of any of the following actions, when carried out with the intention of annihilating part or all of the Jewish people: 1) killing Jews; 2) causing severe bodily or mental harm to Jews; 3) deliberately forcing Jews to live under conditions that could lead to their physical destruction; 4) taking measures to prevent births among Jews; 5) forcibly transferring Jewish children to another religious or national group; 6) destroying or desecrating Jewish religious or cultural treasures or values; and 7) inciting others to hate Jews.

"Crimes against the Jewish People" involve the Jewish people only, and relate to a totally unique and unparalleled case. However, the crimes perpetrated against the Jewish people in the context of the HOLOCAUST were also crimes that negated the basic principles and values of all humanity. Thus, they affected not only the Jews but also the entire world, in that they tried to remove from the world one of its many fundamental elements.

Holocaust experts all agree that genocide was a part of the Holocaust. However, some scholars also say that what the Nazis did to the Jewish people went beyond genocide for several reasons. The attempt to dehumanize and then murder every Jew, everywhere, regardless of his activities or beliefs, was unprecedented in history. Moreover, the Nazi belief that Jews had to be murdered for the sake of mankind, is a dimension not present in other acts of genocide that were carried out either before or after the Holocaust. Since the 1980s, the field of genocide studies, which usually includes the Holocaust, has grown considerably.

GENS, JACOB (1905–1943), Chairman of the JUDENRAT in the VILNA Ghetto.

When the Germans occupied Vilna in June 1941, Gens was named director of the Jewish hospital. When the *Judenrat* was set up in September, he was made commander of the GHETTO police. The police participated in the *aktionen* that took place in the ghetto between September and December, in which tens of

Jacob Gens, Head of the Vilna Judenrat

thousands of Jews were killed. Gens tried to help the Jews during the mass slaughters, and became the ghetto's leading personality.

In July 1942 the Germans dissolved the *Judenrat* and made Gens head of the ghetto administration. In that position, Gens initiated his "work for life" plan; he believed that if the Jews could prove themselves to be a productive workforce for the Germans, then the destruction of the ghetto would be delayed. Gens constantly tried to expand the number of Jewish workers—eventually 14,000 out of 20,000 ghetto inhabitants had work. For a time, the ghetto was calm, and Gens established a medical care system and welfare and cultural institutions.

Gens' attitude toward the ghetto's underground was mixed. At first, he cooperated with the United Partisan Organization, Vilna's main resistance group. However, he later decided that their activities endangered the rest of the ghetto population, and gave in to a German

demand to turn in the underground commander, Yitzhak WITTENBERG.

The Germans began liquidating the Vilna Ghetto in August and September 1943. By that time, the ghetto inhabitants no longer trusted Gens. After the underground attacked the Germans, Gens tried to prevent a German backlash by offering to provide Jews for FORCED LABOR in ESTONIA, if the Germans would leave the ghetto. The Germans agreed, and deported all but 12,000 of the ghetto's inhabitants.

Gens' Lithuanian wife and daughter lived outside the ghetto. Gens received many offers to leave the ghetto and join them, but he refused, in favor of staying and helping the Jews of the ghetto. On September 14 he was summoned to the GESTAPO headquarters and shot. The ghetto was completely liquidated 10 days later. (see also RESISTANCE, JEWISH and UNITED PARTISAN ORGANIZATION, VILNA.)

GEPNER, ABRAHAM (1872–1943), Businessman, WARSAW political figure, and member of the Warsaw Ghetto JUDENRAT.

Before WORLD WAR II, Gepner was a member of the Warsaw city council. He was also active in Jewish affairs and charitable activities. When the Germans invaded POLAND in September 1939, Gepner was 67 years old. He and Samuel ZYGELBOJM were the two Jews among 12 hostages taken by the Nazis when they entered Warsaw.

Gepner served on the city's *Judenrat* from the start and was close to the *Judenrat* chairman, Adam CZERNIAKOW. When the Germans established the Warsaw GHETTO in November 1940, he became head of the supply department, which provided food and other vital items. Although Gepner was not able to prevent hunger and death from starvation, the ghetto's inhabitants trusted him and his department worked as efficiently as possible.

Gepner was also involved in assistance and welfare in the ghetto, especially for children and orphans. He supported the ghetto's underground and secret pioneer movements. When the WARSAW GHETTO UPRISING broke out on April 19, 1943, Gepner initially refused to hide in a bunker. However, he finally gave in and entered a bunker on Franciszkanska Street. On May 3 the Germans pulled Gepner and others out of the bunker and murdered them.

GERMAN ARMAMENT WORKS (*Deutsche Ausrustungswerke,* DAW), one of the ss's leading economic enterprises. DAW was founded in May 1939 with SS-*Standartenfuehrer* Walter Salpeter as its executive director. The company's main offices were in BERLIN.

DAW's mandate was to manage the factories that had been established by the SS to take advantage of the slave labor of prisoners interned at CONCENTRATION CAMPS such as DACHAU, SACHSENHAUSEN, BUCHENWALD, and AUSCHWITZ. Later on, similar factories were set up in other camps, including Pulawy, STUTTHOF, Fursten-walde, RAVENSBRUECK, NEUENGAMME, and at the Jewish PRISONER OF WAR camp in LUBLIN. The two biggest plants run on slave labor were those at the JANOWSKA camp in LVOV and at the Lublin prisoner of war camp. In 1940, 1,220 prisoners were forced to work in all the factories put together; that number rose to 15,500 in 1943. Some 8,000 Jews worked at Janowska and Lublin alone.

Most of the prisoners who worked in these DAW-controlled factories perished during the war, either from exhaustion and overwork, or during *aktionen,* in which hundreds of Jews were massacred. The largest of these *aktionen* took place in November 1943, when 2,000 Jewish prisoners of war were taken to the crematoria at MAJDANEK and shot to death as part of Operation ERNTEFEST.

GERMAN VANGUARD, GERMAN JEWISH FOLLOWERS

(*Deutscher Vortrupp, Gefolgschaft Deutscher Juden*), organization established in February 1933 by a group of 150 Jewish university students in GERMANY. The group's goal was to preserve their Jewish religious identity, while at the same time emphasize its fundamental connection to German culture. The Vanguard was headed by a student of religion, Hans Joachim Schoeps.

Schoeps and his followers were extremely patriotic Germans who wanted to be seen as a Jewish political movement within the revival of German nationalism. They looked down on Eastern European Jews, and opposed Zionism, Marxism, and liberalism. Zionism was considered negative because Zionists wanted to become a separate Jewish nation like any other, while the Vanguard believed that German Jews belonged to the German nation, and were only different with regard to their religion. They even saw Zionism as a type of assimilation away from pure German-ness.

Vanguard members failed to understand that the Nazis hated Jews because of their race, and considered them to be non-Aryan, or non-German, to the core. They thought that Jews would eventually be allowed to integrate into the THIRD REICH. Nonetheless, fearing

arrest, Schoeps fled to SWEDEN in 1938, where he kept up contact with German conservatives throughout the war.

GERMANY　　Country in central Europe. During World War I (which lasted from 1914 to 1918), Germany fought alongside Austria-Hungary and ITALY against GREAT BRITAIN, FRANCE, the UNITED STATES, and Russia. After Germany was vanquished by the Allies and the war ended, the democratic Weimar Republic was established (under which the country's Jews enjoyed complete legal equality). However, the Weimar period was fraught with unemployment and economic disaster. The Allies made Germany pay them huge sums of money to make up for their material losses in the war, and the situation got even worse in 1929 when the Great Depression hit. The economic desperation in Germany led to great turbulence: extremist political parties gained in strength, including the NAZI PARTY on one end of the political spectrum and the Communist Party on the other. Both gathered many new followers in the late 1920s and early 1930s, and both proposed radical solutions to the country's economic and social woes.

In January 1933 Adolf HITLER and his Nazi Party rose to national power in Germany. Hitler soon became the country's dictator, and declared the establishment of the THIRD REICH—his name for the new German Empire. During their first years in power, the Nazis tried to redraw the face of Germany. One of their main goals was to erase the line between the government and the party institutions. For example, after 1936 both the police (a government institution) and the SS (a party institution) were directed by the same man, Heinrich HIMMLER. In addition, many police officers were awarded SS ranks. The Nazis also sought to restrict and supervise German art and culture, as evidenced by the 1933 public burning of books that were not approved of by the Nazi Party.

During the first years of the Nazi regime, all those who opposed the Nazis in any way were imprisoned in the newly established CONCENTRATION CAMPS, and were forced to stay there until their opposition had been broken down. Many Germans truly accepted Nazism, while others did not but conformed in public in order to avoid confrontation. Very few Germans actively resisted the Nazis, and on the face of it, at least, Germany became a Nazi society.

Hitler's foreign policy successes amassed before

Nazi mass meeting in Braunschweig before the war

WORLD WAR II even started gained him immense public support. Several regions were either reunited with Germany or annexed to it without war, such as the Saar region in 1935, AUSTRIA and the Sudeten region of Czechoslovakia in 1938, and Bohemia and Moravia in 1939. Then, on September 1, 1939 German troops invaded POLAND, launching a world war. In the spring of 1940 the fighting extended to Western Europe, to the Balkans in the spring of 1941, and to the SOVIET UNION in late June of that year. The Germans gained victory after victory; the Nazis were fighting to ensure their place of dominance in Europe and by extension the world, and to gain living space, or LEBENSRAUM, for the German people. They also meant to reshape the world in their own racial image, which included solving the so-called Jewish problem. However, their fortunes changed after their defeat by the Soviets at Stalingrad in early 1943. The Allied invasions of Italy in 1943 and France in 1944 sealed Nazi Germany's fate, and its final defeat came in May 1945.

Back in 1933 when Hitler came to power, some

566,000 Jews by racial definition were living in Germany, making up less than one percent of the entire population. One-third of those Jews lived in the capital, BERLIN, and another third resided in other big cities. Immediately after the Nazis took control of the government, they began to exclude Jews from German society and strip them of their legal and civil rights. Jews were fired from their jobs, not allowed to study at universities, and were kept out of German cultural life. In September 1935 the Germans passed the racial NUREMBERG LAWS which led to the definition of who was to be considered a Jew, and further isolated Jews from the rest of the society, stripping them of their citizenship. In addition, antisemitic measures continued to be implemented, peaking in the destructive KRISTALLNACHT pogrom of November 1938, during which hundreds of synagogues were burned down, Jewish homes and businesses were attacked and pillaged, and thousands of Jews were abused and sent to concentration camps.

In response to the constantly multiplying anti-Jewish measures, the Jews of Germany set up a comprehen-

A Nazi Party rally in Nuremberg

sive network of self-help associations. Their most important goal was to facilitate emigration, but they also set up organizations for relief within Germany itself. These included adult education centers (see also MITTEL-STELLE FUER JUEDISCHE ERWACHSENENBILDUNG), cultural associations (see also CULTURAL UNION OF GERMAN JEWS), social welfare bodies, and the umbrella organization called the REICH REPRESENTATION OF GERMAN JEWS.

Between 1933 and 1941 about 346,000 Jews emigrated from Germany, most before the outbreak of the war. Between *Kristallnacht* and the outbreak of the war, flight reached panic level proportions.

In September 1941 all Jews in Germany over the age of six were ordered to don the Jewish badge (see also BADGE, JEWISH). The DEPORTATION of German Jews had begun back in 1940, when Jews from Stettin were sent to Poland and Jews from Baden and the Saar region were sent to France. Most were later transported to their deaths at EXTERMINATION CAMPS. Deportations from the rest of Germany began in October 1941; at first, Jews were sent to the GHETTOS of Eastern Europe, but later deportation transports were sent directly to AUSCHWITZ and other extermination camps. All told some 200,000 German Jews died during the HOLO-CAUST. About 137,000 were deported from Germany, of whom 128,000 were murdered. The rest of the murdered German Jews had fled to countries that later fell under Nazi influence. In Germany itself about 20,000 Jews survived, including three-quarters of the MISCHLINGE.

GERSTEIN, KURT   (1905–1945), SS officer who tried in vain to tell the world about the Nazis' murderous activities. Gerstein joined the NAZI PARTY in 1933, but at the same time associated himself with the anti-Nazi Confessing Church. As a result he was sent to a CONCENTRATION CAMP and kicked out of the Nazi Party in 1938. At that point he began studying medicine.

Gerstein's sister-in-law was murdered as part of the EUTHANASIA PROGRAM; Gerstein was determined to discover the truth about the murder of mental patients in "euthanasia institutes" so he volunteered for the *Waffen*-SS and was sent to work at its hygiene institute. In this post, he worked with ZYKLON B, the poison gas used by the Nazis for mass extermination. In August 1942 he visited the TREBLINKA, SOBIBOR, and BELZEC extermination camps, ostensibly to view Zyklon B in action for work purposes. In truth, Gerstein wanted to make sure his facts were accurate so he could tell the world what was really going on.

Gerstein made contact with various diplomats and clergymen, but his efforts to expose the Nazis and stop the mass murder were ignored. After the war he was arrested as a suspected war criminal. He died in jail, apparently as a suicide.

GESTAPO (acronym of *Geheime Staatspolizei*, meaning Secret State Police), the THIRD REICH'S secret political police force, which served as HITLER'S main instrument of torture and terror.

The *Gestapo* was established even before the Nazis came to power as a secret intelligence agency within the Prussian police department. When Hitler rose to power in 1933, he appointed Hermann GOERING interior minister of Prussia. This gave Goering authority over the Prussian political police, including the *Gestapo*. One month later, the *Gestapo* was given the power to impose "protective custody" on whomever it liked. Ultimately, this meant that if a person was arrested by the *Gestapo*, he lost all civil rights and was no longer protected by the law. Legally, the *Gestapo* was completely free to do whatever it wanted to its victims.

In April 1933 the *Gestapo* was totally separated from the rest of the Prussian police, and in 1934, a "Jewish section" was established within the operation. In April of that year, SS chief Heinrich HIMMLER took the *Gestapo* and all the CONCENTRATION CAMPS in GERMANY under SS control. The *Gestapo* now had the power to send its victims to concentration camps and determine their fate there—to live or die, and how. The German criminal code still forbade murder and torture, so the *Gestapo*—which often performed murder and torture—

The Gestapo main office, Berlin, 1941

began using methods, developed in DACHAU, of faking a victim's cause of death.

In June 1936 Himmler reorganized Germany's entire police system in order to free it from the restrictions of government red tape. He divided the police into two main sections, the Order Police (ORDNUNGSPOLIZEI, ORPO), and the Security Police (*Sicherheitspolizei,* SIPO). The ORPO was the "regular" police force, while the SIPO included the *Gestapo* and the Criminal Police (*Kriminalpolizei,* KRIPO). Under Himmler, the *Gestapo* grew exponentially and took control of all of Germany's political police agencies.

Until September 1939, the structure of the *Gestapo* was as follows: Division I, under the direction of Werner BEST, was in charge of organization and financial matters, including legal affairs. Division II, the *Gestapo's* most important section, was under the direct control of Reinhard HEYDRICH. He and his deputy, Heinrich MUELLER, were responsible for destroying the opponents of the Nazi regime. Division III, headed by Guenther Palten, was in charge of counterintelligence. Between November 1937 and October 1938 the *Gestapo* trained special units to terrorize and "nazify" foreign countries. In late 1938, after Adolf EICHMANN led the campaign to expel Jews from the newly-annexed AUSTRIA, Mueller and Eichmann took responsibility for the emigration and DEPORTATION of Jews from all Nazi-occupied areas. After the KRISTALLNACHT pogrom of November 1938, the *Gestapo* became Germany's major executor of its anti-Jewish policies.

When WORLD WAR II began in September 1939 the Security Police (SIPO) was united with the Security Service (*Sicherheitsdienst,* SD) to form the REICHSSICHERHEITSHAUPTAMPT (Reich Security Main Office, RSHA). In the RSHA, Mueller became the official head of the *Gestapo,* while Eichmann headed the agency's Jewish section. Under their lead, the *Gestapo* participated in the arrest of Jews, GYPSIES, and members of "inferior races;" suppressed the territories occupied by Germany with brutal terror tactics; persecuted Jews; and played a major part in the "FINAL SOLUTION."

The *Gestapo* used the "protective custody" method to deal with European Jewry. They betrayed members of the ghettos' JUDENRAETE and took them hostage; created "language regulation" (SPRACHREGELUNG), a type of euphemistic jargon used to refer to their anti-Jewish policies in order to conceal the true nature of those acts; and supervised the liquidation of the GHETTOS. Eichmann's section of the *Gestapo* organized the deportation of Jews to concentration and EXTERMINATION CAMPS, and had direct control over the THERESIENSTADT concentration camp in Czechoslovakia. *Gestapo* officers also headed the EINSATZGRUPPEN units that mass-murdered Jews in the SOVIET UNION.

After the war, most of the *Gestapo's* major players eluded capture and trial.

GETTER, MATYLDA   (d. 1968), Mother superior of a Polish religious order in WARSAW. Sister Matylda saved the lives of hundreds of Jewish children from the Warsaw GHETTO. She was designated as RIGHTEOUS AMONG THE NATIONS by YAD VASHEM for her rescue activities.

GHETTO   A street or city section where only Jews lived. The word ghetto was first used in Venice in 1516,

Entrance to the Lodz Ghetto, the sign reads: "Jewish residential district, entry forbidden"

as part of the phrase "Geto Nuovo" meaning "New Foundry." This referred to the closed Jewish section of the city, which had originally been the site of a foundry. During WORLD WAR II the Jews of Eastern Europe were forced to leave their homes and move to ghettos where they were held essentially as prisoners.

Many Jews died in the ghetto. However, there is no proof that the ghettos were originally created for the distinct purpose of killing Jews, or that as the war continued, the Nazis tried to turn the ghettos into sites at which they could carry out their plan to decimate the Jews of Europe. Nevertheless, the Germans were not troubled by the huge number of Jews dying from hunger and lack of other basics.

There is also no evidence that the Nazi leadership themselves ordered the establishment of ghettos in the exact form they eventually took. Even on September 21, 1939, when Reinhard HEYDRICH called for the centralization of Polish Jews into separate areas of cities and used the term ghetto, he did not mean it in the way it was ultimately carried out. Most likely, ghettos were instituted separately by local officials. Thus, each ghetto was unique in how and when it was set up, how it was sealed off from the rest of the city, and how it was governed.

The first ghetto in POLAND was established in the city of PIOTRKOW TRYBUNALSKI in October 1939, just a month after the war broke out. Next, a ghetto was closed off in the city of LODZ on April 30, 1940. The largest ghetto in Europe, the WARSAW Ghetto, was set up in November 1940. Only four months later, in March 1941, the population of the Warsaw Ghetto reached an all-time high of 445,000. In other areas, ghettos were only instituted later on. For example, the ghettos of Silesia (in what is now southwest Poland) were established at the end of 1942 and beginning of 1943. In the parts of the SOVIET UNION occupied by the Germans, ghettos were usually set up after some of the local Jews

A bridge over an "Aryan" street connecting two sections of the Lodz Ghetto

had been murdered. Ghettos were also constructed in HUNGARY, Amsterdam, and THERESIENSTADT.

Each ghetto was closed off and guarded in its own particular way. The Lodz Ghetto was set off from the rest of the city by a wooden fence and barbed wire. In some spots, a brick wall was also built. Guards stood on both the inside and outside of the line dividing the ghetto from the outside. The Warsaw Ghetto was surrounded by an 11-mile wall. Guards patrolled the wall and were posted at its gates. However, it was possible to smuggle food and other items into the ghetto. The Piotrkow Trybunalski Ghetto did not have a fence or guards. Poles could go in and out of the ghetto freely, and Jews were allowed to leave the ghetto. It was only locked at the end of 1941. In October of that year, Hans FRANK, the head of the GENERALGOUVERNEMENT, ordered the execution of any Jew found outside the ghetto area without permission to be there. Furthermore, most ghettos were locked during DEPORTATIONS.

Each ghetto was also governed uniquely. Because the ghetto was actually a type of city-within-a-city, the Jews were forced to run services and institutions for themselves for which they had no previous experience. In addition to running the JUDENRAETE, which were established before the ghettos and were a separate entity, Jews in the ghetto ran postal services, police forces, and various other services that a city would normally provide. They were also compelled to distribute food rations, and arrange for housing, health care, and jobs. Sometimes, a ghetto was divided into two separate areas: one for the workers, and one for the rest of the population. Some ghettos also contained other types of REFUGEES besides Jews. For example, at one point, GYPSIES were held in the Lodz Ghetto.

Jews living in the ghettos of the east obtained food in two different ways: from official German sources, and from the unofficial black market. Officially, the Jews were given ration cards that allowed them to buy much less than the rest of the local population. By mid-1941, in Poland, the Germans were giving out ration cards that provided only 184 calories per day—7.5 percent of the minimum daily requirement. The Germans themselves received a full ration, while the Poles received a ration of 26 percent of the daily needs. In order to supplement the pitiful rations, the Jews were forced to pay exorbitant prices for food sold on the black market. However, most of the Jews had very little money, so many starved to death. Only wealthy Jews could afford

to buy on the black market. Some Jews who worked in German factories received food on the job.

In some cases, the Germans used different names to refer to the areas in which they forced the Jews to live. Mostly, they used the common term, ghetto. However, sometimes they called those areas "Judischer Wohnbezirk," meaning Jewish residential sections.

Soon after the "FINAL SOLUTION" began, the Germans began to eliminate the ghettos. The first ghettos were liquidated in the spring of 1942. The last Polish ghetto to be destroyed, Lodz, was emptied in the summer of 1944. Most of the Jews taken from the ghettos were deported to EXTERMINATION CAMPS where they were murdered. Only a small number were taken to CONCENTRATION CAMPS and FORCED LABOR camps near the end of the war. Almost all of the Jews of Eastern Europe had been forced to leave their homes for the ghettos of their cities and towns. By the end of the war, however, not one Eastern European ghetto was left in existence. In Hungary, where the last ghettos were established in 1944, most existed for only a few weeks pending the deportation of the Jews to AUSCHWITZ. In January 1945 when Pest was being conquered by Soviet forces, the BUDAPEST Ghetto became the only ghetto to be liberated.

GILDENMAN, MOSHE (nicknamed "Uncle Misha," d. 1958), Jewish PARTISAN commander in the Volhynia region of the UKRAINE.

Gildenman's wife and daughter were killed during the Nazis' first *aktion* in their hometown of Korets, in May 1942. Soon after, Gildenman and his son Simha established a rebel unit. The day before the final liquidation of the Jews of Korets, Gildenman and his men escaped to the forest. Their only weapons were two guns and a butcher knife. They wandered north for about two weeks, where they met and took in the survivors of a group of Jewish fighters. The newly enlarged group set up camp in a swampy area of the forest, and its members armed themselves with weapons they retrieved from battles. They then proceeded to assault Nazi collaborators and attack German farms and Ukrainian Police headquarters.

The group joined up with Gen. Aleksandr Saburov's partisan unit in January 1943. Gildenman set up a fighting company that was originally all Jewish (as time went by, many non-Jews joined). The company was active in the Zhitomir district until the area was liberated in October 1943. Gildenman went on to volunteer

Moshe Gildenman during the war

for the Soviet army; he served as a captain in the engineer corps until war's end. Gildenman settled in Israel in the early 1950s.

GITTERMAN, YITZHAK (1889–1943), Director of the American Jewish JOINT DISTRIBUTION COMMITTEE (JDC) in POLAND and active member of the WARSAW underground.

In 1921 Gitterman became director of the JDC in Warsaw. When WORLD WAR II broke out, Gitterman traveled to VILNA to aid the large number of REFUGEES there. He began a trip to SWEDEN to ask for aid, but the Germans captured his ship and sent him to a PRISONER OF WAR camp. He was returned to Warsaw in April 1940, where he immediately took charge of the Jewish Self-Help Society and the Jewish Mutual Aid Society.

Gitterman supported the underground in the Warsaw GHETTO and was active in underground activities, including secret cultural programs and social work services. Gitterman also served on the executive boards of

the secret ONEG SHABBAT archives and the Yiddish Culture Organization. When the underground first heard about the extermination of European Jews, Gitterman supported the establishment of a fighting alliance, the Jewish Fighting Organization (ZOB), and became a member of the ZOB's financial department, whose main purpose was to find funds to buy weapons.

Gitterman was murdered on January 18, 1943, during the second *aktion* by the Nazis in the Warsaw Ghetto. (see also JEWISH FIGHTING ORGANIZATION, WARSAW.)

GLASBERG, ALEXANDRE (1902–1981), French priest who saved the lives of many Jews during the HOLOCAUST.

Born a Jew in Zhitomir, in the UKRAINE, Glasberg traveled around Central Europe, converted to Catholicism, and ultimately became a Catholic priest in FRANCE. After the Germans invaded and occupied France in May 1940, Glasberg set up a charity, called Christian Friendship (*Amitie Chretienne*), to help Jews who were being persecuted by the Nazis. Christian Friendship was supported by Cardinal Pierre-Marie Gerlier, the head of the Catholic church in France; under his sponsorship, the organization established shelters that took in hundreds of Jews who had been released from French internment camps.

The Nazis began the mass arrest and DEPORTATION of French Jews in the summer of 1942. At that point Glasberg took his rescue activities underground. He worked with Jewish rescue associations, and made sure that the Jews living in his shelters were not pressured to convert to Catholicism. The GESTAPO found out about Glasberg's rescue activities in December 1942. Glasberg then joined the French PARTISANS under a different name. After the war ended, he participated in the activities of the ALIYA BET, helping Jews in France and Iran "illegally" immigrate to Palestine.

GLAZMAN, JOSEF (1913–1943), Jewish underground and PARTISAN leader in LITHUANIA. Active in the *Betar* Zionist YOUTH MOVEMENT, Glazman became the head of *Betar* Lithuania in 1937. In July 1940 the SOVIET UNION took control of Lithuania, and banned all Jewish political movements, such as *Betar*. At that point, Glazman joined the underground.

In June 1941 GERMANY invaded the Soviet Union and Soviet-occupied territories, including Lithuania. Glazman was in VILNA at that time; he was arrested and sent to do FORCED LABOR. In November 1941 Glazman returned to Vilna, where a GHETTO had been established. He both organized an underground group comprised of *Betar* members, and joined the Jewish ghetto police to be in a better position to carry out his underground activities. He also participated in the ghetto's educational and cultural programs.

In January 1942 Glazman helped found an underground militia called the United Partisan Organization (*Fareynegte Partizaner Organizatsye*, FPO). He was named deputy commander of the FPO, was in charge of its intelligence department, and commanded two of its battalions. In June Glazman left the police and became the head of the ghetto's housing department.

Because of his underground activities, Glazman had a very poor relationship with the head of the JUDENRAT, Jacob GENS. Gens ordered Glazman's arrest in October 1942, and in June 1943, he had Glazman sent to a labor camp. Glazman returned to the ghetto several weeks later. After Gens surrendered FPO leader Yitzhak WITTENBERG to the Germans, Glazman left the ghetto for the forest with a group of FPO fighters; their objective was to set up a partisan base there. On the way they were ambushed by the Germans and lost one-third of their men. In July Glazman and the remaining fighters reached the forest, where they formed a Jewish partisan unit.

In September the Germans began a serious hunt for the partisans in Glazman's area; he and his men tried to escape to a different forest. On October 7, they were attacked by a strong German force; only one member of Glazman's group survived. (see also UNITED PARTISAN ORGANIZATION, VILNA.)

GLIK, HIRSH   (1922–1944), Poet and PARTISAN in LITHUANIA. Glik began writing poetry when he was 13.

The Germans occupied VILNA in June 1941; Glik and his father were sent to a FORCED LABOR camp, where they worked in the peat bogs. Glik continued to write poetry even under those harsh circumstances. He was transferred to the Vilna GHETTO in early 1943. He joined the ghetto's United Partisan Organization (*Fareynegte Partizaner Organizatsye*, FPO), while continuing to write. In September 1943 his FPO unit was caught and Glik was sent to a camp in ESTONIA.

Glik kept writing even while suffering in the camps, and read his works to his fellow inmates. Most of these works did not survive. However, some of his poems, musical in style, were written to be sung. Most were

הירש גליק, — פּאָעט, פּאַרטיזאַנער. דערשאָסן נאָכן אַנטלױפֿן פֿון אַ נאַצישן לאַגער אין עסט־ לאַנד

Hirsh Glick – poet, partisan. Shot after escaping from a Nazi camp in Estonia

הירש גליק —משורר, פּארטיזאן. נורה לאחר שנמלט ממחנה נאצי באסטוניה

Гирш Глик — поэт партизан; застрелен после побега из нацистского лагеря в Эстонии

1944 – 1920

Hirsh Glik

meant to honor the partisans and strengthen their hope and morale. His most famous work was the "Song of the Partisans" which quickly became the partisan anthem and was sung all over Nazi-occupied Europe. After the war it became famous among Jews world over.

In the summer of 1944 Glik and eight of his FPO comrades attempted to break out of the camp; they were all killed during their escape. (see also UNITED PARTISAN ORGANIZATION, VILNA.)

GLOBKE, HANS   (1898–1973), German civil servant who helped write many of the anti-Jewish laws put into effect in GERMANY during the Nazi regime.

A lawyer who never joined the NAZI PARTY, Globke began working for the German government in 1929. In 1933 he helped draw up the emergency law that gave HITLER all-encompassing power. In 1935 Globke helped write the draft of the first two NUREMBERG LAWS, which stripped the Jews of their political rights, and forbade marriages and extramarital sexual relations between Germans and Jews. Along with Wilhelm Stuckart, he wrote an explanation of the racial Nuremberg Laws. Later, Globke penned the laws which forced all German Jews to take on the names Israel or Sarah and gave all property belonging to CONCENTRATION CAMP victims to the German government. During the war, Globke helped SS leader Heinrich HIMMLER enforce these laws all over occupied Europe.

After the war, Globke was not tried because he had only gone along with the Nazis, but was never one of them. He enjoyed a high-ranking job in the German parliament, and was consistently defended by German Chancellor Konrad Adenauer, who believed Globke's claim that he had tried to lighten the ANTI-JEWISH LEG-ISLATION in Germany.

GLOBOCNIK, ODILO

(1904–1945), Senior SS commander who played a major role in the destruction of the Jews of POLAND. Of Austrian-Croat descent, Globocnik joined the NAZI PARTY in AUSTRIA in 1931 and the SS in 1934. He engaged in a number of illegal activities for the Nazi Party, and was imprisoned several times as a result. In 1938 Globocnik began rising through the SS ranks; by May he was made state secretary and party leader of VIENNA. He was stripped of this position just a few months later due to some illegal dealings. Nonetheless, SS Chief Heinrich HIMMLER pardoned Globocnik of all wrongdoing, and in November 1939 he was named SS and Police Leader for the Lublin district of Poland.

In 1941 Himmler, who was quite fond of Globocnik and called him "Globus," charged him with organizing and setting up an SS power base in Poland. In 1942

Odilo Globocnik in SS uniform

Himmler once again gave Globocnik a great deal of responsibility: this time, he was ordered to implement AKTION REINHARD—the systematic extermination of the Jews in Poland. In this capacity, Globocnik was in charge of special SS troops who answered to Himmler only. Globocnik used the EXTERMINATION CAMPS of BELZEC, SOBIBOR, TREBLINKA, and MAJDANEK as killing sites where some two million Jews perished. He also became the executive director of OSTINDUSTRIE GMBH, an organization whose sole purpose was to expand the industrial SS empire and to take advantage of the Jews in the extermination camps who were not immediately gassed by using them as slave laborers. Globocnik also supervised the seizure of the Jews' valuables and property; he even had the gold teeth and fillings of the murdered Jews melted down and reused. In all, during *Aktion Reinhard,* 178 million reichsmarks worth of property was confiscated from the Jews of Poland.

In August 1943, after disagreements with other SS and Nazi Party leaders, Globocnik was transferred to Trieste, ITALY where he was charged with suppressing the PARTISANS. At the end of the war he was captured by British soldiers and in May 1945 he took his own life.

GLUCKS, RICHARD

(1889–1945), SS officer who helped develop the Nazis' CONCENTRATION CAMP system.

Glucks joined the NAZI PARTY after HITLER rose to national power in 1933. In 1936 he became deputy to Theodor EICKE, who at that time was Inspector of Concentration Camps. Soon after WORLD WAR II broke out in September 1939, Glucks succeeded Eicke as inspector.

When Glucks took over the management of the concentration camps, their main purpose was to make use of slave laborers for the war effort. Under Glucks' direction, the number of concentration camps swelled, as did the number of concentration camp inmates. All prisoners, Jews and non-Jews alike, were made to do hard FORCED LABOR, and many died from disease, maltreatment, and starvation.

Glucks was a major contributor to the execution of the "FINAL SOLUTION"—the destruction of European Jewry. He established AUSCHWITZ, where millions of Jews were exterminated; was in charge of the construction of GAS CHAMBERS; and helped develop the MEDICAL EXPERIMENTS program that was carried out in the concentration camps.

In 1942 Glucks was made responsible for a unit of the Economic-Administrative Main Office

(WIRTSCHAFTS-VERWALTUNGSHAUPTAMT), which dealt with industrial companies regarding the use of concentration camp prisoners as slave laborers in their factories. Glucks committed suicide in May 1945.

GOEBBELS, JOSEPH (1897–1945), Nazi minister of Propaganda.

Goebbels was born in Rheydt, GERMANY, to a poor, religious Catholic family. Because he had a clubfoot, Goebbels was unable to serve in World War I. Instead he earned a doctorate in literature and philosophy, hoping to become a writer. He was partly able to fulfill his aspirations by joining the Nazis in 1924 and editing a party journal.

Soon, Goebbels gained a reputation as a dynamic speaker and propagandist. In 1926 he was made district party leader of BERLIN; his assignment was to win over the capital for the party. In 1928 Goebbels became the party's chief of propaganda, and it was he who coordinated the Nazis' election campaign that brought HITLER to national power in January 1933.

In March 1933 Goebbels was made minister of propaganda and public information. His goal was to "Nazify" the art and culture of Germany. Accordingly, he ordered all "un-German" books burnt on May 10, 1933. Goebbels used radio and propaganda films to win over supporters. He was also responsible for creating a cult of personality for Hitler. In November 1938, it was Goebbels' idea to exploit the murder of a German diplomat in FRANCE by a Jewish youth (Herschel GRYNSZPAN), to stage a violent pogrom against the Jews of Germany. He gave this violent outburst its cynical name KRISTALLNACHT.

During the war Goebbels directed the Nazis' psychological warfare propaganda campaign. He turned the Germans against their "enemies" by creating and spreading lies and hatred. He depicted the Jews as subhuman creatures who were the Germans' greatest enemies. Goebbels thought that people would only believe lies if they were repeated often enough, and that the bigger the lie, the greater the chance it would be believed.

Despite the fact that Goebbels was an adoring fan of Adolf Hitler, Hitler did not always return the admiration. Their relationship stabilized, though, when Goebbels supported Hitler after a failed attempt on Hitler's life. As the war was about to end, Hitler named Goebbels his successor, but Goebbels refused. The day after Hitler committed suicide in his bunker, Goebbels and

Joseph Goebbels addressing Nazis

his wife followed suit, after ordering the execution of their six children. Russian troops identified Goebbels' body several hours later. (see also PROPAGANDA, NAZI.)

GOERING, HERMANN (GORING) (1893–1946), Nazi leader, founder of the Nazi GESTAPO, and commander of the German Air Force.

Goering was born in Rosenheim, Bavaria, into a wealthy family. During World War I he served as a fighter pilot and won many medals for bravery. He joined the NAZI PARTY in 1922 after getting to know Adolf HITLER. He was soon appointed commander of the Storm Troopers (SA), the party's private army. In November 1923 Goering joined Hitler in his unsuccessful bid to take over the Bavarian government.

Goering had connections with members of the German aristocracy, so he was sent to BERLIN to procure financial support for the party. In 1928 he convinced Hitler to let him represent the Nazi Party in the German parliament (REICHSTAG); he became speaker of the *Reichstag* in 1932 and helped Hitler to power in 1933.

Goering was given several positions in Hitler's government, and helped create the Nazi *Gestapo*. In 1934,

Hermann Goering (front center) in Linz, Austria, two weeks after the Anschluss, March 25, 1938

he and Heinrich HIMMLER led the "Night of the Long Knives" in which they murdered SA leader Ernst ROHM. Goering was appointed commander of the German Air Force (*Luftwaffe*) in 1935.

In 1936 Goering was put in charge of Hitler's FOUR-YEAR PLAN, an economic program whose goal was to revitalize the German army and economy within four years, in anticipation of war. Thus, Goering was given extensive powers within the economic sphere; one of his responsibilities was the confiscation of Jewish property.

When war broke out, Hitler appointed Goering his successor. On July 31, 1941 Goering set the stage for the "FINAL SOLUTION" when he ordered Reinhard HEY-DRICH to make preparations to resolve the "Jewish question" in Europe.

Goering fell out of Hitler's good graces when the *Luftwaffe* failed to conquer GREAT BRITAIN and protect GERMANY from attack. Goering spent the rest of the war on his estate, until he was completely removed of rank when he declared himself *Fuehrer* during the last days of the Nazi regime. Goering was convicted as a war criminal at the NUREMBERG TRIALS. He was sentenced to death, but poisoned himself in his cell hours before his execution.

GOETH, AMON LEOPOLD   (1908–1946), SS officer and commandant of the CONCENTRATION CAMP at PLASZOW, located outside of CRACOW.

Born in VIENNA, AUSTRIA, Goeth joined the NAZI PARTY in 1932 and the SS in 1940, in which he reached the rank of SS-*Hauptsturmfuehrer*. When the Nazis began deporting Jews from GHETTOS in the GENERALGOU-VERNEMENT to EXTERMINATION CAMPS, Goeth was assigned to serve in the SS command headquarters and in the LUBLIN police. Next, he was relocated to Cracow where he oversaw the liquidation of the ghettos and FORCED LABOR camps at Szebnie, Bochnia, Tarnow, Cracow, and other places.

From February 1943 to September 1944 Goeth served as commandant at the Plaszow camp (as portrayed in the film, *Schindler's List*), which held some 10,000 inmates at its most crowded. Most of these prisoners were from the Cracow Ghetto, and were later sent to their deaths at AUSCHWITZ.

After the war Goeth was extradited to POLAND, and tried before the Polish Supreme Court. He was charged with the mass murder of Jews during the liquidations of the Szebnie and Plaszow camps. He was sentenced to death for his crimes, and hanged in Cracow.

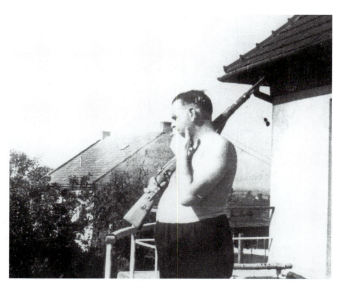

Amon Goeth taking a break from shooting prisoners at random in Plaszow (Photo: USHM, Washington)

GOGA, OCTAVIAN

(1881–1938), One of the leaders of the antisemitic movement in ROMANIA.

Goga's antisemitic ideas were very influenced by the nationalist conflict between the Romanians and Hungarians in TRANSYLVANIA. He believed that the Jews as a group were hopelessly pro-Hungarian, and thus should be removed from Romania. During the 1930s Goga became close to Alexandru CUZA, who touted a similar antisemitic ideology, and began supporting the Nazis. The two men formed the Christian National Party in 1935. The Nazis considered Goga someone worth investing in: like them, Goga always referred to the Jewish problem in his speeches, and his party's thugs attacked Jews and political opponents.

At the end of 1937, Goga became prime minister of a short-lived Romanian government. As the first Romanian leader to come to power on an obviously antisemitic platform like that of the Nazis, Goga focused his energies on carrying out his antisemitic policies. In January 1938 he passed the Law for the Reexamination of Citizenship of the Jews, in which he cancelled the civil rights of one-third of Romanian Jewry. However, he was forced to step down one month later due to French and British pressure. Goga, of course, blamed this on the Jews.

GRABE, HERMANN FRIEDRICH

(1900–1986), German who rescued dozens of Jews during the HOLOCAUST. As a construction worker with the Jung Company, Grabe was asked to establish a company branch in the UKRAINE in October 1941. Grabe hired thousands of Jews to work in the new branch, and made sure that they were treated fairly. He managed to convince the district's Nazi commander to cancel fines that the Jews had been ordered to pay, and rescued his Jewish workers from the murderous *aktionen* in Rovno in November 1941 and July 1942.

Grabe had many Jews working for him in the company's headquarters. In the summer of 1942 they were at risk of being deported. Grabe gave them forged identity papers and sent them to a different city to work in a "new" company branch; in fact, Grabe had established the "branch" without telling his superiors, and supported the Jews there out of his own pocket.

In the NUREMBERG TRIALS, Grabe testified about the persecution of the Jews in his area, including the extermination of the Jews of Dubno which he had seen with his own eyes. Because of this, he was hated in GERMANY, so he moved with his family to California. In 1966 he was designated as RIGHTEOUS AMONG THE NATIONS by YAD VASHEM.

GREAT BRITAIN

Country in northwestern Europe. Before and during WORLD WAR II, Great Britain's policy on intervening in GERMANY'S affairs and its policy on accepting REFUGEES from Nazi-dominated Europe developed and changed based on the course of world events.

Despite Great Britain's victory over Germany in World War I, the British did not come out of the war unscathed: thousands of soldiers had perished and much money and materials had been spent. The British army was nowhere near ready for another world war, while the public was not ready to support a program to rearm the military. Thus, Britain tried to cover up its weakness with a policy of "appeasement." This meant that it tried to keep war at bay by making compromises and letting potentially dangerous countries, such as Germany, do what they wanted without stopping them. Britain also pursued a policy of appeasement because some British authorities felt guilty over the harsh way they had dealt with the vanquished Germans after World War I, and thus wanted to make it up to them. Therefore, when Germany invaded and annexed AUSTRIA in March 1938, Britain did nothing. When it became painfully obvious that HITLER planned to invade Czechoslovakia next, British Prime Minister Neville Chamberlain actively tried to cooperate with and appease him in order to avoid all-out war in Europe. At the MUNICH CONFERENCE of September 1938, Chamberlain met with Hitler in Germany, and officially gave Hitler his consent to annex the Sudeten region of Czechoslovakia. Chamberlain declared that he had achieved "peace in our time" and truly believed that he had actively avoided another world war.

However, Hitler did not live up to his word, and in March 1939 he took the next step in his quest to dominate all of Europe by occupying the rest of Czechoslovakia. By that time, Britain realized that its appeasement policy had been a complete and utter failure, and Chamberlain and his government were forced to find a new way of dealing with Germany. They guaranteed military support to ROMANIA and POLAND, which they expected would be Hitler's next stomping grounds. When Germany did indeed invade Poland in September 1939, Britain stood by its promises, and declared war on Germany. From then on, and especially after Winston CHURCHILL took over the job of prime minister in May 1940, Great Britain was completely committed to once again vanquishing Germany, with "no negotiations" and "unconditional surrender" as its new foreign policies. From the fall of FRANCE in June 1940 until the turn of events in 1941 (the Nazi invasion of the SOVIET UNION and the Japanese attack on Pearl Harbor), Britain faced Nazi Germany and its allies alone. The British played a fundamental role in the defeat of the Axis powers.

Britain's response to Jewish refugees fleeing the Nazis also evolved before and during the war. Soon after Hitler rose to national power in Germany in January 1933, thousands of Jewish and non-Jewish refugees flocked to Great Britain, which had a longstanding tradition of admitting those in need of a safe haven. However, the British government made it rather difficult for refugees to enter. Based on the country's immigration laws of 1919, no distinction was made between the refugees and other immigrants to Britain, so the refugees were not granted any special treatment due to their special situation. Those that were allowed in were only accepted on a temporary basis.

The British public was quite sympathetic to the refugees, as were the Jews of Britain, who quickly began establishing refugee aid organizations, such as the Jewish Refugee Committee. In April 1933 the committee's director, Otto Schiff, and the chairmen of the BOARD OF DEPUTIES OF BRITISH JEWS, Neville Laski and Leonard Montefiore, met with British government authorities; they promised them that the Jewish community would provide financial support for every Jew-

ish refugee that entered Britain, and that no refugee would become a burden on the government. In fact, until the end of 1939, British Jewish organizations fully supported the thousands of Jewish refugees that entered Britain, with money, housing, education, job training, and help with further emigration.

After the KRISTALLNACHT pogrom took place in Germany in November 1938, pro-refugee groups and certain members of Parliament put a lot of pressure on the government to change its immigration policy for refugees, and in fact, unlike other countries at that time, Britain eased its immigration regulations. In all, more than 80,000 Jewish refugees reached Britain by September 1939. However, when World War II broke out, Britain banned all emigration from Nazi-controlled territories. Throughout the rest of the war, only some 10,000 Jewish refugees managed to find their way into Britain. In addition, the British WHITE PAPER OF 1939 further limited European Jewry's chances of finding refuge in that it restricted Jewish immigration to Palestine, which was under the control of the British Mandate authorities.

For the lucky Jews who had successfully reached Britain before it closed its doors at the beginning of the war, life was not easy. Many highly educated people could only find work as domestics. After Germany invaded and conquered several northern and western European countries in mid-1940, the British public began to panic. Fearing that anyone with a German accent might be a spy, the British government began imprisoning Germans and Austrians who had settled in Britain, calling them "enemy aliens." This included Jewish refugees from Nazi-occupied Germany and Austria. About 30,000 were interned in camps in Britain itself (where in some cases Jews and pro-Nazi Germans were put together), while 8,000 were deported to CANADA and Australia (some of whom died when their ships were hit by torpedoes). As the threat of a German invasion passed, the prisoners were released and some of the deportees were returned to Britain.

From 1942 on, the British government knew about the Germans' execution of the "FINAL SOLUTION." However, after winning the war, Britain still did not open the gates of immigration to Palestine, and physically turned away thousands of Holocaust SURVIVORS who wanted to make a fresh start in a Jewish homeland. Only after the Jews in Palestine rebelled against the British Mandate authorities did the British give up their control over the region.

GREECE Country in southeast Europe. The Italians attacked Greece in 1940–1941. The Greeks were able to hold off the Italians, but when the Germans joined the struggle in April 1941, all of Greece soon came under AXIS control. Greece was divided between the Axis countries GERMANY, ITALY, and BULGARIA.

At first, the Germans delayed their attack on the Jews of Greece. One reason was that the Italians did not want to discriminate against the Jews. This prevented the Nazis from separating the Jews from the rest of the population. Jews in the German section recognized this difference, and many escaped into Italian-occupied Greece. The Germans tried to halt this outflow by demanding that Jews wear the yellow badge. The Italians refused to require the Badge. (see BADGE JEWISH.)

The systematic destruction of Greek Jewry, which began in early 1943, had three separate phases. The Jews of SALONIKA in German-occupied Greece were the first to be forced into GHETTOS for DEPORTATION. They were soon followed by the Jews in Bulgarian areas. The Italians repeatedly refused to deport the Jews living in their Greek territories, even though the Germans pressured them. The Italians knew what the Germans planned for the Jews. On a number of occasions, the Italians announced that Jews in their territories would be brought into Italy proper, or could be concentrated together on the Greek islands. However, after Italy broke away from the Axis in September 1943, Germany seized all of Italian Greece.

Dieter WISLICENY and Alois BRUNNER directed the anti-Jewish actions in Greece on behalf of Adolf EICHMANN. In October 1943, the full range of Nazi anti-Jewish laws was extended across the newly occupied territories. Jews were ordered to register themselves and their property–or be shot.

In March 1944, Jews living in Athens were rounded up and deported by the WEHRMACHT and Greek police. They were sent to the EXTERMINATION CAMPS in POLAND. The property of these Jews was distributed to the general population in order to improve relations between the occupiers and the occupied. Many other Jews—perhaps 2,000—had been hidden due to the activism of Rabbi Barzilai and Christian Greeks. Many Jews in smaller towns and on the islands also avoided deportation as the warnings of Rabbi Barzilai and Archbishop Damaskinos echoed across the country. On the island of Volos, for example, 752 Jews were hidden and 130 deported. However, 1,800 to 2,000 Jews from CORFU were deported to their deaths in June 1944, as were 1,700 to 2,200 Jews from Rhodes one month later.

A number of Greek Jews participated in the uprising in AUSCHWITZ-Birkenau in October 1944. Others were among the inmates who blew up a crematorium at the death camp.

Of Greece's prewar Jewish population of some 77,000, at least 60,000 died in the Holocaust.

GREISER, ARTHUR (1897–1946), Governor of the WARTHEGAU, a Polish region attached to the Reich after the invasion of POLAND in 1939.

Greiser was one of the founders of the Steel Helmet nationalist organization of DANZIG in 1924. In 1928 he joined the NAZI PARTY and the Storm Troopers (SA). After a while, he switched over to the SS. He held various positions in the Nazi Party in Danzig and was appointed president of its senate in 1934.

During the German invasion of Poland in 1939, Greiser became the head of the civil management in the Poznan district. By the next month, he was appointed governor of the Warthegau. Unlike other governors of Polish territories, Greiser managed to retain support for himself among Nazi leaders, and maintain a good relationship with Heinrich HIMMLER. As governor, Greiser wanted to rid his region of Poles and replace them with VOLKSDEUTSCHE (ethnic Germans). He took

Arthur Greiser (front center) in Poland, 1939

away Polish property, placed Polish orphans with "Aryan" families, terrorized the clergy, and limited cultural and educational programs. From 1939–1945 he kicked out 630,000 Jews and Poles and replaced them with 537,000 ethnic Germans.

Greiser was tried by a Polish court in 1946. He was hanged in front of the Warthegau governor's mansion.

GROBELNY, JULIAN (1893–1944), Polish Socialist nationalist who headed ZEGOTA, the Polish Council for Aid to Jews. Grobelny provided relief to thousands of needy Jews, especially children, whom he hid in foster homes, public orphanages, and convents.

GRODNO City in western BELORUSSIA. Between the two world wars, Grodno belonged to POLAND. When WORLD WAR II broke out in September 1939, Grodno was annexed to the SOVIET UNION under the terms of the NAZI-SOVIET PACT. At that time, 25,000 Jews lived in the city.

The Germans invaded the Soviet Union in June 1941. They reached Grodno on the first day of the invasion, and immediately seized all Jews aged 16–60 for FORCED LABOR. In July the Nazis killed 80 Jewish intellectuals. In November the Germans established two GHETTOS: "A" for skilled workers, and "B" for "nonproductive" Jews. There was an active cultural and communal life in these two ghettos.

Situated between VILNA and BIALYSTOK, Grodno was a focal point for the Jewish underground. In early 1942 a resistance movement was created there, which unsuccessfully tried to assassinate the ghetto commandants.

DEPORTATIONS from Grodno began in November 1942. Thousands of Jews were sent to AUSCHWITZ; others to Kielbasin, a transit camp on the way to EXTERMINATION CAMPS. Many Jews fled to the forests, but were not accepted by the non-Jewish PARTISANS. Suffering from hunger and cold, some returned to Grodno. Others organized themselves, took revenge on peasant collaborators, and later joined Soviet units.

Soviet troops liberated Grodno on July 14, 1944. About 200 Jews from the city were still alive, including partisans.

GROJANOWSKI REPORT Report on the extermination of Jews in CHELMNO, written in 1942 by the ONEG SHABBAT Archives of the WARSAW Ghetto. The report was based on the statements of Jacob Grojanowski, the first person to escape Chelmno.

In January 1942 Grojanowski was rounded up with other Jews from his hometown and deported to Chelmno, an EXTERMINATION CAMP near LODZ, POLAND. He was forced to work there burying the Jews and GYPSIES who had been murdered in GAS VANS. In February Grojanowski escaped the camp and traveled to the Warsaw GHETTO. He then gave testimony to the ghetto's archives, headed by Emanuel RINGELBLUM, regarding his experiences in Chelmno. This included a detailed description of the way people were murdered in gas vans, and the procedure that followed—including the removal of the corpses from the vans, cleaning the inside of the vans, and burying the bodies in large pits. Grojanowski also described his escape, the bleak condition of the prisoners forced to deal with the dead, and the brutality of the murderers.

Oneg Shabbat wrote up their report in Polish and German; the Polish version was sent to the DELEGATURA, the underground representatives of the POLISH GOVERNMENT-IN-EXILE, while the German copy was meant for the German people, to evoke their compassion for the Jews.

GROSMAN, HAIKA (1919–1993), PARTISAN and underground activist in BIALYSTOK.

Born in Bialystok, Grosman became an active member of the Zionist *Ha-Shomer ha-Tsa'ir* YOUTH MOVEMENT. When WORLD WAR II broke out in September 1939, Grosman moved to VILNA, LITHUANIA, an area that had not yet been overrun by the Nazis. In Vilna, Grosman helped recruit and unite members of the city's pioneering Zionist youth movements.

In June 1941 GERMANY invaded the SOVIET UNION and Grosman returned to Bialystok, where she helped organize an underground movement. Along with five other young women who posed as Poles—Liza Czapnik, Marila Ruziecka, Hasya Belicka (Borenstein), Bronka Winicki (Klibanski), and Ana Rud—she carried messages to various GHETTOS and helped the Jewish underground and the partisans who were then setting up bases around Bialystok. Grosman then became a member of a Jewish partisan unit, and in August 1943 she took part in the Bialystok Ghetto uprising.

After the region's LIBERATION, Grosman worked as the representative of *Ha-Shomer ha-Tsa'ir*. In 1948 she immigrated to Israel, where she joined Kibbutz Evron. She served in Israel's parliament (*Knesset*) from 1969 to 1981 and from 1984 to 1993. Her book, *The Underground Army*, was published in 1988.

GROSSMAN, MENDEL (1917–1945), Photographer in the LODZ Ghetto of POLAND who secretly documented on film the awful situation there during WORLD WAR II. The Germans made it illegal for Jews to photograph in the GHETTO. Grossman, however, worked in the ghetto's statistics department, where he had access to photography equipment and was allowed to keep a camera. He risked his life to shoot more than 10,000 pictures throughout the years that the ghetto existed, from early 1940 to its liquidation in September 1944.

After the ghetto was destroyed, Grossman was deported to the Koenigs Wusterhausen labor camp. Even there, he kept on taking photos in secret, but did not develop and print them. As the Allies approached, the Germans sent the prisoners in the camp on a DEATH MARCH, during which Grossman collapsed and died—with his camera still on him.

Grossman had hid the negatives of his photographs in the ghetto before its liquidation. After the war, they were found and sent to Israel. However, most were lost during the War of Independence in 1948. Those that were saved were put in a book published in 1977, called *With a Camera in the Ghetto*.

GROSS-ROSEN Polish CONCENTRATION CAMP located south of the town of Gross-Rosen (Rogozhnica) in Lower Silesia. Gross-Rosen was established in the summer of 1940 as a satellite labor camp of the SACHSENHAUSEN concentration camp. On May 1, 1941 Gross-Rosen became an independent camp; it functioned as such until its evacuation in February 1945. Altogether, 125,000 prisoners passed through Gross-Rosen; 40,000 perished.

Gross-Rosen was commanded by Arthur Roedl, Wilhelm Gideon, and Johannes Hassebroock. At the beginning, prisoners were forced to work at constructing the camp and in the nearby granite quarry, which was owned by the SS German Earth and Stone Works (*SS-Deutsche Erd- und Steinwerke GmbH*). However, as the Germans' need for armaments grew, Gross-Rosen also grew: arms factories were built, 70 sub-camps (satellite camps) were ultimately added, and the number of prisoners swelled.

Jews made up the largest group of inmates. The first small group of Jews arrived at Gross-Rosen from DACHAU on June 8, 1941. Throughout the rest of 1941 and 1942 several more small groups of Jews were brought from other camps and from Polish GHETTOS. The Jewish prisoners were subjected to extremely hard

work in the quarry and were forced to carry out special assignments during their breaks. Inmates of different blocks were not allowed to talk to each other. They were also denied medical treatment. Some of these Jews were then sent on to Dachau, and 119 were murdered in December 1941 as part of the EUTHANASIA PROGRAM. The last of these Jewish prisoners were transferred to AUSCHWITZ in October 1942; for the following year there were no Jews in Gross-Rosen.

From October 1943 until January 1945, 57,000 Jews were brought to the camp (including 26,000 women). They were mostly from POLAND and HUNGARY, with smaller groups originally from FRANCE, BELGIUM, YUGOSLAVIA, ITALY, SLOVAKIA, and GREECE. Many were placed in the sub-camps where they worked for the German company, I.G. FARBEN and Krupp. Gross-Rosen took over 28 camps from ORGANIZATION SCHMELDT and kept 20 in operation. Fifteen of those were set aside for 6,000–7,000 women prisoners. Altogether, Gross-Rosen had 20 sub-camps for women, which were governed less harshly.

More sub-camps were set up between April and June 1944 to house 13,000 new Jewish arrivals. Most had come from Hungary and were used to build HITLER'S underground home. Prisoners were frequently transferred from one sub-camp to another. In all, the Jews were spread out over 50 sub-camps, where the death rate was extraordinarily high.

In its last stage of existence, the Gross-Rosen compound held 78,000 prisoners, including 52,000 men and 26,000 women. These made up 11 percent of the prisoners in all concentration camps at that time.

The Nazis began evacuating Gross-Rosen at the very end of 1944. The first sub-camps to be destroyed were those on the eastern bank of the Oder River. The prisoners from those camps were sent away on foot in DEATH MARCHES; many died along the way. The main camp was cleared out in February 1945, followed by the rest of the sub-camps. The prisoners of the main camp were evacuated by train rather than by foot, but many died anyway because they were not given any food en route. Altogether, at least 19,500 Jewish inmates were transferred from Gross-Rosen to camps within the German Reich; nothing is known about the fate of the other 37,500. It is also not clear how many Jewish prisoners actually died in the Gross-Rosen camp, but approximately one-half of the prisoners in the sub-camps were left behind during evacuation. About 9,000 survived in 13 of the 20 women's sub-camps.

However, it does seem that many Gross-Rosen inmates did survive long enough to be liberated.

GRYNSZPAN, HERSCHEL (1921–1943?), Jewish assassin of a German diplomat in PARIS. Born into a Polish-Jewish family in Hanover, GERMANY, Grynszpan escaped to FRANCE in 1936. In early November 1938 Grynszpan found out that his family, along with thousands of other Jews born in POLAND, had been deported from Germany back to Poland. As neither country wanted to take responsibility for the deportees, they had dumped them in a no-man's-land on the German-Polish border (see also ZBASZYN). Grynszpan was outraged, and decided to assassinate a German official in protest. On November 7 he entered the German embassy in Paris and after being introduced to Ernst vom Rath, the embassy's third secretary, Grynszpan shot him at close range. Grynszpan immediately turned himself in, and vom Rath died two days later. The Germans used the assassination as an excuse to launch the KRISTALLNACHT pogrom all over Germany and AUSTRIA.

After the German invasion of France in 1940, the French authorities surrendered Grynszpan to the Germans. In 1942 Nazi Minister of Propaganda Joseph GOEBBELS planned a sensational show trial, intending to show the connection between Grynszpan and a Jewish conspiracy to cause war in Europe. However, the trial never took place, and Grynszpan's fate is unknown. However, he probably did not survive the war.

GURS Prison camp located in the Pyrenees Mountains of southwestern FRANCE, 50 miles from the Spanish border. Gurs was originally established in April 1939 by the French government, in order to detain Spanish Republican soldiers running from SPAIN after their defeat in the Spanish Civil War.

After France fell to GERMANY in mid-1940, Gurs was located in the zone unoccupied by the Germans, which was controlled by the Vichy government. At that point, many Jewish REFUGEES fled to southern France hoping to escape the German army. However, the Vichy authorities imprisoned many of those refugees in Gurs and other camps like it. In addition, the German authorities deported to Gurs thousands of Jews from the German regions of Baden and Palatinate. Some of these prisoners were released over the next two years and moved overseas.

In spite of the severe conditions at Gurs, the prison-

Prisoners performing forced labor in Gurs

ers managed to conduct high level cultural activities, education courses, and religious services on a regular basis.

After Germany occupied southern France in November 1942, the Germans began deporting Jews from prison camps like Gurs to EXTERMINATION CAMPS in POLAND. By late 1943 some 6,000 Jews had been deported, and only 48 remained. Gurs was liberated by the Allies in the summer of 1944. (for more on Vichy, see also FRANCE.)

GUSEN Satellite camp of the MAUTHAUSEN concentration camp in GERMANY. Gusen was established in March 1940 to compensate for the phenomenal growth of Mauthausen. It was liberated on May 5, 1945.

During 1940 some 5,000 prisoners arrived at Gusen, where they worked in brickyards and quarries. During that time, more than 1,500 prisoners died or were killed there. During the first half of 1942, over 2,000 Soviet prisoners were brought to Gusen.

Scaffold for executions in Gusen

The living conditions at Gusen were quite brutal. Prisoners were made to work at a backbreaking pace, and those who could not keep up were killed. One of the camp's barracks was designated for prisoners who were to be executed by poisonous injection and was also used for the fatal beatings of those prisoners too weak to work. In addition, groups of prisoners from Gusen were taken to be killed in the GAS CHAMBERS of the nearby Hartheim castle.

Two more satellite camps, Gusen II and III, were instituted in 1944. The prisoners at Gusen II worked on constructing tunnels to underground armaments factories.

Altogther, 67,677 people were interned at the Gusen camps, of whom 31,535 were recorded as having died, not including the 2,500 Jews whose deaths were not recorded, and the 2,630 prisoners gassed at Hartheim—a former EUTHANASIA PROGRAM installation.

GWARDIA LUDOWA   see HOME GUARD, POLAND.

GYPSIES   (*Roma*, *Sinti*), a people who have been living in Europe since the fifteenth century, who share a common language, culture, and until the twentieth century, a wandering way of life. The Gypsies, also called *Roma*, were one of the groups persecuted by the Nazis. About 200,000 Gypsies, and possibly more, were killed throughout Europe.

The Gypsies probably originally came from India, and migrated to Iran by the fourteenth century. They reached HUNGARY, SERBIA, and other Balkan countries by 1438. Next, they spread into POLAND, Russia, SWEDEN, SPAIN, and GREAT BRITAIN. Some Gypsies converted to Islam or Orthodoxy, but most became Catholics, while still observing much of their pre-Christian religion. Their language split into many dialects; only today is it becoming a written language.

Because of their nomadic lifestyle, the Gypsies made a living mainly from trading horses and other animals, peddling, silver and gold work, and music. They were not allowed to own land where they lived, and were often accused of stealing by the locals. Because the Gypsies were deemed different and foreign, they were treated in a hostile manner by their adopted countries.

When the Nazis came to power, they slated the Gypsies for persecution, because the Gypsies represented a contradiction to the Aryan ideal. They were not as bad as Jews, but they were not of pure Aryan blood, they did not live a settled way of life, and they did not fit into the kind of society to which the Nazis aspired. The Nazis sought to determine which Gypsies were most harmful. Their treatment of Gypsies was influenced by whether they were "pure" or of mixed blood, and whether they lived a traditional Gypsy lifestyle or not. Since at various times the Nazis regarded these factors differently, Gypsies were treated inconsistently. Some Gypsies were murdered, others were enslaved, others were to be sterilized and others were largely left alone.

The NUREMBERG LAWS of September 1935 included the Gypsies in their discrimination. In 1936, groups of Gypsies were taken to the DACHAU camp. A Nazi named Richard Ritter set to the task of deciding what to do with the Gypsy population. He called for the separation of Gypsies from Aryans, and MISCHLINGE Gypsies from pure Gypsies, and for the sterilization and imprisonment of the *Mischlinge*. In 1939 Heinrich HIMMLER announced the removal of 30,000 Gypsies from GERMANY to the GENERALGOUVERNEMENT; only 2,500 were deported. On December 16, 1942 Himmler ordered the transfer of the *Mischlinge* Gypsies to AUSCHWITZ, with the exception of a few former German soldiers, important war industry workers, and those who were "socially adapted," who were to be sterilized instead. In 1943 and 1944 thousands of Gypsies were deported to Auschwitz. They lived under horrible conditions. Many died of starvation, illness, and MEDICAL EXPERIMENTS. Others were murdered. In total, about 24,000 Gypsies from Germany and AUSTRIA were sent to CONCENTRATION CAMPS. Approximately 13,500 others were saved. Only a few hundred Czech Gypsies survived.

In German-occupied Europe, Gypsies often were murdered along with the Jews. Generally, the Nazis would imprison the Gypsies and then transport them to Germany or Poland to be killed. In YUGOSLAVIA alone, 90,000 were exterminated. Gypsies from the NETHER-LANDS, LUXEMBOURG, FRANCE, and BELGIUM were arrested and sent to Auschwitz. About 16,000–18,000 Gypsies from non-occupied France were murdered in German camps. Some Italian Gypsies were interned, some were made to perform FORCED LABOR, and others were sent to EXTERMINATION CAMPS. Many Gypsies from Hungary were deported. About 25,000 Romanian Gypsies died, and Slovak Gypsies were forced into labor brigades, expelled, and murdered by their Slovak countrymen. In Poland, Gypsies were put in the GHETTOS, and sent to camps; about two-thirds of the Polish Gypsies died, numbering 25,000. In the SOVIET UNION and the Baltic States, a distinction was sometimes made between settled and nomadic Gypsies. Those Gypsies from BULGARIA, DENMARK, FINLAND, and GREECE were spared.

Gypsies imprisoned by the Nazis

H

HA'AVARA AGREEMENT see TRANSFER AGREEMENT.

HAGUE, THE Capital of the NETHERLANDS.

The Germans occupied the Netherlands in 1940; at that time, 18,000 Jews lived in The Hague. The Germans set up their main government offices in The Hague, meaning that the city's Jews were dealt with directly by the Jewish affairs department of the Reich Security Main Office (REICHSSICHERHEITSHAUPTAMT, RSHA). Thus, the Jews were treated especially badly: as early as September 1940, about 2,000 Jews who did not hold Dutch citizenship were forced to leave the city.

The Germans began deporting the city's Jews in August 1942. About 4,000 were ordered to travel to the Dutch transit camp at WESTERBORK, but only 1,200 appeared. The Germans then began arresting Jews in their homes. Large-scale DEPORTATIONS began again in January 1943. In April 1943 many Jews from The Hague were sent to the camp at VUGHT. Altogether, 15,000 Jews from The Hague were deported to Nazi camps, and only a few survived. About 2,000 Jews remained in hiding in The Hague. Jews married to non-Jews were drafted for FORCED LABOR instead of being deported.

HAHN, LUDWIG (b. 1908), SS officer. Hahn joined the NAZI PARTY in 1930 and the SS in 1933. In 1935 he enlisted in the SS's Security Service (SD). In 1936 he became an SS officer, and quickly rose through the Nazi hierarchy.

When WORLD WAR II broke out in September 1939, Hahn commanded an EINSATZGRUPPE unit in POLAND. In January 1940 he became Security Police (SIPO) and SD commander in CRACOW. In August 1940 he was appointed to serve as the representative of SS chief Heinrich HIMMLER in BRATISLAVA, the capital of SLOVAKIA. A year later Hahn was named SIPO and SD commander in WARSAW. In that post, Hahn was responsible for deporting the city's Jews to TREBLINKA, and arranging the massacre of thousands of Poles in Warsaw's PAWIAK PRISON.

Ludwig Hahn

In December 1944 Hahn was sent to FRANCE to command an *Einsatzgruppe.* He was then sent to the Vistula Army commanded by Himmler. Just weeks before the war ended, Hahn became senior SIPO and SD commander in Westphalia, GERMANY.

After the war Hahn changed his identity and went into hiding. In 1949 he resumed his former life. After two arrests, he was finally sentenced to life imprisonment in July 1975.

HAMBURG Second-largest city in GERMANY and fourth-largest German Jewish community during the early 1930s. In 1933 there were 16,885 Jews living in Hamburg. Most were well-integrated in city life and were quite assimilated. After the Nazis rose to power in January 1933, incidents of persecution increased. During the anti-Jewish boycott of April 1, 1933, some parts of Hamburg's population did not participate in ostracizing the Jews (see also BOYCOTT, ANTI-JEWISH). However, Jews were soon removed from government positions, the court system, health service institutions, and the city's university. Between 1933 and 1937, 5,000 Hamburg Jews left Germany.

During the KRISTALLNACHT pogrom of November 1938, most of Hamburg's synagogues were vandalized. Jewish community organizations were soon shut down, and in April 1939, the two Jewish schools were combined into one, which stayed open until late 1942.

From 1941–1945, Jews were deported on 17 transports to LODZ, MINSK, RIGA, AUSCHWITZ, and THERESIENSTADT. More than 300 of the city's Jews committed suicide; 80 during the height of the DEPORTATIONS in late 1941. By 1943, there were only 1,800 Jews left in Hamburg, most of whom were married to non-Jews. The Jewish community was officially liquidated in June of that year. In all, about 7,800 Hamburg Jews were murdered in the HOLOCAUST.

HASAG (*Hugo Schneider Aktiengesellschaft-Metalwarenfabrik*), one of the privately owned German companies that used CONCENTRATION CAMP prisoners as forced laborers. HASAG, which manufactured armaments, was the third largest of such companies, after I.G. FARBEN and the Herman Goering Works.

In 1932 a NAZI PARTY member and SS officer named Paul Budin became general manager of HASAG. In 1933 the company became the German army's regular ammunitions supplier. In 1934 HASAG was officially designated as a *Wehrmachtsbetrieb,* a company working for the armed forces. In 1939 its classification was raised to that of *Ruestungsbetrieb,* meaning armaments company. In 1940 Budin was made responsible for the production of all light ammunition for the air force and infantry; his responsibilities were expanded in 1942. In 1944 HASAG was assigned a contract to produce infantry rocket launchers.

During WORLD WAR II HASAG had eight factories inside GERMANY. Two types of workers were employed at these factories. The first group included civilian workers from all over Europe, especially the Slavic countries. Some of these employees volunteered to work for HASAG, but most were forced laborers. The second group of workers consisted of concentration camp prisoners. In the summer of 1944 the Nazis set up labor camps next to each HASAG factory. In all, some 41,000 prisoners passed through the HASAG labor camps.

HASAG also opened its doors in POLAND during the war. In 1940 HASAG was put in charge of the ammunitions factories in SKARZYSKO-KAMIENNA, the grenade factory in KIELCE, and the foundry in Czestochowa. In early 1943 HASAG bought those factories from the GENERALGOUVERNEMENT. After Germany invaded the SOVIET UNION in mid-1941, HASAG became the *Generalgouvernement's* main ammunitions supplier. Until 1942 it employed mostly Poles; at that time, HASAG began employing Jewish forced laborers, whose wages were paid directly to the SS. Six forced labor camps were built by HASAG in the Radom district. By June 1943 HASAG's camps held 17,000 Jewish prisoners, who were subjected to terrible conditions and periodic selections (see also SELEKTION). From July 1944 to early 1945, HASAG transferred most of its equipment, materials, and workers from the *Generalgouvernement* factories to its factories within the Reich. (see also FORCED LABOR.)

HASSELL, ULRICH VON (1881–1944), German diplomat who aided the German anti-Nazi resistance movement. Hassell aspired to overthrow the Nazi government and negotiate peace with the Allies, but the GESTAPO discovered his plans and executed him.

HAUPTTREUHANDSTELLE OST (HTO) (Main Trusteeship Office East), office responsible for the confiscation of Polish government property and property belonging to Polish citizens, including Jews, living within the Reich or within territories annexed to the Reich. The HTO was established in October 1939 by Hermann GOERING as part of his implementation of the FOUR-YEAR PLAN, the goal of which was the revitalization of the German army and economy. During the war, Goering created offices such as HTO to rob occupied POLAND and other countries of their property and raw materials in order to accomplish GERMANY's economic goals.

The HTO had its main office in BERLIN, with branches throughout occupied Poland. By 1942 the HTO had repossessed over 200,000 factories, shops, workshops, and businesses, the personal property found in 500,000 apartments, over 290,000 plots of land, and other valuables worth billions of zlotys, in addition to 270 million reichsmarks worth of Polish state and private property. Companies specifically established for this purpose dealt with the stolen property and materials.

HAUSNER, GIDEON (1915–1990), Israeli law expert who served as the chief prosecuting attorney in the riveting trial of senior SS officer Adolf EICHMANN, which took place in Jerusalem, Israel in 1961.

Gideon Hausner during the Eichmann Trial

Hausner was born in LVOV and reached Palestine in 1927. From 1960 to 1963 Hausner served as Israel's attorney general. It was during this term of office that he served as the chief prosecuting attorney in the EICHMANN TRIAL. Many feel that his opening remarks constituted one of the high points of the trial. Based on the incredible volume of evidence presented to the court by Hausner, Eichmann was convicted and sentenced to death—the first time that Israel had ever invoked the death sentence.

Hausner served as a member of the *Knesset* (Israel's parliament) from 1965 to 1981, and from 1972 to 1974 he joined the cabinet as a minister without portfolio. After retiring from the *Knesset*, Hausner became

the chairman of the World Council of YAD VASHEM, and traveled all over Israel and to many other countries, lecturing on the HOLOCAUST. He authored a book on the Eichmann trial called *Justice in Jerusalem,* which has since been translated into several languages

HAUTVAL, ADELAIDE (b. 1906), French doctor who was designated as RIGHTEOUS AMONG THE NATIONS by YAD VASHEM in 1965 for her efforts at helping Jews during the HOLOCAUST.

In April 1942 Hautval was caught trying to cross from the occupied zone of FRANCE into the unoccupied zone for her mother's funeral. She was arrested and put in jail to await her trial. During her detention, Hautval strenuously protested the mistreatment of the Jewish prisoners. As punishment for her outspokenness, she was sent to AUSCHWITZ where she was made to work as a doctor. In that capacity she protected as many prisoners as she could, including a group of women ill with typhus. Hautval hid the women on the top floor of her block, so that the Nazis did not discover the epidemic and murder those infected, as was their usual practice.

Later, one of Auschwitz's head SS doctors asked Hautval to do some gynecology work. Hautval soon found out that SS doctors were using defenseless female prisoners as human guinea pigs in brutal pseudo-scientific MEDICAL EXPERIMENTS; she spoke out against the experiments and refused to participate.

Hautval was transferred to the RAVENSBRUECK women's camp in mid-1944 where she stayed until LIBERATION in April 1945.

HEIL HITLER (in English, "Hail Hitler"), the greeting given as part of the Nazi salute. The salute consisted of raising an arm and saying the phrase "Heil Hitler." When addressing HITLER himself, the greeting "Heil mein Fuehrer" ("hail my leader") was used.

HESS, RUDOLF (1894–1987), Nazi leader and close aide to Adolf HITLER.

During World War I Hess served in the army as an infantry officer and later as a pilot. He was among the first to join the NAZI PARTY in 1920. In November 1923 Hess joined Hitler in his unsuccessful bid to take over the Bavarian government. As punishment, he was imprisoned along with Hitler in Landsberg Prison. During their time there, Hess took dictation for and edited Hitler's book, MEIN KAMPF.

guilty of crimes against peace. He was sentenced to life imprisonment, despite the demands of the Soviet judge, who wanted Hess executed. Hess was incarcerated in the Spandau Prison in West BERLIN, under the joint authority of the UNITED STATES, GREAT BRITAIN, SOVIET UNION, and FRANCE. For years, Hess was the only prisoner at Spandau. He committed suicide in 1987.

HEYDRICH, REINHARD (1904–1942), Nazi SS leader who was a key player in the planning and execution of the "FINAL SOLUTION." Heydrich served as head of the Nazi Security Police (SIPO), the Security Service (SD), and the Reich Security Main Office (REICHSSICHERHEITSHAUPTAMT, RSHA).

Heydrich was born in Halle, GERMANY to a family of musicians. He had a strict upbringing that included near-worship of state authority. He joined the German navy, but was dishonorably discharged in 1931 after being found guilty of misconduct with a female friend. That same year Heydrich became head of the Security Service (SD), the SS's espionage and intelligence organization (originally, he had viewed the SS with disdain, but relented after meeting Heinrich HIMMLER). At that point of his life, Heydrich gave himself over both to his new superiors and to his dark side: he was cruel, cynical, pitiless—and ambitious. This dangerous combination, along with his Aryan looks, allowed Heydrich to thrive in the Nazi hierarchy.

As chief of the SD, Heydrich reigned over the blackmail and information-getting that helped Himmler gain control over the GESTAPO, the German secret police. In 1936 Heydrich himself became executive director of the *Gestapo*, while retaining control of the SD. These two posts gave him unlimited power to send "enemies of the Reich" such as Jews to CONCENTRATION CAMPS. He also pitted his two agencies against each other in a race to see who could better carry out HITLER'S anti-Jewish policies.

By 1938 Heydrich began calling for the "forced emigration" of Jews as a solution to the "Jewish question." He was one of the main planners of the KRISTALLNACHT pogrom of November 9–10, 1938, and presided over the arrests of thousands of Jews.

On January 24, 1939 Hermann GOERING set up the Reich's Central Office for Jewish Emigration (ZENTRALSTELLE FUER JUEDISCHE AUSWANDERUNG) and appointed Heydrich's aide, Heinrich MUELLER, as its head. This meant that the execution of the Germans' anti-Jewish policies would now be in the hands of Heydrich and the SS.

Rudolf Hess in Nazi uniform

When they were let out of jail in 1925, Hess became Hitler's personal aide and private secretary. He held those posts until Hitler rose to power in January 1933. At that point, Hess was appointed deputy leader of the Nazi Party. He later served as a cabinet minister, and signed all laws passed by the Nazi regime.

As a dependable aide, Hitler trusted Hess with the execution of several important missions concerning Germany's annexation of AUSTRIA (ANSCHLUSS) and the Sudeten region of Czechoslovakia. However, he was soon appointed to the Secret Cabinet Council and Reich Ministerial Defense Council, committees with little power or influence. Hess believed that he was being cut out of the loop. This might have been his motivation for flying to England in May 1941, to convince British leaders that peace was possible with GERMANY. It is not known whether Hess undertook this mission alone, or was influenced to do so by Hitler. In any case, Hess was arrested as soon as he reached England, and Hitler denied any involvement. Hess was held in England until the end of the war.

Afterwards, Hess was tried at the main NUREMBERG TRIAL. In October 1946 he was acquitted of CRIMES AGAINST HUMANITY and war crimes, but was found

After the war broke out in 1939, Heydrich took charge of the EINSATZGRUPPEN; on September 21 he ordered them to begin forcing Polish Jews into GHETTOS and establishing Jewish councils called *Judenraete*. He ordered the Jews to concentrate in the large towns near transportation, ready for the next step of the "Final Solution". Heydrich then united the SD and the *Gestapo* into one agency, the RSHA. This allowed merciless SD members like Adolf EICHMANN total authority over Germany's anti-Jewish activities.

In 1941 Germany invaded the SOVIET UNION. Before the invasion, Heydrich ordered *Einsatzgruppen* in Russia to carry out the immediate annihilation of Soviet Jews and officials in the areas about to be occupied.

On July 31, 1941 Goering set Heydrich to the task of coming up with the "Final Solution" to the "Jewish question" of all the Jews in Europe. To successfully coordinate this, Heydrich needed the cooperation of all the government's ministries. Thus, he convened the WANNSEE CONFERENCE in BERLIN on January 20, 1942, to discuss and further organize the mass extermination of all European Jewry.

Later that year Heydrich was appointed acting governor of the Protectorate of Bohemia and Moravia (see

Reinhard Heydrich in Nazi uniform

also BOHEMIA AND MORAVIA, PROTECTORATE OF). This was apparently a reward for his "excellence" in anti-Jewish terror and the extermination campaign. Less than a year later, Heydrich was attacked by Czech resistance fighters in an ambush near PRAGUE. He died of his wounds on June 4, 1942. Five days later, the Germans retaliated by burning the Czech village of LIDICE to the ground and killing all of its men. AKTION REINHARD, which was the operation for the mass murder of the Jews of POLAND, was named for Heydrich.

HICEM   Organization established in 1927 whose goal was to help European Jews emigrate. HICEM was formed with the merger of three Jewish migration associations: HIAS (Hebrew Immigrant Aid Society), which was based in New York; ICA (Jewish Colonization Association), which was based in PARIS but registered as a British charitable society; and Emigdirect, a migration organization based in BERLIN. The name HICEM is an acronym of HIAS, ICA, and Emigdirect.

The agreement between the three organizations stipulated that all local branches outside the UNITED STATES would merge into HICEM, while HIAS would still deal with Jewish immigration to the US. However, Emigdirect was forced to withdraw from the merger in 1934, and later on, British wartime regulations restricted the ICA from using its funds outside Britain. Thus, for a while, HICEM was funded exclusively by HIAS.

By the time WORLD WAR II broke out in September 1939, HICEM had offices all over Europe, South and Central America, and the Far East. Its employees advised and prepared European REFUGEES for emigration, including helping them along during their departure and arrival.

HICEM's European headquarters were based in Paris. After GERMANY invaded and conquered FRANCE in mid-1940, HICEM decided to close its Paris offices and move them to Lisbon, Portugal. Portugal, a neutral country, was friendly with the Allies and had an officially recognized Jewish community. Thus, HICEM simply functioned as the immigration section of the Jewish community council. In addition, because Lisbon was a neutral port, by July 1940 it became the foremost route for Jews to escape Europe for North and South America. Other organizations also moved their European offices to Lisbon at that time, including the American Jewish JOINT DISTRIBUTION COMMITTEE (known as the JDC or Joint) and the AMERICAN FRIENDS SERVICE COMMITTEE.

From 1940 on, HICEM's activities were partly supported by the Joint. Despite the friction between the two organizations, they worked together to provide refugees with tickets, information about visas and transportation, and helped them leave Lisbon on neutral Portuguese ships. In all, some 90,000 Jews managed to escape Europe during the HOLOCAUST with HICEM's assistance.

HILFSVEREIN DER DEUTSCHEN JUDEN (Aid Association of German Jews), German Jewish organization established in 1901 mainly to help Jewish communities in Eastern Europe that had fallen victim to pogroms and wars.

It supported the creation of Jewish education and social welfare institutions in Eastern Europe, as well. After World War I the association also helped Jews emigrate from Eastern Europe through GERMANY to locations abroad.

After HITLER came to power in 1933, the association began to provide assistance for German Jews who wanted to leave Germany for countries other than Pa-

lestine (those immigrating to Palestine were served by the Jewish Agency). In all, it helped 90,000 Jews relocate.

After the NUREMBERG LAWS were passed in 1935, more and more Jews turned to the association for help; they were offered language instruction, job training, and assistance in leaving the country. The association worked with worldwide Jewish organizations such as the JOINT DISTRIBUTION COMMITTEE and HICEM. Closed down in 1939 by the authorities, its activities were taken over by the Reich Association's emigration department.

HILFSWILLIGE ("volunteer helpers"), Soviet civilians and PRISONERS OF WAR employed by the German army to do lower-level jobs. "*Hiwis*" worked as individuals or as groups attached to German military units. Later, their job description expanded to include guarding military objects.

HIMMLER, HEINRICH (1900–1945), Leader of the SS and chief of the German police, an architect of the

Heinrich Himmler reviewing SS troops in Croatia, 1943

"FINAL SOLUTION," and one of HITLER'S main advisors. Next to Hitler, Himmler emerged as the most powerful man in Nazi GERMANY.

Himmler was born in MUNICH to a middle-class Catholic family. His father was a strict authoritarian. At the age of 17 Himmler joined the army, but never saw action in World War I. He attended the Munich School of Technology, where he studied agriculture and economics. During the 1920s he worked as a salesman and a chicken farmer. At that time, Himmler also got involved with the newly formed NAZI PARTY.

In 1923 Himmler participated in Hitler's unsuccessful attempt at taking over the Bavarian government. He then joined a terrorist organization, led by Hitler's ally Ernst ROHM. Himmler enlisted in the SS in 1925. At that point the SS was a group of 200 men who acted as Hitler's bodyguards. By 1929 Himmler took control of the organization; with him at its helm, the SS became the dominating element of the Nazi empire, chiefly responsible for the murder of European Jewry.

After Hitler came to power in January 1933, Himmler was appointed police president in Munich and head of the political police throughout Bavaria. This gave him the authority to enlarge SS membership, organize the Security Service (SD) under the leadership of his protege, Reinhard HEYDRICH, and ultimately subdue the Storm Troopers (SA), a rival Nazi group. Also in 1933, Himmler established DACHAU, the first CONCENTRATION CAMP. Within a few years Himmler was made commander of the entire police force throughout the Reich; he was given the titles *Reichsfuehrer*-SS and Chief of the German Police. In 1938 Himmler organized the KRISTALLNACHT pogrom of November 9–10.

In October 1939, soon after the outbreak of WORLD WAR II, Himmler was appointed Reich *Commissar* for the Strengthening of German Nationhood, and was given control of newly-occupied POLAND. This included being responsible for replacing Poles and Jews with ethnic Germans. By 1941 Himmler was in charge of the Polish concentration and EXTERMINATION CAMPS, the entire police force, intelligence, political administration in occupied areas, and the extensive *Waffen*-SS armed formations. When he became minister of the interior in 1943, he also gained authority over the courts and civil service.

Himmler used his powers, efficient nature, and total lack of morals to pursue his fantastic aspirations for the racial purity of Europe. He believed that the Aryans belonged to a superior race that was destined to rule inferior races and was threatened with contamination by the Jews. Thus, the Jews needed to be annihilated. As means to this end, he established concentration and extermination camps; ordered that MEDICAL EXPERIMENTS be performed on Jews and other camp inmates; brutally used inmates as forced laborers; and encouraged special marriage laws and coupling institutions for the creation of perfect Aryans.

As the war drew to a close, Himmler realized that the Germans would be defeated. At that point, he tried to charm the Allies, while simultaneously continuing the war in the east. He hid evidence of mass murder, and allowed several hundred camp inmates to be transferred to SWEDEN. He attempted peace negotiations through Count Folke BERNADOTTE, head of the Swedish Red Cross, and even suggested surrendering to UNITED STATES General Dwight D. EISENHOWER. This enraged Hitler, who took away all of Himmler's authority.

After the Germans surrendered, Himmler tried to escape Germany, but was caught by British soldiers. He committed suicide on May 23, 1945, before he could be brought to trial as a war criminal.

HINDENBURG, PAUL VON BENECKENDORFF UND VON (1847–1934), German general and president of GERMANY who appointed HITLER chancellor in 1933.

Hindenburg, a career army officer, became chief of staff of the German Army during World War I. He and his aide, General Erich Ludendorff, ruined all efforts to end the war by a peace compromise. Nonetheless, the German people considered him a hero. In 1925 Hindenburg was elected the second president of Weimar Germany as a right-wing candidate. He originally tried to rule according to the Weimar Constitution, which called for democratic government. However, due to the growing unemployment and economic crisis, Hindenburg could not keep to the terms set by the constitution.

Hindenburg was reelected in 1932, this time as a centrist candidate. Although the NAZI PARTY received the most votes, Hindenburg refused to allow Hitler to form a cabinet. New elections were held in November; again the Nazis had a clear majority, but Hindenburg appointed General Kurt von Schleicher as chancellor. However, when Schleicher was unable to create a cabinet, Hindenburg was convinced to appoint Hitler in his stead. Despite his assurances otherwise, Hitler immedi-

President Paul von Hindenburg greeting his Chancellor, Adolf Hitler, at Potsdam, March 21, 1933

ately took complete control of the government. Hindenburg nominally remained president until his death in 1934.

HIRSCH, OTTO (1885–1941), German Jewish leader who chaired the REICH REPRESENTATION OF GERMAN JEWS, the national organization of Jews in Nazi GERMANY. Active in Jewish affairs throughout the 1920s, Hirsch promoted Jewish emigration to Palestine and adult Jewish education, and was one of the leaders of the CENTRAL UNION OF GERMAN CITIZENS OF JEWISH BELIEF.

The Reich Representation was established in 1933, with Hirsch as its executive director. He also acted as the organization's contact with Jewish aid societies in other countries. Hirsch was arrested for the first time in 1935 because of an anti-Nazi speech that the Reich Representation had written to be read in all German synagogues on the High Holidays. He was arrested again after the KRISTALLNACHT pogrom of November 1938, and sent to the SACHSENHAUSEN concentration camp for two weeks. Upon his release, he concentrated his efforts on finding ways for German Jews to escape Germany. One of his main plans was to establish refugee camps in GREAT BRITAIN and other countries; he traveled to Britain and the UNITED STATES several times in 1938 and 1939 to meet with government officials.

Hirsch was arrested again in February 1941 and sent to MAUTHAUSEN, where he was tortured to death.

HIRSCHLER, RENE (1905–1944), Chief rabbi of Strasbourg who engaged in welfare activities in southern FRANCE during WORLD WAR II.

France fell to the German army in mid-1940, and was subsequently divided in two: northern France was occupied by GERMANY, while southern France remained unoccupied, but was taken over by the Vichy government, which collaborated with the Germans. Both when the war first broke out in September 1939 and after the division of France, many Jews from the north fled south, trying to escape the Germans. Hirschler set up a sorely needed welfare system for those Jews. Furthermore, he tried to unite the various Jewish welfare organizations under one umbrella organization, in order to better serve the REFUGEES' needs.

In early 1942 Hirschler established a Jewish chaplaincy program, whose members helped the Jews imprisoned in French internment camps in the south of France. The chaplains visited camps, hospitals, and many other venues, providing Jews with both religious support and general aid. Hirschler worked tirelessly to help his fellow Jews. However, his activities ultimately led to his arrest in December 1943. Along with his wife Simone, Hirschler was sent to AUSCHWITZ in February 1943, where he died. (for more on Vichy, see also FRANCE.)

HIRSCHMANN, IRA   (1901–1989), Jewish American businessman who helped rescue Jews during the HOLOCAUST.

After Hitler's rise to power he was active in the University in Exile, which employed refugee scholars from Germany.

In 1943 Jewish rescue organizations asked Hirschmann to check out the possibility of shuttling Jews from ROMANIA, BULGARIA, and HUNGARY to safety via Turkey, a neutral country. In February 1944 Hirschmann traveled to Turkey on behalf of the American government's WAR REFUGEE BOARD (WRB). He and the American ambassador to Turkey managed to convince the Turkish authorities to allow REFUGEES to land in Turkey, and ensure the rescue of, or at least better conditions for, thousands of Jewish refugees in Romania, Bulgaria, and Hungary. In fact, almost 7,000 Jews reached Turkey and Palestine with the help of Hirschmann and the WRB.

Next, Hirschmann helped convince the Romanian authorities to return to Romania the remaining 48,000 Jews who had been deported to TRANSNISTRIA. During the summer of 1944, Hirschmann influenced Monsignor Angelo Roncalli to provide Hungarian Jews in hiding with baptismal certificates; the Romanian authorities to allow Hungarian Jews to leave Romania for Turkey; and the Bulgarian government to stop persecuting its country's Jews and restore to them their full rights.

In 1946 Hirschmann was sent to inspect the situation of Jewish displaced persons in GERMANY as the special inspector for the UNITED NATIONS RELIEF AND REHABILITATION ADMINISTRATION. (see also DISPLACED PERSONS, JEWISH.)

HITLER, ADOLF   (1889–1945), Dictator (*Fuehrer*) of the Third German Reich. Hitler was born in Braunau, AUSTRIA to a family of small landowners. His father was a customs official. From 1900–1905 Hitler went to secondary school in the Austrian town of Linz; this marked the end of his formal education. His father died in 1903. In 1907 Hitler tried to get into the Vienna Academy of Art's School of Painting, but he failed the entrance exam. That same year, his mother died of breast cancer; her doctor had been a Jew. In 1908 Hitler moved to VIENNA. He survived on the orphan's allowance that he received from the government and from the sale of postcards he painted. At that time, ANTISEMITISM was rampant in Vienna. The city's mayor, Karl Lueger, was rabidly antisemitic, and Hitler embraced his ideology. Hitler later declared that the period during which he lived in Vienna was extremely influential in molding his opinions and views.

Adolf Hitler

Hitler moved to MUNICH in 1913. When World War I broke out the next year, he joined the Bavarian Army. He worked as a message runner in BELGIUM and FRANCE and was quite a good soldier. He was promoted to lance corporal and was awarded medals for his bravery.

After the war, Hitler returned to Munich with much bitterness over GERMANY's defeat. He believed that the Jews were responsible for Germany's loss. At that point, he wrote his first political document, in which he stated

Hitler (front center) at the Nuremberg Rally, 1935

that the final aim of antisemitism should be the "total removal of the Jews." He soon joined the small anti-semitic German Workers' Party which, in 1920, changed its name to the National Socialist German Workers' Party—or the NAZI PARTY, for short. The party's platform called for all German Jews to be denied civil rights, and for some of them to be kicked out of the country. People started recognizing Hitler as an extraordinary and charismatic public speaker. In 1921 he became his party's all-powerful chairman and a cult of personality was created which depicted him as the greatest of Germans, who had infallible judgement. By 1923 the Nazi Party included 56,000 members and a private army of 15,000 Storm Troopers.

In November 1923 Hitler attempted to take over the Bavarian government in Munich during an armed revolt called the Beer Hall Putsch. The bid failed, and Hitler was sentenced to five years in jail. However, he was let out after nine months. While in jail he had

written the first part of his infamous book, MEIN KAMPF (My Struggle).

In 1925 Hitler reestablished the Nazi Party. Its membership continued to grow, especially at the end of the decade, as Germans were hit hard by the Great Depression and needed an outlet and a scapegoat for their troubles. Hitler and his party were seen as dynamic and youthful. In the national elections of 1932, the Nazi Party won 230 seats of a total of 599, giving it 37.3 percent of the vote—making it the largest political party in the German parliament. On January 30, 1933, as a result of backroom deals, Hitler was named chancellor of Germany. Despite the fact that his party did not hold an absolute majority in the government, Hitler was able to gather more and more power into his hands. On February 27 Hitler masterminded a fire in the parliament building—and used it as an excuse to destroy his political opponents in the government. Less than a week later, Hitler had a law passed that annulled German democracy and eventually gave him absolute powers. With the death of the German President Paul Von HINDENBERG on August 2, 1934, Hitler assumed that office as well.

From within his racial view of the world, Hitler sought to revitalize Germany. Thus, among his main goals were building up the army and enacting anti-Jewish measures. On April 1, 1933 an anti-Jewish boycott took place all over Germany (see also BOYCOTT, ANTI-JEWISH), and on April 7, a law was passed that made it legal to fire Jews from their civil service jobs. In September 1935 the racial NUREMBERG LAWS were passed, and from then on, the Nazis introduced a series of anti-Jewish measures that excluded Jews from all facets of German life. Meanwhile the Nazis had also begun establishing CONCENTRATION CAMPS where their political and ideological opponents were imprisoned.

In March 1938 Hitler annexed Austria to Germany. This added almost 200,000 more Jews to Hitler's domain. Later that year, he was given the Sudetenland region of Czechoslovakia as a result of the MUNICH CONFERENCE, and in March 1939, he took over the rest of the Czech lands and established a puppet regime in SLOVOKIA. On September 1 of that same year, Hitler's army invaded POLAND, signaling the beginning of WORLD WAR II and the start of an amazing string of military victories that added greatly to Hitler's aura. The Germans immediately began persecuting Polish Jewry. In the spring of 1940, Hitler's armies took most of Western Europe in a lightning campaign, followed the next spring by the conquest of the Balkans. The systematic mass killing of Jews, also known euphemistically as the "Final Solution," began in June 1941 after Germany attacked its former ally, the SOVIET UNION, and began to conquer large portions of its territory.

Hitler viewed the Jews as his ideological enemies, and as a danger to the "Aryan" race, Germany, and the world in general. He also saw them as the major proprietors of democracy, liberalism, and Socialism—ideological trends directly opposed to his beliefs. Thus, as *Fuehrer* (leader) of Germany, Hitler focused on destroying the Jews and establishing German dominance in Europe, and later the world, based on Nazi racial principles.

The first massacres of Jews in the Soviet Union were carried out by EINSATZGRUPPEN units, regular army units, various police units, and local collaborators. Soon, Hitler decided to extend the mass murder of Jews to all of Europe. His regime established EXTERMINATION CAMPS where millions of Jews were destroyed. However, by the end of 1942, Hitler's luck was changing. The Soviet army began winning battles against the Germans on the eastern front, and in 1943 and 1944 the Western Allies, including the UNITED STATES, which had joined the war in December 1941, were beating the Germans in the southern and western fronts. He blamed others for his failures, and in 1944, some of his generals unsuccessfully tried to assassinate him. As Germany lost more and more battles and military defeat seemed more and more unavoidable, Hitler continued the "Final Solution." By April 2, 1945, Hitler was able to brag about the murder of European Jewry. However, less than a month later, on April 30, 1945, Hitler committed suicide in his Berlin bunker, with his wife Eva Braun. His legacy will live on, however, as the man who perpetuated one of the worst evils in history.

HITLERJUGEND

(HITLER Youth), Nazi youth movement. The Adolf Hitler Boys' Storm Troop, a branch of the Storm Troopers, was established in 1922. In 1926 it changed its name to Hitler Youth. The movement first admitted girls into a separate organization in 1928; it eventually became the League of German Girls (*Bund Deutscher Maedel*, BDM).

The movement's purpose was to shape the young generation, the group that would ensure the continuation of the Nazi revolution. In accordance with Nazi ideology, German youth were to focus on physical development, and sophisticated methods of propagan-

Member of the Hitlerjugend in Vienna, Austria

da were used to gain their support for the movement's ideals. Their movement activities eclipsed their formal education and often turned them into their families' lead Nazis.

Hitler Youth was run by an official government agency, the Reich Youth Leadership. Members were organized into two age groups: 10–14 and 14–18, and divided into military units. Boys were given uniforms and bayonets; when they turned 19, they were drafted into the Reich Labor Service, after which they joined the army. Girls were taught to be the ideal Nazi woman—obedient, self-sacrificing, dutiful, and physically fit. They were also trained to hate Jews and become mothers of superior Aryan children.

HLINKA, ANDREJ

(1864–1938), Slovak clergyman and nationalist political leader for whom the HLINKA GUARD was named.

Czechoslovakia became an independent republic in 1918. Hlinka supported the change and called for his native SLOVAKIA to join the new state. However, he and other Slovak Catholic leaders were unhappy about the new government's policy of division of church and state, and especially disapproved of the laws that removed education from the church's control. Disappointed in Czechoslovakia, Hlinka revitalized the Slovak People's Party, and led it in a campaign for Slovak self-rule within the context of the Czechoslovak government. Hlinka's party soon came into conflict with the Czechoslovak authorities, who promoted the idea of a unified Czechoslovak people. The party also felt that the authorities discriminated against Slovaks with regard to the economy and other matters. Some elements in the party even began advocating Slovak national independence, despite the fact that Hlinka himself still called for Slovak autonomy within Czechoslovakia. In fact, there were several elements in his party that Hlinka could not contain, including those who called for attacks on Jews, while he denounced ANTISEMITISM and called on Slovak Jews to support Slovak nationalism.

After his death in 1938, Hlinka became a symbol of Slovak nationalism and his party became a major force in Slovak politics.

HLINKA GUARD   Militia in SLOVAKIA established by the pro-Nazi Slovak People's Party after the MUNICH CONFERENCE of 1938, in which Western leaders allowed HITLER to occupy the Sudeten region of Czechoslovakia. The Hlinka Guard was named for Andrej HLINKA, a Slovak nationalist who died that same year.

Members of the guard were given military training and were urged to hate Jews, Czechs, and supporters of the left. They wore black uniforms and used the Nazis' raised-arm salute.

The Nazis and the Slovak nationalist Hlinka Guard shared a common goal: the Nazis wanted to dismember Czechoslovakia, lest it oppose them in war, while the Slovak nationalists wanted to dismember Czechoslovakia so they could gain Slovak national independence. After GERMANY took over Bohemia and Moravia in March 1939, Slovakia declared itself an independent country. The guard's leader, Alexander MACH, was named prime minister of the Slovak government, and the guard lost no time in attacking Jews and desecrating Jewish cemeteries and synagogues.

In 1942 the guard helped the Nazis capture Slovak Jews and deport them to EXTERMINATION CAMPS. However, the guard discontinued its participation in those activities after the Vatican representative in Slovakia denounced the DEPORTATIONS. After the 1944 SLOVAK NATIONAL UPRISING, the SS took over the guard, and used it for its own purposes.

HOESS, RUDOLF   (1900–1947), Camp commandant of AUSCHWITZ.

Hoess was born in Baden-Baden, GERMANY. He volunteered for the army during World War I even though he was underage. In November 1922 Hoess joined the NAZI PARTY. In 1928 he got involved with the Artamanen Society, a nationalist group which encouraged work on the land and resettlement on Polish territory. He joined the SS in June 1934, on the advice of SS commander Heinrich HIMMLER, one of the leaders of the Artamanen society.

From 1934–1938 Hoess learned how to run a CONCENTRATION CAMP at DACHAU, where he trained under camp commandant Theodor EICKE. In May 1940 Hoess was transferred to the site of Auschwitz, and made commandant of the new concentration camp there. Hoess played a large role in organizing and setting up the camp to his liking. In May 1941 Himmler ordered Hoess to establish a new camp right near Auschwitz; this became Birkenau, or Auschwitz II. By the summer, Hoess began preparing the camp as a mass extermination site. At that point, Himmler advised Hoess that HITLER had ordered the "final solution" to the "Jewish question" and that the SS was responsible for carrying out that assignment. Auschwitz was chosen as the major site of the "Final Solution"—the mass extermination of all of European Jewry—because it was conveniently located, with respect to transportation and concealment from the outside world.

From summer 1941 to November 1943 Hoess presided over the murder of Jews from Germany, the Protectorate of Bohemia and Moravia, POLAND, FRANCE, NETHERLANDS, BULGARIA, SLOVAKIA, BELGIUM, AUSTRIA, YUGOSLAVIA, ITALY, NORWAY, and GREECE. He was the one who had made the decision to use ZYKLON B gas for that purpose. He left Auschwitz at the end of 1943, but returned to head the extermination of Hungarian Jewry in "Aktion Hoess." In all, he was responsible for the deaths of more than one million people.

After the war, Hoess escaped and assumed a false identity. In March 1946 he was found and arrested. The supreme court in WARSAW sentenced him to death; he was hanged in Auschwitz on April 16, 1947.

HOLOCAUST   (in Hebrew, *sho'ah*), the name used in English to refer to the systematic destruction of European Jewry at the hands of the Nazis during WORLD WAR II. The word Holocaust comes from the Greek word *holokauston*, which is a translation of the

Hebrew word *olah*. During Biblical times, an *olah* was a type of sacrifice to God that was totally consumed or burnt by fire. Over time, the word holocaust came to be used with reference to large-scale slaughter or destruction.

The Hebrew word *sho'ah*, which has the connotation of a whirlwind of destruction, was first used in 1940 to refer to the extermination of the Jews of Europe, in a booklet published in Jerusalem by the United Aid Committee for the Jews in Poland. The booklet was titled *Sho'at Yehudei Polin* (The Holocaust of the Jews of Poland). It included articles and eyewitness reports on the persecution of Eastern European Jewry that began when World War II broke out in September 1939. The reports were written or dictated by Jews who had seen what was going on and escaped, including some prominent Polish Jewish leaders. However, the term *sho'ah* was hardly used until the spring of 1942. Instead, many Yiddish-speaking Jews used the term *churban*, which also means destruction or catastrophe, and historically refers to the destruction of the

ancient Holy Temple in Jerusalem, both in 586 BCE and in 70 CE.

In the spring of 1942 a historian in Jerusalem, Ben-Zion Dinur, used the word *sho'ah* with reference to the extermination of European Jewry, and called it a "catastrophe" that showed how different and unique the Jewish people were from the rest of the world. Other Jews in Palestine soon began using the term *sho'ah* to describe the destruction of the European Jewish community. By the 1950s, the English term Holocaust came to be employed as the term for the murder of the Jews in Europe by the Nazis. Although the term is sometimes used with reference to the murder of other groups by the Nazis, strictly speaking, those groups do not belong under the heading of the Holocaust, nor are they included in the generally accepted statistic of six million victims of the Holocaust.

HOLOCAUST, DENIAL OF THE   Claims that the mass extermination of the Jews by the Nazis never happened; that the number of Jewish losses has been

Demonstrators who deny the Holocaust, their signs read:
"I am an ass because I still believe that Jews were gassed in German Concentration camps."

greatly exaggerated; that the HOLOCAUST was not systematic nor a result of an official policy; or simply that the Holocaust never took place. Clearly absurd claims of this kind have been made by Nazis, neo-Nazis, pseudo-historians called "revisionists" and the uneducated and uninformed who do not want to or cannot believe that such a huge atrocity could actually have occurred.

Holocaust denial was attempted even before WORLD WAR II ended, despite the obvious evidence at hand. The Nazis who attempted to carry out the "Final Solution"—the extermination of European Jewry—used euphemistic language like the terms "Final Solution" and "special treatment" rather than gassing, annihilation, and killing, in order to conceal their murderous activities from the world. During the last two years of the war, SONDERKOMMANDO units, put to work in a secret program called AKTION 1005, were charged with digging up mass graves and burning the corpses. Again, the Nazis' purpose was to hide all evidence of their activities.

In the present day, more than 50 years later, there are still some people who either completely reject the notion that the Holocaust happened or say that the Holocaust was not as widespread as it actually was. "Revisionist historians" and other pseudo-scholars are active in much of the world. In 1978 a revisionist group in California established the Institute for Historical Review. The group, which claims to be scholarly, publishes the Journal of Historical Review and holds international conferences.

Revisionists often say that the Holocaust did not affect as many people as it really did. A Frenchman named Paul Rassinier, one of the original founders of the revisionist school, stated that only 500,000 to one million Jews died during World War II, mostly due to bad physical conditions and gradually—not systematically at the hands of the Nazis. Rassinier also claimed to have found the millions of Jews who disappeared from Europe. He maintains that the large number of North African Jews who moved to Israel both before and after it became a state were not always native North Africans. Rather, they were Jews who had fled Europe before and during the war.

Arthur R. Butz, an American revisionist, alleges that a mere 350,000 Jews are missing. He even goes as far as saying that some of them are not really missing, but rather just fell out of contact with their families, while only about 200,000 were executed by the Germans

during the war. Butz also claims that many Jews were not killed, but rather immigrated to the United States illegally, changed their identities, and were absorbed into American life without leaving a trace of their former selves. Furthermore, he maintains that the number "six million" was created out of thin air by the Zionists, and that YAD VASHEM can only come up with three million names of Holocaust victims.

Revisionists claim that Holocaust diaries, testimonies, and photographs are not credible and are full of lies. Some deniers say that the Nazis could not have physically cremated so many people so quickly, nor could ZYKLON B gas have feasibly been used on a regular basis in one place. With the advent of the Internet, Holocaust deniers have used this medium to spread their messages of hate. Many websites, established by them or by related groups such as white supremacists, offer their skewed version of events.

Important steps have been taken to combat this misinformation. In some countries Holocaust denial has been made illegal and those who perpetuate it are punished. Many Holocaust museums have been established, and Holocaust education has been instituted in many schools—in order to ensure that, despite the efforts of deniers, it will never happen again.

HOME ARMY (*Armia Krajowa*, AK), Polish military resistance organization, active in occupied POLAND from the fall of 1939 to January 1945.

In late September 1939 the Polish Victory Service was established; this evolved into the Union for Armed Struggle, which in turn became the Home Army (AK) in February 1942. Later, most of the other Polish underground armies were assimilated into the AK, and by early 1944 it numbered 250,000–350,000 members.

The AK's main goal was to prepare for action against the Germans, and at the end of the German occupation, carry out general armed revolt until victory. Then the London-based POLISH GOVERNMENT-IN-EXILE would return and assume control.

Although few Jews served in the AK, in February 1942 the AK Information and Propaganda Office created the Section for Jewish Affairs, to collect information about the situation of the Jewish population. The office wrote reports that were sent to government officials in London, and made contact between Polish and Jewish military organizations. The AK also aided the Jews during the WARSAW GHETTO UPRISING.

The AK was responsible for much armed and economic subversion. Most prominently, it led the WARSAW POLISH UPRISING, which broke out on August 1, 1944 and was only put down on October 2, 1944; and participated in PARTISAN battles with the Nazis.

HOME GUARD, POLAND (*Gwardia Ludowa,* also known as *Armia Ludowa,* meaning People's Army), a Polish underground PARTISAN organization active in the GENERALGOUVERNEMENT and areas of POLAND annexed to the Reich. It was created in January 1942 by the Polish Workers' Party (*Polska Partia Robotnicza,* PPR).

A regional commander of the Home Guard, Korchisky, Poland

In the spring of 1942 the PPR established the first Home Guard partisan units. They were run by a supreme command, and divided into many districts and regions. By late 1943 the guard had approximately 15,000–20,000 members and had carried out about 1,700 military actions.

In January 1944 a new Communist organization, the Polish National Council, ordered the Home Guard to change its name to the People's Army (*Armia Ludowa*). It kept the same structure as before. By summer 1944 the army had about 34,000 members, and throughout 1944 had carried out more than 1,500 military actions against the Germans.

Several Jewish partisan units, among them the unit of Yehiel Grynszpan, that originally worked alone, joined the People's Army. The army also provided some weapons for the fighters in the WARSAW Ghetto, and tried to help them during the WARSAW GHETTO UPRISING.

In July 1944 the People's Army merged with the newly formed Polish army, which fought alongside the Soviet army until the end of the war.

HOMOSEXUALITY IN THE THIRD REICH Despite the fact that homosexuality was illegal in GERMANY before the Nazi rise to power, it was generally tolerated. During the 1920s, homosexuality became a subject of public discussion, and a Scientific Humanitarian Committee was instituted for the defense of homosexuals. However, the NAZI PARTY denounced homosexuality as a deviation from normal behavior that was completely antithetical to its fundamental belief in the need to increase the pure, "Aryan" population and proper family life. The Nazis saw the purpose of sexual relations as reproduction, rather than pleasure, and viewed homosexuality as a threat to the superior "Aryan" race.

When Adolf HITLER came to power in 1933, he banned all homosexual groups. Gay bars were raided and many homosexuals were imprisoned. In 1934 Hitler ordered the execution of his loyal aide and known homosexual, Ernst ROHM, along with 300 of Rohm's men, some of whom were also homosexual. In 1935, the law about homosexuality was made even stricter, forbidding even male friendships based on homosexuality without any homosexual acts. Soon, many who were found to be habitual homosexuals were sent to CONCENTRATION CAMPS, where they were forced to wear pink triangular badges, were treated very harshly, and thousands perished.

HORST WESSEL SONG Official anthem of the NAZI PARTY and the second national anthem of the THIRD REICH, whose lyrics were taken from a poem written by Horst Wessel, a member of the Storm Troopers (SA) killed in a 1930 brawl.

Miklos Horthy on a white horse, November 1938

HORTHY, MIKLOS (1868–1957), Leader of HUNGARY from 1920 to 1944. During World War I, Horthy served in the Austro-Hungarian navy. In 1920 he took control of the Hungarian government and adopted the title "regent." Horthy's government was antisemitic and invoked a *Numerus Clausus* (quota) law in September 1920, which restricted the number of Jews who could attend university. In fact, Hungary was the first government in post-World War I Europe to issue such a restriction.

Hungary allied itself with GERMANY and ITALY. In 1938 Horthy began instituting further ANTI-JEWISH LEGISLATION. However, in 1941 and 1942 Horthy refused to succumb to HITLER, who demanded that Horthy introduce even harsher measures, such as ex-cluding Jews from Hungary's economic realm; forcing the Jews to wear the Jewish badge (see also BADGE, JEWISH); constructing GHETTOS; and deporting Jews to concentration and EXTERMINATION CAMPS. Throughout 1943 and 1944 Horthy sought to leave his alliance with Germany. As a result, on March 18, 1944, Hitler sent for Horthy. Hitler warned him that German troops were going to invade Hungary the very next day. Horthy immediately gave in—he accepted the installation of a pro-Nazi government with complete power to institute and carry out anti-Jewish measures, and agreed to deport the Jews.

Just four months later, Horthy changed his mind again. Under pressure from Western governments, the Red Cross, the king of SWEDEN, and the Vatican, Horthy stopped the DEPORTATIONS, and even proposed that a certain number of Hungarian Jews be allowed to leave Hungary for Palestine (see also HORTHY OFFER). At the end of August Horthy appointed a prime minister who re-initiated attempts to get Hungary out of the war. However, the Nazis tried to thwart Horthy's plans in October, when they kidnapped Horthy's son as a pawn. The Germans immediately deposed him and put him in jail. In his place, they appointed Ferenc SZALASI, who completely cooperated with the Nazis.

After the war the Allies refused to surrender Horthy to the Hungarians. Instead, they let him move to Portugal. There he wrote his memoirs.

HORTHY OFFER Proposal made in July 1944 by Hungarian leader, Miklos HORTHY, to allow certain Hungarian Jews to leave HUNGARY, especially for Palestine. Horthy made his offer soon after he halted the DEPORTATION of Hungarian Jews to EXTERMINATION CAMPS.

Horthy proposed that 1,000 children and 8,243 bearers of certificates of immigration and their families be allowed to go to Palestine. On July 17, a Hungarian delegate in GERMANY informed the International Red Cross of the offer, adding that the Germans had agreed to it (see also RED CROSS, INTERNATIONAL).

The American and British governments officially responded in August with a commitment to take care of Hungarian Jewish emigrants. The UNITED STATES tried to convince neutral European and Latin American governments to absorb any Jews who might manage to leave Hungary. The Latin American countries would not commit to helping, but SWEDEN and SWITZERLAND promised to take in several thousand Hungarian Jews. GREAT BRITAIN even agreed to accept into Palestine those Jews with immigration certificates. Tens of thousands of Jews in BUDAPEST received safe-conduct passes from the representatives of the neutral governments. However, despite all these efforts, the Germans did not allow any Hungarian Jews to leave the country. The efforts were not totally worthless, though, because they spurred on the rescue activities in Hungary of neutral diplomats, and greatly enhanced the value of protective papers issued by neutral governments and agencies.

HOTEL POLSKI   Hotel in WARSAW. In mid-1943 the GESTAPO used the Hotel Polski to house Jews who bore citizenship papers of neutral countries—mostly South American countries—and thus were to be exchanged for German citizens imprisoned by the Allies.

Most of these citizenship papers were forged documents prepared by the neutral countries' consulates in Europe, without the knowledge of their home governments. Jews who had gone into hiding risked their lives to obtain the papers. Then they abandoned their hiding places, once again risking their lives, despite warnings by the Warsaw underground, because they no longer felt that they could survive in hiding.

Ultimately, 300 Jews living at the Hotel Polski were deported to the VITTEL camp, while another 2,000–2,500 were sent to BERGEN-BELSEN. The last group of 420 Jews to be taken to Bergen-Belsen was instead unloaded at the PAWIAK PRISON and shot. The South American governments did not regard the citizenship papers as authentic, and thus refused to honor them. As a result, 2,500 Jews who considered those papers their ticket to life were deported to AUSCHWITZ in 1943 and 1944, where they were murdered. Only a few hundred Jews were saved by their documents, most of them exchanged for Germans imprisoned in Palestine.

HUNGARIAN LABOR SERVICE SYSTEM   (*Munkas-zolgalat*), system of labor service in HUNGARY. In March 1939, a law was passed in Hungary requiring the draft of Jews aged 20–48 into labor service units. After the German invasion of the SOVIET UNION in June 1941, the service began to grow. By 1942, 100,000 men had served in these units.

The units were run by Hungarian army officers. The Jews worked mainly at construction, mining, and building military fortifications. At the front lines, they built tank traps and trenches, cleared minefields, and fixed

roads. Originally, these laborers were to be paid the same amount as regular Hungarian soldiers, and receive the same uniforms and rations. However, many of their officers and guards were extremely antisemitic. As time went on, some Jews were deprived of their army boots and uniforms or never received them at all. At the front the officers and guards often stole the Jews' pitiful food rations, forced them to live outside, and subjected them to degradations. Thousands of laborers died from abuse, malnourishment, cold, and disease. Retreating from Bor in YUGOSLAVIA, labor servicemen were massacred and in Doroshich hundreds were burned alive by their Hungarian guards.

After GERMANY occupied Hungary in March 1944, the labor service, somewhat ironically, became a haven for thousands of Jews who otherwise would have been deported to EXTERMINATION CAMPS.

HUNGARY   Country in central Europe. After Adolf HITLER rose to power in 1933, the Hungarian government became interested in making an alliance with Nazi GERMANY. The Hungarians felt that such an alliance would be good for them in that the two governments had similar authoritarian ideologies, and because the Germans could help them regain land they had lost in World War I. Over the next five years Hungary moved ever closer to Germany. The MUNICH CONFERENCE of September 1938 allowed Germany to

Deportation of Hungarian Jews, 1944

Jewish women and girls rounded up in Budapest, fall 1944

annex the Sudeten region of Czechoslovakia. In November Germany carved a piece off of Czechoslovakia—a part that had formerly belonged to Hungary—and handed it back to Hungary to cement relations between the two nations. In August 1940 Germany also gave Hungary possession of northern TRANSYLVANIA. In October 1940 Hungary joined Germany, ITALY, and Japan in the AXIS alliance. Hungary was awarded even more land in March 1941 when, despite its alliance with the Yugoslav government, Hungary joined its new ally, Germany, in invading and splitting up YUGOSLAVIA. By that time, with all its new territories, the Jewish population in Greater Hungary had reached 725,007, not including about 100,000 Jews who had converted to Christianity but were racially considered to be Jews.

Hungary began issuing ANTI-JEWISH LEGISLATION soon after the ANSCHLUSS—the annexing of AUSTRIA by Germany in March 1938. Hungary passed a law whereby Jewish participation in the economy and the professions was cut by 80 percent. In May 1939 the Hungarian government further limited the Jews in the economic realm and distinguished Jews as a "racial" rather than religious group. In 1939 Hungary created a new type of labor service draft, which Jewish men of military age were forced to join (see also HUNGARIAN LABOR SERVICE SYSTEM). Later, many Jewish men would die within its framework. In 1941 the Hungarian government passed a racial law, similar to the NUREMBERG LAWS, which officially defined who was to be considered Jewish.

Despite the hardships caused by these anti-Jewish laws, most of the Jews of Hungary lived in relative safety for much of the war. However, one group of Hungarian Jews was subject to tragedy in the summer of 1941: some 18,000 Jews randomly designated by the Hungarian authorities as "Jewish foreign nationals" were kicked out of their homes and deported to KAMENETS-PODOLSKI in the UKRAINE, where most were murdered in cold blood. Another 1,000 Jews in the section of Hungary newly-acquired from Yugoslavia were murdered in early 1942 by Hungarian soldiers and police in their "pursuit of PARTISANS."

At the same time as they were passing anti-Jewish laws, the Hungarian authorities were getting more and more entrenched in their alliance with Germany. In June 1941 Hungary decided to join Germany in its war against the SOVIET UNION. Finally, in December 1941, Hungary joined the Axis in declaring war against the UNITED STATES, completely cutting itself off from any relationship with the West. But after Germany's defeat at Stalingrad and other battles in which Hungary lost tens of thousands of its soldiers, the regent of Hungary, Miklos HORTHY, began trying to back out of the alliance with Germany.

This move was not acceptable to Hitler, and in March 1944 German troops invaded Hungary in order to keep the country loyal by force. Hitler immediately set up a new government that he thought would be faithful, with Dome SZTOJAY, Hungary's former ambassador to Germany, as prime minister. Accompanying the occupation forces was a SONDERKOMMANDO unit headed by Adolf EICHMANN, whose job was to begin implementing the "Final Solution" within Hungary. Anti-Jewish decrees were passed at lightning speed. JUDENRAETE were set up throughout Hungary with a central *Judenrat* called the *Zsido Tanacs* established in BUDAPEST under Samu STERN.

The Germans isolated the Jews from the outside world by restricting their movement and confiscating their telephones and radios. The Jews were forced to don the Jewish badge for easy identification (see also BADGE, JEWISH). Jewish property and businesses were seized, and from mid to late April the Jews of Hungary were forced into GHETTOS. These ghettos were short-lived. After two to six weeks the Jews of each ghetto were put on trains and deported. Between May 15 and July 9, about 430,000 Hungarian Jews were deported, mainly to AUSCHWITZ, where half were gassed on arrival. In early July Horthy halted the DEPORTATIONS, still intent on cutting Hungary's ties with Germany. By that time, all of Hungary was "Jew-free" except for the capital, BUDAPEST. During spring of 1944 Israel KASZTNER, Joel BRAND, and other members of the RELIEF AND RESCUE COMMITTEE OF BUDAPEST began negotiating with the SS to save lives. Many Jews (perhaps up to 8,000) fled from Hungary, most to ROMANIA, many with the help of Zionist youth movement members.

From July to October, the Jews of Budapest lived in relative safety. However, on October 15 Horthy announced publicly that he was done with Hungary's alliance with Germany, and was going to make peace with the Allies. The Germans blocked this move, and then simply toppled Horthy's government, giving power to Ferenc SZALASI and his Fascist, violently antisemitic ARROW CROSS PARTY.

The Arrow Cross immediately introduced a reign of terror in Budapest. Nearly 80,000 Jews were killed in Budapest itself, shot on the banks of the Danube River, and then thrown in. Thousands of others were forced on DEATH MARCHES to the Austrian border. In December, during the Soviet siege of the city, 70,000 Jews were forced into a ghetto, thousands dying of cold, disease, and starvation.

Tens of thousands of Jews in Budapest were saved during the Arrow Cross reign by members of the Relief and Rescue Committee and other Jewish activists, especially Zionist YOUTH MOVEMENT members, who forged identity documents and provided them with food. These Jews worked together with foreign diplomats such as the Swedish Raoul WALLENBERG, the Swiss Carl LUTZ, and others who provided many Jews with international protection.

Hungary was liberated by the Soviet army by April 1945. Up to 568,000 Hungarian Jews had perished during the HOLOCAUST.

HUSSEINI, HAJJ AMIN AL (1895–1974), Grand Mufti of Jerusalem; prominent Arab-Palestinian leader and Nazi collaborator.

In his position as a Muslim religious leader, Husseini encouraged Arabs in Palestine to riot and commit other acts of violence against Jews. At the beginning of WORLD WAR II, Husseini escaped to Iraq, where he endorsed a pro-Nazi revolt. After the revolt was suppressed, he went to ITALY and then to GERMANY.

From October 1941 onward, Husseini allied himself with the AXIS powers. His motivations were to obtain support from them for Arab nationalistic goals, and lend his support to the "Final Solution."

Husseini contributed to the Nazi war effort by setting up Bosnian Muslim battalions that were attached to the *Waffen-SS*. These soldiers fought PARTISANS in Bosnia and massacred civilians there.

Husseini also tried to convince the Axis authorities to bomb Tel Aviv, and to extend the "Final Solution" to the Jews in North Africa and Palestine. When he was informed of various Nazi plans to exchange Jewish lives for goods or large sums of money, he strenuously lobbied against them.

After the war, Husseini was arrested in FRANCE, but he escaped and found refuge in Egypt. He continued to be active in Arab matters until his death.

Hajj Amin al Husseini reviewing troops fighting for Germany, Croatia, 1943

I.G. FARBEN (IGF)   A corporation of eight of GERMANY'S major chemical companies.

Prisoners from Auschwitz III being taken to work at an I.G. Farben factory

HITLER aspired to create a self-sufficient Germany not dependent on raw materials from the outside world, and thus sought to develop a synthetic-materials industry. IGF produced synthetic rubber and synthetic fuel from coal; Hitler guaranteed large state purchases of these products from IGF. This helped create a strong connection between the corporation and the Nazis. In 1936, when Hitler launched his FOUR-YEAR PLAN under the management of Hermann GOERING, an IGF board member named Carl Krauch was given a leading role. The corporation also contributed huge sums of money to the NAZI PARTY between 1933 and 1944. The poisonous ZYKLON B gas used for mass extermination was first developed by a subsidiary of IGF, DEGESCH, before the war.

As Germany annexed new areas, IGF took over the management of chemical factories located there. In 1941 IGF set up synthetic rubber and gasoline plants at AUSCHWITZ. A new section called Auschwitz III was even added to Auschwitz near the IGF plants to house the prisoners working there. The average life span of prisoners working for IGF in Auschwitz was three months.

After the war, IGF paid reparations to the Jews who had been forced to work for the company at Auschwitz; non-Jews were not compensated. In the late 1990s the issue of reparations was re-opened.

IASI   (in German, Jassy), city in northeastern ROMANIA. In 1941, 51,000 Jews lived in Iasi, including many REFUGEES.

Ion ANTONESCU came to power in Romania in 1940, supported by the fascist, antisemitic IRON GUARD move-

Trainload of 2,430 Jews deported from Iasi to Calarasi on June 29, 1941. During a short stop a survivor stands in front of a car filled with Jews who had died on the way. The 980 survivors of the deportation were returned to Iasi on August 30, 1941.
(Photo: USHM, Washington)

ment. During his reign, Jews were subjected to persecutions such as random arrests, blackmail, torture, and confiscation of property and businesses. In November two synagogues were destroyed. Jewish community leaders bribed the Iron Guard to stop the persecutions, and for a few months the Jews were left alone.

Things changed when the Germans invaded the SOVIET UNION in June 1941. Iasi was a gathering point for German and Romanian troops heading for the front lines. After accusing the Jews of signaling to Soviet planes, Romanian and German government agencies instigated pogroms that began on June 28, 1941. Thousands of Jews were killed on the streets and in their homes, and thousands more were arrested. On June 29, called "Black Sunday" by the Jews, thousands of Jews were gathered in the courtyard of police headquarters. Most were shot by Romanian troops; 4,330 of the survivors, together with Jews from other parts of Iasi, were herded into sealed cattle cars. Of those, 2,650 died of thirst or suffocation. Altogether, over 10,000 Jews were murdered in Iasi.

INSTITUT D'ETUDE DES QUESTIONS JUIVES see INSTITUTE FOR THE STUDY OF THE JEWISH PROBLEM.

INSTITUTE FOR THE STUDY OF THE JEWISH PROBLEM (*Institut d'Etude des Questions Juives,* IEQJ), French anti-Jewish institution that was active from 1941 to 1943. With the financial backing of the German occupation authorities in FRANCE, the IEQJ spread anti-Jewish propaganda among the French, called for the removal of Jews from the economic and cultural spheres of French life, and urged the French people to tell on Jews and surrender them to the authorities. The institute's greatest achievement was an exhibit called "The Jew and France" whose purpose was to show how Jews had allegedly harmed France throughout French history. From the point of view of the IEQJ, the exhibition was a wild success: 500,000 people came to see it in PARIS alone, before it moved on to two other locations.

In May 1942 the Vichy government's OFFICE FOR JEWISH AFFAIRS was put under the direction of Louis DARQUIER DE PELLEPOIX, an infamous antisemite who pledged to collaborate even more closely with the Nazis. This made the IEQJ's activities redundant. In June the director of IEQJ decided to attach it to Darquier's office. The IEQJ was then renamed the Institute for the Study of Jewish and Ethno-Racial Problems; however, it

never got off the ground, and by July 1943, it had been completely dissolved. (for more on Vichy, see also FRANCE.)

INSURANCE COMPANIES AND THE HOLOCAUST
Before the HOLOCAUST many Jews in Europe bought life insurance policies from insurance companies such as Alliance, Axa, Generali, Zurich Financial Services Group, Winterhur, and Baloise Insurance Group. Many of those Jews were then murdered by the Nazis during WORLD WAR II. During the war, some of these insurance companies actively collaborated with the Nazis. After the war they almost never gave the owed monies to heirs of the dead. Instead they claimed that they could not trace the insurance policies back to the owners, or that the Communist governments of Eastern Europe had nationalized all insurance, and thus they could not or did not have to honor the policies.

In 1996, more than 50 years after the war's end, the Italian insurance company, Generali, bought an Israeli insurer, Migdal. Soon after the purchase the Israeli parliament tried to find out how Generali had acted with regard to reimbursing heirs of Holocaust victims. In early 1997 Holocaust SURVIVORS and heirs of Holocaust victims filed a lawsuit in New York against several European insurance companies; soon thereafter, insurance commissioners in several American states began an investigation of the issue. Former United States Secretary of State Lawrence Eagleburger was then given the responsibility of creating a process for compensation, and as a result, in the spring of 1999, several insurance companies agreed to pay the heirs of Holocaust victims who held life insurance policies. The payment process is supposed to begin during the year 2000 (Generali already began the process in Israel in late 1999).

IRON GUARD (*Garda de Fier;* also called *Totul Pentru Tara,* meaning "All for the Fatherland"), fascist and antisemitic movement in ROMANIA, whose members were known as "Legionnaires."

Originally established in 1927 under the name "Legion of the Archangel Michael" and organized into paramilitary units, the Iron Guard soon became a mass political movement. It was officially dissolved in 1933, but continued to function, even receiving the third-largest number of votes in Romania's 1937 election. During the mid-1930s the Iron Guard also established ties with the Nazi regime in GERMANY.

In 1938, Romania's King Carol II again outlawed

the Guard. Nonetheless, in September 1940 he made a deal with the movement and invited its leaders into the government. The Guard immediately launched a wave of terror against Romania's Jews in hopes of removing them from Romanian life. They passed racist laws and revitalized their ties with the Nazis and the fascist government in ITALY.

In January 1941 the Guard unsuccessfully attempted to take over the government completely. The failed coup was accompanied by pogroms, in which 123 Jews were killed. Most of the Iron Guard leaders then fled to Germany. After the war, many of the Guard's members escaped to SPAIN and Portugal, where they avoided trial as war criminals.

IRVING-LIPSTADT TRIAL   Legal proceeding held in London during the first few months of the year 2000. David Irving, a British writer who has published books about the Nazi period, sued Professor Deborah Lipstadt of Emory University, Atlanta, Georgia for writing in her book, *Holocaust Denial, The Growing Assault on Truth and Memory,* that he was a denier of the HOLOCAUST.

The publisher of the book in the United Kingdom, Penguin, was named as a co-defendant. Irving claimed that being classified a Holocaust denier had damaged his reputation and had caused him monetary loss. He sued Lipstadt and the case was brought to trial before Judge Charles Gray of the London High Court. The defense sought to show that in his writings Irving had falsified and manipulated documents in order to diminish HITLER'S role in the destruction of the Jews. Moreover, statements he had made, they argued, such as that the Jews had not been murdered in GAS CHAMBERS, or that more people had died in the back of US Senator Edward Kennedy's car than had been killed in AUSCHWITZ, clearly showed that he denied the Holocaust. Lastly, they sought to prove that Irving was associated closely with those circles that advocate Holocaust denial. Irving defended himself at the trial, claiming that he did not deny the Holocaust, but merely was engaging in legitimate historical debate.

The trial aroused a great deal of public interest, with some saying the case put the truth of the Holocaust on trial, whereas others believed it was more of a case about what is or is not considered reasonable historical debate. The judgement returned by Gray was in favor of Lipstadt, and in it he called Irving an active Holocaust denier, antisemitic and, racist. Judge Gray also said: Irving has for his own ideological reasons persistently

and deliberately misrepresented and manipulated historical evidence.

The importance of the trial, beyond declaring Irving a Holocaust denier, was that it sent a clear message to the public that people like him who represent themselves as engaging in a reasonable and legitimate argument about the events of the Holocaust, are really engaged in the falsification of history. (see also HOLOCAUST, DENIAL OF THE.)

ITALY   Country in southern Europe. By the twentieth century Jews were quite integrated into Italian life, and there was almost no ANTISEMITISM in the country.

Mussolini and Hitler meet at the Brenner Pass, June 2, 1941

Benito MUSSOLINI, the leader of the Italian Fascist movement, took control of the Italian government in October 1922 (see also FASCISM). Antisemitism was not part of Mussolini's political platform; nonetheless, Italy's Jewish community was nervous about the new regime. Mussolini was quick to assure them that the Fascists were not antisemitic and did not seek to harm the country's Jews. For the next ten years, Mussolini and the Jews enjoyed civil relations. In fact, many Jews even joined the Fascist Party, as they supported Mussolini's national agenda.

After the Nazis rose to power in GERMANY in 1933, Mussolini spent several years trying to balance his relationship with the West and his support for Adolf HITLER. However, in 1936 Italy moved away from the Western powers and edged towards Germany: that year, Italy joined Germany in the Spanish Civil War, and soon thereafter, Mussolini first used the term "Rome-Berlin AXIS" to denote the countries' alliance. That fall, Mussolini initiated an antisemitic press campaign to satisfy Hitler. In September 1938 the Italian government committed itself to the "Axis" by issuing racial ANTI-JEWISH LEGISLATION, similar to Germany's NUREMBERG LAWS. Foreign Jews living in Italy were ordered to leave the country.

Italy officially entered WORLD WAR II in June 1940. At that point, Mussolini felt compelled to step up his country's anti-Jewish measures. Masses of foreign Jews who had not left the country in 1938 were thrown in prison. In early September the Italian Ministry of the Interior ordered the establishment of 43 camps, where "enemy aliens" (including foreign Jews) and Italian opponents of the Fascist government were to be detained. These camps, although by no means comfortable, were a far cry from the Nazis' CONCENTRATION CAMPS. In Italy, families were allowed to live together, schools were set up for the children, and there were social and cultural activities for all.

Mussolini was completely dependent on Hitler, both economically and militarily, so he could not afford to stop his program of anti-Jewish persecution within Italy itself (although Mussolini never agreed to deport his country's Jews to EXTERMINATION CAMPS). However, the Italians asserted their independence by helping those Jews living outside Italy, in Italian-occupied territories, such as in FRANCE, YUGOSLAVIA, and GREECE. In 1942, after Germany began deporting Jews to the east in earnest, the Italian military began a serious rescue operation throughout the territories it administered. In all, the Italian authorities saved some 40,000 non-Italian Jews.

In early September 1943 the Italians decided to end their participation in the war and make peace with the Allies. Mussolini was overthrown, and the Allies began liberating Italy, starting with the south of the country. At that point, Germany stepped in to reoccupy all the parts of Italy not already taken by the Allies. A government was set up with Mussolini as a puppet ruler, and the Germans as the real power. This signaled the beginning of the HOLOCAUST for the Jews of Italy.

From mid-September 1943 to the end of the war in April 1945, the Germans hunted down Italian Jews; more than 20 percent of the country's Jewish population was imprisoned in jails and concentration camps, and then sent on to extermination camps. From September 1943 to January 1944, 3,110 Jews were deported to AUSCHWITZ. Throughout the rest of 1944, another 4,056 were deported to the east. Another 4,500 Italian Jews living in territories formerly under Italian rule were also deported. An additional 173 Jews were murdered in Italy itself.

In all, some 15 percent of Italy's Jews perished during the Holocaust. The great majority of the country's Jewish population survived with the help of both Italian civilians and the Italian military.

J

JAEGER, KARL (1888–1959), SS officer. Born in SWITZERLAND, Jaeger joined the NAZI PARTY in 1923 and the SS in 1932. In 1938 he was assigned to serve in Munster, where he worked as chief of the Security Service (SD). Next he served in the occupied NETHERLANDS for a short time, and then became the commanding officer of *Einsatzkommando* 3 of the EINSATZGRUPPE A unit, attached to an army unit in northern Russia.

Jaeger's next assignment was as commander of the SD and Security Police in LITHUANIA. In that post, Jaeger was responsible for the annihilation of Lithuania's Jews. In December 1941 he reported that there were no Jews left in Lithuania except for those in three GHETTOS: Siauliai, KOVNO, and VILNA. Three months later, Jaeger produced a report that included the number of people killed by his unit: 136,421 Jews, 1,064 Communists, 653 mentally ill people, and 134 others. Of these victims, 55,556 were women and 34,464 children.

In the fall of 1943 Jaeger was transferred back to GERMANY, where he became chief of police in the Sudeten city of Reichenberg. After the war, he managed to disguise his identity and became a farmer. He was arrested in 1959; on June 22 of that year he killed himself in his cell.

JANOWSKA Labor camp located on Janowska Road in LVOV (in the UKRAINE), where thousands of Jews were murdered. The Germans established Janowska in September 1941 as an arms factory. Soon, it was expanded into a complex of factories that served the German Armament Works. These factories employed Jews as forced laborers (see also FORCED LABOR). By October, there were 600 prisoners who worked mostly at carpentry and metalwork; some were given meaningless jobs designed to exhaust them before sending them to their deaths. At the beginning of November the Nazis asked the chairman of the Lvov JUDENRAT, Dr. Joseph Parnes, to provide more workers for the camp. He refused and was executed.

The camp underwent a change in March 1942.

When the mass DEPORTATIONS of Jews from Eastern Galicia to the BELZEC extermination camp began, Janowska was used as a transit camp for those prisoners who were still capable of doing hard labor. When they were no longer of any use to the Germans, they were sent to Belzec like the others.

Later in the spring, the Nazis expanded Janowska and turned it into a CONCENTRATION CAMP. The Lvov *Judenrat* tried to help the prisoners there by sending them food, but hardly any of the packages reached them. During the summer of 1942, thousands more Jews arrived.

In mid-1943 Janowska became more and more like an EXTERMINATION CAMP. Fewer prisoners were used as forced laborers, and the amount of time they stayed in the camp was shortened. The Nazis executed prisoners on the outskirts of Lvov; over 6,000 Jews were murdered in May 1943 alone.

The prisoners in Janowska tried to organize resistance actions. Prisoners who worked outside Janowska were able to smuggle weapons into the camp, to be used in the event of the camp's liquidation. However, the date of the liquidation was moved up to November 1943, catching the prisoners unaware. One revolt did break out among the prisoners forced to burn corpses to conceal evidence of mass extermination. The rebels killed some guards, but most were caught and killed. Altogether, tens of thousands of Jews from Lvov and Eastern Galicia were murdered in Janowska.

JASENOVAC Largest concentration and EXTERMINATION CAMP in CROATIA, located 62 miles south of Zagreb. Jasenovac, which was actually a network of several subcamps, was established in August 1941 and dissolved in April 1945. The Nazis gave control of Jasenovac to the puppet Croatian government, which was run by the fascist USTASA movement. A large number of *Ustasa* members served in the camp, most notably Miroslav Filipovic-Majstorovic, who was notorious for killing prisoners with his bare hands.

Altogether, about 600,000 people were murdered at

A view of the Jasenovac camp

Jasenovac, including Serbs, Jews, GYPSIES, and Croats who opposed the *Ustasa* government. Of that number, some 25,000 of the victims were Jews, most of whom had been brought to Jasenovac before August 1942 (at which point the Germans began deporting the Jews of Croatia to AUSCHWITZ).

Jews were brought to Jasenovac from all over Croatia. Most were killed on arrival; a small number of skilled professionals were kept alive to work at the camp. They endured horrible conditions and brutal treatment at the hands of the *Ustasa* guards. Near the end of the war, Jasenovac's administration blew up much of the camp and killed most of the prisoners in an attempt to conceal evidence of the mass murders that took place there.

JEHOVAH'S WITNESSES   Religious sect whose doctrine focuses on the second coming of Jesus. The Jehovah's Witnesses believe that in every generation there will be an "end of days" that is preceded by political disasters, like those that accompanied the Nazi regime. They spread their message primarily through written tracts and door to door canvassing.

The Witnesses were outlawed in GERMANY in April 1933, despite the fact that at first they did not clearly oppose the Nazis. However, by 1935 the Witnesses refused to serve in the German army or perform the "Heil Hitler" salute (they refuse to serve in all armies and refuse to salute flags), and in 1936 an international convention of Witnesses condemned the Nazi regime. As a result, many of the sect's members were arrested during 1936 and 1937. Other widespread arrests took place soon after WORLD WAR II broke out and in 1944.

The Witnesses encompassed only a small group of prisoners within the concentration camp system. The Nazis promised individual Witnesses their freedom if they would renounce their beliefs, but they refused to do so. The SS tried to keep the Witnesses away from other prisoners in order to avoid new converts. Later they attempted to break up the Witnesses by scattering them throughout the camps. In spite of all this, the Witnesses refused to try to escape from the camps or actively resist the Nazis.

JEW HUNTS   Attempts made by the Nazis to search out and kill Jews who had escaped from the GHETTOS of Eastern Europe. In late fall 1941 a police order was issued in the GENERALGOUVERNEMENT which decreed that any Jew found outside the ghetto was to be promptly shot; this order was the premise for the Nazis' attempts to catch Jews who had gone into hiding.

"Jew hunts" were especially prevalent after most of the ghettos of POLAND and the former Soviet territories had been liquidated (a process that was carried out mainly during the second half of 1942 and throughout 1943). The Nazis would scour the "Aryan" sides of cities and towns, the forests and countryside in search of hidden Jews. In general, a small group of Nazis would go in search of a specific Jewish hiding place after getting a lead from local inhabitants. As soon as a Jew was found, he would be shot to death. In some cases, entire forests were combed in order to uncover and root out Jews. Often, local collaborators would help the Nazis in their search.

The so-called "Jew hunts" reflect how seriously and thoroughly the Nazis pursued the Jews after formally adopting the "Final Solution" policy.

JEWISH ANTIFASCIST COMMITTEE   (*Evreiskii Antifashistskii Komitet*), Soviet Jewish organization that operated in the SOVIET UNION from 1942 to 1948.

In April 1942 the Soviet government founded several antifascist committees. The Jewish Antifascist Committee was the only one that represented a national group. The committee's goal was to call on the Jews of the world, mainly American Jewry, to join the struggle against Nazi GERMANY. It used Jewish themes, symbols, and the names of prominent Jews to attract the attention of its target group. The committee was also one of the first institutions to document the atrocities of the HOLOCAUST and the activities of the Jewish resistance. It worked with the Soviet Government

Commission for the Investigation of Nazi Crimes, and put together a major work called the BLACK BOOK OF SOVIET JEWRY, which documented the crimes committed by the Nazis in the Soviet Union.

Besides its anti-Nazi activities, the committee was considered to be the central representative body of the Jews in the Soviet Union, which provided advice and support for its constituents. It was dissolved by the Soviet authorities in November 1948; most of its leaders, among them the actor Shlomo Michoels, were executed by STALIN during his anti-Jewish purges.

JEWISH ARMY, FRANCE   (*Armee Juive*, AJ), French Jewish resistance and fighting organization that was created in January 1942 in the southern French city of Toulouse. Its founders were the Zionist activists Abraham POLONSKI and Lucien LUBLIN, who had decided to create a Jewish militia as a response to the German occupation of FRANCE in mid-1940.

The AJ was a completely secret operation. Its members were recruited secretly, they swore their loyalty to the AJ on the Bible and the Zionist flag, and they even began training to fight before the organization had procured arms. It is unclear how many members the AJ actually had. Not all Zionist groups supported or trusted the AJ.

In the fall of 1943 the AJ began sending members over the Pyrenees Mountains into SPAIN, from where they were to travel to Palestine and join the Jewish units of the British army. Some 300 men successfully made it over into Spain, braving brutal conditions. That number included 80 members of the Dutch *He-Halutz* YOUTH MOVEMENT who had clandestinely entered France. Other AJ members fought in Toulouse, Nice, Lyons, and PARIS. In Nice, they destroyed a deadly group of collaborators who were often able to recognize Jews by their facial features. The AJ members active in Lyons received tens of millions of francs from the Jewish Agency and from the American Jewish JOINT DISTRIBUTION COMMITTEE; they in turn passed out the money to other rescue and fighting organizations. AJ troops also attached themselves to the French resistance fighting in the south of France; four AJ officers fell in battle in Lyons and Toulouse.

The AJ's worst losses came as a result of actions carried out by the GESTAPO. In May 1944 five of the AJ's Dutch members who were working in Paris were tracked by the *Gestapo*, and in July the *Gestapo* arrested 25 AJ fighters in Paris (destroying the AJ's base in the city). The captured soldiers were tortured and then deported to BUCHENWALD with the last transport from DRANCY.

The AJ also participated in the general French revolt against the Germans in August 1944. (see also RESISTANCE, JEWISH.)

JEWISH BRIGADE GROUP   A brigade group of the British army that was made up of Jewish volunteers from Palestine. The Jewish Brigade was formed in 1944 and helped liberate ITALY in 1945.

Previous attempts had been made to incorporate Jews into the Allied forces. At the beginning of WORLD WAR II Zionist leaders proposed the creation of an official Jewish unit within the British army. These talks dragged on until 1941, and were finally discontinued. Meanwhile, some 30,000 Jews from Palestine volunteered for the British army.

After confirming reports about the extermination of European Jewry in 1942 and 1943, the British decided that it would only be fair to give Jews a chance to take revenge on the Nazis in an official capacity. They accepted the Zionist leadership's proposal to create a Jewish fighting force, and on September 20, 1944 the British War Office announced the creation of the Jewish Brigade Group.

The brigade was composed of 5,000 soldiers. The Zionist flag was chosen as its banner—making it not the first Jewish unit to fight in the war, but the first one to be recognized as representing the Jewish people.

At the war's end, members of the Jewish Brigade helped prepare Displaced Persons for "illegal" immigra-

Members of the Jewish Brigade in Bergen-Belsen after the liberation

tion to Palestine. The British disbanded the brigade in July 1946. (see also DISPLACED PERSONS, JEWISH and YISHUV.)

JEWISH CENTER, ROMANIA

(*Centrala Evreilor*), Jewish institution similar to a JUDENRAT, set up in ROMANIA in February 1942 by Romanian leader Ion ANTONESCU, in response to German pressure. The *Centrala* replaced the Union of Jewish Communities, which had long represented the Jews of Romania.

The *Centrala,* run by Nandor Ghingold, was forced to carry out all orders issued by the Romanian and German authorities regarding Jewish affairs. It was charged with carrying out two contradictory tasks: helping the German authorities organize the DEPORTATION of Jews to EXTERMINATION CAMPS in POLAND; and serving the Romanian authorities, who wanted to use the council to steal money and property from the Jews and provide FORCED LABOR. The *Centrala* aided the Germans by making a list of all the Jews in their domain. The group did not participate in Jewish leader Wilhelm FILDERMAN'S struggle to stop the deportation of Romanian Jews to Poland. However, as the Romanian policy shifted in 1943–1944 and the government sought a way out of its alliance with HITLER, the *Centrala* took over the organization of welfare activities and provided spiritual and material care for Romania's Jews. The *Centrala* was dissolved in December 1944 after Romania's LIBERATION, and its leaders, including Ghingold, were given long prison sentences.

JEWISH CENTER, SLOVAKIA

(*Ustredna Zidov*), Jewish institution established by the Slovak government in 1940 to run Jewish affairs.

When SLOVAKIA was given autonomy in 1938, its Jews obtained permission to set up an umbrella Jewish organization, which they named the Central Jewish Office for Slovakia. This office, which excluded Orthodox Jews, ran social, cultural, economic, and religious activities. In mid-1940 GERMANY increased its pressure on Slovakia. This convinced the Jews that the entire Jewish community needed to unite, so a new organization was established that included Orthodox Jews. This organization functioned until late September 1940, when the government dissolved all Jewish agencies. At that point, the authorities set up another institution to administer Jewish affairs, which they called the Jewish Center.

The Jewish Center was headed by a *starosta,* or elder,

who was assisted by a council, but actually held most of the organization's power in his own hands. In addition, many of the center's employees collaborated with the Nazis. Some of those working at the center opposed the way the organization was run; together with Jewish leaders not associated with the center, they set up their own semi-underground agency, the WORKING GROUP, which led the effort to rescue the remaining elements of the Slovak Jewish community.

JEWISH FIGHTING ORGANIZATION, WARSAW

(*Zydowska Organizacja Bojowa,* ZOB; in Yiddish, *Yidishe Kamf Organizatsye*), underground Jewish military group established in the WARSAW Ghetto to resist DEPORTATIONS of Jews to EXTERMINATION CAMPS. The ZOB was formed on July 28, 1942, during a two-month wave of deportations to TREBLINKA.

During the deportations of the summer of 1942, the ZOB appealed to the GHETTO'S Jews to resist. However, the Jews did not heed their call. In addition, the ZOB was made up of different political factions who had trouble cooperating, and the group did not have enough weapons. Thus, the ZOB was unable to execute any effective attacks at that time.

When the deportations ended, ZOB members saw that they needed to settle their differences and organize themselves in order to be of any help to the Jews of the ghetto. Many new members joined under the leadership of Mordecai ANIELEWICZ, who became head of a revitalized ZOB in November 1942. They prepared for the next onslaught by the Germans, and executed those Jews in the ghetto who had helped the Nazis carry out the deportations. In January 1943, they resisted Nazi attempts to round up Jews. The ZOB then organized the WARSAW GHETTO UPRISING, and when the revolt broke out in April 1943, ZOB members fought heroically to the bitter end.

JEWISH MILITARY UNION, WARSAW

(*Zydowski Zwiazek Wojskowy,* ZZW), a military organization active in the WARSAW Ghetto, numbering 250. It was organized by the *Betar* Zionist YOUTH MOVEMENT and the Revisionist Zionist Movement.

A major DEPORTATION of Warsaw Jews took place from July to September 1942. At that time, the main Warsaw *Betar* leaders were not in the GHETTO; they were staying in Hrubieszow. In September there was an *aktion* there. Those *Betar* members who survived returned to Warsaw and created the ZZW.

The ZZW had ties to the Polish HOME ARMY and received arms from some Polish officers. However, the ZZW did not get along well with the Jewish Fighting Organization (*Zydowska Organizacja Bojowa,* ZOB), Warsaw's major Jewish underground organization. The ZZW claimed that the ZOB refused to incorporate them into their group's structure, while the ZOB maintained that the ZZW wanted to take over the operation. In addition, both groups imposed taxes on the ghetto's wealthier Jews, causing more tension between them. Nonetheless, the groups made their peace in time for joint action in the WARSAW GHETTO UPRISING. ZZW members heroically fought one of the major battles of the uprising; afterwards, they fled through a tunnel to the Aryan side, where many died fighting German soldiers. (see also JEWISH FIGHTING ORGANIZATION, WARSAW.)

JEWISH PHILOSOPHICAL AND THEOLOGICAL RESPONSES TO THE HOLOCAUST   During the HOLOCAUST some six million Jews were murdered and Jewish life in Europe was virtually destroyed. The overwhelming nature of the Nazi atrocities and the Jewish losses in the Holocaust has compelled the post-Holocaust generation to search for answers to the following questions: Why did this happen? How could God have let this happen?

Some Jewish thinkers have found meaning in traditional Jewish responses to human suffering. Jewish sources often assert that tragedy happens to the Jewish people as a punishment for their sinfulness. There are several variations on this theme. The first ascribes the cause of the Holocaust to Jewish sin but does not specify which. The second view states that the Holocaust happened as a result of the rise of Reform and other non-Orthodox forms of Judaism. The third position contends that Zionism was the sin that caused the Holocaust, as the Jews should have waited for the Messiah rather than proactively try to build a Jewish state in Palestine.

Four biblical models are often mentioned in response to the existential questions brought on by the Holocaust. The first is the "Binding of Isaac." By comparing the victims of the Holocaust to the biblical Isaac, the Jews are seen not as sinners (as in the aforementioned positions), but rather as innocent victims who were sacrificed as a test of their Jewish faith. The second model is the image of the "Suffering Servant" used by the prophet Isaiah. Those that compare Holocaust victims to God's "Suffering Servant" see them as bearing the weight of the sins of others. God is even viewed as sharing in the torment of those righteous sufferers, and rewarding them in the world to come. The third biblical model calls up the idea of *Hester Panim,* or God's hiddenness. Some believe that God "hides" Himself in order to tolerate sin in the world, and along the way people are hurt by that sin. Others assert that there is no explanation for God's hiding. The last biblical model brought up in response to the Holocaust is the "Job" analogy. Job, who was not a sinner, was dealt great suffering as a test of his belief in God's existence; the Jewish victims of the Holocaust are seen as confronting a similar situation.

Some Jewish thinkers have rejected these traditional responses to human suffering in favor of more original responses. Both Eliezer Berkovits and Arthur A. Cohen adopt the "free-will" defense, which states that humans have free-will to do as they please, whether good or evil, and thus it is not God who caused or even allowed the Holocaust, but human beings. Unlike Berkovits and Cohen, Emil Fackenheim does not remove God from the Holocaust. In effect, he places God at the scene of the crime itself—AUSCHWITZ—but says that he cannot understand exactly what God was doing there. Whatever God's intention, Fackenheim believes that the Holocaust should be considered a new occasion of Divine revelation, and that a proper response to it is the adoption of a 614th Jewish commandment: not to allow HITLER a posthumous victory by letting Judaism die out.

Not only does Richard Rubenstein remove God from the Holocaust, he removes Him altogether, based on the Holocaust. Rubenstein argues that the horrors of the Holocaust prove that God cannot exist. Unlike Rubenstein, Irving (Yitzchak) Greenberg still believes in God. However, he observes that the Holocaust destroyed the traditional covenant between God and the Jews. Greenberg suggests that in its stead, the Jews have taken on a new, voluntary relationship with God in the wake of the Holocaust. Arthur Cohen goes even further than Greenberg and suggests that not only must the Jewish people redefine their relationship with God, but they must redefine their notion of God altogether. Perhaps, claims Cohen, God is not all-powerful and all-knowing, and thus was neither responsible for the Holocaust, nor could He have stopped it from happening.

Finally, there are those Jewish thinkers who have chosen to keep silent, as the only thinkable response to the unthinkable.

JEWISH POLICE (*Juedischer Ordnungsdienst*), Jewish police units set up on German orders in certain locations within German-occupied areas. The JUDEN-RAETE in Eastern Europe were commanded to organize these police units, generally as a prerequisite to the establishment of GHETTOS in their areas.

The duties of the Jewish police included collecting ransom payments, personal possessions, and taxes from their fellow Jews; gathering Jews for FORCED LABOR quotas; guarding the ghetto; and accompanying labor crews that worked outside the ghetto. Early on, the Jewish police also carried out public welfare duties, such as giving out food rations and aid to the poor and dealing with sanitary conditions.

The Germans set guidelines regarding the type of person to be recruited for the police: someone who was physically fit, and had both military experience and an academic degree. However, these guidelines were not actually observed. The Jewish police was officially part of the *Judenrat*, but many *Judenraete* regarded the police suspiciously: they feared that the Germans would have direct control over the police and make them carry out their dastardly policies. Indeed, the German authorities often made sure to appoint Jewish police heads who would follow their orders without question. Thus, many Jews in the ghettos considered the Jewish police to be a danger to the rest of the ghetto population. In addition, many YOUTH MOVEMENTS and Jewish political parties forbid their members from joining the police forces.

As time went on, the Jewish policemen were strongly affected by the mass DEPORTATIONS TO EXTERMINATION CAMPS. Many decided to quit the force, rather than participate in the rounding up of their fellow Jews (most of these policemen were then themselves deported). Other policemen stayed in their posts, following German orders to the very end. This type of behavior came under serious investigation by SURVIVOR groups after the war. In Munich, 40 Jewish policemen were found guilty of improper behavior and ostracized by the Jewish community; in Israel several policemen were charged, but most were acquitted, based on the terrible context in which they had to function during the war.

JODL, ALFRED (1890–1946), Chief of the German Armed Forces High Command Operational Staff during WORLD WAR II. Jodl served as HITLER'S chief advisor on operations and strategy, and commanded all

General Alfred Jodl on his way to Rheims, France to sign the terms of surrender, May 7, 1945

of the WEHRMACHT'S campaigns except the one against the SOVIET UNION. He was sentenced to death at Nuremberg (see TRIALS OF WAR CRIMINALS) and hanged in 1946.

JOINT DISTRIBUTION COMMITTEE (full name: American Jewish Joint Distribution Committee; also known as the JDC or the Joint), American Jewish philanthropic organization, founded in 1914 to send money to needy Jews abroad. During the HOLOCAUST, the JDC served as American Jewry's central relief and rescue body for their European brethren. At its helm during WORLD WAR II was Joseph J. SCHWARTZ, who headed the JDC's European offices (located in neutral Lisbon, Portugal). Schwartz often stretched the limits of what the American JDC headquarters called legal, in order to get the organization's money to where it was truly needed.

Soon after the Nazis rose to power in GERMANY, they began issuing ANTI-JEWISH LEGISLATION that struck at the Jews financially. The JDC took on a major role in helping German Jews find new ways to survive economically. In addition, the JDC helped those Jews who could no longer stay in Germany emigrate.

During the war, JDC funds were used to help French Jews—partly through legal means, and partly through underground channels; small groups of surviving German Jews in BERLIN; and the surviving members of the Jewish community in Zagreb, CROATIA. In addition, aid packages were sent to various CONCENTRATION CAMPS and to the THERESIENSTADT Ghetto. The JDC also sent food and money to POLAND before the UNITED STATES entered the war in late 1941; supported the evacuation of thousands of Polish Jews in LITHUANIA to East Asia; supplied large sums of money to aid Romanian Jewry; raised funds for Jews in the WARSAW Ghetto; and was active in the attempts to save Slovak Jewry. After the Germans occupied HUNGARY in 1944, the JDC supplied large amounts of money to set up shelters for Jewish children and to fund the rescue efforts of neutral diplomats such as Raoul WALLENBERG of SWEDEN and Carl LUTZ of SWITZERLAND. After the war, the JDC was the main Jewish agency supporting Jewish SURVIVORS in Displaced Persons camps. In fact, between 1946 and 1950, a total of $280 million was spent by the JDC on rehabilitating survivors. (see also RESCUE OF POLISH JEWS VIA EAST ASIA and DISPLACED PERSONS, JEWISH.)

JUDENRAT   (in plural, *Judenraete*), Jewish councils set up in the Jewish communities of Nazi-occupied Europe on German orders. The *Judenraete* were given the responsibility to implement the Nazis' policies regarding the Jews. These Jewish councils often performed a balancing act: on one hand, they felt a responsibility to help their fellow Jews as much as possible; on the other, they were supposed to carry out the orders of the Nazi authorities, often at the expense of their fellow Jews. The role played by the *Judenraete* is one of the most controversial aspects of the HOLOCAUST period.

The *Judenraete* were not set up in a consistent manner: in some cases a *Judenrat* was responsible for one city only, while in other cases a *Judenrat* or a body similar to it held authority over an entire district, or sometimes over a whole country, as in GERMANY, FRANCE, BELGIUM, the NETHERLANDS, SLOVAKIA, ROMANIA and the Protectorate of Bohemia and Moravia. (see BOHEMIA and MORAVIA, PROTECTORATE OF.) The first *Judenraete* were established in occupied POLAND in the fall of 1939, just weeks after WORLD WAR II broke out, on orders issued by GESTAPO Head Reinhard HEYDRICH and implemented by GENERALGOUVERNEMENT Head Hans FRANK. They were to be made up of "influential people and rabbis."

Frank ordered that in areas with less than 10,000 Jews, the *Judenrat* would have 12 members, while in larger cities or towns the council would consist of 24 members. The councils were to be elected by the local population and the council itself would elect its chairman and vice-chairman. The Germans then had to approve the selections. In certain cases, Jewish activists refused to participate in the *Judenraete*, as they suspected—correctly—how the Germans intended to exploit the councils, and that they would force them to act against their fellow Jews. However, in general, most Jewish leaders did join the *Judenraete*.

After the *Judenraete* were established the Germans instructed them to carry out various administrative and economic measures that were destructive to the Jews. In most instances, the *Judenraete* tried to delay or lighten the measures. Other *Judenraete* members believed that if they would comply with the Germans' demands, then the Germans would see how productive the Jews could be, and ease the blows. In a few cases, *Judenraete* members took advantage of their privileged positions for their personal gain, which led to much animosity and criticism on the part of the Jewish communities.

The *Judenraete* were put in charge of transferring Jews from their homes to GHETTOS, maintaining the peace, and preventing smuggling. In addition, they were responsible to hand out the meager food rations allowed by the Germans. In some cases, the *Judenraete* tried to alleviate the starvation in their ghettos by procuring food illegally. The councils also set up mutual help organizations, hospitals, medical clinics, and orphanages. From 1940 the *Judenraete* were ordered to provide workers to do FORCED LABOR in labor camps. In most cases the councils complied with the Germans' demand, again causing tension in the community.

When the Nazis embarked upon the "Final Solution"—the annihilation of European Jewry—they demanded from many of the *Judenraete* that they hand over names of Jews to be deported to EXTERMINATION CAMPS. Each council had to decide whether and how much to comply with the Germans. Most looked for ways to prevent or at least decelerate the DEPORTATION process; some did so by adopting a policy of "rescue by labor." They tried to show the Germans that the Jews were vital to the war economy as producers of various important products and armaments, and that the Germans could not afford to exterminate them en mass. Some council leaders decided to sacrifice certain elements of the community for others—cutting off the hand to save the rest of the body. Both during and after the war, this practice provoked great criticism and controversy. In several cases *Judenraete* members planned and took part in armed resistance to the Nazis.

K

KAISERWALD (in Latvian, Meza-Park), CONCENTRA-
TION CAMP in LATVIA, situated in a recreation village near
RIGA. Kaiserwald was established in March 1943; the
first prisoners to arrive were several hundred German
criminals. After June 1943 most of the remaining Jews
deported from Riga were brought to Kaiserwald. In
November of that year the remnant of Latvian Jewry,
along with the survivors of the VILNA Ghetto, were
deported to Kaiserwald, as well. A small group of Jews
were taken to work at nearby FORCED LABOR camps that,
over time, became satellites of Kaiserwald.

In 1944 thousands of Jewish women from HUNGARY
and a group of Jews from LODZ, POLAND were deported
to Kaiserwald. In March of that year the camp housed
almost 12,000 inmates, nearly all Jews. The inmates at
Kaiserwald were used as forced laborers in mines, factories, and farms. They suffered from terrible cold,
hunger, and overcrowding.

In July 1944 the Soviet army was drawing near, so
the Germans began evacuating prisoners from Kaiserwald. First, thousands of Jews who were deemed unfit
were murdered in a series of brutal *aktionen*. The evacuation was over by September 1944; the prisoners were
sent by train or ship to the STUTTHOF camp near DANZIG.
Over time, they were sent to various camps inside
GERMANY.

KALTENBRUNNER, ERNST (1903–1946), Nazi
functionary. Born in AUSTRIA, Kaltenbrunner joined
both the NAZI PARTY and the SS in 1932. In 1934 and
1935 Kaltenbrunner was imprisoned in Austria for high
treason; he then went on to head the SS in that country
from 1935 to 1938.

After the ANSCHLUSS—the annexing of Austria by
GERMANY in March 1938—Kaltenbrunner was ap-
pointed undersecretary of state for public security in
Austria. In that capacity, Kaltenbrunner supervised
Adolf EICHMANN'S Central Office for Jewish Emigration
(ZENTRALSTELLE FUER JUEDISCHE AUSWANDERUNG) in
VIENNA. By April 1939, Kaltenbrunner had helped
force tens of thousands of Jews to leave Austria. As an

SS-*Gruppenfuehrer*, Kaltenbrunner was deeply involved
in the EUTHANASIA PROGRAM.

After Reinhard HEYDRICH was assassinated in mid-
1942, Kaltenbrunner succeeded him as chief of the
Reich Security Main Office (REICHSSICHERHEITS-
HAUPTAMT, RSHA). Along with SS chief Heinrich
HIMMLER, Kaltenbrunner was one of the major initia-
tors and organizers of AKTION REINHARD—the systema-
tic extermination of the Jews in the GENERAL-
GOUVERNEMENT in POLAND.

Despite Kaltenbrunner's attempt to maintain a low
profile, and his behavior at the NUREMBERG TRIALS, where
he claimed no knowledge of the Nazis' plan to kill all
the Jews in Europe, Kaltenbrunner was sentenced to
death, and hanged in October 1946.

KAMENETS-PODOLSKI City in the UKRAINE and site
of a massacre of Jews in August 1941.

In late June 1941 HUNGARY followed GERMANY in
declaring war on the SOVIET UNION. Soon thereafter,
the Hungarian authorities decided to deport Polish
and Russian Jews residing in Hungary. In July, in
addition to Polish and Russian Jews, the Hungarians
also rounded up a large number of native Hungarian
Jews, some of whom could not prove their citizenship
because their identity papers were not readily accessible.
Entire Jewish communities in the Hungarian-con-
trolled TRANSCARPATHIAN UKRAINE were evicted under
the pretext of being "Jewish foreign nationals."

These "aliens," who were arrested very quickly, were
crowded into freight trains and transported to the
Ukrainian border. They were then moved over the
border at a rate of 1,000 per day. By the end of August
1941 some 18,000 Jews had been handed over to the SS.
After being transferred to Kolomyia, the Jews were
marched to Kamenets-Podolski, where 23,600 were
murdered in an *aktion* directed by Friedrich Jeckeln
on August 27 and 28. Between 14,000 and 16,000
victims were from Hungary and the rest were local
Jews. The surviving Jews from Hungary mostly returned home.

KARSKI, JAN (b. 1914), Undercover name for Jan Kozielewski, a Polish non-Jew who brought news of the HOLOCAUST to the West. After WORLD WAR II broke out, Karski joined the Polish underground and served as a messenger for the POLISH GOVERNMENT-IN-EXILE. In 1942 he was to be sent to London, where the Polish government-in-exile sat, to issue a report on the situation in Nazi-occupied POLAND, specifically regarding the status of the Jews. Karski wanted to provide an accurate report, so he visited the WARSAW Ghetto on two occasions and a transit camp for deportation to TREBLINKA, probably Izbica. During his visits Karski met with Jewish leaders who asked him to tell the West about the Jews' dire situation.

Karski arrived in London in November 1942. He made his report to the Polish government-in-exile, and then met with Prime Minister Winston CHURCHILL and various other politicians, public figures, and journalists. In December, based on Karski's testimony, the Polish government asked the Allies to intervene on behalf of Polish Jewry and stop GERMANY from carrying out mass murders. After his stay in London, Karski traveled to the UNITED STATES, where he met with President Franklin ROOSEVELT and others, and tried to rally the public against the Germans.

In 1982 Karski was designated as RIGHTEOUS AMONG THE NATIONS by YAD VASHEM.

KASZTNER, REZSO (also known as Rudolf or Israel; 1906–1957), Hungarian Zionist leader. Kasztner was a Labor Zionist activist in his native TRANSYLVANIA and then in BUDAPEST after Transylvania was annexed by HUNGARY in 1940. In late 1944 he helped found the RELIEF AND RESCUE COMMITTEE OF BUDAPEST. Until spring 1944, the committee successfully smuggled into Hungary REFUGEES from POLAND and SLOVAKIA.

GERMANY invaded Hungary in March 1944. Kasztner believed that the best way to save Hungarian Jewry—the last Jewish community in Europe—was to negotiate with the German authorities. Thus, the rescue committee contacted the SS officers in charge of implementing the "Final Solution" in Hungary. Soon thereafter, Adolf EICHMANN made his offer to exchange "Blood for Goods" whereby a certain number of Jews would be spared in exchange for large amounts of goods, including trucks. An emissary, Joel BRAND, was sent to Turkey to bring this offer to the attention of the Allies and Jewish leaders. When he did not return to Hungary, Kasztner took over direct negotiations with

Rezso (Israel) Kasztner (on the left)

Eichmann and later with Kurt BECHER. In late June 1944 Kasztner convinced Eichmann to release some 1,700 Jews. Kasztner and other Jewish leaders drew up a list of Jews to be released, including leading wealthy Jews, Zionists, rabbis, Jews from different religious communities, and Kasztner's own family and friends. After being detained in BERGEN-BELSEN, the members of the "Kasztner train" eventually reached safety in SWITZERLAND. Kasztner and Becher continued negotiating for an end to the murder and later for the surrender of various Nazi camps to the Allies. These negotiations may have led to the order to stop the murder in AUSCHWITZ and to stop the DEPORTATIONS from Budapest in fall 1944.

After the war, Kasztner moved to Palestine. In 1954 he sued a journalist named Malkiel Grunwald, who had accused Kasztner of collaborating with the Nazis. However, Grunwald's lawyer turned the trial into an indictment of Kasztner, and in fact, the judge summed up the trial by saying that Kasztner had "sold his soul to the devil"—by negotiating with the Nazis, by favoring his friends and relatives, and by not doing enough to warn Hungarian Jews about their fate. Kasztner appealed this verdict and the Israeli Supreme Court cleared Kasztner of all wrongdoing. However, before the new decision could be announced, Kasztner was assassinated by extreme right-wing nationalists.

KATZENELSON, ITZHAK (1886–1944), Jewish poet, playwright, and educator. Born in the Minsk district of Russia, Katzenelson moved to LODZ with his family in 1886. He began writing poetry at a young age, and throughout his life he wrote in both Hebrew and Yiddish.

In November 1939 Katzenelson escaped Lodz for WARSAW. He lived and wrote in Warsaw until the WARSAW GHETTO UPRISING. For the first year and a half of the Nazi occupation of Warsaw, Katzenelson tried to encourage the GHETTO'S Jews by saying that just like other bleak times in Jewish history, "this too shall pass." However, when Katzenelson realized that the Nazis intended to destroy every last Jew in Europe, he lost his optimism. His writings began to focus on confronting the mass death of Polish Jewry. His poems dealt with Jewish heroism, and mourned the Jews who had been sent to their deaths, including his wife and two of his sons.

After the outbreak of the ghetto revolt in April 1943, Katzenelson hid for weeks on the Polish side of Warsaw. He was discovered by the Germans in May. Because he possessed a Honduran passport, he was sent to the VITTEL camp in FRANCE. There he wrote a diary which is an important document about the HOLOCAUST. A year later, he and his surviving son were deported to AUSCHWITZ, where they were executed.

KATZMANN, FRITZ

(1906–1957), SS officer. Katzmann joined the NAZI PARTY in 1928 and the SS in 1930. From November 1939 to August 1941 he served as SS and Police Leader in the Radom district of the GENERALGOUVERNEMENT. Next, he was appointed SS and Police Leader in the Galicia region, a post he held until the fall of 1943. In this capacity, Katzmann was in charge of the implementation of the "Final Solution" for the Jews of Galicia. Under his direction, most of the Jews of Eastern Galicia were exterminated. On June 30, 1943 Katzmann submitted a report to his superiors, in which he described in great detail how he and his men had eliminated almost all of the Jews who lived in the region, either by shooting them on the spot, or by deporting them to their deaths at FORCED LABOR or EXTERMINATION CAMPS. His report also made mention of cases of Jewish resistance to his actions.

In 1944 Katzmann was appointed SS and Police Leader in Military District XX, whose main offices were located in the city of DANZIG. After the war, Katzmann falsified his name and went into hiding; he died in 1957. No other details are known about his post-war life.

KAUFERING

Network of 15 camps located around the German village of Kaufering, about 25 miles southwest of MUNICH. The Kaufering camps, which were satellites of the DACHAU concentration camp, were established between June and October 1944. Those prisoners brought to Kaufering were used as part of the Ministry of Armaments' plan to transfer Jews to GERMANY to build underground fighter plane factories that could not be harmed by Allied bombs. This plan was called the *Jagerstab* program.

The first prisoners at Kaufering were Lithuanian Jews who arrived in June 1944. In October large groups of Hungarian, Polish, Czechoslovak, and Romanian Jews arrived; most had been transferred to Kaufering from AUSCHWITZ. The prisoners were housed in semi-underground huts, and were badly maltreated. They were given insufficient food rations, no medical care, and were made to do extraordinarily hard work for the armaments industry and construction companies. This resulted in a very high death rate.

The Germans began evacuating the Kaufering prisoners to Dachau in April 1945, a week before American troops arrived to liberate the camp complex. When the Americans arrived, they found the camps empty, but for a few prisoners who had hidden in the woods during the evacuation. It is unclear how many prisoners perished at Kaufering.

KEITEL, WILHELM

(1882–1946), Chief of Staff of the German Armed Forces High Command from 1938 to 1945. In this capacity, Keitel was responsible for the

Field Marshal Wilhelm Keitel walking one pace behind Hitler as they review troops

shooting of hostages and the massacre of PRISONERS OF WAR and civilians in German-occupied territories. After the war, at the NUREMBERG TRIAL, he represented the army's High Command, which was on trial as a criminal organization. He was sentenced to death and hanged.

KIDDUSH HA-HAYYIM (literally, "sanctifying life"), Hebrew term used with regard to the HOLOCAUST to indicate types of Jewish resistance to the Nazis that glorified the value of Jewish life, as opposed to the value of martyrdom. (see also KIDDUSH HA-SHEM.)

KIDDUSH HA-SHEM (literally, "sanctifying the Name [of God]"), Hebrew term used to indicate Jewish martyrdom, i.e. a Jew choosing to die for the sake of his religion or in the case of the HOLOCAUST, a Jew being murdered simply for being a Jew.

KIELCE City in southeast POLAND and site of a post-war pogrom that triggered the exodus of many Jews.

Kielce was occupied by German troops just days after WORLD WAR II broke out. The Germans immediately began persecuting the city's Jews, who numbered some 24,000. A GHETTO was set up in April 1941, and the able-bodied Jewish men were made to do FORCED LABOR. The Nazis began liquidating the Kielce Ghetto on August 20, 1942. Sick Jews and orphans were executed, while all but 2,000 of the city's Jews were deported to TREBLINKA. The remaining 2,000 were sent to forced labor camps; in August 1944 the surviving prisoners were sent to BUCHENWALD or AUSCHWITZ.

The Soviet army liberated Kielce in January 1945; at that point, only two Jews were left in the city. Over the next 18 months, about 150 Jews gathered in the city's former Jewish community building. Despite all that had happened, a blood libel was made against the Jews. On July 4, 1946 an angry mob attacked the Jewish group, massacring 42 Jews and wounding about 50. When order was finally restored, seven of the main rioters were executed. The Kielce pogrom is considered a catalyst for the flight of many Holocaust SURVIVORS from Poland.

Survivors of the Kielce pogrom wait to leave the city, July 1946

KLOOGA One of the three largest labor camps in ESTONIA. Klooga, established in the summer of 1943, was a sub-camp of the VAIVARA concentration camp. It held about 2,000–3,000 prisoners, who mainly arrived in August and September 1943 from the VILNA Ghetto. A smaller contingent came from the KOVNO Ghetto, and about 100 Soviet PRISONERS OF WAR were also interned there.

The Germans established camps in Estonia in order to take advantage of the local natural resources. The prisoners were made to manufacture goods for the German war effort and build fortifications against the Soviet army, which was drawing near. At Klooga, most prisoners worked in brick and cement factories and in sawmills, while a smaller group worked in a wooden clog factory. The conditions at the camp were brutal; the prisoners received meager food and water rations and were forced to work even when they were ill. A 75-man underground was active in Klooga, but because prisoners were often transferred out of the camp, the underground was unable to organize itself for an uprising.

The Germans began evacuating Klooga in the summer of 1944. On September 19 SS men shot the last 2,500 prisoners in the camp. Only 85 prisoners managed to hide, and survived.

Jews behind barbed wire in Klooga

KOCH, KARL AND ILSE (1897–1945 and 1906–1967), Commandant of Nazi CONCENTRATION CAMPS and his wife. During the 1930s Karl Koch served in senior positions at several camps. In August 1937 he became commandant at BUCHENWALD and his wife was made a camp overseer. The two soon became infamous for treating the prisoners brutally—Ilse was known for

Ilse Koch

riding through the camp on a horse and whipping prisoners with her horsewhip.

Koch was transferred to MAJDANEK in September 1941. During the couple's stay there, they amassed a collection of tattooed human skin and shrunken skulls. Before their extermination, Ilse would choose the living prisoners whose skin she coveted.

In July 1942 Koch was removed from Majdanek in the wake of a mass prisoner escape. He was arrested in August 1943 for forgery, embezzlement, threatening officials, and other charges (including their skin collection). Ilse was arrested as an accomplice. In April 1945 Koch was executed by the SS; Ilse was acquitted. After the war she was arrested by the Americans and sentenced to life imprisonment. In 1949 she was pardoned, but then re-arrested. In 1951 she was again sentenced to life in jail; in 1967 she committed suicide in her cell.

KOMOLY, OTTO (also known as Nathan Kahn; 1892–1945), A Zionist leader and one of the heads of the RELIEF AND RESCUE COMMITTEE OF BUDAPEST.

In late 1941 Komoly joined the activities of Rezso (Rudolf) KASZTNER, who was providing assistance for

Jewish REFUGEES in HUNGARY. In early 1943 Komoly and Kasztner officially established the Relief and Rescue Committee of Budapest. One of the committee's early achievements was the smuggling of over 1,000 Polish Jews into Hungary. In the spring of 1943 the committee began sending emissaries to POLAND to search for any surviving Jews. Those that were found were smuggled into Hungary.

GERMANY invaded Hungary in March 1944. At that point, Komoly concentrated on trying to convince the more liberal Hungarian authorities to protect Hungary's Jews from the Nazis. He also participated in various negotiations with the Germans regarding the exchange of Jewish lives for money or goods. In late summer 1944 Komoly became the head of an International Red Cross department in charge of helping Jewish children (see also RED CROSS, INTERNATIONAL). He began organizing safe houses for children, accelerating his efforts after the brutal and antisemitic ARROW CROSS PARTY took over the government in October. In retaliation for these rescue activities, Komoly was executed by the Arrow Cross right before the Soviet army arrived in BUDAPEST.

KORCZAK, JANUSZ (pen name of Henryk Goldszmit; 1878 or 1879–1942), Polish Jewish doctor, author, and educator. Born in WARSAW to an assimilated Jewish family, Korczak dedicated his life to caring for children, especially orphans. He believed that children should always be listened to and respected, and this belief was reflected in his work. He wrote several books for and about children, and broadcast a children's radio program.

Janusz Korczak (center)

In 1912 Korczak became the director of a Jewish orphanage in Warsaw. When WORLD WAR II broke out in 1939, Korczak first refused to accept the German occupation and heed their regulations (and consequently spent time in jail). However, when the Jews of Warsaw were forced to move into a GHETTO, Korczak refocused his efforts, as always, on the children in his orphanage. Despite offers from Polish friends to hide him on the "Aryan" side of the city, Korczak refused to abandon the children.

On August 5, 1942, during a two-month wave of DEPORTATIONS from the ghetto, the Nazis rounded up Korczak and his 200 children. They marched in rows to the UMSCHLAGPLATZ with Korczak in the lead; he never abandoned his children, even to the very end. Korczak and the children were sent to TREBLINKA, where they were all murdered.

KOVNER, ABBA (1918–1988), Underground leader and PARTISAN commander; a leader of the BERIHA movement; and Hebrew poet and writer.

Born in Sevastopol, Russia, Kovner attended Hebrew high school in VILNA, where he became a member of the *Ha-Shomer ha-Tsa'ir* Zionist YOUTH MOVEMENT. After Vilna was occupied by the Germans in late June 1941, Kovner decided that the only thinkable response was active resistance. He focused his efforts on creating an underground Jewish fighting force, and inspired other young Jews throughout Eastern Europe to stand up against the Nazis. On January 21, 1942 a Jewish military organization was created in Vilna, called the United Partisan Organization (*Fareynegte Partizaner Organizatsye,* FPO). Kovner was one of the FPO's leaders, and became its commander in July 1943. During the final DEPORTATION from Vilna in September 1943, Kovner directed the FPO's activities and the escape of the GHETTO fighters to the forests. Kovner then commanded a Jewish partisan unit in the Rudninkai Forest.

After the war, Kovner helped organize the *Beriha* movement, in which hundreds of thousands of SURVIVORS made their way west in order to reach Palestine. Kovner and his wife, Vitka Kempner—also his partner in the underground movement—settled in Palestine, where Kovner became a distinguished writer. (see also UNITED PARTISAN ORGANIZATION, VILNA.)

KOVNO (in Lithuanian, Kaunas; in Polish, Kowno), city in LITHUANIA. In 1939 about 40,000 Jews lived in Kovno.

Local collaborators escorting Kovno Jews to an execution site

GERMANY invaded the SOVIET UNION in June 1941; Kovno was occupied on June 24. Even before the Germans entered the city, antisemitic Lithuanians went on wild killing sprees directed against the Jews. When the Germans arrived, they took charge of the killings. Thousands of Jews were transferred to locations outside the city, including the Seventh Fort, which was one of a chain of forts built around Kovno during the nineteenth century. The Jews brought there were brutally abused and then shot by the Lithuanian guards. In all, some 10,000 Jews were murdered within the first six weeks of the Germans' arrival.

Soon, the Germans established a civilian administration, which issued a series of anti-Jewish decrees. The Jews were given one month to move into a GHETTO. When the ghetto was closed off from the outside world in August 1941, it contained 29,670 Jews. During the next 10 weeks 3,000 Jews were murdered. The Germans staged a mass killing operation—the "big *aktion*"—on October 28, during which 9,000 Jews were taken to the NINTH FORT and murdered. Life in the ghetto, including much cultural activity, was administered by the JUDENRAETE under Dr. Elchanan ELKES.

Until March 1944, relative quiet reigned in Kovno. However, the quiet was shattered on March 27, 1943 when 1,800 babies, children, and old people were dragged out of their homes and murdered. At that time, underground groups increased their resistance activities. A joint body of Zionists and Communists, the General Jewish Fighting Organization, worked on an escape plan. In all, some 350 Kovno Jews escaped the ghetto to join the PARTISANS.

In early July 1944, as the Soviet army drew near, the Germans began transferring the Jews of Kovno to CONCENTRATION CAMPS in Germany. Many Jews tried to hide; the Germans literally smoked them out with grenades and firebombs, and some 2,000 Jews died. About 4,000 Jews were taken to camps in Germany, where they were joined by Kovno Jews who had been detained in camps in ESTONIA.

Kovno was liberated on August 1, 1944. At the war's end, almost 2,000 Kovno Jews had survived.

KRAKOW see CRACOW.

KRAMER, JOSEF (1906–1945), SS official who served as the commandant at NATZWEILER from April 1941 to May 1944, and at BERGEN-BELSEN from December 1944 until the camp's LIBERATION in April 1945. He was tried and executed by the British.

KRIPO (*Kriminalpolizei*), German criminal police; section of the REICHSSICHERHEITSHAUPTAMT (Reich

Security Main Office). Usually, KRIPO dealt with nonpolitical crimes, while the GESTAPO handled political matters. On occasion, KRIPO assisted the *Gestapo* in its operations against Jews and other political opponents.

KRISTALLNACHT ("Crystal Night" or "Night of the Broken Glass"), pogrom carried out by the Nazis throughout GERMANY and AUSTRIA on November 9–10, 1938. The name *Kristallnacht* refers to the glass of the shop windows smashed by the rioters. Officially, *Kristallnacht* occurred in retaliation for the assassination in PARIS on November 7 of a German embassy official named Ernst vom Rath by a young Jewish REFUGEE named Herschel GRYNSZPAN. On November 9 vom Rath died of his injuries.

Smashed windows of a Jewish store after Kristallnacht

That same night, a group of Nazi leaders gathered in MUNICH to commemorate the anniversary of HITLER'S (failed) attempt to take over the Bavarian government in 1923. The Nazi Minister of Propaganda, Joseph GOEBBELS, told the other participants that the time had come to strike at the Jews. The Nazi leaders then sent instructions to their men all over the country: they were not supposed to act as if they had launched the pogrom, but were to participate all the same. In hours, crazed rioting erupted. The shop windows of Jewish businesses were smashed and the stores looted, hundreds of synagogues and Jewish homes were burnt down, and many Jews were physically assaulted. Some 30,000 Jews, many of them wealthy and prominent members of their Jew-

ish communities, were arrested and deported to the CONCENTRATION CAMPS at DACHAU, SACHSENHAUSEN, and BUCHENWALD, where they were subjected to inhumane and brutal treatment and many died. During the pogrom itself, about 90 Jews were murdered.

After the pogrom was over, the Nazis followed it up with other types of severe anti-Jewish measures. The ARYANIZATION process of seizing Jewish property was intensified; the Jewish community was forced to pay a fine of one billion reichsmarks, ostensibly as a payback for the death of vom Rath; and the Germans set up a Central Office for Jewish Emigration (ZENSTRALSTELLE FUER JUEDISCHE AUSWANDERUNG) to "encourage" the Jews to leave the country.

Western countries and even the SOVIET UNION were shocked by the *Kristallnacht* pogrom, and some governments began allowing in more refugees as a result. However, the Nazis were not deterred, and forged ahead in their plan to do away with European Jewry.

KUBE, WILHELM (1887–1943), NAZI PARTY official and governor of various Nazi-occupied territories.

Kube was one of the first members of the Nazi Party, and he served in numerous positions within the party ranks. In 1928 he became party head in the German *Gau* Ostmark, and in 1933 he filled the same post in the *Gau* Kurmark. From 1924 to 1928 and again in 1933 he represented his party in the Prussian provincial legislature and in the German parliament (REICHSTAG). In 1933 he was named governor of the Brandenburg-Berlin district. However, due to disagreements with other party leaders—and because they suspected him of embezzlement—Kube was dismissed from all his positions.

In 1941 Kube was given another chance—he was assigned to serve as governor of BELORUSSIA, which was part of the German administrative unit known as REICHSKOMMISSARIAT OSTLAND. However, he once again fought with senior SS and police commanders over their policies; Kube felt that they were excluding him from important decision-making. He even tried to bring his complaints to the very top by writing to the *Fuehrer's* bureau.

Kube was assassinated on September 22, 1943. His maid—an undercover Soviet PARTISAN—had planted a bomb under his bed.

KULTURBUND DEUTSCHER JUDEN see CULTURAL UNION OF GERMAN JEWS.

L

LATVIA Country on the Baltic Sea. After WORLD WAR II broke out Latvia was first occupied and later annexed by the SOVIET UNION, according to the terms of the NAZI-SOVIET PACT. However, in June 1941 GERMANY attacked its former ally, the Soviet Union. Soviet-held territories like Latvia were immediately occupied by German troops. Incorporated into the REICHSKOMMISSARIAT OSTLAND, Latvia became known as *Generalbezirk Lettland*. A civil administration was appointed under D. Heinrich Drechsler and was made up of Latvians. At that point, some 70,000 Jews lived in Latvia.

At the end of July 1941, the mobile killing units of EINSATZGRUPPE A carried out the first mass murder of Jews in Latvia. From July to October 1941 some 34,000 Jews were massacred, including 4,000 inhabitants of Latvia's capital, RIGA. At the end of October about 32,000 Jews from Riga were forced into two GHETTOS. At the same time, Higher SS and Police Leader Friedrich Jeckeln arrived to take over the extermination of the remaining Jews in Latvia. His orders, straight from SS chief Heinrich HIMMLER, were to "empty the ghetto." On November 30 and again on

Jewish women and girls gathered before their execution, Liepaja, 1941

December 7, thousands of Jews were taken from the ghetto and shot to death in the RUMBULA Forest. About 25,000 Jews were murdered in this *aktion,* nicknamed the Jeckeln *Aktion.* The Jews imprisoned in the ghettos in Dvinsk and Liepaja were also annihilated in November and December 1941. A commando of Latvians under Viktor Arajs was responsible for the murder of many Latvian Jews.

In November about 20,000 Jews from Germany, AUSTRIA, and Czechoslovakia were brought to Latvia and moved into the Riga Ghetto in place of the Riga Jews who were being killed. A small number were used by the Germans as forced laborers, but the majority— some 14,000—were killed in the forests from January to July 1942, just like the Jews of Latvia.

By the beginning of 1943 only 5,000 Jews remained in Latvia, either in the ghettos or in a few FORCED LABOR camps, such as KAISERWALD. That fall, the Jews that were left in the ghettos were moved to Kaiserwald. In the late summer of 1944, as the Soviet army drew near, the last Jews in Latvia were sent to camps in Germany; many died en route. By war's end, nearly all of the 70,000 Jews living in Latvia in 1941 had perished.

LAVAL, PIERRE
(1883–1945), Head of the collaborating Vichy government in FRANCE from 1942 to 1944.

Laval served as French prime minister from 1931 to 1932 and from 1935 to 1936. After the Nazis occupied the northern part of France in June 1940, Laval became the second in command to Philippe PETAIN, the French war hero who agreed to collaborate with the Nazis and set up a government in southern France. However,

Petain was afraid that Laval would seize power away from him, so he fired Laval in December 1940. In spite of Petain's decision, the Nazis called for Laval to be reinstated, and in May 1942 he returned as prime minister.

Laval was more interested in being practical than in ideology. He wanted peace for France at any price—so he agreed to cooperate with the Nazis in full. He helped the Nazis arrest thousands of Jews for DEPORTATION to their deaths, while in public, he stuck to the story that they were just being sent to labor camps in the east.

After the war, Laval was sentenced to death for collaboration and treason against France. He was executed in PARIS in the fall of 1945. (for more on Vichy, see also FRANCE.)

LEBENSRAUM
(German for "living space"), the term used by the Nazis to denote their supposed need to expand GERMANY'S borders, mostly eastward, and install their world order in the acquired territories.

LE CHAMBON-SUR-LIGNON
Town in southern FRANCE whose inhabitants protected some 3,000–5,000 Jews from the Nazis between 1941 and 1944. The rescue activities that took place in Le Chambon were initiated and led by the town's pastor, Andre Trocme, and his wife Magda. Trocme encouraged his constituents to assist Jews who were fleeing the Nazis by

Pierre Laval talking with Hermann Goering

Monument at Yad Vashem to the rescuers from Le Chambon

hiding them in their private homes and farms. Other Jews were given refuge in children's homes and public institutions in Le Chambon. Some were then smuggled over the border into SWITZERLAND. Volunteers from Le Chambon, such as Pastor Edouard Theis, took these Jews on dangerous journeys through French towns and villages; when they reached the Swiss border, they handed the Jews over to Protestant volunteers on the other side.

A cousin of Pastor Trocme named Daniel Trocme was the director of a children's home in Le Chambon. In that capacity, he rescued many Jewish children. However, he was found out by the Germans in June 1943, and sent to the BUCHENWALD concentration camp, where he perished. Andre Trocme was also arrested, but he was released. After the war, Andre Trocme, Daniel Trocme, Edouard Theis, and 32 other inhabitants of Le Chambon were designated as RIGHTEOUS AMONG THE NATIONS by YAD VASHEM.

LEVI, PRIMO (1919–1987), Italian Jewish Holocaust SURVIVOR and author. Born in Turin, Levi was awarded a doctorate in chemistry in September 1943. Soon thereafter, the Italians surrendered to the Allies and GERMANY quickly took control of much of ITALY.

Primo Levi

Levi fled to the mountains in the north of the country, but he was caught, and in February 1944 he was deported to AUSCHWITZ.

Levi was imprisoned in Auschwitz for 10 months, and was in fact one of the few Italian Jews to survive the camp. When he returned to Italy he resumed his life as a chemist, married, and had children. However, his experiences at Auschwitz never left him alone. In 1947 Levi wrote *Survival in Auschwitz: The Nazi Assault on Humanity,* which described his stay at Auschwitz and his observations on life there. He depicted his horrific experiences authentically and humanely without anger or generalizations. However, it took years for his writing talents to be fully appreciated. Over time, Levi came to be known as an author with remarkable talent, and one of the best Italian writers of his time, whose works continued to focus on Auschwitz and the human condition after Auschwitz. Levi took his own life in 1987, leaving behind no explanation.

LIBERATION The freeing of prisoners from Nazi CONCENTRATION CAMPS and EXTERMINATION CAMPS, and from Nazi-ruled areas.

As the Allies retook control of lands that had been occupied by the Germans, Jews in hiding suddenly found themselves free. The Allies also came across many Nazi camps. In some instances, the Nazis had tried to destroy all evidence of the camps, in order to conceal from the world what had happened there. In other cases, only the buildings remained, as the Nazis had sent the prisoners elsewhere, often on DEATH MARCHES. However, in many camps the Allied soldiers found hundreds or even thousands of emaciated SURVIVORS living in the most horrific of conditions, many of whom were dying of malnourishment and disease.

The liberation of the Nazi concentration and extermination camps began in Eastern Europe when Soviet troops reached MAJDANEK in July 1944. Soon they found many other camp sites, some of which were camouflaged from the outside. Oftentimes the Soviet authorities did not reveal their findings to the rest of the world. The British and American troops who were approaching from the west did not reach the concentration camps of GERMANY until the spring of 1945. What they found was unspeakable—tens of thousands on the verge of death, as well as piles upon piles of corpses. The Allied liberators tried very hard to help the survivors, but many died anyway in the weeks after liberation.

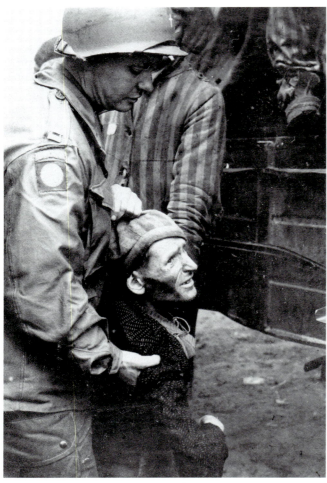

American liberator helping survivor in Wobbelin, 1945

After the war's end, most of the non-Jewish survivors returned to their homes. However, for the Jews, liberation was a mixed blessing. On the one hand, they were now free from Nazi tyranny, free to move on. On the other hand, many of them had nowhere to go and no compelling reason to leave—often, these Jews were the only survivors from their entire families, sometimes from their entire community. Many had no homes left; others began to search desperately for any remnant of family or friends. Many of the Jews ended up in Displaced Persons (DP) camps, sometimes in the company of their former persecutors. Over the next few years the DPs rebuilt their lost lives, usually moving to a place where they had located a relative or friend. Many of the Jews eventually moved to Israel. (see also DISPLACED PERSONS, JEWISH.)

LIBYA Country in east-central North Africa. From 1911 to 1943 Libya was under Italian control; in 1951 it became an independent kingdom. In 1969 the Libyan monarchy was overthrown by a group of army officers, who then instituted a new regime.

In September 1938 the Italian government committed itself to its alliance with GERMANY by issuing racial ANTI-JEWISH LEGISLATION, similar to Germany's NUREMBERG LAWS. The Jews in Italian-controlled Libya, however, were not as badly affected by these laws as the Jews of ITALY, because the governor of Libya, Marshal Italo Balbo, succeeded in lessening their impact. He also took the wind out of the local Fascists, who wanted to enforce harsher anti-Jewish measures. In fact, the Jews in Libya had more to fear from their Muslim neighbors than the Fascists; the Muslims were quite hostile and tormented the Jews.

The Jews' situation deteriorated after Marshal Balbo died in an airplane crash in June 1940. British, Italian, and German troops vied for dominance in the region, and their seesaw battles for Libya affected the Jews. In early 1941 the Italians regained control over Libya; they quickly accused the Jews there of having collaborated with the British. The Jews who held French citizenship were transferred to TUNISIA, while the Jews with British citizenship—some 300—were moved to Italy, where they were detained in CONCENTRATION CAMPS. In 1944, after the Germans took control of northern Italy, they sent those British Jews to BERGEN-BELSEN.

In December 1941 and January 1942 the British retook the Cyrenaica region of Libya; the Italians succeeded in driving them away again during May and June 1942. At that point the Italian authorities carried out many new harsh anti-Jewish measures. They instituted several FORCED LABOR camps for Jews, including Giado, Gharyan, Jeren, and Tigrinna, all of which were located about 45 miles south of Tripoli. Some 3,000 Jews were imprisoned in Giado on the orders of MUSSOLINI himself, while many other Jews were sent to the villages outside Giado, and interned in Gharyan, Jeren, and Tigrinna. Giado was the worst camp in Libya: some 500 Jews died there of weakness, hunger, and disease, especially typhus and typhoid fever.

From June to December 1942 the authorities instituted even more anti-Jewish decrees. Jews were not allowed to make real-estate deals with "Aryan" Italians or with Muslims; they were forbidden to do import, export, or retail trade with Italy; or engage in any activity that could affect the defense of Libya. Next, all Jewish males between the ages of 18 and 45 were drafted for forced labor. In August a camp was established at Sidi Azaz (located some 62 miles east of Tripoli) for the Jews of the Tripolitania region. On October 9, 1942 a decree was issued whereby the racial laws of Italy were to be enforced in Libya, and on October 23 some 350 Jews were deported to the Tobruk area.

By December the battle over Libya was nearly over: all of Cyrenaica had been liberated and the British were nearing Tripolitania (Tripoli was liberated on January 23, 1943). After its LIBERATION the Italians no longer ruled Libya, and all of their racial laws were repealed. However, the Jews of Libya were not left in peace: in November 1945, the Muslim population carried out a three day pogrom against the Jews, one of the most vicious pogroms in the country's history. One hundred and twenty-one Jews were murdered, hundreds more were wounded, synagogues were completely ruined, and hundreds of Jewish homes and places of business were ransacked and destroyed. This pogrom came as a great shock to the Jews, and as a result, many revitalized their sense of Jewish identity, as well as their wish to settle in Palestine. After the establishment of the State of Israel, more than 30,000 Jews left Libya for the new Jewish homeland.

LIDICE   Village in Czechoslovakia that was completely destroyed by the Germans during WORLD WAR II.

In September 1941 senior SS officer Reinhard HEY-DRICH was appointed acting governor of the Protectorate of Bohemia and Moravia. After much deliberation, the London-based CZECHOSLOVAK GOVERNMENT-IN-EXILE decided to assassinate him. On October 4, 1941 a number of two-man PARTISAN teams parachuted into the Protectorate. By May 27, 1942 they were ready for the hit. One of the teams hid in a bend in the road where Heydrich passed daily on his trip to PRAGUE. As the car drove by, they pelted it with hand grenades, wounding Heydrich severely. A few days later, Heydrich died of his wounds.

In retaliation, HITLER ordered the execution of 10,000 Czechs. This order was not carried out; instead, the Germans entered the village of Lidice on the morning of June 10, and executed all of the vil-

Murdered inhabitants of Lidice shot in retaliation for the murder of Reinhard Heydrich, June 1942

lage's men, 192 altogether, along with 71 women. The rest of the women, 198 in all, were deported to the RAVENSBRUECK concentration camp, and 98 children were sent to be "reeducated" by the Germans. No more than 16 of the children survived.

After the war Lidice was rebuilt. It became the symbol of both the Nazis' reign of terror and of the heroism of the Czech resistance. (see also BOHEMIA AND MORAVIA, PROTECTORATE OF.)

LITERATURE ON THE HOLOCAUST   The depiction of the events of the HOLOCAUST through fiction, drama, and poetry. Some literature about the Holocaust is written as historical fiction that closely follows actual events, adding only imaginary dialogue that is consistent with those events. Other writing is much more removed from the actual course of events, and uses allegory and other non historical literary devices to get its point across.

Both Jews and non-Jews have written about aspects of the Holocaust in the French language, especially about the camps. Charlotte Delbo and Jorge Semprun are among the best known non-Jews who have written in this vein. The works of Elie WIESEL are probably the best known pieces of Holocaust literature written in French by a Jewish writer. His first publication, actually written in Yiddish and published in French in 1958, was *La Nuit* (published in English in 1964 as *Night*). This novel, which has since been translated into many additional languages, is almost autobiographical. Wiesel's later works transcend the real-life Holocaust experience and depict a poetic universe rooted in Jewish tradition. Another important French Jewish author is Anna Langfus who, in *The Whole Land Brimstone* (published in English in 1962), is extremely realistic in her depiction of the CONCENTRATION CAMP universe. One of the most significant allegorical works about the Holocaust, *The Last of the Just* (published in English in 1961), was written by Andre Schwarz-Bart. Using the Jewish folk tradition concerning the role of 36 righteous people in maintaining the world, he explores the significance of the sanctification of God's name. Other important French Jewish writers who began publishing about the Holocaust in the first three decades after the war include Romain Gary, Jean-Francois Steiner, and Henri Raczymov. In the last decade of the twentieth century several new authors published fiction in French about the Holocaust, including Johan Bourret, Jean Malaquais, Fanny Levy, and Yael Hassan.

Through the end of the 1980s, most German fiction writers chose to avoid Holocaust themes. Prior to the 1980s, the best known author to have dealt with the Nazi regime (although not directly with the Holocaust) was probably Guenther Grass. Somewhat less known was Jacov Lind, who dealt more directly with Jewish themes in his writing. Until the 1970s those Germans who wrote about the Nazi period generally portrayed both perpetrators and victims in a two-dimensional fashion. This rather black and white presentation of events is evident in Rolf Hochhuth's *The Deputy* (published in English in 1964). Hochhuth's work, a damning fictional presentation of the moral failure of Pope PIUS XII to help the Jews, incited much discussion when it first came out. In Peter Weiss's drama, *The Investigation* (published in English in 1964), the theme raised about the personal responsibility of the perpetrators is heavy, but does not really probe the depths of Nazi criminality. In the 1990s many literary works were published in German about the Holocaust, both original German works and translations into German. Some, like *The Reader* by Bernhard Schlink, reached a wide audience, and were made into films. German language poets have also addressed the Holocaust. One of the most powerful poems ever written about the murder of the Jews is Paul Celan's "Todesfuge," or "Death Fugue", with its haunting refrain: "death is the master in Germany."

It is not surprising that the Holocaust is the main theme or a secondary theme in hundreds of works of literature in Hebrew. Some of Israel's most highly regarded and best-selling authors have written about the Holocaust, including Dan Ben Amotz, David Grossman, Haim Guri, Savyon Liebrecht, Aharon Meged, Uri Orlev, Amos Oz, and Dan Pagis. Others, such as Yehiel Dinur (known as Ka-Tzetnik) and Aharon Appelfeld, are famous specifically for their Holocaust writings. In addition, many Hebrew works about the Holocaust have been translated into other languages. The Holocaust has also made its imprint on the Hebrew drama. Hebrew playwrights such as Motti Lerner and Yehoshua Sobol have addressed controversial issues, such as collaboration with the Nazis and the existence of theatres in the GHETTOS.

Hebrew poetry on the Holocaust has been created by three generations of poets. The first generation—the poets of the 1940s—was far removed from the scene of the crime. These poets did not write firsthand; they wrote on the basis of what they sensed of the dread of the Holocaust. The second generation witnessed the creation of the state of Israel. Most of these poets abandoned the direct approach of the first generation of Hebrew Holocaust poets, and instead searched for indirect means of expressing the horror. Poets like Abba KOVNER, Dan Pagis, Itamar Yaoz-Kest, and Yaakov Besser, who personally experienced WORLD WAR II in their early childhood or youth, express both the personal and the national trauma of the Holocaust. The third generation of Hebrew poets to write about the Holocaust consists of children of Holocaust survivors.

In POLAND, there was a wave of writing about the Holocaust immediately after the war, but during the Stalinist period that lasted until 1956, these writers were essentially silenced. After a wave of Polish ANTI-SEMITISM in the late 1960s, Polish literature devoted greater attention to the subject of Jewish-Polish relations during the Holocaust. The major figure that has preoccupied Polish Holocaust literature is that of Janusz KORCZAK. Since the fall of the Communist regime, many works of fiction and poetry have been published. Among the most heart-wrenching works to appear in Polish in the last decade (also translated into English and Hebrew) are those of Ida Fink. Her short stories discuss the terrible choices, or lack thereof, which Jews faced during the Nazi period. In works written in Polish, as well as in Yiddish and occasionally in Hebrew, the borderline between literature and historical documentation is often blurred, especially when those works were created during or immediately after the war. The Polish writings of Tadeusz Borowski, such as *This Way for the Gas, Ladies and Gentlemen* (published in English in 1967), are especially noteworthy.

The amount of literature on the Holocaust that has appeared in English (both as original works and in translation) is immense. It reflects the tremendous surge of interest that began in the UNITED STATES in the last three decades of the twentieth century. As a group, Americans have confronted the Holocaust through the eyes of others, with only immigrant SURVIVORS and some soldiers having had direct contact with its horror. The first American encounter with the Holocaust can be found in the writings of returning American soldiers. The horror of their encounter so exceeded the grasp of the imagination that the language that tried to contain it was often stretched to its limits. This can be seen in the works of John Hersey (*The Wall,* 1950), Bernard Malamud (*The Assistant,* 1957), and Lewis Wallant (*The Pawnbroker,* 1961). In the two

decades following the EICHMANN TRIAL, a kind of "fascination with Nazism" led to the flourishing of an American literature on the Holocaust. Around this time, but more so from the mid-1970s onward, the voices of the survivors began to be heard. Elie Wiesel, whose works were translated into English, has arguably made the greatest impact on the American reading public. Primo LEVI's writings have also been widely read. In addition, best-selling writers, Jews and non-Jews, have used the Holocaust or the Nazi camps as a theme in their works. Among them are Saul Bellow (*Mr. Sammler's Planet,* 1972), William Styron (*Sophie's Choice,* 1979), Cynthia Ozik (*The Shawl,* 1989), Louis Begley (*The Man Who Was Late,* 1993), Pat Conroy (*Beach Music,* 1996), and Belva Plain (*Legacy of Silence,* 1998). In the last decade of the twentieth century the impact of Holocaust literature has been so great that its study has become a staple course at many universities and colleges in the United States.

The flourishing of modern Yiddish literature was halted by the Holocaust. Nevertheless, Yiddish literature continued to be written in the ghettos and camps, and it played an important public role in providing spiritual sustenance to the ghetto population. Little is known about the Yiddish literature created in the EXTERMINATION CAMPS, as it was hard to find a hiding place for literary works in the camps, and even those authors who survived came back empty-handed. Still, a few of the works created in the camps were saved, such as Zalman Gradowski's *In Harts fun Gehenem* (*In the Heart of Hell*). The texts of songs sung in CHELMNO, TREBLINKA, AUSCHWITZ, and other extermination camps were published by Nahum Blumenthal.

Literature and poetry on the Holocaust have appeared in many other languages, as well, both as original creations and in translation. There is a significant body of books in Czech, Dutch, Hungarian, Italian, Russian, and Serbo-Croatian. Books have also appeared in most of the other European languages, including Finnish, Ladino, and Greek.

LITHUANIA Largest and southernmost of the Baltic states. Jews lived in Lithuania since the fourteenth century. From the seventeenth century Lithuania's rabbinical academies were world-renowned, and during the nineteenth century the country was a center of Jewish culture, religion, and Zionism. After World War I Lithuania became an independent state.

In the non-aggression and territorial agreements

Lithuanians beating Jews under the gaze of German soldiers, summer 1941

made by Nazi GERMANY and the SOVIET UNION just days before WORLD WAR II broke out in September 1939, Lithuania was relegated to the Soviet sphere (see also NAZI-SOVIET PACT). On October 30 of that year control over VILNA was returned to Lithuania from POLAND. At that time, Lithuania's Jewish population grew by about 100,000 to 250,000. This number included about 15,000 Jewish REFUGEES who had fled to Vilna from Nazi-occupied Poland. Most of Lithuania's population was angered by the Nazi-Soviet pact, which took away their country's independence. They let out their anger on the country's Jews with attacks on them and their property.

On June 15, 1940 the Soviet army moved in and took control of Lithuania; about seven weeks later Lithuania was officially annexed to the Soviet Union. Lithuania's Jews were affected profoundly when it became a Soviet republic. On one hand, Jewish representatives were asked to join the government, and Jews were allowed to attend institutions of higher learning

without restriction. On the other hand, many of their businesses were nationalized, and Jewish political, cultural, and welfare organizations were closed down. On June 14, 1941 the Soviets expelled tens of thousands of Lithuanians whom they considered to be "enemies of the people." Among them were some 7,000 Jews. Although the Jews suffered very greatly under the Soviets, their fellow Lithuanians considered them to be supporters of the Soviets. As a result, many Lithuanians, including members of the nationalist Lithuanian Activist Front, harassed the country's Jews.

On June 22, 1941 Germany invaded its former ally, the Soviet Union, and Soviet-held territories such as Lithuania. Most of the Lithuanian population welcomed the Germans, as they felt that the Germans would grant them independence, and many willingly collaborated with the German invaders. Even before the Germans finished conquering Lithuania, the Lithuanians carried out pogroms against the Jews in at least 40 localities. Jews were killed, injured, and raped, and rabbis were brutalized. However, the Germans never intended to award Lithuania its independence: Lithuania was made part of the REICHSKOMMISSARIAT OSTLAND administration, and its name was changed to *Generalbezirk Litauen* (General District of Lithuania).

Just weeks after the Germans arrived, they instituted a systematic campaign to exterminate all of Lithuanian Jewry, led by *Einsatzkommando* 3 of EINSATZGRUPPE A. Many of the stages of the annihilation, including rounding up the Jews, guarding them, and transporting them to the extermination sites, were performed by Lithuanian soldiers and police.

During the summer of 1941 most of the Jews of the provinces were murdered. From September to November most of the Jews in the big cities (who had been imprisoned in GHETTOS when the Germans arrived) were also slaughtered. By late 1941 only 40,000 Jews were left in Lithuania; these were localized in four ghettos (in Vilna, KOVNO, Siauliai, and Svencionys) and several labor camps. During the summer and fall of 1943 the ghettos in Vilna and Svencionys were liquidated, while those in Kovno and Siauliai became CONCENTRATION CAMPS. Approximately 15,000 Jews were sent to labor camps in LATVIA and ESTONIA, where they perished, and some 5,000 Jews were sent to EXTERMINATION CAMPS.

Before the Germans retreated from Lithuania in the summer of 1944, they transferred about 10,000 Jews from the Kovno and Siauliai camps to concentration camps in Germany. Those who tried to resist were murdered. By the time Germany surrendered to the Allies in 1945, only a few thousand Lithuanian Jews had survived.

LODZ City in POLAND. An important center of Jewish culture, Lodz was home to 223,000 Jews on the eve of WORLD WAR II.

The Germans entered Lodz on September 8, 1939. They designated the city as part of the WARTHEGAU, a Polish region that was annexed to the Reich. As soon as they occupied Lodz the Germans began to persecute the city's Jews. They organized riots and kidnapped Jews for FORCED LABOR. Jews were confined to their homes from

Deportees saying goodbye to those left behind in the Lodz Ghetto

5:00 p.m. to 8:00 a.m., and were restricted economically. The Germans even outlawed synagogue services. On November 9 Lodz was formally annexed to the Reich, and from November 15–17 the Germans razed all the synagogues in the city. At the same time, the Jews were ordered to don the Jewish badge (see also BADGE, JEWISH). In October 1939 the Germans appointed a JUDENRAT (known in Lodz as an *Altestenrat,* or Council of Elders), with Mordechai Chaim RUMKOWSKI as its chairman.

Bekanntmachung Nr. 355.

Betr.:

AUSSIEDLUNG
aus Litzmannstadt-Getto

Hiermit fordere ich die zur Aussiedlung bestimmten Personen auf, sich **unbedingt pünktlich** zu der ihnen bekanntgegebenen Zeit am Sammelpunkt zu stellen.

Diejenigen, die sich nicht freiwillig stellen, werden **zwangsweise geholt,** auch wenn sie sich nicht in ihrer eigenen Wohnung aufhalten, da sie überall gefunden werden.

Bei dieser Gelegenheit beziehe ich mich auf meine Bekanntmachung Nr. 347 v. 30. 12. 1941 **und warne die Gettobevölkerung letztmalig.**

Personen, die in ihren Wohnungen nicht gemeldet sind, bei sich aufzunehmen und übernachten zu lassen.

Sollten sich für die Aussiedlung bestimmte Personen bei anderen Familien aufhalten, um sich dadurch der Aussiedlung zu entziehen, werden nicht nur die zur Aussiedlung bestimmten Personen, sondern auch die Familien, die diese Personen aufgenommen haben, sowie die Hauswächter der betreffenden Häuser **zwangsweise ausgesiedelt.**

Dieses ist meine LETZTE WARNUNG!

Litzmannstadt-Getto, den 14. Januar 1942.

(-) CH. RUMKOWSKI
Der Aelteste der Juden in Litzmannstadt

Announcement of deportations, June 14, 1942

From the beginning of the German occupation, the Jews of Lodz were subjected to periodic expulsions. By March 1940 some 70,000 Jews had left the city. Some had fled of their own will, but most had been deported by the Germans. A GHETTO was set up in February and sealed off in late April; approximately 164,000 Jews were packed into it. The ghetto administration was headed by Hans BIEBOW, whose major concern was making money for the SS; he established factories in the ghetto where cheap Jewish labor was exploited for the German war economy. The *Altestenrat* clung to these factories as a means of proving Jewish productivity, with the hope that this would save Jewish lives, so it energetically found work for more and more Jews.

Throughout 1941 and 1942 some 38,500 Jews were moved into the Lodz Ghetto, including Jews from GERMANY, AUSTRIA, Czechoslovakia, LUXEMBOURG, and from other towns in the Warthegau. By the end of 1942, some 204,800 people had passed through the ghetto. About 43,500 people died there as a result of starvation, disease, and cold.

DEPORTATIONS from the Lodz Ghetto began in December 1940. At first, Jews were transferred from the ghetto to forced labor camps outside the city. From January 1942, Jews were deported from the ghetto directly to the CHELMNO extermination camp. From January to May 1942, 55,000 Jews and 5,000 GYPSIES (who had been held in Lodz temporarily) were sent to their deaths at Chelmno. Another deportation *aktion* was carried out in early September of that year: almost 20,000 Jews were sent to Chelmno, and hundreds were killed on the spot during the deportation process.

From September 1942 to May 1944, there were no more deportations and life in Lodz was relatively calm for the 77,000 remaining ghetto inmates. During that time, underground political parties and YOUTH MOVEMENTS contributed much to the ghetto in the way of (illegal) political, public, and cultural activities. However, these groups could not help their fellow Jews when the Germans decided to liquidate the Lodz Ghetto once and for all in May 1944. The Nazis renewed transports to Chelmno, and by July more than 7,000 Jews had been deported. In early August the Nazis rerouted the deportations to AUSCHWITZ in order to accelerate the extermination process. By August 30, the date of the last transport to Auschwitz, about 70,000 Jews had been sent to the infamous EXTERMINATION CAMP. Only 1,200 Jews were left in Lodz; 600 were sent to labor camps in Germany, while the other 600 were put in a camp inside Lodz (Radogoszcz prison). The Nazis intended to kill all the prisoners in that camp before they withdrew, but the prisoners managed to escape to the ghetto area, where they were liberated by the Soviet army on January 19, 1945. At the war's end, no more than 7,000 Jews from the Lodz Ghetto had survived the CONCENTRATION CAMPS.

LOHSE, HINRICH (1896–1964), German politician who served as the Reich Commissioner for the *Ostland* (the Baltic and Belorussian areas) from 1941 to 1944. A

Hinrich Lohse (right) seated with Heinrich Himmler (center) and Martin Bormann (left of Himmler)

member of the Prussian Chamber of Deputies from 1928 and the REICHSTAG from 1932, Lohse was promoted to the Prussian State Council in 1933 and elected president of the province of Schleswig-Holstein. In 1934 he became an officer in the Nazi Storm Troopers (SA).

As Reich Commissioner of the *Ostland,* he was responsible for the total extermination of the Jews in those areas. He directed his underlings to only give GHETTO inmates the most miniscule of food rations—just enough to keep them alive until the "Final Solution" could officially get underway. After the mass executions in the VILNA Ghetto and other places, Lohse questioned whether all Jews should be exterminated, including those who could be useful to the German economy (such as skilled workers in armaments factories, etc.). However, when he was instructed that all Jews should be killed without exception, he cooperated.

Lohse was arrested in 1945 and sentenced to 10 years of hard labor in 1948. He was released in 1951 due to health problems.

LOWENHERZ, JOSEF (1884–1946), Head of the Jewish community of VIENNA during the HOLOCAUST. A lawyer and Zionist activist, Lowenherz was elected annually from 1929 as deputy chairman of the city's Jewish community. In 1936 he became director of the Jewish community. In March 1938 GERMANY annexed AUSTRIA to the Reich (see also ANSCHLUSS). At that point, the Jewish community's offices were closed down, and Lowenherz and other Jewish leaders were arrested. Lowenherz, however, was spared DEPORTATION to DACHAU due to his status as a paid, rather than honorary, official. In May 1938 SS leader Adolf EICHMANN ordered Lowenherz to reorganize the community council. Between 1938 and 1940 Lowenherz focused on helping his constituents emigrate, and even convinced Eichmann to renew emigration after it had been halted in October 1939. However, from 1941 on, Lowenherz was forced to cooperate with the Nazis by providing names of Jews for deportation.

Lowenherz stayed in Vienna until the city was liberated by the Soviet army in 1945. After the war he was arrested and interrogated, but was ultimately released by his son, an officer in the United States army. Lowenherz and his wife immigrated to the United States soon thereafter, but less than a year later, Lowenherz died.

LUBETKIN, ZIVIA (1914–1976), A leader of the Jewish underground in POLAND and one of the founders of the Jewish Fighting Organization (*Zydowska Organizacja Bojowa,* ZOB) in WARSAW.

Born in eastern Poland, Lubetkin joined the pioneering *Dror* Zionist YOUTH MOVEMENT as a young woman. When WORLD WAR II broke out in September 1939, Lubetkin found herself in the part of Poland occupied by the SOVIET UNION. As soon as she could, she made her way to German-occupied Warsaw, in order to participate in her movement's underground activities. At that time, she also met and fell in love with fellow underground leader Yitzhak ZUCKERMAN. The couple later married.

By 1942 the Germans were deporting Jews from Warsaw to EXTERMINATION CAMPS at an extremely fast rate. At that point, Lubetkin helped found the Antifascist Bloc. This was the first organization set up in the Warsaw GHETTO whose express purpose was armed resistance. In July 1942 Lubetkin also helped establish the ZOB. She became a member of its political council (called the Jewish National Committee), and also served on the Coordinating Committee, which acted as a contact between the ZOB and the Jewish Socialist BUND movement.

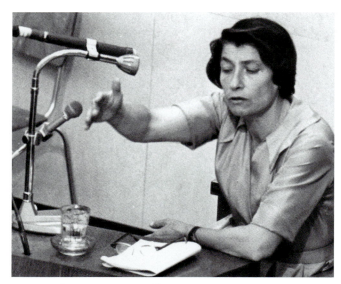

Zivia Lubetkin testifying at the Eichmann Trial

In January 1943 the Germans launched a wave of DEPORTATIONS from the Warsaw Ghetto. The ZOB, thinking that this was to be the final liquidation of the ghetto, sent its two armed units to stage an uprising. Lubetkin fought in this revolt, and was one of the few ZOB fighters to survive. In April 1943, when the actual final liquidation of the ghetto began, Lubetkin participated in the WARSAW GHETTO UPRISING. She sur-

vived by escaping through the sewers to the "Aryan" side of Warsaw. During the summer of 1944, Lubetkin also fought with the ZOB units that took part in the WARSAW POLISH UPRISING.

After the war, Lubetkin was active in the organization of Holocaust SURVIVORS, and helped organize the BERIHA, an organization that helped European Jews "illegally" immigrate to Palestine. She herself settled in Palestine in 1946, where she helped found the Ghetto Fighters' Kibbutz and the Ghetto Fighters' Museum. (see also JEWISH FIGHTING ORGANIZATION, WARSAW.)

LUBLIN   City in POLAND and capital of the Lublin district. Right before WORLD WAR II some 40,000 Jews lived in Lublin. During the first weeks of the war, before the German army reached Lublin, thousands of Jews arrived in the city seeking refuge. The Germans occupied Lublin on September 18, 1939, and immediately began persecuting the city's Jews: many were sent to do FORCED LABOR, some were physically attacked by the Germans, and Jewish property was confiscated. In November 1939 Jews were forced to wear the Jewish badge (see also BADGE, JEWISH), their movement was restricted, and those Jews living on the city's main street were evicted from their homes.

Soon the Germans began implementing a grand

SS men terrorize an elderly religious Jew in Lublin

plan to deport all of the Jews in Poland and the Reich to the Lublin district. This program, known as the NISKO AND LUBLIN PLAN, was ultimately scrapped, but by February 1940 some 6,300 Jews had been brought to the area.

In January 1940 the Germans instituted a JUDENRAT in Lublin. The *Judenrat* set up welfare institutions, soup kitchens, health services, and orphanages. However, when the Germans began arresting Jews for forced labor, the *Judenrat* was ordered to provide lists of even more Jewish names. The council eventually succumbed to German pressure, horrifying the city's Jews.

In the spring of 1941 the Germans ordered the establishment of a GHETTO in Lublin. In preparation, they thinned out the city's Jewish population by deporting some 10,000 Jews to nearby towns. The ghetto was instituted in March 1941; it housed over 34,000 Jews.

The DEPORTATION of Jews to the BELZEC extermination camp began on March 17, 1942; up to 1,400 Jews were deported daily. This deportation *aktion* ended on April 20 after 30,000 Jews had been deported to their deaths, leaving only 4,000 in the city. The remaining Jews were moved to a Lublin suburb; over the next few months, they were subjected to periodic selections (see also SELEKTION). By October, 3,800 Jews had been selected for deportation to MAJDANEK, near the city. In July 1944 the last Jews from Lublin were murdered by the Germans. The city was liberated that same month.

LUBLIN, LUCIEN (b. 1909), Underground activist in FRANCE. Born in Brest-Litovsk, Lublin moved to France where he earned a degree in electrical engineering. When WORLD WAR II broke out in September 1939, he joined the French army. An active member of the Zionist Labor Movement, Lublin helped found an underground Jewish militia called the *Armee Juive*, or Jewish Army, in January 1942. As a member of its supreme command, Lublin put the Jewish Army under the authority of the YISHUV, the organized Jewish community in Palestine, and the *Hagana*, the *Yishuv's* secret army. Lublin found funding for the Jewish Army with the help of Zionist Labor Movement leaders, and staffed it with the best of the French Zionist YOUTH MOVEMENTS and with Zionist youth who had smuggled themselves into France from the NETHERLANDS. During the winter of 1943–1944, the Jewish Army's escape network helped some 300 of its members successfully flee to SPAIN, from whence most immigrated to Palestine. Many of the army's other members fought in battles alongside the PARTISANS in France.

After the war, Lublin created the Society for Protecting Jewish Children, which assisted children who had survived the HOLOCAUST and helped them reach Palestine. (see also JEWISH ARMY, FRANCE.)

LUDIN, HANS ELARD (1905–1946), German ambassador to SLOVAKIA from 1941 to 1945. Ludin joined the NAZI PARTY in 1930 and the Storm Troopers (SA) in 1931. He was one of several SA men who were not executed during the "Night of the Long Knives" in June 1934, and were then made GERMANY's ambassadors to its Eastern European allies and satellite countries during WORLD WAR II.

Ludin did not have many responsibilities as ambassador to Slovakia, because before he took the position, a system had been set up whereby various SS officers served as advisors to the Slovak government. These advisors were the real "ambassadors" to Slovakia; they bypassed the embassy and reported right to the top of the Nazi hierarchy.

However, Ludin did fulfill one important task for Germany in February 1942: he passed a message to the Slovak government requesting 20,000 young, strong Jews for work in the east. The government cooperated, and in March, he again passed on a message, this time requesting the DEPORTATION of the remaining Slovak Jews. Ludin reported that the government agreed without any "pressure." Ludin also provided diplomatic support for the renewed deportations after the SLOVAK NATIONAL UPRISING was put down in 1944.

Ludin was tried and executed in 1946.

LUDWIGSBURGER ZENSTRALSTELLE see CENTRAL OFFICE OF JUDICIAL ADMINISTRATION, LUDWIGSBURG.

LUTHER, MARTIN (1896–1945), Head of the German division of GERMANY's Foreign Office from 1940 to 1943. The owner of a furniture-moving business, Luther joined the NAZI PARTY and the Storm Troopers (SA) in 1932. While redecorating his home, Luther became close to German diplomat Joachim von RIBBENTROP. Luther slowly entrenched himself in Ribbentrop's staff, and when Ribbentrop became foreign minister in 1938, Luther was brought into the foreign office.

Luther's career flourished; he became chief of "Division Germany" in 1940 and undersecretary in 1941.

His main goal was to nazify the foreign office, while at the same time defend it against Nazi Party rivals. Therefore, when Luther realized at the end of 1941 that the Nazis' main priority was the "Final Solution"—the DEPORTATION and extermination of Europe's Jews— he made sure that it became a priority for the foreign office, too. After Luther attended the WANNSEE CONFERENCE in January 1942, where the implementation of the "Final Solution" was discussed, the foreign office fully cooperated with the SS regarding the deportations.

Luther gradually got fed up with Ribbentrop's inadequacies as foreign minister, and tried to unseat him. However, the coup backfired and Luther was arrested. He spent the rest of the war at SACHSENHAUSEN, and died soon after the war's end.

LUTZ, CARL   (Charles; 1895–1975), Swiss diplomat who saved thousands of Jews in HUNGARY. Lutz arrived in BUDAPEST in January 1942 to serve as SWITZERLAND'S vice-consul, and was put in charge of representing the UNITED STATES, GREAT BRITAIN, and other countries that had cut off ties with Hungary.

Carl Lutz in his office in Budapest

Several weeks after the Germans occupied Hungary in March 1944, they began deporting Jews to EXTERMINATION CAMPS. Lutz tried to persuade the Hungarians to stop the DEPORTATIONS. After the HORTHY OFFER, which was to allow Jews to leave Hungary for Palestine, Lutz issued four group certificates of *aliya,* each for 1,000 persons. It was Lutz who issued these because, as Swiss

consul, he represented British interests in Hungary, including issues regarding the British Mandate in Palestine. Soon, the certificates were augmented so that not only the person on the list could immigrate, but his family, too. By that time, almost 50,000 Jews had been put under Swiss protection as potential immigrants to Palestine. All of these Jews were also given letters of protection that guaranteed their safety until they left for Palestine.

After the ARROW CROSS PARTY came to power in Hungary in October 1944, Zionist Youth activists, housed in Lutz's office, forged 100,000 more of these documents. The authorities demanded that Lutz and Raoul WALLENBERG separate the legitimate from the false papers and, to protect the delicate rescue operation, they gave in. When the Germans established two GHETTOS, one for document-holders, Lutz obtained buildings to house 3,000 more Jews under his protection. All but six survived.

In November 1944 Adolf EICHMANN ordered the forced march of Budapest's Jews to the Austrian border. Lutz and other diplomats rushed to rescue as many Jews as possible; he, like his colleagues, plucked Jews out of the marching columns and returned them to Budapest.

When the Soviets invaded Budapest in January 1945, Lutz and his wife fled. After the war they returned to Switzerland, and in 1965, Lutz was designated as RIGHTEOUS AMONG THE NATIONS by YAD VASHEM.

LUXEMBOURG   Small country in Western Europe bordered by BELGIUM, FRANCE, and GERMANY. On the eve of WORLD WAR II, 3,500 Jews lived in Luxembourg, 30 percent of whom were REFUGEES who had arrived since the Nazi rise to power in 1933.

The Germans invaded Luxembourg in May 1940, and immediately set up a military administration. In August 1940 a civil government was established under the leadership of a Luxembourg Nazi. A month later, the administration put the racial NUREMBERG LAWS into effect and began ARYANIZATION—the confiscation of Jewish property. In September 1941 the Jews of Luxembourg were ordered to wear the Jewish badge (see also BADGE, JEWISH), and many were placed in a GHETTO-like camp which soon became the assembly point for DEPORTATIONS to the east.

By October 1941, 750 Jews had left Luxembourg, and most of those who remained were 50 or older. That

Jews being deported from Luxembourg

month, the deportations began: on October 16, 324 Jews were sent to LODZ. In all, 674 Jews were deported in eight transports—the last of which left in September 1943—and only 36 survived. Many had been sent directly to EXTERMINATION CAMPS. Of the 3,500 Jews in Luxembourg before the war, 1,945 perished. Luxembourg was liberated by the Allies on September 9, 1944.

LVOV (in Polish, Lwow; in Ukrainian, Lviv; in German, Lemberg), city in East Galicia, now part of the UKRAINE. Before WORLD WAR II Lvov was under Polish control, but was also claimed by Ukrainian nationalists. In 1939 there were 110,000 Jews in Lvov, making up one-third of the city's total population.

Based on the terms of the NAZI-SOVIET PACT signed just before the war broke out, the Soviets occupied Lvov in September 1939. Soon, 100,000 Jewish REFUGEES arrived from the German-occupied areas of western POLAND.

GERMANY attacked the SOVIET UNION, its former ally, in June 1941. As soon as the Germans entered Lvov, Jews were murdered. By early July 4,000 Jews had been killed, mostly by Ukrainian collaborators. A few days later the Ukrainians carried out another pogrom, killing 2,000 Jews.

By the end of July a JUDENRAT was established. Its chairman, Joseph Parnes, refused to surrender Jews to be sent to CONCENTRATION CAMPS, and in late October was killed for his efforts. Throughout the summer Jews were sent to do FORCED LABOR, synagogues were burnt, and Jewish property was pillaged.

A GHETTO was established in November 1941. Tens of thousands of Jews were packed inside; about 5,000 sick and elderly Jews were killed first so as not to "crowd" the ghetto. In March 1942 the *Judenrat*

Nazi propaganda team filming in Lvov, July 1941

helped the Germans prepare lists of Jews to be deported. Over the next month, 15,000 Jews were sent to BELZEC.

Throughout the summer of 1942, 50,000 Jews were sent to Belzec and JANOWSKA, a camp right inside the city. In September the remaining Jews were moved into a smaller ghetto, and in November, "unproductive" Jews were either sent to Janowska or Belzec to be murdered.

In January 1943 the *Judenrat* was dissolved, the ghetto was turned into a labor camp, and 10,000 Jews without work cards were killed. In May and June the Germans began murdering Jews with work cards. A small underground group tried to defend itself and killed several Nazis. A few of its members managed to reach the PARTISANS in the forest.

Lvov was liberated in 1944; several hundred Jews came out of hiding.

MACEDONIA AND THRACE   Macedonia is a region in southern YUGOSLAVIA, and Thrace, located to the east of Macedonia and south of BULGARIA, is a region in the eastern Balkan peninsula which, today, is divided between Greece and Turkey. Before WORLD WAR II there were some 7,800 Jews in Macedonia and over 5,100 in Thrace.

Jews being deported from Thrace

In April 1941 GERMANY invaded Yugoslavia and divided it amongst its allies. Bulgaria received Macedonia; that same year, Bulgaria also annexed most of Thrace. In both areas, already existing Bulgarian ANTI-JEWISH LEGISLATION was applied. At first, the anti-Jewish measures basically affected the Jews' economic situation. Jewish professionals were no longer allowed to have dealings with non-Jews, shopkeepers lost their businesses, and the Jewish communities were forced to pay large fines. In addition, the Jews were restricted regarding where they could travel and live.

In the fall of 1942, while the rest of the population was given Bulgarian citizenship, the Jews were denied citizenship. Next, they were forced to register their homes and places of business. Finally, all Jews over the age of 10 were made to wear Jewish badges (see also BADGE, JEWISH).

The next step was DEPORTATION. In February 1943 the Bulgarians signed a pact with Germany, in which they agreed to deport to the east 20,000 Jews from their territories. Since nowhere near 20,000 Jews lived in the newly annexed territories of Macedonia and Thrace combined, the Bulgarian authorities intended to include Jews from Bulgaria itself in the deportations.

In March 1943 almost all of the Jews in Bulgarian-occupied Thrace (some 4,000) were arrested and surrendered to the Germans, who then deported them to their deaths at TREBLINKA. Another group of about 1,200 Thrace Jews was moved to SALONIKA and then sent to AUSCHWITZ. At the same time, all of the Jews of Macedonia were rounded up by the Bulgarian authorities; all but 165 were deported to Treblinka. Some 200 Macedonian Jews survived the war, along with some 250 Jews from Thrace, who either joined the PARTISANS or hid with their Christian neighbors. Other Thrace Jews managed to escape to Italian-held territories during 1941–1942.

MACH, ALEXANDER   (1902–?), Slovak leader who headed the fascist HLINKA GUARD and held various positions in the Slovak government; Mach was one of the main supporters of the DEPORTATION of Slovak Jewry.

In the summer of 1940 Mach became minister of internal affairs in the Slovak government, which was a satellite of Nazi GERMANY from 1939–1945. In July, Mach, Slovak President Jozef TISO, and Prime Minister Vojtech TUKA met with Adolf HITLER to set up a Nazi regime in SLOVAKIA. For the rest of the war, Mach and Tuka led a bloc in the government that was even more extreme than the Tiso bloc.

In September 1941 Mach and Tuka called for the deportation of 10,000 Jews from BRATISLAVA, Slovakia's capital, to eastern Slovakia. The deportations began in March 1942 and were carried out by Mach's ministry. Almost 58,000 Jews were deported over the next seven months. In February 1943 Mach tried to restart the deportations. However, he was unsuccessful due to the efforts of the Jewish WORKING GROUP and because the Germans were not interested in renewing the deportations at that point.

Mach stayed in his ministerial position until the SLOVAK NATIONAL UPRISING. After the war, he was sentenced to 30 years in prison.

MADAGASCAR PLAN   Plan to deport the Jews of Europe to Madagascar, a French island colony off the southeast coast of Africa, that was briefly brought up in the summer of 1940 as a solution to the "Jewish question."

The idea of sending European Jewry to Madagascar was not new: British, Dutch, and Polish antisemites had been suggesting a similar plan since World War I. In 1937 the Polish government sent a three man commission to Madagascar to explore the possibilities of settling Jews there. In early 1938 Adolf EICHMANN was asked to prepare a report on the subject of Madagascar. However, it was not until more than two years later that the idea caught on in the upper echelons of the Nazi regime.

In the spring of 1940 it became obvious that the NISKO AND LUBLIN PLAN—which called for the DEPORTATION of all the Jews in the annexed parts of POLAND to the GENERALGOUVERNEMENT—was not going to work. The Germans were also about to invade Western Europe, which would potentially bring hundreds of thousands more Jews under German control. In late May while FRANCE, which controlled Madagascar was being taken, HITLER approved the idea of sending Jews to an African colony.

The Madagascar Plan became technically unfeasible later that year when the Germans lost the Battle of Britain.

MAJDANEK   CONCENTRATION CAMP located in a suburb of LUBLIN which, during WORLD WAR II, was part of the GENERALGOUVERNEMENT. The camp's official purpose was to destroy enemies of the THIRD REICH, help carry out the extermination of the Jews, and take part in the DEPORTATION and "resettlement" of the Poles living in the Zamosc region of the *Generalgouvernement*. In all, some 360,000 victims perished at Majdanek.

Majdanek covered 667 acres of land on the highway connecting Lublin, Zamosc, and Chelm. It had a highly electrified double barbed-wire fence and 19 watchtowers, where guards stood watch and made sure that no one escaped. The camp was made up of five sections, which included 22 prisoner barracks, seven GAS

Piles of shoes that had belonged to victims of the Majdanek camp, 1945

CHAMBERS, two wooden gallows, a small crematorium, and various other necessary buildings such as storehouses, workshops, laundries, and coal storehouses. Up to 45,000 prisoners could be housed at Majdanek at a time. The section set aside for the SS was comprised of their living quarters, the camp commandant's offices, and a casino. A larger crematorium was added in September 1943. Majdanek also had many satellite camps, such as BUDZYN and camps in RADOM and WARSAW. The Nazis had grand plans to expand Majdanek; they wanted to build barracks for 250,000 prisoners, industrial factories, more gas chambers, and a more effective crematorium. However, their full plans were never realized.

From its opening in September 1941 to its LIBERATION in July 1944, five different camp commandants ran Majdanek. These were Karl KOCH, Max Koegel, Herman Florsted, Martin Weiss, and Arthur Liebehenschel.

The first prisoners arrived at Majdanek in October 1941. Throughout the next two and a half years, many groups followed. These included inmates from Soviet PRISONER OF WAR camps and from other concentration camps, such as SACHSENHAUSEN, DACHAU, BUCHENWALD, AUSCHWITZ, NEUENGAMME, GROSS-ROSEN, GUSEN, and Flossenberg; Polish civilians who had been arrested in German raids or had been prisoners elsewhere; Jews from POLAND, GERMANY, Czechoslovakia, the NETHERLANDS, FRANCE, HUNGARY, BELGIUM, and Greece; non-Jews from BELORUSSIA and the UKRAINE; and Polish farmers from the Zamosc region who had been kicked out of their homes. Tens of thousands of Jews were deported to

Majdanek from Warsaw after the WARSAW GHETTO UPRISING in April 1943, and thousands of Jews from BIALYSTOK were brought to the camp after the liquidation of the GHETTO there in August 1943.

Altogether, nearly 500,000 people of 54 different nationalities, from 28 different countries, passed through Majdanek; of those, about 360,000 perished at the camp. Sixty percent died as a result of the camp's woeful conditions, whether by disease, starvation, exposure, overwork, and exhaustion, or by beatings at the hands of the camp guards. The other 40 percent were murdered in the gas chambers or executed in some other fashion, such as mass shootings, which were carried out either in the camp itself or nearby. In 1941 and 1942 the Germans shot sick Soviet prisoners of war; in April 1942 they shot 2,800 Jews; that spring, thousands of other prisoners were also shot to death; 300 Soviet army officers were executed in that way in the summer of 1943; and on November 3, 1943, some 18,000 Jews were shot to death in one single day. That last massacre was part of the ERNTEFEST operation. The Jews were shot into giant pits, while in the background, the Germans blared dance music to drown out the sounds of the killing and the dying. Most of those gassed to death in the gas chambers were Jews. In fact, some of the Jewish prisoners were immediately taken to the gas chambers upon arrival at Majdanek. In this regard, some historians consider Majdanek to be an EXTERMINATION CAMP, and not just a concentration camp.

Several resistance movements existed at Majdanek, and from time to time, groups or individuals attempted to escape the camp. The Polish prisoners at Majdanek were aided by the Polish resistance movement and Polish aid organizations, such as the Polish Red Cross or the Central Welfare Council (see also CENTRAL WELFARE COUNCIL, POLAND).

By July 1944 the advancing Soviet army was very close by, so the Germans liquidated Majdanek. Approximately 1,000 prisoners were evacuated; only half of them reached Auschwitz. Before they left the camp, the German staff destroyed incriminating documents and burnt down the large crematorium and other buildings. However, they were in such a hurry to vacate the camp that they neglected to destroy most of the prisoners' barracks and the gas chambers. The Soviet army liberated the camp on July 24. Only a few hundred Jewish prisoners remained.

Right after the camp's liberation, a joint Polish-Soviet commission began looking into the war crimes that had been committed at Majdanek. Less than two months later it published its report; however, only a very small number of the 1,300 staff members who had worked at Majdanek were even brought to trial. In November 1944 six SS men were tried for their service at Majdanek. Four were sentenced to death, while the other two took their own lives before they could be sentenced. From 1946–1948 another 95 SS men from Majdanek, mostly guards, were put on trial. Seven were given the death sentence, while the rest were sentenced to jail. From 1975–1980 an additional 16 Majdanek staff members were tried in Germany.

Today, Majdanek remains one of the best-kept examples of what a Nazi camp looked like. Several major sections of the camp are still standing; they constitute a museum that memorializes those who perished there at the hands of the Nazis. The original gas chambers and crematoria are now a silent tribute to the 360,000 victims of Majdanek. Next to the gas chamber building stands a dome-shaped structure that shrouds a colossal pile of ashes taken from the camp's crematoria.

MALY TROSTINETS   Village in eastern BELORUSSIA located 7.5 miles east of MINSK; camp and site of mass murder of Jews. About 200,000 people were murdered in the Trostinets area. About 65,000 were killed in Maly Trostinets, including over 30,000 from the last major *aktion* in Minsk.

Between July 28–31, 1942 and on October 21, 1943 the last Jews from Minsk were murdered and buried in Maly Trostinets and Bolshoi Trostinets.

During 1942, Jews from GERMANY, the NETHERLANDS, POLAND, AUSTRIA, and the Protectorate of Bohemia and Moravia were brought by train to be killed in Maly Trostinets (see BOHEMIA AND MORAVIA, PROTECTORATE OF.). Most of the victims were lined up in front of large pits and shot. Tractors then flattened the pits out. The prisoners in the camp were forced to sort through the victims' possessions and maintain the camp. They occasionally underwent selections (see also SELEKTION). This happened more frequently during 1943.

In the fall of 1943 the Nazis began to destroy all evidence of mass murder by burning bodies. Soviet PRISONERS OF WAR were forced to rake through the ashes looking for gold. As the Soviet army approached in June 1944, the Germans killed most of the remaining prisoners. On June 30 the Germans completely destroyed the camp. When the Soviets arrived on July 3, they found a few Jews who had escaped.

MAURITIUS   Tropical island in the Indian Ocean. During WORLD WAR II, 1,580 European Jews who had tried to immigrate "illegally" to Palestine were deported to this British colony as part of a British policy to deter immigration.

MAUTHAUSEN   CONCENTRATION CAMP located near an unused stone quarry about three miles from the town of Mauthausen in Upper AUSTRIA. Mauthausen was opened in August 1938, just a few months after the ANSCHLUSS—the annexing of Austria by GERMANY. The first prisoners to arrive were forced to build the camp and work in the quarry. The work in the quarry proved deadly for many inmates.

The infamous quarry in Mauthausen where thousands of prisoners were worked to death

During its opening year, the 1,100 prisoners brought to Mauthausen were common criminals, people deemed "asocial" and unfit to live in German society, and political opponents of the Reich, including a group of political prisoners transferred from DACHAU. Throughout the war, the camp was mainly used for political or ideological opponents of the Nazi regime.

Mauthausen was divided into three sections: the prison camp, the administrative area, and SS housing. The prison camp was Mauthausen's main area, and it itself was made up of three sections. The prisoners lived in the 20 huts of Camp No. 1. Each hut was supposed to hold only 300 prisoners, but in most cases more than 600 were jammed in. Four of the huts were quarantine huts, where new prisoners lived for three weeks. Afterwards, they were moved into other huts. Camp No. 2 was a workshop area that contained four huts. From the beginning of 1944, it was also a quarantine area. Camp No. 3, built in the spring of 1944, originally contained six huts. Beginning in the summer of 1944, sick and weak prisoners were brought there before being killed.

The camp complex was guarded by the brutal SS DEATH'S HEAD UNITS. Prisoners held various positions of authority, such as camp elder, the elder's deputies, and camp registrar. The work in the camp was overseen by *Kapos* and the camp blocks were handled by the block elder, block registrar, and room elders. All of the prisoners in authority positions were given special privileges.

Until WORLD WAR II broke out, Mauthausen was similar to other concentration camps in Germany: mostly German prisoners were made to do terribly harsh FORCED LABOR, but besides that, the conditions at the camp were not so brutal. When the war started, things changed at Mauthausen. It expanded to become both a concentration camp and a killing center for political and ideological opponents from within the Reich and from other Nazi-occupied countries. Food rations were decreased and the prisoners lived in terribly crowded and unsanitary conditions. This led to the outbreak of typhus and dysentery epidemics, weakening and killing many.

By the end of 1939, the camp had more than doubled its prisoner population to 2,666. During 1940, the number of arriving prisoners grew exponentially: about 11,000 new inmates were sent to Mauthausen that year, leading the camp authorities to establish the first of several satellite camps nearby. Among the prisoners who arrived in 1940 was a group of Republican Spaniards who had fled SPAIN after General Francisco Franco won the Spanish Civil War. They had sought refuge in FRANCE only to be arrested there by the Nazis after the German invasion in May 1940.

A total of 18,000 new prisoners arrived at Mauthausen in 1941, including the camp's first group of Jews, who came in May from the NETHERLANDS. Other new arrivals included many new Spanish prisoners, Czech

The Mauthausen prisoner orchestra accompanies inmates being led to execution

political prisoners, and more than 4,000 Soviet PRISON-ERS OF WAR. Most of the Czech prisoners were murdered that summer, in retaliation for the death of SS leader Reinhard HEYDRICH at the hands of Czech resistance fighters. The Soviet prisoners lived in separate huts called the "Russian camp." Despite the large number of incoming prisoners, there were only 11,135 left by the end of 1941 due to the camp's extremely high mortality rate.

In 1942, in addition to more prisoners from the Netherlands, the SOVIET UNION, Czechoslovakia, and YUGOSLAVIA, transports also arrived from France, BEL-GIUM, GREECE, and LUXEMBOURG. During 1943, 21,028 new internees arrived from all over Europe. Only a few were Jews. That year, more than 8,000 prisoners died in Mauthausen and its sub-camp, GUSEN.

So many new prisoners arrived in 1944 that the German authorities ordered the construction of several satellite camps to control the overflow. Altogether, more than 65,000 new prisoners were recorded, and the maximum population that year was 114,524. In May 1944 Mauthausen admitted large transports of Jews from AUSCHWITZ. The number of Jews who died in Mauthausen that year topped 3,000. Many groups of Poles also arrived in Mauthausen in 1944, after the WARSAW POLISH UPRISING was put down in October 1944. Many Polish students and underground members were killed soon after they arrived.

Almost 25,000 new prisoners came to Mauthausen in 1945, including a stream of Jewish prisoners from HUNGARY who had been previously interned in camps along the Austrian-Hungarian border, where they had been forced to build a line of fortifications. As the battle front drew closer, their camps were emptied out and the prisoners were marched on foot to Mauthausen. Many died en route.

The Jews interned in Mauthausen were treated much worse than the other prisoners. They were forced to dig tunnels at the sub-camps for underground ammunition factories and were expected to do so at an unbearably fast pace. After a month or so, the Jewish workers were so physically broken and exhausted they could hardly move.

On May 3, 1945 a police unit from VIENNA took over the camp's security. The next day, all work stopped at the camp and the SS officers left. On May 5 American troops arrived and liberated the camp. Altogether, 199,404 prisoners passed through Mauthausen. Approximately 119,000 of them, including 38,120 Jews, were killed or died from the harsh conditions, exhaustion, malnourishment, and overwork. That number also included the sick, weak, and "undesirable" prisoners who were taken to the nearby Hartheim castle to be exterminated in the GAS CHAMBER there during the periods of August 1941 to October 1942 and April to December 1944.

MAYER, SALY (1892–1950), Swiss Jewish leader and representative of the JOINT DISTRIBUTION COMMITTEE (JDC). From 1936–1942 Mayer served as president of the Federation of Swiss Jewish Communities; his responsibilities included working with the Swiss government on the issue of Jewish REFUGEES in SWITZERLAND. Many blamed him for Switzerland's prohibitive policy regarding Jewish immigration.

In 1940 Mayer volunteered to act as JDC representative in Switzerland. During his first two years in this position, Mayer had very little money at his disposal. His main responsibilities included getting information from occupied Europe and passing it on to the JDC headquarters in Portugal, and assisting Jewish refugees in Switzerland. When the UNITED STATES entered the war in December 1941, Mayer devised a way to side-step American restrictions on sending funds to occupied Europe. Thus, he received $235,000 from the US in early 1942 and $1,588,000 in late 1943. However, for the year and a half in between, he received no funds due to Swiss restrictions. He received another $11,000,000 during the last year and a half of the war. However, these amounts were not nearly enough to help the Jews in occupied Europe.

During the summer of 1942, the Slovak WORKING

GROUP, a semi-underground rescue committee, came to Mayer with a request for ransom money to save Slovak Jews. Soon, they began negotiations for a larger ransom; this was termed the EUROPA PLAN. At first Mayer regarded these negotiations with suspicion, but he later changed his mind, and sent Swiss money to SLOVAKIA. He also asked the Jewish Agency to provide money. In 1944 Rezso KASZTNER, the Hungarian Jewish negotiator, asked Mayer to join his negotiations with the SS regarding the rescue of Hungarian Jews. Despite the JDC's refusal to participate, Mayer went ahead as the supposed representative of the US and Swiss authorities. From August 1944 to February 1945 Mayer conducted deft negotiations with SS-*Obersturmbannfuehrer* Kurt BECHER, during which Heinrich HIMMLER apparently agreed to stop the DEPORTATION of the Jews of BUDAPEST. However, many accused Mayer of not demanding enough for the Jews during these negotiations or involving other Jewish organizations in the talks.

MCDONALD, JAMES GROVER   (1886–1964), The League of Nations' High Commissioner for REFUGEES from GERMANY.

A history and political science professor, McDonald became interested in the refugee issue in 1933. That same year, he became the head of the newly formed League of Nations' Office of the High Commissioner for Refugees from Germany, which included a Jewish affairs department.

McDonald was plagued with obstacles from the start. The UNITED STATES government did not belong to the League of Nations, while the French and British governments were not supportive of his activities. He was not given adequate funding, so the JOINT DISTRIBUTION COMMITTEE allocated monies for most of the office's expenses.

In 1935 the racial NUREMBERG LAWS were passed in Germany. McDonald realized that as a result of these laws, many new German refugees would need assistance. Thus, he decided to resign his position as high commissioner, but in a dramatic way that would call attention to the growing refugee problem. On December 3, 1935 McDonald publicly resigned his post; in his statement he accused the German government of planning racial extermination, and denounced the members of the League of Nations for their apathy and indifference to the issue.

Germany annexed AUSTRIA in March 1938. Just months later, President Franklin D. ROOSEVELT con-

vened the EVIAN CONFERENCE to discuss the refugee problem. As a result of the conference, Roosevelt created the President's Advisory Committee on Political Refugees (PAC), and named McDonald chairman. McDonald soon realized that he was facing the same obstacles that had stumped him as high commissioner. In 1940 he fought with the State Department when it denied a PAC request for special visas into the United States for outstanding European political, cultural, and labor leaders. McDonald was soon disillusioned. In 1943, he turned down an offer to lead the US delegation to the BERMUDA CONFERENCE.

McDonald was also deeply troubled by the restrictions on Jewish immigration to Palestine. In 1945 he served on the Anglo-American Committee of Inquiry on Palestine, which recommended that 100,000 Jewish SURVIVORS be admitted into Palestine immediately. In 1949 McDonald became the first American ambassador to Israel.

MECHELEN   (in French, Malines), city in BELGIUM located halfway between ANTWERP and BRUSSELS, and site of an assembly camp for Belgian Jews from which they were deported to the east. During the summer of 1942 the German occupation authorities took over barracks in Mechelen's old city and turned them into an assembly camp. As railroad tracks led right up to the camp, Mechelen was a convenient spot for an assembly point for DEPORTATION.

Beginning on July 25, 1942 some 200 Jews arrived at Mechelen per day. These Jews were divided into groups, including Jews who were deported as soon as possible; Jews coming from neutral countries or countries that were allied with GERMANY, who were not always deported; Jews married to non-Jews or half-Jews, who were sent on to the DRANCY camp in FRANCE; and those considered politically "dangerous" who were transferred to prison. Later on, groups of GYPSIES were also brought to the camp.

From August 1942 two transports of Jews, each carrying 1,000 people, departed the camp each week. During 1943 the rate of deportation was somewhat slower. By July 1944, however, 25,257 Jews had left Mechelen for the east on 28 trains. Most were taken to their deaths at AUSCHWITZ.

MEDICAL EXPERIMENTS   Series of brutal pseudo-scientific medical experiments performed in Nazi camps from 1939–1945. Approximately 7,000 Jews, GYPSIES, and PRISONERS OF WAR were used as human guinea pigs in these experiments, conducted by trained Nazi medical doctors.

The Nazis' penchant for medical experiments and operations came to light as soon as Adolf HITLER rose to power in 1933. Between 1933 and 1937, some 200,000 young Germans were sterilized after the Nazis supposedly found that they suffered from genetic diseases. In Nazi ideology, purity of the superior German race was of utmost importance, and any sign of bad "blood" was cause for immediate destruction. In addition, approximately 200,000 chronically and mentally ill patients were exterminated as part of the EUTHANASIA PROGRAM—hiding behind the innocent, even kind term "mercy killing" was the cold-blooded murder of regular German citizens who did not fit in to the Nazis' social or racial code. Finally, the Nazis also set up genetic research departments to identify people with pure Aryan "blood."

From 1942 to 1945 some 70 medical research projects were carried out in Nazi camps. About 200 doctors were posted at the camps; their job was to conduct SELEKTIONEN and participate in these medical experiments, which were initiated by German and Austrian universities and research institutes. Each medical experiment needed to be approved by SS chief Heinrich HIMMLER, who was especially interested in them.

The medical experiments carried out in the camps can be divided into two major categories. The first category includes experiments that were not ethically problematic in and of themselves—in fact, their aims might have been acceptable under other circumstances—but the way in which they were carried out violated ethical codes. The second category includes experiments that both violated medical ethics in the way they were conducted and in their very purpose of being.

The first category consisted of two types of experiments: experiments dealing with survival and rescue, and experiments dealing with medical treatment. Survival and rescue experiments tested the abilities of a human being to survive under harsh conditions and to adapt to those conditions, and figured out how to save lives in various situations. Conducted on prisoners at DACHAU by the SS and German air force, these included testing human potential for survival at high altitudes and at freezing temperatures, and seeing whether and how long humans could survive by drinking seawater.

Prof. Holzlöhner (links) und Dr. Rascher bei einem Unterkühlungsversuch

Bei sinkendem Luftdruck   Übergang zur schlaffen Lähmung

Die Abbildungen sind einem fortlaufenden Filmstreifen entnommen. Der Filmstreifen wurde durch den Abteilungsleiter an der Deutschen Versuchsanstalt für Luftfahrt, Dr. Hans Wolfgang Romberg, identifiziert. (Dokument NO 610 – Prozeß gegen SS-Ärzte in Nürnberg am 9. Dezember 1946)

381

Photographs of medical experiments presented at the Medical Case trial in Nuremberg, December 1946

Medical treatment experiments—still part of the first category—tried to figure out how to treat certain battle injuries and victims of gas attacks, and tested various medicines and vaccination techniques, to learn more about preventing or treating contagious diseases. The chemical warfare experiments were sponsored by the German army.

The second major category of experiments, which violated medical ethics by both their means and their ends, included experiments that tried to prove the Nazis' racist ideas through biology. Those experiments seeking biological proof of the Nazis' racist beliefs included tests on dwarfs and twins, and the study of Jewish skeletons. Those experiments seeking to advance the destruction of the Jews included mass sterilization, meant as an alternative to immediate extermination.

After the war, one of the NUREMBERG TRIALS, called The Medical Case, dealt with these medical experi-

Twenty-three doctors and medical officials were tried and convicted of planning and implementing experiments on human beings against their will in a brutal fashion that included horrific torture, and of planning to murder some of the victims. Seven of the accused were sentenced to death, nine were sentenced to prison, and seven were acquitted. Other major players in the Nazi medical experiments were not tried, as they either committed suicide or escaped Europe.

MEIN KAMPF   Translated as "My Struggle," a book written by Adolf HITLER while in jail in 1924. According to his introduction, Hitler's purpose in writing *Mein Kampf* was to present his goals and philosophy. The major themes of the book are the superiority of the Aryan race, Hitler's plan for Aryan world rule, and the guilt of the Jews as the destroyers of the world.

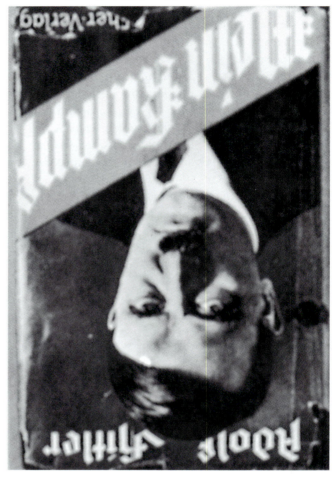

The cover of an edition of "Mein Kampf"

Mein Kampf was written in two volumes. The first volume, called *Eine Abrechnung* ("A Reckoning"), was

published in July 1925. The second, *Die Nationalsozialistische* ("The National Socialist Movement"), was issued in December 1926. After 1930 the two volumes were combined into one.

The book focuses on Hitler's political ideas and plans. He wrote about his foreign policy goals, which highlighted the capture of land in Eastern Europe and Soviet Russia to be used as "living space" for the German people. He also used the book as a forum for espousing his anti-Jewish program. Before he wrote *Mein Kampf* Hitler had advocated the removal of Jews from GERMANY. However, in the book he used veiled terms to call for the actual murder of the Jews.

Much of the autobiographical information Hitler provided in Volume 1 is untrue. He probably changed the data so as to make it look like his political views were based on experiences in his early life. In the second volume, Hitler wrote about the history of the NAZI PARTY, but obscured the facts with ideological statements.

Although not written very well, *Mein Kampf* was a wild success. By 1939, 5.2 million copies had been sold and it had been translated into 11 languages; by 1945, about 10 million copies were in publication and it had been translated into an additional five languages. Since then even more translations have been done, but it has not been published again in German.

Some scholars believe that *Mein Kampf* is an important work that clearly states Hitler's goals, which he then actually pursued when he came to power. Others see it simply as propaganda. (see also PROPAGANDA, NAZI.)

MELNYK, ANDREI   As head of the ORGANIZATION OF UKRAINIAN NATIONALISTS, Melnyk called on Ukrainians to collaborate with the Germans against the SOVIET UNION, and formed a Ukrainian division within the SS in 1943.

MEMEL   (in Lithuanian, Klaipeda), port city on the Baltic Sea. Until 1919 Memel belonged to GERMANY. After World War I the city was taken away from Germany, and in 1923 it was annexed to LITHUANIA. In 1939 there were 9,000 Jews living in Memel, constituting 18 percent of the city's population.

The Jews in Memel were strongly affected by the tension between the Lithuanians, who ran the city's government, and the Germans, who were a majority. After HITLER rose to national power in Germany in 1933, the Nazis began campaigning for the city's return to Germany. This campaign included anti-Jewish riots and other antisemitic actions. In October 1938 the local Nazis called for the implementation of the NUREMBERG LAWS in Memel; at the end of that year the Nazis won 26 of 29 seats in the city's parliament, effectively making Memel part of Germany.

Jewish family fleeing Memel after the Germans occupied the city on March 22, 1939

German troops entered Memel in March 1939. Luckily, many Lithuanians and almost all of the city's Jews had managed to escape to KOVNO and other nearby towns before the invasion. However, after the Nazis took over Lithuania in mid-1941, they destroyed those Jews along with the rest of Lithuanian Jewry. When Memel was liberated by the Soviet army in January 1945, not one Jew remained.

MENCZER, ARON (1917–1943), YOUTH ALIYA activist.

After the ANSCHLUSS—the annexing of AUSTRIA by GERMANY in March 1938—Menczer began working for Youth Aliya in VIENNA. In March 1939 he accompanied a group of Youth Aliya children to Palestine. Although he could have stayed there, Menczer felt a responsibility towards the young Jews still in Austria, so he returned to Vienna.

In September 1939 Menczer became the head of the Vienna branch of Youth Aliya. In 1940 the Germans would no longer allow anyone to leave the country, so Menczer turned his efforts to the 400-student Youth Aliya school in Vienna. In addition, he managed to unite the many Zionist YOUTH MOVEMENTS in Austria into one umbrella organization.

The Youth Aliya offices in Austria were closed in 1941 and Menczer was sent to a FORCED LABOR CAMP.

He was returned to Vienna on September 14, 1942, but transferred to THERESIENSTADT just 10 days later. In Theresienstadt Menczer served as a youth leader and a member of the *He-Halutz* youth movement central council. In August 1943 Menczer helped take care of a group of 1,200 children deported to Theresienstadt from BIALYSTOK. In October Menczer accompanied the children to AUSCHWITZ-Birkenau, where they were all murdered.

MENGELE, JOSEF (1911–1978?), German doctor and SS officer who served as chief physician at AUSCHWITZ from 1943–1944. Mengele was in charge of the camp's selection process, choosing who would live and who would die (see also SELEKTION). In all, he sent about 400,000 people to their deaths in the GAS CHAMBERS. He was also responsible for horrific pseudo-scientific MEDICAL EXPERIMENTS performed on camp prisoners, whose purpose it was to prove the superiority of the Aryan race. Mengele used human beings as guinea pigs to study their resistance and reaction to heat, cold, sterilization, and pain. He was mostly interested in babies, young twins, and dwarfs.

Born in Guenzburg, GERMANY, Mengele earned a doctorate in philosophy and a medical degree. He joined the NAZI PARTY in 1937 and the SS in 1938. Starting in June 1940, Mengele served in the *Waffen-SS* Medical Corps. In May 1943 he was stationed at Auschwitz where he worked until the camp's evacuation in January 1945. He then moved to MAUTHAUSEN, after which he disappeared to South America. Despite concerted efforts to track him, Mengele never resurfaced. He may have drowned in Brazil in 1978. In 1985 a public trial of Mengele was held at YAD VASHEM, in his absence.

MERIN, MOSHE (1906–1943), Chairman of the JUDENRAT in Eastern Upper Silesia, a part of Poland annexed to the Reich by the Germans.

Before the war, Merin was a Zionist activist in the town of Sosnowiec. In September 1939 the Germans invaded Poland. When they entered Sosnowiec, Merin presented himself as the leader of the local Jewish community. In January 1940 the Germans set up a *Judenrat* and named him chairman. The council was not only responsible for Sosnowiec, but also for 100,000 Jews living in 45 nearby communities.

Like all *Judenrat* chairmen, Merin was torn between serving the needs of his fellow Jews, and obeying the

Nazis. However, he executed his responsibilities efficiently and was in close contact with his Nazi administrators. Merin controlled the JEWISH POLICE and labor office, and used them to carry out the Nazis' orders to round up Jews from the entire area for FORCED LABOR. By 1941 Merin's *Judenrat* had 1,200 employees working in various municipal departments. Most of the experienced community leaders left the *Judenrat*, while Merin's cronies took its top positions.

Merin was liked by some and hated by others of his constituents. Although he flamboyantly used his influence to get permission to travel, he also used it to keep his region's Jews out of GHETTOS for a long time. In addition, most of the Jews in his area had jobs and better conditions than Jews elsewhere. On the other hand, Merin complied with German demands in May 1942 to deport the Jews of Eastern Upper Silesia to EXTERMINATION CAMPS. Merin believed that if he doomed some to death, others could be saved. He also thought that if the Jews worked in Nazi factories, they could avoid DEPORTATION.

Zionist youth group members opposed Merin's policies, and branded him a collaborator. In 1943 he turned two Zionists over to the Nazis. They also fought over using South American passports for protection, which Merin thought was dangerous.

Despite his cooperation with the Germans, Merin was sent to AUSCHWITZ in June 1943. The rest of his region's Jews were deported soon after.

MINSK Capital of BELORUSSIA. On the eve of the German invasion of the SOVIET UNION in June 1941, 80,000 Jews lived in Minsk, representing one-third of the city's total population.

Minsk was one of the first cities in the Soviet Union to be occupied by the Germans, so few of its Jews managed to escape to the Soviet interior. The Germans quickly launched the organized persecution of the city's Jews. On July 8 an EINSATZGRUPPE unit began taking Jews out of Minsk to the nearby woods and shooting them. A GHETTO was established on July 20; Jews from Minsk and nearby towns were herded in, as were non-Jews married to Jews and their children. All in total 100,000 Jews lived in the ghetto. A JUDENRAT was formed in July under Eliyahu (Ilya) Mushkin. Soon, an underground group was established as well, under Hersh Smolar.

In November 1941 the Germans initiated an *aktion* in which 12,000 Jews were murdered. Soon after, Jews from the Reich were deported to Minsk; over the course of the next year, 35,442 had come. They were put into a separate ghetto, divided into sections according to their home cities in the Reich. The Germans launched another *aktion* later that month in which 7,000 Jews were murdered. The underground responded to the extermination by expanding its activities.

In March 1942 the Germans ordered the *Judenrat* to surrender 5,000 Jews, but the council refused. In retaliation, the Nazis attacked Jews coming home from work and killed more than 5,000. They also carried out murder operations at night throughout the spring of 1942.

At the end of July 1942 the Germans exterminated more than 30,000 Jews, including the German Jews from the second ghetto. When the *aktion* was over, only 9,000 Jews were left, and the *Judenrat* was dissolved.

The nearly 450 member ghetto underground sought to flee to the forests and become PARTISANS. This flight gained momentum after the March 1942 *aktion*. Eventually seven partisan units were founded by Minsk Jews. In March 1943 more German Jews were murdered, and in August, Jews from Minsk were deported to SOBIBOR. In September 2,000 Jews were sent to a FORCED LABOR camp. The Germans carried out the final *aktion* in Minsk in October, murdering the last 4,000 Jews. Minsk was liberated on July 3, 1944. Only a handful of Jews who had hidden during the final *aktion* were left.

MIR Town in BELORUSSIA, and home to one of the most famous *yeshivas* in Eastern Europe. In September 1939 Mir was annexed by the SOVIET UNION. At that point, 2,500 Jews lived there. The *yeshiva* was moved to VILNA and most of the students eventually escaped to SHANGHAI (see also RESCUE OF POLISH JEWS VIA EAST ASIA).

In June 1941 GERMANY invaded the Soviet Union. German troops entered Mir on June 26; on November 9, the Germans launched an *aktion* in which 1,500 Jews were murdered. Next, they established a GHETTO and crammed 850 people inside.

Soon, an 80-man underground was formed in the ghetto, whose goal was to defend the Jews of the ghetto in case of another *aktion*. Oswald RUFAJZEN, a Jew posing as a VOLKSDEUTSCHE who had been appointed district commander of the German police, helped supply the underground with arms.

On August 6, 1942 Rufajzen was informed that an

aktion would take place in the ghetto on August 13. He gave the information to the underground, and told them that on August 9, he and the rest of the police would be out of town on a "raid against the PARTI-SANS"—providing the Jews with a perfect opportunity for escape. When the time came, only 180 Jews actually fled the ghetto. All those who remained were exterminated during the *aktion*.

MISCHLINGE (German for "hybrid"), part Jews. The racial NUREMBERG LAWS of September 1935 did not actually define who was legally to be considered a Jew. Thus, an additional decree was made in November 1935 which provided detailed definitions of Jew, Aryan, and Mischling.

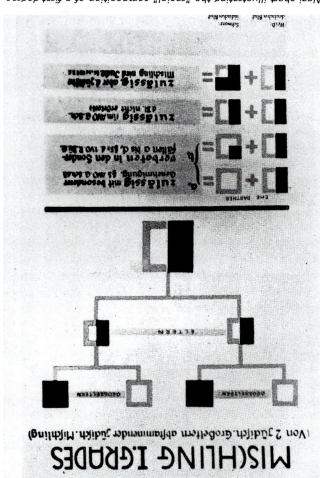

Nazi chart illustrating the "racial" composition of a first-degree Mischling—a person with two Jewish grandparents

Jews were defined as people with at least three full Jewish grandparents. A *Mischling* of the first degree, or half-Jew, was a person with two Jewish grandparents who did not belong to the Jewish religion or who was not married to a Jew as of September 15, 1935. A *Mischling* of the second degree, or quarter-Jew, was someone with one Jewish grandparent or an Aryan married to a Jew. In 1939, 72,000 first degree *Mischlinge* and 39,000 second degree *Mischlinge* were still living in GERMANY.

The *Mischlinge* issue was very important to Adolf HITLER. The policy in Germany was to assimilate second degree *Mischlinge* into the Aryan nation, while first degree *Mischlinge* were to be considered like Jews. In other countries, policies differed. Over the winter of 1941–1942, some Nazis proposed that all *Mischlinge* of the first degree be sterilized; however, nothing ever came of this because the Nazis feared the reactions of the many Germans related to the *Mischlinge*.

MITTELSTELLE FUER JUEDISCHE ERWACHSENEN-BILDUNG (Jewish Center for Adult Education), Jewish educational agency in GERMANY, active from 1934–1938. The center was founded by the REICH REPRESENTATION OF GERMAN JEWS after the rise of Nazism in Germany, on the initiative of Jewish philosopher and educator Martin Buber. Its main goal was to give German Jews the opportunity to strengthen their sense of Jewish identity, especially when the Jewish world as they knew it was falling down all around them. This is reflected in the center's slogan, coined by Buber: "arming for existence." It is also reflected in the words of another center leader, who called the center a form of "moral resistance."

The center's main education technique was the *Lernzeit*, or study period, which was a group study seminar that was held out in the country and usually lasted for several days. Sometimes the seminars were geared towards specific groups, such as youth leaders or teachers, and sometimes they were open to the general Jewish community. Some seminars dealt with one major theme, while others dealt with several subjects at once. Buber was the center's spiritual leader: he chose the seminar themes, usually finding topics in the Bible with relevance to modern times. The center also counseled Jews on a variety of topics.

MOGILEV-PODOLSKI Town in the TRANSNISTRIA region of the UKRAINE. Mogilev-Podolski was occupied by German and Romanian troops in July 1941. Soon thereafter, thousands of Jews in the town were murdered by the occupiers.

Mogilev-Podolski soon became a transit camp for Jews expelled from BESSARABIA and BUKOVINA to Transnistria. From September 1941 to February 1942 more than 55,000 deportees came through the town. Thousands of people were jammed into the transit camp and treated cruelly by the Romanian guards. Many Jews were not allowed to stay in Mogilev-Podolski; thousands were forced to travel by foot to nearby villages and towns. The 15,000 who were initially permitted to stay in the town organized themselves into groups. Some 2,000–3,000 were given residence permits, while the rest lived in constant fear of being deported into the Transnistrian interior for FORCED LABOR.

In December 1943 over 3,000 Jews were allowed to return to ROMANIA, and in March 1944, Jewish leaders in BUCHAREST got permission to bring back 1,400 orphans. Mogilev-Podolski was liberated that month; many Jewish men were immediately drafted by the Soviet army. Many who stayed in the city were killed by German bombs. Most of the deportees were allowed to return to Romania in the spring of 1945.

MOLOTOV, VIACHESLAV MIKHAILOVICH (1890–1987), Soviet leader who signed the NAZI-SOVIET PACT. From 1930 to 1941 Molotov was the official head of the Soviet government. In May 1939 he was appointed peoples' *Commissar* (minister) for foreign affairs. In this capacity, Molotov signed his country's non-aggression pact with Nazi GERMANY just days before WORLD WAR II broke out (the pact is also known as the Molotov-Ribbentrop Pact, named after the two foreign ministers who signed it). This alliance shocked the world because until that time, Germany and the SOVIET UNION had behaved as mortal enemies.

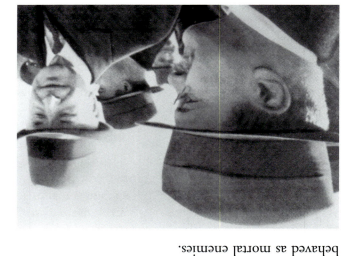

Viacheslav Molotov (front left)

In May 1941 Joseph STALIN took over as official head of government. Molotov stayed on as his deputy and as foreign minister. After Germany turned on its short-lived ally in June 1941, Molotov took an active role in negotiations with the Allied powers. After the war Molotov, whose wife was Jewish, was the man behind the Soviet Union's support of a Jewish state in Palestine. In 1949 Molotov began to lose power. However, after Stalin died, he once again became a Soviet leader. In 1957 Molotov took part in a failed bid to overthrow Nikita Khrushchev; he was stripped of all his senior positions and was publicly condemned. He retired in 1962.

MONTELUPICH PRISON Jail, located on Montelupich Street in CRACOW, which was used by the GESTAPO throughout WORLD WAR II. Prisoners in Montelupich included political prisoners, members of the SS and Security Service (SD) who had been convicted and given prison terms, British and Soviet spies and parachutists, victims of *Gestapo* street raids, soldiers who had deserted the *Waffen-SS*, and regular criminals. Only male prisoners were held at the Montelupich prison; females were housed in a nearby convent. One thousand men and 300 women could be detained at a time; altogether, 20,000 prisoners passed through the prison.

The Jewish political prisoners in Montelupich were treated much worse than the other prisoners. They lived in the cellar, were given paltry food rations, and were frequently tortured. After weeks or months in the prison, they were transferred to PLASZOW to be killed or sent to AUSCHWITZ or GROSS-ROSEN.

In late April 1943 a group of prisoners, members of Cracow's Jewish Fighting Organization, were being sent from Montelupich to Plaszow. They attacked their German guard and tried to escape; most were killed in the struggle, but a few managed to escape and join the underground. Only two prisoners, Shimon and Gusta Draenger, successfully made it to the Wisnicz forests.

MORGENTHAU, HENRY, JR. (1891–1967), American statesman and secretary of the treasury during WORLD WAR II. In that post, Morgenthau was the most important Jew in the government of President Franklin D. ROOSEVELT, and he used his influence to try to mobilize the American government to rescue Jewish REFUGEES in Europe.

Morgenthau was brought into Roosevelt's cabinet as secretary of the treasury in 1934. In his department's

Secretary of the Treasury Henry Morgenthau (left) with President Franklin D. Roosevelt, promoting the sale of Saving Bonds

dealings with the new Nazi government in GERMANY, Morgenthau began to sense early on just how dangerous Adolf HITLER really was, and he consistently pushed for a strong, prepared American armed forces—just in case.

In July 1938 President Roosevelt convened an international meeting, the EVIAN CONFERENCE, to deal with the refugee problem in Europe. The only result of the conference, which was quite ineffective, was the creation of the President's Advisory Committee on Political Refugees. Roosevelt requested that Morgenthau head the new committee, but Morgenthau refused.

By mid-1942 the UNITED STATES government had confirmed the news that the Germans were exterminating European Jews en mass. Morgenthau was quite moved by the information, and he supported Roosevelt's idea to resettle Jews outside of Europe. In late 1943 he managed to convince the State Department to allow the American Jewish JOINT DISTRIBUTION COMMITTEE to send funds to Europe to help rescue Jews in FRANCE and ROMANIA. However, by early 1944 Morgenthau became very critical of the State Department's unwillingness to initiate or even participate in rescue activities. In January one of Morgenthau's assistants handed him a report which documented the State Department's active subversion of rescue activities and refusal to absorb refugees into the United States. Morgenthau toned down the report a bit, and then pre-

sented it to Roosevelt. To a large degree, owing to the possibility of imminent scandal and Morgenthau's urgent demands, Roosevelt quickly created the WAR REFUGEE BOARD, a government agency dedicated to rescuing and assisting World War II victims.

After the war Morgenthau left his post in the government and dedicated himself to Jewish causes until his death in 1967.

MOROCCO Country in North Africa governed by FRANCE from 1912–1956; a small part of the country was ruled by SPAIN. On the eve of WORLD WAR II, about 200,000 Jews lived in Morocco, most in the French-held part. During the 1930s, both French right-wing and Arab Muslim groups in Morocco began anti-Jewish propaganda campaigns that led to violent clashes between them and the Jews. In spite of that, however, many Jewish REFUGEES fled to Morocco after the war broke out in September 1939.

After GERMANY occupied northern France and a pro-German regime was established in southern France, at Vichy, most of the French administration in Morocco declared allegiance to the Vichy government. By October 1940, they instituted the same anti-Jewish laws (STATUT DES JUIFS) that were being enacted in France, but adapted them for the special circumstances in Morocco. Unlike in Europe, Jews in Morocco were defined as such by religion, so as not to offend the Muslim majority by targeting Jews who had converted to Islam. Also, the Vichy anti-Jewish decrees mainly affected Jews in urban areas.

In 1941 many Jewish refugees fled occupied France for Morocco. At the same time, the French administration in Morocco established over 30 FORCED LABOR and detention camps, where Jews were sent to work in an insufferable climate for more than 10 hours per day. The largest Moroccan forced labor camp was Djelfa, which contained 700–1,000 prisoners, many of whom were those same refugees who had come to Morocco seeking a safe haven.

The UNITED STATES army liberated Morocco on November 11, 1942. Technically, the Jews in Morocco were free, but it was several months until all anti-Jewish decrees were cancelled and prisoners interned in camps were actually let out. Furthermore, French right-wing groups and some Muslims once again organized violence against the Jews. Even the police persecuted the newly-"liberated" Jews; tens of Jews were randomly arrested in the streets and given heavy punishments. This type of cruel treatment lasted for many months. (for more on Vichy, see also FRANCE.)

MOSLEY, SIR OSWALD

(1896–1980), British Fascist leader. After serving for a short time in the British Labor Government of 1929, Mosley left to help found the New Party. However, the New Party did not win even one seat in the 1931 elections. In 1932 Mosley visited ITALY, where the Fascist Benito MUSSOLINI was in power. With that as inspiration, he established the British Union of Fascists (BUF).

Sir Oswald Mosley, leader of the British Union of Fascists

Like the Fascists in Italy, the British Fascists marched in formation and wore black shirts as their uniform. Their demonstrations, staged in Jewish neighborhoods, soon became violent; BUF members attacked Jews and their property. By 1934 this type of antisemitic violence caused reputable British groups to withdraw their support from the BUF and kept it from becoming a major political party. However, the violence continued: in 1936 Fascists and Jews came to blows in the East End of London in the "Battle of Cable Street." As a result, the commissioner of the London Police called for the banning of political armies, or at least the banning of their uniforms.

When WORLD WAR II broke out Mosley and other BUF leaders were put in prison and the movement was outlawed. After the war Mosley unsuccessfully tried to revitalize his political organization.

MUDRIK DAVID

(1913–1987) Commander of a Jewish PARTISAN unit of about 250 persons, part of them armed and others old women and children. They operated in the Vinnitsa district of the Ukraine as part of the second Stalin brigade.

MUELLER, HEINRICH

(1900–?), Chief of the GESTAPO.

In 1919 Mueller began working at the MUNICH police headquarters. When Reinhard HEYDRICH was appointed Bavarian police chief in 1933, Mueller became one of his closest aides. His job performance even caught the eye of SS leader and Chief of German Police, Heinrich HIMMLER. Mueller became controller of the criminal police in 1935. Although not a member of the SS until 1939, Mueller was made a member of the SS's Security Service (SD).

Heydrich was named *Gestapo* chief in 1936; he brought Mueller along with him, and appointed him co-director of a subsection responsible for investigating possible enemies of the Reich, including Jews. By January 1937 Mueller had been promoted to SS-*Standartenfuehrer,* and in June he was awarded the rank of senior administrative councilor and criminal police councilor.

From September 1939 to the end of the war in 1945, Mueller was the head of the *Gestapo.* At the same time, he also served as deputy commander of the Security Police and the SD. He answered directly to Heydrich, and after Heydrich's assassination, to his successor, Ernst Kaltenbrunner. Under Mueller's leadership, the *Gestapo* evolved into the most fear-inducing secret police in Europe.

Mueller played a major role in organizing the atrocities of the HOLOCAUST, but he tended to work behind the scenes. He was boss to Adolf EICHMANN, who organized the DEPORTATIONS of Jews to their deaths in EXTERMINATION CAMPS in POLAND. He represented the *Gestapo* at the January 1942 WANNSEE CONFERENCE in BERLIN. He himself approved executions. In June 1942 Mueller ordered that all evidence of mass murder in Eastern Europe at the hands of the EINSATZGRUPPEN mobile killing units be destroyed.

Mueller was loyal to HITLER to the end. He destroyed

Heinrich Mueller, Chief of the Gestapo

the participants in the plot on Hitler's life, including personal friends of his. He was last seen on April 29, 1945 in Hitler's command bunker. Then he disappeared, leaving no trace.

MUNICH   Capital of the Bavaria region of GERMANY. In 1933, 9,005 Jews lived in Munich. Jews played an important role in Munich life. At the same time, Munich was the center of the NAZI PARTY, founded there in 1922. Because of this, the Jews of Munich were subjected to especially harsh torment during the Nazi regime.

The Nazis rose to national power in January 1933. In May police confiscated property belonging to 50 Jewish organizations. Members of the SS, Storm Troopers (SA), Hitler Youth (HITLERJUGEND), and employees of the Nazi newspaper, *Der* STUERMER, attacked Jewish-owned businesses and beat up Jews. Jewish business owners were pressured to dissolve their enterprises, and Germans were discouraged from patronizing those still in business. The Jewish Community Organization responded proactively to the persecution by setting up hospitals and welfare services, schools, an orchestra and

theater, clubs, and an adult education institute. However, many Munich Jews responded differently: from March 1933 to May 1938, 3,574 Jews left the city, 3,130 of them moving abroad.

In June 1938 HITLER decided to tear down Munich's Great Synagogue because it was situated next to the German Art House. During the KRISTALLNACHT pogrom of November 9–10, 1938, a synagogue, chapel, and Jewish library were burnt down and many Jewish businesses, homes, and institutions were harmed. About 1,000 Jewish men were arrested and sent to DACHAU. The next day, the municipal government stepped up the ARYANIZATION process.

By the fall of 1941, 1,500 Jewish homes had been confiscated. Their occupants were forced to build an assembly and transit camp in a Munich suburb to accommodate Jews before their DEPORTATION. In November 1941, 980 Jews were deported from there to RIGA and in April 1942, 343 were sent to a GHETTO near LUBLIN. That summer, the remaining 300 Jews were sent to the Berg-am-Leim Ghetto. From May to August 1942, 1,200 Jews from Munich were sent to THERESIENSTADT. Another 200 Jews were deported to Theresienstadt from June 1943 to February 1945. In all, 2,991 Munich Jews were deported. Of those who were sent to Theresienstadt, only 297 survived the war.

MUNICH CONFERENCE   Conference held in MUNICH on September 28–29, 1938, during which the leaders of GREAT BRITAIN, FRANCE, and ITALY agreed to allow GERMANY to annex certain areas of Czechoslovakia.

The Munich Conference came as a result of a long series of negotiations. Adolf HITLER had demanded the Sudetenland in Czechoslovakia; British Prime Minister Neville Chamberlain tried to talk him out of it. When Hitler would not back down, and even extended his demands, Chamberlain decided to follow a policy of "appeasement" and give in to Hitler on this issue, in the hope that Hitler would not make any more demands. Thus, Chamberlain, French leader Eduard Daladier, and Italian dictator Benito MUSSOLINI met in Munich with Hitler and officially agreed to the annexation of the Sudeten region to Germany. Czechoslovakia was not invited to attend. Chamberlain returned to Britain and announced that he had achieved "peace in our time." However, just five months later, Hitler broke the spirit of the agreement by dismembering the rest of Czechoslovakia. Hitler's true intentions for Europe

Participants in the Munich Conference, September 1938. Front row from left to right: Neville Chamberlain, Eduard Daladier, Adolf Hitler, Benito Mussolini, Galeazzo Ciano

were made very clear, and France and Britain ended up looking foolish and being discredited. Forever after, the term "Munich" became a symbol of appeasement that only hurts in the long run.

MUNKASZOLGALAT   see HUNGARIAN LABOR SERVICE SYSTEM.

MUSELMANN   German term widely used among CONCENTRATION CAMP inmates to refer to prisoners who were near death due to exhaustion, starvation, or hopelessness. The word *Muselmann* literally means "Muslim." Some scholars believe that the term originated from the similarity between the near-death prone state of a concentration camp *Muselmann* and the image of a Muslim prostrating himself on the ground in prayer.

Many victims, totally lacking the wherewithal to adapt, reached this stage soon after arrival in a camp. Other prisoners succumbed to sickness, physical abuse, hunger, and overwork. One could identify *Muselmaenner* by their physical and psychological decline; they were lethargic, indifferent to their surroundings, and could not stand up for more than a short period of time. Most other prisoners avoided contact with *Muselmaenner,* in fear of contracting the condition themselves.

The Nazis running the camps considered the *Muselmaenner* undesirable, because they could not work or endure camp rule. Thus, during selections, these victims were the first to be sentenced to death. A person at the *Muselmann* stage had no chance for survival; he or she would not live for more than a few days or weeks. (see also SELEKTION.)

MUSEUMS AND MEMORIAL INSTITUTES
(HOLOCAUST Museums and Memorials), in 1999, there were 169 institutions that belonged to the Association of Holocaust Organizations, located all over the world, the bulk in the UNITED STATES. Most Holocaust organizations are resource centers that contain collections of books and teaching materials, recorded testimonies of Holocaust SURVIVORS, and other documentation related to the subject. Many emphasize both Holocaust education and commemorative activities.

The three most important Holocaust museums in America focus on other issues. The Simon Wiesenthal Center/Museum of Tolerance, opened in Los Angeles in 1993, challenges visitors to think about how the Nazis could have done such evil and stresses the need for a pluralistic and tolerant society. The United States Holocaust Memorial Museum, located on the mall in Washington D.C., was also opened in 1993. The focus in that museum is on the Americans—the liberators, and the bystanders. Visitors in Washington are con-

The Last March. Relief work appearing in the Warsaw Ghetto Square, Yad Vashem, Jerusalem

Over 30 Holocaust organizations have museums, each with its own focus and specialty. In Israel, the two largest Holocaust museums are at YAD VASHEM, the Holocaust Martyrs and Heroes Remembrance Authority in Jerusalem, which was established in 1953, and *Beit Lohamei Haghetaot,* the Ghetto Fighter's House in the Galilee, opened in 1949. These museums, more than those in other countries, accentuate the commemoration of the murdered Jews. They emphasize seeing the events through Jewish eyes, and view Jews not as helpless victims who were simply led to the slaughter, but rather as active people who responded to the persecution and did the best they could under the circumstances.

fronted with the question of how Americans could have known about the exterminations in Europe, and yet allowed them to continue; how much was really known, by whom, and what was their response. This museum, situated right near the American government, implies that the lessons of the Holocaust are relevant to all Americans. The Museum of Jewish Heritage/A Living Memorial to the Holocaust, located in New York City, depicts the events of the Holocaust in the context of Jewish culture and Jewish experience in the twentieth century.

In GREAT BRITAIN Beth Shalom offers an exhibit about the Holocaust as does a wing of the Imperial War Museum. Among the former EXTERMINATION

The United States Holocaust Memorial Museum, Washington, DC (Photo: USHM, Washington)

CAMPS, AUSCHWITZ-Birkenau, MAJDANEK, and TREBLINKA have become sites of pilgrimage for people from all over the world. In GERMANY, many of the former CONCENTRATION CAMPS, among them BERGEN-BELSEN, BU-

Memorial at Buchenwald

CHENWALD, DACHAU, and SACHSENHAUSEN, are sites of visitation and commemoration.

MUSIC, THE HOLOCAUST IN   The suffering of the Jews at the hands of the Nazis has been a widely-explored musical subject both during and after the HOLOCAUST. Music has provided an outlet both for the expression of the pain caused by the Nazis, and for the hope that endured even during the darkest years of Jewish history.

Soon after HITLER came to power in 1933, the Nazis instituted a central music office to control all musical activity in GERMANY. Richard Strauss, the composer, was made its president, and the conductor Wilhelm Furtwaengler was made vice-president. Performing the works of Jewish composers was not allowed, and all professional Jewish musicians in Germany were fired. In July 1933 the Jews established the CULTURAL UNION OF GERMAN JEWS, which furthered the cause of music and the arts among German Jews. The society was very successful; over eight years, its members performed 500 performances of 25 operas and hundreds of other concerts. Many Jewish musicians fled Germany, some for Palestine. There they joined the Palestine Symphony Orchestra (today's Israel Philharmonic Orchestra), which was founded for the purpose of saving German-Jewish musicians.

Inmates orchestra, Theresienstadt

When the war began and Jews in POLAND were transferred to GHETTOS, musical life continued and flourished. Old songs were sung and new were written. Among the most famous songs composed in the ghettos of Poland were the "Song of the PARTISANS," "Es Brent" ("A Fire Is Raging"), and "Shtiler, Shtiler" ("Quiet, Quiet"). An 11-year-old living in the VILNA Ghetto wrote the music for "Quiet, Quiet." The WARSAW Ghetto had a Jewish symphony orchestra that even played in the coldest of conditions. The Nazis shut down the Warsaw orchestra on April 16, 1942, as a punishment for having defied orders not to play works by German composers. Chamber and liturgical music were often performed in the CRACOW Ghetto. The LODZ Ghetto had a community center specially built for music and theater performances, a symphony orchestra, the Zamir choir, and a theater group. A symphony orchestra, a theater group, and several choirs were active in the Vilna Ghetto. Vilna also housed a music school with 100 students. Music flourished in the THERESIENSTADT Ghetto, with orchestras, choirs, community singing, and opera productions. One opera composed in the ghetto was about to be performed in October 1944 when most of the ghetto's musicians were sent to AUSCHWITZ. Many years after the war the manuscript was finally rediscovered and the opera performed.

Music was also part of life in the camps. In this case, the Jews themselves did not form orchestras or choirs; in most of the large CONCENTRATION CAMPS and EXTERMINATION CAMPS, the Nazis set up music groups and forced the Jewish prisoners to play at their whim. Music was performed when new trains arrived, when the new arrivals were on their way to the GAS CHAMBERS, during selections, during marches, and for the entertainment of the SS (see also SELEKTION). The extermination camps— TREBLINKA, BELZEC, SOBIBOR, and MAJDANEK—had orchestras. Auschwitz had six. Some musical creations were also composed in the camps.

Both during and after the war, numerous musical compositions were created on the subject of the Holocaust. Among the many topics covered in these operas, choral pieces, oratorios, symphonies, marches, and other types of music are the WARSAW GHETTO UPRISING, the gas chambers, Anne FRANK, Auschwitz, BABI YAR, and the children of the Holocaust. Composers from all over the world and from many different backgrounds have contributed to the music of the Holocaust. Some experienced the Holocaust personally and some were even born after the fact. Israeli institutions, such as YAD VASHEM and *Yad Letzlilei Hashoah* (the Institute for Conservation and Research of Jewish Music of the Holocaust), collect and put out musical works and songs from the Holocaust.

MUSSERT, ANTON ADRIAN   (1894–1946), Founder of the Dutch National Socialist Movement. Not particularly antisemitic, Mussert unsuccessfully promoted a Greater Dutch State (to include the NETHERLANDS, BELGIUM, and northern FRANCE) within a Union of German States. (see also NATIONAL SOCIALIST MOVEMENT, NETHERLANDS.)

MUSSOLINI, BENITO   (1883–1945), Italian dictator from 1922 until the end of WORLD WAR II.

Before World War I, Mussolini was a radical Socialist, and during the war he was anti-German. After the war, he founded the Fascist movement, based on a platform of Italian nationalism and anti-Communism. In October 1922 Mussolini and his followers took control of the Italian government, and by 1925, Mussolini became ITALY'S dictator, calling himself *Il Duce*— the Leader.

Mussolini was not strongly antisemitic. He had close

Mussolini and Hitler, Germany, 1934

ties to Italian Jews, including several early founders and members of the Fascist movement. He was also strongly affected by two Jewish women: Angelica Balabanoff, from Russia, and Margherita Sarfatti, an Italian. After Mussolini rose to national power, he reassured Italian Jewry of their safety in an interview with the chief rabbi of Rome. From 1922 to 1936, Mussolini summed up his policy towards the Jews in his country with the statement: "The Jewish problem does not exist in Italy." However, off the record, Mussolini verbally attacked Jews and Zionism. During Italy's war against Ethiopia in 1935–1936, Mussolini ranted against "international Jewry." Finally, when GERMANY and Italy started getting friendly in 1936, Mussolini began rethinking his Jewish policy. At first, he tried to deal with the Jews by forcing them into becoming Fascists; in 1938 he decided to issue racial laws in an attempt to remove Jews from public life in Italy. However, he refused to implement the brutal anti-Jewish measures used by the Germans, and even allowed Jews a safe haven in areas of Europe controlled by Italy.

Until 1943, HITLER allowed Mussolini to shape Italy's racial policy without any interference. However, in September 1943 Mussolini's Fascist Grand Council decided to make peace with the Allies. They overthrew and imprisoned Mussolini. At that point, Hitler jumped in. The Germans rescued Mussolini, and made him the head of a puppet government in the parts of Italy occupied by Germany. Heinrich HIMMLER was charged with implementing the "Final Solution" in those areas. At the end of the war, Mussolini tried to escape the country, but was caught and killed by Italian PARTISANS.

N

N.V. GROUP   (in Dutch, *Naamloze Vennootschap,* meaning "Anonymous Company"), an underground group in the NETHERLANDS, also known as the Limited Group, that saved the lives of 250 Jewish children during WORLD WAR II.

Most of the children rescued by the N.V. Group were smuggled out of the Dutch Theater in Amsterdam, where they and other Jews had been assembled for DEPORTATION to the WESTERBORK camp. They were then taken from Amsterdam by different routes to safe havens in various areas, especially the southern Dutch province of Limburg. Nearly 50 of these children were accompanied to safe hiding places by Baroness Anne Marie van Verschuer, one of the group's members. The group also supplied children in hiding with false identity papers and ration cards, clothes, and other necessary items.

The N.V. Group was made up of more than a dozen members, including a taxicab company owner named John Theo Woortman and a laboratory worker named Jaap Musch. Woortman was arrested for his underground activities and sent to BERGEN-BELSEN, where he perished; Musch was also arrested and deported to the Ommen camp, where he was tortured to death. Sixteen members of the N.V. Group were designated as RIGHTEOUS AMONG THE NATIONS by YAD VASHEM.

NACHT UND NEBEL   see NIGHT AND FOG.

NARODOWE SILY ZBROJNE   see NATIONAL ARMED FORCES, POLAND.

NATIONAAL SOCIALISTISCHE BEWEGING (NSB) see NATIONAL SOCIALIST MOVEMENT, NETHERLANDS.

NATIONAL ARMED FORCES, POLAND   (*Narodowe Sily Zbrojne,* NSZ), nationalistic and antisemitic Polish underground military organization established in 1942. The NSZ did little to fight the Nazis; rather, it mostly fought the Polish leftist underground and Soviet and Jewish PARTISAN groups.

NATIONAL SOCIALISM   (Nazism; NS), German political movement led by Adolf HITLER. The notion of combining the concepts of "national" and "social" became popular in GERMANY before World War I. In 1919 an antisemitic right-wing political party called the German Workers' Party (*Deutsche Arbeiterpartei*) was founded in MUNICH; this party adopted the combined "national-social" ideology. In 1920 the party added "National Socialist" to its name and thus became the National Socialist German Workers' Party (*Nationalsozialistische Deutsche Arbeiterpartei,* NSDAP or NAZI PARTY). A year later Adolf Hitler, a man who started out as a public speaker for the party, became its undisputed leader, or *Fuehrer.*

The National Socialist ideology was an outgrowth of earlier political theories that also gave birth to FASCISM—a political movement that became popular in ITALY some years before the Nazis took over Germany. Nazism brought together the ideas of racial ANTISEMITISM (that Jews were inferior by virtue of their race, or genetic makeup), Social Darwinism (that certain individuals or ethnic groups are dominant because of their inherent genetic superiority), and LEBENSRAUM (the belief that Germans needed more "living space," i.e. more territory, particularly in Eastern Europe). Nazism also embraced the attitude of total anti-Bolshevism, and demanded revenge against those people—especially Jews—who, they claimed, had "betrayed" Germany during World War I and caused it to be vanquished by the enemy (see also STAB IN THE BACK MYTH).

During its first three years of existence, the NAZI PARTY was mainly active in Bavaria. However, its members used emotional appeals and violence to attract many new members. On November 8–9, 1923 Hitler attempted to take over the Bavarian government, but failed. The Nazi Party was outlawed and Hitler was thrown into jail. During his nine months in prison, Hitler penned much of MEIN KAMPF (My Struggle), a book that would soon become the National Socialist bible. It included what Hitler alleged to be his life story and his public declarations regarding Nazi ideology.

Hitler at a mass meeting of the Nazi Party, 1934

Soon after Hitler was released he revitalized the Nazi Party, and it quickly spread to western and northern Germany.

As the humiliated social and economic state of German society in the wake of World War I was compounded by the Great Depression, more and more people were attracted to Nazism. Germans from all walks of life were drawn to the Nazis, for all sorts of reasons. Some saw it as a young, dynamic, proactive force that could fix the country's social and economic problems. Others liked its antisemitic and anti-Communist ideology. Still others could relate to the party's call for violent, revolutionary change, while even others were drawn to the Nazis' vision of a superior society in which every pure-blooded "Aryan" German would have his own place. Party adherents included a range of Germans—from unemployed ex-soldiers, to lower middle class Germans, to moderates from the Young Conservative and Christian Socialist movements. Hitler became a cult figure to the followers of Nazism: as the *Fuehrer*—simply meaning leader—he was seen as the ultimate German who could do no wrong.

By 1932 the Nazi Party boasted a total of 800,000 members and 14 million voters. During the 1932 and 1933 elections it was the largest party in Germany, although it never won a majority of votes in a democratic election. After months of refusing to put Hitler into the government, German President Paul von HINDENBURG named him chancellor of a coalition government in January 1933.

Over the first year of their power, Hitler and the Nazis worked on obtaining absolute, authoritarian rule for their party. By the summer of 1934 Hitler had disposed of his enemies from within the party, such as Ernst ROHM (see also SA). That same year, President von Hindenburg died, and Hitler took on the additional title of president. A few months later, Hitler passed a law giving him absolute power over Germany.

The Nazis destroyed the line between their particular party and the general institutions of state. They smashed any inkling of opposition by sending their opponents to CONCENTRATION CAMPS set up for that purpose. Those Germans not completely enamored with Nazism usually pretended to be in public, so as to avoid problems with the government.

After the Nazis attained their initial power in 1933 and 1934, there were four years of relative quiet. The Nazis concentrated their power, took credit for a somewhat improved economy, lowered unemployment rates substantially, and began revitalizing the German military. Much of what many Germans had hoped for had come to be: Germany was no longer an isolated pariah country and the economy was on the rise.

However, Hitler had much bigger achievements in mind: he wanted to conquer much of Europe for the German Empire, which he called the THIRD REICH. In March 1938 the Germany army entered AUSTRIA and annexed it to Germany in a move known as the ANSCHLUSS. In October 1938 Hitler took over the Sudeten region of Czechoslovakia. By now, Hitler could legitimately call himself *Fuehrer* of the "Greater German Reich." But he had more in mind. National Socialism took on an ever more radical tune, which was manifested in the awful violence directed towards the Jews of Germany and Austria in the KRISTALLNACHT pogrom of November 8–9, 1938, 15 years to the day that Hitler tried to overthrow the Bavarian government. This new extremism could also be seen in the violent activities of the Nazi Party's sub-organizations, such as the SS.

Hitler launched WORLD WAR II in September 1939 as a means to achieve the National Socialist dream of a Europe dominated by Germany, in which a new racial order would prevail. However, by 1943 these dreams began to crumble, when the war turned in favor of the Allies. The Nazi regime came to an undignified close when Hitler took his own life in April 1945, but Hitler remains a cult figure even today for extremist groups world over. In his name and in the name of National Socialism, they continue to spout hatred.

NATIONAL SOCIALIST MOVEMENT, NETHERLANDS

(*Nationaal Socialistische Beweging*, NSB), Nazi movement in the NETHERLANDS. The NSB was established in 1931 by the Dutch nationalist Anton Adriaan MUSSERT. Its platform borrowed full paragraphs from that of the German NAZI PARTY, but left out all paragraphs referring to Jews.

In 1934 the NSB had 21,000 members; by 1936 it claimed 52,000. In the 1935 Dutch provincial elections, the NSB received eight percent of the country's vote. This stunned the traditional Dutch political parties, who could not believe that the Nazi Party would gain so much support, and the Catholic church, who could not believe that so much of that support came from the Catholic sector. During the next elections, all other parties vocally opposed the NSB, as did the Catholic church.

Despite Mussert's original refusal to associate himself with ANTISEMITISM, extremist elements in his party forced him to change his views. In 1938 Jews were no longer allowed to be NSB members.

When GERMANY occupied the Netherlands in 1940, Mussert hoped to be made prime minister, but he was ignored. Additionally, many of his party members began supporting the idea of annexing the Netherlands to the Reich. After the war, the NSB's leaders were tried and imprisoned; Mussert was sentenced to death and executed.

NATZWEILER-STRUTHOF

German CONCENTRATION CAMP near Natzweiler, south of Strasbourg. The site was chosen because it contained granite quarries, mined for German construction projects.

The first 500 prisoners arrived at Natzweiler in May 1941. A year later the camp was ready to house a large number of prisoners. By the end of 1943 the main camp contained 2,000 inmates who worked at arms production and in the quarries. Prisoners also built deep underground tunnels to make space for factories that would be safe from air attacks.

Natzweiler was expanded in 1944 as part of the underground factory plan by adding several satellite camps. By that time, there were 7,000–8,000 inmates in the main camp and 19,000 in the satellite camps. A special category of prisoners was brought to Natzweiler, called NIGHT AND FOG. These were Western European resistance fighters who were punished by being placed in terribly harsh working conditions.

A GAS CHAMBER was built at Natzweiler in August 1943. Jews and GYPSIES brought from AUSCHWITZ were gassed there as part of pseudo-scientific MEDICAL EXPERIMENTS conducted on behalf of the University of Strasbourg.

The main camp was emptied in August–September

1944; most of the satellite camps were evacuated in March 1945. Prisoners were sent on DEATH MARCHES towards DACHAU.

NAZI PARTY (*Nationalsozialistische Deutsche Arbeiterpartei;* National Socialist German Workers' Party), German political party founded on January 5, 1919. The Nazi Party was an outgrowth of the Political Workers' Circle, a small, extremely antisemitic right-wing group that began meeting in November 1918. In 1919 the circle developed into the German Workers' Party; this was the first time that the ideology of NATIONAL SOCIALISM was touted by an official political party. Adolf HITLER joined the party that same year.

In early 1920 the party was renamed the National Socialist German Workers' Party; in 1921 Hitler became the party's undisputed leader. The party was banned in 1923 when Hitler attempted to take over the Bavarian government and failed. It was revitalized in February 1925.

The Nazi Party structure was based on the FUEH-RERPRINZIP, or leadership principle. At the heart of the party stood extreme ANTISEMITISM and racist ideology. Hitler was the *Fuehrer,* the ultimate, authoritarian party leader. The party was managed by 18 high-ranking officials and 32 territorial party leaders; sub-organizations associated with the party included the Storm Troopers (SA), the SS, the HITLERJUGEND youth movement, and worker and teacher unions. The Nazi Party multiplied exponentially during its years of existence, growing from 6,000 members in 1922 to 8.5 million in 1945.

NAZI-SOVIET PACT Agreement made between Nazi GERMANY and the SOVIET UNION right before WORLD WAR II. It was signed by German Foreign Minister Joachim von RIBBENTROP and Soviet Foreign Minister Viacheslav MOLOTOV, giving the agreement its nickname: Molotov-Ribbentrop Pact. This pact shocked the world because until that time Germany and the Soviet Union had acted like mortal enemies.

The countries actually made two agreements: the

Nazi Party rally, 1935

Foreign Minister Molotov signing the Nazi–Soviet Pact

first dealt with economic relations, while the second was a non-aggression pact. The economic agreement, signed on August 19, 1939, called for an exchange of goods worth 200 million reichsmarks. Four days later, Ribbentrop went to Moscow to sign the non-aggression pact. The two countries agreed not to attack each other or help another party attack the other side for a period of 10 years. The pact also included a secret attachment concerning the division of various territories. The Baltic States (ESTONIA, LITHUANIA, and LATVIA) and BESSARABIA were to be part of the Soviet sphere, while Lithuania's claim of VILNA and its surroundings was acknowledged by the Germans. POLAND was to be divided between the two countries.

A week after the second agreement was signed, Germany invaded Poland. The Soviet Union took over the eastern part of the country, including western BELORUSSIA and the western UKRAINE, while Germany occupied the rest. In 1940 the Soviets annexed the Baltic States, Bessarabia, and northern BUKOVINA. However, the pact was abruptly broken by the Germans when they invaded the Soviet Union in June 1941.

NEBE, ARTHUR   (1894–1945), Head of the German Criminal Police and commander of an EINSATZGRUPPE unit.

In 1920 Nebe was accepted into the criminal police, and in 1923, he became a criminal police commander. Nebe joined the SS, the NAZI PARTY, and the SA in 1931. In April 1933 Nebe was moved to the GESTAPO, and over the next few years he rose rapidly through the ranks of the SS. In June 1937 he became director of the Reich

Criminal Police (KRIPO) for all of GERMANY. Nebe continued to rise in rank; at the same time, he got involved with the secret anti-Hitler opposition movement, for which he became an important informer.

In mid-1941 Nebe volunteered to head an *Einsatzgruppe*—one of the mobile killing units that led the extermination of more than one million Jews in the SOVIET UNION. Nebe commanded *Einsatzgruppe* B until October 1941. He played a significant role in making killing methods more efficient. Under his command the unit killed over 45,000 people.

After a bid to assassinate HITLER failed in July 1944, Nebe helped round up the schemers, but three days later he himself disappeared. In January 1945 he faked suicide, but was soon arrested for his part in the assassination attempt. He was sentenced to death, and hanged on April 3.

NEO-NAZISM   Post-WORLD WAR II brand of Nazism embraced by various antisemitic and racist groups the world over. Neo-Nazis use Nazi symbols such as the SWASTIKA and glorify HITLER and the horrific crimes carried out by his Nazi regime. (see also HOLOCAUST, DENIAL OF THE.)

NESVIZH   (in Polish, Nieswiez), town in BELORUSSIA and site of one of the first GHETTO uprisings. In September 1939 Nesvizh was annexed by the SOVIET UNION. At that point, 4,500 Jews lived there. In June 1941 GERMANY invaded the Soviet Union. German troops entered Nesvizh on June 27, and immediately began killing Jews. The Jews responded by establishing an underground organization.

On October 30, 1941 the Germans launched an *aktion* in which 4,000 Nesvizh Jews were murdered and the remaining 585 were locked into a ghetto. The underground began planning an uprising in case of another *aktion* that would completely liquidate the ghetto.

After learning of the liquidation of a nearby ghetto in July 1942, the underground increased its efforts by digging bunkers, preparing homemade weapons, and organizing fighting teams. Their plan was to set fire to the ghetto, and fight their way to the forest. On July 20 the Germans announced that a SELEKTION would take place. The Jews declared that they would put up an armed defense. Fighting broke out, and some Jews fled to the forest. However, many were killed en route or turned over to the Germans by local collaborators. Some groups did reach the forest where they set up Jewish PARTISAN groups.

NETHERLANDS, THE
Country in Western Europe, also known as Holland.

SS man beating a Jewish woman in the Netherlands

When HITLER rose to power in GERMANY in 1933, many German REFUGEES moved to the Netherlands. Those that entered the country illegally were interned in camps. In 1939 a central camp was put up in WESTERBORK for this purpose. After the outbreak of WORLD WAR II in 1939, approximately 34,000 refugees entered the Netherlands, and more than 15,000 were still there in May 1940.

Germany invaded the Netherlands on May 10, 1940; four days later, the Dutch army surrendered. Queen Wilhelmina fled to GREAT BRITAIN, where she set up a government-in-exile. The heads of the government ministries stayed behind, forming a substitute cabinet. Hitler soon ordered the establishment of a German civil administration, led by Reich Commissioner Arthur SEYSS-INQUART. At that time, the Netherlands had a Jewish population of 140,000; 75,000 Jews lived in Amsterdam.

When the Germans invaded, many Jews tried to escape the country. A series of anti-Jewish measures began in the fall of 1940. In September, almost all Jewish newspapers were shut down, and in November, all Jewish civil servants were fired, including Lodewijk Ernst VISSER, the president of the supreme court. Soon the Germans began "aryanization" by ordering all Jewish business owners to register their enterprises. In January 1941 the Jews themselves were ordered to register with the government.

In response to these anti-Jewish measures, the Jewish community decided to institute a committee which would serve as their leadership; the Jewish Coordinating Committee, chaired by Visser, was established in December 1940. Two months later, the Germans set up a JUDENRAT called the *Joodse Raad;* it was chaired by Abraham ASSCHER and David COHEN. Several days later, the Germans arrested 389 young people and sent them to BUCHENWALD (and from there to MAUTHAUSEN) in response to a fight in a cafe between Jews and German police. In a singular act of solidarity with the deported Jews, strikes broke out throughout the Netherlands, beginning on February 25, 1941. Responding to pressure put on the Jews by the Nazis, the strikes ended after three days. It was clear to the Nazis, however, that most of the Dutch would not be converted to Nazism.

Nevertheless, while some Dutch were inclined to sympathize, others collaborated. Ever since the NAZI PARTY had risen to power in Germany in the early 1930s, the Netherlands had had its own antisemitic, right-wing movements, whose members strongly resented incoming Jewish refugees. On the other hand, many Dutch citizens, including many intellectuals, strenuously criticized the anti-Jewish measures being enacted.

The Jews' situation deteriorated throughout 1941. Reinhard HEYDRICH set up a Central Office for Jewish Emigration in the Netherlands. During the summer, Jews were banned from public places, subjected to a night curfew and travel restrictions, and thrown out of schools and universities. Operational Staff Rosenberg (EINSATZSTAB ROSENBERG) began plundering Jewish art and property. In late 1941 the Germans opened FORCED LABOR camps, and charged the *Joodse Raad* with finding workers to fill ever-increasing labor quotas.

In January 1942 the Germans began removing the Jews from the provinces and concentrating them in Amsterdam, and in March, the German administration started confiscating Jewish property. A month later the Jews were ordered to wear the Jewish badge (see also BADGE, JEWISH). Many non-Jews protested this decree, and some even wore Jewish badges in solidarity with their country's Jews.

DEPORTATIONS began in the summer of 1942. Jews were taken to Westerbork, and from there to AUSCHWITZ. By October, deportation was accelerated: Jewish men in Dutch labor camps were sent to Westerbork, where they were joined by their families, and all were sent to Auschwitz.

During that summer the Germans also began confiscating Jewish money. Jews had to put all their money in blocked bank accounts; those accounts were soon cancelled and all the money was deposited into one general account which was used to fund the *Joodse Raad*.

By April 1943 Jews were only allowed to live in Amsterdam, in the VUGHT and Westerbork camps. Deportations were again accelerated in May 1943. By the summer of that year, only a small number of Jews were left in the Netherlands; on the eve of the Jewish New Year, in September, most of the remaining Jews—including the *Joodse Raad*—were deported to Westerbork. Most of the Jews deported from the Netherlands did not survive.

Some 25,000 Dutch Jews managed to go into hiding after being ordered to report for forced labor or deportation; about one-third were eventually discovered by the Germans. One famous case is that of the family of Anne FRANK, who lived in a secret annex for two years before being found by the Germans. The Franks, like other Jews, were helped into hiding by non-Jewish contacts. These non-Jews would help Jews move from hideout to hideout, and provide food, ration cards, and forged identity documents. Many non-Jews selflessly helped hidden Jews without asking for any money. Some, however, took advantage of the situation. Nonetheless, all those who helped Jews were in danger of being deported to CONCENTRATION CAMPS. Later on, organizations were set up to help Jews in hiding, and in early 1944 the national underground organization set up a section to assist Jews in hiding. Many children were also hidden with non-Jewish families; in all, 4,500 children were taken in, and very few were found by the Germans.

Some Jews tried to escape the country altogether, but this proved a very difficult task. Most Jews who tried to reach Britain failed, and movement through FRANCE and BELGIUM was very dangerous. Some Jews did manage to reach SWITZERLAND, and some even reached SPAIN. Several hundred Dutch Jews escaped by being exchanged for Germans, while others were let out of BERGEN-BELSEN because they held Latin American passports.

No specifically Jewish resistance movement was established in the Netherlands, but many Jews joined in general resistance activities. The Netherlands was liberated on May 6, 1945. After the war, the Dutch Jewish community tried Asscher and Cohen of the *Joodse Raad* for collaboration; they were removed from communal posts. The two were later exonerated, but they never returned to Jewish public life.

NEUENGAMME CONCENTRATION CAMP located right outside HAMBURG, GERMANY. Altogether, about 106,000 prisoners were sent to Neuengamme, and 55,000 perished there.

Prisoners performing forced labor in Neuengamme

Originally, Neuengamme was a satellite of the SACHSENHAUSEN concentration camp. The first prisoners arrived in December 1938 in order to build the camp. They lived in an old brick factory. In fact, it was because of that factory that a concentration camp was established in Hamburg in the first place: the SS wanted to reopen the brick factory and use its products for construction of the new public buildings planned for the city.

In April 1940 the German Earth and Stone Works, an SS-owned corporation, signed a contract with the city of Hamburg regarding various construction works, including the expansion of the brick factory, making a canal that would connect the factory to the river, and building a connection for the factory to the railroad. All this work was to be done by prisoners at Neuengamme. Barracks were set up and more prisoners were brought to the camp. By June 1940 Neuengamme achieved independent concentration camp status, and in the fall of 1941, thousands of Soviet PRISONERS OF WAR were brought there. Eventually, there were 34,500 Soviet citizens at Neuengamme, making them the largest national group at the camp.

In 1942 private German firms set up subdivisions at Neuengamme. Many satellite camps were established at armament production sites, such as in the Bremen and Hamburg machine and shipbuilding works, in Hanover, and in the industrial zone in Brunswick. By 1945, Neuengamme had 70 satellite camps; most of the new prisoners who arrived at the camp were interned in those sub-camps. In 1944 the main camp held 12,000 prisoners while the satellites had more than 25,000. In the summer of 1944 large groups of Jews were brought to Neuengamme, mostly from HUNGARY and POLAND. From 1944–1945 approximately 13,000 Jewish prisoners passed through the main camp or satellites.

The main camp at Neuengamme was evacuated in late April 1945, soon after most of the satellite camps were evacuated.

NEURATH, KONSTANTIN FREIHERR VON (1873–1956), Foreign Minister of GERMANY from 1932–1938 and Reich Protector of Bohemia and Moravia from 1939–1941.

Neurath joined the foreign diplomatic service in 1901. In June 1932 he was made foreign minister,

Foreign Minister Konstantin von Neurath waving to the crowd along with Hitler

and held that position under Adolf HITLER until 1938. He led the negotiations that resulted in the alliance of Germany and ITALY. Hitler used Neurath to keep up the appearance of respectability in his foreign policy, but replaced him in February 1938 with Joachim von RIBBENTROP when he was ready to shed appearances and show his true aggressive nature.

After Czechoslovakia was dissolved in March 1939, Hitler appointed Neurath the Reich Protector of Bohemia and Moravia. In this case, Hitler once again hid behind Neurath's respectability in order to carry out dastardly activities. As Reich Protector, Neurath nominally supervised the execution of the same anti-Jewish measures already in effect in Germany and destroyed the region's political and cultural institutions. However, when Hitler was once again ready to implement even harsher measures, Neurath was dropped in favor of Reinhard HEYDRICH.

After the war, Neurath was found guilty of war crimes at the NUREMBERG TRIALS and sentenced to 15 years imprisonment; he was freed after eight years due to illness. (see also BOHEMIA AND MORAVIA, PROTECTORATE OF.)

NEVEJEAN, YVONNE (d. 1987), Belgian who rescued Jewish children during the HOLOCAUST. Nevejean chaired the National Agency for Children (*Oeuvre Nationale de l'Enfance,* ONE): an organization, sponsored by the Belgian government-in-exile, that managed children's homes throughout BELGIUM. In 1965 she was designated as RIGHTEOUS AMONG THE NATIONS by YAD VASHEM.

The Nazis began to deport Belgian Jews in the summer of 1942. At that time Nevejean was contacted by Belgium's main Jewish underground organization, the Committee for the Protection of Jews in Belgium, and asked to rescue Jewish children separated from their parents. Nevejean did not consult her board of directors; she immediately agreed to place children, through ONE, with families and in institutions. Ultimately, she saved the lives of 4,000 Jewish children, nicknamed "Yvonne's children."

The Jewish underground financed Nevejean's extensive rescue operation, but when their funds were not sufficient, Nevejean found funding from banks and from the London-based Belgian government-in-exile. The GESTAPO tried to undo Nevejean's good works, and arrested some rescuers and rescuees. However, it was generally unsuccessful due to the brave stand made by Nevejean and other Belgians, such as the Queen Mother Elizabeth and Leon Platteau of the Belgian Ministry of Justice, also designated "Righteous among the Nations" by Yad Vashem.

NIEBUHR, REINHOLD (1892–1971), American theologian who opposed the Nazis during the HOLOCAUST.

Niebuhr was a pastor in Detroit and a professor at Union Theological Seminary in New York. In both these posts, Niebuhr used the moral and ethical wisdom of the Hebrew biblical prophets in his teachings. He often spoke at colleges and universities, and was a leader in the World Student Christian Federation. As a theologian, Niebuhr revitalized the idea that the Bible is the basis of Christian theology.

During the Holocaust, Niebuhr wrote and spoke expansively about the issue of the German church's conflict with the Nazis. He condemned the Nazi persecution of Jews, denounced ANTISEMITISM, and called for the church to drop its attitude about being right in its beliefs and all others, including Jews, being wrong. In addition, Niebuhr was the first distinguished Christian theologian to reject those Christian missionaries who tried to convert Jews.

In 1943 Niebuhr wrote a series of articles in *The Nation* calling for the establishment of a Jewish state in the British Mandate of Palestine after the war's end. He actualized his support of this goal by taking a leading role in the American Christian Palestine Committee.

NIEMOLLER, MARTIN (1892–1984), German Protestant pastor who headed the anti-Nazi Confessing Church during the Nazi regime. During World War I Niemoller distinguished himself in the German navy. He was ordained as a minister in 1924; in 1931 he became the pastor of an important parish in BERLIN, where his fame as a naval hero and his preaching drew large crowds.

Niemoller was not a supporter of the Weimar government, and in fact, originally welcomed the Nazis. However, he soon saw how dangerous they were. In 1934 he established the Pastors' Emergency League, and in 1937 he became the head of the Confessing Church. At that point, he was arrested for "malicious attacks on the state," assigned a symbolic sentence, and made to pay a small fine. However, after he was released, he was re-arrested based on direct orders from HITLER. For the next seven years, Niemoller was detained in the

CONCENTRATION CAMPS of SACHSENHAUSEN and DACHAU, where he was often kept in solitary confinement. Despite this, at the beginning of WORLD WAR II, the patriotic Niemoller volunteered to help the German navy—but he was refused. In 1945 he was released by the Allies, and became an avowed pacifist who supported a neutral, disarmed, and unified Germany.

NIGHT AND FOG (*Nacht und Nebel*), German term used in a secret order issued by Adolf HITLER on December 7, 1941. The order stated that any underground resistance activities against the Reich carried out in Western Europe would be punished in the most severe ways. The term "Night and Fog" referred to those underground activists from Western Europe who, as a result of this order, were to disappear into the "fog of the night" without leaving a trace.

The order was issued as a result of the situation in Nazi-occupied northern FRANCE, where resistance activities were on the rise after the German invasion of the SOVIET UNION in June 1941. Hitler and Wilhelm KEITEL, the WEHRMACHT chief of staff who signed the order, wanted to discourage resistance activities, so they made them severely punishable. The order applied to underground activists in France, the NETHERLANDS, BELGIUM, DENMARK, and NORWAY.

According to the order, special military courts could impose the death sentence without a unanimous decision. If not sentenced to death, the defendants were to be deported to GERMANY, where they would disappear without a trace into CONCENTRATION CAMPS or prisons.

The few surviving "Night and Fog" prisoners were liberated in April and May 1945.

NINTH FORT Site of mass execution of Jews in KOVNO, LITHUANIA. In the nineteenth century the Ninth Fort was one of a group of forts built around Kovno. Over 50,000 people were killed there during the German occupation, from June 1941 to the summer of 1944. Many were Jews from Kovno or Jews who had been deported from GERMANY.

The Ninth Fort was located four miles from the center of Kovno, and it had served as a prison between the two world wars.

In the fall of 1943 the Germans began to destroy all evidence of mass murder by burning bodies. This operation was kept completely secret. It was executed by the SONDERKOMMANDO serving in AKTION 1005. Thirty-four prisoners from the Kovno Ghetto who had tried to escape, 26 Soviet PRISONERS OF WAR, and four non-Jews were forced to participate in the operation.

The Ninth Fort prisoners were strictly guarded and kept chained after work. Nevertheless, 64 escaped on December 24, 1943. Some reached the Kovno Ghetto, from which they were taken to join the PARTISANS. Thus, the horrors committed by the Germans in the Ninth Fort became known a year before the war ended. Today, the fort houses a museum.

NISKO AND LUBLIN PLAN   Plan developed by the Germans at the beginning of WORLD WAR II for the expulsion of Jews living in German-occupied areas to the LUBLIN region of POLAND. Adolf EICHMANN and Franz STAHLECKER initiated the plan. They chose Nisko, near the eastern Galician border, as the site for a transit camp for the Jews, from which the Jews would be resettled in the Lublin district of the GENERALGOUVERNEMENT. The Lublin Reservation was slated to be "a Jewish state under German administration." Near the end of 1939, this plan was accepted among SS leaders.

The first transport of 901 Jews from the Protectorate of Bohemia and Moravia set off for Nisko on October 18 (see also BOHEMIA AND MORAVIA, PROTECTORATE OF). When they arrived, the Jews were forced to set up barracks in a swampy field. Another 1,800 Jews from Katowice and VIENNA arrived a few days later. However, despite Eichmann's long-term plans for the site, the transports were soon stopped, and the camp was shut down in April 1940.

Officially, the Nisko and Lublin Plan was cancelled due to "technical difficulties" which probably referred to the difficulties Heinrich HIMMLER had in finding jobs for those ethnic Germans he had resettled in Poland in place of the Jews. Additionally, HITLER lost interest in a Jewish reservation—and turned his attention to deadlier means of solving the "Jewish question."

NORWAY   A country in Scandinavia. Right before WORLD WAR II broke out in 1939, Norway, along with the rest of Scandinavia, proclaimed itself strictly neutral in the event of war. Nonetheless, Germany invaded Norway on April 9, 1940. At that time, about 1,700 Jews were living in Norway, including about 200 Jewish REFUGEES from Central Europe. Most of Norway's Jews lived in the capital, Oslo, and about 300 lived in the city of Trondheim.

The Germans proved much stronger than the Nor-

wegians, who were forced to surrender on June 9. King Haakon VII, his family, and staff escaped to London, where they established a government-in-exile. A Norwegian collaborator named Vidkun QUISLING of the National Unity Party declared himself prime minister, but his government lasted only six days. The Germans then appointed Josef Terboven Reich Commissioner of occupied Norway. He did not pass any official laws against the Jews, but began to place restrictions on them and their property.

As the Germans began preparing in early 1941 to invade the SOVIET UNION, the Jews of Norway began to suffer more arrests and imprisonment. Four Jews were shot in Trondheim in March 1941, and in April the Germans expropriated the Trondheim synagogue. In June, 60 Jews were imprisoned in the camp of Grini. Although the Jews of Oslo were less affected, nine of its Jews were arrested in August 1942. In addition, by early 1942 Jewish identity papers had to be stamped with the word "Jew."

By that time, Quisling was once again prime minister; he and Reich Commissioner Terboven launched the main persecution of Norwegian Jewry in the fall of 1942. In early October, all Jewish males in Trondheim were arrested; on October 26–27, 260 male Jews were arrested in Oslo. Additionally, Jewish property was confiscated. A month later, the rest of Oslo's Jews were arrested by the Norwegian police and SS units. Some were able to escape after being warned by policemen and the underground. However, all those who had been arrested were deported to AUSCHWITZ.

The Nazis carried out the DEPORTATION of the Jews in spite of strenuous protests made by the rest of the Norwegian population, led by their church leaders. On November 11, 1942 the bishops of Norway, along with other Protestant congregations, sent a letter to Prime Minister Quisling objecting to his treatment of their country's Jews. On December 6 and 13, the letter was read aloud by clergy in all religious establishments; the congregations stood in support. The letter was also quoted in the official New Year message broadcast by the church. These protests, however, had no effect on the Nazi regime. Less than two months later, another 158 Norwegian Jews were deported to Auschwitz.

A total of 763 Norwegian Jews were deported. Of that number, 739 were killed (including 101 of those Jewish refugees who had fled to Norway in the hope of finding a safe haven). Only 24 survived to return to

Norway after the war. In Norway itself, 23 Jews died at the hands of the Nazis. About 900 Jews were able to escape to SWEDEN with the help of the Norwegian underground. Fifty Jews who had family in Sweden were taken in by the Swedish consul, Claes Adolf Hjalmar Westring, and were sent to Sweden in February 1943.

More than 5,000 non-Jewish Norwegians were also deported to CONCENTRATION CAMPS; 649 died there. Most were saved through the efforts of Count Folk BERNADOTTE and his Red Cross activities. In addition, about 50,000 Norwegians escaped to Sweden.

The Germans gave up their control over Norway in May 1945. Soon after, King Haakon VII returned after five years in exile.

NOSSIG, ALFRED   (1864–1943), Writer, sculptor, and Zionist, whose interest in Jewish emigration led him to collaborate with the Germans. A member of Warsaw's JUDENRAT, Nossig was assassinated by the Jewish Fighting Organization in retaliation for his collaborative efforts.

NOVAK, FRANZ   (b. 1913), One of Adolf EICHMANN'S helpers in the DEPORTATION of Jews to their deaths at EXTERMINATION CAMPS. Novak joined the Hitler Youth (HITLERJUGEND) in 1929 and the NAZI PARTY in 1933. In July 1934 he was forced to flee his native AUSTRIA for GERMANY after participating in a Nazi coup in which the Austrian chancellor was assassinated.

After the ANSCHLUSS—the annexing of Austria by Germany in 1938—Novak returned to VIENNA to serve in the SS's Security Service (SD). He soon became an important staff member at the ZENTRALSTELLE FUER JUEDISCHE AUSWANDERUNG (Central Office for Jewish Emigration), an office headed by Eichmann whose goal was to force the Jews within the Reich to emigrate. Later, Novak helped Eichmann establish similar offices in BERLIN and PRAGUE.

When Eichmann took over the Jewish affairs department in the Reich Security Main Office (REICHSSICHERHEITSHAUPTAMT, RSHA), Novak was made responsible for the transportation sub-department; in this position, he was in charge of the trains that took Jews from GHETTOS and Western Europe to extermination and CONCENTRATION CAMPS. In 1944 he played a large part in the deportation of Hungarian Jewry.

Novak was finally arrested in 1961 and sentenced to jail, but on appeal he was acquitted and set free.

NOVAKY   Labor camp in central SLOVAKIA. The first Jews were brought to Novaky in late 1941, but the camp began operating in earnest in mid-1942, when the Germans began the mass DEPORTATION of Slovak Jewry. Novaky was created due to the efforts of the Slovak Jewish Center, which had asked the Slovak government to establish camps where the Jews could work and thus be spared from deportation.

Novaky, one of the largest labor camps in Slovakia, held 1,600 Jewish prisoners. Most were skilled craftsmen and carpenters who worked in workshops. The products they produced were high-quality and made the camp an economic success. Novaky was run by a JUDENRAT that managed to manipulate the Slovak camp commandant, who was a drunk. The conditions at the camp were not bad: food rations were adequate, the prisoners ran their own school, medical clinics, and welfare institutions, and cultural activities such as drama, religious studies, and sports were allowed. In fact, the camp even had a swimming pool. An underground was also in existence at Novaky.

Novaky was liberated in August 1944 during the SLOVAK NATIONAL UPRISING. Over 200 men from the camp joined the rebels, and 35 were killed in the fighting. (see also JEWISH CENTER, SLOVAKIA.)

NUREMBERG   City in Bavaria. In 1922 Nuremberg's Jewish community was the second largest in Bavaria, with 9,280 Jews, many of whom were wealthy bankers, professionals, and businessmen.

In 1923 NAZI PARTY leader Julius STREICHER founded the infamous Nazi newspaper, *Der* STUERMER, in Nuremberg. The violence and hatred incited by the newspaper greatly harmed the Jews of Nuremberg. Young Nazis attacked hundreds of the city's Jews and broke into the Jewish cemetery. The Jews felt the need to protect themselves by posting armed guards at community institutions. Riots started up again in Nuremberg after the Nazis' gains in the 1930 elections.

The Nazis rose to national power in 1933. The resulting attacks on Jews were worse in Nuremberg than in other places. In July 1933 Storm Troopers (SA) broke into 400 Jewish homes and stole money and possessions, and 300 Jews were arrested and beaten.

From the rise of the Nazis in January 1933 to March 1934, almost 1,500 Jews left Nuremberg. Soon thereafter, many of the Jews of Nuremberg decided to change their approach and stay in the city. They reorganized their cultural, educational, religious, and social life in order to make themselves independent of the rest of their environment.

However, antisemitic acts continued in Nuremberg. In August 1938 Streicher ordered the arson of the Great Synagogue and the Jewish community building next door. During the KRISTALLNACHT pogrom of November 9–10, 1938, SA men assembled in the city center and set fire to various synagogues. Gangs of thugs ran through the streets attacking Jews; 160 Jews were arrested and beaten in the city hall. The rioters, aided by passersby, broke into and pillaged hundreds of Jewish homes and businesses. After the pogrom, most of the city's Jews fled Nuremberg.

The DEPORTATION of Nuremberg's Jews began in November 1941. That month, 535 Jews were sent to RIGA; in March 1942, 650 were transported to Izbica, near LUBLIN. Another 200 were deported over the next months. By the fall of 1942, the only Jews left in Nuremberg were those married to non-Jews.

NUREMBERG LAWS   Racial laws put into effect by the German parliament in NUREMBERG on September 15, 1935. These laws became the legal basis for the racist anti-Jewish policy in GERMANY. Thirteen additional decrees were added to the Nuremberg Laws over the next eight years; these included the first official definition of who was to be considered a Jew and who an Aryan, and methodically ostracized the Jews from German life. Jews with three or four Jewish grandparents were considered full blooded Jews.

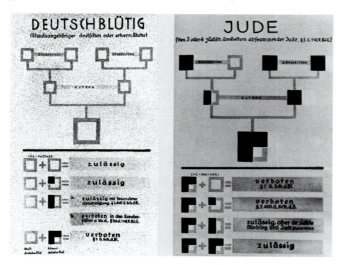

Chart showing definitions of Germans and Jews by the Nuremberg Laws and its amendments. The "German Blooded" are those with four Aryan grandparents and "Jews" are those with at least three Jewish grandparents

The first of the two Nuremberg Laws was called the "Reich Citizenship Law," which declared that only Aryans could be citizens of the Reich. This stripped the Jews of their political rights, and reduced them from *Reichsbuerger* (citizens of the Reich like the Aryans), to *Staatsangehoerige* (state subjects). The second law, called the "Law for the Protection of German Blood and Honor," forbade marriages and extramarital sexual relations between Germans and Jews; the employment of German maids under the age of 45 in Jewish homes; and the raising of the German flag by Jews.

In early anti-Jewish policy, exceptions were made for Jewish World War I veterans and state officials who had worked for the government before the war's outbreak in 1914. The Nuremberg Laws nullified those exceptions; Jewish war heroes were to be treated just as badly as any other German Jew.

By the summer of 1935 the need for laws like these had become urgent. The NAZI PARTY had no clear policy on the status of the Jews in Germany, and party leaders and state officials were in conflict with each other about the "Jewish Question." Anti-Jewish rioting had broken out, the party and public were demanding some clarification, and HITLER felt pressed to provide a response to the subject. The Nuremberg Laws appeased those Nazi officials who had been calling for virulent anti-Jewish wording in the party's platform.

The Nuremberg Laws not only provided a "legitimate" legal mechanism for excluding the Jews from mainstream German culture, but also supplied the Nazi Party with a rationalization for the antisemitic riots and arrests they had carried out over the previous months.

NUREMBERG TRIALS   Major trials of leading Nazis accused of war crimes. The first Nuremberg Trial was conducted by the International Military Tribunal (IMT), a court made up of eight judges, two from each of the four powers occupying postwar Germany (the UNITED STATES, SOVIET UNION, FRANCE, and GREAT BRITAIN). The trial took place in Nuremberg; it lasted from October 18, 1945 until October 1, 1946.

Twenty-two of Nazi GERMANY'S political, military, and economic leaders were put on trial. These included HITLER'S deputies Rudolf HESS and Martin BORMANN *in absentia;* German air force commander Hermann GOERING; army chief Wilhelm KEITEL; army chief of operations Alfred JODL; naval commander Erich

Raeder; commander of the navy and Hitler's appointed successor Karl DOENITZ; chief of the Security Police Ernst KALTENBRUNNER; Minister of the Eastern Occupied Territories Alfred ROSENBERG; Governor-General of POLAND Hans FRANK; Governor of the NETHERLANDS Arthur SEYSS-INQUART; governor of Bohemia and Moravia Konstantin Freiherr von NEURATH; Armaments Minister Albert SPEER; Foreign Minister Joachim von RIBBENTROP; Interior Minister Wilhelm FRICK; Minister of Economics Hjalmar SCHACHT; Bank of Germany president Walther FUNK; ambassador to AUSTRIA and Turkey Franz von Papen; Plenipotentiary-General for Labor Mobilization Fritz SAUCKEL; HITLERJUGEND leader Baldur von Schirach; broadcasting head Hans Fritzsche; and Nazi newspaper editor Julius STREICHER. These defendants were accused of crimes against peace, war crimes, and CRIMES AGAINST HUMANITY. In addition, the tribunal found that participating in a criminal organization, such as the GESTAPO or the SS, was a crime against humanity, and thus declared the NAZI PARTY leadership, the SS, the SA, and the *Gestapo* to be criminal organizations.

The IMT found three of the defendants "not guilty," sentenced 12 to death, and the rest to jail. In its verdict, the IMT stressed the persecution of the Jews as a reflection of the Nazis' grave inhumanity.

Twelve subsequent trials were also including under the "Nuremberg Trials" heading. Notable among them were the EINSATZGRUPPEN Case (which dealt with the *Einsatzgruppe* mobile killing units), and the Medical Case (which addressed the brutal MEDICAL EXPERIMENTS carried out by the Nazis). These trials ended in 1949, with the conviction of 177 Nazi criminals. (see also TRIALS OF WAR CRIMINALS.)

A scene from the International Military Tribunal at Nuremberg, November 20, 1945

O

OBERG, CARL ALBRECHT (1897–1965), SS and Police Leader in the Radom district of the GENERAL-GOUVERNEMENT and Higher SS and Police Leader in occupied FRANCE. Oberg was among those responsible for the mass extermination of Jews in both areas.

ODESSA Port city in the UKRAINE, situated on the shores of the Black Sea. During the nineteenth and early twentieth centuries, Odessa was an important Jewish and Zionist center. In 1939 some 201,000 Jews lived in the city.

GERMANY and ROMANIA established a siege on Odessa on August 5, 1941; the city surrendered on October 16. Before the siege, about half of Odessa's Jews had man-aged to escape, and by October the Jewish population had dwindled to about 90,000. *Einsatzkommando* 11B and a group of Romanian troops immediately mas-sacred over 8,000 of the city's inhabitants; most were Jews.

As soon as the Germans and Romanians took con-trol of Odessa, they designated the city as the capital of the newly-coined TRANSNISTRIA region, which the Ger-mans turned over to Romania. On October 22 the Romanian military headquarters were blown up, kill-ing 66 officers and soldiers. In retaliation, the leader of Romania, Ion ANTONESCU, ordered the execution of thousands of Communists. He also ordered that one member of every Jewish family in Odessa be taken

Jews wearing the Jewish badge, Odessa, October 1941

hostage. The next day, 19,000 Jews were taken to the harbor, where they were burnt alive. Another 20,000 Jews were gathered and taken to a nearby village, where they were shot or burnt to death. In addition, many Jews were sent to camps throughout Transnistria.

Between October 25 and November 3, 1941, the remaining Jews in Odessa—some 40,000—were taken outside the city to the Slobodka GHETTO. They were left outside for 10 days; many old people, women, and children froze to death. On November 7 the men were gathered in the local jail. On January 12, 1942 the Romanians began deporting them to camps throughout Transnistria. By February 23 over 19,000 Jews had been deported. Most of those Jews who had not been deported were either killed by Germans who had resettled the area, or died from starvation, exposure, and disease.

Odessa was liberated by the Soviet army on April 10, 1944. Out of the original 201,000 Jews, 99,000 of the city's Jews had perished.

OEUVRE DE SECOURS AUX ENFANTS (OSE)

(Children's Aid Society), worldwide Jewish organization for children's welfare and health care. During WORLD WAR II, the OSE established a rescue network for children in Nazi-occupied FRANCE called *Circuit Garel.*

OFFICE FOR JEWISH AFFAIRS

(*Commissariat General Aux Questions Juives*), agency established by the collaborating Vichy government on March 29, 1941 to coordinate FRANCE'S anti-Jewish policies and prepare and carry out ANTI-JEWISH LEGISLATION.

The *Commissariat* was founded when the Vichy government heard that the Nazis intended to set up an office for Jewish affairs in PARIS; the French did not want to lose control of this area, so they offered to set up their own. The first director of the *Commissariat* was the antisemitic Xavier VALLAT.

Vallat sought to consolidate the anti-Jewish activities of both the occupied and unoccupied (Vichy) zones of France. On June 2, 1941 he issued a new STATUT DES JUIFS in order to tighten the decrees set forth in the first one. He also announced a census of all the Jews in the Vichy (unoccupied) zone. This census, which shocked French Jewry, later facilitated DEPORTATION. The *Commissariat* confiscated Jewish property, and tried to sell all Jewish holdings—the money earned was intended for France.

In May 1942 Vallat was replaced by Louis DARQUIER DE PELLEPOIX, an ardent pro-Nazi. He instituted a police-like organization to carry out acts of repression, and cooperated fully with the Nazis during the roundups of summer 1942. From late 1943 he was replaced by Charles Mercier du Paty de Clam who was able to somewhat reverse the office's antisemitic direction. (for more on Vichy, see also FRANCE.)

OFFICE OF SPECIAL INVESTIGATIONS

Agency set up in the UNITED STATES Department of Justice to investigate and take legal action against Nazi war criminals living in the United States. It was created in 1979 after information came to light that hundreds of Nazi war criminals had immigrated to the US after WORLD WAR II.

American courts are not allowed to put people on trial for crimes committed outside the US unless they were committed against American citizens. The OSI circumvented this by prosecuting Nazi war criminals for lying about their wartime activities during the immigration process. Had those activities been revealed, the war criminals would not have been permitted to enter the country.

During its first twenty years, the OSI investigated hundreds of cases which led to the removal of 48 Nazi war criminals from the US. Most of these cases involved ethnic German, Latvian, Lithuanian, and Ukrainian collaborators. The war criminals were divided into various levels of categories, ranging from top-level decision-makers to German scientists who used CONCENTRATION CAMP prisoners as forced laborers in special projects. Two special inquiries were made at the request of the American government, regarding Klaus Barbie and Josef MENGELE. (see also BARBIE TRIAL.)

OHLENDORF, OTTO

(1907–1951), Commander of EINSATZGRUPPE D, a mobile killing unit that carried out the mass extermination of tens of thousands of Jews and other Soviet civilians and PRISONERS OF WAR after GERMANY invaded the SOVIET UNION in mid-1941.

A cultured academic who had earned degrees in economics and law, Ohlendorf joined the NAZI PARTY in 1925 and the SS in 1926. He joined the Security Service (SD) in 1936, and when WORLD WAR II broke out in September 1939 he was appointed the head of the SD's inland section in the Reich Security Main Office (REICHSSICHERHEITSHAUPTAMT, RSHA).

In June 1941 Ohlendorf was named commander of *Einsatzgruppe* D. In that capacity, Ohlendorf was re-

Neo-Nazis fire weapons in salute to the late Otto Ohlendorf

sponsible for the murder of at least 90,000 people. By June 1942 Ohlendorf's unit had rampaged through the Crimea and Ciscaucacas, exterminating Jews and other Soviet citizens. This brutal behavior won Ohlendorf a Military Service Cross.

After the war, Ohlendorf was the main defendant in the *Einsatzgruppen* case at the NUREMBERG TRIALS. He openly and unabashedly admitted his murderous actions during the war, and even explained why he thought his actions were justified. He was sentenced to death and hanged in 1951.

OLYMPIC GAMES OF 1936   Olympic Games held in GERMANY in 1936, often called the "Nazi Olympics." The winter games took place in Garmisch-Partenkirchen and the summer games in BERLIN.

In 1931 the International Olympic Committee assigned the 1936 games to Germany. However, when Adolf HITLER rose to power in 1933, it was unclear whether he would go ahead with the plan. Ultimately swayed by the opportunity to show off the new Ger-

Postcard celebrating the Olympic Games in Berlin, August 1936

many to the world and use the Olympics for their propaganda value, Hitler finally agreed to host the games. Germany went all out in preparation for the big event: a new stadium was built, Berlin was cleared of its antisemitic billboards, and anti-Jewish persecution was even decelerated.

For the West, the hero of the 1936 Olympics was the African-American runner, Jesse Owens, who won four gold medals (much to the chagrin of Hitler and his racist associates). However, Germany still outscored the UNITED STATES. On the whole, Hitler succeeded in hiding the terrible truth about the Nazi regime and its persecution of Jews during the games, and his routine appearances at the Olympic stadium and the reverence and adoration from the German crowds made a very strong impression on visitors from all over the world.

ONEG SHABBAT   Code name for a secret archive in the WARSAW Ghetto, which was founded and run by historian Emanuel RINGELBLUM. In Hebrew, the phrase *Oneg Shabbat* literally means "Sabbath delight" and usually refers to a Sabbath eve gathering. Ringelblum's archive was given the name *Oneg Shabbat* because the archive staff held its secret meetings on the Sabbath.

Ringelblum instituted the archive in October 1939. As an historian, he understood that history was about to be made for the Jews, and he felt that it was extremely important to document their experiences. In November 1940 the Jews of Warsaw were forced into a GHETTO. At that point, Ringelblum and his colleagues decided to turn the archive into an organized operation that would include tens of historians, writers, and teachers. The group's main goals were to document the events taking place within the Warsaw Ghetto and all over POLAND; to gather items of historical value; and to record the personal testimony of Jews who had been released from PRISONER OF WAR and FORCED LABOR camps, and that of Jewish REFUGEES from all over Poland who had reached Warsaw. The archive members also tried to get their hands on as many German documents as possible that related to the DEPORTATION of Jews and their extermination. In addition, they made huge efforts to send the information they had amassed to the free world. They managed to send reports to Jewish organizations and to the POLISH GOVERNMENT-IN-EXILE in London via the Polish underground.

In August 1942, March 1943, and again in April 1943, the archivists began sealing the contents of the *Oneg Shabbat* Archives in metal containers and hiding

Recovering part of the hidden *Oneg Shabbat* archives

them in various places in the ghetto. The first group of documents—made up of 1,209 items hidden tin milk containers—was discovered in September 1946, and the second group of 484 items in December 1950. The third group has never been found. The *Oneg Shabbat* Archive is the single most important historical source from the era of Nazi occupation in Poland. Much of what has been found so far has been published by YAD VASHEM in Hebrew translation.

ORADOUR-SUR-GLANE   Village in the Limoges area of FRANCE whose entire population was massacred by SS men in June 1944.

After the Allies landed at Normandy on June 6, 1944, PARTISAN operations all over France were intensified. As a result, convoys of German troops traveling on French roads were faced with widespread resistance; in

The remains of Oradour-sur-Glane after the Nazi reprisal against the town in June 1944

frustration, the Germans began taking revenge on the partisans by attacking French citizens. In one case of retaliation that took place on June 10, a unit of SS men stormed the village of Oradour-Sur-Glane, rounded up its entire population of 634 men, women, and children, and drove them into the village church, which they then set on fire. Every single person inside the church was burnt to death—not one inhabitant of Oradour-Sur-Glane survived. After the war, Oradour was rebuilt and settled with new residents. The village's name became a symbol of the horrifically brutal manner in which the Germans treated France and the French people during WORLD WAR II.

ORANIENBURG CONCENTRATION CAMP located near BERLIN, in the Potsdam district of GERMANY. Oranienburg was one of the first camps to be instituted by the Nazis.

The first group of prisoners arrived at the camp on March 31, 1933, less than three months after the Nazis rose to national power in Germany. This trans-

port was made up of 40 Communists and Social Democrats.

Just a few weeks after Oranienburg had been set up, the camp commandant, an officer in the SA, submitted his command to the Potsdam chief of police, who agreed to take responsibility for the camp's costs. Soon, the number of prisoners began to rise, and by August 1933 there were 900 people interned at the camp. This made Oranienburg one of the three largest concentration camps in Germany, besides DACHAU and Esterwegen.

Oranienburg quickly became infamous as a camp where the prisoners were treated very harshly. Because of that stinging reputation, and because the facility was rather limited in size, Hermann GOERING (at that time Prussian Minister of the Interior) decided to close down the camp. During the summer of 1933 Goering and the chief of the GESTAPO at that time, Rudolf Diels, concluded that the facilities set aside for political prisoners were too disorganized, and that they should be replaced with a few large camps that would be controlled by the

Prisoners in Oranienburg

government. In November 1933 some 300 prisoners from Oranienburg were moved to camps at Sonnenberg, Brandenburg, Moringen, and at other locations within the Reich.

On June 30, 1934 many SA men, including SA leader Ernst ROHM, were murdered by the SS in a massacre called the "Night of the Long Knives." At that point, the SS took over the administration of Oranienburg, and Goering stepped up his efforts to shut the camp down. That September, he ordered that the camp should only be used in a case of overflow from other camps. The last report about the camp was issued in March 1935.

ORDNUNGSPOLIZEI   (Order Police, ORPO), reorganized German police force formed in 1936, based on orders from SS Chief Heinrich HIMMLER. The new Order Police was a merger of the conventional police (*Schutzpolizei*) and the *Gendarmerie*. In fact, the *Schutzpolizei* operated as the national police in urban areas, while the *Gendarmerie* functioned as such in rural areas. However, both groups were organized the same way, had the same weapons, and wore the same uniforms.

In 1938 the professional German firefighters were united into the Fire-fighting Police, and joined the ORPO as its third branch. In 1942 the civil-defense police and the urban and rural supplementary police were also put under the control of the ORPO.

From 1938 on, various police units were formed and put under the ORPO's authority. These units were supposed to perform regular police jobs, but in actuality fought PARTISANS and sometimes helped German military units. Collaborators in countries under Nazi domination also joined *Schutzpolizei* units. By 1944 the ORPO had 3.5 million members. Many ORPO units also helped the Security Police carry out the persecution of the Jews, including DEPORTATIONS to EXTERMINATION CAMPS and shooting massacres, and they were notorious for their cruel methods and behavior.

ORGANIZATION OF UKRAINIAN NATIONALISTS
(*Orhanizatsyia Ukrainskykh Natsionalistiv,* OUN), a nationalist Ukrainian organization established in 1929. During the 1930s the OUN came under the influence of Nazi ideology, and even moved its headquarters to BERLIN.

After WORLD WAR II broke out in September 1939, the OUN coordinated underground activities in the Soviet-occupied western UKRAINE, and operated openly in German-occupied POLAND. In 1940 the group split into two; the majority wanted to organize an uprising in the Soviet-occupied Ukraine, while the other group wanted to keep cooperating with the Germans for the time being.

During the German invasion of the SOVIET UNION in mid-1941, OUN members formed two Ukrainian battalions within the German army, acted as interpreters, and attacked retreating Soviet troops. They then set up a Ukrainian civil administration and police in now German-occupied Ukraine. After the Germans invaded the city of LVOV, OUN members proclaimed the establishment of a national Ukrainian government. However, the Nazis quickly foiled their plans by arresting the members of the so-called government. OUN leaders were forced to hide, but its members still collaborated with the Germans.

The OUN hoped to establish an independent Ukrainian state after the war, but the group was destroyed by the Soviet police in the 1950s.

ORGANIZATION SCHMELT   Program of FORCED LABOR first imposed upon the Jews of Eastern Upper Silesia and later extended to other areas. In effect from 1940 to 1944, Organization Schmelt was named for its director, SS-*Oberfuehrer* Albrecht Schmelt.

Organization Schmelt began establishing forced labor camps for Jews in 1940. The camps were built next to factories where war materials were manufactured, so that Jewish labor could be exploited. In March 1941 SS chief Heinrich HIMMLER decided to use Jews from Organization Schmelt camps to construct even more factories. While previously there had been 1,500 Jews working for Organization Schmelt, now there were 4,000. As the program's factories became more important to the army, Jews from Silesia were joined by Jews from the GENERALGOUVERNEMENT. In mid-1942 some 10,000 Western European Jews were taken out of transports to AUSCHWITZ and brought to work for Organization Schmelt.

Altogether, Organization Schmelt established 160 labor camps, and by early 1943, the program included more than 50,000 Jewish forced laborers. However, later that year the Germans began liquidating the organization's factories and camps and deporting workers to Auschwitz. Only those prisoners working for indispensable armaments and ammunitions factories were allowed to remain. Eventually, the remaining camps were attached to Auschwitz, GROSS-ROSEN, and BLECHHAMMER. (see also SILESIA, EASTERN UPPER.)

ORGANIZATION TODT Organization for large-scale construction work in Nazi GERMANY, named after its founder, the engineer Dr. Fritz Todt (1891–1942). The organization employed many foreign workers, PRISONERS OF WAR, and CONCENTRATION CAMP inmates to build military factories and fortifications.

Todt was made road construction inspector-general in 1933. In 1938 he became the head of coordination of the building sector, as part of Hitler's FOUR-YEAR PLAN. He was responsible for the construction of the West Wall (the fortifications along Germany's western border), and expanded the defense of the western coast from NORWAY to the Bay of Biscay after Germany defeated FRANCE in 1940. In March 1940 he became the minister for armaments and munitions, but was mysteriously killed in a plane crash in 1942.

After Todt's death, the organization expanded and was divided into units attached to different army groups. By 1944 it had 1,360,000 employees, who worked on projects such as the construction of Mittlewerk (the largest underground factory in the world, it produced missiles and plane engines); air force fortifications; and at least six underground factories with takeoff and landing strips. Tens of thousands of Jews transported from HUNGARY helped build large bunkers and a defensive structure called the Southeast Wall.

ORHANIZATSYIA UKRAINSKYKH NATSIONALISTIV see ORGANIZATION OF UKRAINIAN NATIONALISTS.

OSTBATAILLONE (Eastern Battalions), German army units, made up of Soviet civilians and PRISONERS OF WAR, which served in German-occupied Europe. The Germans employed Soviets in their army due to their heavy losses early on in the war against the SOVIET UNION.

OSTINDUSTRIE GMBH (East Industry, Inc., Osti), company established by the SS in March 1943 to capitalize on Jewish labor in the GENERALGOUVERNEMENT, as long as there were enough Jews living there to make it profitable.

At the WANNSEE CONFERENCE of January 1942, it was made clear that Jews in the *Generalgouvernement* would be sent from GHETTOS to EXTERMINATION CAMPS. In the meanwhile, those Jews who were strong enough would be made to work. Thus, the SS set up its own economic firm (Osti) and labor camps under its jurisdiction, in order to be the main recipient of the Jews' work. The connection between Osti and the German intention to ultimately murder the Jews is reflected in who was chosen to head Osti: Odilo GLOBOCNIK, who was also in charge of carrying out AKTION REINHARD—the Nazis' program for exterminating all the Jews in the *Generalgouvernement*. In addition, the labor camps served as gathering points for transports being sent to the extermination camps.

Osti's main office was in LUBLIN, because most of the remaining Jews in the *Generalgouvernement* lived in the Lublin district. Osti took control of various businesses in the area, including brush factories, peat works, a fur plant, and ironworks. Until November 1943, some 16,000 Jews and 1,000 Poles were employed by Osti.

OVERDUIJN, LEENDERT (1901–1976), Dutch pastor who saved the lives of at least 461 Jews during WORLD WAR II.

Reverend Overduijn led an organization of more than 40 people in the eastern Dutch town of Enschede, which helped find hiding places for Jews in various parts of the NETHERLANDS. Most of the safe havens provided by Overduijn's organization were in the towns and villages in the northern Dutch province of Friesland, where the Nazi occupation was somewhat looser than in the more crowded industrial towns of the country's southern regions.

Most often, Overduijn's daughter and his other aides traveled around the Netherlands, looking for appropriate hiding places. Overduijn himself often visited the Jews in hiding, bringing them ration cards, cigarettes, and news from their relatives and friends. However, his movements were noticed and tracked by the authorities, and eventually he was brought in and interrogated. He was then put in jail for an extended period of time.

After the war, Overduijn refused to accept any awards or honors for his lifesaving work. In 1973, though, he was designated as RIGHTEOUS AMONG THE NATIONS by YAD VASHEM in Jerusalem.

P

PAPON TRIAL   War crimes trial of Maurice Papon, who served as the Vichy government's secretary-general in the Bordeaux region of FRANCE during WORLD WAR II. Papon was the highest ranking Vichy official ever to be convicted by a French court of CRIMES AGAINST HUMANITY. In his position in the collaborating Vichy government, Papon was responsible for the DEPORTATION of about 1,600 Jews from Bordeaux to Nazi EXTERMINATION CAMPS, including more than 220 children. Almost all of the deportees were exterminated at AUSCHWITZ. After the war, Papon went on to enjoy an illustrious career: from 1958 to 1967 he served as chief of the Paris police, and during the 1970s he was budget minister of France.

In 1981 Papon was accused of being a war criminal;

in April 1988 he was convicted of crimes against humanity and sentenced to 10 years in prison. Throughout the trial, Papon made dubious assertions about his innocence, claiming that he had helped the French Resistance, and that he was no worse than French Jewish leaders of the time. He protested his conviction, and in 1999 he lost his final appeal. At that point, Papon fled to SWITZERLAND, but was found and returned to France to serve his sentence. (for more on Vichy, see also FRANCE.)

PARACHUTISTS, JEWISH   A group of Jewish volunteers from Palestine sent on missions in Nazi-occupied Europe between 1943 and 1945.

In 1942 the *Hagana* (the Jewish underground army

Jewish parachutists with partisans in Yugoslavia

of the YISHUV in Palestine) came up with a plan to send messengers into Nazi-occupied countries to raise Jewish morale, organize resistance, and rescue Jews. As the *Hagana* had no way to transport their emissaries to Europe, it turned to the British government for help. The British refused the Jewish Agency's proposal to send hundreds of volunteers. However, they did agree to drop trained individual parachutists, who would work both as Jewish emissaries and British agents.

The candidates were mostly recent immigrants who were members of the *Palmah,* the *Hagana's* strike force. Ultimately, only 37 were chosen—32 parachuted in, and five sneaked into the target countries. Of the 37, 12 were captured by the Germans and seven died in captivity or were executed. Some were caught while fighting in the SLOVAK NATIONAL UPRISING, while others, like Hannah SZENES, were found in HUNGARY. Others landed in FRANCE, ITALY, AUSTRIA, ROMANIA, YUGOSLAVIA, and BULGARIA.

These missions were meant to be just the beginning for Jewish groups infiltrating Nazi-occupied Europe. However, later missions never happened, due to British hesitations and technical difficulties.

PARIS   Capital of FRANCE and in 1939, home to 200,000 Jews. Most of those were Eastern Europeans immigrants who had recently moved to France. In all, about 50,000 Parisian Jews died in the HOLOCAUST.

GERMANY invaded France in May 1940. By June, France had surrendered and signed a truce agreement. Paris then became the capital of German-occupied France. At that time, hundreds of thousands of Frenchmen who had fled southward returned to the occupied zone. Among those were about 20,000–30,000 Jews. Jewish life began to be revived, despite the fact that much Jewish property was confiscated and Jews suffered many restrictions.

Many Jewish organizations were revitalized or established in the summer of 1940. The Jewish Communists of Paris formed an underground resistance organization called *Solidarite* (meaning Solidarity). Groups of Zionists, Jewish-Socialists (Bundists), and immigrant community activists got together to institute the AMELOT Committee. The CENTRAL CONSISTORY OF THE JEWS OF FRANCE reopened its synagogues, and other French-Jewish associations opened their doors, as well. In September 1940 there were 150,000 Jews in Paris.

However, in October of that year, the Vichy government began to pass anti-Jewish laws. Also at that time,

Hitler in Paris, June 1940

the Nazis' "Jewish expert" in Paris, Theodor DANNECKER, began to pressure the Jews to organize all Jewish organizations under one umbrella agency. Thus, in January 1941, the Coordinating Committee of Jewish Welfare Societies (*Comite de Coordination des Oeuvres Israelites de Bienfaisance,* CC) was formed. Dannecker appointed two men from VIENNA to run the CC; the Jews struggled to keep a hand in controlling the Jewish organization.

In May 1941 Dannecker called for the first group of Jews to be arrested; 3,700 Jewish men were sent to French internment camps. The CC refused to hand over 6,000 Jewish men for FORCED LABOR, so Dannecker ordered the imprisonment of 4,300 French and immigrant Jews in the CONCENTRATION CAMP located in the northeastern Paris suburb of DRANCY.

Seven synagogues were bombed in October 1941 and the Jews were ordered to turn in their bicycles, telephones, and radios. The Nazis responded to French resistance activities in December 1941 by punishing the Jews: they were fined one billion francs, and 750 French Jews were arrested. A new Jewish umbrella organization, the UNION OF FRENCH JEWS, which had been established by the Vichy government in November, was made responsible to pay the huge fine. By the end of 1941 Jews were forbidden to leave Paris or change their address.

January 1942 opened with a law that forbid Jews from being outside their homes at night. In March the first group of Jews was deported, and in June all Jews over the age of six living in the occupied zone were ordered to wear a yellow star of David marked with the word "*Juif*," meaning Jew.

At the beginning of July 1942 Adolf EICHMANN visited Paris to make final decisions regarding a major DEPORTATION of Jews. On July 16 some 12,000 foreign Jews were arrested and brought to the *Velodrome d'Hiver* sports stadium, from where they were to be taken to Drancy, and then on to AUSCHWITZ. About 15,000 others had escaped arrest by fleeing to the Vichy zone, hiding, or procuring a special protective identity card.

By early 1943, 30,000 Jews had been deported and thousands of others had gone into hiding or escaped. There were only 60,000 known Jews left in Paris. The Germans began to have troubling feeding their insatiable desire to deport Jews; they thus began arresting Jews living in children's homes, old-age homes, and the Jewish hospital. Soon, even Jews born of mixed marriages were arrested. By early 1944 less than 15,000 Jews still lived openly in Paris, and the Germans were rounding up anyone they could find. Deportations continued until Paris was liberated on August 25, 1944. (for more on Vichy, see also FRANCE.)

PARTISANS Groups of organized guerilla fighters operating in enemy-occupied territory. During WORLD WAR II, partisans in Nazi-occupied Europe were mainly active in Eastern Europe, but there was also partisan activity in YUGOSLAVIA, GREECE, SLOVAKIA, and Western European countries such as FRANCE and ITALY.

The rise of the partisan movement in Eastern Europe was gradual. On July 3, 1941, just days after GERMANY invaded the SOVIET UNION and Soviet-held territories, Joseph STALIN called for the establishment of an underground that would help the Soviet army fight the enemy. However, early efforts to set up partisan units were not particularly successful. About a year

after Stalin's original order, centralized headquarters were established for the whole partisan movement, and the number of Soviet partisans grew exponentially. By the last year and a half of the war, the partisans were integrated into military operations on the warfront, and took part in the effort to liberate regions before the Soviet army arrived.

Despite the fact that there was no independent Jewish partisan movement in Europe during the Nazi reign of terror, many Jews did operate as partisans, whether as part of individual Jewish units or as members of non-Jewish units. Jewish and non-Jewish partisans were different in several ways. Non-Jewish partisans joined the fight either as ultra-nationalists, who wanted to rid their countries of all foreigners (Nazis and Jews), or as socialist-leftists, who wanted to combat FASCISM. They had left their families at home in a relatively safe environment, generally expecting to return to them after the war. The Jewish partisans were not fighting for an ideal, such as nationalism or antifascism—the Jewish partisans were fighting for their lives. Jewish partisans believed that they would never

Jewish partisans from the Kovno area

Greek partisans captured by German soldiers

see home or family again, especially since most of their families had already been slaughtered by the Nazis. Furthermore, non-Jewish partisans had support, and believed that as patriotic citizens doing their duty for their country, they could rely on local farmers to provide them with food and supplies. Not so the Jews. Jewish partisans could not rely on the locals, who often hated the Jews as much as the Nazis did. The Jewish partisan was a stranger, and had a very slight chance of actually surviving in the forest.

Just to become a partisan, a Jew had to overcome all sorts of hurdles. First, he had to escape from a GHETTO. After a successful getaway, he had to enter the forest, and locate a partisan base whose members may or may not have been willing to accept him. Even if the partisan group did agree to accept him into its ranks, the Jew, being a Jew, was not always treated as an equal (outside of Eastern Europe, Jews were generally accepted into partisan units as equals). Despite all these obstacles, Jewish partisan activity in Eastern Europe swelled to considerable proportions. Scholars believe that some 20,000–30,000 Jews participated in the partisan units in the forests, where they carried out daring raids and rescue operations.

The Eastern European forest was a natural place for Jews running from the Nazis to hide and regroup for partisan activity. First, the territory was full of thick woodlands and many swamps, which provided ample cover. Second, many of the Jews had lived in nearby areas before the war and were familiar with the terrain, and thus were able to adapt to life in the forests. After the Germans launched mass murder campaigns in BE-LORUSSIA and the UKRAINE during the second half of 1941, many Jews felt that their only choice was to flee to the forests. From that time on, Belorussia had the largest concentration of partisans in Eastern Europe. By late August 1941 there were some 230 partisan units in the region, with about 5,000 fighters (Jewish and non-Jewish). Just two years later the numbers had multiplied greatly, with 243,000 partisans in 1943 and 374,000 in 1944.

Many Jewish partisans in Belorussia had their own units that operated as part of the general Belorussian partisan movement, although some of these Jewish units lost their Jewish character over time. The largest Jewish unit in Belorussia was led by the Bielski brothers; operating in the Naliboki Forest, it consisted of 1,200 people, including partisans and a family camp (see also BIELSKI, TUVIA). The Zorin unit, led by Shalom ZORIN, included 800 Jews. Many other Jewish partisan units were active in the Lipiczany Forest.

The partisan movement in Lithuania developed much later than the one in Belorussia. It was in VILNA, Lithuania that Jewish YOUTH MOVEMENT leader Abba KOVNER called for his fellow Jews to resist the Germans in the ghettos and escape to the forests to form a Jewish partisan movement. Ultimately, there were about 850 Jewish partisans active in the forests of Lithuania (mainly the Rudninkai Forest), making up one-tenth of the entire Lithuanian partisan movement.

A large Soviet partisan movement was also active in the Ukraine where, from the earliest days of the German occupation, Jews fled to the forests and swamps in search of refuge. In the summer of 1941 they began to form partisan units. Some groups like that of Moshe GILDENMAN or Sofievka-Kolki later joined Soviet units. A Jewish partisan company of 120 under D. Mudrik operated in the Vinnitsa district.

Jewish partisan activity in POLAND was much smaller in scale, as the Polish underground HOME ARMY did not use guerilla tactics for most of the war; Poland is not highly forested; Jews who did manage to escape to the forests were often murdered by the fascist, antisemitic National Armed Forces underground militia (see also NATIONAL ARMED FORCES, POLAND); and by the time the partisan movement in the GENERALGOUVERNEMENT region was strong enough to fight, most Jews in the area had already been wiped out.

Jews also became partisans in Slovakia, where more than 1,500 participated in the SLOVAK NATIONAL UPRISING. In Yugoslavia, BULGARIA, and Greece, Jews were accepted into partisan units as equals; however, and perhaps because of that acceptance, there were no separate Jewish partisan units in those countries. (see also FAMILY CAMPS IN THE FORESTS.)

PAVELIC, ANTE (1889–1959), Leader of the fascist puppet state in CROATIA from 1941–1945. Pavelic began his political career as a member of the Croatian Justice Party. In 1929 he was elected to the Yugoslav government. However, when King Alexander instituted a dictatorship in YUGOSLAVIA that same year, Pavelic escaped to ITALY, where he founded an underground nationalist organization called USTASA. Ustasa's goal was to achieve Croatia's independence from Yugoslavia. Pavelic directed the terrorist activities of his followers in Croatia from Italy. He modeled *Ustasa* on the Italian Fascist movement, and when Adolf HITLER rose to power in GERMANY in 1933, Pavelic added ANTISEMITISM to *Ustasa*'s platform.

Yugoslavia was conquered by Germany in 1941. The regions of Croatia, Bosnia, and Herzegovina were united into the Independent State of Croatia. Pavelic was appointed *poglavnik,* or leader, of Croatia's government. Pavelic set up a fiercely cruel regime: hundreds of thousands of Serbs and tens of thousands of Jews were murdered in death camps and in other awful ways such as being thrown off cliffs or burned alive in their homes.

After the war, Pavelic escaped to Argentina, where he continued to advocate Croatian independence. In 1957 he was hurt in an assassination attempt, and died two years later from his injuries.

PAWIAK PRISON Main prison in the WARSAW district, used by the German Security Police and Security Service (SD) from October 1939 to August 1944. Located in Warsaw's Jewish quarter, Pawiak was mainly a prison for men, but it also included a section for women known as "Serbia." It was guarded by SS men and Ukrainian collaborators.

Altogether, some 65,000 prisoners passed through Pawiak, most of whom were Poles from Warsaw. It is unclear how many Jews were interned there. The Jewish prisoners were generally people who had been caught outside the GHETTO. There was also a group of Soviet PRISONERS OF WAR imprisoned in Pawiak. As a rule, both the Jews and Soviets were shot soon after arriving at the prison. In all, about 32,000 prisoners were shot to death (sometimes in public executions), 23,000 prisoners were transferred to various camps, and several thousand were released. A few prisoners managed to escape from Pawiak, but an attempted revolt against the guards in July 1944 was a failure. Pawiak also had a strong underground that kept in contact with the outside world.

The last transports left Pawiak on July 30, 1944. The remaining prisoners were either released or shot. On August 21 the Germans blew up the prison.

PECHERSKY, ALEKSANDR (1909–1990), Leader of the uprising at the SOBIBOR extermination camp. Pechersky was born in the UKRAINE. As an officer in the Soviet army, he was called up for service when the Germans attacked the SOVIET UNION in June 1941. In October he was taken prisoner by the Germans. In August 1942, after the Germans discovered that he was Jewish, Pechersky was moved to an SS camp in MINSK.

In September 1943 Pechersky was sent to Sobibor along with 2,000 Jews from the Minsk GHETTO and from the SS camp. Soon after his arrival he was contacted by the camp's underground. As an officer, he accepted the position of underground commander and agreed to lead its members in an uprising. On October 14, 1943 the prisoners at Sobibor revolted under Pechersky's command. They succeeded in killing most of the SS men and many prisoners were killed, but some escaped, including Pechersky. He joined a Soviet PARTISAN unit, and fought with it until the summer of 1944, when the Soviet army reached the area and the partisans joined regular military units. After being badly wounded, Pechersky returned to his hometown.

After the war, Pechersky served as the main witness at the trial of 11 Ukrainians who had worked as guards at Sobibor.

PETAIN, PHILIPPE (1856–1951), French World War I military hero and head of the collaborating Vichy government during WORLD WAR II.

During World War I, Petain distinguished himself as a hero while defending the fortresses of Verdun. In 1917 he was made commander-in-chief of the French armies under Marshal Ferdinand Foch, and a marshal of FRANCE in 1918. The French people viewed him as a symbol of their military victory.

French propaganda poster in which Marshal Philippe Petain makes a plea: "Frenchmen, you have not been sold out, nor betrayed nor abandoned. Follow me with confidence"

When German forces succeeded in crushing the French army in June 1940, Petain called for the cessation of armed conflict against GERMANY. On June 16 he was invited to head the new French government, which would rule over the southern part of France—the area not occupied by the Germans—from the town of Vichy. Petain negotiated a truce with the Germans, and was wholeheartedly accepted as prime minister by the French people. They believed in his allegiance to France and his devotion to its honor. At that time, Petain was 84 years old.

Under the leadership of Petain and his assistant, Pierre LAVAL, the Vichy government collaborated fully with the Nazis. They supported the Nazi regime's anti-Jewish policies, including the DEPORTATION of French Jews to CONCENTRATION CAMPS. Petain was motivated to comply with the Nazis by his "National Revolution" agenda. This was a program intended to transform France into a totalitarian, strictly unified country within the framework of the Nazi plans for a New World Order in Europe. Included within the outline of the "National Revolution" was the plan to eliminate Jewish influence in France. Petain was apathetic to the fate of the French Jews whom he handed over to the Nazis.

After France was liberated in 1944, Petain was convicted of treason by a French court, and was sentenced to death. However, General Charles de GAULLE commuted his sentence to life in prison due to his heroic World War I military record. He was banished to the island of Yeu, off the coast of Brittany in northern France. Petain died there at the age of 96. (for more on Vichy, see also FRANCE.)

PIOTRKOW TRYBUNALSKI   Central Polish town 16 miles south of LODZ; the site of the first GHETTO in Nazi Europe. In 1939 there were about 18,000 Jews in Piotrkow Trybunalski.

The Germans occupied Piotrkow in September 1939. The Nazis treated the Jews to cruel beatings, murdered many, and pillaged their property. They imprisoned Jews in FORCED LABOR camps. They also broke into the town's beautiful synagogue, stole its ritual objects, beat the worshippers, and destroyed the building. About 2,000 Jews were able to escape, while many REFUGEES from nearby towns streamed in, inflating Piotrkow's population.

On October 8 the city's commander ordered the establishment of a ghetto—the first in POLAND. The town's Jews were commanded to move into the specified area with none of their personal items except bedding. All Jews were compelled to wear the Jewish badge on pain of death (see also BADGE, JEWISH). Next, the Jews were subjected to a number of decrees, soon to become the norm for all of Poland. They were not allowed to own more than 2,000 zlotys; they had to give up all their silver and gold; they were not allowed to work in industry or in public service; Jewish doctors were not permitted to treat Aryans and vice versa. No Jew was allowed to leave Piotrkow without permission. The Germans also set up a JUDENRAT which, among its other responsibilities, had to hand over workers daily and build lodgings in the ghetto for 4,000 Jews from nearby towns.

The Piotrkow Trybunalski Ghetto was liquidated on October 13–21, 1942. Local collaborators surrounded the ghetto, while SS soldiers assembled the Jews into two lines: one for those 2,000 Jews with work cards (who were allowed to stay), and one for the 20,000 Jews without cards, who were deported to TREBLINKA. About 500 Jews escaped to the forests, while some Jews hid, only to be rounded up and murdered.

By July 1943 all remaining workers had been moved to other labor camps or to AUSCHWITZ. At that point Piotrkow was declared "cleansed of Jews." Only 1,400 Piotrkow Jews survived in the forests or in the camps.

PIUS XII   (Eugenio Pacelli; 1876–1958), Pope from 1939–1958. As Pope throughout WORLD WAR II, Pius XII was controversial for his failure to publicly condemn the extermination of Europe's Jews.

During the 1920s, Pacelli was the papal ambassador to GERMANY. In 1933, while serving as the Vatican's secretary of state, he signed a pact with Nazi Germany. This was considered a diplomatic triumph for HITLER.

Cardinal Pacelli was elected Pope on March 2, 1939, and took the name Pius XII. Under his leadership, the Vatican was mixed about its attitude towards helping Jews. Right after his election, Pius XII stepped in to obtain 3,000 visas to Brazil (a Catholic country) for Jews who had been baptized. However, just a year later, the Pope ignored requests made by the chief rabbi of Palestine, Isaac Herzog, to intercede on behalf of Jews in SPAIN so that they would not be sent back to Germany. A similar request was made concerning Jews in LITHUANIA; this was also neglected by the Pope.

The Vatican's Secretariat of State was one of the first groups in the world to receive reports about the extermination of the Jews. In early 1941 Cardinal Theodor Innitzer of VIENNA told Pius XII about the DEPORTATION of Jews. A representative of the Vatican in SLOVAKIA, Giuseppe Burzio, informed the Vatican about the systematic murder of Jews in his area. On October 7, 1942 the chaplain of a hospital train in POLAND told the Vatican about "mass assassination" and mentioned the number two million as the count of those already killed. However, when in September 1942 the UNITED STATES' representative to the Vatican, Myron Taylor, sent a note to the Vatican secretary of state, Cardinal Maglione, declaring that the Jews were being deported to the east to be murdered, Maglione feigned innocence. He innocuously replied that it was impossible to confirm such rumors.

Three months later, right before Christmas Eve, many advocates sent the Pope telegrams begging him to save the Jews of Eastern Europe. At that point, Pius XII decided to take something of a stand. On his December 24 radio broadcast, he hinted of the Jews' plight when he spoke about the hundreds of thousands of Europeans being murdered simply due to their racial origin. However, he only hinted, and never mentioned the Jews outright. Although the Pope himself never spoke out against the atrocities being committed, other members of the Church did get involved in rescue work. Angelo Rotta the Nuncio did his part to protest the persecution of the Jews in HUNGARY. Angelo Roncalli, another Nuncio, engaged in rescue work from Turkey; he later became Pope John XXIII. In addition, even though the Pope may not have issued protests and condemnations aloud when the Jews of Rome were deported, it is possible he ordered Catholic institutions to provide aid to Jews.

Why Pope Pius XII never spoke out publicly against the persecution of the Jews is a matter of great debate. Some say that he believed that nothing could stem the tide of the Nazis' violent plan, and in fact speaking out publicly could endanger other rescue activities still possible. Others say that the Pope actually wanted to help the Jews, and that speaking out could only end up hurting them. Perhaps he thought that the victims who could be saved would be best helped by private intervention. Some Catholic writers maintain that the Pope was afraid that public protest would cause a split among German Catholics, or even lead the Nazis to seek reprisals against him personally, against other Church leaders, or against Catholics in occupied countries. Some point to the Pope's terrible fear of Communism as a reason for not attacking Hitler. In the 1990s Pope John Paul II began the process of making Pius XII a saint.

PLASZOW FORCED LABOR camp located in a suburb of CRACOW. Plaszow was established in the summer of

Prisoners engaged in forced labor in Plaszow

1942; in January 1944 it became a CONCENTRATION CAMP.

Plaszow was situated within Cracow's city limits, on land made up of two Jewish cemeteries, other property belonging to the Jewish community, and the private property of Poles who had been evicted from their homes. Plaszow was divided into various sections: housing for the Germans; factories where the prisoners were forced to work; and the prisoners' living quarters, divided into sections for men and women and subsections for Jews and Poles. Every once in a while the camp was expanded; at its largest, in 1944, it covered 200 acres. The campsite was surrounded by an electrified barbed-wire fence 2.5 miles long.

The Germans liquidated the Cracow GHETTO on March 13–14, 1943. Some 2,000 Jews were murdered in the streets of Cracow, and buried in a mass grave at Plaszow. Of the surviving Jews, most were deported to BELZEC, while about 8,000 were imprisoned in Plaszow.

In July 1943 the Germans set up a separate camp at Plaszow for Polish prisoners who had been arrested for disciplinary or political violations. According to the Germans, these prisoners were to be "retrained by work." In fact, those prisoners who had been charged for discipline were kept at the camp for a few months, while the political prisoners were kept there indefinitely. This Polish camp also held dozens of GYPSY families, including their small children.

The number of prisoners interned at Plaszow went up over the years: before the liquidation of the Cracow Ghetto there were 2,000 prisoners, while during the second half of 1943 there were 12,000 prisoners. By May and June 1944 Plaszow contained its peak number of prisoners: 22,000–24,000, including 6,000–8,000 Jews from HUNGARY. The number of Polish prisoners also rose, from 1,000 early on to 10,000 after the WARSAW POLISH UPRISING in late summer 1944.

Some German criminal prisoners were also detained at Plaszow; they were made to do various jobs around the camp. Of those, some 25,000 were considered to be "permanent prisoners" and given personal numbers. Beyond that, there was an unknown number of other "temporary" prisoners.

Five men served as camp commandant at Plaszow during its two and a half years of existence. Amon GOETH, who held the position from February 1943 to September 1944, was considered to be the most cruel and inhumane. He encouraged SELEKTIONEN, mass murders, and working the prisoners so hard that they died.

He was also personally responsible for the deaths of many prisoners.

From 1942 to 1944, when Plaszow was a designated forced labor camp, most of the camp's guards were Ukrainians working for the Nazis. When Plaszow became a concentration camp, 600 SS men from the DEATH'S HEAD UNITS stepped in. After the SS men came in, while most prisoners still worked at forced labor, mass numbers of Jews were murdered. In addition, Poles who had been condemned for participating in patriotic Polish activities were brought to Plaszow and shot. In all, about 8,000 people were murdered at Plaszow, whether as individuals or as groups. Some 900 prisoners worked for Oskar SCHINDLER, in whose factory they were protected from the horrors of the camp.

By the summer of 1944 the Soviet army was approaching. The Germans began taking apart the camp and sending prisoners to other camps, including EXTERMINATION CAMPS. Among those, 2,000 Jews were sent to their deaths at AUSCHWITZ in May 1944. In September the Polish section of Plaszow was also eliminated. The Germans then tried to destroy the evidence of mass murder at the camp: they dug up mass graves, took out the corpses, and burned them in huge piles. The last prisoners were removed from Plaszow on January 14, 1945 and deported to Auschwitz.

PLOTNICKA, FRUMKA (1914–1943), A leader of the *He-Halutz* underground in occupied POLAND.

Born in a village near Pinsk, Plotnicka was a member of the *Dror* Zionist YOUTH MOVEMENT. In 1938 she went to work at the *Dror* headquarters in WARSAW. When WORLD WAR II broke out in September 1939 and the Germans occupied Poland, Plotnicka, along with many other young Zionists, moved to eastern Poland which was still occupied by the Soviets. From there, they hoped to make it to Palestine. In 1940 Plotnicka returned to the German-occupied zone to reorganize *Dror* as an underground movement. From Warsaw, Plotnicka attempted to unify and bolster the Zionist *He-Halutz* youth movement undergrounds.

In September 1942 Plotnicka was sent to Bedzin by the Jewish Fighting Organization of Warsaw, in order to help establish a self-defense organization there. She also made contact with organizations in SWITZERLAND and SLOVAKIA and the RESCUE COMMITTEE OF THE JEWISH AGENCY in Turkey; she sent them information about the dire situation in Poland.

Plotnicka refused to escape and save her own life, in favor of staying and helping her fellow Jews. She perished in battle on August 3, 1943, along with the last remaining fighters in Bedzin. (see also JEWISH FIGHTING ORGANIZATION, WARSAW.)

POHL, OSWALD (1892–1951), Head of the SS's Economic-Administrative Main Office (WIRTSCHAFTS-VERWALTUNGSHAUPTAMT, WVHA). Pohl joined the NAZI PARTY in 1926 and the SS in 1929. His talents as an organizer caught the eye of SS chief Heinrich HIMMLER, who made Pohl chief of administration in the SS Main Office in 1935.

Oswald Pohl, head of the WVHA

In 1939 Pohl was appointed ministerial director of the ministry of the interior. In that position he quickly built up SS companies with the help of Nazi supporters from various German industries. In 1942 Pohl's activities were brought together under one new roof: the WVHA, which was responsible for the CONCENTRATION CAMP inspectorate, and for the work projects of more than 500,000 concentration camp inmates, who were sometimes hired out to work for German companies. This made Pohl one of the most powerful and prominent men in the SS.

Pohl also came up with the idea of sending back to GERMANY all personal possessions of Jews who had been gassed—including hair, gold teeth, clothes, wedding rings, and other jewelry, etc.—and using them or turning them into cash. This operation was all part of the SS's emphasis on being efficient and financially independent of other countries.

After the war Pohl was arrested and sentenced to death. He was executed in 1951.

POLAND Country in Eastern Europe. On September 1, 1939 GERMANY attacked Poland, launching WORLD WAR II. Poland's allies, GREAT BRITAIN and FRANCE, immediately declared war on Germany. Despite this, Poland fell to the Germans in just weeks, its capital, WARSAW, capitulating on September 28.

A POLISH GOVERNMENT-IN-EXILE was quickly established in France (when France fell to the German army in mid-1940, the government-in-exile moved to London). This government, represented in Poland by the underground DELEGATURA and the Polish National Council, continued to wage war against Germany for the duration of World War II.

According to the terms of the NAZI-SOVIET PACT, signed in August 1939, Germany and the SOVIET UNION eagerly divided up the newly-conquered Poland: Germany annexed the western third to the Reich, a region that included 600,000 Jews; the Soviet Union annexed the eastern third to its Soviet republics of BELORUSSIA and the UKRAINE, adding 1.2 million Jews to its population; and the middle third was put under the control of a German civil administration, called the GENERALGOUVERNEMENT. Approximately 1.5 million Jews found themselves under the *Generalgouvernement*'s jurisdiction.

The Nazis had a plan for Poland: to turn it into LEBENSRAUM ("living space") for Germans. To do so, they first had to destroy the Polish society and people. Thus, some two million Poles with German blood were given special privileges, while the rest of the Polish population was treated with great brutality and suppression. Many Poles were displaced to make room for ethnic Germans (VOLKSDEUTSCHE), while leaders of the Polish people and resisters were killed, often in Nazi camps. There was a broad resistance in Poland that took the form of an underground state. Contact from Poland was maintained with the Polish government-in-exile in London. The two largest armed resistance organizations in Poland were the HOME ARMY and the Home Guard (see also HOME GUARD, POLAND).

The single most defining feature of the history of Polish Jewry under the Nazis is the appearance of the "Final Solution." The history must be viewed in each community as two distinct periods—before and after the start of the murders. Immediately after the Germans occupied Poland, the country's Jews were subjected to a two-month wave of random murders. After the Germans and Soviets carved up Poland, some 300,000 Jews fled to the Soviet-occupied region from the German areas, leaving 1.8–2 million Jews in German-ruled Poland.

Among the first sets of official anti-Jewish measures in Poland was that issued by GESTAPO chief Reinhard HEYDRICH on September 21, 1939: he demanded that the Jews living in areas annexed to the Reich be expelled to the *Generalgouvernement;* that they be concentrated in large cities near major railroad junctions; and that JUDENRAETE be established. In late fall the governor of the *Generalgouvernement,* Hans FRANK, decreed that in his jurisdiction all Jews over the age of 10 must wear a white armband with a blue Star of David (see also BADGE, JEWISH). In October he issued a decree whereby all Jewish males of a certain age could be sent to do FORCED LABOR. In addition, the Nazis began seizing and liquidating Jewish businesses with the exception of small shops. Jews were only allowed to keep small amounts of money, making it very hard to buy or sell anything. In January 1940 Jews were forbidden to use trains, except by special permit, and they were ordered to register their property with the authorities. Many Jews were attacked, rounded up randomly and made to do various jobs, and robbed.

The first Polish GHETTO was established in October 1939 in PIOTRKOW TRYBUNALSKI. The first large ghetto, in the city of LODZ, was decreed in February 1940 and was closed off from the outside world in May 1940. Ghettos were set up in Warsaw in November 1940, in LUBLIN and CRACOW in March 1941, and in the Zaglembie region as late as 1942 and 1943, after mass extermination had begun.

In some ghettos, Jews had the ability to leave, which helped them smuggle in food and supplies. Other ghettos were hermetically sealed, letting no one in or out—subjecting the Jews to starvation and epidemics. Jews in all the ghettos, however, were determined to survive. The *Judenraete* and Jewish community organizations tried their hardest to procure and distribute food and medicine to the ghetto population, provide some semblance of schooling for the children, and cultural activities for all. ZEGOTA (the Polish Council for Aid to Jews), the Jewish Self-Help Organization, the YOUTH MOVEMENTS, and political undergrounds all strove to help their fellow Jews survive, both physically and emotionally.

In June 1941 Germany turned on its ally, the Soviet Union, and began a massive invasion. The Germans created a new territorial district called BIALYSTOK, and accorded it a status similar to that of the Polish areas that were incorporated into the Reich earlier on. Other areas taken from the Soviet Union by Germany became part of the REICHSKOMMISSARIAT UKRAINE and the REICHSKOMMISSARIAT OSTLAND administrations. German mobile killing units called EINSATZGRUPPEN immediately embarked upon the mass extermination of the Jews living in the newly conquered areas.

Just months after the slaughter began in the Soviet Union, the Germans launched a mass murder campaign in Poland, as well. The first of six EXTERMINATION CAMPS on Polish soil, CHELMNO, was established on December 7, 1941. During the spring of 1942, three other extermination camps began to function—SOBIBOR, BELZEC, and TREBLINKA—as part of AKTION REINHARD, the plan to liquidate all Jews in the *Generalgouvernement.* In addition, the CONCENTRATION CAMPS at AUSCHWITZ and MAJDANEK were expanded to function as extermination centers, as well. Those Jews who had been interned in ghettos were now sent to their deaths in these camps. The liquidation of ghettos in the *Generalgouvernement* continued throughout 1943, and by summer 1944 only the Lodz Ghetto was left.

The Germans did not immediately kill all the Jews, however, because they wanted to exploit Jewish slave labor for the war economy. In early 1943 some 250,000 Jews were still being kept as slave laborers in the *Generalgouvernement.* But the killing continued, and by late 1944, when SS chief Heinrich HIMMLER ordered a halt to the murders in Auschwitz, only tens of thousands of Jews were left.

Some ninety percent of Polish Jewry, about three million, were murdered by the Nazis; approximately three million non-Jewish Poles, soldiers and civilians, also met their deaths during the war.

POLICINIAI BATALIONAI (Lithuanian Police Battalions), paramilitary group made up of Lithuanians who collaborated with the Germans.

GERMANY occupied LITHUANIA in the summer of 1941 as part of its invasion of the SOVIET UNION and Soviet-held territories (like Lithuania). Various groups of Lithuanian ex-soldiers and ex-officers, police, and all sorts of nationalists (including many high school and university students) began persecuting and murdering Lithuanian Jews and joined the Germans in attacking the withdrawing Soviet army. At the end of 1941 those groups were reorganized into an official framework of battalions, renamed *Policiniai Batalionai.* By August 1942 there were 20 battalions comprised of 8,388 men: 341 were officers, 1,772 were noncommissioned officers, and the rest were privates. Most of the commanders had previously served in the Lithuanian army. The higher-ranking officers had German officers as mentor-liaisons, while the highest levels of Lithuanians reported directly to the district SS and Police Leader.

The *Policiniai Batalionai,* specifically Battalions 1 and 2, played a large role in the mass extermination of the Jews in Lithuania and in nearby parts of POLAND and BELORUSSIA. After the war, several members of the battalions were identified and put on trial. Some were found guilty of murdering both civilians and PRISONERS OF WAR.

POLISH GOVERNMENT-IN-EXILE New Polish government established after GERMANY and the SOVIET UNION occupied POLAND in September 1939. The Polish government-in-exile was first based in FRANCE, but moved to London after the French army surrendered to the Germans in mid-1940. The Allies accepted the government-in-exile as the legitimate representative of the Polish people soon after it was created.

The government-in-exile allied itself with the West, as its members believed that only a total military victory over Germany would restore Poland's independence and freedom. In addition, it amassed its own land, air, and naval forces.

In 1942 reports about the mass murder of Jews in Poland reached London; at that point, the Polish government-in-exile made several public declarations on the subject, and officially demanded that the Allied powers stop the Germans from their murderous crusade. In early 1943 the Polish government-in-exile begged Pope PIUS XII to condemn the Nazis' actions. From December 1942 onward, the government-in-exile backed the rescue work of ZEGOTA, which offered aid to Jews throughout occupied Poland.

POLONSKI, ABRAHAM (b. 1913), A founder of the French Jewish underground. Born in Russia, Polonski moved to Toulouse, FRANCE, where he worked as an electrical engineer.

The Germans invaded France in May 1940, and by June, the French army surrendered to them. Polonski responded to the dire situation by founding an underground military organization called *La Main Forte,* meaning "The Strong Hand." The organization's goal was to organize a worldwide fighting force that would conquer and take Palestine from the British.

In January 1942 Polonski and Labor Movement Zionist activists helped establish an underground Jewish militia called the *Armee Juive,* or Jewish Army. Polonski and another underground activist named Lucien LUBLIN led the Jewish Army, which was composed of the cream of the Zionist YOUTH MOVEMENTS. During the winter of 1943–1944, the Jewish Army's escape network helped some 300 of its members successfully flee to SPAIN, from whence most immigrated to Palestine.

Polonski and Lublin trained their soldiers as PARTISANS, who then fought in Toulouse, Nice, Lyons, and PARIS. These soldiers attacked French informers who had collaborated with the GESTAPO and helped liberate France in the summer of 1944.

After the war, Polonski helped Jews "illegally" immigrate to Palestine from France. (see also JEWISH ARMY, FRANCE.)

PONAR (PONARY) Site of mass extermination in LITHUANIA, located 6.2 miles from VILNA. From early summer 1941 to July 1944, 70,000–100,000 people were murdered at Ponar; most were Jews.

In 1940 and 1941 the Soviet government dug large pits at Ponar for fuel storage tanks, but they evacuated before they could complete the project. When the Germans occupied Lithuania in mid-1941, they used the pits for the mass murder of Jews from Vilna and the surrounding area, Soviet PRISONERS OF WAR, and other enemies of the Nazis. The victims were brought to Ponar by the hundreds or thousands, by foot, truck, and train. SS men, German police, and Lithuanian collaborators then shot them to death in the pits.

In the early phases of the Ponar exterminations, the victims were buried in the same pits where they had been shot. However, in September 1943, the Nazis began digging up the pits and burning the bodies in order to destroy all evidence of mass murder (see also AKTION 1005). About 80 Jewish prisoners were forced to do the job for them. On April 15, 1944 these prisoners heroically attempted to escape Ponar. Most were killed, but 15 successfully fled to the PARTISANS in the Rudninkai Forest.

Jews being led blindfolded to their execution in Ponary by Lithuanian militiamen

PONIATOWA   FORCED LABOR and PRISONER OF WAR camp, located in the Polish town of Poniatowa, near LUBLIN. Poniatowa was established in September 1941 as a camp for Soviet prisoners of war. By December, 24,000 Soviet prisoners were interned there. The conditions were so harsh that hundreds of prisoners died daily; by early spring 1942, some 22,000 prisoners had died or had been executed. During that summer the German army gave the SS control of the camp. Soon, the SS began using Poniatowa as a forced labor camp for Jews.

The first Jews arrived in October 1942. By January 1943 some 1,500 Jews were interned there. After the WARSAW GHETTO UPRISING in April 1943, 16,000–18,000 more Jews were brought to Poniatowa. Ten thousand prisoners were made to work in a textile factory that had been transferred from the Warsaw GHETTO. The rest worked at various outdoor jobs. Hundreds of prisoners were executed or tortured to death by the SS staff and the Ukrainian guards.

On November 4, 1943, the Germans began destroy-ing Poniatowa: some 15,000 Jews were shot to death in a one-day massacre as part of Operation "ERNTEFEST." Prisoners who resisted were burnt alive inside their barracks. Only a few survivors escaped the camp before it was totally liquidated.

PRACOVNA SKUPINA   see WORKING GROUP.

PRAGUE   Capital of Czechoslovakia, and during WORLD WAR II, the capital of the Protectorate of Bohemia and Moravia. During the early 1930s some 35,000 Jews lived in Prague. After HITLER rose to national power in GERMANY in 1933, many German Jews fled to Prague. Many more REFUGEES arrived in Prague in 1938, after Hitler conquered AUSTRIA and the Sudeten region of Czechoslovakia. This increased the city's Jewish population to about 56,000.

German troops invaded Prague in March 1939, and declared the entire western region of Czechoslovakia to be a German protectorate, called the Protectorate of Bohemia and Moravia. The word protectorate was ac-

Czech citizens react as German troops occupy Prague, March 1939

tually a euphemistic term that meant that Bohemia and Moravia were totally subjugated to Germany. Soon after the occupation, Adolf EICHMANN arrived to establish a branch of the ZENTRALSTELLE FUER JUEDISCHE AUSWANDERUNG (Central Office for Jewish Emigration), whose goal was to "encourage" the Jews of the protectorate to leave the country.

When World War II broke out in September 1939, many of Prague's Jewish leaders were taken hostage. Despite this, Jewish organizations continued their work in secret. Prague's Palestine Office succeeding in helping some 19,000 Jews escape the country for Palestine by the end of 1939.

Between October 1941 and March 1945, the Nazis deported 46,067 Jews from Prague. Most were first sent to the THERESIENSTADT Ghetto, and then deported to their deaths at AUSCHWITZ. The Nazis established a department that was responsible for the apartments and possessions of the deported Jews. The Germans needed 54 warehouses to store all the property they had pillaged from the Jews. In addition, they made a collection in Prague of thousands of religious and ritual items from the Jewish communities all around Prague. The Nazis intended to use this collection as the basis of a "Central Museum of the Extinguished Jewish Race." However, after the war it became part of the Jewish Museum of Prague. Today, the names of the Jews from the Protectorate of Bohemia and Moravia who were killed by the Nazis are displayed on the walls of Prague's Pinkas Synagogue. (see also BOHEMIA AND MORAVIA, PROTECTORATE OF.)

PRIEBKE TRIAL   Trial of former SS captain Erich Priebke, who was convicted in July 1997 of ordering the massacre of 335 men and boys during WORLD WAR II. Priebke ordered the slaughter, which took place in the Ardeatine caves near Rome, in retaliation for the bombing death in Rome of 33 German soldiers. The bomb had been set by the Italian resistance, so most of Priebke's victims were anti-fascist prisoners whom he took from the city's jails. However, Priebke also included 75 Jews in the massacre, who had had nothing to do with the bomb. The victims were brought to the caves, where they were shot.

After the war Priebke moved to Argentina, where he lived openly until he was discovered by ABC News. In 1995 he was extradited to ITALY. In a trial that took place in 1996, an Italian court decided to drop the charges against Priebke, claiming that his crimes were not bad enough to disregard Italy's 30-year statute of limitation. Many Italians vehemently protested the decision, especially the Jewish victims' families. The first verdict was overturned and a retrial was held in 1997. Priebke was convicted and sentenced to 15 years in prison, of which only five were to be served.

PRISONERS OF WAR   (Jewish and Soviet prisoners of war), two hundred thousand Jewish soldiers of the various Allied armies and more than five million Soviet soldiers taken prisoner by the Germans during WORLD WAR II. The Jewish POWs were treated differently based on which army they belonged to.

Jewish soldiers from the armies of Western countries, including the UNITED STATES, FRANCE, CANADA, Australia, GREAT BRITAIN, and its Jewish units from Palestine, were generally treated the same as any other POWs from those countries. The policy was very different for Jews serving in the Polish and Soviet armies. About 65,000 Polish-Jewish soldiers were taken prisoner by the Germans. The Germans separated out the Jewish prisoners; they tortured them, gave them meager food rations, and made them do hard labor. By mid-1940, 25,000 Jewish prisoners of war had perished. Prisoners of war from the German-occupied territories of POLAND were sent to GHETTOS, where they shared the fate of the rest of the Jews there. Jews from the Soviet-occupied parts of Poland were sent to camps in the LUBLIN district, where no more than a few hundred survived. About 85,000 Jewish soldiers from the Soviet army were taken prisoner; all of them were killed by the Germans, no matter what their rank.

After the Jews, the largest group murdered by the Nazis was Soviet prisoners of war. About 5.7 million soldiers of the Soviet army were captured by the Germans; 3.5 million perished. Given starvation rations and treated brutally, many succumbed, while others were murdered outright. This treatment was a direct result of Nazi ideology which considered Slavs (including Russians) to be subhuman. Russian soldiers were seen as especially dangerous because they were supposedly imbued with Bolshevism. Among other places, thousands of Soviet POWs were imprisoned in AUSCHWITZ and MAJDANEK. In Auschwitz, they were

Soviet prisoners of war in a camp in Poland, 1941

the first victims of murder experiments using ZYKLON B gas. In order to escape this terrible treatment, many Soviet POWs volunteered to become guards in the CONCENTRATION CAMPS, where some became notorious for their cruelty. A Jewish Soviet POW, Aleksandr PECHERSKY, led the SOBIBOR uprising.

PROPAGANDA, NAZI   Systematic promotion of certain ideas and practices in order to further one's cause. The Nazis were among the most sophisticated and innovative users of propaganda in history. Before they rose to national power in GERMANY, they used propaganda to attract the attention of the public and gain support among the German people. In particular, they created and sold the myth of HITLER'S infallibility and dynamism. After the NAZI PARTY took control of the German government in January 1933, propaganda was used to reinforce Adolf Hitler's hold over Germany and to secure his dictatorship in the public eye and mind.

In his book, MEIN KAMPF, Hitler described his perspective on propaganda. He explained that propaganda is not meant to be used on scientifically trained intellectuals because, as propaganda is not logical, rational, or scientific, the intellectuals will not be swayed by it.

Nazi antisemitic propaganda from the newspaper Der Stuermer

Rather, he said, propaganda is meant for the masses who cannot comprehend logic and intellect, but can be convinced of anything if their emotions are manipulated. Hitler further stated that since the masses have very little intelligence and are quite forgetful, the key to propaganda is to keep repeating the same ideas over and over again until they are understood by and engraved on the mind of even the slowest person.

Hitler believed that the only way to get across his ideas was to keep the propaganda simplistic and create the illusion that the German people had but one enemy: the Jews. Thus, he combined both RACISM and ANTISEMITISM in Nazi propaganda, telling the German people over and over how parasitic and racially inferior the Jews are, and how they must be removed for Germany to achieve its goal of becoming a superior, racially pure nation.

Hitler used all sorts of means to hammer home his message. In March 1933, just two months after he came to power, Hitler created the Reich Ministry of Public Enlightenment and Propaganda, and appointed Joseph GOEBBELS propaganda minister. The ministry was divided into seven sections, mirroring the methods used by the Nazis to spread their ideas: radio; the press; films; theater; adult education (which included literature); administration and organization; and propaganda. They masterfully utilized Nazi Party rallies and parades to attract the attention of the German people and appeal to their need to be part of something larger than themselves, something to which they could belong. The Nazis also published antisemitic literature, such as the weekly newspaper *Der* STUERMER. The paper included hostile, infantile articles which described Jews as inferior

and sexually perverse, while its drawings depicted contorted, ugly Jews with hooked noses, huge ears and lips, hairy bodies, and crooked legs. *Der Stuermer* succeeded in fostering an aura of hatred around Jews by distorting and mocking them—pure propaganda. The Ministry of Propaganda also had antisemitic films produced in order to visually convince Germany that the Jews were so awful that they deserved to be persecuted. *Jued Suss* was a film that came out in Germany in 1940 as one of a series of three antisemitic movies. It told the story of an immoral Jewish banker who rapes a blond "Aryan" woman. All the other Jews in the film are shown to be dirty, immoral, and ugly. Another film, *Der ewige Jude* (The Eternal Jew), promoted by the Nazis as a documentary, "revealed" the Jews to be a disgusting group that used the blood of Christian children for their religious rituals, thereby bringing up a piece of medieval propaganda. The Nazis also made films about the great 1937 Nazi Party rally at NUREMBERG, which glorified Germany and racism.

Goebbels himself stated the fundamental idea behind the Nazis' propaganda machine: "the great mass

Nazi antisemitic exhibit "The Jew and France," Bordeaux, France

of people in the simplicity of their hearts are more easily taken in by a big lie than by a little one." (see also FILMS, NAZI ANTISEMITIC.)

PROTOCOLS OF THE ELDERS OF ZION

Forged document that claims to reveal a Jewish plot to take over the world. The *Protocols* were based on a satire of the French regime by Maurice Joly that had been published in BELGIUM in 1864. The adaptation was first distributed in Russia. Eventually, the *Protocols* were used by the Nazis as "proof" of the Jews' wickedness and greed. Groups still publish the *Protocols* today with the intention of hurting the Jews and denying the HOLOCAUST (see also HOLOCAUST, DENIAL OF THE).

The *Protocols* state that the Jews will use weapons to achieve control over the world. It claims that the Jews brought about the French Revolution, Liberalism, Socialism, Communism, and anarchy in order to weaken European society. Jews also control the price of gold and have the power to evoke economic crises, rule the media, create religious and tribal feuds, and destroy cities if the need arises. Once they gain world power, they would demand total obedience to a Jewish king. Finally, the FREEMASONS would act as their collaborators in these conspiracies.

The forged claims made by the *Protocols* were not original. By the mid-eighteenth century, similar stories were published in the German media. Such ideas were also being published in Russia at the end of the century. Pyotr Ivanovich Rachkovsky, head of the foreign branch of the Russian secret police in PARIS, was probably responsible for forging the *Protocols* during the Dreyfus Affair of 1894. Rachkovsky hoped to accomplish two goals: to provide a document for the French that would "implicate" Alfred Dreyfus, a Jewish military officer, of his alleged crimes, and a document for the Russians to support their antisemitic policies.

Other versions of the *Protocols* were published in Russia at the turn of the century. When opponents of the Revolution fled Russia, they took the *Protocols* with them to the West; versions of the document appeared in GERMANY by the 1920s. Soon the Nazis began to use the *Protocols*—they were often quoted in Nazi newspapers. The *Protocols* quickly spread all over the world, including the UNITED STATES and GREAT BRITAIN, and were translated into dozens of languages.

PRUETZMANN, HANS-ADOLF

(1901–1945), SS officer. Born in East Prussia, Pruetzmann joined the NAZI PARTY in 1929 and the SS in 1930. He quickly shot up through the SS's ranks: in 1934 he was promoted to the rank of SS-*Gruppenfuehrer;* he became a senator in HAMBURG in 1938; and soon thereafter was named Higher SS and Police Leader in the Nordsee district of GERMANY. In April 1941 Pruetzmann was promoted once again, this time to the rank of lieutenant-general in the police.

On June 22, 1941, the day that the German army invaded the SOVIET UNION, Pruetzmann was named Higher SS and Police Leader for the areas occupied by the German Army Group North, including the Baltic States (LITHUANIA, LATVIA, and ESTONIA) and the area between their eastern borders and Leningrad. On October 31, 1941, he was moved to the Southern Command (UKRAINE) region. Two years later, in October 1943, he was also appointed Higher SS and Police Leader for all of REICHSKOMMISSARIAT UKRAINE.

In late 1944 Pruetzmann was put in charge of various special assignments. He was also named commander in chief of CROATIA. At the end of the war he was captured by the British; he subsequently took his own life.

Cover of a French version of the Protocols of the Elders of Zion, entitled "The Jewish Peril"

Q

QUISLING, VIDKUN (1887–1945), Norwegian fascist leader and head of the Nazi-controlled puppet government in NORWAY from 1942–1945.

From 1922–1930 Quisling worked for the League of Nations providing aid to starving peasants in the UKRAINE and on similar projects in BULGARIA, the Balkans, and Armenia. By the time he left the SOVIET UNION in 1929, he had decided that Communism and Bolshevism were threats to Norway.

In 1931 Quisling co-founded the Nordic Folk Awakening movement, which mirrored Nazi ideology. He believed that Norway needed strong leaders to protect individual rights, and that the Jews were impure and a threat to his ideal society. From 1931–1933 he served as minister of defense; in May 1933 he founded a fascist political party called National Unity with its own youth movement and bodyguard corps called the "*Hird.*" However, Quisling was not elected to the parliament. Thus, he soon turned to Nazi GERMANY for support.

In December 1939 Quisling met with Adolf HITLER and Nazi ideologist Alfred ROSENBERG. He was guaranteed German funds and moral support. In exchange, Quisling invited the Nazis to occupy Norway. The Germans invaded Norway in April 1940; Quisling openly met them and declared a new government with himself as prime minister. His traitorous behavior prompted the *London Times* to use his name as a synonym for all treason and collaboration.

However, the Germans rapidly became discontented with Quisling and kicked him out of office after just a week. The new government retained many of Quisling's people but was really run by the Germans. Quisling maintained leadership of the National Unity Party and for two years, he unofficially worked behind the scenes. In February 1942 a national government was established with Quisling as minister-president. However, his actual powers were limited. He aspired to make a treaty with Germany that would give his government true authority and independence. However, he never succeeded, and was always dependent on the Germans.

After the LIBERATION of Norway, Quisling was arrested and put on trial. He was found guilty, sentenced to death, and executed on October 24, 1945.

Vidkun Quisling saluting a Nazi officer
(National Archive, Washington)

R

RAB Italian internment camp on the Yugoslav island of Rab, located in the Italian-occupied zone of YUGOSLAVIA. Rab was established in July 1942 for the detention of Slovenians who opposed the Italian occupation. The Slovenians were treated very harshly; some 4,000 died.

In early 1943 the Italians decided to establish a camp for the Jews of Italian-occupied Yugoslavia next to the Slovenian camp. This decision was not based on the Italians' desire to persecute the Jews. On the contrary: the Italian occupiers refused to surrender the Jews under their control to the Germans, and as a result they feared a German attack. Thus, they decided to concentrate the region's Jews in one place (Rab), close to the Italian border, so they could escape into liberated areas when the time was right. The day after ITALY surrendered to the Allies, on September 8, 1943, Rab was liberated and most Jews were taken to the liberated areas. Those who were strong enough joined the PARTISANS. Several hundred Jews refused to leave for the liberated areas; some made it to liberated southern Italy later on by themselves, while the rest were arrested when Germans troops conquered the island of Rab in March 1944. They were then sent to AUSCHWITZ, where they were exterminated.

RACE AND RESETTLEMENT MAIN OFFICE (*Rasse- und Siedlungshauptamt*, RuSHA), Nazi office that dealt with racial matters. Established in 1931, RuSHA was designated as an SS Main Office (the central office of an SS organization) in 1935. The office's tasks included doing research and providing instruction on race issues, including special training courses for elite Nazi groups; making sure that SS men and their wives were racially pure; carrying out the resettlement of SS men in Nazi-occupied countries as part of the global Nazi plan for expanding the German Reich throughout Europe; and encouraging them to settle on farm lands near cities. RuSHA's staff included many determined and industrious young men who either had medical or some other professional eligibility. Some were later promoted to senior SS positions.

The RuSHA began evicting landowners from their homes and settling Germans in their place in mid-1939. RuSHA offices established in the parts of Poland annexed to the Reich were in charge of confiscated Jewish- and Polish-owned land. In 1940 RuSHA came up with the plan to "Germanize" Poles who had the appropriate racial qualities. Possible candidates were screened and interviewed by "race experts and qualifications examiners." These experts also checked out the racial authenticity of Poles who registered themselves as "ethnic Germans" (VOLKSDEUTSCHE). In addition, RuSHA made plans to "Germanize" the Ukrainian people.

RACISM Philosophy that attributes a person or group's character, abilities, appearance, intelligence, and behavior to race—usually defined as a population with traits in common. Racists divide the world into "superior" and "inferior" races, and believe that, by nature and fate, the superior peoples have the right to dominate the inferior. Before WORLD WAR II racism began to exert great influence on the policies of political movements in Europe, especially those of the NAZI PARTY in GERMANY. The persecution of specific racial groups during the HOLOCAUST, particularly the Jews, was a product of the Nazi racial view of the world.

In the mid-1850s Comte Arthur de Gobineau published his "Essay on the Inequality of Human Races." Before Gobineau, racism was mostly a subject for scientists. He turned racism into a cultural and political issue, by saying that the deterioration of the modern age resulted from the mixing of superior and inferior races. He divided humanity into the black, yellow, and white races, and claimed that only the pure white, or Aryan, race was and could be truly noble.

Antisemites used racist theory to prove the morality of their hatred of Jews. Houston Stewart CHAMBERLAIN pitted Germans against Jews in his writings. Germans were seen as the highest cultural achievers and the saviors of humanity; Jews were a "bastard race" of greedy, inferior foreigners who lived in the midst of Europe, but behaved differently than their neighbors.

Neben sie heften wir das Bildnis eines deutschen Menschen. Dann schauen wir ein paar Minuten lang und vergleichen die Bilder der Juden mit jenem des Deutschen. Es wird nicht lange währen, da wird es Antworten hageln: „Die Juden haben andere N a s e n, andere O h r e n, andere L i p p e n, ein anderes K i n n, ein ganz anderes G e s i c h t, wie wir deutschen Menschen." Wer seinen Kindern den Auftrag gibt, den Juden draußen im Leben zu beobachten, wie er auf der Straße geht, wie er vor seiner Ladentüre steht, wird ein paar Tage später folgende Auskunft von den Kindern erhalten: „Die Juden laufen anders wie wir. Sie haben Sentfüße. Ihre Körperhaltung ist eine andere wie die unsrige. Ihre Haare, ihre Augen, ihre Augenbrauen sind anders wie die unsrigen. Sie haben längere Arme wie wir. Sie reden anders wie wir." Alle diese Beobachtungen läßt der Lehrer in das neu angelegte „J u d e n m e r k h e f t" eintragen. So zum rassischen Sehen erzogene Kinder werden aus tausend Menschen den Juden auf den ersten Blick herausfinden.

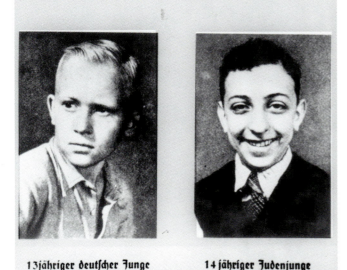

1 3jähriger deutscher Junge   *1 4 jähriger Judenjunge*

Nazi racial propaganda comparing a "typical" German youth to a "typical" Jewish youth

Both groups had entered history at the same time, and thus had to compete to the bitter end for domination. In fact, all of human history was a struggle between the races, and the Germans were fated to destroy the Jews. Other antisemites blamed Jews as the middle class that devoured money and kept others in poverty.

The Nazis sharpened political racist philosophy for their own purposes and turned theory into practice in their attempt to destroy all of European Jewry. Racism was a major element in Nazi ideology; the Nazis were able to "justify" their horrible actions by making the Jews seem less human. Thus, by the time physical attacks were initiated against the Jews, it seemed they even deserved what was coming to them. Dietrich Eckart, one of HITLER'S early political advisors, said that no one would have left the Jews alive throughout history

had they known what their true nature really was, and what their evil plans for the world were. Hitler truly believed these ideas; he said that an inferior race, like the Jews, had more in common with the apes than with superior human races. Heinrich HIMMLER motivated his soldiers to carry out his murderous orders by dehumanizing the Jews completely. He claimed that the Jews were similar to fleas and mice—disgusting lower forms of life that deserved to be exterminated. The Nazis tried to convince the German people of the truth of their claims by creating propaganda films that visually proved racist theory.

Another way the Nazis made racism look honorable was to propagate it, not through obvious violence, but through the cooperation of government agencies. Hitler gradually promoted racism through "legitimate" laws that his government made, chief among them the NUREMBERG LAWS of 1935. These laws legally called for the separation of Jews from Christians, and also defined for the first time who was to be considered a Jew, and who was to be considered an Aryan. A Jew, according to this legislation, was someone with at least three Jewish grandparents. An Aryan was a person whose four grandparents all belonged to the Aryan race. In order to become a member of the elite SS troops, however, a person had to prove that his ancestors were pure Aryans in the period before 1800 (at which time the Jews were given greater freedoms and thus had more of a chance to mix with Aryans, thereby polluting the gene pool). Someone with only two Jewish grandparents was defined as a MISCHLING, meaning a person of mixed heritage. *Mischlinge* were not allowed to have sexual relations with either Jews or Aryans, so they were doomed to have no children and die out. Thus, these laws brought racism legally out into the open.

As the Germans occupied different European countries during World War II and expected collaboration toward the reordering of society in accordance with their racial views, they put European racism to the test. Many of those countries' leaders, especially those who were politically conservative, were ambivalent about Hitler's demand to hand over their Jews. Marshal Ion ANTONESCU of ROMANIA originally agreed to deport and exterminate his country's Jews. He later changed his mind when he saw where the war was heading. In HUNGARY, Admiral Miklos HORTHY did not succumb to Nazi pressure until they occupied his country. Marshal Philippe PETAIN of FRANCE agreed to give up the non-French Jews who had sought refuge there, but

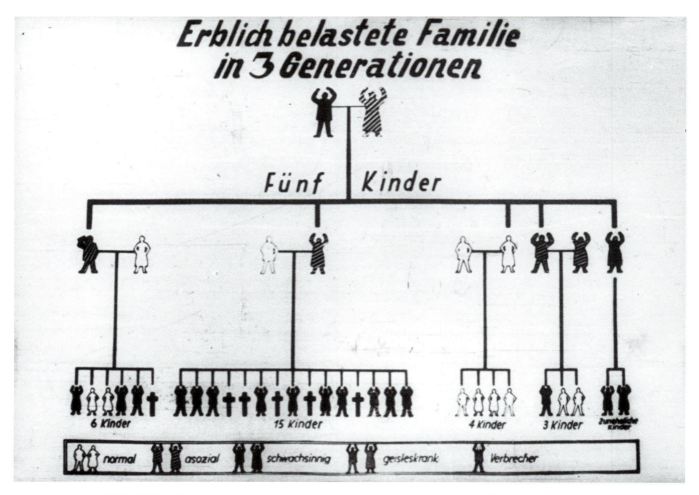

Racist chart showing what will happen over three generations to a family tending to racial weakness

tried to save his country's native Jews. In ITALY, racism was never successfully spread to the masses.

The countries allied against Germany during the war, namely the UNITED STATES, GREAT BRITAIN, and the SOVIET UNION, loudly condemned racism and used it as a motivation to win the war and destroy the Nazi regime; this despite their racist activities at home against blacks, colonial populations, and Jews, respectively.

Today, the Holocaust is used as the prime warning against the advancement of racism. However, racism still continues to exist. The Internet has provided a free forum for expression of racist ideas, and less-educated groups use stereotypes as the foundations of their beliefs. Some people still fear those who are different, and some countries still utilize the racist myths of the past to shape their modern policy. (see also PROPAGANDA, NAZI.)

RADA GLOWNA OPIEKUNCZA see CENTRAL WELFARE COUNCIL, POLAND.

RADEMACHER, FRANZ (1906–1973), Nazi official. Rademacher joined the NAZI PARTY in March 1933. He was recruited to work in the Foreign Office in 1937, and served abroad for several years. In May 1940 Rademacher became the head of the Foreign Office's Jewish desk. Rademacher wanted to attain prominence in this post as the man who came up with a "final solution" to the Jewish question. One of the ideas he presented was the expulsion of European Jewry to the French island colony of Madagascar. High-ranking Nazis expressed their approval for this idea, so Rademacher set out to develop the MADAGASCAR PLAN, which was also being prepared by Adolf EICHMANN. However, the plan hit a dead end when the Germans failed to defeat the British in the Battle of Britain. Nonetheless, Rademacher did play a role in the "Final Solution": he was in charge of making sure that there were no foreign policy issues that could delay or threaten the DEPORTATIONS of Jews to

EXTERMINATION CAMPS, and he performed this task very well.

After the war, Rademacher was convicted of war crimes, but he jumped bail and escaped to Syria. He returned to Germany in 1966 and was once again tried and convicted before he died in 1973.

RADOM   City in central POLAND, 62 miles south of WARSAW. In 1939, 30,000 Jews lived in Radom, making up one-third of the city's total population.

The Germans occupied Radom on September 8, 1939. The GENERALGOUVERNEMENT was created that October, and Radom became the capital of one of its districts. In December the Germans formed a JUDENRAT and a JEWISH POLICE force. Soon, many Jews were deported to FORCED LABOR camps.

By April 1941 all of Radom's Jews were herded into one of two GHETTOS, a large one in the city center and a small one in a nearby suburb. The Jews living in the ghettos suffered from hunger and unsanitary conditions. During the first half of 1942, small murder *aktionen* took place and hundreds were deported to AUSCHWITZ.

The Nazis liquidated the small ghetto on August 5, 1942 with the help of Ukrainian collaborators. Some Jews were shot, others were sent to do forced labor, and the rest were deported to TREBLINKA. From August 16–18 the large ghetto was also destroyed. A forced labor camp was set up on the site of each ghetto.

Several underground resistance groups were active in Radom. During the DEPORTATIONS, hundreds of Jews from these groups escaped to the forest; some participated in the WARSAW POLISH UPRISING in late summer 1944.

RASCH, EMIL OTTO   (1891–1948), Commander of EINSATZGRUPPE C, a mobile killing unit that helped carry out the mass extermination of hundreds of thousands of Jews and other Soviet civilians and PRISONERS OF WAR after GERMANY invaded the SOVIET UNION in mid-1941.

Rasch joined the NAZI PARTY in 1931 and the SS in 1933. When the Nazis rose to national power, Rasch was made mayor of Radeberg and then of Wittenberg. For the next few years he moved up the Nazi hierarchy, holding posts in the Reich Security Main Office, the State Police, the Security Police, and the Security Service (SD).

In May 1941 Rasch was named commander of *Einsatzgruppe* C, which was attached to Army Group South and covered the northern and central UKRAINE. Rasch and his unit were responsible for many *aktionen,* in which tens of thousands of Jews were massacred. The most notorious *aktion* carried out by Rasch's *Einsatzgruppe* was in BABI YAR, where over 33,000 Jews were killed in two days of shooting.

In September 1941 Rasch was ordered to return to BERLIN. After the war, he was arrested and tried in the *Einsatzgruppen* case at the NUREMBERG TRIALS. He died before the case ended.

RASSE-UND SIEDLUNGSHAUPTAMT   see RACE AND RESETTLEMENT MAIN OFFICE.

RAUFF, WALTHER   (1906–1984), Nazi official. Rauff had his future set out for him as a professional naval officer, until a nasty divorce ruined his chances for career advancement and caused him to leave the navy in December 1937. At that point, he was accepted into the Security Service (SD), the SS's intelligence service, which was under the command of Reinhard HEYDRICH.

Jews in the Radom Ghetto

Eventually, Rauff became the head of the technical affairs section of the Reich Security Main Office (REICHSSICHERHEITSHAUPTAMT, RSHA). In this position, he was responsible for equipping and issuing about 20 GAS VANS, in which some 200,000 people were exterminated.

In late 1942 Rauff went to Tunis where he led an EINSATZGRUPPE unit for the SD. In September 1943 he became the district SS and Police Leader in northern ITALY, after German forces occupied that area.

After the war ended, Rauff was detained in a prisoner of war camp. He escaped in December 1946 and hid in a monastery in Rome for a year and a half. He then managed to travel abroad, finally settling down in Chile. In 1963 West Germany tried to convince the Chilean authorities to send Rauff back to Europe, but they refused. Rauff died in 1984 in Santiago, Chile.

RAUSCHNING, HERMANN (1887–1982), Nazi politician who broke away from HITLER and Nazism before WORLD WAR II.

Born in West Prussia, Rauschning studied history and music before volunteering during World War I. After the war, he was active in ethnic German organizations. In 1926 Rauschning bought an estate in DANZIG, a city on the Baltic Sea that for centuries had been a point of conflict between GERMANY and POLAND, and after World War I was designated as a "free city" that did not belong to any specific country. In 1931 Rauschning joined the NAZI PARTY.

In June 1933 the Nazi Party won a majority in Danzig's parliamentary elections and Rauschning was named president of the Danzig senate, making him the city's governor. However, Rauschning quit the post in November 1934; he had lost his enthusiasm for Nazism after getting to know HITLER and the local Nazi leader, Albert Forster. In 1936 Rauschning fled to SWITZERLAND; two years later the Danzig senate stripped him of his Danzig citizenship.

At that point, Rauschning began writing books in which he hoped to reveal the true character of Nazism, and warn the world about Hitler's evil plans. In 1948 Rauschning moved to the UNITED STATES, where he continued writing about German politics.

Women prisoners engaged in forced labor, Ravensbrueck

RAVENSBRUECK CONCENTRATION CAMP in eastern GERMANY, located near the town of Ravensbrueck. The only major women's camp established by the Nazis, Ravensbrueck was opened in May 1939. In all, some 132,000 women from all over Europe passed through the camp, including Poles, Germans, Russians, Ukrainians, Jews, French, GYPSIES, and others. Of that number, 92,000 perished.

Ravensbrueck was staffed both by SS men, who served as guards and administrators, and by 150 women, who served as supervisors. These female supervisors were either SS volunteers or women who had taken the job for the good pay and work conditions. Ravensbrueck also housed a training camp for female SS guards. About 3,500 women trained there, and went on to serve either at Ravensbrueck or at other concentration camps.

The first group of prisoners arrived at Ravensbrueck on May 18, 1939; the group consisted of nearly 900 women who had previously been imprisoned at the Nazi concentration camp at Lichtenburg. At the end of 1939, 2,000 women were interned at Ravensbrueck; in late 1942 there were about 10,800. By 1944 Ravensbrueck had 34 satellite camps, many of which were located nowhere near Ravensbrueck itself; some were situated as far away as Bavaria and the Protectorate of Bohemia and Moravia. During that year there were 26,700 prisoners living at the Ravensbrueck main camp, while another 70,000 prisoners were brought to the camp and parceled out among the satellite camps. Several thousand girls were housed in a detention camp for minors located near the main camp.

The main camp at Ravensbrueck and most of its satellite camps were attached to military factories where the prisoners were made to do FORCED LABOR. Many of the prisoners manufactured Nazi uniforms. The working conditions at Ravensbrueck were brutal: the women worked 12 hours a day and were subjected to outdoor roll calls in any kind of weather. In addition, they were given meager food rations. The Jewish prisoners were made to do the hardest labor and were treated with intense cruelty.

While the great majority of prisoners at Ravensbrueck were women, there were also some men detained there. In April 1941 a camp for men was built near the Ravensbrueck main camp. Officially, this camp was a satellite of SACHSENHAUSEN. In its four years of existence, about 20,000 men passed through, including more than 3,000 Jews.

In the summer of 1942 the Nazis began conducting pseudo-scientific MEDICAL EXPERIMENTS at Ravensbrueck. In one experiment, 74 Polish women were used as human guinea pigs in a test to check the effectiveness of a sulfa drug called sulfonamide in treating infected and swollen wounds and bone transplants. In another experiment, carried out by the SS doctor Professor Carl CLAUBERG, 35 women, mostly Gypsies, were brutally sterilized.

During its first years of operation, prisoners at Ravensbrueck were exterminated by being shot in the back of the neck. By 1942 the prisoners selected for destruction were either sent to AUSCHWITZ-Birkenau or to EUTHANASIA PROGRAM killing centers. Later, prisoners were killed by poisonous injection at Ravensbrueck itself, and their bodies were cremated at a crematorium nearby. However, when the killings at Ravensbrueck increased, it became inconvenient to transfer the corpses to a different location. Thus, the Nazis built a crematorium at Ravensbrueck in April 1943. In early 1945 they also constructed GAS CHAMBERS there, and by late April of that year, some 2,300 prisoners had been gassed to death.

The Germans began evacuating Ravensbrueck in March 1945; thousands of starving prisoners were sent on DEATH MARCHES to other camps in Germany. In early April 500 prisoners were handed over to the Red Cross, while 2,500 German prisoners were released. Ravensbrueck was liberated by the Soviet army on April 29–30; only 3,500 prisoners remained in the camp.

RAYMAN, MARCEL (1923–1944), French Jewish underground fighter who took part in attacks on German soldiers and army installations in PARIS. In 1943 Rayman participated in the killing of the German administrator responsible for recruiting French workers for labor in GERMANY.

RAYSKI, ABRAHAM (also known as Adam; b. 1914), Jewish Communist who was active in the anti-Nazi resistance in FRANCE during WORLD WAR II.

Rayski was born to a traditional, middle-class Jewish family in BIALYSTOK. He got involved with Communism at a young age. When he was 18 he left home for PARIS, and within just two years he became a full-time reporter for a Communist newspaper called *Neie Presse*.

From July 1941 until the war's end Rayski worked as national secretary of the French Communist Party's Jewish section. He made several important contributions to Jewish survival in France during the war: he helped develop French Jewish resistance; wrote articles for the underground press; and assisted in the establishment of the REPRESENTATIVE COUNCIL OF FRENCH JEWS (an umbrella organization of French Jewish associations, established in January 1944, which unified the long-divided native French Jewish and immigrant Jewish organizations).

Many years after the war, Rayski wrote and published a striking autobiography called *Nos illusions perdues* (*Our Lost Illusions*, 1985).

RED CROSS, INTERNATIONAL

(International Committee of the Red Cross, ICRC), private non-governmental humanitarian organization, founded in 1863, staffed by citizens of neutral SWITZERLAND. The ICRC's goals included maintaining contact between national Red Cross societies, acting as a neutral go-between for enemy countries during war, and ensuring the development and implementation of humanitarian law.

By the time WORLD WAR II broke out in 1939, the ICRC had extended its domain from helping wounded troops on the field of war to protecting PRISONERS OF WAR, as well. However, it had not yet extended this protection to civilians during times of war. The ICRC used this as an excuse for not aiding the millions of HOLOCAUST victims who were civilians.

By the spring of 1942, the ICRC was made aware of the true meaning of the "Final Solution." However, it did not publicly condemn the atrocities committed by the Nazis against the Jews, and never even asked the German government to respect the human rights the ICRC supposedly stood for. Furthermore, the ICRC did not want to bring up the subject of discrimination based on race. As a rule, the ICRC did not try to rescue the Jewish victims of the Nazis or even intercede on their behalf. Individual representatives of the ICRC sometimes made efforts to help, but achieved little on their own.

At the end of 1942 and the beginning of 1943, as the ICRC decided that rescue was impossible to achieve, they chose instead to send aid packages of food, medicine, and clothing to deportees in Nazi-dominated countries. However, the ICRC never obtained the necessary documents from the Allies to pass through their war blockade, so the results of their efforts were quite limited.

In spring 1944 the Germans launched the DEPOR-TATION of the Jews of HUNGARY. At this late point, the ICRC, led by representative Friedrich Born, finally interceded on the Jews' behalf. In early 1945 the ICRC also attempted to negotiate with the German authorities regarding the exchange of civilian prisoners. However, their activities were woefully few in the face of the Nazis' flouting of human rights—which on paper, at least, were the ICRC's domain.

RED ORCHESTRA

Code name for a Russian spy network that infiltrated German intelligence during WORLD WAR II. The Red Orchestra was established in 1937 on behalf of Soviet Military Intelligence by Leopold Trepper (Leib Domb), a Polish Jew.

The Germans occupied FRANCE in 1940; soon the Red Orchestra moved its headquarters to PARIS and set up offices around Western Europe. The network managed to infiltrate main German offices in Paris, including the German air force and high command, and even tapped the phones at the French branch of German intelligence.

The Red Orchestra successfully found out about the imminent German invasion of the SOVIET UNION and passed on detailed information to Joseph STALIN who, for whatever reason, refused to acknowledge it. The network also gave advance warning of the German attacks on Moscow, Stalingrad, and the Caucasus. However, German counterintelligence began tailing the Red Orchestra in late 1941, and members were arrested in spring 1942. By November, the Paris headquarters were liquidated and Trepper arrested. He escaped less than a year later. After the war Trepper was flown to Moscow, where instead of receiving the hero's welcome he expected, he was framed and thrown into jail. He was released in 1955, and in 1973 immigrated to Israel.

REFUGEES

People fleeing from the land of their birth because of war or political, social, religious, or economic persecution.

As soon as the Nazis rose to national power in 1933, Jews began fleeing GERMANY en mass. Between 1933–1938, about one-quarter of Germany's 525,000 Jews left the country. In 1934 and most of 1935, emigration slowed down; it accelerated again after the NUREMBERG LAWS were passed in September, which stripped Jews of their German citizenship and excluded them from many aspects of economic and communal life.

Most of these Jews went to nearby countries, such as FRANCE, the NETHERLANDS, SWITZERLAND, Czechoslova-

Einschiffung

Jewish refugees embarking on a ship to the United States, 1939

kia, and AUSTRIA. Sometimes, immigrants found it hard to cope in the new country, prompting them to return to Germany. However, the Nazis did not want any returning Jews, so in 1935 they decreed that all returnees would be imprisoned in CONCENTRATION CAMPS. Some Jews stayed in Germany because the emigration taxes were too high, or because they were forbidden to take any substantial amounts of money out of the country with them.

In 1938 Nazi persecution got even worse. In March 1938 Germany annexed Austria, bringing approximately 200,000 more Jews under German control. From April–November 1938, 50,000 Jews left German-occupied Austria; in all about 150,000 Jews fled the Reich after the KRISTALLNACHT pogrom of November 1938. More would have left had the countries of the world been willing to take them in. The American-initiated EVIAN CONFERENCE of July 1938 had done nothing to enlarge the world's immigration quotas. Many Western countries enacted further immigration limitations at the end of the 1930s as a result of their deep-seated ANTISEMITISM; their concern that the tens of thousands of Jews from the Reich would soon be joined by millions of refugees from Eastern Europe; and their desire, after the Great Depression, to keep their countries' jobs for themselves.

WORLD WAR II broke out in September 1939. At that point, 110,000 Jewish refugees were spread out all over Europe. Some 71,500 more Jews fled the Reich before the Germans totally forbade Jewish emigration in October 1941. As the German army moved across Europe, Jews continued to flee persecution. About 300,000 Polish Jews left German-occupied POLAND for Soviet territories. However, when the Nazis invaded the SOVIET UNION in the summer of 1941, most Soviet and Polish Jews living in Soviet territories were murdered by EINSATZGRUPPEN and other units before they had a chance to flee.

ITALY protected many Jews who entered its domain. Some Jews were able to escape to neutral countries. About 21,600 Jews reached Switzerland, but thousands more were turned away during much of the war. Others reached SPAIN and many were immediately sent on to Portugal, from which thousands left for America. SWEDEN served as a refuge for many Scandinavian Jews, including the 7,200 Jews who were saved by the Danish people in October 1943.

The UNITED STATES, despite its long-held reputation of a safe haven for refugees, did not open its doors to Jewish refugees during World War II. The BERMUDA CONFERENCE of April 1943 was just an attempt to quiet public opinion, without having to actually make a serious effort to save any Jews. Only in January 1944, with a scandal looming after it was discovered that the United States State Department was sabotaging rescue efforts, did President Franklin D. ROOSEVELT establish an official government agency, the WAR REFUGEE BOARD (WRB), to deal with the Jewish refugee problem. It managed to save thousands of Jews—but began its good work too late, when most of European Jewry had already been massacred.

REICH REPRESENTATION OF GERMAN JEWS

(*Reichsvertretung der Deutschen Juden*), central representative organization of German Jewry. The Reich Representation was founded on Jewish initiative in September 1933, several months after Adolf HITLER rose to power in GERMANY. Spearheaded by its president, Rabbi Leo BAECK, and its executive director, Otto HIRSCH, the organization's goal was to confront the grave problems facing German Jewry under the antisemitic Nazi regime.

As its name implied, the Reich Representation was to serve as the representative of German Jewry both in dealing with the German authorities and with Jewish organizations outside of Germany. Though it had no official status, the organization was recognized by the Nazi authorities. Thus, the Reich Representation was responsible for administering all aspects of German Jewish life, including education, both for young people and adults; job training and retraining for the many Jews who had lost their means of livelihood as a result of ANTI-JEWISH LEGISLATION; support for the poor; general economic assistance, which included establishing employment offices and loan funds; and emigration. All these methods of assistance helped the Jews of Germany cope with the serious problems they faced as a result of the Nazis' anti-Jewish decrees and measures.

In 1935 the authorities forced the Reich Representation to change its name to "Reich Representation of Jews in Germany" (as opposed to "German Jews"), and in 1939, following changes in its structure, the organization's name was changed once again to "Reich Association of Jews in Germany."

From late 1938 until its dissolution in July 1943, the Reich Representation/Association was the only organization in Germany itself that dealt with the issue of Jewish survival. By that time its main goal was Jewish emigration, and it continued in its efforts to help Jews leave the country until all emigration was banned by the authorities in October 1941. In addition, when all Jewish students were expelled from German public schools, the organization set up a widespread Jewish school network, which functioned until it was shut down by the government in June 1942.

The last of the organization's leaders were deported to the THERESIENSTADT Ghetto in 1943, and in July of that year, the Reich Representation/Association was officially abolished

REICHSBUND JUEDISCHER FRONTSOLDATEN see REICH UNION OF JEWISH FRONTLINE SOLDIERS.

REICHSKOMMISSARIAT OSTLAND (Reich Commissariat for Ostland), one of two major administrative units in the German civil administration that controlled the occupied territories of the SOVIET UNION during WORLD WAR II.

In mid-1941 the Nazis decided to establish a Ministry for the Occupied Eastern Territories under Alfred ROSENBERG, which would administer the territories newly-conquered from the Soviet Union. That July, they further decided to divide the territories in two, REICHSKOMMISSARIAT UKRAINE and *Reichskommissariat Ostland*, and assigned each a civilian administration. From 1941–1944 Henrich LOHSE was the *Reichskommissar*.

Reichskommissariat Ostland covered the Baltic states (LITHUANIA, LATVIA, and ESTONIA) and parts of western BELORUSSIA. Accordingly, it was divided into four "General Commissariats" (Lithuania, Latvia, Estonia, and Belorussia), each headed by a German official. In turn, these were also comprised of smaller units. The Germans made future plans to settle the three Baltic states with ethnic Germans (VOLKSDEUTSCHE) and incorporate the areas into the Reich. Belorussia was to be a separate administrative entity.

The Jews living in the *Reichskommissariat Ostland* were exterminated by the mobile killing units of EINSATZGRUPPEN A (in the Baltic states) and B (in Belorussia), along with members of the SIPO, SD, and local collaborators. All of *Ostland* was liberated by the Soviet army during the summer of 1944.

REICHSKOMMISSARIAT UKRAINE (Reich Commissariat for the Ukraine), the German civil administration in the UKRAINE during WORLD WAR II.

In mid-1941 the Nazis decided to establish a Ministry for the Occupied Eastern Territories under Alfred ROSENBERG, which would administer the territories newly-conquered from the SOVIET UNION. That July, they further decided to divide the territories in two, REICHSKOMMISSARIAT OSTLAND and *Reichskommissariat Ukraine,* and assigned each a civilian administration. Erich Koch served as *Reichskommissar.*

HITLER officially transferred the Soviet districts of Volhynia, Rovno, and KAMENETS-PODOLSKI to the authority of *Reichskommissariat Ukraine* in August 1941. As the German army advanced further and further into the Soviet Union, more areas were put under the administration's control. Certain districts, however, stayed under the control of the German military as long as it occupied the Soviet Union.

By the beginning of 1943, *Reichskommissariat Ukraine* covered 130,994 square miles and included almost 17 million inhabitants. Its capital was Rovno. The administration's Higher SS and Police Leader, Hans-Adolf PRUETZMANN, had his headquarters in Kiev. EINSATZGRUPPEN C and D, two of the mobile killing units that exterminated hundreds of thousands of Jews in the Soviet Union, were active in both the *Reichskommissariat Ukraine* and in the part of the Ukraine that was controlled by the German military administration.

REICHSSICHERHEITSHAUPTAMT (RSHA) (Reich Security Main Office), the central office through which the Nazis dealt with their political and ideological enemies. It was established in September 1939, as a combination of the Security Service (SD) and the Security Police (SIPO), which included the GESTAPO and the Criminal Police (KRIPO). Under the leadership of Reinhard HEYDRICH, the RSHA grew enormously, until it was the Nazis' most utilized terror organization.

The RSHA encompassed seven departments. Department IV, under the control of Heinrich MUELLER, was the *Gestapo.* It was divided into 14 divisions, each dealing with matters such as political enemies, treason, and counterintelligence. Subsection IV B-4, also called the Jewish affairs department, was headed by Adolf EICHMANN. From late 1941 on, this section dealt with the "Final Solution" including the DEPORTATION of European Jews to GHETTOS, FORCED LABOR camps, and EXTERMINATION CAMPS.

The RSHA was also responsible for all security work within the Reich, the occupied territories, and behind the army's front lines. It supplied the soldiers who manned the EINSATZGRUPPEN units that carried out the mass extermination of Jews in the SOVIET UNION, and planned the postwar resettlement of POLAND with Germans and ethnic Germans, called GENERALPLAN OST.

REICHSTAG GERMANY'S parliament from 1871 to 1945. According to the constitution of the democratic Weimar Republic (which lasted from 1919 to 1933), the *Reichstag* was supposed to be elected by all citizens every four years. However, in reality, the German president had the right to dissolve the parliament of his own accord. In addition, the Weimar law allowed proportional representation, meaning that even parties with a small number of supporters were represented in parliament. During the late 1920s more and more small parties were taking part in the parliament, and as a result, it became increasingly difficult to form a government with a majority of votes. In fact, by 1930 the president mostly governed by himself, issuing emergency decrees as he saw fit.

In January 1933 Adolf HITLER and the Nazis rose to national power without a majority of votes or seats. Then, in order to gain better control, the Nazis burnt down the *Reichstag* building in late February and pinned the arson on their Communist opponents.

On March 23, 1933 the *Reichstag* surrendered its authority to the Nazis. Until 1942 the *Reichstag* continued to exist as a one-party parliament, but with no lawmaking powers. In 1999 the *Reichstag* building again became the seat of the German government.

REICHSVERTRETUNG DER DEUTSCHEN JUDEN see REICH REPRESENTATION OF GERMAN JEWS.

REICH UNION OF JEWISH FRONTLINE SOLDIERS (*Reichsbund Juedischer Frontsoldaten,*RJF), union of German Jewish war veterans, created in February 1919 by 40 Jewish soldiers who had served on the frontlines of the German army during World War I. One of their main purposes in forming the union was to disprove the popular belief that during World War I, Jews had either only held desk jobs or had avoided

serving in the army altogether. One of their proofs of Jewish service was the fact that 12,000 Jewish soldiers had died fighting for GERMANY. The members of the RJF wanted to assimilate completely into German society, and thus considered the Zionists, who emphasized their uniqueness as Jews in their desire for a Jewish homeland in Palestine, to be their political enemies.

By 1933 the RJF had grown to include 30,000 members in 360 local union branches. After HITLER rose to national power, the RJF tried to avoid being affected by the Nazis' anti-Jewish policies and attempted to win themselves a privileged status. They were able to maintain their unique status until the racial NUREMBERG LAWS were passed in 1935, at which point they lost their preferential treatment and were considered to be Jews, just like the rest.

REIK, HAVIVA   (1914–1944), One of the Jewish parachutists from Palestine sent by the leadership of the YISHUV and the British on military and then rescue missions in Nazi-occupied Europe.

Born in SLOVAKIA, Reik was a member of the *Ha-Shomer ha-Tsa'ir* Zionist YOUTH MOVEMENT. In 1939 she moved to Palestine, where she joined Kibbutz Ma'anit and later enlisted in the *Palmah,* which was the fighting branch of the *Hagana* (the *Yishuv's* underground military organization). At the end of her *Palmah* service, Reik found out about and joined the new parachutists' unit; her hope was to be sent to her native Slovakia to help rescue Jews there.

On September 21, 1944 Reik parachuted into Slovakia—right in the middle of the SLOVAK NATIONAL UPRISING. Her assignment was to reach Slovakia's capital, BRATISLAVA, and connect there with the leaders of the semi-underground Jewish rescue organization called the WORKING GROUP. A week earlier, three other parachutists, Rafael Reiss, Zvi Ben-Yaakov, and Chaim Hermesh (Kassaf), had infiltrated Slovakia. At the end of September, a fifth parachutist arrived, Abba Berdiczew, carrying radio transmitters for the rest of the group. However, Reik and the other Palestinian emissaries were unable to even begin rescue operations, as they were totally occupied with fighting for their own lives.

Intending to establish a Jewish PARTISAN unit, Reik and her comrades managed to gather about 40 Jewish partisans who had been fighting in the non-Jewish partisan units in the area. When the Slovak National Uprising was suppressed in October, Reik's group with-

A commemorative display for Haviva Reik. On the right is Solo Peled from the Slovakian army

drew into the mountains, where they gathered weapons and tried to set up a small fortification. However, on the sixth day in the camp, they were caught and taken prisoner by a group of Ukrainian *Waffen*-SS soldiers. On November 20 the Germans executed the captive Jews, among them Reik, Ben-Yaakov, and Reiss. Later Abba Berdiczew also was killed.

Haviva Reik is considered to be a Zionist hero and consequently, she is memorialized by Kibbutz Lahavot Haviva, the ship *Haviva Reik,* which brought Jewish "illegal" immigrants to Palestine after WORLD WAR II, and the Israeli educational center Givat Haviva. (see also PARACHUTISTS, JEWISH.)

RELIEF AND RESCUE COMMITTEE OF BUDAPEST
(*Va'adat ha-Ezra ve-ha-Hatsala be-Budapest,* known as the *Va'ada*), committee founded to provide aid for

Jewish REFUGEES in HUNGARY. Composed of representatives of various Hungarian Zionist groups, the committee was headed by Otto KOMOLY and Rezso (Israel) KASZTNER. Late in 1941, Komoly, Kasztner and others began helping refugees, and in 1943 they formed a committee aligned with the Jewish Agency in Palestine.

The committee's original goals included rescuing Jews by smuggling them into Hungary (which, until 1944, was a relatively safe place to be); helping refugees within the country; and preparing for the self-defense of Hungarian Jewry. Among its earlier achievements, the committee managed to smuggle some 1,100 Polish Jews out of POLAND before the German occupation of Hungary in March 1944. It also helped support Jewish refugees inside Hungary. Additionally, the committee served as an important contact between the Jews in the West and the persecuted Jewish communities in Poland and SLOVAKIA.

When GERMANY occupied Hungary, the committee's leaders divided up responsibilities in an attempt to save Hungarian Jews. Komoly worked on procuring support for the Jews from Hungarian political and church leaders, while Kasztner and Joel BRAND began negotiating with SS officers Adolf EICHMANN and Kurt BECHER. The rescue deals they discussed were based on the Slovak WORKING GROUP'S EUROPA PLAN. While Brand traveled to Turkey to convince the Allies of the Germans' proposition, Kasztner immersed himself in one specific part of the negotiations: the Germans' offer to let hundreds of Hungarian Jews leave Hungary by train, as a show of the Nazis' goodwill. Eventually, over 1,600 Jews left on the "Kasztner train" and ultimately reached safety in SWITZERLAND.

Although negotiations with the SS continued until early 1945, a bargain was never reached. Nonetheless, along the way, 21,000 Hungarian Jews were transferred to a safer camp in STRASSHOF, AUSTRIA in mid-1944, where most survived. After the violent ARROW CROSS PARTY took over the Hungarian government in October 1944, the committee was involved in protecting Hungarian Jews within BUDAPEST. Working with the International Red Cross and Zionist YOUTH MOVEMENTS, Komoly helped provide food, shelter, heat, and protection for the beleaguered Jews. Early in 1945 Kasztner and Becher traveled to several CONCENTRATION CAMPS where Becher convinced the commanders to hand over the Jews to the Allies without harming them.

RELIEF COMMITTEE FOR THE WARSTRICKEN JEWISH POPULATION (RELICO)

Organization established in Geneva in September 1939 by Dr. Abraham Silberschein. Mainly funded by the WORLD JEWISH CONGRESS, RELICO's original goals were to search for missing relatives and provide monetary and legal assistance to Jewish REFUGEES. However, Silberschein soon concentrated his efforts on refugee activities.

In the early days of the war Silberschein was informed that the Germans were willing to release Polish Jews from SACHSENHAUSEN, DACHAU, and BUCHENWALD if they would leave GERMANY immediately. With help from a Jewish immigrant organization in America, Silberschein succeeded in getting several groups out of Germany in 1940 and into Bolivia and Palestine. RELICO also helped organize the emigration of Jewish refugees from VILNA and KOVNO to Japan, SHANGHAI, and to the Dutch colonies. It also aided Polish refugees in ROMANIA, SLOVAKIA, HUNGARY, and ITALY, in addition to refugees from the NETHERLANDS, BELGIUM, and northern FRANCE, who had reached the unoccupied (Vichy) zone of France.

In all his refugee activities, Silberschein used the services of various bodies to transmit information and deliver packages of food and medicines; these included the International Red Cross, the Polish, Czechoslovak, and Dutch consuls in SWITZERLAND, representatives of the Vatican, the Protestant Church Council, and the Quakers. Due to its many contacts and its ability to transmit information quickly, RELICO was one of the first sources to break the news about the CHELMNO and TREBLINKA extermination camps.

After squabbling with the World Jewish Congress' Swiss representatives, Silberschein divided RELICO into two sections: one, headed by Silberschein, continued relief activities for the Jews of POLAND and of Eastern and Southern Europe, while the other searched for missing relatives, rescued children in Western Europe, and sent food packages to THERESIENSTADT. Silberschein's attempts to rescue bearers of South American passports by seeking validation for the documents from the South American governments were ultimately unsuccessful. However, in 1944 he did manage to carry out rescue activities for certain Hungarian Jews.

After the war Silberschein worked with Holocaust SURVIVORS in Poland, Germany, AUSTRIA, and Italy; was active in the hunt for war criminals; and helped young survivors with tuberculosis in Switzerland.

REPARATIONS AND RESTITUTIONS Financial compensation for Jewish suffering during the HOLOCAUST and reimbursement for Jewish property that was stolen by the Nazis. From 1953 to 1965, West GERMANY paid the State of Israel, Jewish SURVIVORS, and German REFUGEES hundreds of millions of dollars in a symbolic attempt to make up for the crimes committed by the Nazis during the Holocaust.

While WORLD WAR II was still raging, Jews around the world began making plans to demand financial indemnification for Holocaust victims. Just months after the war ended, the Jewish Agency made its first formal claim for reparations and property reimbursement to the four Allied powers that controlled Germany: the UNITED STATES, GREAT BRITAIN, FRANCE, and the SOVIET UNION. The agency proposed that a certain amount of Germany's money be allotted for the settlement of Jewish claims for reparations and the resettlement of Holocaust survivors in Palestine.

After the State of Israel was established in mid-1948, it became clear that the Jewish country should be authorized to represent the Jewish people in submitting restitution claims. In 1951 the Israeli authorities made a claim to the four occupying powers regarding compensation and reimbursement, based on the fact that Israel had absorbed and resettled 500,000 Holocaust survivors. They calculated that since absorption had cost 3,000 dollars a person, they were owed 1.5 billion dollars by Germany. They also figured that six billion dollars worth of Jewish property had been pillaged by the Nazis, but stressed that the Germans could never make up for what they did with any type of material recompense.

The West German government was quite willing to pay reparations to the Jewish people. Chancellor Konrad Adenauer and other politicians admitted Germany's guilt and wanted to take this chance to atone for it. In addition, they realized that paying reparations would help accelerate West Germany's acceptance by the Western powers.

Also in 1951, 22 Jewish organizations met in New York to set up the Conference on Jewish Material Claims against Germany. The purpose of the conference was to support Israel's claims and represent the claims of Holocaust victims living outside Israel.

Within Israel, the reparations issue provoked heated debate. Many survivors strenuously opposed accepting any money from Germany, claiming that nothing could ever even begin to atone for the suffering imposed on them by the Nazis. There were many Israelis, however, who supported the talks, among them Prime Minister David BEN-GURION. He claimed that huge amounts of money were needed to properly rehabilitate the survivors who had immigrated to Israel, and that it was only natural and fair that German money be accepted in order to further that goal. The negotiations began in March 1952. A year later, the German parliament approved the agreements made between Israel and Germany. These included Germany's commitment to pay Israel 845 million dollars in the form of goods. Of that sum, 110 million dollars would be passed on to the Claims Conference. West Germany carried out its commitment in full. The money given to the Claims Conference helped Jewish communities and institutions in 39 countries reestablish themselves.

Since 1956, the original Reparations Agreement has been greatly expanded, and over the years, Germany has paid billions of dollars to the victims of the Holocaust. In the 1990s, Jews began making claims for property stolen in Eastern Europe. Various groups also began investigating what happened to money deposited in Swiss banks by Jews outside of SWITZERLAND who were later murdered in the Holocaust, and what happened to money deposited by various Nazis in Swiss banks. In addition, individual companies (many of them based in Germany) began to be pressured by survivor groups to compensate former forced laborers (see also FORCED LABOR). Among them are Deutsche Bank, Siemens, BMW, Volkswagen, Ford, and Opel. In response, early in 1999, the German government proclaimed the establishment of a fund with monies from these companies to help needy Holocaust survivors. A similar fund was set up by the Swiss, as was a Hungarian fund for compensation of Holocaust victims and their heirs.

At the close of the 1990s, discussions of compensation by insurance companies that had insured Jews before the war and who were later murdered by the Nazis were held. These companies include Alliance, Axa, Generali, Zurich Financial Services Group, Winterhur, and Baloise Insurance Group. With the help of information about Holocaust victims made available by YAD VASHEM, an international commission under former US Secretary of State Lawrence Eagleburger has been trying to uncover the names of those who had been insured and died in the Holocaust. The World Jewish Restitution Organization was created to organize these efforts. On behalf of US citizens, the US Foreign Claims Settlement Commission reached agreements with the German government in 1998 and 1999 to compensate Holocaust victims who immigrated to the US after the war.

REPRESENTATIVE COUNCIL OF FRENCH JEWS

(*Conseil Representatif des Juifs de France,* CRIF), umbrella organization of French Jewish associations, established in January 1944. CRIF was innovative in that it unified the long-divided native French Jewish and immigrant Jewish organizations.

The president of the Zionist Federation, Joseph Fischer, began working on the unification process in mid-1943. By August, he managed to unite the many immigrant organizations under one roof, the *Comite General de Defense* (CGD). He then moved on to the more difficult task of allying the immigrant organizations with the CENTRAL CONSISTORY OF THE JEWS OF FRANCE (CC), the association that represented French-born Jews.

The CC and CGD began negotiations in late 1943. By early 1944 they had agreed on basic issues, but were still debating three matters: the closure of the UNION OF FRENCH JEWS, the organization established by the Vichy government to represent French Jewry; resistance activities; and the establishment of a Jewish state in Palestine. The group dealt with the first two issues in part, but continued to argue about Palestine. Finally, they agreed to move on anyway, despite their differences, and CRIF was created. After the LIBERATION of FRANCE, CRIF was able to represent a united Jewish community and bring its needs to the attention of the French provisional government. (for more on Vichy, see also FRANCE.)

RESCUE COMMITTEE OF THE JEWISH AGENCY IN TURKEY

(in Hebrew, *Va'ad ha-Hatsala be-Kushta*), representatives of the Jewish Agency's Joint Rescue Committee who were active in Istanbul, Turkey from late 1942 through 1944. All of the Jewish political movements in Palestine participated in this committee. Its goals were to make and maintain contact with the Jewish communities in Nazi-occupied Europe and communicate to them how concerned the Jews in Palestine were about them, and to implement aid and rescue operations. The committee worked out of Turkey because of that country's close proximity to the Balkan region where, when operations were started in late 1942, there were still Jews to be rescued—Jews who had not yet been slated for extermination by the Nazis.

The committee's work was divided into three areas of operation: making contact with Jews in occupied territories and exchanging information with them; transferring funds to the Jewish communities for various uses (such as for the EUROPA PLAN, in which the Jewish communities of Europe tried to ransom Jewish lives by paying the Germans large amounts of money); and carrying out both "legal" and "illegal" immigration to Palestine. The committee considered any type of movement to Palestine to be the most reliable way of rescuing Jews.

RESCUE OF CHILDREN

Efforts to rescue Jewish children who were living in areas under Nazi domination. Soon after Adolf HITLER and the Nazis came to power in early 1933, they began persecuting the Jews of GERMANY. During the late 1930s the Nazis took control of several new territories, including Bohemia and Moravia and AUSTRIA; the Jews in those areas were also subjected to severe anti-Jewish measures. In response, great efforts were made to help get Jewish children out of Europe even before WORLD WAR II broke out in the fall of 1939. (see also BOHEMIA and MORAVIA, PROTECTORATE OF.)

Most of the children's rescue operations were conducted by Jewish groups. One of the earliest rescue efforts was YOUTH ALIYA, a program that took children out of Europe and brought them to Palestine. Youth Aliya, which was launched in 1932 by Recha Freier, the wife of a BERLIN rabbi, was later taken over by the Jewish Agency. Before the war broke out, Youth Aliya succeeded in helping more than 5,000 Jewish children make it to Palestine. Youth Aliya continued its efforts throughout the war as well: more than 9,000 children reached Palestine in spite of the British Mandate immigration restrictions, while another 15,000 were sent to Western European countries, most notably via the *Kindertransport* to GREAT BRITAIN.

Other Jewish groups also facilitated the rescue of Jewish children in the pre-war years. One example was the German Children's Jewish Aid. This group, which was set up in 1934 in New York, succeeded in bringing several hundred children into the UNITED STATES, despite the US government's strict immigration regulations.

After the war broke out in Eastern Europe, many parents were desperate to save their children from Nazi persecution. Often, these parents made plans to save their children on an individual, informal basis, smuggling them out of the GHETTO and hiding them with non-Jews who promised to take care of the children until the war's end. Of course, leaving their children with strangers was probably one of the hardest things Jewish parents were forced to do. Besides the misery of being separated from their children and feeling uncertain about their fate, the parents feared that their children might be raised as Christians, abandoned, or even worse—turned over to the Nazis by fake rescuers. However, in most cases the rescuers were truly motivated to help the children for humanitarian or moral reasons, and they put their lives in serious danger by doing so, as hiding a Jewish child was a crime punishable by death.

Besides this type of individual rescue effort, there were many networks and organizations that attempted large-scale rescue efforts. In POLAND, the Council for Aid to Jews (known as ZEGOTA) took care of some 2,500 Jewish children. *Zegota* was founded in WARSAW and later spread to other Polish towns. Its major goals were to help Jews living in non-Jewish areas and to supply Jews in hiding with forged identity papers. In July 1943 *Zegota* established a special department dedicated to helping children; the children's department placed Jewish children in non-Jewish homes or in institutions.

In FRANCE some 7,000 Jewish children were saved during the HOLOCAUST due to the efforts of various groups. One major rescuer of children was the international children's health care and welfare society the OEUVRE DE SECOURS AUX ENFANTS, which set up an underground children's rescue network known as *Circuit Garel*. In addition, when the Nazis began deporting the Jews of France in 1942, many local groups also helped in the rescue of Jewish children. Catholic and Protestant church leaders, regular French citizens, and underground groups rescued children from internment camps and placed them in the safe havens of private Christian homes or in institutions. They provided the children with necessary supplies, including false identity papers. From 1942 to 1944 many children were smuggled into neutral SWITZERLAND and SPAIN.

After the Germans occupied HUNGARY in the spring of 1944, Zionist activists set up children's homes which were under the protection of the International Red Cross and several of the neutral countries with representatives in BUDAPEST (see also RED CROSS, INTERNATIONAL). Over 6,000 children were safeguarded in these homes and lived to see Budapest liberated by the Soviet army in early 1945. Thousands of other children were rescued in Budapest by members of the Protestant and Catholic churches; many of them were hidden in convents until the war's end.

In the NETHERLANDS and BELGIUM resistance movements also managed to rescue thousands of Jewish children by hiding them in monasteries, hospitals, and boarding schools.

Hiding children from the Nazis was an extremely difficult feat—both for the rescuer and for the child. As mentioned above, hiding a Jewish child was punishable by death. In general, the child had to be hidden from the rest of the world, so as not to cause any suspicion amongst outsiders. Children who came from afar and could not speak the local language, boys who were circumcised, proving their Jewish identity, and children without forged identity papers were at great risk of being discovered and turned in to the Nazis. (Rescue organizations tried to provide the children with new papers, especially birth certificates that used a new name and stated that the document's bearer was Christian.) The children themselves were often very disoriented and quite miserable about having to leave their parents. They needed to pretend all the time and memorize new facts about themselves, sometimes even new names. In many cases the children became very close to the families with which they lived, creating great problems after the war when their real parents or relatives came to claim them. Much effort was made to locate Jewish children who had been placed in the hands of Christian rescuers. Although most of these children eventually returned to Jewish family or friends, some rescuers and even some children refused to give up their new families, having gone through so much together.

RESCUE OF POLISH JEWS VIA EAST ASIA Soviet troops invaded VILNA on September 19, 1939. On October 10 they transferred the city to the independent republic of LITHUANIA. Soon, about 14,000 Polish Jews fled to Vilna, hoping to escape both the Nazis and the Soviets. These included Jewish leaders such as Menachem Begin (later prime minister of Israel), about 2,000 members of the Zionist YOUTH MOVEMENTS, and students of more than 20 Polish yeshivas.

In June 1940 the Soviets reoccupied Lithuania; many of the REFUGEES searched for a way to get out. That summer, they were given an opportunity to flee to other countries via East Asia. The Dutch consul in KOVNO began issuing many refugees visas to Curacao,

Jewish refugees who had survived the war in Shanghai arrive in Israel, 1949

a Dutch colony in the Caribbean. Subsequently, the refugees asked the local Japanese consul, Sempo SUGI-HARA, for transit visas that would allow them to get to Curacao via Japan. Of his own accord, Sugihara granted thousands of visas—against the instructions of the Japanese government—until he and other consuls were expelled by the Soviets. Zorah WARHAFTIG, the head of the local Palestine Office for Polish Refugees, helped the refugees in the final step of the emigration process: applying for Soviet exit permits. They were finally allowed to leave the country after refugee leaders convinced the Soviets to grant them the necessary documents. The first group arrived in Japan in October 1940.

Other refugees received visas to Curacao from the Dutch consuls in Stockholm, SWEDEN and Kobe, Japan. They procured Japanese transit visas from consuls in Russia and were aided by the Japanese N.Y.K. shipping line, which provided visas for those who had bought boat tickets. Hundreds of refugees reached the UNITED STATES, Palestine, and other countries by traveling through Japan.

In the spring of 1941, the Japanese authorities tried to stop Jewish refugees from entering Japan. However, over 500 Jews managed to enter between April and August. That summer, the Japanese sent those Jewish refugees with nowhere else to go to Shanghai, China, where they stayed for the rest of the war. From October 1940 to August 1941, 3,489 Jewish refugees entered Japan.

RESISTANCE, JEWISH   Planned or spontaneous opposition to the Nazis and their collaborators by Jews. During the HOLOCAUST, Jewish resistance came in many forms. In some cases, the resistance was organized and obvious, such as the armed struggles carried out in GHETTOS, camps, and by PARTISAN units. In other cases, individuals resisted the Nazis' plan to dehumanize the Jews in hundreds of little ways, such as keeping themselves clean in the terribly unsanitary conditions in the CONCENTRATION CAMPS, or by making sure to pray despite the threat of being shot if discovered. In all cases of resistance, the Jews were fighting against almost impossible odds, and the fact that any resistance took place at all is one of heroic proportions. After the Holocaust, many asked how the Jews could have let themselves be destroyed, and why there was so little resistance action. In fact, many instances of armed and other resistance did take place.

Within the ghettos and camps, non-armed resistance against the Nazis was widespread and part of everyday life. Jews resisted the Nazis' unbearable economic and social restrictions in order to survive: they smuggled food, clothing, and medicine into the ghettos and camps to preserve their physical strength, and founded Jewish newspapers, schools, theaters, and orchestras to keep up their spiritual and mental strength. The cultural and communal aspects of the ghettos and camps helped the Jews maintain their dignity despite the Nazis' systematic efforts to dehumanize them; those aspects also helped boost their morale in the face of uncertainty and death. The Jews called this attempt to maintain their humanity "KIDDUSH HA-HAYYIM," meaning "sanctification of life."

Rescue and partisan activities also come under the heading of Jewish resistance. These include activities organized and carried out by Jews themselves or in conjunction with non-Jews. In FRANCE and BELGIUM, children were a special focus of rescue actions, and heroes such as Yvonne NEVEJEAN saved many children by placing them with foster families or institutions. In POLAND, the Council for Aid to Jews (ZEGOTA) hid thousands of Jewish children in foster homes, public orphanages, and convents. In Eastern Europe, many Jews resisted by joining partisan units, while in Western Europe, many participated in the French and Belgian undergrounds.

Individuals and groups physically resisted the Nazis by escaping to safer regions. Over 300,000 Polish Jews fled to the SOVIET UNION as the Nazis advanced towards their homes, while tens of thousands from the western Soviet Union fled eastward. Thousands of Jews managed to escape from the WARSAW Ghetto to the Polish side of the city; these were among the many who hid throughout Poland. Thousands escaped SLOVAKIA and fled to HUNGARY when DEPORTATIONS began in Slovakia,

Jewish partisans from Vilna. Standing fourth from the left is Abba Kovner.

and thousands more escaped Hungary for ROMANIA when Hungary was occupied by the Germans. Jewish YOUTH MOVEMENTS helped plan the escape of Jews in France to SPAIN, and Jews in France and ITALY to SWITZERLAND.

Despite the almost impossible conditions, there were many cases of Jewish armed struggle during the Holocaust. The Jews of the different ghettos and camps had little or no contact with each other, no outside support, were physically debilitated, had few weapons and little training at armed warfare, and were going up against the might and wrath of the German war machine. In many cases, they were even resisting the policies of the JUDENRAETE, which sometimes tried to save Jews by cooperating with the Nazis. Most of the fighters also knew that they had no real chance of beating their oppressors, and yet they fought as hard as they could. They wanted to show the world that they did not sit back and wait for the end, but instead took a stand at defending Jewish honor. These Jews resisted for resistance's sake.

Underground organizations were formed in about 100 ghettos in Poland, LITHUANIA, BELORUSSIA, and the UKRAINE, whose purpose was to stage armed uprisings or break out of the ghetto by force in order to join the partisans on the outside. Resistance actions were usually timed to coincide with the dates chosen by the Nazis for deportations to EXTERMINATION CAMPS. In some cases, the uprisings were spontaneous. The most famous ghetto revolt was the WARSAW GHETTO UPRISING. The Nazis entered the ghetto on April 19, 1943 in order to resume deportations to extermination camps. The Jews, led by the Jewish Fighting Organization, then began their revolt, and bravely held off the Germans until June. Dozens of survivors managed to escape to the partisans.

Armed revolts took place in many other ghettos, as well. In CRACOW, the Jewish resistance felt that they had no chance fighting inside the ghetto, so they moved the fight to the "Aryan" side of the city and staged attacks against the Germans there. In VILNA, the Jews were not content to resist locally; they vainly attempted to enlist the involvement of Jews all over Eastern Europe. In KOVNO the underground members tried to reach the partisans. In BIALYSTOK, as the uprising faltered, a planned escape to the partisans was foiled and the fighters were killed.

All reason opposed physical resistance within the camps: the Jews there had no weapons, they were at the mercy of their guards, they were starving, exhausted, and sick, and they knew that if one person resisted, many others would be punished. And yet, revolts took place in a number of camps, including TREBLINKA, SOBIBOR, AUSCHWITZ, and Birkenau. In the latter, SONDERKOMMANDO members succeeded in killing several SS members and set fire to a crematorium. (see also JEWISH FIGHTING ORGANIZATION, WARSAW, JEWISH MILITARY UNION, WARSAW, and UNITED PARTISAN ORGANIZATION, VILNA.)

RHODES   Island in the Aegean Sea, today a part of GREECE. Beginning in 1912, Rhodes was under Italian control. In 1934 some 3,700 Jews lived on the island. In 1938 the Italian authorities introduced anti-Jewish laws to Rhodes; at that point, 55 Jews who had moved there after World War I were expelled, and over the next two years another 1,300 Jews moved away. The Jews that remained were isolated from the general population and the island's well known rabbinical college was shut down. The Jews' conditions improved somewhat when the antisemitic governor was replaced with a more moderate ruler.

The Allies invaded ITALY in September 1943; just days later the German army occupied Rhodes. In June 1944 Anton Burger, one of Adolf EICHMANN'S assistants, arrived in Rhodes to supervise the DEPORTATION of the island's Jews. The Jews were ordered to appear at various assembly centers by mid-July. On July 20 the Jewish males were arrested (only a few avoided arrest and joined the PARTISANS). Accompanied by their wives and children, the prisoners were sent to ATHENS, and then on to AUSCHWITZ. Upon arrival, 400 of the 1,800 Jews were chosen for hard labor; the rest were executed immediately. Only 150 survived the war. Another 42 Jews from Rhodes were rescued by the Turkish consul, Selahattin Ulkumen.

RIBBENTROP, JOACHIM VON   (1893–1946), Foreign Minister of Nazi GERMANY from 1938 to 1945.

A wine and spirits exporter who paid a distant relative for permission to add the noble "von" to his name, Ribbentrop joined the NAZI PARTY in 1932. In January 1933 HITLER used Ribbentrop's home to hold some of the strategy meetings that led to his rise to national power at the end of that month. Ribbentrop quickly became Hitler's foreign-policy advisor, in which capacity he negotiated Germany's naval agreement with GREAT BRITAIN in 1935 and its alliance with ITALY and Japan in 1936 (see also AXIS). From 1936 to 1938 Ribbentrop served as Germany's ambassador to England. Despite the fact that he originally supported the idea of having a diplomatic relationship with England, he became more and more anti-British during his stint as ambassador.

Ribbentrop was named foreign minister in February 1938. In August 1939, just days before the German army invaded POLAND kicking off WORLD WAR II, Ribbentrop reached the peak of his career with the signing of the NAZI-SOVIET PACT. It was also known as the Ribbentrop-Molotov Pact, named for the two foreign ministers who made the deal. After that point, Ribbentrop became less and less influential within the Nazi hierarchy, as Hitler was no longer interested in diplomacy. Ribbentrop's attempt to convince Hitler not to betray the Nazi-Soviet Pact fell on deaf ears, and less than two years after signing the agreement, German troops invaded the SOVIET UNION in June 1941.

Unlike many other Nazis, Ribbentrop was not an extreme antisemite, and did not completely understand how serious Hitler was about solving the "Jewish question" in Europe until early 1943. At that point, trying to curry favor with the *Fuehrer,* Ribbentrop embarked upon a personal campaign to pressure Germany's allies and satellite states to allow the DEPORTATION of their local Jews.

After the war, Ribbentrop was convicted at the NUREMBERG TRIAL and sentenced to death. He was hanged in 1946.

RICHTER, GUSTAV   (b. 1913), Aide to Adolf EICHMANN and SS advisor in ROMANIA.

Richter worked in Eichmann's Jewish affairs department in the Reich Security Main Office (REICHSSICHERHEITSHAUPTAMT, RSHA). In April 1941 he was sent to Romania as an advisor on Jewish matters. He soon left, but returned to Romania in September 1941 at the request of political leader Mihai ANTONESCU. He then stayed until August 1944.

Richter called for the establishment of a JUDENRAT called the Jewish Center (see also JEWISH CENTER, ROMANIA). Soon, he helped plan to put Romanian Jews in GHETTOS; make them wear the Jewish badge (see also BADGE, JEWISH); confiscate their property; and ban immigration to Palestine. Richter then convinced Mihai Antonescu to prepare to deport Romanian Jews to BELZEC. However, many of Richter's plans were foiled. Ghettos were generally not established in Romania; Jewish leaders managed to get the Jewish badge decree cancelled; and Romania gradually changed its mind about sending the Jews to EXTERMINATION CAMPS and

finally broke off its alliance with Germany. Over time, Richter became less influential. After the war, Richter spent 10 years in PRISONER OF WAR camps in the SOVIET UNION. In 1981, he was finally put on trial for planning to deport Romanian Jewry, and sentenced to four years in prison.

RIEFENSTAHL, LENI   (b. 1902), German filmmaker who made propaganda films for the Nazis. Her most famous work, *Triumph of the Will,* documented the 1934 NAZI PARTY rally in NUREMBERG. Riefenstahl claimed that she was just an artist, not a Nazi, but she remains a symbol of artistic collaboration with the Nazis.

RIEGNER CABLE   Telegram that is considered the first documented report of the "Final Solution" to reach the West. It was sent on August 8, 1942 by Dr. Gerhart Riegner, the WORLD JEWISH CONGRESS representative in

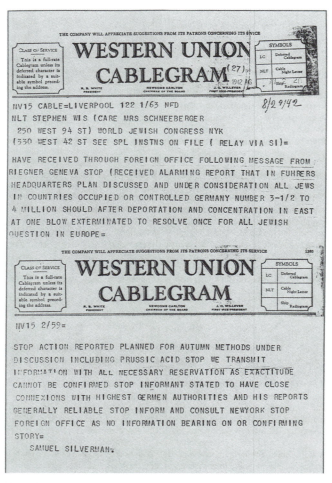

Text of the Riegner Cable, uncovering the Nazi plan to murder the Jews, sent by Sidney Silverman to Stephen Wise

SWITZERLAND, to Rabbi Stephen S. WISE in the UNITED STATES and Sidney Silverman, a Member of Parliament, in GREAT BRITAIN.

The cable indicated that HITLER and his aides had decided to exterminate all the Jews in Europe. The information came from a successful German businessman named Eduard Scholte whose identity was only released to the public decades later. In fact, Scholte's information was not completely accurate. The mass extermination of European Jewry had already been going on for more than a year, and it was an ongoing process, not a one-time "blow" as written in the telegram. However, the general idea was accurate.

The cable was supposed to be transmitted to Wise through the US State Department, but department officials refused to pass it on. Silverman contacted Wise himself, and Wise approached the Secretary of State demanding action. The government refused to publish the information until it was confirmed. On November 24, the American government finally received convincing confirmation of the terrible information, and Wise was allowed to release the news to the press.

RIGA Capital of LATVIA and cultural center of Latvian Jewry. In 1935 there were 43,000 Jews in Riga.

In June 1940, Riga was annexed, along with the rest of Latvia, by the SOVIET UNION. A year later the Germans invaded the Soviet Union; they occupied Riga on July 1, 1941. Throughout July thousands of Jews were killed or imprisoned. Between July and October, the Germans issued a series of anti-Jewish decrees: 32,000 Jews were herded into a GHETTO and a Council of Elders was formed under Michael Elyashov.

In November the Germans separated the ghetto inhabitants into two groups: the working Jews were put into the "small ghetto" while the non-working Jews remained in the "large ghetto." The large ghetto was liquidated in late November and early December and some 20,000 Jews were shot and buried in the Rumbula forest. During the first half of 1942, 16,000 Jews from the Reich were brought to the "large ghetto." Fourteen thousand were later murdered.

An underground was established in early 1942. Later that year, underground members tried to escape the ghetto and reach the PARTISANS. They were discovered, and most were killed. In addition, many alleged underground members were murdered in retaliation.

In November 1942 the "small" and "large" ghettos were combined and re-divided into two sections, one

A street in the Riga Ghetto

for Jews from the Reich and one for Latvian Jews. The reshuffling in the ghetto caused much tension between the two groups.

During the summer of 1943 the Germans moved some of the ghetto inhabitants to the KAISERWALD camp. That November they launched *aktionen* in the ghetto and the Jews' workplaces. By December, the ghetto was completely destroyed.

In 1944 some of the remaining Riga Jews were forced to participate in the gruesome work of digging up mass graves and burning the bodies to conceal evidence of mass murder (see also AKTION 1005). After they finished, they too were murdered. In June 1944 the Germans killed many of the prisoners in Kaiserwald and its sub-camps. The surviving Jews were transferred to CONCENTRATION CAMPS outside Latvia.

The Soviet army liberated Riga on October 13, 1944. A few days later, about 150 Jews came out of hiding.

RIGHTEOUS AMONG THE NATIONS Official title given to non-Jews who risked their lives in order to rescue Jews during the HOLOCAUST. The name comes from a Talmudic phrase: "The righteous among the nations of the world have a place in the world to come."

In 1953 Israel's parliament passed the Martyrs' and Heroes' Remembrance (Yad Vashem) Law, which gave YAD VASHEM in Jerusalem the responsibility to set up awards and a memorial for those "righteous among the nations who risked their lives to save Jews." Since the early 1960s, a Commission for the Designation of the Righteous has worked under the Yad Vashem Remembrance Authority. This committee is in charge of bestowing the "Righteous among the Nations" title. In its early years of existence, the committee was chaired by Moshe Landau, who later became the president of Israel's supreme court.

When the name of a rescuer is submitted for recognition, the committee carefully investigates evidence of the rescuer's actions and motivations. The survivor or group of survivors involved must testify as to the rescuer's deeds, and the committee gathers corroborative documentation from European historical institutions regarding the course of events in question. The original law itself did not specify an exact definition of the term "Righteous among the Nations." As it has been used throughout Jewish history, the title refers to a moral person who offers empathy, compassion, and aid to Jews in times of trouble and persecution. However, with regard to the Martyrs' and Heroes' Remembrance Law, it is clear that a person had to have been extraordinary to receive the official title, "Righteous among the Nations." Thus, the committee tries to determine the candidate's motivations for rescuing Jews, and asks questions such as: Was the rescuer given money to help Jews? What sorts of risks and dangers did the rescuer face? Did the rescuer's motivations include friendship, religious belief, etc.? In general, to qualify for the title, a person had to have risked his or her life, safety, or personal freedom to rescue a Jew from DEPORTATION without asking for money in exchange.

In some cases, the issue of "risk" or "danger" is a difficult one for the committee, because there were rescuers who had diplomatic immunity from persecution in the countries where they were working, and thus did not put themselves in actual life-threatening situations. For example, Aristides de SOUSA MENDES, the Portuguese consul in FRANCE who gave Jews entry visas to his country; Sempo SUGIHARA, the Japanese consul in KOVNO who did the same; and Paul Gruninger, the Swiss police captain on the Austrian border who let hundreds of Jewish REFUGEES enter SWITZERLAND, all disobeyed the official instructions of their governments in order to save Jewish lives. However, they also all had a special diplomatic status that made sure they were not in danger. Even so, they did lose jobs or reputations and suffered because of their humane activities, so the committee chose to honor them. Raoul WALLENBERG, the Swedish diplomat who saved tens of thousands of Hungarian Jews, also had diplomatic immunity, but that did not keep him from being arrested by the Soviets after the LIBERATION of BUDAPEST.

In many cases, it was not diplomats, but ordinary people who saved Jewish lives during the Holocaust. They chose, against all odds, to hide one or more Jews in their homes or yards. Often, the rescuer would build a bunker for the Jew, who would stay there for weeks, months, or years, hardly ever seeing the sun. Food was very scarce during the war, and the rescuer would share the few pieces of bread he had with the Jews he was hiding from the Nazis.

There are also cases where groups of people, rather than individuals, rescued Jews. In the NETHERLANDS, NORWAY, BELGIUM, and France, underground resistance groups helped Jews, mainly by finding them hiding places. One very special group of people lived in the small Dutch village of Nieuwlande. In 1942 and 1943, the villagers decided together that every household would conceal one Jewish family or individual. All 117 inhabitants of Nieuwlande were designated as "Righteous among the Nations." Another instance of a group of rescuers was in the French village of LE CHAMBON-SUR-LIGNON. The village's pastor, Andre Trocme, prevailed upon his constituents to provide hiding places and assistance for Jews running from the Nazis. In DENMARK, ordinary Danes transported 7,200 of the country's 8,000 Jews to SWEDEN in a daring fishing boat operation.

Some other famous cases of rescue acts perpetuated by Europeans during the Holocaust are those of Oskar SCHINDLER, the German businessman who rescued thousands of Jews from the PLASZOW camp by employing them in his factory; and Miep GIES, one of the non-Jews who helped the family of Anne FRANK while they hid in the "secret annex."

The number of Jews saved by non-Jews during the Holocaust is not clear. Some Jews helped by a non-Jew died later during the war, and thus no one remains to give testimony or even submit the rescuer's name to the committee. Sometimes, the rescuer himself died along with those Jews he saved. In other cases, rescuers chose to remain anonymous even after the war—just having done what their consciences told them was the right thing to do, while millions of other Europeans stood by and did nothing. By 2000, over 17,000 men and women had received the honor and title. Until the mid 1990s many "Righteous among the Nations" planted trees to commemorate their acts. In 1996 a special memorial garden was founded that includes the names of all the recipients of the award and to which recipients' names are added as the people are accorded recognition.

The many instances of rescue perpetuated by those designated as "Righteous among the Nations" shows that rescue was indeed possible, despite the dangerous circumstances. The recipients of the title not only saved Jewish lives, but help restore our faith in humanity.

RINGELBLUM, EMANUEL (1900–1944), Jewish historian and founder and director of the secret ONEG SHABBAT Archive in the WARSAW Ghetto.

Ringelblum was born in Buczacz, POLAND (now UKRAINE). He earned a doctorate in history at the University of Warsaw in 1927. From a young age, Ringelblum belonged to the *Po'alei Zion* left and was active in public affairs. For a while he taught high school; he then took a job with the JOINT DISTRIBUTION COMMITTEE in Poland. In November 1938 the JDC sent him to the border town of ZBASZYN, where 6,000 Jewish REFUGEES from GERMANY were gathered. These people had been pushed out of Germany, but not allowed into Poland. Ringelblum spent five weeks in Zbaszyn as the person in charge of the refugees; his experiences there made a great impact on him.

After the Germans invaded Poland in September 1939, Ringelblum continued working for the JDC. He ran welfare programs and soup kitchens for the Jews of the Warsaw GHETTO. He instituted House Committees, which attempted to deal with the growing deprivation within the Ghetto. Along with his friend Menahem Linder, Ringelblum also founded a society for the advancement of Yiddish culture (*Yidishe Kultur Organizatsye*) in the ghetto.

Back in 1923, several Jewish historians in Poland had formed a historical society, with Ringelblum as one of its leaders and prominent scholars. The group was eventually associated with the Institute for Jewish Research (*Yidisher Visenshaftlikher Institut,* YIVO). Ringelblum was one of the editors of the society's publications, and by 1939, he himself had published 126 scholarly articles. His efforts within that group were just a preview of what he would accomplish in the Warsaw Ghetto.

Within the first few months of the war, Ringelblum launched his greatest feat: the secret *Oneg Shabbat* Archive. The name means "Sabbath pleasure" and usually refers to cultural gatherings taking place on the Sabbath. Thus, Ringelblum's archive was aptly named because its members met in secret on Saturday afternoons. At the beginning, the archivists would collect reports and testimonies by Jews who had come to the ghetto to seek help from the self-aid organizations. Ringelblum would collect information during the day, and write notes at night. He knew that what was happening to the Jews was unprecedented, and he was determined to record a complete description of the time and place for future historians. He and his colleagues collected data on and wrote articles about towns, villages, the ghetto, and the resistance movement. They also documented the DEPORTATION and extermination of Polish Jewry. Near the end of the ghetto's existence, the archivists sent every bit of information they had about the murders to the Polish underground, which in turn smuggled it out of the country. Thus, Ringelblum helped expose the Nazis' atrocities.

The *Oneg Shabbat* materials were preserved in three milk cans. One of the cans was uncovered in 1946 and a second in 1950; the other has yet to be located. The archive materials and Ringelblum's own written chronicles constitute the most comprehensive and valuable source of information we have concerning the Jews in German-occupied Poland and the significance of the events taking place.

In March 1943 Ringelblum and his family escaped the ghetto and went into hiding in the non-Jewish area of Warsaw. During Passover of that year, he returned to the ghetto, which was in the midst of an uprising. He was deported to the TRAWNIKI labor camp, but escaped with the help of a Polish man and Jewish woman. He went back into hiding with his family, but in March 1944 their hide-out was discovered. Soon after, Ringelblum, his family, and the other Jews he had been hiding with were taken to the ruins of the ghetto and shot to death.

ROBOTA, ROSA (1921–1945), Jewish underground activist in AUSCHWITZ. Robota was born in Ciechanow, POLAND, and was a member of the town's *Ha-Shomer ha-Tsa'ir* Zionist underground movement. In 1942 Robota was taken to Auschwitz on a transport from Ciechanow; she was one of the first inmates to be placed in the women's camp in Birkenau (also know as Auschwitz II). In 1943 a Jewish underground group was established in Auschwitz. Robota quickly joined the group and solicited support for it from many women inmates.

In 1944 Robota helped smuggle tiny amounts of explosives from the ammunition factory in Birkenau where she worked. They were given to the underground in Auschwitz I and to the SONDERKOMMANDO

Rosa Robota

men working in the Birkenau crematoria. In October of that year the *Sonderkommandos* revolted; during the investigation of the mutiny Robota and three other young women from the factory were arrested. Robota was the only one who had any useful information about the underground, its main members, and how it functioned, but in spite of the torture inflicted upon her, she did not reveal a single name. On January 6, 1945, just a few weeks before Auschwitz was evacuated, Robota and three fellow underground members were hanged.

ROHM, ERNST   (1887–1934), Nazi leader and head of the Storm Troopers (SA). Originally, Rohm was an

Ernst Rohm (standing, second from left) with other prominent members of the SA

ally of Adolf HITLER. He was one of the first members of the NAZI PARTY, and joined the SA when it was established in 1921. In 1923 Rohm fought alongside Hitler in his unsuccessful bid to take over the Bavarian government. Rohm was found guilty of treason but was freed the same day.

After the coup, Rohm began calling for a violent seizure of power, while Hitler condoned using legal means. This disagreement led Rohm to resign the SA leadership and move to Bolivia. After the Nazi victory in the 1930 elections, Hitler called Rohm back to GERMANY to revitalize the SA. In less than four years Rohm helped it grow from 70,000 to 4.5 million members.

After Hitler rose to power in 1933, Rohm wanted to incorporate the SA into the German army. Many army officers opposed this plan, and Hitler feared that Rohm would try to seize power as the head of a military government. Thus, Hitler ordered the liquidation of the SA. On June 30, 1934 Rohm and other SA leaders were arrested and shot—this purge was later called "The Night of the Long Knives."

ROMANIA   Eastern European country established in 1859 with the union of the former Walachia and Moldavia principalities. These two areas together were called the Regat. During and after World War I, Romania was enlarged significantly by annexing Southern Dobruja from BULGARIA, TRANSYLVANIA from HUNGARY, and BESSARABIA from Russia. These new areas had a very high percentage of Jews, sometimes up to 30 percent of the population.

Between the two world wars, the lack of political stability in Romania led to the creation of right-wing nationalist and antisemitic political parties such as the IRON GUARD, and to the growth of ANTISEMITISM. After the Nazis came to power, they also encouraged anti-Jewish measures in Romania. In late 1937 the Nazis' Foreign Policy Office, headed by Alfred ROSENBERG, helped form the short-lived Goga-Cuza government. Octavian GOGA and Alexandru CUZA only ruled Romania for 40 days, but they did their best to turn their antisemitic ideals into reality. The parliamentary government established next was so weak that King Carol II instituted a dictatorship in February 1938. The Jews' situation became even worse under this regime; Romania's new constitution included several sections that allowed racial discrimination against them.

In March 1939 Romania signed a trade agreement with GERMANY. This was followed by several other deals giving Germany power over the Romanian economy. In addition, when Germany and the SOVIET UNION made their non-aggression pact during the summer of 1939, Germany agreed to take Bessarabia and northern BUKOVINA from Romania and return them to the Soviet Union. Germany also forced Romania to return Northern Transylvania to Hungary, and southern Dobruja to Bulgaria. These withdrawals caused severe problems for the Jews of those areas. In Bukovina and northern Moldavia, villagers and withdrawing Romanian troops took out their fury on the Jews, killing hundreds. Also at that time, the Romanians wanted to please the Germans, so they instituted laws that canceled the citizenship of most Jews and forbade marriages between Jews and Romanians. With the return of lands to the Soviet Union, Hungary, and Bulgaria, the Jewish population of Romania was reduced from 760,000 to 342,000.

In September 1940 General Ion ANTONESCU asked King Carol II to set up a new pro-German cabinet. Carol fled Romania and his son nominally became king. Antonescu took over as a fascist dictator and destroyed any remnant of democracy. He instituted a government that consisted of Iron Guard members and army officers. Under Antonescu, there was mass plundering of Jewish property, Jews lost the right to vote, and were barred from doing business.

In January 1941 the Iron Guard tried to take over the government completely. This revolt was put down by Antonescu's army, but was also accompanied by anti-Jewish riots—127 Jews were murdered. After the rebellion was crushed, the government passed more anti-Jewish laws that aimed to eliminate Jewish involvement in Romanian life. Antonescu, aided by the office of Adolf EICHMANN, set up a "National Romanianization Center" which officially organized terror acts against Jews. The police and a special intelligence unit persecuted those who opposed Antonescu's regime, including Communists and Jews.

The Germans turned on their Soviet allies in June 1941. The Romanians sided with the Germans, hoping to reannex the land they had been forced to give back to the Soviet Union. In fact, Romania did regain some of its land, but lost it again in 1944 to the Soviets. During this time, Antonescu ordered the expulsion of 40,000 Jews from their villages and towns. Some were sent to detention camps, while others were transferred to other areas.

Antonescu treated Jews of different areas in different ways. He called for the extermination of the Jews of Bessarabia and Bukovina, but not of the Jews of the Regat. When Romania joined Germany in fighting the Soviet Union, HITLER informed Antonescu of his plan to exterminate Europe's Jews; Antonescu agreed to go along with Hitler's designs. The Romanian army was commanded to imprison city Jews, while the police were ordered to kill any Jew found in rural areas. German and Romanian army units, aided by EINSATZGRUPPEN, carried out the extermination of Romania's Jews. About 160,000 were killed in the first phase, with local Romanians and Ukrainians joining in the murders; tens of thousands of Ukrainian Jews were also killed by the police and Romanian army. In September 1941 Antonescu ordered that the 150,000 remaining Jews be banished to TRANSNISTRIA. Tens of thousands died on the way.

During 1942 Antonescu began to doubt that Germany would win the war. In addition, the Jewish leadership of Romania was exerting great pressure on him to help the Jews. These elements convinced Antonescu to cancel the next phase to which he had originally agreed: the DEPORTATION of most of the remaining 292,000 Jews to BELZEC. Instead, he decided that the solution for Romania's Jews was to leave Romania. He agreed to the emigration of 70,000 Jews in exchange for a large payment. However, Eichmann blocked the plan and less than 5,000 Jews reached Palestine. Once the plans for extermination were aborted, Jewish organizations fought hard for the return of the Jews who had been deported to Transnistria. In late 1943 the first of the surviving deportees were brought home, and the rest returned in 1945 and 1946.

Antonescu's government was overthrown on August 23, 1944 by an anti-fascist group called the National Democratic Bloc. In September the new government

Jewish identity card used in Romania during the war

signed an agreement with the Soviet Union that formally acknowledged that Romania was no longer allied with Germany.

In all, about 420,000 Jews who had been living in Romania in 1939 died in the HOLOCAUST. This includes those killed by the Romanian army, those who died in or on the way to Transnistria, the victims of pogroms, and the Jews of Hungarian-occupied Northern Transylvania who were murdered at AUSCHWITZ. This number does not count those Jews living in the Soviet territory taken over by Romania during the war who also died during the Holocaust.

ROOSEVELT, FRANKLIN DELANO (1882–1945), President of the UNITED STATES from 1933–1945. Roosevelt was the only president to have served four terms. Although he probably could have done more than any other leader during WORLD WAR II to help save the Jews of Europe, many historians believe that he did not try hard enough.

When Franklin D. Roosevelt came into office, the most pressing problem in America was the terrible poverty and hopelessness produced by the Great Depression. In his "New Deal" program, Roosevelt created welfare programs to help desperately poor Americans.

President Franklin Delano Roosevelt and his wife Eleanor

This won the support of many American Jews, who agreed with Roosevelt's social-democratic tendencies. By the election of 1940, Roosevelt's third, nine out of ten Jews were voting for him. Many American Jews stayed loyal to Roosevelt throughout his presidency despite his inactivity concerning the Jewish situation in Europe.

In fact, Roosevelt did instruct American consuls in Europe to try and help Jewish REFUGEES who were seeking visas to the United States. He also recalled his ambassador to GERMANY in a gesture of objection after the KRISTALLNACHT pogrom of November 9–10, 1938. In addition, he allowed Jews who were in the United States on visitor's visas to extend their stay. However, he would not significantly change the country's strict immigration laws to allow more refugees. He may have succumbed to the pressure of anti-immigrationists who feared that new immigrants would take away jobs from "real" Americans. Roosevelt also allowed consular officials to refuse visas to anyone who might, at a later time, need public assistance. This excuse was often used to keep Jewish refugees out of the United States. This type of inaction slipped down a slippery slope that continued into the next stage of the HOLOCAUST: mass murder of Europe's Jews. As time went on, suggestions made about helping the Jews in Europe were routinely rejected by various government agencies.

After Germany annexed AUSTRIA in March 1938, Roosevelt made a weak attempt to deal with the growing Jewish refugee problem by calling the EVIAN CONFERENCE. Thirty-two countries were invited to meet in FRANCE in July to discuss possible solutions. However, one by one, each country's representative announced that his country was filled to the brim with refugees and could not admit any more. In all, the conference failed when the US refused to set a humanitarian example.

Two agencies were created as a result of the Evian Conference—the Intergovernmental Committee on Refugees (IGCR), and the President's Advisory Committee on Political Refugees (PAC). However, these committees were essentially for show; like the conference, they were intended to keep rescue activists quiet, rather than actually help any Jews.

When the "Final Solution" was at its most horrifying in 1943, and the rest of the world was aware of it, Roosevelt convened a second refugee conference in Bermuda along with the British, called the BERMUDA CONFERENCE. This, too, accomplished nothing. Only as the result of a special entreaty made by Secretary of the Treasury Henry MORGENTHAU (who informed the president that the State Department had been systematically sabotaging the rescue effort) did Roosevelt create the WAR REFUGEE BOARD in 1944. However, by the time of its creation most of European Jewry had already been murdered.

Some believe that Roosevelt simply did not want to help Europe's Jews. However, it is more likely that he was distracted by the war and his health problems, and just did not comprehend the extent of the Holocaust's horrors.

ROSENBERG, ALFRED

ROSENBERG, ALFRED   (1893–1946), Nazi ideologist and head of the NAZI PARTY'S foreign-affairs department. Rosenberg was born in ESTONIA to a family of Baltic Germans, but moved to MUNICH in 1918.

Rosenberg was an antisemitic and anti-Bolshevik ultra-nationalist who shared his views in two books

Alfred Rosenberg (in the foreground) visiting troops in Kiev, Ukraine

published in 1919: *Die Spur der Juden im Wandel der Zeiten* (*The Track of the Jews Through the Ages*), and *Unmoral im Talmud* (*Immorality in the Talmud*). He joined the Nazi Party in its early stages, and in 1921, became chief editor of the party's newspaper. In 1923 Rosenberg participated in HITLER'S unsuccessful bid to take over the Bavarian government. While Hitler sat in jail for the next two years, Rosenberg was entrusted with the Nazi Party leadership. Other leading Nazis denounced Rosenberg for his Baltic roots, but Hitler was impressed with his intellectual theories about RACISM. Rosenberg soon became the head ideologist of the Nazi Party.

In 1929 Rosenberg established the Fighting League for German Culture, and wrote his most important work, *Der Mythus des 20. Jahrhunderts* (*The Myth of the Twentieth Century*). In this book, Rosenberg stated that art, science, culture, and world history are all determined by race. He also denounced Christianity for not controlling the Jewish takeover of the world. The work had great influence over Nazi philosophy and was a best-seller, approaching the popularity of Hitler's MEIN KAMPF.

From 1933–1945 Rosenberg headed the party's foreign-policy department, and in 1934 he was also appointed the head of the Center for Nazi Studies. In 1939 he founded the Institute for the Investigation of the Jewish Question; he declared that every single Jew living in Greater GERMANY would have to leave in order for the "Jewish question" to be considered solved.

After the fall of FRANCE, Rosenberg headed Operational Staff Rosenberg (EINSATZSTAB ROSENBERG), an organization that systematically plundered the art and cultural objects of French and other Jews. In November 1941 Rosenberg was nominated Minister of the Occupied Eastern Territories, where he oversaw the murder of the Jews.

Rosenberg was convicted as a war criminal at the NUREMBERG TRIALS, and hanged in 1946.

ROWECKI, STEFAN

ROWECKI, STEFAN   (1895–1944), Polish army officer who served as the commander of the HOME ARMY, a military resistance organization that constituted the most important part of the Polish underground.

When the Germans invaded POLAND in September 1939, Rowecki commanded a tank brigade. The Polish army surrendered by the end of that month; Rowecki then received orders to go underground and form a secret resistance organization that would report to the POLISH GOVERNMENT-IN-EXILE. Rowecki's militia was first called "Service for the Victory of Poland," renamed "Union for Armed Struggle" in 1940, and was finally dubbed "Home Army" (*Armia Krajowa*) in 1942.

In his post as Home Army commander, Rowecki came up with the idea of limiting actual fighting against the German army until it was sufficiently weakened, at which time the Home Army could stage a successful revolt. In preparation, Rowecki worked to fortify the underground. However, when the time came, the concept was unsuccessful.

After being contacted by members of the Jewish resistance, Rowecki provided limited aid to the Jewish underground militia in WARSAW, the Jewish Fighting Organization. In June 1943 Rowecki was arrested and deported to SACHSENHAUSEN, where he was subsequently executed. (see also JEWISH FIGHTING ORGANIZATION, WARSAW.)

RUFAJZEN, OSWALD (1922–1999; originally named Shmuel Rufeisen, later known as Brother Daniel), Jew posing as an ethnic German who helped save Jews during the HOLOCAUST.

Born near CRACOW, Rufajzen was a member of the *Akiva* YOUTH MOVEMENT as a young man. When WORLD WAR II broke out in September 1939, Rufajzen escaped to VILNA, LITHUANIA where he met up with other Zionists who had gathered there. In June 1941 GERMANY invaded the SOVIET UNION and Soviet-occupied territories, including Lithuania. Rufajzen managed to procure false identity papers that "confirmed" that he was a VOLKS-DEUTSCHE (ethnic German) named Josef Oswald. Rufajzen then moved to MIR, a town in BELORUSSIA, where he began working for the local police chief. Soon, under the name Oswald, he was appointed district commander of the German police.

While in Mir, Rufajzen met up with two Zionist friends from his Vilna days, who were now leaders of the Mir GHETTO underground. Unbeknownst to the German police, he cooperated fully with the underground, giving them information about the Germans' plans and providing them with weapons. On August 6, 1942 Rufajzen told the underground leaders that a date had been set for the liquidation of the ghetto: August 13. He also told them that on August 9, he and the rest of the police would be out of town on a "raid against the PARTISANS"—providing the Jews with a perfect opportunity for escape. When the time came, 180 Jews fled the ghetto for the forests.

After the escape, the German authorities began to suspect that Rufajzen had been assisting the Jews. He was arrested, but managed to escape to a monastery, where he hid for 16 months, at which point the Germans were hot on his trail. Rufajzen fled to the forests, where he was almost arrested by the partisans for being a German, until Jewish partisans from Mir recognized him.

After the war, Rufajzen helped identify Mir locals who had collaborated with the Germans. He then moved on to Cracow, where he converted to Christianity. He later moved to Israel, where he joined a monastery.

RUMBULA (also called Rumbuli), site of a 1941 massacre, located five miles from RIGA, LATVIA. From November 29 to December 9, 1941, some 38,000 Jews were executed at Rumbula, a woodsy area situated near a train station. These included 28,000 Jews from the Riga GHETTO and 10,000 from GERMANY, AUSTRIA, and the Protectorate of Bohemia and Moravia, who had been brought to Riga by train. (see BOHEMIA AND MORAVIA, PROTECTORATE OF.)

Temporary monument set up to the Jews murdered at Rumbula, the text reads "Away with Fascism"

After WORLD WAR II, the massacre site lacked a sign memorializing the massacre victims. In 1962 a group of Jewish activists erected a wooden sign at Rumbula, which read: "On this site the voices of 38,000 Jews of Riga were stilled, November 29–30, 1941 to December 8–9, 1941." However, the Soviet authorities refused to sanction any memorial that singled out Jewish victims, and took down the sign. The Jewish activists refused to back down; as a result, the authorities agreed to erect a non-specific memorial at Rumbula. The inscription, written in Russian, Latvian, and Yiddish, read: "To the memory of the victims of the Nazis, 1941-1944."

Rumbula has since developed into a place of Jewish gathering, especially on the Jewish High Holidays and on the yearly observances of the Rumbula massacre and the WARSAW GHETTO UPRISING.

RUMKOWSKI, MORDECHAI CHAIM (1877-1944), Chairman of the JUDENRAT in the LODZ Ghetto in POLAND. Formerly an unsuccessful businessman and an orphanage director, Rumkowski was appointed *Judenrat* chairman on October 13, 1939, soon after the German invasion of Poland that launched WORLD WAR II.

Like all *Judenrat* heads, Rumkowski was torn between helping his constituents survive, and giving in to the demands of the German authorities. Rumkowski, however, is considered to be one of the most controversial of all *Judenrat* leaders, in that he often cooperated with the Germans and treated the Jews of his GHETTO dictatorially.

Rumkowski reported directly to the German ghetto administration, which was headed by Hans BIEBOW. He was completely responsible for everyday life in the ghetto: he had to provide food, housing, heat, work, and health and welfare services for the suffering ghetto population. Rumkowski controlled all aspects of the ghetto, even its cultural life. When rabbis were forced to stop working, he himself began performing marriages. His picture even appeared on the ghetto's money. Rumkowski was also charged with setting up factories for the Germans inside the ghetto. He established 120 of them, where he could employ thousands of the ghetto's Jews: Rumkowski believed that if he could create a productive and vital work force for the Nazis, then they would not destroy the ghetto.

Rumkowski also believed that in order to save the ghetto as a whole, he would have to cooperate with the Nazis and give in to their DEPORTATION demands. By the end of 1941, the EXTERMINATION CAMP at CHELMNO had been instituted and the Germans forced Rumkowski to organize the deportation of some of the ghetto population. At first, Rumkowski tried to convince the Germans to cut down the number of Jews to be deported. However, the Germans refused and made Rumkowski responsible for deciding who was to be deported. During the first five months of 1942, 55,000 Jews from Lodz were sent to their deaths at Chelmno.

Another deportation was carried out during the second week of September 1942. The Nazis demanded that Rumkowski turn over all children and old people. He cooperated with their demand, and even calmly asked families to surrender their own children. Twenty thousands Jews were brutally rounded up and sent to Chelmno. For the next while, there was a respite from the deportations, encouraging Rumkowski in his belief that keeping the peace and working for the Germans would help prevent further deportations. In fact, during that period of time, the Lodz Ghetto was left alone while other ghettos all over Poland were being destroyed.

However, by the late spring of 1944, the Soviet army was advancing towards Lodz. At that point, the Ger-

mans decided to liquidate the Lodz Ghetto once and for all. They made Rumkowski arrange the deportation. From June 23 to July 14, 1944, about 7,000 Jews were sent to Chelmno. The Jews of Lodz resisted the deportations passively, leading the Nazis to decide to liquidate the ghetto immediately, with SS and German police units carrying out the evacuation. The Germans closed the ghetto's factories and dissolved all *Judenrat*-run institutions. They also changed the Jews' destination from Chelmno to AUSCHWITZ. Rumkowski encouraged the Jews to calmly report for deportation, but they ignored his request. The Germans completed the liquidation of the ghetto in late July and August, sending the Jews to their deaths. Only a few hundred Jews managed to hide successfully.

Rumkowski and his family were not spared—they were deported to Auschwitz on August 30, 1944, and were soon killed there. Lodz was liberated by the Soviet army on January 19, 1945.

Some historians view Rumkowski as a collaborator and traitor. Others believe he made a serious, yet flawed, attempt to rescue as many Jews as possible.

Miniature bound leather bible presented in the Lodz Ghetto to Mordechai Chaim Rumkowski by Shlomo Knobel

S

SA (*Sturmabteilung,* Storm Troopers), also known as "Brown Shirts," the NAZI PARTY militia that helped Adolf HITLER rise to power in GERMANY.

SA men in Berlin during the anti-Jewish boycott, April 1, 1933

Created in 1922, the SA's supposed purpose was to guard Nazi Party meetings, but in actuality, Hitler meant for the group to serve as the Nazi army. The SA was extremely antisemitic and antidemocratic in its military activities. Its members were mainly lower-middle class Germans who had lost their jobs due to the country's economic problems. The SA gave them something to be part of and proud of. They engaged in street fights with their political enemies, practiced pseudo-military exercises, and terrorized Germany.

Ernst ROHM became the Supreme Commander of the SA in 1924. Around that time, Hitler began calling for the use of legal means to take control of Germany. Rohm was not satisfied with this: he wanted the SA to be the basis of a revitalized German army that would take power by force. Hitler rejected Rohm, and in 1925, Rohm stepped down. However, Hitler invited him back to his old job in 1930 after the Nazis' electoral victory, and ordered him to rebuild the SA.

Rohm took to the task with a vengeance. In just a few short years, the SA's membership grew from 70,000 to more than four million. Rohm divided Germany into 21 military-like districts, created flying squads and the Nazi Motor Corps, and reorganized the SA high command. When Hitler rose to national power in 1933, the SA became an official government organization. SA soldiers joined the regular police in order to arrest and torture ideological, political, and even personal enemies, including many Jews. They set up CONCENTRATION CAMPS for this purpose. However, when Rohm showed signs of wanting to take control of the army and rebel against Hitler in a military coup, the SS massacred him and other SA leaders in the "Night of the Long Knives"—June 30, 1934. From then on, the SA was no longer a dominant organization within the Reich, but it continued to exist, its members guarding concentration camps and terrorizing enemies of the Nazi regime.

SACHSENHAUSEN German CONCENTRATION CAMP located in Oranienburg, 20 miles north of BERLIN. Sachsenhausen was built in July 1936 by groups of prisoners who had previously been interned at other German camps. Sachsenhausen was established more than three years before WORLD WAR II broke out, but in fact, according to SS chief Heinrich HIMMLER, it was built with war and a large number of prisoners in mind. Over the almost nine years of the camp's existence, all sorts of inmates were imprisoned there, including political

Prisoners' roll call in Sachsenhausen

prisoners, common criminals, GYPSIES, JEHOVAH'S WIT-
NESSES who refused to support the German war effort,
homosexuals, and Jews. The different groups of
prisoners were made to wear different colored badges
for easy identification of their status. Jews wore yellow
stars, while homosexuals wore pink triangles (see also
BADGE, JEWISH). Jews lived in separate barracks from the
rest of the inmates, and were treated worse than the rest,
as well. Prominent prisoners such as the anti-Nazi
German Protestant pastor Martin NIEMOLLER were also
housed separately.

In November 1938, after the KRISTALLNACHT pogrom, 1,800 Jews were brought to Sachsenhausen;
450 of them were murdered soon thereafter. During
1940 some 26,000 mainly Polish prisoners arrived in
the camp. Most were soon transferred to other camps.
During the summer of 1941 the Nazis set up a system at
Sachsenhausen for mass extermination by shooting;
over the next few months, 13,000–18,000 Soviet PRIS-
ONERS OF WAR were shot to death. In 1943 the Nazis

installed a GAS CHAMBER, which was only used on certain
occasions. One of these "special" occasions was in February 1945 when the SS gassed thousands of sick and
weak prisoners right before they began evacuating the
camp.

Sachsenhausen had 61 satellite camps which functioned as FORCED LABOR camps. The prisoners were
made to work long hours for private German companies that paid the prisoners' salaries directly to the SS.
One of the biggest work projects at Sachsenhausen—
and probably one of the most brutal places to work in
the entire camp complex—was a brick factory located
near the camp. About 2,000 prisoners worked on the
project every day, and by April 1941 the Germans built
a special satellite camp for them. Those prisoners assigned to work there had a very short life expectancy.
After 1943 most of the prisoners worked in armaments
factories where they produced engines for planes, tanks,
and other vehicles. In 1944 the brickyard was converted
into a grenade factory.

Prisoners engaged in forced labor, Sachsenhausen, 1940

Throughout the war, conditions at Sachsenhausen deteriorated. Originally, the camp had been built to hold 10,000 prisoners, but by April 1945 it housed over 50,000. In addition, the SS performed horrible pseudo-scientific MEDICAL EXPERIMENTS on Gypsy, Jewish, and homosexual prisoners. Dr. Werner Fischer conducted experiments in which he tried to prove that Gypsy blood was different from "Aryan" blood. For other experiments, Jews and Gypsies were murdered so that their skeletons and organs could be sent to German universities for research purposes.

It is estimated that some 200,000 prisoners passed through Sachsenhausen and that 30,000 perished there. That number does not include the Soviet prisoners of war who were exterminated immediately upon arrival at the camp, as they were never even registered on the camp's lists. The number also does not account for those prisoners who died on the way to the camp, while being transferred elsewhere, or during the camp's evacuation.

In February 1945 Red Cross representatives arrived at Sachsenhausen and offered to take control of the camp. However, the Nazis refused, and instead sent most of the camp's prisoners on a DEATH MARCH through GERMANY. Many died along the way. Sachsenhausen was liberated by Soviet troops on April 27, 1945. They found only 3,000 prisoners who had been too ill to leave on the death march.

SAJMISTE   Fairground site located in the Yugoslav town of Zemun, near BELGRADE, which was used as an internment camp for some 8,000 Jews from SERBIA before they were killed by GAS VAN in the spring of 1942.

During the fall of 1941, WEHRMACHT firing squads murdered most of Serbia's male Jews and GYPSIES. However, they had refused to shoot women and children. Thus, in December 1941 the Germans imprisoned the surviving Jews and Gypsies in Sajmiste, mostly women and children but also some men, until such time when they could be deported to their deaths in EXTERMINATION CAMPS in POLAND.

The former fairground of Sajmiste was quickly converted into a camp, its large, open buildings turned into barracks by adding wooden scaffolding. The camp did not have heat, and the prisoners had to crawl on their hands and knees through the scaffolding to reach their living quarters.

The Gypsy prisoners were released in the spring of 1942. Despite their plan, the Germans did not send the Jews to Poland. Instead, in early March, they brought in a gas van from GERMANY in order to finish the job of exterminating the rest of Serbia's Jews right then and there. Over the next nine weeks, groups of Jewish prisoners from Sajmiste were told that they were being relocated, and then loaded on to the gas van. As the van drove through Belgrade, the passengers were suffocated to death and then buried at Avala, south of the city. Altogether, 6,280 Jews from Sajmiste were killed in the gas van, while another 1,200 died from starvation or exposure to the cold.

After all the Jews had been done away with, the German authorities refilled Sajmiste with political prisoners. Despite complaints from the German plenipotentiary (representative) to the Balkan region that the camp was a political eyesore and caused discomfort among the inhabitants of Belgrade, Sajmiste was used until the Germans left YUGOSLAVIA. In all, some 47,000 people perished there during the war.

SALIEGE, JULES-GERARD   (1870–1956), Archbishop of the southern French city of Toulouse who actively opposed the anti-Jewish steps taken in FRANCE during WORLD WAR II.

Before World War I, Saliege was strongly affected by Catholic theologians who believed that the church should begin rethinking some of its theological stands and get more involved in social issues. During the 1930s Saliege condemned RACISM as an un-Christian concept, and persisted in his opposition even after the Vichy government came to power in southern France in 1940.

In August 1942 the Vichy authorities began full-scale DEPORTATION of Jews. At that point, Saliege wrote

a letter condemning the deportations and demanded that Christians acknowledge Jews as their "brothers." Saliege then sent the letter out to all the parishes under his authority. The letter was part of a revolution in Catholic thinking regarding Jews. As a result, many Catholics in southern France lent their support to the Jewish cause. (for more on Vichy, see also FRANCE.)

SALONIKA   Main city and port on the northeastern mainland of GREECE, located in the MACEDONIA region. The Germans invaded Greece in April 1941. On April 9 they conquered Salonika; at that point, there were 50,000 Jews living in the city. Within a week, the Nazis arrested the Jewish community leaders, confiscated Jewish apartments, shut down Jewish newspapers, and took over the Jewish hospital for the use of German troops. During April and May, EINSATZSTAB ROSENBERG, an organization established for the systematic plunder of the art and cultural objects belonging to Jews in Europe, methodically looted the Jewish libraries and cultural treasures of Salonika. Most of the pillaged items were sent to FRANKFURT, where the Nazis were setting up a Jewish research library.

Over the next 14 months, the Nazis did not call for any specific anti-Jewish measures. However, the winter of 1941–1942 was extremely harsh, and the Jewish community of Salonika was threatened with starvation. Over 600 Jews died of cold and disease. In addition, the Jews of Salonika were not prepared for what was to come next.

On July 11, 1942, 9,000 Jewish males from the ages of 18–45 were forcibly assembled at Liberty Square (*Plateia Eleftheria*), the city's central square. About 2,000 were sent to do FORCED LABOR for the German

Nazis terrorize Jews in Salonika, July 11, 1942

army. By October, 250 had died. The rest of the men were brought back home in exchange for a ransom handed over to Dr. Maximilian Merton, the advisor to the German military administration in Macedonia. The Jewish communities of Salonika and Athens paid some of the ransom; the rest came from the transfer of the Jewish cemetery in Salonika to the city's municipality, which used the stones of the 500-year-old cemetery for building materials. Eventually, a university was built over the cemetery's ruins.

A JUDENRAT was established in December 1942. Dr. Zvi Koretz, the chief rabbi of Salonika, was named *Judenrat* president—he represented his community in negotiations with Dieter WISLICENY and Alois BRUNNER, the SS officers sent by Adolf EICHMANN in February 1943 to supervise the DEPORTATION of Salonika's Jews. Scholars have debated Koretz's actions as *Judenrat* chairman, expressing contradictory views.

Beginning on February 8, 1943, Merton published several decrees that put the NUREMBERG LAWS into effect. Jews were forced into a GHETTO in the city's Baron Hirsch quarter, located near the railway station, in preparation for convenient deportation. About 20 transports, carrying 43,850 Salonikan Jews, arrived in AUSCHWITZ-Birkenau between March 20 and August 18, 1943. Most of the new arrivals were immediately gassed. Of the 1,200 who survived the initial selections, most died later. Some of the women were used as subjects for pseudo-scientific sterilization experiments (see also SELEKTION and MEDICAL EXPERIMENTS). Rabbi Koretz, the *Judenrat,* and the Jewish police were taken to BERGEN-BELSEN in August.

Some Salonikan Jews were spared: those who held Spanish, Italian, Turkish, or other passports; 367 Jews who were given Spanish citizenship and reached SPAIN via Bergen-Belsen; and those few hundred Jews helped by the Italian government to escape to Italian-occupied territory or given Italian citizenship, causing conflict between the Italians and their German allies. In addition, some Salonikan Jews managed to reach Palestine with the help of PARTISANS.

Hundreds of Salonikan Jews survived the extermination and labor camps. After the war, many returned to the city, along with those who had hidden in the mountains and those who had joined the partisans. In 1945, there were 1,950 Jews in Salonika. Many, attacked as "Communists" during the ensuing Greek civil war, immigrated to Israel, the UNITED STATES, and South America.

SAUCKEL, FRITZ (1894–1946), Nazi official who, from 1942 to 1945, was responsible for recruiting forced laborers from Nazi-occupied territories to work in the German armaments industry.

Sauckel joined the NAZI PARTY in 1921. In 1925, he was appointed *gauleiter* (party leader) of Thuringia, and in 1933 became its governor.

When WORLD WAR II broke out, Sauckel was named Reich defense commissioner for the German military district of Kassel. In 1942 he was appointed "plenipotentiary-general for labor mobilization." This meant that he was in charge of finding and supplying laborers to work in the German armaments industries. To fulfill the quotas, Sauckel ordered the DEPORTATION of millions of workers from the territories occupied by the Nazis, and exploited them ruthlessly. As a result, thousands of Jewish forced laborers from POLAND died while in his employment.

After the war, Sauckel was tried at the NUREMBERG TRIALS and convicted. He was hanged in 1946. (see also FORCED LABOR.)

SCHACHT, HJALMAR (1877–1970), German economist, president of the German State Bank (*Reichsbank*), and minister of economic affairs.

Schacht was very involved in getting HITLER appointed as chancellor of GERMANY in 1933. He became *Reichsbank* president in March of that year and minister

Hjalmar Schacht (at the top of the steps) greeting Hitler in Nuremberg, 1935

of economic affairs in August. Despite the fact that Schacht guided the recovery of the German economy during Hitler's early reign, he never joined the NAZI PARTY.

In November 1937 Hitler sought to focus the economy on preparation for war. At that point, Schacht resigned as minister. In January 1939 he also left his job as *Reichsbank* president. After an attempt was made on Hitler's life in July 1944, Schacht was put in a CONCENTRATION CAMP due to his relationship with Hitler's opponents. Because of his incarceration during the war years, Schacht was acquitted fully at the NUREMBERG TRIALS.

Scholars have long questioned Schacht's position regarding the persecution of the Jews. While he claimed to have protected Jews by helping them maintain their economic activities while he was economics minister, it seems that he had a vested interest in keeping certain Jews involved in Germany's economy. He denounced KRISTALLNACHT, but allowed anti-Jewish boycotts and did not protest the removal of Jews from economic life. (see also BOYCOTT, ANTI-JEWISH.)

SCHELLENBERG, WALTER (1910–1952), Head of the THIRD REICH'S espionage services. Schellenberg joined the NAZI PARTY and the SS in 1933 and the head office of the Security Service (SD) in 1934. In September 1939 he organized the creation of the Reich Security Main Office (REICHSSICHERHEITSHAUPTAMT, RSHA) through the combination of the SD and the Security Police (SIPO). At that point, he took over direct control of the RSHA section that dealt with anti-German secret agents active in GERMANY and in Nazi-occupied countries.

Schellenberg was promoted in November 1939, after successfully kidnapping two British agents in the NETHERLANDS. He was then made responsible to prepare the SIPO for an invasion of GREAT BRITAIN. When that plan was dissolved, Schellenberg was put in charge of foreign intelligence. In this capacity, he set up information centers in all the European capitals.

In mid-1942 Schellenberg took part in Operation Zeppelin, in which Soviet PRISONERS OF WAR were retrained as anti-Communists and parachuted into Soviet territory in order to fight the anti-Nazi PARTISANS. However, most of the parachutists were caught and executed. In 1944 Schellenberg became chief of the merged SS and WEHRMACHT intelligence services.

After the war Schellenberg was tried and sentenced to prison. He was released early due to health problems.

SCHINDLER, OSKAR   (1908–1974), Businessman who protected Jews during the HOLOCAUST. Schindler was designated as RIGHTEOUS AMONG THE NATIONS by YAD VASHEM, and made famous by Steven Spielberg's award-winning film, *Schindler's List.*

Oskar Schindler was born in Sudetenland, Czechoslovakia. After GERMANY invaded POLAND in 1939, Schindler went to CRACOW to take over two enamelware factories that had previously been owned by Jews. Both were successful ventures, and he operated one as an agent for the German occupiers. Schindler later opened a third factory outside Cracow, in which he employed mainly Jews, saving them from DEPORTATION.

The Cracow Ghetto was liquidated in early 1943; many of its Jews were sent to the PLASZOW labor camp nearby. Schindler, greatly affected by the Jews' plight, used his good connections with important German officials in the Armaments Administration to establish a branch of the Plaszow camp inside his factory compound. Nine hundred Jewish workers, some unfit for hard labor, were employed in the factory. They were thus rescued from the terrible conditions at Plaszow.

By October 1944 Schindler's factory was no longer in use, and the Russian army was advancing towards Poland. Schindler got permission to move his factory to Sudetenland and reestablish it as an armaments production company. He once again used his contacts to arrange to take his Jewish workers with him. He successfully transferred 700–800 men from the CONCENTRATION CAMP at GROSS-ROSEN and about 300 women from AUSCHWITZ. The names of these workers were recorded on a list, earning the name "Schindler's List."

Schindler's Jews were treated in the most humane way possible. He and his wife, Emilie, provided them with food and medical care. Those Jews who died were buried in proper Jewish funerals. Schindler consistently used his charming personality and good connections to befriend and extract favors from important SS officials in Poland (they even got him out of jail several times when the GESTAPO accused him of corruption).

In all, Schindler saved about 1,100 Jews from almost certain death. He is buried in a Christian cemetery in Jerusalem.

SCHIPER, IGNACY (YITZHAK)   (1884–1943), Jewish historian and public figure. Born in Eastern Galicia,

Oskar Schindler (second from left) with Jews who worked for him, Cracow, 1942

Schiper was a member of the *Po'alei Zion* Zionist Socialists; he represented his party in the Polish parliament from 1919–1927. Schiper was also one of the two most important Jewish historians of his time in POLAND.

Schiper was very active in public affairs in the WARSAW Ghetto; he participated in public meetings, took part in the Jewish Culture Organization's activities, and gave lectures. He also continued his scholarly work in the GHETTO. He was critical of the ghetto's JUDENRAT; for a time, Schiper served on an ultimately unsuccessful committee that tried to suggest ways for the *Judenrat* to improve itself.

At first, Schiper was convinced that the Jews should actively resist the Nazis. Nevertheless, when the Germans launched DEPORTATIONS from the ghetto in July 1942, Schiper objected to a policy of resistance. He stated his belief that the Jews had suffered before, but by accepting their losses, had managed to preserve their identity as a people and ensure Jewish continuity.

After the January 1943 deportation, Schiper tried to escape to the "Aryan" side of Warsaw. He was arrested during the WARSAW GHETTO UPRISING, and deported to MAJDANEK where he was killed.

SCHMID, ANTON

SCHMID, ANTON (1900–1942), German soldier who rescued Jews during WORLD WAR II. While serving in VILNA as a sergeant in the WEHRMACHT, Schmid came in contact with a group of Jews from the Vilna GHETTO who were assigned to work for his unit. Schmid treated them kindly, and they grew to trust him.

After hearing about the massacres at PONARY in late 1941, Schmid decided to do whatever he could to rescue Jews. He released Jews who were being detained in the Lakishki jail, secretly brought food and supplies to Jews in the ghetto, and hid Jews in the cellars of three houses under his supervision. He also worked with the Jewish underground in Vilna. He even transported some underground members to WARSAW and BIALYSTOK in his truck, so that they could warn the Jews there about the mass executions in Ponary. Underground members had meetings and even slept in his home. Schmid also sent groups of Jews to other ghettos, which at that time were still safe.

In January 1942 Schmid was arrested and executed by a military court. In 1964, 22 years after his death, Schmid was designated as RIGHTEOUS AMONG THE NATIONS by YAD VASHEM.

SCHONFELD, SOLOMON

SCHONFELD, SOLOMON (1912–1982), English rabbi and educator who rescued Jews during the HOLOCAUST.

In early 1938 Schonfeld created a rescue organization called the Chief Rabbi's Religious Emergency Council, whose purpose was to bring Orthodox rabbis and teachers to England who were not sponsored by other refugee organizations in GREAT BRITAIN because they were considered to be "unproductive" citizens. That winter, Schonfeld brought to London 250 children from VIENNA who were not receiving support from the Jewish community there. Until he could find permanent homes for them, he housed them in his own home and in his schools. Next, he instituted a rabbinical academy as a way of bringing some 120 REFUGEE students into England.

By appealing to various prominent British figures and government officials, Schonfeld was able to procure entry permits for some 3,700 Jews, who arrived in England before and right after WORLD WAR II. During the war, Schonfeld also came up with several rescue plans that were not implemented by the authorities.

After the war, Schonfeld worked with Jewish DISPLACED PERSONS in the British zone of GERMANY. He also traveled to POLAND and Czechoslovakia to bring war orphans to England.

SCHWARTZ, JOSEPH J.

SCHWARTZ, JOSEPH J. (1899–1975), European director of the JOINT DISTRIBUTION COMMITTEE (JDC) from 1940–1949. Schwartz joined the JDC in his native UNITED STATES. He was soon sent to PARIS to serve as European deputy director; in 1940 he became director. When the Germans occupied FRANCE in 1940, Schwartz moved the JDC's offices to Portugal.

As JDC director, Schwartz directed many rescue and aid operations. He supervised the emigration of Jews who could still get visas to Western countries. He allotted funds for rescue activities all over occupied Europe, where JDC workers rescued and hid many Jews. He supported armed Jewish resistance, despite the policy of the American JDC. Schwartz endorsed illegal Jewish emigration to Palestine in 1940 and 1941. He established another JDC office in Istanbul. He sent thousands of aid packages to the SOVIET UNION via Tehran, which saved thousands of starving Jewish REFUGEES in Soviet Central Asia. In addition, Schwartz allocated moneys for the upkeep of Jewish religious institutions in Palestine.

After the war, Schwartz sent JDC workers to help

run Displaced Persons' camps in GERMANY. He also sent teams to help Jews in Eastern Europe, and aided refugees who wanted to go to Palestine. Schwartz continued working for Jewish organizations until his retirement in 1970.

SCHWARZBART, IGNACY ISAAC (1888–1961), Zionist activist and politician. Born in Galicia, Schwarzbart was a lawyer who served as an officer in the Austro-Hungarian army during World War I. In 1918 he enlisted in the Polish army. After the war he returned to his law practice and began writing for various Zionist newspapers. He also served as a delegate from the General Zionist movement to most of the Zionist Congresses and was a member of the WORLD JEWISH CONGRESS'S executive committee. In addition, he was a member of the Jewish faction in CRACOW'S city council, and one of the leaders of Cracow's Jewish community. In 1938 Schwarzbart was elected to the Polish parliament as a representative of the Cracow district.

When WORLD WAR II broke out in September 1939 Schwarzbart, as a member of the Polish government, fled Poland for FRANCE, where the POLISH GOVERNMENT-IN-EXILE was established. At that point, he became a member of the Polish national council-in-exile. After France fell to GERMANY in mid-1940, Schwarzbart moved with the government-in-exile to London.

In early 1940 Schwarzbart created a publication on Polish Jewish affairs called *The Future*. In January of that year he also instituted the Organizing Committee of the Polish Jewish Representation in France.

Over the next six years, Schwarzbart served on the National Council of the Polish Republic and the Delegation of Polish Jewry. Over time, he also wrote a war diary and collected a wealth of documents about the history of Polish Jewry during the HOLOCAUST and the interactions between Jews and Poles during World War II. This archive has since been maintained as an important collection of Holocaust testimony and documentation; it was brought to YAD VASHEM in the early 1960s.

After the war, Schwarzbart continued writing and stayed active in the Zionist movement, including the World Jewish Congress. From 1946 to 1961 he lived in the UNITED STATES, where he published several booklets about the WARSAW GHETTO UPRISING, including *The Story of the Warsaw Uprising: Its Meaning and Message,* and a book in Yiddish on Jewish life in Cracow between the world wars, called *Between the Two World Wars.*

SD (*Sicherheitsdienst des Reichsfuehrers-SS,* Security Service of the SS), the SS's intelligence service and one of the major agents of the "Final Solution."

The SD was created as the SS's intelligence service in 1931, and put under the command of Reinhard HEYDRICH. Its purpose was to expose enemies of the NAZI PARTY and keep them under observation.

After HITLER brought the Nazi Party to national power in GERMANY in 1933, the SD was given official government responsibilities, such as creating and operating a widespread spy network among the German people. It reported on the activities of political and racial enemies of the Reich, mainly Jews, and kept Hitler informed of public opinion.

In 1934 the SS took over the GESTAPO, the Reich's secret political police. Soon thereafter, the SD was declared the party's exclusive intelligence service. However, the line between the two intelligence branches—the SD and the *Gestapo*—was quite blurry. The two agencies were headed by the same people and had similar responsibilities, namely, dealing with the "Jewish question." This did not prevent rivalry, however. Soon, SS Chief Heinrich HIMMLER clarified the division of labor: the SD was to serve as an intelligence and counterintelligence service whose job was to identify state enemies; once they were exposed, the *Gestapo* would deal with those enemies. The SD also attempted to get into international espionage and military intelligence. Regarding the Jewish issues, the SD and *Gestapo* shared responsibilities.

At the end of 1936 the SD's Jewish section adopted an official policy of ridding Germany of Jews. From then on, the SD harassed German Jews in order to get them to leave the country. The SD used confiscation of property, public pressure, and terror to achieve its goal. With the establishment of the Reich Security Main Office (REICHSSICHERHEITSHAUPTAMT, RSHA) in 1939, SD functions were divided between two of the newly created offices. Certain individual staff members in other RSHA offices continued to be considered SD personnel. Many of them played a major part in planning and executing the "Final Solution." Many served in the EINSATZGRUPPEN units that carried out the systematic mass murder of Jews in the SOVIET UNION in the summer of 1941.

After the war, the SD was declared to be a criminal organization by the International Military Tribunal at NUREMBERG, and its members subject to punishment as war criminals.

SD man humiliating an observant Jew by cutting off his beard, Warsaw, October 1939

SECURENI   Transit camp for 30,000 Bessarabian Jews. Secureni, located in northern BESSARABIA, was established in July 1941 and evacuated on October 3, 1941, when all the Jews in the camp were deported to TRANSNISTRIA.

SELEKTION   (literally, selection; in plural, *selektionen*), term used by the Nazis to denote the sorting of deportees or prisoners into two groups—those who were to do FORCED LABOR, and those who were to be killed. (see picture on page 405).

SENDLER, IRENA   (b. 1916), Nicknamed "Jolanta," one of the most active members of the Council for Aid to Jews (ZEGOTA), a Polish underground organization that provided assistance for Jews. From the start of Germany's occupation of POLAND, Sendler helped her many Jewish friends and acquaintances. She worked for the social welfare department of the WARSAW municipality, so she could obtain a permit to visit the city's GHETTO at all hours. Thus, she managed to supply many

Jews with clothing, money, and medicine. Sendler wore an armband with the Star of David while working in the ghetto, both to show her support for the Jews and so as not to call attention to herself.

During the summer of 1942, Sendler was asked to join a new organization called the Council for Aid to Jews; she became one of its most important members. She brought with her a large group of people who already assisted her in her work. One of Sendler's specialties was sneaking Jewish children out of the ghetto and placing them in the care of non-Jewish families in the Warsaw area. The families were funded by the *Zegota*. Each of her colleagues was put in charge of several apartment blocks where Jewish children were hidden, and she herself took responsibility for 8–10 apartments where Jews were hiding.

In October 1943, Sendler was arrested by the GESTAPO. They took her to the notorious PAWIAK PRISON, where she was tortured brutally in order to make her give up information about her activities. In spite of the agony of torture, Sendler surrendered nothing, leading

The process of selektion begins for Hungarian Jews who have reached Auschwitz, 1944

her interrogators to tell her that she was to be executed. However, her underground comrades bribed a *Gestapo* agent, and on the day she was supposed to be killed, Sendler was set free. She was officially listed as executed and thus had to stay hidden for the rest of the occupation. However, she continued working behind the scenes for *Zegota*. In 1965, she was designated as RIGHT-EOUS AMONG THE NATIONS by YAD VASHEM.

SERBIA   Region of YUGOSLAVIA. Before Yugoslavia was established in 1919, Serbia was an independent country. On the eve of WORLD WAR II, some 16,000 Jews lived there. Of that number, about 14,500 were exterminated during the war.

GERMANY invaded Yugoslavia in April 1941, and divided the country amongst its allies, keeping Serbia for itself. The Germans then set up a military adminis-tration to control the region. Very quickly, the new authorities began issuing anti-Jewish laws. First, they defined exactly who was to be considered a Jew. Next, the Jews of Serbia were made to wear the Jewish badge (see also BADGE, JEWISH), and were kicked out of certain professions. In addition, they were restricted to living in certain areas. By the summer of 1941, some 900 Jewish businesses had been taken away from their owners, Jewish bank accounts were blocked, and the Jewish community was forced to pay three large fines. In addition, all Jewish men from the ages of 16 to 60 were rounded up for FORCED LABOR.

In July 1941 a general revolt broke out in Serbia. In retaliation, the German military authorities came up with a policy whereby 100 Serbs would be executed for every German soldier killed during the revolt, and 50 would be executed for every German injured. How-ever, instead of antagonizing the local population too much, the Germans filled their quotas with Jews. In this fashion, the Germans also did away with much of the "Jewish problem" in Serbia.

By early fall 1941, most of the Jewish men of Serbia had been imprisoned in local CONCENTRATION CAMPS, and the Germans began carrying out mass executions. By December, most of the Jewish males—about 5,000—had been killed, except for those needed for forced labor. That same month, about 8,000 Jewish women, children, and old people were sent to a fair-ground-turned-internment camp at SAJMISTE, near BEL-GRADE. From March to May 1942, more than 6,000 were killed by GAS VAN, while another 1,200 died of exposure or starvation.

By the summer of 1942, only a few Jews remained in

Serbia. These Jews had either been hidden or joined the PARTISANS.

SERED FORCED LABOR and CONCENTRATION CAMP in SLOVAKIA. During the spring and summer of 1942, the authorities began using Sered as a labor camp. In fact, the idea of establishing such labor camps had come from the Jews themselves: during the height of the mass DEPORTATIONS, the Slovak Jewish rescue organization called the WORKING GROUP came up with a plan to save Jews from being deported by sending them to work in forced labor camps instead. However, not all Jews were spared. During that summer, some 4,500 Jews from Sered were sent to POLAND on five transports.

After the last transport, the conditions at Sered improved greatly. The laborers produced an impressive number of quality goods, and as a result they received more food and even leave passes. There were school services for the children and cultural activities for all. A Jewish Council under Alexander Pressburger even helped run the camp.

During the August 1944 SLOVAK NATIONAL UPRISING, the camp was opened and many prisoners left to participate in the revolt. However, after the Germans put down the uprising, Sered was taken under their control. From October 1944 to March 1945, 13,500 Jews were deported from Sered to THERESIENSTADT and AUSCHWITZ. The camp was liberated by the Soviet army in April 1945.

SERENI, ENZO (1905–1944), One of the Palestinian parachutists sent into occupied Europe by the YISHUV.

Born in Rome, Sereni became a Zionist activist at a young age. In 1925 he earned a doctorate in philosophy. Two years later he settled in Palestine, eventually helping to found Kibbutz Givat Brenner. During the early 1930s, Sereni traveled to GERMANY several times, first to help the Zionist YOUTH MOVEMENTS there, and then to work on YOUTH ALIYA and the Jewish Agency's TRANSFER AGREEMENT, which helped German Jews immigrate to Palestine.

When WORLD WAR II broke out, Sereni volunteered for the British army. In 1941 he was sent to Iraq, where he prepared young Jews for underground work and for immigration to Palestine. In 1943 Sereni was appointed intermediary between the Palestinian parachutists and their British trainers. Despite the fact that he was almost 40, Sereni insisted on being one of the parachutists

himself, and not just a behind the scenes organizer. In May 1944 he parachuted into northern ITALY, where he was caught by the Germans. They imprisoned him in DACHAU, where he became a leader among the prisoners. He was executed in November 1944. (see also PARACHUTISTS, JEWISH.)

SEYSS-INQUART, ARTHUR (1892–1946), Austrian Nazi. Throughout the years of Nazi power, Seyss-Inquart was very loyal to HITLER, and was rewarded accordingly with various important positions.

Arthur Seyss-Inquart (center) speaking to Hitler in Vienna

Originally, Seyss-Inquart was not an antisemite, but over time, he became interested in the NAZI PARTY. Hitler was impressed with Seyss-Inquart, so he pressured the Austrian chancellor into appointing Seyss-Inquart Austrian Minister of the Interior and Public Security in February 1938. Soon, Hitler pushed the chancellor into resigning, and gave Seyss-Inquart his job. Seyss-Inquart immediately invited the German army into AUSTRIA, setting the stage for the ANSCHLUSS—the annexing of Austria by GERMANY in March 1938. In reward, Hitler named Seyss-Inquart Reich Commissioner of Austria, and SS Chief Heinrich HIMMLER gave him the rank of SS-*Obergruppenfuehrer*. In May 1939 Seyss-Inquart was made minister without portfolio in the German cabinet, and that October, he was appointed deputy governor-general in POLAND, where he was charged with inspecting the land to be used in the NISKO AND LUBLIN PLAN.

In May 1940 Hitler once again gave Seyss-Inquart a new, challenging job: he appointed him Reich Commissioner of the Occupied NETHERLANDS, with the task of creating friendly relations between the Dutch and the Germans. In fact, for the first few months in his new position, Seyss-Inquart did not make any radical moves, in order to make the Dutch think that the Germans would not persecute them. However, it soon became obvious to him that the Dutch did not accept his efforts at friendship. Thus, he launched a campaign of oppression against the Dutch. He instituted anti-Jewish measures, which in turn made the Dutch reject him even more. In punishment, Seyss-Inquart initiated the plunder of Jewish property and the DEPORTATION of Jews to EXTERMINATION CAMPS, instead of letting the local SS control the "Final Solution" themselves.

In the last months of the war, Seyss-Inquart saw that Germany would never emerge victorious, so he began negotiating with the Allied armies. After the war, Seyss-Inquart was indicted for CRIMES AGAINST HUMANITY, and at the NUREMBERG TRIALS, he was sentenced to death.

SHANGHAI A port city in China occupied by Japan from 1937. Shanghai was a haven for Jewish REFUGEES from GERMANY, AUSTRIA, and POLAND during WORLD WAR II, as it was the only place in the world where one could enter without a visa. By 1941, 17,000 Jews had moved to East Asia.

After the KRISTALLNACHT pogrom of November 9–10, 1938, many refugees began to arrive in Shanghai. They were aided by the small, wealthy community of 400–500 Iraqi Jews that had been living in Shanghai since the mid-nineteenth century, and by the American Jewish JOINT DISTRIBUTION COMMITTEE. These groups set up five large refugee camps for more than 3,000 people.

Despite their economic constraints, the refugees were able to create an active social, religious, and cultural existence with religious services, schools, cultural productions, and three German-language newspapers. The refugee community included Polish intellectuals,

Hasidic Jews on a street corner in Shanghai

Zionist leaders, and rabbis and students of the MIR Yeshiva. In February 1943 the Germans forced the Japanese to establish a Jewish GHETTO. The conditions there were miserable, but not nearly as bad as those of the European ghettos. At the end of the war, most of the refugees left Shanghai for Palestine and other Western countries. (see also RESCUE OF POLISH JEWS VIA EAST ASIA.)

SHEPTYTSKY, ANDREI (1865–1944), Head of the Greek Catholic church in southeast POLAND, and one of the leaders of the Ukrainian nationalist movement.

Between the two world wars, Sheptytsky was active in the struggle of Poland's Ukrainian population for national rights. During the 1930s, the Ukrainian nationalist movement became increasingly extremist, and adopted a pro-German, antisemitic ideology. Sheptytsky did not approve of the movement's terrorist activities, but he did not denounce them, either.

Sheptytsky had always had a good relationship with the Jewish leaders of Eastern Galicia. In July 1941 he even promised one rabbi that he would stop the Ukrainians from killing Jews. However, the Ukrainians continued their attacks. In February 1942 Sheptytsky asked Heinrich HIMMLER to forbid the Ukrainian police from participating in the murder of Jews. Over the next few months, Sheptytsky helped dozens of Jews find refuge in his monasteries and even in his own home. At the same time, however, he supported the German army as the savior of the Ukrainians from the Soviets, and endorsed the formation of a Ukrainian division within the SS. One of Sheptytsky's closest aides served as the division's chief chaplain. Despite his sympathy for the Jews, Sheptytsky did nothing to stop the Ukrainian nationalists from backing GERMANY.

SHOAH   see HOLOCAUST.

SIKORSKI, WLADYSLAW EUGENIUSZ   (1881–1943), Polish general and statesman. After the Germans invaded POLAND in September 1939 and WORLD WAR II broke out, Sikorski fled the country as head of the POLISH GOVERNMENT-IN-EXILE. He was also named commander in chief of the Polish armed forces in November 1939.

From 1940–1943 Sikorski served as Polish Prime Minister and Chief of General Staff. He devised Poland's war objectives, planned the deployment of Polish troops outside of Poland, and organized a resistance movement inside occupied Poland. In statements made in 1939 and 1942, Sikorski described his plans for the future of Poland: he hoped that changes would be made after the war, making Poland more like the democratic countries in the West. In July 1941 Sikorski signed a diplomatic agreement with the SOVIET UNION. However, the Soviets broke ties with Poland in 1943 after Sikorski demanded that the International Red Cross be allowed to look into the murder of thousands of Polish officers on Soviet soil (see also RED CROSS, INTERNATIONAL).

Sikorski did not always have a positive attitude towards European Jewry. However, on several occasions, he condemned the annihilation of the Jews and unsuccessfully begged Western leaders to take a stand against the murder.

Sikorski was killed in a plane crash in July 1943.

SILESIA, EASTERN UPPER   Region of POLAND annexed by GERMANY during WORLD WAR II.

Soon after the Germans occupied Silesia, they began instituting anti-Jewish decrees, such as the confiscation of Jewish property, drafting Jews for FORCED LABOR, and making the Jews wear the Jewish badge (see also BADGE, JEWISH). However, for the first years of the war, conditions in Silesia were not as bad as in other parts of Poland. Closed GHETTOS were not established until 1943 and food rations were more substantial.

The Germans set up a central JUDENRAT in early 1940 under the leadership of Moshe MERIN. Merin believed that if the Jews worked in Nazi factories, they could avoid DEPORTATION. He also theorized that if he doomed some to death, others could be saved. Thus, he aided the Germans during deportations. During the summer of 1942 most of the small communities in Silesia were liquidated. By August, 25 percent of Silesia's urban Jews had been deported to AUSCHWITZ.

In 1943 ghettos were established in the big cities. By that summer, most of the region's Jews had been deported, including Merin. In some cases, Jews rebelled during the liquidation of the ghettos. Some members of Zionist YOUTH MOVEMENTS managed to hide from the Germans and escape to SLOVAKIA, and from there to HUNGARY.

SILVER, ABBA HILLEL   (1893–1963), American rabbi and community leader who helped organize the American Jewish anti-Nazi boycott. In 1947 Silver played a title role in the Jewish Agency's campaign at

Abba Hillel Silver, American Zionist leader

the United Nations to get the Palestine partition plan approved. (see also BOYCOTTS, ANTI-NAZI.)

SIMA, HORIA (1906–1990), Romanian fascist leader. Born in BUCHAREST, Sima joined the fascist, antisemitic IRON GUARD movement in 1927, and became the movement's leader in 1938. King Carol II outlawed the Guard soon thereafter, so Sima fled to YUGOSLAVIA and then to GERMANY. He returned to ROMANIA in 1940; the king, trying to retain some power, invited Sima to join the cabinet. On September 6 Sima and Ion ANTONESCU established a "National Legionary Government" based on the Iron Guard's nickname, the "Legionnaires."

As deputy prime minister, Sima sought to take revenge against Iron Guard opponents and exclude Jews from Romania's economy. He provoked terror attacks on Jews and forcibly confiscated their property. He created a "Legionary Police" to accomplish his goals, and personally supervised the murder of 11 Jews in Ploiesti.

After a split between Sima and Antonescu over Sima's policies, Sima tried to take over the government by staging an Iron Guard revolt. A pogrom broke out in Bucharest during the revolt and 123 Jews were murdered. Antonescu quickly put down the revolt, and Sima fled to Germany. Despite being sentenced to death at two trials, Sima ultimately escaped to SPAIN where he lived as the leader of an exiled Iron Guard breakaway group until his death.

SIMAITE, ONA (1899–1970), Lithuanian librarian who helped Jews in the VILNA Ghetto.

Simaite, who worked at Vilna University, got involved with aiding Jews after seeing firsthand how the Germans and their Lithuanian collaborators were persecuting them. She used the excuse that she had to retrieve overdue library books that had been borrowed from her library by Jewish students in order to get into the GHETTO. While inside, she took the responsibility of preserving important historical and literary materials that were given to her by private individuals and public institutions for safe keeping.

Simaite also helped the Jews in the ghetto by retrieving some of the valuables that they had left with non-Jews. These possessions were needed by the ghetto Jews so that they could buy food. Simaite, who visited the ghetto everyday, also brought them food and other necessary items. In addition, she enlisted other Lithua-

nians to help hide Jews outside the ghetto. She herself adopted a Jewish girl in 1944; when she was discovered, Simaite was arrested and tortured. She was deported to DACHAU, and then exiled to southern FRANCE.

After the war, Simaite refused to accept any honors for her aid activities. She was designated as RIGHTEOUS AMONG THE NATIONS by YAD VASHEM in 1966.

SIXTH SLOVAK BRIGADE Brigade in the Slovak army that included special companies of Jewish laborers during WORLD WAR II. Based on a law issued in SLOVAKIA in January 1940, Slovak Jews, GYPSIES, and others were taken out of their regular army units and placed in special labor units. The Jews were transferred to the Twenty-first, Twenty-second, and Twenty-third Companies of the Sixth Brigade. These men built roads, regulated rivers, and did excavations. For a while, the Twenty-first Company was moved to POLAND, where its men repaired roads.

The Nazis launched large-scale DEPORTATIONS from Slovakia in March 1942. At that time, many of the men serving in the Sixth Brigade deserted the army; some returned to their families in order to be deported together with them, while others escaped to HUNGARY or obtained forged "Aryan" identity papers. Despite pressure on the army from the Slovak Ministry of the Interior to deport the Jews of the brigade to Poland, the army refused, saving the lives of hundreds of Jewish soldiers.

In May 1943 the brigade was dissolved; its soldiers were either moved to labor camps or formed into work gangs employed by private builders. Many of the Sixth Brigade's men participated in the SLOVAK NATIONAL UPRISING of August 1944; 52 perished in battle.

SKARZYSKO-KAMIENNA (Kamienna in German sources), FORCED LABOR camp for Jews, located in the Polish town of Skarzysko-Kamienna. The camp belonged to the German HASAG concern. It was established in August 1942 and was liquidated on August 1, 1944. Altogether, 25,000–30,000 Jews were brought to Skarzysko-Kamienna, and between 18,000–23,000 perished there.

The camp was divided into three separate factory camps, known as *Werke* A, B, and C. The three camps were located next to the factories where the prisoners worked, and were guarded by the Ukrainian factory police. Of the three factory camps, *Werk* A was the largest. *Werk* B shared an administration and security

Jews forced to "bathe" in a sewer, Skarzysko-Kamienna

with Camp A, but had its own Council of Elders. The prisoners of both *Werke* A and B worked at producing ammunition. *Werk* C was attached to a filling plant, where underwater mines filled with picric acid were produced. This was the worst of the three camps, because the acid poisoned the prisoners there within three months. All of the factories had two 12-hour shifts. Men and women, working together, were obliged to fill quotas they could not possibly fill. The sanitary conditions were unspeakable, and there was not nearly enough food. Prisoners were left to wear the same clothes for weeks. There were also terrible epidemics in the camps. Every once in a while there were selections—those prisoners chosen to die were killed by factory police. Only due to a great manpower shortage in the spring of 1944 did the living conditions get a bit better.

Mass executions of prisoners from GESTAPO jails took place in Camp C in late 1943 and early 1944. Right before Skarzysko-Kamienna was to be destroyed in the summer of 1944, the SS forced Jewish inmates to dig up the bodies of those victims and cremate them, in order to conceal evidence of mass murder. In late July many prisoners were massacred, and the 6,000 that remained were sent to BUCHENWALD and other German camps.

Many of the German camp staff were tried in 1948; four were sentenced to death, while the rest were put in prison with varying sentences. (see also SELEKTION.)

SKOBTSOVA, ELIZAVETA (MOTHER MARIA)
(1891–1945), Nun in FRANCE who helped Jews during the HOLOCAUST. Skobtsova was born in LATVIA. Before

WORLD WAR II, she organized welfare activities for Russians who had immigrated to France; her aide was Father Dimitri Klepinin, another Russian refugee. When the Nazis began persecuting Jews in France, Mother Maria decided that as a devoted Christian, she was required to do whatever she could to help the Jews. First, she opened the church's free kitchen to needy Jews; she then arranged temporary housing for them. Father Klepinin issued forged baptismal certificates for Jews who needed new identities. They were shocked when, in 1942, the Nazis decreed that all Jews must wear the yellow Jewish badge (see also BADGE, JEWISH).

In July 1942 the Nazis rounded up thousands of Jews for DEPORTATION. Mother Maria managed to enter the stadium where they were being held, and with the help of garbage collectors, smuggled out several children in garbage bins. The Nazis soon warned her to stop helping Jews, but she did not listen.

Mother Maria and Father Klepinin were arrested in February 1943 and sent to CONCENTRATION CAMPS, where they both perished. Both were designated as RIGHTEOUS AMONG THE NATIONS by YAD VASHEM.

SLOVAK NATIONAL UPRISING
A revolt that broke out in SLOVAKIA in late August 1944 and lasted until October 1944. Groups including the Communist Party, Slovak nationalists, and a group of Slovak army officers planned the rebellion. Their common goal was to overthrow the pro-Nazi government of Jozef TISO.

On August 28, 1944 German troops invaded Slovakia to suppress the country's PARTISANS. At that point, the uprising erupted. The Germans thought that they would curb the rebellion in just a few days, but the rebels—the Slovak army and partisan units—proved to be much hardier than they had estimated. More than 2,000 Jews also participated in the revolt, including underground fighters from the Jewish labor camps at NOVAKY, SERED, and VYHNE. These Jews hoped that by vanquishing the pro-Nazi government, the remaining 20,000 Jews in Slovakia would be rescued. However, by October the Nazis sent in thousands of soldiers to destroy the rebellion. On October 27 the uprising headquarters were crushed, signaling the end of the uprising.

In punishment, the Germans began rounding up thousands of Jews and partisans. Some were killed immediately, while another 13,500 were sent to AUSCHWITZ and THERESIENSTADT. Because the war was almost over, 10,000 Slovak Jews survived in the camps. Another 4,000–5,000 survived by hiding in Slovakia.

SLOVAKIA   Country in east central Europe. Until 1918 Slovakia belonged to HUNGARY. Between the two world wars it belonged to the independent Czechoslovak republic. From 1939–1945 Slovakia was a satellite of Nazi GERMANY. After the war it again was a part of Czechoslovakia until that country's breakup in 1993. Since 1993 Slovakia has been an independent country. On the eve of WORLD WAR II, there were 88,951 Jews in Slovakia.

In 1938 Slovak nationalists demanded more independence within the Czechoslovak republic; in October, Slovakia became an autonomous region. These antisemitic nationalists attacked Jews, looted their homes, and banished them to the no-man's land between Slovakia and Hungary.

In March 1939, Slovakia became an independent state. It was ruled by a totalitarian government called the Slovak People's Party, headed by the pro-Nazi Catholic priest, Jozef TISO. Tiso was an extreme nationalist who called for Christian solidarity. When he came to power, Jews were subjected to more attacks, and new Jewish restrictions were put into effect. These were augmented in July 1940, when at a conference attended by HITLER and Tiso, it was decided to establish a Nazi regime in Slovakia and begin executing severe ANTI-JEWISH LEGISLATION. In August SS officer Dieter WISLICENY came to Slovakia to be an "advisor on Jewish affairs" and Jewish men were drafted into labor units of the Slovak army. In addition, the Central Economic Office was established to ban Jews from the economy and seize their property.

In September 1940 the government instituted the Jewish Center (*Ustredna Zidov,* UZ) to answer to the

Deportation of Jews from Slovakia, 1942

Central Economic Office and act as an intermediary between the government and the Jews. The UZ was slated to retrain Jews for physical work, promote Jewish emigration from Slovakia, and run Jewish schools and charities.

In the summer of 1941 the Slovaks entered the war as Germany's ally against the SOVIET UNION, and anti-Jewish legislation became even worse. Basing its laws on the racial NUREMBERG LAWS, Slovakia banned Jews from many public places and forced them to wear the Jewish badge (see also BADGE, JEWISH). Many Jews were sent to labor camps, and the Slovak government decided to begin deporting Jews. From March to October 1942, about 58,000 Jews were deported to AUSCHWITZ, MAJDANEK, and the LUBLIN area. Their property was taken by the government and distributed to the Slovak people. From autumn 1942 until late summer 1944, there was a long lull in the transports.

In reaction to the DEPORTATIONS, members of the UZ created the WORKING GROUP. Led by Rabbi Michael Dov WEISSMANDEL and Gisi FLEISCHMANN, the group tried to stop the deportations in any way they could. They bribed Dieter Wisliceny with US $40,000–50,000 to stop the transports. This lasted from 1942–1944, during which time the Working Group also attempted to negotiate the rescue of other European Jews, later to be called the EUROPA PLAN. They also realized that if they helped establish labor camps in Slovakia itself, some Jews would be spared from deportation; three labor camps were soon built at NOVAKY, SERED, and VYHNE. The Working Group also helped some Slovak Jews escape over the border to Hungary. In addition, they tried to make contact with leaders in the West to let them know about the extermination of Europe's Jews, and beg their help.

In the summer of 1944, various nationalist groups decided to overthrow the Nazi government. The SLOVAK NATIONAL UPRISING lasted from August–October 1944. More than 2,000 Jews, belonging to PARTISAN groups and the Jewish armed cells that developed in labor camps, participated in the uprising. In October the Germans put down the revolt; as they occupied land, they arrested and deported about 13,000 Jews to Auschwitz, SACHSENHAUSEN, and THERESIENSTADT. Many hundreds of Jews were killed by the Germans in Slovakia itself.

In total, about 100,000 Slovak Jews (including those who had fled before the war) were murdered in the HOLOCAUST. About 15,000 survived, including 4,000–5,000 who hid with the partisans or in cities and towns. After the war, most Slovak Jews immigrated to Israel. (see also JEWISH CENTER, SLOVAKIA.)

SOBIBOR   EXTERMINATION CAMP located in the LUBLIN district of POLAND, near the village of Sobibor. The camp was established in March 1942 as part of AKTION REINHARD, and shut down at the end of 1943 after a prisoners' uprising. About 250,000 Jews were killed at Sobibor.

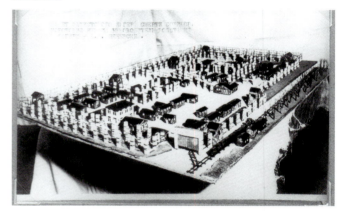

Model of Sobibor made by Sasha Pechersky for a school in Rostow

The Germans constructed Sobibor as a rectangle, 1,312 by 1,969 feet. The camp was surrounded by a barbed-wire fence woven with tree branches meant to hide what was inside. It was divided into three sections: the administration area, reception area, and extermination area. Jews brought in by transport were taken directly to the reception area. The extermination area held GAS CHAMBERS, burial trenches, and housing for the Jewish prisoners who worked there. The gas chambers, built to look like shower rooms, could hold 160–180 people each and were fueled by carbon monoxide gas.

Sobibor was run by SS-Obersturmfuehrer Franz STANGL, appointed camp commandant in April 1942. His staff included 20–30 SS soldiers, many of whom had worked on the EUTHANASIA PROGRAM, and 90–120 Ukrainians.

The strongest Jews who arrived in Sobibor were appointed to Jewish work teams. Their job was to serve the camp staff and carry out duties related to the processing of new arrivals. Eventually, about 1,000 prisoners worked in these teams.

However, most of the Jews brought to Sobibor were murdered immediately. As they arrived by train, they were told that they had reached a transit camp in route to labor camps. Before embarking on the next part of their journey, they were to take showers and have their clothes disinfected. The men and women were separated. Children were sent with the women. The Germans ordered the victims to remove their clothing and hand over their valuables. The Jews were then marched on the run to the gas chambers. They were beaten, screamed at, and warning shots were fired at them. About 450–550 Jews were forced into the chambers at a time.

The gas chambers were sealed when they were jam-packed with Jews. Poisonous gas was then piped in. Within 20–30 minutes, all those inside were dead. Jewish work teams removed the bodies, pulled out any gold teeth, and buried the dead. The whole process, from arrival to burial, took only two or three hours. During that time, prisoners were forced to clean the railroad cars, after which the trains left and another 20 cars entered the camp.

Those Jews who were not sent to the gas chambers immediately underwent a SELEKTION process almost every day. Only a few survived for more than a few months.

The murder of Jews at Sobibor actually began before the camp was even completed. In mid-April 1942, 250 Jews were brought from the Krychow labor camp and killed in the gas chambers. The first stage of the extermination process after Sobibor was built lasted from early May to late July 1942. Jews were brought in from Czechoslovakia, GERMANY, AUSTRIA, and the Polish district of Lublin. Between 90,000–100,000 were murdered. At the end of July the transports stopped temporarily, in order to repair the railway line from Lublin to Chelm. The Germans used the break to build three more gas chambers, because they had found that the existing chambers could not hold enough people per gassing and were slowing down operations. The new chambers allowed for twice the amount of victims at one time. During that period, Stangl was transferred to TREBLINKA and Franz Reich-sleitner took over.

The transports to Sobibor were renewed by the beginning of October 1942. At the end of that year, the Germans tried to hide the killings done so far by digging up the bodies and cremating them. In March 1943 four transports from FRANCE arrived carrying 4,000 Jews. By June 70,000–80,000 Jews from Lublin and the Eastern Galicia districts and 145,000–150,000 from the GENERALGOUVERNEMENT had been deported to Sobibor. About 35,000 Jews from the NETHERLANDS arrived between March and July. They were forced to write letters to their relatives to let them know that they had arrived at a labor camp. However, after writing the letters, they were murdered just the same. By the end of October 1943, 25,000 Jews from SLOVAKIA had been murdered at the camp. The last victims, about 14,000 in all, arrived in September 1943. They came from the VILNA, MINSK, and Lida GHETTOS.

During the year and a half that Sobibor was operative, several attempts were made at prisoner escape. Some were successful, but the Germans executed many prisoners as punishment. In July and August 1943 the prisoners organized an underground group, led by Leon Feldhendler, who had been the head of the JUDENRAT in Zolkiew. Their plan was to arrange an uprising and mass escape from Sobibor. At the end of September, Soviet Jewish PRISONERS OF WAR were brought to Sobibor from Minsk. Included in that group was Lt. Aleksandr PECHERSKY, who was brought into the underground group and made its commander, with Feldhendler as his second-in-command. The group's plan was to kill the SS soldiers, take their weapons, and fight their way out of the camp. The uprising took place on October 14, 1943. The prisoners managed to kill 11 SS men and several Ukrainians. Approximately 300 prisoners were able to escape, but most of them were chased down and killed. Those prisoners who had not joined the escape were also killed. About 50 of the escapees survived the war.

In February 1943 Heinrich HIMMLER had visited Sobibor and viewed its extermination process. He then decided to transform it into a CONCENTRATION CAMP. However, after the October uprising, those plans were changed. The Germans decided to destroy Sobibor. They plowed the whole area and planted crops. A Ukrainian camp guard moved onto the site.

In 1965 eleven of the SS men who helped run Sobibor were brought to trial in Hagen, West Germany. One was sentenced to life in jail, five were given three to eight year sentences, four were acquitted, and one committed suicide. The Polish government turned Sobibor into a national memorial site.

SONDERKOMMANDO German term meaning "Special Commando," which referred to several types of "special" units during WORLD WAR II.

Originally, the term *Sonderkommando* referred to a German SS unit that carried out special tasks or mis-

"Barbers" at Birkenau sorting the hair of victims. Paris, 1945, ink and wash, David Olere. Yad Vashem Art Museum Collection, Gift of Miriam Novich

sions. Some 10 *Sonderkommando* units were also dedicated to the goal of killing Jews as sub-units of the EINSATZGRUPPEN or as a unit in CHELMNO. Those units in charge of destroying all physical evidence of the mass murders as part of AKTION 1005 were called *Sonderkommando* 1005.

The name *Sonderkommando* was also assigned to those groups of Jewish prisoners in the Nazi EXTERMINATION CAMPS who were forced to work in the GAS CHAMBERS and crematoria. *Sonderkommando* members helped prep the Jews who were about to be gassed. They cut the women's hair (sometimes doing this after the gassing). Others removed the corpses from the gas chambers, removed gold teeth and fillings, and transferred the bodies to pits or to the crematoria. Some *Sonderkommandos* cleaned the gas chambers, while others dealt with the victims' personal possessions, sorting them and readying them for shipment to GERMANY. After a few months of such gruesome work, the *Sonderkommando* men were themselves executed and replaced with new prisoners.

In October 1944 the *Sonderkommando* unit that worked in the crematoria of AUSCHWITZ-Birkenau staged its own revolt. They managed to burn down one of the crematoria and kill some of their German guards. All of these prisoners were caught and killed. However, some had authored diaries that were later found in the ruins of the crematoria. The diaries described the daily anguish of being in constant contact with murder, and begged the world to understand how the *Sonderkommando* prisoners had not willingly done

their jobs, but had been forced by the Nazis to participate in the extermination process.

A Jewish *Sonderkommando* unit was also active in the LODZ Ghetto. This group was part of the Jewish GHETTO police.

SOUSA MENDES, ARISTIDES DE (1885–1954), Portuguese diplomat in FRANCE who rescued thousands of Jews during WORLD WAR II.

In May 1940 GERMANY invaded France. Tens of thousands of REFUGEES escaped to the south of France; their hope was to cross into Portugal via SPAIN, and from there leave Europe by ship. However, to enter Portugal, the refugees needed Portuguese visas. On May 10 the Portuguese government ordered its diplomats in France to stop issuing visas to refugees trying to escape the Nazis, especially Jews.

At that point, Sousa Mendes was serving as Portugal's consul general in the southern French city of Bordeaux, where some 10,000 Jewish refugees were in need of Portuguese visas. Sousa Mendes decided to defy his government's orders and issue Portuguese transit visas—some 10,000—to all refugees who needed them. When his government discovered what he was

Aristides de Sousa Mendes

doing, Sousa Mendes was immediately recalled to Portugal.

After his return home, Sousa Mendes was stripped of his job and benefits. With no pension and 13 children to feed, he died miserable and penniless. In 1966 he was designated as RIGHTEOUS AMONG THE NATIONS by YAD VASHEM, and in 1988 the Portuguese government posthumously restored his good name.

SOVIET UNION   Country extending from Eastern Europe to easternmost Asia. As of January 1939, about three million Jews lived in the Soviet Union; about one million were murdered in the HOLOCAUST.

Following HITLER'S rise to power, GERMANY and the Soviet Union behaved as mortal enemies. One month prior to the outbreak of WORLD WAR II, however, the two countries surprised the world by signing a "non-aggression pact" (NAZI-SOVIET PACT), in which they agreed to abstain from attacking each other. This pact allowed the Germans free reign to invade POLAND without Soviet

intervention. In exchange, the Soviets were given the eastern parts of Poland and the Baltic countries of LATVIA, LITHUANIA, and ESTONIA. Over the next year the Soviets also annexed BESSARABIA and BUKOVINA, which had been under Romanian rule since World War I. Altogether, these new territories had a Jewish population of about two million. In addition, about 250,000–300,000 Jewish REFUGEES from German-occupied western Poland had fled to the Soviet Union after the war broke out. The Jews in these territories did not live under the best conditions, but at this point were spared the systematic extermination suffered by Jews under the Germans.

However, the relatively good status of the Jews in the Soviet Union did not last long. In mid-1941 the Germans decided to betray their pact with the Soviets— they secretly planned to attack the Soviet Union in Operation "Barbarossa." In preparation for their invasion, the Nazis ordered the extermination of all Jews living in those areas annexed by the Soviet Union in

Soviet recruits in Moscow

1939–1940. The Germans attacked on June 22, 1941. After the invasion, more than five million Jews came under Nazi rule—over half of Europe's Jewish population. EINSATZGRUPPEN followed the advancing army and, assisted by local collaborators and various police and regular army (WEHRMACHT) units, quickly massacred most of the Jews of the Baltic states, BELORUSSIA, and the UKRAINE by open-air shooting. The remaining Jews were put into GHETTOS, and most were murdered within 12–18 months.

The German army quickly overran the Soviet Union, which was unprepared for the onslaught. The Soviet people began to flee eastward, away from the advancing army. Those Jews who fled had a much better chance of avoiding extermination. However, most Jews could not escape. The Nazis considered the killing of the Jews within pre-1939 Soviet Union to be a military priority. As they occupied a new area, they would begin the extermination of its Jewish population, and finish the job within two–three months, at most.

The destruction of the Jews in the Soviet Union was carried out in one of several ways. Generally, the German occupiers appointed a JUDENRAT with three or four members who were important constituents of the Jewish community. A few days later the Jews were ordered to register with this council, and within a few more days or weeks, they were ordered to appear at a certain spot in town, from which they would be leaving, supposedly, for a labor camp or for Palestine. When they arrived, Germans and local Jew-haters would beat them and shoot anyone who protested or walked slowly. The Jews were then led to nearby ditches where they were to be killed. Just before the spot, they were split into groups and made to undress. Then the Jews were forced into the ditches and fired at, from all directions, by Germans with machine guns. After one group was exterminated, another would be brought in. In some cases the Germans immediately rounded up and shot the Jews, without all the interim steps. In other cases, Jews were put into lightly guarded ghettos and made to wear the Jewish badge, while the young, skilled workers would be put to hard labor outside the ghetto. These ghettos generally lasted no more than a few weeks or months—the Jews were soon taken out and shot. Sometimes, an area's Jews were forced into a temporary CONCENTRATION CAMP and forced to wear the Jewish badge. Then they would be massacred by the thousands at nearby sites (see also BADGE, JEWISH).

After the Jews of the Soviet Union were exterminated, the Germans still continued to hunt for the few who had escaped and hidden. Those that were found were immediately shot. Very few non-Jews were willing to risk their lives to help Jews because they knew that they would be punished by death. Many non-Jews collaborated with the Nazis and took part in the mass murders.

Organized Jewish resistance in the Soviet Union was limited mostly to the territory annexed from Poland in 1939. Since the Russian Revolution, all Jewish organizations were forbidden in the Soviet Union, so they did not have a basic structure for cooperation. Also, the murders took place so quickly that the Jews had no time to band together against the Germans. In addition, hundreds of thousands of Jewish men were away serving in the Russian army (many Jews who had been drafted distinguished themselves in the army; more than 160,000 won military awards), and thus were simply not around to coordinate resistance against the Germans. The only major possibility for resistance was to escape and join the Russian PARTISANS. About 10,000 Jews fought in that way. Some families also escaped to the forests and established FAMILY CAMPS.

At the end of 1942 the Soviets' luck turned with their victory over the Germans at Stalingrad; over the next two years they took back lands that had been occupied by the Nazis. For political reasons, STALIN established the JEWISH ANTI-FASCIST COMMITTEE, which became the first representative body of the Soviet Jews since the revolution. However, Jews returning to their homes in the Soviet Union were met with destruction, ANTISEMITISM, and news that their neighbors had collaborated with the Nazis. They quickly realized that the Soviet boast of having destroyed antisemitism was a fiction. This led to a growth of Jewish identity and interest—a force that eventually led to the mass immigration of Soviet Jewry to destinations world over.

SPAIN Country in Western Europe. As a non-belligerent country during WORLD WAR II, Spain became a possible refuge for Jews fleeing the Nazis. Indeed, within two years of HITLER'S rise to power in GERMANY in 1933, some 3,000 Jews had entered Spain in search of a safe haven. When the Spanish Civil War broke out in July 1936, there were about 6,000 Jews residing in Spain. During the war, which lasted until April 1939, most of the Jews left Spain. After the Civil War ended with a victory for General Francisco Franco, all Jewish organizations in Spain were shut down.

Although Hitler's army had helped Franco's Fascist forces defeat the Republicans in the Civil War, and although Spain was a member of the Anti-Comintern Pact (along with Germany), other than a few members of the Spanish legion who joined the SS, Spain did not take part in the fighting during World War II.

After FRANCE surrendered to Germany in June 1940, tens of thousands of REFUGEES flocked to the Spanish border, hoping to reach Spanish or Portuguese ports from which they would try to leave Europe by ship. In spite of strict rules about entry into Spain that were issued in 1940 and 1941, tens of thousands of refugees managed to cross the border—even if they did not possess a visa to a final destination. Refugees who missed their boats or had entered Spain without a visa were detained in the Miranda de Ebro concentration camp or transferred back to France. Jewish refugees from Germany continued to pass through Spain by train until the German authorities banned all emigration from the Reich in October 1941. During the first half of the war, some 20,000–30,000 Jews were given permission to pass through Spain.

During the summer of 1942 the Nazis began deporting Jews from France, BELGIUM, LUXEMBOURG, and the NETHERLANDS. At that point, many Jewish refugees crossed into Spain illegally. Those who were caught were arrested, and the Spanish government planned to return them to France, where they would face almost certain death. The Allies warned that the fate of these refugees would have a major impact on Allied policy on Spain. As a result of that warning, Spain announced in April 1943 that it would admit refugees, as long as some other party would provide for their care and the refugees would leave the country as fast as they could. The refugees were mainly provided for by the JOINT DISTRIBUTION COMMITTEE in Spain. Between the summer of 1942 and the fall of 1944, some 7,500 Jews fled to Spain and were given temporary refuge.

During the war, more than 4,000 Spanish Jews found themselves living in German-occupied territories; as Spanish nationals, these Jews were given protection by the Spanish government, which instructed its representatives abroad to report any situations in which Spanish citizens were mistreated, and to intervene on their behalf. However, as long as Spanish laws were not violated, the representatives were not supposed to insist that Spanish citizens be exempt from local laws. Thus, in many cases, Spanish Jews depended on the goodwill of the representatives of the Spanish government to deliver them from danger. In HUNGARY in 1944, Georgio Perlasca, an Italian national, rescued Jews in the name of Spain.

In January 1943 the German embassy in Spain told the Spanish government that it had two months to remove all of its Jewish citizens from Western Europe. Spain now had an opportunity to save the lives of 4,000 Spanish Jews—but instead of rising to the task, the government severely regulated who was to be given entry visas. As a result of these restrictions, only 800 Spanish Jews were allowed to enter Spain. After the war the Spanish government claimed that it had protected all of its Jews, and the truth about its real actions was hidden from the Spanish public.

SPEER, ALBERT (1905–1981), HITLER'S architect and German Minister of Armaments from 1942 to 1945.

Speer joined the NAZI PARTY in 1931. Soon after the Nazis rose to national power in 1933, he was given his first large contracts from the party. His work caught Hitler's eye; the *Fuehrer* personally gave Speer assignments. Soon, the two developed a special relationship.

Albert Speer (on right) visiting forced laborers from Mauthausen in the Hermann Goering Works, Linz

Hitler gave Speer great freedoms, and Speer gave Hitler his complete allegiance.

In 1934 Speer became Hitler's personal architect. He was charged with creating architectural plans for BERLIN (Hitler and Speer seemed to have the same taste in grandiose monuments) and building a permanent structure for party events. In 1937 Speer was named inspector general of construction in Berlin. In this position, he gained access to the apartments vacated by Berlin's Jews in 1939 and again in 1941, after DEPORTATIONS began to the east.

In 1942 Speer was named minister of armaments and in 1943 minister of armaments and war production. In both these posts, he utilized forced laborers and confiscated Jewish property to achieve his goals. He raised armaments production to an extraordinary level, even as Allied air attacks were increasing.

By the end of the war, Speer and Hitler had fallen out. Speer even claimed that he planned to assassinate Hitler; however, he probably did not mean to go through with it.

After the war, Speer was put on trial by the International Military Tribunal at Nuremberg. He was charged with war crimes and for using forced laborers and CONCENTRATION CAMP prisoners in his work. Unlike most other war crimes defendants, Speer admitted responsibility for the actions of the Nazis, even those he claimed he was not directly aware of. Although he claimed that he knew nothing about the mass exterminations in Eastern Europe, Speer expressed regret for his crimes. He was found guilty of war crimes and CRIMES AGAINST HUMANITY, and sentenced to 20 years in prison—presumably, a light sentence due to his admission of guilt and regret. After his release, Speer published his memoirs, in which he once again expressed remorse for his actions.

SPORRENBERG, JACOB (1902–1952), SS and Police Leader in the Lublin district who organized "ERNTEFEST"—the operation in which some 43,000 Jews imprisoned in the camps of MAJDANEK, TRAWNIKI, and PONIATOWA were massacred.

SPRACHREGELUNG (lit. "language regulation"), euphemistic language used by the Nazis to refer to their anti-Jewish policies in order to conceal the true nature of those acts. For example, the neutral term "Final Solution" actually referred to the annihilation of European Jewry.

SS (*Schutzstaffel*, Protection Squad), elite organization within the THIRD REICH that was responsible for the "Final Solution" and other acts of terror and destruction.

The SS was originally instituted in March 1923 as Adolf HITLER's personal bodyguard corps. It was an exclusive group of fighters that competed with the NAZI PARTY's other militia, the Storm Troopers (SA), for superiority. SS members were subject to strict military discipline and were expected to swear complete loyalty to Hitler and the Nazis.

In January 1929 Nazi leader Heinrich HIMMLER became the national head of the SS, or "Reich Leader of the SS." Under his leadership, the SS increased fantastically in size and strength. By the time Hitler rose to national power in GERMANY in 1933, Himmler had made the SS the dominant organization within the Reich. He created many new departments within the SS organization, such as an intelligence department called the Security Service (SD), which he put under

SS commander Heinrich Himmler with senior SS officers, Dachau, January 20, 1941

the authority of Reinhard HEYDRICH; and the RACE AND RESETTLEMENT MAIN OFFICE, which was in charge of all racial purity issues. Himmler also took charge of the security of the Nazi Party headquarters and leaders.

Himmler transformed the SS into the most elite group within the Reich. In order to become an SS officer, a person had to prove his "racial purity" and that of his wife back to the eighteenth century; had to look appropriately Aryan; and had to commit unconditional allegiance to Hitler. SS members wore uniforms that helped cloak them in a dark aura of fearlessness: black uniform, black cap, death's head badge, death's head "ring of honor," and officer's dagger, which was engraved with the SS's motto: "Loyalty is My Honor."

In 1934 Himmler concentrated the power of the SS. He crushed the original SA leadership, taking the militia under SS command, and took control of the GESTAPO (the Reich's secret political police) and all CONCENTRATION CAMPS in Germany. He put the camps under the authority of Theodore EICKE, the head of the SS Guard and DEATH'S HEAD UNITS. The Death's Head Units were the source of SS military units that later became known as the *Waffen*-SS. Himmler also developed a strategy for bringing key Germans into the SS as "honorary leaders" and recruiting low-level police officers.

Over the next few years, Himmler instituted young officers' schools and special SS police units, known as EINSATZGRUPPEN. In 1939 he created special SS courts, which legally allowed the SS to ignore established German law.

After WORLD WAR II broke out in September 1939, the SS grew enormously. SD units, *Einsatzgruppen,* and local SS offices carried out the Reich's anti-Jewish policies all over occupied Europe. The Reich Security Main Office (REICHSSICHERHEITSHAUPTAMT, RSHA) was soon established, which was in charge of internal Reich security, killing enemies of the Nazis, and sending prisoners to concentration camps.

SS officers were in charge of the planning of the "Final Solution" — the extermination of European Jewry. When Germany invaded the SOVIET UNION in June 1941, the *Einsatzgruppen* mobile killing units spearheaded the execution of hundreds of thousands of Jews. The RSHA's Jewish affairs expert, Adolf EICHMANN, planned and supervised the DEPORTATION of Jews from their homes to GHETTOS, and then on to their deaths at concentration or EXTERMINATION CAMPS. SS officers were also directly responsible for the management of those camps, where millions of Jews were murdered by poison gas. Eventually, the SS included millions of soldiers and officers.

After the war, the SS was declared to be a criminal organization by the International Military Tribunal at NUREMBERG. Members of all its sub-organizations, including the *Gestapo*, SD, Death's Head Units, *Waffen*-SS, and others were tried as war criminals. Some were sentenced to death or life imprisonment, but many were let free.

ST. LOUIS German ship carrying Jewish REFUGEES to Cuba in 1939. Before the refugees could land, the Cuban government voided their landing permits and denied them entry.

The "St. Louis"

The *St. Louis* left HAMBURG for Cuba on May 13, 1939 with 936 passengers, most of them Jewish. All possessed landing certificates for Cuba, arranged for by Manuel Benitez Gonzalez, the Cuban Director General of Immigration. Legally, the certificates were free, but Gonzalez took money for them. Jealousy of Gonzalez's gain, local dislike of Jewish immigration, and the government's fascist tendencies led them to cancel the certificates on May 5, 1939, after they had been purchased, but before the departure of the ship. Thus, many passengers hoped the Cubans would continue to honor the certificates.

When the ship reached Havana on May 27 its passengers were denied entry. The American Jewish JOINT DISTRIBUTION COMMITTEE (JDC) tried to negotiate on their behalf, but the Cuban president insisted that the ship leave. The ship left Havana on June 2, and steered in circles while negotiations continued. An agreement was reached whereby the JDC would pay $453,000 in exchange for entry into Cuba. The JDC could not meet its deadline, however, and the ship returned to Europe, where the refugees were taken in by other European countries. Most were later murdered by the Nazis.

STAB IN THE BACK MYTH (*Dolchstosslegende*), groundless myth claiming that the German army had not been defeated militarily in World War I, but rather

Süddeutsche Monatshefte
Heft 7. Jahrg. 21   April 1924

DER DOLCHSTOSS

Süddeutsche Monatshefte G. m. b. H., München
Preis Goldmark 1.10.

Illustration depicting the stab in the back legend, Suddeutschen Monatsheftel, April 1924

was forced to stop fighting by the defeatist activities of the liberals, Socialists, and Jews.

STAHLECKER, FRANZ WALTER   (1900–1942), ss officer and commander of an EINSATZGRUPPE.

Stahlecker joined the NAZI PARTY in 1932. He then served in the police, and in 1934, became chief of police in the Wuerttemberg region. Soon he moved to the Security Service (SD) main office, and in 1938—after GERMANY annexed AUSTRIA—he became the SD chief of the Danube (VIENNA) district. He kept this position even after he was promoted to the rank of *Standartenfuehrer* and became the Higher SS and Police Leader of the Protectorate of Bohemia and Moravia (see BOHEMIA AND MORAVIA, PROTECTORATE OF.) In 1940 Stahlecker was sent to NORWAY to serve as Higher SS and Police Leader there; he was also promoted to SS-*Oberfuehrer*.

When Germany invaded the SOVIET UNION in June 1941, Stahlecker became a *Brigadefuehrer* in the SS and a major general in the police. He was appointed com-

manding officer of *Einsatzgruppe* A, which functioned in the Northern Command—an area consisting of the Baltic States and the region west of Leningrad. His killing unit massacred Jews and other Soviet citizens. In November 1941 Stahlecker was made Higher SS and Police Leader of REICHSKOMMISSARIAT OSTLAND, an area including ESTONIA, LATVIA, LITHUANIA, and BELORUSSIA. He was killed on March 23, 1942 in a battle with Soviet PARTISANS.

STALIN, JOSEPH VISSARIONOVICH   (1879–1953), Ruler of the SOVIET UNION. After the Russian Revolution of 1917, Stalin became a prominent member of the Bolshevik Party. When Lenin died in 1924, Stalin fought tooth and nail to replace him as Soviet premier. By 1928, he rose to undisputed leadership.

As soon as he came to power, Stalin called for a Soviet industrial revolution. In 1929 he took control of the secret police. Stalin used "total terror" to impose his radical policies on his constituents. Anyone suspected of disagreeing with him was put in jail. Beginning in 1935, Stalin subjected many of his opponents to "show trials" in order to discourage opposition—based on trumped up charges, these former Communist leaders were tried for conspiracy, and many were executed. During the late 1930s, Stalin launched a purge of millions of alleged opponents. An entire generation of Communists was destroyed. ANTISEMITISM became a secret, yet major, part of their ideology.

In August 1939 Stalin shocked the world by signing a non-aggression agreement with his country's former enemy, GERMANY, called the NAZI-SOVIET PACT. In June 1941 HITLER betrayed that alliance and invaded the Soviet Union. During 1941 and 1942, the Soviet army suffered colossal defeats at the hands of the Germans, but Stalin eventually turned the war around. Between 1943 and 1945, Stalin met with Western leaders at conferences in Tehran, Yalta, and Potsdam, where, as imminent victors, they shaped Europe's future map.

In 1947 Stalin extended his support to the establishment of a Jewish state in Israel; apparently, he hoped that it would become a Soviet satellite state. However, when that did not come true by the end of 1948, Stalin withdrew his support and began implementing antisemitic measures in the Soviet Union. All Jewish organizations were dissolved, Jewish leaders were rounded up and executed, and many Jews were deported to Siberia. In 1953 Stalin dreamed up the "Doctors' Plot," in which he accused several Jewish doctors of trying to

Joseph Stalin

poison him. Stalin began preparing for the deportation of Soviet Jewry—but died before the expulsion could be implemented.

STANGL, FRANZ (1908–1971), Nazi police officer and commander of EXTERMINATION CAMPS. Born in AUSTRIA, Stangl joined the Austrian police in 1931 and became a criminal investigations officer in the political

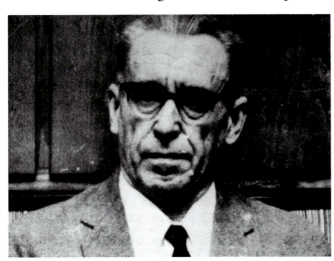

Franz Stangl during his trial, December 1970

division. In 1940 Stangl joined the EUTHANASIA PRO-GRAM at its Hartheim castle institute—one of six centers where handicapped, mentally disabled, and other "asocial" Germans were killed.

In March 1942 Stangl became commandant of the SOBIBOR extermination camp in POLAND. Later that year he became commandant of TREBLINKA where he was responsible for the deaths of 870,000 Jews. After the prisoner revolt in Treblinka in September 1943, Stangl and his staff were transferred to Trieste, ITALY to organize anti-partisan actions. He also spent time at the San Sabba CONCENTRATION CAMP.

After the war Stangl returned to Austria, where he was arrested by the Americans for being an SS member (they did not know that he had participated in the extermination of Jews). However, Stangl was found out when the Americans began investigating the Euthanasia Program. About to be charged in May 1948, Stangl escaped to Rome, Syria, and eventually Brazil where he and his family lived under their own names until discovered in 1967. Stangl was tried in GERMANY and sentenced to life in prison, where he died in 1971.

STARACHOWICE Labor camp located in the Polish town of Starachowice.

Before WORLD WAR II, Starachowice housed armaments factories and an iron-ore mine. When the Germans occupied Starachowice on September 9, 1939, they took over the factories and the mine and renamed them the Hermann Goering Works (*Hermann Goering Werke*). They then rounded up the town's Jewish males from the ages of 17–60, and used them as forced laborers on the site. The workers were given an extremely low pay of 55 groszy an hour, plus a bowl of soup during work hours.

In February 1941 the Germans established an open GHETTO in Starachowice that also took in Jews from the towns of Plock and LODZ. The ghetto was liquidated on October 27 of that same year; approximately 200 Jews were shot on the spot. Of those that remained, the stronger ones were moved to a nearby labor camp that had already been prepared for their coming, *Julag* I. The rest were deported to the EXTERMINATION CAMP at TRE-BLINKA. Those Jews who had been working in the armaments factories were also moved to *Julag* I.

About 8,000 Jews passed through *Julag* I. Nine percent died in rampant typhus epidemics, or were shot as the result of a SELEKTION. The camp had about 5,000 prisoners at a time; every once in a while prisoners from MAJDANEK, PLASZOW, and other places would be brought to work there to replenish the manpower.

In the summer of 1943, the prisoners working in the factories were moved to yet another camp, called *Julag* II. About 5,000 prisoners passed through *Julag* II altogether and seven percent were shot or died of typhus. This camp averaged about 3,000 prisoners at a time.

In July 1944 the Germans began to liquidate the labor camp. When the prisoners saw what was happening, many tried to escape; the Ukrainian guards killed 300 immediately, and caught and executed those who had escaped. The other 1,500 prisoners were deported to AUSCHWITZ.

STATUT DES JUIFS

STATUT DES JUIFS (Jewish Law), anti-Jewish laws passed by the collaborating French Vichy government in two stages in October 1940 and June 1941. These laws were created purely on the initiative of the French government and not by the Nazis themselves.

On October 3, 1940 the government passed its first widespread ANTI-JEWISH LEGISLATION. This included an even stricter definition of who was a Jew than the Nazis allowed: under Vichy, someone was Jewish if he or she had three Jewish grandparents, or two Jewish grandparents if his or her spouse was also Jewish. The first Jewish Law also called for the drastic cutback of Jewish involvement in French society. Jews were to be excluded from the army officer corps and noncommissioned officer posts, top government administration positions, and any other job that influenced public opinion. They were only allowed to hold low-level public-service jobs if they had fought in World War I or distinguished themselves in battle in 1939–1940, and they were limited within liberal professions.

The second Jewish Law was issued on June 2, 1941. It made the definition of a Jew even more rigid, and called for the removal of Jews from industry, business, and liberal professions. Only a few Jews were exempted from these cutbacks. (for more on Vichy, see also FRANCE.)

STAUFFENBERG, CLAUS COUNT SCHENK VON

STAUFFENBERG, CLAUS COUNT SCHENK VON (1907–1944), Key figure in the German assassination plot against Adolf HITLER.

A career soldier, Stauffenberg was at first fascinated by NATIONAL SOCIALISM. However, after the terribly destructive KRISTALLNACHT pogrom of November 1938, he began to question Hitler's persecution of German Jewry. His disgust for Hitler's treatment of Jews and Slavs grew after the German invasion of the SOVIET UNION in 1941. In April 1943 Stauffenberg was badly wounded while serving as a lieutenant colonel in Africa. During his recovery, he came to the conclusion that Hitler needed to be done away with.

In October 1943 Stauffenberg was appointed chief of staff at the General Army Office. In that position, Stauffenberg was able to bring together many of Hitler's opponents and plan a coup. After being promoted to colonel and placed on the staff of the Reserve Army Commander Friedrich Fromm, Stauffenberg decided that the time was now right to eliminate the *Fuehrer*. On July 20, 1944 Stauffenberg brought a briefcase with a time bomb into Hitler's command barracks of the "*Wolfsschanze*" (in east Prussia) where Fromm was supposed to be meeting Hitler. Since Stauffenberg left the room and flew to BERLIN before the bomb exploded, he did not know that the assassination bid failed. Stauffenberg and his co-conspirators were arrested and promptly executed.

STERN, SAMU

STERN, SAMU (1874–1947), Jewish community leader in HUNGARY. Born in Janoshaza, Stern was a very successful banker. In addition, he held the title of advisor to the Hungarian royal court. He served for many years as the president of the Jewish community in Pest, which was the largest Jewish community in Hungary, and as the head of the National Bureau of the Jews of Hungary, which was the chief umbrella organization of Hungary's Neolog (Conservative) congregations. As a rich, upper-class Jewish Hungarian, Stern had very good dealings with the Hungarian aristocracy, including the noble and ruling class. He considered himself to be a "*Magyar* (Hungarian) of the Israelite faith," putting his Hungarian identity before his Jewish one; thus, he was very patriotic to his country and did not support the Zionist idea of establishing a Jewish state in Palestine.

After GERMANY occupied Hungary in March 1944, Stern was appointed the head of the country's central JUDENRAT (in Hungarian, *Kozponti Zsido Tanacs*). He held this post until late October 1944, at which time he went into hiding.

Although Stern was clearly a supporter of Jewish causes, when the Germans invaded Hungary, he was not up to the challenge. He dealt with them and with their Hungarian collaborators in an unimaginative and compliant manner. After the war he wrote his memoirs.

STERNBUCH, RECHA (1905–1971), Swiss Jewish rescue activist who served, along with her husband, Isaac, as Swiss representative of the VA'AD HA-HATSALA—the rescue committee of the American Union of Orthodox Rabbis.

The Sternbuchs began their rescue activities by helping Jewish REFUGEES in SWITZERLAND. Next, they headed the "Relief Organization for Jewish Refugees in Shanghai" set up in 1941 to help rabbis and *yeshiva* students who had escaped to SHANGHAI, China (see also RESCUE OF POLISH JEWS VIA EAST ASIA). Later they changed the organization's name to "Relief Organization for Jewish Refugees Abroad." Under that heading, they sent aid packages to Jews in POLAND and Czechoslovakia; tried to rescue Jews by obtaining Latin American passports for them; kept in close contact with Jewish leaders in occupied HUNGARY and SLOVAKIA; and kept tabs on what was happening throughout occupied Europe.

In September 1942 the Sternbuchs gave information to Jewish leaders in the UNITED STATES about the mass DEPORTATIONS from the WARSAW Ghetto and begged them to get help from the American authorities. Later, the couple participated in negotiations with the Nazis that ultimately led to the transfer of 1,200 Jews from THERESIENSTADT to Switzerland in February 1945. After the war, Recha Sternbuch devoted herself to retrieving surviving Jewish children from non-Jewish orphanages, convents, and private homes.

STRASSHOF CONCENTRATION CAMP located near VIENNA. In June 1944 almost 21,000 Jews from HUNGARY were brought to Strasshof as a result of an agreement made between Senior SS Officer Adolf EICHMANN and the leaders of the RELIEF AND RESCUE COMMITTEE OF BUDAPEST. This agreement came about in mid-June 1944, when Eichmann offered to put 30,000 Hungarian Jews "on ice" in AUSTRIA, as a gesture of his good will in order to help facilitate the exchange offer he had made called "Blood for Goods." According to the "Blood for Goods" offer, Eichmann was to spare "one million" Hungarian Jews in exchange for certain goods, including 10,000 trucks. The deal ultimately failed; but while it was still a possibility, five million Swiss francs were paid to the SS in exchange for the 21,000 Jews sent to Strasshof. They were transferred from the GHETTOS of Baja, Debrecen, Szeged, and Szolnok, and made to work as forced laborers in industry and agriculture in eastern Austria. Almost all of the Jews at Strasshof, including old people and children, survived the war.

STREICHER, JULIUS (1856–1946), NAZI PARTY leader and founder of *Der* STUERMER, the Nazi weekly newspaper.

Antisemitic placard bearing Julius Streicher's portrait

Streicher was born in Augsburg, Bavaria. He became an elementary school teacher, and distinguished himself during World War I for brave military service. He was eventually removed from his teaching position for inappropriate behavior; among other things, Streicher had his students shout "HEIL HITLER" when he entered the classroom.

Streicher was one of the founders of the German Socialist Party, which soon united with the Nazi Party. He then served as a member of the Bavarian legislature from 1924–1932. When HITLER came to power in January 1933, Streicher was elected to represent the Nazi Party in the German parliament (REICHSTAG). He soon held the rank of general in the Storm Troopers (SA). Streicher used his influence to keep Jews out of public places, and tried to convince the authorities to institute GHETTOS.

Streicher, a rabid antisemite, founded his newspaper, *Der Stuermer,* in 1923. The name *Der Stuermer* means "The Attacker" and Streicher used the paper as a forum for violently attacking Jews. Every issue contained stories about how Jews had attacked and stolen from Germans, killed Jesus, raped young girls, and other such antisemitic, pornographic drivel. Some Nazi leaders felt the need to disassociate themselves from Streicher, who was constantly plagued with libel suits, bad business deals, and pornographic scandals. They even closed down the newspaper in NUREMBERG, where Streicher had his main following. In 1939 Hitler forbade him from making public statements representing the Nazis and in 1940 Hermann GOERING launched an investigation into Streicher's dealings. As a result of this investigation, Streicher was removed from all party positions.

After the war Streicher was discovered and arrested by American soldiers. He was convicted at the NUREMBERG TRIALS of CRIMES AGAINST HUMANITY and sentenced to death. As Streicher was about to be hanged on October 16, 1946, he shouted out the words "*Heil Hitler*" and "*Purimfest*," alluding to the Jewish festival of Purim, which recalls the Jews' victory over their enemy Haman, who was also hanged.

STROOP, JUERGEN

(1895–1951), Higher SS and Police Leader responsible for crushing the WARSAW GHETTO UPRISING. Stroop joined the NAZI PARTY and SS in 1932. He quickly rose through the ranks, and by 1939 was commander of a police unit. When GERMANY invaded the SOVIET UNION in 1941, Stroop volunteered for combat. After being wounded, he moved to the police in the occupied Soviet Union, where he focused

Higher SS and Police Leader Juergen Stroop (second from left) with a Jew caught during the Warsaw Ghetto Uprising, spring 1943

on persecuting the population, especially local PARTISANS.

In April 1943 Stroop was sent to WARSAW to participate in the liquidation of the GHETTO—he took over as commander when the ghetto's Jews launched an uprising. Stroop treated the action against the uprising as if it were a military campaign. He brought in massive amounts of troops and sent reports to Nazi headquarters daily. On May 16 Stroop ended the "Great Operation" by destroying the main Warsaw synagogue. According to his final report, 56,065 Jews had been caught, of whom 13,929 were exterminated and 5,000–6,000 killed in the bombing and burning.

After Warsaw, Stroop left for GREECE, where he served as Higher SS and Police Leader, and supervised the DEPORTATION of Greek Jews to AUSCHWITZ. After the war, he was tried and condemned by two different courts. Stroop was hanged in Warsaw in 1951.

STRUMA

Boat that attempted to bring Jewish REFUGEES to Palestine in late 1941.

On December 12, 1941, 769 Jews boarded the *Struma* in the Romanian port of Constanta. They had been witness to the massacre of Jews in BESSARABIA and BUKOVINA, and were desperately trying to escape Europe. The *Struma*'s first stop was to be Istanbul, Turkey—despite the fact that the passengers had no visas for Turkey. The boat was hardly seaworthy, and barely reached Istanbul. When it finally arrived, the passengers were not allowed to disembark. For ten weeks, they were restricted to the boat. The Turks refused to transfer them to a transit camp on land, even though the camp would have been funded in complete by Jewish organizations. In addition, nothing could convince the British authorities to admit these refugees into Palestine, because they did not want to set a precedent for similar escapes.

O amabilă invitație la moarte. (Copyright)

O amabilă invitație la moarte. (Copyright)

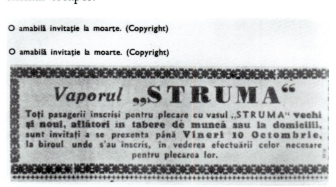

Obituary notice for the drowned Struma passengers

On February 23, 1942 the Turkish authorities took matters into their own hands: they towed the old ship to the open sea, without fuel, food, or water. Within hours, the ship was torpedoed, most probably by a Soviet submarine that mistook it for an enemy German ship. All but one refugee drowned. (see also ALIYA BET.)

STUERMER, DER   (The Attacker), Nazi weekly newspaper founded by Julius STREICHER. It was first published in the spring of 1923, and shut down on February 1, 1945, after a major drop in circulation.

Issue of Der Stuermer focusing on the slur that Jews commit "Ritual Murder," April 1937

Originally, Streicher used the newspaper to attack his local party enemies. In the years before HITLER came to power, the paper dealt mostly in sex scandals, crime, and political sensationalism. Over time, *Der Stuermer* became more antisemitic. By the time Hitler took power in 1933 the newspaper had a following of 25,000 and was virulently anti-Jewish. By 1938 the paper was selling 500,000 copies a week. Germans would gather around newspaper displays protected by *Stuermer* guards.

The paper included easy-to-read articles that were low-level and hostile. However, the highlight of *Der Stuermer* was the antisemitic cartoons drawn by Philipp Rupprecht ("Fips"), which depicted contorted, ugly Jews with hooked noses, huge ears and lips, hairy bodies, and crooked legs. He also portrayed the Jews as sexually perverted. Fips succeeded in creating an aura of hatred around Jews by distorting and mocking them.

Nine special editions were put out after 1933, coinciding each year with the annual NUREMBERG rally. These editions helped strengthen the Nazi claim that the Jews were less than human.

STULPNAGEL, KARL HEINRICH VON   (1886–1944), German general who participated in the conspiracy against Adolf HITLER in 1944.

Stulpnagel began his army career in 1904. By 1935 he had reached the rank of general-major, and when WORLD WAR II broke out, he became a general. After GERMANY vanquished FRANCE in mid-1940, Stulpnagel was in charge of the cease-fire negotiations between the two countries.

In February 1942 Stulpnagel was appointed military governor of France. Stulpnagel was a harsh ruler who wanted to suppress the French Resistance; he often had hostages and their families killed. However, he had never committed himself totally to Nazism, and as early as 1939, Stulpnagel had been in on a plot to overthrow Hitler. In 1944 Stulpnagel became a leader of the group of army officers who opposed the Nazis and wanted to overpower them before the Allies invaded Europe. In conjunction with an assassination attempt on Hitler's life, Stulpnagel arrested in PARIS some 1,200 members of the GESTAPO, SD, and SS. However, the bomb plot failed, ruining Stulpnagel's plans. He was stripped of his position, and called back to BERLIN. On the way, Stulpnagel tried to take his own life, but was unsuccessful. Instead, he was hanged by the Nazis in August 1944.

STUTTHOF   CONCENTRATION CAMP in northern POLAND, located 22 miles east of DANZIG. Stutthof was first set up in September 1939 as a civilian prison camp. In January 1942 its status changed to that of a concentration camp. Altogether, some 115,000 prisoners passed through Stutthof; 65,000 of them perished, while another 22,000 were transferred to other concentration camps.

Stutthof, which eventually included several dozen

The crematoria at Stutthof after the liberation, August 1945

FORCED LABOR sub-camps all over northern and central Poland, was guarded by members of the SS DEATH'S HEAD UNITS and Ukrainian collaborators (see also UKRAINIAN AUXILIARY POLICE).

At the beginning of its existence, there were very few Jewish prisoners at Stutthof. Most of the prisoners were non-Jewish Poles from Danzig and Pomerania. Later, more Poles arrived from WARSAW and from all over northern Poland. Large groups of Soviets, Norwegians, Danes, and others soon joined them. Large numbers of Jews began arriving in 1944. These were mainly women who had been transferred from labor camps in the Baltic states or from AUSCHWITZ.

The conditions at Stutthof were unbearable; starvation and disease were rampant, and the prisoners were made to do hard labor. In fact, so many of the prisoners died at Stutthof that it was almost like an EXTERMINATION CAMP. In addition, prisoners were often executed, usually those who had taken part in the resistance movement. Selections would also take place from time to time (see also SELEKTION). Those prisoners who were found to be too sick to work anymore were exterminated in the camp's GAS CHAMBER. Wounded or sick prisoners recuperating in the camp infirmary were often killed by the doctors there.

By late 1944 the Soviet army was approaching. At that point, in the dead of winter, the SS sent some 50,000 prisoners on forced DEATH MARCHES towards the west.

Tens of thousands of the prisoners died or were murdered en route. Other groups of prisoners were evacuated by sea in small boats; many drowned along the way. The main camp at Stutthof was liberated by the Soviet army on May 9, 1945.

SUGIHARA, SEMPO   (1900–1986), Japanese consul in KOVNO, LITHUANIA, who rescued Jewish REFUGEES during WORLD WAR II.

Sugihara became consul in Kovno in the fall of 1939, soon after GERMANY had invaded and conquered nearby POLAND. Thousands of Jewish refugees fled to Lithuania, which at that point was still operating as an independent country. However, in June 1940 the SOVIET UNION took control of Lithuania, prompting many refugees to seek some means of escape.

In early August 1940, just weeks before all foreign diplomats were supposed to leave Lithuania on the orders of the Soviet authorities, Sugihara was contacted by Dr. Zorah WARHAFTIG, the director of the Jewish Agency's Palestine Office in Kovno. Warhaftig described an escape plan to Sugihara, whereby Jewish refugees would travel to Curacao, an island in the Caribbean controlled by the Dutch, where permits were not needed in order to enter. To get to Curacao, the refugees would need to travel through the Soviet Union and Japan. Thus, Warhaftig asked Sugihara to give the refugees the necessary transit visas so that they could travel via Japan. The Soviet authorities had already agreed to let the refugees leave and travel through the Soviet Union—if the refugees could obtain visas for Japan.

Japan, which was a German ally, refused to approve

Sempo Sugihara

the plan. However, in a bold and rare act of diplomatic resistance, Sugihara decided to go against his government's orders and begin issuing transit visas. Over the next few weeks, he handed out some 1,600 visas, saving as many lives. Some of the most famous refugees to use Sugihara's visas were the rabbinical students from the MIR yeshiva, who traveled through Japan to SHANGHAI, China, where they spent the rest of the war in safety.

By the end of August Sugihara was kicked out of Lithuania, and transferred to another Japanese consulate. When he returned to Japan in 1947, he was asked to leave the Foreign Service because of his act of defiance in 1940. In 1984 Sugihara was designated as RIGHTEOUS AMONG THE NATIONS by YAD VASHEM. (see also RESCUE OF POLISH JEWS VIA EAST ASIA.)

SURVIVORS   Jews who survived the HOLOCAUST period in Nazi-occupied Europe. It is obvious that Jews who managed to live through the mass exterminations carried out by the Nazis are "Survivors." However,

sometimes the term "Survivor" also includes Jews who did not actually come into direct contact with the Nazi murder machine: some Jews fled GERMANY before the Nazis rose to national power; others escaped Germany after Adolf HITLER came to power but before he and the Nazis put the "Final Solution" into effect; while others were persecuted not by the Nazis themselves, but by the partners of the Nazis (in Nazi satellite countries or by Nazi collaborators). All of these are often considered to be survivors as well.

Because it is difficult to define the term "Survivor," it is extremely hard to say exactly how many Jews survived the Holocaust. It is possible, nonetheless, to make an estimation by working backwards. Right before the Nazis began carrying out the "Final Solution," some 9.8 million Jews lived in areas dominated by the Nazis and their partners. Approximately six million of them were murdered, leaving less then four million Jews who could be considered survivors.

Jews who survived the Holocaust carried the baggage

Child survivors in the Feldafing Displaced Persons' camp

Two survivors in Buchenwald, 1945

of very painful memories, especially if their lives had been in direct danger or if they had lost family and friends. Despite this, many survivors built new lives for themselves, establishing new families and careers. Some Holocaust survivors have contributed much to society at large and have lived full post-Holocaust lives. However, there are also survivors so haunted by their Holocaust experiences that they needed serious psychological help, and even then some could not move past their trauma.

For many years after WORLD WAR II many survivors felt that they could not describe their experiences to those who had not gone through the Holocaust. Some were able to record testimony about their experiences or publish their memoirs. The writing of such memoirs became more widespread during the 1970s, and continued to increase in the past two decades. These accounts are essential to our understanding of the Holocaust experience.

SURVIVORS, SECOND GENERATION OF
Children born after WORLD WAR II to parents who survived Nazi persecution during the HOLOCAUST.

During the 1960s and 1970s, children of Holocaust SURVIVORS began exploring what it meant to be "children of Holocaust survivors." Psychological studies were done on this "second generation of survivors" to determine how their parents' nightmarish experiences affected their lives. At the same time, awareness groups developed, in which children of survivors could explore their feelings in a group that shared those feelings. In November 1979 the "second generation" met nation- ally at the "First Conference on Children of Holocaust Survivors", which generated the creation of support groups all over the United States.

Many members of the "second generation" have gone beyond the suffering they experienced as children of Holocaust survivors, to proactively commemorate the lives and way of life lost during the Holocaust. They do historical research on Jewish life in pre-war Europe and on the Holocaust itself; educate people about the Holocaust and combat Holocaust denial, RACISM, and ANTISEMITISM; revitalize Yiddish culture; become politically active, whether with regard to finding and prosecuting Nazis, or by taking up some Jewish or humanitarian cause; and creatively explore the effect of the Holocaust on themselves and their families through art, literature, and theater. (see also HOLO-CAUST, DENIAL OF.)

SUTZKEVER, ABRAHAM
(b. 1913), Yiddish poet and PARTISAN fighter from BELORUSSIA. Sutzkever moved to VILNA in 1922. He authored poetry from the age of 14; his first poem was published in a literary magazine in 1934. From 1934–1941, Sutzkever contributed much to Yiddish literature.

The Nazis invaded Vilna in June 1941 and established the Vilna GHETTO soon thereafter. Sutzkever lived in the ghetto until September 1943, during which time he wrote more than 80 poems. Many of these poems focus on the events that Sutzkever himself experienced in the ghetto, and its communal and cultural life. Sutzkever was very involved in choosing the material to be performed in the ghetto theater and ran a literary circle there for young people. While doing FORCED LABOR, he was made to sort through the collections of books and manuscripts in the library of the Yiddish Institute (YIVO), which was located outside the ghetto. Along with Shmaryahu Kaczerginski and others, Sutzkever took the opportunity of being outside the ghetto to obtain weapons and smuggle them in. He also composed many of his wartime poems while working at the YIVO building. He won the Writers' Association literary prize in July 1942 for his dramatic poem, "Child of the Tomb." In February 1943 he penned the famous poem "Kol Nidre," that described the liquidation of Vilna's "small ghetto" on the High Holy Day of Yom Kippur, 1941.

On September 12 he and his wife, along with Shmaryahu Kaczerginski, fled the ghetto for the forest, where they joined the partisans. Sutzkever served with the Voroshilov Brigade in the Naroch Forest; at that time he kept a record of testimonies about the crimes committed by Nazis. He also chronicled the partisan movement's history in the area.

On March 12, 1944 Sutzkever was flown from the Naroch Forest to Moscow, where he stayed until he testified on behalf of the Soviet prosecution at the NUREMBERG TRIAL of 1946. The next year, Sutzkever immigrated to Israel. He continued to write both poetry and prose, with the HOLOCAUST and Israel as his major themes.

SWASTIKA   The twisted cross, which served as the symbol of the NAZI PARTY.

An ancient symbol, the swastika has been discovered by archeologists in the ruins of Egypt, Troy, China, and India. It was even used as a decoration in the synagogues of ancient Israel. The name swastika comes from the Sanskrit language of India, where the symbol was

The German eagle holding the Nazi swastika

used as a sign of fertility. German *volkist* activists regarded the swastika as a symbol of the Germanic past.

The idea of taking on the swastika as the symbol of the Nazis came from Adolf HITLER himself. In fact, as a representative symbol, the swastika wielded a huge amount of power throughout Europe and all over the world: it roused and galvanized the masses of Nazi followers, and terrified both the Nazis' victims and the innocent bystanders of the world.

SWEDEN   Scandinavian country. Sweden had been neutral since the mid-nineteenth century, and wanted to remain neutral during WORLD WAR II. In fact, it successfully avoided entering the war. However, depending on the course of the war, the Swedes sometimes tended to act more pro-German, while at other times they supported the policies of the Allies. This affected their attitude towards Jewish REFUGEES.

At the beginning of the war, Sweden's neutrality swayed in GERMANY'S favor. After the Germans invaded NORWAY and DENMARK in April 1940, Sweden was surrounded by Germans. Furthermore, the British sea blockade cut Sweden off from the rest of the world. As a result, the Swedish government was forced to depend on Germany for necessary materials, while they gave Germany iron ore, a vital war industry product. Throughout 1940 Sweden allowed Germany the use of its railroads and coastal waters to move soldiers and war materials to Norway; in exchange, Germany did not try to directly influence Swedish rule. By the spring of 1941, because of their plans to invade the SOVIET UNION, Germany tightened its rein on Sweden. After the German attack on the Soviet Union in June, the Swedes felt compelled to give in to German demands to let them transport soldiers and materials through Sweden to Germany's ally, FINLAND.

By the winter of 1942–1943, the Allies defeated Germany in battles at North Africa and Stalingrad. This empowered Sweden to tip their policy away from Germany, in favor of the Allies. In May 1943 Sweden reopened trade relations with the Allies, and in July, the Swedish government announced that it would no longer permit Germany to transfer soldiers or war materials across their country. By 1944 Sweden was clearly favoring the Allies, without halting their trade with Germany.

Before World War II, there were 7,000 Jews in Sweden, most of them living in the capital, Stockholm. However, when Jewish refugees wanted to enter the country, Swedish authorities limited immigration. Thousands of Jewish refugees asked to be allowed to enter on a temporary basis, but most were refused. The Swedish Jewish community tried to help these Jewish refugees by establishing several refugee relief committees, some in conjunction with non-Jews.

As Sweden's attitude towards the Germans changed during the war, so did their attitude towards refugees. Sweden took in tens of thousands of Norwegians and Finns, including 20,000 Finnish children. When the Nazis began to persecute Norwegian Jews in 1942, the Swedes were shocked into action. About 900 Norwegian Jews, more than half of Norway's Jewish community, fled Nazi DEPORTATIONS and were taken in by Sweden. The Swedish foreign ministry accepted Jews and non-Jews who had Swedish relatives.

In the fall of 1943 Georg DUCKWITZ, a German official in Copenhagen, met with the Swedish prime minister regarding the rescue of Danish Jewry. The Swedish government announced that it was ready to accept all Danish Jewish refugees. About 7,000 Danish Jews and 9,000 Danish Christians entered Sweden and were thus rescued from the Germans.

The Swedish government also initiated an operation to rescue Hungarian Jewry. In 1944 Swedish diplomat Raoul WALLENBERG was sent to BUDAPEST to save Jews on their way to deportation. He and his staff, along with the Swedish Red Cross, rescued thousands of Hungarian Jews.

Near the end of the war, Sweden sent food packages to Jews in CONCENTRATION CAMPS, such as BERGEN-BELSEN. Additionally, Count Folk BERNADOTTE of the Swedish Red Cross managed to transfer the last 14,000 women in the RAVENSBRUECK camp, including 2,000 Jews, to Sweden.

After the war, Sweden absorbed thousands of SURVIVORS and did everything possible to help them start new lives. By the late 1950s, half the Jewish refugees had been integrated into the Swedish community; the rest emigrated to the UNITED STATES, CANADA, and Israel.

In the late 1990s the Swedish government came to the realization that many young people knew little about the HOLOCAUST and that others did not believe it had even happened. Led by Prime Minister Goren Perssons, Sweden organized a campaign to foster education about the Holocaust within its own borders and throughout the world. This initiative resulted in a special international task force on Holocaust education.

SWITZERLAND   Country in central Europe. Since the early nineteenth century, Switzerland was a neutral country with a tradition of providing a safe haven for REFUGEES. During WORLD WAR II, however, Switzerland floundered in its attitude towards immigration and refugees: at some points, it practiced a strict immigration policy, while at other times many Jews were allowed into the country. This was influenced by the course of the war. In all, over 300,000 refugees passed through Switzerland during the Nazi period; 30,000 were Jews.

Right before World War II, there were 18,000 Jews living in Switzerland. Its Jewish communities were organized into the Federation of Swiss Jewish Communities. During the years of Nazi power, Swiss Jewish aid institutions joined under one umbrella organization, the Swiss Aid Society for Jewish Refugees. Immediately after the Nazis came to power in GERMANY in January 1933, thousands of Jewish refugees tried to enter Switzerland. The government then decided to distinguish between different types of refugees: political refugees, who were allowed in; immigrants, who were given residence for a limited time only; and refugees, whom the government tried to kick out as soon as possible. During the war, non-Jewish refugees also fled to Switzerland.

After Germany annexed AUSTRIA in March 1938, thousands more Jews tried to enter Switzerland. The Swiss government, not wanting such a large group of refugees entering their country, asked Germany to mark the passports of German and Austrian Jews with a special sign. In this way, the Swiss could tell which German and Austrian tourists were Jews, and thus turn them away. In the fall of 1938, Switzerland and Germany agreed that every German and Austrian Jew would have a "J" marked on his or her passport.

During the war, the Swiss government tried to curb the number of Jews it allowed into the country so as not to offend Germany, on whose economy Switzerland depended. In October 1939, just a month after the war began, the Swiss created new limitations on the entry of foreigners—especially Jews—into Switzerland. In 1940, after Germany occupied many other countries in Northern and Western Europe, the Swiss authorities were terrified that Germany would invade their country, as well. Thus, they tried to appease Germany by putting their refugees into camps, and prohibited the entry of refugees from FRANCE.

In 1941, the Swiss government was much less strict

regarding the refugees from the NETHERLANDS and BEL-GIUM. This saved the lives of several hundred Jews. However, their policy changed once again as the tide of the war changed: when Germany occupied southern France in November 1942, the rules for entry into Switzerland were made much stricter. Several dozen refugees were even sent to Swiss labor camps. Despite the stringent regulations, though, several thousand refugees managed to enter the country illegally.

Germany invaded central and northern ITALY in September 1943. At that point, Switzerland relaxed its rules somewhat, and allowed many refugees to enter. About 20,000 Italians, including 10,000 PARTISANS, crossed over the border into Switzerland. Among those were several thousand Jews. Some groups of Jews also arrived legally as a result of negotiations with the German authorities. In 1944, 1,684 Hungarian Jews arrived in Switzerland from BERGEN-BELSEN as part of the KASZTNER transport, and in 1945, 1,200 Jews arrived from THERESIENSTADT. By February 1945 there were 115,000 refugees of all types in Switzerland, about half of them military deserters who had fled the countries bordering Switzerland.

During the war, many international organizations used neutral Switzerland as their headquarters, and as a center of information from German-occupied Europe. Reports on the mass extermination of European Jewry reached Switzerland first, and were then passed on to the rest of the free world. Some Swiss agencies also tried to rescue Jews from the Nazis.

During the HOLOCAUST years the Swiss banking community worked closely with many Nazis. Large quantities of pilfered gold and currency were deposited in Swiss banks. After the war most of this remained in Switzerland, as did money deposited by thousands of Jews from outside of Switzerland who had been murdered in the Holocaust. In the late 1990s international pressure on the Swiss led to the investigation of these issues. A committee was established under former chairman of the US Federal Reserve, Paul Volcker, which uncovered much information; a process of restitution and painful confrontation with this difficult period in history was begun.

SZALASI, FERENC (1897–1946), Leader of the Hungarian ARROW CROSS PARTY and head of the Hungarian government from October 1944 until the end of WORLD WAR II.

A former major in the Hungarian army, Szalasi

joined an extreme right-wing, secret organization called Hungarian Life League in 1930; the league's purpose was to "protect the superior race." During the 1930s Szalasi wrote several pamphlets describing his ideology, which borrowed ideas from the Italian Fascist movement and the German NAZI PARTY. Szalasi played a leading role in several extreme right-wing parties, such as the Nation's Will Party, the Hungarian National Socialist Party, and the National Socialist Hungarian Party-Hungarist Movement. At one point, Szalasi was thrown into jail for spreading treasonous ideas.

In 1940 Szalasi was let out of jail. He immediately established the Arrow Cross Party, an antisemitic, fascist party that used the arrow cross as its symbol. Many of his followers were either unemployed or poor landowners, but there were also some intellectuals and aristocrats who followed his racist lead.

On October 15, 1944 HITLER overthrew the leader of the Hungarian government, Miklos HORTHY, and installed Szalasi in his stead. Just days later, Szalasi and his Arrow Cross henchmen began a reign of terror against the Jews in BUDAPEST—the only Jews left in HUNGARY. Some 76,000 Jews—men, women, and children—were arrested and forced on a DEATH MARCH towards the Austrian border. Those who lagged behind were shot to death by the accompanying guards; others

Ferenc Szalasi, Arrow Cross leader (center, front), Budapest, October 16, 1944

perished from starvation or exhaustion. The Jews left in Budapest were subjected to increasing Arrow Cross violence. Some 20,000 Jews were marched to the Danube River and shot.

The Nazis in Hungary surrendered to the Soviet army on February 13, 1945. Szalasi tried to flee by joining the withdrawing German forces. However, he was caught in Germany by American troops, and sent back to Hungary in 1945 to stand trial. Szalasi was convicted of war crimes and crimes against the people, and sentenced to death. The former government head was hanged in public on March 12, 1946.

SZENES, HANNAH (1921–1944), One of the Jewish parachutists from Palestine sent by the YISHUV leadership on rescue missions in Nazi-occupied Europe.

Born in BUDAPEST to an assimilated Jewish family of writers, musicians, and poets, Szenes too became a poet at a young age, writing in Hungarian at first and later in Hebrew. Soon she also became a Zionist, and in 1939 she immigrated to Palestine. Two years later she joined Kibbutz Sedot Yam, near the coastal town of Caesarea.

In 1943 Szenes volunteered for a newly founded group of parachutists who were to be sent on rescue missions behind enemy lines in occupied Europe. Her hope was to reach her native HUNGARY and help aid Jews there. However, she also felt that even if she did not end up rescuing Jews, she and her fellow parachutists would be an inspiring and morale-raising symbol of hope to the Jews of Europe. In March 1944, just a week before the Germans occupied Hungary, Szenes parachuted into YUGOSLAVIA. For the next three months, she and other Palestinian parachutists lived with Yugoslav PARTISANS. In early June Szenes crossed over the border into Hungary with a radio transmitter. She was caught immediately. The Germans put her in prison where they tortured her brutally to find out the code for her radio transmitter. However, Szenes did not break, even when the Germans threatened the life of her mother.

After five months in prison, Szenes was put on trial. She defended herself bravely; however, she was convicted of treason against Hungary, and executed by firing squad.

The life of Hannah Szenes, a modern Jewish hero, has been chronicled in plays, books, and even a movie. Her poems and writings have been widely published, and they are still often read or sung when memorializing the HOLOCAUST. A village in Israel, Yad Hannah, is named for her. (see also PARACHUTISTS, JEWISH.)

Hannah Szenes in uniform before being sent to Hungary

SZLENGEL, WLADYSLAW (d. April 1943), Jewish poet and songwriter who wrote many of his poems in the WARSAW Ghetto.

Before the war, Szlengel was a very active writer, composing satiric poems for newspapers and theaters. When he was interned in the Warsaw GHETTO, he began creating both prose and poetry for *Sztuka,* a club for the ghetto's wealthier Jews. During that period, he wrote about his views of the Germans and his apprehension about the ghetto's administration. His poems were very popular in the ghetto, and were read out loud at meetings.

When the Germans began deporting the ghetto's Jews to EXTERMINATION CAMPS, the tone of Szlengel's poetry changed. He began writing about the fear felt by the ghetto's inhabitants, now that death was knocking at their doors, and about the relationship between man and God in such a situation. His last poems deal with the deterioration of the ghetto during its final weeks of existence. Even at that point, Szlengel continued to share his poetry with the public—in small, secret get-togethers.

Szlengel was killed in April 1943 during the WARSAW GHETTO UPRISING. Some of his poetry and prose were saved, and a collection of his writings was published in Polish under the title, *What I Read to the Dead.*

SZTEHLO, GABOR   (1909–1974), Christian minister in BUDAPEST who rescued hundreds of Jewish children during the HOLOCAUST.

After GERMANY invaded HUNGARY in March 1944, Sztehlo and his Protestant Good Shepherd Committee began rescuing abandoned Jewish children. In October 1944, after the antisemitic, fascist ARROW CROSS PARTY took control of the Hungarian government and embarked upon a reign of anti-Jewish terror, Sztehlo decided to extend his rescue activities to all Jewish children. This included young Jews who had been forced into the HUNGARIAN LABOR SERVICE SYSTEM and, having deserted their units, needed a place of refuge.

By the end of 1944 the Soviet army had besieged Budapest. Many of Sztehlo's institutions were bombed in the battle between the Germans and the Soviets, and thus could no longer be used as shelters. Sztehlo then moved 33 children to the basement of his home. For 20 days, he and his family hid with the children in the cellar, while bombs exploded right above their heads. When Budapest was liberated in February 1945, Sztehlo moved the children to new accommodations, and took care of them until their families or Jewish organizations came to claim them.

In 1972 Sztehlo was designated as RIGHTEOUS AMONG THE NATIONS by YAD VASHEM.

SZTOJAY, DOME   (also called Sztojakovics; 1883–1946), Pro-Nazi military leader in HUNGARY.

From 1925 to 1933 Sztojay served as Hungary's military attaché in BERLIN. Next, he worked in the Hungarian ministry of defense, and in 1935 he was named Hungarian minister in Berlin.

GERMANY occupied Hungary on March 19, 1944. Three days later, Sztojay was appointed prime minister and foreign minister of the puppet Hungarian government installed by the Nazis. Under his reign, the Hungarian authorities issued ANTI-JEWISH LEGISLATION that called for the isolation of the Jews of Hungary, putting them in GHETTOS, pillaging their property, and deporting them to their deaths in Polish EXTERMINATION CAMPS.

In July 1944 Sztojay fell ill, and was forced to give up his position as prime minister to Lajos Remenyi-Schneller. By that time, the entire Jewish population of Hungary outside of BUDAPEST had been deported, under his orders.

As the Soviet army approached Budapest, Sztojay fled Hungary with the Nazis. However, he was caught by American troops who returned him to Hungary in October 1945. On March 22, 1946 Sztojay was found guilty of war crimes and crimes against the people by a Hungarian court, sentenced to death, and shot.

Dome Sztojay

TALLINN (in Russian, Revel), capital of the Baltic state of ESTONIA. In 1939 some 2,300 Jews lived in Tallinn, making up almost half of Estonia's entire Jewish population. In 1940 Estonia was annexed by the SOVIET UNION. The Soviet authorities arrested and expelled hundreds of Tallinn's Jews to remote parts of the Soviet Union, along with many other Tallinn residents.

In June 1941 GERMANY invaded the Soviet Union and Soviet-held territories, including Estonia. At that point, many Jews from Tallinn voluntarily joined Estonian defense units. The Soviets began evacuating the city's residents, and despite the German siege and bombing, about half of Tallinn's Jews managed to escape.

German troops conquered Tallinn on July 25, 1941. The Jews were immediately commanded to wear the Jewish badge (see also BADGE, JEWISH) and their lives were harshly restricted. Many women and children were made to do FORCED LABOR, while most of the men were imprisoned in the city jail. During September and October these men were executed by Estonian Nazi collaborators under the supervision of a SONDERKOMMANDO unit. By December 19, 610 Jews had been murdered. The rest of the city's Jews were killed during early 1942.

Soviet troops liberated Tallinn on September 22, 1944. Only five Jews had survived in the city.

TEHRAN CHILDREN Group of Polish Jewish children who reached Palestine in February 1943 via Tehran, Iran.

When WORLD WAR II broke out in September 1939, some 300,000 Jews fled POLAND for the SOVIET UNION. This flight included grave hardships, such as illness, starvation, and cold, and many children lost their parents along the way.

In 1942 the POLISH GOVERNMENT-IN-EXILE and the Soviet authorities agreed to allow the emigration of some 24,000 of these Polish REFUGEES. Included were 1,000 Jewish children, mostly orphans, and 800 Jewish

Tehran Children, arriving in Palestine, February 1943

adults. From April to August 1942 the entire group was taken to Tehran. When they arrived, the adult Jewish refugees set up an orphanage with the help of the Jewish community there.

As soon as the Jewish Agency heard about the Jewish refugees in Iran, they sent emmisaries to help run the orphanage and set up a Palestine Office in Tehran. By January 1943 the Jewish Agency had procured a ship and immigration permits from the British authorities, so the children and their attendants sailed to Suez, and then transferred to trains. On February 18, 1943, some 861 children and 369 adults reached Palestine, where they were welcomed with great joy and fanfare. Ultimately, most were taken to live on *kibbutzim* (communal settlements).

TENENBAUM, MORDECHAI   (1916–1943), A leader of the VILNA, WARSAW, and BIALYSTOK undergrounds. A member of the *Dror* Zionist YOUTH MOVEMENT, Tenenbaum joined the staff of the *He-Halutz* head office in Warsaw in 1938. Soon after the war broke out in September 1939, Tenenbaum and some comrades fled Warsaw for Vilna, hoping to reach Palestine. However, Jewish immigration to Palestine was restricted. Tenenbaum gave his friends forged documents, but decided himself to stay behind in Vilna.

Mordechai Tenenbaum

The Germans occupied Vilna in June 1941. Tenenbaum provided comrades with forged work papers, saving some from the Nazis. He then moved comrades who had survived the Vilna *aktionen* to Bialystok, which was still pretty quiet. In January 1942 Tenenbaum himself left for Bialystok. In March he returned to Warsaw. At a meeting of all the Jewish political parties, Tenenbaum declared that the events in Vilna proved that the Germans intended to kill all Jews in their domain.

Tenenbaum often left Warsaw for nearby GHETTOS to gather information and organize underground activities. In July 1942 he helped found the Jewish Fighting Organization (*Zydowska Organizacja Bojowa*, ZOB), Warsaw's major underground alliance. In November he again left Warsaw for Bialystok to organize a resistance movement there. Upon arrival, he found the ghetto surrounded. Tenenbaum was shot in the leg when the Germans realized his papers were forged. He escaped, and after recovering, returned to Bialystok to unite the ghetto's underground movements and prepare them for rebellion.

In early February 1943 the Germans began deporting the Jews of Bialystok. Tenenbaum sent messengers to obtain arms from the PARTISANS, and had his soldiers steal weapons and hoard food. They decided that when the Germans would begin liquidating the ghetto, they would first fight in the ghetto and then escape to the forest. On August 16, 1943 Tenenbaum saw that the ghetto's liquidation was imminent, so he launched an uprising. His soldiers were not able to break out of the ghetto for the forest, but some fighters held out for a month. It is unclear what happened to Tenenbaum himself—he may have died in battle or committed suicide. (see also RESISTANCE, JEWISH and JEWISH FIGHTING ORGANIZATION, WARSAW.)

THADDEN, EBERHARD VON   (1909–1964), German Foreign Office official who, from April 1943 to the end of WORLD WAR II, was in charge of Jewish affairs and served as the intermediary between the Foreign Office and the SS.

Thadden joined the NAZI PARTY in 1933 and the SS in 1936. At that point, a question was raised about whether Thadden had a Jewish ancestor, but the problem was solved when his old family friend, Hermann GOERING, testified that the ancestor in question was not Jewish, but rather the illegitimate son of a Russian noble. Thadden entered the Foreign Office in 1937. He then enlisted in the *Waffen*-SS, and was subsequently wounded in battle. In 1942 he returned to work for the Foreign Office in GREECE, and in April 1943 he was appointed head of the Foreign Office's Jewish desk. In this capacity, he was involved in the DEPORTATION of Jews from all over Europe. He was particularly involved in the mass deportation of Hungarian Jewry during the summer of 1944.

In 1950 Thadden was indicted by a German court, but the charges were eventually dropped. The investigation into his crimes was reopened in 1958, but Thadden was killed in a car accident before he could be put on trial.

THERESIENSTADT   (in Czech, Terezin), GHETTO in Czechoslovakia. The Nazis built Theresienstadt for the purpose of concentrating most of the Jews of the Protectorate of Bohemia and Moravia (see also BOHEMIA AND MORAVIA, PROTECTORATE OF), as well as certain categories of Jews from GERMANY and Western Europe, such as famous or wealthy Jews, those with special talents, and old people. Ultimately, the Nazis intended to mask the extermination of European Jewry by presenting Theresienstadt as a model ghetto, but at the same time, slowly deport the Jews at Theresienstadt to EXTERMINATION CAMPS.

The first Jews arrived in Theresienstadt in November 1941. Czech Jewish leaders had supported the idea of a "model Jewish settlement" at Theresienstadt, thinking it would keep the Jews from being deported. However, upon arrival, it was plain to see that conditions at Theresienstadt were like at a CONCENTRATION CAMP, and that the ghetto would not save them from DEPORTATION. The first 2,000 Jews were deported to RIGA just two months later.

By September 1942 the ghetto reached its peak with 53,004 prisoners, with Jews continuing to arrive until war's end. At the same time, deportations continued: at first, to ghettos in POLAND and the Baltic States; by October 1942 until the end of the war, to the TREBLINKA and AUSCHWITZ extermination camps. By that time, only 11,068 people remained in Theresienstadt.

Theresienstadt was run by the SS; Czech police acted as ghetto guards. The internal affairs of the ghetto were run by the *Aeltestenrat* (Council of Elders), whose first chairman was Jacob EDELSTEIN. The council was responsible for making the lists of those to be deported. However, it also helped the ghetto's Jews a great deal: members gave out work, housing, and food; supervised health and sanitation services, cultural activities, and public order; and took care of the old and young. The council also secretly supported schooling, and due to the large number of scholars, artists, and writers in Theresienstadt, there were many cultural activities there.

The physical conditions in Theresienstadt were intolerable. This led to the breakout of epidemics, killing many. By the end of 1943, the ghetto's health department had managed to establish a hospital, leading to a drop in the mortality rate.

Placard advertising a performance of the puppet theater, Theresienstadt

By the end of 1943, people in the outside world were becoming more aware of what was happening in the Nazi camps. Thus, the Germans decided to permit a visit at Theresienstadt by an International Red Cross investigations committee (see also RED CROSS, INTERNATIONAL). First they had to prepare the ghetto: the Germans alleviated some overcrowding by deporting more prisoners to Auschwitz; they built a fake cafe, stores, bank, kindergartens, and school; they planted flower gardens; and they made a propaganda film that portrayed life in Theresienstadt as idyllic and comfortable. The committee arrived on July 23, 1944. The prisoners who met with committee members had been warned beforehand how to behave and what to say. The visit was a success—the SS had the committee completely duped.

During the ghetto's last six months, many more Jews arrived from SLOVAKIA, HUNGARY, the Protectorate of Bohemia and Moravia, Germany, and AUSTRIA. Near the end of the war, the Red Cross transferred some of them to neutral countries. In April 1945 the Germans brought in thousands of prisoners who had been evacuated from concentration camps. This led once again to the outbreak of epidemics. On May 3 the Nazis handed Theresienstadt over to the Red Cross; the ghetto was liberated on May 8 by Soviet troops. The last Jew left Theresienstadt on August 17.

In all, 140,000 Jews were brought to Theresienstadt: 33,000 died there, 88,000 were deported to extermination camps, and 19,000 survived either in the ghetto or among the groups that had been transferred to SWEDEN or SWITZERLAND. Of those deported, 3,000 survived.

THIERACK, OTTO   (1889–1946), Nazi judge and later Reich Minister of Justice.

A lawyer from Saxony, Thierack was named public prosecutor in Leipzig in 1921 and in 1926, in Dresden. He joined the NAZI PARTY in 1932, at which point he began his career as a leading Nazi judge. He held various high-ranking posts in Nazi courts, which prosecuted people accused of crimes against the THIRD REICH in closed sessions and without the right of appeal.

In 1942 Thierack was named Reich Minister of Justice. He used his position to twist laws into what the Nazis wanted them to be, and actively supported their murderous activities through his rulings. He made it legal to send certain types of foreign prisoners or forced laborers to CONCENTRATION CAMPS, where they would be "exterminated through work." He also made it legal for Jews, Poles, GYPSIES, Russians, and Ukrainians *not* to be sentenced by regular courts, but to be taken care of directly by the SS—meaning, of course, that they would be sent to their deaths at Nazi camps in the east.

At the end of the war Thierack was arrested and imprisoned, but took his own life in jail before he could be put on trial.

THIRD REICH   (in German, *Drittes Reich*), Nazi term for GERMANY and its regime during the period of Nazi reign, from 1933 to 1945. The German word *reich* means kingdom or realm, and is used in a fashion similar to the word "empire."

The "Third Reich" term alludes to two different series of three. The first series is that of the three German empires: the Holy Roman Empire of the German People, which formally lasted until 1806, was considered the First Reich; the German Empire, which lasted from 1871 to 1918, was the Second Reich; while the Third Reich was the empire that the Nazis aspired to set up. The second series is a "spiritual" one that comes from the ideas of a twelfth century Christian mystic. He envisioned the history of man as a series of three thousand-year kingdoms: the "kingdom of the Father" the "kingdom of the Son" and the "kingdom of the Holy Spirit." This third kingdom (which the Nazis translated as the "Third Reich") was supposed to be actualized in the perfect world of the end of days, and as the Nazis came to power in the last century of the millenium, Hitler predicted that the Nazis' "Third Reich" would continue on for a thousand years.

TISO, JOZEF   (1887–1947), Slovak politician and Catholic priest who ran SLOVAKIA from 1939 to 1945. After Czechoslovakia became independent in 1918, Tiso began calling for an independent Slovakia under an authoritarian, Catholic government. In 1925 he was elected to Czechoslovakia's parliament and in 1927 was named minister of health. However, his ideology was so radical that he was dismissed from his post.

Tiso was a member of the Slovak People's Party, run by Andrej HLINKA. After Hlinka's death in 1938, Tiso became the party's leader. A few weeks later, the MUNICH CONFERENCE took place, in which Western leaders al-

Dr. Jozef Tiso at his postwar trial in Slovakia, 1945

lowed HITLER to occupy parts of Czechoslovakia. Subsequently, Slovakia was awarded autonomy, and Tiso became its president.

In March 1939 Tiso declared Slovakia an independent country and made it a satellite of the Nazi regime. Even after the SLOVAK NATIONAL UPRISING in 1944, in which thousands of Slovaks rebelled against the Nazis, Tiso stayed loyal to Hitler and his murderous activities. He had the ability to exempt people from DEPORTATIONS, but he only used this to help some 1,100 wealthy Jews or Jews-turned-Catholics.

In April 1945 Tiso escaped to AUSTRIA. He was caught and sent back to Czechoslovakia, where he was tried and executed.

TITO

(Josip Broz; 1892–1980), Yugoslav leader and statesman. Born in CROATIA, Tito joined the Soviet army in 1917 after being captured during World War I. He returned to YUGOSLAVIA in 1920 and was imprisoned from 1928 to 1934 for Communist activities. An activist in Communist International, Tito was elected secretary-general of the Yugoslav Communist Party in 1937, despite its outlawed status.

In spring 1941 GERMANY invaded Yugoslavia. In July a revolt broke out against the Nazis in the Yugoslav region of SERBIA. Soon, Tito and his Communist followers took the lead in fighting the Nazis, and the rebellion spread to the rest of the country. Despite very harsh conditions, Tito created an effective fighting force of almost 300,000 men. As part of the struggle with the Germans, Tito ordered his fighters to help Jews trying to escape the Nazis in any way they could. In fact, both during the war and after, Tito was always compassionate towards the Jews in Yugoslavia and was supportive of the fight to establish a Jewish state.

Following WORLD WAR II, Tito became the premier of Yugoslavia, and in 1953, its president. One of the world's most prominent leaders, Tito ruled Yugoslavia until his death in 1980.

TOTENKOPFVERBAENDE   see DEATH'S HEAD UNITS.

TOUVIER TRIAL   Trial in 1994 of Paul Touvier, who served as the intelligence chief of a pro-Nazi militia (*Milice*) active in FRANCE during the final year of the Nazi occupation. Some 50 years after the fact, a French court convicted Touvier of ordering the execution of seven Jewish hostages in Rilleux-la-Pape during the war. The execution was an act of retaliation for the murder of a Vichy regional minister named Philippe Henriot.

An extreme antisemite, Touvier had been convicted of war crimes in 1946 and 1947. During the 1970s he was pardoned by French president George Pompidou; this led French courts to reopen the case in 1973. Originally, Touvier had been accused of 11 different crimes, but none besides the murder of the seven hostages could be proved so long after they had occurred. Touvier was found guilty and sentenced to life in prison. He died in jail of cancer in 1996.

Touvier's trial was followed carefully throughout France, and brought up many issues that were debated by the French public, such as the responsibility of the Vichy government for the DEPORTATION and murder of French Jewry, and the accountability of many Frenchmen in standing by while innocent people were annihilated. (for more on Vichy, see also FRANCE.)

TRANSCARPATHIAN UKRAINE (CARPATHORUS)

Region in the Carpathian Mountains that now belongs to the UKRAINE. Before World War I the Transcarpathian Ukraine was part of HUNGARY; after the war, it was taken over by Czechoslovakia. Just months before WORLD WAR II broke out, the region was returned to Hungary. After the war, it was annexed to the SOVIET UNION, and made part of the Ukraine.

In 1939 some 500,000 people lived in the region; about 15 percent were Jews. The Jewish community, known for its strict religious observance, was very poor. Despite this, the Jews in the Transcarpathian Ukraine administered a large network of Jewish and Hebrew educational institutions and sponsored a great amount of Zionist activity.

Until GERMANY occupied Hungary in 1944, the Jews in the Transcarpathian Ukraine were basically able to maintain their way of life. They even aided many Jews who had come to the region from SLOVAKIA and POLAND seeking refuge. Although Jewish business owners were forced to hand over their enterprises to non-Jews, this generally happened in name only.

One group of Jews, however, was singled out by the authorities; some 18,000 "Jewish foreign nationals" whose families had actually been living in the Transcarpathian Ukraine for generations, were kicked out of the region. Most were then exterminated by the SS in German-occupied POLAND. Another group of Jews was also affected by the war before the Germans ever invaded; these were the young Jews who were drafted into the

HUNGARIAN LABOR SERVICE SYSTEM, many of whom died or were murdered while serving as laborers for the Hungarian army.

Germany occupied Hungary in March 1944. The Nazis began their campaign to annihilate Hungarian Jewry in the Transcarpathian Ukraine. They quickly set up GHETTOS, and brought the Jews from small towns and villages to the large population centers. By May, the Germans began deporting the Jews to the east. In general, the Hungarian authorities themselves were in charge of the DEPORTATIONS. In all, about 80 percent of the Jews of the Transcarpathian Ukraine perished during the HOLOCAUST. A few Jews managed to survive by fleeing to the mountains or hiding.

TRANSFER AGREEMENT (*Ha'avara*), agreement made in August 1933 between the Nazi regime and the German Zionist Federation that encouraged the immigration of German Jews to Palestine by allowing them to transfer some of their funds from GERMANY to Palestine. The Hebrew word *ha'avara* means transfer.

The pact allowed would-be immigrants to place at least 1,000 pounds sterling—the amount the British charged for an immigration certificate to Palestine— in a German bank, and upon arrival in Palestine, to collect either that same amount of money or its equivalent in goods.

The Zionists were interested in the agreement because it attracted wealthy German Jews to Palestine. However, they were severely criticized by Jews who felt that the pact was a transgression of the anti-Nazi boycott and a rupture in Jewish unity (see also BOYCOTTS, ANTI-NAZI). The Germans liked the agreement for those very reasons, and because it would help get rid of German Jews.

By 1938, the agreement became the only possibility for large-scale emigration from Germany to Palestine. It operated until a few months after WORLD WAR II broke out in September 1939, when it was cancelled because of the Allies' economic blockade on Germany. In all, several thousand immigrants took advantage of the Transfer Agreement to help them successfully reach Palestine.

TRANSNISTRIA An artificial geographic term created during WORLD WAR II, which refers to a region in the UKRAINE. Before World War II, there were 300,000 Jews living in the area.

In June 1941 GERMANY attacked its former ally, the SOVIET UNION. Germany quickly conquered Transnistria and gave it to its ally, ROMANIA. Many Jews managed to escape the area before German troops arrived. However, tens of thousands of Jews were massacred during the first few months of German occupation by EINSATZGRUPPEN units, and by German and Romanian troops.

Ion ANTONESCU, the leader of Romania, soon decided that the Jews of the BESSARABIA, BUKOVINA, and northern Moldavia regions of Romania were an "enemy population" and thus were to be deported to Transnistria, his newly-gained dumping ground. These DEPORTATIONS began on September 15, 1941 and lasted until October 1942. Most of the Jews who had survived mass killings in Bessarabia and Bukovina were expelled to Transnistria by the end of 1941, as were Romanian political prisoners (mostly Jewish), and Jews who had avoided the FORCED LABOR draft. Altogether, approximately 150,000 people were sent to Transnistria.

Many deportees died en route to Transnistria. Thousands were jammed into freight trains without food or water, causing many deaths. Others were marched to Transnistria by foot in the severe winter cold, many dying along the way. In both cases, the Romanian guards accompanying the prisoners randomly shot at them as well.

Those Jews that reached Transnistria alive were packed into camps and GHETTOS, which were run by the Romanian authorities and police. They were made to do backbreaking forced labor. During the winter, tens of thousands of prisoners died from starvation or typhus, because none of their basic needs were provided for.

After Antonescu ordered a mass slaughter in ODESSA (the capital of Transnistria), the survivors were brought to Transnistria and interned in three camps: BOGDANOVKA, Akhmetchetka, and DOMANEVKA. In Bogdanovka all the Jews were shot to death by Romanian and Ukrainian police and a SONDERKOMMANDO unit made up of ethnic Germans. During January and February 1942, many thousands of Jews were murdered in Akhmetchetka and Domanevka. 12,000 Jews from the Ukraine were exterminated in Akhmetchetka and Domanevka. Another 28,000 were murdered by SS and German police in southern Transnistria. By March 1943, a total of 185,000 Ukrainian Jews had been murdered by Romanian and German soldiers in Transnistria.

In December 1941 Romanian Jewish leader Wilhelm FILDERMAN managed to get permission from Antonescu to send aid packages to the Jews in Transnistria. Despite the fact that the Romanian authorities put all sorts of hurdles in Filderman's way, the first shipment reached the Jews in Transnistria by the beginning of winter 1942–1943, and it helped some of them survive. By that time, the Romanian government had begun shifting its policy away from Germany, and thus stopped the deportations to Transnistria. Representatives of the AUTONOMOUS REFUGEE AID COMMITTEE were also allowed to visit the Jews in the area. By the end of 1943, the Jews of Transnistria began receiving assistance packages from the American Jewish JOINT DISTRIBUTION COMMITTEE, the Jewish Agency, the WORLD JEWISH CONGRESS, and the OEUVRE DE SECOURS AUX ENFANTS.

During 1943, Romanian Jewish groups concentrated their efforts on securing permission for the deportees to return home. Permission was finally granted when the Soviet army began closing in on Transnistria. Many of the survivors returned at that point, although others were only allowed to go home after the war ended. Of the 150,000 Jews who had been deported to Transnistria, a total of 90,000 perished there. In addition about 185,000 local Ukranian Jews also were murdered.

TRANSYLVANIA   Region in Central Europe that belonged to HUNGARY until 1920, at which time it was given to ROMANIA. On August 30, 1940, Northern Transylvania was transferred back to Hungary, as a reward for siding with GERMANY.

Northern Transylvania had a population of 2.5 million, including 165,000 Jews. Most lived in the areas of Dej, Cluj, Sighet Marmatiei, Tirgu Mures, Oradea, and Satu-Mare. Many Transylvanian Jews were happy to join Hungary after 20 years under Romania; however, they were soon subjected to Hungary's anti-Jewish regulations.

The Germans occupied Hungary in March 1944, and quickly began readying the Jews for the "Final Solution." They divided Northern Transylvania into two districts. Jews were not allowed to travel or communicate with Jews in other areas, so each community was left isolated. The only way to make contact was through the Jewish Council of BUDAPEST, which usually just passed on instructions from the German and Hungarian authorities. On May 2 Jews were forbidden to leave their homes, except for one short hour in the morning to shop. The next day, the Nazis began trans-

ferring Jews to GHETTOS; the operation ran smoothly and took only 10 days. There was hardly any resistance. Some Jews did not realize what was going to happen to them, others thought they were being sent away to work, and some hoped the Allies would soon win the war. In the villages and smaller towns, the Jews were gathered in their synagogues and community buildings; after a few days, they were moved to the ghettos located in larger cities. In Dej, the Jews were moved to the forest. Each ghetto had its own JUDENRAT, which carried out the instructions given them by the main Jewish Council or by the Hungarian or German authorities. Each ghetto also had a building, nicknamed the "mint," where Jews were tortured into revealing the whereabouts of their valuables.

The Jews did not stay long in the ghettos—131,641 Jews were soon deported to AUSCHWITZ. The transports lasted from May 16 to June 27, 1944. Only the Jews working in labor units and a few exemptions were left behind.

Romania retained control of Southern Transylvania. In 1941 there were 40,937 Jews living there. During the reign of the "National Legionary Government" in 1940, local authorities terrorized the Jews of Southern Transylvania. Their property was systematically looted and they were kicked out of their homes. Hundreds of Jews were tortured into "selling" their property to the authorities. However, when the Legionary government toppled in January 1941, the situation improved slightly. The conditions in the FORCED LABOR units were somewhat alleviated, and few Southern Transylvanian Jews were sent to labor battalions.

During the summer of 1941, Ion ANTONESCU, the head of the Romanian government, ordered all Romanian Jews—including those in Southern Transylvania—expelled from their villages and towns. The operation was executed haphazardly, causing the Jews much distress. During the expulsion, the authorities found that the large cities where they had planned to station the Jews were not suitable. Thus, in late 1941 and early 1942, the Jews who had already been sent to the larger towns were now moved to makeshift ghettos. By the summer of 1942 they were faced with another threat: DEPORTATION. Southern Transylvanian Jewish leaders traveled to BUCHAREST to enlist the help of Romanian Jewish leader Wilhelm FILDERMAN.

By the summer of 1943, the Jews' situation had improved somewhat. In 1944 they themselves were able to rescue thousands of Jews from Northern Transylvania and Hungary, where Jews were being arrested and deported. However, the circumstances of the Jews of Southern Transylvania changed in September 1944, soon after the Romanian army surrendered to the Soviets. The Hungarian army occupied an area along the northern border of Southern Transylvania. Most Jews fled the region, but the Hungarians murdered any they could find. The area was liberated that month, but when the Romanian army reoccupied most of Southern Transylvania, no Jews were left.

TRAWNIKI   FORCED LABOR camp located southeast of LUBLIN. Trawniki was established in 1941; some 20,000 Jews passed through the camp during its two years of existence.

The first prisoners in Trawniki were Soviet PRISONERS OF WAR and Polish Jews. In mid-1942 Jews from GERMANY, AUSTRIA, and Czechoslovakia arrived. Many died due to the harsh conditions, were sent to their deaths at the BELZEC extermination camp, or were shot in the forest nearby.

In late 1942 the Germans transferred a factory to Trawniki from the nearby Miendzyrzec Podlaski GHETTO, and the camp's prisoners were forced to work there. After the WARSAW GHETTO UPRISING in April 1943 and the subsequent destruction of the ghetto, WARSAW factories were transferred to Trawniki, along with 10,000 workers (including ghetto archivist Emanuel RINGELBLUM and 33 fighters from the Jewish Fighting Organization). In May 1943 Jews from the NETHERLANDS, BIALYSTOK, MINSK, and Smolensk were brought to Trawniki.

In the fall of 1943 the Nazis carried out Operation ERNTEFEST, in which some 43,000 Jews were exterminated, including 10,000 Jews from Trawniki. In the spring of 1944 the surviving prisoners were transferred to the STARACHOWICE camp in the Radom district. Trawniki also served as a training camp for Soviet POWs who volunteered to become SS guards. (see also JEWISH FIGHTING ORGANIZATION, WARSAW.)

TREBLINKA   EXTERMINATION CAMP in the northeastern part of the GENERALGOUVERNEMENT, located 2.5 miles from the train station of Malkinia on the main line running from WARSAW to BIALYSTOK. Treblinka was established in early summer 1942 as part of AKTION REINHARD—the Nazis' plan to exterminate the Jews in the *Generalgouvernement* area. In all, some 870,000 people were murdered at Treblinka.

The first transports reached Treblinka on July 23, 1942; these included Jews from the Warsaw GHETTO. From that day until September 21, 1942, some 254,000 Jews from Warsaw itself and 112,000 Jews from other places in the Warsaw district were murdered at Treblinka. Hundreds of thousands of Jews from the Radom and Lublin districts of the *Generalgouvernement* were also executed there. In all, approximately 738,000 Jews from the *Generalgouvernement* perished at Treblinka, as well as 107,000 Jews from the Bialystok district. Thousands of Jews from outside POLAND were also brought to Treblinka; these included Jews from SLOVAKIA, GREECE, MACEDONIA AND THRACE, and some who had previously been interned at THERESIENSTADT. Altogether, 29,000 Jews from outside Poland were murdered at Treblinka, as were 2,000 GYPSIES. The mass extermination program was in operation at Treblinka until April 1943, after which only a handful of transports arrived.

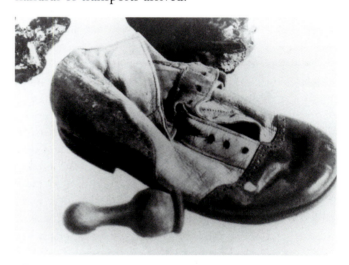

The shoe of a murdered child found in Treblinka after the war

From August 1942 Treblinka was run by camp commandant SS-*Obersturmfuehrer* Franz STANGL, who had previously served as commander of the SOBIBOR extermination camp. Stangl's deputy was Kurt FRANZ. They were assisted by 20–30 SS men (who had participated in the EUTHANASIA PROGRAM), and 90–120 Ukrainian soldiers who worked as camp guards.

Treblinka was situated in a sparsely populated area that was heavily wooded; this site was chosen in order to conceal the atrocities taking place there. Treblinka contained living, reception, and extermination areas. The extermination area included a brick building that housed three GAS CHAMBERS. A diesel engine was housed in an adjoining shed; this engine produced the carbon monoxide that fueled the chambers. The gas flowed through pipes attached to the ceiling of the chambers that ended in what looked like showerheads. The Germans arranged the gas chamber in this way in order to create the impression that the Jews were merely entering the building to take showers—not to be murdered. A hallway in the building led to each of the three gas chambers, and in each chamber was another door through which the corpses were removed. About 200 yards away lay the huge trenches where the corpses were buried.

The extermination process at Treblinka was based on experience gained by the Nazis in BELZEC and Sobibor—the two other *Aktion Reinhard* camps. When a train, made up of 50–60 cars and holding some 6,000–7,000 people, arrived at the nearby train station, 20 cars were brought into the camp, while the rest were made to wait in the station. The car doors were opened, and SS men ordered the Jews to disembark. Next, a camp officer would announce to the new arrivals that they had reached a transit camp where they would take showers and have their clothes disinfected, and then travel on to various labor camps. After this announcement, the Jews were taken to "deportation square." Men and women were then separated (children going with the women). The women and children were made to undress in a barrack, and the women's hair was cut. Naked, they were forced to leave the barrack and enter the "pipe"—a narrow, fenced-in, camouflaged path that led to the gas chambers. After the victims were locked into the chambers, the engine was started and poison gas poured in. Within half an hour, all inside were dead, and the next group of victims would prepare to enter. Meanwhile, the bodies were removed and taken for burial in the trenches. This last job was done by a team of Jewish prisoners called SONDERKOMMANDO. These prisoners were not immediately executed upon arrival at the camp; rather, they were selected to do horrific jobs such as cleaning the train cars, preparing the victims for their execution, dealing with the possessions and clothing of the victims, and of course, handling the dead. When the Nazis decided to cremate the corpses in the spring of 1943, rather than just burying them, these prisoners were made to do that, as well. Most of these Jews were exterminated themselves after a few days or weeks of work, newer arrivals taking their places.

After a while, the Germans decided that the exter-mination process at Treblinka was not efficient enough. Thus, between August and October 1942 ten new gas chambers were constructed there. In addition, the Germans added another improvement to their extermination system: those new arrivals who were too weak to walk to the gas chambers unaided were told that they were being sent to the infirmary. They were taken to a closed-in area with a Red Cross flag adorning it; inside were SS men and Ukrainian guards who murdered them on the spot.

AKTION 1005—the campaign to destroy all evidence of the Nazis' murderous activities—was launched at Treblinka in March 1943, and lasted until July. After this operation was completed, Treblinka was shut down. Most of the camp structures were destroyed, the ground was plowed and planted over, and the site was turned into a farm that was given to a Ukrainian family.

Hundreds of Jews tried to escape the trains on their way to the camp, but most failed in their attempts. Others attempted to escape the camp itself, but almost all were caught and hanged. Jews from several transports offered resistance in which German and Ukrainian guards were wounded or killed. An uprising was planned when the prisoners found out that the Germans were planning to liquidate the camp; however, the uprising was suppressed and most of the 750 prisoners who tried to escape were caught.

After the war, many of the SS men who worked at Treblinka were put on trial. Both commandant Franz Stangl and deputy commandant Kurt Franz were sentenced to life imprisonment.

TRIALS OF WAR CRIMINALS   The prosecution of political and military leaders for war crimes. After WORLD WAR II, those Germans and Japanese accused of war crimes against citizens of the Allied countries were put on trial in various courts. The accused criminals were divided into two large categories: "major" war criminals were those political and military leaders whose crimes knew no geographical boundaries, and "minor" war criminals were civilians or former soldiers whose crimes were committed in specific locations. Major war criminals were tried in Nuremberg or Tokyo by courts that were established based on international agreements made by the Allies. The overwhelming majority of accused war criminals, however, were those in the "minor" category. Their trials were run by military courts in the various occupied zones of GERMANY

The Bergen-Belsen Trial, Luneburg, fall 1945

(whether American, British, French, or Soviet); in ITALY and AUSTRIA; and by special courts set up for this purpose in Allied countries. In addition, war criminals were also tried in countries that had been occupied by or satellites of Germany during the war, such as POLAND, HUNGARY, ROMANIA, NORWAY, the NETHERLANDS, LITHUANIA, CROATIA, and FRANCE—some even very recently. After West Germany was created, German courts initiated proceedings against Nazi war criminals. Over the last 20 years, courts in the UNITED STATES, CANADA, and Australia have also begun trying war criminals who entered their countries after the war.

The first trial of Nazi war criminals was held even before World War II had ended. This trial took place in Krasnodar, Russia, from July 14–17, 1943; it meted out justice to 13 Soviet citizens who had served in EINSATZGRUPPE D. Eight of the accused were sentenced to death, and three others to 20 years in prison.

Between October 1945 and October 1946 an International Military Tribunal (IMT) tried 22 of the most infamous major Nazi figures in proceedings that came to be known as the NUREMBERG TRIAL. Twelve defendants were sentenced to death, three were acquitted, and the rest were sentenced to jail.

During that trial, the four occupying powers in Germany passed a law that allowed them to conduct criminal trials on charges of aggression, war crimes, CRIMES AGAINST HUMANITY, and membership in a criminal organization. Subsequently, the US authorities in Germany set up six military courts that were made up of American civilian judges. From December 1946 to April 1949, these courts tried and convicted 177 persons in 12 trials—known as the Subsequent Nuremberg Trials. The defendants included leaders of the Nazi government, the SS, the German army, and German industry, medical, and legal establishments.

The British occupying authorities in Germany also set up military courts to try war criminals. However, as distinct from the American trials, the British only tried those accused of committing crimes against British subjects, especially British soldiers, and those who committed war crimes against Allied citizens in British zones. The British did not specifically deal with crimes against Jews, unless the Jewish victims were also citizens of Allied countries.

A British military court also tried the staff of the BERGEN-BELSEN concentration camp. This trial was held in Luneburg, Germany, from September to November 1945. Forty-five defendants stood on trial, among them camp commandant Josef KRAMER. Eleven of the accused were sentenced to death by hanging, while 14 were acquitted.

Another trial put in front of a British military court was the March 1946 trial of the owners and executives of Tesch and Stabenow—a company that manufactured ZYKLON B. Two of the three defendants were sentenced to death. In the 1990s two criminals were subjected to preceedings in Britain.

In Poland, where almost all of the Nazi EXTERMINATION CAMPS were located, special courts were established in September 1944 to try Nazi war criminals—more than half a year before the war came to a close. These courts, which allowed no appeals, functioned until 1949. Their first trial involved the staff of the MAJDANEK camp. They then went on to try 5,450 war criminals. Among the war criminals tried in Poland were Amon GOETH, the commandant of PLASZOW, and Rudolf HOESS, the commandant of AUSCHWITZ.

By the end of 1946, most of the leading Hungarian politicians who had collaborated with Nazi Germany had been tried and punished, including many of the ministers of the Dome SZTOJAY and Ferenc SZALASI governments (including, of course, those prime ministers as well). Almost 40,000 suspected war criminals were investigated and tried in Hungary, more than 19,000 of whom were found guilty.

The punishment of Romanian war criminals was carried out within the context of severe political struggle between the traditional leaders of Romania and the Communist Party. From March 1945, those Nazi criminals involved in the extermination of the Jews of BESSARABIA, BUKOVINA, and TRANSNISTRIA were put on trial, including Prime Minister Ion ANTONESCU, who was executed in 1946.

In the Netherlands, special courts were set up in late 1945 to deal with Nazi war criminals who had been active there, as well as with Dutch collaborators. A total of 14,562 people were convicted and sentenced by the time the courts ceased operations in 1950. In Norway,

Nazis and Nazi collaborators were put on trial, most notably Norwegian Prime Minister Vidkun QUISLING, who invited the German army into his country in 1940. Most leading war criminals in Norway were sentenced to death.

The West German authorities began investigating Nazi crimes in a serious way in the late 1950s. In 1958 the CENTRAL OFFICE OF JUDICIAL ADMINISTRATION IN LUDWIGSBURG was established to uncover any available information on Nazi crimes and to initiate criminal proceedings against those responsible. To date, Germany has tried over 90,000 individuals and meted out over 6,400 severe sentences.

During the late 1990s both Lithuania and Croatia attempted to try war criminals. In Lithuania, the trials never got off the ground, due to the poor health of the defendants. In Croatia, the commandant of JASENOVAC was found guilty of crimes against humanity and sentenced to 20 years imprisonment. In the 1990s investigations and legal preceedings have also been carried out in Australia and Canada against war criminals who reached those countries after the war. (Regarding the United States, see OFFICE OF SPECIAL INVESTIGATIONS; regarding Israel, see EICHMANN TRIAL and DEMJANJUK TRIAL; regarding Italy, see PRIEBKE TRIAL; and regarding France, see BARBIE TRIAL, PAPON TRIAL, and TOUVIER TRIAL.)

TRUMAN, HARRY S. (1884–1972), Thirty-third president of the UNITED STATES, in office from 1945–1953. Before he reached the White House, Truman

President Harry S. Truman (left) with the first president of Israel, Chaim Weizmann, Washington, DC, July 18, 1948

was a judge and a senator from Missouri, and in 1944 became the vice-presidential running mate of President Franklin D. ROOSEVELT. Truman became president upon Roosevelt's death in April 1945. Less than a month later the Germans surrendered to the Allies and the war in Europe ended.

Already as a senator, Truman took a strong stand in favor of helping the persecuted Jews of Europe. As president at the war's end, he was candidly supportive of helping Jewish SURVIVORS and Displaced Persons (DPs, see also DISPLACED PERSONS, JEWISH). In July 1945 he changed certain aspects of the Displaced Persons Act that were discriminatory against Jews. In 1946 he publicly asked the British government to allow 10,000 DPs into Palestine, as he was convinced that Palestine was the best place to resettle Jewish REFUGEES. As a result, he also supported the establishment of a Jewish state in Palestine, and on November 29, 1947 he had the United States vote affirmatively for the United Nations' Partition Plan, whereby Jews would be given a state in Palestine. In May 1948 Truman's government was the first to recognize the newly established State of Israel.

TUCHIN   (in Polish, Tuczyn), small town in the UKRAINE. When WORLD WAR II broke out in September 1939, Tuchin was annexed by the SOVIET UNION. At that point, 3,000 Jews lived there. In mid-1941 GERMANY invaded the Soviet Union. Soon, the Jews in Tuchin were subjected to heavy anti-Jewish measures.

After hearing about the annihilation of the Jews in nearby Rovno in July 1942, the Jewish leaders of Tuchin decided to resist the Nazis. They came up with a plan to set fire to the houses in the GHETTO, shoot at the Germans, and make a mass run for the forest. On September 24, when German and Ukrainian troops moved into the ghetto, the resisters struck. They set fire to the ghetto and began shooting, while the rest of the ghetto population began running. Two-thirds of the Jews made it to the forest, while the rest died in battle, along with several Germans and Ukrainians. The revolt ended on September 26 when the lead resisters turned themselves in to the Germans.

Those who reached the forest found themselves in a terrible situation. About half were caught within three days, while 300 women with babies could not handle being in the forest, so they returned to Tuchin, where they were shot. Many other escapees died or were killed by peasants. When Tuchin was liberated in January 1944, only 20 Jews from the town remained in the region.

TUKA, VOJTECH   (1880–1946), Prime minister of the Nazi satellite state of SLOVAKIA during WORLD WAR II. A Slovak nationalist, Tuka worked as a law professor in the southwest Hungarian city of Pecs and later at the University of Bratislava. He also served as the secretary of the Slovak People's Party, which called for an independent Slovak state, and edited the party's periodical, *Slovak*.

Vojtech Tuka (front center)

After World War I Tuka worked together with the Hungarian Irredenta movement with regard to their joint anti-Czech platform. In 1923 he set up the fascist Home Guard military organization, and in 1929, a Czechoslovak court convicted him of high treason against the Czechoslovak government. Over the next decade, Tuka became a major supporter of an independent Slovakia, and acted as a leader of the extreme right-wing pro-German elements of the Slovak People's Party, which was now under the command of the Catholic priest, Andrej HLINKA.

As prime minister of Slovakia during World War II, Tuka strongly advocated the DEPORTATION of his country's Jews to the east—in other words, to their deaths at Nazi EXTERMINATION CAMPS in POLAND. After the war,

Tuka was sentenced to death by a court in BRATISLAVA, Slovakia, but he died in prison.

TUNISIA   Country in North Africa under French rule. Right before WORLD WAR II, 85,000 Jews lived in Tunisia.

During the first few weeks of the war, anti-Jewish feeling increased in Tunisia. In many areas, Jewish homes and stores were attacked. When FRANCE fell to GERMANY in May 1940, the Tunisians' longing for independence was stirred up, so they took their frustration out on the Jews.

In late 1940, there were calls to implement race laws in Tunisia. However, the governor-general, Vice Adm. Jean-Pierre Esteva, was sympathetic to the Jews, so he implemented only some of the STATUT DES JUIFS (Jewish Law). In addition, the Italian authorities also helped prevent the implementation of anti-Jewish laws: they demanded that the French refrain from confiscating the property of the 5,000 Jews in Tunisia who held Italian passports.

In November 1942 German and Italian troops invaded Tunisia in reaction to the invasion of ALGERIA and MOROCCO by the Allies. The Germans soon began initiating anti-Jewish measures. On November 23 they arrested four Jewish community leaders, including its president. On December 6 the Germans dissolved the Jewish Community Board and ordered the creation of a new one, whose first responsibility was to round up 2,000 Jews for FORCED LABOR. Eventually, 5,000 Jews were made to do forced labor under harsh conditions. In the Italian forced labor camps, the Jews were treated much better.

The Germans also carried out other anti-Jewish actions. Twenty Jewish political activists were arrested and deported to EXTERMINATION CAMPS in Europe, where they all died. Much Jewish property was seized, and heavy fines were exacted from the Jews. In certain places, Jews were forced to wear the Jewish badge (see also BADGE, JEWISH). These steps were meant to be the beginning of the destruction of the Tunisian Jewish community.

However, the Allies entered the capital, Tunis, on May 7, 1943, and quickly vanquished the Germans. The Jews were saved from annihilation at the hands of the Germans, but they were also subjected to harsh treatment by the returning French authorities, who arrested and imprisoned dozens of Jews with Italian passports as "collaborators." Several weeks went by before those Jews were released.

U

UKRAINE   Formerly a republic in the southwestern SOVIET UNION, and today an independent country. In 1920 most of the Ukraine was incorporated by the Soviet Union, while portions of the western Ukraine were annexed to POLAND (Volhynia and Eastern Galicia) and ROMANIA (BUKOVINA). On the eve of WORLD WAR II, there were 1.5 million Jews living in the Soviet Ukraine.

When war broke out in September 1939, the Soviet Union annexed the western (Polish) Ukraine, according to the terms of the NAZI-SOVIET PACT. In June 1940 the Soviet Union also took control of Bukovina and BESSARABIA and annexed them to the Soviet Ukraine. With its new, wider borders, the Ukraine now housed 2.4 million Jews.

GERMANY attacked its former ally, the Soviet Union, in June 1941. By October of that year the German army had occupied almost all of the Ukraine. Many

Execution carried out by SD men, Vinnitsa, Ukraine, 1942

Ukrainian citizens, mostly from the western Ukraine who were extremely antisemitic and had always seen the Soviet authorities as unlawful occupiers, happily welcomed their German "saviors" whom they thought would grant them full independence. Many Ukrainians volunteered to join the German army and police, and a Ukrainian SS division was even created as part of the *Waffen*-SS. However, the Germans never had any intention of allowing the Ukraine to become an independent country. The Nazis put most of the Ukraine under a civil administration called REICHSKOMMISSARIAT U-KRAINE, and the rest under a military administration. Eastern Galicia was added to the German administration in central Poland, known as the GENERALGOUVERNEMENT; the Jews there shared the fate of the rest of the Jews of Poland. Bukovina and Bessarabia were turned over to Romania, at that time allied with Germany. Many of the Jews in those areas were deported to the Ukrainian region of TRANSNISTRIA, where tens of thousands died of disease, malnourishment, exposure, and ill treatment, or were murdered.

Persecution of Jews began just as soon as German troops reached the Ukraine in mid-1941. In Bukovina and the western Ukraine, the local Ukrainians, led by the UKRAINIAN AUXILIARY POLICE, launched pogroms in which thousands of Jews were massacred and much Jewish property was either destroyed or looted. The Germans were more than happy to take advantage of Ukrainian ANTISEMITISM, and they encouraged the Ukrainian savagery.

In addition, along with the German army came EINSATZGRUPPEN—mobile killing units whose main task was to annihilate Jews and Communists. In the region that had been the Soviet Ukraine before the war, the *Einsatzgruppen* initiated a pattern of events, leading up to the extermination of the Jews, that were generally followed. Soon after the Germans arrived in each city or town, the Jews living there were ordered to don the Jewish badge for easy identification (see also BADGE, JEWISH); a JUDENRAT was established; the Jews were confined to certain streets or a GHETTO and some were sent to do FORCED LABOR. After a short time, the executions began: Jews were rounded up by German and Ukrainian police and sometimes German army units, and taken to empty quarries, ravines, or antitank ditches. When they arrived, they were shot to death by the *Einsatzgruppen.* Those Jews who tried to escape on the way were murdered on the spot, as were Jews who could not keep up with the rest. In some cases, the Germans used GAS VANS to murder the Jews in the Ukraine. The largest murder operation carried out by the *Einsatzgruppen* took place in a ravine called BABI YAR, outside of the city of Kiev. In two days at the end of September 1941, 33,371 Jews were shot to death. In many communities Jews offered resistance or fled to the forests and swamps where they engaged in PARTISAN activities.

The LIBERATION of the Ukraine by the Soviet army began when the German forces were defeated in the Battle of Stalingrad, and was completed in August 1944 with the liberation of the western Ukraine.

UKRAINIAN AUXILIARY POLICE
(*Ukrainische Hilfspolizei*), Ukrainian military units that were set up in the UKRAINE at the beginning of the German invasion of the SOVIET UNION in mid-1941. The job of these collaborating Ukrainians was to aid German troops in various operations, such as fighting the Soviet PARTISANS.

During the first week of the German occupation of the Ukraine, members of the Ukrainian Auxiliary Police took part in pogroms against the Jews. Later, they escorted Jews to their FORCED LABOR sites and guarded the GHETTOS. In those capacities, the Ukrainians stole from the Jews, harassed them, and often shot Jews at random. When the Germans began liquidating the ghettos of the Ukraine, the notoriously brutal Ukrainian policemen participated in those *aktionen.* They besieged the ghettos in order to prevent any escapes, searched for Jews who had gone into hiding, and chased down those who had managed to get away. They also accompanied the Jews to their executions, killed thousands of Jews who did not walk to their deaths fast enough, and guarded the execution sites so no one could get in or out.

In mid-1943 many Ukrainians abandoned the police to join the UKRAINIAN INSURGENT ARMY. Others withdrew from the Ukraine with the German army.

UKRAINIAN INSURGENT ARMY
(*Ukrainska Povstanska Armyia,* UPA), military wing of the ORGANIZA-TION OF UKRAINIAN NATIONALISTS. During WORLD WAR II, the UPA fought both Soviet and Polish troops in an effort to achieve Ukrainian independence; along the way they murdered Jews and 40,000 Poles.

UKRAINISCHE HILFSPOLIZEI
see UKRAINIAN AUX-ILIARY POLICE.

UKRAINSKA POVSTANSKA ARMYIA
see UKRAINIAN INSURGENT ARMY.

UMSCHLAGPLATZ
(transfer point), the departure point in WARSAW from which hundreds of thousands of Jews were deported to Nazi EXTERMINATION CAMPS.

The *Umschlagplatz* was actually the area that separated the Warsaw GHETTO from the Polish part of the city. It was the only official junction where goods could be transferred in and out of the ghetto.

When the Germans began mass DEPORTATIONS from the ghetto in July 1942, the site no longer served as a point of transfer between the ghetto and the outside; instead, it was used as the assembly site for the ghetto Jews who were to be deported. These Jews were arrested in the streets of the ghetto and marched to the *Umschlagplatz.* They were made to sit on the ground in the *Umschlagplatz's* courtyard or on the floor inside an empty building on the site, where they waited for the daily train to pull in. When it arrived they were packed in, 100–120 persons to a freight car. SS men, Ukrainian and Baltic troops, and the Polish police were all on hand to ensure that nothing went awry.

In 1988 a monument was dedicated at the *Umschlagplatz* to commemorate the more than 300,000 Warsaw Jews who were deported from there to their deaths. (see picture on page 449)

UMWANDERERZENTRALSTELLE
see CENTRAL RE-SETTLEMENT OFFICE.

UNION DES JUIFS POUR LA RESISTANCE ET L'ENTR'AIDE
see UNION OF JEWS FOR RESISTANCE AND MUTUAL AID.

UNION GENERALE DES ISRAELITES DE FRANCE (UGIF)
see UNION OF FRENCH JEWS.

UNION OF FRENCH JEWS
(*Union Generale des Israelites de France,* UGIF), organization established by the Vichy government's Office of Jewish Affairs to

The Umschlagplatz, point from which Jews were deported from Warsaw, summer 1942

consolidate all the Jewish organizations of FRANCE into one single unit.

The UGIF was set up on November 29, 1941 in response to German demands. The organization actually consisted of two autonomous councils, one in the occupied zone under Andre Baur and one in the unoccupied Vichy zone under Raymond Raoul Lambert.

The Jews of France were assured that the purpose of the UGIF was to furnish social aid for the Jews—and indeed the union set up orphanages and other social services. However, it was frequently forced to yield to German and French demands for money, cooperation with mass arrests, and names of Jewish resistance activists. Those leaders who refused to cooperate were arrested themselves and sent to CONCENTRATION CAMPS. Despite this, some members of the UGIF, especially in the unoccupied zone, took upon themselves to proactively resist German policy. For example, the southern UGIF intervened to halt the DEPORTATION of foreign Jews seeking refuge in their zone. It succeeded in illegally evacuating many children and adults from French internment camps. Welfare and other forms of assistance were provided by the UGIF until it was dissolved in 1944. (for more on Vichy, see also FRANCE.)

UNION OF JEWS FOR RESISTANCE AND MUTUAL AID (*Union des Juifs pour la Resistance et l'Entr'aide*), a secret resistance organization, originally called *Solidarite* (Solidarity), formed by Jewish Communists in PARIS after the German invasion in August 1940.

In January 1941 *Solidarite* refused to join the Coordinating Committee of Jewish Welfare Societies, suspecting the Nazis would take control. In May almost 4,000 Parisian Jews were arrested, which took *Solidarite* and others by surprise. After the Germans invaded the SOVIET UNION in June, *Solidarite* began to sabotage German industry. In early 1942 they opposed the UNION OF FRENCH JEWS, claiming that its members were collaborators. At the same time *Solidarite* created the National Movement against Racism, hoping for non-Jewish support.

After the mass DEPORTATIONS of July 1942, *Solidarite*

formed more partisan groups. In their secret press they publicized the Nazi program for mass gassing, and called for the Jews to hide and fight, not work for German industry. However, by summer 1943, *Solidarite* changed its name and strategy after the Germans had devastated the group and the French-Jewish population. It then turned to its members in southern FRANCE to lead fighting efforts. By war's end, the organization had saved 900 children, but lost more than 500 of its members. (see also RESISTANCE, JEWISH.)

UNION OF ROMANIAN JEWS

(*Uniunea Evreilor Romani*, UER), ROMANIA'S oldest and most important Jewish organization. In 1938 Romania's King Carol II dissolved all of his country's political organizations, including the UER. Until that time, the UER worked at defending Jewish interests; instituted and maintained civil rights for Jews; fought official and unofficial ANTISEMITISM; and encouraged the incorporation of Jews into Romanian life.

The union was headed by Wilhelm FILDERMAN, considered by many to be the leading Jew in Romania. During the war, Filderman managed to convince his contacts in the Romanian government not to deport the Jews living within pre-World War I Romania and in Southern TRANSYLVANIA to the EXTERMINATION CAMPS in POLAND.

After Romania's LIBERATION, the UER concentrated on defending the human rights of Romanian Jews. Union members worked very hard to reintroduce Holocaust SURVIVORS into Romania's economic life and restore Jewish property that had been confiscated during the war. However, the Jewish Communists considered the union to be a threat, and union leaders an impediment to their Communist programs among the Jews. They managed to divide the union and form a breakaway organization with the help of some of Filderman's closest assistants. The UER's activities were cancelled in late 1947.

UNITED NATIONS RELIEF AND REHABILITATION ADMINISTRATION (UNRRA)

Organization created by the Allies to assist REFUGEES who were displaced as a result of WORLD WAR II and to aid countries in poor economic shape due to the war.

The UNRRA was established in November 1943. It was run by a council that consisted of one delegate from each of the United Nations' member states, and a Central Committee that was made up of representa-

UNRRA orphanage, Bad Reichenhall, Germany

tives from the UNITED STATES, GREAT BRITAIN, the SOVIET UNION, and China. The four member states of the Central Committee committed themselves to funding 75 percent of the UNRRA's budget, while the United States assumed the responsibility of providing a director-general for the agency.

The UNRRA council held its first meeting in mid-November 1943, at which its members set up advisory committees for Europe and East Asia based on region, as well as committees to deal with finance control, agriculture, health, rehabilitation of industry, welfare, and displaced persons (DPs). Until the war ended in 1945, the UNRRA was unable to accomplish much in the way of restoration and rehabilitation. It had to get the approval of the Allied Forces Supreme Command before moving into liberated areas, and the operation was slow going.

In May 1944 UNRRA teams were able to begin fulfilling their function of rehabilitating refugees and displaced persons; at that time they joined the administration of refugee camps in Palestine, Syria, and Egypt, which were filled with some 37,000 refugees from GREECE, Albania, ITALY, and YUGOSLAVIA. By the end of 1944 the UNRRA was taking care of 74,000 refugees located in refugee camps all over the Mediterranean, Africa, and the Middle East. In Italy, the UNRRA was responsible for two hospitals and 6,000 refugees in four camps.

When the war ended in 1945, the UNRRA was faced with overwhelming responsibilities. Millions of homeless refugees and DPs were lost in Europe and needed care, both physical and emotional. Thousands of children had been orphaned, and families had been torn apart. There were great shortages of clothing and food, the possibility of disease loomed, and UNRRA workers and the DPs had trouble communicating due to the language barrier. After months of enlisting the appropriate staff, the UNRRA found that those they had hired were not nearly prepared enough to deal with the SURVIVORS.

After several months, the UNRRA became better organized and was able to assist the DPs. Based on agreements with the American, British, and French authorities in Europe, the UNRRA was put under the control of each country's military command in the zone it occupied. The military occupiers and the UNRRA then divided responsibilities: the military was in charge of housing, maintaining the peace, and obtaining and giving out basic supplies, while the UNRRA was responsible for running the DP camps, providing welfare and health services, entertainment, and job training, and contributing whatever supplies the military did not. By the end of 1945, the UNRRA was running two-thirds of the transit centers and DP camps in West Germany.

The UNRRA also provided food, clothing, raw materials, medical supplies, farming machinery, and more to various recovering countries and regions. These included Czechoslovakia, Yugoslavia, Italy, POLAND, AUSTRIA, the UKRAINE, BELORUSSIA, Albania, Greece, China, the Dodecanese islands and, to a smaller extent, FINLAND, HUNGARY, Ethiopia, and the Philippines. In addition, the UNRRA was responsible for the operation of 23 volunteer welfare agencies, including various Jewish organizations (such as the JOINT DISTRIBUTION COMMITTEE and HIAS). By September 1946 the UNRRA had spent about $3.67 billion.

In 1947 the UNRRA's role in Europe was gradually dissolved; the responsibility for some 643,000 DPs was assumed by the Preparatory Commission for the International Refugee Organization. By 1948 the UNRRA closed its remaining offices in Europe, Asia, Australia, and Central and South America. (see also DISPLACED PERSONS, JEWISH.)

UNITED NATIONS WAR CRIMES COMMISSION (UNWCC)

International committee established by the Allies in October 1943 to find and prosecute war criminals. Representatives of Australia, BELGIUM, CANADA, China, Czechoslovakia, FRANCE, GREECE, India, the NETHERLANDS, LUXEMBOURG, New Zealand, NORWAY, POLAND, South Africa, the UNITED STATES, YUGOSLAVIA, and Ethiopia participated in the UNWCC. The SOVIET UNION did not join, but cooperated with the group in spirit.

The UNWCC was made responsible for investigating Nazi crimes, recording them, and helping prepare indictments; making sure the war criminals were arrested and the evidence of their crimes was exposed; finding the legal basis for the punishment and extradition of the criminals; and figuring out which actions should be included under the heading "CRIMES AGAINST HUMANITY," including the crime of GENOCIDE.

Based on the UNWCC's recommendations, Centers of Documentation of Nazi War Crimes were set up throughout GERMANY to aid research into their crimes. The UNWCC also called for the institution of the International Military Tribunal at NUREMBERG and other courts, and helped establish the official lists of war criminals—registering 36,000 suspected war criminals.

The UNWCC was dissolved in 1948 as the Cold War heated up, due to the failure of various countries to cooperate with their obligations to extradite suspected war criminals.

UNITED PARTISAN ORGANIZATION, VILNA

(*Fareynegte Partizaner Organizatsye,* FPO), underground Jewish organization active in the VILNA Ghetto. The FPO was established in January 1942; it consisted of members of the GHETTO's Zionist YOUTH MOVEMENTS. The FPO's first commander was Yitzhak WITTENBERG.

FPO members mined railroad tracks used by trains going to the front lines; sabotaged weapons and equipment in German factories where underground members worked; and forged documents for fellow Jews. They also focused on obtaining weapons, which were very hard to come by. They bought some weapons from the local population, and FPO members who worked at the Germans' captured-weapons warehouse managed to smuggle some from there, too. The organization also assembled primitive Molotov cocktails and hand grenades inside the Ghetto itself.

The FPO sent messengers to nearby ghettos to establish contact, warn them about the mass extermination of the Jews of Vilna and the rest of LITHUANIA, and spread the idea of armed revolt and resistance. The group also tried, unsuccessfully, to make contact with the Polish HOME ARMY.

The FPO soon found itself at odds with the Vilna JUDENRAT. Jacob GENS, the *Judenrat* chairman, believed that the FPO endangered the ghetto with its activities. Based on a German order, Gens arrested Wittenberg in July 1943. Wittenberg managed to escape, but surrendered after he saw that most of the ghetto's inhabitants sided with Gens. Wittenberg committed suicide that night, and Abba KOVNER took over the FPO's command.

In September 1943 the Nazis began liquidating the ghetto. The FPO prepared to fight and called on the ghetto's inhabitants to join the revolt. However, the inhabitants did not respond, thinking they were being sent elsewhere to work. The FPO then gave up on a ghetto uprising for lack of support, and began sending its members to the forest. Most managed to reach the Soviet PARTISANS, and establish themselves as Jewish battalions in the Soviet partisan movement. FPO members-turned-partisans participated in the LIBERATION of Vilna by the Soviet army on July 13, 1944.

UNITED STATES OF AMERICA   Long considered to be a country that could be counted on as a place of refuge for the "tired, poor, huddled masses yearning to breathe free," the United States did not live up to those expectations during the HOLOCAUST. The US government would not change its immigration quotas to allow in more Jewish REFUGEES from Europe, nor did it embark on extensive rescue operations. Despite relatively early knowledge of the true meaning of the "Final Solution" the Americans refused to bomb the railroad tracks leading to the AUSCHWITZ extermination camp. President Franklin D. ROOSEVELT, long supported by most American Jews, would not allow the war with the Germans to be depicted as a battle to save European Jewry.

The United States' ambivalent policy regarding Nazi ANTISEMITISM can be viewed as a result of several factors. The country was slowly recovering from the crippling Great Depression, which had left many Americans in poverty. Public opinion condemned the notion of allowing in European refugees who were liable to take away jobs from Americans who really needed them. Many Americans also called for isolationism, with an emphasis on America first. They did not want the government to adopt a policy of intervention in the affairs of other countries. Furthermore, there were strong antisemitic elements within the American government. Right-wing politicians criticized both Roosevelt's New Deal programs and American Jews, whom they associated with the liberal president. Laws calling

US soldier and survivor, Buchenwald, 1945

for rescue operations were not passed because those politicians refused to support them. In addition, the State Department itself was responsible for the prevention of the rescue of European Jews from the Nazis.

During the 1930s, American immigration quotas were very low, and even those were prevented from being filled. In July 1938 President Roosevelt convened the EVIAN CONFERENCE with delegates from 32 countries to discuss the growing European refugee problem. However, not one country, including the United States, was willing to selflessly take in any refugees. All the American delegate would commit to was making the previously unfilled quota for Germans and Austrians available to the new refugees. The American-initiated conference did nothing to help those refugees desperately trying to get out of Europe before it was too late.

After the KRISTALLNACHT pogrom of November 1938, the American ambassador to GERMANY was recalled in a gesture of disapproval. However, the United States continued to ignore the refugee problem by refusing to take in or even intercede on behalf of the 937 Jewish refugees sailing on the ST. LOUIS, a ship that had left Germany in May 1939. Those Jews were subsequently turned back to Europe, where most perished in the Holocaust. In 1939 and 1940, a bill to allow

10,000 Jewish children into the United States was never even put to discussion in Congress.

The United States entered WORLD WAR II in December 1941. From then on, the government's main priority was winning the war, not saving Europe's Jews. The anti-refugee activists in the government also began spreading the fear that if refugees would be allowed to enter the country, the Germans would plant spies among them. Thus, they felt that no refugees should be admitted. Roosevelt did not want to alienate those elements of the government by making it look like the war was about the Jews. Thus, at the Allies' war conferences, the mass annihilation of European Jewry was not even mentioned—despite the fact that the United States had received reliable reports about the dire situation in Europe.

As further reports of Nazi atrocities reached the West by the end of 1942, the British government was put under pressure to do something to help the Jews. They decided to make a small gesture in order to assuage the British public. On December 17, 1942 the United States joined GREAT BRITAIN, NORWAY, the SOVIET UNION, and various governments-in-exile in loudly condemning the Nazis' "bestial policy of cold-blooded extermination." Nevertheless, this was just a gesture.

Another meaningless gesture was made in April 1943, at the BERMUDA CONFERENCE, convened by the United States and Great Britain. Ostensibly, the conference was called to deal with the refugee problem again, now that the world knew what was really happening in Europe. However, the organizers designed the conference to be as unsuccessful as possible. The venue of Bermuda itself was remote and hard to reach, almost no reporters were admitted in, and no Jewish representatives were invited. The Jewish aspect of the issue was forbidden to be discussed, along with the words "Final Solution." In the end, the conference was called to shush the growing public outcries for the rescue of European Jewry without actually having to find any solutions to the problem.

During the winter of 1942–1943, the opposite ends of the spectrum in the American government were revealed: certain government officials began pressuring President Roosevelt to issue a rescue proclamation, while the State Department continued to sabotage rescue efforts. When Henry MORGENTHAU, the Jewish secretary of the treasury, found out about the State Department's activities, he immediately reported them to the president. Fearing a scandal, the president decided to establish an agency for the rescue of Jewish refugees. This was called the WAR REFUGEE BOARD (WRB).

Fighting America's previous policy on Jewish refugees, the WRB tried to do its best to rescue Jews. It sponsored the activities of diplomats like Raoul WALLENBERG, who saved thousands of Hungarian Jews, and it pushed for the establishment of a safe haven for refugees in FORT ONTARIO, New York. However, Roosevelt would not support the institution of other such havens, nor would he agree to the board's recommendations to publicly condemn the mass murder of Jews by the Nazis and bomb Auschwitz. Thus, the success of the WRB proved to be too little, too late. Only after the war did President Harry S. TRUMAN enlarge America's immigrant quotas to allow in Holocaust SURVIVORS and support the establishment of a Jewish state in Palestine. (see also AUSCHWITZ, BOMBING OF.)

UNIUNEA EVREILOR ROMANI   see UNION OF ROMANIAN JEWS.

USTASA   ("insurgent" in plural *ustase*), Croatian nationalist, fascist, terrorist movement created in 1930. *Ustasa* was led by Ante PAVELIC.

The *Ustasa* opposed YUGOSLAVIA as a national entity, which was ruled by a Serb royal family, as *Ustasa* members fiercely hated Serbs. They also hated Jews, Communists, and non-Catholics. Until 1941, fascist ITALY acted as the group's political sponsor. In the mid-1930s the *Ustasa* began to woo Nazi GERMANY by adopting various aspects of Nazi ideology, including its anti-Jewish sentiments. When WORLD WAR II broke out, the *Ustasa* began hating Jews as much as they hated Serbs. However, the Germans ignored the *Ustasa* until their invasion of Yugoslavia in April 1941.

At that point, the Nazis created a Croatian satellite state, and allowed the *Ustasa* to run a puppet government with Pavelic at its head. During their four years in power, the *Ustasa* carried out a Serb GENOCIDE, exterminating over 500,000, expelling 250,000, and forcing another 250,000 to convert to Catholicism. The *Ustasa* also killed most of CROATIA'S Jews, 20,000 GYPSIES, and many thousands of their political enemies.

The *Ustasa* government was dissolved in May 1945. After the war, most of the *Ustasa* leaders escaped to South America and SPAIN.

USTREDNA ZIDOV   see JEWISH CENTER, SLOVAKIA.

V

VA'AD HA-HATSALA Rescue Committee of UNITED STATES Orthodox Rabbis, established in November 1939 by the Union of Orthodox Rabbis of the United States and CANADA. Its goal was to rescue rabbis and *yeshiva* students who had fled POLAND for LITHUANIA after WORLD WAR II broke out.

For the first two years of its existence, the *Va'ad* sent aid to 2,500 rabbis and students in Lithuania, at that time under Soviet control. The committee helped 650 of these REFUGEES emigrate during the first half of 1941. Some made it to the United States or Palestine, but most ended up in SHANGHAI, China, where they stayed for the rest of the war. Some of the rabbis who arrived in the United States became active in the *Va'ad*'s activities.

After the United States entered the war in December 1941, the *Va'ad* focused on helping the refugee scholars in Shanghai and hundreds of scholars who had sought refuge in Soviet Central Asia. The committee sent them money and packages, which helped them continue their study routines despite the difficult conditions.

In 1942 the news of the mass extermination of European Jewry was made public. The *Va'ad* then turned its attention to the rescue of Jews in Eastern Europe. They pressured the US government to help save the Jews; one of the committee's major activities was a protest march of 400 Orthodox rabbis to the White House on October 6, 1943. This effort helped contribute to the creation of the WAR REFUGEE BOARD.

From 1939–1943, the *Va'ad* had concentrated on rescuing *yeshiva* students and rabbis only. In January 1944, when the extent of the destruction in Eastern Europe was made known to committee leaders, they decided to work on rescuing all types of Jews. Throughout 1944 and 1945 the *Va'ad* engaged in relief and rescue activities through its offices in SWITZERLAND, SWEDEN, Turkey, and Tangier. The committee also kept in contact with Orthodox leaders in SLOVAKIA and HUNGARY. In February 1945 the *Va'ad* succeeded in rescuing 1,200 prisoners from THERESIENSTADT and sent them to Switzerland.

After the war, the *Va'ad* assisted SURVIVORS of the HOLOCAUST.

VAIVARA Transit and CONCENTRATION CAMP in northeast ESTONIA. Vaivara was established by the SS in 1943 as a camp for Soviet PRISONERS OF WAR. From August 1943 to February 1944 it served as the main branch of 20 FORCED LABOR camps located throughout Estonia. Some 20,000 Jews from LATVIA and from the Lithuanian GHETTOS of VILNA and KOVNO were brought to Vaivara, where they were kept before being sent on to the labor camps. For that reason, Vaivara was considered a transit camp. In addition, as a concentration camp, Vaivara housed 1,300 prisoners at a time. These prisoners were mainly Jews, with smaller groups of Russians, Dutch, and Estonians.

The prisoners worked at various types of hard labor, including railroad construction, digging antitank ditches, quarrying, and cutting down trees in forests and swamps. They lived in wooden huts that let in the brutal cold, and they received meager food rations. In addition, water was scarce, while lice and illness were widespread. The prisoners were subjected to selections every two weeks, as a result of which many were murdered, while others died from SS beatings (see also SELEKTION).

As the Soviet army drew closer, hundreds of the surviving prisoners were sent westward on DEATH MARCHES.

VALLAT, XAVIER (1891–1972), Coordinator of Jewish affairs in FRANCE's Vichy government during 1941 and 1942. Vallat was first elected to France's parliament in 1919. His ideology was strongly influenced by ACTION FRANCAISE, the radical, nationalist, right-wing, antisemitic movement, and he often attacked Jews in parliament.

In March 1941 Marshal Philippe PETAIN, the head of the Vichy government, named Vallat director of the government's OFFICE FOR JEWISH AFFAIRS. As such, Vallat was responsible for instituting and carrying out France's

ANTI-JEWISH LEGISLATION. In late 1941 he created the UNION OF FRENCH JEWS, on the initiative of Adolf EICHMANN'S representative, Theodor DANNECKER. However, despite the fact that Vallat fully believed in the need to exclude Jews from French society, he did not want to be subservient to the Nazis nor further a program that would bolster the German economy. He refused to carry out the Germans' more extreme requests such as the DEPORTATION of Jews. In May 1942 the Germans stripped Vallat of his position, because they considered him too moderate. After the war, Vallat was sentenced to 10 years in jail, but was released after two. (for more on Vichy, see also FRANCE.)

VAN DER VOORT, HANNA
Dutch woman who rescued Jewish children during WORLD WAR II.

During the HOLOCAUST, van der Voort and a man named Nico Dohmen were associated with a widespread underground network. The two worked together to find hiding places for 123 Jewish children in the southern NETHERLANDS. Dohmen and van der Voort organized both temporary and permanent safe havens for the children in private homes. In addition, they transferred the children from place to place when they were in danger of being discovered. The underground provided funds for the children, and stole food coupons for them from the Germans. Dohmen acted as a messenger between the underground and the families who were providing refuge. He kept in close contact with the children, and became very familiar and devoted to them, acting as sort of a substitute father. He spent much time trying to cheer them up and give them hope.

Van der Voort's activities were eventually discovered by the Germans. She was arrested and tortured, but she refused to reveal any information about her co-workers or their activities. The brutal treatment she received in jail permanently damaged her health. Both she and Dohmen were designated as RIGHTEOUS AMONG THE NATIONS by YAD VASHEM.

VAPNIARKA
Ukrainian town attached to TRANSNISTRIA for most of the war, and site of a detention camp established by the Romanians in October 1941.

The first prisoners brought to the camp were Jews from ODESSA. In 1942 Jewish prisoners arrived from BUKOVINA and ROMANIA. At the end of that year, Vapniarka became a CONCENTRATION CAMP for political prisoners under the direct control of the Romanian government. The camp was actually designated for Jews, since no other "political prisoners" were held there. There were 1,179 Jews in the camp, including 107 women. The inmates established a camp committee to help each other survive the terrible conditions. The camp also had an underground.

The prisoners overcame typhus by keeping the camp immaculately clean. However, they were fed horse fodder, which caused hundreds to contract a paralysis-inducing disease that affects the bone marrow. The inmates demanded medical help; the authorities permitted the Jewish Aid Committee to provide medicine, and finally stopped feeding the Jews animal food.

As Soviet troops approached in October 1943, the authorities decided to liquidate the camp. Some Jews were sent to GHETTOS in Transnistria, but most prisoners were moved to another Romanian camp until the National Legionary Government toppled in the summer of 1944.

VEESENMAYER, EDMUND
(1904–1977), German diplomat in the Balkan region during WORLD WAR II. Veesenmayer joined the NAZI PARTY in 1925. By the end of the war he had reached the rank of *Brigadefuehrer* in the SS. In 1932 Veesenmayer joined the diplomatic service and was sent to serve in the Balkans. He became a prominent member of economic circles and had a lot of important friends in high places.

At the beginning of 1941 Veesenmayer was attached to the German diplomatic staff in Zagreb, CROATIA. He played a role in the persecution and murder of Croatian and Serbian Jewry.

In 1944 Veesenmayer was sent as the Reich plenipotentiary (representative) to HUNGARY, where he worked very hard at furthering the "Final Solution" in conjunction with SS officer Adolf EICHMANN. In fact, Veesenmayer acted as diplomatic camouflage for Eichmann's murderous activities.

After the war Veesenmayer was convicted of war crimes and sentenced to 20 years in prison. However, in 1951 he was released by the United States High Commissioner in Germany.

VICHY
see FRANCE.

VIENNA
Capital of AUSTRIA. Despite a long antisemitic tradition, Jews played an important role in Viennese life as composers, writers, thinkers, and scientists. In 1923 there were 201,513 Jews in Vienna. By the late 1930s, 30,000 Jews had fled the city.

After the ANSCHLUSS—the Nazi takeover of Austria in March 1938—the Germans began implementing anti-Jewish measures. At first, the Germans' goal was to pressure the Jews into emigrating. They shamed the Jews by making them wash the streets. They closed the Jewish community and Zionist organization offices, and sent their board members to DACHAU. Those offices were reopened in May to take care of emigration and social aid. From mid-October, almost every night in Vienna was punctuated with attacks on Jewish stores, synagogues, and schools. Then the KRISTALLNACHT pogrom took place in November, which aggravated the situation: 49 synagogues were destroyed, and 3,600 Jews were deported to Dachau and BUCHENWALD. Those Jews were only released when they could show proof that they were going to emigrate.

After the Germans invaded POLAND in September 1939, DEPORTATIONS began from Vienna. In early October, 1,048 Polish and stateless Jews were sent to Buchenwald, and later that month, 1,584 Jewish professionals were deported to the Nisko region. By early 1941, SS leader Adolf EICHMANN was still willing to allow emigration. Jews desperately searched for places to go, to very little avail.

In July 1941 there were still 50,000 Jews living in Vienna. Emigration of Jews between the ages of 18–45 was outlawed on August 5, and full-fledged deportations to EXTERMINATION CAMPS began on October 15, 1941. Tens of thousands of Jews were sent to THERESIENSTADT, LODZ, RIGA, MINSK, and Izbica (in the LUBLIN district). Most were later shot to death or gassed.

By the end of 1944 less than 6,000 Austrian Jews were left in Vienna. Most of these were partners in "privileged mixed marriages" or in regular mixed marriages. Vienna was liberated by Soviet troops on April 12, 1945. At that time, 150 Jews came out of hiding. Another 150 had survived as workers in the warehouses of confiscated Jewish possessions, or as laborers in homes of SS leaders.

Jews waiting in line after the Anschluss to register with the police, Vienna, 1938

VILNA (in Lithuanian, Vilnius; in Polish, Wilno), capital of LITHUANIA. Before WORLD WAR II, Vilna was a major center of Jewish scholarship and culture. Under Polish rule from 1920–1939, Vilna had a population of 200,000, including 55,000 Jews. On September 19, 1939 the Soviets entered Lithuania; about 15,000 Jewish REFUGEES from POLAND fled to Vilna soon after. A few weeks later, the Soviets delivered Vilna to the Lithuanians. In July 1940 Vilna, along with the rest of Lithuania, was annexed to the SOVIET UNION. From September 1939 to June 1941, 6,500 Jewish refugees left Vilna for the UNITED STATES, Palestine, the Far East, and elsewhere.

On June 24, 1941 the Germans occupied Vilna as part of their invasion of the Soviet Union. A few days later, the German and Lithuanian authorities began instituting anti-Jewish measures. On July 4 the Germans ordered that a JUDENRAT be established. During July 5,000 Jewish men were arrested by EINSATZGRUPPEN and Lithuanian collaborators, and shot in the PONARY Forest outside of Vilna. At the beginning of September, two GHETTOS were established with two *Judenraete* and a Jewish police. Over the next few months, thousands of Jews were exterminated at Ponary in a series of *aktionen*. By the end of 1941, the smaller ghetto had been liquidated and 33,500 Jews had been murdered. Another 3,500 had fled or hidden outside the ghetto.

For most of 1942 there were no further *aktionen*, and the Jews in the ghetto were able to develop a rich communal life. They established schools, a health-care system, cultural activities, and social-aid institutions. The *Judenrat* was chaired by Jacob GENS, who believed that if the ghetto was economically worthwhile for the Germans, they would not destroy it. Thus, the council provided jobs for as many Jews in the ghetto as possible. The United Partisan Organization (*Fareynegte Partizaner Organizatsye*, FPO) was also established during the quiet of 1942.

The situation deteriorated in the spring of 1943. Nearby small ghettos and labor camps were liquidated, and the mass killings began again. The FPO and the *Judenrat* had several major clashes, because Gens believed that the FPO's underground activities were endangering the rest of the ghetto. In July, the Germans demanded the arrest of the FPO leader, Yitzhak WITTENBERG, under the threat that the entire ghetto would be destroyed. Wittenberg turned himself in, hoping to avoid further bloodshed. However, the ghetto was destined for destruction.

Mass DEPORTATIONS took place in August and September; thousands of men and women were sent to CONCENTRATION CAMPS in ESTONIA. During these deportations, the FPO called on the inhabitants of the ghetto to revolt. However, the Jews did not heed the call. The FPO began attacking German troops themselves; Gens, believing that armed revolt would just lead to the total destruction of the ghetto, offered to hand over the required number of Jews for deportation. This ended the clashes. Gens himself was shot by the GESTAPO on September 14.

The final liquidation of the Vilna Ghetto took place on September 23–24, 1943. Over 4,000 children, women, and old men were deported to SOBIBOR; 3,700 Jews were sent to camps in Estonia and LATVIA; and hundreds of women, children, and old men were shot at Ponary. About 2,500 Jews were left in labor camps in Vilna. About 1,000 Jews had gone into hiding inside the ghetto; most were caught over the next few months. A few hundred FPO members joined the PARTISANS. Eighty Jews were kept in Ponary to open the mass graves and burn the bodies to destroy the evidence of mass killings. Ten days before Vilna was liberated, the Jews in the local labor camps were killed in Ponary; 150–200 managed to escape.

Vilna was liberated on July 13, 1944. Only 2,000–3,000 of the city's original Jewish population had survived. (see also UNITED PARTISAN ORGANIZATION, VILNA.)

VISSER, LODEWIJK ERNST (1871–1942), Dutch judge active in Jewish affairs. Visser was appointed to the Dutch Supreme Court in 1915 and became chief justice in 1939. During the 1930s he helped aid Jewish REFUGEES and protested the persecution of German Jewry. When the Germans occupied the NETHERLANDS in May 1940, Jews were removed from government jobs; Visser was suspended from the supreme court.

In December 1940 Holland's Jewish organizations convened to establish the Jewish Coordinating Committee, in an attempt to provide a united leadership for the Jewish community and face the Germans' anti-Jewish policies. Visser was appointed chairman. He strongly criticized the establishment of the Nazi-appointed Jewish Council and its cooperation with the Nazis. The Germans annulled Visser's Coordinating Committee in October 1941, and recognized the Jewish Council as the only official representative of Dutch Jewry. Nonetheless, Visser continued to criticize the council's policies.

Portrait of the Dutch Supreme Court Justice,
Lodewijk Ernst Visser

Visser believed that the Dutch government should take responsibility for Dutch Jews, as Dutch citizens with full rights. He even took specific appeals to government officials and asked them to oppose the Germans' anti-Jewish orders. However, he was warned to stop his activities at the threat of being sent to a CONCENTRATION CAMP. Several days later, Visser died of a heart attack.

VITTEL Detention camp located in northeastern FRANCE. Vittel was established by the Germans in 1940 to house citizens of neutral or enemy countries whom they wanted to exchange for German prisoners. Vittel did not look like other Nazi camps: it was made up of luxurious hotels situated inside a park. Of course, the park was surrounded by three rows of barbed wire and guarded by German patrols.

In early 1943 the internees at Vittel included British and American citizens and a group of Polish, Belgian, and Dutch Jews. Some of these prisoners were holders of Latin American passports or visas. In January 1944 the SS sent a special delegation from BERLIN to check the validity of the Latin American passports held by prisoners at Vittel. The delegation decided that the passports were invalid, and as the Latin American governments

themselves did not recognize the passports, the bearers of the documents were then in mortal danger. Humanitarian and Jewish organizations begged the American and British authorities to pressure the Latin American countries to honor the documents. The passports were finally validated in late March 1944, but this was too late: about 250 Jews at Vittel had already been sent to their deaths at AUSCHWITZ. Among them was the poet Yitzhak KATZENELSON.

Children in Vittel who were later murdered in Auschwitz

Vittel was liberated by the Allies on September 12, 1944.

VLASOV, ANDREI (1900–1946), Soviet army general who collaborated with the Germans against the Soviet regime. Vlasov trained anti-Soviet propaganda agents in GERMANY, instituted the Committee for the Liberation of the Peoples of Russia, and organized two Russian divisions in Germany. The Soviets executed Vlasov in 1946.

VOLDEMARAS, AUGUSTINAS (1883–1942), Fascist and antisemitic Lithuanian politician. Voldemaras's supporters—backed financially by the German Foreign Office—were some of LITHUANIA'S foremost Nazi collaborators, and actively participated in the murder of Jews in Lithuania and in other countries.

VOLKSDEUTSCHE Nazi term, literally meaning "German-folk," used to refer to ethnic Germans living outside of GERMANY. *Volksdeutsche* did not hold German or Austrian citizenship, but the Nazis felt it important to strengthen their communities throughout east-central Europe.

Ethnic Germans (Volksdeutsche), Warsaw, 1939

In 1936 the Nazis set up an office to act as a contact for the *Volksdeutsche*. After the Germans occupied PO-LAND in September 1939, they established a central registration bureau, called the German Folk List (*Deutsche Volksliste,* DVL), where they registered Polish citizens of German origin as *Volksdeutsche*. Poles were greatly encouraged to register themselves, and were sometimes forced to do so. Those who joined this group were given benefits, including better food, and were accorded a special status. They were given apartments, farms, workshops, furniture, and clothing—all stolen from Jews and Poles sent to Nazi camps.

In early 1940, the Nazis divided the *Volksdeutsche* into four categories: ethnic Germans who supported the THIRD REICH; other ethnic Germans; Poles who had German ancestors; and Poles who were related to Germans.

After the Nazis occupied YUGOSLAVIA, they introduced the *Volksliste* there; they also registered ethnic Germans living in the SOVIET UNION. Many were resettled in the GENERALGOUVERNEMENT or in parts of Poland occupied by the Nazis, and many served in the German army.

VUGHT   Transit camp for Jews, located in the southern part of the NETHERLANDS, which was established in late 1942. The first Jewish prisoners arrived at Vught in January 1943. By May there were 8,684 Jews in the camp, plus a number of non-Jewish prisoners. The conditions at Vught were quite bad until David COHEN of the Dutch JUDENRAT intervened; at that point, the living and sanitary conditions at the camp improved to a certain degree.

From April 1943 the male prisoners at Vught were sent to work outside the camp. The rest of the prisoners worked at Vught itself, where they manufactured furs and clothing. Some 1,200 prisoners were employed at workshops of the Philips Company; this was considered the best place to work, as the company insisted that its Jewish workers be given better living conditions and a hot meal every day, and made sure that they were not deported.

The Dutch Prince Bernard visiting Vught after the war

Throughout the transit camp's existence, prisoners at Vught were transferred to the WESTERBORK camp, from which they were deported to their deaths at AUSCHWITZ and SOBIBOR. The last group of Jews deported from Westerbork included the prisoners from Vught who had worked at Philips; ultimately, despite its efforts, the company was unable to save its Jewish employees.

VYHNE Labor camp in SLOVAKIA. Vyhne was established in early 1940 to house 326 Jewish REFUGEES from PRAGUE who had been imprisoned in Sosnowiec, POLAND. The group was brought to Slovakia by the Slovak Jewish Center, especially through the efforts of Gisi FLEISCHMANN. Ultimately, most of the 326 successfully reached Palestine.

In March 1942 the Germans began the mass DEPORTATION of Slovak Jewry. At that point, the Jewish Center asked the Slovak government to establish camps where Jews could work and be spared from deportation. The first two camps to be used as such were NOVAKY and SERED; soon Vyhne was also turned into a Jewish work center. The Jews at these camps showed the Germans how valuable they were as workers; in Vyhne they developed a productive textile industry. In addition, the conditions at the camp were not bad: the prisoners received adequate food rations, the children there had a school, and the inmates were even allowed to leave the camp from time to time.

When the SLOVAK NATIONAL UPRISING erupted in August 1944, Vyhne was liberated. Many of the young inmates left to join the revolt, while most others found refuge in the areas of Slovakia liberated during the uprising. (see also JEWISH CENTER, SLOVAKIA.)

W

WAFFEN-SS   see SS.

WAGNER, HORST   (1906–1977), Nazi official who headed the "Interior II" section of GERMANY'S Foreign Office from April 1943 until the war's end. In that position, Wagner oversaw Foreign Office matters regarding the SS and police, Jews, and ethnic Germans (VOLKSDEUTSCHE).

WALDHEIM, KURT   (b. 1918), Austrian soldier who served in the German WEHRMACHT. Despite the fact that Waldheim appeared on the United Nations' list of war criminals, he was elected United Nations Secretary-General in 1971 and president of AUSTRIA in 1986.

Kurt Waldheim in uniform, Podgorica, Yugoslavia, May 1943

WALLENBERG, RAOUL   (1912–?), Swedish diplomat, RIGHTEOUS AMONG THE NATIONS who saved the lives of Jews in BUDAPEST, HUNGARY.

In March 1944 the Germans occupied Hungary, and began deporting Jews to AUSCHWITZ in May. Between mid-May and July some 435,000 Hungarian Jews were deported; by the time the DEPORTATIONS ended, only about 200,000 Jews remained in Budapest. Soon after the invasion, the Swedish diplomatic representatives in Budapest began a rescue operation. The Swedish Foreign Minister, Ivar Danielsson, suggested that they issue temporary Swedish passports to Hungarian Jews who had some connection to Swedish citizens. In July, based on the recommendation of the Swedish branch of the WORLD JEWISH CONGRESS and with the support of President Roosevelt's WAR REFUGEE BOARD, the Swedish Foreign Ministry sent Wallenberg to Budapest to take over the passport operation.

The deportations halted in the summer of 1944, but by October they began again in full force. Then the ARROW CROSS PARTY took over the government, putting the Jews in further danger. At this point, Wallenberg also stepped in in full force. Over the next three months, he issued thousands of impressive looking "protective passports." When Adolf EICHMANN ordered the DEATH MARCH of Budapest's Jews to the Austrian border, Wallenberg chased the convoys in his car, removed those Jews who held his passports, and took them back to Budapest. He was even able to remove passport holders from trains that were about to depart for Auschwitz, and rescue Jews from being sent to FORCED LABOR camps.

Wallenberg also spared Jews from the danger of the Arrow Cross by setting up special hostels—protected houses—as safe havens for them. Other diplomatic delegations created their own protected houses in a part of the city which came to be known as the "international ghetto." Approximately 600 Jewish employees helped manage Wallenberg's operation, which included providing food, health services, and sanitation for the protected Jews.

Raoul Wallenberg (seated), Budapest, 1944

The Soviet army entered Budapest on January 16, 1945. The first part of the city that they liberated was Pest, where both the main GHETTO and the "international ghetto" were located. Wallenberg attempted to negotiate with the Soviets and make sure that they would take good care of the liberated Jews. However, the Soviets suspected Wallenberg and the other Swedish diplomats in Budapest of spying for the Germans. They asked Wallenberg to report to their army headquarters in Debrecen, where he went, believing that his diplomatic immunity would protect him. He returned to Budapest the next day, accompanied by two Soviet soldiers. Wallenberg was overheard saying, "I do not know whether I am a guest of the Soviets or their prisoner." After that, Wallenberg disappeared without a trace.

For several years after Wallenberg's disappearance, the Soviets claimed that they knew nothing of his whereabouts. However, German PRISONERS OF WAR returning from the SOVIET UNION swore that they had met Wallenberg in prison. On the basis of these testimonies, the Swedish government demanded that the Soviets release any information they had on Wallenberg. After the death of Joseph STALIN, the Soviet government announced that Wallenberg had indeed been arrested, but had died in a Soviet prison in 1947. Nonetheless, Wal-

lenberg's family did not believe this story, as they had received other reports from Soviet prisoners who claimed to have seen Wallenberg alive at various later dates. There is no definitive proof of his death.

As years passed, many people criticized the Swedes for mishandling the situation. Wallenberg had become a legendary name; films were made about him, streets were named for him, and the UNITED STATES awarded him honorary citizenship. He was also designated as Righteous among the Nations by YAD VASHEM in Jerusalem.

WANNSEE CONFERENCE   Meeting held at a lakeside villa in Wannsee, BERLIN, on January 20, 1942, whose purpose was to discuss and coordinate the "final solution" to the "Jewish Problem"—the mass extermination of all European Jewry.

The Wannsee Conference was organized by Reinhard HEYDRICH, Heinrich HIMMLER'S deputy and head of the REICHSSICHERHEITSHAUPTAMT (Reich Security Main Office, or RSHA). The attendees included the state secretaries of those German government offices that carried out HITLER'S anti-Jewish policies, and some SS leaders. Adolf EICHMANN, the director of Heydrich's Jewish office, was one of those included; he later wrote the conference report. At the meeting Heydrich announced that the official policy of the German government regarding the Jews would be total annihilation. The men invited to the meeting all knew about the Jewish policy; they were either involved in or directly aware of the murder of Jews already taking place across Europe. The question at hand was not whether to implement the policy, but *how* to implement it.

In July 1941 Hermann GOERING had ordered Heydrich to coordinate a plan for the "Final Solution." Heydrich's EINSATZGRUPPEN had been murdering Russian Jews by firing squad since the war against the Soviets broke out in 1941. However, this was not a suitable way to kill the Jews outside the war zone. Thus, Heydrich had to create something new. In November EXTERMINATION CAMPS in CHELMNO and BELZEC were already being built with facilities for murder by poison.

The Wannsee Conference was originally called for December 9, but was pushed off until January 20, 1942. Heydrich opened the conference with a long speech. He first repeated that he had authorization from Goering to coordinate the "Final Solution." Then he reviewed the Nazis' previous, temporary solution to the Jewish problem—the forced emigration of Jews from the areas under German control, until Himmler forbade any more emigration in the fall of 1941. Next, he announced the new policy that was taking the place of emigration: the "Final Solution." The program would begin with the "Evacuation of the Jews to the East" a thinly veiled term for DEPORTATION of the Jews to camps. This phase would include all "11 million" Jews in Europe, even those living in countries not yet occupied by the Germans. However, the camp phase was only to be a temporary one, which would lead finally to the annihilation of all European Jewry. He allowed that the strong and healthy Jews would be used as laborers, but that most would not survive. Heydrich concluded his speech by describing some of the specific problems facing the program, such as what to do with Jews in mixed marriages and their part-Jewish children. The attendees spent much time discussing this issue. Different possible solutions were mentioned, but nothing was decided, so the problems were discussed at two later conferences in March and October 1942.

The next part of the meeting was less structured. The attendees drank and discussed the general issues at hand. At some point, they got down to the business of suggesting various methods of mass destruction. At his war crimes trial in Jerusalem, Eichmann testified that "during the conversation, they minced no words about it at all. They spoke about methods of killing, about liquidation, about extermination." At that stage of the war, the Germans still had little experience in mass murder on such a large scale.

Heydrich closed the meeting with an appeal for cooperation among the participants. Afterwards, Heydrich seemed satisfied that all had gone according to plan, and that the government secretaries were in full agreement about what had to be done. Soon after the Wannsee Conference, the construction of the rest of the extermination camps began.

WARHAFTIG, ZORAH (b. 1906), Zionist leader who helped many Jewish REFUGEES during WORLD WAR II. Born in western BELORUSSIA, Warhaftig studied in WARSAW. He was very involved in Jewish public life there, and was an active member of the religious Zionist *Mizrahi* movement.

Because of his role in an anti-Nazi boycott committee, Warhaftig was forced to flee the advancing German troops when war broke out. He escaped to LITHUANIA and immediately began helping Jews there by taking charge of the Palestine Committee for Polish Refugees. In that capacity, he took care of other Polish refugees who had escaped to Lithuania, and made efforts to get them to Palestine. Most notably, Warhaftig helped many refugees reach the safe haven of East Asia by convincing the Soviet authorities to grant them transit visas through the SOVIET UNION (see also RESCUE OF POLISH JEWS VIA EAST ASIA). Warhaftig himself left for Japan soon thereafter, where he continued working on behalf of the refugees there, especially rabbis and *yeshiva* students. In 1942 he went to the UNITED STATES, where he was elected to the executive board of the WORLD JEWISH CONGRESS.

After the war, Warhaftig moved to Palestine, where he became a leading member of parliament and, later, minister of religious affairs. He published his memoirs, *Refugee and Survivor,* in 1988.

WAR REFUGEE BOARD (WRB) UNITED STATES government agency dedicated to rescuing and assisting WORLD WAR II victims. The WRB was established by President Franklin D. ROOSEVELT in January 1944, and ultimately helped to save about 200,000 Jews.

At the end of 1942 the American State Department confirmed reports of the systematic mass murder of European Jewry. Roosevelt was put under pressure by certain government officials to issue a rescue proclamation; in November 1943 Congress debated passing an official resolution. Also at that time Secretary of the Treasury Henry MORGENTHAU, was informed of attempts by the State Department to obstruct the rescue process and discourage the absorption of REFUGEES into the United States. Due to the possibility of imminent scandal, Morgenthau's urgent demands, and because Roosevelt did not want Congress to get the credit instead of him, he quickly established the WRB.

Roosevelt made the WRB responsible for carrying out the United States' new government policy of taking all measures within its power to rescue the victims of enemy oppression in imminent danger of death. The agency, run by executive director John Pehle and a staff of 30, made plans to evacuate Jews and other endangered people from enemy territory, find safe havens for them, send relief supplies to CONCENTRATION CAMPS, and use psychological threats such as war crimes trials against the Germans to stop DEPORTATIONS. The rescue programs were put into effect by a small number of WRB workers stationed in Europe.

Officially, the WRB was given much authority. All US government agencies were supposed to cooperate with it, most importantly the State, Treasury, and War Departments. However, only the Treasury Department, led by Morgenthau, did its part. In addition, the WRB was strapped for money: Roosevelt only allocated $1 million for organizational costs. The board had to collect money from private Jewish organizations like the American Jewish JOINT DISTRIBUTION COMMITTEE to fund the actual rescue programs. American Jews contributed almost $17 million to the WRB.

In 1944 the WRB set out to rescue Hungarian Jewry. By focussing international attention on the Hungarian government and putting pressure on them, the WRB was able to stop the deportations before all 230,000 Jews of BUDAPEST were swallowed up by the Nazi regime. The board also sent the Swedish diplomat, Raoul WALLENBERG, and others to protect the Jews of Budapest. The WRB funded Wallenberg's rescue work there.

In August 1944 the WRB brought 982 Jewish refugees from ITALY to a safe haven in Oswego, New York. The board intended to create other such places of asylum, and thus also influence other countries to provide sanctuary for World War II victims. Roosevelt, however, disabled one of the board's most important rescue programs by refusing to establish any other havens besides Oswego.

The board lobbied Roosevelt to publicly condemn the mass murder of Jews by the Nazis. Members also argued that the US army should bomb AUSCHWITZ. This, however, was never done.

By the end of the war in 1945 almost 200,000 Jews had been rescued by the War Refugee Board. About 15,000 Jews and more than 20,000 non-Jews had been evacuated from Nazi domain. At the very least, about 10,000 Jews were protected within Nazi-controlled territory by underground programs funded by the WRB. The board removed the 48,000 Jews in TRANSNISTRIA to safe areas of ROMANIA. About 120,000 Jews from Budapest also survived due in part to the WRB's activities.

Despite its best intentions, the War Refugee Board was never able to accomplish what it was charged with doing because of the lack of cooperation of the United States government and even President Roosevelt. WRB director Pehle described their work as too little, too late. (see also AUSCHWITZ, BOMBING OF.)

WARSAW   Capital of POLAND and site of the largest GHETTO in Europe during WORLD WAR II. An important

Jewish center, 375,000 Jews lived in Warsaw just before the war (constituting almost 30 percent of the city's total population).

GERMANY invaded Poland on September 1, 1939. Within a few days the Polish government fled Warsaw, and on September 28 the capital capitulated to the Nazis. In late October Warsaw became a district center of the new GENERALGOUVERNEMENT civil administration, with Ludwig FISCHER serving as district governor.

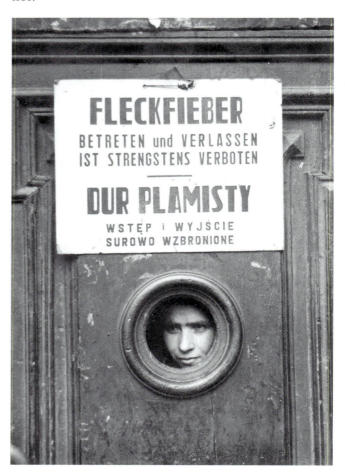

Jew quarantined in the Warsaw Ghetto. The sign reads: "Typhus, entry and exit are strictly forbidden," July 1941

As soon as Poland fell to the Germans, the Jews of Warsaw were subjected to brutal attacks and FORCED LABOR. In November 1939 the German authorities issued the first ANTI-JEWISH LEGISLATION. This included the order for Jews to don a white armband with a blue Star of David (see also BADGE, JEWISH) and various economic restrictions. As a result, many Jews lost any means of supporting themselves and their families.

A JUDENRAT was also set up under the chairmanship

of Adam CZERNIAKOW, and no Jewish institutions besides the *Judenrat* and welfare organizations were permitted to function. The Jewish Mutual Aid Society (ZTOS) was outstanding in its aid distribution activities. Funded by the American Jewish JOINT DISTRIBUTION COMMITTEE, ZTOS ran over 100 soup kitchens, created House Committees to help alleviate the crowding, set up youth clubs and kindergartens, and arranged cultural activities.

In October 1940 the Jews were informed that a ghetto was to be established in Warsaw. The ghetto was sealed off on November 16; at its peak, it housed some 445,000 Jews. From the start the living conditions in the ghetto were insufferable. Six or seven people lived in one room, the food rations supplied by the Germans were a tenth of what they should have been, and many people died of disease, cold, and malnourishment. The ghetto's legal economic exchanges with the outside world were regulated by the German Transfer Office, but most economic activity conducted by the ghetto Jews was illegal, including the smuggling of food. Most Jews who survived in the ghetto either subsisted on their savings or participated in "illegal" economic activities.

Despite the grave hardships, life in the Warsaw Ghetto was rich with educational and cultural activities, conducted by its underground organizations. There were secret libraries, classes for the children, and a symphony orchestra. In addition, prominent writers and poets continued to create. The ONEG SHABBAT Archive, an underground enterprise led by the historian Emanuel RINGELBLUM, worked on documenting the history of the Warsaw Ghetto and other communities in Nazi-occupied Poland.

Many of the underground organizations were offshoots of various Jewish political parties and YOUTH MOVEMENTS. In March 1942 Yitzhak ZUCKERMAN of the *Dror He-Halutz* Zionist youth movement tried to unite the various movements into one self-defense organization. However, not all groups wanted to join, so the leftist Anti-Fascist Bloc was created instead. This organization lasted but two months, and collapsed in May 1942 when its Communist leaders were jailed.

During the first half of 1942 there was growing panic in the ghetto, as reports began to come in about DEPORTATIONS from other ghettos. In addition, the Germans began carrying out night raids in which Jews were plucked from their houses at random and murdered. Then, in late July, the Germans launched a two month long wave of deportations from the Warsaw Ghetto.

Children caught smuggling food into the Warsaw Ghetto

Judenrat chairman Czerniakow committed suicide, as he was unwilling to help the Nazis decide whom to deport, as they had ordered. By September 12 about 300,000 Jews had been deported, some 254,000 of them to the TREBLINKA extermination camp.

The 60,000 Jews left in the ghetto soon went through a great psychological shift. At the beginning of the deportations, a cross-movement self-defense group had finally been organized, under the command of Mordecai ANIELEWICZ. Known as the Jewish Fighting Organization (*Zydowska Organizacja Bojowa*, ZOB), many of its members were galvanized to fight the Nazis when they realized that the deportations meant death.

A second wave of deportations was launched in January 1943. Believing that this was to be the final liquidation of the ghetto, the ZOB sent its armed fighters to resist the Germans. The deportations were halted after just five days (some 6,000 Jews having been deported), leading the Jews to believe that it was their resistance that had stopped them. In fact, the German plan had only been to deport a few thousand Jews at that time. Whatever the truth was, however, the ghetto Jews now believed that they had a chance of survival. The ZOB fighters had no such illusions: they knew that they would have to fight to their last man, and that their goal was not survival, but resistance for resistance's sake.

The final liquidation of the Warsaw Ghetto began on April 19, 1943. The Jews had been warned and they were ready and waiting in their bunkers, which they had built in anticipation over the previous months. As the general population hid from the Germans who entered the ghetto, the ZOB fighters attacked, launching the WARSAW GHETTO UPRISING—the first uprising of an urban population in occupied Europe. Days of guerilla-type warfare stumped the Germans, who then resorted to searching for the Jews, bunker by bunker, and burning down the ghetto. The members of the ZOB and the smaller Jewish Military Union (aligned with the *Betar* movement) fought heroically, but in the end, they were no match for the Germans. By May 8 the ZOB leaders were discovered in their bunker, and by May 16 the Germans felt that the operation was over. Nonetheless, individual Jews hid in the ghetto for well over a year, and thousands crossed over to the Polish side of Warsaw in search of refuge. Indeed, many were killed in the general Polish uprising that broke out in Warsaw in August 1944 (known as the WARSAW POLISH UPRISING). Warsaw was razed to the ground after the failed revolt, and more than 150,000 Poles were sent to labor or CONCENTRATION CAMPS.

Warsaw was liberated by the Soviet army on January 17, 1945. Some 300 Jews were found hiding in the Polish part of the city. (see also JEWISH FIGHTING ORGANIZATION, WARSAW and JEWISH MILITARY UNION, WARSAW.)

WARSAW GHETTO UPRISING

Last attempt at resistance of Nazi DEPORTATIONS by the Jews of the WARSAW Ghetto. The uprising broke out on Passover Eve, April 19, 1943, and lasted until mid-May.

By the spring of 1942, reports had confirmed that the Nazis were conducting a campaign to exterminate

Jews discovered at the time of the Warsaw Ghetto Uprising trying to flee the ghetto by way of the sewers, spring 1943

all of European Jewry. Within the Warsaw GHETTO, members of the Jewish underground—mainly members of the Zionist YOUTH MOVEMENTS—decided that they needed to take action by establishing an effective defense organization. This became a reality on a small-scale during the summer of 1942, in the midst of a two-month long wave of deportations to TREBLINKA. The Jewish Fighting Organization (*Zydowska Organizacja Bojowa,* ZOB) was created on July 28, consisting of the members of only three Zionist movements. At that time, the ZOB was powerless to stop the deportations, which finally ended in mid-September, leaving only 55,000–60,000 Jews in the ghetto.

Altogether, some 300,000 Jews had been deported, including older people and children. The survivors of the *aktion* were mainly young people who blamed themselves for not having saved their families by standing up to the Nazis. These strong feelings spurred many of the underground groups into joining the ZOB. Ultimately, the only Zionist movement that did not join the ZOB was the Revisionists, which created its own fighting organization called the Jewish Military Union (*Zydowski Zwiazek Wojskowy,* ZZW). ZOB members began preparations for a serious confrontation with the Nazis in the case of more deportations. They made contact with the Polish HOME ARMY, which recognized the new resistance organization and sent it a small number of weapons.

On January 18, 1943 the Germans initiated the second wave of deportations from the ghetto, called the "January *Aktion*." The ZOB, which had not yet finished preparing for battle, assumed that this *aktion* was to be the final deportation of Warsaw's Jews. The two units that had weapons attacked the Germans on the streets of the ghetto. Mordecai ANIELEWICZ led the ZOB fighters, of whom many were killed. The *aktion* was only halted after four days. The Jews in the ghetto—both the underground and civilians—saw this as a victory for the ZOB, whose resistance seemed to have been the cause of an early end to the deportations.

This new feeling of strength galvanized the ZOB. Under Anielewicz's leadership, the group spent three months intensely preparing for the final battle against the Germans. Twenty-two fighting units were formed, each one representing a different youth movement. In all, the ZOB consisted of 500 fighters, while the ZZW had another 200–250 fighters. More members could have been recruited, but the ZOB did not make an effort to do so because there were not enough weapons

The Warsaw Ghetto in flames, spring 1943

to go around. Its own fighters had just a few pistols and automatic weapons. The ZOB had learned two important lessons from the events in January: they needed to be on constant alert, because the Germans could take them by surprise again, and they themselves had to surprise the Germans with attacks launched from strong positions within the ghetto. Thus, they spent their time training, obtaining weapons, and mapping out a strategy for the ghetto's defense.

The civilian population of the ghetto also prepared itself for the next wave of deportations. They saw the events during the "January *Aktion*" as proof that Jewish resistance could derail the Germans. They also believed that an uprising within the ghetto could provoke rebellion throughout POLAND, creating serious problems for the Nazis. Thus, the civilians cooperated with the underground fighters by preparing underground bunkers and hiding places for themselves where they could survive even if they were cut off from each other during the fighting.

On April 18, 1943, the fighters received information that the final liquidation of the ghetto was to begin the next day. By the time the Germans marched into the ghetto on the morning of April 19, the entire Jewish population was ready and waiting. The German troops did not find one Jew on the streets; they had all taken to their bunkers and hiding places. Then the fighting began. That first day, the Germans were forced to retreat from the ghetto.

The ghetto fighters fought the Germans face to face for several days. After each encounter, the Jewish fighters withdrew via the rooftops; the Germans were thus unable to strike at them, nor could they uncover the Jews hidden inside bunkers. The Germans next decided

Jews during the Warsaw Ghetto Uprising who have been burned out of their hiding places, surrendering to German troops, spring 1943

to burn the ghetto, building by building. The fighters then had to retreat to the bunkers and carry out scattered attacks.

The Germans continued their search for the Jewish fighters by burning out the bunkers. This proved to be much more difficult than the Nazis had planned: every day, SS and Police Leader Juergen STROOP reported that his troops had conquered the underground fighters, only to report the next day that there was no end in sight to the fighting. However, the Jewish fighters did not have enough arms to hold out for much longer. They fought desperately and heroically, but their small cache of weapons was no match for the German war machine.

By May 8, most of the ZOB fighters had retreated to their headquarters bunker at 18 Mila Street. The bunker fell to the Germans that day, and ZOB commander Anielewicz and many of his fighters and commanders perished. ZOB members had not made plans for a retreat from the ghetto; they simply planned to go on fighting until the last man had fallen. However, several dozen fighters managed to escape with the help of ZOB members on the Polish side of the ghetto who led them through the city's sewer system.

On May 16 Stroop reported that the fighting was over, and that 56,065 Jews had been destroyed. However, even after that date there were still hundreds of Jews hidden in the ghetto's underground bunkers. The

Warsaw Ghetto Uprising had been the first uprising of an urban population in occupied Europe. (see also RESISTANCE, JEWISH, JEWISH FIGHTING ORGANIZATION, WARSAW, and JEWISH MILITARY UNION, WARSAW.)

WARSAW POLISH UPRISING   Polish revolt against the Germans that broke out in WARSAW in August 1944. The uprising was launched by the Polish HOME ARMY, the largest Polish resistance organization, based on orders from the London-based POLISH GOVERNMENT-IN-EXILE. Their goal was to take control of Warsaw from the Germans before the Soviet army reached the city, which was expected to happen soon.

Poles shooting at Germans during the Warsaw Polish Uprising, August 1944

The rebels originally consisted of 23,000 young fighters with few weapons who stood up to tens of thousands of well-equipped German soldiers and police. The Poles launched the uprising on August 1. On August 4 the rebels freed hundreds of Greek and Hungarian Jews imprisoned at the CONCENTRATION CAMP on Gensia Street; the prisoners immediately joined the uprising. Members of the Jewish Fighting Organization (ZOB) who had survived the WARSAW GHETTO UPRISING also took part in the fighting. The civilian citizens of Warsaw were very supportive of the rebels: they published rebel newspapers, supplied first aid to the fighters, and organized mail services and supplies. On August 5 the German troops, heavily reinforced, began a counterattack and soon put the city center under siege.

On September 14 Polish army units that had parachuted into Warsaw took control of the right bank of the Vistula River; they also managed to transfer several battalions to the left bank, suffering heavy casualties. Despite their efforts, though, they could not help the rebels. The city center fell to the Germans on October 2, signaling the end of the Warsaw Polish Uprising.

In all, about 16,000–20,000 Polish fighters were either killed or went missing and 7,000 were wounded. Approximately 150,000 civilians were also killed, including several thousand Jews who had hidden with Poles in Warsaw after the GHETTO was liquidated in May 1943. About 16,000 German soldiers were killed or went missing and 9,000 were wounded. Most of Warsaw's surviving civilians were deported by the Germans to nearby camps, and 65,000 were soon transferred to concentration camps. About 100,000 were taken to do FORCED LABOR in the Reich, while the rest were spread out over the GENERALGOUVERNEMENT. The Germans burned and destroyed those parts of Warsaw that were still standing, including many of POLAND'S cultural and spiritual treasures. (see also JEWISH FIGHTING ORGANIZATION, WARSAW.)

WARTHEGAU   (Wartheland), territory established by the Germans in October 1939 in the part of POLAND that was incorporated into the Reich; the Warthegau existed until it was liberated in January 1945. It was the largest administrative unit in the Reich, covering a total of 16,966 square miles. At the beginning of WORLD WAR II, 4,922,000 people lived in the area, including 385,000 Jews and 325,000 Germans.

The Warthegau was run by Arthur GREISER, who intended to turn the region into a model of racial purity. He divided the population into superior persons—the Germans—and inferior persons, including Poles, Jews, and GYPSIES. Within weeks, the superior group had taken all the high posts in the business, political, and economic administration of the region, and received many privileges.

Members of the "inferior group" were badly persecuted. More than 70,000 Poles were murdered and others were sent to FORCED LABOR and CONCENTRATION CAMPS. The Germans also persecuted Poles by restricting their movement, expelling many, giving them the most meager of food rations, welfare, and health services, and preventing certain couples from getting married. The Germans confiscated 95.5 percent of Polish property, closed down their schools, and forbid Poles from devel-

Jews being deported from the Warthegau to the Generalgouvernement

oping their cultural and social lives. Even using the Polish language was restricted.

As soon as the Warthegau was established, the Germans began instituting anti-Jewish measures. Jews were forced to wear Jewish badges (see also BADGE, JEWISH), sent to labor camps, and were forbidden to use public transportation. Jewish property was confiscated, and Jews were banned from cultural, educational, and political activities. Some Jews were also murdered.

From early 1940 to late 1941, the Jews were herded into 173 GHETTOS and forced labor camps. Many died of starvation, overwork, and unsanitary conditions; several thousand were murdered. Beginning in December 1941, most of the Jews were exterminated. During the last few months of the war the Germans slowed the rate of extermination, so that the remaining Jews could be exploited for their work abilities. Altogether, 380,000 Warthegau Jews were killed, and only 5,000 survived. In addition, hundreds of Gypsies living in the Warthegau were also murdered.

WDOWINSKI, DAVID (1895–1970), One of the founders and leaders of the Jewish Military Union in the WARSAW Ghetto. Born in Bedzin, Wdowinski studied at the universities of VIENNA, Brno, and Warsaw, and became a psychiatrist. However, at the request of Zionist Revisionist leader Vladimir Jabotinsky, he gave up his practice to devote himself full time to working for the Revisionist movement.

During the war, Wdowinski was an operative mem-

ber of the underground in the Warsaw GHETTO. He also served in the Jewish Mutual Aid Society as the Revisionists' representative. In the summer of 1942 Wdowinski helped create the Jewish Military Union (*Zydowski Zwiazek Wojskowy, ZZW*), an underground militia led by members of *Betar,* the Revisionist movement's youth group. After the WARSAW GHETTO UPRISING, Wdowinski was sent to various CONCENTRATION CAMPS, which he survived.

After the war, Wdowinski settled in the UNITED STATES, where he wrote a book entitled *And We Are Not Saved,* which described his life and activities in the *Betar* movement in the Warsaw Ghetto. In 1961 Wdowinski served as a witness in the trial of senior SS officer, Adolf EICHMANN. He died in 1970 after suffering a heart attack during a memorial gathering for the Warsaw Ghetto Uprising. (see also JEWISH MILITARY UNION, WARSAW.)

WEHRMACHT (Armed Forces of GERMANY), name of Germany's armed forces from 1935–1945. The name *Wehrmacht* was taken on in March 1935 after a mandatory military draft was introduced in Germany. In April 1938 the *Wehrmacht's* land forces consisted of 28 divisions. Less than a year and a half later, when WORLD WAR II broke out in September 1939, the *Wehrmacht* had grown exponentially to 75 divisions, consisting of 24,000 officers and 2.7 million military personnel. Before 1935, the German army included only 100,000 soldiers and 4,000 officers.

In 1938 HITLER instituted the Armed Forces High Command (OKW). The OKW, an advisory organization, was intended to coordinate the activities of the Army High Command, the Air Force High Command, and the Navy High Command. When World War II began, most of the fighting was done by the army because the war's main venue was land.

The *Wehrmacht* was quite "nazified" by 1938, after Hitler gained the respect and fear of the armed forces by taking over territories, such as AUSTRIA and parts of Czechoslovakia, without having to resort to war. In addition, by that time, many young soldiers had joined the armed forces straight out of the Hitler Youth movement (HITLERJUGEND) and the Reich Labor services. Some officers may have disapproved of the atrocities carried out by the Nazis when Germany invaded PO-LAND in September 1939; however, they kept quiet after Germany vanquished FRANCE in May and June 1940 in a striking display of military strength and

Soldiers of the Wehrmacht executing civilians, Lithuania, 1941

might. Almost no officers voiced objections to Hitler's barbaric orders regarding the "ideological war" initiated against the SOVIET UNION when Germany invaded in June 1941. The main criticism *Wehrmacht* officers had about Hitler was about not being able to keep to the original schedule for the invasion of the Soviet Union.

Members of the *Wehrmacht* stood by as EINSATZ-GRUPPEN units attached to the army carried out the mass murder of Jews. Some *Wehrmacht* units even gave the *Einsatzgruppen* military support. A very few *Wehrmacht* officers objected to the extermination of Europe's Jews. Those that did were immobilized or dismissed from the army.

WEILL, JOSEPH   (1902–1988), French Jewish physician who was active in the underground and in welfare organizations during WORLD WAR II.

GERMANY attacked FRANCE in May 1940; in June, France surrendered. Germany then established a German administration in northern France and installed a puppet French government in the southern French town of Vichy. Because of his good government connections, Weill was allowed into the detention camps in southern France where the Vichy authorities had interned tens of thousands of Jews. Weill sent reports to American and Swiss humanitarian agencies about the terrible conditions at the camps, and as a result, thousands of children and old people were released.

When the Germans began deporting the Jews of France, Weill and his aides saved the lives of hundreds of Jewish children by providing them with forged papers which concealed their Jewish identity. He also helped establish an underground organization, called the Garel Network, which found places of refuge for the children among non-Jewish families. In all, some

4,000 children were cared for by this network, including 1,000 who were smuggled into SWITZERLAND.

In 1943 Weill himself fled to Switzerland, where he continued his work on behalf of refugee children. After the war, he served as president of the Jewish communities of ALSACE. (for more on Vichy, see also FRANCE.)

WEISSMANDEL, MICHAEL DOV (1903–1956), Slovakian rabbi and a leader of the WORKING GROUP (*Pracovna Skupina*), a semi-underground rescue organization.

From March–October 1942, the Germans deported about 58,000 Jews from SLOVAKIA. The Working Group was established during the peak of the DEPORTATIONS as a rescue agency. Weissmandel and other Working Group leaders toiled night and day, devising ways to save Jewish lives. He begged for assistance from every possible source, in Slovakia and elsewhere.

In the summer of 1942 Weissmandel initiated the plan to bribe SS officer Dieter WISLICENY, Slovakia's advisor on Jewish affairs, in exchange for halting the deportation of Slovakian Jews to EXTERMINATION CAMPS. The Working Group paid Wisliceny between US $40,000–$50,000 in two installments. When the deportations did in fact stop, Weissmandel and the Working Group believed that it was because of their bribe.

The Working Group next decided to try and repeat their success with the rescue of Jews from all over occupied Europe. This was termed the EUROPA PLAN. The group agreed to amass about two–three million US dollars, and to provide a down payment of $200,000; however, they were unable to do so. In March 1944 Weissmandel wrote to friends in BUDA-PEST about making contact with Wisliceny, who by that time had been transferred to HUNGARY. However, just two months later, the Germans launched the deportation of Hungarian Jewry. By then, Weissmandel had changed his mind and advised his friends not to get involved with bribing the Nazis, but rather to try to escape and set up resistance.

In the spring of 1944 four Jewish escapees from AUSCHWITZ told the Working Group about the mass exterminations going on there. Weissmandel broadcast this information to Jewish organizations abroad, the Slovak government, and the country's Catholic Church. He begged the Allies to bomb Auschwitz and the railways leading to it, but there was no response.

After the SLOVAK NATIONAL UPRISING was crushed in October 1944, the Germans resumed deportations from Slovakia. Weissmandel was sent to Auschwitz, but managed to escape en route. He eventually reached SWITZERLAND, and after the war, he settled in the UNITED STATES. (see also AUSCHWITZ PROTOCOLS and AUSCHWITZ, BOMBING OF.)

WEIZMANN, CHAIM (1874–1952), Scientist and Zionist statesman who served as the first president of the State of Israel.

Chaim Weizmann (standing) and other Zionist leaders, Jerusalem, 1945

Born in Russia, Weizmann studied chemistry in both GERMANY and SWITZERLAND. He moved to England in 1904 to work at the University of Manchester. During his early years in GREAT BRITAIN, Weizmann became very active in the World Zionist Organization and the English Zionist Federation. He played a key role in British war production in World War I, having developed a way to produce acetone. During World War I, Weizmann came to the conclusion that it was not the crumbling Ottoman Empire that should be depended on to further the Zionist goal of establishing a Jewish state in Palestine, but rather the British Empire, which soon took control of Palestine as a British colonial "mandate." In November 1917 Weizmann played a major role in securing the Balfour Declaration, the British government's promise to support the creation of a Jewish homeland in Palestine. In 1920 Weizmann was elected president of the World Zionist Organization, and in 1929 he helped establish an expanded Jewish Agency.

After HITLER'S rise to power in 1933, Weizmann took over the Jewish Agency's Department for the Settlement of German Refugees. He used his diplomatic contacts with various world leaders to try to ease the persecution of Jews in Germany and other Nazi-dominated areas and to try to get as many Jews as he could out of Germany and into Palestine. After WORLD WAR II broke out, Weizmann called for the creation of a Jewish fighting unit within the British army; this was finally achieved in 1944. Weizmann also tried to organize various rescue efforts, but the British government consistently refused to help him in his struggle. They declined to suspend the WHITE PAPER OF 1939, which severely restricted Jewish immigration to Palestine, and denied a proposal to pay the Germans large amounts of money in exchange for Jewish lives. Weizmann also asked the British government to bomb the EXTERMINATION CAMPS, to no avail (see also AUSCHWITZ, BOMBING OF).

After the war, Weizmann continued working for the Zionist cause. In February 1949 he was elected the first president of the newly established State of Israel.

WEIZSACKER, ERNST VON   (1882–1951), Secretary of State in the German Foreign Office from 1938–1943 and German ambassador to the Vatican from 1943–1945.

Weizsacker was extremely ambivalent regarding his government's actions. He hated Nazi extremism, yet he never expressed his opposition strongly or impressively. He opposed GERMANY'S invasion of POLAND, but he never spoke up or resigned his post in protest. He wanted to get rid of Adolf HITLER, but he wanted Germany to win the war and thus supported the *Fuehrer's* aggression. He was quite aware of the persecution of European Jewry, having received reports about the EINSATZGRUPPEN and the WANNSEE CONFERENCE, and probably regretted the annihilation, but he failed to object to the DEPORTATION of Jews to their deaths in EXTERMINATION CAMPS. Apparently, Weizsacker wanted to serve both his country and his moral code, but could not satisfy both at the same time.

After the war, Weizsacker was convicted of crimes

Ernst von Weizsacker's portrait on a campaign poster for the German People's Party

against peace and CRIMES AGAINST HUMANITY. He appealed the first conviction and won, but was sentenced to seven years for the second conviction. He served only 18 months in prison. Thirty years later, his son Richard was elected president of Germany. Richard consistently condemned Nazi atrocities committed during the HOLOCAUST, and spoke of the obligation to "never forget."

WESTERBORK   Transit camp located in the northeastern NETHERLANDS through which most of Dutch Jewry passed on their way to Nazi EXTERMINATION CAMPS in Eastern Europe. Westerbork had been established originally in October 1939 by the Dutch government to detain German Jewish REFUGEES who had entered the Netherlands illegally.

In late 1941 the Germans decided to use Westerbork as one of the three transit camps in Western

Europe where Jews would be assembled for DEPORTATION. The Nazis took control of the camp on July 1, 1942. The first Jews arrived on July 14, and the first deportation transport left for AUSCHWITZ the next day. In all, nearly 100,000 Jews were deported from Westerbork to Nazi extermination and CONCENTRATION CAMPS, including Auschwitz, SOBIBOR, and BERGEN-BELSEN, and the THERESIENSTADT Ghetto.

Jews being deported from Westerbork, 1942

Not all Jews brought to Westerbork were automatically deported. While many Jews were brought into the camp and sent away after a week or two, there was also a "permanent" population that was made to work in the camp, performing jobs such as metalworking, outdoor tasks, and various services for the camp staff and population.

Westerbork was liberated by the Allies in mid-April 1945. At that point, 876 prisoners remained in the camp, of whom 569 were Dutch nationals.

WESTERWEEL, JOOP (1899–1944), Dutch teacher who rescued Jews during the HOLOCAUST. After his death, Westerweel was designated as RIGHTEOUS AMONG THE NATIONS by YAD VASHEM, and a forest was planted in Israel in his name in 1954.

Around the time that the German occupiers began deporting Dutch Jews to their deaths in EXTERMINATION CAMPS in 1942, Westerweel got to know a group of young Zionists (*halutzim*) living at a farm near his home. He and their counselor, Joachim ("Schuschu")

Simon, joined forces to organize an underground movement in order to hide the young people and spare them from being deported. In early August they found hiding places for 60 of the *halutzim*. Then Westerweel and Schuschu began organizing an escape route for them, through BELGIUM and FRANCE to SWITZERLAND and SPAIN.

In the fall of 1942 Schuschu traveled to France to make contact with the Jewish underground there. In December 1942 and January 1943 the first groups of *halutzim* were smuggled into France via Belgium; they were then able to move on to freedom in Spain. In January Schuschu was arrested by the Nazis in the south of the NETHERLANDS during one of his many trips to France to set up escapes. While in prison, he managed to inform his co-activists of his arrest, and then took his own life. After this loss, Westerweel's rescue operation increased to 20 members.

In February 1944 Westerweel himself accompanied a group of *halutzim* to the border between France and Spain in the Pyrenees Mountains. In a moving farewell,

Joop Westerweel, 1940

he asked that upon their arrival in Palestine, they remember and commemorate those of their comrades who had not made it. Less than a month later, Westerweel was caught by the Germans while trying to sneak two young *halutzim* over the Dutch border into Belgium. He himself did not make it: he was taken to the CONCENTRATION CAMP at VUGHT, where he was tortured but never revealed any information about his fellow rescuers. On August 11 he was executed. However, his group continued on, smuggling nearly 200 Jews into France, including 70 *halutzim*.

WHITE PAPER OF 1939   British government statement regarding its policy on Palestine, issued in May 1939, which limited Jewish immigration to Palestine and Jewish land acquisition in Palestine, and declared its intention of establishing an Arab state there in 1949.

Elie Wiesel visiting Yad Vashem

WIESEL, ELIE   (b. 1928), Holocaust SURVIVOR, world-famous writer, and Nobel Peace Prize recipient. Wiesel has worked tirelessly to educate the world about the HOLOCAUST, to ensure that it never happen again.

Elie Wiesel was born in Sighet Marmatiei, TRANSYLVANIA to a religious family. In 1944, he and his family were deported to AUSCHWITZ. He was then transferred to BUCHENWALD, from which he was liberated in 1945. He later attended the Sorbonne in PARIS and began a career as a journalist; he worked as a foreign correspondent for the Israeli daily newspaper, *Yediot Aharonot*.

In 1956 Wiesel published his most famous work, originally called *Un di Velt Hot Geshvigen* in Yiddish, the language in which it was written. The memoir was subsequently adapted and translated into 18 languages, and is known in English as *Night*. It tells the story of a CONCENTRATION CAMP inmate, based on Wiesel's own experiences, and has served as an important resource on the Holocaust.

Wiesel has since written his memoirs and 25 novels on Jewish subjects; most, however, focus on the Holocaust. He has made the Holocaust accessible to millions by describing his experiences and feelings in vivid, human detail. He mourns the losses of the Jewish People: the destruction of what existed before the war, and the innocence and life-affirming beliefs stolen from those who survived. He has also dealt with the moral difficulties of faith in God after the Holocaust.

Between 1980–1986 Wiesel served as chairman of the US Holocaust Memorial Council; he instituted National Days of Remembrance in the UNITED STATES and inspired schools all over the country to offer Holocaust studies. In 1985 he received the Medal of Honor of the United States Congress for his work, and was awarded the Nobel Peace Prize in 1986.

While reserving a special place for the victims of the Holocaust, Wiesel is also famous for fighting against human rights transgressions around the world.

WIESENTHAL, SIMON   (b. 1908), Nazi hunter. Born in Galicia, Wiesenthal studied architecture in PRAGUE and was living in LVOV, POLAND when WORLD WAR II broke out. He was arrested with his family, and spent the rest of the war in FORCED LABOR and CONCENTRATION CAMPS, including JANOWSKA, PLASZÓW, GROSS-ROSEN, BUCHENWALD, and MAUTHAUSEN. He survived, and on May 5, 1945 was liberated from Mauthausen by American troops.

After the war Wiesenthal decided to dedicate himself to hunting down Nazi war criminals so that they could be brought to justice. At first he worked for the United States army's War Crimes department in AUSTRIA. In 1947 he founded the Jewish Historical Documentation Center in the Austrian city of Linz. However, over the next few years, the public lost interest in tracking down former Nazis, so Wiesenthal was forced to close the center in 1954.

In 1961 public interest in catching Nazis and putting them on trial was again peaked when Senior SS Officer Adolf EICHMANN was captured by Israeli secret service agents in Argentina and brought to trial in Jerusalem. At that point, Wiesenthal reopened the Jewish Documentation Center in VIENNA and continued his investigation of former Nazis. During the 1960s and 1970s he hunted down many Nazis, some well known, some less so. Among the more notorious Nazis caught by Wiesenthal were Franz STANGL, the commandant of SOBIBOR and TREBLINKA; Gustav Wagner, the deputy commandant of Sobibor; Franz Murer, the commandant of the VILNA Ghetto; and Karl Silberbauer, the police officer who arrested Anne FRANK and family.

In 1977 the Simon Wiesenthal Center for Holocaust Studies was instituted in Los Angeles, and in 1980 the US Congress awarded Wiesenthal a gold medal for his work. Besides Nazi-hunting, Wiesenthal has also devoted himself to memorializing the victims of the Nazis. He has written many works on the HOLOCAUST, including *The Murderers Among Us; Sunflower; Max and Helen;* and *Every Day Remembrance Day: A Chronicle of Jewish Martyrdom.* Wiesenthal's memoirs, *The Murderers Among Us,* has been made into a film about Wiesenthal's life, starring Ben Kingsley.

WILNER, ARIE   (1917–1943), One of the founders of the Jewish Fighting Organization (ZOB) in WARSAW.

Before WORLD WAR II, Wilner belonged to the *Ha-Shomer ha-Tsa'ir* Zionist YOUTH MOVEMENT in Warsaw. When the war broke out in September 1939, Wilner, along with many other young Zionists, escaped from Nazi-occupied western Poland to VILNA, LITHUANIA. However, the Germans invaded Lithuania in June 1941, and began massacring Jews there. Wilner managed to escape; instead of running eastward, Wilner returned to Warsaw to warn the Jews there about the mass murders in Lithuania.

Back in Warsaw, Wilner became a leader of the Jewish underground. Because of his Polish looks, he was able to travel to other GHETTOS to encourage underground resistance activities. During the summer of 1942 the Germans launched a two-month long wave of DEPORTATIONS. At that point, Wilner and his comrades decided that armed resistance was the only answer. On July 28 they founded the Jewish Fighting Organization (*Zydowska Organizacja Bojowa,* ZOB), and Wilner became the ZOB's representative outside the ghetto. He soon made contact with the HOME ARMY, the main Polish underground militia. The Home Army officially recognized the ZOB and supplied the Jews with a limited number of weapons, as did the Communist underground militia (see also HOME GUARD, POLAND).

Although he lived outside the ghetto, Wilner still took part in the ZOB's important decision making. In January 1943 he participated in the fighting between the ZOB and the Nazis when the Nazis initiated a short wave of deportations.

In March the Germans searched Wilner's apartment on the Polish side of Warsaw. They found weapons and arrested him, assuming that he was part of the Polish underground. However, they soon found out that he was Jewish, and sent him to a CONCENTRATION CAMP. Wilner was rescued a short time later by the Polish Catholic Scouts movement, and he returned to the Warsaw Ghetto to participate in the last stand against the Nazis—the WARSAW GHETTO UPRISING. When the ZOB headquarters were discovered by the Germans, Wilner called on his comrades to commit suicide, and he himself died in the bunker. (see also JEWISH FIGHTING ORGANIZATION, WARSAW.)

WIRTH, CHRISTIAN   (1885–1944), SS officer and designer of Polish CONCENTRATION CAMPS. Trained as a carpenter, Wirth distinguished himself in World War I. After the war he joined the German police; he became infamous for his brutal interrogation methods. Wirth joined the NAZI PARTY in 1931. In 1939 he transferred to the GESTAPO.

By the end of 1939 Wirth moved on to the EUTHANASIA PROGRAM. At that point he also took part in the first gassing experiments on certifiably insane Germans. In 1940 Wirth became an inspector of Euthanasia Program facilities within the Reich, and in 1941 he was posted in LUBLIN, where he was charged with instituting a new euthanasia facility. This was the first euthanasia center to be established outside Greater GERMANY.

Next, Wirth set up three EXTERMINATION CAMPS in

POLAND—BELZEC, SOBIBOR, and TREBLINKA—where he introduced new gassing methods. With the help of Odilo GLOBOCNIK and Lublin's SS police headquarters, Wirth supervised the murders of more than 1.5 million Jews.

Belzec was closed in fall 1943, at which point Wirth was sent to Trieste, ITALY, to accelerate Jewish DEPORTATION. He was killed by PARTISANS while on a trip to Fiume.

WIRTSCHAFTS-VERWALTUNGSHAUPTAMT (WVHA)

(Economic-Administrative Main Office), central administration for SS economic activities. Located in BERLIN, the WVHA was established in February 1942. It included the SS's office of CONCENTRATION CAMP inspectors.

The reason the concentration camps were incorporated into the WVHA was that, as of 1942, concentration camp prisoners were expected to play a larger role in the manufacture of armaments. The WVHA negotiated contracts with industrial companies regarding the use of concentration camp prisoners in their factories; the number of prisoners to be employed; the type of work they would do; the food and lodging they would receive; and the amount of money the firms would make per prisoner per day.

At first, because the WVHA's main goal was to expand the SS's contribution to the war effort, prisoners working for them were given better conditions than usual. However, this improvement was short-lived. The WVHA then sought to increase the amount of work done by the prisoners without increasing the amount of food provided or creating reasonable sanitary living conditions for the prisoners. As a result, they had to turn to brutality to make the prisoners work, and of course, replacement workers were always readily available. Prisoners working for the WVHA were terribly exploited and abused.

WISE, STEPHEN SAMUEL

(1879–1949), American Jewish leader, Zionist activist, and champion of social causes.

In 1907 Wise founded the Free Synagogue in New York, and in 1915 established the American Jewish Congress, which aimed to protect Jewish rights and oppose discrimination against Jews, blacks, and other minorities. In 1922 he founded the Jewish Institute of Religion, which later merged with Hebrew Union College.

Wise was also a key player in establishing the American Zionist movement. He and Louis D. Brandeis helped convince President Woodrow Wilson to support the Balfour Declaration—Britain's pledge to establish a Jewish state in Palestine.

During the 1920s and 1930s, Wise's speeches and sermons dealt with all sorts of social issues. He clashed with Franklin D. ROOSEVELT, then governor of New York, over Wise's campaign against the corrupt mayor of New York, James Walker. The discord between them lasted until Roosevelt's presidential election in 1936, when Wise gave Roosevelt his support.

Wise actively opposed HITLER'S policies from the start. The rabbi organized the movement to boycott German products and spoke out against Hitler's behavior at the 1936 OLYMPIC GAMES in BERLIN. He was indecisive, though, about whether to support the Jewish Agency's TRANSFER AGREEMENT, which allowed them to help German Jews leave for Palestine at the expense of being able to protest the Germans' activities.

Wise's leadership role became increasingly difficult as the Nazis gained power. American Jewry was weak and divided over how to respond. Wise tried to use his influence to save Jews from the Nazis by serving on the President's Advisory Committee on Political REFUGEES, but his efforts were often frustrated by the obstacles created by the State Department, War Department, and even by President Roosevelt himself. He also found it hard to appeal to the president about European Jewry when America itself faced great danger. In 1943 Wise organized the "Stop Hitler Now" demonstration at Madison Square Garden, but by 1944 he was deeply disillusioned. The establishment of the State of Israel in 1948 was a relief to Wise, but he never recovered from the great losses suffered by European Jewry. (see also BOYCOTTS, ANTI-NAZI.)

WISLICENY, DIETER

(1911–1948), SS officer and deputy to Adolf EICHMANN in the Jewish affairs department of the Reich Security Main Office (REICHSSICHERHEITSHAUPTAMT, RSHA).

Wisliceny joined the SS and became part of the Security Service (SD) in 1934. By 1940 he was acting as advisor on Jewish affairs to the Slovakian government, and took part in the DEPORTATION of Jews from SLOVAKIA, GREECE, and HUNGARY between 1942–1944. At the beginning of that period, the Slovakian Jewish underground WORKING GROUP tried to bribe Wisliceny into delaying Jewish deportation. Led by Rabbi Michael

Dov WEISSMANDEL, the Working Group initiated the so-called EUROPA PLAN in an attempt to rescue the remaining Jews of Europe. The contact with Wisliceny, however, petered out when Wisliceny was posted to Greece. In March 1944, while helping Eichmann organize the deportation of Hungarian Jewry, Wisliceny took part in the negotiations with the RELIEF AND RESCUE COMMITTEE of BUDAPEST. These negotiations focused on the rescue of Hungarian Jews in exchange for goods.

After the war, Wisliceny served as a witness at the NUREMBERG TRIALS and wrote several sworn statements about SS activities; his testimony was used at Eichmann's 1961 trial in Jerusalem (see also EICHMANN TRIALS). Wisliceny himself was sentenced to death and hanged in BRATISLAVA in 1948.

WITTENBERG, YITZHAK (LEO ITZIG) (1907–1943), First commander of the United Partisan Organization (*Fareynegte Partizaner Organizatsye*, FPO), a Jewish resistance organization in the VILNA Ghetto.

Wittenberg was born into a working class family and became a tailor by trade. He joined the Communist party at a young age, and distinguished himself as a Communist activist during the short time a Soviet government ruled in LITHUANIA (from June 1940 to June 1941). After the Germans occupied Vilna and deported its Jews to the GHETTO, Wittenberg became a leader of the ghetto and the Communist resistance movement.

The FPO was founded in January 1942, and Wittenberg was chosen as its commander. He was the obvious choice to lead the group because of his personal qualities, his experience with the underground, and his Communist contacts outside the ghetto. He was also well liked by his soldiers.

However, Wittenberg was betrayed by one of his contacts who had been captured by the Germans, despite the fact that the contact did not really know about the FPO's activities. The Nazis demanded that the JUDENRAT hand Wittenberg over. The chairman of the *Judenrat*, Jacob GENS, was willing to give up Wittenberg because he thought that the FPO and its underground activities only made matters worse for the rest of the ghetto population, but the FPO resisted surrendering their leader. The Lithuanian police then arrested Wittenberg, but armed FPO soldiers set him free and hid him in the ghetto. The tension peaked when the Germans threatened to destroy the rest of the ghetto if

Wittenberg was not given up. Gens appealed to the ghetto population, many of whom who turned against the FPO. This pressure, and the realization that the time was not right for an organized uprising, convinced the FPO to surrender their leader. When Wittenberg learned that the Communist ghetto leaders supported his surrender, he accepted their decision and gave himself up to the JEWISH POLICE. That day—July 16, 1943—was named "Wittenberg Day." Wittenberg was imprisoned, where he killed himself by taking poison. (see also UNITED PARTISAN ORGANIZATION, VILNA and RESISTANCE, JEWISH.)

WOLFF, KARL (1900–1984), Senior SS officer who served as Heinrich HIMMLER'S deputy. Wolff was in charge of procuring trains used for deporting Jews to TREBLINKA, and thus was directly responsible for the DEPORTATION of some 300,000 Jews.

WOLINSKI, HENRYK (1901–1986), Polish RIGHTEOUS AMONG THE NATIONS who, as head of the Jewish affairs section in the Polish HOME ARMY, begged his commanders to help rescue Jews. Wolinski also participated in the ZEGOTA and helped hide many Jews.

WORKING GROUP (*Pracovna Skupina*, in German *Nebenregierung*), Jewish semi-underground group in SLOVAKIA heroically dedicated to rescuing Jews from the Nazis. The group was active until the last DEPORTATION of Slovakian Jews, after the SLOVAK NATIONAL UPRISING failed in the autumn of 1944.

The Working Group was led by Rabbi Michael Dov WEISSMANDEL and Gisi FLEISCHMANN. It consisted mostly of members of the Jewish Center (*Ustredna Zidov*, UZ), and developed out of the Committee of Six. This committee was founded after the UZ received reports of imminent deportations. After unsuccessful attempts to garner support from Slovakian government officials and the Catholic Church, the deportations began, and the committee expanded into the Working Group.

The most famous Working Group effort was the bribing in 1942 of SS-*Sturmbannfuehrer* Dieter WISLICENY in exchange for halting the deportation of Slovakian Jews. The negotiations evolved into the EUROPA PLAN, which aspired to rescue much of European Jewry. The Europa Plan occupied the Working Group from summer 1942–autumn 1943.

The group also called for the escape of Slovakian Jews to HUNGARY. Late in 1942 they joined the efforts of the

Zionist YOUTH MOVEMENTS and various Orthodox Jews to fund the escape of 6,000–8,000 Slovakian Jews. They also helped about 1,200 Polish Jews reach Hungary.

Another rescue activity run by the group included establishing and expanding Jewish labor camps at SERED, VYHNE, and NOVAKY. The plan was instituted in 1942 at the height of the deportations. These camps were run partly by Jews, and were to allow Jews to work instead of being deported and murdered. Although not all inmates were saved from deportation, most survived. About 4,000 Jews lived in these three camps until September 1944.

Finally, the Working Group also gathered and distributed information about the Jews who had been deported. In July 1942 messengers reported a high rate of death among deportees. The group then sent this information to their Western connections. They also found out about mass murders in BELZEC, TREBLINKA, and AUSCHWITZ, and broadcast that information. They begged their contacts abroad to bomb Auschwitz and the railroad tracks leading to it, to no avail. (see also JEWISH CENTER, SLOVAKIA and AUSCHWITZ, BOMBING OF.)

WORLD JEWISH CONGRESS (WJC)
International Jewish organization officially founded in 1932, but actually operative from 1936. The WJC was closely linked to the American Jewish Congress (AJC), both of which were headed by the American rabbi and Zionist, Stephen S. WISE. Both congresses were among the first organizations to actively oppose Nazism.

After WORLD WAR II broke out, the WJC moved its offices from Europe to the UNITED STATES. However, the WJC's aid and relief efforts were hindered by the US government's refusal to allow them to send money or food to Nazi-occupied countries. In addition, the WJC's funds were rather limited. Despite this, the WJC and the AJC repeatedly organized mass demonstrations and lobbied the US government and the Allied embassies to take action and provide relief for the Jews in Europe. In August 1942 the WJC representative in Geneva, Dr. Gerhart Riegner, sent a cable to Rabbi Wise describing the Nazis' plans for the "Final Solution"—the extermination of all the Jews in Europe. Known as the RIEGNER CABLE, this telegram finally made American Jewry much more aware of what was happening to their brethren. As a result, Rabbi Wise helped spur Secretary of the Treasury Henry MORGENTHAU to action, who in turn was instrumental in the creation of the US government's WAR REFUGEE BOARD.

WORLD WAR II
War involving most of the world's nations that was launched in 1939 and lasted until 1945. It began with the German invasion of POLAND on September 1, 1939, and ended in Europe with the German surrender on May 7, 1945 and in the Pacific with the Japanese surrender on September 2, 1945. Alongside GERMANY fought ITALY and Japan, known as the AXIS powers. Fighting against them were FRANCE and GREAT BRITAIN, and later on the SOVIET UNION and the UNITED STATES, or the Allied powers.

The destruction and devastation caused by World War II were mammoth in breadth. It is difficult to say how many people perished during the war. The estimates for Europe run between 30–35 million deaths, while nearly 55 million people died world over. Included in that number are six million Jews who were murdered in the HOLOCAUST.

World War II was the result of Nazi Germany's desire to take control of Europe and establish the dominance of the "Germanic-Nordic Aryans." The Nazi ideals of racial ANTISEMITISM and LEBENSRAUM (the desire for more "living space" for the German people) were closely linked. Although the Nazis had no functional plans for a total annihilation of the Jewish people before 1941, the seeds of the Holocaust were contained in Nazi ideology.

British artillery at Tobruk, January 1941

Soon after he rose to national power in Germany in early 1933, Adolf HITLER took steps to acquire territory and prepare the German economy and army for war. He entered into alliances with Italy and later with Japan and other countries. By the time Hitler had taken over and carved up Czechoslovakia in March 1939 (after promising the Western powers that he would refrain from doing so), most of the world realized that it was just a matter of time until the outbreak of war.

German troops crossing the Polish border at the outbreak of World War II, September 1, 1939

In late August 1939 Germany and the Soviet Union, formerly enemies, shocked the world by signing a non-aggression agreement called the NAZI-SOVIET PACT. This opened the door to the outbreak of war: on September 1, 1939 Germany invaded Poland. Two days later Great Britain and France, whose governments had promised to defend Poland, declared war on Germany. However, they never sent troops to Poland, so Germany and the Soviet Union greedily divided up the newly conquered territories of Poland as stipulated in their pact.

After the fall of Poland at the end of September, several months passed with no active fighting on the part of the Germans; this period was called the Phony War. The only real fighting to take place during the Phony War was in FINLAND, which was invaded by the Soviet Union on November 30, 1939. The Finns put up a staunch fight, but they were ultimately defeated in March 1940 (although Finland remained an independent state).

The Nazis waited until April 1940 to make their next major move: the invasion of several Western European countries. German troops invaded NORWAY and DENMARK on April 9; Denmark surrendered almost immediately, while Norway resisted but could not hold out for more than a few weeks (although the port of Narvik continued to be held by the Allies until June 10). On May 10 the Germans attacked the NETHERLANDS, BELGIUM, LUXEMBOURG, and France using the BLITZKRIEG strategy of war. They conquered the Netherlands in five days, while Belgium surrendered on May 28. In France, the fighting raged until early June. At the Battle of Dunkirk in northern France, some 350,000 Allied troops, British, French, and Belgian, managed to evacuate as France fell to Germany. PARIS fell to the Germans on June 14, and a new government under World War I hero Marshal Philippe PETAIN was set up to negotiate a French surrender. Italy had officially joined the war on June 10 and became a co-victor with

Germany. France signed armistice agreements with Germany on June 22 and with Italy on June 24. As a result, France was divided up: its northern zone was occupied by the Germans, while most of its southern zone was put under the control of a French administration that was based in the spa town of Vichy. Another small section in the south was put under Italian control. By late June 1940 Germany and its partners dominated Europe.

During the fighting in France, British Prime Minister Neville Chamberlain had resigned his post and Winston CHURCHILL took his place. British troops in Oran, ALGERIA attacked French naval forces to make sure the area did not fall into German hands, while other French naval forces outside of Europe were put under British control.

In the meantime, the Soviet Union entered the Baltic states—LATVIA, LITHUANIA, and ESTONIA—and over the course of two months stripped them of their independence. On June 28 the Soviets occupied BESSARABIA and northern BUKOVINA. In August 1940 Germany mediated between HUNGARY and ROMANIA. As a result, Germany gave northern TRANSYLVANIA to Hungary, winning Hungary's loyalty, and the royal Romanian government was dissolved and an authoritarian regime under Ion ANTONESCU took its place. Both Romania and Hungary were now firmly under German influence. Not to be outdone, Italy attacked GREECE from Albania in October 1940, but did not make many breakthroughs.

Originally, the Germans planned to conquer their major opponent—Britain—and end the war in the early fall of 1940. However, the date was pushed off again and again due to growing technical difficulties. The German Air Force could not make any headway against the British Royal Air Force, so it changed tactics: bombing British cities to break the citizens' morale in assaults that came to be known as the "Blitz." However, that strategy did not work either, and by the spring of 1941 it looked like neither the Germans nor the British could beat the other.

In the meantime, in September 1940 Italian troops invaded Egypt, which was under British control. The Italians failed to conquer the country and were even put under attack by the British. At that point, Germany sent troops to help its ally in North Africa, where the war was to continue in a seesaw fashion for almost two years. Until early 1941 the British had the upper hand after gaining control of Cyrenaica in LIBYA. This changed

when Germany's Gen. Erwin Rommel and his forces entered the scene. The British were pushed back to Tobruk, but then managed to retake Cyrenaica. Meanwhile, in Iraq, British forces clashed with the pro-Nazi Rashid Ali al-Gaylani. The British successfully took control of Baghdad on May 30, 1941; by doing so, they also stopped the anti-Jewish pogrom that had broken out there.

Meanwhile, in Europe during the second half of 1940 Hitler had begun planning an attack on his ally, the Soviet Union. This was part of his ideological desire to obtain living space for Germany by conquering the Soviet Union. Preparations for this attack, code-named "Operation Barbarossa," went on throughout the winter of 1940–1941 and the spring of 1941. An order issued in March 1941, known as the *Kommissarbefehl,* called for the murder of all political officers of the Soviet armed forces, as well as all Communists. Since Hitler equated Jews with Communists, some historians see the *Kommissarbefehl* as an order by Hitler to murder the Jews.

Romania, BULGARIA, and YUGOSLAVIA officially joined the Axis alliance in early 1941, but the Yugoslav government was overthrown by an anti-Nazi military group under Gen. Dusan Simovic. As a result, in April 1941 Germany invaded Yugoslavia and Greece—Yugoslavia to topple the anti-German government, and Greece to bail out the Italian forces who were floundering there in their fight against the British. Once again using the *Blitzkrieg* strategy, Germany defeated Yugoslavia and Greece easily.

Next, after postponing the attack several times due to the situation in the Balkans, Germany launched its surprise invasion of the Soviet Union on June 22, 1941. The German forces consisted of some three million men, including Finnish, Romanian, and Hungarian units. Despite brave resistance in some areas, millions of Soviet soldiers were soon killed. German forces overran the Baltic states in July, with the local populations actively helping the Germans (although the Soviets managed to stop the Germans before they reached Leningrad). In the south, the Germans moved in on the UKRAINE in September, conquering Kiev and then ODESSA and Kharkov in mid and late October. They invaded and conquered the Crimea in November, and laid siege to the Crimean city of Sevastopol on November 15. The Germans' main attack in July 1941 brought them to MINSK and then Smolensk. Both in the Ukraine and in the Briansk-Viazma region, huge Soviet armies were defeated and most of their soldiers were taken prisoner. In November the Germans continued their advance on Moscow, and by December 1941 they had nearly reached the Russian capital. However, at that point there was a turnaround: the Soviets launched a counteroffensive on December 6 and pushed the Germans back, away from Moscow. It is possible that this was the war's turning point. The Germans were no longer as confident, and they were forced to fight throughout the winter in the bitter Russian cold.

In the spring of 1942 the Germans managed to rekindle their offensive. Conquering the Don River basin, they reached the outskirts of Stalingrad—a strategically crucial city from their standpoint—on August 20, 1942. In September they broke out of the Crimean peninsula and soon occupied the Caucasian oil fields. By mid-September they had penetrated Stalingrad it-

self; the Soviet troops there held on desperately. On November 19, the Soviets renewed their counteroffensive, and closed in on 22 German divisions that included 300,000 soldiers. In January 1943 the Soviet offensive in Leningrad relieved the 17-month German siege of the city. On February 2, 1943 the German Sixth Army, fighting at Stalingrad, surrendered to the Soviets. Some 91,000 German soldiers were taken prisoner.

In spite of mutual distrust, the British, Americans, and Soviets agreed to work together against the German threat. At first the Americans only meant this in terms of aiding the British and Soviets with war materials. In March 1941 the US Congress had approved the Lend-Lease Act, and the Soviet Union became the recipient of massive American assistance. However, on December 7, 1941 the Japanese (German allies) attacked the US naval base at Pearl Harbor, Hawaii, causing great loss

General Alfred Jodl signing the terms of surrender, Rheims, France, May 7, 1945

of life and equipment. The United States declared war on Japan, and a few days later Germany and Italy declared war on the United States. Now that the war had expanded to the Far East, it had truly become a "world war." Like the Germans in Europe, the Japanese wanted to become the dominant power in East Asia, and the United States, greatly weakened by Pearl Harbor, was unable to stop them. The US was powerless to defend Guam and the Wake Islands, which fell to the Japanese on December 13 and 20, respectively. The Japanese then invaded the Philippines in late December and vanquished them in January (although US troops held out on the Philippines' Bataan peninsula and Corregidor until May 1942).

Also in December 1941, the British surrendered to the Japanese in Hong Kong, and in January the Japanese conquered the Dutch East Indies. Next, Malaya was overrun, Singapore fell on February 15, and Thailand allied itself with Japan. In March the Japanese conquered Burma and threatened India, but were halted by the British. In addition, the Allies (mainly Australians and New Zealanders) stopped the Japanese advance in New Guinea, and in the Battle of the Coral Sea in May, some 100,000 tons of Japanese materials were sunk.

The turning point on the Pacific front came in June 1942 when the US defeated the Japanese in the battle for the Island of Midway. American troops then landed on the Solomon Islands in August. In November a Japanese fleet was defeated there, while the Battle of Guadalcanal cost the lives of large numbers of both Americans and Japanese. In 1943 American and British Commonwealth troops slowly retook control of the Pacific Islands and invaded Burma. Allied soldiers taken as PRISONERS OF WAR and jailed Allied civilians were subjected to extreme brutality at the hands of the Japanese.

Back in North Africa the seesaw battles continued. The British lost ground in Cyrenaica in January 1942, and in June Tobruk was taken by the Germans under Rommel. However, in July German tanks were stopped at El Alamein. The British then launched their major offensive on October 23, 1942. Less than two weeks later Rommel's troops were in full retreat; they had fallen back to TUNISIA by January 1943. On November 8, 1942 American and British troops invaded North Africa. Algiers was occupied by a local anti-Nazi militia composed mainly of Jews. The pro-German French administration in North Africa arranged to surrender

to the Allies, and was given the right to continue its rule (and kept the Vichy government's anti-Jewish laws intact for another few months). In Tunis, the Axis forces surrendered on May 12, 1943 after a bitter fight. Thus, the first region to be cleared of Axis troops was North Africa.

In July the Allied forces under General Dwight D. EISENHOWER invaded Sicily in southern Italy. This resulted in the resignation and imprisonment on July 25 of Benito MUSSOLINI and the establishment of a military government, which surrendered to the Allies. However, the Germans freed Mussolini and set up a Fascist puppet government in northern Italy. While the Allies liberated Rome on June 4, 1944 and Florence on August 12, the Germans held onto northern Italy until April 1945.

During 1943 the Soviets liberated most of the Ukraine, and in the spring of 1944 they liberated much of Poland. In their advance southward they caused the Romanian king to change his colors and overthrow the pro-Nazi dictator, Ion Antonescu. Soon, Romania surrendered to the Allies and joined the fight against Germany on August 23. On September 5 the Soviet Union declared war on Bulgaria; Bulgaria soon surrendered and the Soviets occupied the capital, Sofia, on September 16. In March 1944 Hungary, a German ally, tried to make peace with the Allies. In response, Germany invaded Hungary and appointed a pro-German government that collaborated in the DEPORTATION of most of the country's Jews. In October, Hungarian Regent Miklos HORTHY again tried to arrange a peace agreement with the Allies; Germany responded by toppling Horthy's government and setting up an antisemitic, Fascist, collaborative government under the ARROW CROSS PARTY. Now, most of the remnant of the Hungarian Jewish community was destroyed.

Meanwhile, the British and American air forces worked together to strategically bomb the German enemy: the Americans concentrated on daytime bombings of military and industrial targets, while the British devastated German cities at night. In 1944 the Allied air forces, now operating from Italy, achieved complete supremacy in the air. By June, the Allies were ready for their major offensive. On June 6, 1944 (known as D-Day), some 250,000 Allied soldiers landed on the shores of Normandy in northwestern France. By July 31 American forces broke through the German lines of defense, and by the end of August they had liberated France. By the fall of 1944 the Allies were poised to defeat Germany. However, German resistance continued for eight more months: the Allies were held back in the southern part of the Netherlands in September, and were taken by total surprise in December when German forces tried to break through American lines in Belgium. The Allies finally managed to push the Germans back in this battle that came to be known as the "Battle of the Bulge."

On January 12, 1945 the Soviets began a powerful offensive, taking WARSAW just five days later (the Poles had tried to defend Warsaw in August of the previous year, but the Soviets refused to help them, so Warsaw was ravaged and many Poles were killed). BUDAPEST, Hungary was also liberated in January and February. In March 1945 the final Allied offensive was launched both in the east and in the west. Allied troops made their way through Germany (discovering the Nazi CONCENTRATION CAMPS in the process), and in April, met at the Elbe River. The Germans were surrounded, and on April 30 Hitler committed suicide in his BERLIN bunker (Mussolini had been shot by anti-Fascist PARTISANS on April 28). Soviet troops liberated Berlin in early May, and on May 7 the Germans surrendered. May 8 was proclaimed to be Victory in Europe Day (V-E Day).

The war in the Pacific lasted another three months. American Gen. Douglas MacArthur had advanced from one chain of Pacific islands to another, while in October 1944 American forces had begun liberating the Philippines, and at the end of that month they sank a large part of the Japanese fleet. Air raids on Japan itself began in November, while British forces began to retake Burma. After bitter battles that cost the lives of many Americans (especially on the islands of Iwo Jima and Okinawa), the US government decided to end the war, once and for all, by dropping an atomic bomb on Hiroshima, Japan on August 6, 1945. Over 80,000 people were killed on the spot, and many more died later from the aftereffects of the atomic radiation. Three days later another equally devastating bomb was dropped on Nagasaki. On August 8 the Soviet Union joined the war against Japan in order to gain control of certain territories they were fighting over. Japan finally surrendered on August 11, and Victory in Japan (V-J Day) was celebrated on August 15, 1945. With the formal signing of the Japanese surrender on September 2, 1945, the war had finally come to an end.

WURM, THEOPHIL   (1868–1953), German Protestant theologian who was appointed bishop of Wurttemberg in 1933. At the very beginning of the Nazi regime, Wurm was a supporter of the "German Christians," a Protestant group that endorsed the NAZI PARTY. However, in late 1933 the Nazis began the process of *Gleichschaltung,* meaning Coordination under Nazism. For the churches, the gist of this process was to put their institutions under the control of Nazi organizations and subject them to Nazi ideology. Wurm strenuously opposed the notion that the Nazis would officially be in charge of what the church could say and do, so he joined the anti-Nazi Confessing Church. He also strongly protested the appointment of Nazi supporter Ludwig Mueller as "Reich bishop" of the Evangelical (Protestant) Church—a move that would make sure that the Protestant church would back the Nazis and oppose the Confessing Church. Because of his strong views and outspokenness, Wurm was placed under house arrest in 1934. However, the Nazis could not keep Wurm down. After a public protest, Wurm condemned the EUTHANASIA PROGRAM and the persecution of Jews at the hands of the Nazis.

After the war Wurm helped author the "Stuttgart Confession," an admission that the church had not done enough to fight the Nazis.

Y

YAD VASHEM THE HOLOCAUST MARTYRS' AND HEROES' REMEMBRANCE AUTHORITY, Israel's national Holocaust memorial. The name *Yad Vashem* comes from a verse in the biblical book of Isaiah that refers to an everlasting memorial. Located on Jerusalem's *Har HaZikaron* (Remembrance Mountain) near the Mt. Herzl complex, Yad Vashem was officially established by Israel's parliament in 1953 in accordance with the Martyrs' and Heroes' Remembrance Law. The authority was charged with commemorating the six million Jews who were murdered by the Nazis and Nazi collaborators; the Jewish communities of Europe that were destroyed; the heroism of the soldiers, underground fighters, PARTISANS, and prisoners of the GHETTOS; and the RIGHTEOUS AMONG THE NATIONS. The law also made the authority responsible to establish memorial projects; gather, research, and publish educational materials about the Holocaust and its lessons; award honorary Israeli citizenship to the victims; and represent Israel internationally with regards to Holocaust commemoration.

Yad Vashem consists of various special areas. The Historical Museum tells the story of the Holocaust chronologically, beginning with Adolf HITLER and his rise to power in GERMANY in 1933, moving on to the persecution of Jews within the THIRD REICH, the mass annihilation of European Jewry, armed resistance by the Jews, and the last stages of the Holocaust. The Museum of Art houses an important collection of pieces created during the Holocaust.

The Hall of Remembrance has a tent-shaped roof and a mosaic floor engraved with the names of the 22 largest Nazi CONCENTRATION CAMPS. The hall's Eternal Light is flanked by a vault that holds the ashes of Holocaust victims, brought to Israel from the EXTERMINATION CAMPS in Europe. Commemoration ceremonies are held in the Hall of Remembrance.

The Hall of Names serves as a register of the names of millions of Jews who were killed, while the Children's Memorial commemorates the one and a half million children who died during the Holocaust. The latter consists of a dark building lit by five memorial candles that are multiplied exponentially with the use of mirrors. These lights represent the children whose names are continually read aloud in the background.

There are also many outdoor sites at the Yad Vashem facility. The Garden of the Righteous honors those non-Jews, officially designated by Yad Vashem as "Righteous among the Nations," who risked their lives to rescue Jews during the Holocaust. The awardees are entitled to plant trees along the garden's Avenue of the Righteous among the Nations. Another compelling outdoor site is the authentic German cattle car that

A courtyard in the Valley of Jewish Communities at Yad Vashem

Pope John Paul II at Yad Vashem, March 2000 (Photo: Y. Harari)

represents the victims' final journey. Along the western end of Yad Vashem's memorial hill is the Valley of the Destroyed Communities. This exhibit includes the names of approximately 5,000 Jewish communities that were destroyed or severely hurt by the Nazis during the Holocaust. The southern section of the hill contains WARSAW Ghetto Square and a monument to the WARSAW GHETTO UPRISING, where Israel's official state ceremony of Holocaust Remembrance Day is held each year.

Yad Vashem also includes an archives and a library, representing the world's most important collection of Holocaust information. The archives contain roughly 50 million pages of testimonies and documents; the library has over 80,000 books by title and 4,500 periodicals that deal with all aspects of the Holocaust. Yad Vashem has published hundreds of books and recorded the testimonies of tens of thousands of Holocaust survivors. Yad Vashem's International School for Holocaust Studies holds study seminars for many audiences in many languages. It places a strong emphasis on teacher training and curriculum development.

As befits an important national shrine, about two million people visit Yad Vashem each year, from both Israel and abroad, Jews and non-Jews alike. Official guests on state visits to Israel go to Yad Vashem as part of their customary program.

YISHUV The Jewish community in Palestine. Right before WORLD WAR II, the relations between the *Yishuv* and the British Mandate authorities were strained due to restrictions made on Jewish immigration to Palestine. Despite the friction, the *Yishuv* considered itself an obvious ally of those countries fighting the Nazis, and 30,000 Palestinian Jews joined the British army.

By the time the Nazis began implementing the "Final Solution" in 1941, the *Yishuv* had set up communication pipelines to Europe; nonetheless, information was not yet clear about what was going on. Specific reports about the horrors of the HOLOCAUST began arriving in early 1942. The *Yishuv* itself faced mortal danger at that time: the Germans in North Africa were advancing towards Palestine. Only when that threat was destroyed in mid-1942 could the *Yishuv* begin to deal with the issue of European Jewry.

In the fall of 1942 a group of Palestinian Jews returned to Palestine from Europe bearing terrible reports of mass atrocities. This shocked the *Yishuv* into mourning, and then into action. In January 1943 the Joint Rescue Committee of the Jewish Agency was founded. From then on, the *Yishuv* initiated many programs for rescuing European Jews.

At the end of 1942 ROMANIA suggested a deal whereby thousands of Jews would be returned home from exile in TRANSNISTRIA in exchange for millions of dollars. The Jewish Agency kept in contact with Romanian representatives and provided financial help for the Jews in Transnistria. In 1944 the SURVIVORS began to return to Romania. Another rescue scheme was the EUROPA PLAN, initiated by the Slovakian Jewish community's WORKING GROUP. This called for the payment of large sums of money in exchange for the lives of Jews who had been deported to POLAND. In June 1943, after considering the offer's legitimacy, the Jewish Agency agreed to help pay the Germans $200,000 as a down payment. However, transferring large sums during wartime proved impossible. Another Jewish Agency plan included parachuting young Palestinian Jews behind occupied lines to boost the Jews' morale and convince them to participate in armed resistance. In the end, 37 young people actually took part in this venture.

The Jewish Agency adopted other rescue proposals, such as giving out "protective passports" to Jews in German-occupied countries; according the Jews PRISONER OF WAR status; exchanging them for German prisoners of war; transferring them from Europe to North Africa; or keeping them in transit camps in their own countries, under the protection of the International RED CROSS. The most important, and perhaps boldest proposal, was that the Allies demand that the Germans immediately stop the annihilation of European Jewry. However, the Allies did not seriously consider any of these proposals.

After the BERMUDA CONFERENCE of April 1943, the *Yishuv* realized that there was very little chance of a mass rescue. Instead, they would have to direct their efforts toward "small rescue" operations. This meant smuggling Jews across borders; organizing the exchange of small groups of Jews for Germans; sending packages of food, medicine, money, and documents to Jews in the occupied countries; and maintaining mail contact in order to boost the morale of European Jewry.

Protesting the British immigration policy to Palestine, Italy, 1947

In the spring of 1944, soon after the Nazis began deporting Hungarian Jews to AUSCHWITZ, they made a proposal to the *Yishuv* regarding the release of one million Jews. The *Yishuv* leaders did not believe the Germans were really interested in sparing Hungarian Jewry, but they hoped that negotiations could help halt the DEPORTATIONS. However, the Allies were not able to cooperate with the *Yishuv* in getting the plan together. That summer, the Jewish Agency begged the Allies to bomb the train tracks leading to Auschwitz and its extermination area. These appeals were also rejected. (see also PARACHUTISTS, JEWISH and AUSCHWITZ, BOMBING OF.)

YIZKOR BOOK   A book commemorating a European Jewish community that was destroyed during the HOLOCAUST. Generally, a *Yizkor* book will concentrate on a large community, but may include chapters on smaller communities located nearby. The first *Yizkor* book was published in New York in 1943; entitled *Lodzer Yizkor Buch,* it was dedicated to the Jews of LODZ. Since then, more than 900 *Yizkor* books have been produced.

Most *Yizkor* books cover the Jewish communities in Eastern Europe. However, there have also been *Yizkor* books written about the Jewish communities in Western Europe, especially those that thrived in GERMANY before the Nazi rise to power. Since the late 1970s some non-Jews in Germany have assembled books about the Jews who had lived among them; these often take the form of *Yizkor* books.

Yizkor books generally include articles on a community's history from before the war, but mainly focus on the war years, including details about life in the GHETTOS and the camps, resistance activities, Nazi collaborators and RIGHTEOUS AMONG THE NATIONS, and the annihilation of the community members. They also include articles about the post-war years, and may provide information about victims and SURVIVORS. Many books also include personal diaries, poems, and other documents written by Jews during the Holocaust.

YOUTH ALIYA (Youth Immigration), program run by the Zionist movement to rescue Jewish youth in Europe by sending them to Palestine. The Youth Aliya project was started in 1932 in GERMANY by Recha Freier, the wife of a BERLIN rabbi. After the Nazis rose to power in 1933, Youth Aliya was adopted by the Jewish Agency. A Youth Aliya Office was created and put under the direction of American Zionist Henrietta Szold.

By the time WORLD WAR II broke out in 1939, 5,012 children had been taken to Palestine by Youth Aliya. During the war, Youth Aliya pressured the British authorities to increase the number of Jews allowed into Palestine. However, the British refused to increase their immigration quotas substantially, so only 9,342 Jewish children entered Palestine during the war years of 1939–1945. Youth Aliya sent another 15,000 to Western European countries, most notably GREAT BRITAIN.

Youth Aliya continued its aid and rescue activities after the war as well. From 1945 to 1948, 15,999 Jewish youth immigrated to Palestine; most had to do so "illegally" as the British Mandate authorities would still not increase their immigration quotas. By that time, children arriving in Palestine under the sponsorship of Youth Aliya were taken to live at well-established youth villages and educational institutions.

YOUTH MOVEMENTS Jewish youth organizations that came into being in Europe between the two world wars. These movements had different motivations, whether religious, social, cultural, or political. Some were Communist or Socialist, others were Zionist, and some movements were both Zionist and Socialist. Others were not associated with any political movement or ideology. However, as the Nazis began persecuting Jews throughout Europe, members of all the Jewish youth movements took a leading role in resisting the Nazis and assisting their fellow Jews.

In Eastern Europe, many of the youth movements were Zionist in nature. Among the first youth movements in Eastern Europe was *Ha-Shomer ha-Tsa'ir,* which combined both Zionism and radical Socialism in its ideology. The *Dror* movement was similar to *Ha-Shomer ha-Tsa'ir,* but its members came from poorer circles. The *Gordonia* movement promoted a more moderate Zionist-Socialist platform, while the *Ha-No'ar ha-Tsiyyoni* and *Akiva* youth movements encouraged Zionism and Hebrew culture. The *Betar* group was actually the youth wing of the Zionist Revisionist political movement, and thus had specific political goals in mind.

Many of the Zionist movements, except *Betar,* were connected to specific *kibbutz* (collective settlement) movements in Palestine, and part of their ideologies was to send members off to settle in Palestine. Thus, many of the movements' members participated in agricultural training programs in preparation for immigration. The connection between members of youth movements was very strong, as was their belief that what they were preparing for was very worthwhile and important. This attitude was probably one of the great reasons why during the war, youth movement members, despite their age, took a leading role in resisting the Nazis.

Right before WORLD WAR II broke out in the fall of 1939, some 100,000 young Jews were involved in the various youth movements. Despite the fact that the Nazis outlawed Jewish youth movements and their activities early on, the movements continued in secret. After Germany invaded POLAND, signaling the beginning of the war, many youth movement leaders fled the cities of western and central Poland for Soviet-held eastern Poland, hoping to make it from there to Palestine. Soon, however, some of the youth movements decided to send some of their senior members back to German-occupied territory to help their fellow young people trapped by the Nazis, and reorganize them for a viable existence as secret, underground organizations. Among such leaders who returned home in 1940 were Yitzhak (Antek) ZUCKERMAN of the *Dror-he-Halutz* movement and Mordecai ANIELEWICZ of the *Ha-Shomer ha-Tsa'ir* movement.

The youth movements active in the various GHETTOS of Poland embarked upon serious activities, such as organizing study courses, seminars, ideological workshops, and other such programming. They were also in charge of publishing the underground newspapers, and in WARSAW, the youth movements set up a courier network to keep in contact with other ghettos.

Unlike many of the older, more established Jewish communal leaders, who felt that "this too shall pass," the leaders of the youth movements saw the future with surprising clarity. They were convinced that they had no real chance of survival under the Nazis, and that their only chance was armed resistance, even until the death of their last man. Thus, after the "Final Solution" was put into effect, the youth movements began organizing themselves for resistance against the Nazis. In the Warsaw, VILNA, and other ghettos, youth movements established militias to carry out uprisings within the ghettos. In other ghettos, such as in KOVNO, the young resisters made plans to escape to the forests and join the PARTISANS. In FRANCE, Jewish youth movements were involved in armed resistance (see also JEWISH ARMY, FRANCE) and in rescue activities (see also FRENCH JEWISH SCOUTS). In BUDAPEST, HUNGARY, youth movement members saved thousands of their fellow Jews mostly by handing out forged identity documents. (see also RESISTANCE, JEWISH.)

YUGOSLAVIA   Country in southeastern Europe, established after World War I with the union of several territories housing many different ethnic groups. Yugoslavia's hub was SERBIA, joined by Montenegro, CROATIA, Bosnia and Herzegovina, MACEDONIA, and other areas.

Before the outbreak of WORLD WAR II, 15.5 million people lived in Yugoslavia. Of that number, 43 percent were Serbs, 34 percent were Croats, seven percent Slovenes, and seven percent Macedonians. The rest of the population consisted of Germans, Hungarians, Albanians, GYPSIES, and approximately 80,000 Jews.

Before HITLER came to power in GERMANY, there was not much ANTISEMITISM in Yugoslavia. However, as Nazi Germany began to systematically persecute German

Jews, antisemitism in Yugoslavia also mounted. After the war broke out, the Yugoslav government wanted to appease the Germans, so it passed two anti-Jewish laws in October 1940. The first law fixed a quota for Jews entering secondary schools and universities; the second banned Jews from buying and selling certain food items. Intellectuals and the Serbian public strenuously objected to these laws, to no avail.

On April 13, 1941 Germany, along with ITALY, HUNGARY, and BULGARIA, invaded Yugoslavia. By April 18 the Yugoslav army surrendered. Hitler decided to do away with the political entity of Yugoslavia, and divide it among his allies. Germany took Serbia; Bulgaria annexed Macedonia; and Hungary took the BACKA region. Italy was given Montenegro and most of Yugoslavia's Adriatic coast. Croatia, Bosnia, and Herzegovina were united into the Independent State of Croatia, under the control of the USTASA Fascist nationalist movement.

Yugoslavia's population of 80,000 Jews consisted of 40,000 in Croatia, 16,000 in Serbia, 16,000 in the Backa region, and 8,000 in Macedonia. How they were treated after the Germans invaded in 1941 depended on the region.

In Serbia, the Germans dealt with the region's Jews thoroughly, quickly, and cruelly. Right after they took over Serbia, they ordered the Jews to register themselves, and enacted anti-Jewish laws. For the next few months, most male Jews were forced to work at hard labor. After a Serbian revolt broke out in July 1941, all male Jews were put in CONCENTRATION CAMPS. Over the next year, all of the region's Jews were deported or murdered.

The Jews of Croatia were persecuted as part of a general GENOCIDE of foreigners, including Serbs, Jews, and Gypsies. Jewish property and money were taken away, and by the end of 1941 about two-thirds of Croatia's Jews had been imprisoned. Many were killed by the *Ustasa* government. Most of the rest of Croatia's Jews were deported to AUSCHWITZ or other concentration camps in the east. Some were able to escape to the Italian zone of Yugoslavia.

Macedonia was ruled by Bulgaria. In March 1943 Germany convinced Bulgaria to arrest the region's Jews and deport them to TREBLINKA. More than 7,000 Macedonian Jews were killed, and less than 1,000 survived.

Hungary had annexed the Backa region, and subjected it to its own anti-Jewish laws. In January 1942 the Hungarian army and police went on the "great raid" in which they murdered and plundered Backa's Jews. They then forced the young Jews to work at hard labor, and concentrated the rest of the Jews in three camps. In 1944 more than 10,000 Jews were deported to Auschwitz.

Those Jews who lived in Montenegro or on Yugoslavia's Adriatic coast were the lucky ones. The Italian government, army, and foreign ministry worked together to protect their Jews from the Germans. They did so on principle, because they realized that the Germans were losing the war, and because they wanted to preserve their admired status in Yugoslavia. About 5,000 Jews were saved by the Italians.

Altogether, about 66,000 Yugoslav Jews were killed in the HOLOCAUST, and altogether about one million Yugoslavians died in World War II.

Z

ZBASZYN (ZBONSZYN)   Polish border town used, between November 1938 and August 1939, as a REFUGEE camp for thousands of Jews who had been expelled from GERMANY.

On October 27, 1938 the Germans began arresting Jews with Polish citizenship who had been living in Germany, with the intention of kicking them out of the country. Their pretext was a decree made by the Polish Ministry of the Interior earlier that month, which declared that Polish citizens living abroad needed to get their passports checked and re-stamped. Those who had not done so by October 29 would no longer be allowed to return to POLAND. Germany used this as an excuse to deport thousands of Jews who had been living on German soil.

Most often, only the head of the family was banished, but in some cases the whole family was sent off. A son of one of these families, Herschel GRYNSZPAN, was outraged by their DEPORTATION, so he shot a German diplomat in PARIS, inciting the KRISTALLNACHT pogrom. The Polish authorities had not been forewarned about the thousands of refugees being sent into their country. Thus, they placed them in the border town of Zbaszyn, and forbade them from leaving in the hope that the

Jewish deportees in Zbaszyn lining up to receive food, November 1938

large number of Jews near the border would pressure the Germans into beginning negotiations to allow them back into Germany.

For the first few days, the Polish citizens of Zbaszyn heeded the call of their authorities and gave the Jewish refugees food and warm water. By October 30, the Warsaw-based JOINT DISTRIBUTION COMMITTEE sent Emanuel RINGELBLUM and Yitzhak GITTERMAN to organize an aid committee for the refugees, which provided for their basic needs.

As negotiations lingered on, the Polish authorities let the refugees leave the town. Many were taken in by friends and family in Poland, and were aided by Polish Jewish communities. Others managed to leave the country. Negotiations finally ended on January 24, 1939. The Germans allowed the deportees to return to Germany to wind up their affairs, while the Poles agreed to absorb the deportees and their families. The arrangements lasted until the summer of 1939.

ZEGOTA (*Rada Pomocy Zydom,* Council for Aid to Jews; *Tymczasowy Komitet Pomocy Zydom,* Provisional Committee for Aid to Jews), Polish code name for the underground Council for Aid to Jews. *Zegota* operated from December 1942 until the LIBERATION of POLAND in January 1945.

Zegota originated as the Provisional Committee for Aid to Jews, initiated by writer Zofia Kossak-Szczucka, and consisted of democratic Catholic activists. It was soon revamped as *Zegota,* an organization which included both Jews and non-Jews from many different political movements. Despite their differences, they were motivated to fight the injustices perpetrated by the Nazis.

Zegota was funded by the DELEGATURA, the BUND, and the Jewish National Committee. By the summer of 1944, *Zegota* was helping 4,000 Jews. However, they were unable to provide aid for more people due to a chronic shortage of funding.

Zegota furnished many Jews with false identification papers, money, and safe hiding places. Despite the death penalty imposed on people who hid Jews, *Zegota* members successfully placed thousands of Jewish children in foster homes, public orphanages, and convents. They also provided medical care to Jews in hiding. In addition, *Zegota* tried very hard to convince the POLISH GOVERNMENT-IN-EXILE and the *Delegatura* to implore the Polish people to help the Jews.

ZEITLIN, HILLEL (1871–1942), Religious thinker, scholar, and writer who forecast the extermination of European Jewry in his writings. Born in BELORUSSIA, Zeitlin settled in WARSAW, where he founded and wrote for two major Yiddish newspapers. He was a student of Jewish mysticism who tried to interest other thinkers of his time in the classical Jewish sources.

As early as 1917, Zeitlin began writing about dreams and visions in which he clearly saw the impending annihilation of Europe's Jews. In one dream he saw his own death, while in another he saw a ship sinking, the Jews on it dying as martyrs. In a later dream Zeitlin envisioned a DEPORTATION train carrying Jews to their deaths. In July 1939, less than two months before WORLD WAR II broke out, Zeitlin described, in great detail, a vision he had had that included the total liquidation of the European Jewish community. He told a group of friends and students about his vision, and published a description of it in a Jewish periodical.

After the war did indeed break out, Zeitlin was moved to the Warsaw GHETTO, where he worked feverishly, and took no part in public life. He was probably shot to death on the UMSCHLAGPLATZ in 1942.

ZENTRALAUSSCHUSS DER DEUTSCHEN JUDEN FUER HILFE UND AUFBAU see CENTRAL COMMITTEE OF GERMAN JEWS FOR HELP AND RECONSTRUCTION.

ZENTRALSTELLE FUER JUEDISCHE AUSWANDERUNG (Central Office for Jewish Emigration), organization originally established in August 1938 by the SS's Security Police and Security Service to supervise the emigration and expulsion of the Jews of AUSTRIA. Later, the *Zentralstelle* also dealt with the Jews of the Protectorate of Bohemia and Moravia (see also BOHEMIA AND MORAVIA, PROTECTORATE OF).

The Vienna office was set up on August 26, 1938; it was headed by Adolf EICHMANN. The methods instituted by Eichmann in the *Zentralstelle* were later used as models for the expulsion of the rest of European Jewry. He moved all of the Jews of Austria into VIENNA and established quotas for the number of Jews who had to emigrate. Then Eichmann made the Jewish community responsible for filling those quotas and for paying for the expulsion themselves. Jews with more money were forced to pay for Jews who could not finance themselves.

On January 24, 1939 Hermann GOERING was told to set up an organization in GERMANY similar to the *Zen-*

tralstelle. This organization, headed by Reinhard HEYDRICH, was called the *Reichzentralstelle fuer Juedische Auswanderung* (Reich Central Office for Jewish Emigration). Another *Zentralstelle* was instituted in PRAGUE on July 26, 1939, after the Nazis occupied Bohemia and Moravia. This office was also headed by Eichmann, and it ultimately dealt with the expulsion of the Jews of the Protectorate of Bohemia and Moravia to THERESIENSTADT.

After the Germans occupied POLAND in September 1939, Eichmann was put in charge of banishing the Jews who lived in those parts of western Poland that had been annexed to Germany. On December 21, 1939 he was appointed the "officer in charge of all Security Police Affairs relating to the clearance of the eastern areas." He moved to BERLIN to run the Reich Central Office for Jewish Emigration, and consolidated the Vienna and Berlin offices into one. This office soon became a department of the Reich Security Main Office (REICHSSICHERHEITSHAUPTAMT, RSHA), and later helped supervise the DEPORTATION of European Jews to the EXTERMINATION CAMPS.

ZIMAN, HENRIK　(also known as Genrikas Zimanas; 1910–1987), Lithuanian Jewish Communist leader and PARTISAN commander.

Born in southern LITHUANIA, Ziman, nicknamed "Hanak," became a very active member of the Communist party in 1932. After the SOVIET UNION annexed Lithuania in the summer of 1940, Ziman was put in charge of making Lithuania's culture more Soviet. He also helped dissolve the country's Zionist and Hebrew language organizations.

GERMANY invaded the Soviet Union and Soviet-held territories, including Lithuania, in June 1941. At that point, Ziman escaped to Moscow, where he directed anti-Nazi propaganda for the Soviet Lithuanian government. In November 1942 he was named deputy chief of the Lithuanian partisan movement. In mid-1943 Ziman parachuted into BELORUSSIA, close to the Lithuanian border. He made his way to the Rudninkai Forest in Lithuania, where he took charge of a large partisan brigade that included Jewish partisans who had escaped the GHETTOS of VILNA and KOVNO.

After the war, Ziman returned to work for the Communist party in Soviet Lithuania. He occupied several high-ranking positions in the party, and edited the party's daily newspaper and its periodical. Over the years, Ziman wrote hundreds of articles on various political and cultural subjects; in some, he strongly criticized the Zionist movement.

ZIMETBAUM, MALA　(1922–1944), Escapee from AUSCHWITZ. Originally from POLAND, Zimetbaum grew up in BELGIUM. In September 1942, during deportations from Belgium, she was deported to Auschwitz, where she was transferred to a women's camp in Birkenau. Since she could speak several languages, Zimetbaum became an interpreter. This accorded her a special status in the camp, but unlike other privileged inmates, Zimetbaum managed to gain the trust of her fellow prisoners.

During her time at the camp, Zimetbaum came to know a young Polish inmate named Adek Galinski. Galinski, who was planning his escape from Auschwitz, invited Zimetbaum to come with him, and in June 1944 the two fled. In fact, Zimetbaum was the first woman to escape Auschwitz. The two managed to reach the Slovak border, but were caught and sent back to the camp. Both were sentenced to death by hanging—as a punishment and a warning to the other prisoners. However, on the way to the gallows, each committed suicide. Zimetbaum took her own life with a hidden razor blade, which she used to cut an artery in her wrist. The SS guard who was holding her tried to grab the razor away from her—and in an ultimate act of defiance, she slapped his face with her bloody hand.

ZORIN, SHALOM　(1902–1974), Jewish PARTISAN commander in MINSK.

The Germans invaded Minsk in late June 1941 and transferred the city's Jews, Zorin included, to a GHETTO. Zorin worked in a local PRISONER OF WAR camp, where he met a captured Soviet officer named Semyon Ganzenko. In late 1941 Zorin and Ganzenko escaped to the forests in the Staroe Selo region, about 19 miles southwest of Minsk. While hiding in the forest, the two established a partisan unit called *Parkhomenko.* The unit consisted of 150 members, including many Jews.

As more and more Jews joined *Parkhomenko,* many conflicts arose between the Jewish and non-Jewish fighters. Zorin defended his fellow Jews, leading Ganzenko to recommend that he establish a new Jewish partisan unit to take in Jews who had escaped the ghetto, called "Unit 106" (later the unit was referred to as the "Zorin Unit"). The Zorin Unit began with 60 men and 15 guns, but over time, it grew to 800 people. After the Zorin Unit was attacked by the Belorussian

Shalom Zorin

police and the Nazis situated in the Staroe Selo area, it moved its headquarters to the Naliboki Forest. The unit stayed in contact with the Minsk Ghetto through teenage boys who helped Jews who had escaped the ghetto reach the forest.

The Zorin Unit also had a camp for Jewish artisans who set up workshops in the forest, and thus served partisan units all over the area (see also FAMILY CAMPS IN THE FORESTS). There was a sewing workshop, a shoemaker's workshop, a flourmill, a bakery, a sausage factory, a weapons repair and bomb production shop, and a big hospital with doctors from Minsk. They also created a school that served 70 students. The camp members celebrated both Soviet and Jewish holidays. Zorin had about 100 fighters in his combat unit whom he treated with fatherly care. He believed that saving Jewish lives was his most important goal.

In July 1944 Zorin was wounded in his leg during a battle with a retreating German unit; seven of his men were killed. In 1971, about 25 years after the war, Zorin immigrated to Israel.

ZUCKERMAN, YITZHAK (ANTEK) (1915–1981), One of the leaders of the Jewish Fighting Organization (*Zydowska Organizacja Bojowa,* ZOB) in WARSAW. Born in VILNA, Zuckerman moved to Warsaw in 1938 to work for the *Dror He-Halutz* Zionist YOUTH MOVEMENT.

When WORLD WAR II began in September 1939, Zuckerman fled to Soviet-occupied eastern POLAND, where he organized Zionist youth groups. In April 1940 he returned to German-occupied Poland to encourage underground activities. At that time, he also met and fell in love with fellow underground leader, Zivia LUBETKIN. The couple later married.

When the Germans launched mass DEPORTATIONS from Warsaw during the summer of 1942, Zuckerman called for armed resistance against the Germans. On July 28 he and other youth movement leaders established the ZOB, an underground resistance organization. That December, Zuckerman was sent by the ZOB to CRACOW to meet with resistance fighters. During that mission, Zuckerman was wounded in the leg, and barely made it back.

When the Nazis initiated a second wave of deportations in January 1943, Zuckerman led a group of fighters in armed battle with the Germans. The ZOB spent the next three months preparing for a revolt. Zuckerman became commander of one of the three main areas of the GHETTO. However, as it got closer to the uprising, the ZOB ordered Zuckerman to cross over to the Polish side of Warsaw to represent the organization there. During the WARSAW GHETTO UPRISING, Zuckerman tried to supply his comrades with arms, and in the revolt's final leg, Zuckerman and others set up a rescue team that saved fighters by leading them through the sewer system.

After the uprising, Zuckerman joined the Jewish National Committee (*Zydowski Komitet Narodowy*), an organization which provided aid for Jews. He wrote a summary report about the ZOB that he sent to London. He also commanded a group of Jewish fighters in the WARSAW POLISH UPRISING.

After the war, Zuckerman and his wife got involved in the BERIHA movement, helping Jews reach Palestine. They immigrated to Palestine themselves in 1947, where Zuckerman helped found the Ghetto Fighters'

Yitzhak Zuckerman (front at center), commemorating fallen comrades, Warsaw, 1945

Kibbutz and the Ghetto Fighters' House. (see also JEW-ISH FIGHTING ORGANIZATION, WARSAW and RESISTANCE, JEWISH.)

ZYDOWSKA ORGANIZACJA BOJOWA   see JEWISH FIGHTING ORGANIZATION, WARSAW.

ZYDOWSKI ZWIAZEK WOJSKOWY (ZZW)   see JEWISH MILITARY UNION, WARSAW.

ZYGELBOJM, SAMUEL ARTUR   (1895–1943), A leader of the Polish BUND (Jewish-Socialist) Party who tried to tell the world about the mass murder of Jews in Europe during the HOLOCAUST.

When WORLD WAR II broke out in September 1939, Zygelbojm was one of 12 Poles taken hostage by the

Samuel Artur Zygelbojm

Germans in WARSAW. After he was released, Zygelbojm helped organize a *Bund* resistance cell. He was also chosen to represent his party in the city's JUDENRAT. However, fearing arrest due to his underground activities, Zygelbojm fled to Western Europe, where he told a Socialist International meeting about the persecution of Polish Jewry. In September 1940 Zygelbojm left FRANCE for New York. In 1942 he returned to Western Europe when he was made a member of the National Council of the London-based POLISH GOVERNMENT-IN-EXILE.

When Zygelbojm received early reports of the Germans' murderous crusade in POLAND, he took responsibility for telling the world. As a member of the Polish government-in-exile, he begged the governments of the free world to launch rescue operations.

In May 1942 Zygelbojm received a new report from the *Bund* in Warsaw about the mass extermination of Polish Jewry. This was one of the first official reports to define the scope of the killing and provide names and sites of EXTERMINATION CAMPS. Zygelbojm went on a BBC broadcast on June 2, 1942 to spread the horrific news and appeal for public support to stop the annihilation.

In October of that same year, Zygelbojm met with a Polish underground representative, who brought him a message from two Jewish underground members living on the Polish side of Warsaw. The message begged Zygelbojm to take immediate steps to save his fellow Jews. Zygelbojm, growing more and more desperate, appealed to anyone and everyone for help, including Prime Minister CHURCHILL and President ROOSEVELT. However, no one heeded his anguished call.

In May 1943 Zygelbojm was told that the last Jews of Warsaw—including his wife and sixteen-year-old son—had been murdered. This was the last straw: Zygelbojm committed suicide in despair and protest of the world's apathy to the fate of the Jews.

ZYKLON B   Highly poisonous gas used for extermination in the EUTHANASIA PROGRAM and later in the GAS CHAMBERS of the Nazi EXTERMINATION CAMPS, particularly AUSCHWITZ. Zyklon B is the commercial name of hydrogen cyanide (HCN).

Originally, the Germans used carbon monoxide in GAS VANS and in sealed rooms, such as at CHELMNO, BELZEC, SOBIBOR, and TREBLINKA. The Nazis realized, however, that carbon monoxide gassing was not efficient for the large-scale killing they were planning for Auschwitz.

Zyklon B pellets

Adolf EICHMANN then went in search of a different poisonous gas that would be more appropriate. On September 3, 1941 the Nazis experimented on a group of Russian PRISONERS OF WAR; they wanted to see whether Zyklon B, used in the camps for fumigation purposes, was an effective means of mass murder. The experiment was successful. From then on, Zyklon B was used in Birkenau (Auschwitz II) for the mass gassing of Jews brought there from all over Europe.

Zyklon B was delivered to the camps in crystal pellet form. As soon as the pellets were exposed to air they turned into poisonous gas. A Nazi equipped with a gas mask would empty the crystals into the packed gas chamber through a small opening. Within minutes, the victims were dead.

Majdanek camp staff holding canisters of Zyklon B

CHRONOLOGY

February 24, 1920: The Nazi Party platform is written.

November 9, 1923: Beer-Hall Putsch: Adolf Hitler and the Nazis fail in their attempt to overthrow the Bavarian government in Munich.

July 31, 1932: The Nazis win over 37% of the vote in a *Reichstag* election.

1933

January 30: Hitler becomes chancellor of Germany after the Nazis win 33% of the vote in a *Reichstag* election.

February 27: The *Reichstag* building is set on fire; on February 28 a national emergency is declared.

March 20: The first concentration camp is established at Dachau; on March 21 the first prisoners arrive.

March 24: The *Reichstag* passes the Enabling Law; Hitler uses it to help set up a dictatorship in Germany.

April 1: A one-day anti-Jewish boycott is carried out in Germany; unofficial boycotts continue afterward.

May 10: Public book-burnings take place all over Germany.

August 25: Jewish leaders from Palestine and Nazi authorities sign the Transfer (*Ha'avara*) agreement.

September 22: In Germany, Jews are excluded from the fields of literature, art, music, broadcasting, theater, and the press.

1934

June 30: Night of the Long Knives: Under Hitler's orders, Heinrich Himmler and the SS destroy the SA leadership. Many are murdered, including Ernst Rohm.

July 25: The Nazis fail in their attempt to seize power in Austria; Austrian Chancellor Engelbert Dollfuss is murdered in the fray.

August 2: German President Paul von Hindenburg dies, paving the way for Hitler to assume the presidency and become dictator.

1935

January 13: Germany retakes the Saarland.

September 15: The Nuremberg Laws are issued at a Nazi Party rally.

October 3: Italy attacks Ethiopia.

December 31: In Germany, Jews are dismissed from the civil service.

1936

March 7: German forces enter the Rhineland.

May 5: Ethiopia surrenders to Italy.

October 25: Nazi Germany and Fascist Italy sign the Rome-Berlin Axis agreement.

1937

March 21: Pope Pius XI issues an official statement against racism and nationalism.

November 25: Germany and Japan make a military and political alliance.

1938

March 13: Anschluss: German forces occupy Austria.

April 24: In Germany, all Jewish property must be registered.

April 26: In Austria, authorities call for the seizure of all Jewish property.

May 29: The First Anti-Jewish Law is issued in Hungary, restricting Jewish involvement in the economy to 20%.

June 15: Fifteen hundred German Jews are imprisoned in concentration camps.

June 25: German Jewish doctors are only allowed to treat Jewish patients.

July 6–15: Evian Conference: Representatives from 32 countries meet in France to discuss the refugee problem, but do almost nothing to fix it.

July 8: The Great Synagogue in Munich is razed on Nazi orders.

August 17: All Jews in Germany are forced to add a Jewish name to their own; men must take on the name "Israel" and women "Sarah."

August 26: The *Zentralstelle fuer Juedische Auswanderung* (Central Office for Jewish Emigration) is established in Vienna under Adolf Eichmann.

September 27: In Germany, Jews are prohibited from practicing law.

September 29: The Munich agreement is signed.

October 5: The passports of German Jews are stamped with the letter J for Jew.

October 6: Based on the Munich agreement, Germany annexes the Sudetenland, the Czechoslovak Republic is established, and Slovakia is given autonomy.

October 28: Between 15,000–17,000 Jews are kicked out of Germany and sent to Poland; most are detained in the border town of Zbaszyn.

November 2: Hungary annexes parts of Slovakia and the Transcarpathian Ukraine.

November 9–10: A young Jew named Herschel Grynszpan assassinates Ernst vom Rath, a German embassy worker, in Paris. Subsequently, the *Kristallnacht* pogrom is carried out throughout Germany and Austria. About 30,000 Jews are imprisoned in concentration camps and scores are killed.

1939

January 1: Jews are legally banned from working with Germans.

March 2: Cardinal Eugenio Pacelli becomes Pope Pius XII.

March 14: Slovakia is declared an independent state.

March 15: German forces enter Prague; Jews, German emigres, and Czech intellectuals are arrested throughout the Protectorate of Bohemia and Moravia.

March 22: Germany annexes Memel, Lithuania.

April 7: Italy invades Albania.

May 5: The Second Anti-Jewish Law is issued in Hungary, defining who is a Jew and restricting Jewish involvement in the economy to 6%.

May 17: White Paper of 1939: The British government restricts Jewish immigration to Palestine.

August 23: Germany and the Soviet Union sign the Nazi-Soviet Pact.

September 1: The German army invades Poland.

In Germany, Jews are forbidden to be out of doors after 8:00 p.m.

September 3: France and Great Britain declare war on Germany.

September 17: The Soviet Union annexes parts of eastern Poland.

September 21: Reinhard Heydrich meets with Adolf Eichmann and *Einsatzgruppen* commanders; he orders them to establish *Judenraete* in Poland, to concentrate and count Polish Jews, and to take a survey of the Jewish work force and Jewish property throughout Poland.

September 27: The Reich Security Main Office (*Reichssicherheitshauptamt,* RSHA) is instituted.

September 28: Germany and the Soviet Union divide up Poland; German forces occupy Warsaw.

October 8: The first Nazi-established ghetto is set up in Piotrkow Trybunalski, Poland.

October 18–27: Over 4,800 Jews from Maehrisch Ostrau, Katowice, and Vienna are deported to the Lublin area.

November 12: The Nazis begin to deport Jews from Lodz to other parts of Poland.

November 15–17: The German authorities destroy all the synagogues in Lodz.

November 23: Hans Frank, governor-general of the *Generalgouvernement,* orders that all Jews in his jurisdiction must don the Jewish badge by December 1, 1939.

November 28: The establishment of *Judenraete* in the *Generalgouvernement* is decreed.

November 30–March 13, 1940: The Soviet Union invades Finland, launching the Winter War.

December 5–6: In Poland, Jewish property is confiscated by the German authorities.

1940

February 8: Authorities order the establishment of a ghetto in Lodz. It is closed off on April 30.

April 9: German forces invade Denmark and Norway.

April 12: Hans Frank orders that Cracow must be "Jew-free" by November 1940. By March 1941, 40,000 of the city's 60,000 Jews have been deported.

April 27: Himmler orders that a concentration camp be set up at Auschwitz. In early June the first prisoners, mostly Poles, arrive.

May 10: German forces invade Belgium, Luxembourg, and the Netherlands.

British Prime Minister Neville Chamberlain resigns; Winston Churchill takes over the post.

May 12: German forces cross into France.

May 14: The German airforce bombs Rotterdam heavily; the Dutch surrender to the Germans.

May 17: German forces occupy Brussels.

May 26–June 4: British forces retreat from France to Great Britain.

May 28: Belgium surrenders to Germany.

June 10: Italy enters the war as a German ally, declares war on Great Britain and France, and invades France.

June 14: German forces occupy Paris.

June 15: The Soviet Union occupies the Baltic states (Lithuania, Latvia, and Estonia).

June 22: Germany and France sign a peace agreement.

June 24: Italy and France sign a peace agreement.

June 27: Romania hands over Bessarabia and Bukovina to the Soviet Union.

July 9: The Blitz: The German bombing of London begins.

July 16: Jews from Alsace-Lorraine are expelled to southern France.

August 2: In Luxembourg, a civilian administration is set up under Nazi official Gustav Simon.

August 3: Hungary annexes northern Transylvania.

September 6: King Carol II flees Romania; his son Michael I becomes king and the "National Legionary Government" is established under Ion Antonescu.

September 7: Romania hands over southern Dobruja to Bulgaria.

September 26: The Jewish Center (*Ustredna Zidov*) is set up in Bratislava.

September 27: Pact of Berlin: Germany, Italy, and Japan sign the 10-year Tripartite Pact.

October 3: The first *Statut des Juifs* (Jewish Law) is issued in Vichy France.

October 5: The Romanian government legalizes the confiscation of Jewish property.

October 7: In Bulgaria, the Law for the Protection of Nations is issued, restricting the rights of Jews.

October 22–25: The Jews of Baden, the Palatinate region, and Wurttemberg are sent to the Gurs camp in France.

October 28: Italy invades Greece.

November 4: Throughout the Netherlands, Jews employed in the civil service are fired.

November 15: The Warsaw Ghetto is closed off.

November 20–25: Hungary, Romania, and Slovakia join the Tripartite Pact.

1941

January 10: In the Netherlands, all Jews are registered by the authorities.

January 21–23: In Romania, the Iron Guard unsuccessfully attempts to overthrow the government; riots against the Jews are rampant.

February 13: The Jewish Council (*Joodse Raad*) convenes for the first time in Amsterdam.

February 22: A total of 389 young, Jewish men from Amsterdam are deported to Buchenwald.

February 25: A general anti-Nazi strike is observed in Amsterdam.

March 1: Bulgaria joins the Tripartite Pact.

Himmler orders the construction of a camp at Birkenau (to be Auschwitz II). Construction begins in October 1941 and continues until March 1942.

March 3–20: The Cracow Ghetto is ordered, set up, and closed off.

March 11: The United States government authorizes the Lend-Lease Act.

March 25: Yugoslavia joins the Axis alliance.

March 27: In Yugoslavia, pro-Allied forces overthrow the government.

April 1: In Iraq, a pro-Nazi government is set up by Rashid Ali al-Gaylani.

April 6: German forces invade Greece and Yugoslavia.

April 9: German forces occupy Salonika.

April 10: In Antwerp, riots break out against Jews.

April 13: Japan and the Soviet Union sign a neutrality agreement.

April 18: Yugoslavia surrenders to Germany.

April 24: The Lublin Ghetto is closed off.

May 11: Hitler's deputy, Rudolf Hess, arrives in Glasgow, Scotland for what he calls "a private peace mission."

May 19: In Baghdad, Iraq, a pogrom is carried out against the Jews.

May 30: British forces capture Baghdad.

June 1: British forces retreat from Crete.

June 2: The second *Statut des Juifs* (Jewish Law) is issued in Vichy France.

June 6: Kommissarbefehl: In preparation for the invasion of the Soviet Union, the Nazis issue an order for the execution of all political officers in the Soviet army.

June 8: British forces invade Vichy-controlled Syria.

June 18: Turkey and Germany sign a friendship treaty.

June 21: In Romania, Jews are expelled from the villages and towns of southern Bukovina.

June 22: Operation Barbarossa: German forces invade the Soviet Union. They capture Kishinev, Kovno, and other places.

Jews from Zagreb, Croatia are arrested and sent to the Pag and Jadovno concentration camps.

June 23: The *Einsatzgruppen* begin the mass murder of Jews in the Soviet Union; they report on their activities almost daily.

June 24: German forces occupy Vilna.

June 27: Hungary enters the war as a German ally.

German forces occupy Bialystok and kill 2,000 Jews.

June 28: In Iasi, some 15,000 Jews are murdered in a pogrom.

German forces occupy Minsk.

June 29: Black Sunday: In Iasi, thousands of Jews are shot in the police headquarters courtyard.

June 30: German forces occupy Lvov.

July 1: German forces occupy Riga.

July 1–August 31: In Bessarabia, *Einsatzgruppe* D, *Wehrmacht* troops, and a Romanian unit murder some 150,000–160,000 Jews.

During July, some 5,000 Jews from Vilna are murdered by *Einsatzkommando* 9 and local collaborators.

July 10: In Syria, Vichy French forces surrender to the British.

July 16: By this point, 2,700 Jews have been shot to death outside Riga.

July 16–29: The Germans and Soviets fight at Smolensk; the Germans win the battle.

July 20: The Minsk Ghetto is established.

July 21: Romanian forces occupy Bessarabia.

July 24: The Kishinev Ghetto is established; by this time some 10,000 Kishinev Jews have been killed.

July 25–27: The Petliura Days: Local Ukrainians carry out a pogrom against the Jews in Lvov.

July 31: Hermann Goering gives Heydrich the written go-ahead to prepare a "total solution" to the "Jewish question" in Europe.

August 1: The Bialystok Ghetto is established.

August 4–5: In Kovno, a Jewish Council is set up under Elchanan Elkes.

August 5–7: Over 10,500 Jews from Pinsk are killed.

August 14: Roosevelt and Churchill sign the Atlantic Charter—a declaration of peace goals and conditions.

August 19: In Mogilev, *Einsatzkommando* 8 and local collaborators kill 3,726 Jews.

August 21–August 17, 1944: Seventy thousand Jews pass through the Drancy transit camp near Paris.

August 25: Soviet and British forces enter Iran.

August 27–28: In Kamenets-Podolski, 23,600 Jews are murdered by German forces under Friedrich Jeckeln; at least 14,000 of the victims had recently been deported from Hungary.

August 31–September 3: Eight thousand Jews from Vilna are murdered in Ponary.

September 1: The Euthanasia Program is "officially" closed down; killings continue, however, and in total, some 200,000 people fall victim to the program before the war ends.

September 3: First gassing experiments are performed in Auschwitz on Soviet prisoners of war.

September 3–6: Two ghettos are set up in Vilna.

September 9: The "Jewish Code" is issued in Slovakia; this defines who is a Jew.

September 15: In the Netherlands, Jews are legally banned from many public places.

Some 18,600 Jews are killed outside Berdichev.

September 15–October 13, 1942: At least 150,000 Jews from Bessarabia and Bukovina are deported to Transnistria; about 90,000 die there.

September 19: In the Reich, Jews are required to wear the Jewish badge in public.

September 27: Heydrich arrives in Prague as acting governor of the Protectorate of Bohemia and Moravia.

September 29–30: At Babi Yar, *Einsatzkommando* 4a murder 33,771 Kiev Jews.

October 1–December 22: In Vilna, 33,500 Jews are murdered in *aktionen.*

October 6–March 16, 1945: In all, 46,067 Prague Jews are deported to Theresienstadt and the "east."

October 8: The Vitebsk Ghetto is liquidated; over 16,000 Jews are killed.

October 12: German forces nearly reach Moscow; the city is partly evacuated.

October 13: In Dnepropetrovsk, 20,000 Jews are murdered.

October 15: Jews are deported from Germany and Austria to Kovno, Lodz, Minsk, and Riga.

October 16: German forces occupy Odessa.

October 19: Jews are murdered in Belgrade.

October 19–September 28, 1943: Luxembourg Jews are deported to Lodz in eight transports.

October 23: Jews are forbidden to emigrate from Germany.

In Odessa, 19,000 Jews are murdered.

October 24: German forces occupy Kharkov.

October 28: Some 9,000 Jews are murdered at the Ninth Fort outside Kovno; 17,412 Jews remain in the Kovno Ghetto.

November 1: In Poland, construction of an extermination camp at Belzec begins.

November 7: At Tuchinka, 12,000 Jews from Minsk are murdered.

November 7–8: Some 21,000 Jews are murdered in the Sosenki pine grove outside Rovno.

November 8: An order is issued for the establishment of a ghetto in Lvov.

November 10: The Nazis put the finishing touches on their plans for Theresienstadt.

November 15–July 2, 1942: Sevastopol falls to the Germans after a seven-month battle.

November 20: Twenty thousand Minsk Jews are killed at Tuchinka.

November 20–December 7: Jeckeln Aktion: Thirty thousand Jews are killed in the Rumbula Forest outside Riga.

November 24–April 20, 1945: In all, 140,937 Jews are deported to Theresienstadt; 33,539 die and 88,196 are later deported from Theresienstadt.

November 25: The Association of Jews in Belgium (*Association des Juifs en Belgique*) is formed.

November 29: The Union of French Jews (*Union Generale des Israelites de France*) is formed.

December 6: Great Britain declares war on Romania.

Soviet forces launch a counteroffensive outside Moscow.

December 7: Night and Fog Decree: Hitler orders the suppression of anti-Nazi resistance in occupied Western Europe.

Japanese forces attack the American naval base at Pearl Harbor, Hawaii.

December 8: Japanese forces invade Malaya and Thailand.

First transport of Jews arrives at the Chelmno extermination camp; transports continue to arrive until March 1943. Chelmno reopens in April 1944. In all, some 320,000 Jews are murdered at the camp.

December 10: Germany and Italy declare war on the United States and vice versa.

December 13: Bulgaria and Hungary declare war on the United States.

December 21–31: Some 54,000 Jews are murdered in the Bogdanovka camp; 200 are left alive.

December 22: Japanese forces invade the Philippines.

Churchill comes to Washington to meet with Roosevelt.

December 25: Hong Kong surrenders to the Japanese.

1942

January 10–11: Japanese forces invade the Netherlands East Indies.

January 14: Dutch Jews begin to be gathered in Amsterdam.

January 16: Deportations from Lodz to Chelmno begin; they continue until September 1942.

January 20: Wannsee Conference: Top Nazi officials attend a conference in a Berlin suburb in order to coordinate the "Final Solution."

January 21: German forces launch a counteroffensive in North Africa.

Jews in Vilna create the United Partisan Organization (*Fareynegte Partizaner Organizatsye*, FPO).

February 1: The SS Economic-Administrative Main Office (*Wirtschafts-Verwaltungshauptamt*, WVHA) is instituted.

In Norway, a nationalist government is formed under Vidkun Quisling.

February 15: The British surrender Singapore to the Japanese.

February 23: The *Struma:* A Jewish refugee-laden ship that was not allowed entry into Palestine sinks off the coast of Turkey; only one of 769 passengers survives.

March 1: In Poland, construction of an extermination camp at Sobibor begins; the first Jews are killed there in May 1942.

March 2: Five thousand Minsk Jews are murdered.

March 7: British forces evacuate Rangoon.

March 12–April 20: Thirty thousand Jews are deported from Lublin to Belzec.

March 17: Mass murder begins at Belzec, the first of the *Aktion Reinhard* extermination centers to begin operations.

March 19–end of March: Fifteen thousand Jews are deported from Lvov to Belzec.

March 26: Adolf Eichmann's office sends the first transport of Jews to Auschwitz.

March 26–October 20: Over 57,000 Jews from Slovakia are deported.

March 28: First transport of French Jews is sent to Auschwitz.

April 9: American forces surrender to the Japanese at Bataan.

April 29: In the Netherlands, Jews are ordered to wear the Jewish badge.

April 30: In Pinsk, the Jews are ordered to set up a ghetto in one day; some 20,000 Jews move in.

In Diatlovo, 1,200 Jews are murdered in an *aktion;* the Jews resist, but to no avail.

May 7: Battle of the Coral Sea: The Allies sink more than 100,000 tons of Japanese goods.

May 27: In Belgium, Jews are ordered to wear the Jewish badge; the decree goes into effect on June 3.

Heydrich is fatally wounded by Czech partisans in an attack near Prague; he dies on June 4.

June 4: The United States declares war on Romania.

June 4–7: In the Pacific front, US forces defeat the Japanese at Midway.

June 7: In occupied France, Jews are required to wear the Jewish badge.

June 10: The Czech village of Lidice is destroyed in retaliation for Heydrich's assassination.

June 11: Eichmann's office issues an order for the deportation of Jews from the Netherlands, Belgium, and France.

June 21: German forces capture Tobruk from the British.

June 22: The first transport from the Drancy transit camp leaves for Auschwitz.

June 25: Churchill and Roosevelt meet in Washington.

June 26: In the Netherlands, regular deportations begin to Westerbork, and from Westerbork to Auschwitz.

July 11: Nine thousand Jewish men from Salonika between the ages of 18 and 45 are made to do forced labor in Greece for Organization Todt.

July 16–17: In Paris, 12,887 Jews are rounded up and sent to Drancy. In total, some 42,500 French Jews are sent to Drancy during this *aktion.*

July 19: Himmler orders that the liquidation of the Jews in the *Generalgouvernement* be completed by the end of 1942.

July 20: In Nesvizh, an armed Jewish uprising takes place.

July 22: The extermination camp at Treblinka is ready for operation; by August 1943 about 870,000 have been murdered there.

July 22–September 12: Some 300,000 Jews are deported during a mass deportation from Warsaw, 254,000 of them to Treblinka. Some 60,000 Jews are left in the Warsaw Ghetto.

July 23: The head of the Warsaw *Judenrat,* Adam Czerniakow, takes his own life rather than help the Nazis in deporting his fellow Jews.

July 27, 31; August 3: Over 10,500 Jews from Przemysl are deported to Belzec on three separate days. On the first day, *Wehrmacht* lieutenant Dr. Alfred Battel saves Jews who work for the *Wehrmacht.*

July 28: In Warsaw, the Jewish Fighting Organization (*Zydowska Organizacja Bojowa,* ZOB) is formed.

July 28–31: Thirty thousand Jews from Germany who have been deported to Minsk are murdered at Maly Trostinets.

August 6–December 29, 1943: Jewish prisoners from the Gurs camp in France are sent to Auschwitz and Sobibor via Drancy.

August 8: Riegner Cable: In Geneva, Gerhart Riegner sends a cable to Rabbi Stephen S. Wise in New York and Sidney Silverman in London regarding the extermination of European Jewry. The US State Department, however, does not deliver the message to Wise; he only receives it from Silverman on August 28.

August 9: Jews actively resist the Nazis during the liquidation of the Mir Ghetto.

August 10–23: Fifty thousand Jews are deported from Lvov to Belzec.

August 12: Churchill, Stalin, and Averell Harriman meet in Moscow and declare their joint goal of destroying Nazism.

August 12: Most of the remaining Jews of Croatia are deported to Auschwitz.

August 16–18: The large ghetto in Radom is liquidated; 18,000 Jews are deported to Treblinka and 1,500 who resist are executed on the spot. Four thousand Jews are imprisoned in a labor camp in Radom.

August 20–24: Eighteen thousand of the 24,000 Jews in Kielce are deported to Treblinka.

September 2: German forces surround the Lachva Ghetto; an uprising breaks out and 6,000 Jews flee, but most are quickly caught and executed.

September 4: In Macedonia, the Jews are required to wear the Jewish badge.

September 12: German forces reach the outskirts of Stalingrad and the Battle of Stalingrad begins.

September 24–26: The Germans begin liquidating the Tuchin Ghetto; an uprising breaks out and most of the Jews escape, but they are quickly caught and executed.

October 2: The deportation of Dutch Jewry is stepped up.

October 9: The Italian racial laws are put into force in Libya.

October 13–21: Twenty thousand Jews from Piotrkow Trybunalski are deported to Treblinka; 500 escape to the forest. The Germans liquidate the Piotrkow Ghetto in July 1944 and the remaining Jews are sent to labor camps or Auschwitz.

October 29–November 1: Nearly all the Jews of Pinsk are murdered.

November 1: The deportation of Jews from the Bialystok district to Treblinka begins.

November 2: British forces capture El Alamein from the Germans.

November 8: American and British forces invade North Africa, launching Operation "Torch."

November 9: German and Italian forces occupy Tunisia.

November 11: The Germans and Italians occupy southern France.

November 19: Soviet forces launch a counterattack near Stalingrad.

November 20: Nine hundred and eighty Munich Jews are deported to Riga.

November 24: Rabbi Stephen S. Wise publicizes the information contained in the Riegner Cable.

December 4: In Poland, *Zegota* (the Council for Aid to Jews) is formed.

December 6: In Tunisia, the German authorities order Jewish leaders to gather 2,000 Jews for forced labor. Eventually, 5,000 Jews are detained in labor camps.

December 10: The Polish government-in-exile asks the Allies to launch reprisals against the Nazis for killing civilians, especially Jews.

December 16: In Kharkov, a ghetto is set up. Three weeks later about 15,000 Jews are murdered in the Drobitski Ravine.

December 17: The Allies officially condemn the Nazis' "bestial policy of cold-blooded extermination."

December 23: In Pinsk, the remaining Jews are murdered.

1943

January 12: About 10,000 Jews are murdered in the Lvov Ghetto and the ghetto becomes a *Judenlager* (*Julag*), or camp for Jews.

January 14–24: Roosevelt and Churchill meet at Casablanca; they declare Germany's unconditional surrender to be a major war aim.

January 18–22: Over 5,000 Jews are deported from Warsaw and murdered. The first Warsaw Ghetto Uprising breaks out.

January 23: In Libya, British forces liberate Tripoli.

February 2: At Stalingrad, 91,000 German soldiers under Field Marshal Friedrich von Paulus surrender to the Soviet army.

February 5–12: In Bialystok, 2,000 Jews are murdered and 10,000 are deported to Treblinka. Jews actively resist the Germans.

February 13: In Tunisia, the Jews of Djerba are forced to pay the German authorities 10 million francs.

February 24: In Salonika, a ghetto is set up.

February 26: The first groups of Gypsies reach Auschwitz; they are placed in a special camp section known as the Gypsy Camp.

March 4–9: Almost all of the 4,000 Jews from Bulgarian Thrace are arrested and deported to Treblinka.

March 11: A total of 7,341 Macedonian Jews are gathered in Skopje; most are soon deported to Treblinka.

March 20–August 18: Transports from Salonika arrive at Auschwitz.

April 19–30: Bermuda Conference: British and American representatives meet in Bermuda to discuss rescue options, but fail to come up with any significant possibilities.

April 19–May 16: The Warsaw Ghetto Uprising takes place and the Warsaw Ghetto is destroyed.

May 5–10: The last two transports of Jews are sent from Croatia to Auschwitz.

May 8: Mordecai Anielewicz and other leaders of the Warsaw

Ghetto Uprising are killed during the fighting in their bunker at 18 Mila Street.

May 11–27: Churchill and Roosevelt meet in Washington.

May 12: Samuel Zygelbojm, a Jewish representative of the Polish government-in-exile in London, takes his own life to protest the world's silence with regard to the fate of the Jews in Nazi-occupied Europe and in solidarity with the Warsaw Ghetto fighters.

May 13: Tunisia is liberated by the Allies.

June 25: Jews in Czestochowa actively resist the Germans with arms.

July 5: Himmler orders that the Sobibor extermination camp be made into a concentration camp.

July 9–10: Allied forces invade Sicily.

July 21: Himmler orders the liquidation of the ghettos in the *Reichskommissariat Ostland;* Jewish workers are sent to labor camps and the rest of the Jews are killed.

July 25: Benito Mussolini is overthrown; Pietro Badoglio sets up a new government in Italy.

August 1: The Nazis begin the final liquidation of the Bedzin and Sosnowiec ghettos; Jews actively resist and most are deported to Auschwitz.

August 2: An uprising takes place at Treblinka.

August 4–September 4: Seven thousand Jews are deported from Vilna to Estonia for forced labor.

August 15–20: Nazi forces led by Odilo Globocnik surround the Bialystok Ghetto. The ghetto's remaining 30,000 Jews are ordered to report for evacuation; a Jewish uprising breaks out in the ghetto.

August 18–21: The last Jews of Bialystok are deported.

September 1: The Jews in the Vilna Ghetto attempt to revolt but are suppressed; throughout the rest of the month the fighters escape to the partisans.

September 2: The Nazis begin the final liquidation of the Tarnow Ghetto. Jews actively resist; 7,000 Jews are deported to Auschwitz and 3,000 to Plaszow. The 300 workers who remain in Tarnow are sent to Plaszow at the end of the year.

September 3–4: The last transport of Jews leaves Belgium.

September 3: The Allies invade southern Italy.

September 8: German forces occupy Athens; Italian forces surrender to the Germans in Rhodes.

September 11–14: The Minsk Ghetto is liquidated and nearly all of its Jews are murdered.

September 23–24: The Nazis liquidate the Vilna Ghetto; 3,700 Jews are sent to labor camps in Estonia and 4,000 are deported to Sobibor.

September 28: The Jews of Rome pay a tax of 50 kilograms of gold to the *Gestapo.*

September 29: The remaining 2,000 Jews in Amsterdam are sent to Westerbork.

October 1–2: In Denmark, German police begin rounding up Jews for deportation; the Danish population launches the rescue of 7,200 Danish Jews.

October 13: Italy declares war on Germany.

October 14: An uprising takes place in Sobibor.

October 16: In Rome, mass arrests of Jews are launched.

October 18: In Rome, 1,035 Jews are deported to Auschwitz.

October 21: During the final liquidation of Minsk, 4,000 Jews are murdered at Maly Trostinets.

October 25: Dnepropetrovsk is liberated.

November 3: Erntefest/Operation "Harvest Festival": The Nazis liquidate the Poniatowa and Trawniki camps and murder the remaining Jews in Majdanek. Other Jews brought to Majdanek from the Lublin area are also killed. In total, some 42,000–43,000 Jews are murdered.

November 9: The United Nations Relief and Rehabilitation Agency (UNRRA) is established.

November 19: The *Sonderkommando* 1005 prisoners in the Janowska camp revolt; dozens escape, while the rest are killed.

November 28–December 1: Churchill, Roosevelt, and Stalin meet in Tehran.

November 30: The Nazis order all Italian Jews concentrated in camps.

1944

January 15: Soviet forces liberate Berdichev.

January 25: The Allies cause considerable damage to the German war effort by successfully bombing the Schweinfurt ball-bearing factory.

March 15: Soviet forces begin the liberation of Transnistria. They cross the Bug River and reach the Dniester River by March 20.

March 17: A group of 99 prisoners breaks out of the Koldichevo camp; 75 reach partisan units such as the Bielski unit, while 24 are recaptured.

March 19: Hungary tries to withdraw from the eastern front; as a result, German forces occupy Hungary.

April 5: Jews in Hungary begin wearing the Jewish badge.

April 7: The Auschwitz Protocols: Two Jewish prisoners, Alfred Wetzler and Rudolf Vrba, escape Auschwitz and reach Slovakia with detailed information about the mass murder of Jews in the camp. Their report (supplemented by information brought by two more escapees) reaches the free world in June.

April 15: Jewish prisoners employed in burning corpses attempt to escape Ponary; 15 get away successfully, while 65 others are killed.

April 16: In Hungary, the concentration of Jews begins.

May 15–July 9: Over 435,000 Hungarian Jews are deported to Auschwitz; half are gassed soon after their arrival.

May 23: The Allies launch an offensive at Anzio, Italy.

June 4: The American Fifth Army captures Rome.

June 6: D-Day: Allied forces land in Normandy, France with the largest force in history to come by sea.

June 17–24: The Jews of Budapest are restricted to specially marked "Jewish buildings."

June 23–July 14: Transports from Lodz reach Chelmno.

July 7: Miklos Horthy, the Hungarian regent, orders a halt to the deportations from Hungary; they cease on July 9.

July 8: The Nazis liquidate the Kovno Ghetto.

July 13: Soviet forces liberate Vilna.

July 20: An assassination attempt on Hitler's life is unsuccessful.

July 23: A delegation from the International Red Cross visits Theresienstadt.

July 25: Soviet forces liberate Lublin.

July 27: Soviet forces liberate Dvinsk; 20 Jews remain in the city.

July 28: The Gesia Street camp in Warsaw is evacuated, beginning the first major death march; 3,600 prisoners leave on foot for Kutno, and 1,000 are murdered on the 81-mile trip.

July 31: In France, American forces break through German lines. France is liberated by the end of August.

August 1: In Warsaw, the Polish Uprising begins.

Soviet forces liberate Kovno.

August 7–30: Deportations from Lodz to Auschwitz take place.

August 11: American forces capture Guam from the Japanese.

August 12: Allied forces occupy Florence.

August 23: Paris is liberated.

The government of Ion Antonescu is overthrown; Romania joins the Allies.

August 28–29 to October 27: The Slovak National Uprising takes place and is put down by the SS.

September 3: The last transport of Jews leaves Westerbork.

September 4: Antwerp is liberated.

September 5: The Soviet Union declares war on Bulgaria.

September 9: Churchill and Roosevelt meet in Quebec.

September 12: Soviet forces begin their attack on Budapest.

September 16: Bulgaria surrenders to the Soviet Union.

September 28: Soviet forces liberate the Klooga camp; 85 prisoners, having survived in hiding, are found alive.

October 2: The Warsaw Polish Uprising is suppressed.

October 6–7: Sonderkommando prisoners in Auschwitz revolt; a gas chamber is destroyed before the uprising is suppressed.

October 13: Soviet forces liberate Riga.

October 15: In Hungary, Ferenc Szalasi and his Arrow Cross Party take over the government.

November 8: Deportations from Budapest are resumed.

November 13: In Budapest, a ghetto is set up for Jews without international protection.

December 16: Battle of the Bulge: German forces launch an offensive in the Ardennes Forest.

December 26: The Soviet siege of Budapest, which began on September 12, 1944, is complete.

1945

January 9: American forces land in Luzon.

January 16: Soviet forces liberate Kielce; 25 Jews remain in the city.

January 17: The SS is ordered to leave Auschwitz; on January 18 the evacuation begins. About sixty thousand prisoners are force-marched toward Wodzislaw to be sent from there to other camps. Fifteen thousand die en route.

Soviet forces liberate Warsaw.

Raoul Wallenberg is arrested by the Soviets.

January 18: Soviet forces liberate Pest.

January 19: Soviet forces liberate Lodz.

January 25: Four thousand Jews are force-marched from the Blechhammer camp in the direction of the Gross-Rosen camp; 1,000 die en route.

January 25–April 25: Fifty thousand Jews are sent on death marches from the Stutthof camp and its satellites; tens of thousands die en route.

January 27: Soviet forces enter Auschwitz; they find 7,650 prisoners.

February 3: American forces invade Manila.

February 4–12: Churchill, Roosevelt, and Stalin meet at Yalta.

February 5: The International Red Cross helps 1,200 Jews from the Protectorate of Bohemia and Moravia reach Switzerland.

February 19: American marines invade Iwo Jima.

March 7: American forces cross the Rhine River.

April 1: American forces invade Okinawa.

April 4: All German forces are kicked out of Hungary.

April 5–6: Over 25,000 prisoners are evacuated from Buchenwald; between 7,000–8,000 are killed.

April 9: The Nazis begin the evacuation of Mauthausen.

April 11: American forces liberate the Buchenwald camp.

April 12: Roosevelt dies; Harry S. Truman becomes president.

April 15: The International Red Cross helps 413 Danish Jews in the Protectorate of Bohemia and Moravia make it to Sweden.

British forces liberate Bergen-Belsen; they find a raging typhus epidemic.

April 25: The United Nations meets in San Francisco.

April 28: Italian partisans shoot Mussolini as he tries to escape to Switzerland.

April 29: The American Seventh Army liberates Dachau.

The Soviet Union occupies Slovakia.

April 30: Hitler and Eva Braun commit suicide in Hitler's Berlin bunker.

May 2: Soviet forces capture Berlin.

German forces in Italy surrender to the Allies.

May 3: The Nazis hand over Theresienstadt, including 17,247 prisoners, to the International Red Cross.

May 4: The SS leave Mauthausen.

May 7: The Germans surrender to the Allies.

May 8: V-E Day: The war in Europe is officially over.

June 26: The United Nations charter is signed in San Francisco; it goes into effect on October 24, 1945.

August 6: The United States drops a nuclear bomb on Hiroshima.

August 8: The Soviet Union declares war on Japan.

August 9: The United States drops a second nuclear bomb, on Nagasaki.

August 14: Japan accepts the Allies' terms of surrender; World War II is completely over.

September 2: In the Tokyo harbor, the Japanese sign the American and British terms of surrender aboard the *USS Missouri*.

September 9: Japan signs the Chinese terms of surrender.

BIBLIOGRAPHY

1. Comprehensive Histories of the Holocaust

Bauer, Yehuda. *A History of the Holocaust.* New York: Franklin Watts, 1982.

Berenbaum, Michael, ed. *The Holocaust and History: The Known, the Unknown, the Disputed, and the Reexamined.* Bloomington, IN: Indiana University Press, 1998.

Dawidowicz, Lucy. *The War Against the Jews, 1933–1945.* New York: Holt, Rinehart and Winston, 1975.

Gilbert, Martin. *The Holocaust: A History of the Jews in Europe during the Second World War.* New York: Holt, Rinehart and Winston, 1985.

Gutman, Israel, editor in chief. *The Encyclopedia of the Holocaust.* New York: Macmillan, 1990.

Gutman, Israel, and Chaim Shatzker. *The Holocaust and Its Significance.* Jerusalem: The Zalman Shazar Center, 1984.

Hilberg, Raul. *The Destruction of the European Jews.* Chicago: Quadrangle Books, 1961 (definitive edition, New York: Holmes and Meier, 1985).

Marrus, Michael. *The Holocaust in History.* Hanover, NH: University Press of New England, 1987.

Poliakov, Leon. *Harvest of Hate.* London: Best Seller Library, 1960 (French edition, copyright 1954).

Reitlinger, Gerald. *The Final Solution.* New York: Beechurst Press, 1953 (second revised and augmented edition, London: Vallentine-Mitchell, 1968).

Yahil, Leni. *The Holocaust: The Fate of European Jewry 1932–1945.* New York: Oxford Press, 1990.

2. Antisemitism

Cohn, Norman. *Warrant for Genocide: The Myth of the Jewish World-Conspiracy and the Protocols of the Elders of Zion.* London: Eyre and Spottiswoode, 1967.

Katz, Jacob. *From Prejudice to Destruction: Anti-Semitism 1700–1933.* Cambridge, MA: Harvard University Press, 1980.

Massing, Paul W. *Rehearsal for Destruction: A Study of Political Anti-Semitism in Imperial Germany.* New York: Harper and Brothers, 1949.

Mosse, George Lachmann. *The Crisis in German Ideology.* New York: Schocken Books, 1981 (first published in 1964).

Parkes, James. *Antisemitism.* London: Vallentine, 1963.

Poliakov, Leon. *The History of Anti-Semitism.* 4 vols. London: Elek Books, 1966–1985.

3. Racial Antisemitism

Mosse, George Lachmann. *Toward the Final Solution: A History of European Racism.* London: JM Dent, 1978.

Stern, Fritz. *The Politics of Cultural Despair: A Study in the Rise of the Germanic Ideology.* Berkeley: University of California Press, 1974.

4. Nazism and Fascism

Allen, William Sheridan. *The Nazi Seizure of Power: The Experience of a Single German Town, 1930–1935.* Chicago: Quadrangle Books, 1965 (revised edition, New York: Franklin Watts, 1984).

Bracher, Karl Dietrich. *The German Dictatorship: The Origins, Structure and Effects of National Socialism.* New York: Praeger, 1972.

Mosse, George Lachmann. *The Fascist Revolution: Toward a General Theory of Fascism.* New York: H. Fertig, 1999.

Neumann, Franz. *Behemoth: The Structure and Practice of National Socialism.* New York: Harper, 1966 (originally published in 1944).

Sternhell, Zeev. *The Birth of Fascist Ideology: From Cultural Rebellion to Political Revolution.* Princeton, NJ: Princeton University Press, 1994.

Weiss, John. *Ideology of Death: Why the Holocaust Happened in Germany.* Chicago: Ivan R. Dee, 1996.

5. Hitler

Bullock, Allan. *Hitler: A Study in Tyranny.* London: Odhams, 1965.

Fest, Joachim. *Hitler.* London: Weidenfeld and Nicolson, 1974.

Jaeckel, Eberhard. *Hitler in History.* Hanover, NH: University Press of New England, 1984.

———. *Hitler's Weltanschauung: A Blueprint for Power.* Middletown, CT: Wesleyan University Press, 1972.

Kershaw, Ian. *Hitler.* London: Longman, 1991.

———. *Hitler, 1889–1936, Hubris.* London: Allen Lane, 1998.

———. *The Nazi Dictatorship.* London: Edward Arnold, 1985.

Lukacs, John. *The Hitler of History.* New York: Knopf, 1997.

Rosenbaum, Ron. *Explaining Hitler: The Search for the Origin of His Evil.* London: Macmillan, 1998.

6. Development of the "Final Solution"

Aly, Goetz. *"Final Solution": Nazi Population Policy and the Murder of the European Jews.* London: Arnold, 1999.

Breitman, Richard. *The Architect of Genocide: Himmler and the Final Solution.* London: The Bodely Head, 1991.

Browning, Christopher. *Fateful Months: Essays on the Emergence of the Final Solution.* New York: Holmes and Meier, 1985.

———. *The Path to Genocide: Essays on Launching the Final Solution.* New York: Cambridge University Press, 1992.

Cesarani, David, ed. *The Final Solution: Origins and Implementation.* London: Routledge, 1994.

Friedlander, Henry. *The Origins of Nazi Genocide: From Euthanasia to the Final Solution.* Chapel Hill, NC: The University of North Carolina Press, 1995.

Friedlaender, Saul. *Nazi Germany and the Jews.* New York: HarperCollins, 1997.

Goldhagen, Daniel Jonah. *Hitler's Willing Executioners: Ordinary Germans and the Holocaust.* New York: Knopf, 1996.

Herbert, Ulrich. *National-Socialist Extermination Policies.* Oxford: Berghahn Books, 1999.

Schleunes, Karl. *The Twisted Road to Auschwitz.* London: Deutsch, 1972.

7. The Murderers

Arendt, Hannah. *Eichmann in Jerusalem: A Report on the Banality of Evil.* New York: The Viking Press, 1963.

Benz, Wolfgang. *The Holocaust: A German Historian Examines the Genocide.* New York: Columbia University Press, 1999.

Browning, Christopher. *Ordinary Men: Reserve Police Battalion 101 and the Final Solution in Poland.* New York: HarperCollins, 1992.

Hoehne, Heinz. *The Order of the Death's Head: The Story of Hitler's SS.* London: Secker and Warburg, 1969.

Klee, Ernst, Willi Dressen, and Volker Riess. *Those Were the Days: The Holocaust Through the Eyes of the Perpetrators and Bystanders.* London: Hamish Hamilton, 1991.

Krausnick, Helmut, and Martin Broszat, et al. *The Anatomy of the SS State.* London: Collins, 1968.

Lifton, Robert. *The Nazi Doctors: Medical Killing and the Psychology of Genocide.* New York: Basic Books, 1986.

Sereny, Gitta. *Into That Darkness: From Mercy Killing to Mass Murder.* New York: McGraw-Hill, 1974.

Sereny, Gitta, *Albert Speer: His Battle with Truth.* New York: Knopf, 1995.

8. Nazi Camps

Arad, Yitzhak. *Belzec, Sobibor, Treblinka: The Operation Reinhard Death Camps.* Bloomington, IN: Indiana University Press, 1987.

Des Pres, Terrence. *The Survivor: An Anatomy of Life in the Death Camps.* New York: Oxford University Press, 1976.

Dwork, Deborah. *Auschwitz: 1270 to the Present.* New York: W.W. Norton, 1996.

Feig, Konnilyn. *Hitler's Death Camps: The Sanity of Madness.* New York: Holmes and Meier, 1981.

Frankl, Viktor. *From Death Camp to Existentialism: A Psychiatrist's Path to a New Therapy.* Boston: Beacon Press, 1959 (revised and reissued as *Man's Search for Meaning.* New York: Washington Square Press, 1968).

Gutman, Israel, and Michael Berenbaum, eds. *Anatomy of the Auschwitz Death Camp.* Bloomington, IN: Indiana University Press, 1994.

Gutman, Israel, and Avital Saf, eds. *The Nazi Concentration Camps: Structure and Aim—The Image of the Prisoner—The Jews in the Camps.* Jerusalem: Yad Vashem, 1984.

Karay, Felicja. *Women in the Forced-Labor Camps.* New Haven, CT: Yale University Press, 1998.

Kogon, Eugene. *The Theory and Practice of Hell: The German Concentration Camps and the System Behind Them.* London: Secker and Warburg, 1950.

Sofsky, Wolfgang. *The Order of Terror: The Concentration Camp.* Princeton, NJ: Princeton University Press, 1997.

9. The Ghettos

Trunk, Isaiah. *Judenrat: The Jewish Councils in Eastern Europe under Nazi Occupation.* New York: Macmillan, 1972.

10. The Polish Government-in-Exile

Engel, David. *Facing a Holocaust: The Polish Government-in-Exile and the Jews, 1943–1945.* Chapel Hill, NC: University of North Carolina Press, 1993.

———. *In the Shadow of Auschwitz: The Polish Government-in-Exile and the Jews, 1939–1942.* Chapel Hill, NC: University of North Carolina Press, 1987.

11. Jewish Response in Eastern Europe

Altshuler, Mordechai. *Soviet Jewry on the Eve of the Holocaust: A Social and Demographic Profile.* Jerusalem: Hebrew University Center for Research of East-European Jewry, 1998.

Arad, Yitzhak. *Ghetto in Flames: The Struggle and Destruction of the Jews in Vilna in the Holocaust.* Jerusalem: Yad Vashem, 1980.

Cholavsky, Shalom. *The Jews of Bielorussia during World War II.* Amsterdam: Harwood Academic Publishers, 1998.

———. *Soldiers from the Ghetto.* San Diego: AS Barnes, 1980.

Gutman, Israel. *The Jews of Warsaw, 1939–1943: Ghetto, Underground, Revolt.* Bloomington, IN: Indiana University Press, 1982.

Krakowski, Shmuel. *The War of the Doomed: Jewish Armed Resistance in Poland 1942–1944.* New York: Holmes and Meier, 1984.

Levin, Dov. *Fighting Back: Lithuanian Jewry's Armed Resistance to the Nazis 1941–1945.* New York: Holmes and Meier, 1985.

12. The Ukraine and Belarus

Aster, Howard, ed. *Ukrainian-Jewish Relations in Historical Perspective.* Edmonton, Can.: Canadian Institute of Ukrainian Studies, 1990.

Dean, Martin. *Collaboration in the Holocaust: Crimes of the Local Police in Belorussia and the Ukraine, 1941–1944.* New York: St. Martins Press, 2000.

Ehrenburg, Ilya, and Vasily Grossman. *The Black Book.* New York: Holocaust Library, 1981.

Kuznetsov, Anatoly. *Babi Yar.* London: MacGibbon and Kee, 1967.

Spector, Shmuel. *The Holocaust of Volhynian Jews 1941–1944.* Jerusalem: Yad Vashem, 1990.

13. France

Adler, Jacques. *The Jews of Paris and the Final Solution: Communal Response and Internal Conflicts 1940–1944.* New York: Oxford University Press, 1987.

Cohen, Richard. *The Burden of Conscience: French Jewish Leadership during the Holocaust.* Bloomington, IN: Indiana University Press, 1987.

Lazare, Luciene. *Rescue as Resistance: How Jewish Organizations Fought the Holocaust in France.* New York: Columbia University Press, 1996.

Marrus, Michael, and Robert Paxton. *Vichy France and the Jews.* New York: Basic Books, 1981.

Zuccotti, Susan. *The Holocaust, the French and the Jews.* New York: Basic Books, 1993.

14. The Netherlands and Belgium

Colijn, G. Jan, ed. *The Netherlands and Nazi Genocide: Papers of the 21st Annual Scholars Conference.* Lewiston, NY: The Edward Mellen Press, 1992.

de Jong, Louis. *The Netherlands and Nazi Germany.* Cambridge, MA: Harvard University Press, 1990.

Michman, Dan, ed. *Belgium and the Holocaust: Jews, Belgians, Germans.* Jerusalem: Yad Vashem, 1998.

Moore, Bob. *Victims and Survivors: The Nazi Persecution of the Jews in the Netherlands 1940–1945.* London: Arnold, 1997.

Presser, Jacob. *The Destruction of the Dutch Jews.* New York: EP Dutton, 1969.

15. Scandinavia

Abrahamsen, Samuel. *Norway's Response to the Holocaust: A Historical Perspective.* New York: Holocaust Library, 1991.

Rautkallio, Hanno. *Finland and the Holocaust: The Rescue of Finland's Jews.* New York: Holocaust Library, 1987.

Yahil, Leni. *The Rescue of Danish Jewry: Test of a Democracy.* Philadelphia: Jewish Publication Society, 1969.

16. Italy

Carpi, Daniel. *Between Mussolini and Hitler: The Jews and the Italian Authorities in France and Tunisia.* Hanover, NH: Brandeis University Press, 1994.

Michaelis, Meir. *Mussolini and the Jews: German-Italian Relations and the Jewish Question in Italy, 1922–1945.* Oxford: Clarendon Press, 1978.

Zuccotti, Susan. *The Italians and the Holocaust: Persecution, Rescue and Survival.* New York: Basic Books, 1987.

17. The Balkans

Bar-Zohar, Michel. *Beyond Hitler's Grasp: The Heroic Rescue of Bulgaria's Jews.* Holbrook, MA: Adams Media Corporation, 1998.

Chary, Fredrich. *The Bulgarian Jews and the Final Solution 1940–1944.* Pittsburgh: University of Pittsburgh Press, 1972.

Mazower, Mark. *Inside Hitler's Greece: The Experience of Occupation, 1941–1944.* New Haven, CT: Yale University Press, 1993.

18. German Jewry

Angress, Werner. *Between Fear and Hope: Jewish Youth in the Third Reich.* New York: Columbia University Press, 1988.

Baker, Leonard. *Days of Sorrow and Pain: Leo Baeck and the Berlin Jews.* New York: Macmillan, 1978.

Barkai, Avraham. *From Boycott to Annihilation: The Economic Struggle of German Jews, 1933–1943.* Hanover, NH: University Press of New England, 1989.

——. *Renewal and Destruction, 1918–1945.* New York: Columbia University Press, 1998.

Gay, Peter. *Freud, Jews and Other Germans: Masters and Victims in Modernist Culture.* New York: Oxford University Press, 1978.

Kaplan, Marion A. *Between Dignity and Despair: Jewish Life in Nazi Germany.* New York: Oxford University Press, 1998.

Kulka, Otto Dov, and Paul Mendes-Flohr, eds. *Judaism and Christianity Under the Impact of National Socialism, 1919–1945.* Jerusalem: The Historical Society of Israel, 1987.

Mosse, George Lachmann. *German Jews Beyond Judaism.* Bloomington, IN: Indiana University Press, 1985.

Mosse, Werner Eugene. *The German-Jewish Economic Elite 1820–1935: A Socio-Cultural Profile.* Oxford: Clarendon Press, 1989.

Niewyk, Donald. *The Jews in Weimar Germany.* Baton Rouge, LA: Louisiana State University Press, 1980.

Poppel, Stephen. *Zionism in Germany 1897–1933: The Shaping of a Jewish Identity.* Philadelphia: Jewish Publication Society, 1977.

Pulzer, Peter. *Jews and the German State: The Political History of a Minority, 1848–1933.* Oxford: Blackwell, 1992.

Reinharz, Yehuda. *Fatherland or Promised Land: The Dilemma of the German Jew, 1893–1914.* Ann Arbor, MI: University of Michigan Press, 1975.

Reinharz, Yehuda, and Walter Schatzberg, eds. *The Jewish Response to German Culture: From the Enlightenment to the Second World War.* Hanover, NH: University Press of New England, 1985.

Richarz, Monika, ed. *Jewish Life in Germany: Memoirs from Three Centuries.* Bloomington, IN: University of Indiana Press, 1991.

Schorsch, Ismar. *Jewish Reactions to German Anti-Semitism, 1870–1914.* New York: Columbia University Press, 1972.

Tal, Uriel. *Christians and Jews in Germany.* Ithaca, NY: Cornell University Press, 1975.

19. Hungary and Romania

Ben-Tov, Arieh. *Facing a Holocaust in Budapest: The International Committee of the Red Cross and the Jews in Hungary 1943–1945.* Geneva: Henry Dunant Institute, 1988.

Braham, Randolph L., ed. *The Destruction of Romanian and Ukranian Jews during the Antonescu Era.* Boulder, CO: The City University of New York, 1997.

——. ed. *The Holocaust in Hungary: Fifty Years Later.* New York: Columbia University Press, 1997.

——. *The Politics of Genocide: The Holocaust in Hungary.* New York: Columbia University Press, 1981 (revised edition, 1994).

Cesarani, David, ed. *Genocide and Rescue: The Holocaust in Hungary 1944.* Oxford: Berg, 1997.

Cohen, Asher. *The He-Halutz Underground.* Boulder, CO: Social Science Monographs, 1986.

Katzburg, Nathaniel. *Hungary and the Jews: Policy and Legislation 1920–1943.* Ramat Gan, Isr.: Bar-Ilan University Press, 1981.

20. Slovakia

Frieder, Emmanuel. *To Deliver their Souls: The Struggle of a Young Rabbi during the Holocaust.* New York: Holocaust Library, 1987.

Fuchs, Abraham. *The Unheeded Cry.* Brooklyn: Mesorah Publications, 1984.

Toth, Dezider, ed. *The Tragedy of Slovak Jews: Proceedings of the International Symposium, Banska Bystrica, 25th to 27th March, 1992.* Banska Bystrica: Datai, 1992.

21. Czech Republic

Bondy, Ruth. *"Elder of Jews" Jacob Edelstein of Theresienstadt.* New York: Grove Press, 1989.

22. Jewish Rescue Attempts

Bauer, Yehuda. *American Jewry and the Holocaust: The American*

Joint Distribution Committee, 1939–1945. Detroit: Wayne State University Press, 1981.

———. *The Holocaust in Historical Perspective.* Seattle: University of Washington Press, 1978.

———. *The Jewish Emergence from Powerlessness.* Toronto: University of Toronto, 1979.

———. *Jews For Sale? Nazi-Jewish Negotiations, 1933–1945.* New Haven, CT: Yale University Press, 1994.

Jewish Resistance during the Holocaust: Proceedings of the Conference on Manifestations of Jewish Resistance, Jerusalem, April 7–11, 1968. Jerusalem: Yad Vashem, 1971.

Morrison, David. *Heroes, Antiheroes and the Holocaust: American Jewry and Historical Choice.* 2nd ed. Jerusalem: Gefen, 1999.

Patterns of Jewish Leadership in Nazi Europe, 1933–1945: Proceedings of the Third Yad Vashem International Historical Conference, Jerusalem, April 1–7, 1977. Jerusalem: Yad Vashem, 1979.

Rescue Attempts during the Holocaust: Proceedings of the Second Yad Vashem International Historical Conference, Jerusalem, April 8–11, 1974. Jerusalem: Yad Vashem, 1977.

23. Jewish Partisans

Tec, Nechama. *Defiance: The Belski Partisans.* New York: Oxford University Press, 1993.

24. Allied Response

Abella, Irving, and Harold Troper. *None is Too Many: Canada and the Jews of Europe, 1933–1948.* New York: Random House, 1983.

Baumel, Judith Tydor. *Unfulfilled Promise: Rescue and Resettlement of Jewish Children in the United States, 1934–1945.* Juneau: Denali Press, 1990.

Breitman, Richard. *Official Secrets: What the Nazis Planned, What the British and Americans Knew.* New York: Hill and Wang, 1998.

Breitman, Richard, and Alan Kraut. *American Refugee Policy and European Jewry, 1933–1945.* Bloomington, IN: Indiana University Press, 1987.

Cohen, Michael. *Palestine Retreat from the Mandate: The Making of British Policy, 1936–1945.* London: P. Elek, 1978.

Feingold, Henry. *The Politics of Rescue: The Roosevelt Administration and the Holocaust 1938–1945.* New Brunswick, NJ: Rutgers University Press, 1970.

Gilbert, Martin. *Auschwitz and the Allies.* New York: Holt, Rinehart and Winston, 1981.

Kushner, Tony. *The Holocaust and the Liberal Imagination: A Social and Cultural History.* Oxford: Blackwell, 1994.

Laqueur, Walter. *The Terrible Secret: An Investigation in the Suppression of Information about Hitler's "Final Solution."* London: Weidenfeld and Nicolson, 1980.

Lipstadt, Deborah. *Beyond Belief: The American Press and the Coming of the Holocaust, 1933–1945.* New York: The Free Press, 1986.

Nicosia, Francis. *The Third Reich and the Palestine Question.* London: I.B. Taurus, 1985.

Ofer, Dalia. *Escaping the Holocaust: Illegal Immigration to the Land of Israel, 1939–1944.* New York: Oxford University Press, 1990.

Porat, Dina. *The Blue and the Yellow Stars of David: The Zionist Leadership in Palestine and the Holocaust, 1939–1945.* Cambridge, MA: Harvard University Press, 1990.

Sherman, A. J. *Island of Refuge: Britain and Refugees from the Third Reich, 1933–1939.* London: P. Elek, 1973.

Sompolinsky, Meier. *Britain and the Holocaust: The Failure of Anglo-Jewish Leadership?* Brighton: Sussex Academic Press, 1999.

Wasserstein, Bernard. *Britain and the Jews of Europe, 1939–1945.* London: Institute of Jewish Affairs, 1979.

Wyman, David. *The Abandonment of the Jews: America and the Holocaust.* New York: Pantheon Books, 1984.

———. *Paper Walls: America and the Refugee Crisis, 1938–1941.* Massachusetts: University of Massachusetts Press, 1968.

Zweig, Ronald. *Britain and Palestine during the Second World War.* Woodbridge, Suffak, UK: The Boydell Press, 1986.

25. Neutral Governments and the Holocaust

Favez, Jean-Claude. *The Red Cross and the Holocaust.* Cambridge: Cambridge University Press, 1999.

Haessler, Alfred. *The Lifeboat is Full: Switzerland and the Refugees, 1933–1945.* New York: Funk and Wagnalls, 1969.

Koblik, Steven. *The Stones Cry Out: Sweden's Response to the Persecution of the Jews, 1933–1945.* New York: Holocaust Library, 1988.

Levin, Itamar. *The Last Deposit: Swiss Banks and the Holocaust Victims' Accounts.* Westport, CT: Praeger, 1999.

Ziegler, Jean. *The Swiss, the Gold, and the Dead: How Swiss Bankers Helped Finance the Nazi War Machine.* New York: Harcourt Brace and Co., 1998.

26. Churches and the Holocaust

Cornwell, John. *Hitler's Pope: The Secret History of Pius XII.* New York: Viking, 1999.

Friedlaender, Saul. *Pius XII and the Third Reich: A Documentation.* New York: Knopf, 1966.

Hochhuth, Rolf. *The Deputy.* New York: Grove Press, 1964.

Morley, John. *Vatican Diplomacy and the Jews during the Holocaust, 1939–1943.* New York: Ktav, 1980.

27. Righteous Among the Nations

Fogelman, Eva. *Conscience and Courage: Rescuers of Jews during the Holocaust.* New York: Anchor Books, 1994.

Oliner, Samuel. *The Altruistic Personality: Rescuers of Jews in Nazi Europe.* New York: The Free Press, 1988.

Paldiel, Mordecai. *The Path of the Righteous: Gentile Rescuers of Jews during the Holocaust.* Hoboken, NJ: Ktav, 1993.

Tec, Nechama. *When Light Pierced the Darkness: Christian Rescue of Jews in Nazi-Occupied Poland.* New York: Oxford University Press, 1986.

28. Selected Diaries and Memoirs

The Diary of Eva Heyman. Jerusalem: Yad Vashem, 1974.

Fenelon, Fania. *The Musicians of Auschwitz.* London: M. Joseph, 1977.

Friedlaender, Saul. *When Memory Comes.* New York: Farrar, Straus and Giroux, 1979.

Geva, Thomas. *Youth in Chains*. Jerusalem: R Mass, 1958.

Hart, Kitty. *I Am Alive*. London: Abelard-Schuman, 1961.

Hillesum, Etty. *Etty: A Diary 1941–1943*. London: J. Cape, 1983.

Lengyel, Olga. *Five Chimneys*. London: Hamilton, 1963.

Levi, Primo. *Survival in Auschwitz: The Nazi Assault on Humanity*. New York: Collier Books, 1971.

Mechanicus, Philip. *Waiting for Death: A Diary*. London: Calder and Boyars, 1968.

Mueller, Filip. *Auschwitz Inferno: The Testimony of a Sonderkommando*. London: Routledge and Kegan Paul, 1979.

Notes from the Warsaw Ghetto: The Journal of Emmanuel Ringelblum. New York: McGraw-Hill, 1958.

Nyiszli, Miklos. *Auschwitz: A Doctor's Eyewitness Account*. London: Hamilton, 1964.

Rousset, David. *The Other Kingdom*. New York: Reynal and Hitchcock, 1947.

Scroll of Agony: The Warsaw Diary of Chaim Kaplan. New York: Macmillan, 1965.

Surviving the Holocaust: The Kovno Diary, Avraham Tory. Cambridge, MA: Harvard University Press, 1990.

The Terezin Diary of Gonda Redlich. Lexington, KY: University Press of Kentucky, 1992.

The Warsaw Diary of Adam Czerniakow. New York: Stein and Day, 1979.

Wiesel, Elie. *Night*. New York: Hill and Wang, 1960.

Zuckerman, Yitzhak. *A Surplus of Memory: Chronicle of the Warsaw Ghetto Uprising*. Berkeley: University of California Press, 1993.

29. Selected Literature and Poetry

Appelfeld, Aharon. *The Age of Wonders*. Boston: David R. Godine, 1981.

——. *The Immortal Bartfuss*. New York: Weidenfeld and Nicolson, 1988.

——. *Katerina*. New York: Random House, 1992.

——. *Unto the Soul*. New York: Random House, 1994.

Begley, Louis. *The Man Who Was Late*. New York: Knopf, 1993.

——. *Wartime Lies*. New York: Knopf, 1991.

Bellow, Saul. *Mr. Sammler's Planet*. London: Penguin, 1972.

Borowski, Tadeusz. *This Way for the Gas Ladies and Gentlemen*. New York: Viking Press, 1967.

Fink, Ida. *The Journey*. New York: Farrar, Straus and Giroux, 1992.

Hersey, John. *The Wall*. London: H. Hamilton, 1960.

Levi, Primo. *The Drowned and the Saved*. New York: Summit Books, 1988.

——. *If Not Now When*. New York: Summit Books, 1985.

——. *The Mirror Maker*. New York: Schocken Books, 1989.

——. *The Periodic Table*. New York: Schocken Books, 1984.

Plath, Sylvia. *Crossing the Water*. London: Faber and Faber, 1971.

——. *Winter Trees*. London: Faber and Faber, 1971.

Wiesel, Elie. *The Accident*. New York: Hill and Wang, 1962.

——. *Dawn*. London: MacGibbon, 1961.

——. *The Fifth Son*. New York: Warner Books, 1985.

——. *The Gates of the Forest*. New York: Holt, Rinehart and Winston, 1966.

——. *Legends of Our Time*. New York: Holt, Rinehart and Winston, 1968.

30. The Holocaust in Literature and the Arts

Amishai-Maisels, Ziva. *Depiction and Interpretation: The Influence of the Holocaust on the Visual Arts*. Oxford: Pergamon Press, 1993.

Ezrachi, Sidra Dekoven. *By Words Alone: The Holocaust in Literature*. Chicago: University of Chicago Press, 1980.

Flam, Gila. *Singing for Survival: Songs of the Lodz Ghetto*. Urbana, IL: University of Illinois Press, 1992.

Karas, Joza. *Music in Terezin 1941–1945*. New York: Beaufort Books, 1985.

Langer, Lawrence. *Admitting the Holocaust: Collective Essays*. New York: Oxford University Press, 1995.

——. *The Holocaust and the Literary Imagination*. New Haven, CT: Yale University Press, 1975.

——. *Holocaust Testimonies: The Ruins of Memory*. New Haven, CT: Yale University Press, 1991.

——. *Preempting the Holocaust*. New Haven, CT: Yale University Press, 1998.

——. *Versions of Survival: The Holocaust and the Human Spirit*. Albany: State University of New York Press, 1982.

Rosenfeld, Alvin. *A Double Dying: Reflections on Holocaust Literature*. Bloomington, IN: Indiana University Press, 1980.

Roskies, David. *Against the Apocalypse: Responses to Catastrophe in Modern Jewish Culture*. Cambridge, MA: Harvard University Press, 1984.

Steiner, George. *Language and Silence: Essays, 1958–1966*. London: Faber and Faber, 1967.

——. *The Portage to San Cristobal of AH*. New York: Simon and Schuster, 1981.

Young, James Eduard. *Writing and Re-Writing the Holocaust: Narrative and the Consequences of Interpretation*. Bloomington, IN: Indiana University Press, 1990.

31. Collective Memory

Friedlaender, Saul. *Memory, History and the Extermination of the Jews of Europe*. Bloomington, IN: Indiana University Press, 1993.

Katz, Steven. *The Holocaust in Historical Context, Vol. 1*. New York: Oxford University Press, 1994.

Novick, Peter. *The Holocaust in American Life*. Boston: Houghton Mifflin, 1999.

Young, James Eduard. *The Texture of Memory: Holocaust Memorials and Their Meaning*. New Haven, CT: Yale University Press, 1993.

32. Philosophy and Theology

Berkovits, Eliezer. *Faith After the Holocaust*. New York: Ktav, 1973.

——. *With God in Hell: Judaism in the Ghettos and the Death Camps*. New York: Sanhedrin Press, 1979.

Braiterman, Zachary. *(God) after Auschwitz: Tradition and Change in Post-Holocaust Jewish Thought*. Princeton, NJ: Princeton University Press, 1998.

Cohen, Arthur A. *The Tremendum: A Theological Interpretation of the Holocaust*. New York: Crossroad, 1981.

Fackenheim, Emil. *God's Presence in History: Jewish Affirmations and Philosophical Reflections*. New York: New York University Press, 1970.

———. *The Jewish Return into History: Reflections in the Age of Auschwitz and the New Jerusalem.* New York: Schocken Books, 1978.

———. *The Jewish Thought of Emil Fackenheim: A Reader.* Detroit: Wayne State University Press, 1987.

———. *To Mend the World: Foundations of Post-Holocaust Jewish Thought.* Bloomington, IN: Indiana University Press, 1994.

Katz, Steven. *Post-Holocaust Dialogues: Critical Studies in Modern Jewish Thought.* New York: New York University Press, 1985.

Rubenstein, Richard. *After Auschwitz: Radical Theology and Contemporary Judaism.* New York: Bobbs-Merrill, 1966.

Schweid, Eliezer. *Wrestling until Day-Break: Searching for Meaning in the Thinking on the Holocaust.* Lanham, MD: University Press of America, 1994.

33. Holocaust Denial

Lipstadt, Deborah. *Denying the Holocaust: The Growing Assault on Truth and Memory.* New York: Plume Books, 1994.

Vidal-Naquet, Pierre. *Assassins of Memory: Essays on the Denial of the Holocaust.* New York: Columbia University Press, 1992.

34. War Crimes Trials and Criminals

Finkielkraut, Alain. *Remembering in Vain: The Klaus Barbie Trial and Crimes Against Humanity.* New York: Columbia University Press, 1992.

Gilbert, Gustave Mark. *Nuremberg Diary.* New York: Farrar, 1947.

Harel, Isser. *The House on Garibaldi Street.* New York: Bantam Books, 1976.

Ryan, Allan. *Quiet Neighbors: Prosecuting Nazi War Criminals in America.* San Diego: Harcourt, Brace, Jovanovich, 1984.

Taylor, Telford. *The Anatomy of the Nuremberg Trials: A Personal Memoir.* New York: Knopf, 1992.

Wiesenthal, Simon. *The Murderers Among Us.* London: Heinemann, 1967.

Zuroff, Efraim. *Occupation: Nazi-Hunter, The Continuing Search for the Perpetrators of the Holocaust.* Hoboken, NJ: Ktav, 1994.

35. Holocaust Survivors, Their Post-War Experiences and Psychology

Bar-On, Dan. *Fear and Hope: Three Generations of the Holocaust.* Cambridge, MA: Harvard University Press, 1995.

Baumel, Judith Tydor. *Kibbutz Buchenwald: Survivors and Pioneers.* New Brunswick, NJ: Rutgers University Press, 1997.

Gilbert, Martin. *The Boys: Triumph over Adversity.* London: Weidenfeld and Nicolson, 1996.

Gill, Anton. *The Journey Back from Hell: Conversations with Concentration Camp Survivors.* London: Grafton Books, 1988.

Hass, Aaron. *In the Shadow of the Holocaust: The Second Generation.* New York: Cambridge University Press, 1996.

Karpf, Anne. *The War After: Living with the Holocaust.* London: Heinemann, 1996.

Yablonka, Hanna. *Survivors of the Holocaust: Israel after the War.* London: Macmillan, 1999.

INDEX

Bold numbers indicate an entry on the subject